Ireland

THE ROUGH GUIDE

D1513795

There are more than one hundred Rough Guide titles
covering destinations from Amsterdam to Zimbabwe

Forthcoming titles include
Chile • Indonesia • Laos • New Orleans • South India

Rough Guide Reference Series
Classical Music • European Football • The Internet • Jazz
Opera • Reggae • Rock Music • World Music

Rough Guide Phrasebooks
Czech • Egyptian Arabic • French • German • Greek
Hindi & Urdu • Hungarian • Indonesian • Italian • Japanese
Mandarin Chinese • Mexican Spanish • Polish • Portuguese
Russian • Spanish • Swahili • Thai • Turkish • Vietnamese

Rough Guides on the Internet
www.roughguides.com

ROUGH GUIDE CREDITS

Text editor: Ruth Blackmore

Series editor: Mark Ellingham

Editorial: Martin Dunford, Jonathan Buckley, Jo Mead, Kate Berens, Amanda Tomlin, Ann-Marie Shaw, Paul Gray, Chris Schüler, Helena Smith, Judith Bamber, Kieran Falconer, Orla Duane, Olivia Eccleshall, Sophie Martin, Jennifer Dempsey, Sue Jackson, Geoff Howard, Claire Saunders, Anna Sutton, Gavin Thomas (UK); Andrew Rosenberg, Andrew Taber (US)

Production: Susanne Hillen, Andy Hilliard, Link Hall, Helen Ostick, James Morris, Julia Bovis, Michelle Draycott, Cathy Edwards

Cartography: Melissa Flack, Maxine Burke, Nichola Goodliffe

Picture research: Eleanor Hill

Online editors: Alan Spicer, Kate Hands (UK); Geronimo Madrid (US)

Finance: John Fisher, Celia Crowley, Neeta Mistry, Katie Miesiaczek

Marketing & Publicity: Richard Trillo, Simon Carloss, Niki Smith (UK); Jean-Marie Kelly, SoRelle Braun (US)

Administration: Tania Hummel, Alexander Mark Rogers

ACKNOWLEDGEMENTS

Special thanks to contributors to previous editions of this guide: Frances Power, Sarah Foster, Roderick O'Connor, Debbie Almond, John S. Doyle, Paul Power, Gerry Smyth, Nuala O'Connor, Hilary Robinson, Luke Dodd, Seán Doran, Joe O'Connor, Killian Robinson, Tom Joyce and Richard Nairn. Thanks also to Nick Thomson and Cameron Wilson for extra Basics research, Russell Walton for proofreading, James Morris for typesetting and Kingston Presentation Graphics for cartography.

Margaret Greenwood would like to thank John Lahiffe at Bord Fáilte, Anne and Frank Greenwood; Jenny and Brian Nuttall; Con, Rosie and Siobhan Lynch and Orla; Sinead Slattery; Nial and Ger Shanahan; Mary White and John Bolger; Marleena dry Koningen; Andy Thompson; Chris Murphy and Nicole Matthews.

Mark Connolly would like to thank all at no. 11 Belvedere Road, Niall Kennedy of Dublin Tourist Board,

Peter Friel for his help reviewing the maps, Eoin Alexander for proofreading, Cecil Xavier for her research help in Navan, Nell Killian for her help in Mullingar, Sean Faherty for all his assistance in the Aran Islands, the Killough family and Mr and Mrs Connolly for the use of their phone and fridge.

Geoff Wallis wishes to thank the following for their support, advice and assistance: staff at Bord Fáilte, especially John Lahiffe in London, North West Tourism staff in Donegal town and Letterkenny, Eamon Jordan, Fergal Kearney, Sean MacLoskey, Anton Meenan, Frank and Rita Mellon, Majella and Nick Newton, the Northern Ireland Tourist Board (especially Orla Farren in Belfast), the Northern Ireland Youth Hostel Association, Ray and Joan O'Hoireachtaigh, Mary Reynolds, the South Armagh Tourism Initiative (especially Michelle Boyle) and Stena Line.

PUBLISHING INFORMATION

This fifth edition published February 1999 by Rough Guides Ltd, 62–70 Shorts Gardens, London WC2H 9AB.

Distributed by the Penguin Group:

Penguin Books Ltd, 27 Wrights Lane, London W8 5TZ.

Penguin Books USA Inc., 375 Hudson Street, New York 10014, USA.

Penguin Books Australia Ltd, 487 Maroondah Highway, PO Box 257, Ringwood, Victoria 3134, Australia.

Penguin Books Canada Ltd, 10 Alcorn Avenue, Toronto, Ontario, Canada M4V 1E4.

Penguin Books (NZ) Ltd, 182–190 Wairau Road, Auckland 10, New Zealand.

Typeset in Linotron Univers and Century Old Style to an original design by Andrew Oliver.

Printed in England by Clays Ltd, St Ives plc.

Illustrations in Part One and Part Three by Ed Briant;

Basics illustration by Gila. Contexts illustration by Andrea McMordie.

© Margaret Greenwood, Mark Connolly and Geoff Wallis 1999

No part of this book may be reproduced in any form without permission from the publisher except for the quotation of brief passages in reviews.

720pp – Includes index.

A catalogue record for this book is available from the British Library.

ISBN 1-85828-400-7

Ireland

THE ROUGH GUIDE

written and researched by

Margaret Greenwood,
Mark Connolly and Geoff Wallis

THE ROUGH GUIDES

THE ROUGH GUIDES

TRAVEL GUIDES • PHRASEBOOKS • MUSIC AND REFERENCE GUIDES

 We set out to do something different when the first Rough Guide was published in 1982. Mark Ellingham, just out of university, was travelling in Greece. He brought along the popular guides of the day, but found they were all lacking in some way. They were either strong on ruins and museums but went on for pages without mentioning a beach or taverna. Or they were so conscious of the need to save money that they lost sight of Greece's cultural and historical significance. Also, none of the books told him anything about Greece's contemporary life – its politics, its culture, its people, and how they lived.

So, with no job in prospect, Mark decided to write his own guidebook; one that aimed to provide practical information that was second to none, detailing the best beaches and the hottest clubs and restaurants, while also giving hard-hitting accounts of every sight, both famous and obscure, and providing up-to-the-minute information on contemporary culture. It was a guide that encouraged independent travellers to find the best of Greece, and was a great success, getting shortlisted for the Thomas Cook travel guide award,

and encouraging Mark, along with three friends, to expand the series.

The Rough Guide list grew rapidly and the letters flooded in, indicating a much broader readership than had been anticipated, but one which uniformly appreciated the Rough Guide mix of practical detail and humour, irreverence and enthusiasm. Things haven't changed. The same four friends who began the series are still the caretakers of the Rough Guide mission today: to provide the most reliable, up-to-date and entertaining information to independent-minded travellers of all ages, on all budgets.

We now publish more than one hundred titles and have offices in London and New York. The travel guides are written and researched by a dedicated team of more than one hundred authors, based in Britain, Europe, the USA and Australia. We have also created a unique series of phrasebooks to accompany the travel series, along with an acclaimed series of music guides, and a best-selling pocket guide to the Internet and World Wide Web. We also publish comprehensive travel information on our Web site:

www.roughguides.com

HELP US UPDATE

We've gone to a lot of effort to ensure that this edition of The Rough Guide to Ireland is accurate and up-to-date. However, places get "discovered"; telephone numbers change; restaurants, hotels and other tourist facilities raise prices or lower standards. If you feel we've got it wrong or left something out, we'd like to know, and if you can remember the address, price, the time, the phone number, so much the better.

We'll credit all contributions, and send a copy of the next edition (or any other Rough Guide if you prefer) for the best letters.
Please mark letters: "Rough Guide Ireland" and send to:
Rough Guides Ltd, 62–70 Shorts Gardens, London WC2H 9AB, or
Rough Guides, 375 Hudson St, 9th Floor, New York, NY 10014.
Or send email to: mail@roughguides.co.uk
Online updates about this book can be found on Rough Guides'
Web site at www.roughguides.com

THE AUTHORS AND CONTRIBUTORS

Margaret Greenwood graduated from the University of Kent at Canterbury in 1981. Since then she has worked as a welfare rights campaigner and an English teacher. She has written extensively on Spain and has also worked on childrens' comics. She is a keen hill walker and has been a regular visitor to Ireland since the early 1980s.

After embarking on more careers than he cares to remember, **Geoff Wallis** now works as a free-lance writer. He has been contributing to the Rough Guides since the early 1980s and has recently worked on *The Rough Guide to Dublin* and *The Rough Guide to Europe*. In his spare moments he hunts for rare records and tries to treat his addiction to Nottingham Forest.

After graduating from Queen's University Belfast, **Mark Connolly** taught English in Poland, Israel and Japan. He has worked as a radio journalist for BBC Radio Ulster and BBC Radio 5 and is currently based in Dublin.

READERS' LETTERS

Thanks to all the readers who have taken the time and trouble to write in with comments and suggestions:

Antonio Fineschi and Sandra Mastacchini, Elizabeth Bayati, Elma Brazel, Tracey Hardwick, Ian Herne, Susan O'Halloran, Paul Crimes, Julie Reed, Christopher Hole, Eric and Sally Rowland, Michael Andrews, Thomas Heneaghan, Dr C.O. Óhaiseadha, Bruce Houldsworth, Daniel McDonnell, Mark Grinnell, Peter Smith, Darcy A. Freeman, Jonathan Dalton, Declan McSweeney, Gwendoline Bennett, Pam and Rog Wortley, Monica Medina, Mikkel Brix Finsen, Marjorie Threm, N. Kelley, A. Justin Bell, Mr and Mrs Paul F. Bellnier, Joanne Linder, Dick Bogash, Micheál Finucane, Hans Skotte, Karen Richardson, G. and E. Wiley, Kath Neil, Marian Cavanagh, Chris Himsworth, Ian Lane, Patricia Lewis, Sue Ramsay, Everett, Pat and Luke Lindsey, Nancy S. Haas, Sarah Pepper, Jayne D. Procter, Dr David and Mrs Lynne Lawrence, G. Paul Clark, Mervyn Kingston, Kathleen McGroarty, Jean Sinclair, J.S. Fleming, Molly Potter, Andy Kirkham, Blair O'Connor, Matt Fabian, Anne Purvis, Heather Elliott, Robert Armitage, Liz Statham, Ingrid Björkman, Bridgette Sorensen, D.J. Lewis, Hector Salgado, Richard and Christine Billinghurst, G.W. Telford, Lyn Harber, Patricia Joyce, Brian Fitzpatrick, Marc Trommelmans, Ann Day, M.J. Harper, Claire Gorman, Alison Kevan, Jim Wells, Daniel Lynch, Jo Thomas, Mary Reynolds, Laura Coles, Grace Meenan, C. McBride, Steve Pearson, Barry Humphries, Anne Wichmann, Alberto Crespi, Nicoltetta Gemmi, Aian Buckley, Kate Barnard, Tim Padmore, Lorna Sumsion, Kate Orpwood, V. Coffey, Tony Partridge, Susan Van Benthuysen, Bill Kerr, Ton Vendel, Glen Gibb, D.J. Corney, Meryl Emmerton, Geraldine Morris, Lynda Smith, David Moane, Niamh Shaw.

CONTENTS

Introduction xi

INTRODUCTION

L andscape and people are what bring most visitors to Ireland – the Republic and the North. And once there, few are disappointed by the reality of the stock Irish images: the green, rain-hazed loughs and wild, bluff coastlines, the inspired talent for talk and conversation, the easy pace and rhythms of life. What is perhaps more of a surprise is how much variety this very small land packs into its countryside. The limestone terraces of the stark, eerie Burren seem separated from the fertile flatlands of Tipperary by hundreds rather than tens of miles, and the primitive beauty of the west coast, with its cliffs, coves and strands, seems to belong in another country altogether from the rolling plains of the central cattle-rearing counties.

It's a place to explore slowly, roaming through agricultural landscapes scattered with farmhouses, or along the endlessly indented coastline. Spectacular seascapes unfold from rocky headlands, and the crash of the sea against the cliffs and myriad islands is often the only sound. It is perfect if you want space to walk, bike or (with a bit of bravado) swim; if you want to fish, sail, or spend a week on inland waterways. In town, too, the pleasures are unhurried: evenings over a Guinness or two in the snug of a pub, listening to the chat around a blood-orange turf fire.

This said, there are sights enough. In every part of the island are traces of a culture established long before the coming of Christianity: sites such as Newgrange in County Meath or the clifftop fortress of Dún Aengus on Inishmore (the biggest of the Aran Islands) are among the most stupendous Neolithic remains in Europe, while in some areas of Sligo almost every hill is capped by an ancient cairn. In the depths of the so-called Dark Ages the Christian communities of Ireland were great centres of learning, and the ruins of Clonmacnois in County Offaly, the Rock of Cashel in Tipperary and a score of other monasteries are evocative of a time when Ireland won its reputation as a land of saints and scholars. Fortifications raised by the chieftains of the Celtic clans and the Anglo-Norman barons bear witness to a period of later turbulence, while the Ascendancy of the Protestant settlers has left its mark in the form of vast mansions and estates.

But the richness of Irish culture is not a matter of monuments. Especially in the Irish-speaking *Gaeltacht* areas, you'll be aware of the strength and continuity of the island's oral and musical traditions. Myth-making is for the Irish people their most ancient and fascinating entertainment. The ancient classics are full of extraordinary stories – Cúchulainn the unbeatable hero in war, Medb the insatiable heroine in bed, or Fionn Mac Cumhaill (Finn Mac Cool) chasing Diarmuid and Gráinne up and down the country – and tall tales, superstition-stirring and "mouthing off" (boasting) play as large a part in day-to-day life as they did in the era of the Táin Bó Cuailngè, Europe's oldest vernacular epic. As a guileless foreigner enquiring about anything from a beautiful lake to a pound of butter, you're ideally placed to trigger the most colourful responses. And the speech of the country – moulded by the rhythms of the ancient tongue – has fired such twentieth-century greats as Yeats, Joyce and Beckett.

Music has always been at the centre of Irish community life. You'll find traditional music sessions all around the touristed coasts and in the cities, too – some of it might be of dubious pedigree, but the *Gaeltacht* areas, and others, can be counted on to provide authentic renditions. Side by side with the traditional circuit is a strong rock scene, that has spawned Van Morrison, U2, Sinéad O'Connor and more recently Ash and The Divine Comedy. And ever-present are the balladeers, fathoming and feeding the old Irish dreams of courting, emigrating and striking it lucky; there's hardly a dry eye in the house when the guitars are packed away.

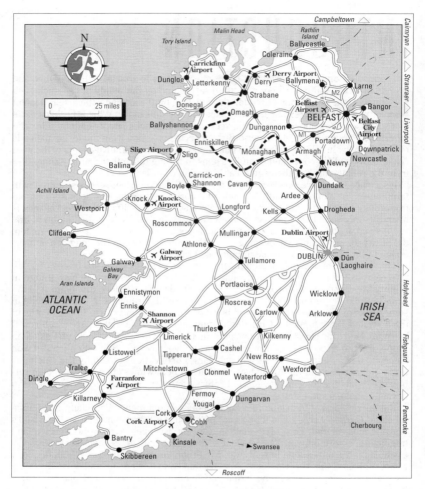

The lakes and rivers of Ireland make it an angler's dream, but the sports that raise the greatest enthusiasm amongst the Irish themselves are speedier and more dangerous. Horse racing in Ireland has none of the socially divisive connotations present on the other side of the Irish Sea, and the country has bred some of the world's finest thoroughbreds. While association football has become remarkably popular since the reign of Jack Charlton as manager of the Republic's national team, Gaelic football, which bears only a superficial resemblance to the British version, still commands a large following. Hurling, the oldest team game played in Ireland, requires the most delicate of ball skills and the sturdiest of bones.

No introduction can cope with the complexities of Ireland's politics, especially the dramatic changes in Northern Ireland over the last couple of years. However, throughout the guide we have addressed the issues wherever they arise, and at the end of the book, in the "Contexts" section, we have included pieces that give a general overview of the current situation. Suffice it to say that, just about everywhere hospitality is as warm as the brochures say, on both sides of the border.

Where to go

It's arguably the west coast that has the most appeal, where the demonically daunting peninsulas of the northern reaches are immediately contrasted a little inland by the mystical lakes of the Donegal highlands. The midwest coastline is just as strangely attractive, combining vertiginous cliffs, boulder-strewn wastes, and violent mountains of granite and quartz. In the south, the melodramatic peaks of the Ring of Kerry fall to lake-pools and seductive seascapes. Less talked about, but no less rewarding in their way, are the gentle sandy coves that Cork and Kerry share.

In the north of the island, the principal draw is the weird basalt geometry of the Giant's Causeway, not far from the lush Glens of Antrim. To the south of Belfast lies the beautiful walking territory of the softly contoured Mountains of Mourne, divided by Carlingford Lough from the myth-drenched Cooley Mountains.

The interior is nowhere as spectacular as the fringes of the island, but the southern heartlands of pastures and low wooded hills, and the wide peat bogs of the very centre are the classic landscapes of Ireland. Of the inland waterways, the most alluring are the island-studded Lough Erne complex of Fermanagh, and the River Shannon, with its string of huge lakes.

Some of the country's wildest scenery lies just offshore: the west-coast Aran Islands are the best known of the islands, but equally compelling are storm-battered Tory Island, to the far northwest and the savage Skelligs, off the southwest coast.

For anyone with strictly limited time, one of the best options must be to combine a visit to Dublin with the mountains and monastic ruins of County Wicklow. Dublin is an extraordinary combination of youthfulness and tradition, a modern European capital on a human scale with elegant Georgian squares and a vibrant cultural life. Belfast vies with Dublin in the vitality of its nightlife, while the cities of Cork and Galway have an energy and bustle that makes them a pleasure to visit.

When to go

Ireland's climate, determined by the pressure-systems of the Atlantic, is notoriously variable, and cannot be relied upon at any time of the year. Each year produces weeks of beautiful weather – the problem lies in predicting when they are likely to arrive. In recent years late spring and early autumn have seen some of the best of the weather, with May and September as the most pleasant months.

Geographically, the southeast is the driest and sunniest part of the country, and the northwest is the wettest. But regional variations are not particularly pronounced, the overall climate being characterized by its mildness – the country benefiting from the warming effects of the Gulf Stream. Even in the wetter zones, mornings of rain are frequently followed by afternoons of blue sky and sun – and besides, a downpour on a windswept headland can be exhilarating, and provides as good a pretext as any for repairing to the local pub, the hub of Irish social activity.

See overleaf for climate chart.

IRELAND'S CLIMATE

Average maximum and minimum daily temperatures (°C) and monthly rainfall (mm)

	Jan	Feb	Mar	Apr	May	Jun	Jul	Aug	Sep	Oct	Nov	Dec
Cork												
Max	9	9	11	13	16	19	20	20	18	14	11	9
Min	2	3	4	5	7	10	12	12	10	7	4	3
Rainfall	119	79	94	57	71	57	70	71	94	99	116	122
Dublin												
Max	8	8	10	13	15	18	20	19	17	14	10	8
Min	1	2	3	4	6	9	11	11	9	6	4	3
Rainfall	67	55	51	45	60	57	70	74	72	70	67	74
Valentia												
Max	9	9	11	13	15	17	18	18	17	14	12	10
Min	5	4	5	6	8	11	12	13	11	9	7	6
Rainfall	165	107	103	75	86	81	107	95	122	140	151	168

PART ONE

THE

BASICS

GETTING THERE FROM BRITAIN

Choosing how to travel to Ireland depends heavily on the amounts of time and money available for your trip. Unless you live near a ferry port the cheaper options of train and coach travel can involve a lengthy and sometimes arduous journey. Flying is the quicker alternative and there are usually cheap tickets available to most of the Republic's airports and, somewhat less so, to Northern Ireland. However, at the peak times of Easter, July, August and Christmas many of the low-cost fares may not apply or the few cheap seats may have been booked long in advance. It's worth looking out for deals advertised in one of the weekly newspapers catering for the Irish in Britain, such as the *Irish Post* or *Irish World*.

FLIGHTS

Flight time from London to the **Republic** is between an hour (to Dublin) and ninety minutes (to Cork, Knock, Shannon, Waterford and Kerry). The main carriers are Aer Lingus, which flies from ten UK airports, and its main Irish competitor, Ryanair, which flies from seven. **Northern Ireland** is similarly well served: British Airways and British Midland run frequent daily flights from London to Belfast (1hr 15min), and there are services from eighteen regional airports. You can also fly to Derry from Manchester and Glasgow. Bord Fáilte and the Northern Irish Tourist Board (see p.22 for details) provide information on all available routes – well worth getting before you plan your trip.

There are usually reductions for mid-week travel, though the astonishingly complex fare structures are constantly changing, so it's always a good idea to check the latest special deals direct with the airlines or with your local travel agent. After these, the cheapest fares are the ones usually called **Apex** (Advanced Purchase Excursion), available year round from most airlines. The conditions governing these tickets vary from airline to airline; however, most require that you stay one Saturday night, allow no changes and offer no refunds if you cancel your flight. A number of airlines have also introduced cheaper deals for two people flying together, for instance, Cityjet companion tickets from East Midlands Airport to Dublin can cost as little as £89 for two people. In general, it's a good idea to book as far in advance as possible, and especially so if you intend to travel during peak times and/or to one of the regional airports.

Return fares from **London to Dublin** with British Midland and Aer Lingus (from Heathrow) can cost as little as £79; with Cityjet (from London City Airport) from £85; with British Airways (from Gatwick) £81; and with Ryanair (from Gatwick, Stansted and Luton) £60. Flights from **London to Irish regional airports** are also good value. Tickets for Aer Lingus's Heathrow–Cork flights start at £89, Heathrow–Galway at £109, and Ryanair from Stansted to Knock or Cork from £80. AB Airlines flights from Gatwick, Stansted and Birmingham to Shannon start from £85.

Aer Lingus operates services from all the main **UK regional airports to Dublin**, from Newcastle for as little as £59 and from Birmingham, Leeds-Bradford, Manchester and Glasgow for £69 upwards. Ryanair also offers some good fares: from Liverpool or Prestwick from £55; from Manchester or Birmingham from £60. APEX tickets for Cityjet flights from East Midlands Airport to Dublin cost from £79. Suckling Airways flies twice weekly from Luton and three times a week from Cambridge to Waterford from late-July to the beginning of September with tickets costing from £115. Manx Airlines flies all year from Cardiff to Dublin from £70.

Flights from **London to Belfast** are also competitively priced. You can expect to pay £85 for a return flight from Heathrow to Belfast International with British Midland and a similar price with

British Airways. Additionally, Jersey European Airways runs services from Stansted to Belfast International from £85, from Gatwick to Belfast City from £84. They also fly Gatwick to Derry for around £130. A British Airways' standard return flight from Luton to Belfast City costs £90. From the **north of England**, British Airways operates flights from Manchester to Belfast International and to Derry both from £89. Gill Airways flies Newcastle–Belfast City from £99, and British Airways Liverpool–Belfast City from £80. From **Scotland**, British Airways flies Edinburgh–Belfast City from £108, Glasgow–Belfast City from £57 and Glasgow–Derry from £79.

AIRLINES

AB Airlines, Enterprise House, Stansted Airport, Essex CM24 1QW (☎0345/464748 or 0800/4588111).

Aer Lingus, 223 Regent St, London W1R 6LB (☎ 0645/737747). Other offices in Birmingham, Glasgow and Manchester.

British Airways, 156 Regent St, London W1R 6LB (☎0345/222111). Other offices in Birmingham, Manchester, Glasgow and Edinburgh.

British Midland Airways, Donington Hall, Castle Donington, Derby DE74 2SB (☎0345/554554).

Cityjet, London City Airport, The Royal Docks, London E16 2PX (☎0171/474 8888 or 0345/445588).

Gill Airways International, New Aviation House, Newcastle Airport, Newcastle-upon-Tyne NE13 8BT (☎0191/214 6666).

Jersey European Airways, Exeter Airport, Exeter, Devon EX5 2BD (☎0990/676676).

Manx Airlines, Ronaldsway Airport, Ballasalla, Isle of Man (☎0345/256256).

Ryanair, Enterprise House, Stansted Airport, Essex CM24 1QW (☎0541/569569).

Suckling Airways, Cambridge Airport, Newmarket Road, Cambridge CB5 8RT (☎01223/293393).

SPECIALIST TRAVEL AGENTS

Birmingham and West Midlands
Claddagh Travel, 199 High St, Erdington B23 6SY (☎0121/382 4803) and Fountain Court, Streethouse Lane B4 6DR (☎0121/200 3320); Ireland Direct, 115 Radford Rd, Coventry CV6 3BQ (☎0500/026385).

Bristol Thorntons Travel Service, 48/54 Baldwin St, BS1 1QP (☎01179/293211).

Edinburgh Sibbald Travel, 86 South Clerk St, EH8 9PT (☎0131/667 9172) and five other branches.

Glasgow Going Places, 66 Gordon St, G1 3TG (☎0141/221 5715); William Martin Travel, 184 Ingram St, G1 1ND (☎0141/552 5871).

Greater London Pat Carroll Travel, 260 Kilburn High Rd, NW6 2BY (☎0171/625 9669); Gerry Feeney Travel, 8 Centre Way, High Rd, Ilford IG1 1ND (☎0181/514 5141); Tara Travel, 240–242 High Rd, Kilburn NW6 2BS (☎0171/625 8601) and several other branches, including 758 Holloway Rd, N19 (☎0171/281 4171) and 75 High St, Lewisham SE13 (☎0181/318 7633).

Liverpool Towns Travel, 114 County Rd, L4 3QW (☎0151/733 1476); Wise Travel, 66 Allerton Rd L18 1NA (☎0151/733 1476).

Manchester Curry Travel, 139 Wilbraham Rd, Fallowfield M14 7DS (☎0161/225 1133); Irish Travel Bureau, 1 Marsland Rd, Sale Moor M33 3HP (☎0161/976 3887).

TOUR TRAVEL AGENTS

Usit Campus, 52 Grosvenor Gardens, London SW1W 0AG (☎0171/730 3402); other branches in Bristol, Birmingham, Brighton, Cambridge, Edinburgh, Manchester, Oxford and in YHA shops and on university campuses all over Britain. Also USIT offices in Ireland. *Student/youth travel specialists.*

STA Travel, 86 Old Brompton Rd, London SW7 3LH (☎0171/361 6161); other offices in Bristol, Cambridge, Manchester, Oxford, Leeds, Birmingham, Canterbury, Cardiff, Coventry, Durham, Glasgow, Loughborough, Nottingham, Warwick and Sheffield. *Specialists in low-cost flights and tours for students and under-26s.*

If you want to bring a **bike** with you, most airlines will allow you to do so and don't charge (except Ryanair; £15 extra each way), as long as you don't exceed your baggage allowance. It makes sense to ask if the airline carries bikes before buying your ticket. It's also worth informing them in advance and to check in early – particularly if you are travelling to a small regional airport or during peak times, since carrying bikes is subject to available space.

YOUTH AND STUDENT FARES

Although there are few reductions on offer and the definition of "youth" varies between airlines (anything from under-20 to under-25), it is always worth asking, especially if you want a return period of longer than a month or a one-way ticket only. Ryanair offers a good deal to any student with an International Student Identity Card (ISIC; see p.19 for more on special passes): you can buy a confirmed ticket on any of their routes for just £30.

If you are a student or **under 26** it's also worth checking fares through a specialist agency like STA or Usit Campus (see opposite for addresses).

FERRIES

In an attempt to compete with cheap air travel, ferry services have been considerably upgraded during the last few years. There are also catamaran or high-speed services on each of the main routes, Holyhead–Dún Laoghaire, Fishguard–Rosslare, Liverpool–Dublin, Cairnryan–Larne and Stranraer–Belfast, which cut sailing times almost in half (see box overleaf for companies, routes and times). If you need a car when you get to Ireland, bringing your own is the best option – car rental in Ireland is among the most expensive in Europe (see "Getting Around"; p.27).

Ferry prices vary enormously depending on the time of year and even the day and hour you travel. Most ferry companies have **peak seasons** of July, August and Christmas and some also operate higher fares on bank holidays. In summer, in particular, car and foot passengers should always book in advance or risk turning up and not getting on the boat. Generally, midweek crossings are cheaper throughout the year, and many companies offer special **off-peak deals**. Also bear in mind that prices are higher for the night-time crossings on some routes. In virtually all cases, bicycles are conveyed free of charge.

Generally, combined bus/ferry or train/ferry tickets (see pp.6–8) are good value.

The main crossing points to the Republic are from Holyhead on the Isle of Anglesey in North Wales and from Fishguard and Pembroke in southwest Wales. A standard return ticket for a car and five passengers on Stena Line's HSS service from **Holyhead to Dún Laoghaire** ranges from £208 to £408 in peak season and from £54 to £72 return for foot passengers. Stena's slower Superferry service and Irish Ferries also run from **Holyhead to Dublin Port**, both charging return fares from £158 to £318 for a car and five passengers. However, foot passengers are only carried on the Irish Ferries service – a return ticket costs £30. Again, Stena Line has two services plying the longer **Fishguard–Rosslare** route – the high-speed Lynx service (£178 to £418) and the Superferry (£108 to £298). Foot passenger tickets cost from £54 to £72 and £40 to £60 respectively. The range for the Irish Ferries service from **Pembroke to Rosslare** is again identical to Stena's Superferry, though its foot passenger rate is a standard £30 return.

The Isle of Man Steam Packet Company's Seacat catamaran service plies regularly between **Liverpool and Dublin Port**. Standard return fares for a car and four passengers range from £238 to £418. Foot passengers are charged from £50 to £70. Lastly, there's a ten-hour sailing between **Swansea and Cork** operated by Swansea–Cork Ferries. Return fares for a car and four adults cost from £150 to £378 and for foot passengers from £44 to £64. The fare for bicycles is £14 return. As ever, it's worth looking out for special offers – as little as £139 during off-peak times.

Most of the departure points for Northern Ireland are in southwest Scotland. The quickest option is the Seacat service from **Stranraer to Belfast** and standard return fares for a car and five passengers cover a range from £276 to £379. Stena Line also operates on this route, charging £240 to £320 for cars with prices varying according to season and whether you take the speedier HSS service. A little further north, P&O runs a service from **Cairnryan to Larne** in County Antrim, costing from £260 to £380 for a car and five passengers, with a similar seasonal variance and higher prices if you take the quicker Jetliner. Foot passenger rates for all of these services range between £45 and £55 return. The newest Scottish service is the Argyll and Antrim Steam Packet Company trip from **Campbeltown on the Mull**

FERRY COMPANIES, ROUTES AND TIMES

Argyll and Antrim Steam Packet Company,
Ballycastle Harbour, County Antrim
(☎0990/523523).
Campbeltown–Ballycastle (2 daily; 2hr 45min).

Irish Ferries, Reliance House, Water St,
Liverpool L2 8TP (☎0990/171717); 150 New Bond
St, London W1Y 0AQ (personal callers only).
Holyhead–Dublin Port (2 daily; 3hr 15min);
Pembroke–Rosslare (2 daily; 4hr).

Isle of Man Steam Packet Co., Room 323,
Third Floor, India Buildings, Water St, Liverpool
L2 0QN (☎0151/236 3411).
Liverpool–Dublin (1–2 daily; 3hr 55min).

Norse-Irish Ferries, North Brocklebank Dock,
Bootle, Merseyside L20 1BY (☎0151/944 1010).
Liverpool–Belfast (1 nightly; 1 Tues/Thurs/Sat
daytime; 11hr).

P&O European Ferries, Cairnryan, Stranraer,
Wigtownshire DG9 8RF (☎0990/980777).
Cairnryan–Larne (3–9 daily; Jetliner 1hr; Ferry
2hr 15min).

Seacat Scotland, Seacat Terminal, West Pier,
Stranraer, Wigtownshire DG9 7RE
(☎0990/523523).
Stranraer–Belfast (4–5 daily; 1hr 30min).

Stena Line, Charter House, Park St, Ashford,
Kent TN24 8EX (☎0990/707070).
Holyhead–Dún Laoghaire (4–5 daily; 1hr 40min);
Holyhead–Dublin Port (1–2 daily; 3hr 45min);
Fishguard–Rosslare (4–6 daily; Lynx 1hr 40min;
Ferry 3hr 30min); Stranraer–Larne (7–11 daily;
HSS 1hr 45min; Ferry 3hr 15min).

Swansea Cork Ferries, King's Dock, Swansea,
West Glamorgan (☎01792/456116).
Swansea–Cork (1 daily; 10hr).

TRAIN AND BUS COMPANIES

CIE, 185 London Rd, Croydon CR0 2RJ
(☎0181/686 0994). *Provides information on train*
and bus services in the Republic.

National Express Eurolines, 52 Grosvenor
Gardens, London SW1 (☎0171/730 8235).

National Rail Enquiry Service
(☎0345/484950).

Rail Europe Enquiry Service (☎0990/848848).

Ulsterbus Travel Centre, Europa Buscentre,
Belfast BT12 5AH (☎01232/337002; ☎028/9033
7002 from April 2000).

Yorkshire Bikeliner, Box 1, Carlton House,
307–311 Annlaby Rd, Kingston-upon-Hull, HU3
2SB (☎01482/222122).

of Kintyre to Ballycastle in County Antrim.
There are two departures daily in each direction
from the middle of June to the middle of October,
but only at weekends at other times, and in winter services may be restricted by treacherous
tides. Prices begin at £99 for a car and two adults
in low season rising to £323 for a car and five
adults in high season. Foot passenger rates are
between £46 and £50 return. Finally, Norse Irish
Ferries operates an overnight service from
Liverpool to Belfast. Fares for a car and four
adults cost from £210 to a hefty £596 in high season, though for this you get a cabin, four-course
dinner and breakfast. Foot passengers are
charged from £78 to £106 return with supplementary charges for cabins, if required. Prices on the
daytime sailing are significantly cheaper (£170 to
£310 for a car and four adults, £60 to £70 for foot
passengers) and there are special deals for
Tuesday and Thursday sailings. Advance booking
is usually essential for this route.

Student reductions on ferries can be considerable. P&O charge only £22 to £40 for the
Cairnryan–Larne crossing, Stena Line £34 to £40
and Seacat £28 to £31 for Stranraer–Belfast.
Savings on fares from Holyhead, Liverpool,
Pembroke and Fishguard are generally between
£6 to £8 on the standard fare. Lastly, student fares
from Campbeltown to Ballycastle range from £28
to £30. Reductions are also available for members
of youth hostel organizations (see pp.31–32).

TRAINS

Prices of combined train/sea tickets vary according to departure time and season. It's usually
more expensive to travel in the daytime and during the peak periods of Easter, July, August,
Christmas and bank holidays. The return fare
from **London to Dublin** ranges from £41 up to
£61; from Manchester prices start at £31 and
from Glasgow at £51. **London to Belfast** via

Dublin is £53 to £83 return; **Birmingham to Belfast** is £48 to £73. Simply book at a mainline station or travel agent.

Anyone **under 26** can get one-third off standard train fares by buying a Young Person's Railcard (£18) from any train station or at branches of Usit Campus (see p.4).

An **InterRail** pass (£259 for a month) is unlikely to be worth buying when travelling to Ireland; although the pass gives free train travel in the Republic, it doesn't include trains in mainland Britain or Northern Ireland. For train passes valid for travel in Ireland only, see "Getting Around", p.24.

TOUR OPERATORS

Aer Lingus Holidays (☎0181/899 4747 London; ☎0645/737747 outside London). *Dublin, Cork and Galway city holidays, coastal and country weekend breaks with accommodation, ranging from B&Bs to four-star hotels. Good fly-drive deals.*

Celtic Journeys, 6 Turnberry Mews, Portstewart, Co. Derry BT55 7SA (☎01265/836448; ☎028/7083 6448 from April 2000). *Six- to nine- day walking, conservation and study trips in the north and west of Ireland.*

Conservation Volunteers Northern Ireland, 159 Ravenhill Rd, Belfast BT6 0BP (☎01232/645169; ☎028/9064 5169 from April 2000). *Spend a week or weekend learning conservation skills, such as dry-stone walling, woodland management and wildflower planting.*

Cresta Holidays, Tabley Court, Victoria St, Altrincham, Cheshire WA14 1EZ (☎0161/926 9999). *Vast range of hotel and cottage holidays, river cruising, horse-drawn caravans, walking and golfing packages.*

Drive Ireland, 311 Tower Building, Water St, Liverpool L3 1AS (☎0151/231 1480). *Combined flight/accommodation/car rental deals.*

Flanagan & Sons World Travel, 115 Radford Rd, Coventry CV6 (☎0500/026385). *Specialists in angling holidays at competitive rates. They also arrange combined ferry/flight and accommodation.*

Gerry Feeney Travel Ltd, 8 Centre Way, High Rd, Ilford, Essex IG1 1ND (☎0181/514 5141). *Fly- and ferry-drive packages, self-catering and coach tours.*

Go Ireland, Killorglin, Co. Kerry (☎66/976 2094 or 0800/371203). *Guided walking holidays in Kerry, Connemara, Donegal and elsewhere; semi-guided cycling tours; specialist golfing holidays.*

Ireland Golf, Clogherbrien, Tralee, Co. Kerry (☎66/23733). *Upmarket golfing holidays.*

Irish Cycling Safaris, 7 Dartry Park, Dublin 6 (☎1/260 0749). *Well-organized one-week guided tours for cyclists of all abilities in prime areas along the west coast from Cork to Donegal, with luggage van and hotel/guesthouse accommoda-*

tion.

Irish Ferries Holidays, Reliance House, Water St, Liverpool L2 8TP (☎0990/170000). *Competitively priced car rental available in its sail-drive and fly-drive packages, with a broad range of accommodation options. Also golfing, fishing and cruising all-in holidays. Under-16s travel free.*

Leisure Breaks, 33 Dovedale Rd, Liverpool L18 5EP (☎0151/734 5200). *Very good range of activity holidays including riding, cycling, horse-drawn caravanning. Also accommodation and ferry deals and fly-drive packages.*

Murphy's Way, 12 Belvoir Close, Belfast BT8 4PL (☎01232/693232; ☎028/9069 3232 from April 2000). *Walking and specialist wildlife holidays in Northern Ireland.*

Rural Cottage Holidays, St Anne's Court, 59 North St, Belfast BT1 1NB (☎01232/241110; ☎028/9024 1110 from April 2000). *Northern Ireland Tourist Board subsidiary offering reasonably-priced, high standard, self-catering accommodation, often traditional cottages, in the Glens of Antrim, the Mournes, the Sperrins and Fermanagh Lakelands.*

Slattery's, 162 Kentish Town Rd, London NW5 2AG (☎0171/485 1438 or 0800/515900). *Full range of transport (flight, ferries and bus travel, plus motoring holidays) and accommodation deals (hotels, country houses and self-catering). Also horse-drawn caravans and rambling with a donkey.*

Stena Line Holidays, Stena Line Ltd, Charter House, Park St, Ashford, Kent TN24 8EX (☎0990/747474). *Full range of ferry, fly-drive, accommodation and self-catering packages. Under-16s travelling with a family in a car go free.*

Swansea Cork Ferries, King's Dock, Swansea, West Glamorgan (☎01792/456116). *Activity holidays, self-catering packages in Cork and Kerry, go-as-you-please tours.*

BUSES

Getting to Ireland by bus is a slog, but very cheap. The main services are provided by National Express Eurolines which operates a daily and nightly service from **London to Dublin** via Birmingham throughout the year with extra departures from May to October and over the Christmas period. The trip takes between eleven and thirteen hours, depending on the speed of the ferry, and costs from £29 return rising to £39 at peak times for the daytime service and from £36 increasing to a maximum £49 for the night trip. A host of **connecting services** is available from Dublin (costing from £46 to £55 no matter how far you travel) or there are daily direct services from London via Birmingham to Galway, Westport, Ballina and Sligo (all £49 to £59 return). Other Eurolines services to Dublin run daily from: Leicester via Nottingham; Leeds via Manchester and Liverpool; Bristol via Wolverhampton. There are also daily runs from London and Birmingham to Cork, Limerick and Tralee using the Pembroke crossing (£49 to £65), and connections are available at Rosslare (to Dublin), Waterford (to Kilkenny and Carlow) Cork (to Kinsale) and Limerick (to Roscrea and Ennis). There are reductions for **under-25s** on all night-time services, varying between £3 and £8 depending on the departure point and time of year. Tickets for Euroline services can be bought from the head office (see p.6), National Express Coach Stations in Birmingham, Leeds, Liverpool and Manchester, or from any travel agent acting as a National Express agent. Yorkshire Bikeliner runs a weekly Friday evening service from the end of May to mid-September from **Hull to Dublin**, Galway, Ennis and Limerick costing £98 to £110 per passenger and cycle.

Getting to the North by bus is a little more expensive. Ulsterbus operates the following routes via Stranraer: from **London to Belfast** via Birmingham (£48 return; 11–12 hr); from Birmingham via Manchester (£47; 11hr); from Edinburgh via Glasgow (£36 return; 7hr). Tickets can be purchased from National Express at Victoria Coach Station, London or UK travel agents acting as National Express or Scottish Citylink agents.

PACKAGE HOLIDAYS

If you are looking for a specific holiday activity (such as angling, cycling, walking or golfing), heading for a busy festival or simply want to avoid the hassle of making your own arrangements, there are numerous package deals available from tour operators. If you intend to rent a car, it's worth considering the various fly-drive and sail-drive offers available and the ferry companies often offer good packages including accommodation.

GETTING THERE FROM THE USA AND CANADA

Ireland is easily accessible from the USA by a number of airlines that offer direct flights to the major gateways of Dublin, Shannon and Belfast. From Canada only indirect flights are available. Ferries and cheap flights also make Ireland easily accessible as part of a wider European travel itinerary.

SHOPPING FOR TICKETS

Leaving aside discounted tickets, the cheapest way to go is with an **Apex** (Advance Purchase Excursion) ticket, although these carry certain restrictions: you will probably have to book – and pay – 21 days before departure (though to get the very cheapest fares on certain routes, you may need to book ninety days in advance, spend at least seven days abroad (maximum stay three months), and you tend to get penalized if you change your schedule. There are also winter **Super-Apex** tickets, sometimes known as Eurosavers – slightly cheaper than an ordinary Apex, but limiting your stay to between seven and 21 days. Some airlines also issue **Special Apex** tickets to those under 24, often extending the maximum stay to a year. Many airlines offer youth or **student fares** to under 25s; a passport or driving licence is sufficient proof of age, though these tickets are subject to availability and can have eccentric booking conditions. It's worth remembering that most cheap return fares involve spending at least one Saturday night away and that many will only give a percentage refund if you need to cancel or alter your journey, so make

sure you check the restrictions carefully before buying a ticket. Any local travel agent should be able to access up-to-the-minute fares, although in practice they may not have time to research all the possibilities – you might want to call the airlines directly.

Discount outlets, however, can usually do better than any Apex and most student fares. They come in several forms. **Consolidators** buy up large blocks of tickets that airlines don't think they'll be able to sell at their published prices, and sell them at a discount. Besides being cheap, consolidators normally don't impose advance purchase requirements (although in busy times you'll want to book ahead just to be sure of getting a ticket), but they do often charge very stiff fees for date changes. Also, these companies' margins are pretty tiny, so they make their money by dealing in volume – don't expect them to entertain lots of questions. **Discount agents** – such as STA, Council Travel, Nouvelles Frontières, or others listed on p.10 – also wheel and deal in blocks of tickets off-loaded by the airlines, but they typically offer a range of other travel-related services such as travel insurance, train passes, youth and student ID cards, car rentals and tours. These agencies tend to be most worthwhile to students and under-26s, who can often benefit from special fares and deals.

Travel clubs are another option for those who travel a lot – most charge you an annual membership fee, which may be worth it for discounts on air tickets, car rental and the like. You should also check the travel section in the Sunday *New York Times*, or your own major local newspaper, for current bargains, and consult a good travel agent.

AIRLINES IN NORTH AMERICA

Air Canada ☎1-800/776-3000.

Aer Lingus ☎1-800/223-6537 or 212/557-1110.

American Airlines ☎1-800/433-7300.

British Airways US ☎1-800/247-9297; Canada ☎1-800/668-1059.

Delta Airlines US ☎1-800/241-4141 or 404/765-5000.

United Airlines ☎1-800/538-2929.

Virgin Atlantic Airways ☎1-800/862-8621.

DISCOUNT AGENTS, CONSOLIDATORS AND TRAVEL CLUBS

Air Brokers International, 150 Post St, Suite 620, San Francisco, CA 94108 (☎1-800/883-3273 or 415/397-1383; *www.airbrokers.com*). *Consolidator and specialist in RTW tickets.*

Airtech, 588 Broadway, Suite 204, New York, NY 10017 (☎1-800/575-8324 or 212/219-7000; *www.airtech.com*). *Standby seat broker; also deals in consolidator fares and courier flights.*

Air Courier Association, 191 University Blvd, Suite 300, Denver, CO 80206 (☎1-800/282-1202 or 303/215-0900; *www.aircourier.org*). *Courier flight broker.*

Council Travel, Head Office, 205 E 42nd St, New York, NY 10017 (☎1-800/226-8624, or 212/822-2700). Other offices in San Francisco, Los Angeles, Washington, Boston. *Nationwide US organization. Mostly, but by no means exclusively, specializes in student travel.*

Educational Travel Center, 438 N Frances St, Madison, WI 53703 (☎1-800/747-5551). *Student/youth discount agent.*

International Association of Air Travel Couriers, 8 South J St, PO Box 1349, Lake Worth, FL 33460 (☎561/582-8320; *www.courier.org*). *Courier flight broker.*

High Adventure Travel, 353 Sacramento St, Suite 600, San Francisco, CA 94111 (☎1-800/350-0612 or 415/912-5600; *www.highadv.com*). *RTW tickets. Web site features interactive database that lets you build and price your own RTW itinerary.*

New Frontiers/Nouvelles Frontières, 12 E 33rd St, New York, NY 10016 (☎1-800/366-6387 or 212/779-0600); 1001 Sherbrook East, Suite 720, Montréal, PQ H2L 1L3 (☎514/526-8444). *French discount travel firm, mostly to Europe. Other branches in LA, San Francisco and Quebec City.*

Now Voyager, 74 Varick St, Suite 307, New York, NY 10013 (☎212/431-1616). *Courier-flight broker and consolidator.*

STA Travel, 10 Downing St, New York, NY 10014 (☎1-800/777-0112 or 212/627-3111). Other offices in Los Angeles, San Francisco, Boston, Chicago, Philadelphia, Minneapolis, etc. *Specialists in independent travel.*

TFI Tours International, 34 W 32nd St, New York, NY 10001(☎1-800/745-8000 or 212/736-1140). *Consolidator.*

Travac, 989 Sixth Ave, New York, NY 10018 (☎1-800/872-8800). *Consolidator and charter broker mostly to Europe; has another office in Orlando.*

Travel Avenue, 10 S Riverside, Suite 1404, Chicago, IL 60606 (☎1-800/333-3335). *Discount travel company.*

Travel Cuts, 187 College St, Toronto, ON M5T 1P7 (☎1-800/667-2887 or 416/979-2406). Other offices in Calgary, Montréal, Vancouver, Winnipeg, etc. *Canadian student travel organization.*

Uni Travel, 11737 Administration Drive, St Louis, MO 63146 (☎1-800/325-2222 or 314/569-0900). *Consolidator.*

Be advised also that the pool of travel companies is swimming with sharks – exercise caution with any outfit that sounds shifty or impermanent, and *never* deal with a company that demands cash up front or refuses to accept payment by credit card.

Regardless of where you buy your ticket, the **fare** will depend on **season**. Although these may vary from airline to airline, as a general rule, fares to Ireland are highest from the beginning of June through September and from December 12 to 31; they drop during the "shoulder" seasons, the beginning of October to around December 12; and you'll get the best deals during the low season, January through May. If you want to travel during the Christmas–New Year period, book at least two or three months ahead.

A further possibility is to see if you can arrange a **courier flight**, although the hit-or-miss nature of these makes them most suitable for the single traveller who travels light and has a very flexible schedule. In return for shepherding a parcel through customs and possibly giving up your baggage allowance, you can expect to get a heavily discounted ticket. The duration of your stay is also likely to be restricted. A couple of courier "associations" (courier-flight brokers) are listed in the box above.

Prices quoted are round-trip, assume midweek travel (add on $50–75 for weekends), exclude taxes (around $50–100) and are subject to availability and change.

Flying time from New York is approximately five hours thirty minutes to Dublin and seven hours to Belfast.

FLIGHTS FROM THE USA

Aer Lingus, the national airline of Ireland, flies direct out of **Boston** and **New York** to both **Dublin** and **Shannon**. The APEX fares out of the East Coast to both these cities are roughly the same: starting at approximately $320 (low season) or $530 (high season). **From Chicago** the fares are around $430 (low season) or $650 (high). Also be on the lookout for Aer Lingus' special limited promotional fares, such as their two seats for the price of one offer, which crop up from time to time, most likely in the off-season, and are advertised in national newspapers. As always, a reputable discount agent, such as Council Travel or STA, should be able to sift through all the available fares and find one that best suits your particular travel requirements.

Of the **US airlines** that operate services direct to the Republic, Delta flies from **Atlanta** to both Shannon and Dublin. Their cheapest Apex fares range from approximately $525 (low season) to $860 (high).

SPECIALIST TOUR OPERATORS

All prices quoted exclude taxes and are subject to change. Accommodation is based on single person/double occupancy. Unless stated otherwise, round-trip flights are from New York.

Aer Lingus Vacations ☎1-800/223-6537. *Airline tour department.*

Adventures Abroad ☎1-800/665-3998 or 604/303-1099; www.adventures-abroad.com. *Specialists in small group tours. One week in Northern Ireland or the Republic from $1895; two week combo from $2996.*

Art Horizons International ☎212/969-9410. *Customized art and architecture tours.*

Backroads ☎1-800/GO-ACTIVE,462-2848 or 510/527-1555; www.backroads.com. *Eight days cycling in Co. Cork and Co. Kerry from $2798 plus $150 bike rental; six days walking from $2398 (both land only).*

Brian Moore International Tours ☎1-800/ 982-2299. *Wide range of products. Fly-drives, escorted tours plus customized chauffeur-driven tours, weddings, honeymoons, St Patrick's Day parades, gourmet, walking, horseback-riding etc.*

Castles, Cottages and Flats ☎1-800/742-6030 or 617/742-6030. *Realize your fantasies of living in a medieval castle for roughly $750–1000 per person, per night (land only). Plus other less exotic options.*

Celtic International Tours ☎1-800/833-4373. *Customized packages, motor coach tours, fly-drives etc.*

CIE Tours International ☎1-800/CIE-TOUR or 973/292-3899. *Fly-drives, city breaks, coach tours etc. Three nights in Dublin from $319 (land only). Six-night "Irish Welcome" B&B/hotel and coach trip from $1258 (land/air).*

Classic Adventures (formerly Classic Bicycle Tours & Treks) ☎1-800/777-8090. *Fully escorted biking tours in the southwest from $1449 for one week plus $100 bike rental (land only).*

Contiki Holidays ☎1-800/CONTIKI or 466-0610. *Group tours for 18–35 year-olds. Nine days in the Republic of Ireland with optional two-night London add-on from $1235 (land/air).*

Destinations Ireland & Great Britain ☎1-800/832-1848. *Flexible range of travel products. Five nights B&B/guesthouse plus car hire in Belfast from $319 or in Dublin from $465.*

Distinctive Journeys ☎1-800/922-2060. *Customized deluxe packages to Ireland.*

Fishing International ☎1-800/950-4242 or 707/542-4242. *Three nights/two days salmon fishing in the Moy River with deluxe castle accommodation, breakfast, licence, instruction and fishing gear for $980 (land only).*

Golf International ☎1-800/833-1389. *Several packages, including seven days golfing in Ballybunion and Lahinch from $1500 (land only).*

International Gay Travel Association ☎1-800/448-8550. *Trade group with lists of gay-owned or gay-friendly travel agents, accommodation and other travel businesses.*

Irish American International Tours ☎1-800/633-0505. *Group and individual customized packages, car rental, hotels, B&B, airline tickets, family reunions, winter pub tours etc.*

Irish Festival Tours ☎1-800/441-4277. *Tours hosted by entertainers, winter pub crawls etc.*

Isle Inn Tours ☎1-800/237-9376. *Irish travel specialists. Cycling, walking, cruising, B&B etc. Two-berth boat on the River Shannon from $639 per week rental. Seven-day/six-night B&B plus car rental from $269 (both land only).*

Owenoak International ☎1-800/426-4498. *Customized tours and golf trips.*

Saga Holidays ☎1-800/343-0273. *Specialists in group travel for seniors. "Around the Emerald Isle" fifteen-night escorted coach tour from $2599; "Romantic Ireland" eight-night escorted coach tour from $1599 (both land only).*

A number of carriers also fly **direct to Belfast**. Aer Lingus flies several days a week from New York. Fares start at approximately $350 in low season, $550 in high season.

From the **West Coast** there's less choice direct to the Republic or the North and you might find it cheaper and more convenient flying via London. The big airlines fly at least three times a week (sometimes daily) from Los Angeles, San Francisco and Seattle. British Airways has plenty of flights and is competitive, with fares starting at around $750 (low season) or $1050 (high season) to London. However, Delta does have a service from LA to Dublin or Shannon costing approximately $580 (low season) or $960 (high season).

FLIGHTS FROM CANADA

Aer Lingus does not fly out of **Canada**, but **Air Canada** flies indirect (with a change of plane in London) out of Toronto, Montréal and Vancouver to Dublin, Shannon and Belfast. Apex-type tickets from Toronto and Montréal to Dublin and Shannon are around Can$900 (low season) or Can$1190 (high season) and Can$1015 (low) or Can$1345 (high) to Belfast. From Vancouver, expect to pay around Can$1170 (low) or Can$1460 (high) to Dublin or Shannon and Can$1245 (low) or Can$1615 (high) to Belfast.

For more options and potential for bargain fares, it may be worth considering flying to London first. British Airways flies from Toronto to London for around Can$725 (low season) or Can$975 (high season) and from Vancouver to London for roughly Can$960 (low) or Can$1200 (high). The add-on to the Republic or the North is around Can$150. But be warned that the fares for this last leg of the journey may come with more restrictions than the transatlantic tickets, especially with regard to changing your travel plans.

The actual flying time to Dublin from Toronto is approximately eight hours and from Vancouver between ten and eleven hours.

EUROPEAN RAIL PASSES FOR NORTH AMERICAN AND AUSTRALASIAN TRAVELLERS

There are a number of European rail passes that can only be purchased before leaving home, though consider carefully how much travelling you are going to be doing: these all-encompassing passes only really begin to pay for themselves if you intend to see a fair bit of Ireland and the rest of Europe.

The best-known and most flexible is the **Eurail Youthpass** (for under-26s) which costs US$376/A$678 for fifteen consecutive days, and there are also one-month and two-month versions; over-26's can buy a first-class version for US$538/A$970 for the fifteen-day option. You stand a better chance of getting your money's worth out of a **Eurail Flexipass**, which is good for a certain number of travel days in a two-month period. This, too, comes in under-26/first-class versions: ten days cost US$444/A$800 for under-26s, US$634/A$1143 for over 26s, though it also comes in fifteen-day formats. These passes can be bought from the agents listed below and also from many regular travel agents, especially youth and student specialists (see listings on p.10 and p.14).

North Americans and Australasians are also eligible to purchase **more specific passes** valid for travel in Ireland only – see "Getting Around", pp.25, for details.

RAIL CONTACTS IN NORTH AMERICA

CIE – Irish Rail and Bus Line (☎1-800/CIE-TOUR or 973/292-3899).

CIT Tours, 9501 W. Devon Ave, Suite 502, Rosemont, IL 60018 (☎1-800/223-7987).

Euro Vacations (☎1-888/281-EURO).

Rail Europe (☎1-800/438-7245 in US; ☎1-800/555-2748 in Canada).

RAIL CONTACTS IN AUSTRALASIA

CIT, 263 Clarence St, Sydney (☎02/9267 1255 or 9299 4754); offices in Melbourne, Adelaide, Brisbane and Perth Comprehensive range of rail passes. No NZ office – enquiries and reservations via Australian offices.

PACKAGES

Package tours may not sound like your kind of travel, but don't dismiss the idea out of hand. It's true that tours arranged in North America tend to be of the everybody-on-the-bus group variety, but many agents can put together very flexible deals, sometimes amounting to no more than a flight plus car or train pass and accommodation. If you're planning to travel in moderate or luxury style, and especially if your trip is geared around special interests, a package can work out cheaper than the same arrangements made on arrival. A package can also ensure a worry-free first week while you're finding your feet on a longer tour (of course, you can jump off the itinerary any time you like). Most companies will expect you to book through a local travel agent, and, since it costs the same, you might as well do that.

A variety of short excursions and specialized tours to Ireland are available from a number of organizations, including Aer Lingus, which offers a range of **fly-drive packages**. CIE Tours International is a good general operator to Ireland and also sells train passes. Other special-interest operators are listed on p.11.

For students, programmes combining work and study with travel to Ireland are available from: The Irish American Cultural Institute, 1 Lackawanna Place, Morristown, NJ 07960 (☎1-800/232-ERIN or 973/605-1991); The Council on International Education Exchange, 205 East 42nd Street, New York, NY 10017 (☎1-888/COUNCIL); The Humanities Institute, 533A Putnam Ave, Cambridge, MA 02139 (☎1-800/754-9991); and The American Institute for Foreign Study, College Division, 102 Greenwich Ave, Greenwich, CT 06830 (☎1-800/727-2437 or 203/869-9090. For general information and publications about studying abroad, try contacting the Institute of International Education, 809 UN Plaza, New York, NY 10017 (☎212/883-8200).

GETTING THERE FROM AUSTRALIA AND NEW ZEALAND

There are no direct scheduled or charter flights to Ireland from Australia or New Zealand; all require a transfer, often at a London terminal. Fares from both Australia and New Zealand are "common rated", so there's no price difference between the main airlines, but they do vary significantly with the seasons. For most major airlines, low season is from mid-January to February

28 and October to November 30, and high from mid-May to August 31 and December 10 to mid-January (shoulder seasons cover the rest of the year). There's no variation in price during the week. The prices quoted below are low-season discounted fares. On top of these you can expect to pay between A$200 and A$400 in shoulder season and A$500 and A$700 in high season.

From **Australia** there are numerous indirect flights to Ireland via Heathrow: Singapore Airlines-British Midland/Aer Lingus offer several flights a week to **Dublin** and **Belfast** from Sydney, Melbourne, Brisbane and Perth for around A$1885. At the time of writing, KLM (to Dublin, Belfast and Cork from Sydney via Amsterdam) is offering a special of A$1320 and a regular low-season fare of A$1650. Malaysia Airlines-British Midland operate services several times a week to Belfast from Sydney, Melbourne, Brisbane and Perth via Kuala Lumpur (around A$1875), and British Airways via Singapore (around A$1885).

From **New Zealand**, indirect flights from Auckland to Dublin are offered by Singapore Airlines-Aer Lingus via Singapore several times a week (around NZ$2600); and via the US, Air New Zealand-Aer Lingus fly to Dublin four times a week (around NZ$2300). Malaysia Airlines-British Midland run services to **Belfast** twice weekly via Kuala Lumpur and Heathrow (around NZ$2300).

In addition to these airlines Qantas, Thai Airways, Japan Airlines and Cathay Pacific include free European **side trips** that can be used to get to Ireland from Australia or New Zealand. **Flying to London** is a worthwhile option, if you pick up one of the cheap deals offered by some carriers in low season – for example, A$1400 from Australia with Malaysia Airlines. The add-on fare to destinations in Ireland is around

AIRLINES

Aer Lingus, World Aviation Systems, 64 York St, Sydney (☎02/9321 9123); 6th Floor, 229 Queen St, Auckland (☎09/379 4455).

Air New Zealand, 5 Elizabeth St, Sydney (☎02/9223 4666; reservations ☎13/2476); Queen St, Auckland (☎09/366 2424).

British Airways, 64 Castlereagh St, Sydney (☎02/9258 3300); 154 Queen St, Auckland (☎09/356 8690).

British Midland, US Airways (agent in Australia), 140 Arthur St, North Sydney (☎02/9959 3922); Discover the World Marketing (agent in New Zealand), no address, Auckland (☎09/623 4294).

Cathay Pacific, Sydney Airport (☎02/9931 5500; reservations ☎13/1747); 11th Floor, 205–209 Queen St, Auckland (☎09/379 0861 or 0800/800 454).

Japan Airlines, 14th Floor, 201 Sussex St, Sydney (☎02/9272 1111); Floor 12, Westpac Tower, 120 Albert St, Auckland (☎09/379 9906).

KLM, Level 6, 5 Elizabeth St, Sydney (☎02/9231 6333 or 1800/505747). No NZ office.

Malaysia Airlines, 16 Spring St, Sydney (☎02/9364 3535; reservations ☎13/2627); 12th Floor, The Swanson Centre, 12–26 Swanson St, Auckland (☎09/373 2741).

Qantas, 70 Hunter St, Sydney (☎02/9951 4294; reservations ☎13/1211); Qantas House, 154 Queen St, Auckland (☎09/357 8900 or 0800/808 767).

Singapore Airlines, 17–19 Bridge St, Sydney (☎02/9350 0121; reservations ☎13/1011); Lower Ground Floor, West Plaza Building, cnr Customs and Albert streets, Auckland (☎09/379 3209 or 0800/808 909).

Thai Airways, 75–77 Pitt St, Sydney (☎02/9251 1922; reservations ☎13/1960); Kensington Swan Building, 22 Fanshawe St, Auckland (☎09/377 3886).

DISCOUNT AGENTS

AUSTRALIA

Anywhere Travel, 345 Anzac Parade, Kingsford, Sydney (☎02/9663 0411).

Flight Centres, 82 Elizabeth St, Sydney (☎02/9229 6611), plus branches nationwide. For nearest branch call ☎13/1600.

Northern Gateway, 22 Cavenagh St, Darwin (☎08/8941 1394).

Passport Travel, 401 St Kilda Rd, Melbourne (☎03/9867 3888).

STA Travel, 855 George St, Sydney (☎02/9212 1255; toll-free or 1-800/637 444), plus branches nationwide. For nearest branch, call ☎13/1776.

Thomas Cook, 175 Pitt St, Sydney (☎02/9229 6611).

Topdeck Travel, 65 Grenfell St, Adelaide (☎08/8232 7222).

Tymtro Travel, 428 George St, Sydney (☎02/9223 2211).

UTAG Travel Agents, 122 Walker St, North Sydney (☎02/9956 8399); branches throughout Australia.

NEW ZEALAND

Budget Travel, Floor 5, Waterhouse Centre, 66 Wyndham St, Auckland (☎09/307 1888); branches throughout New Zealand.

Gulliver's Travel, Floor 5, Waterhouse Centre, 66 Wyndham St.

Flight Centres, National Bank Towers, 205–225 Queen St, Auckland (☎09/309 6171); other branches countrywide.

STA Travel, Traveller's Centre, 10 High St, Auckland (☎09/309 0458); offices throughout New Zealand.

Thomas Cook, 159 Queen St, Auckland (☎09/379 3924); other branches nationwide.

TOUR OPERATORS

Adventure World (wholesaler), 73 Walker St, North Sydney (☎02/9956 7766 or 1800 221 931); 101 Great South Rd, Remuera, Auckland (☎09/524 5118). *Agents for CIE bus tours, motoring holidays, Dublin city breaks and a range of car-accommodation packages.*

European Travel Office (wholesaler), 122 Rosslyn St, West Melbourne (☎03/9329 8844); 407 Great South Rd, Remuera, Auckland (☎09/525 3074). *Tours, car rental and accommodation for the independent traveller.*

Eblana Travel, Level 4, 67 Castlereagh St, Sydney (☎02/9232 8144). *A wide selection of Irish accommodation packages and tours.*

Wiltrans Australia, Level 10, 151 Macquarie St, Sydney (☎02/9255 0899). *Agents for Maupintour's luxury all-inclusive fifteen-day bus tours of Ireland, staying in premier hotels and medieval castles.*

A\$150/NZ\$170. See p.14 for details of discount agents who supply low-cost tickets.

If you are considering a **package holiday**, many agents can put together very flexible deals (amounting to no more than a flight plus car or train pass and accommodation) and special-interests **tours** (such as walking, cycling or staying in historic country houses). See above for details of tour operators.

For information on **European train passes** that you buy before you leave, see the box on p.12.

VISAS, CUSTOMS REGULATIONS AND TAX

British nationals born in the UK do not need a passport to enter the Republic or the North, but it is useful to carry one in case you use the medical services, and for cashing travellers' cheques. If you don't take a passport, be sure to have some other form of convincing ID. UK passport holders *not* born in Great Britain or Northern Ireland must have a valid passport or national identity document. If you are a British national of Indian, Pakistani, Bangladeshi, Far Eastern or African descent, it is advisable to take along your passport (or your birth certificate), in spite of the fact that, technically speaking, you don't need one.

If you are an EU national, you can enter the **Republic** with either a national ID card or a passport, and you are entitled to stay for as long as you like. Travellers from the USA, Canada, Australia and New Zealand are simply required to show a passport and can stay for up to three months. After this you'll need to apply to the nearest superintendent's office in the Garda Siochana (police) in the district in which you intend to stay; in Dublin apply to the Aliens Registration Office, Harcourt Street (☎01/475 5555). All other visitors to the Republic should contact the Irish Embassy in advance as regulations vary.

In the **North**, British regulations apply. This means that citizens of all the countries of Europe (except Albania, Bulgaria, Romania and the republics of the former Soviet Union, with the exception of the Baltic states) can enter Northern Ireland with just a passport or national ID card for up to six months. UK and Irish citizens need no ID or passport. US, Canadian, Australian and New Zealand citizens

EMBASSIES AND CONSULATES

IRISH

Britain, 17 Grosvenor Place, London SW1X 7HR (☎0171/235-2171).

Australia, 20 Arkana St, Yarralumla, Canberra, ACT 2600 (☎02/62733022).

Canada, 130 Albert St, Suite 1105, Ottawa, ON K1P 5G4 (☎613/223-6281).

New Zealand, 2nd Floor, Dingwall Building, Queen St, Auckland (☎09/302-2867).

United States, 2234 Massachusetts Ave NW, Washington, DC 20008 (☎202/462-3939); 345 Park Ave, 17th Floor, New York, NY 10154 (☎212/319-2552); 535 Boylston St, Boston, MA 02116 (☎617/267-9330); 400 N Michigan Ave, Chicago, IL 60611 (☎312/337-1868); 44 Montgomery St, Suite 3830, San Francisco, CA 94104 (☎415/392-4214).

BRITISH

Australia, (High Commission), Commonwealth Ave, Yarralumla, Canberra, ACT 2600 (☎02/6257 1982).

Canada (High Commission), 80 Elgin St, Ottawa, ON K1P 5K7 (☎613/237-1530).

Ireland, 29 Merrion Rd, Dublin 4 (☎01/205-3700).

New Zealand (High Commission), 44 Hill St, Wellington (☎04/472-6049 or 472-6056).

United States, 3100 Massachusetts Ave NW, Washington, DC 20008 (☎202/588-6500).

---

can enter the country for up to six months with just a passport, provided they have an onward or return ticket and evidence of sufficient funds to support themselves for the duration of their stay. Citizens of all other nationalities require a visa, obtainable from the British Consular office in the country of application. For stays of longer than six months, US, Canadian, Australian and New Zealand citizens should apply to the British Embassy or High Commission (see above). If you wish to extend your visa, you should write, before the expiry date given on the endorsement in your passport to: The Undersecretary of State, Home Office, Immigration and Nationality Department, Lunar House, 40 Wellesley Rd, Croydon CR9 2BY.

Travellers coming into the Republic or the North directly from another EU country do not have to make a declaration to **customs** at their place of entry and can effectively bring almost as much wine or beer as they like. However, there are still strict restrictions – details of which are prominently displayed in all duty-free outlets – on tax- or duty-free goods, so you can't invest in a stockpile of cheap cigarettes, wherever you're coming from.

There are import restrictions on a variety of articles and substances, from firearms to furs derived from endangered species, none of which should bother the average tourist. Visitors from mainland Britain can bring pets into the North and the Republic; animals brought from elsewhere overseas are subject to tight quarantine restrictions.

Throughout Ireland most goods are subject to **Value Added Tax** (VAT) at 17.36 percent in the Republic and 17.5 percent in the North. Visitors from non-EU countries can save a lot of money through the Retail Export Scheme, which allows a refund of VAT on goods to be taken out of the country – though savings will usually be minimal, if anything, for EU nationals, because of their own VAT rates. Note that not all shops participate in this scheme – enquire before you make your purchase – and you cannot reclaim VAT charged on hotel bills or other services.

In order to make a claim you have to leave the Republic within two months and the North within three months of purchase. Some shops offer the lower price directly to the customer, and all you are required to do is hand in a receipt to customs as you leave the country, but this procedure does vary, so check at the time of purchase.

COSTS, MONEY AND BANKS

The currency in the Republic is the Irish pound, also known as the *punt*, which is divided into 100 pence as in Britain. Exchange rates vary, but currently the punt is worth a little less than the pound sterling. For the best rates you should change money either in banks or bureaux de change. The currency in the North is sterling, as in Britain, though the notes are different and are not readily acceptable in mainland Britain. Prices quoted in this guide are in punts for the Republic and pounds sterling for Northern Ireland.

It may be a surprise to find that the **Republic** is not a cheap place to travel. The least expensive hostel bed will rarely cost less than £6 a night, while bed and breakfast generally works out at £14–17 per person, £20 in Dublin. Reckon on about £5 for a basic, filling meal, and on spending more than you expect on drink, partly because it's expensive and partly because so much social life and entertainment revolves around the pubs. In short, you're likely to spend an absolute minimum of £20 a day, even if you're being very careful, and it's easy to find yourself getting through £30 or more if you plan to live it up in the slightest. As always, if you're travelling in a group you may be able to save some money by sharing rooms and food. Prices for travellers in the **North** are much the same as in the Republic, although B&B accommodation, basic groceries and consumer goods are cheaper.

If you are planning on visiting a lot of **historic monuments** in the **Republic**, it may be worth buying a **Heritage Card** (£15; children/students

£6), valid for one year from the date of purchase. This gives you unlimited admittance to sites cared for by **Dúchas**, the Heritage Service, which runs many parks, monuments and gardens. Cards can be bought from the first Dúchas site you visit, or in advance from their main office at 51 St Stephen's Green, Dublin 2 (☎01/661 3111). Monuments for which the card is valid are indicated throughout this book; membership of An Óige also includes discounts on access to certain sites (see **hostels** on p.31). In the **North**, the **National Trust** offers a similar deal, but there are a lot fewer sites. If, however, you are also visiting Britain, membership (£28; under-25s £13; family £54) may be worth it. Write to Rowallane, Saintfield, Co Down BT24 7LH (☎01238/510721; ☎028/9751 0721 from April 2000) or 36 Queen Anne's Gate, London SW1H 9AS (☎0171/222 9251).

Throughout this guide, the full entry price for museums, art galleries and other sights has been given. Many places will also offer a **concessionary** price for children, students and those over sixty, which is usually at least a third off the full amount.

CARRYING MONEY

If you have a PIN, the easiest way to draw cash is with a **cashpoint card or credit card**. If you are from the UK, cashpoint cards allow you to withdraw money directly from your account. NatWest customers can use any Ulsterbank ATM free of charge, while Midland Bank customers incur no charge using Ulsterbank or National Irish Bank. Most sizeable towns throughout Ireland have at least one bank with a cash dispenser that will accept Visa/Barclaycard and/or Mastercard/Access and most also accept Plus and Cirrus. Most large department stores, filling stations, hotels and upmarket restaurants in both the Republic and Northern Ireland accept the major credit cards – Access/MasterCard, Visa/ Barclaycard, though Diners' Club and American Express are not widely accepted. However, credit cards are less useful in rural areas; smaller establishments all over the country, such as B&Bs, will often accept cash only. Of course, if you are travelling from mainland Britain to the North, you can use your cashpoint card since Northern Irish banks are linked to the major British ones (see overleaf).

Another easy and safe way to carry your money is in **travellers' cheques**, available for a small commission from any major bank. The most commonly accepted travellers' cheques are American Express, followed by Visa and Thomas Cook – most cheques issued by banks will be one of these brands. You'll usually pay commission again when you cash each cheque, or a flat rate – though no commission is payable on Amex cheques exchanged at Amex branches and the same goes for Thomas Cook cheques exchanged at Thomas Cook branches. Make sure you keep a record of the cheques as you cash them, so you'll be able to get the value of all uncashed cheques refunded immediately if you lose them.

BANKS AND BUREAUX DE CHANGE

Almost everywhere banks are the best places to change money and cheques; outside banking hours you'll have to use a bureau de change, widely found in most city centres and at international airports. Avoid changing money or cheques in hotels, where the rates are normally very poor.

The main high-street **banks** in the **Republic** are Allied Irish Bank and Bank of Ireland; two smaller clearing banks are Ulster Bank and National Irish Bank. All are open Mon–Fri 10am–12.30pm and 1.30–3pm; banks in larger cities stay open all day and are open until 5pm one day a week, usually Thursday. It makes sense to change your money while in the cities since many small country towns are served by sub-offices open only certain days of the week. **Foreign exchange counters** are open at Dún Laoghaire, Dublin Port and Rosslare **ferry terminals** and at all main **airports**: Dublin daily from 6am to 8pm year round, staying open later during the summer; Shannon daily from 6.30am to 5.30pm and catering for London flights at 9pm; Cork Monday to Friday 9am–5pm, Sat & Sun 11am–5pm; Knock International daily year round. In Dublin city, there are several outlets where you can change money, including a branch of Thomas Cook at 51 Grafton St, and American Express branches at 41 Nassau St and 14 Upper O'Connell St.

In the **North**, the main high-street banks are linked with British **banks**: National Irish Bank with Midland; Ulster Bank with NatWest; and Bank of Ireland with Barclays. Main banks in large towns are open Mon–Fri 9.30am–4.30pm, with some opening for longer hours and on Saturdays;

outside the cities some may close between 12.30pm and 1.30pm. In very small villages the bank may open on only two or three days a week – so, as in the Republic, aim to get your cash in the bigger centres. Belfast International **airport** has a branch of Thomas Cook, there's a bureau de change at City of Derry Airport, but no **foreign exchange facilities** at Belfast City airport. In Belfast itself, you can change money at the Post Office, 7 Shaftesbury Square, or at Thomas Cook, 11 Donegall Place; they also have a branch in Derry at Unit 7, Quayside Strand Road. There are also American Express branches at 4 Castle Lane and at Castlecourt Shopping Centre, Royal Ave.

EMERGENCIES

If, as a foreign visitor, you run out of money or there is some kind of emergency, the quickest way to get **money sent out** is to contact your bank at home and have them wire the cash to the nearest bank.

For **Americans and Canadians** – or any Amex cardholder – one of the quickest ways to get money from home is through American Express. The company allows cardholders to draw cash from their checking accounts, up to $1000 every 21 days (over the counter) or seven days (from an ATM), as well as offering its own Moneygram Service (☎1-800/543-4080), through which money can be sent to Europe (fees commensurate with amount of money being sent). Another option is to have cash sent out through Western Union (☎1-800/395395) to a nearby bank or post office (this service is available to any traveller, not just North Americans). Make sure you know when it's likely to arrive, since you won't be notified by the receiving office. Remember, too, that you'll need some form of identification when you pick up the money.

Finally, Americans in dire straits can arrange to have money sent to them via the State Departments' Citizen's Emergency Center (☎202/647-5225 during business hours, otherwise ☎202/647-7000)

For **Australians and New Zealanders**, your best bet is to take a Visa or Mastercard with you. Otherwise you have to make arrangements for a possible international money transfer before you leave by nominating a bank and account number in Ireland, entrusting your bank account number with someone at home and paying a fee of A$25/NZ$30.

YOUTH AND STUDENT DISCOUNTS

There are various official and quasi-official youth/student ID cards available that soon pay for themselves in savings.

Full-time students are eligible for the **International Student ID Card** (ISIC). This entitles the bearer to discounts at some museums, theatres and visitor centres, but is perhaps most useful with an additional Travelsave Stamp (£8), available at any USIT office in Ireland, giving reductions on some bus fares and half-price train fares. For Americans there's also a health benefit, providing up to US$3000 in emergency medical coverage and US$100 a day for sixty days in the hospital, plus a 24-hour hotline to call in the event of a medical, legal or financial emergency. The card, which costs £5 in Britain, £6 in Northern Ireland, £7 in the Republic, US$20 in the US and around A/NZ$15 in Australia and New Zealand, is available from branches of USIT in Ireland and Council Travel, STA and Travel Cuts around the world.

The **European Youth Card** is available to any European under 26 and can be obtained at any USIT office (£6, Republic £7); take along valid ID and a passport photo. The card gives discounts on flights, and in the Republic, for an additional £7, entitles you to a fifty percent reduction on train fares.

You only have to be 25 or younger to qualify for the **Go-25 Card**, which costs the same as the ISIC and carries the same benefits. It can be purchased through Council Travel in the US, Hostelling International in Canada (see "Accommodation"), and STA in Australia and New Zealand.

STA also sells its own ID card that's good for some discounts, as do various other travel organizations. A university photo ID might open some doors, too.

Also see p.17 for Heritage and National Trust cards.

HEALTH AND INSURANCE

There are no inoculations required for travellers to Ireland, nor any particular health hazards to beware of beyond those of taking care when travelling in an unknown place. Certainly you're unlikely to suffer sunstroke, and the water is safe almost everywhere. Still, you're as likely to fall ill or have an accident here as anywhere else, so it's as well to make sure you're covered by adequate travel insurance.

A decent policy will cover not just medical costs but also loss or theft of baggage or money; and in real trouble it should get you home. For the peace of mind it offers, it's well worth having. In **Britain**, schemes – from around £23 a month for Ireland – are sold by almost every travel agent or bank and by specialist insurance companies. If you are buying a policy from a travel agent, do read the small print to make sure that the cover is adequate and appropriate. You must make sure you keep all medical bills, and, if you have anything stolen, get a copy of the police report when you report the incident – otherwise you won't be able to claim.

In the **US and Canada** you should also check the insurance policies you already have carefully before taking out a new one. You may discover that you're covered already for medical and other losses while abroad. Canadians especially are usually covered by their provincial health plans. American holders of official student/youth cards (see above) are entitled to accident cover and hospital in-patient benefits. Students may also find their health coverage extends during vacations, and many bank and charge accounts (particularly American Express) include some form of travel cover; insurance is also sometimes included if you pay for your trip with a credit card.

TRAVEL INSURANCE COMPANIES

BRITAIN

Usit Campus, 52 Grosvenor Gardens, London SW1W 0AG (☎0171/730 3402); other offices throughout the country.

Columbus Travel Insurance, 17 Devonshire Square, London EC2M 4SQ (☎0171/375 0011).

Endsleigh Insurance, 97–107 Southampton Row, London WC1B 4AG (☎0171/436 4451).

Frizzell Insurance, Frizzell House, County Gates, Bournemouth, Dorset BH1 2NF (☎01202/292333).

STA Travel, 86 Old Brompton Rd, London SW7 3LH (☎0171/361 6161); other offices throughout the country.

NORTH AMERICA

Access America, PO Box 90310, Richmond, VA 23230 (☎1-800/284-8300).

Carefree Travel Insurance, PO Box 9366, Garden City, NY 11530-9366 (☎1-800/323-3149).

STA Travel, 10 Downing St, New York, NY 10014 (☎1-800/777-0112 or 212/627-3111).

Travel Assistance International, 1133 15th St NW, Suite 400, Washington, DC 20005 (☎1-800/821-2828).

Travel Guard, 1145 Clark St, Stevens Point, WI 54481 (☎1-800/826-1300).

Travel Insurance Services, 2930 Camino Diablo, Suite 200, Walnut Creek, CA 94596 (☎1-800/937-1387).

AUSTRALIA AND NEW ZEALAND

Australian Federation of Travel Agents Ltd (AFTA), 144 Pacific Highway, North Sydney (☎02/9956 4800).

Ready Plan, 141 Walker St, Dandenong (☎1300/555 017) and 10th Floor, 63 Albert St, Auckland (☎09/379 3208).

United Travel Agent Group (UTAG), 122 Walker St, North Sydney (☎02/9956 8399).

If you do want a specific travel insurance policy, there are several to choose from. The best deals are usually through student/youth travel agencies – STA policies, for example, cost $35–45 (depending on cover) for up to seven days; $45–60 for eight to fifteen days; $85–110 for one month; $115–140 for 45 days; $135–165 for two months; $35–50 for each extra month. If you are planning to do any "dangerous sports" (watersports, climbing etc), be sure to ask whether these activities are covered; some policies add a hefty surcharge. One thing to bear in mind is that none of the currently available policies covers theft; they only cover loss while in the custody of an identifiable person – though even then you must make a report to the police and get their written statement.

In **Australia and New Zealand**, travel insurance is offered by airlines and travel agent groups. A typical insurance policy for Ireland will cost A$180/NZ$200 for a month and A$279/NZ$300 for two months.

HEALTH CARE

Visitors from **EU countries** are entitled to medical treatment in the **Republic** under the EU Reciprocal Medical Treatment arrangement. EU visitors should collect a form E111 from their Social Security office (or in Britain from any Post Office). Although an E111 is technically not a requirement for people from the UK, in reality it's essential to get the entitlement to free treatment and prescribed medicines. Even then, you can run into problems, and it makes sense to take your NHS card, too. Armed with these documents, check that the doctor or dentist you use is registered with the Health Board Panel, and make it clear you want to be treated under the European Union's social security arrangements. Similarly if you are admitted to hospital, make it clear you want to be treated within the EU Reciprocal Treatment scheme. The only other real problem is that in rural areas you may find yourself miles from the nearest doctor or hospital, and possibly even further from one prepared to treat you under the reciprocal arrangements.

British citizens need no documentation to be treated in the **North**; for non-British EU travellers, the requirements are the same as for the Republic.

Citizens of **non-EU countries** will be charged for all medical services except those administered by accident and emergency units at health service hospitals. Thus a US citizen who has been hit by a car would not be charged if the injuries simply required stitching and setting in the emergency unit, but would if admission to a hospital ward were necessary. Health insurance is therefore extremely advisable for all non-EU nationals.

Citizens of some countries may also enjoy a reciprocal agreement; in Australia, Medicare has such an arrangement with Ireland and Britain. Check before you leave. And remember that whatever your legal rights, the local doctor may not necessarily know anything about them.

INFORMATION AND MAPS

There's no shortage of information published on Ireland, much of it free; it's well worth contacting the local office of the Irish Tourist Board (Bord Fáilte) and/or the Northern Ireland Tourist Board before you leave.

Bord Fáilte and NITB offices outside Ireland are listed overleaf. Once **in Ireland**, you'll find some kind of tourist office in nearly all towns with a reasonable number of tourists passing through: either a branch of Bord Fáilte or the NITB, or a locally run information centre, many of which open only for the summer. Most of these are listed in the relevant sections of the Guide and are usually extremely helpful, providing local maps and leaflets as well as information on where to stay (booking charge £1–2). It has to be said, though, that they only give details on services which they have approved, thereby excluding some excellent hostels, campsites and private bus services, and they tend to be reluctant to show favouritism among hotels and restaurants, so always go to them for information, not advice. A Bord Fáilte or NITB recommendation implies a certain standard of service, however, so if you don't think your approved B&B comes up to scratch, they are the people you should complain to.

MAPS

A variety of large-scale **road maps** covering the whole of Ireland are available for general touring, such as the Michelin 1:400,000 (no. 405) or the AA 1:350,000. The four Ordnance Survey Ireland Holiday Maps, covering the North, West,

BORD FÁILTE OFFICES ABROAD

Australia, Level 5, 36 Carrington St, Sydney NSW 2000 (☎02/9299 6177).

Britain, 150 New Bond St, London W1Y 0AQ (☎0171/493 3201). See also All Ireland Desk addresses given below.

New Zealand, c/o Walshe's World Ltd, Dingwall Building, 87 Queen St, Auckland 1 (☎09/379 3708).

USA and Canada, 345 Park Ave, New York, NY 10154 (☎1-800/223-6400 or 212/418-0800).

NORTHERN IRELAND TOURIST OFFICES ABROAD

Australia, at the same address as the Bord Fáilte office above.

Britain, All Ireland Desk, British Travel Centre, 1 Lower Regent St, London SW1 (drop-in only); 3rd Floor, 24 Haymarket, London SW1Y 4DG (☎0541/555250); 135 Buchanan St, Glasgow G1 2JA (☎0141/204 4454).

Canada, 111 Avenue Rd, Suite 450, Toronto, ON M5R 3J8 (☎416/925-6368).

New Zealand, at the same address as the Bord Fáilte office above.

USA, 551 Fifth Ave, Suite 701, New York, NY 10176 (☎1-800/326-0036 or 212/922-0101).

East and South at a scale of 1:250,000, give more contour details and are probably the best all-purpose maps on offer. These and others are widely available in Ireland.

For more detail, and for **walking**, the **Ordnance Survey** Discovery Series (1:50,000; a little over 1 mile: 1 inch) is generally the best option and now covers the whole island. Additionally, there are 1:25,000 maps on offer for certain tourist areas: the Fermanagh Lakeland and Mourne Country. The old OS half-inch maps were surveyed in the nineteenth century and can be inaccurate over 1000 feet, so a certain amount of caution is advisable if using them.

For specialist interest maps it makes sense to check locally, as tourist boards or bookshops will often have something better than the above. For walking maps see "Sports and Activities" p.39.

MAP OUTLETS

BRITAIN

Edinburgh, The Stationery Office Ltd, 71 Lothian Rd, EH3 9AZ (☎0131/228 4181).

Glasgow, John Smith and Sons, 57–61 St Vincent St, G2 5TB (☎0141/221 7472).

London, Daunt Books, 83 Marylebone High St, W1 (☎0171/224 2295); National Map Centre, 22–24 Caxton St, SW1 (☎0171/222 2486); Stanfords, 12–14 Long Acre, WC2 (☎0171/836 1321); The Travellers Bookshop, 13 Blenheim Crescent, W11 (☎0171/229 5260).

*Maps by **mail or phone order** are available from Stanfords.*

THE US

Book Passage, 51 Tamal Vista Blvd, Corte Madera, CA 94925 (☎415/927-0960).

The Complete Traveller Bookstore, 199 Madison Ave, New York, NY 10016 (☎212/685-9007); 3207 Fillmore St, San Francisco, CA 92123 (☎415/923-1511).

Elliot Bay Book Company, 101 S Main St, Seattle, WA 98104 (☎206/624-6600).

Forsyth Travel Library, 226 Westchester Ave, White Plains, NY 10604 (☎1-800/367-7984).

Map Link Inc, 30 S La Patera Lane, Unit 5, Santa Barbara, CA 93117 (☎805/692-6777).

The Map Store Inc, 1636 First St NW, Washington, DC 20006 (☎202/628-2608).

Phileas Fogg's Books & Maps, #87 Stanford Shopping Center, Palo Alto, CA 94304 (☎1-800/533-FOGG).

Rand McNally, 444 N Michigan Ave, Chicago, IL 60611 (☎312/321-1751); 150 E 52nd St, New York, NY 10022 (☎212/758-7488); 595 Market St, San Francisco, CA 94105 (☎415/777-3131) etc.

Travel Books & Language Center, 4437 Wisconsin Ave, Washington, DC 20016 (☎1-800/220-2665).

MAP OUTLETS (continued)

THE US (continued)

Sierra Club Bookstore, 6014 College Ave, Oakland, CA 94618 (☎510/658-7470).

Travelers' Bookstore, 22 W 52nd St, New York, NY 10019 (☎212/664-0995).

Note: Rand McNally now has more than twenty stores across the US; call (☎1-800/333-0136 ext 2111) for the address of your nearest store, or for direct mail maps.

CANADA

Open Air Books and Maps, 25 Toronto St, Toronto M5R 2C1 (☎416/363-0719).

Ulysses Travel Bookshop, 4176 St-Denis, Montréal H2W 2M5 (☎514/843-9447).

World Wide Books and Maps, 1247 Granville St, Vancouver V6Z 1G3 (☎604/687-3320).

AUSTRALIA AND NEW ZEALAND

Adelaide, The Map Shop, 16a Peel St, SA 5000 (☎08/8231 2033).

Auckland, Speciality Maps, 58 Albert St (☎09/307 2217).

Brisbane, Hema, 239 George St, (☎07/3221 4330).

Melbourne, Mapland, 372 Little Bourke St, VIC 3000 (☎03/9670 4383).

Perth, Perth Map Centre, 884 Hay St, WA 6000 (☎08/9322 5733).

Sydney, Travel Bookshop, 6 Bridge St, NSW 2000 (☎02/9241 3554).

GETTING AROUND

Travel between major centres in the Republic is generally straightforward, with reliable – albeit infrequent and slow – public transport operated by the state-supported train and bus companies Iarnród Éireann (Irish Rail) and Bus Éireann. There are, however, glaring anomalies, and you should never assume that two major, local towns are necessarily going to be connected. It pays to think and plan ahead. Once off the main routes this becomes particularly important since it's quite usual for small towns and villages to be served by a couple of buses a week and no more. Transport in the North is similarly infrequent in rural areas. Ulsterbus is generally regular and dependable, as is the (limited) train network.

TRAINS

In the **Republic**, Irish Rail (Iarnród Éireann – ☎01/836 6222) operates **trains** to many major cities and towns en route; on direct lines it's by far the fastest way of covering long distances, but the network is by no means comprehensive – Donegal, for instance, has no service at all. In general, train lines fan out from Dublin, with few routes running north–south across the country. So although you can get to the west easily by train, you can't sensibly use the train network to explore the west coast.

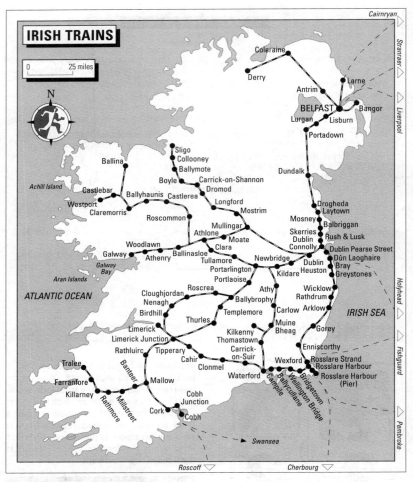

IRISH TRAINS

0   25 miles

N

Cairnryan
Stranraer
Liverpool
Holyhead
Fishguard
Pembroke

Coleraine
Derry
Antrim
Larne
BELFAST
Bangor
Lurgan   Lisburn
Portadown
Dundalk

Sligo
Collooney
Ballymote
Carrick-on-Shannon
Ballina
Boyle   Dromod
Castlebar   Ballyhaunis   Castlerea
Achill Island
Westport   Longford
Claremorris   Mostrim
Drogheda
Laytown
Roscommon   Mosney
Mullingar   Skerries
Woodlawn   Athlone   Moate   Balbriggan
Galway   Clara   Dublin   Rush & Lusk
Athenry   Ballinasloe   Connolly
Galway   Tullamore   Newbridge   Dublin Pearse Street
Bay   Portarlington   Kildare   Dún Laoghaire
Aran Islands   Portlaoise   Dublin   Bray
Heuston   Greystones
ATLANTIC OCEAN
Roscrea   Athy   Wicklow
Cloughjordan   Ballybrophy   Rathdrum
Nenagh   Carlow   Arklow
Birdhill   Templemore   IRISH SEA
Thurles   Muine
Limerick   Kilkenny   Bheag   Gorey
Limerick Junction   Thomastown
Rathluirc   Tipperary   Carrick-   Enniscorthy
on-Suir
Tralee   Cahir   Wexford   Rosslare Strand
Clonmel   Rosslare Harbour
Farranfore   Mallow   Waterford   Rosslare Harbour
Killarney   Bridgetown   (Pier)
Cobh   Wellington Bridge
Junction   Ballycullane
Cork   Campile
Cobh
Swansea
Roscoff   Cherbourg

Train travel is not particularly cheap, either. Prices are usually cheaper midweek; and, if possible, it's best to buy a return ticket as singles cost nearly as much. As a general example, an off-peak Dublin–Galway single ticket costs £15, rising to £25 on either a Friday or Sunday, a five-day return, excluding Friday and Sunday costs £21, a return ticket valid for a month £35. It's always worth asking about any special fares that may be on offer; or if you're doing a fair amount of travelling, it may be worth buying a **train pass**. Irish Rail's Irish Rover ticket, valid in the Republic and

the North, costs £75 (child £37) for five days out of fifteen. A further option open to 16–26 year olds is the Faircard which gives a fifty percent discount on tickets. Available from any Iarnród Éireann office, it costs £8 and is valid for a year.

Given the limited reach of the rail system, one of the most useful options is the Irish Explorer Ticket, a **combined rail and bus pass**, covering all intercity state and private rail and bus lines in the Republic (but no city transportation except DART, see p.56) and costing £60 for any five days' travel out of fifteen consecutive days, and

£90 for eight out of fifteen days. For **unlimited train and bus travel** in the Republic and the North, an Emerald Card costs £105 for eight days out of fifteen, £180 for fifteen days out of thirty (same prices in Northern Ireland). Bear in mind, though, that the nature of travel in Ireland is such that you very rarely stick to your carefully drawn itinerary, and you may not get the value from your pass that you hope for. A Freedom of Northern Ireland Ticket, for daily (£9) or weekly (£32) unlimited travel on trains and all scheduled Ulsterbus services, is available at main bus and railway stations. The only service **between the Republic and the North** is the Dublin–Belfast express (6 each way daily, 2hr; £17 single, £26 return); this is quite an expensive option but is by far the most comfortable train in the country. Once **in the North**, you'll find only three short train routes, but these are efficient and reasonably cheap: a Belfast–Derry ticket will cost you £6.10 single, £9.90 return. If you are looking for a **train pass** a Runaround ticket is valid on all Northern Irish trains for one week and costs around £35.

Students in possession of an ISIC card can buy a Travelsave stamp (£7 from any USIT office – Dublin, Cork, Galway, Limerick, Maynooth, Waterford, Belfast, Coleraine, Jordanstown and Derry), which entitles you to discounts of 50 percent off standard train fares and 30 percent off bus fares in the Republic. In the North, you'll get a return ticket for the price of a single and single fares for half-price.

The cost of taking **bikes** on trains varies between £2 and £6 per single journey in the Republic. In Northern Ireland it costs a quarter of the single fare.

For **North American** visitors who anticipate covering a lot of ground in Ireland, a rail and bus pass is a wise investment; both the Irish Explorer and Emerald passes (see above) are also available to buy in voucher form before you leave for the same time periods and commensurate prices.

Travellers also taking in Great Britain might benefit from the **Britain and Ireland Pass**, which entitles the holder to five days' unlimited travel within a month ($473 first class, $359 standard) or ten days within a month ($698 first class, $511 standard). The pass, which must be purchased before departure from North America, is available from Rail Europe and some travel agents (see p.12 for details of agents selling Irish and British passes).

For **Australians and New Zealanders**, several bus/train passes are available from travel agents (see p.12 and p.14) before you leave: the Irish Explorer train pass costs A$144/NZ$177 for five days' travel out of fifteen; a combined train/bus pass for eight days out of fifteen costs A$217/NZ$265. The Irish Rambler bus pass costs A$67/NZ$83 for three days' travel in eight; A$164/NZ$200 for eight days in fifteen; and A$236/NZ$288 for fifteen days in thirty. The Emerald Card train-and-bus pass includes Northern Ireland: eight days out of fifteen A$253/NZ$309; fifteen out of thirty A$433/NZ$529.

For information on **Eurail** passes see "Getting There from North America" p.12.

BUSES

Bus Éireann operates throughout the **Republic**, and its services are reliable, if infrequent. It's possible to travel by bus between all major towns, but routings can be complex, involving several connections, and hence very slow. Fares are generally far lower than the train, especially in mid-week – a single, Boomerang ticket bought on Tuesday, Wednesday or Thursday gives you the return journey free (if you travel again Tues–Thurs). This system operates on short local journeys too, so it's always worth hanging on to your midweek bus tickets, even if you don't think you'll use them – they remain valid for a month. Occasional special fare offers are also worth looking out for.

Rambler tickets (around £28 for any three days out of eight; £68 for any eight days out of fifteen; £98 for fifteen days out of thirty) all give unlimited bus travel throughout the Republic; **students** can get reductions on standard fares if they have a Travelsave stamp (see p.19). It makes sense to pick up the relevant information for the area you intend to explore before you leave; remote villages may only have a couple of buses a week, so knowing when they are is essential.

Carrying a **bike** on a bus will cost you £5 single regardless of length of journey, though be warned that the driver is under no obligation to take them and in any case usually only has room for one bike.

Private buses, which operate on many major routes, are often cheaper than Bus Éireann, and sometimes faster. They're very busy at weekends, so it makes sense to book ahead if you can; during the week you can usually pay on the bus. Prices for parts of the journeys are often negotiable, and bikes can be carried if booked with your seat.

If you are backpacking round the Republic you might want to consider travelling on **The Slow Coach** (Round-Ireland-Budget-Bus), which for £119 will pick you up at ferry ports and drop you off at towns, sights (often with free guided tours) and hostels along an extensive route. Each ticket allows you a full circuit, and you can take up to six months to complete it. Contact The Slow Coach office at First Floor, 6 South William St, Dublin 2 (☎01/679 2684) or at the YHA Hostel, 38 Bolton Gardens, Earls Court, London SW5 0AQ (☎0171/373 7283).

In the **North**, Ulsterbus runs regular and reliable services throughout the six counties, particularly to those towns not served by the train network. Students can get a fifteen percent discount on certain services with an ISIC card.

Details of bus services connecting principal towns and cities are given in "Travel Details" at the end of each chapter in this guide.

For details of **joint train and bus passes** see "Trains", p.24.

DRIVING

In order to **drive** in Ireland you must have a current driving licence; foreign nationals will need to supplement this with an international driving permit available from national motoring organizations for a small fee. If you're bringing your own car into the country you should also carry your vehicle registration or ownership document at all times. Furthermore, you must be adequately insured, so be sure to check your existing policy.

The **Republic's** uncongested roads make driving a very relaxing option. It also remains (along with Britain) one of the few countries in the world where you drive on the left, a situation that can lead to a few tense days of acclimatization for many overseas drivers. Unleaded petrol is about 55–60p per litre; the national **speed limit** is 55mph/88kph, except where posted otherwise. Front-seat occupants must wear seat belts, and motorcyclists and their passengers must wear helmets. In remote areas, wandering cattle, unmarked junctions, and appallingly potholed minor roads are all potential dangers, particularly for motorbikes. Other hazards to watch out for include drunk drivers late at night, a continuing problem in spite of high accident rates and a concerted police crackdown. A cause of some confusion are "passing

lanes" or "slow lanes", indicated by a broken yellow line, where you can pull over to the left for the car behind to overtake. However, they should be used with care as many have poor surfaces and can suddenly end with little or no warning. Be careful if you take a car to Dublin – theft and vandalism rates are high, and you're best advised to leave your car in a supervised car park.

Ireland is very slowly converting to metric measures, and on the main roads the new (green) signs are in **kilometres**. In rural areas, however, you'll find mostly the old black-and-white fingerpost signs in miles. Most people continue to think and talk in miles too. There is also such a thing as an "Irish mile" – longer than the standard imperial measure – though this is rare and found only on very old signposts. **Unleaded petrol** is available almost everywhere. In all large towns a **disc parking** system is in operation: discs can be bought in newsagents and have to be displayed on the vehicle when parked in a designated area.

Roads in the **North** are in general notably superior to those in the Republic. Driving is on the left and rules of the road are as in Britain: speed limits are 30–40mph/50–60kph in built-up areas, 70mph/110kph on motorways (freeways) and dual carriageways and 60mph/100kph on most other roads. Car seat-belt and motorbike-helmet rules are the same as in the Republic (see above). Cars bearing large red "R" (Restricted) plates identify drivers who have passed their driving test within the past twelve months and are meant to keep to low speeds. Although security is not as rigorous as it was during the IRA's campaign, controlled parking is still in effect in some towns; a parked car in a control zone is considered a security risk and may result in a security alert. **Petrol prices** in the North are about 70–74p a litre.

In the Republic, the **Irish Automobile Association** (IAA) operates 24-hour emergency breakdown services. They also provide many other motoring services, including a reciprocal arrangement for free assistance through many overseas motoring organizations – check the situation with yours before setting out. You can ring the emergency numbers (see opposite) even if you are not a member of the respective organization, although a substantial fee will be charged. In the North, the **Automobile Association** (AA) and the **Royal Automobile Club** (RAC) both offer the same services as the IAA.

MOTORING ORGANIZATIONS

American Automobile Association, 4100 E Arkanas Ave, Denver, CO 80222 (☎1-800/222-4357). *Most member services apply only in the US and Canada, but the AAA can refer members to the AA and also provide international drivers' licences.*

Australian Automobile Association, 216 Northbourne Ave, Canberra, ACT 2601 (☎02/6247 7311).

Automobile Association, Fanum House, Basingstoke, Hants RG21 2EA (☎0990/448866); 36 Wellington Place, Belfast (☎01232/232131 or 028/9023 2131 from Aug 2000). Emergency number: ☎0800/887766.

Irish Automobile Association, 23 Suffolk Rd, Dublin (☎01/667 9481); Cork (☎021/276922). Emergency number: ☎1-800/667788.

Canadian Automobile Association *Each region has its own club – check the phone book for local address and phone number. Benefits are comparable to the AAA's.*

New Zealand Automobile Association, Floor 17, 99 Albert St, Auckland (☎09/377 4660).

Royal Automobile Club, PO Box 100, RAC House, 7 Brighton Rd, South Croydon CR2 6XW (☎0181/686 0088); 79 Chichester St, Belfast (☎01232/232640; ☎028/9023 2640 from April 2000). Emergency number: ☎0800/828282.

CAR RENTAL FIRMS

IRELAND

Avis Dublin ☎01/677 6971; Belfast ☎01232/240404; ☎028/9024 0404 from April 2000.

Budget Rent-A-Car Dublin ☎01/837 9611; Belfast ☎01232/230700; ☎028/9023 0700 from April 2000.

Cahill Car Hire Dublin ☎01/831 1944.

Dan Dooley Dublin ☎01/677 2723.

Europcar Dublin ☎01/668 1777; Belfast ☎01232/450904; ☎028/9045 0904 from April 2000.

Hertz Dublin ☎01/676 7476; Northern Ireland ☎0990/996699.

Holiday Autos Dublin ☎01/454 9090.

Thrifty Rent-A-Car Dublin ☎01/679 9420.

BRITAIN

Avis ☎0181/848 8733.

Budget ☎0800/181181.

Eurodollar ☎01895/233300.

Europcar/InterRent ☎01345/222525.

Hertz ☎0345/555888.

Holiday Autos ☎0171/491 1111.

NORTH AMERICA

Alamo domestic ☎1-800/354-2322; international ☎1-800/522-9696.

Avis domestic ☎1-800/331-1212; international ☎1-800/331-1084.

Budget ☎1-800/527-0700.

Europe By Car ☎1-800/223-1516.

Hertz domestic ☎1-800/654-3131; international ☎1-800/654-3001; in Canada ☎1-800/263-0600.

Holiday Autos ☎1-800/422-7737.

National Car Rental ☎1-800/CAR-RENT.

AUSTRALIA

Avis ☎1800/225 533.

Budget ☎13/2727.

Hertz ☎13/3039.

Eurodrive ☎02/9299 3344.

NEW ZEALAND

Avis ☎09/526 2847.

Budget ☎03/375 2222.

Fly and Drive Holidays ☎09/366 0759.

Hertz ☎09/367 6350.

CAR RENTAL

Large international **car rental companies** such as Hertz have outlets in all major cities, airports and ferry terminals in the **Republic**: they're expensive at around £150–300 a week, and, especially if you're travelling from North America, you'll proba-

bly find it cheaper to arrange things in advance. Booking a fly-drive or a train-sail-drive package is one of the cheapest ways to arrange car rental, or if you don't want to be so tied down, try an **agency** such as Holiday Autos, who will arrange advance booking through a local agent and can usually undercut the big companies considerably.

If you haven't booked, then the smaller local firms can almost always offer better deals than the well-known names. You must produce a full valid driving licence (which you must have held without endorsement for at least two years); most companies will only rent cars to people over 23 years of age, though you might find some that will rent to drivers over 21; it will generally be more expensive if they do. It's advisable to take out a collision damage waiver with your car rental – otherwise expect to be liable for around £1000 damages in the event of an accident. If you intend to drive **across the border**, you should inform your rental company beforehand to check that you are fully insured.

Renting a car in the **North** involves much the same cost and age restrictions as in the Republic. There are fewer outlets, but rental is available in all major cities and at Belfast airport. Again, the cheapest deals are booked ahead, and here too you must inform the car rental company if you plan to cross the border.

HITCHING

In the **Republic** hitching is commonplace; for locals it's almost as much a normal part of getting around as using the bus and train networks, and for the visitor the human contact makes it one of the best ways to get to know the country. Knowing the shortcomings of public transport, many drivers readily give lifts, and it's not unusual to see single women with babies and the shopping or whole families waiting for a ride. It has to be borne in mind, however, that local people experience no real problems in getting lifts since they usually know just about everybody on the road; visitors can have a less easy time of it.

The chief problem if you plan to hitch extensively is lack of traffic, especially off the main roads, and if you are travelling around one of the tourist-swamped areas of the west, you may find there's a reluctance to pick up foreigners. That said, without transport of your own you are probably going to *have* to hitch if you want to see the best of Ireland's wild, remote places. Just be sure to leave yourself plenty of time.

Although it's probably safer than just about anywhere else in Europe, it goes without saying that hitching is never entirely risk-free, and on the whole it's best for women to avoid hitching alone.

Hitching a lift in the **North** is rather less straightforward and probably easiest for pairs of women who are obviously tourists. Men travelling alone or in pairs can still be viewed with suspicion and may find it impossible to get a lift. Men and women travelling together are at least in with a chance.

CYCLING

If you are lucky enough to get decent weather, cycling is one of the most enjoyable ways to see Ireland, ensuring you're continually in touch with the landscape. Roads are generally empty, though very poor surfaces may well slow you down.

Most airlines carry **bicycles** free as long as you don't exceed your weight allowance; but be sure to check the regulations in advance (charters may be less obliging) and let them know when you book your ticket that you plan to carry a bike. Always deflate the tyres to avoid explosions in the unpressurized hold.

If you don't want to cycle long distances, it's easy and relatively cheap to **rent a bike** in most towns in the **Republic** and at a limited number of places in the **North** (most outlets are listed in the text); you can't take a rented bike across the border. Raleigh, who operate a national rental scheme and a choice of drop-off options, are the biggest distributors (£7 per day, £35 per week plus around £30 deposit; collection and delivery service £6–12; in the North £6.50 a day, £27 a week). You can call their main office at Raleigh House, Kylemore Road, Dublin 10 (☎01/626 1333) to find out details of their agents throughout Ireland. Local dealers (including some hostels) are often less expensive. Wherever you rent your bike, it makes sense to check the tyres and brakes immediately and demand a pump and repair kit before you set off. You should also consider the terrain: if you plan on mountain riding, make sure your machine has enough gears to cope. **Cycle helmets** are available for rent at some shops, but if you want to be certain of wearing one, bring your own along.

In tourist spots at high season it's best to collect a bike early in the day (or book it the day before) as supplies frequently run out. If you arrive with your own bike, it's easy enough to carry it across long distances by train, less so by bus (see p.25). Finally, a problem you may encounter – for some reason particularly in the west – is that of farmers' dogs chasing and snarling at your wheels. Should you be fortunate enough to be heading downhill at the time, freewheeling silently past cottages and farm entrances is perhaps the only humane way of minimizing the risk of savaged wheels and ankles.

ACCOMMODATION

Ireland offers a wide range of accommodation, from the spartan – camping for free in a farmer's field (usually possible if you ask permission first) – to the sybaritic: many of Ireland's elegant old country houses take bed-and-breakfast guests. There's also a huge number of hostels, which vary enormously, but all have at least the essentials of a bed and somewhere to cook, and some offer a great deal more. A notch up in price, in more or less the following order, come bed and breakfasts, guesthouses, town houses, country houses, and hotels, the majority officially graded by the tourist boards on a set formula which, most of the time, gives a fair idea of what to expect. Prices quoted throughout this book indicate the price you can expect to pay for a double room in high season. The cost of a dormitory bed in a hostel in high season is generally around £7. Where it exceeds £10, this is indicated in the text. In B&Bs and hotels, rates for single rooms are generally considerably higher.

ACCOMMODATION BOOKINGS

Accommodation in the Republic and Northern Ireland can be booked in advance through the Tourist Board-approved agency, Gulliver Infores. The cost of the service is £3 and there is a non-refundable £10 deposit taken on your credit card as soon as you make the reservation. All calls to these numbers are free:

from within **Ireland** ☎1800/668668;

from the **UK** or **Northern Ireland** ☎0800/668 668 66 or 0800/783 5740;

from **USA** ☎0011/800 668 668 66.

Whatever your budget, remember that accommodation can be difficult to find in **Dublin** at any time of year; in **July and August** accommodation in the cities and big tourist centres gets booked up well in advance, and during **festivals** things get even more hectic. For the really big festivals – like the Fleadh Cheoil and the Cork Jazz Festival (see p.39 for a full list of events) – there's often an extra accommodation office trying to cope with the overload, but you may still end up sleeping in a different town, or perhaps just revelling your way through to morning. The less famous festivals can be equally difficult for the spontaneous traveller. Since festivals take place all over Ireland throughout the summer, it's worth checking out where and when they are before you head off – simply pick up an events calendar from any major tourist office.

B&B, GUESTHOUSES AND HOTELS

B&Bs in the Republic vary enormously, but most are welcoming, warm and clean, with huge breakfasts including cereal, massive fry-ups of bacon, egg, sausage and tomato, and toast and tea. Afternoon tea can usually be arranged and can be delicious, with home-made scones and soda bread – it will cost you around £3 or £4; evening meals in guesthouses tend to be expensive – around £15 – and generally need to be pre-booked. Bord Fáilte-registered and approved B&Bs are generally pretty good, though it's not an absolute guarantee. Don't assume that non-registered places will be less good – inclusion in the official guide is voluntary, and a fair few simply choose not to bother. Many historic buildings are run as B&Bs, and they too can be surprisingly cheap. Many are managed by extremely good cooks, with some of the best and most inventive examples of new Irish cuisine on the menu.

You can expect to pay from around £14–17 per person sharing, £20 in Dublin (from £13 for non-registered houses). **Bookings** for registered B&Bs can be made through tourist offices (£1–2) – well worth considering at busy periods, or you can do it yourself. Many phone numbers and addresses are given in the text of this guide, but if you want the complete list then buy *The Accommodation Guide* published by Bord Fáilte (£5), which has comprehensive, graded lists of B&Bs, hotels and campsites. The Family Homes of Ireland is a smaller organization, their B&Bs tend to be a pound or so cheaper, and are particularly worth considering if you require single rooms; their brochure (£2) is available from The Family Homes of Ireland, Oughterard, Co. Galway (☎091/550055; www.family-homes.ie) Alternatively, finding accommodation is simple enough in just about any town or touristy village – simply go into a pub and ask.

In the **North**, B&B accommodation costs much the same as in the Republic, perhaps a pound or two cheaper in country areas. It's worth ringing ahead if you're planning to stay in Belfast, Derry or one of the main resorts during festivals or high season. Addresses and phone numbers for B&Bs in all of the main centres are given in the *Guide*, and the Northern Ireland Tourist Board's *Where to stay in Northern Ireland* (£3.99) gives extensive, highly detailed lists.

Accommodation in a **farmhouse** or in a cottage can be arranged through the tourist board; for all their simple rooms and turf fires, many "Rent-an-Irish-Cottage" cottages cluster in tiny tourist villages, so it's worth checking out exactly what the set-up is if you're after real solitude. This said, some are very good value. The Family Homes of Ireland (see above) also offers a good range, and if you are travelling from the UK it is well worth checking out combined cottage and

ferry deals from the major ferry companies.

Inns and **Travel Lodges** are a recent innovation providing good quality, if often rather characterless, accommodation, and for families and small groups often work out less expensive than B&Bs: a typical room sleeping three adults or two adults and two children costs around £48 per night.

Hotels are generally more expensive, particularly in the cities; however, many of the swanky hotels slash their tariffs at weekends when the business types have gone home or offer competitively priced low season deals. In smaller towns and villages, hotels are not always so pricy and may well be a lively social focus. Virtually all hotels have bars and provide meals to residents and non-residents alike.

HOSTELS

Hostel accommodation in Ireland has grown hugely in breadth and quality recently, and staying in a hostel no longer means subjecting yourself to the rigours of old-fashioned hostelling – although **An Óige** (the official Irish Youth Hostel Association) and the **Youth Hostel Association of Northern Ireland** (YHANI) still manage to satisfy more spartan tastes. Hostels in the more popular areas tend to fill up very quickly in July and August, so booking in advance is strongly advised.

YOUTH HOSTEL ASSOCIATIONS

Australia: Australian Youth Hostels Association, 422 Kent Rd, Sydney (☎02/9261 1111). *Adult membership costs A$44 for a year (annual renewal is $27); under-18s' membership costs $13.50. Members are entitled to discounts on some air and land travel, travel insurance, car rental, entrance fees to museums and historical sights.*

Canada: Hostelling International–Canadian Hostelling Association, Room 400, 205 Catherine St, Ottawa ON K2P 1C3 (☎1-800/663-5777 or 613/237-7884). *Annual membership for adults $26.75, children under 18 free when accompanied by parents; 2-year membership costs $35.*

England and Wales: Youth Hostel Association (YHA), Trevelyan House, 8 St Stephen's Hill, St Albans, Herts AL1 2DY (☎01727/855215). *Membership costs £5 for under 18s, £10 for over 18s. There are fifteen other YHA city locations throughout England.*

Ireland: An Óige, 61 Mountjoy St, Dublin 7 (☎01/830 4555, www.Irelandyha.org).

New Zealand: Youth Hostels Association of New Zealand, 173 Gloucester St, Christchurch (☎03/379 9970). *Adult membership costs NZ$34 for a year; under-18s pay NZ$12, with the same discounts as the Australian Association.*

Northern Ireland: Youth Hostel Association of Northern Ireland, 22 Donegall Rd, Belfast BT12 5JN (☎01232/324733).

Scotland: Scottish Youth Hostel Association, 7 Glebe Crescent, Stirling FK8 2JA (☎01786/891400). *Membership costs £2.50 for under 18s and £6 for over 18s.*

USA: Hosteling International–American Youth Hostels (HI–AYH), 773 15th St NW, Suite 840, PO Box 37613, Washington, DC 20005 (☎1-800/444-6111; www.hiayh.org). *Annual membership for adults $25, youths (under 18) $10, seniors (55 or over) $15, families $35.*

ACCOMMODATION PRICE CODES

Throughout this book, prices of hotels, guesthouses and B&Bs have been graded with the codes below, according to what you can expect to pay for a double room in high season.

① Under £26
② £26–33
③ £33–40

④ £40–55
⑤ £55–70
⑥ £70–90

⑦ £90–110
⑧ £110–130
⑨ Over £130

Independent hostels are generally run along more relaxed lines, and as well as having traditional dormitory accommodation, a growing number have many private, double and family rooms. Some new city hostels compare favourably in terms of comfort with B&Bs. The majority are classed as **Independent Holiday Hostels** (IHH) and are recommended by Bord Fáilte, but you will also find some excellent (usually small) hostels that don't belong to An Óige, YHANI or IHH; many of these are part of the Independent Hostel Owners organization (IHO). All independent hostels are privately owned, and they're all different, each reflecting the character and interests of its owner. Some are tucked away in such beautiful countryside that they're worth staying in for the setting alone. Very often the atmosphere is cosy and informal: you can stay in all day if you want, and there are no curfews or chores. On the downside, such is their popularity that some hostels cram people in to the point of discomfort. July and August are particularly bad, especially in the major cities and on the west coast, as are festival times. If you're relying on them it's worth ringing ahead to check what the situation is; or better still use the book-a-bed-ahead scheme. This allows you to book from one IHH hostel to another, usually for a charge of 50p; the hostel owner will phone through your booking and on payment of £6 will issue you with a ticket that guarantees your bed at the next hostel. Some hostels offer bike rental, some food: details are given in the text. Expect to pay around £7 for a dormitory bed; £8–12 per person for private rooms where available (more in Dublin). Many hostels are open all year round. Where this is not the case, we have specified which months they are open in the text. If you are planning on using hostels extensively, it's worth calling for their detailed lists in advance: for the IHH call ☎01/836 4700, (*www.iol.ie/hostel*), for the IHO call ☎073/30130 (*www.eroicapub.com/ihi*).

An Óige and YHANI hostels are run more traditionally: many are closed during the daytime and enforce evening curfews, at least officially. Thanks to competition from other hostels, you'll find many far more flexible than the rule book would suggest, particularly in out-of-the-way places. Smaller dorms and private rooms are available in certain hostels. Some are worth visiting for the location (which can often make up for the lack of facilities); others, especially in the mountains, may be the only place to stay. In the Republic, **An Óige membership** – which includes membership of the umbrella organization, **Hostelling International** (HI), and therefore also membership of YHANI – costs £4 for under 18s and £10 for over 18s, and can be obtained by visiting or writing to An Óige's main office in Dublin (see box opposite for details). In Northern Ireland, YHANI membership (including membership of HI and therefore An Óige) costs £3 for under 18s, £7 for over 18s. Visitors from elsewhere in Britain, and foreign nationals, who wish to join HI once in the Republic or the North can do so. It is worth remembering that if you buy membership before leaving home some transport companies offer discounts; from Britain Stena and Irish Ferries offer a twenty percent reduction on foot passenger fares, and certain car rental companies also offer discounts. The members' handbook also lists discounts available at a range of historic sites, and in shops and visitor centres. If you turn up at an An Óige hostel as a non-member, you will be charged a nightly supplement of £1, which accumulates so that after paying six you become a temporary member, though you are not eligible for the discounts that full membership entitles you to.

Hostels are graded according to the quality of facilities, and **prices** in the **Republic** vary accordingly, ranging between £6.50 and £10 for a dorm in high season; city hostels are generally the most expensive. It's worth getting a copy of the *An Óige Handbook*, which clarifies the intricacies of the system, lists every hostel in the association and gives details of YHANI hostels; it's available from the address on p.30. An Óige also offers special accommodation-and-travel deals, which you should check out in advance – for instance, its combined transport to Ireland, hostel and train ticket is often very good value. In the **North**, charges for an overnight stay range from £7.50 to £10 and include linen.

CAMPING

The cheapest way to sleep in Ireland is to **camp rough**, although the distinct possibility of rain, without the facilities of a campsite, may put you off. You'll also find that some of the terrain is very tricky, especially in the areas of bog and rock in Clare, Galway, Mayo and Donegal. There's usually no problem if you ask to camp in a field, and in out-

of-the-way places nobody minds where you pitch a tent (the only place you definitely can't camp in the Republic is in a state forest – but these are usually dark pine woods anyhow). You may find that the farmer will ask you for a pound or two if the field happens to be in a heavily touristed region such as Kerry, and if there's an organized site nearby you'll probably be directed to it, but other than this you can often camp for free. The cost of staying in **organized campsites** varies depending on the facilities offered, the number of people sharing etc; expect to pay £5–8 for two people in a small tent. Sites are listed throughout the *Guide*. It's also worth bearing in mind that many of the **hostels** will let you camp on their land for £3–4 a night, with the use of kitchen facilities and showers.

FOOD AND DRINK

Ireland has no real tradition of eating out, but the range and quality of food has increased enormously in recent years, especially at the top end of the market, and this edition of the *Guide* includes the most luxurious and expensive of eating places, along with more everyday establishments. Outside smart restaurants the best of Irish food is to be found in seafood bars on the west coast and the all-too-rare vegetarian cafés dotted around the country. These aside, the fresh, though rather plain, selection of vegetables,

breads and Irish-made cheeses available in the shops make self-catering a reasonable option. If your budget is restricted, the best bet is to fill up with a hearty breakfast and/or a good lunch from a pub or coffee shop in the middle of the day, and then concentrate on drinking in the evening – few pubs serve food at night.

FOOD

Irish food is generally highly meat-oriented, and you don't have to be a vegetarian to find this wearing after a while. Meat in Ireland is generally of a good standard – steaks, in particular, are excellent – but after a while you begin to long for some variety in your diet and for something which hasn't been fried.

If you're staying in B&Bs, it's almost impossible to avoid the "traditional" Irish **breakfast** of sausages, bacon and eggs, which usually comes accompanied by generous quantities of delicious soda bread. Pub **lunch** staples are usually meat and two veg, with plenty of gravy, although you can usually get freshly made sandwiches (sometimes excellent, but often sliced white bread and processed cheese); home-made soups can be very good too. Most larger towns have good, simple **coffee shops** (open daytime only) where you can get soup, sandwiches, cakes and the omnipresent apple pie as well as slightly more ambitious and filling dishes. In the North, in particular, expect enormous portions of meat and thoroughly over-cooked vegetables that will ground you for the rest of the afternoon. It's worth remembering that **hotels** are obliged to offer food to all comers – so you can always find a sandwich and a cup of coffee, at any reasonable hour; you can generally order a plate of sandwiches and a pot of tea in pubs, too. This said, huge areas of the countryside offer no places to eat or drink at all – and many cafés and restaurants outside the cities close from September through to May. If you are going to explore the best of the landscape, you'll probably need to take your own provisions.

Many traditional Irish dishes are based on the **potato** and you certainly do get an awful lot of them – often served up in several different forms in the same meal. Potato cakes can be magnificent – a flour and potato dough fried in butter – as can potato soup. **Irish stew** of varying qualities will be available almost everywhere; and **colcannon**, cooked potatoes fried in butter with onions and cabbage, or leeks, can also be very good. Colcannon is a traditional dish for Hallowe'en, as is **barm brack**, a sweet yeast bread with spices and dried fruits.

RESTAURANTS AND ALTERNATIVES

Much is made of Ireland's recent **gastronomic revolution**, with new Irish cuisine, consisting of elegant meals using local produce that are often adaptations of traditional recipes, very much in vogue. Some **guesthouses**, particularly if they're historic buildings, serve very good food, in what can be very grand surroundings, and a growing number of excellent vegetarian and wholefood cafés offer a good budget alternative. There are also some impressive **seafood restaurants**, particularly along the west coast, which serve freshly caught fish and seafood along with homegrown vegetables. Irish **oysters** are famous; the season opens with an oyster festival at Clarinbridge on Galway Bay. **Salmon** and trout can also be fabulous, but be warned that away from the coast fish-farming is the norm.

Catering for yourself, at least some of the time, may be the best option. Produce available in Ireland is usually fresh and excellent, but – aside from in the cities and some tourist towns on the west coast – it is limited in range (you won't find exotic fruits and vegetables, for instance). Irish

potatoes, cabbages and carrots are delicious, though surprisingly hard to buy in rural areas, where the population may be too small to support even a grocer's shop. Meat is very good; bread and scones are wonderful; and if you're travelling around the coast, you can often buy seafood cheaply direct from the fishermen. Sometimes you'll come across more unusual things in this way – spider crabs and monkfish, for example – that you would never find in local fish shops; it's all exported. In many places you can gather your own mussels from the rocks – but be sure to check locally in case there's a sewage outlet nearby.

Dairy products, especially cheese, can also be excellent. The past decade has seen an upturn in the Irish cheese business, which now produces many delicious, often unpasteurized cheeses. Look out for the creamy Cashel Blue, St Killian brie, and Gubbeen Farmhouse in West Cork as well as countless more idiosyncratic cheeses from smaller makers, many of whom like to experiment. There's no need to go to a smart restaurant to taste these – you can often find them in grocer's shops and markets.

DRINK

To travel through Ireland without visiting a **pub** would be to miss out on a huge chunk of Irish life, some would say the most important. Especially in rural areas, the pub is far more than just a place to drink. It's the social and conversational heart of any Irish village, and often the cultural centre too. If you're after food, advice or company, the pub is almost always the place to head for; and very often they'll also be the venues for local entertainment, especially traditional and not so traditional music (see "Festivals and Entertainment", p.38).

Along with Mass and market day, the pub is the centre of Irish social activity: a cultural cliché, perhaps, but one that wears very well. Talking is an important business here, and drink is the great lubricant of social discourse. That said, it doesn't pay to arrive with too romantic a notion of what this actually means. Away from the cities and the touristed west coast, there are plenty of miserable, dingy bars where the only spark of conviviality is the dull glow of the TV. But in most big towns and cities you'll find bars heaving with life, and out in remote country villages it can be great fun drinking among the shelves of the ancient grocery shops-cum-bars you'll find dotted around.

While women will always be treated with genuine (unreconstructed) civility, it's true to say that the majority of bars are a predominantly male preserve. In the evening, especially, women travellers can expect occasional unwanted attention, though this rarely amounts to anything too unpleasant. Should your first encounters be bad ones, persist – the good nights will come, and will probably rank amongst the most memorable experiences of your trip.

In the Republic, **opening hours** are (in summer) Monday to Saturday 10.30am–11.30pm, on Sunday 12.30–2pm & 4–11pm – they close at 11pm in winter; illegal lock-ins remain something of an after-hours institution in rural parts. In the **North** pubs are open Monday to Saturday 11am–11pm, on Sunday 12.30–10pm.

WHAT TO DRINK

The classic Irish drink is, of course, **Guinness** ("a Guinness" is a pint; if you want a half of any beer, ask for "a glass") which, as anybody will tell you, is simply not the same as the drink marketed as Guinness outside Ireland. For one thing, good Guinness has to be kept properly, something non-Irish pubs abroad tend not to do; it has to be poured gradually (the ultimate gaffe in a pub is to ask them to hurry this process); and even across Ireland you'll taste differences – it's best in Dublin where it's brewed. A proper pint of Irish Guinness is a dream, far less heavy than you may be used to, though still a considerable, filling drink. Other local stouts, like Beamish and Murphy's (a Cork stout, far sweeter and creamier), make for interesting comparison: they all have their faithful adherents.

If you want a pint of English-style **bitter**, then Smithwicks is your only option, though it has none of the flavour of a decent real ale. As everywhere, of course, **lager** is also increasingly popular: mostly Harp (made by Guinness) or Heineken. Whatever your tipple, you're likely to find drinking in Ireland an expensive business at around IR£1.80–2.30 a pint.

Irish **whiskeys** – try Paddy's, Powers, Jameson's or, from the North, Bushmills – also seem expensive, but in fact the measures are far larger than those you'll get in mainland Britain. If you've come in from the cold you can have your whiskey served warm with cloves and lemon – just ask for a hot whiskey. Asking for Scotch in an Irish pub is frowned on, and in any case anyone here will tell you that the Irish version is infinitely superior.

Wine is expensive in the Republic – expect prices in supermarkets to start at around £5 a bottle (and in small villages in the west you can expect to pay £7 at the very least), so if you are planning a self-catering holiday and travelling from Britain, it's worth bringing your own; in the North prices are similar to those in the rest of Britain.

Non-alcoholic drinks are limited to an uninspiring array of the usual soft drinks and bottled fruit juices, plus Ireland's own, aggressively fizzy mineral water, which is now available in a number of pleasantly un-sweet, fruity flavours. Unless the bar is extremely busy, you can always get **coffee** (generally served with a dollop of full cream) or **tea**. You can usually get **Irish coffee** too (with whiskey and cream), which is delicious if not very traditional – it was invented at Shannon airport.

POST AND PHONES

In towns throughout Ireland you'll find fully automatic payphones in kiosks; instructions for use are on display, and internal and international calls can easily be made. A local call generally costs 30p minimum but, as you might imagine, long-distance daytime calls are expensive. International calls are cheapest if dialled direct after 6pm. Cardphones, found in towns all over the country, are by far the most convenient way of making long-distance calls, avoiding the chugging of coins interrupting your call; they're also cheaper than coin-operated phones. Phonecards can be bought at newsagents and post offices – it's worth carrying one with you since cash-operated phones are rare in remote areas. If you make calls from a hotel or the like, expect a hefty premium charged on top of the normal price.

International dialling codes in the United Kingdom (including Northern Ireland) and Ireland follow the European standard – to call Ireland the code is 353, and for Northern Ireland, as part of the UK, it's 44. If you're calling the North from the Republic, however, the code is 080.

There are few **fax bureaux** outside Dublin or Belfast. If you need to use a fax, ask at one of the swankier hotels – they're usually pleased to help and are unlikely to charge you an unreasonable rate.

Post to or from the Republic is generally reasonably fast and efficient. If it's something important, it's worth spending the extra for recorded or registered mail. An Post (the postal service) has three different charges: letters and postcards to Ireland or Britain cost 30p; those going to any other European country cost 32p; cards or letters outside Europe cost 45p. Main post offices are open Monday to Friday 8.30am–5.30pm, Saturday 9am–noon. From the North, letters and postcards travel anywhere in the EU for 30p, for the rest of the world postcards are 37p and letters cost a minimum of 43p. Post office hours in the North are Monday, Tuesday, Thursday & Friday 9am–5.30pm and Wednesday & Saturday 9am–12.30pm.

OPERATOR SERVICES

In the Republic:
Operator ☎10
Directory Enquiries within Ireland including Northern Ireland☎1190
International Directory Enquiries☎1198
International Operator Services☎114
Telegrams☎196

In the North:
Operator ☎100
Directory Enquiries☎192
International Directory Enquiries☎153
International Operator Services☎155
Telegrams☎190/193

CHANGES TO PHONE NUMBERS IN IRELAND

As from June 1 1999, a new code, 028, will replace all existing area codes in **Northern Ireland**. In addition, a new two-digit prefix will be placed after the area code and before the first digit of the current number.The new prefixes are shown in boxes in the relevant chapters. New and old numbers will run in parallel between June 1 1999 and April 22 2000. After this date, only the new number will be operational. In August 1999, some phone numbers in the **Cork** area will change. See box on p.259 for details.

THE MEDIA

NEWSPAPERS AND MAGAZINES

The most widely read **papers** in the **Republic** are the heavyweight *Irish Times* and the lighter *Irish Independent*. High-quality but remarkably slim papers, they really bring home just how small the population is. The *Times* is the more upmarket, a liberal newspaper with comparatively good foreign news coverage and plenty of feature material on home news and sport. *The Cork Examiner* is another well-regarded national daily (although mainly distributed around Munster), and the *Star* is Ireland's tabloid. Sunday newspapers include The *Times* and *Independent* equivalents, the liberal *Sunday Tribune* and the more sensational *Sunday World*. British newspapers are generally available the same day in Dublin and other cities. Mostly conservative and varying widely in quality, there's a local daily paper in every county; some of the best are *The Kerryman*, *The Donegal Democrat* and *The Kilkenny People*.

In the **North**, all the main British papers are sold. Of the newspapers produced in Northern Ireland, the biggest seller is the evening paper, the middle-of-the-road *Belfast Telegraph*, which is consumer-led and has little to say on politics or culture. The morning papers are the *Irish News*, read by the Nationalist community, and the Unionist tabloid *News Letter*.

TELEVISION AND RADIO

In the **Republic**, RTE (Radio Telefís Éireann) runs two state-sponsored **television** channels: RTE 1 and Network 2. RTE 1 reflects the state broadcasting policy with an emphasis on public information and a commitment to Irish-language and bilingual programmes. Network 2 is more upbeat, with plenty of chat shows and youth-oriented programmes. The new Irish-language channel, Telifís na Gaelige, has sought to use the contemporary medium of television to reinvigorate the language and this is reflected in much of its programming which is youth-oriented, upbeat and visually progressive. Ireland's most popular, long-running and often controversial chat show is Gay Byrne's much-loved *The Late Late Show* on Friday evenings; very much a voice box for the nation, it's probably the best, and most entertaining, indicator of current issues and concerns. In the **North** you get the BBC and Ulster Television, and you can also pick up broadcasts from the Republic. Throughout Ireland the four major English terrestrial TV channels are available on cable, as are satellite channels such as Sky One and Skysport.

RTE also runs three **radio** stations – Radio 1, 2 and FM3. Radio 1 is devoted to middle/highbrow music and cultural and political programmes. RTE 2 is a pop channel, and FM3 is the national Irish-language station, Radio na Gaeltachta, which shares the frequency with classical music programming. Today FM 100–104 was recently launched as an ambitious attempt to rival the state-owned media, and although its daytime output is rather uninspiring, its evening broadcasting, a mix of politics, satire and informed musical opinion is by far the best in the country: *The Last Word*, weekdays from 5 till 7pm, a current affairs programme hosted by the outspoken Eamonn Dunphy, is followed by the musically unpredictable *Eclectic Ballroom* from 7 to 9pm, with John Kelly, a man who revels in his persona as the antithesis of the smiley mid-Atlantic DJ. The evening finishes with Donal Dineen, an authority on contemporary electronic music. Deregulation of the radio has resulted in the growth of local radio on the FM airwaves. The quality varies, but you'll find some interesting fare, including all-Irish stations in Connemara and Ring, Co. Waterford, that are worth listening to for traditional music, country and western and insights into local issues.

OPENING HOURS AND HOLIDAYS

Business and shop opening hours in both Northern Ireland and the Republic are very similar to Britain's: approximately 9am to 5.30pm, Monday to Saturday. Many places in the towns stay open until 8pm or later on Thursdays and Fridays and an increasing number are open on Sundays from around noon until 6pm. The midweek half-day closing tradition survives in some of the smaller towns though even then you're likely to find somewhere open.

In the Republic, however, particularly away from the bigger towns, hours are more approximate, with later opening and closing times. In rural areas you can generally find someone to sell you groceries at any reasonable hour, even if they have to open their shop to do it – and very often the village shop doubles as the local pub. For banking hours see "Costs, Money and Banks" on p.18. On the main **public holidays** (see below),

outside the cities virtually everything will be closed except the garages and pubs. Should St Patrick's Day or Orange Day happen to fall on a Saturday or Sunday, the holiday is carried over to the Monday.

There's no pattern to the opening and closing of **museums**, **archeological sites** and the like, though many close altogether for at least one day a week. Wherever possible, hours and prices are listed in the *Guide*. The bigger attractions will normally be open throughout the day, while smaller places may open only in the afternoon. Many sites away from the main tourist trails – especially houses or castles which are also private homes – are open only during the peak summer months.

Churches, at least if they're still in use, are almost always open, and if they're locked there's usually someone living nearby (often the priest) who will have the keys; otherwise, opening times will follow religious activity fairly closely.

PUBLIC HOLIDAYS

IN THE REPUBLIC:
New Year's Day
St Patrick's Day, March 17
Easter Monday
First Monday in May
First Monday in June
First Monday in August
Last Monday in October
Christmas Day
December 26

IN THE NORTH:
New Year's Day
St Patrick's Day, March 17
Easter Monday
First Monday in May
Last Monday in May
Orange Day, July 12
Last Monday in August
Christmas Day
December 26

FESTIVALS AND ENTERTAINMENT

Virtually every village and town in Ireland seems to have a festival of some kind or other each year. Whatever the pretext for the celebration, it's usually also an excuse for serious partying. Well-established ones like the Cork Jazz Festival and the Wexford Opera Festival are big international events, and getting tickets for top performances can be well nigh impossible without advance planning. The very word "festival" seems to act as a magnet for all sorts of musicians, and many events are wonderfully overwhelming. No matter the size of the town, there's rarely enough room for all that's happening, with music and dancing bursting out of the official venues into surrounding streets and bars. The biggest of the annual events are listed here, but pick up a calendar of events at any major tourist office and you'll soon get a picture of the huge range of celebrations.

MUSIC

Apart from their sheer exuberance, the most enjoyable aspect of Irish festivals is, without doubt, the traditional music. Many festivals (known as *Fleadh* – pronounced fla) are devoted almost exclusively to this: the biggest of them is the **Fleadh Cheoil na hÉireann** (see opposite), which includes the finals of the All Ireland music and dance contests.

However, if you can't make it to a festival, there's usually plenty going on in the pubs and bars, especially in high season in the popular tourist spots. Music in Irish pubs is legendary, and

there's lots on offer, though only a relatively small proportion of it is "traditional". Country and western, for example, is extremely popular with a host of regular sessions across Ireland. You'll still find that Irish staple, the showband, too, and there's a myriad of middle-of-the-road pop bands lurking in country areas. Ballads are another well-developed Irish music form though the term "ballad" is a bit of a catch-all and open to countless interpretations – it's generally some form of dull crooning, often accompanied by just a guitar and monotonous beatbox. Brace yourself for the worst, and from time to time you'll be very pleasantly surprised.

The cream of pub music, however, has to be the **traditional sessions** of fiddles, accordions, bodhrán (a drum) and singing. Interest from abroad and the tourist industry has much to do with the resurgence of this musical culture – but this hardly matters, since the music can be phenomenal. The west coast (especially around Clare and Galway) has the best of the traditional scene. There's plenty in all the major cities, and pointers to the best sessions are given in the text. However, these locations are hard to pin down for long and it's wise to ask around and keep your ears open for local tips.

Traditionally Sunday evening was the night for sessions, and in rural areas this is still often the case (a throwback to restrictions on holy days that meant partying on Saturdays had to stop at midnight), but increasingly Friday and Saturday have become just as important, and, in Summer, you may find something happening any night of the week. Things generally don't get going till late, and a bar that's still empty at 10pm may be a riot of music by half-past. While it's all extremely convivial and relaxed, if you're a musician yourself and want to join in, then do so tactfully. The first thing to do is sit and listen for a while – to make sure you can play to a high enough standard – and then work out who the leader is and ask. If you're not playing, don't crowd the musicians; the empty seats around them are reserved for others who may arrive later.

Comhaltas Ceoltóiri Éireann is an organization that exists purely to promote traditional music and culture, and evenings organized by them (not always in bars), though by their nature not spontaneous, are well worth looking out for. They are run by real enthusiasts, and the standard of playing is usually pretty high.

MAJOR ANNUAL FESTIVALS AND EVENTS

Saint Patrick's Day (March 17): celebrations all over Ireland, including a national festival in Dublin and major events in all the larger towns and cities.

Irish Grand National (April): horse racing at Fairyhouse (Meath).

Cork International Choral Festival (April/May): one of the big ones.

Foyle Film Festival (April/May): the best of new Irish and international film, Derry.

Music Festival in Great Irish Houses (June): just what it says, classical music at venues around the country.

Irish Derby (June): and other important races at the Curragh (Kildare).

James Joyce Summer School (July): strictly for Joyce buffs; Dublin.

Galway Arts Festival (July): festival of music, theatre and general partying; one of the best.

Galway Races (July/August): another important race meeting, very popular.

Yeats International Summer School (August): this Sligo event has often courted controversy through its exploration of nationalistic themes.

Rose of Tralee International Festival (August): a massive event, centred round a beauty contest.

Fleadh Cheoil na hÉireann (August): the most important of all the traditional music festivals, held in a different town every year.

Kilkenny International Arts Week (August): includes recitals, poetry readings, art exhibitions.

Lisdoonvarna Matchmaking Festival (September): plenty of traditional entertainment accompanies the lonely hearts side of the festivities.

All Ireland Hurling and Football Finals (September): the biggest events of the year, separated by a fortnight, in Dublin.

Cork Film and Jazz Festivals (October): Ireland's major film event and an enormously popular jazz festival.

Derry Halloween Carnival (October/November): street theatre, music and mayhem, especially during the fireworks display on October 31.

Wexford Opera Festival (October/November): a large gathering of international renown.

SPORTS AND ACTIVITIES

Ireland has two hugely popular indigenous sports, hurling and Gaelic football, with important matches attracting big crowds and passionate support. **Hurling** is a stick game, a precursor of hockey and lacrosse, but much faster and more competitive than either and there are fifteen players a side. Like rugby, there's an H-shaped set of goalposts and each team aims to score as many points as possible by either hitting the leather, baseball-sized ball (*sliotar*) over the crossbar for one point or into the net below for three points. The game's skill lies in control of the broad, wooden hurley stick (*camán*) and players can knock the ball along the ground, hit it through the air or run knocking the ball up and down on the hurley. The ball can be caught by hand or with the hurley. The hurling season begins with local games in the early summer, progressing through county and then provincial championships to reach its climax in the All Ireland Hurling Final on the first Sunday in September at Croke Park in Dublin (see p.108). Cork, Kilkenny, Offaly and Tipperary are the most successful counties. **Camogie**, the women's version of hurling, is becoming increasingly popular, and well worth watching, if there's a match in the area.

Gaelic football is played on the same pitches as hurling and shares the same scoring system and team size. It has similarities with both rugby and association football, as the round, soccer-sized ball can be kicked, caught and passed by either boot or hand. However, running with the ball is only allowed if a player keeps control by tapping the ball from foot to hand every five steps. The season, which runs from mid-February, is organized like hurling's, culminating in an All

Ireland final at Croke Park on the third Sunday in September. Details of fixtures for hurling and gaelic football can be obtained from the Gaelic Athletic Association (☎01/836 3222).

Rugby union and soccer are also extremely popular and tickets for international matches much in demand, especially in the Republic. The international **rugby** team is a joint Republic/Northern Ireland side, with home matches played at Dublin's Lansdowne Road Stadium (see p.76 and p.109). The main event of the year is the Five Nations Championship, a series of international games against France, England, Scotland and Wales played in Spring. **Soccer** is organized on a professional basis in both the North and the Republic, though the majority of players are semi-professional, with teams competing in the Irish League and League of Ireland respectively. Standards are not especially high and Irish teams rarely progress beyond the preliminary rounds of the European competitions. Northern Ireland's international matches are played at Windsor Park, Belfast (see p.508), and the Republic's at Lansdowne Road. Both international teams draw the overwhelming majority of their players from the English and Scottish leagues. The Northern Ireland side has not seen any degree of success since the 1980s, but the Republic gained a high profile and creditable international reputation under the managership of the Englishman "Big Jack" Charlton in the 1990s – it's undoubted high point was the 1–0 defeat of Italy during the 1994 World Cup Finals. There's hope for the future too, as the Republic's youth team gained a remarkable third place in the 1997 World Finals and, uniquely, won both the under-16 and under-18 1998 European Championships. However, the most popular clubs here (and in the North) are Manchester United and Liverpool. Glasgow Celtic and Rangers are also popular in the North with support following sectarian Catholic and Protestant divisions.

Horse racing unites two Irish passions, horses and betting, and is carried out with a relaxed good humour that you shouldn't miss. Racing is concentrated around the Curragh, a grassy plain in Co. Kildare (see pp.124–126), where the classic flat-race course of the same name is located, along with Punchestown race course and many of Ireland's famous stud farms. The Irish Grand National is run at Fairyhouse in Co. Meath in April, the Irish Derby at the Curragh in June. The flat-racing season runs from mid-March to early November while National Hunt racing over jumps takes place throughout the year. For details of the

fixtures at Dublin's race course, Leopardstown, see p.108. Just as much fun is **greyhound racing**. There are two tracks in Dublin and another sixteen across the country. Information on meetings is available from Bord na gCon, the Irish Greyhound Racing Board (☎061/316788).

Cycling is a hugely popular sport in Ireland, exemplified by the large crowds all the way along the route of the Irish sections of the 1998 Tour de France, a race won in 1987 by one of the country's sporting heroes, Stephen Roche. Another, Sean Kelly, was world number one from 1984 to 1988. There's an enormous number of **golf** courses here too, with major championships like the Irish Open in July. Both tourist boards produce information on where you can play and have details of holiday packages and accommodation.

Naturally, as this is an island, there are innumerable opportunities for sea **angling** and hundreds of lakes and rivers for fishing of the fly and game varieties. In general, the best of the sea angling takes place on the south and west coasts and Bord Fáilte can help with information. The high spot of the fly fishing season is the emergence of the mayfly around mid-May when anglers flock to the best brown trout spots such as Lower Lough Erne (Co. Fermanagh), Lough Derg (Co. Clare) and the Corrib system (Co. Galway). There are plenty of other possibilities, however, and, again the tourist boards can assist.

The relatively sheltered waters of the east coast see most of the **sailing** activity, especially in Dublin Bay and further south around Arklow and Wexford, though there are excellent opportunities, too, in West Cork and on Lough Derg, Co. Clare. The south and southwest are most popular for cruising, though the Cork coast offers many possibilities for yachting. The rougher waters of the west coast restrict the options to the areas more protected from the elements, such as Galway Bay or Killybegs (Co. Donegal). On the north coast, Lough Swilly is increasingly popular, while on the other side of the border, there are numerous boating possibilities on Strangford Lough. For further information contact the Irish Sailing Association (☎01/280 0239). Inland waterways also offer **canoeing**, ranging from touring to rough- and white-water racing. **Windsurfing** and **water-skiing** are usually possible wherever there are good sailing waters and there are some fabulous beaches for **board surfing**. Some of the best are Barleycove beach (Co. Cork), Inch Strand and Castlegregory beach on, respectively, the south and north sides of the Dingle

Peninsula. Further north, Easky (Co. Sligo) offers perhaps the best of the lot, though Bundoran and Rossnowlagh beaches (Co. Donegal) are close contenders. The Northern Ireland coast between Castlerock (Co. Derry) and Portrush (Co. Antrim) attracts hordes of board fanatics.

Situated in the path of the Gulf Stream, there are stupendous opportunities for **diving** off the Irish coast, from protected harbours for beginners to rocky cliff faces for the more experienced. There are plenty of places where you can learn to dive too. The Irish Underwater Council can provide details of clubs and courses (☎01/284 4601).

The Ulster Way was the first waymarked **walking** trail in Ireland and it's still the longest, running a 560-mile circuit of Northern Ireland and linked to trails from Donegal and Cavan. If you don't fancy the complete trek, the Northern Ireland Tourist Board publishes information on specific shorter walks, and the route guides published by the Sports Council for Northern Ireland (House of Sport, Upper Malone Rd, Belfast BT9 5LA; ☎01232/381222; ☎028/9038 1222 from April 2000) are also useful. A variety of similar trails now exist in the Republic, ranging from walks through glens and mountains, such as the Wicklow Way, or around entire peninsulas, like the Beara and Dingle Ways. Although the walks are waymarked, you'll always need a good map as a standby. Local tourist offices and councils have produced map guides for some of the ways, as has East West Mapping (Ballyredmond, Clonegal, Enniscorthy, Co. Wexford; ☎054/77835), which also sells trail guidebooks. Bord Fáilte's publication *Walking Ireland* is a handy introduction. Particularly useful walking guides are listed in "Contexts", p.678.

The number of rare species visiting Ireland makes the country a **birdwatching** paradise. Again, the tourist boards can provide details and Birdwatch Northern Ireland has been established specifically to assist ornithologists visiting the North (☎01232/693232; ☎028/9069 3232 from April 2000). Though Ireland's mountain ranges are not especially high, there are numerous opportunities for **rock-climbing**, expecially in Counties Cork and Kerry – the latter's Macgillycuddy's Reeks make up for their lack of height by spectacular settings. To the east, the Wicklow Mountains are hugely popular, while the craggy splendour and coastal setting of the Mourne Mountains in County Down are hard to beat. The Mountaineering Council of Ireland (☎01/450 1633) publishes a number of guides and offers advice on the variety of peaks.

WALKING SAFETY

Though one of the joys of hill- and mountain-walking in Ireland is the sheer solitude of the experience, bear in mind that the lack of other people in your vicinity can be a significant drawback if a mishap occurs. The Irish climate can seem pretty mild, but the temperature drops two to three degrees Celsius for every thousand feet climbed and a strong wind can make it seem even colder. Mist can suddenly transform your surroundings too, so a pleasant day at sea-level can rapidly become perilous higher up. If you're planning any walk, especially on high ground, consider the following:

1. Always plan your route carefully beforehand and ensure, especially, that it can be finished before nightfall. Average walking speed is around two and a half miles an hour. A map is essential and, if you're unfamiliar with your route, carry a compass too. A torch, small first aid kit and whistle are useful and the mountain distress signal is six blasts of a whistle per minute, followed by a pause.

2. Check weather forecasts in advance and, no matter the weather when you set out, ensure you have clothing suitable for changes – warm, windand water-proof. Walking boots are essential for all but the shortest and easiest of walks.

3. Always carry a reserve supply of high energy food, e.g chocolate, and hot drink.

4. Walking alone is inadvisable, except in populated areas or where there are plenty of other walkers. Even when walking in a group, it's advisable to let someone (your hostel, B&B, etc.) know where you're going and when you're likely to return. If you drive to your starting point, a note left visible in your car is another alternative.

5. Exercise caution when walking along cliff tops – some 'safe' walks can become perilous in high winds. Streams in flood are particularly dangerous too and bear in mind that most accidents occur on the way back when you're fatigued, especially on descents.

6. If an accident does happen and urgent assistance is needed, telephone 999 and ask for the Mountain Rescue, if you're on high ground, or the local Garda station.

7. Follow the Farmland Code of Conduct – remember that often as not you'll be crossing someone's land, so respect the environment and leave everything as you found it.

SECURITY AND THE POLICE

The Republic is one of the safest countries in Europe in which to travel. This said, don't let the friendliness of people as a whole lull you into a general carelessness; like anywhere else visitors are seen as easy targets for petty thieves (particularly in the bigger cities) and women especially should always take note of our advice on choosing accommodation. Some areas of Dublin are dangerous late at night and it's a good idea to take local advice about safety on the streets from your hostel or B&B. Although the North has opened up a lot in the last few years, there is still a security presence, and you should be careful in certain city areas. Personal security, and crimes against the individual, are not a major worry. You're probably less likely to be robbed or mugged here than elsewhere in Britain.

In the Republic, people generally have a healthy indifference to law and red tape, perhaps in part a vestige of pre-Independence days, when any dealings with the police smacked of collusion with the British. The **police** – known as **Garda** or **Gardai** (pronounced "gar-dee") – accordingly have a low profile. In rural areas the low level of crime is such that policing is minimal and, should you need them, you might spend an entire afternoon waiting for the Garda to arrive. If you have

The emergency number in both the North and the Republic is ☎999 or 112.

any dealings with the Garda at all, the chances are that you'll find them affable enough.

In the **North** the **Royal Ulster Constabulary** (RUC) deal with all general civic policing and are the people you should go to if in difficulties. Police stations are heavily fortified and security inside is tight, but whatever their reputation, you'll find that the RUC are helpful in matters of everyday police activity.

Security measures have been considerably relaxed during the last few years. Many of the border controls have been dismantled and it's unlikely that you'll encounter either a police roadblock or an army foot patrol. However, at the time of writing, it is impossible to assess the impact of new measures introduced by both British and Irish governments in the wake of the bombing of Omagh town centre in August 1998. It does seem likely, however, that the security presence at certain key border crossings will have been reinforced. If you do find yourself being quizzed about your movements and plans, simply be polite and cooperative and you should experience no problems.

Obviously politics remains a sensitive subject in the North, and you should use your common sense about what you say to whom.

SEXUAL HARASSMENT, PREJUDICE AND RACISM

For women Ireland is wonderfully relaxing: the outlandish sexism of Irish society manifests itself in a male courtesy that can range from the genuine and delightful to the downright insufferable, but you are unlikely to experience any really threatening behaviour. Most uncomfortable situations can be defused by a straightforward, firm response.

That said, don't believe the general view that *nothing* can happen to you. It is worth remembering that outside the cities, communities are very small, and local women you see hitching alone do so in safety because they know and are known by just about everybody on the road. Foreign travellers don't have that added security, and, though it is very unlikely, you could be unlucky. In particular, if you are travelling alone use only the budget accommodation that is listed in this guide or recommended by the tourist office, don't go with touts at stations, and exercise the kind of care in cities at night that you would in any other European country. In the case of serious assault, if possible contact a Rape Crisis Centre before going to the police (telephone numbers are given in chapter listings). Attacks are rare and the Garda, though well-meaning, have little experience of handling distressed women.

Black travellers may have a less easy time of it. The Republic of Ireland, and, to an extent, the rural North are fiercely conservative and shamefully intolerant of minority groups. If you are black you may well experience a peculiarly naive brand of ignorant racism. Open comment on the colour of a person's skin isn't uncommon outside the major cities, especially in the remote west, where people simply aren't used to seeing black people, though here there's no need to anticipate any real malice. In the cities, there does seem to have been a marked change for the worse in recent years, and, along with increased aggression evident in society as a whole, verbal abuse would also seem to be on the increase.

The **gay** community is both the biggest and least visible minority in Ireland. Although part of the UK, Northern Ireland was excluded from the 1967 Act that legalized homosexuality for consenting adults in Britain. This led one individual to take his case to the European Court of Human Rights in 1982, which brought the legal status of gays in Northern Ireland into line with the rest of the UK. In the Republic, homosexuality has been legal since 1990, and a nominally wide-ranging Incitement Against Hatred Act was passed in 1994 specifically prohibiting discrimination against people on the grounds of sexual orientation as well as race. However, public indecency charges are still pursued – such as surveillance and arrest of gays cruising Dublin's Phoenix Park, and censorship laws are used to exclude gay material. Outside the big cities homosexuality is not at all socially accepted, and public displays of affection are out of the question.

TRAVELLERS WITH DISABILITIES

The disabled traveller in Ireland is not well served, and wheelchair users in particular are not likely to find ramps, lifts and wide doors commonly available. With this in mind, it is well worth contacting the National Rehabilitation Board (NRB) in the Republic and the Northern Irish Tourist Board (NITB) for information before you travel.

CONTACTS FOR TRAVELLERS WITH DISABILITIES

IN IRELAND

Disability Action, 2 Annadale Ave, Belfast BT7 3JH (☎01232/491011; ☎ 028/9049 1011 from April 2000).

Disability Federation of Ireland, 2 Sandyford Office Park, Sandyford, Dublin 18 (☎01/295 9344).

Irish Wheelchair Association, Blackheath Drive, Clontarf, Dublin 3 (☎01/833 8241).

Mental Health Association of Ireland, Mensane House, 6 Adelaide St, Dún Laoghaire, Co. Dublin (☎01/284 1166).

National Rehabilitation Board, 44 North Great George's St, Dublin 1 (☎01/874 7503) ; Access Dept., 25 Clyde Rd, Dublin 4 (☎01/608 0400).

Northern Irish Tourist Board, St Anne's Court, 59 North St, Belfast BT1 1NB (☎01232/246609; ☎028/9024 6609 from April 2000).

IN BRITAIN

Disabled Drivers Association, Ashwellthorpe, Norwich NR16 1EX (☎01508/489449).

Disabled Drivers Motor Club, Cottingham Way, Thrapston, Northamptonshire NN14 4PL (☎01832/734724).

Holiday Care Service, 2nd floor, Imperial Building, Victoria Rd, Horley, Surrey RH6 7PZ (☎01293/ 774535). *Information on all aspects of travel.*

Royal Association for Disability and Rehabilitation (RADAR), 250 City Rd, London EC1V 8AF (☎0171/250 3222). *All kinds of info and advice.*

IN NORTH AMERICA

Directions Unlimited, 720 N Bedford Rd, Bedford Hills, NY 10507 (☎1-800/533-5343). *Tour operator specializing in custom tours for people with disabilities.*

Jewish Rehabilitation Hospital, 3205 Place Alton Goldbloom, Chomedy Laval, PQ H7V 1R2 (☎514/688-9550 ext 226). *Guidebooks and travel information.*

Mobility International USA, PO Box 10767, Eugene, OR 97440 (Voice and TDD: ☎503/343-1284). *Information and referral services, access guides, tours and exchange programmes. Annual membership $25 (includes quarterly newsletter).*

Society for the Advancement of Travel for the Handicapped (SATH), 347 Fifth Ave, New York, NY 10016 (☎212/447-7284). *Non-profit-making travel industry referral service that passes queries on to its members as appropriate.*

Travel Information Service (☎215/456-9600). *Telephone-only information and referral service for disabled travellers.*

Twin Peaks Press, Box 129, Vancouver, WA 98666 (☎206/694-2462 or 1-800/637-2256).

Publisher of the Directory of Travel Agencies for the Disabled ($19.95), listing more than 370 agencies worldwide; *Travel for the Disabled* ($19.95); *Directory of Accessible Van Rentals* ($9.95) and *Wheelchair Vagabond* ($14.95), loaded with personal tips.

IN AUSTRALASIA

ACROD, PO Box 60, Curtin, ACT 2605 (☎02/6282 4333); 24 Cabarita Rd, Cabarita (☎02/9743 2699). *Compiles lists of organizations, accommodation, travel agencies and tour operators.*

Barrier-Free Travel, 36 Wheatley St, North Bellingen, NSW 2454 (☎02/6655 1733). *Fee-based travel access information service.*

Disabled Persons Assembly, 173 Victoria St, Wellington (☎04/801 9100).

The NRB publishes very useful and comprehensive **survey guides** of **accommodation, tourist amenities** and **restaurants/pubs** in the Republic. They also have listings of accessible toilets and provide the keys to them. Another useful publication is their *Dublin: A Guide for People with Disabilities*, which has detailed information on access to transport, toilets, public buildings, accommodation, shops and nightlife etc in the capital (all of the above publications are free). Even if you don't intend staying in Dublin, it's worth getting for its advice on transport to Ireland and how to get the best service from airlines and ferry companies.

Certain **ferry companies** offer good reductions to disabled travellers coming from mainland Britain. For members of the Disabled Drivers Association (DDA) or the Disabled Drivers Motor Club (DDMC), Irish Ferries offer a return fare of £80 for the driver and vehicle (£30 for additional passengers). In high season, however, these rates are only available from Tuesday to Thursday, and at any time you need to book fourteen days in advance. Stena offers a ten percent reduction off all sailings, and off-peak you can get a reduction of up to fifty percent for a car and up to five people; booking in advance is advisable.

In **Northern Ireland**, NITB (also very helpful) publish a guide to accessible accommodation, and their general guide to restaurants throughout the North highlights those with wheelchair ramps and facilities for disabled people (a nominal fee is charged for both publications). It is also worth contacting Disability Action for their holiday fact sheets.

DIRECTORY

CHILDREN Children are generally liked and indulged in Ireland, even if there are few places actually designed to cater for them. Baby supplies are sold everywhere, and children are generally welcome at B&Bs (though few have cots or special facilities), in pubs during the daytime, and almost anywhere else.

CONTRACEPTIVES Throughout Ireland anyone over 18 can buy condoms at pharmacies (though in the Republic, where legal contraception was only introduced in 1992, you may still find places which don't sell them – or don't approve). The pill is available on prescription only.

ELECTRICITY In the Republic, electricity is 230V AC, in the North 240V AC. Plugs everywhere are British-style three square pins (just occasionally you may still find old round ones). In other words British appliances will work everywhere; North American ones will need both a transformer and a plug adapter; Australian and New Zealand appliances only an adapter.

LAUNDRY You'll find laundries only in the bigger towns and on large caravan/campsites. Hostels, though, will often have a washing machine for residents' use, and at many B&Bs they'll do your washing for you. Elsewhere it's worth taking along a tube of Travel Wash – designed to be used in hotel washbasins – which makes a lot less mess than powder.

TOILETS Public toilets are reasonably common in all the big towns, and generally acceptably clean, if no more. Or you can pop into the local pub, and stop for a drink while there. The Irish labels to look out for are *Fír* (Men) and *Mná* (Women).

WORK Although EU citizens are legally allowed to live and work in Ireland, local unemployment is extremely high, and your chances of finding a decent job are slim. If you intend to stay in Dublin, there are plenty of jobs for waiters/waitresses, especially in the Temple Bar area. Another option for travellers is seasonal work in resorts or perhaps helping out in a hostel in return for board and pocket money. You'll need to search locally.

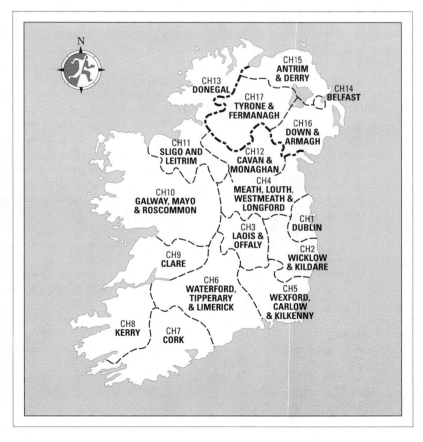

N

CH15 **ANTRIM & DERRY**

CH13 **DONEGAL**

CH14 **BELFAST**

CH17 **TYRONE & FERMANAGH**

CH16 **DOWN & ARMAGH**

CH11 **SLIGO AND LEITRIM**

CH12 **CAVAN & MONAGHAN**

CH10 **GALWAY, MAYO & ROSCOMMON**

CH4 **MEATH, LOUTH, WESTMEATH & LONGFORD**

CH1 **DUBLIN**

CH3 **LAOIS & OFFALY**

CH9 **CLARE**

CH2 **WICKLOW & KILDARE**

CH6 **WATERFORD, TIPPERARY & LIMERICK**

CH5 **WEXFORD, CARLOW & KILKENNY**

CH8 **KERRY**

CH7 **CORK**

DUBLIN

E mphatically the Republic of Ireland's capital, **DUBLIN** is a focus for the energy of a country now redefining itself as a modern European nation and is earning itself a reputation as a cosmopolitan young city. Of roughly one and a half million people in greater Dublin, more than fifty percent are under 25, and the relative prosperity of many of them is making its impact on a rapidly changing urban landscape. New shops are everywhere, and restaurants, cafés, bars and clubs are opening in abundance, bringing an unmistakable buzz to the capital, especially at night. The city's emergence from provincialism is, however, only part of the truth, as Dubliners will be quick to tell you. With the continuing drift of population from the land to the capital, Dublin is bulging at the seams, which, of course, brings its problems – spend just a couple of days here and you'll come upon inner-city deprivation as bad as any in Europe. The spirit of Dublin has its contradictions, too, with youthful enterprise set against a leaden traditionalism that harks back nostalgically, as in the words of one popular folk song, to "Dublin city in the rare old times". However, the collision of the old order and the forward-looking younger generations is an essential part of the appeal of this extrovert and dynamic city.

If you approach Dublin by sea, you'll have an opportunity to appreciate its magnificent physical setting, with the fine sweep of **Dublin Bay** and the weird, conical silhouettes of the Wicklow Mountains providing an exhilarating backdrop to the south. Central Dublin is not big, and it's easy to find your way around. One obvious axis is formed by the river, the **Liffey**, which runs from west to east and acts not only as a physical, but also a social and, at times, psychological dividing line. The **North Side**, distinctly working class, with some areas blighted by unemployment and drugs, stands in stark contrast to the affluent neighbourhoods of the **South Side**.

The metamorphosis from Europe's economic dunce to top of the class has cast the city economically and culturally into the heart of the continent. This new-found cosmopolitan chic has its home in the vibrant **Temple Bar** area, "Dublin's Left Bank", with its numerous pubs, clubs, galleries and restaurants. For many visitors, however, the city's heart lies around the best of what is left of Georgian Dublin – the grand set pieces of **Fitzwilliam** and **Merrion** squares, with their graceful red-brick houses with ornate, fan-lighted doors and immaculately kept central gardens, and the wide but strangely decorous open space of St Stephen's Green. The elegant South Side is also the setting for Dublin's august seat of learning, Trinity College and its famous library; **Grafton Street**, the city's upmarket shopping area; and most of the city's museums and art galleries.

ACCOMMODATION PRICE CODES

Throughout this book, prices of hotels, guesthouses and B&B's have been graded with the codes below, according to what you can expect to pay for a double room in high season. For more details on accommodation, see p. 29.

① Under £26	④ £40–55	⑦ £90–110
② £26–33	⑤ £55–70	⑧ £110–130
③ £33–40	⑥ £70–90	⑨ Over £130

North of the Liffey, the main thoroughfare is **O'Connell Street**, on which stands the **General Post Office**, the scene of violent fighting in the Easter Rising of 1916. Further north, among Georgian squares older and seedier than the ones you'll see on the South Side, are the **Dublin's Writers' Museum** and the **Hugh Lane Municipal Museum of Art**. West again, and you come to Dublin's biggest open space – indeed, one of the world's largest city parks – **Phoenix Park**, home of both the President's Residence and the zoo.

The urban sprawl stands in sharp contrast to the countryside around – trains make access easy to the whole curve of Dublin Bay, from the fishing port of **Howth** in the north to the southern suburbs of **Sandycove** with its James Joyce connections, Dalkey, made famous by the comic writer Flann O'Brien, and salubrious **Killiney**, now colonized by the rich and famous. And further: Dublin must be one of the world's easiest capitals to get out of, making it a good base for exploring the hills and coastline of Wicklow to the south and the gentler scenery to the north that leads up to the megalithic monuments of the verdant **Boyne Valley**.

Some history

> *Fort of the Saxon*
> *Garrison of the Dane*
> *Augustan capital*
> *Of a Gaelic nation*
>
> Louis MacNeice

Although the earliest evidence of a settlement beside the Liffey is Ptolemy's celebrated map of 140 AD, which shows a place called Eblana, it's as a Viking settlement that Dublin's history really begins. The Norse raiders sailed up the Liffey and, destroying a small Celtic township, set up a trading post on the south bank of the river at the ford where the royal road from the Hill of Tara in the north crossed the Liffey on its way to Wicklow. The Vikings adopted the Irish name, Dubh Linn or Dark Pool, for their settlement, which soon amalgamated with another Celtic settlement, Baile Átha Cliath ("town of the hurdles", pronounced *Ballya-aw-kleea,* and still the Irish name for Dublin), on the north bank.

The next wave of invaders were the **Anglo-Normans**. In the twelfth century, the opportunistic Strongbow and a band of Welsh knights were sent over by Henry II in response to the beleaguered King of Leinster Dermot McMurrough's request for help to regain his throne – in return he gave an oath of fealty. The invasion was successful, and the English king, concerned that Strongbow and his Welsh adventurers were becoming too powerful, fixed a court at Dublin. The city was thereby established as the centre of British influence in Ireland and set the precedent for the annual social and political Seasons, which were to shape Dublin's role and character for the next seven centuries.

Because most of the early city was built of wood, only the two cathedrals, part of the Castle and one or two churches have survived from before the seventeenth century. What you see today, in both plan and buildings, dates essentially from the **Georgian period**. By this time, soldiers in the service of the English monarchs, who had been rewarded with confiscated land, had begun to derive income from their new estates. As they began to replace their original fortified houses with something more fashionable, they wished also to participate in the country's burgeoning economic and political life, which was centred on Dublin. Their town houses (along with those of the growing business and professional classes), and the grandeur of the public buildings erected during this period, embodied the new confidence of the **British ruling class**: a group that was, however, starting to regard itself not as British, but as Irish.

In the second half of the eighteenth century the wealth of this Anglo-Irish class was reflected in a **rich cultural life** – Handel's *Messiah*, for instance, was first performed in Ireland, and the legacy of architecture, furniture and silverware, though now much diminished, speaks for itself. Growing political freedom was to culminate in the parliament of 1782 in which Henry Grattan made a famous **Declaration of Rights**, modelled on the recent American example, which came very close to declaring Irish (by which he meant Protestant Anglo-Irish) independence. A severely limited and precarious enterprise, the Irish bid for self-government was to collapse very soon, with the abortive **uprising of 1798** and the **Act of Union** which followed in 1801.

The Act of Union may have shorn Dublin of its independent political power, but the city remained the centre of British administration, in the shape of the Vice Regent, and the Seasons continued to revolve around the Viceroy's Lodge (now the President's Residence) in Phoenix Park. Along with the rest of Ireland, Dublin entered a long **economic decline** and became the stage for much of the agitation that eventually led to Independence. In 1829, the Catholic lawyer (and Kerryman) Daniel O'Connell secured an important advance by achieving limited Catholic emancipation, allowing Catholics to play some part in the administration and politics of their capital city and, in a signal victory, was elected Lord Mayor of Dublin. Dublin was also the centre of the **Gaelic League**, which, founded by Douglas Hyde in 1893, encouraged the formation of an Irish national consciousness through efforts to restore the native language and culture. This paved the way for the **Celtic literary revival** under W.B. Yeats and Lady Gregory and the establishment, in 1904, of the Abbey Theatre.

Poverty and **violence** were the other side of the political coin, and the early years of the twentieth century saw the fight for the establishment of trade unionism in Ireland. In 1913, this came to a head in the **Great Lock-Out**, when forcibly unemployed workers and their families died of hunger and cold. Open violence hit the streets during Easter Week of **1916** in the uprising that was the main event in the long struggle for Irish independence. The prominent battles were fought in and around the centre of Dublin, and the insurgents made the General Post Office their headquarters (see p.86). The city's streets were the scene of violence once more during the brief **Civil War** that broke out after the creation of the Irish Free State in 1921, when supporters and opponents of the **partition** of Ireland fought it out across the Liffey, and the Four Courts, one of Dublin's great Georgian buildings, went up in flames after being bombed by opponents of the Anglo-Irish Treaty.

The history of Dublin since Independence has been the history of the capital of a young-old nation endeavouring to leave behind its colonial past. It's to this, as well as the appalling condition of many of the old tenements, that the destruction of much of the Georgian city can be attributed. Today areas of the inner-city, especially on the North Side, remain fractured and decaying, despite the decanting of people from the tenements to – as it turned out rather inadequately planned – suburban estates during the 1960s and 1970s, and more recent corporate plans to attract investment and build new housing rather than the previous high-rises. On the South Side Georgian streets have been replaced in many places by modern offices – you can see how human civic planning has given way to corporate exhibitionism.

One of the outstanding successes of recent years has been the **new development** at **Temple Bar** (see p.76), which has done much to enhance the image and atmosphere of the city. Indeed Dublin now has a new feel to it, a sense that the legacy of its colonial relationship with Britain has finally been put to one side, as the capital, with the rest of the Republic, looks increasingly to Europe and America, rather than across the Irish Sea.

Arrival, information and transport

Buses from out of town, the airport included, will drop you at or close by the **Central Bus Station**, or Busáras (☎874 6301), in Store Street, behind the Custom House. Right by the river, this is dead central for almost anywhere in the city and is one of the few places you can leave luggage during the day (£1.50–2). The city is served by two main **train stations**, Connolly and Heuston. The former is on Amiens Street, behind the bus depot, while Heuston Station is in the west of the city just south of the river from Phoenix Park.

The telephone code for Dublin is ☎01.

Coming in from the **airport**, six miles north of the centre, you can take the official airport bus for £2.50, or a scheduled city bus (#41A or #41C) will do the same job for £1.10. Either takes around half an hour to reach the bus station; a taxi will cost you around £10. If you arrive by **ferry**, you'll come in at one of two harbours: Dún Laoghaire (pronounced *Learey*; for Stena Line services), six miles out, is on the efficient DART (Dublin Area Rapid Transport) city train network, which will whisk you into town in about twenty minutes; Dublin Port (Irish Ferries/B&I), nearer in, is served by local buses #53 and #53A, though it is common for coaches from the UK to continue to Busáras in Store Street. For information on leaving the city see "Listings".

Information

The obvious first stop for information is **Dublin Tourism's main office**, which is housed in a converted church on Suffolk Street and has all the usual booking facilities, as well as a bookshop and café (July–August Mon–Sat 9.30am–8.30pm, Sun 11am–5.30pm; Sept–June Mon–Sat 9am–6pm, except Tues 9.30am–6pm). The office is always incredibly busy, but it has much of the most frequently needed information posted on the walls and has a vast collection of literature and maps (not all of it free). There's a room-booking service, which costs £1 for accommodation in Dublin and £3 for anywhere else. Since the staff aren't allowed to make recommendations, all you're paying for is a phone call. Other branches are at Dublin Airport (8am–10pm; ☎844 5977), the port at Dún Laoghaire (opening times vary according to ferry times, minimum hours 9am–8pm; ☎284 6361) and at Dublin Port (June–Aug for ferry arrivals). Bord Fáilte has a much smaller office at Baggot Street Bridge (9am–5.15pm; ☎676 5871). There's a Northern Ireland Tourist Board office in 16 Nassau St (☎878 6055), which provides a high standard of service.

There's an **USIT office** on Aston Quay, just opposite O'Connell Bridge (Mon–Fri 9am–5.30pm, Sat 10am–1pm; ☎677 8117). USIT not only books bed and breakfasts during the summer but also has its own hostel and a travel agency offering student discounts on ferries and flights. Call in here for Travelsave stamps (see p.19), ISIC cards and information on everything that's going on in Dublin.

For listings of Dublin events, the best sources are either the fortnightly magazine *In Dublin*, which you can pick up from any newsagent, or the *Dublin Event Guide*, free from the tourist office and most cafés around the city. *The Irish Times* and *Evening Herald* have theatre and cinema listings daily; the former also does a good weekly overview in its Saturday edition.

City transport

It's customary to say that the way to get to know Dublin is to walk. It's true that the city's size makes this a practical possibility, but equally true that walking the city streets can quickly become a tiring slog. Luckily there's an extensive and reasonably priced local bus network that makes it easy to hop on a **bus** whenever you want. Buses start running between 6am and 6.30am, and the last city-centre buses leave town around 11.30pm. After midnight a limited night bus service takes over and runs every hour. Maximum fare on the daytime bus system is £1.10. A one-day bus-only pass costs £3.30; an Explorer Ticket, a one-day bus-and-train pass (including DART) costs £4.50; a four-day version of the latter is still better value at £10. Passes are available from most newsagents. Finding your way around the bus system may prove more of a problem, although most stops do now have timetables and routes for the buses that stop there. If you don't know which stop to go to in the first place, though, either ask a bus inspector – there usually seems to be one around, dispensing directions – or invest in a bus timetable, which includes a Dublin bus map, for £1.20 from

Ashbourne, Slane & Derry △   △ The Airport   Malahide & Howth △

Prospect Cemetery

Botanical Gardens

INGLAS ROAD

CABRA

DRUMCONDRA

MARINO

NAVAN ROAD

PHIBSBOROUGH

CLONLIFFE ROAD

CABRA ROAD

Mountjoy Prison

Croke Park Stadium

PHIBSBOROUGH RD

PORTLAND ROW

Phoenix Park

NORTH CIRCULAR ROAD

Zoo

Cathedral (pro.)

Connolly Station

Bus Station

CONYNGHAM RD

EDEN Q. CUSTOM HOUSE QUAY NORTH WALL QUAY

CHAPELIZOD ROAD

Heuston Station

St Patrick's Hospital

PARKGATE ST WOLFE TONE ST ELLIS Q. ARRAN Q. INNS Q. UPR. ORMOND Q. WELLING. ESTON. Q.

BURGH Q. GEORGE Q. CITY QUAY

TARA ST.

LINK ROAD

ISLANDBRIDGE

Kilmainham Gaol

Christ Church Cathedral

Trinity College

PEARSE STREET

Pearse Street Station

SOUTH LINK

Irish Museum of Modern Art

Guinness Brewery

Dublin Castle

MOUNT ST.

SHELBOURNE RD

BEACH STREET

INCHICORE

KILMAINHAM

St Patrick's Cathedral

ST STEPHEN'S GREEN

HADDINGTON RD

DOLPHIN ROAD

Grand Canal

DOLPHIN'S BARN

Irish Jewish Museum

MESPIL RD

LANSDOWNE ROAD

BALLSBRIDGE

PARNELL ROAD

GROVE ROAD   CANAL RD

LEESON'S ST.

SANDYMOUNT

CRUMLIN

RATHMINES

WESTBURY RD

DONNYBROOK

HAROLD'S CROSS ROAD

UPR. MOREHAMPTON RD

MILLTOWN

TERENURE

RATHGAR

University College (U.C.D.)

GREENTREES RD

DODDER PARK RD

Pearse Museum

TEMPLEVILLE ROAD

BRAEMORE ROAD

SPRINGFIELD AVENUE

RATHFARNHAM

CHURCH TOWN ROAD

TANEY ROAD

Rathfarnham Castle

MAIN ST.

SANDYFORD ROAD

▽ Dublin Mountains

Mullingar, Athlone, Galway, Sligo & Westport ◁   Naas, Kilkenny, Waterford, Limerick, Cork & Killarney ◁   Blessington ◁

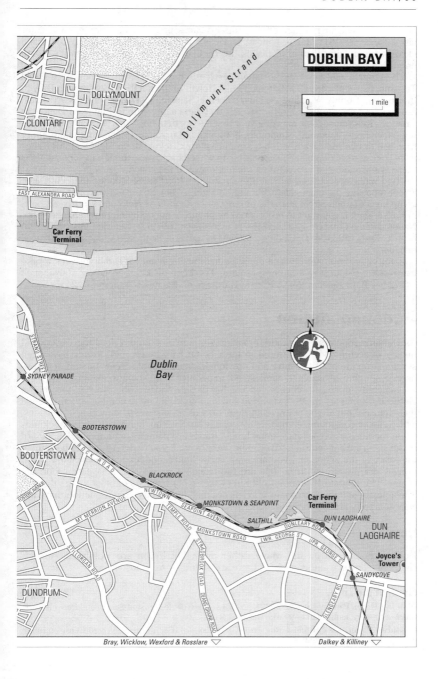

DUBLIN BAY

0   1 mile

DOLLYMOUNT

CLONTARF

Dollymount Strand

EAST ALEXANDRA ROAD

Car Ferry Terminal

N

Dublin Bay

STRAND STREET

SYDNEY PARADE

BOOTERSTOWN

BOOTERSTOWN

ROCK ROAD

BLACKROCK

FOSTERS AVENUE

NEWTOWN

MT MERRION AVENUE

SEAPOINT AVENUE

TEMPLE ROAD

MONKSTOWN & SEAPOINT

MONKSTOWN ROAD

SALTHILL

Car Ferry Terminal

DUN LAOGHAIRE

STILLORGAN ROAD

STRADBROOK ROAD

DEANS GRANGE ROAD

LWR GEORGE ST

DUNLEARY ROAD

UPR GEORGE ST

DUN LAOGHAIRE

Joyce's Tower

GLENGEARY RD

SANDYCOVE

DUNDRUM

Bray, Wicklow, Wexford & Rosslare ▽   *Dalkey & Killiney* ▽

Dublin Bus, 59 Upper O'Connell St (Mon–Fri 9am–5pm, Sat 9am–1pm; ☎873 4222 for city buses, ☎836 6111 for provincial services). Dublin Bus also runs city tours and cheap trips outside Dublin to places the regular services don't visit, so it's worth enquiring about these.

The other useful city transportation service is the **DART**, the Dublin Area Rapid Transport system (☎836 3333), which links Howth to the north of the city with Bray to the south in County Wicklow, via such places as Sandycove. DART services are quick, efficient and easy to use, and the stretch that runs along Dublin Bay from Dalkey to Killiney gives you such an amazing view that it's worth taking the train just to see it. It's not expensive – maximum single fare is £1.50 – but if you're considering taking more than one or two trips, it's worth buying an Explorer Ticket (see p.53). The DART runs from 6.55am to 11.30pm and is accessible to wheelchair users, though in some stations there is a pronounced gap between the platform and the coach.

Taxi ranks are situated outside the *Shelbourne Hotel* on St Stephen's Green, Dame Street (opposite the main gate of Trinity College), Abbey Street (on the right-hand side going up O'Connell Street from the bridge), or close to *Jurys Hotel* and *The Towers* hotel in Ballsbridge. If you want to order a taxi by phone, some of the more reliable firms are National Radio Cabs (☎677 2222; 24hr), City Cabs (☎872 7272), Central Cabs (☎365 555) or ABC Taxis (☎285 5444). Finding a taxi after 11pm is difficult, so if you know you'll need one, book it.

If you're brave enough to face the often hair-raising habits of Dublin drivers, a **bike** can make a useful way of getting around. Try Rent-A-Bike at 58 Lower Gardiner St (☎872 5399), or Raleigh Rent-a-Bike at Hardings on Bachelor Walk (☎873 2455).

Accommodation

As Dublin's popularity as a tourist destination increases so too does the variety and quality of accommodation offered in the city. Of late, hotels and hostels have been springing up in both the centre and previously unfashionable areas. In summer, however, it is highly advisable to book ahead, imperative to do so on weekends.

Generally, prices are cheaper on the North Side and anywhere out of the centre. Hotels in Dublin are mostly expensive and sometimes no more comfortable than good guesthouses, but if you're travelling out of season, it's worth checking reductions, which can be considerable. Also, many swanky hotels drop their tariffs at the weekends when the business types have gone home. B&Bs are plentiful, and of a high standard in the suburbs, but central B&Bs can be overpriced. If you're determined to be right at the heart of the action and you are on a fairly limited budget, various well-organized official and private youth hostels are the cheapest option; most have some private rooms. The tourist office in Suffolk Street (see p.53) has lists of most things that are available, though there are many good places that, for various reasons, neither have nor want tourist board recommendation.

Hotels

Dublin's hotels are on the whole rather pricy, but if you are looking for luxury, Georgian elegance and good food, there are a number to choose from.

North of the Liffey

Aishling Hotel, Parkgate St (☎677 2324, fax 679 3783). Near to Heuston Station and Phoenix Park, this is a friendly, family-run hotel with disabled access. ⑦.

Cassidy's Hotel, 7–8 Cavendish Row (☎878 0555, fax 878 0687). Fine converted Georgian house with good car parking facilities. ⑥.

Gresham, Upper O'Connell St (☎874 6881, fax 878 7175). Traditionally regarded as Dublin's second-best hotel after the *Shelbourne*, and considerably flashier. ⑨.

Holiday Inn, 99–107 Pearse St (☎670 3666, fax 670 3636). Good facilities with parking but not the greatest location. ⑦.

Hotel Isaacs, Store St (☎855 0067, fax 836 5390). Modern, friendly hotel near to bus and train stations. ⑤.

Jurys Custom House Inn, Custom House Quay (☎607 5000, fax 829 0400). As with all hotels in this chain, it's family-friendly with first-rate disabled access. Parking is available in the nearby car park. ⑤.

Maple Hotel, 75 Lower Gardiner St (☎874 5239, fax 874 0225). Reasonably comfortable, small, central hotel – handy for the airport and bus station – with budget rates. ④.

Royal Dublin Hotel, Upper O'Connell Street (☎873 3120, fax 873 3666). A modern hotel on the north side of the main thoroughfare opposite the traditional *Gresham*. ⑧.

Wynn's Hotel, 38–39 Lower Abbey St (☎874 5131, fax 874 1556). An old-fashioned hotel recently refurbished and a traditional stopover for Irish from outside the capital. Close to the Abbey Theatre. ⑥.

St Stephen's Green area

Buswell's, 23–27 Molesworth St (☎676 4013, fax 676 2090). Comfortable, well-run hotel in a Georgian terrace near St Stephen's Green. ⑦.

The Georgian House, 18 Lower Baggot St (☎661 8832, fax 661 8834). One of the few period buildings in Dublin where you can actually stay; five minutes' walk from St Stephen's Green, with a good seafood restaurant. ⑧.

Grafton Plaza, Johnson's Place (☎475 0888, fax 475 0908). A centrally located hotel offering high-standard accommodation. ⑧.

Longfield's Hotel, 9–10 Fitzwilliam St Lower (☎676 1367, fax 676 1542). A small, friendly hotel, right in the heart of Georgian Dublin, with an excellent restaurant serving French and Mediterranean cuisine. ⑦.

Mont Clare, Merrion Square (☎607 3800, fax 661 5663). Another hotel in the Merrion Square area that exudes Georgian elegance and charm. Good weekend offers. ⑨.

Shelbourne Hotel, St Stephen's Green (☎676 6471, fax 661 6006). Widely acknowledged to be Dublin's best hotel, and an old-money society watering hole. Has elegantly furnished period interiors and a buzzing social life, plus an excellent restaurant and bar. Be prepared to pay, though. ⑨.

The Westbury Hotel, Henry St (☎679 1122, fax 679 7078). Five-star flashiness, just off Grafton Street. ⑨.

Temple Bar and around

Aston Hotel, 7–9 Aston Quay (☎677 9300, fax 677 9007). Good-value hotel in Temple Bar with full disabled access. No parking. ⑥.

Adams Trinity, 28 Dame Lane (☎670 7100, fax 670 7101). A small hotel near Dublin Castle. ⑧.

Bewley's, 19–20 Fleet Street (☎670 8122, fax 670 8103). Friendly hotel right at the heart of the action. Breakfast is an extra £6. ⑦.

Bloom's Hotel, Anglesea St (☎671 5622, fax 671 5997). Another new hotel in Temple Bar offering fine rooms; breakfast is extra. ⑥.

Central Hotel, 1–5 Exchequer St (☎679 7302, fax 679 7303). Bright pink walls and colourful modern Irish art save it from overpowering tastefulness. Does excellent breakfasts. ⑧.

The Clarence Hotel, Wellington Quay (☎662 3066, fax 662 3077). U2-owned hotel overlooking the Liffey designed in the manner of the *Royalton Hotel* in New York. It makes no secret of its ultra-stylish aspirations and neither do many of its guests. ⑧.

George Frederick Handel Hotel, Fishamble St (☎670 9400, fax 670 9410). Fine hotel on the edge of Temple Bar, with a lively bar attached. ⑦.

Harding Hotel, Copper Alley, Christchurch (☎679 6500, fax 679 6504). Right by Temple Bar, this bright, modern USIT hotel offers en-suite rooms, many of which accommodate up to three people, at a competitive flat rate; the restaurant serves food all day. ⑤.

Jurys Hotel, Christchurch Place (☎874 0225, fax 874 5239). A rather ugly new building opposite Christchurch. On the plus side, it's close to St Patrick's Cathedral, Guinness and the Irish Museum of Modern Art, and the flat rate for rooms makes it a good option for anyone travelling with small children. ⑤.

Parliament Hotel, Lord Edward St (☎670 8777, fax 670 8787). Large red-bricked hotel opposite Dublin Castle, with parking and close to some of the best entertainment in the city. ⑨.

Riverhouse, 23–24 Eustace St (☎670 7655, fax 670 7650). Small family-friendly hotel in one of the area's quieter streets. ④.

Temple Bar Hotel, Fleet St (☎677 3333, fax 677 3088). Modern hotel, ideally placed for exploring the Temple Bar area. Disabled access. ⑧.

Wellington Hotel, 21–22 Wellington Quay (☎677 9315, fax 677 9387). Small modern hotel with bar and nightclub at the north end of Temple Bar, with competitive flat-rate rooms. ⑥.

Ballsbridge

Berkeley Court, Lansdowne Rd (☎660 1711, fax 661 7238). Five-star elegance in quiet area. ⑨.

Jurys Hotel, Pembroke Rd (☎660 5000, fax 660 5540). Huge complex with all manner of facilities including a round-the-clock coffee bar. ⑨.

Lansdowne, 27 Pembroke Rd (☎668 2522, fax 668 5585). Popular with the rugby and, more recently, football crowds because of the proximity of Lansdowne Road Stadium, this comfortable hotel is two miles from the city centre in leafy surroundings. ⑥.

The Towers, Lansdowne Rd (☎667 0033, fax 660 5540). Another *Jurys* hotel with huge bedrooms; generally attracts a business clientele. ⑧.

Dalkey and Killiney

The Court Hotel, Killiney Bay, Killiney (☎285 1622, fax 285 2085). Large Victorian-style hotel near the DART station, with seafood and French restaurants. ⑦.

Fitzpatrick Castle Hotel, Killiney (☎284 0700, fax 285 0207). A four-star ex-stately home with fine views of the Bay. Breakfast not included in the price. ⑨.

Dún Laoghaire

Kingston Hotel, Adelaide St (☎280 1810, fax 280 1237). Family-friendly hotel that can prove a bargain if you book one of the rooms that sleep five people. ⑥.

Rochestown Lodge, Rochestown Ave (☎285 3555, fax 285 3914). Child- and pet-friendly hotel near the ferry terminal. ⑥.

Royal Marine Hotel, Royal Marine Rd (☎280 1911, fax 280 1089). A top-of-the-range hotel reflecting the town's slightly faded identity as a seaside resort. ⑧.

Bed and breakfast

Bed and breakfast places abound, with the cheapest clustered around Connolly Station, especially on Gardiner Street, on the North Side. In the south there are more salubrious, and more expensive, guesthouses in the Ballsbridge area, still within easy walking distance of the centre. The best balance between price and quality, though, generally involves staying further out in the suburbs. Given the relatively small scale of the city and the excellent public transport, these places are definitely the better option.

Gardiner Street and around

This area has the advantage of being close to both the bus and train (Connolly) stations, and bus #41 from the airport stops on the street. However, it is prone to car theft and anyone with a car should consider whether or not secure car parking is available. Formerly, Lower Gardiner Street had a poor reputation and, although some pretty dingy places still remain, there is also a lot of excellent accommodation at reasonable prices.

Anchor Guest House, 49 Lower Gardiner St (☎878 6913, fax 878 8038). Refurbished Georgian house. Discounts for children, infants free. ⑤.

The Abbot Lodge, 88 Lower Gardiner St (☎836 5548). Bright guesthouse offering special family rates. Car parking available. ④.

Carmel House, Upper Gardiner St (☎874 1639). High-quality guesthouse. ④.

Clifden House, 32 Gardiner Place (☎874 6364, fax 874 6122). A refurbished Georgian house with secure parking. Child reductions and baby-sitting available. Breakfast not included. ⑦.

Fatima House, 17 Upper Gardiner St (☎874 5292, fax 872 7674). Family-friendly guesthouse allowing children over 7 at half price and below that age free. Offers single rooms for £20, though these are not en suite. ④.

Georgian Court Guesthouse, 77–79 Lower Gardiner St (☎855 7872). A flashy new guesthouse with all the services you'd expect plus a car park. ③.

Harvey's Guesthouse, 11 Upper Gardiner St (☎874 8384). A good value option on Gardiner Street with secure parking. ③.

Lyndon House, 26 Gardiner Place (☎878 6950). A well-run, friendly Georgian guesthouse. The young owners have done a great job with the house, though it's a pity they couldn't refurbish the street as well. ⑤.

Marian Guesthouse, 21 Upper Gardiner St (☎874 4129). A clean and friendly place with good breakfasts and no exploitive price hikes at peak times. ②.

The Talbot, 95–98 Talbot St (☎874 9202). Large, modern guesthouse just off Gardiner Street. Prices rise at the weekend but it's good value during the week. ④.

The Townhouse, 47–48 Lower Gardiner St (☎878 8808, fax 878 8787). Set in a refurbished Georgian house, once the home of playwrights Dion Boucicault and Lafcadio Hearn, *The Townhouse* is more like a hotel in terms of ambience and service. There is secure parking, great breakfasts and all rooms are en suite with TV, fridge and tea maker. ⑥.

St Stephen's Green area

Fitzwilliam, 41 Upper Fitzwilliam St (☎660 0448, fax 676 7488). Upmarket southside guesthouse near Merrion Square. Has car park but no breakfast. ⑥.

Grafton Guesthouse, 26–27 South Great Georges St (☎679 2041, fax 677 9715). Perfectly located, this is a fine, family-friendly place to stay. ⑥.

The Grey Door, 23 Upper Pembroke St (☎676 3286, fax 676 7488). If you have come to Ireland to pamper yourself, and quality, not price, is your concern, then look no further than this classy establishment. ⑦.

Staunton's on the Green, 83 St Stephen's Green (☎478 2300, fax 478 2263). Posh southside place with prices that match the standards. ⑦.

Trinity Lodge, 12 South Frederick St (☎679 5044, fax 679 5223). A fine Georgian townhouse on South Frederick Street, right in the heart of the city. ⑧.

Ballsbridge

Directly south of the centre, about two miles out, the better-heeled inner suburb of Ballsbridge (on bus routes #5, #6, #6A and #7) has high-standard B&Bs on offer.

Aberdeen Lodge, 53–55 Park Ave, off Ailesbury Rd (☎283 8155, fax 283 7877). Large Edwardian house offering all kinds of comforts. Has gardens and secure parking. ⑦.

Anglesea Townhouse, 63 Anglesea Rd (☎668 3877, fax 668 3461). Upmarket guesthouse with reductions for pensioners and children. ⑦.

Mrs Bridget Brady, *Northumberland Lodge*, 68 Northumberland Rd (☎660 5270). A spacious Victorian house in pleasant suburban street. ⑥.

Mrs Cathy Cotter, *Lansa House*, 68 Merrion Rd (☎668 0416, fax 660 0803). Non-smoking mock-Tudor house opposite the Royal Dublin Society. Parking and child-minding available. ⑤.

Mrs Sheila Matthews, *Elva*, 5 Pembroke Park (☎660 2931). Convenient location at the centre-of-town end of Ballsbridge. ②.

Merrion Hall, 56 Merrion Rd (☎668 1426, fax 668 4280). Another swanky establishment in the embassy belt. ⑦.

Number Eighty-Eight, 88 Pembroke Rd (☎660 0277, fax 660 0291). This place is hard to beat and has all the extras. ⑦.

Sandymount

Sandymount (buses #1, #2, #3 and #6, and a short walk from DART stations Sandymount and Sydney Parade) is slightly further out again, but the attraction here is that you're near the sea, it's also fairly handy for the ferry and the accommodation is good value.

Mrs M. Bermingham, 8 Dromard Terrace (☎668 3861). Old-fashioned comfort, with child reductions and baby-sitting facilities, but no ensuite facilities. Good-value single price available. Open May–Sept. ②.

Kane's, 49 Beach Rd (☎660 2969). Standard B&B, right on the seashore. ④.

Mrs M. Smyth, 21 Sandymount Rd (☎668 3602). Quiet location close to the seafront.③.

Northwest

Glasnevin (to the north and west of the centre), Cabra (on the northern fringes of Phoenix Park) and Castlenock (to the west of the park) are all reasonable places to stay and not too far from the centre.

Mrs E. Delahunty, *Marymount*, 137 New Cabra Rd, Cabra (☎868 0026). Just a twenty-minute walk from the centre, with TVs in all the rooms. ③.

Egan's Guest House, 7–9 Iona Park, Glasnevin (☎830 3611). Fine family-run guesthouse in a pleasant area. Breakfast is extra. ④.

Iona House, 5 Iona Park, Glasnevin (☎830 6217). Family-friendly guesthouse with good facilities. Charges the same price for a single as per person sharing. There's no car park but the area is pretty safe. ④.

Mrs Mary McKay, *Deerpark House*, Castlenock Rd, near Phoenix Park gates (☎820 7466). To the west of the park, beside Castlenock riding school, this comfortable B&B has en-suite rooms, most with TVs. ③.

Northeast

Northeast, in Clontarf, you're into suburbia again, but you'll be close to the sea. Here rates are generally reasonable, with lots of places to choose from, particularly along the Clontarf Road, which runs right by the seafront. The only drawback to staying here is that Clontarf buses terminate around Talbot Street in the north of the city, so getting to the South Side can be time-consuming. Inland from Clontarf, Drumcondra, although less salubrious than its neighbour, is well served by bus routes (#11, #13 and #16, as well as airport buses) and has a similarly high number of places to stay.

Nuala Betson, *The Villa*, 150 Howth Rd, Clontarf (☎833 2377). Easily accessible by buses #29, #31, #32 and #42A, this is a friendly place with good breakfasts. ④.

Bernie Byrne, *Casino View*, 88 Malahide Rd, Clontarf (☎833 6988). Nice house on the main road, so there are no problems with transport into the city. There is car parking in the grounds. ③.

Mrs C. Canavan, 81 Kincora Rd, off Vernon Ave, Clontarf (☎833 1007). An easy walk from the wildlife reserve on North Bull Island, this house is both friendly and cheap. ③.

Janice Conboy, *Autumn Leaf*, 41 St Lawrence Rd, Clontarf (☎833 7519). Victorian house with a friendly atmosphere. ③.

Copper Beach Court, 16 Hollybrook Park, Clontarf (☎833 3390). Large Victorian guesthouse in a fine location with secure parking. ④.

John Devlin, *Arnagh House*, 301 Clontarf Rd (☎833 8841). A good-value option in a non-smoking Victorian house. ③.

GAY FRIENDLY ACCOMMODATION

The Alternative Guesthouse, near Connolly Station (☎855 3671, fax 855 3655). En-suite twin rooms available, some with kitchenettes. ③.

Inn on the Liffey, 21 Ormond Quay (☎677 0828). Centrally located, this place offers small, reasonably priced rooms. ③.

Frankies, 8 Camden Place (☎478 3087). A friendly place, though the rooms are small; try to secure one with a shower. ⑤.

The Horse and Carriage Hotel, 15 Aungier St (☎478 3537 or 3087). Largest pink hotel in the city, but expect no frills or value for money. ⑤.

Tig na mBan – *The Women's House* (☎473 1781). Offers self-catering or B&B near the city centre. ③.

Mrs Carmel Drain, *Bayview*, 265 Clontarf Rd (☎833 9870). A bright, non-smoking house. Fine vegetarian breakfasts. ③.

Carmel Geoghegan, *The White House*, 125 Clontarf Rd (☎833 3196). Close to Dublin Bay and on the #30 bus route, this house is friendly and very reasonable. Book early if you intend to visit in the high season. ③.

Hedigans, 14 Hollybrook Park, Clontarf (☎853 1663). Top-notch nine-bedroom, family-friendly guesthouse. ⑤.

Eileen Kelly, *Torc House* 17 Seacourt (off St Gabriels Rd), Clontarf (☎833 2547). A detached Georgian house with car parking, in a quiet area. ④.

Helen Stafford, 96 Clontarf Rd (☎833 5893). Good-value option on the main Clontarf road. Parking is available and there are separate lounges for smokers and non-smokers. ③.

Drumcondra

Auburn Guesthouse, Navan Rd, Castlenock (☎822 3535, fax 822 3550). Large, well-equipped modern guesthouse near Castlenock village. ②.

Mrs Maureen Black, 35 Ormond Rd, Drumcondra (☎837 0299). Standard B&B with four double rooms, two of which are en suite. ③.

Charleville Lodge, 268–272 North Circular Rd, Phibsborough (☎838 6633). Impressive guesthouse in a Victorian terrace, close to Phoenix Park. Secure car park. ④.

Mrs R. Gibbons, 24 Alphonsus Rd, Drumcondra (☎830 3221). Just a mile from the centre, with one double room, three singles and shared bathroom. ②.

Kathleen Hurney, 69 Hollybank Rd, Drumcondra (☎837 7907). Comfortable en-suite rooms with TVs, and near the bus stop for easy access to the centre of town. ③.

T. Ryan, 15 Iona Drive, Drumcondra (☎830 5724). A fine detached Edwardian house in a quiet neighbourhood. ③.

St Andrew's Guesthouse, 1 Lambay Rd, Drumcondra (☎837 4684). Large guesthouse with parking and limited disabled access. ⑤.

Hostels

Of late, Dublin has seen a plethora of new upmarket hostels being built. They tend to market themselves as budget accommodation rather than hostels and it is fair to say that there is a difference between these and old-fashioned hostels, not only in the generally higher standard of accommodation, but also in their emphasis on the individual rather than the communal. Many have private and double rooms, for example. The hostels in the centre, especially around Temple Bar, tend to be very lively, so if you need a good night's rest it would be advisable to take one further out.

North of the Liffey

Abraham House, 82–83 Lower Gardiner St (IHH; ☎855 0600). Like all hostels in Lower Gardiner Street, this is handy for Busáras, and in addition, bus #41 from the airport stops outside. It's friendly and clean, with a self-catering kitchen, a launderette, bureau de change, free hot showers and no curfew. There's also a secure car park. Four-bed and private rooms available.

Abbey Hostel, O'Connell Bridge, 29 Bachelors Walk (☎878 0700). You can't get more central than this, just off O'Connell Street Bridge on the north side of the river. All rooms are en suite with great showers. There is no curfew, good security, a large dining room and barbeque area. £14.

Backpackers Citi Hostel, 61–62 Lower Gardiner St (☎855 0035). Basic hostel only worth considering if you want to save a couple of pounds. Breakfast not included. Open 24 hours all year round.

Backpackers Euro Hostel, 80–81 Lower Gardiner St. The down-and-out older brother of the *Backpackers Citi Hostel*. There are rumours of a refit; the sooner the better. Pricing is capricious and exploitive, but starts at around £7.

Cardijn House (or **Goin' My Way**), 15 Talbot St (IHH; ☎878 8484). Above a newsagent's, this family-run hostel is one of Dublin's oldest. Curfew but no lockout. Closed Dec 20–Jan 4.

Celts House, 32–33 Blessington St (☎830 0657). Friendly hostel in the north of the city off Dorset Street.

Charles Stewart, Parnell Square (☎878 0350 or 1767). Another fine north side option with good security and group discounts. Car parking is available on weekends and after 6pm. Good breakfasts. £18.

Dublin International Youth Hostel, 61 Mountjoy St (An Óige; ☎830 1766, fax 830 1600). The hostel is an ex-convent and still retains the austere feel of its former incarnation. There are 363 beds, but it is well run and offers laundry and car parking facilities.

Globetrotters Tourist Hostel, 46 Lower Gardiner St (IHH; ☎874 0592, fax 878 8787). Superlative hostel with security-coded doors, first-rate showers and a breakfast that really sets you up for the day. The dining area is light and spacious with a small garden, great in summer. £10–12.

Isaac's, 2–5 Frenchman's Lane, just round the corner from Busáras (IHH; ☎874 9321, fax 874 1574). Otherwise known as the *Dublin Tourist Hostel*, *Isaac's* is housed in an eighteenth-century wine warehouse, offering a mix of accommodation, from dormitory bunks to single and double rooms. Breakfast isn't included in the price, but there's a good restaurant. Room lockout is from 11am–2.30pm. No curfew. Blankets cost 50p, sheets £1.

Jacob's Inn, 21–28 Talbot Place (☎855 5660). Flashy budget accommodation with swipe card security system. All rooms are en suite with good lockers and there's a decent kitchen.

MEC Hostel, 44 North Great George's St (☎878 0071). A recently renovated hostel on possibly the finest Georgian street on the North Side. The friendly staff and the impressive Georgian building make this a great place to stay. In addition to dorm beds, self-catering apartments are available for around £250 a week.

Temple Bar area

Barnacles Temple Bar House, Temple Lane (☎671 6277, fax 671 6591). Modern, well-equipped hostel in the centre of Temple Bar. There is no curfew and no lockout and breakfast is included in the price. It's becoming increasingly popular, so be sure to book in advance.

Kinlay House, 2–12 Lord Edward St (IHH; ☎679 6644, fax 679 7437). This relaxed, friendly USIT hostel is well run and has good laundry and kitchen facilities. There's no curfew and it can be noisy at night. Breakfast is included in the price.

Oliver St John Gogarty's, 18–21 Anglesea St (☎671 1822, fax 671 7637). Stylish accommodation, including rooftop apartments for four people at £100. There's a pub attached, so this is not the place for quiet contemplation. Dorms from £15 during the week, £16 at weekends.

Strollers, 29 Eustace St (☎677 5614). Not as swanky as the other hostels in the area, *Strollers* is adequate, though not great value for money. £11.

St Stephen's Green area and The Liberties

Ashfield House, 19–20 D'Olier St (☎679 7734). A new well-run and well-equipped hostel in a converted church. Family rooms are available, with under-10's staying for free. It has full disabled access and the staff are very accommodating.

Avalon House, 55 Aungier St (IHH; ☎475 0001, fax 475 0303). Impressive red-brick Victorian ex-medical school close to St Stephen's Green and a stroll from Temple Bar. Fine, if not substantial, breakfasts, kitchen, good common room and restaurant. No curfew.

Brewery Hostel, 22–23 Thomas St (☎453 8600 or 8616). Set in a converted library near the Guinness brewery, this hostel offers clean rooms with sturdy wooden bunks. Breakfast is included and there's secure car parking.

South of the city

Morehampton House, 78 Morehampton Rd (☎668 8866, fax 668 8794). On bus routes #10, #46A and #46B, a few miles out of the centre in leafy Donnybrook, this spacious Victorian house provides hostel accommodation in 4–8-bedded rooms. Breakfast costs an extra £1.50.

Belgrave Hall, 34 Belgrave Square, Monkstown (☎284 2106, fax 280 5838). Impressive accommodation, with off-street parking, next to the Irish Cultural Institute in Monkstown. The area is easily accessible both by DART train, buses #7, #7A or #8 and the Nitelink Bus to Monkstown Road. £10.95.

The Old Schoolhouse, Eblana Ave, Dún Laoghaire (☎280 8777). Adequate hostel with a good-sized kitchen.

Student accommodation (available during the summer)

Trinity Hall, Dartry Rd, Rathmines (☎497 1772). On bus routes #4 and #14A, three miles out of town. There are some family rooms where children under 10 can stay for free. Sports facilities are available. £20 for a single, £15 per person sharing.

UCD Village, Belfield (☎269 7111, fax 269 7704). UCD is a soulless modern campus outside the city centre on bus route #10. A complex of modern self-catering apartments about five miles south of the centre. Accommodation is in single rooms with shared kitchen, dining area and shower room. It's a bit pricey at £22, but a family might be interested in the three-room apartment at £66.

Camping

There's no central campsite in Dublin, but several on the outskirts, including one south of Dún Laoghaire.

Comac Valley Caravan & Camping Park, Corkegh Regional Park, off the Naas Rd, Clondalkin, (☎464 0644; bus #68, #68A or #69). Pleasant site set in landscaped grounds with views of Dublin Mountains. Open all year round.

Donabate, on the North Side, a few miles beyond Swords (☎843 6008; bus #33B from Eden Quay). Fairly basic site with only limited space for tents, so phone in advance.

Shankill, close to the DART stop at Shankill (☎282 0011; bus #45, #45A, #46 or #84). South of Dún Laoghaire by the sea, within reach of secluded beaches.

The City

Although almost all of Dublin's cinemas, two of its most important theatres, the Gate and the Abbey, and one of its busiest shopping areas are on the North Side around O'Connell Street, the majority of the city's historic monuments, including its ancient centre, are south of the river. As you'll probably be spending most of your time on the South Side – also the hub of the newer, more upmarket centres for shopping and socializing – Trinity College, linked to St Stephen's Green by the pedestrianized shopping street, Grafton Street, seems as good a place as any to start.

College Green and Trinity College

In some ways the topography of Dublin has stayed remarkably constant since the city was founded, when the Vikings sited their Haugen or Thengmote, the central meeting place and burial ground, on what is now **College Green**. Formerly known as Hoggen Green, it remained the centre of administrative power in Ireland until the Act of Union.

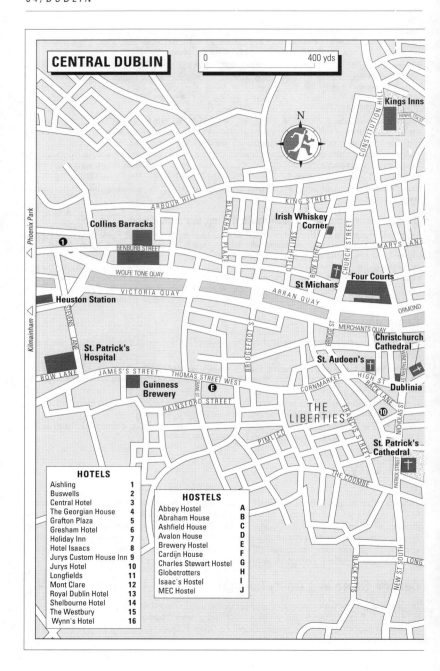

CENTRAL DUBLIN

0   400 yds

N

Kings Inns

HENRIETTA ST

CONSTITUTION HILL

ARBOUR HILL

KING STREET

Collins Barracks

Irish Whiskey Corner

BLACKHALL PLACE

SMITHFIELD

BOW STREET

CHURCH STREET

MARYS LANE

BENBURB STREET

WOLFE TONE QUAY

St Michans

Four Courts

VICTORIA QUAY

ARRAN QUAY

ORMOND

Heuston Station

STEVENS LANE

BRIDGEFOOT ST

BRIDGE ST

MERCHANTS QUAY

Christchurch Cathedral

St. Patrick's Hospital

BOW LANE

JAMES'S STREET

THOMAS STREET WEST

St Audoen's

HIGH ST

BACK LANE

Dublinia

Guinness Brewery

CRANE ST

CORNMARKET

NICHOLAS ST

RAINSFORD STREET

THE LIBERTIES

FRANCIS STREET

PIMLICO

St. Patrick's Cathedral

PATRICK STREET

THE COOMBE

Phoenix Park

Kilmainham

HOTELS

Aishling	1
Buswells	2
Central Hotel	3
The Georgian House	4
Grafton Plaza	5
Gresham Hotel	6
Holiday Inn	7
Hotel Isaacs	8
Jurys Custom House Inn	9
Jurys Hotel	10
Longfields	11
Mont Clare	12
Royal Dublin Hotel	13
Shelbourne Hotel	14
The Westbury	15
Wynn's Hotel	16

HOSTELS

Abbey Hostel	A
Abraham House	B
Ashfield House	C
Avalon House	D
Brewery Hostel	E
Cardijn House	F
Charles Stewart Hostel	G
Globetrotters	H
Isaac's Hostel	I
MEC Hostel	J

BLACK PITTS

NEW ST SOUTH

LONG

Celts House and Dublin International Youth Hostel

Municipal Art Gallery
Irish Writers' Museum
James Joyce Centre
SUMMERHILL
Black Church
Wax Museum
PARNELL SQ N
ST GEORGE'S PL
PARNELL SQ E
PARNELL STREET
PARNELL SQ W
GARDINER STREET
AMIENS STREET
Gate Theatre
Rotunda Hospital
St. Mary's Pro-Cathedral
MOORE ST
O'CONNELL STREET
MARLBOROUGH STREET
Connolly Station
PARNELL STREET
DORSET ST
KINGS INN S
WOLFE TONE ST
HENRY ST
TALBOT STREET
Busáras
BERESFORD PLACE
HENRY ST
ABBEY STREET LOWER
Custom House
St Mary's
MARY STREET
ABBEY STREET UPPER
EDEN QUAY
Abbey Theatre
CUSTOM HOUSE QUAY
CAPEL STREET
see 'Temple Bar' map for detail
HA'PENNY BRIDGE
BACHELORS WALK
O'CONNELL BRIDGE
Tara St. Station
MATT TALBOT BRIDGE
QUAY
WOOD QUAY
ASTON QUAY
WESTMORELAND ST
COLLEGE ST
TOWNSEND STREET
PEARSE STREET
TEMPLE BAR
Bank of Ireland
DAME STREET
COLLEGE GRN
Trinity College
Pearse Street Station
LORD EDWARD STREET
City Hall
EXCHEQUER ST
SUFFOLK ST
WICKLOW ST
NASSAU STREET
LINCOLN PL.
WERBURGH ST
Dublin Castle
STEPHEN ST
GT GEORGES ST
WILLIAM ST
Civic Museum
GRAFTON STREET
DAWSON STREET
National Library
KILDARE STREET
National Gallery
BRIDE S
Marsh's Library
AUNGIER STREET
Royal College of Surgeons
Mansion House
Leinster House
MERRION SQUARE
National Museum
St. Stephen's Green
BAGGOT ST
Huguenot Cemetery
MERRION ST
FITZWILLIAM STREET EAST TOWER
No. 29
CAMDEN ROW
LANE
CAMDEN STREET LOWER
HARCOURT S
Newman House
Royal Hibernian Academy
Bank of Ireland
FITZWILLIAM SQUARE
FITZWILLIAM STREET EAST
National Concert Hall
LEESON STREET LOWER

Trinity College

In comparison to the mighty facade of the Bank of Ireland opposite, the modest portico of **Trinity College** seems almost domestic in scale. Founded in 1591 by Queen Elizabeth I, it played a major role in the development of an **Anglo-Irish tradition**, with leading families often sending their sons to be educated here rather than in England. The statues outside represent Edmund Burke and Oliver Goldsmith, two of Trinity's most famous graduates. The philosopher and statesman Burke (1729–97) adopted an interesting political position, simultaneously defending Ireland's independence and insisting on its role as an integral part of the British Empire (see p.661); Goldsmith (1728–94) was a noted wit and poet (see p.661). Other illustrious alumni include Jonathan Swift, author of *Gulliver's Travels* and many other satirical works (see p.661), and Wolfe Tone, leader of the United Irishmen and prime mover of the 1798 uprising, as well as Bram Stoker, of Dracula fame, the playwright J.M. Synge and playwright and novelist Samuel Beckett.

Until recently, Trinity's Anglo-Irish connections gave it a strong **Protestant bias**. At its foundation, the college offered free education to Catholics who were prepared to change their religion, and right up to 1966 – long after the rule on religion had been dropped by the college itself – Catholics had to get a special dispensation to study at Trinity or risk excommunication. Nowadays, roughly seventy percent of the student population is Catholic, and Trinity is just one of Dublin's universities; University College Dublin is based just south of Donnybrook and forms part of the National University of Ireland; Dublin City University is in Glasnevin.

Simply as an architectural set piece, Trinity takes some beating. It served as an English university in the film *Educating Rita* – bizarre but understandable, given that it looks the way a great university should. Its cream stone college buildings are ranged around cobbled quadrangles in a grander version of the arrangement at Oxford and Cambridge (the cobbles apparently have to be relaid every seven years as the land, reclaimed from the sea, subsides).

With the frenetic city left behind, the first building that catches your eye as you enter is the **Chapel**, reflected in the windows of the Theatre or examination hall, whose elegant, stuccoed interior makes a fine setting for the concerts sometimes held here (check the notice boards in the main entrance). Both were designed by Sir William Chambers, a Scottish Neoclassical architect who never visited Ireland. Beyond the chapel on the left is the **Dining Hall**, also used for exams, built by the German architect Richard Cassels in 1743. The bell tower, or **Campanile**, in the middle of the square, was put up in 1853 and is believed to mark the site of the priory which long predated the university. A startling element of colour is introduced by the red brick of the Rubrics, student accommodation dating from 1712 and one of Trinity's oldest surviving buildings.

THE LIBRARY AND THE BOOK OF KELLS

The other early survivor is the famous **Library** (Mon–Sat 9.30am–5pm, June–Sept also Sun 9.30am–5pm; £3.50), which is meant to receive a free copy of every book published in Britain and Ireland and also contains a famous collection of priceless Irish manuscripts, above all the celebrated **Book of Kells**. Some 200,000 of the total collection of three million books are held here in the old library: the rest are stored off site, where over half a mile of new shelving is needed every year to accommodate new volumes. It's a long – 209ft in all – tall, aristocratic room, flooded with light, with books housed on two storeys of shelves. As designed by Thomas Burgh in the early eighteenth century, the library originally had just one floor, but in 1859 the roof was raised and the upper bookcases were added.

At the entrance to the library is a well-conceived exhibition called "Picturing the Word", which provides some background information on the *Book of Kells* and the other important Irish manuscript held here, the *Book of Durrow*. Here you learn that the illuminated manuscripts are derived from the Celtic ecclesiastical tradition of St Columba, which embraced not only Ireland but also Scotland and the north of England and had a strong influence on monastic institutions in mainland Europe. There's still some debate over whether the eighth-century Book of Kells was really copied and illuminated in Ireland at all; the location may have been Scotland – maybe Iona, St Columba's first Scottish port of call – or even Lindisfarne in northern England. At all events, the book was taken to the monastery of Kells in County Meath for safekeeping during the Viking raids of the ninth century, and, after a chequered history – during which it spent some time buried underground and some thirty of its pages disappeared, it was brought to Dublin in the seventeenth century. Totalling 680 pages, the Book of Kells consists of the four gospels of the New Testament, written in Latin. The book was re-bound in the 1950s into four separate volumes, of which two are on show at any one time: one open at a completely illuminated page, the other at a text page, itself not exactly unadorned, with patterns and fantastic animals intertwined with the capitals.

Famous as the Book of Kells is, the **Book of Durrow** is in many ways equally interesting. It is the first of the great Irish illuminated manuscripts, dating from between 650 and 680AD, and has, unusually, a whole page (known as the carpet page, for obvious reasons) given over to ornament. It's noticeable in all these early manuscripts that the depictions of the human form make no attempt at realism – St Matthew in the *Book of Durrow*, for instance, is apparently wrapped in a poncho, with no hands. The important thing is the pattern, which is derived from metalwork (as in the amazing Ardagh Chalice and Tara Brooch, which you can see in the National Museum close by). The characteristic spirals are always slightly asymmetrical – apparently another trick to ensure that the eye doesn't tire – and it's believed that the ornamentation in general had a symbolic meaning, although its full significance is now unknown.

After examining the books, you climb the stairs to the magnificent Long Room, at the far end of which are two early Irish **harps**, one of them traditionally known as Brian Boru's harp although it's been dated to the fifteenth century, some four centuries after Boru defeated the Vikings at Clontarf in 1014. Also on display is an original copy of the 1916 **Proclamation of the Irish Republic**.

THE DUBLIN EXPERIENCE AND THE DOUGLAS HYDE GALLERY
In summer, visitors to the college tend to be steered towards the **Dublin Experience**, a forty-minute audiovisual display, which uses a combination of archive and new material to trace Dublin's and, to a lesser extent, Ireland's history. It's unlikely that it will give, as it claims, a "complete orientation to the city", but if you're footsore and still have money in your pocket, it may warrant a visit (June–Sept every hour from 10am to 5pm; £3).

If you have time to explore, it's worth having a look at the carvings of animals, birds and foliage around the exterior and much of the interior of the museum on the right-hand side of New Square. They were executed by the O'Shea brothers who were hired and given free licence by the famous firm of architects, the Deanes. The brothers certainly didn't shrink from their task and produced a riot of eccentric ornamentation that earned them the displeasure of their employers and subsequent dismissal. Set just behind this is what is seen as the finest example of modern architecture in the city. Certainly not to everyone's taste, the Berkely Library wears its 60's Brutalist style firmly on its sleeve, though curiously it tends to complement, rather than jar, with its more antiquated neighbours. Behind the library stands the **arts and science block**, which is the centre for student life on campus. The **Douglas Hyde Gallery of Modern Art**, in the same complex, is one of the city's few experimental art venues and always worth checking out; it also has a good bookshop.

The Bank of Ireland

Across the busy traffic interchange from the college, the massive Bank of Ireland has played an even more central role in the history of Anglo-Irish Ascendancy. When originally begun in 1729 by Sir Edward Lovett Pearce, it was envisaged as a suitably grand setting for the parliament of a nation, as the Anglo-Irish were coming to regard themselves, although Jonathan Swift, for one, had some typically tart opinions as to its worth:

> *As I stroll the city, oft I*
> *Spy a building large and lofty*
> *Not a bow-shot from the college*
> *Half the globe from sense and knowledge.*

The Ascendancy's efforts to achieve self-government culminated in the famous Grattan parliament of 1782, in which **Henry Grattan** – whose gesturing statue stands outside on College Green – uttered the celebrated phrase, "Ireland is now a nation". The Protestant, Anglo-Irish parliament endorsed the country's independence unanimously.

This period of nominal self-government was, however, short-lived; with the passing of the Act of Union in 1801, Ireland lost both its independence as a nation and its parliament (which acquiesced by voting itself obediently out of existence). With its original function gone, the building was sold to the Bank of Ireland for £40,000 two years later. Though not exactly geared up for coach parties, the bank does admit sightseers during normal banking hours (Mon–Fri 10am–12.30pm & 1.30–3pm; Thurs closes 5pm; guided tours Tues 10.30am, 11.30am, 1.45pm). Its interior is magnificently old-fashioned – you are shown around by ushers wearing costumes seemingly unchanged since the nineteenth century – and in winter, coal fires glow in the entrance hall's massive grates. In the atmospheric former **House of Lords**, with its coffered ceiling, oak surrounds and eighteenth-century Waterford glass chandelier, you can see the mace from the old House of Commons and two 1733 Thomas Baille tapestries celebrating Protestant victories of the previous century, the Siege of Derry of 1689 and the Battle of the Boyne of 1690.

Grafton Street to the National Museum

The streets that surround pedestrianized Grafton Street frame Dublin's quality shopping area. Boasting no fewer than two shopping malls – the converted Georgian Powerscourt Town House and an extraordinary 1980s confection on the corner of St Stephen's Green, exhibiting a confusion of cultural references that have been variously described as French, Indian, Renaissance and Georgian – it's a totally different Dublin from that which you'll find on the North Side: chic, sophisticated and expensive.

Grafton Street

Grafton Street itself is unabashedly commercial, but it's a pleasant enough place to while away some time – here as in most metropolises, shopping is a way of life, and people come here as much to see and be seen as to buy. Cafés and restaurants of all sorts abound; shops are middle-of-the-road and upward (see "Shopping" p.106). Dublin's leading department store, Brown Thomas, is a classy location for some retail therapy, while Powerscourt Town House is similarly upmarket and set back a little on Clarendon Street. As well as simply wandering in and out of its retail palaces, you can also take in the street life. Since its pedestrianization, Grafton Street has become the centre of Dublin's burgeoning street theatre, and this is one of the few places where you'll find buskers, including poetry buskers.

Unmissable in Grafton Street, even if you have no other business in the area, is **Bewley's coffee house** (daily 7am–1am; Thurs–Sat until 2am). In its dark wood and marble-tabled interior, *Bewley's* does all-day tea, coffee and food ranging from meals to cakes and sticky buns, along with the best potato soup in the universe. It's an extraordinary atmosphere and unbeatable value – a great place to sit and watch people, read a book or write your novel (no one will try to hurry you, even if you've only bought a cup of tea). A testament to the vigour of the café tradition in the city, *Bewley's* is a place where everyone goes – you'll see a range of people from students and old ladies to high-powered businessmen. On the top floor, a small museum traces the history of this Dublin institution. Founded in the 1840s by the Quaker Bewley family, it became a workers' co-operative in 1971 and subsequently almost folded in 1986, provoking a national crisis until the government stepped in and offered to help before a buyer was secured. There are two other central branches of *Bewley's*, each with a slightly different character: in Westmoreland Street, which has wonderful Art Nouveau fireplaces (daily 7.30am–9pm), and South Great George's Street, a smaller and more subdued incarnation (Mon–Sat 6.45am–6pm).

Close to Grafton Street is the **Dublin Civic Museum** at 58 South William St (Tues–Sat 10am–6pm, Sun 11am–2pm; free), a tiny establishment that is probably strictly for museum and history buffs. The display consists of a garbled but oddly intriguing collection of artefacts relating to the history of the city from Viking times to the present.You can see, among other things, the head of the statue of Lord Nelson that used to stand outside the General Post Office in O'Connell Street and was blown up by the IRA in 1966, one of the original 1916 proclamations of the Republic of Ireland, and fascinating minutiae such as timetables detailing the excruciatingly slow progress of that state-of-the-art mode of transport, the canal-boat, across Ireland in the late eighteenth and early nineteenth centuries.

Dawson Street

Dawson Street, just east of Grafton Street, is altogether quieter than its neighbour, and is home to some of Dublin's better **bookshops** (see p.107) as well as a number of august institutions. Chief among these is the **Mansion House**, a delicate building of 1710 weighed down by heavy Victorian wrought iron. This has been the official residence of the Lord Mayor since 1715 and was also where the *Dáil Éireann*, the Irish parliament, met in 1919 to ratify the independence proclamation of 1916. The Mansion House isn't generally open to the public, but in any case there's not a great deal to be seen inside.

Next door, the decorous red-brick house containing the **Royal Irish Academy** is also closed to the public. One of the great learned institutions of Europe, it publishes books of Irish interest and has a weighty collection of Irish manuscripts. Next door again, St Anne's (Church of Ireland) church has an amazingly ornate Italianate facade which is a real surprise when you catch sight of it along Anne Street. Inside, behind the altar, are wooden shelves that were originally designed to take loaves of bread for distribution among the poor of the parish under the provisions of a 1720s bequest. On Thursday lunchtimes, St Anne's hosts a series of recitals and other cultural activities – check *In Dublin* for details.

Kildare Street: Leinster House

Moving east again, and marking the point where what's left of the Georgian city begins, Kildare Street is the really monumental part of the Grafton, Dawson, Kildare trio. The most imposing building is undoubtedly **Leinster House**, built in 1745 as the Duke of Leinster's town house. At that time, the fashionable area of Dublin was north of the river, and there were those who mocked him for building a town house in the south on what was then a greenfield site. The Kildare Street facade, facing the town, is built to look like a town house; the other side, looking out on to what is now Merrion Square, resembles a country house.

Today, this is one of the most important buildings in Dublin, housing the **Irish parliament** – the *Dáil Éireann*, or House of Representatives, and the *Seanad Éireann*, or Senate – as well as the **National Museum** and **National Library**. The Dáil (pronounced *Doil*) has 166 representatives – *Teachtaí Dála*, usually shortened to TDs – elected by direct proportional vote, representing 41 constituencies. The Senate is proposed on a vocational basis, with six members elected by the universities and eleven nominated by the Taoiseach (pronounced *Tee-shuck*), or Prime Minister. General elections take place at least every five years; presidential elections, which are also direct, are held every seven years. Mary Robinson, elected in 1990 as Ireland's first woman president, breathed welcome new life into this formerly symbolic role by speaking out for women and the political left. She was succeeded in 1997 by the current president, Mary McAleese, a Nationalist and devout Catholic.

There are tours of the Government Buildings on Saturdays from 10.30am to 3.30pm. Although admission is free, you'll need to get a ticket, available from the ticket office in the National Gallery, at the back of Leinster House; the tour lasts forty minutes and takes in the Taoiseach's office, the ceremonial stairs and the cabinet room. As the tour is popular, the best thing to do is get there early and put your name down for later in the day. If you go to the Kildare Street Entrance to Leinster House, present your passport or prove you are a tourist and the guard is in a good mood, you should be able to gain entry to the Dáil. The Parliament sits for ninety days a year, mostly from November to May on Tuesday 2.30–8.30pm and Thursday 10.30am–5.30pm.

The National Library and National Museum

Whether or not the massive twin rotundas, housing the entrances of the National Library on the left and the National Museum on the right, do anything to complement the Georgian elegance of Leinster House is debatable; they were added in 1890. The **National Library** (Mon 10am–9pm, Tues & Wed 2–9pm, Thurs & Fri 10am–5pm, Sat 10am–1pm; free) is, however, worth visiting for its associations alone: it seems that every major Irish writer from Joyce onwards used it at some time, and the **Reading Room** is also the scene of Stephen Dedalus's great literary debate in *Ulysses*. The Library has a good collection of first editions and works of Irish writers, including Swift, Goldsmith, Yeats, Shaw, Joyce and Beckett. It's also often used for temporary exhibitions on Irish books and authors.

The **National Museum** (Tues–Sat 10am–5pm, Sun 2–5pm; free) is the place to go to see the treasures of ancient Ireland, as well as a small collection of artefacts – mainly silver, glass and ceramics – from Dublin's eighteenth-century heyday. It is national policy to gather treasures found all around the country in this one museum, so the place is a real treasure trove of wonderful objects. The really venerable exhibits, dating from the Irish **Bronze** and **Iron** ages, bear eloquent testimony to the ancient high culture of Ireland: there's **jewellery** ranging from the eighth to the first centuries BC, mainly the twisted gold bars known as torcs, cloak-fasteners and collars, and the beaten gold lunulae that are characteristic of the period.

The **medieval antiquities** are more spectacular still and include the Tara Brooch and the Ardagh Chalice, found in County Limerick in 1868, both of which date from the eighth century. The twelfth-century Cross of Cong, an ornate reliquary of wood, bronze and silver, is said to contain a fragment of the True Cross; and there's also an eleventh-century shrine, made of gold wire, that houses a bell said to have belonged to St Patrick. The **Tara Brooch** is regarded as perhaps the greatest piece of Irish metalwork, and it's thought that the patterns of manuscript illuminations such as the Book of Kells, which you can see in Trinity College Library, may be derived from this rich craft tradition. Remarkably, the Tara Brooch is decorated both on the front and the back, where the intricate filigree work could be seen only by the wearer – the brooch is displayed above a mirror so that you can see both sides.

One of the more recent finds is the **Derrynaflan Hoard**, a testament to the Irish enthusiasm for metal-detecting. This collection of eighth- and ninth-century silver objects, including a chalice and a paten, was discovered in February 1980 in County Tipperary by amateur treasure hunters using a metal detector that one of them had got for Christmas.

To discover more about the **Viking** tradition, go round the corner into Merrion Row (past the *Shelbourne Hotel*) for the **National Museum Annexe**, which exhibits the results of digs at the Christchurch Place, Winetavern and Wood Quay sites around Christchurch, carried out between 1962 and 1981. The complexity of the culture (Norse invaders first arrived in 795AD) is evident in artefacts such as eleventh-century combs and carrying cases carved from bones and antlers, scales for weighing precious metals together with accurate lead weights, and iron swords.

Right at the top of Kildare Street, at the point where it intersects with Nassau Street, the fussy, Venetian-inspired red-brick building on the corner used to house one of the major institutions of Anglo-Irish Dublin, the **Kildare Street Club** – the carved billiard-playing monkeys on the pillars hint toward the past use of the building as a gentlemen's playground. The place now houses the **Genealogical Office**, where you can trace the history of Irish names (call ☎661 4877 for details), the Heraldry Museum and the Alliance Française. The **Heraldry Museum** gives a general account of the development of its subject in Ireland and Europe (Mon–Fri 10am–12.30pm & 2–4.30pm).

St Stephen's Green

Walk to the bottom of Kildare Street and you'll emerge on the northwest side of **St Stephen's Green**, the focus of central Dublin's city planning. It's an oddly decorous expanse, neat and tidy with little bandstands and pergolas, laid out as a public park in 1880 by Lord Ardilaun (Sir Arthur Edward Guinness). It was an open common until 1663, and the final buildings ringing it went up in the eighteenth century; unfortunately, very few of these have survived, and their replacements speak eloquently of the failure of 1960s planning regulations. The **gardens**, with their ornamental pond, can be a pleasant place to while away some time on a sunny day, but in terms of architecture, or even city life, there's not a lot to see. The statue in memory of Wolfe Tone, backed by slabs of granite, is nicknamed "Tone-henge".

The north side of the square, known in the eighteenth century as the "Beaux Walk" for the dandies and glitterati who used to promenade there – is dominated by the **Shelbourne Hotel**. Fittingly, the *Shelbourne* – which boasts that it has "the best address in Dublin" – continues to be a focus for the upper echelons of the city's social life. It's worth bearing in mind that, as with all Irish hotels, you can wander in for a drink and something to eat in the lobby at any time of day, even if you're not staying. The hotel's afternoon teas (from 3pm) are wonderful; but the airy, chandeliered lobby and the *Horseshoe* bar come into their own in the early evening, when the hotel is a great place for both celebrity-spotting and watching the parade of young Dubliners who are there to be seen. The *Shelbourne* is too well bred to pass comment on jeans and trainers in the lobby, but you'll feel out of place if you penetrate to the excellent (but expensive) restaurant (see p.57) unless you dress up a bit.

Just past the hotel, to the left of a shuttered garden, lies the **Huguenot Graveyard**, which dates from 1693. The Huguenots – French Protestants who fled persecution under Louis XIV, after the repeal of the Edict of Nantes in 1685 took away the religious privileges they had previously enjoyed – enriched cultural life all over Europe with their craftsmanship (their silverwork was particularly valued). Ireland was no exception, and this quiet burial place, with its understated French headstones, seems a particularly fitting tribute to their quietly industrious way of life; for more on the Huguenots in Dublin see p.83.

Linked to the east side of the Green by Hume Street is **Ely Place**, where you can see some of the best-preserved Georgian domestic buildings in Dublin. The sober exteriors conceal some extraordinary flights of fancy: no. 8, for instance, has an amazing staircase with elaborate stuccowork telling the story of the labours of Hercules. Unfortunately, though, it isn't open to the public.

The Catholic University of Ireland: Newman House

University College, Dublin's second-oldest university (after Trinity), is now at Belfield in the suburb of Donnybrook, but the first premises of its predecessor, the **Catholic University of Ireland**, are at nos. 85–86 on the south side of the Green and are now being restored to something approaching their original appearance (the phased restoration scheme is due for completion in 1999). The aim of the foundation was to provide a Catholic answer to the great academic traditions of Oxford and Cambridge, but, despite the appointment of John Henry Newman (who had famously converted from High-church Anglicanism) as its rector, the new university was initially denied official recognition in Britain. Eventually, in 1853, it was successfully established as a University College. The poet and Jesuit priest Gerard Manley Hopkins (1844–89) had a chair here; the 1916 Republican leader Pádraig Pearse, prime minister Éamon de Valera and James Joyce are among its more famous graduates.

The original, newly restored university buildings, collectively known as **Newman House** (guided tours only; hourly June–Sept Mon – Fri noon to 4pm; Sat 2–4pm; Sun 11am–1pm; £2), provide an unparalleled opportunity to get a taste of what the Georgian town houses of St Stephen's Green must have originally been like. No. 85 is a small, early Georgian villa built about 1738 for Hugh Montgomery, a wealthy Ulster landowner and member of parliament for County Fermanagh. This was one of the first town houses built by Richard Castle, or Cassels, the fashionable German country-house architect (who also designed Leinster House, and later the Dining Hall at Trinity College), and shows his mastery of the more intimate scale of urban building.

Inside, this remarkable interior is worth visiting just to see the **Apollo Room**, with its stucco reliefs of the nine muses made by the brilliant Swiss stuccadores Paolo and Filippo Lanfranchini. Upstairs on the first floor, a fine double-cube room with ceiling reliefs celebrating the subjects of good government and prudent economy awaits restoration. The Lanfranchinis boasted that their work was so good that it didn't need colour, so the ghastly colour scheme imposed in the 1940s is completely wrong, destroying the delicacy of the mouldings (compare the simple grey of the restored Apollo room). Notice also the extraordinarily ham-fisted additions made by the nineteenth-century Jesuits, who decided that the ceiling showed far too many naked female bodies and helpfully added what look like fur suits to protect the morals of their students.

In 1765 the small villa was joined by a bigger town house, which is still undergoing restoration. The original house was then extended with an additional room at the back, later to become the physics theatre, where James Joyce lectured to the "L & H" (the "Literary and Historical Society") and which features in his *Portrait of the Artist as a Young Man*. The new house was built by Richard "Burnchapel" Whaley, a virulent anti-Catholic who swore never to let a Papist across his threshold and earned his sobriquet by burning chapels in County Wicklow. His son, "Jerusalem" Whaley, was a founder of the Hellfire Club. Legend tells that he threw a crucifix through the front window on Maundy Thursday, and ever afterwards on the same day its image is still to be seen there. The newer house is characterized by lighter, airier plasterwork (the main staircase, decorated with musical instruments and flowers, is particularly beautiful) and is to be restored to its mid-nineteenth-century appearance, with some of the interventions made by the university prelates.

Next door, **University Church** is an amazingly prolix Byzantine fantasy of 1854–56, with an interior decorated with coloured marble – more familiar from the cloudburst patterns on country bungalows – quarried in Armagh, Offaly and Kilkenny as well as at the better-known quarries of the far west, Mayo and Connemara; it's now a chic location for Dublin weddings.

West of the Green

Harcourt Street, leading off from the southwest corner of St Stephen's Green, is a graceful Georgian street that has survived relatively unscathed. There's nothing much to do here (though there is a good Celtic bookshop), but it's worth strolling down a little way to admire the graceful proportions and elegant town planning.

On the west side of the Green is the **Royal College of Surgeons**, which during the events of Easter Week in 1916 was held by the Irish Citizen Army with Constance Markiewicz as second-in-command; the facade is still pocked with stray bullet-marks. Interrupting the skyline around St Stephen's Green is the shopping mall on the corner with Grafton Street, its white wrought-iron detailing intended, presumably, to echo the Georgian balconies of Merrion and Fitzwilliam squares. In the years since it was built, its flashy architecture has made its peace extraordinarily well with its surroundings, something perhaps not so surprising, given that the famous good taste of Georgian building conceals much the same kind of boom-time, get-rich-quick expansionism.

The Shaw birthplace

A short walk up Harcourt Street, which leaves St Stephen's Green at its southwest corner, will bring you to Harrington Street. Turn right, then left into Synge Street, a modest street of patchy Georgian houses, for the **birthplace of George Bernard Shaw**

GEORGE BERNARD SHAW

Born in Dublin in 1856, **George Bernard Shaw** was technically a member of the privileged Ascendancy, but his father's failed attempt, after leaving the civil service, to make money as a grain merchant, meant that Shaw grew up in an atmosphere of genteel poverty and, by the age of sixteen, was earning his living in a land agency. When his mother left his father for her singing teacher and took her two daughters with her to London, Shaw soon joined them and set about the process of educating himself. Subsidized by his mother's meagre income as a music teacher, he spent his afternoons in the British Museum's reading room and his evenings writing novels. He also became a vegetarian, a socialist, and a public speaker of some note.

Shaw's novels were unsuccessful, but his plays were a different matter entirely: in a way that perhaps underlined the flamboyant young man's wholehearted involvement with his new London environment, he was acclaimed the most important British playwright since the eighteenth century. However, Shaw recognized his foreignness as being a big part of his success: "the position of foreigner with complete command of the same language has great advantages. I can take an objective view of England, which no Englishman can." In the 1890s, influenced by the new drama represented by Ibsen, he began to write plays hinged on moral and social questions rather than romantic or personal interests. In play after play – his best-known dramas include *Man and Superman*, *Caesar and Cleopatra*, *Major Barbara*, *St Joan*, and, of course, *Pygmalion*, from which the musical *My Fair Lady* was adapted – he expounds a progressive view of humanity. For Shaw, the "life-force" is evolving toward an ever-higher level, and his plays successfully mix the accompanying moral fervour with high social comedy. As well as a dramatist, he was an active pamphleteer, critic, journalist and essayist, on subjects ranging from politics and economics to music. Shaw was awarded the Nobel prize for literature – which he refused – in 1925, after the ecstatic reception of *St Joan*. In his old age, he was famous almost as much for his dandified persona as his work. He died in 1950.

(May–Oct Mon–Sat 11.30am–6pm; £2). For playwright Shaw (see overleaf) this house, where he lived until he was ten, was not exactly a cause for celebration; Shaw remembered that "neither our hearts nor our imaginations were in it" and recalled the "loveless" atmosphere: you certainly get a vivid impression of the claustrophobic surroundings of the house and its tiny, neat garden. The terse inscription on the facade, "Bernard Shaw, author of many plays", is as Shaw wished.

Merrion Square and Georgian Dublin

Merrion Square, Fitzwilliam Square and the streets immediately around them form the heart of what's left of **Georgian Dublin**. Representing the latest of the city's Georgian architecture – decrepit Mountjoy Square and Parnell Square, north of the river, are almost all that's left of the earlier Georgian city – their worn, red-brick facades are a brilliant example of confident, relaxed urban planning. The overall layout, in terms of squares and linking streets, may be formal, but there's a huge variation of detail. Height, windows, wrought-iron balconies, ornate doorways, are all different, but the result is a graceful meeting of form and function that's immensely beguiling.

The apogee of the Georgian area, imbued with an atmosphere of grandeur and repose, **Merrion Square**, which was built around 1770, has been home to a lot of well-known people – Daniel O'Connell, the Wildes and W.B. Yeats as well as, less predictably, the Nobel prize-winning physicist Erwin Schrödinger, who lived here between 1940 and 1956. However, it hasn't always been an area only devoted to gracious living: during the Famine, between 1845 and 1849, the park in the centre of the square was the site of soup kitchens to which the starving and destitute flocked. Today, the buildings are mainly occupied by offices, but the square still retains a residential feel, and a hard core of people still live here. The park railings are used on Saturdays and Sundays by artists flogging their wares; the area is also a centre for most of Dublin's private galleries.

Looking along the south side of the square, you experience one of the set pieces of Dublin's architecture: the hard outlines – pepperpot tower, Ionic columns and pediment – of St Stephen's Church (1825). If you want to know more about Ireland's architectural heritage, Georgian in particular, call at the Irish Architectural Archive at no. 63 (Mon–Fri 10am–1pm & 2–5pm). The house is a particularly tatty one, but it will give you some idea of what the interiors of these elegant buildings are like.

The National Gallery and the Natural History Museum

At the northeast of the square, alongside the back of Leinster House – its country-house facade – is Ireland's **National Gallery** (Mon–Wed, Fri & Sat 10am–5.30pm, Thurs 10am–8.30pm, Sun 2–5pm). It's a place that has a real feeling of activity, mainly because of all the people dropping in to eat at the excellent restaurant and as a gallery it's also a delight. The collection is not huge, though there are more than 2000 paintings on show, but the intimacy of its scale gives it a particular charm.

The gallery is divided into three sections. The Dargan Wing – named after the nineteenth-century railway magnate and benefactor William Dargan, who organized the 1853 Dublin Industrial Exhibition here and used the proceeds to start the gallery – houses the collections of **European art** from the Renaissance to the present day. Among the artists represented are Fra Angelico, Titian, Tintoretto, Rembrandt, Pissarro and Monet. There's also a sumptuous, recently rediscovered Caravaggio, *The Taking of Christ* (1602), which hung on the dining-room wall of the Jesuit community on Leeson Street for many years before it was identified. Once they realized the artistic and financial worth of the painting, the Jesuits lent it to the gallery for safekeeping and public view.

The Milltown Rooms house **Irish art** and a small British collection; they were built at the turn of the century to display the collection of Russborough House, which was donated to the gallery in 1902. **British art** on show includes work by Hogarth, Reynolds, Gainsborough, Turner and Landseer. The Irish section, inevitably, is heavy on the art of the Anglo-Irish, and you can trace in the paintings the pattern of their history from the formal portraits of the early seventeenth century to the beginnings of interest in the life of ordinary people, which is to say the native Irish. Some of these pictures seem shockingly sentimental – one, by Edwin Hayes, is a calmly beautiful depiction of an emigrant ship at sunset in Dublin Harbour. Exotica, in the shape of such subjects as Indians and Mandarins, also make their appearance, presumably through the involvement of the Anglo-Irish in British military and trading activities. In room 6, Jack B. Yeats predominates and there are plans to convert the adjoining room into a museum dedicated to the work of the Yeats family. For anyone who's travelled around Ireland before arriving in Dublin, some of the most fascinating items have to be the gallery's **topographical paintings**. These landscapes of estates, commissioned by their owners, show much more than a true portrayal of what was actually there: rather they're aspirational portraits, images of how their owners wanted them to be. There's an amazingly evocative painting of the estates at Lucan in County Dublin, and a group of depictions of Ballinrobe in County Mayo – a place that today, though it exudes a tantalizing sense of past glory, gives no indication of the pleasure gardens depicted in these paintings.

The **North Wing** houses Flemish, German and Dutch art and a particularly impressive **Spanish** collection, including works by Picasso, Velázquez, Goya and Murillo.

Flanking Leinster House on the opposite side of the National Gallery is the **Natural History Museum** (Tues–Sat 10am–5pm, Sun 2–5pm; free), which has been dubbed the "Dead Zoo" by one Dublin writer (the "live" version being in Phoenix Park, see p.91). A wonderful illustration of intact Victorian architecture, it's also a kind of museum of a Victorian museum – the place has hardly changed since it opened in 1857. There are plenty of stuffed animals and skeletons, including a giant Chinese panda, rhinoceroses, two whale skeletons and three examples of the Irish giant elk, which died out some 10,000 years ago.

No. 29 Lower Fitzwilliam Street

At the opposite end of Merrion Square, at no. **29 Lower Fitzwilliam Street**, is what's billed as a "faithfully recreated Georgian family home" (Tues–Sat 10am–5pm, Sun 2–5pm; £2.50). Recreated is the word – the house fell down and has been rebuilt, brick by brick, by the Electricity Board, whose offices adjoin it at the back. Considering that the Electricity Supply Board was responsible, in the 1960s, for knocking down 26 Georgian houses and destroying the longest unbroken row of period houses then surviving, this act of homage is perhaps the least that could be demanded of it. If you want a postmodern take on the Georgian, this is it, furnished in a notional style of between 1790 and 1820. Viewing the house is an extraordinary experience, a bit like being an alien on a visit to earth. There's little feeling that you'd have anything in common with the people who once lived here: rather you're told that these creatures "only drank wine and beer" and that the women "did nothing but write letters to themselves". Georgian life is turned into a cabinet of curiosities, a weird kind of sideshow which does, admittedly, have its fascination. For an idea of "real" eighteenth-century Dublin life, Newman House (see p.72) is far superior; but if you have a taste for kitsch, you may find some grotesque humour at no. 29.

Fitzwilliam Square, south of Merrion Square along Fitzwilliam Street, is another elegant example of a late Georgian square – it was built between 1791 and 1825 – with some of the city's finest Georgian doors and fanlights. The dwindling number of residents still hold keys to the central garden.

Baggot Street and the Grand Canal

Crossing over Fitzwilliam Street, **Baggot Street** – with its multitude of lively pubs – starts out Georgian, but the street plan is pretty soon broken by the great black metal-and-glass bulk of the Bank of Ireland building, enlivened only by a few brightly coloured metal constructivist sculptures. Just afterwards, you reach the Grand Canal, one of Dublin's two constructed waterways: the Royal Canal runs through the north of the city. True Dubliners, or "Jackeens", are said to be those born between the two waterways.

The **Grand Canal** was the earlier and more successful of the two: started in 1756 and reaching the Shannon by 1803 (the Royal Canal was begun in 1790), it carried passengers and freight between Dublin, the midland towns and the Shannon right up to the 1960s, despite competition from the railways. Its total length, including stretches of the rivers Barrow and Shannon, was 340 miles. The potential for tourism in re-opening the canals has only recently been realized; consequently some patches are clean, free-flowing and beautiful while around the bend the vista is a picture of economic decline. Perhaps the best stretch of the canal to visit is the section around Baggot Street Bridge, where the water is fringed by trees. Baggot Street and a Dublin institution, the late, lamented **Parson's bookshop**, were haunts of many of Dublin's celebrated writers in the 1950s, including the poet Patrick Kavanagh and the playwright Brendan Behan. Kavanagh lived in a flat nearby in Pembroke Road and produced a "journal of literature and politics", entitled *Kavanagh's Weekly* and written largely by himself (with a few contributions from Behan and Myles na Gopaleen, aka Flann O'Brien). It ran to a total of thirteen issues before folding, with pieces about anything and everything – professional marriage makers, visits to the bookies, weeks when nothing happens.

The Grand Canal reaches the River Liffey at Ringsend (about a mile northeast of Baggot Street Bridge), through its original locks, constructed in 1796. You can find out more about the history and use of all of Ireland's canals and waterways at the Waterways visitors centre, a little upstream from the Grand Canal Dock.

Ballsbridge

If you walk for just over half a mile west of Baggot Street Bridge (buses from the centre of town: #5, #6, #6A, #7A, #8, #10, #46 or #46A) you'll get to Ballsbridge, a respectable, essentially Victorian suburb with some pleasant guesthouses (see "Accommodation", p.59, as well as many of the foreign embassies and smarter hotels – and, for soccer and rugby fans, the essential Lansdowne Road Stadium.

The showgrounds of the **Royal Dublin Society** (off the main Pembroke/Merrion Road) – the first of its kind in Europe, founded in 1731 to promote improvements in agriculture, stock breeding and veterinary medicine – are also here. The Society was highly instrumental in the development of Dublin as a modern metropolis, and encouraged the foundation of the National Museum, the National Library, the National Gallery and the Botanic Gardens. If you're in town for the Spring Show in May, don't pass it by; the Dublin Horse Show (usually in August) is even more impressive – its international showjumping draws the horsey elite (human and equine) from both Ireland and Britain. Details and tickets from the Royal Dublin Society, PO Box 121, Ballsbridge, Dublin 4 (☎669 2386).

Temple Bar

Staying south of the river, the main thoroughfare west from College Green is **Dame Street**. Immediately north, the area between the modern Central Bank and the Liffey is known as **Temple Bar**. Until the dissolution of the monasteries in 1537, the land on

RESTAURANTS AND CAFÉS

Auriga	1
Bad Ass Café	2
Café Irie	3
Chameleon	4
Dish	5
Elephant and Castle	6
Gallahers Boxty House	7
Irish Film Centre	8
Il Baccarro	9
La Med	10
La Paloma	11
Le Vigneron	12
Luigi Malones	13
Mongolian Barbeque	14
Sushi	15
Tante Zoe's	16
Well Fed Café	17

ACCOMMODATION

Aston	A
Barnacles Temple Bar House	B
Bewley's	C
Bloom's	D
The Clarence	E
George Frederick Handel	F
Harding	G
Kinlay House	H
Oliver St.John Gogarty's	I
Parliament	J
Riverhouse	K
Strollers	L
Temple Bar	M
Wellington	N

which Temple Bar stands was the property of the Augustinian order. Originally built on marshy land reclaimed from the Liffey, Temple Bar owes its name not to the friars, as you might expect, but to a seventeenth-century owner, Sir William Temple. During the eighteenth century, the place was a centre for Dublin's low life, in the shape of brothels and pubs (the pubs are still there), while in the nineteenth century it attracted the small businesses and tradesmen who gave it its character.

Bought up in the 1960s by CIE (formerly the state transport company), which wanted to build a new central bus terminal to replace the one on the other side of the river, it suffered for many years from a benign sort of planning blight: even after the bus station idea was abandoned in the 1980s, shops, studios and offices in the area continued to be rented out on short leases and as a result the streets are full of art galleries, restaurants and cultural centres. However, over recent years the area has been extensively redeveloped and has lost much of the bohemian and anarchic feel that was its appeal to begin with. Many of the galleries, restaurants and bars have gone upmarket and smaller businesses have been forced out. All the same, Temple Bar still remains one of the liveliest and most interesting parts of town, often compared with Covent Garden in London or Les Halles in

Paris. The area is especially lively in the evenings. The U2-owned *Clarence Hotel* as well as some of the hippest clubs in town are here (see p.104); for movies, eating, or people-spotting try the bar at the super-cool Irish Film Centre (see below). You can bone up on the more official side of Temple Bar life at the **Temple Bar information centre**, Eustace Street (☎671 5717), which publishes a Temple Bar Guide with a useful map; or consult *In Dublin* for a more general guide to what's on.

One of the best places to see work by contemporary Irish artists is **Temple Bar Gallery and Studios**, 5–9 Temple Bar (Mon–Sat 10am–6pm, Sun 2–6pm), consisting of thirty studios in all and two exhibition spaces, the biggest complex of its kind in the country. Next door is the Original Print Gallery where both Irish and international prints are displayed. Walking away from the river and onto Crow Street, you can't fail to notice **The Green Building**, an experiment in energy-efficient building in a dense urban area. The roof is made up of propellers and solar panels, while the facade is decorated with artworks on the theme of recycling and includes balcony balustrading by James Garner, made from disused bicycle frames. Tracing your steps back down Crow Street, Curved Street, off Temple Lane, is home to **Temple Bar Music Centre** (Mon–Fri 10am–5.30pm), a major concert venue and showcase for new Irish musical talent. The building consists of recording studios in the basement, a 340-seat venue on the ground floor, an information centre on the first and second floors and a music school on the third. Curved Street leads on to Eustace Street where you'll find The Ark Children's Cultural Centre (Mon–Sat 10am–6pm), a theatre specially designed for children with a child-size auditorium, child-height windows and a stage backed by a vertically revolving wall that opens out into Meeting House Square to allow for outdoor performances.

At the back of Eustace Street, Meeting House Square is the second of the main squares in the Temple Bar area and is surrounded by cultural centres. At the south end of the square stands the **Gallery of Photography**; its main exhibition space is reached via an opaque-glass stair tower, and on top there's a roof terrace with views of the square. At the other side of the square you can access the **Irish Film Centre**, but, if you want to really appreciate the building, it's best to retrace your steps and use the entrance on Eustace Street. The IFC was, in many ways, the inspiration for much of the architecture in the area. It is a coolly minimalist conversion of an old Quaker meeting house and as you enter through a long corridor lit from beneath your feet, you feel you're making a symbolic passage between reality and the surreal world of celluloid. Inside, you meet with a courtyard with a film bookshop, and an excellent restaurant and bar, plus two screens where you can catch an interesting repertory of art-house movies: there are seasons of world cinema and gay cinema, children's film festivals and other seasons of special-interest films. The National Film Archive and Film Base, an independent co-operative of Irish film-makers, is housed here. A worthwhile introduction to Irish film is screened every afternoon. Taking the Sycamore Street exit from the IFC and walking towards the river, you'll come to the **DESIGNyard**, a space for showing contemporary Irish jewellery, furniture and interior design. The building itself is a converted eighteenth-century china warehouse and the mosaic-patterned floor is designed to represent the River Poddle which flows beneath the building.

The elegant, arching pedestrian bridge that leads from Temple Bar to the north bank of the Liffey is known as the **Ha'penny Bridge**, from the toll which was charged until early this century. Close by, on the north side of the river, is The Winding Stair (40 Lower Ormond Quay), a kind of northerly outpost of the anarchic spirit of Temple Bar as it used to be before the money-men arrived: an excellent second-hand bookshop with plenty of good remaindered paperbacks, and a café where you can sit and stare peacefully through the grimy windows while the Liffey oozes past the Ha'penny Bridge.

Dublin Castle and around

Dublin Castle (Mon–Fri 10am–5pm, Sat & Sun 2–5pm; £2.00) is just a short walk along Dame Street. Outside its gates are the lime-green headquarters of the Sick and Indigent Roomkeepers Society, founded in 1790 and still going strong; the building has recently been bought by a conservationist who intends to preserve the facade while converting the inside into a family home.

Once inside the castle precinct, you're confronted with a real pig's breakfast of architectural styles: an ugly modern tax office stands to your left, an over-precise Gothic fantasy of a church of 1803 adorns the ridge straight ahead, and to your right is the worn red brick of the castle itself.

The castle dates from King John's first Dublin court of 1207, so it's a surprise to find that today it has the appearance of a graceful eighteenth-century building, with only the massive stone **Record Tower** giving the game away – although, in the nineteenth century, this too was heavily rebuilt. Originally there were four such towers (the base of the Bermingham Tower, to the southwest, also survives), and the castle was a real fortified building; but it later became more an administrative rather than a military centre. The simplicity of the inner courtyard, all warm old red brick and stone facing, with a little clock tower on one side, is evocative of the grace and elegance with which, by the eighteenth century, the British had learned to cloak their hegemony over the country. As the heart of British power – the castle continued as the Viceroy's seat after the Act of Union at the beginning of the nineteenth century – the place stands as a symbol of 700 years of British power in Ireland.

Sometimes, however, the intended symbolism is subverted by Dublin humour: the figure of Justice that stands at the top of the **Bedford Tower**, on the north side of the yard, turns her back to the city – which shows, it was said, just how much justice Dubliners could expect from the English. Further, the scales she holds used to tilt when it rained; to ensure even-handedness, the problem was solved by drilling holes in the scale-pans.

The castle hosted the European Parliament in 1990, and massive amounts of EU funds were spent on refurbishing it in honour of the occasion. The **State Apartments** are now used by the president to entertain foreign dignitaries (so at times they will be closed to visitors) and there's a great deal of pomp and circumstance. It's these, including the **State Drawing Room** and the **Throne Room**, that you'll see on the official tour. The grandeur of the furnishings takes a bit of adjusting to – for instance, all the rooms have Donegal hand-tufted carpets mirroring the eighteenth-century stuccowork, which may be superb examples of craftsmanship but really are quiet revolting. This opulence must always have been in stark contrast to the surrounding reality of the city: the high wall that you'll notice at the end of the castle's garden is said to have been built to shield the delicate sensibilities of Queen Victoria from the appalling condition of the slums on St Stephen Street.

Given the anonymous grandeur of the interior, it's sometimes difficult to appreciate the age and interest of some of the buildings that go to make up the compound. Excavations for the new conference centre built in 1990 revealed perhaps the most interesting part of the tour, the **Undercroft**. Here you can see remains of an earlier Viking fort, part of the original thirteenth-century moat plus the base of the Powder Tower, a section of the old city wall and the steps that used to lead down to the Liffey.

Wood Quay

Directly down towards the Liffey from the castle is **Wood Quay**, site of the Viking and Norman settlements that have yielded amazing quantities of archeological finds (on show in the National Museum Annexe). The excavations were never completed and there's undoubtedly more to be discovered on the site, but despite a lot of argument the corporation of Dublin was able to go ahead and put up two massive Civic Offices, known to one and all as "The Bunkers", destroying what may have been the most important early Viking archeological site in Europe.

St Werburgh's Church

Going westwards, the historical mosaic becomes both increasingly rich and increasingly chaotic. Werburgh Street (left as you come out of the castle, and then left again) was the site of Dublin's first theatre; today, it's home of Leo Burdock's, the legendary fish-and-chip shop (see p.98) as well as **St Werburgh's Church**. Reputedly, by origin, the oldest church in Dublin, its plain exterior, with peeling paint in motley shades of grey, conceals a flamboyant and elegant 1759 interior built in the height of Georgian style, which is well worth seeing. Unfortunately, as with a lot of Dublin's Church of Ireland churches, you'd better resign yourself to the fact that it nearly always seems to be closed (this one open by arrangement; Mon–Fri 10am–4pm; ☎478 3710). Lord Edward Fitzgerald, one of the leaders of the 1798 Rebellion (see p.388), is buried in the vault; Major Henry Sirr, who captured him for the British, is interred in the churchyard. Also John Field, the early nineteenth-century Irish composer and pianist who is credited with having invented the nocturne, later developed by Chopin, was baptized here and in the church records there is mention of one "Molly Malone, fishmonger" who died in 1734.

The cathedrals

The area west of Dublin Castle is the site of the **original Viking settlement** and represents the most ancient part of the city: the old Tholsel, or town hall, used to stand here, as did the original Four Courts. Today, this historic place is remarkable for its strange combination of urban desolation (haphazardly built housing and shops with bag ladies, drunks and beggars on the streets) and urban renewal (generous tax concessions are ensuring that there's plenty of new building), and the massive, over-restored grey bulks of not one but two **cathedrals**. Both date originally from the twelfth century – Christchurch from 1172 and St Patrick's, designed to supersede it, from 1190. The reason why both have survived appears to be that one (Christchurch) stood inside the city walls, the other outside. Both cathedrals remain dedicated to the Church of Ireland, their huge bulks once a symbol of the dominance of the British – but now manifestations of what is very much a minority religious denomination.

Christchurch Cathedral and around

Christchurch (daily 10am–5pm; £1 donation) stands isolated by the traffic system. Like St Patrick's, it suffered at the hands of Victorian restorers, but is still very much a resonant historic site. Dublin's first (wooden) cathedral was founded here by Sitric Silkenbeard, first Christian king of the Dublin Norsemen, in 1038; that church was demolished by the Norman Richard de Clare – Strongbow – who built the new stone cathedral in 1172. This building didn't fare very well, either: it was built on inadequate foundations on a peat bog, and the south wall fell down in 1562. The building you see now is the result of an 1870s restoration; even the flying buttresses are a figment of the imagination of its architect, G.E. Street.

Despite all this, the building remains a monument to that first serious British incursion into Ireland, in the twelfth century. Strongbow himself is interred here (or part of him, most likely his bowels), underneath an effigy which quite possibly depicts an Earl of Drogheda.

Like many of Dublin's larger monuments, Christchurch keeps packing 'em in with multimedia evocations of history: styling itself "a bridge to the medieval past", **Dublinia** (April–Sept daily 10am–5pm; Feb–March Mon–Sat 10am–4.30pm; last admission one hour before closing; £3.95, includes admission to Christchurch) offers a series of presentations of medieval Dublin, including Strongbow's arrival, a full-size reconstruction of a merchant's house and a grotesque depiction of the Black Death. The Viking and Norman artefacts dug up at nearby Wood Quay are also on display here.

Close by, the augustly monumental **St Audoen's church** (entry is on Sunday mornings), the oldest of Dublin's parish churches, was founded by the Normans. Today, it's a strange hybrid: the original church, part of which dates from the twelfth century, is now a Protestant church; but it is grafted on to a much larger, nineteenth-century, Catholic one. The arch beside the church, dating back to 1215, is the only surviving gate from the old city walls.

Not all is as old as it seems hereabouts; for all its air of authenticity, the pub, Mother Redcap's (a little further west on Back Lane, off High Street), is a modern creation amid the open spaces left by the clearance of the inner-city slums. Nearby, however, the **Tailors' Guild Hall** (1706) is the city's last surviving guildhall, with an assembly room that includes an eighteenth-century musicians' gallery where Wolfe Tone and Napper Tandy spoke to the revolutionary "Back Lane Parliament" in the run-up to the 1798 uprising. Tailors' Hall is now the headquarters of An Taisce (pronounced *On Tashka*), a pioneering conservation organization. The restoration of the building was carried out in conjunction with the Irish Georgian Society, and the two groups join forces to lobby the government to devote more funds to caring for Ireland's architectural heritage. With the setting up of a National Heritage Committee in 1988, funded from the National Lottery, that aim came one step closer to fulfilment.

St Patrick's Cathedral

South down Patrick Street from the Guild Hall, **St Patrick's Cathedral** (Mon–Fri 9am–6pm, Sat April–Oct 9am–5pm, Nov–Mar 9am–4pm, Sun 10am–4.30pm; £1.20; bus #50, #54A, #56A from Eden Quay) is now the national cathedral of the Church of Ireland, and is a much more elegant place inside than the grey tank-like exterior leads you to expect. Legend has it that St Patrick baptized converts within its grounds; but its most famous association is with the writer Jonathan Swift, who was dean of St Patrick's in the eighteenth century (see overleaf).

At the west end of the church is an old wooden door with a roughly hewn aperture, formerly the chapter door of the south transept. Anecdote claims this to have brought a new phrase into the English language when, in 1492, the feuding earls of Kildare and Ormonde met here. Ormonde's supporters were barricaded inside the cathedral; Kildare, eager to end the struggle, cut a hole in the door and put his arm through it, inviting Ormonde to shake hands. He did, peace was restored, and the phrase "chancing your arm" was born.

There are plenty of interesting tombs and memorials in the cathedral. One of the most elaborate, at the west end of the church, is a seventeenth-century **monument to the Boyle family**, earls of Cork, teeming with painted figures of family members. The tomb originally stood beside the altar; but a year after being installed in 1632, it was moved, when Thomas Wentworth, Earl of Strafford and the British Viceroy in Dublin, objected that churchgoers were forced to pray "crouching to an Earl of Cork and his lady... or to those sea nymphs his daughters, with coronets upon their heads, their hair dishevelled, down upon their shoulders." This was not the end of the argument, and it was the Earl of Cork who won: he later had Wentworth executed. Robert Boyle (who, as the only son, has pride of place in a niche of his own in the centre of the lowest tier) went on to become a scientist who established the important relationship, still known as Boyle's Law, between the pressure, volume and temperature of a gas.

At the east end of the church a series of three Elizabethan brasses tells the plaintive stories of some of the early English settlers in Ireland. There's a small, plain monument in the north transept to one Alexander McGeek, a servant of Swift, erected by the dean in what was clearly an unusual gesture – all the other tablets are to people of property. A message from one William Taylour strikes a chilling note:

JONATHAN SWIFT

Best known for his satires, including the classic *Gulliver's Travels*, **Jonathan Swift** (1667–1745) was born at Hoey's Court, close to St Werburgh's Church. He could read by the age of three, and at fifteen got a place at Trinity College. On graduating, he worked for the diplomat Sir William Temple, after whom Temple Bar is named, and subsequently for the Church of England. He was appointed Dean of St Patrick's in 1713, where he remained until his death.

Swift began publishing political pamphlets in 1704, and was forced to return to Ireland, after spending some time in London, because his pen had made him enemies among the Whigs. Over the next couple of decades, both his commitment to Ireland and his social conscience grew. He was among those who advocated Irish economic independence: in 1720 his *Proposal for the Universal Use of Irish Manufactures*, published anonymously, suggested that the Irish burn everything English except its coal. More notorious is his *A Modest Proposal* of 1729, a bitter satire in which he suggested that the Irish could solve their problems by selling their babies to the English for food.

Swift's presence is everywhere in the cathedral, giving hints of both his often vitriolic interventions in Dublin's public life and his own mysterious and contorted private life. Immediately to the right of the entrance are memorials to both him and Esther Johnson (1681–1728), the "Stella" with whom he had a passionate, though apparently platonic, relationship. Stella was the daughter of Sir William Temple's housekeeper; in 1701, after Temple's death, Swift brought her to Dublin and lived near her for the rest of her life.

Elsewhere in the church there's a tribute from the sharp-quilled English poet Alexander Pope:

> *Let Ireland tell how Wit upheld her cause,*
> *Her Trade supported and supplied her Laws*
> *And leave on Swift this grateful verse engraved*
> *"The rights a Court attack'd a Poet sav'd."*

The two men were good friends and used to plan sharing a home in retirement (the correspondence is an interesting one, particularly for the gentle light it casts on Pope).

The north pulpit contains Swift's writing table, chair, portrait and death mask. He died at 78 after years of agony from an ailment, unidentified at the time, whose symptoms – giddiness and deafness – terrified him with the possibility that he might be going mad. (It's thought that his malady was Méunière's disease, a degenerative disease of the middle ear that was finally identified in 1861.) He left money to build a hospital for the insane – Swift's Hospital, now St Patrick's, close to the Royal Hospital Kilmainham – which, opening in 1757, was one of the first psychiatric institutions in the world.

Swift's epitaph, which he wrote himself, appears in simple gold lettering on a plain black slab:

> *Here is laid the body of*
> *Jonathan Swift, Doctor of Divinity,*
> *Dean of this Cathedral Church,*
> *Where fierce indignation can no longer*
> *Rend the heart*
> *Go, traveller, and imitate, if you can*
> *This earnest and dedicated*
> *Champion of liberty.*

> *As You are, so were Wee*
> *And as Wee are, so shall You be.*

Finally, near the entrance, it comes as a surprise, among all the relics of the Anglo-Irish, to find an inscription in Irish: to Douglas Hyde, founder of the Gaelic League, first president of Ireland and son of a Church of Ireland clergyman.

Archbishop Marsh's Library

Just outside the main entrance is a compact Georgian building, faced in brick at the front but, tactfully, in the same unrelenting grey stone as the cathedral on the side that faces the church. This is **Archbishop Marsh's Library** (Mon & Wed–Fri 10am–12.45pm & 2–5pm, Sat 10.30am–12.45pm; £1 donation is expected), Ireland's first public library, built in 1701 (by Sir William Robinson, who also designed the Royal Hospital Kilmainham) and given to the city by the wonderfully named Archbishop Narcissus Marsh. Inside, the tiny reading cubicles and the dark carved bookcases carrying huge leather-bound tomes – some 25,000 of them, most dating from the sixteenth to the eighteenth centuries; the earliest a Latin manuscript of 1400 – can hardly have changed since the library was built. The library was peppered with bullets during the 1916 rising, and some of the seventeenth-century volumes are marked by British Army bullets intended for the nearby Jacob's factory, which was a rebel stronghold. The single most important collection in the library is that of one Edward Stillingfleet, Archbishop of Worcester. His 10,000 books were bought for £2,500 and include works from some of the earliest English printers, including Berthelet, Daye and Fawkes. Archbishop Marsh – of whom Swift remarked that "no man will be either glad or sorry at his death" (the dean believed that it was Marsh's fault he had not risen higher in his ecclesiastical career) – was responsible for the preparation of the first translation of the Old Testament into Irish, and two of the volumes survive in the library. The chains that once protected the books from theft are long gone, but three lock-in cages for readers of rare books survive – however, today readers sit in the main office under the watchful eye of the librarian.

The Liberties, the Guinness brewery and Kilmainham

Heading westwards along High Street, you'll enter **The Liberties**, an area spreading out to the south which was once outside the legal jurisdiction of the city and settled by French Huguenot refugees escaping religious persecution in their own country. They set up home, and poplin- and silk-weaving industries, in the southern part of The Liberties known as the Coombe (there is now a street named after it). The 10,000 **Huguenots** who arrived between 1650 and the early eighteenth century had a great civilizing effect on what was then a small and underdeveloped city; they founded a horticultural society and encouraged the wine trade. The Liberties have maintained the characteristics of self-sufficiency that the Huguenots brought with them, and there are families able to trace their local roots back for many generations. In the nineteenth century, local rivalries frequently erupted into violence between the Liberty Boys, the tailors and weavers of the Coombe, and the Ormond Boys, butchers who lived in Ormond Market (to the north of the Liffey at Ormond Quay).

Today, this colourful history is not immediately obvious to the visitor. The Liberties are a hotch-potch of busy streets full of barrows and bargain- and betting-shops. Government tax incentives and low property prices have encouraged speculators to build blocks of high-security luxury apartments, which sit oddly among the urban jumble.

The main road leading west of Christchurch (High Street leading to James's Street), interspersed with grim corporate housing and deserted factories, is dominated by the **Guinness brewery** – a setting out of Fritz Lang's *Metropolis*, with huge dark chimneys belching smoke, tiny figures hurrying along grimy balconies and the smell of malt heavy in the air. For all the seediness of its surroundings, however, Guinness is one of Ireland's biggest commercial successes. Founded in 1759, the St James's Gate brewery covers 64 acres and has the distinction of being the world's largest single beer-export-ing company, exporting some 300 million pints a year; 2.5 million pints are brewed here every day, more than half the total amount of beer drunk in Ireland. Unfortunately you can't go round it, but the former Guinness Hop Store in Crane Street houses an exhi-bition centre (Mon–Fri 10am–4pm; £2; buses #21A, #78, #78A and #78B from outside the Virgin Megastore opposite O'Connell Bridge). You may feel disappointed at having to pay for what is essentially a souvenir shop, but for almost the same price as a pint in the city, you can at least taste what is arguably the best Guinness in Dublin – arguably because the honours traditionally went to Mulligan's in Poolbeg Street (northeast of College Green near George's Quay, see p.102), which still has its supporters. In addi-tion, the upper floors of the airy, four-storey building are given over to exhibitions of contemporary art and offer fine views over Dublin.

The Royal Hospital Kilmainham and the Irish Museum of Modern Art

If you get off the bus (including the #21A, #78, #78B, #79 and #90) where Bow Lane joins James's Street, you'll walk past Swift's Hospital, now known as St Patrick's, on your way to the **Royal Hospital Kilmainham** (just five minutes walk further west). The hospital was extensively and well restored between 1980 and 1984, and the result is that Ireland's first Classical building – its date is 1680 – is a joy to look at, from the outside at least. The name doesn't imply a medical institution of any kind: it was built as a home for wounded army pensioners, like Chelsea Hospital in London or Les Invalides in Paris. The plan is simple: a colonnaded building around a central court-yard, erected with cool restraint so that the sober stone arcading creates a lovely, unadorned rhythm.

The use of the hospital to house the **Irish Museum of Modern Art** (Tues–Sat 10am–5.30pm, Sun noon–5pm; free), which opened in 1991, has caused a great deal of controversy, not least because the reconversion has eaten up funds that might have been better used elsewhere. Almost half the inside has been depersonalized and paint-ed white to provide gallery space of the correct, "modern" kind in a conversion which has led one commentator to quote the Flann O'Brien story about a man born at the age of 25 with a consciousness but no history: the clean white spaces, and the art hung in them, certainly betray no awareness of the hospital's past.

More critically, the museum has been seen as an effort on behalf of the Irish gov-ernment – and, behind it, the figure of the then prime minister, Charles Haughey, who some felt cut an unlikely figure as a patron of the arts – to "buy into" the modernist tra-dition in art.There is no permanent exhibition in the museum (consult *In Dublin* for current exhibitions), which so far owns few works of its own, but instead a regularly changing collection of works mainly borrowed from European collections, hung along-side Irish ones. Whatever else, it is always stimulating; and there's an excellent restau-rant in the basement under the north wing.

Kilmainham Gaol

Outside the hospital, a small formal garden runs down to the Liffey, and a long, tree-lined avenue leads out to the front gates, beyond which looms the grim mass of **Kilmainham Gaol** (April–Sept daily 9.30am–4.45pm; Oct–March Mon–Fri 9.30am–4pm, Sun 10am–4.45pm; £2; Heritage Card). Built in 1792, the jail was com-pleted just in time to hold a succession of Nationalist agitators, from the United Irishmen of 1798, through Young Irelanders, Fenians and Land Leaguers (including Parnell and Davitt) in 1883, to the leading insurgents of the 1916 Easter Rising – Pádraig Pearse and James Connolly were executed in the prison yard. Eamon de

Valera, subsequently three times prime minister and later president, was the very last prisoner to be incarcerated here; he was released in July 1924.

The complex is a great introduction to the history of Republicanism in Ireland, though don't expect any revisionism here, as the history has a real green tint. Not all the prisoners were political: an indication of the severity of punishments is given by a document recording a sentence of seven years' transportation for stealing a piece of printed calico. The guided tours (included in admission price) give an emotionally coloured impression of the place, climaxing in the low lighting of the chapel, where, on May 4, 1916, Joseph Plunkett, one of the leaders of the Easter Rising of 1916, was married by candlelight to Grace Gifford while twenty British soldiers stood to attention, bayonets fixed. They were married at 1.30am; he was executed at 3.30am, after just ten minutes in his wife's company. Until the executions of most of the leaders of the Easter Rising, the insurrection commanded little popular support in Dublin. The rebels had held notable buildings, among them the General Post Office (see p.86) and the Jacob's factory, for five days until British artillery pounded them into submission. was only after James Connolly, already almost mortally wounded. It was executed at Kilmainham (he had to be tied to a chair so they could shoot him) that a wave of support gathered behind the Nationalist cause – leading, ultimately, to the withdrawal of British troops, the partition of Ireland, and civil war.

The North Side: O'Connell Street and around

Crossing over O'Connell Bridge you reach the North Side's main thoroughfare and once the most grandiose of Dublin streets. However, before wandering up what is still the city's busiest, although less salubrious, centre for shopping, it's worth taking a detour eastwards along Eden Quay to the famous Abbey Theatre and the elegant Custom House.

The Abbey Theatre

Not far along Eden Quay, turn left up Marlborough Street to the **Abbey Theatre** on the corner of Lower Abbey Street. Ireland's national theatre, it was opened in 1904 (nearly 20 years before Independence), with co-founders and Celtic literature revivalists W.B. Yeats and Lady Gregory as its first directors. The Abbey soon gained worldwide prestige for its productions of Irish playwrights such as Yeats, J.M. Synge and Sean O'Casey. At home, it also caused great controversy – even riots. Indicative of how much the theatre in Ireland has always been a platform for political dialogue, Synge's *Playboy of the Western World*, and much more directly O'Casey's *The Plough and the Stars* (1926), which questioned the motivations of the by-now haloed martyrs of 1916, so undercut and discredited the romanticized vision of Ireland that Yeats had helped to create – and the Nationalists had encouraged – that Dubliners took to the streets to protest. Today the new Abbey (its predecessor was destroyed in a fire in 1951) holds two theatres, the main one devoted to the Irish classics and new work by such as Brian Friel and Frank McGuinness, while the Peacock Theatre downstairs often shows new experimental drama. For details of what's on, see *In Dublin*.

The Custom House

It's easy enough to overlook the **Custom House**, lying in the shadow of the metal railway viaduct that runs parallel to O'Connell Bridge, east along the river. But, as one of the great Georgian masterpieces built by James Gandon, it's an impressive reminder of the city's eighteenth-century splendour. It is principally Gandon's public buildings that put Dublin ahead of other great, and better-preserved, Georgian cities such as Bath and Edinburgh. The Custom House was the first of them, completed in 1791 (the Four Courts, although started in 1786, were not completed until 1802, and the King's Inns were designed in 1795). It burned for five days after it was set alight by Republicans in 1921, but was thoroughly restored (and has just been refurbished again) and now houses government offices.

The best view of the building is from the other side of Matt Talbot Bridge, from where you can admire the long, regular loggia, portico and dome, all reflected in the muddy waters of the Liffey. This elegance conceals a story of personal ambition and dirty tricks. The building was originally planned by John Beresford, chief commissioner of revenue, and his friend Luke Gardiner. A large stone in the bed of the Liffey was preventing some boats from reaching the old customs point, further upstream, and this was ostensibly the argument for building a new one; but Beresford and Gardiner's prime reason for backing the scheme was that it served their own purposes to shift the commercial centre of the city east from Capel Street to the area where O'Connell Street now stands. Their plans were opposed through parliamentary petitions, personal complaints, even violence, and the hostile party was delighted to discover that the site for the new building was the muddy banks of the Liffey where, they thought, it would be impossible to build foundations. Gandon, however, confounded the scheme's critics by building the foundations on a layer of pine planks – which seems to have done the job.

O'Connell Street
Most things of historical interest on O'Connell Street – now lined by fast-food restaurants, shops, cinemas and modern offices – have long since been submerged under the tide of neon lights and plate glass, but one major exception is the **General Post Office** (GPO), which stands at the corner of Henry Street. It was opened in 1818, and its fame stems from the fact that almost a century later it became the rebel headquarters in one of the most significant battles in the fight for independence (see p.621). The entire building, with the exception of the facade, was destroyed in the fighting; it was later restored and reopened in 1929. From the street you can still see the scars left by bullets: inside (Mon–Sat 8am–8pm, Sun 10.30am–6.30pm) the reconstructed marbled halls are also worth a look. In the window is one of the finest sculptures anywhere in the city – *The Death of Cúchullain* by Oliver Sheppard. The exquisite bronze sculpture was commissioned in 1935 and represents the moment when the raven rests on the shoulder of Cúchulainn, the mythical warrior, before he finally dies. O'Connell Street itself is reputedly one of Europe's widest, and there's a paved stretch down the middle with a series of **statues**. Until 1966 one of them, directly in front of the GPO, depicted Nelson on top of a column; it was blown up by IRA sympathizers in March 1966 (you can inspect the statue's head in the Civic Museum (see p.69). Millennium year saw a notoriously expensive new addition to the gallery: an angular recumbent woman bathed by a fountain representing Joyce's Anna Livia, the personification of the river Liffey, and quickly nicknamed "the floozie in the jacuzzi", or "the whore in the sewer" (this rhymes in a Dublin accent).

Beside the GPO, Henry Street leads to **Moore Street Market**, where you'll find some of the disappearing street life that people are apt to get misty-eyed about. Truth is that the same activities continue to flourish in the less romantic settings of the Illac shopping centre, round the corner, or in the new mall on St Stephen's Green; that doesn't alter the fact that Moore Street's brightly coloured stalls and banter are a lot of fun. A little further up, a turning to the right, Cathedral Street, leads to the Greek Revival **St Mary's Pro-Cathedral** (1816–25), Dublin's most important Catholic church. Due to fears that the originally planned position on O'Connell Street would incite anti-Catholic feeling among the English, the cathedral is hidden away here. Consequently, getting a good view of its six Doric columns – based on the Temple of Theseus in Athens – is nigh on impossible. Inside, every Sunday at 11am, you can hear the famous Palestina Choir, started in 1902; John McCormack, the respected and popular tenor, began his career here in 1904.

THE EASTER RISING

The **Easter Rising** of 1916, which resulted in pitched battles in the streets of Dublin, is remembered as one of the key events leading to Irish self-government.

In fact, at the time, it seemed to most Nationalists a botched and inconclusive event. Leaders of the **Irish Volunteers**, a Nationalist group that had been founded in 1913, secretly planned a nationwide uprising for Easter Sunday 1916. The insurrection was to be staged with the help of a shipment of arms from Germany which were to be picked up by Sir Roger Casement (a British official who became a fervent Nationalist supporter; see p.521). Things began to go wrong almost immediately: the arms arrived a day too early, and the British apprehended Casement and hanged him.

So secret had the preparations for the uprising been that the Irish Volunteers' leader, Eoin MacNeill, knew nothing of them. A week before Easter, the extremist plotters, led by **Pádraig Pearse**, showed MacNeill a forged order, purporting to come from the British authorities at Dublin Castle, for the suppression of the Irish Volunteers. MacNeill consented to give the order for the uprising. Then, the day before it was due to happen, he learned that the document was a forgery, and placed advertisements in the Sunday papers cancelling the insurrection.

Pearse and his allies, however, pressed ahead, in Dublin only, the following day – Easter Monday. They took, among other public buildings, the General Post Office (GPO) in O'Connell Street, and Pearse walked out onto the steps of the GPO to read the historic **Proclamation of the Irish Republic** (see p.621). Fighting continued for five days before being put down by the British authorities.

It was not the rising itself, but the British reaction to it, that was significant for the Republicans. The authorities executed a total of fifteen leaders of the rebellion, including Pearse and another patriot, James Connolly, at Kilmainham Gaol (see p.84). The result was to turn these men, in the eyes of the public, into martyrs to the Nationalist cause. When, a year later, the British attempted to introduce conscription to the trenches of World War I, the public mood turned sharply away from accommodation with the ruling powers – and toward independence, which was finally achieved in 1921.

The final statue at the top of O'Connell Street commemorates the nineteenth-century politician Charles Stewart Parnell (see p.620), quoting his famous words, "No man has a right to fix the boundary to the march of a nation. No man has a right to say to his country, Thus far shalt thou go and no futher...."

Parnell Square to Mountjoy Square

At the top of O'Connell Street, behind Parnell's statue in the square named for him, stands the **Rotunda Maternity Hospital**, dated 1752. This was the very first purpose-built maternity hospital in Europe: the barber-surgeon Bartholomew Mosse funded the enterprise by organizing events including fancy dress balls, recitals and concerts – one of these was the first performance of Handel's *Messiah*, which took place on April 15, 1742. There's a superb chapel with a stucco ceiling by Bartholomew Cramillion. The Rotunda Room itself houses The Ambassador cinema (see p.105). Part of the remainder of the building is still a maternity hospital, while another section – the old Assembly Rooms – houses the **Gate Theatre**, which was opened by the legendary actor Micheál MacLiammóir and Hilton Edwards in 1929.

Behind the Rotunda, bordering on Parnell Square, is all that remains of the pleasure gardens, yet another of Dr Mosse's successful fund-raising ventures. This little open space is now a **Garden of Remembrance** for all those who died in the independence struggle, with a sculpture by Oisin Kelly of the *Children of Lir* (see p.186).

Parnell Square, originally called Rutland Square, was one of the first of Dublin's Georgian squares and still has its plain, bright, red-brick houses, broken by the grey stone mass of the **Hugh Lane Municipal Art Gallery** (Tues–Fri 9.30am–6pm, Sat

9.30am–5pm, Sun 11am–5pm; free; buses passing include #10, #11, #13, #16 and #22). This was originally the town house of the Earl of Charlemont, built for him by the Scottish architect Sir William Chambers in 1762 and the focus of fashionable Dublin – the north side of the square was known as Palace Row – before the city centre moved south of the river. Chambers was also the architect of the delightful Casino, built to embellish the aesthetic Lord Charlemont's country house a few miles away at Marino (see p.94).

The house works well in its revised role as an art gallery, with plenty of good lighting and an intimate scale that complements the pictures. The gallery was set up in 1908 with funds donated by Sir Hugh Lane (nephew of Lady Gregory of Abbey Theatre fame), who died when the *Lusitania* was torpedoed in 1915. He left his collection – centred round the French Impressionists – to "the nation", and with Ireland's independence the problem arose of which of the two nations he might have meant. In 1960 the two governments agreed to exchange halves of the collection every five years, but in 1982 the British government put in a claim for the lot; the matter has recently been settled, with half the collection permanently in residence at Hugh Lane. All the same, it makes interesting viewing, with work from the pre-Raphaelites onwards added to by more modern Irish painters such as Jack B. Yeats and Paul Henry; of particular note is a stained glass window by Harry Clarke, who was also responsible for the Birds of Paradise window in the Westmoreland Street *Bewley's*. There are sometimes free recitals on Sunday lunchtimes (see *In Dublin* for details), and downstairs there's a good-value café/restaurant.

Two doors down, at nos. 18 – 19, a pair of modest Georgian houses are the home of the **Dublin Writers' Museum** (Mon–Sat 10am–5pm, Sun 11.30am–6pm; £2.60, or £3.95 including Shaw's birthplace). There's certainly plenty of material to draw on: apart from its three Nobel laureates – George Bernard Shaw, W. B. Yeats and Samuel Beckett – Dublin nurtured a host of other writers, including Joseph Sheridan le Fanu, Jonathan Swift, Sean O'Casey, Brendan Behan and, of course, James Joyce. However, the exhibits are on the dull side – there's a predictable range of memorabilia, including Brendan Behan's typewriter – and the free audio guide does little to enliven the proceedings. The exhibition begins with a reference to early Irish poetry and the English poet Edmund Spenser's *Faerie Queen*, weaves rapidly through Jonathan Swift's *Modest Proposal* of 1729 and the romantic fiction of the mid-nineteenth century to Oscar Wilde and the playwright George Bernard Shaw. Joyce shares a cabinet with Sean O'Casey – this really is a whistle-stop tour – and the exhibits wind up with material on Samuel Beckett, Brendan Behan and the comic writer Flann O'Brien. Upstairs is a fine 1760s library with rather oppressive colour added in the nineteenth century, now somewhat sententiously dubbed the Gallery of Writers. There's a good bookshop with an intelligent selection of books, including contemporary authors, plus a café with a modest selection of salads; the restaurant below the museum is excellent, however, and if you are in the area, you could do worse than try their pre-theatre menu. Next door is the **Living Writers' Centre**, with work rooms, a couple of apartments and a lecture room, and an ongoing programme of literary lectures and seminars. Ring the museum for further details (☎872 2077).

Mountjoy Square

As you head northeast toward Mountjoy Square, the streets are a little run-down but are, however, being slowly regenerated. Appropriately enough given the presence of the Writers' Museum, the area also has plenty of **literary associations**: Belvedere College in Great Denmark Street is where James Joyce went to school; Sean O'Casey wrote all his plays for the Abbey Theatre – *The Shadow of a Gunman, Juno and the Paycock, The Plough and the Stars* and *The Silver Tassie* – at 422 North Circular Rd (a few streets north of the square), and Brendan Behan grew up nearby at 14 Russell St.

JAMES JOYCE

Author of *Ulysses* (1922), the ultimate celebration of his native city, **James Joyce** – who spent most of his adult life in voluntary exile from Ireland – was born in 1882. After an impoverished childhood, he went to University College, a place of learning then staffed by Jesuit priests, where he led a dissolute life and began to experiment with writing short pieces of prose which he called "epiphanies". In 1904 he started writing the short stories that were eventually published as *Dubliners*. On June 10 of that year, Joyce met Nora Barnacle, and, on their next meeting, June 16, he fell in love with her; it's on this day that the entire epic narrative of *Ulysses* is set. They finally got married some 27 years later.

With the exception of two brief visits to Dublin in 1909, when he attempted to set up a chain of cinemas, and a final visit in 1912, Joyce never again lived in Ireland. All the great works, including *A Portrait of the Artist as a Young Man* (1916) and his late masterpiece, *Finnegans Wake* (1939), were written in various European cities – Zurich, Paris, Trieste – where Joyce and his family eked out a penurious existence supported mostly by donations from rich patrons. At the time of Joyce's death in 1941, *Ulysses* was banned in Ireland, condemned as a pornographic book; it wasn't published in the Rebublic until the 1960s.

Joyce once remarked that he was "more interested in the street names of Dublin than in the riddle of the universe", and boasted that Dublin could be rebuilt from scratch using the information contained in his books. The **Bloomsday** pilgrimage – on June 16 every year people from all over the world meet in Dublin to retrace the action of the novel – starts at the Martello Tower at Sandycove (see p.92, and then progresses through the streets of Dublin, taking in lunch at *Davy Byrne's* pub (see p.102), where Leopold Bloom's lunch of a glass of burgundy and a gorgonzola-and-mustard sandwich is served, then the National Library, the *Ormonde Hotel* (Ormond Quay, north Dublin) and all the other locations made iconic by this great novel.

For serious Joyceans, the **James Joyce Centre** at 35 North Great Georges St (Tues–Sat 10am–4.30pm, Sun noon–4.30pm; £2; ☎873 1984), not far from the Irish Writers' Centre, has a museum with documents of his life and work, and an excellent bookshop. It also has information on lectures, walking tours, and Bloomsday events.

Mountjoy Square itself is Dublin's earliest Georgian square, now in an advanced state of decay. Although there are some signs of revitalization, there's little left of the elegance described by Thomas Cromwell in his *Excursions through Ireland* in 1820: "Taste and opulence have united to embellish; the streets in the vicinity are all built on a regular plan; the houses are lofty and elegant; and neither hotels, shops, nor warehouses, obtruding upon the scene, the whole possesses an air of dignified retirement – the tranquillity of ease, affluence and leisure. The inhabitants of this parish are indeed almost exclusively of the upper ranks."

The King's Inns, the Four Courts and St Michan's

Leaving Parnell Square at the northwest, you come to Dublin's – indeed, the nation's – **Wax Museum** (Mon–Sat noon–5.30pm; £3.50) at the corner of Granby Row and Dorset Street. If you like that sort of thing, and if you have children to entertain, it's a good way of whiling away a wet afternoon: there are more than 300 exhibits of Irish and international interest. In addition to a chamber of horrors, plentiful rock stars, and a curious representation of Leonardo da Vinci's *The Last Supper*, there are topical inclusions such as Jack Charlton, the much-loved former national football team manager, and the popular country and western singer Garth Brookes, who topped a recent survey in the museum for the likeness people most wanted to see.

Across Dorset Street, the **Black Church** (or St Mary's Chapel of Ease) in St Mary's Place is a sinister, brooding building with spiky finials. Legend has it that St Mary's and other similar massive Protestant churches built during the 1820s were designed so that they could be turned into defensive positions should the Catholics attack.

As you walk down Dorset Street and into Bolton Street, everything speaks of urban deprivation: rubbish blowing in the gutters, broken glass, barred shop windows. Henrietta Street, dowdy as it is now, was once the most fashionable in Dublin and was one of the first sites of really big houses in the city, two of which (nos. 9 and 10, at the far end) were designed by Sir Edward Lovett Pearce. These adjoin the impressive **King's Inns** – home of the Irish Bar – designed by James Gandon, architect of the Four Courts and the Custom House. During the daytime you can walk through into the courtyard, though the building itself is not open to the public.

The Four Courts

Making your way south from the King's Inns to the Four Courts (about a ten-minute walk), you're assailed by more blighted urban landscapes. If you walk down **Capel Street**, once one of Dublin's most fashionable addresses, you'll see few signs of modishness now – it's full of cut-price furniture stores and pawnbrokers. More streets full of rubbish and rotting vegetables from the early-morning fruit and vegetable market in Mary's Lane do nothing to prepare you for a solid example of Georgian architecture and urban planning: the **Four Courts** (Mon–Fri 9.30am–5pm), designed by Gandon between 1786 and 1802 as the seat of the High Court of Justice of Ireland and a sort of chambers for barristers.

From the outside the Four Courts have a grim perfection. Inside, the courts – Exchequer, Common Pleas, King's Bench and Chancery – radiate from a circular central hall. The building was completely gutted during the civil war but has been thoroughly restored.

St Michan's Church

Though it doesn't look much now – only the tower and a few other fragments are original – **St Michan's Church** (Mon–Fri 10am–12.45pm & 2–4.45pm, Sat 10am–12.45pm; £1.50), founded in 1095, is the oldest building on the North Side. Turn right up Church Street just west of the Four Courts and you'll find the church a short walk along near the junction with St Mary's Lane. The reason it's on the tourist trail is that the crypt's combination of dry air and constant temperature, together with methane gas secreted by rotting vegetation beneath the church, keeps corpses in a state of unnatural, mummified preservation: some of the "best" are on display, with skin, fingernails and hair all clearly identifiable, sometimes after 300 years. Depending on the mood of the guide, different crypts are opened, and among the dead are a nun, a crusader and a thief – this last identified as such because of a missing hand, amputated as penance for an earlier offence. None of the bodies was originally stored in the church, and how this odd collection of corpses got here is still a mystery. One of the crypts contains the death mask of United Irish leader, Wolfe Tone, and the bodies of two of his compatriots, the Sheare brothers. St Michan's also boasts an early eighteenth-century organ, still with its original gilding on the case, which Handel played and admired during a visit to Dublin.

Towards Phoenix Park

As you head west from St Michan's towards Phoenix Park, the street scene remains desolate, though there are signs of reconstruction and the whole area has been earmarked for redevelopment. At the moment, the main tourist attraction is the old **Jameson Distillery** (year round 9.30am–6pm; £3.50). The price includes a guided tour (tours last

40–45 minutes; last tour leaves between 5 and 5.30pm). There's an audiovisual show on the history and manufacture of Irish whiskey, working models of the distilling process and artefacts associated with it. The tour ends with a complimentary Jameson's.

Smithfield Horse Sales and Collins Barracks

The cobbled expanse of **Smithfield**, just west of Bow Street, seems like an opening without a purpose unless you're there on the first Sunday of a month, when it's the scene of horse sales. There's nothing remotely glamorous about it, but the event does possess a certain fascination. Apparently an entirely male activity, it consists of a load of horse boxes carrying filthy ponies, and deals being struck through the ritual of spitting into the palm and clapping the hands together. Many of the buyers and sellers are travellers, once known as itinerants, and before that gypsies: people who speak their own language, shelta. In fact, shelta has nothing to do with Romany (the most common theory is that the travellers are of purely Irish origin, and took to the roads at the time of the Famine), but the travellers do share with gypsies an impressive knowledge of horses. After the sales you'll see ragged ponies being ridden away bareback towards the grim northern suburbs, where impromptu pony races are held. A few roads west of Smithfield stand **Collins Barracks**, a series of imposing grey stone buildings formerly known as the Royal Barracks. Founded in 1704, their chief claim to fame is as the oldest continuously occupied purpose-built barracks in the world. They are currently being revamped to house the National Museum's decorative arts collection, and are scheduled to open in summer 1996.

Phoenix Park

If you have walked through the urban confusion of the North Side, the open spaces of **Phoenix Park**, Dublin's playground – which begins a few minutes walk west of Collins Barracks – come as a welcome relief. A series of pillars stand across the road and suddenly you're surrounded by grand clipped hedges and tended flowerbeds in what is one of the largest city parks in the world – it's more than twice the size of London's Hampstead Heath or New York's Central Park, for example. The name is a corruption of the Irish *fionn uisce*, or clear water; the park originated as priory lands, which were seized after the Reformation in the seventeenth century and made into a royal deer park. The Viceroy's Lodge – now *Áras an Uachtaráin*, the President's Residence – is here, as well as a 205-foot obelisk erected in 1817 in tribute to the **Duke of Wellington**. Wellington was born in Dublin, but was less than proud of his roots – when reminded that he was Irish by birth, the duke replied tersely, "Being born in a stable doesn't make one a horse."

The park was also the scene of two politically significant **murders** in the late spring of 1882, when two officials of the British parliament, Lord Frederick Cavendish, the chief secretary, and T.H. Burke, the under-secretary, were killed by an obscure organization known as "The Invincibles". At first it seemed that the motivation for the crime – long-standing bitterness over the landlord-and-tenant relationship in post-Famine Ireland – was directly connected with the Anglo-Irish politician Charles Stuart Parnell's ongoing agitation for reform on behalf of the Irish tenancy (see p.620). It seemed to Parnell that he would have to withdraw from public life due to the implication – however ill-founded – that he was connected with these murders, but his obvious sincerity in denouncing them, and the effect that the event had on British policy regarding the tenancy issue, was in fact to make his position in Ireland stronger than ever.

Phoenix Park also contains Dublin's **zoo** (Mon–Sat 9.30am–6pm; Sun 11am–6pm; adults £5.50; at the southeast corner of the park; buses #10, #25, #26), the second oldest in Europe – it was opened in 1830. Its claim to fame used to be that this is where the MGM lion was bred; the zoo now has a programme for breeding endangered species for subsequent release into the wild.

The old duelling grounds, or Fifteen Acres, are also to be found here – now the venue for gaelic football, cricket, soccer and, occasionally, polo – as well as a racecourse where a flea market is held every Sunday from noon onwards. The quality of what's available can vary tremendously, and there seems no way of knowing what it will be like until the day.

The outskirts

Even without going as far as the Wicklow Mountains, whose unlikely, conical outlines you encounter every time you look to the south, there are a number of rewarding trips beyond the city centre which are well worth making time for. The best of these are out along Dublin Bay, using the frequent DART services. These trains will take you southwards to **Sandycove** – a mile beyond **Dún Laoghaire** – and the James Joyce Tower; to the pretty village of **Dalkey**, with its incongruously continental atmosphere; and to the magnificent views across Dublin Bay between Dalkey and **Killiney**. Although the journey north on the DART is nothing like as spectacular as the southward trip – once the industrial city ends, it gives way to suburbia, and it's only when you get as far as **Sutton** (a much sought-after address) that you even see the sea – it takes you to the popular seaside resort of Howth (the DART terminus at the northern end of Dublin Bay), with its rugged hill and long views south. Further out, Malahide and its castle and the charming villages of Donabate and Skerries are accessible both by commuter train and bus. For the worthwhile stops closer in to the city – **Glasnevin**, **Marino** and **Dollymount Strand** – it's easier to take the bus.

Dún Laoghaire and Sandycove

Taking the DART south out of Dublin, you very quickly have the feeling that you're leaving the grime of the city far behind. Almost immediately, the track starts to run along the coast, past **Booterstown Marsh**, a designated bird sanctuary protected against a proposed motorway development, and out to **DÚN LAOGHAIRE**, where the Stena Line car ferries come in from Britain. At this distance, Dún Laoghaire manages to retain some of its flavour as a superior kind of Victorian resort, full of wide tree-lined avenues, promenades and wedding-cake architecture. Its port is still the base for Irish lightships and the biggest Irish centre for yachting (call the National Sailing School for details; ☎280 6654). This aspect of its history is chronicled in the National Maritime Museum, Haigh Terrace (☎280 0969), housed in the Mariners' church and containing, among other things, a longboat sent by the French in support of the United Irishmen, two years before the 1798 rebellion.

A mile south of Dún Laoghaire, **SANDYCOVE**'s Martello Tower (see box opposite) is its main claim to fame: James Joyce spent some time here with his friend Oliver St John Gogarty, whom he later transformed into Buck Mulligan in *Ulysses*. Although for some reason not signposted from the station, it's not hard to find. Turn right down the street into what appears to be the centre of this sleepy suburb, then left at the lights for the seafront. On your right you'll see the tower, next to an extraordinary bit of 1930s modern seaside building – "Geragh", a house built for his family by the late Michael Scott, architect of Busáras and some of the small, and still vanishing, number of Dublin's other modernist buildings. On the seaward side of the tower is the Forty Foot Pool (named not for its size but because the 40th Regiment of Foot of the British army used to be stationed in a battery above it), for many years a men-only swimming hole where nude bathing was the rule. Now that women are allowed – although you seldom see them – it's strictly "togs required – by order", as the notice says. The

---

THE JAMES JOYCE TOWER

The reason the **Martello Tower** has become a place of pilgrimage for Joyce fans is not so much the association with the author's life – the 22-year-old writer spent barely a week here in August of 1904, a month before he left the country with Nora Barnacle – as the fact that it features so prominently in the opening chapter of *Ulysses* (for more on Joyce and Bloomsday see p.89). Joyce's stay wasn't a particularly happy one: Gogarty's other guest was one Samuel Chenevix Trench who, on their sixth night, had a nightmare, grabbed a gun and let off some shots into the fireplace of the room where they were sleeping. Gogarty then seized the gun and shot a row of saucepans that were hanging above Joyce's head, shouting, "Leave him to me!" Joyce left the following morning.

The tower (April–Oct Mon–Fri 10am–1pm, 2–5pm; Sun 2–6pm; £2.40) was opened as a museum in 1962 by Sylvia Beech, who first published *Ulysses*. The exhibits inside amount to little more than a collection of memorabilia – the author's guitar, cigar case and cane are on display – which, with one or two exceptions, offer no great insights into his life. Perhaps most interesting are the letters, including a plaintive note to Nora Barnacle on September 10, 1904, accusing her of "treating me as if I were simply a casual comrade in lust"; there's also a delicious edition of *Ulysses* illustrated by Henri Matisse. But it's the atmosphere of the place that really makes it worthwhile, particularly when you climb up the narrow staircase to the open top of the tower where stately, plump Buck Mulligan performs his ablutions at the beginning of *Ulysses*.

---

hardier swimmers use this rocky, natural swimming pool all year round. Sandycove is also good for canoeing, wind-surfing and water-skiing. For all watersports, check Oceantec, 10–11 Marine Terrace (☎280 1083), a diving equipment shop that will also arrange local diving.

Dalkey and Killiney

Further south along the coast lies the little town of **DALKEY**. Immortalized, if that's the word, in Flann O'Brien's satirical *The Dalkey Archive*, Dalkey (pronounced *Dawkey*) is nowadays a charming little seaside town, and nothing much besides. Its origins as a walled medieval settlement and important landing place for travellers from England are evident, though, especially in the massive Archibold's Castle which dominates the main street. There are narrow lanes with fine, bourgeois residences and, back in the main street, a really excellent new and second-hand bookshop, with plenty of recent review copies. John Dowland, the melancholy Elizabethan lutenist and composer, may have been born here, and George Bernard Shaw certainly lived at Torca Cottage on Dalkey Hill: he later claimed to be "a product of Dalkey's outlook". When the sun is shining, Dalkey has an almost Mediterranean holiday atmosphere, and it's thoroughly pleasant just to stroll about and drink it all in.

In the summer you can rent a boat to take you out to **Dalkey Island**, where you'll find a bird sanctuary, another in the series of Martello towers that were built to defend the coast from Napoleonic attack, and the ruins of the early Irish St Begnet's Church. A curious ritual involving the "King of Dalkey", complete with crown and sword, is still occasionally enacted here: originating in the eighteenth century, it started out as a student joke, but became increasingly political until it was stamped out by Lord Clare in 1797. If you are here around lunchtime, *Finnegans*, Sorrento Rd (☎285 8505), has a great seafood menu (noon–3pm), freshly caught from nearby Coliemore Harbour, served in a beautiful mahogany lounge bar. If you miss lunch, you can dine on the excellent Guinness.

Dublin Bay, views and fishing

From Dalkey Hill a ridge leads to the public park laid out atop **KILLINEY HILL** (pronounced *Kill-eye-nee*), with terrific views of Dublin Bay and the Wicklow Mountains. The stretch south from Dalkey Head is as beautiful a piece of scenery as you'll come across anywhere. As good a way as any to see it is from the DART line (if you walk, you're restricted to the road until you round Sorrento Point, so you're probably better off taking the train to Killiney): as you come out of Dalkey hilltop tunnel you're overwhelmed by the sweep of the bay, the blue sea on one side and on the other the weird bulk of the Sugarloaf mountain.

The entire coastline from Dún Laoghaire to Bray is good for fishing. Off Dalkey Island the dominant catches are conger, tope, pollock, skate and coalfish; further out, on the Burford and Kish banks, turbot, brill, dab and plaice are common. Fishing from the rocks and piers at Dún Laoghaire is free, and you can rent boats at Bullock and Coliemore harbours.

Glasnevin, Marino and Dollymount Strand

The suburb of **GLASNEVIN**, a couple of miles north of O'Connell Street (take bus #13, #19 or #19A, or from Abbey St Middle #34 or #34A), has two attractions to recommend it. The **National Botanic Gardens** (March–Oct Mon–Sat 9am–6pm, Sun 11am–6pm; Nov–Feb Mon–Sat 10am–4.30pm, Sun 11am–4.30pm), founded in 1795, is a quiet open space with a couple of large greenhouses dating from the mid-nineteenth century – their designer, Richard Turner, also constructed the glasshouse at Belfast's Botanic Gardens and the magnificent Palm House at Kew Gardens in London. Ireland's mild climate makes it an excellent place for growing exotic species – witness all those palm trees you see in front gardens along the seafront – and the Botanic Gardens were the first place in the world to raise orchids from seed, in 1844, and the first place in Europe to grow pampas grass and the giant lily successfully.

Close by is **Prospect Cemetery**(8.30am–4pm; free; guided tours Sun 11.30am), started as a burial place for Roman Catholics in 1832, and a jungle of patriotic iconography – shamrocks, high crosses, harps – still eerily surveyed by the watch-towers in the walls, from which sentries would endeavour to deter body-snatchers in the nineteenth century. The Prospect is, in many ways a good place to end a trip to Dublin as so many of the city's important historical figures are buried here: the politicians Daniel O'Connell (see p.619), who died in 1847 but whose body was brought here in 1869; Charles Stewart Parnell (see p.620); Sir Roger Casement, who was executed as a traitor by the British government in 1916 and the independence fighter Michael Collins. Countess Markievicz and Maud Gonne MacBride were both laid to rest here, as was the poet Gerard Manley Hopkins. After a trip to the graveyard, drop in for a pint at nearby *Kavanagh's* (commonly known as *The Gravediggers*), one of Dublin's finest old pubs, where mourners have sought solace since 1833.

Marino

MARINO, just off the Malahide Road three miles north of the city centre (#20A or #24 bus from Eden Quay), is the home of the eighteenth-century Casino, one of the most delightful pieces of Neoclassical lightheartedness you could hope to see anywhere. The bus will let you off next to some playing fields, from where the Casino, exuberantly decorated with urns and swags of carved drapery, is clearly visible to the left.

Needless to say, the **Casino** (mid-June to Sept daily 9.30am–6.30pm; Oct daily 10am–5pm; Nov & May to mid-June Sun & Wed only noon–4pm; closed Dec–April; last admission 45 minutes before closing; £2; Heritage Card) has nothing to do with gambling. Commissioned by Lord Charlemont (whose town house in Parnell Square is now the home of the Municipal Art Gallery), it was designed in the 1750s by Sir William

Chambers, the leading Neoclassical architect of the day, to accompany a villa which would in turn house some of the priceless works of art he had brought home from his grand tour of Europe. Marino House – the building of which spared no expense, and is said to have crippled Lord Charlemont's estate – was demolished long ago, but the Casino, restored in 1984, survives in perfect condition, crowded with witty and unlikely architectural features: the urns, for example, conceal chimneys.

As you go back into town, try to sit upstairs on the left-hand side of the bus. As it turns from the Malahide Road into Fairview, you can see Marino Crescent, an elegant row of Georgian town houses, once nicknamed "Ffolliot's revenge" after a painter who built the crescent out of spite to block the view from Marino House to the sea. Ffolliot's final twist of the knife in the flesh of the aesthetic Lord Charlemont was to make the backs of the houses, which faced Marino House, an unsightly jumble of chimneys, ill-placed windows and sheds.

Dollymount Strand

Immediately north of Dublin Harbour, **DOLLYMOUNT STRAND**, or Bull Island (bus #30 will take you out here, up the Clontarf Road), is one of the seaside areas most readily accessible to Dubliners. Designated, like Booterstown Marsh (in the south bay), a UNESCO Biosphere Reserve, Dollymount Strand is a spit of low sand dunes linked to the shore by a turn-of-the-century wooden bridge. Apart from holidaying Dubliners, it's host to thousands of overwintering wildfowl and wading birds and provides a stopping-off point for Arctic migrants. Birds are not the only interesting wildlife of Dollymount Strand: just a couple of miles from the centre of Dublin, there are foxes, shrews, badgers and rabbits, as well as a wide range of grass and plant species. You can find out more at the new **interpretative centre**, where the causeway road meets the island.

Howth

HOWTH (the name derives from the Danish *hoved*, or "head", and is pronounced to rhyme with both) lies at the northernmost point of both Dublin Bay and the DART line. Arriving in Howth, turn right out of the DART station for the castle, left for the village, abbey and cliff walks. You can also get here on the #31 bus, which passes not far from Marino on its way out.

Howth Head is a natural vantage point giving views right across Dublin Bay to the Wicklow Mountains and at times, so they claim, even as far as the distant Mountains of Mourne in the north and those of Wales across the Irish Sea. Not surprisingly, it has been a strategic military point for centuries, and its history involves a long line of fearful incumbents on the lookout for raiders. The legendary copper-mining Parthalons and Firbolg were the first to come, later conquered by the Gaelic chieftain Criomthain, whose grave is reputedly marked by a cairn on the summit. The Gaels, in turn, were ousted by the Vikings in the eighth century, and they were overthrown by the technologically and strategically superior Normans, led by Sir Almeric Tristram. His descendants, bearing the surname St Lawrence, continue to live at Howth Castle today.

Howth is a popular day-trip destination for Dubliners, and it has the happy and bracing air of a seaside resort, even off-season. There's a **harbour** on the north side, dating from the days when it, rather than Dún Laoghaire, was the main packet station for Dublin. At the jetty at the end of the West Pier you can see the footprint of King George IV, who landed here in 1821 instead of at Dún Laoghaire (which was expecting to rename itself Kingstown in honour of the event; he made up for it later by going home that way). It was from the same jetty, in July 1914, that the Irish Volunteers succeeded in landing 900 rifles and 25,000 rounds of ammunition from Erskine Childers' yacht *Asgard*, which you can see at Kilmainham Gaol. The harbour, full of working boats, is nowadays sited alongside a marina crowded with less practical craft. You can fish from the harbour pier; and, if you're in Howth on a Thursday evening, it's worth staying to see the spectacle when the herring boats come in. Michael Wright, on the quay, sells freshly caught fish and seafood from his shop all week.

Opposite the harbour, the rock-encrusted island is **Ireland's Eye**. A bird sanctuary, this uninhabited expanse of scrub grass and ferns sports yet another Martello tower and the ruins of a sixth-century monastic church, St Nessan's. In summer, you can cross by boat (Frank Doyle & Sons; ☎831 4200; return trip £4) to explore the island.

Much of the interior of Howth Head is built up, but a **footpath** runs all the way round the coast. There are impressive cliffs and amazing views – south past the mouth of the Liffey to the Wicklow Mountains and beyond, north to the flatlands of the Boyne. To get to the cliffs, either carry straight on along the shore road, or take the #31B bus up to the summit and cut down from there.

Howth village itself is a slow, suburban place full of steep streets and sudden views. Its one monument, on a quiet site overlooking Ireland's Eye, is the ruined Howth Abbey, the first church founded by Sigtrygg, Norse king of Dublin, in 1042. In one of the later phases of a chequered history, it was used by smugglers for storing contraband. The abbey is kept locked, but it is possible to get the keys from the caretaker: inside you'll see the fifteenth-century tomb of Christopher St Lawrence and his wife. Just below the abbey is the *Abbey Tavern*: bare, stone-walled, with stark wood furniture, turf fires and gas lighting. The air of authenticity can seem overdone, but it's worth visiting, as long as you don't mind the tourist bus-trip approach to Irish wit and music. The *Abbey Tavern* **restaurant** specializes in fish (best to book; ☎839 0307), and there is music in the evenings from around 9pm, for which there's a £3 cover charge. The other good eating place, if you've money to burn, is the excellent *King Sitric's Tavern*, East Pier (☎633 5235) with main courses at £20.

To get to **Howth Castle**, backtrack a few hundred yards along the road to Dublin and turn left. The castle itself isn't open to the public, but you pass it on the way to the unlovely and expensive *Deer Park Hotel*, and there's a small transport museum (June–Aug 10am–6pm, Sept–May 2–5pm; £1.50). It's an impressive building, even from the outside – a true, battlemented castle, partly ruined, partly inhabited – and one that architects from Francis Bindon to Edwin Lutyens have had a hand in restoring. The gardens are famous for their azaleas and rhododendrons in May and June.

Malahide

The easiest way to get to **MALAHIDE** from the centre of town is to take the suburban train service from Connolly Station (you can also take the #42 bus from Talbot Street or the #47 bus from Marino Casino). Either way, **Malahide Castle** makes for an enjoyable day out (April–Oct Mon–Fri 10am–5pm, Sat 11am–6pm, Sun 11.30am–6pm; Nov–March Mon–Fri 10am–5pm, Sat & Sun 2–6pm; park open daily June 10am–9pm, July–Aug 10am–8pm, Oct 10am–7pm, Nov–Jan 10am–5pm, Feb–March 10am–6pm; adults £2.95). When the last Lord Talbot died in 1973, his family home was taken over by the state. Much of the grounds has since been given over to playing fields but, unpromising as these look, the castle itself is terrific.

Dating in parts from 1174, when a marauding Norman, Richard Talbot, seized the lands and made it his fortress, the castle has been added to haphazardly over the ensuing centuries to make it look just how you think a castle ought to: turrets, Gothic windows, battlements and all. As well as being satisfyingly picturesque, what's fascinating about Malahide Castle is that you can follow its progress from a simple defensive tower – the first room you see inside, with amazing black carved panelling, is within the original square tower – to the addition of embellishments such as battlemented walls and turrets and, later still, its transformation into a country house, all fortifications now strictly decorative, with a mock-Gothic entrance.

Inside, a remarkably successful attempt has been made to show the best Irish furniture and pictures in good period settings: much of what you see is on loan from the National Portrait Gallery of Ireland. In case you're in need of refreshment, there's also an excellent tea room. It's indicative of the complex history of the Anglo-Irish that the rich and powerful Anglo-Norman Talbot family didn't actually turn Protestant until the eighteenth century. The castle even passed out of the hands of the family for ten years during the Cromwellian wars, but they managed to get it back. In the dining room is a large picture of the Battle of the Boyne; as Catholics, the Talbots fought not for Prince William but on the losing side. It's said that of the fourteen members of the family who sat down to breakfast in the dining room before setting out to fight, not one returned alive. For miniature-train buffs, Malahide also has the Fry Model Railway, a working O-gauge layout (April–Sept Mon–Thurs 10am–1pm, Sat 11 am–6pm, Sun 2–6pm; £2.75).

Malahide village, which must once have been little more than a crossroads at the gates of the castle, has long since outgrown its estate village status. It's a delight, one of those places where there's nothing much to write about, but which for some reason is really pleasant to be in: just a few grandish houses, some more modest colour-washed ones, the most spick-and-span train station you've ever seen and quiet streets sloping gently down to the golden strand and wild sea beyond.

Donabate and Skerries

A stop northward from Malahide on the commuter train (or the #33 bus from Dublin) is **DONABATE**, another trim town, worth visiting for **Newbridge House** (April–Sept Tues–Fri 10am–1pm and 2–5pm, Sat 11am–1pm and 2–6pm, Sun 2–6pm; Oct–March Sat & Sun 2–5pm; £2.45), signposted from the station, at the end of a twenty-minute ramble through woodlands, or a car journey from the main road. Built in 1737 for the Cobbe family, who came to Ireland in 1717 and rose rapidly through the Church of Ireland, it's a solid Georgian mansion whose main draw is the extraordinary **Museum of Curiosities**, a rare and marvellous family museum, started in 1790 and almost intact. Decorated with elegant representations of the "labours of China", it includes everything from exotic weapons and fish to an African chief's umbrella and the mummified ear of an Egyptian bull. The house remained unelectrified until the 1960s, when it was wired up for the filming of *The Spy Who Came in from the Cold*, which starred Richard Burton and Clare Bloom. There's a cosy coffee shop with soup and cakes, and the courtyards have been converted into a traditional farm with wandering goats and publicity-shy pigs.

SKERRIES, on the coast a few miles further north on the rail line, is close enough to Dublin to have a prosperous suburban hinterland; but the long main street, and the brightly painted huddle of houses on the spit of land that forms the harbour, preserve the romantic air of a remote fishing village. Atmospheric when it basks in the westering sun, and yet more so when the rain lashes down, this is a place to hole up and write your masterpiece – and, if your publisher's advance is big enough, to enjoy the **seafood** at the *Red Bank Restaurant* (☎849 1005) in Church Street.

Cafés and restaurants

Dublin may not be the gastronomic capital of the world, but there's plenty of choice – nearly all of it south of the Liffey – for both lunchtime and evening eating. **Café society** has reached Dublin in a big way in recent years, providing a new range of chic and trendy locations – in and around Grafton Street and Temple Bar – for all-day eating and drinking, and on Sundays many more places open up for sustaining brunches. At least once, you should experience one of the three *Bewley's* coffee houses. Try the table-service section on the second floor of the Grafton Street branch for elegance and potted palms at much the same prices. At lunchtime, Dublin's many **pubs** traditionally offer the best value: you can usually get soup and sandwiches and often much more substantial, traditional meals. The cheapest **fast-food** outlets – everything from *Pizzaland* and *Wimpy* to cheap Chinese and the ubiquitous kebab houses – are centred around O'Connell Street, but are generally, with one or two exceptions such as *Beshoff Ocean Foods*, pretty unpleasant.

In the evening there's no shortage of **restaurants** either; although on the North Side, places where you'll want to spend any time are thin on the ground. The spectrum of cuisines on offer is impressively wide, ranging from Egyptian, Lebanese, Russian and Cajun to the more familiar dishes from France, Italy and China. There are several restaurants offering **traditional Irish** fare, a number of good **seafood** places and plenty of **vegetarian** options. The cheaper, livelier restaurants are concentrated around the Temple Bar area, between Dame Street and the Liffey, while more expensive establishments are scattered throughout the city, with a concentration around St Stephen's Green.

Cafés

Alpha Café, corner of Clarendon and Wicklow Sts. Traditional fare at a great price served by waitresses that resemble your favourite auntie.

Bad Ass Café, 9 Crown Alley, Temple Bar (☎671 2596). Once the hippest of Dublin's pizza joints. Sinead O'Connor was waitressing here when she cut her first disc with *Ton Ton Macoute*; now distinctly unhip for adults, but great fun for kids. Daily 11am–11pm.

Beshoff Ocean Foods, 14 Westmoreland St & 7 Upper O'Connell St. Superior fish and chips, with bistro-type decor. Daily 11am–3am.

Bewley's, 78 Grafton St (daily 7am–1am, Thurs–Sat till 2am), 12 Westmoreland St (daily 7.30am–9pm) & 13 South Great George's St (Mon–Sat 6.45am–6pm). A Dublin institution, serving everything from drinks to sticky buns and full meals, and its delicious, renowned potato soup, in an elegant ambience.

The Bite of Life, corner of Patrick St and Bull's Alley. Small café with great toasted ciabatta sandwiches.

Café Irie, Fownes St. Possibly the best sandwiches in Dublin served by staff so laid back, they're virtually horizontal.

Café Java, 5 South Anne St. Good for breakfasts and coffees. Mon–Fri 7.45am–6pm, Sat 9am–5pm, Sun 10am–5pm.

Cobalt Café, North Great George's St. Good food in a café-cum-gallery. The space is light, the displays are exemplary, all of which makes this one of the most pleasant places to enjoy a coffee in the city. If you visit the James Joyce centre or stay in the *MEC Hostel* opposite, this cafe is a must.

Cornucopia Wholefoods, 21 Wicklow St (☎677 7583). Vegetarian shop and café. For anyone who has pigged out on one traditional Irish breakfast too many, *Cornucopia* offers a vegetarian alternative, including vegetarian sausages, between 8 and 11am. Café open daily until 9pm.

The Globe, 11 South Great George's St. A bar by night (see p.102), this is a buzzing café by day, serving cappuccinos and herbal teas.

Harveys, 14 Moira House, Trinity St. Good-value breakfast, excellent coffee and exceptional if pricy sandwiches; Mon–Sat 8am–7pm, Sun 11am–5pm.

The Hugh Lane Gallery, Parnell Square. A decent café, good for relaxing in after the delights of the Gallery.

Image Gallery, 25 East Essex St. Photographic gallery plus café, opposite the Irish Design Centre.

Juice, South Great George's St. Imaginative macrobiotic food, mix of oriental and Californian; a chic vegetarian eating place for the '90s, not a sweaty sandal in sight. Daily 8am–11pm.

Leo Burdock's, 2 Werburgh St. Dublin's legendary fish-and-chip shop, now modestly wondering whether its fish and chips are the best not only in Dublin, but maybe in the world. Carry-out only. Mon–Fri 12.30–11pm, Sat 2–11pm.

Marks Bros, 7 South Great George's St. A vibrant café with a good choice of vegetarian eats. Open

Mon–Sat 10am–5pm.

Odessa, 13/14 Dame Court. Exotic snacks and outré decor make this one of the trendiest new cafés; downstairs is good for gossiping in big squashy sofas. Noon–midnight daily; breakfast served noon–4pm.

Simon's Place, South Great George's St beside George's Arcade. With possibly the friendliest staff in the city, this is a great hang-out.

Well Fed Café, Dublin Resource Centre, 6 Crow St. Run by a workers' co-operative, this restaurant does truly excellent vegetarian cooking and has a small alternative bookshop at the front. Daily 10am–8.30pm.

Winding Stair Café, 40 Lower Ormond Quay. This vast second-hand book emporium also has a café serving soup, salads, sandwiches and cakes. Sit by the window and watch the Liffey ooze by. Open till 6pm only.

Moderate (main courses under £10)

Il Baccaro, Diceman's Corner, Meeting House Square. Old-style Italian serving up hearty dishes such as Sicilian aubergine stew. Wine is served by the litre. Open till late.

Blazing Salads II, Powerscourt Townhouse Centre, Clarendon St (☎671 9552). Marvellous vegetarian food in a Georgian townhouse turned shopping centre. Open Mon–Sat.

The Cedar Tree, 11 St Andrew's St (☎677 2121). A dazzling array of Lebanese meze dishes served in a cavernous basement. Open Mon–Sat 5.30–11.45pm, Sun until 11.30pm.

The Chameleon, 1 Fownes St (☎671 0362). Award-winning and highly regarded Indonesian on the northern edges of Temple Bar.

Da Pino, 38 Parliament St (☎671 9308). Marvellous fresh pasta and huge pizzas at low prices. Daily noon–11.30pm.

Elephant and Castle, 18 Temple Bar (☎679 3121). Cross between a New York diner and a brasserie. Will do you anything from a drink to dinner. Main courses can be pricy (£10–15), while burgers start from around £8. Best place by far for Sunday brunch, but make sure you book. Open Mon–Thurs 8am–11.30pm, Fri till midnight, Sat 10.30am–midnight, Sun noon–11.30pm.

Fitzer's, 51 Dawson St (☎660 1644). Cool, airy café/restaurant serving a Californian-style, new-wave menu of soulful food, including pasta, salads, seafood and chargrills, or you can just drop in for a coffee. Outdoor seating on busy Dawson St. Branches in Temple Bar Square and National Gallery. Open Mon–Sat 8am–11pm.

Gallagher's Boxty House, 20 Temple Bar (☎677 2762). A boxty is an Irish potato pancake cooked on a griddle, and stuffed with meat or vegetables. Filling, if bland, food in a pleasant and friendly atmosphere. It's known familiarly as GBH and is somewhat looked down on by Dubliners, who probably regard its menu as strictly tourist fodder. A wonderful aroma is given off by the open peat fires. Daily noon–11.30pm.

Irish Film Centre, 6 Eustace St (☎677 8788). Coolly minimalist designer bar and restaurant in what used to be a Quaker meeting house. Serves delicious food – including highly sinful cakes and pastries – all day. Plenty of vegetarian choice on an eclectic menu: vegetable pâtés, burgers, chicken, jambalaya with bananas. Open according to programme.

Kilkenny Design Centre Restaurant, 6 Nassau St, first floor. Great place for lunch but always packed, so be prepared to queue. Open Mon–Sat 9am–5pm.

Luigi Malones, Fownes St. The menu is pretty bland but if you find something you like you won't go away hungry.

Mao Café and Bar, 2–3 Chatham Row (☎670 4899). The communist chic theme has really taken off in Dublin and nowhere more successfully than *Mao*. The dishes are rice- or noodle-based, the vegetables as fresh as you get and the service is first rate. Highly recommended. 9.30am–10.30pm.

La Med, Temple Bar. Cosy Mediterranean restaurant with great calamari, though desserts don't quite match up to the standard of the mains.

Milano, 61 Dawson St (☎677 8611). First venture of the British *Pizza Express* chain in Ireland – swish surroundings with the familiar and affordable range of pizzas. Daily 6.30–11pm.

Mongolian Barbeque, 7 Anglesea St (☎670 4154). The Genghis McKhan jokes aside this can be a fun place for a group party. You choose your meats, noodles and sauce and the chefs cook them in front of you on a large grill.

Nicos, 53 Dame St (☎677 3062). Italian restaurant popular as much for its atmosphere as for its food.

La Paloma, 17B Temple Bar (☎677 7392). Saturated yellows and hot pinks offer a suitably un-Irish backdrop for good, cheap tapas with a pricier evening menu. The descriptions of the meals, however, are so over the top the food can only be an anticlimax. Open daily till midnight.

Pasta Fresca, Chatham St (☎879 2402). Ireland's first fresh pasta shop. Its restaurant is consistently busy so get there early or book ahead.

Il Pasticcio, 12 Fownes St. Cosy Italian restaurant, pasta from £5.00, great desserts and salads. Open Mon–Sat till 11pm, Sun 10pm.

Romano's, 12 Capel St. Excellent Italian, though somewhat neglected, being on the "wrong" side of the river. Main courses start at around £7, pizzas at £8 and there's a great £6.95 three-course lunch special.

South Street Pizzeria, South Great George's St (☎475 2273). Great pizzas in a relaxed and friendly atmosphere. Look out for the excellent lunchtime specials. Daily noon–8pm.

Sushi, Fownes St. The name gives it away; good selection of fresh fish in friendly surroundings.

Tante Zoe's, 1 Crow St (☎679 4407). Cajun/Creole restaurant with good food at decent prices. Very popular, so best to book. Daily noon to midnight.

Tosca, 20 Suffolk St (☎679 6744). Excellent new-wave Italian cooking in a cool halogen-lit interior guarantees this restaurant's continuing fashionability. There are piles of newspapers for slow browsing during the day but it can get quite hectic at night. Daily noon–3.30pm & 5.30pm to midnight, Fri & Sat until 1am.

Yamamori Noodles, 71–72 South Great George's St (☎475 5001). Popular Japanese restaurant; the sushi is fine, teriyaki great but avoid the tempura.

Moderate to expensive (main courses £10–15)

101 Talbot, 101–102 Talbot St (☎874 5011). One of the very few good restaurants north of the Liffey, this spacious dining room, close to the Abbey Theatre, is worth visiting for its excellent, eclectic menu and relaxed conviviality. Pasta bar open daily noon–11pm; main restaurant Mon–Sat lunch noon–3pm, dinner 6–11pm.

Auriga, Temple Bar Square (☎671 8228). Overlooking Temple Bar Square, *Auriga* serves high-quality food at competitive prices. Try the delicious chicken *confit*.

Dish, 2 Crow St (☎671 1284). Progressive international cuisine by two young Dublin chefs.

Jacob's Ladder, 4–5 Nassau St (☎670 3865). Highest quality Irish food with some Mediterranean variations and a good selection of New World wines. One of the finest dishes on the main menu is the roast breast of duck with caramelized chicory, stuffed potatoes and honey and ginger syrup.

Le Vigneron, 6 Cope St (☎671 5740). The best French restaurant in Dublin with an excellent wine list. Try the lively bistro downstairs if funds are low.

Expensive (main courses at £15 and over)

Chapter One, Parnell Square (☎873 2266). A classy establishment located in the basement of the Dublin Writers' Museum. The pre-theatre menu is good value at £14.50 for three courses.

Cooke's Café, 14 South William St (☎679 0536). Accomplished cooking in cool, terracotta surroundings. Very fashionable, very new wave. Mon–Sat 10am–5pm, Sun 11am–4pm.

Grey Door Irish Restaurant, 23 Upper Pembroke St (☎676 3286). High standards of Irish food served with care in a pleasant atmosphere. The four-course lunch at £14.50 is well worth investigating.

Imperial Chinese Restaurant, 12A Wicklow St (☎677 2580). Popular with the Chinese community and that should be recommendation enough for anyone. If the prices are prohibitive then try the Sunday brunch.

Lord Edward Seafood Restaurant, 23 Christchurch Place (☎454 2420). Around the corner from *Leo Burdock's*, the legendary chippie, the *Lord Edward* represents the other end of the scale.

Located above a very ordinary pub, it's been going for decades and is a Dublin tradition with a terrific reputation for simple cooking using the very freshest fish. Set lunch from £5, set dinner around £25. Open Mon–Sat 12.30–3pm & 6–10.45pm.

The Old Dublin, 90–91 Francis St (☎454 2028). Superb Russo-Irish food amid the dusty junk shops and markets of The Liberties area; borscht, gravadlax (*The Old Dublin*'s definition of Russia seems to include most of Scandinavia), coupled with hearty Irish meat and veg. Cheap menu early evenings. Booking advisable. Open Mon–Sat 12.30–2pm & 6–10.30pm; no Sat lunch.

The Tea Rooms, *The Clarence Hotel*, 6–8 Wellington Quay (☎670 7766). Ultra-stylish restaurant with an eclectic menu.

Trocadero, 3 St Andrew St (☎677 5545 or 679 2385). Pleasant and friendly trattoria with excellent food. It's one of Dublin's oldest Italian restaurants, and the walls are hung with plaudits in the form of signed photographs of visiting showbiz luminaries. Pre-theatre menu for £9.75. The place really comes into its own late at night when it fills up with theatre folk. Daily 6pm–12.15am.

The Unicorn, off Merrion Row in an unpromising little courtyard that leads off to the right a few paces down from St Stephen's Green (☎676 2182). Plain, no-nonsense interior and an extensive Italian menu including pasta and pizzas as well as the standard meat-and-sauce dishes. With *Doheny and Nesbitt*'s pub (see overleaf), across Lower Baggot St, it forms a focus for the more intellectual side of Dublin life, frequented by journalists, economists, campaigners and musicians. Daily noon–3pm & 6–11pm.

Pubs and music

Pubs are an integral part of Dublin's social life and an essential part of any visit. Guidebooks are apt to write as if there's a great mystery about them, or as if they're somehow dangerous places where you shouldn't venture alone, and certainly not without a recommendation from this or that authority. Neither is true, and the charm of most of Dublin's older pubs derives from the fact that they're simple, no-nonsense places, the better ones unchanged for decades, where you can get a good pint of Guinness and the people are friendly. There are over 800 pubs and bars in the city, so what follows doesn't try to be anything like a comprehensive, or even a representative, guide. Instead it's a small – and very personal – selection of Dublin's traditional pubs and new drinking places, with some indication of where you're likely to find music and other entertainment.

The **music scene** is volatile, though, so if you're after something in particular – jazz, folk, traditional – the best place to check is yet again the listings magazine *In Dublin*. *Hot Press*, the national music paper, is another useful source of information. For traditional music, contact the traditional music society, Comhaltas Ceoltóirí Éireann (also known as Cultúrlann) at 32 Belgrave Square, Monkstown (☎280 0295). Their offices are, in any case, worth a visit almost any night for their programmes of traditional music and theatre.

Two general points of **etiquette**: pubs in Dublin tend to be fairly male preserves, but if you're a woman don't be put off – you're unlikely to be made to feel uncomfortable, even if you're alone. And many Dublin pubs have snugs, or small private rooms, which can be the cosiest places to drink if you're in a group. There's nothing exclusive about these – just go in and stake your claim if you find one empty – and drinks cost the same as in the main bar.

Pubs and bars

The Baggot Inn, 143 Lower Baggot St (☎676 1430). Ageing rock clientele congregates to hear rock music nightly.

Café en Seine, 40 Dawson St. Cavernously lively and hip café/bar with extraordinary Celtic/Art Nouveau murals. Good place to drop in for a cappuccino or espresso during the day.

La Cave, 28 South Anne St. This is really a wine bar that opens so late that you even leave of your own volition.

Clarence Hotel, Wellington Quay. U2-owned hotel, that is as designedly cool/uncool as its owners and is loved and hated in equal measure. Its bar is well worth a visit if only to use the wood-panelled toilets.

Davy Byrne's, 21 Duke St, off Grafton St (☎677 5217). Here, in *Ulysses*, Leopold Bloom stopped to eat a gorgonzola sandwich and quaff a glass of burgundy; and here, on Bloomsday (June 16) every year, numerous pilgrims stop to do exactly the same thing. Now decked out in tasteful shades of lemon and grey, *Davy Byrne's* no longer looks exactly Joycean.

Doheny and Nesbitt, 5 Lower Baggot St. Archetypal Dublin pub – the tiny, atmospheric, smoke-filled room looks as if it has hardly changed since the beginning of the century. Always packed, cosy snugs. Upstairs is a slightly less hectic lounge if you can't stand the pace. Much frequented by *Irish Times* hacks.

The Ferryman, 35 Sir John Rogerson Quay (☎671 7053). A walk along the South Quay, or a short #3 bus ride toward Ringsend. This is the place where serious musicians go to play and listen.

The Front Lounge, Parliament St. The spacious interior is always full of the city's most beautiful people. Gay-friendly, great cappucinos, but can get very crowded at weekends.

The Globe, 11 South Great George's St. Mecca for the terminally hip, this is a big airy bar that pulls in large numbers of young drinkers for a pre-dance beer.

Grogan's, 15 South William St. Smoky haunt of literary types down through the years where conversation dominates. Good drinks at relatively reasonable prices, this is the place if you like your beer without the frills.

Gravediggers, Glasnevin. Also known as *Kavanagh's*, this bar has a delightful wooden interior and benches to match.

The International Bar, 23 Wicklow St. Another great drinking establishment that has changed little over the decades. Upstairs hosts comedy and music in a small room that can get very hot in the summer.

The Irish Film Centre, 6 Eustace St, Temple Bar. This designer bar is one of the places to see and be seen. Open according to programme (also see p.105).

Keogh's, 9 Anne St South, off Grafton St. Wonderful snugs if you want to curl up in comparative privacy to sip your pint.

The Long Hall, 51 South Great George's St. Victorian pub with an astonishing array of antiques on show.

McDaid's, 3 Harry St. A literary pub, this is where Brendan Behan used to drown his talent in Guinness – there's a photograph of him with a tiny typewriter wedged between two glasses of the black stuff, one full, one empty.

Mulligan's, 8 Poolbeg St. Mulligan's traditionally served the best Guinness in Dublin; many people now acknowledge that honour to have passed to Guinness's own visitor centre, but *Mulligan's* still has its partisans.

The Palace, 21 Fleet St. Wood-and-glass interior, crowded and friendly pub much loved by Dubliners.

The Porter House, 16–18 Parliament St. Given its location among bars trading in cod tradition, the *Porter House*, is an admirable attempt to present the pub in a modern form. It brews its own drinks and attracts a transitory crowd more interested in the concept and design than aficionados of its various beers.

Pravda, Lower Liffey St. The design motif is communist chic and this huge bar has been a great success since it spearheaded trendiness' colonizing of the northside. The top floor is immersed in daylight and has great couches conducive to daytime coffee and chat.

Ryan's, Parkgate St, across the river from Heuston Station. Another pub famous for its cosy, wood-lined snugs; considered the finest Victorian pub in Dublin.

Sackville Lounge, Sackville St, off O'Connell Street. Quiet watering hole if you need a pint and a chat while north of the river.

Stag's Head, 1 Dame Court, a tiny turning off Dame St almost opposite the Central Bank. Hard to find – a mosaic set in the pavement on Dame St alerts you to the tiny alleyway it's located in – but worth it when you get there: inside it's all mahogany, stained glass and mirrors. Good pub lunches, too, and friendly atmosphere.

Thomas Read's, 79 Dame St. Trendy new pub with good food at lunchtime; a lively spot in the evenings.

Toners Victorian Bar, 139 Lower Baggot St. Dark, cosy pub with a refreshingly plain interior. Snugs, with glazed partitions, for making and breaking confidences.

Pubs with music

Bad Bob's Backstage Bar, East Essex St, Temple Bar (☎677 5842). Still Dublin's central late-night music venue, known to one and all as the "Backside Bar". Traditional and contemporary music.

Brazen Head, 20 Lower Bridge St. Possibly the oldest pub in the city, the *Brazen Head* is situated on the road that leads downhill from Christchurch to the river. It is said to be the last place Robert Emmet had a drink before his abortive rebellion and some drinkers have sworn to have met the former patriot's ghost after a long night. Its courtyard makes a great place to have a beer on a summer's evening.

Hughes', 19 Chancery St. If you're in the vicinity of the Four Courts this is a great place for a drink. If you stay until the day wears off then you could find yourself in the midst of as fine a music session as you're likely to come across in the city.

The International Bar, 23 Wicklow St. (☎677 9250). Great singer-songwriter nights most Tuesdays where young Dubliners cut their musical teeth.

The Mean Fiddler, 26 Wexford St (☎475 8555). A seriously cool interior and a good line-up of live acts have made this venue a strong competitor with *Whelans* (see below), next door.

The Merchant, Lower Bridge St, opposite the *Brazen Head*. Traditional music most nights with impromptu sessions in between.

Mother Redcap's Tavern, Back Lane, off High St (☎453 8306). Traditional and country music – Ireland's other folk tradition – in an old shoe factory in one of the oldest parts of Dublin. A pint of Guinness here, fried fish and a poke of chips from *Leo Burdock's* famous fish-and-chip shop around the corner (see p.98), and your night's made. Big-name billing on Fri and Sat nights for a £6 cover charge.

The Norseman, 29 Essex St, Temple Bar. Formerly a popular haunt of Dublin's bohemia, now more of a tourist hang-out, the *Norseman* has traditional music some evenings.

O'Donoghues, 15 Merrion Row. Seen by many as the home of Dublin folk music. Get here early, get a seat and a pint and the fun will soon follow.

Oliver St John Gogarty's, Anglesea St. "Traditional" music every night though it's a bit of a tourist trap.

Slattery's, 129 Capel St. Good drink and great music are the two essential ingredients for a night's *craic* and *Slattery's* provides both in abundance.

Whelans, 25 Wexford St (☎478 0766). Very lively pub with bands and bar extensions most nights; an eclectic line-up of acts, sometimes Irish traditional or "world music".

Other music venues

The DA Club, 3–5 Clarendon Market, off North William St (☎671 1130). Must be one of Dublin's best venues. This intimate space has a great atmosphere and sound system to match. The first-rate booking policy means that some of the country's finest musicians could be playing to you and a few other discerning punters.

The Furnace, 2 Aston Place (☎671 0088). Student heaven – Doc Martens, plastic glasses and beer-splattered floor.

The Music Centre, Curved St, Temple Bar (☎679 0533). The venue here holds 650 people and has acoustics unrivalled in the city. The booking policy is eclectic, though of a generally high standard.

The Olympia, 74 Dame St, off Temple Bar (☎677 7744). When the evening performance ends in this tinselly ex-music hall on Fri & Sat nights, the theatre closes down for half an hour; at 11.30pm the doors open and the late-night music spot, *Midnight at the Olympia*, begins. As a music venue it's a strange place – you sit in plush theatre seats and dance in the aisles – but it's unbeatable for its line-up of both up-and-coming and established performers. Bar open till 2am.

Red Box, 35 Harcourt St (☎478 0225). Upstairs from *The POD* club, this is a well-designed venue that holds 1000 people.

Clubs and discos

Clubs are by nature volatile, so you should check the latest *In Dublin* listings to see which club nights are still in operation. There are two distinct club scenes in Dublin. The first (and the one listed here) is an eclectic collection – including the new, much talked-about chic clubs – scattered around the city centre, many of which offer special interest and theme nights. Most are hard to get into – that's part of their cachet – and expensive at the weekends.

The second, and distinctly less appealing, is based in and around Leeson Street, southeast of St Stephen's Green. The clubs here do, however, serve a purpose: a string of basement places busy after everything else has shut, these are the clubs to hit at two or three in the morning if you're really desperate to go on partying. Most have no entry fee but very expensive drinks – they're at their dubious best Thursday to Sunday from around 1am till dawn.

Break for the Border, Lower St Stephen's St. The music here only provides a soundtrack to the courting rituals. If you want to meet a Dubliner of the opposite sex, drink lots of beer and have a laugh, this may be the place for you.

Blue Note Club, Bedford Lane, Temple Bar (☎671 9354). Acid jazz and rare grooves for the younger crowd that missed this music first time around.

Club M, Cope Street, Temple Bar. Music is pretty mainstream, and the clothes are generally minimalist.

The Gaiety Theatre, South King St. Friday and Saturday nights see the *Gaiety* hold the popular *Velure* and *Mambo* clubs which are multi-event shows with jazz, samba and reggae rooms, plus live bands and film screenings. Can get a little crowded at times with a clientele more interested in the late bar than the entertainment.

The Kitchen, East Essex St, Temple Bar. Worth getting here early to check out the interior design where the curved walls and dipping ceiling gives a premature feeling of intoxication. Be warned that entry can be difficult but if you do get in expect to hear some of the best dance music in the city.

Lillie's Bordello, Adam Court, Grafton St. A strict door policy means that you may find it difficult to get in but the best advice is to get there before pub closing time.

The POD, 35 Harcourt St. Formerly the place to go dancing in the city, though it's losing its grip a little. There is a draconian door policy that looks for sartorial smartness rather than trendiness. It's more relaxed on Thursdays when the music is a little softer too.

Rí-Rá, South Great George's St (☎677 4835). Compared to other clubs in town the doormen are almost courteous, the music is variable and the crowd fun. Like most clubs, don't expect to get in if you stagger up to the door after pub closing.

System 21, South Anne St. If you like your techno hard and fast this is the place to go.

Theatre and cinema

As seems fitting for a city with Dublin's rich literary past, **theatre** flourishes. The traditional diet of Irish classics at the "establishment" theatres is now spiced by experimental or fringe programmes at newer, smaller venues; tickets are cheap – averaging £9–10 – and drama is accessible, and popular.

Dublin has a large number of **cinemas** – almost all of them on and around O'Connell Street – showing mainstream films. All Dublin's cinemas operate an enlightened policy of cheap seats before 5pm (6.30pm in some cases), seven days a week. The peculiarities of the film distribution system mean that new movies are often released earlier in Ireland than in Britain. There are two art-house cinemas, both showing a changing repertoire of films.

You'll find details of all theatre performances and cinema programmes in the fortnightly listings magazine, *In Dublin*.

Theatre

Abbey Theatre, Lower Abbey St, just off O'Connell St (☎878 7222). The grim concrete building housing the famous Abbey Theatre gives little away about its illustrious past (see p.805). On its rebuilding in 1952, however, Patrick Kavanagh was scathing, writing in his eponymous *Kavanagh's Weekly*: "The Abbey Theatre is the opposite of what it set out to be. The Abbey Theatre was never much good. The life it portrayed was not Irish, but a convention invented by Synge mainly." The theatre is still known for its productions of older Irish plays (by playwrights such as Boucicault and Richard Brinsley Sheridan), but does encourage younger writers. One of the most acclaimed productions of the 1990s was Brian Friel's *Dancing at Lughnasa*. In addition to the main auditorium, the building houses the smaller Peacock Theatre, which sometimes has more experimental shows.

Andrews Lane Theatre, Andrews Lane (☎679 5720). Theatre and studio, just off Dame St in what appears to be the middle of a car park, concentrating on the latest Irish writing. One of Dublin's new performance spaces, under the same management as the remarkable Gate Theatre (see p.87).

City Arts Centre, Moss St, off George's Quay (☎677 0643). A venue that usually features community-based drama.

Crypt Arts Centre, Dublin Castle (☎761 3387). In the crypt of the Chapel Royal, this venue has an eclectic mix from drama to rock concerts and is used by Amharclann na Hide, the Irish language theatre group.

Gaiety Theatre, South King St (☎677 1717). Dublin's oldest theatre stages a mix of musical comedy, revues, occasional opera, and, every now and then, something really worth seeing.

Gate Theatre, Cavendish Row, next to the Rotunda (☎874 4045 or 674 6042). Another of Dublin's literary institutions, it stages more modern Irish plays and can be lively and atmospheric.

Olympia Theatre, Dame St (☎677 8962 or 8147). Formerly Dan Lowry's Music Hall, and that's exactly how it looks: raffish, down-at-heel, with an air of faded, once tinselly glamour. It now puts on (no surprises) vaudeville, comedy, ballet and drama, sometimes packing in two completely different shows in one evening with a late-night music spot to round things off.

Peacock Theatre, Lower Abbey St (☎878 7222). The Abbey's smaller sibling features more progressive theatre and acts as a springboard for some of the country's best talent.

Project Arts Centre at The Mint, Henry Place off Henry Street, beside the GPO (☎671 2321). This is where you're most likely to find experimental or politically sensitive work. The home of the Project for many years in Temple Bar is currently under reconstruction so performances are being held temporarily at the intimate Mint venue, although bookings are still being taken at the old Temple Bar venue.

Tivoli Theatre, Francis St (☎454 4472). A modern theatre near The Liberties that doubles as a rock venue.

Cinemas

Irish Film Centre, 6 Eustace St, Temple Bar (☎679 5744). Art-house cinema with two screens and an excellent restaurant (see p.99), as well as a film-related bookshop and dance-club nights on Fri & Sat (see p.102). Films include new, low-budget Irish work plus seasons of world, gay and children's cinema; a worthwhile survey of Irish film-making is shown every afternoon.

Light House Cinema, 106 Abbey St. Middle (☎873 0438 or 671 0546). Tiny cinema with two screens showing art-house films; mostly continental European.

The Screen, College St. (☎671 4988). Shows a less commercial selection than most Dublin cinemas and has good afternoon prices.

Mainstream cinemas include: The Ambassador, 1 Parnell Square (☎872 7000; one screen); The Savoy, O'Connell St Upper (☎874 6000; five screens); Screen, D'Olier St (☎671 4988; three screens); and Virgin, Parnell St (☎872 8400; nine screens).

Gay life

Although Ireland's celebrated gays include Oscar Wilde, Somerville and Ross, Eva Gore-Booth and Brendan Behan, prejudice remains considerable. In 1988 the European Court of Human Rights decreed that Ireland's anti-gay law contravened the European Convention on Human Rights, and in 1990 the law was repealed and the age of consent lowered to seventeen. The result is that, despite the hegemony of the Catholic Church, gay voices are increasingly making themselves heard in public debate, and Dublin now has a visible gay scene. A good starting point for any gay travellers to Ireland is *Outhouse*, 6 South William St, which has a gay community centre and a café/restaurant (☎670 6377). Alternatively, you can ring Gay Switchboard Dublin (daily 8–10pm, except Sat 3.30–6pm; ☎872 1055) or the 24-hour info and events line (☎1550/122 345). Lesbian travellers may wish to contact Lesbians Organizing Together, which has a drop-in centre at 5 Capel St (Mon–Thurs 10am–6pm, Fri 10am–4pm) or telephone (☎872 7770). It's also a good idea to get a copy of the excellent freebie *Gay Community News* – which you can pick up at the Temple Bar information centre or Books Upstairs.

Gay and mixed meeting places include, *Marks Bros, Juice* and the *Well Fed Café* (see "Cafés and restaurants"). A lot of mainstream venues have themed nights and gay events, and many of the city-centre pubs have a very mixed clientele. More specifically gay places include:

Front Lounge, Parliament St. More a mixed than an exclusively gay venue, its atmosphere is certainly camp which appeals to quite a large gay crowd.

The George Bar and Bistro, 89 South Great George's St (☎478 2983). Three bars in total: the *Loft* disco, a trendy bar with music and a quiet bar. Wed–Sun there's also a lively and vibrant club; dress code, no effort, no entry, it opens until 2.30am.

Hogans, (*The Globe and Hogans*; see p.98), 11 South Great George's St. Busy and stylish mixed crowd.

Out on the Liffey, 27 Upper Ormond Quay. More relaxed than the *George*, this pub is popular with gays and lesbians alike.

Shopping

Around Grafton Street and O'Connell Street, the business of buying and selling rates second only to pub life for vigour, humour and sheer panache. Although many of the store chains – Next, Marks & Spencers, Waterstones – will be familiar to British visitors, the importance of seeing and being seen, and above all of conversation, makes shopping a spectator and participant sport of a high order. The **O'Connell Street** area represents the more ordinary, high-street end of the market, with cut-price shops, chain stores, and a boisterous street market concentrated on nearby Henry Street. Clery's, the august department store, and Eason's bookshop are two of the highlights; the Ilac centre, behind Moore Street, is probably the nadir.

South of the river are the smarter outlets and the tourist shops, as well as the kaleidoscopic and rapidly changing range of "alternative" boutiques that characterizes the fashionable **Temple Bar** area (the place to go for club gear and street fashions). Pedestrianized **Grafton Street** contains Dublin's swankiest department store, Brown Thomas. Just off Grafton Street, the 200-year-old Powerscourt Town House has been converted into a covered mall, with plenty of expensive clothes shops.

As a visitor, you'll find it difficult to escape the range of shops touting "typically" **Irish goods** aimed at tourists, mainly wool, ceramics and crystal. You may well come away with the impression that these are universally depressing and overpriced, but there are some exceptions, and you can occasionally pick up some real bargains.

Antiques

Sullivan Antiques, 43 Francis St in The Liberties, is one of the best established antique shops specializing in *objets d'art* and furniture. Shops in Molesworth Street – including Alexander Antiques at no. 16, which has a wide range of antique clocks, pictures and period furniture – South Anne Street and Kildare Street are all worth a browse.

Bookshops

General bookshops include Eason's, 40–42 Lower O'Connell St (beside the GPO); Waterstones at 7 Dawson St; and Hodges Figgis, nearby at 56–58 Dawson St, which has a particularly extensive stock of **Irish books**, a good remainder bookshop downstairs and a pleasant café on the first floor. Dublin Bookshop, 24 Grafton St, is one of the better mainstream bookshops, while Books Upstairs, 36 College Green (just outside the gates of Trinity College), is still Dublin's major alternative bookshop and has a good selection including feminist and gay fiction, women's studies, poetry and cinema, and magazines and reviews. For all manner of books, including second-hand, academic and Irish-related books, follow Trinity students to the excellent Fred Hanna's, 29 Nassau St. Greenes, 16 Clare St, an academic topsy-turvy second-hand bookshop is also worth a look, and The Winding Stair, 40 Ormond Quay, is an excellent and pleasantly shabby second-hand bookshop with an unhurried café where you can peruse your finds, before or after purchase. If it's sci-fi, fantasy or horror you're after then Forbidden Planet, 36 Dawson St is the place to find it, while Connolly Books, 43 East Essex St, stocks a wide range of books on the political sciences.

Clothes

Brown Thomas, Grafton Street, offers smart designer wear from Irish labels such as Paul Costelloe, Louise Kennedy and John Rocha; while the Irish Fashion Design Centre (Powerscourt Town House), Clarendon Street, has a changing range of stalls by young designers who work mainly in natural materials such as linen, silk and wool. For second-hand clothes, Flip at 4 Fownes St specializes in Americana, jackets, shirts and jeans; at Eager Beaver, The Crown Alley, you can find a wider range of good-quality used clothing. You could also try the George's St Market Arcade, off South Great George's Street, which has a range of stalls selling second-hand clothing (plus jewellery and records).

Irish goods

Kilkenny Design Centre, 6 Nassau St, originally set up by the government to promote good design, is now privately run and stocks high-quality Irish goods: clothes (mainly linen and knitware), crystal and ceramics, which come significantly reduced in price at sale-time. The Blarney Woollen Mills, College Park House, Nassau Street, offers a more traditional range of Irish crystal and china, plus the obligatory woolly pullovers and linen blouses; again, some bargains if you are prepared to sift. House of Ireland, also in Nassau Street, has fancy Irish crystal ranging from Belleek to Waterford, as well as the sweetly sentimental Lladro ceramics. At 41 Lower Ormond Quay, The Dublin Woollen Company sells a huge range of cut-price Irish knitwear, tweeds and lace. Weir and Sons, 96 Grafton St, has antique silver and jewellery plus a good selection of Irish crystal. If you are keen on genealogy, Clans of Ireland, 2 Kildare St, is able to trace the location and significance of most Irish family names.

Music

Claddagh Records, 2 Cecilia St, Temple Bar, stocks a good range of traditional Irish and "world music". Also in Temple Bar, Comet Records, 5 Cope St, sells new indie CDs and second-hand records, and dispenses useful information on current bands and where to see them; Freebird, 1 Eden Quay, specializes in second-hand indie music while Celtic Note on Nassau Street stocks a wide range of Irish-related music. Both HMV, 65 Grafton St, and Virgin Megastore, 14 Aston Quay, offer mainstream sounds.

Listings

Airlines Aer Lingus, 41 Upper O'Connell St and 42 Grafton St (☎844 4777); British Airways, 60 Dawson St (☎1800/626742); British Midland, Merrion Centre (☎283 8833; Dublin Airport ☎677 4422); Ryanair, 3 Dawson St (☎677 4422).

Banks Banking hours are Mon–Fri 10am–4pm, except Thurs when they stay open until 5pm. Main high-street banks are the Allied Irish and Bank of Ireland; branches throughout the city centre.

Car rental Budget, 29 Lower Abbey St (☎878 7814 or 874 7816); Dan Dooley Kenning, 42/43 Westland Row (☎677 2723); Thrifty Rent-a-Car, 14 Duke St (☎679 9420); plus all the usual desks at the airport.

Counselling Samaritans, 112 Marlborough St (☎872 7700); Well Woman's Centre, 73 Lower Leeson St (☎661 0083); Rape Crisis Centre, 70 Lower Leeson St (☎661 4564 or 4911).

Departures Buses to the airport set off from Eden Quay (not all of them go into the airport compound, so check with the driver). For the ferries, take the DART service to Dún Laoghaire; or a bus (#53 or #53A) to Dublin Port from Eden Quay. Buses to all parts of the country (Bus Éireann) leave from Busáras or the streets immediately around (Eden Quay/Abbey St/Talbot St); enquiries all handled at the information office located at 59 Upper O'Connell St, opposite the main tourist information office (Mon–Fri 9am–5pm, Sat 9am–1pm; ☎836 6111). Officially approved private buses are generally cheaper: ask to see the bus information file at the tourist office. Unofficial buses may be cheaper still; they leave from various points around the city, especially on Fri & Sun evenings. Check the *Evening Herald* for advertisements – weekend buses generally need advance booking. Trains to the limited parts of Ireland served by the national train system leave from Heuston Station (still sometimes known by its old name of Kingsbridge) on the South Side (Cork, Waterford, Limerick, Killarney, Tralee, Athlone, Galway, Westport, Ballina, Claremorris) or Connolly Station (aka Amiens St Station) on the North Side (Belfast, Derry, Portadown, Dundalk, Sligo, Arklow, Wexford, Rosslare Harbour). Mainline commuter trains serving coastal towns north and south of Dublin call at Connolly, Tara St and Pearse St stations. For train information call ☎836 6222.

Embassies Australia, Fitzwilton House, Wilton Terrace (☎676 1517); Britain, 31–33 Merrion Rd (☎269 5211); Canada, 65 St Stephen's Green (☎478 1988); Denmark, 121 St Stephen's Green (☎475 6404); France, 36 Ailesbury Rd (☎269 4777); Netherlands, 160 Merrion Rd (☎269 3444); Norway, 34 Molesworth St (☎662 1800); Sweden, Sun Alliance House, Dawson St (☎671 5822); United States, 42 Elgin Rd, Ballsbridge (☎668 8777).

Exchange Thomas Cook, 118 Grafton St, give a fair rate; although the best exchange rates are given by banks (see above).

Ferry companies Irish Ferries, 16 Westmoreland St (☎661 0511); Stena Line, 15 Westmoreland St (☎204 7777).

Gaelic football All the major games of the season are played at Croke Park (☎831 2099). The championship season runs from mid-February, culminating in the All Ireland finals on the third Sun in September. Prices reflect the status of the match, with stand tickets starting from £16 for semi-finals and £19 to £30 for finals (terraces £7 to £10). For more on gaelic football see "Sports and Activities" in Basics.

Gay Switchboard (☎872 1055). Also see "Gay life" p.106.

Horse racing You shouldn't leave Dublin without experiencing Irish horseracing (and betting). Many of the bigger races are run out in Co. Kildare (see p.126), but check for more local events at Leopardstown (☎289 3994); its major jump-race festival is held on the four days after Christmas, while its most important flat races are the Heinz 57 Phoenix Stakes (mid-Aug) and the Guinness Champion Stakes (mid-Sept). Dublin Bus (see p.52 for details) run a special service to Leopardstown on race days. Tickets range from £6 to £8, with an extra £3 to £5 for admission to the enclosure.

Hospitals South Side: Meath Hospital, Heytesbury St (☎453 6555); North Side: Mater Misericordiae Hospital, Eccles St (☎830 1122).

Hurling As with gaelic football (see above for ticket prices) the important games are played at Croke Park; the championship season which begins in early summer finishes with the All Ireland final on the first Saturday in September. For more on hurling see "Sports and Activities" in Basics.

Laundry Exel Launderette, 12 Main St, Donnybrook (☎269 7172); Nova Launderette, 2 Belvedere St, just off Dorset St; Powder Launderette, 42a South Richmond St (☎478 2655); Shirley's, 141

Rathmines Rd (☎962 2228).

Left luggage There are left luggage offices at Busáras (Mon–Sat 8am–8pm, Sun 10am–6pm), Heuston Station (Mon–Sat 7.15am–8.35pm, Sun 8am–3pm & 5–9pm) and Connolly Station (Mon–Sat 7.40am–9.30pm, Sun 9.15am–1pm & 5–9pm).

Legal advice Free Legal Advice Centre, administration office, 49 South William St (☎679 4239).

Pharmacy O'Connell's, 55 Lower O'Connell St (☎873 0427), is open till 10pm daily.

Phones At least half of Dublin's public phones now operate on CallCards, available from newsagents, garages etc. International payphones are available in the GPO.

Police The main metropolitan Garda station is in Harcourt St, just off St Stephen's Green (☎873 2222). In an emergency dial ☎999.

Post office General Post Office, O'Connell St (☎705 7000). Open Mon–Sat 8am–8pm, Sun 10.30am–6.30pm.

Rugby The big games – the Five Nations Championship matches held between January and March – are played at the Lansdowne Road Stadium in Ballsbridge (☎668 9300).

Travel agents USIT, 19–21 Aston Quay, O'Connell Bridge (☎679 8833), are experts in student/youth travel; Thomas Cook, 118 Grafton St (☎677 1721), offers good general services; CIE Tours, 35 Lower Abbey St (☎830 0777), is the biggest internal tour operator, if you want a bus trip around Ireland.

travel details

Trains

Dublin Connolly to: Arklow (4 daily; 1hr 45min); Belfast (6 daily; 2hr 15min); Derry (5 daily; 5hr); Dundalk (9 daily; 1hr–1hr 25min); Portadown (6 daily; 1hr 50min); Rosslare (3 daily; 2hr 50min); Sligo (3 daily; 3hr 15min); Wexford (3 daily; 2hr 30min).

Dublin Heuston to: Athlone (7 daily; 1hr 40min); Ballina (3 daily; 3hr 40min); Claremorris (3 daily; 3hr); Cork (9 daily; 3hr); Galway (4 daily; 3hr); Killarney (4 daily; 3hr 30min); Limerick (11 daily; 2hr 15min); Tralee (4 daily; 4hr); Waterford (4 daily; 2hr 30min); Westport (3 daily; 3hr 40min).

Buses

Dublin to: Belfast (6 daily; 3hr); Cork (4 daily; 4hr 25min); Derry (4 daily; 4hr 25min); Donegal (4 daily; 4hr 15 min); Galway (9 daily; 3hr 45min); Limerick (6 daily; 3hr 30min); Waterford (6 daily; 2hr 45min); Westport (3 daily; 5hr).

In addition to Bus Éireann, scores of private companies connect Dublin with the rest of the country. Routes are too numerous to detail here – we've listed the most useful in the text of the relevant chapters.

WICKLOW AND KILDARE

K ildare and Wicklow, both easily accessible from Dublin, provide a welcome respite from the capital's urban bustle. As central counties of the Pale region, each is heavily resonant with the presence of the Anglo-Irish, yet scenically they are in complete contrast. **County Wicklow** has some of the wildest, most spectacular mountain scenery in Ireland, as well as some impressive monuments: the early

Celtic monastery of Glendalough and the Neoclassical splendours of the great houses of Russborough and the ruined Powerscourt.

County Kildare's charms are more understated: a gently undulating landscape of farming land punctuated only by the great horse-racing plain of the **Curragh**, where the National Stud and Japanese Gardens are well worth making time to see. Here, too, there are signs of the shifting patterns of settlement and land ownership – Celtic high crosses and pedimented buildings – written into the landscape for you to read as you travel.

Their proximity to Dublin makes **transport** very easy in both counties. The Dublin inner-city railway network, or DART, will take you southwards as far as the dull seaside resort of Bray on the Wicklow coast; the main line continues to the rather more enticing towns of Wicklow and Arklow. The major tourist locations inland in County Wicklow are well served by buses. Wicklow, Arklow and Bray also provide good bases for exploration of the interior of the county in terms of both public transport and bike rental. In County Kildare the major N7 road and the railway line to Limerick offer ready access to most sites. The scenic beauties of Wicklow attract a lot of visitors, principally Dubliners, and the positive spin-off is that **accommodation** is no problem – there are plenty of youth hostels and cheap B&Bs, with many developing along the long-distance walking route, the Wicklow Way, as well as an increasing number of grander country houses and some excellent restaurants. Kildare is less visited, although here too a few pioneers are beginning to offer good food and accommodation in beautiful surroundings; but generally you'll find yourself relying on the standard B&B trade.

COUNTY WICKLOW

Get on a bus in central Dublin, and in half an hour or so you can be deep into **County Wicklow**, high in the mountains among gorse, heather, bracken and bent grass, breathing in clear air with no one in sight. It's great **walking** and **cycling** country – particularly challenging for mountain bikers; the **Wicklow Way** is an obvious focus for hiking and there are plenty of golden sandy **beaches**, too (and some rather stuffy **resort towns** closer to Dublin, best avoided). On a short trip to Ireland, you could do a lot worse than simply combine Dublin with a few days in the wilds of Wicklow; it's also a place to get to grips with two of the dominant themes of Irish history, sometimes strangely superimposed: the **monastic tradition** in the shape of one of its most important and charismatic sites, Glendalough; and that of the **Anglo-Irish**, at the great seats of Russborough and Powerscourt.

Wherever you go, apart from a few obvious centres like Wicklow town and Arklow, you're struck by the sparseness of population. It's the same story as everywhere else in Ireland, and Wicklow is far from being the worst sufferer: first the Great Famine of 1845–49, and then the gradual drift of the rural population to the towns. In 1841 the population of Wicklow was 126,431; the Famine reduced it to 100,000, then steady seepage

---

of the population brought it to a low of 58,473 by 1961. Since then it has recovered to around 100,000, partly through the development of commuter towns, as first the railway, then the suburban DART service have penetrated further into the county.

Heading out from Dublin you could follow the **coast**, but a far more attractive option is to head for the hills stopping off at **Powerscourt House** and **Enniskerry** en route. If you have transport, you could continue on into the valley and join the **Wicklow Way** at the An Óige hostel at **Knockree**, or continue a couple of miles further into the valley for a stopover at similarly isolated **Glencree** hostel.

If you're relying on public transport, **Glendalough** and **Laragh** are both accessible from Dublin by St Kevin's bus service (see p.115), and make excellent bases from which to explore the mountains. If you only have a day to explore the area, it's worth considering a **tour** – the Wild Wicklow Tour leaves Dublin four days a week (☎01/280 1899; £22).

The Wicklow Mountains

The **Wicklow Mountains**, so clearly viewed from Dublin, are really round-topped hills, ground down by the Ice Ages, with the occasional freakish shape like the Great Sugarloaf Mountain, where a granite layer has arrested the weathering. Despite their relatively modest height – Lugnaquillia, the highest peak, only just tops 3000ft – they're wild and uninhabited, with little traffic even at the main passes. Given this, and their proximity to Dublin, it's hardly surprising that the Wicklow Mountains were traditionally bandit territory, and that the last insurgents of the land agitation that spread all over Ireland following the French invasion of County Mayo in 1798 hid out here; the mountains were virtually inaccessible until after the ensuing uprisings, when the army built a road to enable them to patrol effectively. This you can still follow, from Rathfarnham in the Dublin suburbs to Aghavannagh, high in the mountains; the Wicklow Way partly follows the road, too.

Enniskerry and Powerscourt House

ENNISKERRY, the estate village of **Powerscourt House**, is picture-book pretty, with a sloping triangular "square" and plenty of day-trippers from Dublin always in attendance to admire it. But what's more interesting is that the town's reason for existing is its relationship with the great house, just a mile or so to the west. It was here, in the heart of the Pale, that the Anglo-Irish were at their most confident and relaxed. This is a bold statement of a theme repeated all over Ireland: big houses with adjoining tied villages. But in Powerscourt's case, the 14,000-acre estate stands as a sort of metaphor for the passing of the power of the Ascendancy. For Powerscourt is an estate without a heart, the shell of a house, designed in 1740 by the German architect Richard Cassels (later anglicized to Castle) and burnt out in 1974 on the eve of a big party that was to have celebrated the completion of an extensive programme of renovation. From afar, the Palladian mansion still looks impressive set in its rolling parklands. Inside, however, only shadows of its former glory remain. There's fresh hope that it will be fully restored once more, and you can at least get some sense of its past grandeur from the smoky brick-work remains of the double-storey ballroom, based on Palladio's version of the "Egyptian Hall" designed by Vitruvius, architect to the Emperor Augustus. Fortunately, photographs of the room before the fire, with its classical columns and lavish gilt decoration, survive and are on display in the attendant **exhibition** (daily 9.30am–5.30pm, winter times may vary; £1.50). The exhibition also includes some interesting material on Powerscourt's strategic importance from the twelfth century onwards and its role in the constant struggle between the Anglo-Irish and the local Irish clans.

The famous **gardens** (same hours as exhibition; £3.50) attached to the house date from the mid-Victorian period, but echo the earlier classical gardens of Europe. The designer of the upper terraces was one Daniel Robertson, an all-too-human individual with a relaxed approach to his job. Robertson had himself trundled about in a wheel-barrow, clutching a bottle of sherry; when this was exhausted his creative powers waned and he finished work for the day. However unorthodox his working methods, the end result was fine: formal gardens with stepped terracing leading the eye down to a lake, with the weird whipped-cream peak of the **Sugarloaf mountain** as a backdrop. This set piece aside, there's plenty of diversity: neat walled gardens, a pet cemetery, and a very fragrant Edwardian **Japanese garden**. The terrace **café bar** and **restaurant**, overlooking all of this, makes an ideal spot from which to enjoy both house and gardens.

The **Powerscourt waterfall**, a spectacular plunge of 400 feet over rocks, lies three miles from the house: turn right out of the main gate and follow the signs along the road (daily summer 9.30am–7pm; winter 10.30am–dusk; £2).

Practicalities

There are a couple of places to stay on the square in Enniskerry village: the *Powerscourt Arms Hotel* provides comfortable **accommodation** (☎01/282 8903; ④), while *Ferndale B&B* (☎01/286 3518; ④) offers antique-furnished rooms and a great breakfast menu.

A good spot for homemade lunches, pies and puddings is *Poppies Country Kitchen* **café-restaurant** (till 7pm in summer), while the more upmarket *Stepping Stones Restaurant* (☎01/286 5259) serves lunch and evening meals in a cheerful, informal atmosphere. Eighteenth-century *Johnnie Fox's Pub*, three miles from Enniskerry at **Glencullen**, is a time-honoured watering hole and worth negotiating the back roads to find. Daniel O'Connell was a regular here when he lived in the village and fliers of considerable historical interest decorate the walls. From chowders at £2.50 to Russian beluga caviar at £95, the seafood bar menu caters for all purses.

To get to Enniskerry and Powerscourt from Dublin, take the #44 bus from Hawkins Street or the DART **train** to Bray and then the #185 bus.

Glencree

Lying about five miles west of Powerscourt House, the tiny village of **GLENCREE**, with its eponymous valley stretching away southeast to the Wicklow Way, is a quiet place with wonderful views of the Sugarloaf mountains. The An Óige **youth hostel** in Glencree, *Stone House* (☎01/286 4037), is a cosy stone house dating from the construction of the military road in 1798; the barrack buildings opposite now house the Glencree Reconciliation Centre, which attempts to promote dialogue between young people of the north and south. Note that basic provisions only are available in the village and there is no pub. As an alternative, *Lackan House* An Óige **hostel** (☎01/286 4036), halfway up the valley at **Knockree**, three miles west of Enniskerry, is less inviting, but in a much better position for joining the **Wicklow Way**, which passes through its grounds. Glencree was once famous for its **oak woods**, but the small one behind the hostel was actually planted in 1988, in sad commemoration of the fact that broadleaved woodlands now cover barely one percent of the country. Further down the valley a dense conifer plantation has been designated a place for walks, with the misleading name of Old Boley Wood.

Above Glencree the military road ascends through dark, sinister terrain towards one of the two main mountain passes, the **Sally Gap**. Close to the source of the Liffey, it has been heavily invaded by Dubliners seeking peat – a further depredation inflicted upon the landscape. The most spectacular route on from here is to continue along the military road down to Glendalough, which runs over rough country until it joins the

---

THE WICKLOW WAY

Knockree is one of the better places to pick up the **Wicklow Way**, Ireland's first officially designated long-distance walk. Following a series of sheep tracks, forest firebreaks and bog roads, above 1600ft for most of the way, the walk leads from Marlay Park in the Dublin suburbs up into the Dublin mountains, skirts the end of Glencree, cuts across the bleak, boggy hillside below Djouce Mountain, and pushes on to Glendalough and Aghavannagh; it finally ends up 82 miles later at Clonegal on the Wexford border. It's not particularly well organized – one of its chief attractions for many hikers – but the whole route can be walked comfortably in ten to twelve days.

If you want to do this, Marlay Park is accessible via the #47B bus from Hawkins Street, Dublin city centre. If you're short of time, the best part to walk is probably the three-day section between Enniskerry and Glendalough; the path reaches its highest point at White Hill (2073ft), from which you can get a view of the mountains of North Wales on a fine day. Take the #44 bus from Hawkins Street, Dublin to Enniskerry, and pick up St Kevin's Bus Service at Glendalough for the return journey.

Low as they are, the Wicklow Mountains are notoriously treacherous, and even if you're planning on spending no more than a day **walking**, you should make sure you have the Ordnance Survey's map no. 56 (Wicklow/Dublin/Kildare; 1:50,000); the tourist board's information sheet on the Wicklow Way (no. 30) is useful, and if you can pick up a copy of An Óige's excellent *A Walking Guide for Hostellers* (no. 4), so much the better. Advice on routes and conditions is also available from the Wicklow Mountains National Park **information point** in Glendalough (see p.116). Bad weather can close in rapidly, making the going dangerous and frightening if you're far from a road or house. All the customary warnings about mountain walking apply and if you don't have any great experience of map reading, you'd do best to follow the yellow way-marking arrows. Trail walking is fairly new in Ireland; consequently, the paths are far less crowded than their counterparts in, say, Britain.

There are four An Óige **hostels** along the way – Knockree (see p.113), Glendalough (see p.116), Glenmalure (see p.117) and Aghavannagh (see p.117) plus plenty of other places to stay around Glendalough, so accommodation shouldn't be a problem, although it may be wise to book ahead in high season. For these hostels and the one at Ballinclea (see p.117) – not actually on the Wicklow Way but in the locale – you book through the main An Óige office in Dublin (☎01/830 4555, fax 01/830 5808). By a stroke of imagination, two of the hostels – Glencree and Aghavannagh – are housed in the great stone barracks complexes built to serve the military road built after 1798, and you can feel the resonances of those grim times.

Glenmacnass River – at this point there's an extraordinary, extended waterfall. The other road (R759) takes you past Lough Tay as it winds its way down to Sraghmore.

Dramatic, inaccessible **Lough Tay** – whose scree sides plunge straight into the water – is owned by Garech a'Brún, a member of the Guinness family who is also the man behind Claddagh Records in Dublin (see p.107). Access to **Lough Dan**, south of here, with its gentler woodlands, is also barred and visitors are made to feel unwelcome by numerous signs warning against trespassing on private land. However, there's still plenty of good, boggy walking and some spectacular views.

Roundwood

Coming down to Glendalough, you pass through **ROUNDWOOD** (one of the stops on St Kevin's Bus Service, (see opposite), a pleasant enough village, though not in the heart of the mountains. You can get **B&B** accommodation here at *Tochar House* (☎01/281 8247; ③), a good, central option, which also has pleasant dorm bunks (£12). Slightly further out are *Woodside*, (☎01/281 8195; ③), a mile and a half along the Dublin road, and *Ballinacor House* (☎01/281 8168; ②), a mile along the road towards Glendalough. The village also has a **campsite** (☎01/281 8163; Easter–Sept). Your **eating** choices in Roundwood are a fast-food place tucked away on the main street, bar food at *The Coach House* in Main Street or, at the other end of the scale, the excellent restaurant at *The Roundwood Inn* (☎01/281 8107), popular with Dubliners at weekend lunchtimes. However, for a wider range of accommodation and for readier access to lonelier and more impressive scenery, your best bet is probably to head on down to Laragh.

Glendalough

GLENDALOUGH – the valley of the two lakes – is one of the standard and very popular bus tours out of Dublin. Nonetheless, besides being one of the most important, and well preserved, monastic sites in Ireland, it has an amazing, quite tangible quality of peace and spirituality. Access to the site is free, and there are numerous pleasant walks from here into the mountains. **Transport** to Glendalough from Dublin is easy – use the St Kevin's Bus Service (£6 one-way, £10 return; ☎01/281 8119; which leaves from the Royal College of Surgeons on St Stephen's Green Mon–Sat at 11.30am and 6pm, Sun 11.30am and 7pm; departs *Glendalough Royal Hotel* Mon–Fri 7.15am, Sat and Sun 9.45am with an additional 9.45am departure daily during July and August, and from the Glendalough Visitor Centre car park Mon–Sat 4.15pm and Sun 5.30pm). The bus passes through Bray, where you can pick up the train if you're heading south.

Glendalough is amply equipped to receive its many sightseers, with acres of car parking and a huge, modern **visitor centre** (daily: mid-March to end May & Sept to mid-Oct 9.30am–6pm; June–Aug 9am–6.30pm; mid-Oct to mid-March 9.30am–5pm; £2; Heritage Card). This is genuinely helpful, with an excellent exhibition and a video show that sets Glendalough in the context of the monastic ruins elsewhere in Ireland – worth seeing, particularly if you're not visiting any others. The admission charge to the centre includes the video show, exhibition and a guided tour.

The monastery

The **monastery** at Glendalough was founded by St Kevin, a member of the royal house of Leinster, during the sixth century. As a centre of the Celtic Church, it became famous throughout Europe for its learning, and despite being sacked by the Vikings in the ninth and tenth centuries and by the English in the fourteenth century, it was patiently restored each time, and monastic life continued tenaciously until the sixteenth century.

The **cathedral**, dating from the tenth and twelfth centuries (it was built in two phases), has an impressively ornamental east window, while **St Kevin's Cross** is a massive slab of granite, carved in the eighth century, in the Celtic form of a cross superimposed on a wheel. It may have been left unfinished, since the "halo" formed by the wheel has not been pierced. In the **round tower**, the doorway is ten feet above the ground. The traditional explanation, and the one that the guide will undoubtedly give you, is that this design was adopted so that monks could pull up the ladder in times of trouble, turning the tower into an inaccessible treasury and refuge; however, more recent thinking suggests that the reason may be structural. The twelfth-century **Priest's House**, partially reconstructed 700 years later, got its name from being used as a burial place for local priests during the suppression of Catholicism. The carving above the door, so worn as to be indecipherable, possibly shows St Kevin between two ecclesiastical figures.

Glendalough's most famous building is **St Kevin's Church**, a solid, barrel-vaulted stone oratory, also known as St Kevin's Kitchen. Although it may well date from St Kevin's time, the round-tower belfry is an eleventh-century addition, and the structure has clearly been altered many times.

The lakes and surrounding attractions

All these buildings are clustered between the visitor centre and the **Lower Lake**, and you'll be shown all of them unless it's raining hard, in which case the tour gets truncated. But the real delights of Glendalough lie beyond what you get to see on the tour. As you climb above the monastery complex, landscape and architecture combine in a particularly magical way, and you could spend days walking the footpaths that crisscross the upper valley, drinking it all in. The scenery is at its most spectacular at the **Upper Lake**, where wooded cliffs and a waterfall plunge vertically into the water. Also here is the Wicklow Mountains National Park **information point** (June to Aug daily 10am–6.30pm), where you can get details of some of the many **local walks**.

There are plenty more antiquities connected with the monastic life among the cliffs around the upper lake, many of them formerly pilgrim shrines. The site of St Kevin's original church, the **Temple-na-Skellig**, is on a platform approached by a flight of stone steps, accessible only by boat. **St Kevin's Bed** is a rocky ledge high up the cliff, where it's said the holy man used to sleep in an attempt to escape from the unwelcome advances of a young girl. Eventually she found his hiding place and, waking up one morning to find her beside him, he reacted with the misogyny characteristic of the early Church fathers – and pushed her into the lake.

Practicalities

Accommodation in **Glendalough** is plentiful. For a grandstand view of the entire area, stay at *Brockagh Heights* guesthouse (☎0404/45243; ②). There's also the *Glendalough Hotel* (☎0404/45135; ⑥), or for budget travellers, the newly refurbished An Óige **hostel**, *The Lodge*, right by the Lower Lake (☎0404/45342), with plenty of facilities and small dorms.

Offering more amenities, **LARAGH**, just over a mile east of Glendalough, also makes a good place to stay. Modest **B&B** accommodation is available at *Village View*, No. 3 Laragh (☎0404/45458; ②), and Peter and Maura McGrath's, No. 4 Laragh (☎0404/45444; ②). A step up in price are the bright and pleasant *Ailbhe* (☎0404/45236; ③), *Oakview* (☎0404/45453; ③) and *Dunroamin House* (☎0404/45487; ③). About half a mile out of Laragh on the R755 towards Rathdrum is *Derrybawn House* (☎0404/45134; ⑤; dinner £17.50), an elegant late eighteenth-century house tucked into the hillside in extensive, wooded grounds. There's a choice of two hostels – the *Wicklow Way Hostel* (☎0404/45398) and the *Old Mill Hostel* (☎0404/45156), about a mile out along the Rathdrum road, housed in a converted mill beside the river – work was ongoing when we visited, so phone ahead.

You can get decent bar food at *The Laragh Inn,* a lively bar with roaring fires, and traditional fare at *The Wicklow Heather* **restaurant** (open till 9.30pm), but for a real gastronomic treat, head for *Mitchell's Schoolhouse* (☎0404/45302; ③; dinner £18.50), a picturesque stone building, also offering B&B, located just north of the crossroads.

Finally, if you need guidance on how to exploit the **sporting opportunities** of the area, you could check out the rock-climbing, mountaineering, canoeing and kayaking courses offered by the Tiglin Adventure Centre (☎0404/40169), about eight miles east of Glendalough near Ashford. There's also an An Óige **hostel** here (see p.119).

Glenmalure and the Glen of Imaal

Northwest of Glendalough, the main road takes you over the **Wicklow Gap**, whence there's a tolerably tough climb up to the top of **Tonelagee** (2677ft). South and west, the country rises, becoming wilder and more desolate, dominated by **Lugnaquillia**, the highest mountain in the Wicklow range. The military road continues southwest and skirts the An Óige **hostel** at **Aghavannagh** (temporarily closed; call ☎01/830 4555 for developments), a massively grand and remote barracks building on a hill with views all round; experienced walkers and map-readers have the option of trekking to the head of Glendalough and down into the next glen.

Either way, you'll arrive in dark and lonely **GLENMALURE**, half of which is off limits as an army firing range. Perhaps appropriately, Glenmalure was the scene of a decisive victory by the Wicklow Irish under Fiach MacHugh O'Byrne over the English under Elizabeth I. One of the 1798 barracks, now ruined, stands at the point where the military road hits the glen. It's a symbol of decay that somehow sets the tone for the entire valley, with its enclosed, mysterious feel and steep scree sides which scarcely afford a foothold to the heather. The road eventually peters out in a car park, but a track continues up to the very basic An Óige Glenmalure **youth hostel** (book through the Dublin office ☎01/830 4555), which stands at the head of the valley just above the point where the river rushes over a weir. With no other buildings in sight, it's a beautiful and unspoilt setting. Past the hostel, the trail forks right for Glendalough and left, over the Table Mountain, for the Glen of Imaal.

By comparison with Glenmalure, the **Glen of Imaal** is almost inviting. Again, it's dominated by the impressive summit of Lugnaquillia and, likewise, half of it is reserved as an army shooting range. Altogether, it's as wild and desolate as you could wish for, though more open and lighter than Glenmalure. There's an An Óige **youth hostel** at **BALLINCLEA** (☎045/404657; March–Nov), just over two miles southeast of Donard. Alternatively, eight miles southwest of Donard, on the edge of the Wicklow Mountains, *Rathcoran House* **hostel** at **Baltinglass** (IHH; ☎0508/81073) is a decent budget alternative, though ring ahead as they do cater for groups.

At **DERRYNAMUCK**, on the southeast side of the valley, stands a cottage where Michael O'Dwyer, one of the last insurgents of 1798, took refuge when trapped by the British, and escaped because Samuel McAllister drew the enemy's fire and died in his place; it's now run as a **folk museum**, the Dwyer McAllister Cottage (mid-June to mid–Sept daily 2–6pm; £1).

Avondale and The Vale of Avoca

South of Laragh, the **Vale of Clara** leads to **Rathdrum**, a quiet village on the Dublin–Rosslare railway route and the Dublin–Arklow bus route. There is little to detain the visitor here and it's much more worthwhile to press on about a mile and a half south to **AVONDALE** where you can visit Avondale House, home of Parnell (daily June–Sept 10am–6pm, Oct–May 11am–5pm; grounds open daily; house £3). One of Ireland's most influential and important politicians, **Charles Stewart Parnell**, born in Avondale in 1846, was hailed as the "the uncrowned king of Ireland" until his career – and his campaign for home rule – was brought to an end by the scandal of his love for a married woman. A successful businessman – Parnell ran his own local lead mine – he was elected to parliament in 1875. Later, under his leadership, the **Irish Home Rule Party** brought the government down, and Parnell persuaded Gladstone's Liberals to support the idea of home rule for Ireland. Although the first Home Rule Bill was defeated in 1886, prospects seemed bright for its eventual success – but scandal intervened. In 1881 Parnell had met, and fallen in love with, the estranged wife of one Captain O'Shea. Parnell and Kitty O'Shea set up house together and had three children. In 1889 the hitherto complaisant Captain O'Shea sued for divorce. Longing to marry Kitty, Parnell refused to defend himself and the British press destroyed his good name. It was, effectively, the end of Parnell's political career. He died, two years later, in the arms of Kitty O'Shea, to whom he had been married for four months.

The **house**, designed in 1779 by the celebrated English architect John Wyatt, is a modest, box-like building. Inside, there's a delicate, Wedgwood-like blue dining room with plasterwork by the famous Lanfranchini brothers, a striking vermilion library (Parnell's favourite room), and, in the entrance hall, an elegant minstrels' gallery from where Parnell, a nervous orator, used to practise his political speeches.

The Avondale estate has been in the possession of the Irish Forestry Board since 1904, and the grounds are used for silvicultural experiments. As a result, they're filled with rare tree species. There's a coffee shop, and plenty of picnic tables.

The scenic **Vale of Avoca**, two miles south of here, draws scores of bus parties, but don't be put off; its beauty – once you leave the fertilizer plant behind – is genuinely rewarding, with thickly wooded slopes on either side of the river, culminating in the **Meeting of the Waters**, the confluence of the Avonmore and Avonbeg rivers.

The Meeting has attracted its fair share of coffee shops, and there's a pleasant pub, but for a wider choice of daytime **food**, among other things, you're better advised to stop a mile or so downstream at the pleasantly unassuming village of **AVOCA** with its hand-weaving mill. The weavers are housed in a group of whitewashed buildings with steep grey roofs, where the fly-shuttle looms that caused mass unemployment when they were introduced in 1723 are presented as picturesquely traditional. Avoca has abandoned its old range of cloaks, kilts and deerstalker hats in bright, heathery pinks and purples for a more appealing range of woollens and knitwear; there's also a good, cheap lunch room selling sandwiches, soup and cakes. For pleasant **accommodation** try *Riverview House* (☎0402/35181; ②), perched above the opposite bank of the rushing river.

The Wicklow coast

The county's scenic highlights are all inland, and the coast is characterized by a handful of unassuming towns. **Arklow**, with its sandy beach, is probably the best of these, and there are bracing walks at **Wicklow** town, but all in all, the area is not likely to detain you for long when so much mountain beauty lies close at hand.

If you are travelling south from Dublin and along the **Wicklow coast**, the N11 will get you to **Bray**, the first major town; from then on the coastal road offers more picturesque sights down to **Rathnew**, where you join the main road again. By train, the **DART service** from the capital runs as far as Bray – very much a dormitory suburb; to get to Wicklow town or Arklow, catch the Wexford train. Alternatively you could take the Wexford bus, which also runs to Wicklow town but then takes you on a scenic detour inland via the heavily wooded Vale of Avoca to Arklow; from Wicklow the journey to Dublin takes just under an hour.

Bray

BRAY, originally a Victorian resort developed when the railway was extended south of Dún Laoghaire in the 1850s, provides a grotty welcome for the hordes of visitors from Dublin at the weekends. With a seafront full of dingy hotels, video arcades, B&Bs and fast-food shops, Bray – once genteel – has lost most of its charm. Its chief claim to fame is that James Joyce lived here from 1889 to 1891, and its main visitor attraction is the **Bray heritage centre** (Mon–Fri 9am–1pm & 2–5pm, Sat 10am–1pm & 2–4pm; ☎01/286 6796; £1), which includes an exhibition on the town's history, a folklore room and a presentation on the engineer William Dargan (1799–1867). This is also where you'll find the **tourist office**. The other attraction of note is the National Aquarium (April–Sept daily 10am–6pm; Oct–March Tues–Fri 10am–1pm & 2–5pm, Sat & Sun 10am–5pm; £3). However, one of the best things to do here is to walk round **Bray**

Head, a knob of rock pushing into the sea, where a massive cross erected to mark the holy year of 1950 serves as a reminder that you are now in Catholic Europe. There are a few secluded coves in the shadow of the Head where you can **swim**.

Outside Bray, **Killruddery House** and its **garden** are worth seeing (gardens open April–Sept daily 1–5pm; house May, June & Sept daily 1–5pm; £4, gardens only £2), reached by bus #84 leaving from Main Street. Laid out in the seventeenth century, Killruddery's gardens are among the earliest that survive in Ireland. Home of the Brabazon family since 1618, the house was remodelled by Richard and William Morrison in the 1820s.

Bicycle rental in Bray is available from Bray Sports Centre, 8 Main St, and **horse riding** can be arranged with Brennanstown Riding School (☎01/286 3778).

Wicklow

There's nothing much to **WICKLOW**, but it is the first place that wholly escapes the influence of Dublin as you go down the coast, and should you find yourself with time on your hands, it's a pleasant, ramshackle town with plenty of entertainment, one or two good, cheap places to eat, a couple of smarter places on the fringes of the town, and walking and swimming, too. It has none of the presence you might expect of a county town and comes across as a happily disorganized kind of place, full of people chatting on pavements, cars parked on double yellow lines and solidly built little houses in bright marine pastels. Well worth a visit is **Wicklow jail**, originally built in 1702 to hold prisoners under the repressive penal laws, now converted into a museum (March–Oct daily 10am–6pm; £3.50) and offering a very lively re-creation of the life of the prison, looking at the part it played in the lives of those involved in the 1798 Rebellion, and those transported from here to the Penal Colonies, of particular interest to Australians with Irish roots.

Just outside town on the seaward side, a knoll encrusted with some knobbly piles of stone constitutes all that's left of **Black Castle**, one of the fortifications built by the Fitzgeralds in return for lands granted them by Strongbow after the Anglo-Norman invasion of 1169 – and all but demolished by the O'Byrnes and O'Tooles in 1301. **Wicklow Head**, unlike Bray, really is spectacular, and you can walk all the way round (there are two tiny swimming beaches, sunny in the mornings) accompanied by exhilarating views of the open sea and, northwards, the weird silhouettes of the Great and Little Sugarloaf mountains. There's also sociable – if unglamorous – swimming with the harbour breakwater closer to the centre of town in summer. Wicklow – along with Arklow and Bray – provides a convenient point of entry to the hinterland; a minibus service operates from Wicklow to Glendalough, June to August, departing from Bridge Street at 10.30am (return 4.15pm) and 3.30pm daily, though times may vary, so contact the tourist office to check.

Practicalities

The **tourist office** is in the central square (late June to mid-Sept Mon–Sat 9am–6pm; mid-Sept to late June Mon–Fri 9am–1pm & 2–5pm; ☎0404/69117). If you want to **stay**, B&Bs are in good supply – try, for example, *Thomond House* in St Patrick's Road Upper (☎0404/67940; ②) or *Silver Ash*, Ashtown Lane (☎0404/69746; ②). For a bit more comfort in the centre of town, try the slightly tatty but friendly *Bayview Hotel* in the Mall (☎0404/67383; ④). There's also a hostel – *Marine House* (☎0404/69213), an imposing building overlooking the sea; otherwise, the nearest hostel accommodation is the An Óige one at **Tiglin**, six miles away near Ashford (☎0404/40259); to book, contact the main office in Dublin (see p.62). You can **camp** on the beach at Silver Strand, about two miles south of town (☎0404/67615).

One of the best places to eat, and the most expensive, is *The Bakery Café and Restaurant*, Church Street (☎0404/66770; evenings and Sunday lunches only), offering a varied menu of Mediterranean and modern Irish cuisine. Other places include *Hannah's Deli*, Main Street, which does homemade snacks and lunches, *Pizza del Forno*, on Main Street, an inexpensive pizza/steak restaurant (until 11.30pm in summer), and the *Opera House*, Market Square. There are a handful of **pubs**: *Philip Healy's* is a genial bar on the Square, while the *Leinster Lodge* has music nights, as does the bar of the *Bayview*.

Just outside town are a trio of **hotel/restaurants** to hide away in if you're feeling self-indulgent. *The Old Rectory* (☎0404/67048; ⑦; March–Dec), a delicate pink mansion up a lane off the Dublin Road, only five minutes' walk from the town centre, and the more luxurious *Tinakilly House* (☎0404/69274; ⑨), a Victorian pile further up the road just outside Rathnew, both offer tranquil settings and the best of new Irish cuisine. *Hunter's Hotel* at Rathnew (☎0404/40106; ⑦) is a good, old-fashioned hostelry where the nineteenth-century politician Charles Stewart Parnell used to stay. It's worth visiting just for a drink in the bar and a stroll in the gardens which slope down to the River Vartry.

Brittas Bay and Mount Usher Gardens

Heading south towards Arklow on the R750, you'll come to a string of white-sand **beaches**. The one at **Brittas Bay**, just north of Mizen Head (beloved of the fishing forecasts), is particularly good – don't be put off by the caravan site, there's plenty of seclusion to be found.

Horticultural enthusiasts should also know about **Mount Usher Gardens** (mid-March to Oct daily 10.30am–6pm; £3), a few miles inland near Ashford, where rare trees, shrubs and flowers grow in profusion in a narrow strip next to the road. For others, the gardens' main attraction may be the miniature suspension bridges where you can see engineering principles at work as they sway and bounce under your weight.

Arklow

Built on a site sloping gently towards the sea at the mouth of the Avoca river, **ARKLOW** has a long and prosperous history, based on fishing, shipbuilding and the export of copper ore, pyrites and even gold, mined further up the valley. Evidence of continued riches in relatively recent times can be seen in the elegant Art Deco cinema at the top of the main street.

Arklow is no longer a major port, but shipbuilding continues to be a dominant factor – *Gypsy Moth IV*, Sir Francis Chichester's prize-winning transatlantic yacht, moored permanently at London's Greenwich, was built at John Tyrrell's yard here. For a grip on the past, stop off at the **Maritime Museum** (summer Mon–Sat 10am–1pm & 2–5pm; £1): turn left at the top of the main street. A delightfully haphazard collection of local finds, it claims a history for Arklow going back to Ptolemy's celebrated second-century map. It also emerges that Arklow was a major centre for arms-smuggling during the upheavals of 1798. The museum houses such curiosities as a whale's tooth and eardrum and a model ship made with 10,700 matchsticks. Arklow's **beach**, white sand like the rest of this part of the coast, is sandwiched between the docks and a gravel extraction plant – you may prefer to head north to Brittas Bay, or, if you have transport, five miles south to the sheltered sandy **Clogga Beach**.

Practicalities

The **tourist office** (June–Aug Mon–Sat 9am–6pm; Sept–May Mon–Fri 9.30am–1pm & 2–5pm; ☎0404/32484) is located in the Coach House on Upper Main Street. **Accommodation** should be easy enough to find, with plenty of B&Bs – recommended are *Vale View*, Coolgreany Road (☎0402/32622; ③), and *Tara*, Gorey Road (☎0402/39333; ③). *Avonmore House* **hostel**, Ferrybank (☎0402/32825), a handy short walk from the town centre, offers decent budget accommodation and a field for **camping**. Places to **eat** are thin on the ground, but you'll find a good range of inexpensive grills and roasts at *Riverwalk Restaurant*, River Walk, off Main Street (☎0402/31657), and reasonably priced meals at *Christy's*. *Kitty's*, Main Street, serves good bar lunches, and their expensive *Loft* restaurant exudes a wonderful air of opulence (☎0402/71755). If you're picnicking, stock up with sandwich supplies from the Stone Oven Bakery at 65 Lower Main St, where Egon Friedrich, a German baker, sells sourdough bread, sausage rolls and strudels. There are lots of **pubs** – most of which seem to have some kind of entertainment on offer, including traditional Irish music, discos and the odd pub quiz. *Christy's* and *Kitty's* are both good starting points.

Russborough House

The third of Wicklow's great cultural landmarks is in west Wicklow: **Russborough House** and its impressive **art collection** (April & Oct Sun 10.30am–5.30pm; May & Sept Mon–Sat 10.30am–2.30pm, Sun 10.30am–5.30pm; June–Aug daily 10.30am–5.30pm; 45-min tour £3). Designed, like Powerscourt, by the German architect Richard Castle (with the assistance of Francis Bindon), Russborough is one of the jewels of the Pale. A classic Palladian structure whose central block is linked to two wings with curving arms, its design was subsequently repeated throughout Ireland, as a result of Castle's influence and its own suitability as a kind of glorified farmhouse.

In Russborough's case, it's very glorified indeed. The house was constructed for Joseph Leeson, son of a rich Dublin brewer and MP for Rathcormack in the days of the semi-independent Irish parliament: he was created **Lord Russborough** in 1756. Russborough epitomizes the great flowering of Anglo-Irish confidence before the Act of Union deprived Ireland of its parliament, much of its trade and its high society (thereafter, the rich Anglo-Irish spent much of the year in London). No expense was spared. Not only were the fashionable architects of the day employed, but the plasterers, the Francini brothers, were also of the best. The plaster ovals in the drawing room, for instance, were made to order to fit the four Joseph Vernet marine paintings that still occupy them, and the over-the-top plasterwork on the stairs has been described as representing the ravings of a lunatic.

The **lake** in front of Russborough provides the house with an idiomatically eighteenth-century prospect. The impression is a false one, however – it's actually a thoroughly twentieth-century reservoir, created by damming the Liffey, which provides Dublin with twenty million gallons of water a day.

The art collection

Impressive though Russborough is, the chief reason why it is so firmly on the tourist trail is its collection of **paintings**. The German entrepreneur Alfred Beit (1853–1906) was a co-founder with Cecil Rhodes of the De Beer Diamond Mining Company, and he poured the fortune he derived from that enterprise into amassing works of art. His nephew, Sir Alfred Beit, acquired Russborough in 1952, which explains why such an extraordinary collection of famous pictures is kept in this obscure corner of County Wicklow. Whatever you may feel about their irrelevance to the site or the source of the wealth that made the acquisitions possible, there are some marvellous paintings by Goya, Murillo, Velázquez, Gainsborough, Rubens and Frans Hals, to name but a few.

Russborough has been burgled twice: in 1974, when Bridget Rose Dugdale stole sixteen paintings to raise money for the IRA – although her booty, worth £18 million, was recovered undamaged from a farmhouse in County Cork a week later; and in May 1986 – some of the paintings taken in the second heist have since been retrieved in The Netherlands. Nowadays security is tight, and visitors are herded around the house in groups, with little chance to study the paintings – or anything else – in detail.

Practicalities

Getting to Russborough is no problem – **BLESSINGTON**, the pleasant coaching town it adjoins, is forty minutes from central Dublin on the Waterford **bus**. There's a central **tourist office** (June–Aug Mon–Sat 9.30am–5.30pm, Sun 2–6pm; ☎045/865850), which has information on possibilities for **outdoor pursuits**. A wide range of these – including canoeing, sail-boarding, pony-trekking and hill-walking – is available at the Blessington Adventure Centre (☎045/865092), signposted from the centre of town. Blessington's marvellous **location** – close to the shining waters of the **Blessington lakes** and, beyond them, the spectacular heights of the Wicklow Mountains – should make it a good base for exploration – but unfortunately, accommodation and places to **eat** are rather limited: try the *West Wicklow* for **bar food**. A few miles out of town, there's the An Óige *Baltyboys* **hostel**, on the wooded shores of the lake (☎045/867266; March–Nov & weekends throughout the year; book through the Dublin office; see p.62).

COUNTY KILDARE

County Kildare, in the heart of the Pale, forms part of the hinterland of Dublin. Although it lacks the spectacle of Wicklow to the capital's south, or the extraordinary range of ancient monuments of the lush Boyne Valley to the north, it has a quiet charm of its own. The **landscape** is a calm one of rolling farmland for the most part, with open grasslands and rough pasturage, just touching the drab stretches of the monotonous Bog of Allen in the northwest. This is ancient countryside, marked by a string of **Celtic crosses** at Moone, Old Kilcullen and Castledermot; but you're also constantly made aware that you're in Pale country – with big stone estate walls bordering many of the fields and Georgian proportions in the buildings, noticeable features of the landscape, as well as more obvious attractions such as the magnificent **Castletown House** with its model village at Celbridge; the **Grand Canal**, which traverses the county and has a walkable towpath; and the pin-neat **National Stud** at Kildare town and its extraordinarily extravagant Japanese Garden.

Because of its proximity to Dublin, there's no problem about transport in County Kildare. The main **buses** to Limerick ply up and down the N7 trunk road, with the **rail** line running close beside it for most of the way. **Accommodation** is less easy – you're reliant on B&Bs, many of them the more expensive kind, catering for business travellers rather than individual tourists.

Maynooth, Castletown House and around

Both Maynooth – due west of Dublin on the N4 – and Celbridge (for Castletown House) are firmly on the daytrippers' trail from Dublin, so you're unlikely to be on your own here. There really isn't all that much to detain you in **MAYNOOTH** (pronounced *Ma-nooth*, with the stress on the second syllable), pretty though it is. Its main claim to fame is its seminary, **St Patrick's College**, which in addition to training priests now houses two universities. For fans of Victoriana, the square is by Pugin in Gothic Revival style. The ruins beside the entrance to the college are those of the thirteenth-century **Maynooth Castle**, one of the two main strongholds of the Anglo-Norman Fitzgerald family who ruled Kildare and, effectively, most of Ireland from the thirteenth century until the coming of the Tudor monarchs (their other castle is at Kilkea, in the south of the county; see p.130). Maynooth's formal town planning is made sense of by Carton House, a Georgian gem by Richard Castle which lies at the other end of the main street.

Castletown House

Few places give a better impression of the immense scale on which the Anglo-Irish imagination was able to work than **Castletown House**, designed in 1722 for the Speaker of the Irish House of Commons, William Conolly, by the Italian Alessandro Galilei. You enter the grounds through the village of Celbridge, planned to lend importance to the house itself. This exhibits the strictest Classicism: the front facade, facing out over the Liffey, gives little away except for a rigidly repeated succession of windows. It's the only thing about the house that is restrained, though, for Castletown, from the very beginning, was built for show.

William Conolly, who commissioned it, was a publican's son from Donegal who – like many others – owed his success to the changed conditions after the Battle of the Boyne and made his fortune by dealing in forfeited estates. Member for Donegal in the Irish parliament since 1692, he was a staunch supporter of the Hanoverian cause and was unanimously elected Speaker of the Irish House of Commons in 1715. In 1717 the ambassador at Florence noted Conolly's intention to bring to Ireland "the best architect in Europe", a move of some significance to national self-esteem. A letter to the famous metaphysician, Bishop Berkeley, states: "I am glad for the honour of my country that Mr Conolly has undertaken so magnificent a pile of building. . . Since this house will be the finest Ireland ever saw, and by your description fit for a Prince, I would have it as it were the epitome of the Kingdom, and all the natural rarities she affords should have a place there." Although plans for the house were magnificent, work proceeded in a haphazard way. The cellar vaults, begun before the design of the house was finalized, still bear little relation to what's above ground; and the house interior remained unfinished – lacking, for instance, a main staircase – until the end of the long life of William's wife, who preferred building follies.

The fruits of old Mrs Conolly's imagination are most obvious in the **grounds**, where one folly, 140ft of what appears to be a monument to chimney-sweeping, closes the vista to the north, while the **Wonderful Barn** forms a focus for the view to the east. Both projects were set up to provide relief work for estate workers hard hit by the famine-ridden winter of 1739, and Mrs Conolly's sister, for one, disapproved: "My sister is building an obleix to answer a vistow from the bake of Castletown house," she wrote of the folly. "It will cost her three or four hundred pounds at least, but I believe more. I really wonder how she can dow so much and live as she duse." Incidentally, it seems that the ground on which the obelisk stands did not belong to Castletown, not that this bothered Mrs Conolly. The Wonderful Barn is currently occupied by Focus Point, a charity working with homeless people. You can be given access to the staircase that snakes around the barn's belly and up to its top by ringing ☎01/624 5448.

The **interior** decoration was the inspiration of Lady Louisa Lennox, who married into the Conolly family in 1759 at the age of fifteen. The newlyweds might have lived in London (Louisa's brother-in-law described her as wanting "to buy every house she sees"), but the fact that Louisa's elder sister, Lady Emily Kildare, had settled at Carton, close by at Maynooth, decided matters. (The life of the Lennox sisters is vividly chronicled, through their letters and diaries, in Stella Tillyard's novel *Aristocrats*, published by Vintage in 1995.) Although little of the furniture at Castletown is original to the house, you can see some of the results of Louisa's efforts. It was she who, with her sister Lady Sarah Bunbury, created the print room on the ground floor, commissioned the Lanfranchini brothers to produce the hall's extraordinary plasterwork and ordered the long gallery at the back of the house, which she considered "the most comfortable room you ever saw, and quite warm; supper at one end, the company at the other, and I am writing in one of the piers at a distance from them all". Apparently, she ordered the magnificent Murano glass chandeliers on a journey to Venice, but when they arrived they were found to clash with the room's blue, Pompeiian-style decor: it was too late to redecorate, so both decor and chandeliers are still there.

Castletown House has been taken over by Dúchas and, as we go to press, much of the house is under conservation. It's due to reopen in 1999 (phone ☎01/628 8252 for times and entrance fee) and there may well be some changes in the way the place is presented.

Straffan and the Steam Museum

About three miles southwest of Castletown, housed in a neat Victorian church that's been brought stone by stone from Dublin, the **Straffan Steam Museum** (Easter–Aug Tues–Sun 2–6pm; £3) offers a benign view of the driving force behind the Industrial Revolution. There are miniature models of steam trains and four – amazingly quiet – working steam engines, plus a series of wall panels offering a rather rose-tinted account of how steam advanced the way forward to our modern world. They also reflect Ireland's uneven industrialization – in 1838 the North had more steam horsepower than the rest of Ireland put together. There's a coffee shop, and there are plans to start up a small steam railway in the grounds. A big hit with children is nearby **Straffan Butterfly Farm** (May–Sept daily noon–6pm; £3.25): huge exotic butterflies fly freely, while giant insects, reptiles and tarantulas remain safely behind glass.

The local Big House, **Kildare House**, is now an extremely swish country-house hotel (☎01/662 7333; ⑨) – well worth visiting for an example of unreconstructed high living.

Larchill Arcadian Gardens

Larchill Arcadian Gardens (May–Sept noon–6pm; £3.25) at **KILCOCK**, four miles west of Maynooth along the N4, are an extremely rare example of a **ferme ornée**, and an absolute must for anyone interested in the development of landscape gardening in the eighteenth century. A circular walk links recently discovered classical and gothic follies, ten in all, most notably the island folly "Gibraltar" and the "Foxes' Earth". The latter was built on the instruction of a Mr Watson who, convinced he would be reincarnated as a fox, wanted to be sure of a bolt-hole from the hounds in the next life. It appears today as a rough, grass-covered mound with gothic tunnels for escape, topped by a cluster of rubble-rough columns. Rare breeds of farm animals are kept in the new *ferme ornée* currently being developed, and interesting material on the conservation project is to be found in the pleasant tearoom.

Kildare town and the Curragh

If you are heading from Dublin to **Kildare town** and the **Curragh**, the N4, the main Dublin–Limerick road, is a relatively swift but rather dull drive; additionally, there's a new stretch of motorway, the M7, which runs from before Naas for about ten miles, rejoining the N11 near Kildare town (from Maynooth, take minor roads southwards and join the N7 at Naas). A road sign advertises **NAAS** (pronounced *Nace*) as "a nice place to shop", and there's probably not a great deal more to be said. Nás na Rí (Naas of the Kings), once the centre of the extensive kingdom of the Uí Dunlainge and their successors, the Uí Faelain, now seems little more than a battered parade of shops. Its main attraction is **Punchestown Racecourse**, whose main meeting is the three-day steeplechasing festival in late April, when the racecourse itself is greatly celebrated for its flowering gorse; a close second is **Mondello Park** motor-racing circuit, which holds races most weekends. If you're not content with simply spectating, for around £100 you can experience the thrill of driving a racing saloon around the track. The town has little in the way of accommodation, but there's welcoming **B&B** at *Setanta Farmhouse*, four miles away at **Castlekeely** (☎045/876481; ③).

NEWBRIDGE, a nineteenth-century town which grew up around the British barracks there is similarly unmemorable, except for its traffic jams. But after Newbridge the road heads over the grassy, unfenced stretches of the Curragh, and you're into racing country proper.

Kildare town

KILDARE town is a delight: a solid, respectable little place around a sloping triangular square, dominated by the massive, squat Church of Ireland **Cathedral of St Brigid**, who founded a religious house here in 490. The present structure dates originally from the thirteenth century, though the north transept and choir were burned to the ground in the Confederate War of 1641, and the Victorian reconstruction of 1875 is pseudo-medieval. Its round tower, probably twelfth century, has a particularly elaborate doorway twelve feet up; nineteenth-century battlements conceal the original conical roof – which you find yourself standing on once you've climbed to the top. The views from here are fine – rolling farmland to the south, the Bog of Allen to the north and the Curragh racecourse to the east (May–Sept Mon–Sat 10am–1pm & 2–5pm, Sun 2–5pm; £2).

The **tourist office** (mid-June to mid-Sept Mon–Sat 10am–1pm & 2–6pm; ☎045/522696) is sited in the nineteenth-century waterworks building right in the middle of the main square. **Accommodation** is limited to a hotel, the *Curragh Lodge* (☎045/522144; ⑤), Dublin Street, and a handful of **B&Bs**: the friendly *Tara* (☎088/219 5106; ③), signposted off the Dublin road, the comfortable and central *Singleton's* at 1 Dara Park, Station Rd (☎045/521964; ③), and *Fremont*, Tully Road (☎045/521604; ②). In the square beside the cathedral, you'll find *Nolan's*, an old **bar** with cosy snugs and regular traditional music nights. If you want to **eat**, *Georgio's*, on the Square, serves moderately priced pizza and pasta and the *Silken Thomas* does very good bar food and has a restaurant alongside – the bar takes its name from a member of the ruling Fitzgerald family, whom the growing powers of the Tudor monarchy provoked into rebellion in 1536. The uprising was unsuccessful, and a bloody massacre followed at Maynooth, later known, ironically, as "the pardon of Maynooth".

The Curragh and the National Stud

The real reason for spending time in the county town, however, is racing. **The Curragh**, just south of Kildare, is the centre of the Irish racing world, with the racecourse itself and dozens of studs. In early morning you can see strings of slim racehorses exercising on the 6000 acres of grassland. Breeding and training them is one of Ireland's major money-spinners, and much of it is centred on the Curragh. For an idea of the scale of the operation, Goff's Kildare Paddocks at Kill, which sells over half of all Irish-bred horses, has an annual turnover of around IR£20 million. At Kill you can rent a staider kind of steed, at the *Old Mill Riding Centre* (☎045/877053).

Security considerations mean that none of the working stud farms are open to the public. The best place to see the perfectionism that attends the breeding and training of these valuable pieces of horseflesh is the **National Stud** (mid-Feb to mid-Nov daily 9.30am–6pm; £5), just outside Kildare, signposted from the centre of town. You can easily walk out from the town, though the entrance is not the obvious one, through the main gates that you pass on the road from Dublin – instead follow the signs from the centre for the Stud and the Japanese Garden. You can pay to see just the Stud, or buy a joint ticket including the garden. This is well worth it even if you're not interested in horticulture: far more than a collection of rare plants, it's also an extraordinary legacy of Anglo-Irish eccentricity.

RACE MEETINGS

You don't have to know anything about horses to enjoy a day at the races. Irish race-going is quite unlike its English counterpart: there's none of the snobbery attached to who's who or who's allowed in the enclosure, and it's not as expensive – around £10–12. It's also different in that there's just as much excitement attached to steeplechasing as flat racing – steeplechasing, in fact, despite its smaller prize money, is often regarded as the better sport.

The major Irish classic meets are all held at the Curragh: the Airlie/Coolmore 1000 Guineas and Goffs Irish 1000 Guineas in May, the Budweiser Irish Derby in June, the Kildangan Irish Oaks in July, and the Irish St Leger in September. Punchestown is also famous for a three-day jump-race meeting in late April. Details of race meetings can be found in all the daily papers or in the specialist press: *Irish Field* (published Saturday morning) and the *Racing Post* (daily). Bord Fáilte publishes an annual information sheet with the dates of the current year's meetings; you should also be able to get schedules from local tourist offices.

If you are interested in getting to the Curragh (☎045/441205; March–Nov), there are special bus and train services scheduled to fit in with all major meetings; ring Busáras in Dublin for details (☎01/830 2222).

The National Stud itself consists of neat white buildings set in green lawns as close-cropped and well groomed as a Derby-winner's coat: a spick-and-span monument to the greater glory and perfectability of horses. Established in 1900 by Colonel William Hall Walker, who believed that horoscopes affected horses' form, the stud enjoyed a marvellous record of success, and in 1915 was bequeathed to the British Crown, which rewarded Walker by creating him Lord Wavertree. When transferred to the Irish State in 1943, it became the National Stud.

Colonel Hall Walker's belief in the stars is reflected in the **stallion boxes**, built in the 1960s according to his astrological principles, with lantern roofs allowing moon and stars to exert their influence on the occupants. There's a brass plaque on each door giving the stallion's name and details of his racing career. The National Stud's **museum** is an enjoyably chaotic account of the history of horses and horse racing which contains, among other bizarre exhibits, the skeleton of the 1960s champion racehorse, Arkle.

The Japanese Garden

Adjacent to the stud is the rather bizarre **Japanese Garden** (mid-Feb to mid-Nov daily 9.30am–6pm), which was laid out on a drained bog (between 1906 and 1910) by Colonel Hall Walker and two Japanese gardeners. Part of the Edwardian craze for all things Japanese, they're planned to represent the "life of man" – man, emphatically, it has to be said, rather than woman. In a weird kind of enumerated metaphysical joyride, you're led from birth to death via the Tunnel of Ignorance (no. 3) and the Parting of Ways (no. 6), where you're invited to choose between a life of philandering bachelorhood or marriage. Choosing marriage, you step across stepping stones to the Island of Joy and Wonder (no. 7) and meet your wife at the engagement bridge (no. 8; easily confused with the Red Bridge of Life, no. 17) and so on. Finally you pass through the Gateway to Eternity (no. 20), and it's time to go.

The Bog of Allen

The Bog of Allen, which has figured in Irish history and legend since prehistoric times, marks the beginning of a great belt of bogland that stretches westward across the country to the Shannon and beyond. **LULLYMORE**, at the foot of the Hill of Allen, site of

---

ALL ABOUT BOGS

Ten thousand years ago, after the last Ice Age, the melting glaciers and ice sheets left central Ireland covered by shallow lakes. As time went by the lake and lakeside vegetation grew and died and partly decomposed, in a continuing cycle that changed these lakes to fens, and eventually into domed bogs. Ireland now has the finest range of peatlands in Europe.

At one time there were 770,000 acres of raised bog in Ireland; by 1974 there were 160,500; and by 1985 there were just 50,000 acres left. They continue to disappear at a rate of 7500 acres per year. It is only recently that the Irish have awoken to the great natural importance of the boglands. Not only are they home to rare plants, from mosses to bilberries, but they provide a habitat for birds. The bog gases also act as preservatives, and the bogs of Ireland have yielded archeological evidence of botanical and human history up to 9000 years ago in the form of pollens and plant remains, gold and silver artefacts, dug-out canoes and human bodies.

To see a raised bog of international importance, go to **Mongan Bog** in County Offaly. Part of the Clonmacnoise Heritage Zone, it's situated on the banks of the Shannon. And if the bog bug really bites, head for the **Peatland World** in Lullymore (see below), where you can buy a copy of the Irish Peatland Conservation Council's *Guide to Irish Peatlands*.

---

the legendary Finn MacCool's palace, offers a good opportunity to get to grips with the life of the bogs, past and present. The place – its name means "great dairy pasture" – is an island in the bog where St Patrick reputedly appointed Eve, an early convert, to run a training college for monks.

Peatland World (all year Mon–Fri 9.30am–5pm, April–Oct Sat & Sun 2–6pm; £3), housed in the eighteenth-century stable block of Lullymore House, provides a comprehensive introduction to Irish bogs and includes exhibitions on conservation, energy production, plant and animal life, together with a history of the area and the estate itself. Bear in mind, though, that the project is supported by both Bórd na Móna (the Irish Peat Board) and the Electricity Supply Board, whose attitudes to bogland conservation may not necessarily coincide with your own.

Further insights into the area's history are provided by the nearby **Lullymore Heritage Park** (Easter–Oct Mon–Fri 9.30am–6pm, Sat & Sun noon–6pm), set in wooded parkland, with reconstructions of a Mesolithic campsite, a Neolithic farmstead, an exhibition on early Christian history, and displays covering social history from the eighteenth century onwards.

Canal country

Monuments to eighteenth-century confidence in Irish trade, which was to be dashed by the Act of Union, the **Royal** and **Grand canals** flow from Dublin through County Kildare and on into the Irish heartland (see map overleaf). While Ireland had experienced a minor industrial revolution in the mid- to late-eighteenth century, when mines, mills, workshops and canals were created, the Act of Union precluded further development. By walking along the **towpaths**, or cruising on the Grand Canal, you can see how industrialization affected – and failed to affect – the eighteenth-century landscape. **Grand Canal cruises** are based at Tullamore in County Offaly (Celtic Canal Cruisers; ☎0506/21861); from here you can head on to the Shannon, or join the River Barrow, which meets the Grand Canal at Robertstown and is navigable all the way down to Waterford.

The **Grand Canal** was a monumentally ambitious project, running from Dublin to Robertstown, where it forks. The southern branch joins the River Barrow at Athy, effec-

THE CANAL SYSTEM

tively extending the waterway as far south as Waterford, while the western branch runs up to Tullamore in County Offaly and on to join the great natural waterway of the Shannon at Shannon Harbour. As late as 1837 the Grand Canal was carrying over 100,000 passengers a year; it continued to be used for freight right up to 1959. The **Royal Canal** runs past Maynooth and Mullingar before joining the Shannon, many tortuous meanderings later, at Cloondara, north of Lough Rea, for access to the northwest. With the recent reopening of the Shannon–Erne Waterway (see p.430), these southern waterways are linked once more with the Fermanagh Lakes in the North, as they were in the nineteenth century.

Robertstown and Monasterevin

Two locations are particularly evocative of canal life. **ROBERTSTOWN**, due north of Kildare, where the ways divide – the canal arrived here in 1785 – is no more than a village, yet it boasts a canal stop complete with the *Grand Canal Hotel* (☎045/870005), which serves **bar food** and arranges leisurely **barge tours** (summer Sun 2–6pm). It's possible to walk along the towpath from here to **Allenwood**, two miles away, where there's good food and **music** on Saturdays in *Carroll's* bar. If you want to navigate the waterways yourself, **cruiser hire** is available from Canalways in Rathangan, six miles northwest of Kildare (☎045/524646).

At **MONASTEREVIN**, west of Kildare along the N7, there's a truly magnificent example of eighteenth-century state-of-the-art technology. Here the Grand Canal crosses the River Barrow on an aqueduct (in eighteenth-century terms, the equivalent of a motorway flyover), with superseding technologies upstream (a railway bridge) and downstream (the N7 Dublin–Limerick trunk road). Otherwise, Monasterevin follows the set pattern of an Irish Pale town: a big house, in this case **Moore Abbey** (once the home of the Irish tenor John McCormack), a church and the town itself, a street of eighteenth-century houses on one side of the road only, their gardens sloping down to the River Barrow on the other. Almost at the end of the terrace is *Carlow House*, which offers **B&B** (☎045/525211; ②).

South Kildare: ancient remains

It's a mistake to think of County Kildare as a relatively modern landscape, or to see in it only the legacies of the Anglo-Normans and Anglo-Irish. South of Naas on the Carlow Road (N9), three **high crosses** set in the green, rolling farmland attest that settlements and cultural history here are much, much older. **OLD KILCULLEN**, off the road in a field, is the site of an early Celtic monastery with the remains of eighth-century crosses and an evocative round tower damaged during the 1798 rebellion. Further south along the Carlow Road, there are more monuments to Ireland's ancient heritage at Moone and Castledermot, then, taking the R418 northwestwards, at Kilkea; but first it's well worth taking a short detour west before Moone to the village of Ballitore (about seven miles south of Old Kilcullen).

Ballitore

BALLITORE is an old Quaker village where the eighteenth-century Anglo-Irish political philosopher **Edmund Burke** (1729–97) was educated in the school run by Quaker Abraham Shackleton – a good example of the religious toleration that it seems the British government was prepared to grant anyone but Catholics. Born in Dublin of a Catholic mother and Protestant father, Burke went on to attend Trinity College, and, moving to London in 1750, he kept company with some of the leading figures of the time, among them Oliver Goldsmith (also a Trinity graduate), Samuel Johnson and Joshua Reynolds. His most important works are *A Philosophical Enquiry into the Origin of Ideas of the Sublime and the Beautiful*, an essay in aesthetic theory that is still studied by art historians, and *Reflections on the Revolution in France*, published the year after the event in 1790, in which he argued strongly against Jacobinism and for counter-revolutionary conservatism.

The **Ballitore Quaker museum** (Mon–Sat 11am–6pm) above the village library, which is housed in the old Friends Meeting House, gives a vivid picture of what Quaker life was like here: each member of the industrious community plied a trade, and their sober, business-like approach made Ballitore a model village by comparison with the general squalor and poverty of surrounding places. But the dominant impression given by the copperplate handwritten letters on show is the sheer boredom of life in a place where any stranger was cause for excitement. *The Cottage Biography* (on sale at the museum) of one of Ballitore's nineteenth-century residents, Mary Leadbeater, preserves more of the same stultifying atmosphere. Up towards the main road is the walled **Quaker graveyard**, whose plain, dignified tombstones seem suitable monuments to the qualities of the dead. If Ballitore's peaceful simplicity takes hold, you can **stay** at *Griesmount* (☎0507/23158; ④), a fine yellow Georgian house a little way from the village centre.

Signposted from the centre of the village is **Crookstown Mill** (all year daily 10am–6pm; £2.50). Built in the 1840s and still functioning, it contributed to an independence from the potato that, along with the industries introduced by the Quakers, meant that there was strikingly little emigration or starvation here during the Famine.

A mile or so further south is the **Irish Pewtermill** (☎0507/24164); although you can see pewter being worked, the place is primarily a retail experience – fine if you're into the Claddagh rings and ancestral crest-type of export Irishness.

From Moone to Kilkea

Back on the N9, the small village of **MOONE** (three miles from Ballitore) once formed a link in the chain of monasteries founded by St Columba, and the garden of Moone Abbey contains the ruins of a fourteenth-century Franciscan friary and a ninth-century cross. The *Moone High Cross Inn* (☎0507/24112; ④) is a friendly, rambling old pub, serving a good range of bar food, plus a more ambitious menu in the restaurant.

Five or so miles further south at **CASTLEDERMOT** there's more to see: two tenth-century granite high crosses, plus a bizarre twelfth-century Romanesque doorway standing by itself in front of an ugly modern church and a truncated round tower. Castledermot also has a thirteenth-century Augustinian abbey, an example of how the European monastic orders muscled in on the indigenous Irish church. Its substantial remains give a completely different feel to what might otherwise be merely a roadside stop; get the keys from the caretaker, who lives next door. There's a scattering of coffee shops; for evening meals and accommodation, try *Doyle's School House* **B&B** (☎0503/44282; ⑤).

Kilkea Castle, the Fitzgeralds' second Kildare stronghold (after Maynooth), stands a couple of miles up the Athy Road (R418) from Castledermot. It's impressive looking, though largely a sham – originally built in 1180, it was modified in the seventeenth century, and most of it is a mid-nineteenth-century restoration. Massively refurbished again in the 1980s, it's now a luxury **hotel** (☎0503/45156; ⑨) with a leisure centre and sauna which you can use even if you're not staying there. There's a more reasonable **B&B** option at *Kilkea Lodge Farm* (☎0503/45112; ⑤), a modest stone-built farmhouse with a riding centre attached, and it does dinner for around £20.

Athy

On the border with County Laois, close to the point where the Grand Canal meets the River Barrow, sits **ATHY** (rhymes with sty, emphasis on the last syllable), one of those places where a bucketful of imagination is required to envisage it as it once was: prosperity has turned a formerly handsome Georgian town with a fine main square into something much more ramshackle. A massive riverside factory sits oddly with the Georgian fanlights and a hideous modern church: the latter is apparently supposed to make reference to a dolmen, although the Sydney Opera House seems a stronger influence. Athy's designation as a heritage town, however, is bringing its historical resonances to life. By the riverside stands the square tower of the fifteenth-century **White's**

Castle, built by Sir John Talbot, Viceroy of Ireland, to protect the ford across the River Barrow and the inhabitants of the Pale from the dispossessed Irish beyond. The early eighteenth-century town hall houses a **heritage centre** (March–Oct Mon–Sat 10am–6pm, Sun 2–6pm; Nov–Feb Mon–Sat 11am–5pm; £2), with a comprehensive exhibition covering the Great Famine, the 1798 Rebellion, the part played by Athy men in World War I, and the life of Antarctic explorer Sir Ernest Shackleton, who came from nearby Kilkea.

Also in the town hall is the **tourist office** (July & Aug Mon–Sat 10am–5pm; Sept–June Mon–Fri 10am–5pm; ☎0507/31859). Aside from some leisurely **strolls** along the Grand Canal and the heritage centre, however, the town's unlikely to detain you for too long – except to eat or stay at *Tonlegee House* (☎0507/31473; ⑤; dinner £20), signposted off the Kilkenny Road, a solidly built mansion that surveys the countryside just beyond Athy's suburban sprawl.

travel details

Trains

Arklow to: Dublin Connolly (3–4 daily; 1hr 20min).
Bray to: Dublin Connolly (3–4 daily; 25min).
Kildare to: Dublin Heuston (20 daily; 30min).
Maynooth to: Dublin Connolly (4 daily; 30 min).
Wicklow to: Dublin Connolly (3–4 daily; 50min).

Buses

Arklow to: Dublin (6–8 daily; 1hr 30min).
Kildare to: Dublin (15 daily; 1hr 20min).
Wicklow to: Dublin (1–2 daily, 2hr 30min).

LAOIS AND OFFALY

f you've come to Ireland for the scenery, or the wild remote places, or the romance of the far west, then the central counties of Laois and Offaly probably don't hold a great deal to entice you. But this quiet and unremarkable part of the country between Dublin and the Shannon is an excellent place to get to know another Ireland, one not yet much hyped by the tourist authorities. Its gentle, green farming land bears the marks of a complex pattern of settlement: the Celtic Church, Viking invaders, the arrival of the Anglo-Normans and, very strongly in these twin counties, the planted settlements with which the British sought to keep their base in the Pale secure. It's a subtle, detailed landscape, and the destruction of Ireland's foreign trade by the Act of Union in 1801 ensured that it remained virtually untouched by the industrial revolution.

ACCOMMODATION PRICE CODES

Throughout this book, prices of hotels, guesthouses and B&Bs have been graded with the codes below, according to what you can expect to pay for a double room in high season. For more details on accommodation, see p. 29.

① Under £26   ④ £40–55   ⑦ £90–110
② £26–33   ⑤ £55–70   ⑧ £110–130
③ £33–40   ⑥ £70–90   ⑨ Over £130

Transport in Laois and Offaly is easy – the main N7 trunk road and the main railway line to Limerick slice straight through Laois, while the industrial centre of Tullamore makes an obvious transport centre, both road and rail, for Offaly. There's an increasing number of **accommodation** possibilities – some comfortable, mid-price hotels and even the odd hostel – but, with the exception of the Celtic monastery at Clonmacnois, the area remains lightly touristed, and it's wise to plan overnight stops in advance.

COUNTY LAOIS

Laois, or Leix in the more old-fashioned orthography (it's pronounced *Leash*), is in many ways Ireland's least-known county. Most people know it only for the maximum security jail at Portlaoise, or as an ill-defined area you go through on the way to Limerick. While most Irish counties have a strong identity, Laois seems oddly accidental. To the east it's more or less bordered by the **River Barrow**; to the north, it forms a large part of the **Slieve Bloom** mountain range (though some of that is in Co. Offaly); but to the west and south there seems little sense in the borders. Laois smarts from an image problem that's summed up by the adage that its landscape is like the local accent – flat and boring. That unjust reputation seems at last to be fading, as its quiet charms and proximity to Dublin attract a variety of people escaping the pressures of life in the capital.

Some history

Until the mid-sixteenth century, Laois remained under its traditional chiefs, the O'Mores, FitzPatricks, O'Dempseys and O'Dunnes, and posed an increasing threat to the British in the Pale. In 1556, a new county was carved out of these tribal lands, settled (or "planted", in the terminology of the time) and named Queen's County (to Offaly's King's County). A new town, **Maryborough**, named after Mary Tudor, was established at what is now Portlaoise. None of this quelled the O'Mores, but eventually transplantation succeeded where mere plantation had failed. The troublesome clans of Laois were exiled to County Kerry and Laois was left free for the colonizers. Because Laois came under British control so early, there are none of the huge estates that were later dished out, by Cromwell and Charles II, to loyal followers in the far west. Rather, there are smaller landholdings and planned towns, interspersed with some settlements of dissenting religious groups – Quakers and French Huguenots. These groups, unlike the Catholic population, which was being persecuted at the time, were able to find the freedom of worship they desired here. All this makes for an intimate – if unspectacular – landscape, epitomizing a history of colonialism as real as anywhere else in the former British Empire.

Portlaoise and around

PORTLAOISE is best known for its top-security **jail** and mental hospital – they're both on the same street, known to locals as Nuts 'n' Bolts Road. The prison was founded in 1547, when the O'Mores held the fortress of Dunamase to the south, as a fortification under the name of Fort Protector. The town itself is pretty unremarkable, though it does have a useful **tourist office** (May–Sept Mon–Sat 10am–6pm; open sporadically at other times; ☎0502/21178), with information on the whole county, reached by walking down the main street, cutting through the lane at *Dowling's Café* and crossing the car park. If you find yourself needing to stay, there's a comfortable **hotel**, *O'Loughlin's 25* (☎0502/21305; ②) on Main Street. You'll have no trouble finding somewhere to eat, while the drinking possibilities are endless – the town boasts 22 pubs in all. You could also head a few miles out of town on the Dublin Road to the thatched *Treacy's*, supposedly the oldest family-run pub in Ireland (founded in 1780), which now sits somewhat uncomfortably on an island between a motorway and a main road but still fulfils its role of serving travellers on the long haul from Dublin to the west.

What is well worth seeing, though, is the **Rock of Dunamase**, two or three miles east on the Stradbally Road (N80) – the fact that such a sight is not signposted says a lot about the area's attitude to tourism. An extraordinary, knobbly mound encrusted with layer upon layer of fortifications, it's a great place for gazing out, beyond the flat surrounding countryside, to the Slieve Bloom hills to the north and the Wicklow Mountains in the east. There are suggestions that Dunamase was known to Ptolemy under the name of *Dunum*, and Celtic *Dun Masc* was valuable enough to be plundered by the Vikings in 845. Today, the hill is crowned by a ruined castle of the twelfth-century king of Leinster, Dermot MacMurrough. He invited Strongbow to Ireland and married his daughter, Aoife, to him, including Dunamase in her dowry. Explicable only in terms of the complex history of the Anglo-Normans, Dunamase eventually passed from Strongbow – Henry II's right-hand man – to the Mortimers and the O'Mores, bitter opponents of the English. It was finally blown up by Cromwell's troops in 1650. The earthworks 500 yards to the east of the fortress are still known as Cromwell's lines.

STRADBALLY (literally "street-town"), a few miles further west, is notable chiefly for the **narrow-gauge railway** at Stradbally Hall. A nineteenth-century steam locomotive, formerly used in the Guinness brewery in Dublin, runs six times a year; there's also a **traction engine museum** (Mon–Fri 11am–1pm and 2–4pm; £1.50) in the town – strictly for steam buffs – and a steam engine rally on the first weekend in August. You can **stay** in solid comfort at *Tullamoy House*, a stone-built nineteenth-century farmhouse set in its own parkland three miles out of town (☎0507/27111; ③; May–Oct).

Once a busy halt on the Grand Canal, **VICARSTOWN**, north of Stradbally on the R427 (about ten miles from Portlaoise) is now just a few houses and some crumbling stone warehouses clustered round a humpback bridge, although it's showing new signs of life as a result of the increased use of the canal (see the map on p.128). It's chiefly remarkable for the spirited **traditional music** sessions on Monday nights in *Turley's* bar (aka *The Anchor Inn*) – be there by nine and sit tight. Accommodation is available on the other side of the water at *Crean's*, officially known as *The Vicarstown Inn* (☎0502/25189; ②). The green beside *Turley's* is a good spot for camping and this stretch of the canal is ideal for a pleasant stroll.

The South: Abbeyleix and Durrow

The south of County Laois consists of lush farmland, dotted with estate towns and villages. The largest of these and well worth a visit is **ABBEYLEIX** (about ten miles from Portlaoise on the N8), named after a Cistercian abbey founded here by a member of the

O'More family in 1183. In one of those periodic bursts of enthusiasm that seem to be a mark of the Ascendancy, Abbeyleix was entirely remodelled by Viscount de Vesci in the eighteenth century and relocated on the coach road away from the old village to the southwest. The place has been designated a heritage town, and has an excellent heritage centre, housed in the old National School Building just off Main Street.

Unfortunately, the attractive pedimented eighteenth-century **Abbeyleix House** (designed by James Wyatt) isn't open to the public, and the gardens are open just two Sundays a year. In the village, the famous *Morrissey's Bar*, an enormous grocer's shop and pub combined, probably hasn't changed in fifty years, with pew seats and a brazier and old advertisements for beer and tobacco that seem to have been forgotten by time. It's a great place to sit and soak up the atmosphere. **B&B** is offered at Ms Peverell's *Olde Manse* (☎0502/31423; ②), *Preston House* (0502/314332; ③), which boasts good-quality rooms and an impressive restaurant, and the fine *Hibernian Hotel* (☎0502/31252; ④), all on Lower Main Street. For friendly service, filling breakfasts and fine views, head a mile out of town, just past the gates of Abbeyleix House, for the solidly handsome *Norefield House* (☎0502/31059; ③). Back in town on Main Street, *Quinn's Tea and Coffee Room* does cheap and delicious soup, sandwiches and home baking.

If you have a few hours to spare, it's worth considering a short excursion to the tiny village of **Timahoe**, seven miles northeast of Abbeyleix, on the R426 road. The village is the site of a twelfth-century monastery, of which all that now remains is a round tower, its entrance framed with unusual carvings of human faces.

About three miles southeast of Abbeyleix in **BALLINAKILL**, itself a pretty Georgian village on a sloping main street, just north of the town the gardens of **Heywood House** (mid-June to mid-Sept Fri–Mon 1–6pm) are worth a look for their re-creation of a distant Italianate idyll. The house was burned down early this century, but the gardens, with planting by the English garden designer Gertrude Jeckyll and architecture – complete with gazebos and sunken terraces – by Sir Edwin Lutyens, architect to the Empire, have been fully restored.

DURROW, back on the N8, about six miles south of Abbeyleix, is yet another planned estate town, grouped around a green adjoining **Castle Durrow**, which is, its medievalized gateway notwithstanding, the first great Palladian house to be built in this area (1716). It's now a convent, but you can walk up the drive and see it from the outside. The town was owned by the Duke of Ormond, who for reasons of his own had it adopted by County Kilkenny; it took an act of parliament to get it returned to what was then Queen's County in 1834. The *Castle Arms* (☎0502/36117; ③), facing the green, is one of the few places to **stay**, while sturdy **home cooking** can be found at the *Copper Kettle*, two doors up. Excellent independent **hostel** accommodation (IHH; ☎0502/34032; ①) is available in a converted grain loft on a working farm at **BALLACOLLA**, about two miles northwest of Durrow on the R434.

The extreme **southwest** corner of County Laois consists of quiet farming land punctuated by small villages such as Cullahill, Rathdowney and Erill, full of neat colour-washed houses. **Cullahill**, about four miles southwest of Durrow, and its castle, up the road opposite the *Sportsman Inn*, are of little interest in themselves, but if you walk through the farmyard next to the castle and look at the stone protruding high up on the south wall, you'll see a fine example of a Sheila-na-Gig. About eight miles west of Durrow (take the R434 then the R433), **Rathdowney** is altogether a more metropolitan sort of place, with a raffish pride that gives it a continental flavour. The *Central* bar on the main square does B&B (☎0505/46567; ②), plus breakfast, tea and dinner.

Just north of Rathdowney, **DONAGHMORE**'s **Workhouse and Agricultural Museum** (daily 2–5pm; £2) gives some idea of the less picturesque aspects of the area's past. The austere building, formerly the parish workhouse (at some distance from the village itself) is evocative of the lives of the poor – its very size indicates the scale of the problem of rural poverty, even if the exhibits themselves, a selection of mainly agricultural machinery, seem a bit random. Families were frequently broken up on admission and no one was allowed to leave the premises; on average two of the 800 inmates died every week, to be buried in the mass grave behind the workhouse.

The buildings functioned as a workhouse between 1853 and 1886, and the museum exhibits take up the story again with a series of documents relating to the Donaghmore Co-operative, which was founded in 1927. Unfortunately, many of them – one of the cases has an order for sandwiches at a hotel in Birr – are of little more than local interest. The museum practises a strenuous self-censorship over the intervening period, during which the buildings were used as a British army barracks, at one stage housing the notorious Black and Tans – something the authorities deem as wiser not to address.

The village itself – three pubs, a Protestant church and a mill – is a clear statement of the inability of these little settlements to ride out the economic turbulence of the nineteenth century.

Slieve Bloom and North Laois

North Laois is dominated by the **Slieve Bloom Mountains**, which bring some welcome variation to this flat county; Bloom is an anglicized version of the name Bladhma, a Celtic warrior who once sought refuge in the area. Although the highest point, the Alderin Mountain (in the south half of the range, beyond the Glendine Gap, near the border with Offaly) only reaches to 1735ft, they're ruggedly desolate enough to give a taste of real wilderness, even if you follow the **Slieve Bloom Way**. The Way, a little over 31 miles in length, takes you round a complete circuit of the mountains across moorland, woods and bog, along part of one of the old high roads to Tara and through the bed of a pre-Ice Age river valley. Along the way dense conifer plantations attempt to survive, with a little help from the taxpayer, way above the natural tree line. If your time is limited and you have a car, the best place to start is probably at the northern end of the range at **Glen Barrow's** car park (three miles west of Rosenallis). Skirting the mountains, the road from Mountmellick (R422), as it passes through Clonaslee and Cadamstown (strictly speaking in Co. Offaly), offers easy access to some pleasant walking, particularly at Cadamstown. Here a waterfall's icy waters are used for bathing by hardy locals, with the tweely named *My Little Tea and Craft Shop* (actually the front room of a cottage) open for a revitalizing feed afterwards. If you don't have a car, you can catch the Dublin–Portumna **bus** at Birr or Portarlington and start walking at Kinnitty, a couple of miles south of Cadamstown, a delightful upland village, which has an excellent pub. The old custom of walking to the summit of Arderin has recently been revived; if you're here on the last Sunday in July, ask around. If you intend to spend some time in the area then John Feehan's *The Landscape of Slieve Bloom* is a good read while Bord Fáilte's *Holiday Guide to County Laois* details many excellent walks in the mountains.

Unfortunately, there is not a great deal of accommodation in this neck of the woods; you may want to base yourself in Birr (see p.143) or head for the Slieve Bloom's south-eastern foothills. Here, in Coolrain, accommodation can be found at *Pine House Farm*, Annaghmore (0509/37029; ②), an ideal base for walking, while the *Village Inn* is good for traditional music.

If you feel like a real treat, check in at **Roundwood House** (☎0502/32120; ⑥), just outside **Mountrath**, a mid-eighteenth-century Palladian mansion nowadays run as a guesthouse. Built by a Quaker who had made his fortune in America, it's a doll's house of a building decorated in vibrantly authentic Georgian colours, with a double-height hall boasting a Chippendale Chinese-style staircase. It's a relaxed, unceremonious sort of place that seems devoted to the virtues of good food, conversation and alcohol: you are likely to find yourself sitting by the turf fire after an excellent dinner, arguing endlessly with other guests about anything and everything.

Mountmellick, Lea Castle, Portarlington, and Emo

Mountmellick and Portarlington are typical of the few little settlements that grew up independently of the great houses, and both were communities of outsiders. **MOUNT-MELLICK**, about six miles north of Portlaoise on the N80, was founded in the seventeenth century by Quakers and still has a spacious eighteenth-century feel to it. You need imagination to see the houses as the elegant buildings they must once have been, but Mountmellick in its heyday was undoubtedly both cultured and prosperous – it had 27 industries, including brewing, distilling, soap- and glue-making and iron foundries.

It was also famous for **Mountmellick work**, white-on-white embroidery that used the forms of flowers and plants to create elegant designs. Local women are setting up a co-operative to revive the art of Mountmellick work, and it's planned to hold residential and day courses in this old Quaker craft. The Mountmellick Embroidery Group is based at Codd's Mill, a little way out of town on the Portlaoise Road and also home to a small exhibition about the town's Quaker heritage. Mountmellick's embryonic **tourist office** (daily 9am–5pm; ☎0502/24525) is based in Irishtown, just off the main square in town.

Set on the banks of the tranquil River Barrow, between Mountmellick and Monasterevin, the ruins of **Lea Castle** are an impressive sight. The best way to reach the castle is from Monasterevin in County Kildare; cross the canal and the river and take the first road on the right after the bridge. The castle dates back to the thirteenth century when it was the stronghold of Maurice Fitzgerald, a member of the powerful Anglo-Norman family who controlled this area. In 1315, it was burned by Edward Bruce, (brother of King Robert Bruce of Scotland), invited to Ireland by the Irish chieftains to create trouble for the Anglo-Normans. The castle later provided refuge for Silken Thomas, another Fitzgerald, after he rebelled against Henry VIII, and in 1650, like most castles in the area, it fell foul of Oliver Cromwell's forces after they had taken Dunamase.

Six miles northeast of Mountmellick along the R423, **PORTARLINGTON** was founded in 1667 by Sir Henry Bennett, Lord Arlington (for whom Arlington, Virginia, is also named), and settled by a group of Huguenot refugees here in the late seventeenth century; they built elegant Georgian houses with spacious orchards and gardens, which once grew exotic fruit such as peaches and apricots (particularly fine mansions are to be seen in Patrick Street). Some of the inscriptions on the tombstones of St Michael's Church, still known as the French Church, are in French, and surnames such as Champ and Le Blanc survive.

The town's elegant Huguenot menfolk used to sit outside the Tholsel, or Market House, in Market Square, sipping that exotic new beverage, tea, from porcelain cups. This idyll had its darker side: a channel was dug to encircle the town, already surrounded on three sides by the River Owenmass, with water to protect it from the displaced Irish, who had gone to live in the bogs. Today, the town's heritage is celebrated in a French week – complete with snail-eating competition – in July.

The **People's Museum** (Sun 11.30am–1pm & 3–5.30pm; free) in the Catholic Club on Main Street has exhibits ranging from 4000-year-old axe-heads to twentieth-century artefacts.

One of the few really big estates in County Laois is **Emo Court**; take the R419 from Portarlington (or if approaching from Portlaoise it's just off the N7 at New Inn). Designed by James Gandon for Lord Arlington around 1790 (but finished, not entirely according to Gandon's plans, only in the mid-nineteenth century), it's a massive domed building which has been impressively restored by its present owner after years of neglect when it was run as a Jesuit seminary. The house is now administered by the Office of Public Works, and you can wander through the extensive **grounds** during daylight hours; the **house** itself is open for guided tours (mid-June to mid-Sept Fri–Mon 10am–6pm; £2; Heritage Card). The nearby **Coolbanagher Church** is a modest and graceful building by Gandon, but unfortunately, it's almost always locked.

If the charms of Laois's quiet landscape take hold of you, you can discover more in John Feehan's excellent topographical survey, *Laois: An Environmental History* – a good example of the new breed of local history that integrates both the natural and the human-made past.

COUNTY OFFALY

From the Bog of Allen in the east to Boora Bog in the west, **County Offaly** is dominated by bog and peat. It's a low-lying region bounded to the northwest by the meandering Shannon and its flood plain, and it's only in the south that the land rises at all into the foothills of the Slieve Bloom range. The **Bog of Allen**, intensively exploited for peat, has been turned into vast swathes of brown desert. **Boora Bog** is entirely different; it's smaller and less unremittingly flat and bare, and is also the site of an archeological find that proves that there was human life here 9000 years ago. Western County Offaly is also the location of **Clonmacnois**, the greatest monastery of early Celtic Ireland, on the great, watery flood-plain of the Shannon.

The Bog of Allen only really becomes overpowering after Edenderry, which traditionally marked the edge of the Pale. But even here, after miles of dark bogland, it's a distinct relief to reach somewhere with lots of people and an air of prosperity: Edenderry's single wide street is lined with cheerfully painted houses. Pushing on along the Dublin–Portumna bus route towards Tullamore, you pass through Daingean, formerly Philipstown, the provincial capital in the days when Offaly was known as King's County (both county and capital were planted in Mary Tudor's reign and named after her husband, Philip II of Spain).

Tullamore

Coming from either direction, the Bog of Allen to the east or Boora Bog to the west, the bright lights and solid buildings of **TULLAMORE**, astride the Grand Canal, seem welcoming. Its Victorian ambience makes the town look more English than Irish, a result of moving the capital from Philipstown to Tullamore in 1834, following decades in which the British pushed the boundaries of King's County ever further westwards. Apart from the shops and a certain amount of nightlife, there are really only two reasons to come to Tullamore. One is to pay homage to **Irish Mist**, a truly delicious whiskey liqueur. Although the factory has now relocated to Clonmel, there are plans to open a heritage centre in the town celebrating the drink's history.

The other reason is **Charleville Forest Castle** (June–Sept Wed–Sun 11am–4pm; April–May Sat & Sun 2–5pm; Oct–March by appointment on ☎0506/21279; £3.50), an extraordinary Georgian-Gothic mansion ("perhaps the first deliberately formed asymmetrical house in Ireland", wrote Dan Cruickshank in the excellent *Guide to the Georgian Buildings of Britain and Ireland*), built in 1779 to the designs of Francis Johnston. The surrounding estate is wonderfully spooky, with a Gothic element suggestive of a horror movie – castellated turrets, shady trees and clinging ivy – while the house in the centre of the estate, surrounded by a second wall topped by urns, is a secretive place ready-made for diabolical activities. With its splendid old trees, leafy walks and even a grotto, the place has everything you could wish for. To get there, take the Birr road out of Tullamore (the N52): Charleville's gates are on the right as you leave the town – about ten minutes' walk.

Practicalities

Tullamore's **tourist office** (June–Aug Mon–Fri 10am–5pm; ☎0506/52617) is on Bury Quay; to get there, walk down Rahan Road, turn right and head towards the canal. If you want to **stay**, there are numerous B&Bs roundabout, such as *Oakfield House*, Rahan Road (☎0506/21385; ②), and *High House* (☎0506/51358; ②), which serves decent food at reasonable prices. You can feast on baked loin of marinated venison at the more upmarket *Tullamore Court Hotel* (☎0506/46666; ④), while traditional hospitality and hearty cuisine are available at the excellent *Beechlawn Farmhouse* (☎0506/53099; ②) in **Daingean**, a little way out of Tullamore along the canal. Tullamore's location makes it a good starting-point for exploring either the Shannon or Barrow rivers by **boat** – it's linked to both by the Grand Canal – although if you're headed for the Shannon, it's worth considering basing yourself among the quieter charms of Banagher (see p.142); cruisers can be rented from Celtic Canal Cruisers (☎0506/21861). **Bike rental** is available from Buckley Cycles, Brewery Lane.

Durrow Abbey

Four miles north of Tullamore on the N52, beyond some handsome wrought-iron gates to the left of the road, lies the site of **Durrow Abbey** (daily 9am–1pm), one of the monasteries founded by the energetic St Columcille (better known as St Columba), and the place where the *Book of Durrow* – an illuminated late seventh-century copy of the Gospels, now exhibited in Trinity College Library, Dublin – was made.

A long avenue brings you to a typically Irish juxtaposition: a grand Georgian mansion next to a medieval church, which stands on the site of the monastery. A notice at the main gates gives directions to the high cross and tombstones; behind you is the formality of the avenue, ahead the well-tended grounds of the house. Inside the church walls a rather eerie atmosphere is created by the disused churchyard, the masonry strangled with ivy, and gravestones leaning crazily on uneven ground as if the earth has opened and disgorged their contents.

The Shannon: Clonmacnois to Banagher

Western Offaly is dominated by the bog and the **Shannon**, one virtually impassable, the other for centuries a means of communication. Exploring the *esker* ridges (raised paths above the bog) of this drowsy, bog-and-water landscape has a quiet appeal if you hit good weather. It's excellent **cycling** country, and while there may not be much the untrained eye can identify most of the time, the romantic ruins that dot the landscape offer plenty of food for the imagination, and following roads that have for centuries been the only passages through the bog has a resonance of its own.

Although the monastery at **Clonmacnois** has made it onto the bus-tour itinerary, these visitors generally climb straight back on board and head for the west, and in general the area remains pleasantly unfashionable and untouristed. That said, there's an increasing range and number of places to **stay** in the area as the Shannon-based tourist industry expands, with the best base located in the relaxed Georgian town of **Banagher**, basking on the banks of the river. Alternatively, you could stay in the busier town of **Birr**, further south, with its elegant Georgian architecture and impressive Big House (see p.636).

Clonmacnois

Of all the ancient sites along the Shannon, **CLONMACNOIS**, early Celtic Ireland's foremost monastery, in the northwest of the county, is by far the most important. Approaching from Shannonbridge to the south, the first evidence of its whereabouts is a stone wall leaning precariously towards the Shannon. This is actually a remnant of a thirteenth-century Norman **castle**, built to protect the river crossing, which has leaned ever since its wooden foundations were destroyed by fire, and has nothing whatever to do with the monastery.

When you first see the **monastic complex** (daily mid-Sept to Oct and mid-March to May 10am–6pm; Nov to mid-March 10am–5pm; £3.00; Heritage Card) – a huddle of wind- and rain-swept buildings on an open plain in a bend in the Shannon, which can seem almost dwarfed by the sheer volume of non-stop tourist traffic that its gleaming new visitor centre processes – it seems hard to believe that this was a settlement of any importance. Yet this was not just a monastery, but a **royal city** and burial place for the kings of Connacht and Tara, including the last high king of Ireland, Rory O'Conor, buried here in 1198. It stood at what was then the busy junction of *Escir Riada*, the great road from Dublin to the west, and the Shannon; and as the bookshrines, croziers and other richly decorated artefacts on show in the National Museum in Dublin testify, it was also an artistic centre of the highest order. The twelfth-century *Book of the Dun Cow*, now in the Royal Irish Academy Library in Dublin, is only one of many treasures made here.

Founded by **St Kieran** around 548, the monastery was largely protected by its isolation; surrounded by bog, Clonmacnois could only be reached by boat or by one road that ran along what are still called *eskers*. It withstood Irish, Viking and Norman attacks, but in 1552 the English garrison at Athlone looted the monastery and left it beyond recovery. However, plenty remains: a cathedral, eight churches, two round towers, high crosses, grave slabs and a thirteenth-century ring fort.

The admission fee to the complex entitles you to an audio-visual presentation and a guided tour, as well as access to the interpretative centre, exhibition (and cosy coffee shop). Clonmacnois is still a pilgrimage site – St Kieran's festival is in September – and the video is a rather romantic hagiography, detailing the saint's peregrinations through ancient Ireland before he settled at Clonmacnois. More important is the **exhibition**; all the site's carved crosses – it has the richest collection in Ireland – have been moved inside to protect them from County Offaly's incessant wind and rain.

The early tenth-century **Great Cross**, over twelve feet high, is unusual in that it includes a secular scene; it is believed to commemorate King Flann and Abbot Coman; the carvings represent the monastery's foundation and scenes from the passion story. The **South Cross**, dating from the ninth century, is decorated with flower and animal motifs.

The buildings

Seeing any significant differences between these small, gaunt, grey buildings takes a trained eye. The **cathedral**, scarcely bigger than its companions, was built in 904 by King Flann and Abbot Coman Conailleach and rebuilt in the fourteenth century by Tomultach MacDermot; the sandstone pillars of the west doorway may have been incorporated from the earlier church.

Not everything at Clonmacnois, however, is as simple as it seems: to the right of the cathedral, **Teampall** (Temple) **Doolin** carries the elaborate coat of arms of Edmund Dowling of Clondarane, who restored the building in 1689; **Teampall Hurpan**, adjacent, was actually added in its entirety in the seventeenth century. **Teampall Kieran**, on the other side of the cathedral, is the reputed burial place of the founding saint, as well as allegedly the place where he built the first church on the site; the ruined **Teampall Kelly** is probably twelfth-century.

Away from the main group of buildings is **O'Rourke's tower**, a round tower 60ft high, erected just after the cathedral and blasted by lightning in 1134. On the outer boundary of the site, by the Shannon, are the **Teampall Finghin**, with another round tower dating from 1124, and the **Teampall Conor**, which was founded early in the eleventh century by Cathal O'Connor and used as a parish church from around 1790.

The **Church of the Nunnery**, away from the main enclosure, is signposted but difficult to find, and most people lose heart before they reach it. Follow the path across the site and bear left along the lane. The church is a little further along on the right, two lovely Romanesque arches in a field by the Shannon, exuding a feeling of peace. It's hard to imagine Clonmacnois ever feeling crowded, but if your arrival does happen to coincide with a bus party, this is the place to come.

The **boats** you'll see moored at Clonmacnois, incidentally, are all private; to rent a craft, you'll have to go downstream to Banagher or Athlone.

The Clonmacnois **tourist office** is next to the monastery (June–July 9am–7pm; March–May & Aug–Oct 10am–6pm; ☎0906/74134). There's B&B **accommodation** a mile from Clonmacnois on the Shannonbridge Road at *Kajon House* (☎0905/74191; ③); you can also **camp** there. One of the best places to stay, however, is a picturesque nine-teenth-century cottage – white-painted, with red windows and a peat roof – restored and rented out by the Claffeys (☎0905/74149; £10 per person per night).

About five miles east of Clonmacnois, just off the main N62 Athlone–Roscrea road, the An Dún Transport and Heritage Museum (daily 10am–6pm; £2) has a small collec-tion of lovingly tended vintage cars, plus agricultural vehicles and an odd assortment of butter churns, televisions and typewriters. There's also a pleasant coffee shop.

Shannonbridge and Shannon Harbour

From Clonmacnois, the road to Shannonbridge skirts the Boora Bog. **SHANNON-BRIDGE** has a set of traffic lights, but only because the sixteen-span bridge across the river is so narrow. Upstream, the wetlands of the Shannon open up; downstream a power station signifies the exploitation of the boglands. This is the point where coun-ties Offaly, Roscommon and Galway meet and the River Suck joins the Shannon: hence the strategically placed and massive artillery fortification dating from Napoleonic times. There are a couple of **B&Bs** here, including *Racha House* (☎0905/74249; ③) and *Laurel Lodge* (☎0905/74189; ②), a mile out of town towards Banagher, which rent out bikes and boats. The *Shannonside Diner* does snacks and light meals; there's a music pub – *Killeen's Tavern* – on the main street.

Just outside the town on the Tullamore Road (the R357), at Bord na Mona's (the Irish Peat Board) Blackwater power-generating plant, you can explore the bog on the **Clonmacnois and West Offaly Railway**, which will take you on a five-mile circular tour on narrow gauge through the Blackwater Bog. Unlike Clara Bog (see p.143), Blackwater Bog is being exploited hell-for-leather; you can't miss the power station with its thin chimneys belching brown smoke into the air – the irony of touring the bog under the auspices of the organization that's itself helping to destroy it won't be lost on anyone. "A few hundred years from now", says the publicity material, suavely, the bog "will be an integrated tapestry of fields, woodlands and wetlands. The landscape never stands still." The tour, which lasts some 45 minutes, leaves every hour on the hour (April–Oct 10am–5pm; £3) and is preceded by a 35-minute video on the flora and fauna you're about to see.

Also nearby, and of particular interest if you have children to entertain, is the Ashbrook Open Farm and Agricultural Museum (April–Sept 10am–7pm; adults £2, children £1.50, family £7), with plenty of farm animals, donkeys, rare birds and farm implements.

About five miles further south (take the R357 and turn at Clonony), **SHANNON HARBOUR** is where the River Brosna and the Grand Canal meet the Shannon after their journey right across Ireland. As you walk down to the junction, there comes a magical point where the entire landscape seems to become water. **Clonony Castle**, a mile or two further inland, is a ruined sixteenth-century tower house with a nineteenth-century reconstructed barn, scene of a private colonization attempt, in the seventeenth century, by an entrepreneurial German, Matthew de Renzi.

Banagher and around

Another couple of miles downstream, **BANAGHER** consists of one long street sloping down to the Shannon, fortified on the Connacht side by a Martello tower. With the construction of a new marina, it's rapidly turning itself into a relaxed and elegant touring centre for the Irish Midlands. Anthony Trollope was posted here as a Post Office surveyor in 1841, and wrote his first book, *The Macdermots of Ballycloran*, in Banagher; Charlotte Brontë spent her honeymoon here. There's a wayward local variant on Classical architecture: two houses on the main street have pepperpot towers, inside which everything curves – doors, fanlights, pediments, the lot. One of these, dated around 1760, has been transformed into a first-rate **hostel**, *Crank House* (IHH; ☎0509/51458). It houses a **tourist office** (March–Oct Mon–Fri 9.30am–8pm, Sat & Sun 9.30am–5pm) as well as the regional offices of Crann, an organization dedicated to the preservation of Ireland's woodlands, and a fine coffee shop (daily 8am–8pm). There's B&B **accommodation** across the road at the *Old Forge* (☎0509/51504; ③) and a comfortable friendly hotel, *The Brosna Lodge* (☎0509/51350; ③), with rooms at practically B&B prices.

The range of **eating** and **drinking** places reflects the extra visitors the town is getting. For daytime eating, *The Water's Edge* offers coffee and snacks – and a fine view of how the other half lives on the pitch 'n' putt course on the opposite bank. *The Vine House* **restaurant** and music bar, close to the river, has a courtyard garden and elegantly hearty menu with an emphasis on seafood (main courses around £8.75). *The Brosna Lodge*'s restaurant, *Snipes*, has a good menu with main course at around £10 – try the excellent potato and nettle soup. There's a handful of **bars** – the *Shannon Hotel* often has music and also has a pleasant garden where you can sit outside in good weather. *J.J. Hough's*, on Main Street, is a good old singing pub where drinkers are openly encouraged to take the mike. You can **rent bikes** from K. Donegan in the main street (☎0509/51178), **canoes** from Shannon Adventure Canoeing Holidays (☎0509/51411), and **boats** to cruise up the Shannon from Carrick-Craft (☎0509/51189). A Clare Class cruiser, which will sleep up to eight, costs between £800 and £1500 per week, although smaller boats are available from £250. For real luxury, this is one of the points where you can pick up the *Shannon Princess*, an old Dutch barge that plies the river between Killaloe and Lanesborough, offering the services of a first-class hotel, including cordon bleu cooking (☎088/514809).

Cloghan Castle, two miles out of town and signposted from the centre, is a massive Norman tower house with Georgian additions, inside an equally massive enclosure (May–Sept Wed–Sat 2–6.50pm; £4). Inhabited continuously for more than 800 years, it packs a wealth of history, starting with a seventh-century monastery founded by St Cronan on the site. For £40 a night, you can also **stay** there and eat breakfast in the magnificent dining hall, warmed in winter by a massive fire. The Thompsons, who own Cloghan, also have another castle, **Emmell Castle**, thirteen miles to the south, which you can rent. A sixteenth-century keep with a Georgian house attached, it sleeps seven and costs £400–490 a week and £300 for a three-day weekend. When visiting Cloghan Castle, you can also take in Lusmagh Pet Farm (summer daily 2–6pm; £2) for some therapeutic patting of pigs, geese, ostriches and sheep.

Close to the castle, and also signposted, is **Victoria Lock**, understandably something of a local beauty spot, where the Shannon runs into two separate channels. Trollope's biographer, James Pope-Hennessy, found the vegetation "so rich and wild, so tangled and impenetrable", that he was moved to compare it, in unreflective colonial tones, to Jamaica or Dominica. It's certainly a beautiful place; beneath the lock, released from artificial constraints, the river spills over once more across its floodplain – the feeling is one of privation followed by liberation.

Clara Bog

Banagher also provides a good base for exploring **Clara Bog**, a large (665 hectares) and relatively unspoiled tract of raised bog. Bord na Mona planned to develop it for industrial-scale peat-cutting and began draining the eastern section in the early 1980s, but in 1987 public pressure resulted in its takeover by the Office of Public Works. In the bog you can find rare species of lichen, moss and the specialized plants that are able to survive in the intensely acid environment – including, in the hollows and pools, the carnivorous sundews and bladderworts that like to supplement their diet with unwary insects. Check the Banagher tourist office for more details.

Birr

BIRR is a perfect example of a middling-sized town planned round a great house – in this case, Birr Castle, home of the Parsons family (Birr used to be known as Parsonstown), later elevated to the Earls of Rosse. Here, eighteenth-century urban planning has resulted in a truly delightful Georgian town, with wide, airy streets and finely detailed, fan-lit houses. Surprisingly, it's not a prissy place but instead feels slightly seedy, down-at-heel and full of life, but with Birr's recent designation as a heritage town this relaxed feel may well evaporate. One of the many places to be billed as the centre point of Ireland, Birr makes a good base for exploring the wetlands of the Shannon and the Slieve Bloom Mountains.

Habitation at Birr dates back to the sixth century, when there was a monastery here; an Anglo-Norman castle was succeeded by an Irish stronghold of the O'Carrolls and then, after the place was granted to Sir Laurence Parsons in 1619, an English garrison town. The development of the Georgian town dates from the time of another Laurence, who succeeded to the title in 1740 and immediately began to "improve" the town, fired by the architectural enthusiasm he'd gained on his Grand Tour.

The Town

Birr is now a heritage town, and there are plans to open one of its Georgian houses on John's Mall to the public, followed perhaps by a pub, school and shop, which may help penetrate behind the town's elegant facade to the reality of eighteenth-century life.

Already open is the local **heritage centre** on the refined John's Mall (Mon–Sat 2.30–5.30pm, Sun 3–5pm; £1), housed in an impeccably elegant miniature Greek temple, which will fill you in on the town's architectural and social background. In the grounds is a small standing stone, mentioned by Giraldus Cambrensis in the twelfth century as the "navel of Ireland" and used in the early nineteenth century, when it had temporarily migrated to County Clare, for secret celebrations of the Mass.

The Earls of Rosse still live at **Birr Castle**. Although their house isn't generally open to the public, some group visits are possible if arranged well in advance with the Estate Office (☎0509/20056) and occasionally rooms are let to very rich paying guests (contact Elegant Ireland, 15 Harcourt St, Dublin, ☎01/475 1665). However, it is possible to visit the castle **grounds** and Demesne, including the Historic Centre and magnificent Rosse telescope (daily 9am–1pm & 2–6pm or dusk; £3.50). Laid out in the 1830s and 1840s by the second earl, the gardens contain rare plants from all over the world as well as an enormous artificial lake and a really charming suspension bridge over the river.

It is, however, the **Rosse telescope** that is Birr's real claim to fame. In 1845, the third earl built what was then, and remained for three-quarters of a century, the largest telescope in the world – a reflector with a diameter of 72 inches. The instrument was used by the fourth earl (1840–1908) to make the first accurate measurement of the temperature of the moon and to catalogue the spiral nebulae. The telescope has just been restored and plans are afoot to install a replica of the six-foot mirror in the mirror box, the original of which is housed in the Science Museum in London.The recently opened **Historic Centre**, housed in the Stable Block of the Demesne, celebrates the scientific achievements of other family members; there is the Lunar Heat Machine invented by the fourth earl (his younger brother, Charles, invented the steam turbine) and an early darkroom used by the photographer, Mary Rosse, wife of the third earl. The family's talent for invention had its downside too when a family friend and talented microscopist, Mary Ward, became the first motor fatality in Ireland when she was run over in the grounds by an experimental, steam-powered car.

Practicalities

Tourist information is available at the Historic Centre in the stable block of the Demesne (see above). By far the best place to stay in Birr is *Spinner's Town House* (☎0509/21673; ③), an elegant **B&B** carved out of old warehouse buildings grouped around a courtyard. Accommodation is in cosy rooms with bare wooden floors and the price includes a delicious cooked breakfast. The complex is also home to a small theatre, a space for art exhibitions and a bistro that's head and shoulders above anything else in town. Almost opposite is the *Maltings Guest House* (☎0509/21345; ③), with self-catering apartments at £20 per head. *Dooly's Hotel* (☎0509/20032; ⑤), in Emmet Square, recently refurbished and extremely pleasant, is one of the focal points for the town's **social life**. *Dooly's* is where the Galway Hunt acquired the nickname of the Galway Blazers after a hunt in 1809, when their over-enthusiastic celebrations resulted in the gutting of the building by fire. Up another notch in comfort, and perfection for anyone with an expensive taste in interiors, is *Tullanisk*, Birr Castle's Dower House (☎0509/20572; ⑤), which also does a delicious dinner for £20. Set in its own parkland a couple of miles out of town on the Banagher road (R439), *Tullanisk* dates from around 1790 and boasts a huge bay window in the drawing room through which you can contemplate the deer munching the grass.

Back in town, for daytime **eating**, try *The Castle Kitchen*, opposite the castle gates. You'll get sturdy evening meals at *The Stables* (☎0509/20263; also B&B; ③), Oxmantown Mall, and good, if mega-rich, special-occasion food at *The Thatch* (☎0509/20985), a bar and restaurant a little way south out of town at Crinkill. *The Thatch*'s walls are hung with some fascinating photographs of the military architecture of the old British army barracks, blown up in 1922. An alternative is the *Riverbank Restaurant and Coffee Shop*, which overlooks the Little Brosna river and the old stone bridge that will take you over into County Tipperary. For something more exotic, there's a good Chinese restaurant, *Kong Lam* (☎0509/21253), in Bridge Street. As for **pubs**, you'll get a friendly welcome at *Craughwell's*, in Castle Street (just down from *Spinner's Town House*), which often has music and barbecues; or try *Kelly's*, where you can sit outside on the street and watch the world go by.

Excursions

If you're thinking of doing some **walking**, a mile out on the Roscrea Road (the N62), is the Slieve Bloom Interpretive Centre (daily 10am–6pm), which offers some rather dry background on the hills' flora and fauna, land use, architecture and legend. It's also the Birr Outdoor Education Centre (☎0509/20029), which runs courses in canoeing, windsurfing, rock-climbing and so on. For **horse-riding**, ring the Birr Riding Centre (☎0509/20551). You can rent **bikes** from P. Dolan & Sons on Main Street.

Finally, a little excursion for ghostbusters. A few miles southeast of town beyond **Clareen**, as the land rises towards the Slieve Bloom Mountains, the fifteenth-century **Leap Castle** fortifies the valley between Leinster and Munster. Before it was destroyed in 1922, it enjoyed the sinister reputation of being the most haunted house in Ireland, and was particularly famous for an unusual, smelly ghost, which was described both by Yeats and his contemporary Oliver St John Gogarty.

travel details

Trains

Portlaoise to: Cork (9 daily; 2hr); Dublin (8 daily; 1hr); Limerick Junction (13 daily; 1hr).

Tullamore to: Dublin (8 daily; 55min); Galway (5 daily; 1hr 45min).

Buses

Banagher to: Dublin (Sat service only; 3hr).

Birr to: Athlone (1 daily; 50min) Cork (1 daily; 3hr 30min); Dublin (2 daily; 4hr).

Portlaoise to: Abbeyleix (2 daily; 20min); Dublin (6 daily; 2hr); Durrow (1 daily; 30min).

MEATH, LOUTH, WESTMEATH AND LONGFORD

Stretching from the borders of County Dublin to the frontier with the North, and from the coast to the heart of Ireland, the four counties of Meath, Louth, Westmeath and Longford epitomize green and rural Ireland, yet provide a total contrast to the west of the country. It's a region neglected by most visitors, whose impression is one of monotonously similar countryside. Pass through at speed, as most people do, and you'll probably share that impression. But if you slow down and target a small area for more detailed exploration, you'll discover far more. In the east there's a wealth of remains of an exceptionally long, rich history, including the great ritual landscapes flanking the River Boyne, and one or two great beaches on the coast. Further west, you're into the lush, green, agricultural heart of Ireland; it's not spectacular country, but as dense in historical resonance as anywhere else, and largely untouristed, with a slow pace and plain style of living that have a steady charm of their own.

In practical terms, you'll find it easy enough to get about, with most of the sites conveniently strung along major roads well served by public transport. Accommodation is less easy, with only a handful of hostels throughout the four counties, and B&Bs only in the major centres. Still, if you base yourself strategically you'll find that a surprising amount can be seen in a short time.

County Louth, the smallest of the Republic's 26 counties stretches northwards along the coast. Here you'll find the only two towns of any real size in this chapter, **Drogheda** and **Dundalk**. Inland, hilly drumlin country hardens in the northeast to real mountains. Here, on the **Cooley Peninsula**, lies the most exciting part of the coast between Dublin and the border. The peninsula is also the setting of one of the richest and oldest legendary tales of Irish literature, the **Táin Bó Cúailnge** (Cattle Raid of Cooley).

Although it does touch the coast (with a couple of excellent beaches), **County Meath** (*Midhe*, middle) is primarily an inland county, whose exceptionally rich farmland unfurls lazily around its major river, the **Boyne**, and its tributaries. To discover the place you simply follow these waterways – above all the Boyne itself and the **Blackwater** – as thousands of years of civilization have done before. Along its rivers, Meath can boast by far the richest bounty of historical remains in Ireland. This history starts in the Stone Age, with some of the oldest buildings in the world at **Brú na Bóinne** and **Sliabh Na Caillighe**, and other important Neolithic remains still being discovered. Celtic Ireland was ruled from **Tara**, in Meath, and from **Uisneach** in Westmeath. Christian Ireland has left a wealth of early monastic remains, magnificent tenth-century high crosses, and the celebrated illuminated manuscript known as the Book of Kells. The largest Norman fortress in Ireland can be seen at **Trim**, and later

---

ACCOMMODATION PRICE CODES

Throughout this book, prices of hotels, guesthouses and B&Bs have been graded with the codes below, according to what you can expect to pay for a double room in high season. For more details on accommodation, see p. 29.

① Under £26	④ £40–55	⑦ £90–110
② £26–33	⑤ £55–70	⑧ £110–130
③ £33–40	⑥ £70–90	⑨ Over £130

---

castles and mansions – from the Plantation period when the county was wholly confiscated and extensively developed – are everywhere, though only a few (notably **Dunsany Castle**) are open to the public.

County Westmeath is characterized by its lakes – **Lough Sheelin**, **Lough Lene**, **Lough Derravaragh**, **Lough Owel** and **Lough Ennell** cut down through its heart – which go a long way to compensate for the falling off in historical or scenic splendour. In the south it becomes increasingly flat, easing into the bogland of northern Offaly, while in the west the border is defined by **Lough Ree** and the **River Shannon**. The Shannon also forms the western border of **County Longford**, which is about all the county has going for it. There's nothing wrong with the place in a dull and placid sort of way, but placid and dull is what it is, and you're unlikely to want to stay long.

COUNTY LOUTH

The main N1 Dublin–Belfast Road, and the train line, provide rapid access to Drogheda, and on to Dundalk and the North. Here on the coast, Meath is barely more than ten miles across, and you can cross over into Louth hardly noticing you've passed through. If you have any time, though, there are some delightful old-fashioned resorts on the coast and a couple of fine, sandy beaches. Biggest of them is **Bettystown**, where there's plenty of dark sand, a campsite and various B&Bs. Pleasant as it is, however, it's probably not somewhere you would want to spend a lot of time, especially if you're going to be seeing the west coast too.

Pressing on, **Drogheda** – straddling the River Boyne – lies immediately across the county border from Meath.

Drogheda

Aside from its obvious advantages as a base for visiting sites like Monasterboice, Mellifont, and, nearby in County Meath, Newgrange (see p.166) and the location of the Battle of the Boyne (see p.164), **DROGHEDA**, tightly contained between two hills, is an enjoyable place in its own right: easily accessible and surprisingly unused to tourism. The precise grey stone of which the town is built, combined with its post-industrial decay, give it a slightly forbidding air, but it has a vitality that suits it well. The architectural legacy of successive civilizations forms the main attraction. The ancient **Millmount mound** and the Boyne itself echo the early habitation you'll see further upstream, but the history of Drogheda as a town really began with the **Vikings**, who arrived in 911 AD and founded a separate settlement on each bank. By bridging the ford between these two, the Danes gave the place its name – *Droichead Átha*, the Bridge of the Ford. By the fourteenth century, the walled town was one of the most important in the country, where the parliament would meet from time to time: remnants of **medieval** walls and abbeys lie like splinters throughout the town. As ever,

though, most of what you see is from the **eighteenth century** or later, reflecting the sober style of the Protestant bourgeoisie after the horrific slaughter of Drogheda's defenders and inhabitants by Cromwell. The important surviving buildings of this age – the Tholsel, Courthouse and the Church of Ireland St Peter's Church – have mellowed romantically and stand among the **nineteenth-century** flowering of triumphal churches, celebrating the relaxation of the persecuting stranglehold on Catholicism, and the riverside warehouses and huge rail viaduct that welcomed the industrial boom years. More recent development, with riverside laneways and suburban housing estates, has affected the flavour of the place very little: the past somehow seems stronger here than the present.

Arrival, information and accommodation

Drogheda is a pretty easy place to find your way around. The **Bus Éireann** depot is on Donore Road, on the south bank of the river, and is also where you'll find the **tourist office** (June to mid-Sept Mon–Sat 10am–6pm; ☎041/983 7070). The **train** station is also on the south side, a short way east of town just off the Dublin Road. **Taxis** line up on Lawrence Street. If you want to stay, **B&B** is available at *Mrs Caffrey*, 69 Maple Drive (☎041/983 2244; ③), the *Europa Hotel* on the Dublin Road (☎041/983 7673; ⑤) or the elegant Victorian *Boyne Valley Hotel* (☎041/983 7737; ⑥), Dublin Road. If you have a car, Mary Friel's *River Boyne House* (☎041/983 6180; ③) offers good service two miles out of town in an isolated rural location near the Boyne Battlefield. The forty-bed *Harpur House Tourist Hostel* (☎041/983 2736) on William Street has adequate dorms, though some of the private rooms leave something to be desired. If you want to **rent a bike** to explore on your own try P.J. Carolan, 77 Trinity St or Bridge Cycles, 4 North Quay.

The town

The Meath side of town, south of the river, is probably the best place to start exploring Drogheda. Atop the southern hill, Millmount's **Martello tower** offers an excellent overview, both in a literal sense and through the excellent display in the local museum sited here. The tower (key from the museum) was severely damaged by bombardment during the 1922 Civil War (there's a large picture of the attack in the museum), but in any event it is the earthen mound on which it stands that gives the place its real importance. The strategic value of the site was recognized from the earliest times: in mythology the mound is the burial place of **Amergin**, the poet warrior, one of the sons of **Mil** of the Milesians who are reckoned to be the ancestors of the Gaels. He arrived in Ireland from northern Spain around 1498 BC and later defeated the *Tuatha Dé Danann* at Tailtiu (Telltown). Another belief is that the mound houses a passage grave. However, the tumulus has never been excavated to find out which story – if either – is true. Not surprisingly, the Normans chose the same strategic eminence for their motte in the twelfth century, and later a castle was built, standing until 1808 when it was replaced by the tower and military barracks you see today. The quickest way up here on foot is via the narrow flight of steps by Dina's corner shop, directly opposite **St Mary's Bridge**. This is near enough the spot where the original bridge was built by the Danes.

Millmount Museum

The eighteenth-century houses in the barracks' square now shelter various arts and crafts enterprises and, above all, **Millmount Museum** (Tues–Sat 10am–5.30pm, Sun 2.30–5pm; £1.50), one of Ireland's finest town museums, in the best chaotic style of the genre. Within a glass cabinet in the **foyer** hangs a topographical quilt showing much of Ireland's east coast – note the two thousand or so grains of French knots that depict the sandy shores. Next to this is a quilted cummerbund of the Georgian houses in Fair Street, very pleasing and precise in its eighteenth-century detail. When you get out into the town you'll find that the area depicted (Fair Street, along with William, Lower and Upper Magdalene streets and Rope Walk) is still rich in period buildings and architectural detail.

The **Guilds Room** follows, hung with three large drapes (the only surviving Guilds' banners left in the country) celebrating the broguemakers', carpenters' and weavers' trades. The broguemakers' banner – in effect an early advertisement – is particularly wonderful. It depicts St Patrick, who in legend rid the country of snakes, standing with his foot on a serpent: even the saint needs some protection, however, so he is sturdily shod in a pair of good Irish brogues. King Charles I also has a bit part, hiding up an oak tree to symbolize both the use of oak for tanning the leather and the security offered by a good pair of shoes (Charles escaped from Cromwell's troops in 1651 by hiding in an oak tree). The carpenters' and weavers' banners are more straightforward, the former depicting compasses and blades, the latter with shuttles clasped in leopards' mouths. In the next room there's a similar theme, with the trade banners of fishermen, labourers and bricklayers. The bricklayers' shows the **barbican at St Lawrence Gate** as their proudest achievement. This, again, is something worth seeing once you get out into the town: still standing, perfectly preserved, with two round towers flanking a portcullis entry and retaining wall. It is the most significant part of the town walls to have survived (part of the West Gate also exists, and a buttress and embrasure can be seen just south of the gate), and arguably the finest such surviving structure anywhere in Ireland.

Heading down the museum stairs you come to a series of displays of a more domestic and industrial nature. The last heavy manufacturing industry left Drogheda in 1986; the exhibits record the sources of its former prosperity, linen and alcohol – at one time the town had sixteen distilleries and fourteen breweries. Next to a case charting the history of the linen trade and a painting of the ship that used to ply between Drogheda and the English coast is a vessel from a much earlier period in the town's long history: a **Boyne coracle**, a recent example of the type of circular fishing boat in use from prehistoric times right up to the middle of this century. This one has a framework of hazel twigs and a leather hide taken from a prize bull in 1943.

There's also a fully equipped **period kitchen**, pantry and scullery. Among the artefacts displayed are an 1860 vacuum cleaner (a man would wind the suction mechanism from outside the house), a tailor's hen and goose irons (clothes irons named for their various shapes and sizes), which would be heated in the fire (hence the phrase "too many irons in the fire"), a settle bed (preferred by the Irish peasant because it would be next to the warmth of the dying embers and could sleep two adults lengthways and four or five children acrossways) and a vast array of other everyday miscellany, including an eccentric collection of geological samples gathered by a Drogheda resident whose wife finally insisted he should give them to the museum. On the **top floor** are a small picture gallery and some rooms devoted to the Foresters and Hibernian societies, both nineteenth-century benevolent institutions set up to provide sickness benefits, burial expenses and the like for the poor. Perhaps ironically, given Drogheda's manufacturing history, the temperance movement was strong here, and one of the banners carries the exhortation: "Hibernia be thou sober."

The north side

Standing on the Millmount hill, you can enjoy an unimpeded **panorama** of Drogheda, with the bulk of the town climbing up the northern hill-slope opposite. From this standpoint, it's clearly apparent how the tight-fitting street pattern of the medieval town gave scant breathing space for the overcrowding of succeeding centuries. The backs of the houses stagger down to the River Boyne in a colourless wash of daubed mortar, their windows staring blankly back at you. On top of the hill opposite, the fifteenth-century **Magdalene Tower** was once the belfry tower of an extensive Dominican friary, founded in 1224 by Lucas De Netterville, Archbishop of Armagh. The tower rises above a Gothic arch where the transept and nave would have met; inside, a spiral staircase reaches up into its two storeys, but since it is railed off from public access it's probably seen to best advantage from a distance. In March 1395, **Richard II**, King of England, received within the priory the submission of the Ulster Chiefs; and later Thomas, Earl of Desmond, a former Lord Chief Justice, was found guilty of treason and beheaded here in 1467 (with him expired his Act of Parliament for a university in Drogheda).

Lower down, the spire that leaps out from the centre of town belongs to the heavily Gothic-styled nineteenth-century **St Peter's Roman Catholic Church** on West Street, the town's main thoroughfare. It's an imposing building, with a grand double flight of steps, but it's the presence of a martyr's head, on view in a tabernacle-like box that forms part of a small shrine down the left-hand aisle, that transforms the place into a centre of pilgrimage. The severed head is a searing reminder of the days of religious persecution. It once belonged to **Oliver Plunkett**, Archbishop of Armagh and primate of all Ireland in the seventeenth century, when Drogheda was the principal seat in Ireland. On July 1, 1681, Plunkett was executed in London for treason: as the Lord Chief Justice of England explained, "the bottom of your treason was your setting up your false religion, than which there is not anything more displeasing to God". His head and mutilated members were snatched from the fire but were not brought back to Ireland until 1721, a time when persecution had somewhat subsided. Plunkett was canonized in 1975, after miracles were said to have been performed in his name in southern Italy.

Walking east along West Street and turning up Peter's Street you'll find the town's other St Peter's Church (this time Church of Ireland). The original church on the site was a thirteenth-century wooden structure and it is said that many of the town's inhabitants perished here in a fire as they sought refuge from Cromwell's forces. The present Church was erected in 1753, and a porch and spire, designed by the eminent Irish architect Francis Johnston, were added in 1793.

Heading south of here towards the docks, the back alleys and stone warehouses are relics of the short-lived industrial revolution and of the local brewing and milling trades. A few are being done up by a new breed of entrepreneur, but as many are empty and crumbling. The docks themselves seem mostly lifeless and deserted, too, and the Boyne's funereal pace does little to enliven a depleted commercial shipping fleet where once sixty Viking ships are said to have rested at anchor. There is, however, one very bright spot down here in the form of **Mrs Carbery's pub**, as appealing as any in Ireland. This has been a local, family-run institution for over a century, and in the evening or early morning (it is allowed to open at 7.30am to cater for the dockers and the men off the boats) the faint orange glow from the lanterns or fire inside makes a welcome landmark and sign of life.

Beaulieu House

Further downstream, the **viaduct** carrying trains on the Dublin–Belfast line spans what is effectively a 200ft-deep gorge. It's an impressive feat of nineteenth-century engineering by Sir John MacNeill, and you can examine it at closer quarters if you feel like extending your visit to *Carbery's* into a stroll a mile or so east along the Baltray Road. Beyond the viaduct and cement works you reach some pleasant woodland. Part of this belongs to **Beaulieu House**, a private domain that claims to have been Ireland's first unfortified mansion, built during 1660–65 after Cromwell's departure, when the land was confiscated from the family of Oliver Plunkett and given to Sir Henry Tichbourne, whose descendants reside there today. The house has a hipped roof in the artisan style and an almost perfectly preserved interior. Most rewarding of all is a mouthwateringly indulgent picture gallery, with a collection ranging from contemporary portraits of William and Mary on tall canvases by the court painter Van der Wyck to an intense collection of early twentieth-century Irish art. Unfortunately the house is strictly private, but the owners do open their doors to tours by the Drogheda Historical Society, so it's worth checking at the museum to see if your visit coincides with one of these.

Eating, drinking and entertainment

Weavers on West Street is an excellent pub for a cheap lunch, always crowded; *Go Bananas*, a few doors down, serves similar **food** and is also good value; and *King's Café* (popular with truckers), a short way out on the Collon Road, will serve up four courses for around £4. *The Swan House* on West Street is a good Chinese restaurant, with cheap takeaway and sit-down meals; while *La Pizzeria*, an Italian restaurant on Peter Street, is very popular with locals (Thurs–Tues 6–11pm; ☎041/983 4208). The *Westcourt Hotel* on West Street (☎041/983 0965) does a good early-bird menu for £12, while the *Buttergate Restaurant* in Millmount Square (Tues–Sun 12.30–2.30pm, also Thurs–Sat 7–11pm; ☎041/983 4759) is a little more expensive, but is worth it for its fine French cuisine.

As far as entertainment goes, check out the **pubs**, many of which are rich in character. *Carbery's* on the North Strand is probably the best-known gathering place on this part of the east coast, especially for the traditional sessions on Tuesday nights (from 9pm) and Sunday lunchtimes (12.30–2.30pm). To get a seat on Sunday make sure you're there by noon. *Clarkes*, on the corner of Fair and Peter streets, is quiet and old-fashioned during the week, popular with the local literary set, but on Saturday nights is a fashionable meeting place. *The Pheasant Pub* on Duleek Street has a ballad night on a Monday and there is often traditional music in *The Old Wall* on George's Street. *Peter Matthews* on Lawrence Street (known locally as *McPhail's*) is frequented by a younger crowd and has lots of toffee-brown woodwork, partitions and cubicles, and a back room for music. *McHugh's*, just up from here on Lawrence Street, is a friendly place with traditional music on Thursday nights. Less traditional venues include *Reds* on Dominick Street, formerly the *Horse and Hounds*, now a disco-bar, *Branagan's* on Lower Magdalene Street (hot snacks 12.30–2.30pm & 5–11pm), and *Squires* on West Street.

Entertainment outside the pubs is limited. The best bet is to check out what's happening at the Droichead Arts Centre in Bellscourt Lane off West Street, which regularly hosts plays, poetry readings and exhibitions. There's a **cinema** in the Abbey shopping centre and also an occasional **disco** at *Lucianos* in the *Boyne Valley Hotel* (☎041/983 7737), and at *The Place* in the *Rosnaree Park*, each a couple of miles out of town.

Mellifont and Monasterboice

Not far north from Drogheda, in the south of County Louth, lie two of the great historical sites which characterize this part of the country: the monasteries of Mellifont and Monasterboice. Both are easily reached from Drogheda and can be visited on your way to or from the sites of the lower Boyne Valley.

To get to Mellifont from Drogheda (about five miles), turn off the road to Collon at Monleek Cross; alternatively turn off the Slane–Collon Road at the signpost. There is no direct bus service to Mellifont, but Mullens taxis (☎041/983 3377) will bring you for £7 each way. Monasterboice can be reached from the main N1 Dublin–Belfast Road, or by continuing up the Drogheda–Collon Road and following the signs to the right.

Mellifont Abbey

Mellifont (daily May to mid-June & mid-Sept to Oct 10am–5pm; mid-June to mid-Sept 9.30am–6.30pm; £1.50; Heritage Card) was, in medieval times, one of the most important monasteries in Ireland, the Motherhouse of the Cistercian Order and a building of exceptional beauty and grandeur. The ruins you see today in no way do justice to this former glory, but they're pretty impressive even so.

At its foundation in 1142 – the inspiration of St Malachy, Archbishop of Armagh, who did much to bring the early Irish Church closer to Rome – Mellifont was the first **Cistercian monastery** in Ireland. Malachy's friend St Bernard, then abbot of the Cistercian monastery at Clairvaux, did much to inspire the work, and sent nine of his own monks to form the basis of the new community. The abbey took fifteen years to build, and you can gauge something of its original size and former glory by imagining the gargantuan pillars that once rose, finishing high among a riotous sprouting of arches and vaulted ceilings, from the broad stumps remaining today. For nearly 400 years Mellifont flourished, at its peak presiding over as many as 38 other Cistercian monasteries throughout the country, until in 1539 all of them were suppressed by Henry VIII.

One hundred and fifty monks fled from Mellifont, and the buildings were handed over to Edward Moore, ancestor of the Earls of Drogheda, who converted the place into a fortified mansion. In 1603 the last of the great Irish chieftains, **Hugh O'Neill**, was starved into submission here before eventually escaping to the Continent in the Flight of the Earls. Mellifont, meanwhile, went into gradual decline. It was attacked by Cromwellian forces, and then used as William's headquarters during the Battle of the Boyne, before eventually falling so far as to be pressed into service as a pigsty in the nineteenth century.

The ruins

Today the remains rarely rise above shoulder height, with the striking exception of the Romanesque octagonal **lavabo**, built around 1200, whose basins and water jets provided washing facilities for the monks.

The rest of the ruins can be easily identified on the map provided, their ground plan almost perfectly intact. You enter through the **north transept**, which originally had five chapels, three in its eastern and two in its western aisle. Two of the three on the eastern side had apsidal ends, an unusual feature in medieval Ireland, seen here presumably because of the French influence on the builders. The chancel area, or **presbytery**, has the remains of an ornate arch and sedilia where the priests celebrating Mass would sit. The entire **nave** would have been paved in red and blue tiles, some inscribed with the words "Ave Maria" and others decorated with the fleur-de-lis emblem; the **pillars**, too, would originally have been painted in brilliant colours and topped with flowery capitals. At the river end of the nave is a **crypt** – an unusual position which served to level the site on which the church was built. The **chapter house**, beyond the south transept, was once the venue for the daily meetings of the monks. It now houses a collection of medieval **glazed tiles**, moved here from around the site for safety.

Behind the lavabo is the south range, where the **refectory** would have been, and back towards the road you'll find the **gatehouse**, the only surviving part of a high defensive wall that once completely ringed the monastic buildings. Also within the grounds are another ruined church up on the slope (converted to a Protestant one in 1542) and a building that was converted by An Óige into a youth hostel. This is now permanently closed, a shame since the setting is delightful, with the River Mattock gliding through gently wooded country, and it used to make a great base from which to move out to the other places of interest nearby – Monasterboice and the Brú na Bóinne complex.

Monasterboice

Monasterboice (*Mainistir Buite* or "Buite's monastery") is a tiny enclosure, but it contains two of the finest high crosses (both dating from the tenth century) and one of the best round towers in the country – the site is open to all during daylight hours. As you enter, the squat cross nearer to you is reckoned the finer of the two, and certainly its high-relief carving has worn the centuries better. It is known as **Muiredach's Cross** after the inscription in Irish at the base of the stem – *Or do Muiredach i Chros*, "A prayer for Muiredach by whom this cross was made". The boldly ornate stone picture panels retell biblical stories and were designed to educate and inspire the largely illiterate populace. Some of the subjects are ambiguous and open to a certain amount of conjecture (William Wilde, father of Oscar, argued that many relate as strongly to events associated with Monasterboice as to the Bible), but most have been fairly convincingly identified.

The story begins at the bottom of the **east face** of the cross, nearest the wall, with **Eve tempting Adam** on the left and **Cain slaying Abel** on the right. Above this, **David and Goliath** share a panel with **King Saul** and David's son **Jonathan**. The next panel up shows **Moses striking the rock** with his staff to conjure water while the Israelites wait with parched throats, and above this, the **Wise Men** bear gifts to the Virgin Mary and baby Jesus. The centrepiece of the wheel is the scene of the **Last Judgement**, with the multitudes risen from the dead begging for entry to Heaven, their hands holding one another in goodwill and the trumpets playing loudly. Below Christ's foot the Archangel Michael is seen driving a staff through Satan's head after weighing the balance of good and evil in one individual's favour. At the very top, SS. Anthony and Paul are seen breaking bread.

The **west face** of the cross is largely devoted to the **life of Christ**. At the bottom is his arrest in the Garden of Gethsemane, with Roman soldiers and the treacherous kiss of Judas. This is followed by three figures clutching books – thought to represent the dispelling of the **doubts of St Thomas**. The third panel shows the **Risen Christ** returned to meet St Peter and St Paul, their faces bowed in shame at ever having doubted the truth. The hub of the wheel shows the **Crucifixion**, with soldiers below, angels above and evil humanity to the sides. This is surmounted by **Moses** descending from Mount Sinai with the Ten Commandments. The flanks of the cross are also decorated. On the **north side** are SS. Anthony and Paul again, Christ's scourging at the pillar, and the **Hand of God** (under the arm of the cross) warning mankind. On the **south side** is the Flight of the Israelites from Egypt and also possibly Pontius Pilate washing his hands. All this is capped at the top as if under the roof of the church and surrounded with abstract or uninterpreted embellishment.

The West Cross

The **West Cross**, the taller of the two, is made up of three separate stone sections, all of them much more worn. The east face shows **David** killing the lion, then **Abraham** ready to sacrifice his son Isaac, with the ram which became the last-minute substitute. Above this is the worship of the **golden calf**, with Moses coming down from Mount Sinai to catch his people red-handed in idolatry. The panel shows them trembling for forgiveness. The other three panels, before Christ seated in Heaven at the end of the world in the centre of the wheel, are hard to identify, though on the right arm of the wheel you can see the upside-down Satan being speared again by St Michael. The **west face** begins with the **Resurrection**, and the **Baptism of Christ** is shown on the second panel. The four three-figure panels before the wheel are again hard to identify, although the central figure looks a strong candidate for Christ. Again the **Crucifixion** dominates the wheel, with Christ tied to the Cross by rope; the left arm shows him being blindfolded and ridiculed, while the right arm has Judas's kiss of betrayal.

The round tower and two churches

Behind the West Cross stands possibly the tallest **round tower** in Ireland, 110ft tall even without its conical peak. Round towers were adopted between the ninth and eleventh centuries by monks throughout the country as a defence against constant Viking attack. They needed no keystone that enemies could pull out for speedy demolition; their height created a perfect look-out post; and the entrance would be several feet from the ground, allowing a ladder to be drawn in when under attack. The only drawback was that if a lighted arrow were to pierce the inner floorboards the whole column would act as a chimney, guaranteeing a blazing inferno. Sadly, you can't go into the tower, which has been closed for safety reasons.

Finally within the enclosure are two thirteenth-century **churches**, the north and the south church. They probably had no real connection with the monastic settlement, which had almost certainly ceased to function by then, and there's little of great interest within their ruined walls.

North to Dundalk

The main reason to head northwards into County Louth, apart from reaching the border, is to get to the mountains of the **Cooley Peninsula**. You have three routes to choose from. The main Drogheda–Belfast Road, the N1, is the fastest, speeding directly towards the border and passing Monasterboice early on, but with little other reason to stop. An alternative inland route to take is to head towards Collon, taking in Mellifont Abbey, and from there continue to Ardee and Louth town (for **St Mochta's House**) and ultimately on to Dundalk or into County Monaghan. Both these routes give excellent, unhindered cross-country views of County Louth, especially of the drumlins rising inland towards counties Cavan and Monaghan. The third option, to take the bay road out of Drogheda and **follow the coast** north, is the most scenic and the one to choose if you want to dawdle along the way or if you're cycling. In the early stages, there's little point diverting to Baltray: instead, carry straight on for **Termonfeckin**.

Termonfeckin

TERMONFECKIN is a placid country village lying in a wooded dip half a mile from the shore. The village has a small tower house **castle** and a tenth-century **high cross** in the graveyard of St Feckin's Church. The castle (keys from Patrick Duff in the bungalow across the cul-de-sac) dates basically from the fifteenth and sixteenth centuries and has as its most unusual feature a corbelled roof – notably less well constructed than the 4000-year-older one at Newgrange. For **accommodation**, try Mrs Kitty McElvoy at *Highfield House* (May–Sept ☎041/982 2172; ②), where you can have a hearty breakfast for £3. You can get good **food** at *The Triple House* restaurant, whose Italian/French menu offers five courses for £14.95, or four courses for £9.95 before 7.30pm.

Clogherhead, Dunleer and Castlebellingham

CLOGHERHEAD is a far busier place – not difficult to achieve: it's a glum beach resort with ancient mobile homes and windswept beach cabins and a few bars aimed squarely at the holiday trade; their briny names, *The Lobster Inn* for example, give the game away. From here the road to **PORT ORIEL** takes you to **Clogher Head** (one mile) and a tiny fishing harbour tucked hard into the coast's rockface – good mackerel fishing off the pier in summer. It's only beyond here, as you approach **ANNAGASSAN**, that the signposts designating the scenic route begin to earn their keep, with the mountains of Cooley and Mourne, one range south of the border, the other north, spectacularly silhouetted against the sky. It's an enthrallingly unimpeded view of the best that lies ahead in counties Louth and Down. *The Glyde Inn* in Annagassan has food (of sorts) and is a nice reclusive spot to take time out for "a small drop of medicine". There's little else to see around the village, although local archeological explorations are provoking controversy as they lay bare what is claimed to have been the first permanent Norse settlement in Ireland, predating even Dublin. Continuing northwards across the humpback stone bridge, you've a watercolourist's idyll of rowing boats laid out along the bulging ramparts of the canalized river as it meets the sea.

Inland from these villages, just off the M1 motorway on the N1 road, lies the village of **DUNLEER**, formerly a traditional stop on the Belfast to Dublin route. The town has little to offer in terms of tourist attractions, except for White River Mill, a traditional water mill, where wheat has been ground for at least three hundred years. If you decide to spend the night, there is B&B accommodation at the red-bricked *Bramble Lodge* (☎041/685 1565; ③). For food you could follow the locals to the *Grove* restaurant where you can get a substantial meal for less than a fiver.

Travel a further five miles north on the N1 and you will arrive at **CASTLE-BELLINGHAM**. Despite the main Dublin–Belfast Road blundering right through the middle, Castlebellingham remains a pretty village. You can take refuge from the traffic down by the mill, now converted into a restaurant. This has a turning gable-end water wheel and a run of several man-made weirs on the River Glyde up the back through woodland alongside a sugary, castellated hotel (good two-course bar lunches), the *Bellingham Castle*, also the only place to stay in Castlebellingham (☎042/937 2176; ⑤). Moving northwards again, the next significant turning off the N1 (right) takes you to **BLACKROCK** and later allows you to bypass most of Dundalk. Blackrock itself (the

Claremount Arms has good Saturday-night traditional sessions involving the *uilleann* pipes) is an overstretched ribbon of Victorian seaside villas along a mudflat beach. It does, though, offer a handsomely crystalline view across **Dundalk Bay** and on to the Cooley Peninsula, by now looming very close.

Ardee

The inland route is far less travelled, and there's less to see along it. Without transport of your own you'll have difficulty getting anywhere, unless you're prepared for some very leisurely hitching. Nonetheless, it has its rewards, mostly in just this lack of traffic or population; a rural tranquillity unrivalled even in the west. Almost exactly halfway between Drogheda and Dundalk, **ARDEE** (*Baile Átha Fhirdia* or Ferdia's Ford) recalls the tragic legendary duel between Cúchulainn the defender of Ulster and his foster-brother Ferdia, a battle brought about through the trickery of Medb, Queen of Connaught.

> *Ferdia: "Attack then if we must.*
> *Before sunset and nightfall*
> *I'll fight you at Bairche*
> *in bloody battle.*
> *Men of Ulster will cry out:*
> *'Death has seized you!'*
> *The terrible sight*
> *will pierce you through."*
>
> *Cúchulainn: "You have reached your doom,*
> *your hour is come.*
> *My sword will slash*
> *and not softly.*
> *When we meet you will fall*
> *at a hero's hands.*
> *Never again*
> *will you lead men."*

These taunting jibes threw down the gauntlet for their fight to the death, in which eventually Ferdia was fatally wounded by the *gae bolga*, a weapon summoned from the *Tuatha Dé Danann* god Lug, by Cúchulainn during the fight in the stream. Ardee is named after the ford where this great battle was fought.

Today, Ardee reeks far more strongly of the Plantation era, with fortified buildings along the main street and a memorial **statue** to a landlord erected by his thankful tenants in 1861. The thirteenth-century **castle** on the main street, currently being turned into a museum, was built here mainly because the town was at the northern edge of the Pale, and from here the Anglo-Irish made forays into Ulster, or were themselves periodically forced onto the defensive. For B&B accommodation the *Railway Bar* (☎041/685 3279; ②) and *Carraig Mór* (☎041/685 3513; ②) are both fine, but if you want something a little special then try Linda Connolly's *Red House* (☎041/685 3523; ⑤), a country house with indoor swimming pool, sauna and tennis courts.

An interesting short diversion from Ardee takes you to the so-called **Jumping Church** at Kildemock. To get there head east from the junction at the southern end of Ardee's main street and turn right after about a quarter of a mile – the small, ruined church lies a further mile down this road. It gets its name from its end wall having shifted three feet from its foundations, which, according to local lore, it did to exclude the grave of an excommunicated person. Less romantic accounts tell of a severe storm taking place in 1715 at around the time the wall jumped, but either way it's a remarkable sight, with the wall shorn clear of its foundations yet still standing (albeit at a 35-degree angle). In the graveyard are simple, foot-high stone markers, some of the earliest graveslabs for the poor.

Louth Village

Ardee is a major road junction, and moving on you could head northeast to Dundalk, northwest to Carrickmacross or west to Kells. If you want to go on heading north, however, a more interesting route is along the minor roads to **LOUTH VILLAGE**: keep on the left fork at the northern end of Ardee and take an immediate right towards Tallanstown, where you'll need to turn right again for Louth. It's not much in itself (and certainly doesn't seem to deserve sharing a name with the county), but it does have one thing well worth seeing in **St Mochta's Church** – turn left towards Carrickmacross and immediately right onto the Inniskeen Road.

According to legend the church was built in a night to give shelter to its founder, **St Mochta**, who died in 534. Originally part of a monastery, and dating probably from the late twelfth century, it has a high, vaulted roof, beautifully crafted, reached by a constricted stairway. In its early years it was plundered many times; these days they obviously feel safer, since the church is left open to any passing visitor. The fourteenth-century **Louth Abbey** is accessible through the graveyard back up the road, from where, if you look west, you'll notice a motte on the nearby hill.

Dundalk

Although Dundalk has a reputation as a tough border town, home to uncompromising Republicanism, it still has enough interest to justify a visit. Starting life in legendary prehistory as a fort guarding a gap in the mountains to the north (*Dún Dealga,* the Fortress of Dealga), it became in turn a Celtic, Norse, Anglo-Norman, Jacobean and finally Williamite stronghold. This hard tradition seems still to hang over the town, and it never seems a place where you – or for that matter the locals – can feel fully at ease (having said that, the town has some excellent pubs; see "Practicalities" on p.160).

As far as sights go, the outstanding one is the nineteenth-century Neoclassical **Courthouse**, whose open Doric portico leads in to an airy, classically proportioned interior. In the plaza outside, the *Guardian Angel* or motherland statue is unequivocally dedicated to "the martyrs in the cause of liberty who fought and died in the struggle against English Tyranny and foreign rule in Ireland" – a far cry from the monument of gratitude in Ardee. **St Patrick's Cathedral** in Francis Street is also worth a look while you're here: its cornucopia of embellished towers, turrets and crenellated walls is a reasonably successful imitation of King's College Chapel, Cambridge. Inside are some rich mosaics using gold pieces in abundance to depict biblical stories.

Louth County Museum (Tues–Sat 10.30am–5.30pm; Sun 2–6 pm; £2), in a warehouse on Jocelyn Street (next to the tourist office), uses a variety of artefacts and documents to tell the stories of local industries, from coopering to cigarettes. The museum is an uneasy mix of high-tech display and poorly labelled exhibits, but there is a wealth of material here. During the 1960s, Henkel bomber cockpits were sent over to Dundalk to be made into bubble cars – you'll find a 1966 model on the first-floor landing. The top two floors house travelling art exhibitions.

Should you wish to see that rare thing, a well-designed and well-maintained Irish Modernist building, head for the 1970 **Carrolls tobacco factory**, designed by Scott Tallon Walker. A mile south of Dundalk on the Dublin Road (N1), it is fronted by a striking sculpture by Gerda Froemmel reflected in an artificial lake, and contains an impressive collection of **modern Irish art**.

Practicalities

The regional **tourist office**, which also hosts touring art exhibitions, occupies a restored tobacco warehouse on Jocelyn Street (Mon–Fri 9.30am–1pm & 2–5.30pm; July & Aug also open Sat; ☎042/933 5484). Among the best of the town's numerous B&Bs are *Glenn Gat House* (☎042/932 8266; ③) at the top of Stapleton Place, which runs off the Dublin Road, and *Rosemount* (☎042/933 5878; ②) near the Carroll's cigarette factory. **Eating** well and cheaply is not a Dundalk speciality, but there are plenty of fast-food places around the centre of town which will do if you're starving. Slightly better fare can be had at *McKeowns Pub* and *Quaglino's* (☎042/933 8567), both on Clanbrassil Street, or at *La Cantina* (☎042/932 7970) off Park Street (evenings only). *The Fairway's Hotel*'s restaurant *Modi's* (after Modigliani, copies of whose sketches adorn the walls) has one of the best menus in town, but the restaurant's contrived theme and purple and yellow decor detract from this a little. **Bikes** can be rented at the Cycle Centre, opposite the shopping complex.

Pubs that are well worth visiting include *Toal's* on Crowe Street, a sawdust-on-flagstone hide-out and a venue for good traditional music (Thurs, Fri & Sat). *McManus's* pub near the library in Seatown is self-described as "simply a great pub" – there are old-fashioned snugs to drink in, excellent-value soup and sandwiches, guitar folk music on a Sunday night and more bluesy stuff on Monday. *McArdles* on Anne Street hosts *Ceolteóirí* every Thursday night. *Café Metz* on Francis Street is the new fashionable place in town, while there are a couple of more old-style pubs on Park Street: *Tara* and *McDaids*. The Council Arts Office in the Market Square (Mon–Fri 9am–5pm; ☎042/933 2276) provides up-to-the-minute details of music and theatre.

Faughert

From Dundalk, **the border** lies just eight miles on up the N1, and Newry only five miles beyond that. Opposite the turning for the Cooley Peninsula, a couple of miles outside Dundalk, is a lesser road that leads a short distance inland to **FAUGHERT**. A small place of little modern interest, Faughert nevertheless has several older associations worth mentioning as you pass. **Cúchulainn** was born at Castletown Hill on the edge of the plain of *Muirthemne*, which stretches away towards Armagh in the north, and in the legendary account he was sent a false offer of peace by Medb asking him to meet her at Faughert. Instead, fourteen of Medb's most skilful followers awaited him: fourteen javelins were hurled at him simultaneously but Cúchulainn guarded himself so that his skin, and even his armour, was untouched. Then he turned on them and killed every one of the "Fourteen at Focherd".

Faughert is also said to be the birthplace of **St Brigid**, patron of Ireland, whose four-armed rush-cross is so common on the walls of rural Irish households. In the local churchyard you can see her holy well and pillar-stone, as well as the grave of **Edward Bruce**, who was defeated here in 1318 after being sent to Ireland by his brother (Robert the Bruce) to divert the English away from the Anglo-Scottish border. There is a stone nearby which in legend was used for his decapitation.

The Cooley Peninsula

You come to **Cooley** for the raw beauty of its mountains, to walk and to experience a life where the twentieth century intrudes only rarely. Indeed, when you get up among the bare hilltops the peninsula's links with legend seem at least as strong as its grip on modern reality. For above all this is country associated with the **Táin Bó Cúailnge**, and in the mountains many of the episodes of the great epic were played out. Its plot (set around the first century AD) concerns the Brown Bull of Cooley (*Donn Cúailnge*) which is coveted by Medb, Queen of Connaught, in her envy of her husband Ailill's White Bull (*Finnbenach*). In their efforts to capture the bull, Medb and Ailill, who come from the west, effectively declare war on the east in general, and Ulster in particular. All the men of Ulster – save one, Cúchulainn – are struck by a curse which immobilizes them through most of the tale, leaving our hero to face the might of Medb's troops alone. The action consists largely of his (often gory) feats, but the text is also rich in topography and placenames, many of them still clearly identifiable.

A single road runs around the peninsula, leaving the N1 to trace the southern slopes of the Cooley Mountains and then cutting across country to Greenore and Carlingford on the north shore. It is here, facing the Mountains of Mourne across **Carlingford Lough**, that the most beautiful scenes lie, with forested slopes plunging steeply towards the lough. The southern slopes are gentler and lazier, making a far more sedate progress to the water's edge. The exact location of the border, visible on the map as a dotted line bisecting the lough, has been in dispute since 1922. Once, it was continually patrolled by British army helicopters; now, there is little evidence of army presence.

Before you reach any of this, however, only about a mile down the peninsula road, there's a short and rewarding detour. From the back of the *Ballymascanlon Hotel*, a footpath leads to the **Proleek Dolmen**, whose massive capstone balances with far more elegance than its 46 tons ought to allow. If you see smaller stones on top they're recent additions, flung there by visitors who hope to have a wish granted. On the path just before the dolmen, a Bronze Age wedge-shaped **gallery grave** can be seen: both of these monuments may become harder to visit if, as local rumour has it, they are incorporated into holes five and six of a new golf course.

Omeath

Aside from being the more scenic, the peninsula's north shore is also the best place to base yourself for **hill-walking** and the easiest for finding food and a bed. Here at **OMEATH**, the lough has narrowed dramatically, so that the sedate towns of Warrenpoint and Rostrevor on the Mourne Mountain slopes across the border seem only a handshake away. In summer there's a handy passenger **ferry service**, which also takes bikes, between Omeath and Warrenpoint (July & Aug daily till about 6pm, tides permitting; £2.50 return; 5min). Staying in the Republic, you can rent **jaunting cars** for short trips out of town; they run mostly to the open-air **stations of the cross** at the Rosminian Fathers' School down the road. As a village, Omeath, with its widely scattered dwellings, is far from typical of the east coast – it was until recent years the last remaining *Gaeltacht* village of any significance in this part of the country.

You can **stay** cheaply at *Delamore House B&B* (☎042/937 5101; ②), or in slightly more comfort at *Omeath Park* (☎042/937 5116; ④), half a mile out on the other side of town at the end of a long driveway up the hillside. Around the crossroads that mark the centre of town are grouped a few **grocery stores** and **pubs**.

Carlingford

CARLINGFORD, a former fishing village five miles or so back down the lough, makes a considerable contrast to Omeath, both for its neatly ordered network of narrow, whitewashed, terraced streets, often with naive murals, at the foot of the Sliabh Foye Mountain, and in its development as an upmarket resort. Although the latter may take a trained eye to detect – it's discernible perhaps mainly as a sprinkling of craft shops – the place retains real charm as well as some excellent places to eat and drink.

LEGENDARY WALKS

You can walk almost anywhere in the mountains behind Carlingford and Omeath, and once you're up there the heather-tuffeted ground on top offers some of the most beautiful hill-walking imaginable, the setting for many episodes from the *Táin Bó Cúailnge*. It's at its best in the afternoon, with the light bringing out the colours of the Mourne Mountains across the water – in the morning the sun tends to get in your eyes. The road up behind the former youth hostel, a mile or so south of Omeath, a few yards off the main road behind the *Ranch Pub and Restaurant*, offers the best approach, switchbacking its way into the hills with the climb ever increasing the drama of the fjord below. At about 1200ft there's a car park where a map table marks out the major sights, and there's a long spiel on the formation of the lough: a valley gouged out by a glacier which was flooded at the end of the last Ice Age.

With a little imagination, it's not hard to translate the gaps, boulders and fording points of rivers up here into the scenes of Cúchulainn's epic battles. And some of the places are clearly identified. From **Trumpet Hill** (*Ochaine*) he slew a hundred men of Medb's army with his sling on three successive nights as they rested in a plain to the west. This forced Ailill, fearing that his entire force would be destroyed, to offer up champions in single combat. Between Ochaine and the sea Cúchulainn slew the first of these warriors, **Nadcranntail**, by letting his spear fly high into the air so that it dropped down onto Nadcranntail's skull and pinned him to the ground. Then he sprang onto the rim of Nadcranntail's shield and struck his head off and then struck again through the neck right down to the navel so that he fell in four sections to the ground.

From **Slievenaglogh** (*Sliab Cuinciu*) Cúchulainn swore to hurl a sling stone at Medb's head – no easy task as she never moved without her army in front holding a barrel-shaped shelter of shields over their heads. Then one of Medb's bondmaids, Lochu, went to fetch water and, thinking it was Medb herself, he loosed two stones, killing her on the plain in the place known as *Réid Locha*, Lochu's level ground. In fact, when he had the chance, Cúchulainn couldn't bring himself to kill Medb. During the final battle an earthy episode is inserted in which Medb suddenly gets a gush of blood that makes her need to urinate. Fergus, her chief warrior and lover, is furious at her bad timing and takes his place in the army of shields raised to protect her while she relieves herself, creating three great channels known as *Fual Medba*, Medb's foul place. Finding her in this delicate position, Cúchulainn was too honourable to kill her from behind (though he seems happy enough to kill everyone else whenever and wherever he can).

Fual Medba is not clearly identified, but you can find the scene of an earlier episode, the **Black Cauldron** (*Dubchoire*), where Medb divides her armies to search for the white bull, which has last been seen here: it's a recess north of the Glenngat Valley (the valley above Ballymackellet). When the spoils are brought back and the cattle have to be driven over the mountain at the source of the Big River (the River Cronn), Fergus decides that they will have to cut a gap in the hills to get the cattle. This is the *Bernas Bo Ulad*, today known as **Windy Gap**. It's also the point in the story where Fergus and Medb hang back behind the army to make love, and where Ailill, aware of their trysts, sent a spy to take Fergus's sword, thus acquiring proof of his unguarded weakness and providing the basis of a phallic joke which recurs throughout the story.

Windy Gap is also the setting of a far later tale, the tragic legend behind the **Long Woman's Grave**, marked by a pile of stones at the roadside. The story concerns two sons at their father's deathbed: the elder promised to give his younger brother a fair share of the estate, saying he would take him up to a high place in the mountains and give him all he could see. He kept his word, but the place where they stood was Windy Gap, where if you look around you see nothing but the immediate hills rising on all sides. The younger son instead became a trader, and on one trip wooed a Spanish beauty to whom he gave the same promise, tempting her hand in marriage. When he brought her home and took her up to the Windy Gap to show her his estate she dropped dead on the spot from shock. Thus the Long Woman's Grave for the tall Spanish beauty is explained.

Carlingford is also an historic place. St Patrick is said to have landed here briefly on his way to introduce Christianity to Ireland (he finally ended his journey further north, in County Down), and the settlement is ancient enough to have been raided by the Vikings. But the oldest visible remain is the D-shaped ruin of **King John's Castle**, down by the main road on the water's edge. King John is said to have visited in 1210, and the Anglo-Norman castle, guarding the entrance to the lough, may be even older than that. It has its counterpart across the lough at Greencastle. The village in general retains a distinctly medieval feel, and there are a couple of solid fifteenth-century buildings: the **Mint**, in a narrow street off the square, is a fortified town house with an impressive gate tower; **Taafe's Castle**, which stood on the shore when it was built but is now some way from it, is impressively crenellated and fortified but sadly not open to the public. The best and safest **beaches** in the area are at Gyles Quay and Shelling Hill.

Practicalities

Carlingford has a small **tourist office** (Mon–Fri 10am–7pm; ☎042/937 3888) behind *O'Hare's pub*. To find it, turn left at the castle as you enter the village from Dundalk. If you want to **stay**, try B&B at the *Viewpoint* on Omeath Road, whose modern, motel-like flatlets enjoy good views from a little way up the hill (☎042/937 3149; ③). *Mourne View* (☎042/937 3551; ③) is a friendly place right at the foot of the mountains, signposted from the main Dundalk road. For views alone, *Barnave B&B* (☎042/937 3742; ③) on the shores of the lough, is difficult to fault. *McKevitt's Village*, Market Square (☎042/937 3116; ⑤) provides a little more luxury, while *Jordan's* on Newry Street (☎042/937 3223; ⑥) is a real treat. The *Carlingford Holiday Hostel*, Tholsel Street (IHH; ☎042/937 3100; open Feb–Nov) caters for the cheaper end of the market, but, as this is part of the **Carlingford Adventure Centre**, you may have to book early as it is often group booked and can be full of overexcited, noisy teenagers.

Jordan's pub-cum-bistro is easily the best of the places to **eat and drink** in Carlingford. The menu includes some perhaps over-sophisticated variations (mango sauce) on excellent local ingredients, but the food, especially the fish, is good and excellent value (12.30–2.30pm, summer 6–10pm, winter 7–9.30pm; ☎042/937 3223); you'll need to book, weekends especially. There's a small room at the back of the pub which sometimes acts as a pre-dinner theatre. *O'Hare's* (aka *PJ's*), on the corner near the Mint, is an old grocery store and bar and the most entertaining place to drink – its publican has a considerable local reputation as a raconteur of tall tales; they also serve pub grub and oysters in season, which here seems to mean most of the year round. Nearby *McKevitt's Village* serves more substantial food, including filling bar meals from around £5. *Ghan House*, a fine Georgian mansion down near the crab-clawed pier, is yet another place where you can get a meal and a drop to drink.

COUNTY MEATH

The River Boyne has a name redolent of Irish history, for it was on its northern banks that one of the battles which shaped the nation's destiny was fought. If you travel up the river, however, this is not what most occupies your attention. For in the early stages, following the N51 to Navan, is the area known as the **Brú na Bóinne** complex, with some of Europe's finest prehistoric remains. The whole Boyne Valley, in fact, has been heavily populated from the earliest times, and traces of virtually every period of Irish history can be found here.

However, before exploring the sites along the northern shore of the Boyne – and especially as there is no river crossing between Drogheda and Slane – you might want to take in two secondary diversions south of the river, easily reached from Drogheda (or if you're heading up the N2 from Dublin).

THE BATTLE OF THE BOYNE

For all the significance attached to it now (including big Protestant celebrations in the North on July 12), the **Battle of the Boyne** was just one skirmish – and arguably not the decisive one – in the "War of the Kings" between James II of Ireland and William of Orange, King of England. It took place at Oldgrange, less than five miles from Drogheda, on July 1, 1690 (the change of date came with the switch to the Gregorian calendar in the eighteenth century). The deposed James II, retreating southwards, took up defensive positions on the south bank of the river, with some 25,000 men (including 7000 well-equipped French troops, but largely Irish irregulars) holding the last major line of defence on the road to Dublin. William's forces – around 36,000 – occupied a rise on the north bank from where they forced a crossing of the river and put their enemies to flight. In terms of losses, the battle was a minor one – some 1500 Jacobites and 500 of William's men – and James's forces were to regroup and fight on for another year. But in political terms it was highly significant and can legitimately be seen as a turning point. In the complexities of European struggle, the Protestant William was supported by the pope and the Catholic king of Spain, both fearful of the burgeoning power of James's ally, the French King Louis XIV. Although the victory on the battlefield was small, the news gave heart to William's supporters in Europe while making Louis fearful of extending further aid to the Jacobite cause. At the same time, it gave William a breathing space to establish his control back home: in the long run, Protestant ascendancy was assured.

The location of the **battlefield** is directly opposite the turn-off from the N51 to Tullyallen, a couple of miles out of Drogheda. Here a stepped path leads to a viewing point on the site occupied by William's troops before the battle. It's only a slight elevation, but it nevertheless commands a broad swathe of the valley and it's not too hard to conjure up a picture of the armies battling it out in front of you. A panoramic plan marks out the various positions of the opposing forces.

Donore and Duleek

A couple of miles southwest of Drogheda, **DONORE**'s chief interest, apart from having been King James's base at the time of the Battle of the Boyne, lies in its **ten-pound castle**. In 1429 Henry VI promised a grant of £10 to every one of his subjects who, in the next ten years, built a castle 20ft long, 16ft wide and 40ft high within the counties of Meath, Louth, Kildare and Dublin, the area known as the **Pale**. The three-storey castle here is built almost exactly to these measurements, though unfortunately it seems to be permanently locked up.

DULEEK (*An Damh Liag*, the stone church), a few miles further south, on the River Nanny, is an historic little place of considerably more interest. The south-of-the-Boyne equivalent of Kells, it was founded by St Patrick who settled St Ciaran here to build the first stone church in Ireland and found a monastic settlement; it was also an early bishopric. Much later, the Jacobite forces withdrew to Duleek after the Battle of the Boyne and spent the night here, while James himself fled to Dublin and then on to France. The ruined **St Mary's Priory** you see today was probably founded in the twelfth century, and was abandoned after Henry VIII's dissolution of the monasteries: there are some fine tombs in the roofless building, and nearby a squat, tenth-century **high cross**. In the town square is a **wayside cross** of a different nature, erected by Genet de Bathe in 1601 as a memorial to William, one of her husbands, and one of the finest examples of a type of cross that crops up all over the place.

If you want to **stay** in this area there's good, reasonably priced B&B accommodation and home-produced food at the historic house of Annesbrook, a short, well-signposted distance out of town (May–Sept; contact Mrs Kate Sweetman, ☎041/982 3293; ④). William Thackeray in his *Irish Sketchbook* (1842) wrote uninspiringly about Annesbrook, but its most striking asset, the Ionic pedimented portico, has an interesting tale attached. The stately entrance is said to have been hastily affixed onto the box-shaped house when its owner was told to expect a visit from George IV, the first king to arrive from England after the departure of William and James. The portico was felt a necessary addition to bring the house up to the standards expected by royalty. The north wing, housing a Gothic dining room, was also built in the king's honour, but he preferred to dine in the garden.

Brú na Bóinne

The area known as **Brú na Bóinne** comprises a landscape made up of a group of forty or so related prehistoric monuments caught within a curve of the river between Tullyallen and Slane. The three most important of them, Dowth, Knowth and Newgrange, are what are known as **passage graves** – high round mounds raised over stone burial chambers. They predate the pyramids by several centuries, and although there's no comparison in terms of size or architecture, there are certain parallels. Just as the fertility of the Nile floodplain helped create the great Egyptian culture, so the lands of the River Boyne and its watershed have been proved to have had some of the richest soil in Europe (and considerably higher temperatures than today) around 3000 BC. On the banks flourished what seems to have been the most advanced Neolithic civilization in Europe. Physically, the tombs' size and solidity are what impress most; beyond the massive, bare stones there's not much to be seen, but there's plenty of scope to try and disentangle the various theories about these structures, to work out who built them, where they came from and where they went.

It was formerly possible to visit the tombs directly from the northern side of the River Boyne but all has changed in recent years. Access to the site is now via **Brú na Bóinne Visitors' Centre** on the southern side of the river. It's signposted from Slane town centre and is on a minor road off the N2. From the visitors' centre (daily: March, April & Oct 9.30am–5.30pm; June to mid-Sept 9am–7pm; May & mid-to end Sept 9am–6.30pm; Nov–Feb 9.30am–5pm; ☎041/982 4488) tour buses run to Newgrange and Knowth. The third site, Dowth, remains closed to the public while lengthy excavations are carried out. The £3 ticket includes entrance to the visitors' centre and a shuttle bus to either Newgrange or Knowth, plus guided tours. Tickets for both Newgrange and Knowth cost £5. The well-organized centre provides background information on the construction, artwork and religious significance of the tombs and also contains a reconstruction of a passage grave.

It would be an understatement to say that this centre is controversial and there has been much argument about how best to preserve the tombs. One of the main arguments for building the centre was that, with the increase in numbers visiting the site, a scheme had to be devised to protect it from destruction; however, since its opening and the intense marketing of Brú na Bóinne the number of visitors has increased enormously, though the number of people allowed to visit the Newgrange tomb is limited to six hundred per day. Consequently, long delays for the Newgrange tour are common, especially in high season, a problem further compounded by the fact that you can't book a tour in advance of your arrival. The best advice is to come as early in the day as possible, book a place on one of the later tours and, if you have transport, spend the intervening time exploring the sights of the surrounding area.

Dowth

The **Dowth mound** – roughly 50ft high and 200ft in diameter – is closed for conservation work at the time of writing, but you can wander about and see the outside. It's reached by taking the first left off the N51 after the battlesite, a minor road which trails the north bank of the river. Just before you reach the cairn you'll see the tower of **Dowth Castle** on the left, adjoining a rambling red-brick Victorian mansion. John Boyle O'Reilly, a Fenian patriot transported to Australia, who later became editor and part-owner of the *Boston Pilot*, was born in the castle in 1844. At the back of the neighbouring ruined church there's a monument to him that forms the heart of a small **commemorative festival** every year on the Sunday closest to August 10.

When you get to the site, the signs of earlier excavations and of pillaging (in the nineteenth century some of the stones were removed for road-making) are immediately apparent, having left a crater in the top of the mound and a large chunk burrowed out of the side. Around 100 **kerbstones**, perhaps half of which can be seen today, originally marked the edge of the tumulus. Inside are two **passage tombs** and an early Christian chamber. The passages are similar in construction to those at Newgrange (see below), as is the decoration of the standing stones which form the walls of the passage, and the ten-foot-high corbelled roof. One distinction between the two sites, however, are the **sill stones** placed across the passage floor and at the entrance to the chamber.

The name Dowth derives from the Irish for "darkness", and the main chamber faces west to the setting sun (the minor chamber looks southwest, directly towards Newgrange). In myth, the site was built when the Druid Bresal, attempting to build a tower that would reach heaven, contracted all the men of Erin for a single day. His sister worked a spell so that the sun would not set until the mound was built, but the two then committed incest, destroying the magic and causing the sun to set: thereafter the sister declared "Dubad (darkness) shall be the name of that place forever". Today, as the sun sets at the winter solstice, its rays enter the tomb (at about 3pm), lighting up the tall stone slab at the back and then moving across to illuminate a recess in which is a decorated stone precisely angled to catch this moment, before finally sinking below the horizon.

If you want to **stay** close to the site with its fine views over the Boyne Valley, the *Glebe House* offers **B&B** (☎041/983 6101; ③), as well as afternoon tea.

Newgrange

The **Newgrange tumulus** has an average diameter of around 338ft and is some 30ft high at its centre point. It has been so completely restored that at first sight it reminds you of a grounded Fifties sci-fi flying saucer. But once you get over the initial shock, the sparklingly new appearance of it all serves only to heighten the wonder. The quartzite retaining wall is glisteningly white and gives some hint (not revealed at other sites where everything is grey and moss-covered) of the power this particular stone must have had for the builders. The nearest natural source is in the Wicklow Mountains, south of Dublin. You'll notice that the wall is bossed with small, round granite stones, the purpose of which no one knows. Speculation is not helped by the fact that they are probably not in their original positions: during the most extensive of the renovations (1962–75) the original photographs were lost and their placement was therefore a matter of educated guess. Other non-original features worth noting are that the front and most ornate kerbstone was originally placed by the entrance tunnel (it was moved to prevent damage by visitors); that the entrance tunnel itself was closed by a standing slab; and that the concave wall at the entrance is designed to accommodate 100,000-odd tourists each year – originally the wall would have continued directly up to the sides of the spirally decorated kerbstone. It is also believed that an obelisk once stood at the top of the mound, to mark it out from afar.

The outer ring of **standing stones**, of which only twelve uprights now remain, was a feature unique among passage grave tombs, and it may have been the addition of a later civilization. None of the standing stones is decorated, and many show signs of being eroded by water, which suggests that they may have been hauled up here from

NEWGRANGE - MYTH AND SUPPOSITION

The name Newgrange derives from "new granary", simply because that was its function at one stage in its history. This hardly seems an adequate description for one of the most important Stone Age sites in Europe, however, and an alternative derivation ("the Cave of Gráinne") is considerably more satisfying, if less accurate. The site has many associations with **myth**. First among these concern the **Tuatha Dé Danann**, the first Irish gods who descended from the sky and inhabited the land before the Celts. Dagda (the Irish Zeus, chief of the gods) gained possession of the mound by making love to Boand (the white cow goddess who later deliberately drowned herself at the source of the Boyne so as to invest the river with her divinity), first tricking her husband Elcmar by sending him on an errand for a day which took him nine months. From their union **Oengus** was born and called *ac ind Oc* (The Youthful Son). In ancient literature Newgrange is *Brugh Mac ind Oc*, the Brugh of Oengus. Oengus also appears later in the **Fenian Cycle** as the succourer of Diarmuid and Gráinne, carrying the fatally wounded body of Diarmuid to Newgrange "to put aerial life into him so that he will talk to me every day". Other legends make the local mounds the tombs of the Kings of Tara; radiocarbon dating, pinpointing the third millennium BC, disproves this fairly convincingly.

What does emerge is just how little concrete information there is on the people who created Newgrange. Perhaps the more off-beat **theories** regarding the meaning of the monuments is that of the American Martin Brennan in his book *Stars and Stones* (Thames and Hudson, 1983). He claims that the scrollwork, lozenges and lines on the stones, which most archeologists see as abstract decoration, perhaps with religious significance, are in fact all part of a single incredibly involved **astronomical chart** which includes not only Newgrange itself, but the rest of the Brú na Bóinne complex and even sites as far-flung as Loughcrew (see p.174) and those in the Curlew Mountains in south County Sligo. In his book he claims that the scrollwork all relates to a calibration system based on the diameter of the earth. Brennan insists that the Newgrange monument is not only the largest but also the oldest such system in the world: predating and far outranking in sophistication the instruments of the Greek astronomers. It is not a theory you are likely to find espoused by your guide, but it does have its convincing aspects. In the end, though, you have to ask why, if they were so sophisticated, is this the only evidence that survives?

the river. There is an inner ring of 97 **kerbstones** all placed on their sides and touching each other, engineered one supposes as a support for the layers of sod, loose stones, shale and boulder clay (20,000 tons of it) that were laid over the chambers.

Perhaps the most important feature of Newgrange – again unique – is the **roof-box** several feet in from the tunnel mouth. This contains a slit through which, at the **winter solstice**, the light of the rising sun begins to penetrate as soon as its full disc appears above the horizon. The rays edge their way slowly up the passage tunnel and, narrowed into a single shaft, eventually find the back of the cruciform chamber. In minutes the chamber becomes radiant with a glow of orange light which fades as suddenly as it has blazed. The sun actually rises at about 8.20am above a hill known as the Red Mountain: it reaches the chamber a couple of minutes before 9am, and fifteen minutes later the whole thing is over. The guided tour includes a "re-creation" of the phenomenon which involves a flash of orange electric light: if you prefer to rely on your imagination, keep your eyes shut through this performance.

The rest you'll be effectively guided through on the tour. The entry passage, about three feet wide, leads into the **central chamber** where the finest of the work is. Its corbelled roof creates a space some 20ft high, and on the stones everywhere are carved superbly intricate decorations, apparently abstract but perhaps (see above) with some more precise meaning. On the way out, beware the last roof-slab – on which most tall people will graze their heads even after this warning.

Knowth

As with Newgrange, access to Knowth is no longer possible except via the Brú na Bóinne visitors' centre (see p.165). Major excavations have been going on at the Knowth site since 1962 and the discoveries there have already surpassed what was excavated at Newgrange, because unlike Newgrange, the site was continuously inhabited until the fourteenth century, and archeologists have been able to explore four distinct phases of settlement. Because of the excavation work it is only possible to visit the exterior of the site.

Several periods of occupation by different cultures have been identified, from the **Neolithic**, when the original passage tombs were built (3000–2000 BC), through occupation by the Beaker people (2000–1800 BC), so called because of a distinctive beaker left with each of their dead, a late **Celtic** settlement in the early centuries AD, early **Christian** occupation (eighth to twelfth centuries) and finally **Norman** usage (twelfth and thirteenth centuries) that brought an extensive settlement and a glut of souterrains (underground passages and chambers), some bored into the Neolithic mound itself. The main passage tomb is about twice the size of that at Newgrange – with a tunnel over 100ft long leading to the central chamber – and even more richly decorated. At Knowth there is also, so far uniquely, a second, smaller passage tomb within the main tumulus, and up to seventeen **satellite tumuli**. Both main tombs are aligned east–west. In construction the mound is basically the same as Newgrange, with a cruciform chamber, high corbelled roof and richly decorated stones, but here there is also evidence of settlement around the mound. Probably the two were created by two distinct communities of the same culture: a supposition backed by carbon dating that places the Knowth mound some 500 years earlier than Newgrange. At Knowth alone, about 250 decorated stones have been found: over half of all known Irish passage grave art. The most recent discovery is a series of large post-holes arranged in a circle, suggesting the existence of some form of wood-henge.

Slane

SLANE village itself, set on a steep hillside running down to the Boyne a mile or so west of Knowth, is an enchanting little place which packs a surprising amount of interest. The scene is set at the village centre, where four three-storey eighteenth-century houses stand at the four corners of a crossroads, each virtually identical (with arched entrance courtyards to the side) and built of rough-cut grey limestone. The story goes that they were built by four spinster sisters who wanted to keep an eye on one another's comings and goings.

Down by the river, the Georgian theme is continued in the fine **mill**, built in 1766, across the road from which stands a large Gothic gate to Slane Castle, whose lands stretch out westward along the river. **Slane Castle** suffered an enormous fire in the spring of 1992 and is strictly out of bounds to the public. Some restoration work is underway, but money is short and the place is unlikely to open to the public again for several years. During the reconstruction period, the owners have appealed to tourists not to enter the grounds at all, for their own safety. Approximately once a year, however, the castle does open its gates to half of young Ireland for massive, open-air rock concerts promoted by the entrepreneurial Lord Henry Mountcharles, who has a warm relationship with Ireland's rock business – including U2, who recorded *The Joshua Tree* in one of the rooms at Slane. The only other way of getting a glimpse of the castle grounds is to go the tiny **nightclub** held in the castle basement every Saturday night (☎041/982 4207). On a more traditional level, the castle is the seat of the **Conyngham family** and is a classically ordered mass of mock battlements and turrets with a neo-Gothic library. The best architects of the day – Wyatt, Johnston and Gandon – were involved in the design, and the grounds were laid out by Capability Brown. Inside, there's a substantial art collection and many mementos of King George IV, who is said to have spent the last years of his life involved in a heady liaison with the Marchioness Conyngham: some claim that this relationship accounts for the exceptionally fast, straight road between Slane and Dublin. Further out in the castle grounds, and not for public consumption beyond a glimpse from the river towpath, is **St Erc's Hermitage**. Lord Mountcharles recently gave this to the nation, but it will be some time before it opens to the public.

The Hill of Slane

Walking north from the crossroads, uphill, you can climb to the top of the **Hill of Slane**, where **St Patrick** lit his Paschal Fire in 433 AD, announcing the arrival of Christianity. This was in direct defiance of Laoghaire, High King of Tara, who had ordered no fire-making until Tara's own hillside was set alight. Fortunately for St Patrick, Laoghaire was promptly converted, welcoming the new religion throughout the country. The summit commands magnificent views of the whole Boyne Valley. Near the top, the ruined **Friary Church** (1512) and separate college building are worth investigating. The church has a well-preserved **tower**, with a very narrow and steep flight of sixty-odd steps: if you make it up you're rewarded with a broad panorama of the eastern counties, though Slane itself is all but hidden from view. In the graveyard there is a very unusual early Christian tomb with gable-shaped end-slabs. This is supposed to be the final resting place of **St Erc**, Patrick's greatest friend and servant whom he made Bishop of Slane. The **college** was built to house the four priests, four lay-brothers and four choristers there to serve the church; assorted pieces of carved stonework can be found if you mooch round its ruins.

Practicalities

Slane has an exceptionally friendly tourist office on Main Street (April–Oct daily 9am–6pm; Nov–March Mon–Fri 9.30am–5pm; ☎041/982 4010). B&B accommodation is offered at *Castle Hill House* at 2 Castle Hill (☎041/982 4696; ②) and *Boyneview* (☎041/982 4121; ③), one of a row of stone cottages overlooking both the river and the grandiose entrance lodge of the castle. Handily placed just opposite the tourist office, the *Conyngham Arms Hotel* (☎041/982 4155; ⑤) also serves reasonably priced lunches and evening **meals**. Inexpensive food is also served at *Ye Olde Coffee Shop*, Main Street. You can get to Slane by bus from Dublin; the journey takes forty-five minutes.

The Ledwidge Museum

A mile or so east out of Slane is the **Francis Ledwidge Museum** (daily: April–Sept 9am–1pm & 2–7pm; Oct–March closes 4.30pm; £1). This stone-built labourer's cottage was the birthplace, in 1887, of the local poet Francis Ledwidge, who died on a battlefield in Flanders on July 31, 1917. His poems were written on a small scale, and the museum reflects this: a modest, almost spartan house with the poetry daintily hung in miniature picture frames. The lines inscribed on a stone plaque outside the cottage were written when Ledwidge heard of the death of his Irish poet friend Thomas MacDonagh, who was executed by the British for his involvement with the Easter Rising of 1916: it's an echo of MacDonagh's own poetic translation of Cathal Buidhe's *Mac Giolla Ghunna* (The Yellow Bittern):

He shall not hear the bittern cry
In the wild sky, where he is lain,
Nor voices of the sweeter birds
Above the wailing of the rain.

There's a fine parallel to this in the poet Seamus Heaney's *In Memoriam Francis Ledwidge*:

> *I think of you in your Tommy's uniform,*
> *A haunted Catholic face, pallid and brave,*
> *Ghosting the trenches with a bloom of hawthorn*
> *Or silence cored from a Boyne passage-grave.*

Upstream to Navan

In its course upstream to Navan, the **Boyne** runs past the grounds of several great houses. You can't visit any of them, but if you follow the river – a distance of some eight miles from Slane to Navan – you get a real sense of an all but vanished world. The old towpath switches sides from time to time, with no obvious means of crossing: the solution to this apparent mystery is that the horse would step onto the barge and be poled across to the other side. It is just about possible to walk all the way if you're prepared to crash out your own path some of the time, but it's a great deal easier to walk as far as you can from this end, then travel to Navan by road and do the same from the other end. After Slane Castle itself, on the opposite side of the river, comes **Beauparc House**, the mid-eighteenth-century mansion also owned by Lord Mountcharles.

A little further on you pass the remains of **Dunmoe Castle** (signposted off the N51, but accessible from there only by a nightmarish potholed lane), high on the northern bank. All that remains are two sides of a four-storey castle which was square in shape with large rounded turrets at the four corners. Inside you can still see parts of the vaulted ceilings of the lower storeys. Better than the crumbling structure, though, are the views it commands: in the river a diagonally dividing weir breaks the water into a stretch of rapids and another of calm, while on the opposite bank, there's a delightful red-brick mansion with a stretch of garden steps worthy of Versailles breaking through the wooded thickets to reach the river. Finally, shortly before Navan and right by the side of the main road, you pass the **Domhnach Mór** (Great Church), site of a superbly preserved round tower above whose arched doorway is carved a relief figure of Christ.

Navan

At **NAVAN** the **River Blackwater** meets the Boyne. It's an historic crossroads – important in the days when the waterways were the chief means of transport – and also a modern one. The N3 comes up from Dublin to follow the course of the Blackwater to Kells and to the Loughcrew Mountains in the northwestern corner of Meath; the N51 arrives from Drogheda to continue into Westmeath, its interest diminishing rapidly as you go; and to the south you can take the N3 to Tara (see p.176), Dunsany and then go eastwards on minor roads to Bective Abbey and Trim (see p.179).

Although it offers access to a lot of places and has a **tourist office**, located behind the local library on Railway Street (Mon–Sat 10am–5pm, Sun 10am–1pm; ☎046/215181), Navan itself has little to detain you. There are a couple of hotels here and a number of fairly simple B&Bs not far away, should you wish to **stay**, such as *Tower View*, on the Slane Road at Donaghmore (☎046/23358; ②) *Dunlair House*, Old Road (☎046/72551; ③) or the excellent *Athlumney Manor* (☎046/71388; ③), less than a mile out of town on the Duleek Road. A good upmarket option is the modern *Newgrange Hotel* on Bridge Street (☎046/73732; ⑥) which has a fine restaurant with main courses at around £13. You'll find a good cheap **lunch** at *Susie's Cookhouse*, centrally placed on the Market Square, or at *Bon Appetit*, on the square at the corner of Ludlow Street, and there's a nice quiet **pub** nearby, the *Bermingham Bar* opposite the cinema on Ludlow Street. *Peter Kavanagh's* on Trimgate Street is another good, old-fashioned pub, and there are **traditional music** sessions every Wednesday and poetry readings once a month in the *Lantern*, Watergate Street. *Molloys* on Bridge Street, opposite the infirmary, hosts traditional-music sessions on a Thursday.

Athlumney Castle

One local sight worth going out of your way for is **Athlumney Castle**, about a mile's walk from the centre of town – head over the bridge, then turn first right following the signs. Just as you come up to the ruin, veer right into **Loreto Convent** (once the castle's outbuildings) where you can pick up the keys. In the convent grounds you should immediately spot the twelfth-century motte (now surrounded by a ring of trees) that would have had a *Bretesche*, or wooden tower, built on it. This was purely defensive, and the owner would actually have lived closer to the river.

The castle you see now is a fifteenth-century tower house to which a Jacobean manor house was added in the early seventeenth century. The **Tower House** has four floors in excellent condition, the first of which has a secret chamber down the stairs in the wall. The last occupant of the mansion was Sir Lancelot Dowdall, a Catholic who on hearing of the defeat of James II decided to set his home alight rather than see it fall into the hands of William's army. According to the story, he crossed the river and stood all night watching it burn before heading into permanent exile. The interior shows large gaping fireplaces and a horseshoe stone-oven on the bottom floor which would have been the area of the kitchens (the heat from which would rise to warm up the living quarters above). It once had a gabled roof within which the servants were housed, and it still has many impressive mullioned windows as well as a magnificent oriel window overlooking the modern road.

If you head back to the bridge you can take the steps down to the **ramparts**, then follow the canalside all the way to Stackallen, though a certain amount of building work may disrupt your way to begin with. A mile or so northeast of Navan on the Slane Road is a fine 100ft-high round tower at Donaghmore. This stands on an early Christian site, reputedly founded by St Patrick.

Kells and around

Following the Blackwater upstream from Navan, Kells is the obvious place to make for, ten miles up the N3 Dublin–Cavan Road. En route, you'll pass the site of the **Tailteann games** (on the hill above Teltown House), a little over halfway. Here games and ancient assemblies sacred to the god **Lugh** took place in the first days of August (the Irish for the month of August is *Lúnasa*, or *Lughnasa*). As late as the twelfth century the games were still being recorded, and right up to the eighteenth century a smaller celebration took place, in which locals rode their horses across the river for the benefit of the sacred qualities of its waters. Christianity eventually put paid to most of the rituals, but there is still talk of what was known as the **Teltown marriages**, where young couples would join hands through a hole in a wooden door, live together for a year and a day, and then be free to part if they so wished. Today only a very few earthworks remain, and certainly if you have visited Tara, or intend doing so, there's little to be gained in stopping here.

Kells

KELLS itself (*Ceanannus Mór*) is a place of history and monastic antiquities – several high crosses, an eleventh-century oratory, a round tower and an ancient square bell tower – but it is most famous for what is not here, the magnificent illuminated manuscript known as the **Book of Kells**, now housed in Trinity College, Dublin. The **monastery** was founded by St Columba in the sixth century, and from about 807 it became the leading Columban monastery in Ireland, when the monks from the original foundation on the Scottish island of Iona fled here from repeated Viking raids. It is probable that the Book of Kells was actually made on Iona and that they brought it with them when they moved. The new home was little safer than the original one and was attacked time and again by Danes and later the Normans: in the twelfth century the monastic order's headquarters moved on to Derry, and by the time of the Dissolution there was little left to suppress. So most of what you actually see is eighteenth century or later, and although the town's layout still etches out the concentric ridges of the early monastery's plan, it's a surprisingly characterless place. Nonetheless, the little that survives is well worth making the effort to see.

When you arrive, head for the spire of the **bell tower** that stands within the grounds of the modern church where most of the relics are to be seen. In the church itself (if it's not open the key can be got from the gate-lodge outside working hours, otherwise search for the priest) there's a facsimile copy of the Book of Kells, and up in the gallery you'll find a small exhibition of blown-up photos of some of its pages. The **Round Tower** in the churchyard is known to have been here before 1076, for in that year Murchadh Mac Flainn, who was claiming the High Kingship, was murdered within the tower. It's a little under 100ft high, with five windows near the top, and missing only its roof.

Near the tower is the **South High Cross**, the best and probably the oldest of the crosses in Kells, carved as ever with scenes from the Bible. Here you'll see, on the south face, Adam and Eve and Cain and Abel; then the three children in the fiery furnace; then Daniel in the lions' den. On the left arm of the wheel Abraham is about to sacrifice Isaac, and on the right are SS. Paul and Anthony in the desert; at the top is David with his harp and the miracle of the loaves and fishes. There are two other complete crosses in the churchyard, and the stem of a fourth (behind the church back-entrance door) with the inscription *Oroit do Artgal*, A Prayer for Artgal. This has several identifiable panels. The near side shows the baptism of Christ, the marriage feast at Cana, David with his harp again, the presentation in the Temple, and others too worn to make out. On the other side are a self-conscious Adam and Eve, Noah's ark, and others hard to identify accurately. There are sculptured stones embedded in the walls of the bell tower.

St Colmcille's House, probably built by the Columban community, can be found just outside the churchyard walls at the north end – coming out of the main gates take a sharp left uphill, but first obtain the keys from the chocolate-brown house just after the stop sign. It's a beautifully preserved building – thick-walled and high-roofed – and peculiarly in character with the terrace of nineteenth-century workers' houses alongside which it stands. A modern entrance has been broken in at ground level, when originally the door would have been about eight feet off the ground in the west wall (reached, for security, by a removable ladder); you can still see the intended way in round to the left from where you enter now. Inside is a space about 19ft by 16ft, where you emerge into a vaulted room that would have once had two levels (with the present ground floor as a basement). Above were three tiny attic rooms, reached now by a metal ladder, which were probably where the residents slept and also a hideout in times of trouble. Underground tunnels link the oratory and the Round Tower, supposedly running beneath *O'Rourke's* pub on Castle Street.

In the central **market square** there's another fine **high cross**, discoloured by traffic fumes, said to have been placed here by Jonathan Swift. In 1798 it served as the gallows from which local rebels were hanged. Yet again, it is liberally festooned with fine stone carving. The base shows horsemen and animals in a battle scene; on the west face are the adoration of the Magi, the marriage at Cana and the miracle of the loaves and fishes, all surrounding the Crucifixion in the centre of the wheel; on the east are Christ in the tomb, Goliath, Adam and Eve, and Cain and Abel, with Daniel in the lions' den occupying centre stage.

Practicalities

Buses pick up outside *O'Rourke's* lounge in Castle Street – an Expressway bus from Dublin is £8 return and takes around an hour. Kells' **tourist office** is in Headfort Place behind the town hall. For **accommodation**, the *Headfort Arms* hotel (☎046/40063; ⑤) at the beginning of the Dublin Road is a reasonable choice. Kells' independent **hostel** (IHH; ☎046/40100) is part of *Monaghan's* pub, at the top of Garrick Street, a steep street of pastel-coloured flat-fronted houses that leads out of the centre of town. You'll get very tasty **food** during the day at *Penny's Place*, a café/lunch room at the bottom end of Market Street (closes 6pm), but in the evenings there's not much choice outside the pubs. *Magee's* on Farrell Street serves fine snacks, but otherwise good **pubs** are surprisingly scarce. One that's definitely worth a visit, however, is *O'Shaughnessy's* on Market Street (running along the bottom of the church plot), which has Irish ballads and old-time music on Friday, Saturday and Sunday nights at 9pm. The song *The Isle of Inishfree* was actually written there by D. Farley, the former owner who was also once superintendent at Dublin Castle.

The Castlekeeran crosses

From Kells the N3 follows the Blackwater northwest into County Cavan. A considerably more interesting route takes the Oldcastle Road or R163 (the one that passes alongside the round tower) towards the Loughcrew cairns (see overleaf). Only a mile out of Kells a very worthwhile short detour takes you up a winding road to the right that leads, after about another mile, to the **Castlekeeran crosses**. Entry is signposted through the yard of a creamy-orange farmhouse and across a field which will take you into the old monastery enclosure.

Hardly anything of the monastery known as **Díseart Chiaráin**, the Hermitage of Ciaran, has survived, although you can pick out a partially earth-covered arch. The high crosses here, three of them plus a fourth in the middle of the river, are older than those at Monasterboice and Kells and far simpler. But their greatest charm lies in the fact that you'll probably be quite alone as you contemplate their history. The only decoration on the crosses are some simple fringing patterns and boss protruberances in the "armpits" and tops and wheel centres. The story of the cross in the River Blackwater tells how St Columba was caught red-handed by St Ciaran as he carried the cross off to his own monastery. In his shame he dropped the cross where he stood and fled back to Kells.

There is also an **early Christian grave slab** in the graveyard, and a very good example of an **Ogham stone**. Ogham was an early Irish script which was widely used from around the fourth to the seventh century AD, after which it was very gradually replaced by Latin script. Even at the height of its popularity Ogham co-existed with Latin writing: it was used primarily on stones and monuments such as this, while Latin script was found in manuscripts. It is thought that the script was once used for secret communication, part of a signalling or gesture system for magical or cryptic purposes; it can also be found in parts of Devon, Wales and Scotland. As late as the nineteenth century some isolated peasant communities still used Ogham script if they needed to write anything down – it had the advantage that no one from outside would be able to interpret it. On stones like this, the edge is used to help define the characters. Five strokes above the line give you five letters; five below another five letters. Five strokes that cross the line make five more letters and five oblique strokes five more: to these a few less obvious symbols are added to make up the alphabet. The inscription here apparently reads *cov-agni maqi mucoi luguni*, but although the letters can be made out nobody seems to know what these words actually mean.

Sliabh Na Caillighe

SLIABH NA CAILLIGHE, the Mountain of the Sorceress (910ft), is the highest part of the **Loughcrew Mountains**, whose two-mile east–west stretch virtually cuts off the furthest tip of County Meath. From the top there's a wonderfully disparate view, with the Cavan lakelands in one direction and the undulating flow of earthy Meath in the other, blending in the far distance into the mountains of Wicklow and Slieve Bloom. Three major groupings of **Neolithic cairns** were constructed on these summits, no doubt chosen to be seen from afar. The first group (coming from the east) is known as the **Patrickstown Cairns** and has been so thoroughly despoiled, largely for building material in the nineteenth century, that no significant trace remains. The other two summits have one major cairn each: **Cairn T on Carnbane East** and **Cairn L on Carnbane West**. Each of these has a handful of satellite mounds, though these represent only a fraction of what must once have been here. The sites are not easy to get to – you'll need transport and still face a hefty walk at the end – but they are well worth the effort. Little known as they are, the Loughcrew cairns are almost as impressive as the Newgrange mounds (certainly when you take into account the sheer number) and you'll almost certainly be free to explore them entirely alone, and with as much time as you want. Bring a torch if you want to appreciate what lies inside.

The Oldcastle Road runs beneath the northern flank of the mountains, and about four and a half miles before Oldcastle you'll see a broken signpost pointing off to the left, to *Sliabh Na Caillighe*. Follow this road for a mile and then take the right turn (signposted) that clearly heads towards the hill complex. In the first bungalow on the right you will be able to get the loan of keys from the Balfe family (buy a leaflet plan off them for 20p, and to be sure of finding someone in – or if you want to be there for sunrise – ring ahead to arrange to pick up the keys, ☎049/854 1256; a deposit of sorts is required). These open the iron grilles on the few major cairns on top of the hills; the minor ones have either been deroofed or are left open. Alternatively, Sarah Keogh gives guided tours of the cairns in English, Irish, French and German; call to make an appointment (June–Sept ☎046/43635; £3). She also runs tours of the Seven Wonders at Fore (see p.186; a ticket for both, £5).

Carnbane West

Half a mile up the road – a steep climb – you'll come to a small clearing where a stile leads into a field: this path heads to the **Carnbane West** grouping. On your way across you'll notice **Cairn M** off to your left on a high peak – except for its astronomical involvement with Cairn L, this hasn't much of interest and it's not really worth the hike. **Cairn L**, with its wide ring of kerbstones, should be obvious to you immediately. It was most recently explored by Martin Brennan in 1980, after years of relative neglect by archeologists; it is his astronomical theories which are in part set out below: they are far from being generally accepted, but in the absence of other explorations they do at least attempt to answer some of the questions about the sites.

Cairn L has an asymmetrical chamber unique among the Loughcrew cairns, with a white **standing stone**, over six feet high, positioned at the back right. It is probable that the mound was built as a majestic housing for this one special stone. According to Brennan its function is found in the rising sun on the cross-quarter days November 8 and February 4 (the days halfway between the solstices and the equinoxes). On these days a flash of light enters the tomb from the rising sun at about 7.40am and catches the top of the standing stone. The lower edge of the light is formed by the shadow of Cairn M, and other standing slabs in L further shape it so that the ray marks out only the standing stone. If you have a torch, then study the decorated slab by the basin to the left of the stone, facing away from the entrance. There are many designs carved into the various stones, but at the bottom of this one, according to Brennan, you can see a pictorial representation of this astronomical event.

Brennan sees **Cairn H** as a warning of the November cross-quarter day. The rising sun begins to penetrate its chamber from mid-October onwards, with the backstone being touched come November, and then from about the third onwards the sun leaves Cairn H and moves on to Cairns M and L for November 8. **Cairn F**, with several examples of decorative grooves, kicks off another alignment series. The sun begins to enter in late April, ready to mark another cross-quarter day on May 6, when the rays of the setting sun centre on **Cairn S**. Cairn S is also aligned for the final cross-quarter day, August 8. By August 16 they enter F again, and from there move on to **Cairn I** to warn of the autumn equinox. If Brennan's theories are correct (critics tend to claim that if you look long enough, and pick enough times and days, you can prove almost anything this way), then cairns I, T, F and S form the longest such sequence of alignments known.

Carnbane East

To get to **Carnbane East**, return to the hill road and carry on until you reach a large car-parking space where a path leads up the hill to the mounds. If you lose the path, which is vague at times, just keep climbing steeply, steering left if there's any doubt: towards the top follow the barbed wire round and enter by the kissing gate which will put you on the threshold of Cairn T. At Carnbane East Brennan sees three mounds functioning as solar dials. **Cairn T** deals with the spring and autumn equinoxes (March 23 and Sept 22). In its cruciform chamber is a large backstone liberally patterned with chevrons, ferns, petals and moon and sun signs. At the spring equinox a shaped patch of light passes across a passage stone and various of the other designs to focus on the large radial sun sign in the centre of this stone. At the autumn equinox the sun makes a more leisurely progress, rising at about 7.11am, and strikes the backstone just over half an hour later. Once again it crosses the sunwheel emblem. Of the satellite mounds, neither of which has a roof any more, **Cairn S** is said to mark the cross-quarter days on May 6 and August 8, while **Cairn U** is synchronized with Cairn L to mark November 8 and February 4. Cairn S has lots of sun emblems, while Cairn U has a variety of more unusual (and less identifiable) markings. Whatever you make of Brennan's theories in the end, he has at least opened an important new area of exploration; and in the undeniable light of Newgrange's connection with the equinox there are few people any more who would contend that these structures were simply tombs and nothing more.

Oldcastle

OLDCASTLE is a mild-natured, genially ramshackle eighteenth-century town, built around a crossroads. Set in sheep country, it was once the largest yarn market in Ireland, but no longer seems to have much significance. You can get **lunch** at the *Naper Arms Hotel* in the square, and there's traditional music at weekends in the *Céilí House Bar* – but there's not much else to do. The nearest **B&B** (☎049/854 1904; ②) is a mile and a half away on the Kells Road. Three miles out of town (take the Castlepollard Road and turn left at the garage) stands the family church of the (Oliver) Plunketts. Their estate was given by Cromwell to one of his soldiers, named Naper, in payment of salary arrears. You can **stay** in the present-day Charlie Naper's *Loughcrew House* (☎049/854 1356; ⑤).

In terms of interest, you're better off heading on to Castlepollard, ten miles south in County Westmeath (p.185), from where you can explore the Fore Valley, Tullynally Castle and the sights around Lough Derravaragh.

Tara and around

South from Navan down the Dublin–Navan Road, there's a trio of places well worth seeing; the first is one of the most famous historic and mythical sites in Ireland, **Tara** and its eponymous hill. Moving south again is **Dunsany Castle**, where you'll find an interesting art collection. Not far west of the castle, the remains of **Bective Abbey** are beautifully located on the River Boyne and make a pleasant stop on the way to Trim (the R161 from Navan to Trim is just by the abbey).

Tara

TARA, the home of the High Kings of Ireland and source of so many of the great tales, looks nowadays like nothing so much as a neatly kept nine-hole golf course: a gently undulating swath of green marked out by archeological plaques. To re-create the palace, whose wood-and-wattle structures have entirely disappeared, leaving only scars in the earth, takes a fair degree of imagination. But it's an effort worth making, for this was a great royal residence, already thriving before the Trojan Wars and still flourishing as late as the tenth century AD. The origins of the site are lost in prehistory, but it probably originally had a religious significance, gradually growing from the base of a local priest-king to become the seat of the High Kings. Its heyday came in the years following the reign of the legendary Cormac Mac Art in the third century AD – when five great highways converged here: this was a ritual, rather than a residential, centre – and by the time of the confrontation of St Patrick with King Laoghaire in the fifth century, its power was already declining. The title of High King was not, on the whole, a hereditary one: rather the kings were chosen, or won power on the battlefield. So they were not necessarily local – or even permanently based here – but all evoked the spirit of Tara as the basis of their power.

In later history, there was a minor battle at the site during the 1798 revolution, and in the mid-nineteenth century **Daniel O'Connell** held a mass "Monster" meeting – said to have attracted as many as a million people (a quarter of Ireland's population today) – as part of his campaign against union with Britain.

You'll find the **site** signposted just off the N3; from the car park it appears as a wild meadow on a table-top hill, no more than 300ft above the surrounding countryside (just beside the car park is the *Banquet Hall Café*, open daily 9.30am–6pm). There is a plan of the place near the entrance, which will help you to identify the various mounds. The path to the site leads through the yard of the old Church of Ireland church, which is now used as a **visitor centre** (May to mid-June 9.30am–5pm; mid-June to mid-Sept 9.30am–6.30pm; mid-Sept to Oct 10am–5pm; £1.50), with a romantic but reasonably sophisticated audio-visual show that gives some background to Tara's history and also, more valuable, shows a number of aerial views that do a lot to make sense of the design. The **church** itself, dated 1822, is a modest grey building typical of the Anglican churches found all over Ireland; somehow it seems fitting that it should find a role participating in the re-enhancement of a more ancient landscape that its builders once attempted to dominate. The church's only remarkable feature is a bright stained-glass window by the well-known Dublin artist Evie Hone, which was installed in 1935 to commemorate the 1500th anniversary of the visit of St Patrick to the site and thus the coming of Christianity to Ireland. St Patrick challenged the then High King at Tara, Laoghaire, by lighting his paschal (Easter) flame on the nearby Hill of Slane in response to the holy fire at Tara – thereby demonstrating the ritual sympathies of the new religion with the old. Once you are on top of what is actually very rich pasture, the power of the setting immediately becomes clear, with endless views that take in whole counties and their patchwork fields, and a huge sky.

The "Banquet Hall"

Teach Miodhchuarta ("Banquet Hall") is on the northern hill slope and consists of two parallel banks between which runs a long sunken corridor. Its length is about 750ft and the breadth 90ft. An account of it in the medieval book known as the *Dinnshenchas* reads:

> *The ruins of this house are situated thus: the lower part to the north and the higher part to the south; and walls are raised about it to the east and to the west. The northern side of it is enclosed and small; the lie of it is north and south. It is in the form of a long house, with twelve doors upon it, or fourteen, seven to the west, and seven to the east. It is said that it was here the* Feis *Teamhrach was held, which seems true; because as many men would fit in it as would form the choice part of the men of Ireland. And this was the great house of a thousand soldiers.*

Easy as it is to imagine the five ancient highways thronged with people on their way to crowd the hall for the great *Feis*, all this is now known to be fantasy. There was no banqueting hall, and the meaning of the banks remains unclear; they may perhaps have been part of a ceremonial entrance to the site.

Gráinne's Fort and the Sloping Trenches

Northwest of the hall is a smaller group of earthworks, the first of which is **Ráth Gráinne** (Gráinne's Fort). It is surrounded by a fosse and bank and has a low mound at its centre, probably once a burial mound or maybe a house site. From here the tragic love tale of the *Pursuit of Diarmuid and Gráinne* began its journey, although, as a much later invention, it wasn't originally associated with the mound. Gráinne was the daughter of Cormac Mac Art, who had arranged to marry her to his aged commander-in-chief, Finn Mac Cool. Instead she fell in love with Diarmuid, one of Mac Cool's young warriors, and the two of them fled together, relentlessly pursued by Finn Mac Cool. Their various hiding places lie strewn throughout Ireland, marking practically every geological oddity in the country.

Further west lie the **Claoin-Fhearta**, or Sloping Trenches, created, according to the legend, when Cormac Mac Art as a youth in disguise corrected the judgements of the then king, Lugaid MacCon. (Mac Art was also something of an Irish Solomon figure.) The consequence of his justice was that half the house where the false judgements had been given slipped down the hill, creating the sloping trenches. The southern part of the trenches witnessed the murder of the princesses of Tara, some thirty of them in a massacre whose total casualties were said to have been 3000, by Dúnlaing, King of Leinster, in 222 AD.

The major mounds

South of the Banquet Hall lies the main group of mounds, and first of all the **Rath of the Synods**. This is so called because of the various church synods said to have been held here by SS. Patrick, Brendan, Ruadhan and Adamnan, although little archeological evidence has been found relating to this function. Two gold torques (flat strips of gold soldered and twisted together rope-like into a necklace) were found here in 1810. Much of the rath, however, which appears to have originally been a ring fort defended by three concentric banks, has been destroyed over the years: partly by the graveyard which encroaches on it, but more especially by a group of British Israelites who earlier this century rooted around trying to find the Ark of the Covenant. More serious archeologists have discovered four stages in the rath's construction: in the centre was a flat-topped mound known locally as the **King's Chair**. There were timber palisades on the banks, and in the middle a house where five burnt bodies were found, along with Roman artefacts which suggest trading links between Tara and the Romans in Britain or Gaul.

The **Mound of the Hostages** (*Dumha na nGiall*) is the most prominent of the mounds and also the most ancient. It contained a passage grave to which entrance is now barred, though you can look in to see the markings on the upright slab at the threshold. About forty Bronze Age cremated burials were found inside, many in large urns which were then inverted over the remains. Eating vessels and knives were found with them, and an elaborate necklace of amber, jet, bronze and faience round the neck of a fifteen-year-old boy, the only body not cremated. A wealth of goods from the passage grave culture (carbon dated 2000 BC) were also discovered, making it the most comprehensive find rescued from any tumulus in Ireland. The mound, once again, is associated with Cormac Mac Art: here he is said to have imprisoned hostages taken from Connacht, who subsequently died within the chamber.

The **Ráth na Ríogh** (Royal Enclosure), immediately to the south, is a large area surrounded by a bank and ditch, within which are two earthworks, the **Forradh** (Royal Seat) and **Teach Cormaic** (Cormac's House). Both, though they're not contemporary, are typical ring forts, with a central raised area for a rectangular house – Cormac's has two protective fosses and banks, the Royal Seat only one. In the centre of Cormac's House are a grotesque, lichen-scabbed **statue of St Patrick**, entirely inappropriate to the site, and the **Lia Fáil** (Stone of Destiny), a standing stone moved from elsewhere on the site and re-erected here in memory of those who died in 1798. It is marked with a cross and the letters RIP. According to one tradition this stone was the original Jacob's pillow, brought to Ireland by the Milesians from the Island of Fal. It is also said to be the stone used in the inauguration of the High Kings, which would roar three times to signify its approval of the coronation.

The final remaining rath on the site is named after High King Laoghaire, who made the historic meeting with Patrick when he lit his challenging fire on the Hill of Slane.

For accommodation at Tara, there's a modern bungalow B&B, *Seamróg*, right next to the site (☎ 046/25296; ③).

Dunsany

Dunsany Castle (July & Aug Mon–Sat 9am–1pm) is only a few miles south of Tara, just outside the village of Dunsany. This is still a private residence, owned by the Plunkett family (under the title Lord Dunsany) who have lived here since the sixteenth century. The Lord Dunsany who died in 1957 established a dual reputation as an author; he wrote witty sketches of London clubland and also bizarre dream-fantasy tales that influenced such American writers as H.P. Lovecraft. It's worth going to the trouble of arranging a visit, for this is one of the finest, most thriving examples of an Irish castle you're likely to see, and packed with a wealth of art.

The castle was originally built in the twelfth century by Hugh de Lacy, another of his fortresses defending the Anglo-Norman possessions around Dublin. It has been much altered and added to since, but it's still a magnificent building, with grounds to match. Among the family relics kept here – and quite apart from the superb private art collection and the furniture that you'll see on the tour – are the ring and other reminders of Patrick Sarsfield, second-in-command of the Jacobite forces in Ireland and successful defender of Limerick for over a year, and possessions and a portrait of St Oliver Plunkett, who was hanged in London for treason (his offence: being Catholic). The Dunsanys, in fact, seem to have made a habit of being on the wrong side in Ireland's conflicts, and it's remarkable that they have held on here so long.

Neighbouring **Killeen Castle** belonged to another branch of the Plunkett family (when the estate was divided, the boundaries were supposedly set by a race; the wives of the inheritors ran from their castles, and the border was set where they met), and during the long years of Catholic suppression it was kept in trust for them by the (converted) Protestant Dunsanys.

St Patrick's Cathedral, Dublin

Buskers, Temple Bar, Dublin

Fitzwilliam Square, Dublin

Glendalough, Co. Wicklow

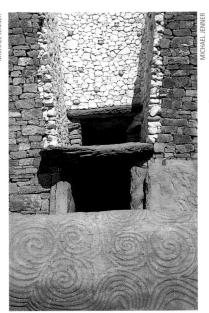

Newgrange (passage tomb), Co. Meath

Bray Head, Co. Wicklow

Practicalities

The **tourist office** is in a glisteningly refurbished Georgian building next to the town's Heritage Centre in Mill Street close to the river (May–Sept; ☎046/37111). For **B&B** try *Brogan's* in the High Street (☎046/31237; ③), also a bar, or *Ms O'Brien's* (☎046/31745; ③). More upmarket accommodation can be found at the *Station House* (☎046/25239; ④), an old cattle-loading bay station six miles or so to the east in Kilmessan, which is almost equidistant from Tara, Bective and Dunsany. If you're hungry, you can get excellent wholefood snacks from the *Salad Bowl Delicatessen* on Market Street, or more substantial **meals** at *Brogan's*, which does a four-course lunch for £5, as well as a range of hefty bar snacks. **Pubs** are as plentiful as ever, but one you should definitely sample is *Marcy Regan's* (see p.180), a tiny, ancient place but remember not to order a pint, for the pub is too old to cope with draught. There is a regular bus service from Dublin to Trim which takes around seventy minutes and costs £7 return.

Around Trim

A couple of miles south of Trim is **LARACOR**, the place where Jonathan Swift lived during his association with Esther "Stella" Johnson and where he was rector (with very little rectitude) from 1699 to 1714. No trace of him, however, remains. Two miles further is **Dangan Castle**, the family home of the Duke of Wellington, now no more than a shell and again with little trace of its past. Ambrosio O'Higgins, father of Bernardo O'Higgins, liberator of Chile, was born here.

Perhaps a more interesting excursion is to the Irish-speaking community at **RATHCAIRN**, near Athboy, eight miles northwest of Trim, where traditional Irish entertainment may well be taking place. The community was uprooted from Connemara by the Land Commission between 1935 and 1940 and replanted here in Meath as a *Gaeltacht*. The population is about 350 and increasing, a unique statistic as most Irish-speaking peoples in their natural habitats are rapidly decreasing in numbers. Not far away, in a field beside the Athboy–Navan Road, is the **Rathmore Church and Cross** (*An Ráth Mhór Teampall agus Cros*). The church was built by the Plunkett family in the fifteenth century, a fine example of the flowering of Irish-Norman culture, with its sympathy towards the native Irish, before the arrival of the Tudor English in the following century, and is full of interesting stone carvings which are worth leaving the road to take a look at. There's an octagonal shaft from a baptismal font, a violated Norman sarcophagus in the fortified tower, a decorated altar stone, the stalk of an ancient cross and other stonework. Note the corbelled roof in the other tower, now trapped as a pigeon-cote.

WESTMEATH AND LONGFORD

As you head west, leaving the Boyne Valley behind, historical interest diminishes rapidly. The attraction of Westmeath lies mainly in its lakes, although in the northeast, around **Castlepollard**, there is an area which deserves more exploration. **Athlone**, in the far west, is an important meeting of the ways near the very heart of Ireland and is a centre for Shannon cruising but, again, it preserves little of interest in itself. Longford, if you visit at all, you'll see only briefly as you pass through on your way to the northwest coast.

The main route into the counties is the N4, following the Royal Canal, and the borders of counties Meath and Kildare, out from Dublin to **Mullingar** and then **Longford town**. As the road enters Westmeath the N6 turns off, to cut across the south of the county to Athlone. If you're coming from Meath, roads from Navan and from Kells converge at Delvin, to run on together towards Mullingar; if you're up by Oldcastle in northwestern Meath, you can cut directly across the border to the most interesting part of Westmeath, the Fore Valley and Castlepollard.

Mullingar and around

MULLINGAR, the chief town of Westmeath, is a raucous, wheeling-and-dealing provincial capital, constantly choked with traffic, that pretty much sums up the things you don't come to Ireland for. It's the centre of a rich cattle-rearing area, and its inhabitants are rural, but the speed and noise of everything is continually wound up by its being a big trading centre on a short lead from Dublin. The first ever **Fleadh Cheoil** (Festival of Music) was held in Mullingar in the late 1960s, but it fell so far short of local expectations that the town has never asked for it back. In short, you're unlikely to fall in love at first sight with Mullingar, but with perseverance you should be able to find a few positive moments before moving on – and there are a couple of good museums.

The first of these, on the corner of the main street at the turn-off to Tullamore, is the **Market House Museum** (July–Sept Mon–Sat 2–5.30pm, at other times ring Paddy Raleigh, ☎044/48152; 50p). Run by local enthusiasts, it doesn't have any one item of outstanding interest (and if it had, it would no doubt be whipped off to the Dublin Museum), but it does have a modest charm in the peculiar wealth of local items on display. There's also the usual quota of Iron Age implements, quernstones and weaponry, together with a potted history of the celebrated local eccentric, Adolphus Cooke (see opposite).

A second museum is attached to Mullingar's **cathedral**, an uninspiring Neoclassical structure whose tapering twin towers – which look like melting candles – you'll be able to spot in the south of town. Inside, behind the side altars of St Patrick and St Anne, are two well-known mosaics by the Russian artist Boris Anrep. To get into the **Ecclesiastical Museum** – whose contents include many wooden penal crosses and the vestments of St Oliver Plunkett – ask for the key at the parochial house, on the right.

The Military Museum

Best of all, however, is the **Military Museum** (☎044/48391) at the Columb Barracks; going southwards, turn right after the bridge over the canal, then swing left and it's 200 yards up on the left, easily walkable. The collection, in the **Old Guard Room**, has a surprisingly broad range of interest. There's all the weaponry you'd expect, of course, with plenty of World War I and II firearms, and uniforms and flags from all over the world. But more intriguing are the sections devoted to the **old IRA**, with various local bands' uniforms and the tunic of Dan Hogan, Chief of Staff after 1929, who was shot by the FBI in 1941. There's also the uniform of Giles Vandeleur, whose role in World War II was portrayed by Michael Caine in the film *A Bridge Too Far*, and a pistol said to be that of **Michael Collins**, who was Chief of Staff throughout the War of Independence and the Civil War – though it's well known that Collins rarely carried a weapon.

More miscellaneous items on display include long, canoe-like boats of bog-blackened oak dredged up from the surrounding lakelands; first thought to be of Viking origin, they have been carbon dated well into the first millennium AD. Similar boats are still being dredged up today, especially in Lough Derravaragh, but are as quickly being wrapped up again in peat and resunk in the middle of the lake. One of the stranger curios is the **military cycling handbook** that was in use until at least 1964. The book instructs the young cadet as to where to put his left foot and where his right and, with even more disciplinary stringency, orders him not to twist the handlebars without the officer's permission. All of this is arranged (or not arranged) amid a fair degree of chaos, though there's usually someone to show you around and attempt to make sense of it all.

Practicalities

The **tourist office** occupies Market House on Pearse Street (daily 9.30am–1pm & 2–5pm ☎044/48650). If you want to **stay** in Mullingar, there are plenty of places to choose from. The best central **B&B** is Gladys Buckley's *Grove House*, Grove Avenue (☎044/41974; ③);

Hilltop (☎044/48958; ③), a mile or so out on the Navan Road, is also good; or you can **camp** at the *Lough Ennell Caravan and Camping Park* (☎044/48101), three miles out on the Tullamore Road. Hotels in town include the *Newbury* (☎044/42888; ⑥), on Main Street, and *Austin Friar's* (☎044/45777; ⑤), on Austin Friar Street. The nearest hostel is just off the N4 road, near the village of Multyfarnham (see p.185).

Good **food** is served in the *Greville Arms* on central Pearse Street (where they also offer slightly more luxurious accommodation; ☎044/48563; ⑥); a wax effigy of James Joyce stands in the foyer, a reminder of a mention of Mullingar somewhere in *Stephen Hero*. There's no shortage of other eating places: *Gallery 29* on Oliver Plunkett Street is probably the best café in town, while *Canton Casey's* café/wine bar on Pearse Street, next to the Market House, has filling portions of spag bol, nachos and baked potatoes at rock-bottom prices; the popular *Oscar's* Italian restaurant, 28 Oliver Plunkett St has a good local reputation, as does *Austin Friar's* hotel restaurant. If you have transport you could consider travelling a little out of town for both food and accommodation; *Woodville House* (☎044/43694; ④) has fine rooms and excellent country cooking (take Lynn Road past the greyhound track and then the first left after O'Brien's garage). A similar standard of accommodation and cuisine are offered at *Crookedwood House*, near the village of Crookedwood (see p.184). Congenial drinking places include *Hughes's* on Main Street, *Caffrey's* on Mount Street, with traditional music sessions, and the more upmarket *Danny Byrne's*, Pearse Street, with good food as well.

Mullingar is on the main Dublin–Sligo railway line, with **trains** accordingly (☎044/48274); **buses** go to Dublin, Sligo, Athlone and Galway.

Around Mullingar

There are a number of minor attractions out from Mullingar; the best of them is **Lough Ennell**, which offers a relaxing mix of aquatic activities and nearby the impressive **Belvedere House and Gardens**.

Cooksborough

COOKSBOROUGH, a hamlet of a few houses strung together about eight miles east of Mullingar on the Delvin Road (N52), might tempt you as a detour before heading south or west. What you're looking for is a tomb in the shape of a beehive in the grave-yard. Neither Cooksborough nor the tomb is signposted but you can find it by looking out for the sign to the *Bee Hive Nite Club*: about thirty yards past this, in the direction of Delvin, enter by an old gate and cross the field to a church and graveyard smothered in bramble, weed and grass. The tomb, which looks like a stone missile warhead poking out of its silo, is that of **Adolphus Cooke** and his nurse Mary Kelly. A famous local eccentric, Cooke was convinced that he would be reincarnated as a bee and he was making sure he was prepared for the event. During his life he was similarly convinced that one of the turkeys scratching around in his yard was his father reincarnated. He also had the windows of his house made into the shape of spoon-backed chairs, in order to reflect the furniture within. There's more information on Adolphus Cooke in the Market House Museum in Mullingar.

Lough Ennell, Kilbeggan, Tyrrellspass and Belvedere House

Lough Ennell, with its low-lying, rushy shoreline, is not an especially dramatic expanse of water, but it is an easy place to go bathing, boating or fishing, especially if you base yourself at the holiday camp, immediately outside Mullingar, or in any of the B&Bs that cluster around the lough – one secluded and rather stately establishment close to the water is *Lynnbury*, a few miles out on the Tullamore Road (☎044/48432; ③). If you do stay here, it's well worth making the short trip to **Belvedere House and Gardens** (May–Oct Mon–Fri noon–4.30pm, Sat, Sun & bank hols noon–6pm; £1), further out on the Tullamore Road just before the turning to the campsite. You're not meant to cut across the fields from the campsite – the way lies across private land – but it does save a lot of walking.

The house was built by **Lord Belfield**, the first Earl of Belvedere, in 1740, and conceived by him as a fishing villa. Much of Belfield's life seems to have been spent feuding with his younger brothers, George and Arthur. In 1736 he married the sixteen-year-old Mary Molesworth, daughter of the third Viscount Molesworth. Within a few years of building Belvedere House he accused her of having an affair with Arthur, and virtually imprisoned her for 31 years at another of his houses. She was eventually released by her son on his father's death in 1774, still protesting her innocence. Meanwhile Arthur had fled to Yorkshire, but when he returned to Ireland in 1759 the earl sued him for adultery and Arthur, unable to pay, spent the rest of his life in jail. An argument with his other brother was responsible for one of the first sights you'll come across in the gardens south of the house, the **Jealous Wall**. This folly is said to be Ireland's largest purpose-built ruin, and was built to block the view of Tudenham House, where George lived, from the earl's own home. Considerable expense went into the construction, including the employment of an Italian architect to design the authentic-looking Gothic facade.

The interior of the **house** is still in the process of renovation, a job which shortage of funds looks certain to make a long one. However, the **rococo plasterwork** of the drawing and dining room ceilings is well worth ducking inside to snatch a look at for a few moments, as is the curved balustrade **staircase** in the entrance recess. Otherwise, the **gardens** are the main attraction. In front of the house three terraces run down to the lake's shore and, behind, woodland stretches along the northeast shore of Lough Ennell. There's also the aforementioned Jealous Wall to see, and a walled garden, gazebo, ice house and stables, where there is a **coffee shop** for refreshments.

Further south at **KILBEGGAN**, and heavily advertised for miles around, is **Locke's Distillery Museum** (April–Oct Mon–Sat 9am–6pm, Sun 10am–6pm; £3). The mill-wheel is still working and the entrance fee now includes a free sample which certainly enhances the tour. The building is suffused with a tantalizing malty smell and there is a small bar that sells some exceptional *uisce beatha* – the Irish for whiskey – which literally means "the water of life"; try either the Locke's single malt or the Connemara single malt for a real treat. The building that looks like a small coal-tip is actually a whiskey warehouse reputedly modelled on a Syrian palace. Recently a restaurant has opened up here serving reasonable food in front of an open fire.

If you need to break your journey on the haul back to Dublin on the N6, you could head for **TYRRELLSPASS** – a tiny cluster of high Georgian and vernacular buildings around a green – just to bask in its delicious prettiness. The *Village Hotel* (☎044/23171; ③), right on the green, is the place to stay. The impressive tower house at the other end of town houses a **museum** and a café that does a range of bar-type lunches for around £4. **St Sinian's**, a Gothic Revival church on The Crescent, has some elaborate Belvedere tombs. One of the simplest commemorates Jane, a countess "gifted with a masculine understanding".

Northern Westmeath

A good portion of the interest of Westmeath lies in the northeast, around the Fore Valley, Lough Lene and Lough Derravaragh. Certainly this is the most beautiful part of the county by some way. It's easily approached from Meath, from the area of Oldcastle and the Loughcrew cairns, or from Mullingar. Coming from Mullingar you'll pass through **CROOKEDWOOD**, near the scenic lower end of **Lough Derravaragh**, set among steep wooded hills that stand out immediately in such flat country. There are two main attractions here: a **restaurant**, *Crookedwood House* (Tues–Sat dinner from £18.50, Sun lunch £12; ☎044/72165; ④), which is far better than you would normally hope to find in such an obscure location (accommodation also offered), and **St Munna's Church**. This beautifully restored fifteenth-century tower-fortified church lies a mile and a half up the road that turns off to the right by the pub; fifty yards before is a butterscotch-coloured bungalow on the left belonging to Seamus O'Simon, who has the key. From the church you can spot a motte on the hill slope, behind which is the Georgian house whose rustic cellar contains the restaurant already mentioned. While in the area, it's worth visiting the village of **MULTYFARNHAM** (*Muilte Farrannáin*, Farrannan's mills) where there is a Franciscan Friary and two excellent pubs, *Weir's* and *Conor Mutagh's*, which have music sessions most weekends. B&B accommodation can be found at the Schoolhouse (☎044/71153; ③); follow the signs out of the village, take a right at the fork and turn left at the T-junction. The nearest hostel is the IHH *Farragh House* (☎044/71466), ideally situated just off the N4 road, overlooking Lough Owel. If you're feeling peckish, the village's restaurant, *An Tintain* ("the fireplace"), has a good menu (main courses around £10).

Castlepollard and Tullynally Castle

Towards the northern end of Lough Derravaragh, **CASTLEPOLLARD** is the most convenient base from which to explore the whole area, handily placed right in the middle of all the attractions. It's not the most exciting of villages, although it clearly sets great store by its picturesqueness, with a vast triangular green surrounded by carefully tended eighteenth- and nineteenth-century dwellings. Many of the visitors are here for the fishing – mainly roach, pike and trout – on Lake Derravaragh, and consequently there are a number of **B&Bs**, of which the *Pollard Arms* is probably the most attractive.

The biggest draw in the immediate vicinity is **Tullynally Castle** (castle daily mid-June to mid-Aug 2–6pm; £3.50; gardens May–Sept; £2; ☎044/61159), whose entrance can be found a half-mile from Castlepollard down the road to Granard (alongside the gable of the *Derravaragh Inn*). From the gatehouse a drive leads across another half-mile of rolling parkland to the castle itself. The home of ten generations of the Anglo-Irish Pakenham family – the Earls of Longford – it's one of the largest and most romantic of castles in Ireland, a vast conglomeration of architectural styles (largely Gothic Revival) with four towers and a long stretch of battlements.

Three hundred years ago the castle was no more than a tower house set amidst the ancient oakwoods which grow around Lough Derravaragh. The park was first laid out, very much along the lines you see today, in 1760 by the first Earl of Longford. His wife founded the family **library** of more than 8000 volumes, which will be in one room on your tour. Their son returned from the French wars to greatly expand the castle to the Gothic designs of **Francis Johnston**, whose work crops up throughout Ireland. The second earl's other claim to fame is to have refused his daughter Kitty's hand in marriage to the young man later to become the Duke of Wellington – they eventually married regardless. One of Kitty's brothers, Edward, fought as Commander-in-Chief of the British Army in America in 1814, and died leading his troops in the attack on New Orleans. His body was sent home pickled in a barrel of rum. In 1840 the third earl added a further 600ft of battlements, a servants' hall for forty, and an immense **Victorian kitchen** which will also make up part of your tour. Later Pakenhams have been less militarily inclined than their forebears: one, Charles Pakenham, forsook the army in the nineteenth century to found the Irish Passionist order of priests; and the present Lord Longford is well known in Britain for his liberal writings and involvement in prison reform.

THE CHILDREN OF LIR

You'll find continually throughout Ireland that physically atmospheric places are the setting for ancient tales or myths, and Lough Derravaragh is no exception. In this case the legend is that of the **Children of Lir** (*oidheadh cloinne Lir*), one of the most tragic of all Irish fables.

Lir had married the daughter of Bodb Derg, King of Connacht. Her name was Aebh and she bore him twins, Fionula and Aodh, and then two more children, Fiachra and Conn. Aebh died and Lir then married her sister, Aoife, who very quickly became jealous of Lir's love for her sister's children. She took them to Lough Derravaragh, and with the help of a druid changed them into swans, condemned to spend 300 years on Derravaragh, another 300 years on the Sea of Moyle, the waters between Ireland and Scotland, and a final 300 on Inis Glóire off Erris Head, County Mayo. In a last-minute pang of remorse she granted them one mercy: that they could have human voices and make the most beautiful music for all humans to hear. When Lir learned of what had happened, in a rage he changed Aoife into an ugly grey vulture. Meanwhile the sons of Bodb Derg, Fergus and Aed, set out to search for the Children of Lir with a host of the *Tuátha Dé Danann*. They eventually found them suffering on the Sea of Moyle, but were helpless to save them from the spell. Left to their destiny the children flew towards Inis Glóire, stopping on the way to search for their father's palace on the plains of Armagh, but finding that only earth mounds remained as they were now 600 years on in their own lives. At the end of the allotted span they died, finally returning to a very aged human form for their last few breaths, and were buried at the onset of the Christian era on Inis Glóire.

In the grounds in front of the castle, a **Garden Walk** leads to a spacious demesne on the left, and the flower garden, River Sham pond and walled gardens off to the right. Passing further to the right, between two stone sphinxes, is the **kitchen garden**, one of the largest in the country and still resplendent with its row of Irish yews. Slightly further afield, the most rewarding walk of all is a forest path which takes you around the perimeter of the spearhead-shaped demesne, with excellent views back onto the castle.

The Fore Valley

East of Castlepollard towards the Meath border, the **Fore Valley** is an area of exceptional natural beauty. It's easy hiking country with a wealth of small-scale interest, especially in the **Seven Wonders of Fore**. There are moves afoot to convert these into some kind of tourist trail, but so far there are few visitors, and the local tradition, strengthened by an early Christian legacy in stone, still seems close to the surface. The wonders are all based on ordinary things which you can find in the valley, and in this perhaps lies the lasting strength of their reputation. They are: the water that will not boil; the wood that will not burn; the monastery built on a quaking sod; the mill without a race; the miraculous emplacement of the lintel stone above the door of St Fechin's Church; the water that flows uphill; and the Anchorite's Cell in the Greville-Nugent family vault.

The village of **FORE** sits at the eastern end of the valley and is the best place to start, discovering the wonders as you walk west. There's a tiny ancient cross on the tiny village green, once part of a stations of the cross, and a couple of pubs are worth visiting. You'll need to pop into the *Seven Wonders* anyway to pick up the key for the **Anchorite's Cell**: the *Abbey* next door has seven old murals depicting the wonders, worth contemplating over a pint. There's usually plenty of ready advice in here for anyone planning to head down the valley; for a guided tour contact Sarah Keogh (see p.174 for details).

If you want to base yourself here for some gentle rambling, there's B&B **accommodation** available nearby at *Hounslow House* (April–Oct ☎044/61144; ③), which is well signposted.

The Seven Wonders

On the valley plain you'll immediately spot the ruined Benedictine priory built on reclaimed bogland (the third wonder), and en route to it you'll pass the first two. The **wood that will not burn** consists of a dead branch of a tree, landscaped into a viewing spot as part of the creation of the tourist trail (from the picture in the *Abbey* pub you'll remember it looking more lively than this); the idea of piercing its bark with coins is also a recent invention. The **well of unboilable water** is handily close by.

The **priory** itself was founded by the De Lacys around 1200, and its remains are the most substantial reminder of the Benedictine Order left in Ireland. It was fortified in the fifteenth century; the towers also served as living quarters. There's a plan in the cloister of the various periods' additions, and some subtly sensitive restoration has been undertaken so that although it's very much a ruin, there's a strong monastic feel to the walls and halls. If you intend to ascend the **tower** at the chancel end, beware that its spiral staircase seems to wind around the diameter of a dinner plate and above all that the steps finish in midair; it should certainly not be attempted in poor light.

On the far hillside from here, the lower of the two buildings is the tenth-century **St Fechin's Church**, which marks the site of the original monastery founded in 630 by St Fechin himself, at one time housing over 300 monks. Note the rare Greek cross on the massive **lintel stone** (which weighs over two tons and was only moved by the miraculous intervention of the saint, hence wonder five), resting on two boulder-sized jambs. Within the ruin is a very weatherbeaten font to your left, a cross slab pinned next to the wall in the chancel at the far end (the chancel was a thirteenth-century addition) and a few other stone slabs, the engravings on which are not clear. From here a ridged path takes you up to the tiny, fortified church known as the **Anchorite's Cell** (wonder seven), decoratively hugged by a low-lying, castellated perimeter wall. The most famous hermit who lived here was Patrick Beaglan, who broke his neck trying to climb out of the window in 1616, thereby fulfilling his vow to stay in the cell till his death. The Romanesque doorway leads into a barrel-vaulted, sandstone interior.

The **water that flows uphill** (wonder six) refers to another of St Fechin's miracles; and the river flowing out of Lough Lene up at the head of the valley does look as if it's flowing upwards. The **mill without a race** (wonder four) is not so easy to trace.

The heart of Ireland: Uisneach to Athlone

As you head west from Mullingar towards Athlone on the R390, you're approaching the middle of Ireland, a spot traditionally identified as the **Hill of Uisneach**. About a mile before Killare (ten miles or so from Mullingar) there are two signposts pointing off the road up to the hill. Follow the second, more westerly one, climb the hill steeply, veering a little to the left, and after crossing a few fields you'll come to the **Catstone** (so called because it resembles the poise of a pouncing cat). More historically known as the *Ail na Mearainn* (the Stone of Divisions), it's a massive boulder (now fragmented a little) set into a circular indentation in the hillside. The stone was said to mark the very centre of Ireland and the division of the five provinces of old. A further and longer walk up the slope will bring you to the summit of a flat-topped hill, barely 250ft above the neighbouring land yet able, on a clear day, to command a view of parts of twenty of the 32 counties of Ireland.

Here, it is recorded, stood the palace of **King Tuathal Techtmar** in the second century AD, and here some claim that the High Kings of Ireland ruled for the two centuries preceding the arrival of St Patrick in 433 AD, when the seat moved back to Tara. On the hill there are two spurs with traces of earthworks, but these are neither easy to find nor to make out if you do, so it's probably easier to accept the history without evidence.

Excavations were made here in the late 1920s, but came up with surprisingly little. No pottery was found, nor any significant trace of permanent occupation. Instead there were great **beds of ashes** which suggested that the place was used for elaborate feasts and ceremonials rather than for defence or peaceful habitation. This accords with the tales of the great pagan festival of *Bealtaine* (Bel's Fire) that was said to be held here in the opening days of the month of May, when vast fires were lit and cattle sacrificed. It was both a religious festival and a market, where traders from the Mediterranean would arrive with their silks and spices in exchange for Irish tools and materials. *Bealtaine*, incidentally, is now the Irish word for the month of May.

As you continue towards Athlone, look out for the tenth-century **Twyford Cross** on a hillside to the left about four miles before you arrive. It was re-erected here after being found sunk in a bog.

Athlone and around

The Hill of Uisneach may be the traditional centre of Ireland, but the busy, apparently thriving, town of **ATHLONE** is a more convincing modern contender. Here, east meets west and north meets south at the midpoint of the River Shannon. This position is its greatest asset, with access by boat upstream to the islands and shores of **Lough Ree** (see p.191), and downstream to the magnificent early Christian site of **Clonmacnois** (see p.139). Either of these trips can easily be done in an afternoon: ask for details at the tourist information office (see p.190).

Not surprisingly, perhaps, given its position, Athlone has quite a history attached, and at least one important legend. The name *Áth Luain*, the **Ford of Luan**, came from (or may perhaps have inspired) the **Snám Dá Én** (Swim of Two Birds), a tale that tells of Estiu, wife of Nár. She had a lover called Buide who used to come and visit her in the form of a bird with his foster-brother Luan. The magic of their song lulled all around to sleep, allowing the lovers to enjoy their trysts undisturbed. Nár, however, questioned a druid about the coming of the birds and on learning the secret he set out for the place on the Shannon (near Clonmacnois) where Buide and Luan could be found and shot both of them with one cast of his sling. Buide was killed instantly, but Luan managed to fly as far north as the ford that marks Athlone today, where he dropped dead from the sky. An alternative derivation of the name comes from the *Táin*, which describes how the remains of the white bull (*Finnbennach*) were deposited throughout the countryside as he died. His loins were left at a place that came to be known as *Áth Luain*, the Ford of the Loins.

In straight historical terms, this ford of the Shannon has always been strategically important. The first castle was erected in 1129 by Toirdelbach Ó Conchobhair, King of Connacht, and replaced in 1210 by the **Norman castle** which, in essence, still stands today. It saw action many times, above all in the seventeenth century in the Cromwellian Wars and the Jacobite invasion. The former put a swift end to the predominantly Catholic nature of the town, placing most of the land and political power in the hands of Protestants. The later battles of 1690–91 saw probably the most vicious fighting in the **War of the Kings**, as the Williamites captured first the Leinster part of town and, after 12,000 cannonballs had reduced much of it to rubble, the Connacht side.

The Town

The few really distinguished old buildings that survive – the castle apart – can be found off Church Street in the **Court Devenish** area. Finest of them is **Court Devenish House**, a seventeenth-century Jacobean mansion now resting ruined in private grounds. Nearby the ruins of the likewise seventeenth-century **abbey** offer perhaps the most peaceful spot in town. There's an intriguing corridor of tombstones leading off the Abbey Road into its graveyard.

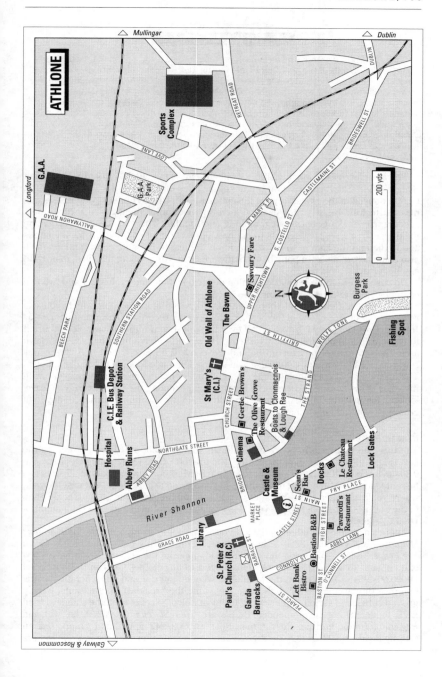

ATHLONE

△ Mullingar
△ Dublin
△ Longford
▽ Galway & Roscommon

DUBLIN ROAD
BRIDESWELL ST
RETREAT ROAD
LOVE LANE
BALLYMAHON ROAD
BEECH PARK
SOUTHERN STATION ROAD
CASTLEMAINE ST
S. COSTELLO ST
ST MARY'S PL
UPPER IRISHTOWN
GRIFFITH ST
WOLFE TONE
THE STRAND
NORTHGATE STREET
CHURCH STREET
ABBEY ROAD
GRACE ROAD
BARRACK ST
PEARCE ST
CONNOLLY ST
BASTION ST
O'CONNELL ST
ABBEY LANE
HIGH STREET
FRY PLACE
CASTLE STREET
MAIN ST
MARKET PLACE
BRIDGE

G.A.A.
Sports Complex
G.A.A. Park
Hospital
C.I.E. Bus Depot & Railway Station
Abbey Ruins
Old Wall of Athlone
The Bawn
Savoury Fare
St Mary's (C.I.)
Gertie Brown's
The Olive Grove Restaurant
Boats to Clonmacnois & Lough Ree
Cinema
Castle & Museum
Sean's Bar
Docks
Le Chateau Restaurant
Lock Gates
Pavarotti's Restaurant
Bastion B&B
Left Bank Bistro
Library
St Peter & Paul's Church (R.C)
Garda Barracks
River Shannon
Burgess Park
Fishing Spot

N

0   200 yds

SHEILA NA GIG

Sheila na Gig sculptures (the term itself is thought to be a corruption of the Gaelic *síla na gcíoch* – "Sheila of the teats") are nude female figures, generally represented face on with their legs splayed and hands placed behind the thighs, the fingers opening grossly oversized vulva. They were thought to be either the symbol of a fertility cult or used to ward off the evil eye, though quite how they managed the latter is not explained. They mainly appear in the walls (usually near the main entrance door) of castles and churches, built between 1200 and 1600. To a lesser extent they are also found in round towers and on standing stones, bridges etc. They are also known in other parts of the British Isles, and even France, but the majority of them by far are in Ireland.

The one place really worth visiting, if only briefly, is the **castle museum** by Market Square (Mon–Sat 10am–4.30pm; the ticket includes entrance to the Visitors' Centre, £2.50), housed in the two storeys of the circular keep. On the upper storey is a section devoted to **folk history**, an Aladdin's cave of rustic implements used in threshing, seeding, ropemaking, harnessing, milking and the like. There's a beautiful article on milking, telling how a few squirts were always dropped first on the grass for the fairies and at the end the sign of the cross made on the teat to bless its consumption. You'll also come across a pair of pony boots that were used when rolling the lawn, to prevent any hoof marks.

Downstairs is a more regular collection on local history and prehistory and two fine examples of **Sheila na Gig** sculptures.

On a quite different level there's an old 78rpm gramophone on which you can request your choice of one of the best lyric tenors ever recorded. The gramophone was John McCormack's own, travelling all over the world with him so that he could use it to test out the quality of his new releases. He is said to have been born in the Bawn area, the old market quarter behind Devenish Gate Street, and in 1928 he was rewarded for his work for Catholic charities by being made a Count of the Papal Court. The one song that even the youngest generations in Ireland are able to associate with his voice is his *Panis Angelicus* – the record may be among the pile. Before you leave, look out for an early Christian grave slab with carvings as beautifully ornate as any high cross that you're likely to have seen.

Practicalities

The **bus** and **train stations** are on Southern Station Road, off Church Street, on the east side of the river, north of the centre. The **tourist office** (May to mid-Oct Mon–Sat 9.30am–5.30pm; ☎0902/94630) is in the castle in Market Square. Boats of all sizes can be rented locally. Much good rod **fishing** can also be done in Athlone, just past the weir, where you'll often see a line of anglers – rent rod and reel from the Strand Tackle Shop in the Strand (£3 per day). **Bike rental** is available from Hardiman's, 48 Connaught St (☎0902/78669).

There's a couple of budget options if you want to stay in Athlone: the IHH *Athlone Holiday Hostel* (☎0902/73399), The Crescent, or the slightly better and bigger *Lough Ree Lodge* (☎0902/76738), on the Dublin Road, opposite the college. If you have a few extra pounds to spend then *The Bastion*, above a trendy clothes shop on Bastion Street (☎0902/94954; ③) is a must; the traditional wooden interior and idiosyncratic decoration give the place a slightly bohemian feel while the breakfast of croissants, freshly ground coffee and various cheeses and fruit is a welcome relief from the standard fried B&B fodder. Other recommended B&B's are *Villa St John* (☎0902/92490; ③) and *Bogganfin House*, both on Roscommon Road (☎0902/94255; ③), and *Cluain Inis* on Galway Road (☎0902/94202; ③). A good bet for lunch or afternoon tea is *Savoury Fare* on Mardyke Street (Mon–Sat), where everything from Turkish flatbread to cheesecake is homemade. The *Left Bank Bistro* on Bastion Street (Mon–Sat; ☎0902/94446), café by day and restaurant by night, serves imaginative, flavoursome Mediterranean dishes at low prices, while *A Slice of Life* on High Street dishes up cheap pasta dishes. In the same street, *Pavarotti's* Italian restaurant has a cosy wine bar (Thurs–Sun 11pm–2am); and there's good lunchtime bar food at *Gertie Brown's*. The new *Olive Grove* restaurant on the east side of the bridge serves excellent food at reasonable prices and if you aren't concerned with cost, investigate the varied menu at *Le Chateau*, in a converted church on St Peter's Port. The best **pub** is probably *Sean's Bar*, tucked away behind the castle and easily identified by its four Ionic columns. It has popular **traditional music** sessions on a Tuesday (pipes and violin), Thursday (violins) and Sunday. You'll find both the **post office** and a **laundry** on Pearse Street.

Lough Ree

If you're taking a trip out to Lough Ree, the islands to ask for are **Inchclearaun** (although this may better be approached from a more northerly point on the lake) and **Inchbofin**. Both islands, especially Inchclearaun, have churches and early Christian grave slabs. Inchclearaun (*Inis Clothrand*) took its name from Clothru, who was murdered by her sister Medb so that she could wed and bed Clothru's husband Ailill and rule Connacht from the island. Medb, goddess of war and fertility, is the most famous of all the legendary and historical characters and a source of continual argument as to which branch of study (legend or history) she truly belongs to. Her life was to end in the waters by the island when Clothru's son Furbaide hurled a piece of cheese from his sling that entered Medb's forehead and struck her dead while she was bathing, thus avenging the murder of his mother.

Goldsmith country

The N55 rushes north from Athlone into **Goldsmith country**, so called after its geographical associations with the works of the eighteenth-century poet, playwright and novelist, Oliver Goldsmith (see overleaf). It's pretty, small-scale countryside, gently rolling and ready-made for cycling through landscaped villages and along aromatic hedge-lined lanes that run off the N55 down to various small boating points on Lough Ree (Killinure, Kileenmore, Muckanagh).

Glassan and around

Ironically enough, **GLASSAN** — identified as "Sweet Auburn", the subject of Goldsmith's celebrated anti-enclosure poem *The Deserted Village* and described as "the village of the roses" — owes its orderly layout of creamy-grey pebbledash cottages to enclosure: it was built by the neighbouring Waterstown estate to provide accommodation for the artisans needed to tend the massive estate with its ten-acre formal garden. The estate was divided by the Land Commission in the 1920s; the house, designed by the eighteenth-century architect Richard Castle, was sold for scrap. As you head north towards Ballitore, there's a profusion of brown "Goldsmith country" signs. Only the front and end walls of Goldsmith's childhood home, the parsonage at **Lissoy**, remain, and still less of the school he attended, or of the "busy mill" that may be the one mentioned in the poem. **Forgney Church**, where Goldsmith's father worked as curate until 1730, was rebuilt in 1810 and is usually locked. Goldsmith's supposed birthplace at **Pallas** has a rather spooky shrine erected by members of the Oliver Goldsmith Society in 1974: a larger-than-life statue of the writer enclosed behind bars in a sort of grotto-prison, as if his poetic spirit is too dangerous to be let out into the world. One wonders what Goldsmith's mocking soul would have made of such funereal pomposity.

OLIVER GOLDSMITH

Best known for his prose, including the comedy *She Stoops to Conquer* and the novel *The Vicar of Wakefield*, **Oliver Goldsmith** (1728–74) was probably born in Pallas, ten miles north of Glassan in County Longford, the son of a Church of Ireland parson; when he was two, he and his family moved to the parsonage at Lisson, just a couple of miles north of Glassan. Goldsmith was also active as a poet, and in travelling through this depopulated landscape, his epic anti-enclosure poem, *The Deserted Village*, helps conjure up the reality of the short-lived heyday of the Anglo-Irish society of which he was a part:

Sweet was the sound, when oft at evening's close
Up yonder hill the village murmur rose;
There, as I passed with careless steps and slow,
The mingling notes came softened from below.

But now the sounds of population fail,
No cheerful murmurs fluctuate in the gale,
No busy steps the grassgrown foot-way tread,
For all the bloomy flush of life is fled.

The poem is a protest against an oppression of the rural poor all over the British Isles, and not just Ireland; whether it can really be traced to Glassan village is uncertain, but its mood of nostalgic regret for a golden childhood past undoubtedly gives it some points of contact with the local landscape. The treasure-hunt for locations mentioned in the poem, all signposted and almost all in ruins, can prove oddly evocative of an absent population – removed not by enclosure but by much more recent economic pressures. The poem also points out some of the internal contradictions of the self-confident Georgian building mania: Goldsmith's lament is for a landscape that disappeared with the building of the great Georgian houses – many of which, like Waterstown at Glassan itself, have now disappeared.

A Goldsmith summer school is held in the area each June. Details from Sean Ryan (☎043/41030 or 46493).

Glassan is probably the best **place to stay** to explore this part of Lough Ree and Goldsmith country. At present, there's little to see of the Goldsmith collection, but an interpretive centre is planned to open in the old school building. There's a scattering of B&Bs – try *Carraun View* in the village (☎0902/85391; ②); and the good, rather elaborate *Village Restaurant* (☎0902/85001), a *Village Inn* and a craft shop that also does teas and sandwiches – in short, a whole range of creature comforts you're unlikely to find further north. Heading back down the road to Athlone you'll find the excellent *Wineport* restaurant on the shores of Lough Ree (open daily from noon in summer, eves only off-season; lunch from £5, dinner from £12.50; ☎0902/85466).

From Glassan, you could do worse than follow the waymarked **Lough Ree tour**, especially if you're cycling. Leaving the village, this takes you down winding lanes for **PORTLICK**, the "local Killarney", set in romantically wooded country and farmland sloping down to the loughside, but without the crowds of Kerry. Portlick's fifteenth-century castle gazes wistfully across the lake, gothically crumbling but still inhabited.

At **KILLINURE**, where there's a spanking new marina, you can rent boats to take you out to the islands of Inchmore or Inchbofin from the local pub *Manto's*, down the road at Killeenmore, which also does B&B (☎0902/85204; ③), with camping and self-catering apartments also available. The *Wineport Sailing Centre*, signposted from the village (☎0902/85466), rents out boats and has a loughside restaurant.

TUBBERCLAIR, a mile up the road offers one of the better panoramic views towards the east of the county. A little further (exactly eight miles from Ballymahon) is the site of the "never failing brook, the busy mill", nowadays no more than a bubbling rivulet, but still easy to identify. The original millstone is now said to be the lintel-stone at the *Three Jolly Pigeons* pub, a quarter of a mile up the road, where the school once stood.

Ballymahon to Lanesborough

Halfway up Lough Ree, Goldsmith Country seeps into **County Longford** through Ballymahon (where his mother lived) and across to Pallas (near Abbeyshrule) where he was born. **BALLYMAHON** is a pretty dull village with an imposingly wide main street, and not somewhere to hang around – aside from a multiplicity of seedy bars, there's nowhere at all to get a meal.

Heading north from Ballymahon to Lanesborough on the N63, you'll pass **CORLEA**. On the edge of the Bog of Allen, it's worth stopping here for the **Corlea Interpretive Centre** (daily May–Sept 9.30am–6.30pm; for winter hours, call the Office of Public Works on ☎01/661 3111 ext 2386; last admission 45min before closing; £2.50), a low, mustard-coloured cruciform building, aligned with a buried *togher*, a trackway of oak planks discovered by turf cutters in 1985. Some of this has been excavated and preserved in an air-conditioned chamber, while the rest still lies beneath the bog. The bog dates from 147 BC, and its construction and the way of life in the bog is examined in a number of displays, while the guided tour includes a walk outside in the bog and a video of the archeological dig.

Alternatively, if you turn off the main road north of Ballymahon (before Corlea) and follow the more minor roads up the lough to the rather nondescript **Newtowncashel**, you'll pass the workshop of the bogwood sculptor Michael Casey, whose raw material is timber many thousands of years old. The wood is dug out of the bog and left for a few years to dry out. On the road north from Newtowncashel to Lanesborough stands **Rakish Paddy's Pub**, worth a visit above all on a Tuesday night for its traditional session: look in for a drink anytime, though, and you can see the three superb modern metal sculptures (by John Mahan) of a seated fiddler, boy and girl dancers and a wooden-flute player evidently playing the well-known reel called Rakish Paddy.

LANESBOROUGH itself, at the head of Lough Ree, is another place to stop off for the boating or fishing (the last bungalow before the bridge has boats for hire) but for no other reason.

Longford

Inland, County Longford doesn't improve, and as far as tourism goes the county is a desert, the half-hearted attempts to promote Goldsmith country notwithstanding. Along with large parts of southern Sligo and Leitrim, Longford has been hard hit by very recent emigration, leaving even the grandest looking houses and mansions deserted by the roadsides. However, if yours is an endlessly indulgent holiday and you have transport of your own, then there are a few things you can catch on your way through. **LONGFORD** itself is a market town that has little to offer beyond convenience as a base. There's a **tourist office** (Mon–Thurs 9.30am–5.30pm, Fri 9.30am–5pm; ☎043/46566) for local information, and if you've time to spare an **ecclesiastical museum** in nineteenth-century St Mel's Cathedral (Mon & Wed 11am–1pm, Sat 1–3pm, Sun 4–6pm). **Accommodation** is plentiful, including the *Longford Arms* on Main Street (☎043/46296; ⑤), which does good food, and numerous B&Bs, especially on Dublin Road, such as *Mrs O'Donnell's* (☎043/41569; ②).

Carriglas Manor

Chief of the surrounding attractions is **Carriglas Manor** (June–Sept Mon, Thurs & Fri 1.30–5pm; Aug same days 1.30–6pm; 40min tours on the hour beginning 2pm; gardens and costume museum cost £2.50 and a visit to the house itself is an extra £3). Situated just three miles out of Longford on the R194 to Granard, it's the seat of the descendants of Huguenot Lefroys. As you go up the avenue, the stables with their classically pedimented and rusticated archways (designed by James Gandon of O'Connell Bridge and Dublin Custom House repute) are on the left. They now house a **costume museum** and tearoom. The yard and buildings are being restored at the moment, but you're free to wander around it and the parkland, within the hours listed above. The costumes in the museum date mainly from the mid-eighteenth century and were found mouldering in trunks in the castle. The castle's architecture is perhaps best described as Tudor-Gothic Revival, and extremely handsome it is, too. It was built in 1837 by Chief Justice Thomas Lefroy, possibly the model for Darcy in *Pride and Prejudice*, as at one stage he enjoyed a romantic liaison with Jane Austen.

The **tour** of the building is directed by the present Lefroys, who are attempting to restore the place to its former majesty. It takes in the dining room, with its set of 1825 Waterford glasses and original ironstone china; the drawing room with its Dutch furniture, one cabinet of which contains an original tea and breakfast set of 1799; a fastidiously well-stocked library; and family portraiture on virtually every wall. All this is explained and expanded on in detail by the present occupier. Carriglas Manor has self-catering apartments in its courtyard that sleep up to five people and cost £50 per night, though you must stay for a minimum of three nights (☎043/45165).

Granard and Edgeworthstown

Continuing on this same road you'll reach **GRANARD**, about fifteen miles from Longford. A famous **harp festival**, originating in 1781, took place here and was revived in 1981. Nowadays it spreads over the second weekend of August, starting on the Friday afternoon with competitions, street entertainment, *seisiúns* and *ceilis*. Lessons on the harp can be arranged on the spot and usually start on the Friday morning. Two **campsites** are set up for visitors, or you can stay at *Houricans Hotel* on Main Street (☎043/86041; ④). The biggest Norman **motte** in Ireland is sited at Granard, with yet another statue of St Patrick on top. The site is said to date back to 5 AD, and to Cairbre, eldest son of Niall of the Nine Hostages.

Finally, it's worth noting a couple of Longford's other literary connections, centred on Mostrim or **EDGEWORTHSTOWN** (about ten miles southeast of Longford town; take the N4), which takes its name from the family name of Maria Edgeworth (1767–1849), who, in her day, was an extremely famous author. *Castle Rackrent*, perhaps her most famous book, was written just before the Act of Union of 1801. Although its caricatures of both the Irish and Anglo-Irish can veer uncomfortably close to stage Irishry, it's a hilariously ironic and oddly prophetic insight into a chaotic Anglo-Irish lifestyle that was disappearing even as she wrote. The town now is little more than a crossroads and **Edgeworthstown House** is used as a nursing home. Maria's father, Richard, was a keen inventor, and the house once boasted central heating and a water pump which dispensed coins to beggars in return for a stint at the handle. The Edgeworth family vault can be seen in the graveyard of St John's Church, on the N4 south to Mullingar. Oscar Wilde's sister Isola is also buried here, and one of his most touching poems, *Requiescat*, was written in her memory:

> *Tread lightly, she is near*
> *Under the snow,*
> *Speak gently, she can hear*
> *The daisies grow.*

> *All her bright golden hair*
> *Tarnished with rust,*
> *She that was young and fair*
> *Fallen to dust.*

Lily-like, white as snow,
She hardly knew
She was a woman, so
Sweetly she grew.

Coffin-board, heavy stone,
Lie on her breast,
I vex my heart alone,
She is at rest.

Peace, peace, she cannot hear
Lyre or sonnet,
All my life's buried here,
Heap earth upon it.

travel details

Trains

Athlone to: Dublin Heuston (11 daily; 1hr 25min); Galway (4 daily; 1hr 10min); Westport (3 daily; 2hr).

Longford to: Dublin Connolly (4 daily; 2hr 10min); Sligo (3 daily; 1hr 20min).

Mullingar to: Dublin Connolly (4 daily; 1hr 10min); Sligo (3 daily; 2hr 10min).

Buses

Athlone to: Dublin (13 daily; 2hr); Galway (9 daily; 1hr 45min); Sligo (2 daily; 2hr 30min); Westport (4 daily; 2hr 45min).

Longford to: Dublin (3 daily; 2hr 10min).

Mullingar to: Dublin (10 daily; 1hr 30min); Sligo (3 daily; 2hr 30min).

WEXFORD, CARLOW AND KILKENNY

The southeast is not the most obvious of areas to visit, especially if this is your first time in the country. There are none of the wild wastes of rock, bog and water, nor the accompanying abandoned cottages that tell of famine, eviction and emigration, so appealing to romantic tastes. It is, however, Ireland's sunniest and driest corner, and what the region does have to offer – whether you're spending a couple of days passing through, or if you simply haven't the time for more distant wanderings – is worth savouring. On the whole, the region's attractions are frustratingly widely scattered, but its medieval and Anglo-Norman history is richly concentrated in the ancient city of Kilkenny – the region's only heavily touristed town – and the lush countryside around it shelters some powerful medieval ruins. Wexford town's conviviality makes up for its disappointingly scant traces of a vigorous Viking and Norman past; Carlow town, sadly, doesn't. While the extreme east is dull and low-lying, and the Blackstairs Mountains open and empty, the southeast is characterized overall by a quality of rich cultivation, as much to do with its history as its natural fertility.

Inland, the region is shaped by three majestic **rivers**: the Nore, the Barrow and the Slaney, and by the empty Blackstairs Mountains which form a rough natural boundary between the counties of Wexford and Carlow. The rivers roll through rich, lush pastures and pretty wooded valleys, past medieval Christian ruins and little towns and villages, whose history belongs to the trade these waterways brought inland. This landscape is at its prettiest in the hills and valleys of the Nore and Barrow, just north of New Ross, and south of Kilkenny town, perfect countryside for leisurely cycling and easy **walking** – an option made all the more attractive by the hostels at New Ross and Kilkenny. The signposted **South Leinster Way** meanders through the heart of this countryside to some of the choicest spots, before heading northeast to the less intimate country of Carlow and the Blackstairs Mountains.

Head for the coast and, to the east, superb sandy **beaches** stretch practically the entire length of County Wexford. While the south coast is less suitable for swimming, its sand banks, shallow lagoons and silted rivers offer great opportunities for **wildlife** enthusiasts: prime spots for **birdwatching** include the Wexford Slobs (around the town itself), the lakes of Lady's Island and Tacumshane, the Saltee Islands off Kilmore Quay

---

ACCOMMODATION PRICE CODES

Throughout this book, prices of hotels, guesthouses and B&Bs have been graded with the codes below, according to what you can expect to pay for a double room in high season. For more details on accommodation, see p. 29.

① Under £26	④ £40–55	⑦ £90–110
② £26–33	⑤ £55–70	⑧ £110–130
③ £33–40	⑥ £70–90	⑨ Over £130

and the Hook Head Peninsula. This low-lying southern coastal region also provides an excellent quick route west to Waterford, since there's a car ferry from Ballyhack across to Passage East on the other side of Waterford Harbour.

Some history

The settled, developed character of this southeastern corner of Ireland owes much to its history of invasion, settlement and trade. The Vikings wrought havoc, but they also built the port of Wexford, which developed steadily, all the while assimilating ideas and peoples from overseas, ensuring the continual cultural influence of Europe. The arrival of mercenaries from Wales, for instance, was common throughout the medieval period, and after Henry II had consolidated the Anglo-Norman victories, Strongbow settled fellow Welshmen in the region: a dialect descended from these people, known as yola, survived in the far southeast of County Wexford right into the nineteenth century.

But it was the power of the English Crown that was to have by far the greatest influence on the character of the region. The towns of Wexford, Carlow and Kilkenny still bear the marks of their **Anglo-Norman** past in city walls and ruined castles; the well-tended farmland of rich surrounding countryside similarly reflects centuries of English settlement. The Anglo-Norman takeover of the southeast was swift, and would have been total were it not for the fiercely Gaelic enclave of counties Carlow and Wexford. There the MacMurrough Kavanaghs became the scourge of the English in Ireland, and they continually thwarted the Crown's attempts to control the entire region. It was Art MacMurrough who defeated Richard II in battles which lost the king not only control of Ireland, but his English throne, too. Only after the arrival of Cromwell was the power of the MacMurroughs broken once and for all.

Colonization was thereafter pursued vigorously: the proximity of the Pale – and of England itself – meant that the Crown's influence was always far stronger here than in the remote west. The English found this area easier to control and administer, and during the growing unrest of the eighteenth century the region remained relatively tranquil. Surprisingly then, by far the most significant uprisings of the **Insurrection of 1798** took place in counties Wexford and Carlow. For nationalists the bloodshed and heroics of that summer form the region's most fêted history and legend.

COUNTIES WEXFORD AND CARLOW

Though the ancient Viking town of **Wexford** bills itself as a tourist centre, you're unlikely to spend more than a day or so here unless you have a car. Sadly, little evidence remains of the town's long and stormy history, and the place is most enjoyable for its small but **lively cultural scene**. The wildfowl **reserves** of the North Slobs are easily accessible, and some marvellous **beaches** are to be found nearby, stretching the length of County Wexford's shoreline north to the popular resort of Courtown. Inland, historic towns like **New Ross**, **Enniscorthy** and **Ferns** merit a visit if you're passing through. To see the best of the south coast, head for quaint **Kilmore Quay**, or rent a bike and explore the isolated and intriguing **Hook Head Peninsula**.

County **Carlow** is less likely to feature on your itinerary, for the good reason that there's little to attract. The **South Leinster Way** trudges at its most lonesome and desolate through the northern half of the Blackstairs Mountains; the county is at its prettiest along the River Barrow, which for much of its length forms the boundary between Carlow and Kilkenny. Carlow town, situated on the Dublin–Kilkenny train route, barely warrants attention.

Wexford town

Apart from the Viking legacy of narrow, quirky lanes, **WEXFORD** town retains few traces of its past, and only the quays suggest that it was once an important trading centre. In fact, the harbour, in business from the ninth century, has now silted up, and Wexford has lost its trade to its old rival Waterford. That's not to say, though, that the town's history stopped with the fall of the Vikings. Settled by the Normans in the twelfth century, it became an English garrison town, brutally taken by Cromwell in 1649, who had 1500 Wexford citizens put to death. In the 1798 Insurrection, the town saw brave rebel fighting against the English Crown (backed by a mainly Protestant yeomanry), which was fearful that the port might be used as a landing place by the French. The rising lasted longer in Wexford than in most places, but the rebels were finally put down and the Crown was quick to exact retribution. Wexford, though, plays down its contribution to Republicanism and has emerged as a positive, forward-looking place, proud of its ethnic and religious mix. It is internationally famous for its prestigious **Opera Festival**, while a more mainstream draw are the town's estimated 93 **bars**, reason enough to give Wexford at least a night.

Arrival, information and accommodation

Wexford's **train** station is at the north end of the quays, just past the bridge over the estuary – which, if you crossed, would take you out to the campsite, the wildfowl reserve (see p.201) and the beaches of the county's east coast. **Bus** Éireann also stops here, while the Ardcavan Coach Company's buses to and from Dublin stop at The Crescent just beside the **tourist office** (April–Oct Mon–Sat 9am–6pm; July & Aug also Sun 11am–5pm; Nov–March Mon–Fri 9.30am–5.30pm; ☎053/23111). **Bike rental** is available at Hayes, 108 South Main St, or The Bike Shop, 9 Selskar St. If you want to get out on the water, **harbour trips** run throughout the summer (£5) and can be booked at the hostel (see below).

   B&Bs in the centre of town include *Westgate House* (☎053/22167; ③) on Westgate, *Bilrene*, 91 John St (☎053/24190; ②), and *John's Gate Street House* (☎053/41124; ④), John's Gate Street. *The Blue Door* (☎053/21047; ④) at 18 Lower George's St is a smart central house with spacious rooms, while more upmarket accommodation is available at *White's Hotel* (☎053/22311; ⑦), George Street. Best of the possibilities further out is the thirteenth-century *Killiane Castle* (☎053/58885; ④) on the Rosslare Road, a B&B with style. Bear in mind that rooms all over town are at a premium during the Opera Festival (see p.200).

   Wexford has a friendly, well-run **hostel**, *Kirwan House* (☎053/21208) in Mary Street, a short walk from the centre of town. You can **camp** at *Ferrybank Camping and Caravan Park* (☎053/42987; Easter–end Sept), immediately over the bridge from Commercial Quay – and there's a swimming pool next to the campsite. Pádraig's Launderette is right next door to the hostel.

The town

Set on the south side of the broad, featureless Slaney estuary, Wexford town sits behind its quays, which drag on relentlessly. A waterfront promenade and marina are planned to cheer things up, but at the moment, the only relief is **The Crescent**, where a statue of **John Barry**, a local who founded the American Navy during their War of Independence, strides against the buffeting wind with cloak billowing. Parallel to the quays runs Wexford's lengthy Main Street, lined with bright shopfronts and creaking bars, a narrow and winding route that gives some idea of the medieval town's layout. Once you've seen it, there is little else left to explore. A monument to the fighting of 1798 briefly draws your attention to the **Bull Ring** (part of Main Street), also scene of a massacre by Cromwell that left all but 400 of the population dead. A lane up behind *Macken*'s off-licence, famous for being both pub and undertakers, leads to the Cornmarket and the parallel streets of the small town centre.

The **Westgate**, built around 1300, is the sole survivor of the medieval walled city's original five gates, and is now designated as West Gate Heritage Tower (May–Oct Mon–Fri 10am–2pm & 2.30–5pm, Sat 10am–2pm; £1.50); you can watch a short film here of the town's history and potter around a craft shop. Nearby are the remains of **Selskar Abbey**, wrecked by Cromwell, where Henry II spent an entire Lent in penitence for the murder of Thomas à Becket in Canterbury Cathedral.

Food, drink and entertainment

There's no shortage of places to get a decent meal in Wexford. Numerous cafés serve lunch from around £3.50, including *Westgate Design Restaurant and Craft Centre*, North Main Street, *Kelly's Deli*, 80 South Main St and *The Backroom* at *Greenacres*, 56 North Main St, probably the best place in town for vegetarian lunches and evening meals. Bar food is even more plentiful: *The Wren's Nest*, *The Centenary Stores* and *Tim's Tavern* are all fine, and for classy meals at bar-food prices try *The Sky and The Ground*, 112 South Main St, also a popular music venue during the summer. The restaurant above it, *Heaven's Above* (☎053/21273), does excellent evening meals at around £25 a head. Equally good is *La Riva,* Crescent Quay (☎053/24330), a lovely, intimate restaurant with main courses at around £7. More run-of-the mill options include *Michael's Restaurant*, 94 North Main St, which dishes up good-value meals daily till around midnight, and *Robertino's* at 19 South Main St, a down-to-earth pizza and pasta house.

The town boasts a vast selection of **pubs** and bars, many featuring live music on one or more days of the week. Start your explorations at *The Centenary Stores*, Charlotte Street, a lively, young spot with traditional Irish music (Mon–Wed nights & Sun mornings). *The Wren's Nest*, Custom House Quay, and *Asples*, The Crescent are also good bets. *Ó Faoláin's*, at 11–12 Moncke St, draws a regular pop-hungry young crowd, but also has traditional music on Monday nights and Sunday mornings. If you just want a quiet drink, try *The Thomas Moore Tavern*, Cornmarket. For after-hours drinking and dancing there are MOR **discos** in *Bodhran's* nightclub behind *Ó Faoláin's* (Thurs–Sat, £3–5), and *The Backroom* behind *The Centenary Stores* (Thurs–Sun; £3–6).

Opera and theatre

The annual three-week long Wexford Opera Festival held in October is long-established and hugely successful, drawing people from all over the world. Each year the festival stages three lesser-known operas by famous composers. If you want to visit the festival it's advisable to book months in advance – the box office usually opens in June; you can get information on ticket availability and programmes from the festival office on High Street (☎053/22400). The festival attracts a range of other performers, too, and you'll find traditional music, blues and jazz in the bars, along with poetry readings and exhibitions. Even out of festival time, Wexford has a lively cultural life, largely generated by a couple of **theatre** venues – the Theatre Royal on High Street (☎053/22144) and the Wexford Arts Centre (☎053/23764), housed in an eighteenth-century market house and town hall in Cornmarket. The latter has a healthy turnover of exhibitions and hosts performance artists, dance groups, drama and music.

Around Wexford town

Within a few miles of Wexford lie plenty of attractions to justify staying around for a day or so. Some, like the wildfowl reserves at the endearingly named **North Slobs**, are of specialist interest. Others, though, could claim anyone's time – not least the excellent sandy beaches as near as Curracloe, five miles to the north, or the resort town of Rosslare to the south.

Birdwatching in the North Slobs

The mud flats sheltered behind the sea walls of the Slaney estuary, known as the North Slobs, are home to the Wexford Wildfowl Reserve. The Slobs are the main wintering grounds for half the world's population of Greenland white-fronted geese, Bewick's swans, pintails and blacktailed godwits; you can also see spotted redshanks, gulls and terns. At the reserve there's a visitor centre (daily: mid–April to Sept 9am–6pm; Oct to mid–April 10am–5pm), a wildfowl collection, a research station, hides, lookout towers and identification charts, all freely accessible.

To reach the North Slobs, take the Dublin Road (the N11) out of Wexford over the bridge, and it's signposted on the right after about two miles.

Ferrycarrig

Just two and a half miles inland from Wexford, the **Irish National Heritage Park** at **FERRYCARRIG** (April–Nov daily 9.30am–6.30pm; £4) plots 9000 years of social change through full-scale models of settlements, homesteads and burial places, from the Stone Age through to Norman times. It's a great place to clarify your knowledge of Ireland's **ancient history**, and helps make sense of the numerous archeological remains dotted throughout the country. The park is also being developed as a **nature reserve**, and the environment has been carefully nurtured to provide the appropriate settings. It works well, so that as you walk through the Mesolithic campsite, the shaggy lichen covering on the hazel trees, the mud and the reeds all help evoke a primeval bog, while the Viking shipyard nestles convincingly on the estuary's banks. Access by public bus is only possible on Fridays; ask at the tourist office about tours from Wexford, or rent a bike.

Johnstown Castle

Four miles southwest of Wexford, off the Rosslare Road, the **Irish Agricultural Museum** (June–Aug Mon–Fri 9am–5pm, Sat & Sun 2–5pm; April, May & Sept–Nov Mon–Fri 9am–12.30pm & 1.30–5pm; Oct–March closed Sat & Sun; £2) is set in the gardens of Johnstown Castle, a Gothic Revival castellated mansion. The museum, which is signposted Research Centre, has good, clear displays on all aspects of rural life, encompassing domestic objects, farming machinery, carts and carriages, reconstructed workshops, and much on dairy farming. In addition, the grounds have mounds of rhododendrons, ornamental lakes, hot houses, dark woodland and walled gardens – all very spruce and well maintained. Again, mini-tours can be arranged from Wexford tourist office.

The beaches

The southeast has more sunshine than any other part of Ireland, and as the entire coastline of the county to the north of Wexford town is made up of safe and sandy beaches, the region is a popular spot in summer for families and caravanners.

From **CURRACLOE**, five miles northeast of town (take the R742), superb, sandy dunes stretch away into the far distance, and though the little villages roundabout are overloaded in July and August, the sands themselves aren't. If you don't have your own transport, then you'll have to rely on the Bus Éireann buses from Wexford to Curracloe, which run highly infrequently.

ROSSLARE HARBOUR TRAVEL INFORMATION

Note that you have to pay £5 **tax** to leave the country on tickets bought in Ireland.

Ardcavan Coach Company (☎053/22561). Buses to Dublin; see "Travel Details" at the end of this chapter.

Bus Éireann (☎053/33114). For local and national bus services, with direct links to Cork, Limerick and Dublin in summer, see "Travel Details" at the end of this chapter.

Irish Ferries (☎053/33158). Services to Pembroke Dock (year round, 2 daily;

4hr), Cherbourg (April–Jan 1–2 a week; 19hr) and Roscoff (April–Jan 1–3 weekly; 16hr 30min).

Irish Rail, Rosslare Harbour (☎053/33114). Rosslare Harbour to Wexford & Dublin (3 trains daily).

Stena Line (☎053/33115). Ferry service to Fishguard (all year, 2 daily; 3hr 30min); their Lynx catamaran (May, 4 days a week; June–Sept 3 daily; 99 min).

Roughly six miles southeast of Wexford is the huge sandy beach at **ROSSLARE**, the county's other main seaside resort, not to be confused with Rosslare Harbour, another five miles further south. Right on the edge of the beach, the best hotel in the southeast, *Kelly's* (☎053/32114; ⑨), has excellent sporting facilities, outdoor hot tubs, and an impressive collection of modern Irish art. Campers can pitch their tents among the caravans at *Burrow Holiday Park* (☎053/32190; mid-March to early Nov).

Rosslare Harbour

ROSSLARE HARBOUR serves ferries to Cherbourg and Roscoff in France, and Fishguard and Pembroke Dock in South Wales. There's a **tourist office** at the harbour terminal (April–Sept open to meet all sailings except the 6.30am sailing; ☎053/33622), or if you are driving, you might use Rosslare Kilrane tourist office just over a mile from the ferry along the N25 (May–Sept daily 11am–8pm; Oct–April Tues–Sun 2–8pm; ☎053/33232).

Ferries aside, there's not much to the place, but if you do need to stay, St Martin's Road, the village's main street, is dotted with several decent **B&Bs**: *Ailsa Lodge* (☎053/33230; ④), *Clifford House* (☎053/33226; ③), *Oldcourt House* (☎053/33895; ③) and *Rock Villa* (☎053/33212; ②). You'll find an An Oige **hostel** nearby in Goulding Street (☎053/33399). You can **camp** down in the dunes by the beach or travel the three miles to Kilrane for *The Holiday Inn Caravan and Camping Park* (☎053/31168; end May–Sept).

The south coast

In the southeast corner of Ireland, the sea has made inroads into an otherwise flat region, forming small lagoons popular with wind-surfers, at **TACUMSHANE** and **LADY'S ISLAND**, both venues for bird enthusiasts. Lady's Island itself sits mid-lagoon at the end of a causeway and has been a place of religious devotion for centuries: an annual pilgrimage is still made here on August 15. On the island are the remains of an Augustinian priory and a Norman castle, both built in the thirteenth century, but the spirit of the place has been destroyed by a large, modern church building that has been tacked onto the side. There are few amenities for travellers in the area, but *The Lobster Pot* bar and restaurant at **CARNE** is a great exception, serving delicious seafood meals.

Kilmore Quay and the Saltee Islands

KILMORE QUAY comes as a real surprise after the largely dull countryside which precedes it. A small, unspoilt fishing and holiday village of thatched cottages and whitewashed walls, it's attractively situated around a stone harbour wall, looking out at the nearby Saltee Islands. County Wexford's **Maritime Museum** is housed in an old lightship alongside the marina (June–Sept daily noon–6pm; £2). There's also a good sandy beach.

Kilmore Quay hosts a **seafood festival**, usually in the second week of July – a fine excuse to eat plenty of seafood, whatever your budget. One of the best seafood restaurants is *The Silver Fox*, with lunch from £4.50 (noon–3pm & 7–9.30pm; ☎053/29888). The village also has a handful of good bars, including *Kehoe's*, which has singalongs, and *The Wooden House*. Both pubs do bar food, and *Walkers*, down by the harbour, is one of the best fish-and-chip shops in Ireland.

Kilmore Quay is also point of departure for visiting the uninhabited **Saltee Islands**, one of Ireland's most important bird sanctuaries, especially for puffins, razorbills, cormorants, shags, gannets, kittiwakes and auks. In the nesting period of late spring and early summer, there are thousands of them; by the end of July they've all left – so time your trip carefully. Boat trips may be available during the summer – contact Declan Bates of *The Saltees Princess* (☎053/29684) or Dick Hayes (☎053/29704), who organizes deep-sea angling trips at around £15 per day.

B&B accommodation can be found at the quaint thatched *Curlew Cottage* (☎053/29772; ②), *Tranquil Sea* (☎053/29658; ②) and *Harbour Lights* (☎053/29881; ②), all a short walk from the harbour. For smart guesthouse accommodation there is *Quay House* (☎053/29988; ④), similarly conveniently situated on the road into the village. Hostel accommodation and camping are available at *Kilturk Independent Hostel* (IHH; ☎053/29883; May to early Oct), about a mile outside the village.

The Hook Head Peninsula

Heading west from Kilmore Quay, the R736/R733 will take you to the Hook Head Peninsula, which forms the eastern side of Waterford Harbour. Only when you reach the peninsula does the flat coastline begin to undulate and the scenery become more attractive. The first town you'll encounter is Arthurstown – probably the best base for exploring the area – and Ballyhack, where you can catch the time-saving ferry across the Barrow estuary to Waterford Harbour.

Arthurstown and Tintern Abbey

ARTHURSTOWN, on the estuary near the neck of the peninsula, has a tiny sandy spot you can swim from, a nice pub that serves seafood, a post office, a shop and several good **B&Bs**, namely *Clogheen* (☎051/389110; ②), the comfortable *Arthur's Rest* (☎051/389192; ③) and spacious *Glendine House* (☎051/389258 or 362276; ③). There's also an An Óige **hostel** (☎051/389411; June–Sept) in the old Coastguard Station – ring ahead to book.

About five miles east of Arthurstown (take the R733), near the muddy Bannow Bay, scene of the first Norman landing in 1169, stands **Tintern Abbey** (mid-June to end Sept daily 9.30am–5.30pm, though times may vary; call ☎01/661 3111 if you want to be sure; £1.50; Heritage Card), built in 1200 by William Marshall, Earl of Pembroke. Another fine Cistercian edifice, it owes its existence in this unprepossessing spot to a vow made by the earl while he was caught in a storm off the south coast. Praying that he might be saved, he promised to build an abbey wherever his boat came ashore. The presbytery is based on the foundation's more famous namesake in Wales.

Ballyhack and Dunbrody Abbey

Just a mile to the north of Arthurstown lies the little village of **BALLYHACK**. From here a useful year-round **car ferry** service runs regularly across the harbour to Passage East in County Waterford, taking just ten minutes (see p.226). Setting off the picturesque scene is **Ballyhack Castle**, a fine five-storey, sixteenth-century tower house. You can climb about halfway up the tower and enjoy a strong sense of its stout proportions (June–Sept Mon–Fri 10am–1pm & 2–6pm, Sat & Sun 10am–6pm). The village's **seafood restaurant**, *The Neptune* (☎051/389284), enjoys a good reputation, while *Byrne's* is a pleasant quayside spot for a drink.

The magnificent ruin of **Dunbrody Abbey** stands at the widening of the Barrow estuary, to the northeast of town off the R733. A thirteenth-century Cistercian foundation, it was altered in the sixteenth century after the Dissolution of the Monasteries, when the large central tower and adjacent buildings were added. There's free parking at the so-called visitor centre (April–Sept only; around £1), but the admission ticket only buys access to a tearoom, a skimpy maze that needs a good twenty years' growth and a similarly thin "museum".

Duncannon to Slade

Unfortunately, the pretty, wooded coastline south of Ballyhack, down to Duncannon, is privately owned, and you can't walk along it. **DUNCANNON** itself is a holiday town, pleasant enough, with a rocky coast to the south that protects its big, sandy Blue Flag beach. Up on the headland, eerie **Duncannon Fort** (June–Sept daily 10am–5.30pm; £1.50) dates back to 1586, when the Spanish Armada was expected to attack. Constantly added to since then, one of its grislier sights is the reputed dungeon of the Croppy Boy, tortured hero of a well-known rebel song. Facilities in Duncannon are minimal: for accommodation, try *Shayanne B&B*, in a great location beside the beach (051/389250; ②). If you're camping, ask to use a local field. A couple of **bars** serve sandwiches and burgers, and *The Strand Seafood Bar* does an all-day menu.

From Duncannon, you can walk wherever you like southwards, but a bike is the ideal way to get down to the very end of the peninsula. Little sandy bays lie concealed behind low cliffs, and there are lovely views across to the broad and beautiful Waterford coastline. Although the Hook Head Peninsula promotes itself as a tourist area, the caravans and kids mostly keep to the areas around Duncannon and Fethard to the east, and there are plenty of isolated spots to be found. A couple of particularly fine, **sandy beaches** are Booley Strand, two miles south of Duncannon, and beyond that the smaller Dollar Bay.

At the peninsula's tip the shoreline is rockier, the limestone rich with fossils, and the land, flat and desolate, just slips away into the sea. The extremity is marked by a **lighthouse** (open to the public in summer) said to be the oldest in Europe – the first on this site was built in the twelfth century. This part of Hook Head is favoured by ornithologists who come to watch the bird migrations, and if you're lucky you can sometimes spot seals. Crashing spray and blow-holes make it a dangerous and dramatic place in a storm – and you certainly shouldn't swim here at any time. For a bracing coastal walk, pick your way east along the coast as far as Slade (see below), about one and a half miles away. The nearest shop to Hook Head is three and a half miles away at the Texaco petrol station at the Fethard–Duncannon junction. Taking the Duncannon Road, *The Templars Inn* (☎051/397162) in Templetown, about three miles from the tip, has a restaurant and bar food, as does the *Naomh Seosamh Hotel* (☎051/397129; ④) in Fethard-on-Sea, where you can also stay. Alternatively, there's accommodation just outside Fethard at the ivy-clad *Innyard House* (☎051/397126; ④), hidden away behind a walled garden.

Tucked away on the east flank of the peninsula, the evocatively crumbling harbour of **SLADE** is a quiet, beautiful place: fishing boats cluster around its quays and slipways, stacked lobster pots lean against a fifteenth-century **castle**, and the whole place is built from stone a nutty brown colour, rich, rusty and warm. If you want to look around the castle, take the lane that runs alongside it and ask at the farm.

New Ross

First impressions of **NEW ROSS** (21 miles west of Wexford on the N25) are not encouraging: a glamourless old port of grubby wharf buildings. However, the place isn't without character, thanks mostly to the river that has long given access to the heart of the Wexford and Kilkenny countryside, and the clutter of narrow lanes that do much to preserve the human scale of the place. In addition, the quayside itself will be greatly enhanced from late 1999 by the presence of the tall-ship *Dunbrody*, a magnificent reconstruction of the original *SS Dunbrody*, a three-masted famine ship which took thousands of emigrants to new lives in America and Canada. On board will be an interactive visitor centre and a comprehensive database of all Irish immigration into the US from 1820 to 1920 (call ☎051/425239 or the tourist office for details; the ship might not remain in port all year round). If you have time to spare, it's worth climbing the steep back alleys to the top of town for views over the river and hills and exploring the thirteenth-century ruins of St Mary's Church, with its graceful, Gothic windows and medieval tombstones in the chancel.

New Ross's **tourist office** (mid-June to Aug Mon–Sat 10am–6pm; ☎051/421857) is located on the quays. Bus Éireann **buses** leave from outside the *Mariner's Inn*, also on the quays. If you are looking for **accommodation**, try *Rossmore B&B*, Priory Street (☎051/421685; ②), or, signposted a short walk uphill from here on Lower William, Street, the comfortable *Riversdale House* (☎051/422515; ③). The friendly *MacMurrough Farm Hostel* (IHH; ☎051/421383) is a comfortable cottage hostel in a beautiful setting a couple of miles out of town; if you're cycling, it makes a good base from which to explore the Nore and Barrow river valleys (see p.213 and p.214). To get there, ask for directions to Kelly's Statoil petrol station on the ring road; the hostel is signposted down the lane alongside.

Down on the quays, *John V's* has an excellent reputation for midday and evening **meals**, while the *Mariner's Inn* is a good spot for lunch. Good-value bar-food is also served at *Crosbies* on North Street, and there's no shortage of coffee shops along South Street. For something different, reserve a table on the *Galley Cruising Restaurant* (☎051/421723), which runs trips up the Barrow and Nore as far as Inistioge and St Mullins and along the Suir to Waterford. Cruises operate from mid-May to late September.

You can sometimes catch live bands at *Crosbies*, while traditional **music** can be heard on a Friday night during summer at both the *Mariner's* and *Mannion's,* a cheerful country pub, about a mile out from the centre along the N30 Enniscorthy Road.

Around New Ross

Four miles north of New Ross along the Enniscorthy Road, take a right turn signposted for the **Berkeley Costume and Toy Museum** (May–Sept Sat 11am–6pm; £3; phoning ahead is a good idea as opening times may vary; ☎051/21361). This private collection of textiles, dolls and toys, dating back to the 1720s, is enthusiastically explained by the owners, allowing the rare experience of seeing Georgian and Victorian dress without glass cases or artificial light. Wedding dresses from three generations of one family, restyled court dresses and French dolls as ambassadors of fashion afford glimpses of social history and how styles were transmitted throughout Ireland from Britain and Europe.

The **arboretum**, five miles south of New Ross, known as the J.F. Kennedy Memorial Park (daily: May–August 10am–8pm; April & Sept 10am–6.30pm; Oct–March 10am–5pm; £2; Heritage Card), contains a collection of around 5000 species of trees and shrubs and affords expansive views of the surrounding countryside. Kennedy's great-grandfather was born close by in Dunganstown, so the place is often frequented by Americans in search of presidential roots. If you have transport, the road south of here will take you to the coast and the Hook Head Peninsula.

Enniscorthy and North Wexford

The market town of **ENNISCORTHY** (14 miles north of Wexford on the N11) is well worth visiting for the **National 1798 Visitor Centre** (March–Nov daily 9.30am–6.30pm; £4), arguably the best interactive centre in Ireland and a must for anyone with an interest in the history of the eighteenth century and the political complexities of contemporary Ireland. Drawing on a rich array of audiovisual techniques, the exhibition brings to life the events surrounding the 1798 Rebellion in Ireland, and sets it in the wider context of revolution in France and the struggle for independence in America. One of the highlights is a tremendously effective audiovisual dramatization of a debate between the English radical Thomas Paine and the Anglo-Irish conservative Edmund Burke.

For a more traditional presentation of the events of 1798 and for material on the 1916 uprising, call in at **The County Museum** (Feb & March daily 2–5pm; April–June & Sept Mon–Sat 10am–6pm, Sun 2–6pm; July & Aug Mon–Sat 10am–8pm, Sun 2–8pm; Oct & Nov daily 2–5pm; Dec & Jan Sun only; £2), housed in a Norman castle overlooking the town. It's crammed with a wonderful mixture of local objects, from an ogham stone to a sedan chair. One gloomy portrait bears the plaintive label, "Information Please". Across the river, covered in mustard and yellow gorse, lies **Vinegar Hill**, the site of the rebels' main encampment during the 1798 Rebellion – and the scene of their final slaughter by Crown forces. If you're around in summer, Enniscorthy hosts the enjoyable "Strawberry Fair", usually held the first or second week in July. If you want to stay, try the recently-built *Enniscorthy Holiday Hostel*, Railway Square (☎054/37766).

The higher countryside to the north and west of Enniscorthy is bald and spartan. There's little in the way of sights on this side of the Blackstairs Mountains, though if you're heading north, **FERNS**, seven miles from Enniscorthy, makes a good lunch stop. One-time seat of the kings of Leinster, it's now a little scrap of a village, top-heavy with history; it was here that Dermot MacMurrough was attacked by Tiernán O'Rourke – whose wife he had abducted fourteen years earlier. MacMurrough sought help from Henry II in France, who lent him Richard Fitzherbert de Clare (Strongbow), and thus an adultery led to the Norman invasion of Ireland. An **abbey** was founded in Ferns in the sixth century, and you can see its remains in St Edan's churchyard and the adjacent field. Most impressive, though, are the ruins of the thirteenth-century **castle**, with its pair of towers – which you can climb – and two curtain walls. When you're feeling peckish, head for *The Courtyard* in the village, which does superb bar food. Decent budget accommodation and camping are to be found at **BUNCLODY**, about twelve miles north of Enniscorthy, at *The Bunclody Hostel* (☎054/76076; March–Sept). The village itself is pretty unremarkable, but it is on the Dublin–Waterford bus route, and just three miles from **CLONEGAL** at the southerly end of the Wicklow Way – the hostel will pick you up from here on request.

Quite the nicest family **seaside town** in the area is **COURTOWN**, around 25 miles north of Wexford (turn off the N11 onto the R742 at Gorey) and plumb in the middle of another excellent, long stretch of sand. Three miles south at **POULSHONE** is the tiny, family-run *Anchorage Hostel* (☎055/25335; May–end Oct), with a nearby shop and a delightful beach just five minutes' walk away.

GOREY, four miles from Courtown, is the main shopping centre for the north Wexford coast, a very cheerful place of brightly coloured stores and numerous interesting bars, among them *Brennan's "64"* on Main Street, popular for bar lunches and evening meals, and *Browne's* and *Quinn's* also on Main Street, a couple of appealing spots for a pint.

COUNTY CARLOW

Northwest of Wexford, tiny **County Carlow** shares little of the appeal of its close neighbours. Much of the terrain is unenticing agricultural land, and none of the few small towns retains much of its history, though the county capital does sport a ruined Norman castle. The most attractive fringes of the county – along the River Barrow and in the Blackstairs Mountains – are covered in the "County Kilkenny" section below, being more approachable from that direction.

Carlow town

For centuries, the town of **CARLOW** was an Anglo-Norman stronghold at the edge of an otherwise fiercely Gaelic county. As such, it has a bloody history, with its most terrible battle during the Insurrection of 1798, when over 600 rebels were slaughtered. Today there's nothing to suggest its former frontier status, and this small, busy town is distinguished only by a fine Classical courthouse with a portico modelled on the Parthenon, an elegant Regency Gothic cathedral – one of the first Catholic churches to be built after Catholic Emancipation in 1829 – and the remains of the once proud Norman **castle**, which lie beside the river at the west end of town. Otherwise, there's plenty on local military, religious and folk history in the **museum**, housed in the town hall (Tues–Fri 11am–5pm, Sat & Sun 2–5pm; £1).

You can get more local information, including a free map and historical guide, from Carlow's **tourist office** at the lower end of the large car park off Kennedy Avenue (May–Sept Mon–Sat 10am–5.30pm; Oct–April Mon–Fri 10am–5.30pm; ☎0503/31554). Bike rental is available during the summer from A.E. Coleman in Dublin Street (☎0503/31273) and you can rent a Canadian canoe from Charlie Horan (☎0509/31307 or 087/529700).

If you want to stay, **B&Bs** include *Westlow*, Green Lane (☎0503/43964; ③), and *Redsetter House*, 14 Dublin St (☎0503/41848; ④), and there are several more out on the Kilkenny Road. By far the nicest budget accommodation in Carlow is the *Ottersholt Riverside Lodge* (☎0503/30404) with camping down by the river.

You'll find the best places to **eat and drink** on Tullow Street: *Tully's* bar has a good atmosphere and is a handy spot for lunch, while *Buzz's* across the street serves a more varied menu in grandiose surroundings. Coffee shops serving light lunches include *Bradbury's* and *Muffins*, also in Tullow Street.

Two miles out of town on the R726 road is arguably County Carlow's most impressive sight: the **Browneshill dolmen**. It's enormous, possibly the largest Neolithic stone formation in Europe, dating from 2500 BC, and the burial place of a local king or prince.

COUNTY KILKENNY

County Kilkenny offers the finest of the southeast's countryside. Mostly it's intensely pretty, rich farmland, especially to the north of New Ross around the confluence of the Nore and Barrow rivers. **Medieval ruins** are scattered all over the county, but they reach their richest concentration in ancient **Kilkenny** city – a quaint but really bustling favourite. The delightful surroundings make it ideal for biking around the river valleys and their medieval ruins, most notably **Kells Priory** and **Jerpoint Abbey**. The cycling is easy: off the main roads there's little traffic, and the minor roads that stay close to the rivers are especially scenic. Alternatively, the heart of this rich, historical farmland can be crossed on foot. As they head south, the Nore and Barrow rivers flow through gentle valleys of mixed woodland: the **South Leinster Way** provides unstrenuous walking, passing through pretty **riverside villages** – Inistioge, Graiguenamanagh, and nearby Borris and St Mullins – before heading north towards the **Blackstairs Mountains**. Immediate access from Kilkenny is by local bus or by taking the train as far as Thomastown and walking. Alternatively, you could see the region from the **cruises** that operate from the river port of New Ross (see p.205).

Kilkenny

KILKENNY is Ireland's finest medieval city. Above the broad sweep of the River Nore sits the castle, while a pretty, humpbacked stone bridge leads up into narrow, cheerful streets laced with carefully maintained buildings. Kilkenny's earliest settlement was a monastery founded by St Canice in the sixth century, but all that remains from those days is the round tower which stands alongside the cathedral. The city's layout today owes more to its medieval history. Following continual skirmishes between local clans, the arrival of the **Normans** in 1169 saw the building of a fort by Strongbow on the site of today's castle. His son-in-law, William Marshall, consolidated Norman power in Kilkenny, maintaining the fortified city and keeping the indigenous Irish in an area of less substantial housing, beyond its walls – of which only the name "Irishtown" remains. In 1391, the Butler family acquired Kilkenny Castle and so ensured the city's loyalty to the English Crown.

In the mid-seventeenth century, Kilkenny virtually became the capital of Ireland, with the founding of a parliament in 1641 known as the **Confederation of Kilkenny** (see "Historical Framework" in Contexts). This attempt to unite resistance to the English persecution of Catholics was powerful for a while, though its effectiveness had greatly diminished by the time Cromwell arrived – in his usual destructive fashion – in 1650. Kilkenny never recovered its former prosperity and importance. The disgrace of the Butler family in 1715, coupled with English attacks upon the rights of Catholics through the Penal Laws, saw the city decline still further, though the towering mill buildings on the river banks are evidence of a considerable industrial history.

Enough medieval buildings remain to attest to Kilkenny's former importance, however, and in a place brimming with civic pride, there's been a tasteful push towards making the town a major tourist attraction. Kilkenny is sometimes known as "the marble city" because of the limestone mined locally, which develops a deep black shine when polished. Echoing this, the town's bar and shop signs all gleam with black and brown lacquer, the names cut in deeply bevelled, stout gold lettering.

Arrival, information and accommodation

The **train** station lies on the north road out of the city, at the top of John Street. Bus Éireann services depart from either the train station or Patrick Street; privately operated **buses** generally depart from The Parade outside Kilkenny Castle. Note that in Irish the city is called Cill Chainnigh, and this is what it says on the front of buses. You can get free maps of the city and plenty of other information from the **tourist office** in Rose Inn Street (April–June & Sept Mon–Sat 9am–6pm; July & Aug Mon–Sat 9am–8pm; May–Sept also open Sun 11am–5pm; Mon–Sat 9am–5pm; Nov–March Mon–Fri 9am–5pm; ☎056/51500).

Kilkenny is well served by **B&Bs**, although in the summer the city can get crowded, and during festival week in August (see p.212) you'll need to book in advance either through the tourist office, or Bed Finders, 23 Rose Inn St (☎056/70088). A good place to start is Dean Street, right in the centre, where your choices are *The Deanery*, 6 Dean St (☎056/52822; ②), the smart *Bregagh Guesthouse*, opposite (☎056/22315; ④), or

KILKENNY

R693 to Freshford — N77 to Ballyragget, — N78 to Castlecomer & Dunmore Caves

St Canice's Cathedral

St Francis Abbey

Watergate Theatre

Black Abbey

Rothe House

St Mary's Cathedral

Market Cross Shopping Centre

The Tholsel

Railway Station

Kilkenny Castle

Castle Gardens

River Nore

Carlow, Dublin & N10

ACCOMMODATION

Berkeley House	1
Bregagh Guesthouse	2
Butler House	3
Danville House B&B	4
The Deanery B&B	5
Fennelly's	6
Kilkenny B&B	7
Kilkenny Tourist Hostel	8
Ormonde Accommodation Centre	9
The Pumphouse	10
Tree Grove Campsite	11

Kilkenny Design Centre

0 — 150 m

Cork N76 — Waterford, N10 — New Ross — Wexford & Rosslare

Kilkenny B&B (☎056/64040; ④). Other central options include *Berkley House* at 5 Patrick St (☎056/64848; ⑤), a comfortable guesthouse over on the other side of town, or *Fennelly's* (☎056/61796; ④), above *Fenelly's* pub on Parliament Street. If you are driving you might consider staying just outside town on the Waterford Road at *Ashleigh* (☎056/22809; ②) or at the delightful *Danville House* (☎056/21512; ②; April–Oct), an eighteenth-century mansion with beautiful gardens, located about a mile out of town along the R700, next door to the well-equipped *Tree Grove Campsite* (☎056/70302). For more upmarket accommodation there's *Blanchfield House* (☎056/27197; ⑥), a Georgian farmhouse five miles out: head out along the Dublin Road and turn right after *The Pike* pub. Alternatively, *Lackan House*, on Dublin Road, offers luxurious B&B (☎056/61085; ⑤).

By far the nicest budget accommodation in Kilkenny is offered by the *Kilkenny Tourist Hostel* at 35 Parliament St (IHH; ☎056/63541), right in the town centre; it has private rooms, a bright airy kitchen and is run by a friendly crowd. Hostel accommodation in dorms and private rooms is also available at *Ormonde Accommodation Centre*, John's Green (☎056/52733). Alternatively, catch a bus out to the An Óige hostel, *Foulksrath Castle*, Jenkinstown (☎056/67144), eight miles north of town along the N77. The setting – a sixteenth-century fort in lush meadows – makes up for the inconvenience. Buggy's buses run from Kilkenny Castle to Jenkinstown; call Buggy's for timetable details (☎056/41264) or ask at the tourist office.

The City

Kilkenny is focused on the hill and its castle. Climbing Rose Inn Street from the river brings you to the tourist office (see p.208), housed in the sixteenth-century **Shee Alms House**, one of the very few Tudor almshouses to be found in Ireland. A walking tour of the city leaves from here six times a day (£3). At the top of Rose Inn Street to the left is the broad stretch known as **The Parade**, which leads up to the castle. Formerly used for military and civic ceremonies, it now serves as a bus park in summer. To the right, the High Street, graced with the eighteenth-century **Tholsel**, once the centre of the city's financial dealings, and now the town hall, soon becomes the busy main thoroughfare of Parliament Street, then continues, crooked and intriguing, with little medieval slips and alleyways ducking off it, through Irishtown towards the **cathedral**.

Of all the surviving buildings from the prosperous Tudor commercial period, the finest is **Rothe House** on Parliament Street (March–Oct Mon–Sat 10.30am–5pm, Sun 3–5pm; Nov–Feb Mon–Sat 1–5pm & Sun 3–5pm; £2). Home to the **Kilkenny Archeological Society museum**, and a **costume** gallery of waistcoats, bonnets and gowns from the eighteenth century onwards, the building itself is a unique example of an Irish Tudor merchant's home dating back to 1594, and comprises three separate houses linked by interconnecting courtyards. There is also a genealogical research centre here for those wanting to trace their roots locally.

Also on Parliament Street you can visit **Kilkenny Brewery** during July and August. Although you won't get a tour, they do at least show a video of the production process, followed by tasting in the cellar bar. It's free, but only fifty tickets are available each day, to be picked up from the tourist office in advance.

Kilkenny Castle

It's the **castle** (April–May daily 10.30am–5pm; June–Sept daily 10am–7pm; Oct–March Mon–Sat 10.30am–12.45pm & 2–5pm, Sun 11am–12.45pm & 2–5pm; guided tours only; £3), an imposing building standing high and square over the river, that really defines Kilkenny. Dating originally from the twelfth century, it was much added to in the seventeenth and nineteenth centuries. While the furnishings and paintings suggest a civilized wealth and domesticity, the scale and grandeur of the rooms, with their deeply recessed windows and robust fireplaces, signify a much cruder political power. The biggest surprise is the flimsy wooden hammer-beam roof of the picture gallery, covered with the folksy, pre-Raphaelite decoration of John Hungerford Pollen – plenty of gold and burnt umber plant life smudging its way across the ceiling. The newly renovated bedrooms of the west wing have recently reopened and house an exhibition of nineteenth-century furniture.

Also within the castle is the **Butler Gallery**, housing exhibitions of modern art, and a tearoom (summer only), in the castle's former kitchen – you don't have to pay the castle entrance fee to visit either the Butler Gallery or the tearoom. The eighteenth-century stables, opposite the castle, have been converted into The Design Centre, an outlet for high-quality Irish crafts.

The cathedral, round tower, churches and brewery

The other must in Kilkenny is **St Canice's Cathedral** (Easter–Sept Mon–Sat 9am–1pm & 2–6pm, Sun 2–6pm; Oct–Easter Mon–Sat 10am–1pm & 2–4pm, Sun 2–4pm). It was built in the thirteenth century, and the purity and unity of its architecture lends it a grandeur beyond its actual size. Rich in carvings, it has an exemplary selection of sixteenth-century monuments, many in black Kilkenny marble, the most striking being effigies of the Butler family.

The **Round Tower** (£1) next to the cathedral is all that remains of the early monastic settlement reputedly founded by St Canice in the sixth century; there are superb views from the top – ask anyone working in the church or churchyard for access (if you want to climb the tower during June, July and August be there before 5.30pm; arrangements are more flexible at other times).

Kilkenny is littered with the remains of other medieval churches. The **Black Abbey**, founded by Dominicans in 1225, has been carefully restored and contains some unusual carvings and sepulchral slabs. On the other side of town, **St John's Priory** has only a roofless chancel, a fine seven-light window and a medieval tomb. Thirteenth-century **St Francis's Abbey** stands in ruins by the river.

Eating, drinking and music

Kilkenny is a very lively small city, and while there's not a huge number of places to eat, there is at least a reasonable range.

Cafés and restaurants

Basement Restaurant, Butler House, Patrick St (☎056/61243). Seafood platters and homemade potato cakes can be enjoyed in the pleasant gardens of the former dower house to the castle; don't be put off by the imposing front door of Butler House – this is the way in and it gives you the chance to sneak a look at the exquisite stucco ceilings en route. Lunch is around £5; evening main courses start at around £7.50.

Café Sol, William St. Does great sandwiches and lunches. The emphasis is on fresh, local ingredients; there's plenty of fish on the menu and always some good vegetarian options; lunches around £4.50; dinner main courses around £13. Lunch daily, evenings Wed–Sat only.

The Caisleán Uí Cuain, Patrick St. Enjoys a good reputation for tasty, good-value bar food (open midday and evenings).

Fléva Brasserie, 84 High St (☎056/70021). Arguably Kilkenny's hippest lunch venue, with a tantalizingly eclectic menu taking in Thai crab cakes and Mediterranean breads via various piquant sauces. Lunch around £3–5, dinner main courses from £7. Evenings Thurs–Sat only.

Italian Connection, Parliament St (☎056/64225). Inexpensive Italian cuisine in a pleasant atmosphere.

Kilkenny Design Centre, The Parade. The centre's café serves excellent homemade soups, salads and quiches.

Lackan House, Dublin Rd (☎056/61085). Kilkenny's finest restaurant. Dinner £22. Tues–Sat.

Lautrec's, 9 St Kieran St (☎056/62720). The best wine bar/bistro in town offering a fusion of Mexican, Italian and French cuisine.

M.L. Dore, 65 High St. Deli and restaurant serving inexpensive hot dinners and salads. Open from breakfast through till 10pm, Sun till 9pm.

Paris Texas, High St. A very popular theme-bar thronged with hungry locals at lunchtime; the evening menu includes cajun and Mexican dishes. Good value.

Restaurant Rinuccini, The Parade (☎056/61575). Expensive Italian-Irish restaurant specializing in homemade pasta, fish and game.

Bars and music venues

Bars are as alluring in Kilkenny as anywhere in Ireland, and you won't be hard pushed to find music here either, though it will be a matter of luck as to what you get.

Biddy Earley's, John St. Local bands and occasional traditional sessions during the summer.

Caisleán Uí Cuain, Patrick St. One of the youngest and liveliest pubs with traditional music (Tues).

Jim Holland's, High St. A traditional bar and something of a favourite with tourists.

John Cleere's, Parliament St. Traditional Irish and folk music on Mondays and bands at weekends from time to time, plus a tiny theatre where they occasionally lay on drama and comedy.

Kyteler's Inn, St Kieran St. A medieval bar associated with tales of cats and witches. Something of a tourist attraction.

Marble City Bar, High St. A traditional bar attracting a young crowd.

Pumphouse, Parliament St. Bands virtually every night during summer and in the winter has country blues (Sun) and rock (Thurs).

Ryan's, Friary St. Traditional music venue (Thurs year round).

Tynan's Bridge Bar, beside John's Bridge. A pleasant spot for a quiet pint.

Widow McGrath's, Parliament St. Hosts live music at weekends. Sit out in the beer garden in summer.

Discos

Expect to pay a cover charge of around £5 in all cases, less mid-week.

Flagstone, Parliament St. Techno music plus live bands on Thurs, usually R&B or traditional. Open Wed–Sun in summer.

Langton's, John St. Disco. Tues, Thurs–Sat.

Nero's, St Kieran St. Extremely popular traditional disco. Thurs–Sun.

Entertainment – Arts Week and The Cat Laughs

Other entertainment is fairly easy to come by in summer. *The Kilkenny People*, published on Wednesday, lists what's on in the city and the surrounding villages; and it is worth checking out the Watergate Theatre, Parliament Street (☎056/61674). One event to try to coincide with is the **Arts Week festival**, held one of the last two weeks in August. The emphasis is on classical music, but alongside this is a fringe festival of literary readings, art exhibitions and jazz and folk sessions. A new festival at the beginning of June, **The Cat Laughs**, brings together comedians from all over the world. Events are held in pubs, clubs and theatres. The programme comes out a month beforehand, and it's worth booking ahead.

Listings

Bank Allied Irish Bank, 3 High St. *M.L. Dore* restaurant, 65 High St (☎056/63374), will cash travellers' cheques, personal cheques and currency, and operates Western Union till 10pm daily. Ulster Bank have an ATM upstairs in the Market Cross Shopping Centre.

Bike rental J.J. Wall, Maudlin St (☎056/21236). Rental is £7 per day, £30 per week.

Books For Irish-interest books, maps and guides, try Dubray Books, Market Cross Shopping Centre or The Book Centre in the High Street – the latter also has a wide selection of foreign newspapers.

Camping supplies Kilkenny Camping and Watersports, Kilkenny Arcade (upstairs), High St (☎056/64025).

Hospital St Lukes, Freshford Rd (☎056/51133).

Laundry Bretts, Michael St (☎056/63200).

Pharmacy Michael O'Connell, High St.

Police ☎056/22222.

Post office High St (Mon–Sat 9am–5.30pm, Tues opens 9.30am).

Swimming pool On the quay (☎056/21380 or 61631 ext 222 for opening times).

Travel agent Mannings Travel, High St (closed 1–2pm; ☎056/22950).

The Dunmore Caves

If you ask about places of local interest, the tourist office will doubtless direct you to the **Dunmore Caves** (mid-March to mid-June & mid-Sept to Oct daily 10am–5pm; mid-

June to mid-Sept daily 10am–7pm; Nov to mid-March Sat, Sun & bank holidays 10am–5pm; £2), situated seven miles north of Kilkenny (take the N77 then the N78) on an isolated limestone outcrop of the Castlecomer plateau. In 1967, Viking coins and the skeletons of 46 women and children were found among the stalactites and stalagmites. It's thought that the Vikings attacked the native Irish, and the women and children hid in the caves for protection. The plan obviously failed, but the fact that the skeletons showed no broken bones suggests that the victims starved to death or were lost, or that the Vikings tried to smoke them out.

To reach the caves, rent a bike in Kilkenny, hitch out on the Castlecomer Road past the train station, or take Buggy's bus from The Parade.

The Nore and Barrow rivers

Two rivers, the **Nore** and the **Barrow**, flowing magnificently through rich countryside, have long been of immense importance to the southeast. Formerly they were the chief means of communication, bringing prosperity to the heart of the region: the Nore brought trade to medieval Kilkenny, the Barrow to Carlow. Today they are treasured for their considerable beauty and are a real treat for anglers. The surrounding countryside is as pretty as you'll find anywhere, perfectly enjoyed on bike or on foot – the South Leinster Way dips down into some of the choicest spots. Plan a leisurely route, and you can meander your way through picturesque ancient villages and take in exceptional medieval ruins.

The Nore Valley

The **Nore Valley** is deservedly renowned for its beauty, the river rolling through lush countryside, past old villages and some engaging ruins. It is perhaps at its finest as it broadens to the south of Kilkenny, where, along the tributary King's River eight miles south of the city (take the R697 or the N10 and turn off at Stonyford), sits medieval **KELLS**. Set amidst lush pastureland, the tiny village is an unexpected sight: its broad bridge is majestically out of scale, an ancient stone water mill stands on the river bank, and the encompassing deep hollow is flecked with mallows, marsh marigolds, docks and irises. Hard by, the magnificent ruin of **Kells Priory** – founded in 1193 – sits like a perfect scale model of a medieval walled city, a clean iron-grey against the surrounding green fields. The ruins consist of a complete curtain wall with square towers and fortified gatehouse, and the remnants of the fourteenth- and fifteenth-century church form one of the most impressive and largest medieval sites in Ireland. This town has nothing to do with the Book of Kells, which is associated with Kells in County Meath, though ironically enough the remains at that far more famous site are considerably less exciting than these.

Signposted from Kells, two miles south, are **Kilkree Round Tower** – just one of the many round towers scattered around this part of the country – and the nearby high cross, decorated with much-eroded biblical carvings. Alternatively, you can take the road east out of Kells and past Stonyford to placid **Jerpoint Abbey** (mid-March to May & mid-Sept to late Oct Wed–Mon 10am–5pm; June to mid-Sept daily 9.30am–6.30pm; £2; Heritage Card). The abbey follows a typical Cistercian layout around an elegant, cloistered garden, and is built of warm, oat-coloured stone, generally visited for its tombs and twelfth-century carvings – especially the animated figures in the cloister.

You can stay at the pleasant *Abbey House* guesthouse (☎056/24166; ④), which is directly opposite the abbey, or at *Belmore* (☎056/24228; ④), Jerpoint Church, Thomastown, an eighteenth-century hunting lodge. If you want to camp, *Nore Valley*

Park (☎056/27229; March to end Oct), about two miles along the Stonyford Road from Bennettsbridge, is a neat, family-geared site with animals for kids to look at.

Thomastown and Inistioge

A mile north of Jerpoint is **THOMASTOWN**. Formerly a medieval walled town of some importance, it's now simply a picturesque country town on the Kilkenny–Waterford train line. Minimal ruins of the walls, a castle and a thirteenth-century church (with some weathered effigies) remain, and in the Catholic church you'll find the high altar from Jerpoint. If you want to stop over, *Burley* (☎056/24297; ③), a short walk along the N9 Dublin road does **B&B**: For a little more, you can stay in a restored medieval tower, *The Tower House* on Low Street (☎056/24500; ④). *The Watergarden* tearoom run by the local Camphill Community makes a refreshing place for a break and several places do a pub lunch. There's also a couple of interesting little bars tucked away on Logan Street – *Carroll's* and *O'Hara's*. Rapid Express Club Coaches operates a cheap bus to Dublin and Waterford, picking up in Thomastown en route.

If you're heading north, it's worth stopping off to visit **Kilfane Glen** and its **woodland garden** (May to mid-Sept Tues–Sun 2–6pm; £3), a steep glen, complete with cottage orné, waterfall and hermit's grotto. It's an example of the Romantic craze for constructing "wild" landscapes in the back garden, and something of a rarity in Ireland. To get to the glen, turn right two miles north of Thomastown on the N9 (before you get to Kilfane), then right again, following the signposts. In **KILFANE** itself, a ruined church holds the fourteenth-century **Cantwell Effigy**, an impressive piece of stone-carving of a knight in full armour.

INISTIOGE, a few miles southeast of Thomastown on the R700, boasts a tree-lined square beside a fine stone bridge. The village is dotted with crumbling stonework, and little eighteenth- and nineteenth-century houses climb the steep lane that twists away from its centre. The grounds of the local estate, Woodstock, are open to the public if you fancy a stroll overlooking the neighbouring countryside, but the house itself was burnt down in 1922 after it had been occupied by the Black and Tans (see "Contexts"). Alternatively, there's a very pleasant walk along the riverbank from the centre of the village. For accommodation, the beautifully situated *Kookaburra House* B&B is on Rock Road (☎056/58519; ②) – head over the bridge towards New Ross, turn left, and follow the lane for just under a mile. There's no pub grub available in the village, but the *Old Schoolhouse Café* serves tea, homemade cakes and local salmon (May–Sept daily 11am–6.30pm; March & April Sat & Sun only).

The Barrow Valley

For walking, the stretch of the South Leinster Way northeast from Inistioge is particularly pretty and offers a couple of pleasant places to rest up. The dusty little market town of **GRAIGUENAMANAGH** (you can also reach here by road from Inistioge and Thomastown) stands in a lovely spot beside the River Barrow, with herons fishing in the rushing weir. The town's great age is indicated by the central **Duiske Abbey** which dominates Graiguenamanagh. Founded in 1204, it was the largest Cistercian abbey in Ireland, and although much has been altered and added outside (including a nineteenth-century clock tower and pebble-dashed walls), the thirteenth-century interior has been lovingly preserved. Besides some original fleur-de-lis tiling and a fine effigy of a knight in chain mail, most impressive is the superb Romanesque processional doorway to the right of the organ – heavily decorated and one of the best to have survived the Reformation. In the churchyard, near the steps outside the south transept, stand a couple of ninth-century stone crosses, and a sixth-century font from Ullard stands outside the north wall of the chancel. The Abbey Centre nearby (all year Mon–Fri 10am–1pm & 2–5pm; summer Sat & Sun 2–5pm) displays interesting contemporary religious art exhibitions. Graiguenamanagh is also a good point from which to walk up **Brandon Hill** (1703ft). The walk is along forest tracks for much of the way, none of it particularly steep, opening out onto a heathery summit and wonderful views. Follow the South Leinster Way Route from town; the route becomes waymarked as the Brandon Way when you reach the hill.

The best place to **stay** and **eat** in Graiguenamanagh is the plush *Waterside B&B* and restaurant (☎0503/24246; ⑥), a beautifully restored stone building overlooking the river. More modestly priced B&B accommodation is offered at *The Anchor Bar* (☎0503/24207; ③), which also serves food daily (Sun till 2pm), and at *Woodside*, Ballynakill (☎0503/24765; ③), about a mile out on the New Ross road. An extensive dinner menu and reasonably priced lunches are available at *The Café Duiske* (Mon–Sat daytime; Wed–Sat evenings; ☎0503/24988), just opposite the abbey.

St Mullins

Five miles south down the towpath (also on the R729), **ST MULLINS** lies tucked away among wooded hills, with the open heights of the Blackstairs Mountains beyond. Strolling through the village, you'll come across the scant remains of a monastery, founded in 696 AD by St Moling, Bishop of Ferns and Glendalough, and alongside them in the churchyard are the base of a round tower and a very worn stone cross. Down beside the stream, at the back of the ruins, a path leads to St Moling's Well, while near the centre of the village stands a defensive earthwork, looking like a sturdy pudding just shaken from its bowl. You might want a break here, too: *Teac Moling* down by the river (follow the steep lane down beside the church) is one of the prettiest places to stop and eat round these parts, offering soups, sandwiches and salads. Similar but less imaginative fare is served at *Blanchfield's* pub and *Teac Moling* also offers **B&B** (☎051/424665; ④). The nearest shop is at Glynn, one and a half miles away.

Borris and Mount Leinster

Following the South Leinster Way north from Graiguenamanagh, along the Barrow, you'll reach tiny **BORRIS**, just over the border in County Carlow. It's not especially attractive aside from its fresh air and one broad (fast) main road, the R729, that sweeps down towards a striking backdrop formed by the ash-mottled Blackstairs Mountains, but it's as good a place as any to stop in the area. Mrs Susan Breen in Church Street does decent, inexpensive **B&B** (☎0503/73231; ②) and *The Step House*, 66 Main St (☎0503/73209; ⑤) is a fine Georgian guesthouse with roaring fires and a very good restaurant. You can camp by the disused train line and get your provisions from *O'Shea's* bar and shop.

The Green Drake Inn serves snacks and lunches every day till 6pm, and more expensive meals until 9.30pm. Considering its size, there's a lot going on in Borris, with live music several nights of the week, mostly in the singalongs and ballads category: try *The Green Drake Inn* (Irish night Wed, MOR music/dancing Sun), *O'Connors* or *O'Shea's*. This last doubles up as a hardware shop so you can sup your pint leaning on a bacon slicer, keeping a weather-eye on the hacksaws and sink plungers dangling from the ceiling.

East of Borris, the South Leinster Way leaves the intimate landscape of the valleys, crossing the open farmland of south Carlow and eventually skirting the bleak height of Mount Leinster. The way finally descends to the lonely cluster of houses which makes up Kildavin, six miles or so from Mount Leinster on the main Carlow–Enniscorthy Road.

travel details

Trains

Carlow to: Dublin (3–6 daily; 1hr 16min); Kildare (3–6 daily; 32min); Kilkenny (3–5 daily; 37min).

Kilkenny to: Carlow (3–5 daily; 35 min); Dublin (3–5 daily, 1hr 40min).

Rosslare Harbour/Europort to: Dublin (3 daily; 3hr 10min).

Wexford to: Dublin (3 daily; 2hr 30min); Rosslare Harbour/Europort (3 daily; 30min).

Buses

Carlow to: Dublin (5–10 daily; 1hr 30min).

Kilkenny to: Dublin (4–7 daily; 2hr 5min); Clonmel (4–5 daily; 1hr 5min).

New Ross to: Dublin (3 daily; 2hr 50min).

Rosslare Harbour to: Cork (late May to mid-Sept only, 3 daily; 3hr 55min–4hr 15min); Dublin (6–8 daily; 3hr 10min); Limerick (2–3 daily; 4hr 15min); Waterford (3–5 daily; 1hr 20min).

Wexford to: Dublin (6–7 daily; 2hr 50min); Rosslare Harbour (3–11 daily; 20min).

WATERFORD, TIPPERARY AND LIMERICK

The route from Waterford through Tipperary to Limerick is the quickest way from the southeast, and the arrival points of the ferries, to the centre of western Ireland, yet it's the area to the south of here that has all the real scenic appeal. All along the Waterford coast, rolling green hills spread down to a fine shore of cliffs interspersed with expansive bays and secluded beaches. There's plenty of history around the county where Lismore and Ardmore preserve extensive early Christian remains, and Waterford city itself has been an important port since the Viking invasions. Nowadays the city preserves an ancient heart, but it's also a thriving modern commercial centre. Inland, rich farming country is contained by mountain ranges that offer excellent opportunities for easy, scenic walking. All of this is contained within a relatively small area, and if you wanted further confirmation that Waterford combines a little of everything, it even has its own tiny Gaeltacht area, around Ring (An Rinn).

Straddling the border with County Tipperary, the **Knockmealdown Mountains** offer similarly attractive walking, as do the **Galtees**, and the landscape reaches its most sumptuous in the velvety slopes of the **Glen of Aherlow**. Scenery aside, Tipperary's farming towns have little to offer the visitor. At the very heart of the county, though, is a site of outstanding interest – the **Rock of Cashel**. A spectacular natural formation topped with Christian buildings from virtually every period, it's effectively a primer in the development of Irish ecclesiastical architecture. The historic sites at **Cahir** and **Carrick-on-Suir** are also well worth taking in.

In **Limerick** you've arrived in the west of Ireland, but the county still has relatively little to tempt you. Industrial and depressed, **Limerick city** has a luckless reputation. Nonetheless, recent efforts do seem to be teasing out strands of elegance and interest in its weather-worn Georgian streets and Norman castle and there's a renewed vibrancy to its cultural life. This said, it still can't compare in terms of enjoyment with the other big towns of the south and west. Inland, the county continues the rich pasture of Tipperary, and perhaps its greatest attraction is the exceptional number of medieval **castles** and towers that dot the landscape; immaculately preserved **Castle Matrix** in the west is one of the finest anywhere. There's also an extremely important Neolithic site at **Lough Gur**, in the heart of the county, and the famously quaint village of **Adare**. In the end, though, Limerick is somewhere you go through to get to counties Clare or Kerry.

ACCOMMODATION PRICE CODES

Throughout this book, prices of hotels, guesthouses and B&Bs have been graded with the codes below, according to what you can expect to pay for a double room in high season. For more details on accommodation, see p.29.

① Under £26	④ £40–55	⑦ £90–110
② £26–33	⑤ £55–70	⑧ £110–130
③ £33–40	⑥ £70–90	⑨ Over £130

△ Athlone

Kildare ▷ Dublin

LAOIS

Riverstown
Lorrha
Terryglass
Borrisokane
Birr

N52

N20

KILDARE

Portlaoise

Roscrea

N7

N78

Nenagh

N7

N62

Carlow

Devilsbit
1571ft ▲

N8

CARLOW

Templemore
Train Station
R498

Templederry

NE
NS

River Suir

Templetouhy

N7

Ballynahow Castle ⌂

Thurles

Urlingford

Kilkenny

N9

Ballycahill

Holy Cross Abbey ⌂

N8

Horse and
Jockey

KILKENNY

T I P P E R A R Y

Limerick
Junction

Hore Abbey ⌂

Rock of Cashel ⌂

N10

New Ross ▷ Wexford

Golden

Tipperary

Cashel

Fethard

N25

Bansha

N8

**Athassel
Abbey**

New Inn

Ahenny

Ballyhack ▷ Wexford

OF AHERLOW

M O U N T A I N S

Cahir

Clonmel

N76

N24

Carrick-
on-Suir

Burncourt

Ardfinnan

Clogheen

**COMERAGH
MOUNTAINS**

● Mitchelstown
Caves

Ballyporeen

Clogheen

Ballymacarbery

East Munster Way

*MONAVULLAGH
MOUNTAINS*

Waterford

Passage
East

Woods-
town

K N O C K M E A L D O W N

N8

W A T E R F O R D

Tramore

Dunmore
East

M O U N T A I N S

Cappoquin

Bunmahon

Annestown

*Waterford
Harbour*

Lismore

Stradbally

N25

Hook Head

Dungarvan

Dungarvan Harbour

IRISH SEA

N25

An Rinn

Helvick Head

Youghal

N25

Ardmore

| 0 | 15 miles |

COUNTY WATERFORD

Photographs rarely do justice to the beauty of **Waterford**. Its strengths lie in a broad grandeur of scale and richness of colour, dark greens and ruddy sandstone reds. In the **south**, grand hills rise gradually from coast and valley, their slopes cloaked with plantations of fir trees. The smoothly sculpted **coastline** is of bold dimensions, low cliffs giving views over large, open bays. The mountains in the north lose the prettiness of their wooded valleys as they rise – not dramatically, but describing gradual, open heights, offering long walks with stupendous views over the plains of Tipperary. Central to the county, Waterford's **river valleys** are luxuriant and fertile, the finest being that of the **Blackwater**, which rolls through rich farmland with a real majesty. Here, it's obvious why the county was so attractive to foreign invaders – Viking, Norman and English. The influence of wealthy colonists is clear, their opulence reflected in remnants of stately, elegant estates.

The county and the city of Waterford developed quite separately. The city was initially a Viking settlement that became a Norman stronghold and thrived as an independent city-state with a major share of Ireland's European trade. While the city prospered as a mercantile centre, the surrounding county lived off farming and fishing, retaining much of its Celtic identity. The Vikings and Normans were not the first newcomers to leave their mark: the area of **Old Parish** around Ardmore gets its name as the arrival point of St Declan in the first half of the fifth century, supposedly the very first of Ireland's proselytizing Christians, preceding St Patrick. The region's early Christian foundations became influential across the country, the most important being that at **Lismore**, founded in 636. It flourished first as a centre of ecclesiastical learning, and later as a secular power rivalling that of Waterford city itself.

Today the distinctions between urban and rural remain marked. Alongside thriving, modern Waterford city, pockets of ancient cultures and histories survive, such as the tiny Irish-speaking community of **Ring** and the historic ecclesiastical foundations of **Ardmore** and **Lismore**. An air of prosperity pervades the county as a whole, in farmland enriched by centuries of cultivation and in the renewed commercial importance of the historic port of Waterford city. The coast offers sandy beaches, a handful of quaint fishing harbours and some great seascapes. It's easily accessible, too – notably good main roads serve city and county, good for long-distance **cycling**.

Waterford

WATERFORD's appearance from the river is deceptively grim: the bare and open stretch of water with the ugly grey wharves and cranes of the working port holds no suggestion of the lively city pulsating beyond its dull quays. This is the commercial capital of the southeast, and yet it retains buildings from Viking and Norman times, and from the eighteenth century, all periods of past eminence. The web of narrow streets that grew up as the focus for commercial activity in the city's earliest days holds the modern city together in compact dynamism. While Waterford has had the modern infrastructure of a mercantile, rather than a rural, centre for decades, the city has developed socially and economically even within the last ten years, and the large number of students here has generated an increasingly upbeat social scene.

Waterford is basically a modern European port wrapped around an ancient Irish city. The **historic town** can happily be explored in a day or so, and the **nightlife** also warrants some sampling. Though a small city by European standards, Waterford has some excellent bars, a small but growing number of decent and imaginative places to eat, and the burgeoning youth/rock scene of an optimistic, albeit small-scale, urban environ-

WATERFORD CITY

Clonmel, Kilkenny & Dublin

New Ross & Wexford

Train & Bus Stations

River Suir

Clock Tower

Holy Trinity Cathedral

Heritage Centre

Chamber of Commerce

The French Church

Reginald's Tower

Christ Church Cathedral

Peoples Park

Waterford Airport, Dumore East & Passage East

Waterford Crystal, Cork, Fermoy, Tramore & Dungarvan

0   200 yards

ACCOMMODATION & BARS

Avondale House (B&B)	1
Barr's Pub	2
Beechwood (B&B)	3
Club L.A.	4
Derrynane House (B&B)	5
Dooley's Hotel	6
Egan's Pub	7
Geoff's Pub	8
Granville Hotel	9
M. Walsh's Bar	10
Muldoon's Bar	11
Portree Guest House	12
T.H.Doolan's Pub	13
The Jazbah	14
The Olde Rogue Pub	15
The Old Stand Pub	16
The Pulpit Pub	17
The Roxy Club	18
The Woodman Pub	19
Viking House Hostel	20

ment. Alongside the city's modernity, though, there's plenty that's traditional, most obviously the place of the pub as a focal point of social activity, and the persistence of music as an integral part of city life.

Some history

The deep, navigable **River Suir** has been the source of the city's importance since the tenth century. Waterford has an excellent harbour; deep inland, and therefore easily defended, it was also perfectly positioned for the internal trading routes of the Barrow and the Nore rivers, reaching into the heart of the southeast's rich farmland. Reliable recorded history of the city starts with the **Viking** settlement founded in the tenth century. The layout of the city (similar to that other Viking town, Wexford) retains its Viking roots, the very long quays and adjacent narrow lanes forming the trading centre. Waterford was the most important Viking settlement in Ireland, and its inhabitants were so feared that even the bellicose Celtic Déisí had to pay them tribute – failure to pay *Airgead Sróine* (Nose Money) resulted in having your nose chopped off. Reginald's (originally Ranguald's) Tower dates from this time, as do some of the remains of the city walls. Nearby, two well-preserved stone arches inside *The Reginald* bar were in fact "sallyports", through which ships entered the fortified city from what is now The Mall but was then water.

The next wave of invaders to leave their mark were the **Anglo-Normans** in the twelfth century. When the King of Leinster, Dermot MacMurrough, made his bid for the High Kingship of Ireland, he knew Waterford was strategically vital for control of the southwest. In 1170, he called on his Welsh Anglo-Norman allies, the most important of these being the Earl of Pembroke, or **Strongbow**, to attack the city. The city walls and towers were formidably strong, but on the third day of attack, August 25, the Normans discovered a weak point, made a breach and flooded in, taking the city with scenes of bloodcurdling violence. Strongbow received his reward: Dermot MacMurrough's daughter Aoife's hand in marriage, and her inheritance. The wedding celebrations took place in Reginald's Tower; the marriage was the first such alliance between a Norman earl and an Irish king, a crucial and symbolic historical event.

The following year, surprised at the Welsh-Norman lords' success, **Henry II** arrived with an awesome display of naval strength (400 ships) and gave the Waterford Normans a charter offering protection – his way of ensuring allegiance to the English crown. Subsequent English monarchs maintained this allegiance, and in 1210 King John arrived with a huge army and enlarged the city with new fortifications. The best-preserved towers of these **Norman walls** are at Railway Square, Castle Street, Stephen Street and Jenkins Lane. During the thirteenth century, the city was the unspoken capital of Ireland. It reaped further royal favour through its part in bringing to ground two would-be usurpers threatening Henry VII: first Lambert Simnel in 1487, then Perkin Warbeck eight years later.

Waterford flourished as an important European port into the sixteenth and seventeenth centuries, **trading** with England, France, Spain and Portugal, and Newfoundland during the eighteenth and early nineteenth centuries, as well as maintaining its inland commerce. It was the only city in Ireland to withstand **Cromwell**, though his forces returned under the command of General Ireton, who took the city without the usual scenes of carnage, giving its citizens honourable terms. The city's importance in trade continued into the eighteenth century, and there's plenty of architectural evidence, both ecclesiastical and secular, of this period's prosperity. The name Waterford is nowadays most famous for its **crystal**, first produced in 1783. The factory closed in 1851 but reopened in 1951 and is now one of the city's major employers.

Arrival, information and accommodation

Roads from the north and the east converge on the river at the **train** and **bus** stations; the city lies over the bridge to the south. Regular daily trains connect Waterford to Clonmel, Tipperary, Limerick, Wexford, Kilkenny and Dublin. In addition to regular Bus Éireann services, Rapid Express Club Travel operates a cheap **bus service** to Dublin and Tramore. Buses leave from outside the Bank of Ireland, Parnell Street. Scheduled **flights** to London depart daily from Waterford Regional Airport, Killowen (✆051/875589). There's no bus to the airport: a taxi will cost you around £8–10.

The **tourist office** is at 41 Merchants Quay, roughly midway between the bridge and the nineteenth-century clock tower (Jan–March Mon–Fri 9am–1pm & 2–5pm; April–Sept Mon–Sat 9am–6pm, Sun 11am–5pm; ✆051/875823). Here you can pick up a comprehensive list of Waterford's **hotels and B&Bs**, many of which are concentrated around The Mall and Parnell Street in the town centre.

For **hostel** accommodation, head for *Viking House*, Coffee House Lane, Greyfriars (IHH; ✆051/853827). If this turns out to be full, and you're contemplating staying in any other hostel accommodation in Waterford, we **strongly** advise you to talk to the tourist office before booking. There's no campsite within walking distance of the city.

Hotels and B&B

Avondale, 2 Parnell St (☎051/852267). A very comfortable city-centre B&B in a Georgian town house. ④.

Beechwood, 7 Cathedral Square (☎051/876677). Standard B&B in a central location. ②.

Brown's Town House, 29 South Parade (☎051/870594). A pleasant Victorian town house decorated with modern Irish paintings and located in a quiet residential street. ④.

The Coach House, Butlerstown Castle, Butlerstown (☎051/384656). Comfortable B&B in a converted coach house, around three miles from Waterford, off the N25. ⑤.

Derrynane House, 19 The Mall (☎051/875179). Good, simple B&B in the centre. ②.

Dooley's, 30 The Quay (☎051/873531). Fine central location for this upmarket hotel. ⑧.

Fernhollow, Cork Rd, Ballinaneeshagh (☎051/358128). Pleasant and comfortable B&B one and a half miles out, just past the glass factory. ②.

Foxmount Farm, Passage East Rd (☎051/874308). Four miles from town, off the Dunmore Rd, this farmhouse B&B also does excellent evening meals. ④.

The Granville Hotel, The Quay (☎051/855111). Swish, well-run hotel in good location. ⑧.

Mrs O'Brien's, 2 New St (☎051/875764). Another good B&B with inexpensive singles. ②.

The Pines, Knockboy, Dunmore Rd (☎051/874452). Clean, comfortable B&B serving excellent breakfasts. ③.

Portree Guest House, Mary St (☎051/874574). Comfortable central guesthouse. ③.

St Martino, Ballinaneeshagh (☎051/374949). Decent B&B just past the glass factory, one and a half miles out of town. ③.

The City

Waterford is centred on a wedge of Georgiana, between the eighteenth-century shops and houses of **O'Connell** and **George** streets, which run behind the modern quays, and the decaying splendour of **Parnell Street** and **The Mall** with their fine doorways and fanlights. These last converge on **Reginald's Tower**, and the angle the two thoroughfares describe is arced by the extensive remains of Viking and Norman city walls. The area immediately behind the quays is still the city's commercial centre. Continue from **Barronstrand Street** through all its changes of name down to where **John Street** meets **Parnell Street**, and you'll find a concentration of fast-food joints and bars. The area of lanes between The Mall and Parade Quay contains some of the city's finest juxtapositions of medieval and eighteenth-century architecture.

Reginald's Tower and the French Church

Waterford's most historic building is Reginald's Tower, a large cylindrical late twelfth-century tower, its design similar to the Scottish broch, with a concealed stairway built within its massive wall; the original Viking tower which stood here was built in 1003. It houses the city's **museum** (April–June, Sept & Oct daily 10am–5pm; July & Aug Mon–Fri 10am–8pm, Sat & Sun 10am–5pm; Nov–March Mon–Sat 10am–5pm; £1.50), which has an impressive collection of royal charters that make quite clear the central role Waterford's allegiance to the English crown played in the city's history. The collection includes the Charter Roll of Richard II (1399), a fabulous transcript of earlier charters.

Wander up Bailey's New Street just behind Reginald's Tower and you immediately come to Waterford's other important medieval building, the **French Church**, or Greyfriars. Founded by Franciscans in 1240, the church served as an almshouse in the sixteenth century, and from 1693 to 1815 was used as a place of worship by French Huguenot refugees, whom the city sheltered in their exile from persecution at home.

It's now a solid, roofless ruin with a complete tower and fine east triple-lancet window. Stones at the base of the outer windows are decorated with comic carved figures, and the church contains some interesting carved slabs, including that of Sir Neal O'Neill, who accompanied James II in his flight from the Battle of the Boyne; collect the key from the Heritage Centre (see below).

Heritage Centre and the cathedral

Occupying a small, old church just off to the right of Bailey's New Street, in Greyfriars Street, the **Waterford Heritage Centre** (April–Oct daily 10am–5pm; Nov–March Mon–Fri 10am–5pm; £1.50) is home to a very exciting collection of artefacts: in 1987–88 extensive excavations of a large portion of the city's old Viking and Norman centre (prior to building development) uncovered finds of quite exceptional quality and variety, dating largely from the early eleventh century. The Heritage Centre displays the best of these, including leather footwear, antler combs, intricately wrought brooches, lathe-turned wooden bowls, weaponry and ceramic vessels. The collection should grow as conservation work continues, and even now it's worth inspecting.

Further up Bailey's New Street, you come to the Church of Ireland **Christ Church Cathedral**. Rebuilt in the 1770s by John Roberts, who did much work in Waterford for both Catholics and Protestants, it's a nicely proportioned building in soothing cream and grey, with a fine steeple and a spacious interior with an elaborate stucco ceiling. The monuments inside the cathedral are worth a look, in particular that of James Rice (Lord Mayor of Waterford), dating from 1482, a gruesome effigy of a corpse in an advanced state of decay, with various creatures crawling in and out of the carcass. The story of Waterford City from the time of the Norman invasion to the present day is relayed in a 45-minute sound and light presentation (April–Oct Mon–Fri at 11.30am, 2.30pm & 4pm; June–Sept additional viewings Sun 2.30pm & 4pm; £2).

Roberts also designed **Holy Trinity Cathedral** in Barronstrand Street. Originally built in 1793, this was greatly altered during the nineteenth century to become the swirling, ornate extravaganza it is today. That the same architect could work on the Protestant and then the Catholic cathedral is evidence of the measure of religious toleration enjoyed by Waterford's citizens at the time. This is further borne out in the little church of **St Patrick's**, tucked away up a lane off Great George's Street. Built in the mid-eighteenth century, it remained a Catholic church throughout penal times and as such is unique. It seems that mercantile strength gave Waterford considerable cultural independence, and Catholics were allowed to hold services here – in stark contrast to the suppression that went on in the rest of the country. Funding came from the sons of Waterford merchants who settled in Spain during the eighteenth century, and dark and dolorous paintings hang either side of the altar, revealing a strong Spanish influence.

City Hall, Georgian architecture and Waterford crystal

Christ Church apart, it's in the city's secular architecture that the best of the eighteenth century is realized. Christ Church Cathedral looks down over The Mall, with its **City Hall** (Mon–Fri 10am–5pm), built in 1788 by John Roberts. Its spacious entrance hall, once used as a meeting place and merchants' exchange, now houses **Waterford Municipal Art Collection**, featuring work by Jack Yeats, Louis Le Brocquy, Paul Henry, Lamb and Keating (Mon–Fri 10am–5pm; tours by arrangement; free). If you are interested in seeing the Waterford crystal chandeliers in the City Hall, ask at the desk. By far the finest eighteenth-century architectural detail in the city, though, is the oval staircase inside the lilac-coloured **Chamber of Commerce** in George Street (open office hours). Once again the work of John Roberts (1785), it's a beautiful cantilevered staircase with fine decorative stucco-work. Georgian housing continues down O'Connell Street, where you'll also find the Garter Lane Arts Centre, at numbers 5 and 22a (see p.226).

If you want to follow up on Waterford Crystal (which is of course for sale all over town), the **Waterford Crystal Glass Factory** offers tours (April–Oct daily 8.30am–4pm; Nov–March Mon–Fri 9am–3.15pm; £3.50) around its glass-cutting and blowing workshops. This is interesting if you've never seen the process before, and a fair way to work up an appetite on a wet day, but not the "absolute must" the publicity tends to suggest. Tours take about forty minutes and in high season it's advisable to book in advance; the tourist office will do this for you free of charge. Buses to the factory leave from beside the clock tower on the quays: ask the driver to put you off at the factory, which is located about a mile from the city centre, on the N25 to Cork.

River cruises

If you want to escape the city for a while, Galley River Cruises' trips to New Ross offer a unique view of the countryside. The cruise includes lunch, afternoon tea or evening meal (June–Aug, £5–24; book at the tourist office or phone ☎051/421723.

Eating, drinking and entertainment

Finding something to **eat** in Waterford is unlikely to prove a problem. There's no shortage of **bar food**: try *Dooley's Hotel*, The Quays, *T.H. Doolan's*, George's Street, also a live music venue, or *Egan's* on Broad Street. You'll find good **café fare** at *Chapman's Pantry*, 61 The Quay, and the café upstairs in *The Design Centre* (next to the tourist office). *Haricot's*, O'Connell Street, serves a good range of vegetarian and wholefood meals (Mon–Sat, last orders 8pm) and *Bean Around The World*, next door, serves sandwiches and a huge range of coffees. *Café Luna*, John Street (Mon & Tues till 2am, Wed–Sun till 3.30am), is a great spot for ciabatta, baguettes, croissants and hot specials. *Coney Island Pizza*, John Street (☎051/850200; Thurs–Sat 5pm–3am, Sun–Wed 5pm–12.30am), is an upbeat, inexpensive pizza place, and one of the cheaper places to eat that also has a wine licence. You can also tuck into pizzas and homemade ice cream at *Gino's*, The Applemarket (daily noon–midnight), or sample more exotic cuisine at *The Happy Garden* Chinese restaurant, 53 High St. For something more upmarket, try *McCluskey's Bistro*, 18 High St (☎051/857766), which offers a diverse and interesting menu, or *Dwyer's*, 8 Mary St; don't be put off by the rather uninspiring exterior, it has an excellent reputation.

Drinking and live music

Waterford has some wonderful **bars**, and there is a steadily growing **music scene** here. John Street is home to two of the city's favourite watering holes – *Geoff's* and *The Pulpit* – both lively young places with a good social mix, and useful for keying into what's happening in the city. *The Olde Rogue*, across the street on Applemarket, is frequented by a good mixed crowd and is another useful place to check out what music is on locally. Other bars with a vibrant atmosphere include *The Old Stand* in Michael Street and *Barr's* on Mayors Walk. *M. Walsh's*, 11 Great George's St, is a wonderful old bar-cum-shop of the type more usually found out in the country.

Traditional music can be heard at a few regular spots: *T & H Doolans*, George's Street; *Muldoon's* (on the corner of Manor Street and Parnell Street), *The Woodman*, John Street (Sun), and *Kitty Kerin's*, Barrack Street. Out of town there's *Meade's Bar* at Halfwayhouse, four miles down the road towards Cheekpoint, with good sessions (Wed & Sun). If jazz is more your thing, make for the trendy *Jazbah*, Parnell Street (Thurs).

As far as **clubs** go, *Preachers*, behind *The Pulpit*, is arguably the liveliest – and most bizarre (the interior is a lavish gothic fantasy) – of Waterford's late-night options, and has discos (Wed–Sun, women free on Thurs). *The Roxy Club*, O'Connell Street, hosts assorted live bands most nights and a disco from Thursday to Sunday (free on Sun &

Tues; till 2am). *Club L.A.* Manor Street, has a disco every night playing mainstream chart music (till 2am).

Arts and theatre

The Garter Lane Arts Centre (Mon–Sat 10am–6pm), housed in two locations – 5 and 22a O'Connell St – has painting and sculpture exhibitions, a theatre and a good current events notice board. It's the place to catch a performance by Red Kettle Theatre Company or various touring companies. Waterford's other theatre is the Theatre Royal, on The Mall (☎051/874402), which stages the city's **Light Opera Festival** in October. The Regional Technical College on the main Cork Road is used for **classical music** recitals, generally advertised in the tourist office.

Listings

Bike Rental Wright's Cycle Depot, 19–20 Henrietta St, off Parade Quay.

Dental emergencies South Eastern Health Board (Mon–Fri 9am–5pm; ☎051/76111). Ask to be put through to Newgate St Dental Clinic.

Hospital Waterford Regional Hospital, Ardkeen, Dunmore Rd (☎051/73321). Medical and dental emergencies out of office hours.

Internet café *Voyager*, Parnell Court, Parnell St (*voyager@iica.net*).

Laundry Washed Ashore, The Quay (Mon–Fri 8am–9pm, Sat 8.30am–6.30pm).

Shopping There's shopping until 9pm every Friday; the Applemarket is a general market held on Saturdays.

Travel agents USIT Youth and Student Travel Office, 36–37 George's St (☎051/872601).

The Waterford coast

Waterford's coastline offers good sandy beaches and some breathtaking coastal walks. The open grandeur of bays like Dungarvan is offset by the intimacy of hidden fishing ports and pockets of ancient history at Ring and Ardmore. The best of the **beaches** are at **Dunmore East**, **Tramore**, **Annestown** and **Ardmore**. Major seaside towns are connected to Waterford by regular bus services, but the choicest spots are best walked, cycled or slowly hitched to; using Bus Éireann to get to these involves a manipulation of the timetable verging on the miraculous.

Passage East and Cheekpoint

Immediately east of Waterford city, at the neck of its long harbour, the pretty ferry village of **PASSAGE EAST** nestles under craggy hills, the estuary slopes aflame with wild gorse. The **ferry** here connects with Ballyhack in County Wexford (Passage East Car Ferry ☎051/382488, continuous services Mon–Sat 7am–8pm & Sun 9.30am–8pm; summer until 10pm; crossing time 10min; car and passengers £4 single, £6 return, pedestrians £1 return) – a particularly useful route east for cyclists, especially if you're making for Rosslare or want to stay with the coast. *The Farleigh Pub* in Passage East does a great range of **bar food** during the summer and sandwiches anytime of year, and if you want to stay there's **B&B** at *Cois Abhann* (☎051/382190; ②). Across the water, less than a mile from Ballyhack, there's an An Óige **hostel** at Arthurstown (June–Sept; ☎051/389411). The tiny fishing village of **Cheekpoint**, to the north of here, sits at the confluence of the rivers Suir, Nore and Barrow, its chief draw the excellent **seafood** at the *Suir Inn*. Coastal paths south of Passage East afford views over the estuary to the Hook Head, Co. Wexford. The long sandy beach flanked by deep woodland at **WOODSTOWN**, just over two miles south of Passage East, takes some beating if you're looking for a quiet stroll or a gentle dip; the *Sartonga* nearby serves **bar food**.

Dunmore East

Further around the Waterford coast, **DUNMORE EAST** settles snugly between small, chunky sandstone cliffs topped by masses of rambling golden gorse. The main street follows a higgledy-piggledy contour from the safe, sandy cove beside which the east village sits, towards a busy harbour full of the rippled reflections of brightly coloured fishing boats and cradled by the crooked finger of the harbour wall. From here, the ruddy sandstone cliffs make bold ribs around the coast. This is still a very active fishing harbour, but has also cashed in on its undeniable picturesqueness, with self-consciously new thatched houses sneaking in alongside the originals.

Quaint as it is, Dunmore East has become very much a playground for affluent Waterford people, and there are three large **hotels** to cater for them – the best being the *Haven* (☎051/383150; ⑥). More moderately priced accommodation is offered by a number of **B&Bs**, including *Church Villa* (☎051/383390; ②) and *Copper Beech*, both on Dock Road (☎051/383187; ③). For sea views stay at *Carraig Liath* on Harbour Road (☎051/383273; ④). **Hostel** accommodation is available at the tourist board-approved *Dunmore Harbour Hostel* (IHH; ☎051/383218; ②; closed Dec), which also does B&B. For **camping**, there's *Strand Caravan Park* (☎051/383174; June to mid-Sept).

Eating is expensive here, and the café down by the beach is just about the only place where you'll get a cheap meal. Good **pub food** is available at *The Ocean Hotel,* near the harbour in the village (☎051/383136). *The Strand Inn* has a very good fish restaurant, and excellent meals are served at the upmarket *Ship* restaurant (☎051/383141).

For **canoeing** and **wind-surfing** contact The Adventure Centre (☎051/383783). Centra **supermarket** on Dock Road operates a **bureau de change**.

Tramore to Dungarvan

Nine miles west of Dunmore East, **TRAMORE** caters for a different type of holiday-maker and a different kind of bank balance. It's a busy, popular seaside resort serving families from Waterford and Cork, and has plenty of amusements, caravans and a huge sandy beach. **B&Bs** are concentrated along Tivoli Road: try the hospitable *Sea Court* (☎051/386244; ③) or the smart *Tivoli House* (☎051/390208; ③). *O'Shea's* is probably the liveliest and most popular **bar** in Tramore, with rock or blues every weekend and good traditional bar food; a good alternative watering-hole is the bar of *The Victoria Hotel.*

The wild and splendid **coast** west of Tramore is one of tussocky grassland, hidden coves and sheer cliffs. Really just a handful of houses, **ANNESTOWN**, six miles from Tramore, is famous for being the only village in Ireland without a pub. It's said that there were once numerous bars catering for the local barracks, but that such was the brawling, the local landowner decided that enough was enough and took away all the licences. There's cosy **B&B** at *Wee Bluin* (☎051/396344; ②), or you can enjoy fabulous views at *Annestown House,* a fine early nineteenth-century building (☎051/396160; ⑤). **Camping** is available overlooking the cliffs one mile west of here at *Boatstrand Camping Park.*

Seven miles further along the coast you'll come to the neat, pretty village of **STRAD-BALLY**. A road leads one mile from here through deep deciduous woods to the fabulous **Stradbally Cove**, a secluded sandy beach flanked by craggy oak and ash-covered slopes. There's hospitable, comfortable **B&B** at *Aisling* (☎051/293264; ③), signposted from the village, with fine views over the coast. Rather more popular, **CLONEA STRAND**, four and a half miles further along the coast and two miles east of Dungarvan, is a broad sandy beach with plenty of space for the holidaymakers at *Casey's Caravan and Camping Park* at its west end. For more comfort, try the nearby *Clonea Strand Hotel* (☎058/42416; ⑤), the pool and bar of which are also open to non-residents.

DUNGARVAN, the major coastal town of County Waterford, has a confident, buoyant air and enjoys a magnificent setting. A wonderful view over the grand, broad bay opens up as you descend to the town, the open heights around topped by pine forests that seem to have been poured on like thick syrup. The **tourist office** on the Square (June–Aug daily 9am–8pm; Sept–May Mon–Sat 9am–6pm; ☎058/41741) can help with **accommodation** and you'll find some decent pubs and restaurants on the square and along the quays. Of more interest and charm, however, are the small communities along the coast to the west.

The An Rinn Gaeltacht

AN RINN, or Ring, is a pocket of Irish tradition hidden away on the modern Waterford coast, signposted off the N25 about six miles outside Dungarvan. It's a tiny **Irish-speaking community** of about 1500 that has somehow survived in what is otherwise one of Ireland's more developed counties, all the more remarkable given the "West Brit" flavour of much of the county's coast. The language survives healthily, as do other traditions, notably music and set dancing.

Like many *Gaeltacht* villages, Ring consists of a community of farms and a handful of bars spread over a wide area, with no real centre. This can be frustrating if you don't have transport, as you have to rely on hitching to and from some of the best bars. *Mooney's* is the first pub on the way into Ring if you are travelling from Dungarvan. It's a great spot for traditional music, and the owners will let you **camp** in their field; another good place to get your bearings is *Tigh an Cheoil*, a bar down by the pier, with traditional sessions on Saturdays throughout the year, and at other times during the summer. Other bars for traditional music are *Murrays*, just over a mile away at Helvick, *The Seanachie*, just off the N25, about six miles west of Dungarvan, and *The Marine Bar*, a mile further on. The **Oyster Festival** over the first weekend in August is a real high point in Ring's music calendar: book accommodation in advance or take a tent. *Ceol na Mara* is a nice little **hostel**, and the owners also offer **B&B** in their spacious nineteenth-century house (☎058/46425; ②). Other options include the welcoming, well-run *Aisling*, Gurtnadiha, Ring (☎058/46134; ②), in a fabulous spot overlooking Dungarvan Harbour, or *Helvick View*, Ring (☎058/46297; ②).

There's nothing specific at Ring beyond the way of life. When the tide's out, you can walk a few miles along the shoreline west of the pier towards Dungarvan, and out along a sand spit. When the tide's in, a walk along the cliffs at Helvick Head gives splendid views of sculpted coastal cliffs and of the mountains inland.

Ardmore

The delightful village of **ARDMORE** is steeped in history and full of character. The fifth century saw the arrival here of St Declan, at least thirty years before St Patrick, and the surrounding area of **Old Parish** is so called because it's supposedly the oldest parish in Ireland. At Ardmore, a medieval **cathedral** and **round tower** stand on the site of the saint's original monastic foundation, commanding stunning views over Ardmore Bay. The long, low twelfth-century cathedral has massive buttresses, its stoutly rounded doors and windows confirming the proud – albeit roofless – Romanesque solidity of the building, while the slender round tower, tall and fine with a conical roof, stands alongside in poignant contrast. There are stones with early ogham inscriptions inside the cathedral, but the most exceptional carvings are on the west external wall. Romanesque arcading, originally from an earlier building, has been set here beneath the window, with boldly carved scenes showing the weighing of souls, the fall of man, the judgement of Solomon and the adoration of the magi: truly impressive, and unique in quality and design. **St Declan's Oratory**, supposedly his burial site, also stands in the graveyard. Earth from the saint's grave is believed to protect against disease.

The village down below – busy in summer – consists of a pleasant row of cottages, a few pubs, a shop, a handful of cafés and a couple of excellent sandy beaches. There's also a small **hotel**, *The Round Tower* (☎024/94494; ⑤), **B&B** at *Byron Lodge* (☎024/94157; ③), and an excellent little **hostel**, *Ardmore Beach Hostel*, Main Street (☎024/94501), with dorms and family rooms. The **caravan** and **camping** site is just beside the beach, and there's a **laundry** in Main Street. The welcoming *Paddy Mac's* pub does good **bar food**, and **traditional sessions** are held on Thursday nights and Sunday afternoons. Myth has it that when St Declan arrived here from Wales, his bell and vestments were magically carried by the large stone that now sits on the beach. This would explain why the boulder is completely different geologically from the surrounding land – though the Ice Age seems a more likely, if comparatively mundane, explanation. Another improbable tale is that crawling under the stone cures rheumatism. It looks unlikely that a fit person could squirm under it, let alone an invalid.

Walking through the village to the east, up the hill you come to a path which leads to the ancient **St Declan's Well** and a steeply gabled **oratory**. It's a moving spot, with fresh water springing beside three primitive stone crosses where pilgrims used to wash, and a stone chair. From here, there's a fine walk around the headland along rocky cliffs for five miles or so, as far as Whiting Bay; alternatively the waymarked path takes you over three miles and brings you back down by the round tower. For longer rambling you can take **St Declan's Way**, a 55-mile route which links Cashel and Ardmore.

The Blackwater Valley and the Comeragh Mountains

Typical of the outstanding beauty of the inland county is the stretch of the **Blackwater Valley** around Cappoquin, where the river makes a sharp westward turn towards County Cork, describing as it goes the southerly limit of the Knockmealdown Mountains (also see p.234). **CAPPOQUIN** itself is prettily situated on a wooded hillside overlooking the river. Despite this beautiful location, the village seems strangely neglected, and there's little attempt to cater for visitors beyond a few B&Bs used mainly by a handful of fishermen at holiday times: if you want to **stay**, *Riverview House* (☎058/54073; ②) is a friendly, central option. *Fawlty's* bar, Mill Street, occasionally does music, and serves lunches. The bar is so called due to the similarities between the owner and Basil Fawlty – though this one has considerably more charm. You'll get good, inexpensive home-cooked **food** at *The Saddlers* (Mon–Sat 8am–6pm), including marvellous breads baked in *Barrons'* Victorian ovens next door. *Richmond House* (☎058/54278; ⑦), on the way to Lismore, is the place for a more extravagant meal (dinner from about £27) and also does B&B.

Although there's little to detain you in the village, the surrounding countryside is lovely. Walk half a mile east, take the right fork by the statue of the Virgin, and you come to the **Glenshelane River walk**. This follows the river through its deep valley banked by pine trees and, after about three miles, brings you to **Mount Melleray**, a Cistercian monastery that welcomes visitors in search of solitude. The trail eventually opens out to more level country, affording great views of the Knockmealdowns and the Galtee Mountains of Tipperary. The walk's a good taster for the varied terrain of the major long-distance walk just north of here in County Tipperary, the East Munster Way (see p.232).

Lismore

Set in the lovely broad plain of the Blackwater Valley three miles west of Cappoquin, **LISMORE**, recently designated a heritage town, is a gem of ecclesiastical history. There's not much sign of this rich history in Lismore's current economically depressed existence, but it does somehow manage to preserve a quiet reverence for its past. Roads approach the town between the river and gentle slopes of mixed woodland – especially beautiful in spring and autumn. The setting is dominated by the romantic towers and battlements of Lismore Castle, whose pale, white-grey stone, set with mullioned windows, rises magnificently on the hill from glorious woodlands and sumptuous **gardens** (May–Sept daily 1.45–4.45pm; £2.50). The castle itself is a successful mid-nineteenth-century imitation of a Tudor castle, remodelled by Joseph Paxton (designer of London's Crystal Palace) around the remains of the medieval fort that originally stood here. The castle's long occupation by the Anglo-Irish aristocracy (and less permanent colonists, including Sir Walter Raleigh) explains why so much of the layout of the parkland and farmland around here is reminiscent of wealthy English shires. The whole setting is strongly evocative of Lismore's former power and glory – even though this building in fact has nothing to do with that era.

In 635 AD St Carthage founded a monastic complex for both monks and nuns in Lismore, and the place so flourished as a centre of learning that in the next century, under the influence of great teachers such as St Colman, it became an important university city. This growth continued into the twelfth century, despite 300 years of sporadic pillage by first Vikings then Normans. Lismore held great political as well as religious power, and the rivalry between the Sees of Lismore and Waterford, which epitomizes the split histories of Waterford city and county, was only resolved in 1363 when the two were united.

Invaders continued to attack the city, and in the late sixteenth century the medieval cathedral was almost totally destroyed by Queen Elizabeth's army. Its site is now occupied by the Church of Ireland **St Carthage's Cathedral**. Although built in 1633, its overall appearance is early nineteenth-century neo-Gothic, the tower and ribbed spire having been added in 1827 by James Pain and the windows of the nave reshaped at the same time. It's a lovely building, sitting in a cobbled churchyard of ancient yews and pollarded limes. Inside is some interesting stonework, including the McGrath family tomb (1548), which has carvings of the apostles, mystical beasts and skulls. The chunky carving of a bishop holding an open book set in the back wall is probably from the ninth-century monastic settlement. In the south transept, just on your left as you enter, there's some striking stained glass by Burne-Jones, the English pre-Raphaelite.

Practicalities

The **tourist office** is in the heritage centre in the courthouse (mid-March to Oct daily 9.30am–6pm; Nov to mid-March Mon–Sat 9.30am–5.30pm; ☎058/54855). If you want to stay in Lismore, you'll find **B&B** in the centre of town at *Alana* (☎058/54106; ②) in Chapel Street, just up behind the tourist office; *Ballyrafter House Hotel*, Vee Road (☎058/54002; ⑥); or *Beechcroft*, Deerpark Road, (☎058/54273; ③), half a mile out of town. Converted Georgian coach-houses provide **hostel** accommodation at *Kilmorna Farm Hostel* (☎058/54315); breakfasts and evening meals are served on request, and they also have room for **camping**.

Eating places are limited to a few pubs along the main street. As for drinking, the town has some fascinating ancient **bars** and grocery stores, a delight to explore in themselves, though there's not much beyond this trip into the past by way of food or entertainment. Try *Foley's*, *O'Brien's*, or *Madden's*, proud of its history as the "local" for castle guests, such as Fred Astaire. For music, try *Rosie's West End Bar* where you might catch traditional, country and western, and ballad sessions on summer weekends.

North of Lismore

The road north from Lismore towards Cahir is typical of this area's gorgeous river valleys, stuffed with rhododendrons, bracken, beech trees and oaks, and dripping feathery pines. The walls are covered with spongy mosses and young ferns. About three miles along the road you can pick up a path leading to higher ground and more open spaces scattered with sheep and fir trees. The path goes through the **Knockmealdowns**, round the huge peat-covered mound of Sugarloaf Hill and after five miles leads to a viewing spot known as **The Vee**. From its steep, heathery V-shaped sides there's a tremendous view of the perfectly flat vale below with its patches of fields and of the town of Cahir at the foot of the Galtee Mountains. If you want to stop off at this point you can follow the road down to Clogheen and hitch to the independent **hostel** at Cahir, County Tipperary (see p.235), or the An Óige **hostel** of *Mountain Lodge*, Burncourt, Cahir (☎052/67277; March–Sept). Alternatively, you can pick up the **East Munster Way** at The Vee. From here it descends to Clonmel, County Tipperary, around seventeen miles further on, taking in the scenic wooded **Nier Valley**.

The Comeragh Mountains

The **Comeragh** mountains, which form the county's central uplands, appear for the most part as heathery, boggy open moorland. They are at their most scenic when explored on foot in the **Nier** valley, which runs from below Knockaunapeebra west to **BALLYMACARBERY**. Walks into the mountains take you up to a fine series of corrie lakes, encircled by high cliffs. Ballymacarbery makes a good base from which to explore the area: *Clonamar Guesthouse* (☎052/36141; ④) offers **B&B**, and there's **traditional music** at *Melody's* bar (Tues, Wed & Sun). The village is also a good stopover if you're walking the **East Munster Way** (see p.232) which crosses the Nier three miles west of the village.

COUNTY TIPPERARY

Tipperary is the largest of Ireland's inland counties, and also the richest. The county's wealth comes from the central **Golden Vale**, a flat limestone plain shared with eastern Limerick that's prime beef and dairy cattle territory. This enormous stretch of farming land is abutted on most borders by crops of mountain ranges, the most beautiful of which are the **Galtee Mountains** and the **Glen of Aherlow**. These are all in the south of the county, and it's this area, without doubt, that packs in the most excitement. The curling course of the **Suir**, Tipperary's principal river, sweeps up most of what there is to see. But for many, Tipperary's attractions hang on one site alone. The **Rock of Cashel** is the county's most dramatic feature by far, its limestone sides rising cliff-like 200ft above the level ground, crowned with the high walls and towers of some splendid medieval ecclesiastical architecture.

Tipperary often has a vaguely familiar ring, thanks to the World War I marching song *It's a long way to Tipperary*. The county was actually picked for the song simply for the rhythmic beat of its name, which dashes the romance somewhat. In fact, Tipperary isn't particularly far from anywhere in southern Ireland, and this is probably its greatest advantage: you can catch the few worthwhile sights on your way through, and still be on the south or west coast within a few hours.

Carrick-on-Suir

Tucked in Tipperary's southeast corner, at the foot of the mountain slopes of neighbouring County Waterford, **CARRICK-ON-SUIR** may well be the first place you see in Tipperary, a slight country town raised a cut above the rest by what is perhaps Ireland's most beautiful Elizabethan mansion: similar examples abound in England but are a rarity here. Set at the very eastern end of the main street, the mansion was built by Thomas, tenth Earl of Ormond ("Black Tom"), in anticipation of a visit from Queen Elizabeth I – and tributes to her are incorporated in the decoration throughout: above all in a fresco over the entrance way and in the superb stucco work of the long gallery. A stunning mansion, with mullioned windows running the length of the building, it's the only major example in Ireland of a completely unfortified dwelling to date from the sixteenth century. It adjoins the remains of an earlier castle built in 1309; the two rectangular towers currently undergoing renovation date from the mid-fifteenth century. There's a collection of magnificent royal charters here, too: the oldest dates from 1661 and granted James Butler the title of Duke of Ormond. A claim is still disputed among historians that Anne Boleyn was born here. The guided tour, available on request, is well worth taking (mid-June to Sept daily 9.30am–6.30pm; £2; Heritage Card).

Regardless of the mansion's splendours, it's as the birthplace of the champion cyclist **Sean Kelly** that the town is most proud of itself, and the tiny main square at the west end of the main street has been renamed in his honour.

Tourist information (June–Sept daily 10am–5pm; ☎051/640200) can be found in the Heritage Centre, just off Main Street. **Accommodation** is fairly limited: in the centre of town are *The Bell and Salmon Arms Hotel*, 95–97 Main St (☎051/645555; ⑤), and *Fatima House* B&B, John Street (☎051/640298; ③). There's also B&B at *Hillcrest*, (☎051/640847; ②), a mile out on the N24 opposite the Sean Kelly Sports Centre. You can **camp** at *Carrick-on-Suir Caravan and Camping Park*, Ballyrichard, Kilkenny Road (☎051/640461), one mile out of town. Cyclists heading for the hostel outside Clonmel (see opposite) are better off leaving the main road at Carrick-on-Suir and heading across country via Rathgormuck.

You'll find good **bar food** at the bar of *The Carraig Hotel*, Main Street (daily till 9.30pm), and *The Park Inn*, New Street, which has a very good local reputation. For fast food head for *The Europa* in Main Street. As for **entertainment**, *The Bell and Salmon Arms Hotel* has a bright modern bar attracting a young crowd, with open Irish sessions (Mon & Wed), live rock and pop bands (Fri & Sun), and discos (summer Sat till 2am). Full of character, *Just Gerry's* and *N.Cooney's* make interesting alternatives, or, for a quiet pint, try the bar of the *Carraig Hotel*.

Five miles north of Carrick, **AHENNY** has two beautiful high crosses in its graveyard. They're thought to be eighth century, and are excellent examples of the transitional style between the early Christian plain shaft crosses and the highly ornate didactic crosses of Monasterboice and Kells.

The East Munster Way

The **East Munster Way** runs from Carrick-on-Suir for 43 miles west to the village of Clogheen, eight miles south of Cahir. The first stretch is easy walking alongside the river Suir as far as Clonmel. From here the Way climbs the heathery, wooded slopes of the Comeraghs, to descend three miles west of Ballymacarbery and the Nier Valley (see p.231). The path soon follows the flank of the Knockmealdown Mountains, affording fine views of the plain below, and winds up at the tiny village of Clogheen, six miles west of Ardfinnian. The walk involves long distances rather than steep, dramatic inclines, and for most of the way you're within a mile or so of habitation. Nevertheless, solitary walkers should bear in mind that much of the route is out of sight of the lowlands, and distress signals won't be noticed. The relevant Bord Fáilte Information Sheet, giving route guidelines for this section of the way, is Carrick-on-Suir–the Vee, Information Sheet No. 26J, and you'll need O.S. **maps** Nos 74 & 75, 1:50,000.

Clonmel

CLONMEL, thirteen miles upstream, is far and away Tipperary's prettiest centre. It's a strangely genteel kind of place and retains something of its flavour as an early coaching town. It was the birthplace in 1713 of Laurence Sterne, philosopher and literary comic genius, and it's not at all difficult to imagine Shandyesque shenanigans in the fine Georgian inns around town. A hundred years later Clonmel became the principal base for Bianconi, the most successful coach business in the country. Bianconi came from Lombardy in Italy and ran his so-called Bians from what is now *Hearn's Hotel* on Parnell Street; if you are here on July 6, expect to find costumed street celebrations of his achievements.

The town is a beautiful place to breeze through: you can't miss Clonmel's finest building, the sorely dilapidated **Main Guard** sagging at the eastern end of O'Connell Street. The oldest public Classical building in Ireland, predating Dublin's Royal Hospital, is now undergoing full renovation. The facade visible today was built by James Butler, first Duke of Ormond, as a courthouse for the Palatinate of the County of Tipperary, and it bears two panels showing coats of arms dated 1675.

Off to the left of the Main Guard runs Gladstone Street; to the right Sarsfield Street runs down to the river, and it's worth wandering here through the town's preserved backstreets and quayside mills. Other examples of period architecture include the nineteenth-century **St Mary's Roman Catholic Church**, with ziggurat tower and portico, in Irishtown, out past the imitation West Gate; the Greek-Revival–styled **Wesleyan Church** on Wolfe Tone Street; and the **Old St Mary's** Church of Ireland church with its octagonal tower and tower house. All of these are impressive from the outside; none offer much if you venture in. The museum in Parnell Street (Tues–Sat 10am–1pm & 2–5pm) records local history in a collection of maps, newspapers, postcards and Bianconi prints, and also has a small gallery of fine paintings.

At Richmond Mill, opposite SuperQuinn, a **Museum of Transport** (June–Sept daily 9.30am–6pm; Oct–May Mon–Sat 10am–6pm; £2.50) houses two rooms of gleaming nostalgia, including Rolls, Jags, Fords from the 1930s on and a 1965 VW Karman Ghia.

Practicalities

Clonmel's **tourist information** point is in the Chamber of Commerce building on Nelson Street down by the quays (Mon–Fri 9.30am–5.30pm; July & Aug also Sat same hours; Oct–April closed 1–2pm; ☎052/22960). There are a few **B&Bs** in the centre of town and plenty more futher out. Good central establishments include *Glenanane*, Wolfe Tone Street (☎052/21950; ②), probably the cheapest, *Mr Bumbles*, Kickham Street (☎052/29188; ④), offering travel-lodge style accommodation, and *Fennessy Hotel*, Gladstone Street (☎052/23680; ④), a newly refurbished traditional **hotel** with bright, comfy rooms and a good breakfast menu. For B&B's outside the centre, follow the Cork road out of town for about one mile and you'll find several signposted up a road that forks to the left, including *Benuala* (☎052/22158; ③) and *Hillcourt* (☎052/21029; ③). Worth the extra journey is the welcoming farmhouse B&B at *Ballyboy House*, Clogheen (☎052/65297; ④), five miles south on the R671 (not to be confused with the town of the same name further west). The nearest **hostel** is *Powers the Pot* at

Harneys Cross, five and a half miles up the slopes of the Comeragh Mountains (☎052/23085). It's probably most popular with **campers**, and there's a cosy **bar** on site. At 1200ft this claims to be the highest house in the country, and it's certainly on the threshold of excellent hill-walking country.

There are several good places to **eat** in Clonmel. At lunchtime *Angela's*, Abbey Street (Mon–Sat till 6pm), off behind the Mainguard, serves excellent good-value vegetarian meals, and *Niamh's* deli and coffee shop, Mitchell Street, is a good spot for light snacks. For **pub lunches** there's the hugely popular *Mulcahy's* – they serve on into the evening, and there is a restaurant if you don't want to eat in the bar. Pizzas are the speciality at *Tom Skinny's*, Gladstone Street (noon–midnight), while *Mr Bumble's* is one of Clonmel's more stylish restaurants.

Good **pubs** for music include *Kitty O'Donnell's* near the station, *Carey's*, Irishtown (through the Westgate towards Cahir) and *Lonergan's*, O'Connell Street. *Fennessy's Hotel* has a cosy bar with a session on a Wednesday night year round. Good for a quiet pint are *Chawke's*, Gladstone Street, and *Phil Carroll's* "antique bar", Parnell Street, both full of character.

Clonmel is the capital of Irish **greyhound racing**, and you can see the sport on Monday and Thursday nights at the local stadium; the surrounding countryside is also famous for racehorse breeding. **Fishing** off the quay is free, otherwise you can get salmon and trout licences from Kavanagh's Sports Shop, Westgate. The river is said to be very good for the late run of the salmon in early September, and trout stocks have risen recently. If you want to **walk** in this lovely area, the *Clonmel and South Tipperary Guide*, available free from the tourist office, details several walks of around seven miles.

Fethard

Leaving Clonmel, you could either head southwest to the plain between the Knockmealdown and Galtee mountains (see below); or north for Cashel, in which case the route via **FETHARD** is the most rewarding. A touchingly plain place to travel through, and rarely sought out by tourists, Fethard has a number of forgotten medieval remains, set at the back of the town towards the river. One of these is a ruined **Templars' Castle**, access to which is through the *Castle Inn* (contact the publican, Mr Keogh). Other remains of old friaries and Iron Age raths can be found in the surrounding land. There's also a **Folk Farm and Transport Museum** at the beginning of the Cashel Road (May–Sept Mon–Sat 10am–6pm, Sun 1.30–6pm). For refreshments, *P.J. Lonegan's* home-cooked lunches are worth stopping off for and *McCarthy's* is a good place for a drink.

The Knockmealdown and Galtee Mountains

Of the mountain ranges in southern Tipperary, the **Galtees** make up one of the most scenic inland ranges in the country and are well worth discovering – the **Glen of Aherlow** makes an excellent base in the heart of it all (see p.241). The **Knockmealdowns** are less interesting, but offer easier hill-walking. The valley plain between the two mountain ranges, which runs for about ten miles east of Mitchelstown (itself over the border in County Cork, see p.236), is not much in itself, but the *Mountain Lodge An Óige Hostel* is a good overnight stop for hikers, and the **Mitchelstown caves** are well worth a visit. Starting from Clonmel you've a choice of two routes west: the main roads via Cahir, or the lesser R665, which cuts straight across to Mitchelstown.

Cahir

You're unlikely to miss **CAHIR**. The town sits on a major crossroads, its square radiating routes from each corner: to Clonmel, Cork, Cashel and Tipperary itself. The **castle** (daily: mid-March to mid-June & mid-Sept to mid-Oct 9.30am–5.30pm; mid-June to mid-Sept 9am–7.30pm; mid-Oct to mid-March 9.30am–4.30pm; £2; Heritage Card), set on a rocky islet in the River Suir, beside the road to Cork, is Cahir's outstanding attraction (even the name Cahir means "fort"). In essence the building is Anglo-Norman, and goes back to the thirteenth and fifteenth centuries, though the virgin appearance of the outer shell is deceptive, with a good deal of the brickwork dating back to the eighteenth and nineteenth centuries. The Irish chieftain Conor O'Brien was the first to build a fortress on the rock; but it was the Anglo-Norman Butlers, the Earls of Ormond, who made this into one of the most powerful castles in the country. The Earl of Essex showered the castle with artillery fire in 1599; it got off lightly during the Cromwellian and Williamite invasions, and gradually fell into ruin until rejuvenated, along with other town buildings, by the Earl of Glengall in the mid-nineteenth century. In modern times, the interior has been uniformly whitewashed and spartanly furnished.

Entrance to the castle is along the side rampart, bringing you into the confined space of the **middle ward**, dominated by the three-storey thirteenth-century **keep**. The keep itself consists of vaulted chambers, a portcullis and a round tower containing a prison, accessible through a trap door. Down to the left, you pass through a gateway topped by machicolations, musket loops to either side, where sixteenth-century invaders could have been bombarded with missiles or boiling oil. Beyond is the much larger **outer ward** and, at its far end, the cottage built by the Earl of Glengall. The cottage now houses a **video theatre** where a twenty-minute film enthuses rhapsodically on the antiquities of southern Tipperary.

In the **inner ward**, two corner towers overlook the road to Cork. The larger was probably designed to be independently defensible once the keep had fallen, and it dates from a mixture of periods – straight, thirteenth-century stone stairs; fifteenth- to sixteenth-century stone vaulting over the ground-floor main room; and nineteenth-century renovation work in the Great Hall, whose stepped battlements reflect sixteenth-century style. The smaller, square tower at the other end of the ward and the curtain wall date from the nineteenth century, though with medieval bases. Just to the left of this second tower, steps lead to the bottom of the well tower, where the castle could safeguard its water supply during a siege. The informative **guided tour** of the castle is well worth taking.

One further building worth seeing is the **Swiss Cottage** (April Tues–Sun 10am–1pm and 2–5pm; May–Sept daily 10am–6pm; Oct, Nov & mid- to end March Tues–Sun 10am–1pm & 2–4.30pm; £2; Heritage Card), a pleasant one-mile walk along the river from the castle or a short drive out of Cahir on the Clonmel Road. This **cottage orné**, probably designed by John Nash, was built in 1810 to provide the Earls of Glengall with a lodge of romanticized – and fashionable – rustic simplicity from which to enjoy their hunting, shooting and fishing. With its thatched roof and ornate timberwork it certainly looks the part, and its status as a unique period piece makes it a popular attraction.

Practicalities

The **tourist office** (April–Sept Mon–Sat 9am–6pm; July & Aug also Sun 11am–5pm; ☎052/41453) is in the car park beside the castle. From the castle you can see another castellated mansion on the hill further along the Cork Road: the *Carrigeen Castle*

(☎052/41370; ③), once the town prison and now a **B&B**. More conventional alternatives are signposted off the N24 Clonmel Road, a short walk from the centre: *Killaun* (☎052/41780; ③), *Silver Acre Guesthouse* (☎052/41737; ③) and *Arden Lodge* (☎052/42338; ③). Basic budget accommodation and camping are available at the welcoming *Lisakyle Hostel* (IHH; ☎052/41963; March–Oct), one mile out of Cahir beyond the Swiss Cottage. Alternatively, the *Kilcoran Farm Hostel* (☎052/41906), something of a rustic idyll, can be reached from Cahir by following the N8 towards Mitchelstown for about four miles and then taking the lane opposite the Tops petrol station for about another mile. You can also phone for a lift from Cahir. Most secluded of all is An Óige *Mountain Lodge Hostel* (see p.231). For those wanting to walk, it is handily located a ten-mile hike from the *Ballydavid Wood* hostel in the Glen of Aherlow, six miles out of Cahir (see p.241). There's **camping** among the fruit trees at *The Apple Farm* (☎052/41459), four miles out of Cahir along the Clonmel road.

Standard café fare is served at the coffee shop above the *Crock of Gold*, opposite the castle, and at *Roma's Café*, on the Dublin side of the square. You can get pasta, pizzas and Irish food at the *Italian Connection*, open every day till 11pm. For good **pub lunches** try the *Galtee Inn* on the square. **Traditional music** is minimal, but sometimes takes place at *Morrissey's*, opposite the castle, and the *Forge Tavern*, beyond the bridges. One of the liveliest pubs in town is *The Stop Inn*, Church Street, just off the square.

Bus Éireann buses to Waterford and Dublin leave from outside the *Crock of Gold*, across from the castle, and those to Cork and Limerick leave from outside the tourist office; there's a timetable posted in the window.

Ardfinnan to the Mitchelstown Caves

Along the minor road from Clonmel to Mitchelstown, you pass through **ARDFINNAN**, where a beautiful fourteen-arched stone bridge crosses the Suir and a private castle stands on the overlooking hillside. Follow along the foot of the Knockmealdowns for several miles and you'll come to Clogheen, where there's the best turn-off route into the mountains, towards the terrific scenic point known as the **Vee** (see p.231).

Back on the R665, you'll come next to **BALLYPOREEN**, a wide-streeted crossroads turned ghost town, whose moment of glory came on June 3, 1984, when **Ronald Reagan** made a prodigal return – his great-grandfather was supposedly born here in 1810. You can read all about it and look at photos of the visit in a specially built centre at the crossroads, opposite the *Ronald Reagan* pub.

Eight miles from Mitchelstown itself, the massive pre-glacial underworld of the **Mitchelstown Caves** (daily 10am–6pm; £3) – signposted north from Ballyporeen down the interlacing lanes of the valley, or south off the N8 – are, aside from walking, the main attraction in the area. By far the most extensive and complicated cave system in Ireland (a couple of miles in all), they have remained, considering their scale, very uncommercialized. The whole underground system was discovered in 1833, when a labourer lost his crowbar down a crevice, though there are records from much earlier of one cave being used as a hiding place, most famously to shelter the Earl of Desmond after his unsuccessful rebellion in 1601.

The caves were formed by the incessant action of rainwater on the limestone over millions of years, and the fantastical stone formations grew out of the calcium carbonate (dissolved limestone) deposited by the dripping water, hardening as it evaporated into gigantic encrustations of stalactites and stalagmites. The temperature in the caves is around 54°F – this can feel chilly in summer, so bring a sweater. The **tours** only take in a few of the major caves but are nonetheless worth taking.

Cashel

Just eleven miles north of Cahir en route to Dublin, **CASHEL** is an obvious next stop. The town has grown around, and is completely dominated by, the spectacular **Rock of Cashel**. No tourist bus will bypass the site – so an early-morning or late-afternoon visit will make an important difference to your first impressions.

In deep contrast to the ecclesiastical splendour of the Rock is the tiny **Bothán Scóir** – a unique one-roomed peasant dwelling that simply has to be seen. For antiquarian booklovers the **GPA Bolton Library** is a must, and the museum at **Cashel Folk Village** will appeal to anyone interested in the old IRA.

The Rock of Cashel

Approached from the north or west, the **Rock of Cashel** (daily: mid-June to mid-Sept 9am–7.30pm; mid-March to mid-June 9.30am–5.30pm; mid-Sept to mid-March 9.30am–4.30pm; £3; Heritage Card) appears as a spectacular mirage of fairytale turrets, crenellations and walls rising bolt upright from the vast encircling plain. It's a tour operator's dream: on one piece of freak limestone outcrop stands the most beautiful and complete Romanesque church in the country, a gargantuan medieval cathedral, a castle tower house, an eleventh-century round tower, a unique early high cross and an exquisite fifteenth-century Hall of Vicars – medieval Irish architecture wrapped up in a morning's investigation. Two more medieval priories lie at its feet.

In **legend** the Rock was formed when the Devil, flying overhead with a large stone in his mouth, suddenly caught sight of St Patrick standing ready to found his new church on the site, and in his shock dropped the rock (in the northeast of the county, a striking gap in a mountain range is known as the "Devil's Bit"). The Rock is also the place where St Patrick is supposed to have picked a shamrock in order to explain the doctrine of the Trinity – God the Father, Christ the Son and the Holy Ghost as three beings of the one stem – since which time the shamrock became Ireland's unofficial emblem.

The Hall of the Vicars

Approaching the Rock from Cashel town, you come first to the **Hall of the Vicars**, built in the fifteenth century to cater for eight vicar *meistersingers*, who assisted in the cathedral services but were later dispensed with because of growing resentment over the power and land that their privileged office entailed. The upper floor of the building is divided between the main hall, with screens and a minstrels' gallery, and what would have been the dormitories. The ground floor, a vaulted undercroft, today contains the original **St Patrick's Cross**, a unique type of high cross. It once stood outside, where there's now a replica. Tradition has it that the cross's huge plinth was the coronation stone of the High Kings of Munster, the most famous of whom was Brian Boru, killed in his tent by a fleeing Viking at the Battle of Clontarf. The cross is simpler than other high crosses, with a carving of Christ on one side and St Patrick on the other. It has an upright supporting its left arm and is without the usual ring-wheel in the centre. It may be that originally the upright and its missing counterpart represented the two thieves crucified with Jesus, and it is also possible that it was never intended as a freestanding cross in the first place, but for erection on a wall.

Cormac's Chapel

Cormac's Chapel (built 1127–34) is the earliest and most beautiful of Ireland's surviving Romanesque churches, and the intricacies of its decoration are as spectacular as they are unique. The architecture has clear continental influences – the twin square

towers, for example, were probably engineered by monks sent from Regensburg, Germany. The **tympana**, or panels, above the grandiose north door (more than likely the original entrance, now leading blindly into the flank of the cathedral) and south door (today's entrance), are also rare in Irish church architecture. Above the north door is depicted a curious carved scene of a large beast ensnaring a smaller one, itself on the point of being speared by a macho centaur in a Norman helmet. The north door is set in six orders of pillars, creating a tunnel-vaulted **porch**, which is sheltered by an outer stone roof porch. Each arch is crowned with capitals, human heads, fantastic beasts, flutings and scallops.

The small size of the chapel is typical of Irish architecture of this period, as are the lack of aisles and the steeply pitched stone roof – you'll find similar-looking buildings at Glendalough and Kells, though Cormac's Chapel is larger than these. The wall opposite you as you walk in has a tall triple arcade, in the centre of which is a large round-headed **window** that would once have lit up the whole interior, illuminating all the painted colour – of which a little remains up at the altar and just above the chancel arch. The **sarcophagus** at the foot of this wall, although fragmented, has an exquisite Scandinavian Urnes design of interlacing serpents and ribbon decoration. It's said to have been the tomb of King Cormac, and is certainly old enough to be so.

The cathedral and round tower

The **cathedral** was begun a century or so after Cormac's chapel. Although Anglo-Norman in conception, with Gothic arches and lancet windows, it's a purely Irish-built endeavour, without help from abroad. A graceful limestone building, it features a series of tall, high-set lancet **windows**, and also some good examples of quatrefoil, or four-petalled, windows, especially above the lancets in the choir space. You'll notice that some of the lancets have been shortened – probably as a measure of fortification. The **choir** is longer than the nave and both are without aisles. The nave was shortened to make room for the **castle tower**, built most obviously for refuge, and also as an archiepiscopal residence. A wooden-floored hall would once have been above the nave (the corbels are still apparent), accessible from the castle tower.

The **central tower**, at the meeting of the transepts, is also on a grand scale and, typically, did not appear until the fourteenth century. It's supported by four Gothic arches rising from very wide piers, their shafts sweeping beautifully into the concave bottom. Access to the tower is by winding stairs from the south transept (this may not be open to the public, so ask). **Passages** also ran through the nave and choir walls, supposedly for the outcasts or lepers of the community, so that they could watch the holy ceremonies without being seen themselves. The **transepts** have shallow chapel altars with some tomb and piscina niches. In the north transept, panels from sixteenth-century altar-tombs survive – one with an intricately carved retinue of saints, the others more broken but just as beautiful.

The **Round Tower** is the earliest building on the rock. Its tapering features have led to suggestions that it's as early as the tenth century, though the officially accepted date is early twelfth century. It's not a typical tower; the entrance door was originally twelve feet above the ground, and various levels of windows ensnare viewpoints in all directions.

Around the Rock

From the grounds of the Rock you can look down at **Hore Abbey** on the plain below, and it's an easy enough walk down, over the fields and jumping the road wall. But there's little to be gained in doing this, beyond escaping the sightseers – you can see just as well from the Rock. The thirteenth-century abbey was the last Cistercian daughter monastery of Mellifont to be completed before the Reformation, and was probably built by those working on the cathedral on the Rock. Originally a Benedictine foundation, it converted after its abbot had a wild dream that his Benedictine monks were plotting to cut his head off; he expelled them and donned the Cistercian habit in 1269. There's yet another abbey ruin, **St Dominic's**, down the south side of the Rock in the town, but this has even less to offer in terms of things to see.

A path known as the **Bishop's Walk** leads from the Rock's rampart entrance down through the back garden of the **Palace Hotel**. The Palace was built in Queen Anne-style by Archbishop Theophilus Bolton in 1730 as a mansion for the archbishops of Cashel (hence the Bishop's Walk to the Rock). It has a simple, red-brick front and a cut stone rear. Cashel owes much to this particular archbishop; it was he who saw the value of Cormac's Chapel and put his wealth into its restoration at a time when the Rock's antiquities were degenerating rapidly towards irrevocable ruin. A further legacy is the **GPA Bolton Library** (June–Sept daily 11am–4.30pm; £2), out on the road opposite the hotel and set in the grounds of the slender-spired eighteenth-century St John's Protestant Cathedral. Its manuscripts (from as early as the twelfth century), rare maps and wealth of literary treasures were principally his bequest when he died in 1744. A selection of the books and maps are on display, changing bi-monthly and well worth viewing.

It's worth the effort of visiting the **Bothán Scóir**: walk up the street past the tourist office, turn first right and look out for a tiny cottage about half a mile up on your right. If there's no one there, ask for Albert Carrie at 6 Ard Mhuire, the first cul-de-sac on the right as you head back down the hill towards town. The Bothán Scóir is a one-roomed peasant dwelling dating from around 1600, the only one of its kind in Ireland. Bothán means "hut", scóir is "score", referring to the score notched up on a tallystick as the peasant worked the 180 days of the year demanded by the landlord in payment for rent of the cottage and a patch of land. The soot-black thatch, the chimneyless roof, the half-door and the jamb wall – layer after layer of authentic detail tell a history of systematic oppression and thorough misery. All this is wonderfully articulated by Albert – a man with an inspiring passion for the history of the common people; it proves a wholly memorable experience.

If you have the time to delve further into Cashel's social history, **Cashel Folk Village** (daily 9.30am–7.30pm; £2), in a lane behind the tourist office, is crammed with interest, including a gruesome traditional butcher's shop guaranteed to turn you vegetarian and a fascinating museum of Republican history.

Practicalities

The **tourist office** (April–Sept Mon–Sat 10am–6pm, July & Aug also Sun 9am–6pm; ☎062/61333) sits in the market house in the middle of the main street. The Cashel of the Kings **heritage centre** alongside gives an overall picture of the history of the town, in particular its ecclesiastical buildings.

If you want to stay, there are several central **B&Bs**, including *Abbey House*, 1 Dominic St(☎062/61104; ③), and *Rockville House* (☎062/61760; ②), both near St Dominic's Friary. Just up the main street there's the welcoming *Maryville*, Bankplace (☎062/61098; ④), and beyond here, a steep lane to the right off the main road leads to *Rockview House* (☎062/62187; ③) and *Twenthe* (☎062/61326; ②), which has fabulous views of the rock. If you favour a more rural setting, several spacious bungalow B&Bs lie out along the Dulla road within a mile of town: *Rahard Lodge*, a modern farmhouse (☎062/61052; ③), *Thornbrook House* (☎062/62388; ③), and *Georgesland* (☎062/62788; ③). Cashel also has two excellent **hostels**. To find *O'Brien's Farmhouse Hostel* (IHH; ☎062/61003), walk to the bottom end of Main Street and turn right at the junction following the Dundrum Road – it's less than a mile. **Campers** can also pitch their tents here. Just off Main Street is *Cashel Holiday Hostel*, 6 John St (IHH; ☎062/62330).

You'll have no trouble finding places to **eat**. There are several coffee shops on Main Street and good-value meals are served at *The Bakehouse* (daily till 8pm in summer). For **pub food** try *Kearney's Castle Hotel*, or *Hannigan's* in Ladyswell Street, the top end of the main road. *Spearman's,* 97 Main St, and *Roasters*, Main Street, are also good bets. If you feel like splashing out, *Chez Hans* (☎062/61177; Tues–Sat 6.30–9.30pm) serves top-notch meals in the unlikely setting of a former Wesleyan chapel.

A great deal of **music** is laid on in the summer, spanning rock, country and western, singalong and traditional Irish. This last tends to move around, but is a regular feature at *Feehan's* (Wed); they also have some sort of live music on every night during the summer. Other bars worth checking out include *Con Gleeson's* and the cosy *Dowling's* – both at the bottom of the main street. For rock bands, try *Knox's* at weekends.

Cycle parts and repairs are available at Burke's, in the centre, and **bike rental** from the hostel in John Street

Golden

Having seen the Rock of Cashel, most people head out of Tipperary for the west, and frankly this isn't a bad idea – the north of the county has little to distract you. Leaving Cashel on the N74, you come after a few miles to **GOLDEN**, where **Athassel Abbey** sits on the banks of the Suir. It was once the largest medieval priory in Ireland, and its ruins even today are fairly extensive – though not dramatic enough to seriously draw you off your route. The west door is the most impressive feature, and the peacefulness of the surroundings the most rewarding. The plain immediately encircling the abbey was once the site of the town, but it was razed to the ground twice during the fourteenth century – enough to obliterate it forever.

Tipperary town and around

A few miles further on, twelve miles from Cashel and less than five from the border of Limerick, the county's honorary namesake, **TIPPERARY** town, lies at the northern side of the Glen of Aherlow. Like many of these namesake county towns, Tipperary is much less important than it sounds. If you've already visited Clonmel, it will come as something of a shock – compared to Clonmel's yuppy prosperity, Tipperary feels out of another era altogether. The town has bold statues sculpted in granite here and there, most notably one to its literary local son, Charles J. Kickham, entitled *Poet, Novelist but above all Patriot*.

You might want to stop over briefly for one of the monthly meetings at the **race-course**, or to take in an intriguing small **museum** (Mon–Sat 9.30am–5pm) hidden away in the foyer of the town swimming pool, by the Cashel Road exit. A tiny store of memorabilia, it exhibits photos, letters and weaponry from the warring years of 1919–23, especially relating to the old IRA. Tipperary was a particularly hot spot during the Anglo-Irish and Civil War strife, especially through its most remembered son, **Seán Tracey**, whose battalion fired the first shots of the Anglo-Irish War (1919–21). There are letters he wrote to his family from prison, some talking about the honour the British had bestowed on him by taking the trouble to get him captured, others of a more domestic nature. A violin belonging to **Joseph Mary Plunkett** (one of the poets executed in the 1916 uprising) hangs beside revolvers, pistols and land mines. Most striking of all, perhaps, are the photographs of the young officers shown clenching their revolvers, either posturing a rebel's stance of defiance or slightly abashed, with innocent-looking smiles.

Practicalities

The **tourist office** is on James's Street (May–Oct Mon–Sat 10am–6pm; ☎062/51457). If you plan to **stay**, try *Central Accommodation*, 45 Main St (☎062/51117; ②), a B&B run by a friendly family. If this is full, there are several pleasant alternatives about one mile out of town on the Galbally road, including *Clonmore House* (☎062/51637; ③) and *Riverside* (☎062/51219; ②).

Places to **eat** are very much geared up to cater for locals working in town. *Seamróg Restaurant*, 1 Davis St, is a traditional café serving good-value hot lunches (Mon–Sat 8am–6pm, Sun 12.30–4.30pm), *The Brown Trout* restaurant, Bridge Street, open daily, serves inexpensive lunches and evening meals, and *The Basement* coffee house, Kickham Place (behind the statue), is similarly cheap and cheerful. You can get **bar food** at *Coughlan's* and *The Kickham House*, both in Main Street. As for drinking, there are plenty of **bars**, including *Corney's*, Davitt Street, which has a mix of traditional and country and western music at weekends, and *The Churchwell Tavern*, also in Davitt Street, where you can sometimes hear rock bands.

The Glen of Aherlow

The luxuriant and majestic **Glen of Aherlow** runs beneath the northern slopes of the Galtee Mountains. The glen itself is only around eight miles long and two miles wide, and its scenic splendour comes as a real surprise, tucked away as it is four miles south of Tipperarary town off the R664. One of the nicest places to stay in the glen is *Ballinacourty House* (☎062/56230; ③; Easter–Sept), offering unusual **accommodation**: seventeenth- and eighteenth-century haylofts have been converted to conceal bedrooms, a wine bar and an inexpensive restaurant, all of which look out over an extremely pretty, cobbled courtyard; **campers** can also pitch their tents here and enjoy fine mountain views. *Homeleigh Farm House* (☎062/56228; ③) offers welcoming B&B and **pony trekking**, and nearby *Aherlow House Hotel* (☎062/56153; ⑤) makes a fine place to stay; non-residents can enjoy **bar meals** and stunning views from their **terrace bar**. For **walkers**, there's the An Óige *Ballydavid Wood* **hostel** (☎062/54148; March–Nov); try to arrive in daylight for this one, for although meticulously signposted, the route has enough twists and turns to get you lost. It's a short day's trek from the *Mountain Lodge* **hostel** (☎052/67277; March–Sept), a spacious, Alpine-style old shooting lodge, offering the bare necessities (including gas lighting).

Thurles and around

Upstream from Cashel, both the Suir itself and the attractions along its banks wane. The river passes through the larger towns of Thurles and Templemore, though its source in the Devil's Bit Mountain falls short of the major town in the northeast, Roscrea. All three centres have train connections.

THURLES is of very little interest in itself, but **Holy Cross Abbey**, just four miles south, sits beside a broad stretch of the Suir and is well worth a visit if you're passing by. Founded in 1180, restored significantly in the fifteenth century and then left derelict for 400 years, the abbey was totally restored between 1971 and 1985 and is now a thriving parish church as well as a tourist attraction. You really need to see photographs of the period before restoration to appreciate its significance; these suggest that every other ruin you've seen could as easily be converted. Holy Cross always had singular importance as a centre of pilgrimage, claiming to possess a piece of the **True Cross**. The splinter was reckoned to have been given to Murtagh O'Brien, King of Munster, by Pope Paschal II in 1110. At the turn of the seventeenth century both O'Donnell and

O'Neill, the Ulster chiefs, stopped off to venerate this relic on their way to Kinsale to meet the French – no doubt hoping they'd be rewarded with a victory over Elizabeth I.

The **interior** of the church has been fully restored, though here there's been no particular attempt at period accuracy; virtually every wall and pillar has been whitewashed, and all the pews have been varnished. Nevertheless, it's rewarding to see the stone ribbing of the vaulted roofs and most particularly the undamaged fifteenth-century **sedilia** in the chancel area, the finest in the country. The sedilia, recessed stone seats for the celebrants of the Mass, is of a hard limestone shaped into cusped arches and crowned with crockets, showing decorative friezework as well as the English royal crest and the escutcheon of the Earls of Ormond. In the transept to the left of the nave, you'll find one of Ireland's rare medieval **frescoes**, this one showing a Norman hunting scene painted in browns, reds and greens. The exterior of the church has a startling full-length slate roof, which reaches down to the cloister pillars. There's a **tourist information centre**, a coffee shop and a religious crafts shop within the abbey complex.

Ballynahow Castle

If you're cycling or driving north towards Thurles you might also think of taking in **Ballynahow Castle**, a circular castle tower built by the Purcell family in the sixteenth century. To get there from Holy Cross, take the road directly opposite the Protestant church, not the Thurles route (even though the signpost says so). From Thurles itself, it's out on the Nenagh Road, right at the Jet Petrol station, and after another mile the castle stands next to a farmhouse – *Ballynahow Castle Farm* (☎0504/21297; ④), where you can pick up the key, or stay in **B&B** accommodation from March to October. The castle is distinguished by its circular plan; inside, entering the lowest of its five storeys is like walking into an igloo, with the corbelled roof curving round almost to the floor. There are many little rooms hidden within the walls and, although undecorated and entirely bare (and quite dark), most of it is in an excellent state of preservation and strongly atmospheric.

Templemore and Cranagh Castle

TEMPLEMORE is even less interesting than Thurles, but it does happen to be within about seven miles of one of the more historical of listed hostels, **Cranagh Castle** (☎0504/53104) – though it's not particularly easy to find; the best thing to do is to phone the hostel direct for directions. The **hostel** occupies parts of the eighteenth-century mansion house attached to the circular Purcell tower house – the family live in the basement. A wide wooden stairway leads to the dorm rooms on the second and third floors, which are extremely spacious, with single beds and left-over period furnishings. Outside, the yard is full of the sounds of an old-fashioned farm: geese, cocks, cows and the gallop of horses first thing in the morning. The produce here is all organic, and there's wonderful fresh milk and bread, though not at all cheap. If you're interested in the working of the farm, then ask about the courses on organic farming that are run off-season. If you can take the silence, it can be a very relaxing place to take time out (though smokers are discouraged). If you have your own transport, the **Devil's Bit Mountain** is within easy reach and is reckoned worth the climb for the views.

Roscrea

ROSCREA sits on a low hillock between the Slieve Bloom Mountains to the northeast and the Devil's Bit to the southwest. It's a charming place, with streets running down the hill slopes and a certain conscious lack of worldliness. However, where the rest of Ireland has secluded river sites and spacious countryside for its abbey ruins, Roscrea has the main Dublin–Limerick Road roaring through the middle of **St Cronan's Monastery**. On one side of the road is the round tower, with a garage shed built into the side of it and the top third removed by the British in 1798. Immediately opposite, virtually on the pavement, is the west gable of St Cronan's church, its yellow sandstone carved out in a twelfth-century Romanesque style reminiscent of Cormac's Chapel in Cashel. The rest of the church was pulled down in the nineteenth century and the stone used as building material elsewhere. **St Cronan's Cross**, just to the right of the gable, must have been a beauty once, but now it's severely weather-beaten and hacked. Up by the centre of the town is a large, sturdy-looking **Gate Tower Castle** from the thirteenth century. Backed by a polygonal curtain wall, it now houses a **heritage centre** (June–Sept daily 9.30am–5.45pm; £2.50). An imposing eighteenth-century town house now used for office purposes stands at the centre of the medieval plot. As both the cross and the castle are on the Dublin–Limerick route, you'd get a reasonable view looking out of a bus window in slow traffic.

Nenagh and Lough Derg

Once again, in comparison with the south of the county, the northwest lacks significant attractions. The remaining crumbs of interest rest on the shores of **Lough Derg**, not far from the sole town of any size, Nenagh.

NENAGH is usually jam-packed with heavy traffic trying to plough its way through. It has one singular historical remain, a colossal round **castle keep** (or donjon) with walls 20ft thick, its five storeys reaching a height of 100ft and topped with nineteenth-century castellations. Totally gutted within, this final retreat tower was originally one of five round towers which, linked by a curtain wall, formed a Norman stronghold. Founded by Theobald Walter, a cousin of Thomas à Becket, the tower was occupied by the Butlers, then captured in turn by the O'Carrols of Eile, Cromwell, went back to James II and then to and fro between Ginckel (King William's chief general) and O'Carrol in the Williamite war. And there the fighting stopped until many centuries later when a farmer, wanting to get rid of a nest of sparrows that were feeding on his crops, stuck some gunpowder in the walls of the donjon and blew another hole in the fortress. A few reinforced concrete steps help you to get near the top, but there's little to be seen.

Across the road from the donjon, the Nenagh **heritage centre** (Easter to mid-Oct Mon–Fri 9am–5pm, Sun 2.30–5pm; £2) is set in the old jail, now a Convent of Mercy school. Housed in the octagonal Governor's House, up the driveway, the museum has a display room housing temporary exhibitions, a mock-up of an old schoolroom with a four-foot mannequin nun (very liberal with her mascara), and a re-created old post office/bar/telephone exchange. In the basement are the usual agricultural items and a realistic but clinical-looking forge. Back at the entrance arch, the cells of the jail have their original hefty iron cell doors, and you can also see the former exercise yard, tiny and cluttered.

The tourist office is on Connolly Street (early May to early Sept Mon–Sat 9.30am–1pm & 2–5.30pm; ☎067/31610). There's the reasonably priced B&B *Sun View*, Ciamaltha Road (☎067/31064; ③), quite close to the bus and train stations, and you can get fairly good snack food at the Foodhall on Pearse Street. At the northern end of this road, the JKC Shopping Arcade provides more substantial lunch venues, or try the *Pantry* on Abbey Street.

Lough Derg

Along the shores of **Lough Derg** lie a number of small villages, none of them really worth making a special trip to visit (unless you're after the fishing), but which may be worth calling at if you're cruising on the lake. **Dromineer** is a small and picturesque yachting harbour, with a tiny castle ruin on its pier; there's food (and drink) at the *Whiskey Still Pub*. **Kilgarvan** has a good antiques shop next to the *Brocka-on-the-water* restaurant. **Terryglass**, where *Paddy's Pub* has a nice interior and **bar food**, offers little else besides a crafts shop in the old church and a good **B&B** nearby – *Tir na Fiuise* (☎067/22041; ④).

COUNTY LIMERICK

To an even greater extent than Tipperary, everyone passes through **County Limerick**, and hardly anyone stays. Once here, you're tantalizingly close to the much more rewarding counties of Cork, Kerry and Clare, and frankly you're not likely to linger. Still, what interest there is lies close to the roads to Cork, Killarney and Tralee, three main routes that run southwards from Limerick city in the northeastern corner. You should try to see at least one of two places: **Castle Matrix**, an authentic, lavishly restored and renovated tower house on the Killarney route, and **Lough Gur**, a Mesolithic-to-Neolithic lake and hill enclave of preternatural beauty. Both can be reached easily no matter what transport you're using.

For **cyclists**, Limerick's terrain is more variable than it's usually given credit for. In its western-to-southwestern corner, the upland bears a likeness to barren stretches of Donegal, whereas the northern estuary stretch is indeed only a slightly bumpy flatland. The centre and east bow in contour towards the eastern frontier of the Tipperary Golden Vale's rich dairy land, but not without gently rising mounds for hills and broadish trickles for rivers. More so than any other county, the land in Limerick is dotted with an array of **tower castles**, some inhabited but most in ruins or no more than stumps.

Historically, Limerick's most notable period arrived with the Norman strongholds, the most dominant family being the Fitzgeralds (or **Geraldines**), also known as the Earls of Desmond – virtually all of Limerick's significant ruins were once this clan's power bases. They quickly became Gaelicized and ruled as independent monarchs, pulling very much away from English rule. The inevitable confrontation with Britain came to a head at the end of the sixteenth century, when in 1571 the Geraldine uprising against Elizabeth I sparked off a savage war, which brought about their downfall and destroyed in its wake much of the province of Munster.

Limerick city

Squarely on the path of all the major routes across the country, and situated pretty much at the head of the Shannon estuary, **LIMERICK CITY** seems a logical place to make for, but it's a disappointment. Though it's the Republic's third city, and heavily industrialized, it somehow falls significantly short of being a metropolis, but also lacks the attractions of a typically relaxed western seaboard town. It's also probably the most Catholic of all Irish cities, its churches regularly full of worshippers.

SPORT IN LIMERICK: THE GARRYOWEN

Even more than most of Ireland, Limerick seems obsessed with sport; horse racing, hurling, gaelic football, soccer and rugby are all avidly followed, and hurling and rugby have particularly strong local traditions. In rugby, the region has passed into immortality with the invention of the **Garryowen** – named after a district of Limerick city which also lent its name to one of Ireland's finest rugby clubs. The move, a high kick upfield pursued by a charging team who hope to hit the opposition as they catch the ball, the equivalent of Rugby League's "up-and-under", is said to have been invented here in the 1920s.

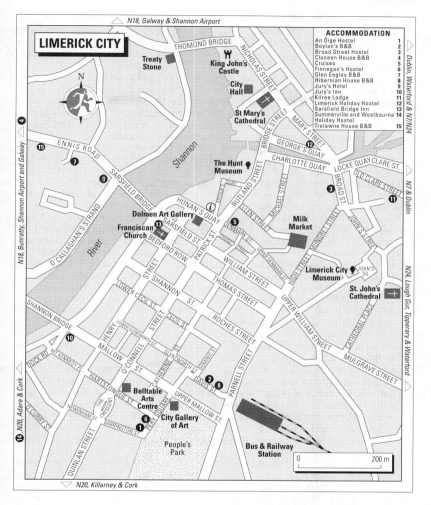

LIMERICK CITY

N18, Galway & Shannon Airport

Treaty Stone

THOMOND BRIDGE

King John's Castle

City Hall

St Mary's Cathedral

The Hunt Museum

Dolmen Art Gallery

Franciscan Church

Milk Market

Limerick City Museum

St John's Cathedral

Belltable Arts Centre

City Gallery of Art

People's Park

Bus & Railway Station

ENNIS ROAD

SARSFIELD BRIDGE

Shannon

River

O'CALLAGHAN'S STRAND

SHANNON BRIDGE

DOCK RD

HARTSTONGUE ST

NEWENHAM ST

O'CURRY ST

QUINLAN STREET

BARRINGTON ST.

THE CRESCENT

MALLOW ST.

HENRY ST.

O'CONNELL ST.

LOWER GLENTWORTH ST.

SHANNON ST.

LOWER CECIL ST.

CECIL ST.

BEDFORD ROW

SARSFIELD ST.

HONAN'S QUAY

ARTHUR'S QUAY

PATRICK ST.

DENMARK ST.

RUTLAND STREET

ELLEN STREET

UPPER DENMARK ST.

WILLIAM STREET

THOMAS STREET

ROCHES STREET

GLENTWORTH ST.

CATHERINE ST.

UPPER MALLOW ST.

PARNELL STREET

DAVIS ST.

DOMINIC ST.

BRIDGE STREET

MARY STREET

GEORGE'S QUAY

CHARLOTTE QUAY

LOCKE QUAY

CLARE ST.

OLD CLARE STREET

BROAD ST.

JOHN'S STREET

HIGH STREET

MUNGRET STREET

CATHEDRAL PLACE

UPPER WILLIAM STREET

MULGRAVE STREET

JOHN'S SQ.

MICHAEL STREET

NICHOLAS STREET

0   200 m

ACCOMMODATION

An Óige Hostel	1
Boylan's B&B	2
Broad Street Hostel	3
Cloneen House B&B	4
Cruises	5
Finnegan's Hostel	6
Glen Eagles B&B	7
Hibernian House B&B	8
Jury's Hotel	9
Jury's Inn	10
Kilree Lodge	11
Limerick Holiday Hostel	12
Sarsfield Bridge Inn	13
Summerville and Westbourne Holiday Hostel	14
Trelawne House B&B	15

N18, Bunratty, Shannon Airport and Galway

N20, Adare & Cork

N20, Killarney & Cork

Dublin, Waterford & N7/N24

N7 & Dublin

N24, Lough Gur, Tipperary & Waterford

Like Derry in the north, Limerick also seems tainted by 300-year-old wars, carrying a stigma that it has still to shrug off. Modern unemployment and economic hard times have also left their mark. It doesn't always seem a friendly town, and certain areas can feel positively intimidating at night. However, recent efforts to clean up Limerick's image are starting to pay off: regeneration, most obvious around Arthur's Quay, King John's Castle and Cruises Street, has blown fresh gusts of optimism into most quarters of the city. While you are unlikely to spend long here, it can be rewarding to explore what the place does have to offer.

The city you see now is predominantly Georgian, but nevertheless Limerick has three distinct historical sectors: **Englishtown**, the oldest part of the city, built on an island in the Shannon with the castle as its focal point; **Irishtown**, which began to take shape in the thirteenth and fourteenth centuries; and within this **Newtown Pery**, the modern centre, made up of beautiful but rather dilapidated Georgian terraces and garish fast-food joints.

Some history

Limerick's history has to be spelt out. Even today, the town is only too aware of spectres from its past. This lowest fording point of the Shannon was first exploited by the **Vikings**, who in the tenth century sailed up the Shannon to *Inis Sibhton* (now Kingstown in Englishtown), an island by the eastern bank formed by a narrow bypass from the main stream now known as Abbey river. Here they established a port, and for a hundred years war after war raged between them and the native Irish. The Vikings were frequently defeated and were finally crushed nationally in 1014 at the Battle of Clontarf, at the hands of Brian Boru, the High King of Ireland. Limerick itself was attacked soon after and burned to the ground. Most of the Vikings didn't actually leave, but from then on they were gradually assimilated into the Gaelic population. The fate of Limerick itself didn't improve much, however, as over the next hundred years the Irish fought amongst themselves, burning the town to the ground again and again.

Some kind of stability was established with the arrival of the **Normans** at the end of the twelfth century. They expanded and fortified the town; King John arriving in 1210 to inaugurate King John's Castle, one of his finest. High walls were built that were now to keep the Gaels out, and because of this exile the first suburb across the Abbey river began to grow into **Irishtown**. There was trouble again with the visits of Edward Bruce in the fourteenth century; but the real emasculation of the city began with the onslaught of Cromwell's forces under the command of his son-in-law, Ireton, in the late 1640s. It was concluded when the city rallied to the Jacobite cause in 1689.

Once James II had lost the Battle of the Boyne in 1690, most of his supporters surrendered quickly – except for the ones at Limerick. As the Williamites advanced, the Jacobite forces within Limerick castle resolved to fight it out under the command of their Irish champion **Patrick Sarsfield**, Earl of Lucan and second in overall command of the Jacobean army. Although the walls of a medieval castle had little hope of withstanding seventeenth-century artillery (one of James's French generals declared that they would not stand up to a bombardment of apples), Sarsfield gained time by sneaking out, with five hundred of his troops, for a surprise night attack on William's supply train. He succeeded in totally destroying the munitions, while William sat waiting for them in front of the castle walls. However, when the Williamites returned the following year, Sarsfield could finally hold out no longer, and he surrendered on October 3, 1691, to the terms of a **treaty** that's so sore an historical point that it's still stuck in the minds of most Limerick people today.

The treaty terms were divided into military and civil articles. Militarily, Jacobeans were allowed to sail to France, which most of them did, along with Sarsfield himself (he died on the battlefield at Landon in Belgium, two years later); the civil agreement promised Catholics the religious and property rights they'd once had under Charles II. Within a couple of months the English reneged on this part of the treaty, and instead enforced extreme **anti-Catholic measures**. There followed civil unrest on such a scale that the city gates were locked every night for the next sixty years, and the betrayal has never been forgotten – it alone may explain the roots of today's element of Republican support in the city. The concordat was supposedly signed upon the **Treaty Stone** that rests on a plinth at the western end of Thomond Bridge. For many years, although this was used as a stepping stone for mounting horses, small pieces continued to be gouged out as souvenirs; one fragment set into a ring is said to have fetched £1000 in the USA.

It was not a promising start for the modern city, and there are those who claim that festering resentment has stunted Limerick's growth ever since. Being also lumbered with a geographical setting that gives it the Irish name *luimneach* ("a barren spot of land") has not helped. One redeeming factor has to lie in its humour; how else could its corporate motto read *An ancient city well studied in the arts of war.*

Arrival and information

Limerick is the nearest big city to **Shannon Airport** (☎061/471444; see p.321) – ten miles away off the Ennis Road. Airport buses (£3.50) run approximately every thirty minutes in the morning, hourly in the afternoon and irregularly after 6pm; a taxi costs around £12–15 (☎061/313131). The **train** and **bus** stations are next door to each other on Parnell Street in Newtown Pery. Some buses also depart from Penney's Store on the corner of Lower Cecil Street and Henry Street.

The excellent **tourist office** (May, June, Sept & Oct Mon–Sat 9.30am–1pm & 2–5.30pm; July & Aug Mon–Fri 9am–7pm, Sat & Sun 9am–6pm; Nov–April Mon–Fri 9.30am–1pm & 2–5.30pm, Sat 9.30am–1pm; ☎061/317522) is at Arthur's Quay, near where the river branches merge and you cross over into Englishtown: easiest found by following O'Connell Street north to the Custom House. Their city map has useful information and phone numbers; you can buy **parking discs** from most local newsagents and shops displaying a green and yellow disc. **Walking tours** of the city are organized by St Mary's Action Centre, 44 Nicholas St, in summer.

For **bike rental** try Emerald Cycles, 1 Patrick St (part of the Raleigh drop-off scheme); or Rent-A-Bike, Barrington Street.

Accommodation

There is a good range of accommodation in Limerick, particularly for budget travellers. If you have a car, secure parking in the centre is a consideration, as Limerick is a modern city with all the problems that go with that. Some areas of town are far better lit than others at night; for women travelling alone the following places are probably the most appealing: *Limerick Holiday Hostel*, the *Sarsfield Bridge Inn, Cruises House* and the B&Bs on the Ennis road.

Hotels and Inns

Jurys Hotel, Ennis Rd (☎061/327777). A small four-star hotel a short walk from the city centre with a gym, pool and tennis courts. Ask for a room away from the main road. ⑨.

Jurys Inn, Lower Mallow St (☎061/207000). Smart, comfortable and inexpensive accommodation for families and groups, though not in the most inspiring part of town. £49 per room sleeping up to two adults and two children or three adults.

Railway Hotel, Parnell St (☎061/413653). A comfortable hotel, but located in a rather lacklustre part of town opposite the train station. ④.

The Sarsfield Bridge Inn, Sarsfield Bridge (☎061/317179). Pleasant, modern inn accommodation. The price includes self-service continental breakfast, though guests can also cook their own food. Some of the rooms have excellent views of the castle and there's a secure car park. ④.

B&Bs

Cloneen House, Ennis Rd (☎061/454461). A smart, large house set back from the main road; all rooms are en suite and there's car parking to the rear. ④.

Cruises House, Denmark St (☎061/315320). Pleasant, functional new city-centre guest accommodation; price includes full cooked breakfast; all rooms are en suite with TVs. ④.

Glen Eagles, 12 Vereker Gardens, Ennis Rd (☎061/455521). A short walk into town, this is a regular B&B in a family home in a quiet cul-de-sac. ③.

Trelawne House, Ennis Rd (☎061/328733). A family house set back from the main road, just under a mile out of town; standard and en-suite rooms available. ③.

Hostels

An Óige Limerick Hostel, 1 Pery Square (☎061/314672). Easy-going regular youth hostel beside the People's Park and handy for the train station.

Broad Street Hostel, Broad St (☎061/317222; single £12, double £14). Crisp new budget accommodation with good facilities and secure car park. Facilities for wheelchair users.

Finnegan's Holiday Hostel, 6 Pery Square (☎061/310308). Beautiful, huge Georgian rooms and relaxed, studenty atmosphere.

Kilree Lodge Budget Accommodation, Old Clare St (☎061/401288; single £13, twin/double £11, 4-bedded family unit £9). Functional budget accommodation offering clean newly-furnished rooms and a self-catering kitchen.

Limerick Holiday Hostel, Barrington House, George's Quay (☎061/415222). Very well run, large hostel with secure parking.

The City

The sometimes incongruous blend of old and new in Limerick is testimony to a city discovering itself after years of neglect. Renovations and new building programmes stand alongside buildings – and indeed whole districts – that seem barely touched by the last fifty years. The best **views** of the city are to be had walking along the banks of the Shannon, especially around Arthur's Quay and the City Hall, or alternatively from the top of King John's Castle. Although virtually all the sights are in the old parts, Englishtown and Irishtown, the modern centre of the city is **Newtown Pery** – where the shops, pubs and restaurants congregate – an area of broad parallel streets scattered with fine Georgian buildings. O'Connell Street is the chief artery of this part of the city, and it's worth wandering down here, checking out the side streets with their characterful pubs and shops. Getting around the centre is easiest on foot.

Englishtown

Englishtown, which still has the narrow curving streets of its medieval origins, if few of the buildings, is the oldest part of the city, north of the modern centre. Crossing Matthew Bridge, the first things you'll see are St Mary's Cathedral ahead of you and the City Hall to your left. If you look down to the embankment of **George's Quay** on the right, your eye should just catch two very fine but armless torsos, metal-sculpted and set upon tall plinths facing one another some forty paces apart. This twentieth-century grotesquerie of war from within and without takes you by surprise – it's an unusually strong statement for Limerick.

The Church of Ireland **St Mary's Cathedral** (June–Sept Mon–Sat 9am–1pm & 2.30–5pm; Oct–May Mon–Sat 9am–1pm; free) was built at the end of the twelfth century, but only the Romanesque doorway facing the Courthouse, the nave and parts of the transepts remain from this period. The chancel, windows and the rest of the transepts date from the fifteenth century. The cathedral's unique feature is its **misericords**, the only set in Ireland: these are choir seats of lovely black oak with reptilian animals – cockatrice, griffins, sphinx and wild boar – carved in bold relief. The area around St Mary's has had a very successful face-lift. As you leave the cathedral, walk down to the Courthouse and stroll around City Hall – a brand-new affair of glass and pink tubing – to appreciate the rushing river and Limerick's buoyant new civic pride. Further into Englishtown is the **city museum** on Nicholas Street (Tues–Sat 10am–1pm & 2.15–5pm; free), displaying coins which date as far back as the Viking period; historic maps showing the old walled towns of Englishtown and Irishtown; memorabilia of various Fenian uprisings (notably a Pádraig Pearse letter from the 1916 Rebellion); and Stone, Iron and especially Bronze Age implements. Many of the Mesolithic items (c.7000–4000 BC) are from the Lough Gur area, and it's worth looking at the excavation photographs of this site before you visit it.

Nearby, overlooking the river at Thomond Bridge, stands **King John's Castle** (mid-April to Oct daily 9.30am–5.30pm; Nov to mid-April Sun noon–4pm; £4). You may well be put off by the newly built entrance hall, a senseless addition of overwhelming vacuity, negating any sense of power as you approach what is in fact one of the most impressive Anglo-Norman castles in Ireland. Built in the early thirteenth century, the castle was originally a five-sided fortress with four stout round towers; these were shortened at a much later stage to accommodate artillery positions – though one was actually replaced as a bastion in 1611. Inside, instruments of medieval siege warfare enliven the castle yard, or you can climb the battlements for superb views; there's an interesting twenty-minute film of the history of Limerick, and a much more detailed history of the Normans in Ireland in the "stand-and-read" **interpretive centre**. Beneath all of this are the foundations of pre-Norman dwellings – the finds of recent excavations. Despite all this, the castle is probably most impressive from the outside, as you stare up at the cliff-like immensity of its walls alongside Thomond Bridge.

The **treaty stone** stands at the far side of Thomond Bridge, on Clancy Strand on the west bank of the Shannon. In recent years it has been moved – only about twenty yards – and sandblasted clean. This, if you want to read symbolic significance into it, can be seen as an attempt to loosen a burden that was preventing the city from developing.

Irishtown

Back across Matthew Bridge you're in **Irishtown**, heading towards the bustle of the modern city centre along Rutland Street and then Patrick Street. Without doubt the most distinguished building here is the **Custom House**, an eighteenth-century structure of harmonious classical balance, and home to the excellent **Hunt Museum** (Mon–Sat 10am–5pm, Sun 2–5pm; Nov–April closed Mon; £3.90). It's an astonishing collection spanning 9000 years, from the Stone Age through to the twentieth century – the personal collection of John Hunt (1900–76), an English antiques dealer who went on to become an expert on medieval art, advising on internationally important collections such as those of William Burrell in Glasgow and the Aga Khan. One of the highlights of the collection is the bronze and enamel Antrim Cross, one of Ireland's most important examples of ninth-century early Christian metalwork and thought to be a precursor of the high cross designs at Monasterboice and Kells. Other highlights include the eleventh-century Beverley crosier, made of exquisitely carved walrus tusk; the dazzling fifteenth-century O'Dea mitre and crosier; and the Late Bronze Age Ballyscullion cauldron. Many of the artefacts are kept in drawers which visitors are free to open and include a thirteenth-century Limoges enamel and drawings by Giacometti.

A series of lanes – Ellen Street, Denmark Street and Cruises Street – run off Patrick Street, just a couple of hundred yards from the museum, worth exploring for their sprinkling of contemporary design shops and fashionable café-bars. The back streets beyond here are somewhat less appealing, the only feature of note being **St John's Cathedral**, a nineteenth-century Gothic Revival monstrosity which boasts the tallest spire in the country (280ft). Outside stands a memorial to Patrick Sarsfield, unsuccessful Jacobite defender of the city.

Back on the city's main thoroughfare, Patrick Street soon becomes **O'Connell Street**, Limerick's main, busy commercial street, with its run-down shops and bars. Heading further south along it, however, the Georgian buildings are better preserved and the Crescent at the far end of the street is rather fine, especially when lit up at night.

Eating, drinking and entertainment

A welcome sign of Limerick's regeneration is the rate at which good new cafés and pubs are appearing. The following list will give you some useful starting points. There's an abundance of bars, and in recent years Limerick has revived its reputation as a musical centre – particularly for contemporary and rock music. Again, a selection of **bars** and places to hear **music** can be found below. *The Belltable*, the *City Gallery* and *Biblio's*, Denmark Street, are good places to make contact with the Irish **arts scene**, and are worth a visit if you've more than half a day in the city; in this last you can pick up a copy of *Drop*, Limerick's free comprehensive fortnightly club/arts listings magazine.

Cafés and restaurants

Belltable Arts Centre, 69 O'Connell St. Good café downstairs with home-cooked lunches and snacks. Daytime only.

Doc's in The Granary, Bank Place (opposite George's Quay). Popular, studenty hang-out with inexpensive lunches. Mon–Fri.

Dolmen Art Gallery & Café, Honan's Quay (opposite the tourist office). Excellent hot lunches and salads in a cheerful art gallery setting.

Fat-zoes's, Rutland St. Popular spot for candle-lit pizzas.

Freddy's Bistro, Theatre Lane (☎061/418749), down an alley off Lower Glentworth St, near the Belltable Arts Centre. Expensive bistro serving steaks and seafood. Tues–Sun 5.30pm till late.

Furze Bush Café Bistro, corner of Glentworth & Catherine Sts. Lively bistro serving delicious crêpes, sandwiches and salads. Mon–Sat lunch; Thurs, Fri & Sat eves.

The Green Onion Caffé, 3 Ellen St (☎061/400710). Adventurous but affordable menu. Daily till 10pm.

The Grove, Cecil St. Health-food shop that does good bar-stool lunches and takeaways.

The Hunt Museum Restaurant, Custom House basement, Arthur's Quay. A stylish spot for lunch, overlooking the river. Opening hours same as museum.

Java's, 5 Catherine St. Delicious breakfasts and lunches, and the best coffee in Limerick. Good for vegetarians. Mon–Sat 8am–4pm, Sun noon–4pm.

Lavazza, Steamboat Quay (☎061/319800). Upbeat, chic bistro serving inexpensive lunches and more expensive dinner menu.

O'Flaherty's Basement Restaurant, 74 O'Connell St (☎061/316311). Expensive restaurant with Georgian brickwork and roaring fires, offering seafood, beef and lamb dishes. Mon–Sat 5.30–11pm.

The Old Quarter Pub & Café, Little Ellen St. Brazenly OTT bar for burgers, bangers, meatballs and New York deli-fare. Open breakfast till 6pm. daily.

Paul's, O'Connell St (☎061/316600). Mouthwatering Italian menu going way beyond the usual pizza brief. Main courses around £8. Lunch Mon–Fri; dinner Tues–Sun 6–10.30pm.

Portlys, Little Ellen St (☎061/313388). Self-consciously stylish café-restaurant serving light pancakes and bagels by day; pricy evening menu.

Thai Gourmet, 18 The Crescent (☎061/312012). Warm and welcoming Thai restaurant. Also does takeaways. Open 6–11.30pm. Closed Tues.

Websters, Thomas St (*webster@iica.net*). Internet café.

Bars and music venues

An Síbín, *Royal George Hotel*, O'Connell St. Traditional music and/or country singalongs every night during the summer.

Charlie Chaplin's, Chapel St. Trendy bar off Cruises Street with live gigs.

Doc's (see above) Upbeat bar in brick-vaulted granary courtyard with all manner of live acts – comedy, rock, reggae, acoustic (Tues, Wed, Thurs, Sun). Separate nightclub to the rear for discos as advertised (Thurs–Sun).

Dolan's, 3–4 Dock Rd. A good atmosphere, with traditional music every night.

James Gleeson, *The White House Bar*, 52 O'Connell St. Ancient ale house, full of character (and characters); packed, but warm and friendly.

The Globe, Cecil St. Trendy bar and nightclub on three floors. Every night till 2am.

The Locke, George's Quay. Traditional music in summer (Sun & Tues); a pleasant place to sit outside on fine evenings.

Nancy Blake's, Upper Denmark St. Lively pub with traditional music Sun–Wed; pleasant beer garden.

The Old Quarter, Cruises St. Airy bar with good daytime food; good for outdoor drinking on hot summer nights.

The Outback, at the back of *Nancy Blake's*; great venue for live blues and rock bands.

Paddy Hogan's, 20–24 Old Clare St. Very much a regular locals' bar with traditional music every Tuesday; spontaneous sessions any time.

Saints and Scholars, 7 Robert St (☎061/417616). Music venue with rave disco Thurs–Sun.

Tom Collins, Cecil St. Quieter bar, popular with local arty types.

The Vintage Club, Ellen St. Lively popular bar attracting a mixed young crowd.

Wicked Chicken, Baker Place. Popular club playing indie music. Until 2am.

Willie Sexton's, Upper O'Connell St. Bar for rugby enthusiasts; big sports events screened. No music.

The Works, Bedford Row. Popular club playing mainly charts, dance and indie music. Until 2am.

Arts centres and galleries

Pick up a copy of *Limerick Corporation Arts Calendar* at the tourist office for listings of theatre, classical music and art exhibitions.

Belltable Arts Centre, 69 O'Connell St (☎061/319866). Interesting mix of performances, including local and international touring companies. The gallery space shows a similarly diverse range of contemporary art.

Biblio's, Denmark St. Irish art and comic-book café.

City Gallery of Art, Pery Square (Mon–Wed & Fri 10am–1pm & 2–6pm, Thurs 2–7pm, Sat 10am–1pm; free). Situated in the People's Park, emphasizes international contemporary art, with a lesser focus on Irish work.

Dolmen Art Gallery, Honan's Quay. Commercial gallery showing interesting exhibitions of contemporary art. The shop alongside also has good quality craft pieces.

National Self-Portrait Collection, Limerick University (Mon–Fri 9am–5pm; free) Small but absorbing collection of Irish self-portraits; the Watercolour Society of Ireland Collection is also housed here. To find the university, head out along the Dublin road; after a few miles, take a left turn immediately after a Maxol petrol station for Plassey; follow the road round for another third of a mile and the entrance is on the left.

The Clare Glens

The **Clare Glens** on the Limerick–Tipperary border is a beautiful area of flowing falls, parts of which you can swim in: it makes a great day's excursion for cyclists. Head for Moroe (sometimes spelt Murroe), east of the city; Clare Glens is two miles north of this. A circular ride of some twenty miles could take this in, along with Glenstal Abbey and the village of **CASTLECONNELL**, a well-known Irish music and Irish-language centre in a scenic setting on the banks of the Shannon some seven miles from Limerick. Coillte Forest Park, sixteen miles west of the city, has a well-equipped campsite, the *Curragh Chase Caravan and Camping Park* (☎061/396349), picnic site, arboretum and the ruins of the home of poet Aubrey de Vere. To the south, it's not much further to Lough Gur (see overleaf) and Adare (p.254).

Lough Gur and around

Leaving Limerick city in the direction of Cork the main route is the N20, a fast and efficient but rather dull route south. If you have time to stop along the way, the smaller R512 road has considerably more to offer – above all Lough Gur, site of a wealth of Neolithic finds and one of County Limerick's chief attractions.

Lough Gur

Seventeen miles south of Limerick city, **Lough Gur** looks as though its waters have been accidentally spilt onto the Limerick soil. It's the only significant lake in the country, and comes as a rare treat in the midst of an otherwise lustreless terrain. The area that surrounds the lake has been an extremely rich source of archeological finds – though what exists now is often an extremely frugal sketch of what took place 5000 years ago. The lake is C-shaped, with a marshy area to the east that would complete the full circle.

In the middle of this circle is a small rise known as **Knockadoon**, whose slopes are studded with faint remains of earthworks showing ring forts and hut foundations dating from 3500 to 1000 BC. The length of its less secure marshy side is naturally forested and guarded at either end by two medieval tower houses, Bouchier's Castle and Black Castle. Mary Carbery's nineteenth-century book, *The Farm by Lough Gur*, gives a vivid contemporary account of life by the lough – the farm still stands up the road from the Neolithic huts known as the Spectacles.

Lough Gur must have been the perfect setting for a **Neolithic settlement**. The lake provided fish, and the gentle hillsides produced berries, nuts and trappings for animal hunting, as well as protection from the elements – and detection. When the lake was partly drained in the middle of the nineteenth century, and its level dropped by three yards, prehistoric artefacts were found in such quantities that stories tell of whole cartloads being hauled away. This may not be such an exaggeration; visit museums across the world today, and you'll discover some find from Lough Gur on display. The most famous discovery was a bronze shield from 700 BC, perfect in its concentric rings of bosses, but for a hacking in two places by the reedcutter who discovered it. The finds here pair well with the Neolithic discoveries made in Meath; this was once a Neolithic living commune, where the Brú na Bóinne site is concerned with ritual and burial. Today there's abundant **birdlife** on the lake; the grazing cattle, antlered goats and lack of modern buildings give you a strong intimation of the life of 5000 years ago.

The Interpretive centre and stone circle

The simplest approach to Lough Gur is to come off the R512 at Holycross. Follow the road to the northernmost section of the lake, keeping an eye out for a wedge-shaped **gallery grave**. The grave, typically, shows a long gallery space where the bodies of eight adults and four children from around 2000 BC were found. The gallery has parallel double walls of stone slabs filled in with rubble and what's called a septal slab at its back. The road then circles on round the marsh to an **interpretive centre** (mid-May to Sept daily 10am–6pm £2.10). Housed in replica Neolithic huts, this attempts to give some idea of what life was like for the early inhabitants. From here the chief attractions on Knockadoon are easily accessible on foot.

A quarter of a mile north of the Holycross turn-off, the first thing you'll see is a gargantuan **stone circle** close to the main road, the most substantial of the area's prehistoric remains. Possibly the grandest example in the country, it has a ring of standing stones (orthostats) marking out an almost perfect circle. A posthole was found at the centre which must have held a stake, from which, with a length of cord attached, the circle could be struck. Some of the stones are massive and are bolstered within their earth sockets by smaller boulders, which were then covered. Flints, arrowheads, blades and bowls were found within the enclosure, but little has been learned about the site's exact function. A circle of this size clearly demanded a good deal of social organization and a strong sense of purpose; the obvious conclusion is that this was a great centre for religious rituals, and frustratingly little else can be said.

The castles and Knockadoon

If you're walking, an alternative approach to Knockadoon is across the stone causeway that leads from near the gallery grave to **Black Castle**. Possibly thirteenth century, the castle is now weighed down by a swarthy camouflage of nettles, brambles and trees. It was once quite extensive, with a high curtain wall and square towers, and acted as a principal seat for the Earls of Desmond. The pathway north to Bouchier's Castle has three **Neolithic hut** remains at various degrees up the hill slope. If you're intent on seeing them, you'll have to forage around among the wooded thickets. A 1681 map shows the Knockadoon Peninsula as an island with a drawbridge sticking out of **Bouchier's Castle**. It's a typical fifteenth-century Desmond tower house of five storeys; but it's still privately owned and can't yet be visited (in any case, there's a better example at Castle Matrix; see p.255).

Turning westwards from the Black Castle towards the lakeshore, you'll see various ring forts and hut traces on the bare grassy slopes. It's not much, but even this scant evidence is enough to conjure up a thriving Stone Age community on **Knockadoon**. Rather than continue round along the bank of the lake, it's best to take this opportunity to cross back along the hilltop centre, where from a point known as **M**, you can get penetrating views into Kerry and Cork, with Limerick spreading towards them in a swath of low hills. **Crock** and **Bolin islands** in the lake are both *crannógs* which the mainland has now caught up with. They were built by laying down a ring of boulders, then the inner space was filled with earth and brushwood. **Garret Island** is a natural island with some stone remains of another Desmond castle.

Kilmallock

Eight miles further down the main road from Lough Gur, **KILMALLOCK** has some good Norman remains: a tower castle, a town gate, a Dominican friary and a medieval stone mansion on the main street. **St John's Tower Castle** stands in the middle of the street and was the town citadel (get the key at the bungalow across the road), but there's little to see here. Turn instead down the lane opposite and you'll find a tiny **museum** (Mon–Fri 1.30–5pm; otherwise contact T. Bohan, Lord Edward St; free) which won't take a minute to get through, unless you lend an ear to the home-made audiovisual history of the town. One interesting fact that crops up, and which goes a long way to explaining the prestigious-looking fortifications and friary bases, is that at the end of the sixteenth century Kilmallock had a population of 2000, compared to Dublin's 5000. Kilmallock's importance was swift to decline – its population today is only 1500.

Bruree

Four miles west of Kilmallock, **BRUREE** was the childhood home of **Eamon De Valera**, familiarly known as the "big man" or "Dev" to a population for whom he's been the most influential political instigator since the birth of the Free State in 1922. He founded the Fianna Fáil (Soldiers of Destiny) party in 1926, acted as premier of Ireland in 1932–48, 1951–54 and 1957–59, and assumed the honorary role of president from 1959 to 1973. This makes up a sizeable chunk of the Republic's history, and his grip on the nation has left an ambivalent attitude to his worth and integrity.

De Valera was the only leader of the 1916 Easter Rising to survive. His initial death sentence was commuted to imprisonment because of his American dual nationality – he was born in New York, and at this time the British were sensitive to American neutrality in World War I. He escaped from prison in England and was unconstitutionally elected the first president of the Irish Republic in 1919; his almost miraculous survival had marked him out as the man to lead Ireland out of seven hundred years of British domination. The Republic immediately declared war on Britain, and when two years of struggle forced the British to negotiate, De Valera's was the leading rebel voice against the signing of the Anglo-Irish Treaty in 1921. He wanted to hold out for an all-Ireland Free State, rather than accept only 26 counties out of 32, as was laid down in the Treaty. This stance divided the Irish and provoked the Civil War of 1921–23. The one war he succeeded in keeping the Irish out of was World War II, at the end of which he had the gall to send official commiserations to the Reichstag on Hitler's death, so profound was the bitterness of his battle with the British.

De Valera was brought up just outside Bruree in a small **cottage**, which has now been turned into a modest memorial of the family's household possessions, including a bulky trunk that was used for their return from exile in New York. The cottage is signposted nearly a mile down the road to the right at the eastern end of Bruree village (key from next house on the right, 150 yards further down the road). At the western end of Bruree village itself is the old schoolhouse, which has been turned into a **museum and heritage centre** (Tues–Fri 10am–5pm, Sat & Sun 2–5pm; £3), stocked with memorabilia of the ex-premier and president, plus a few rural items of general interest.

South and west of Limerick

The road southwest to Killarney is by far the most interesting route out of Limerick, catching the prim English beauty of thatched cottages in **Adare** and, much more importantly, taking in **Castle Matrix**, a Desmond tower house that has been brilliantly restored and gives a unique insight into life as it might have been lived in these castles. The road west to Tralee, the N69, is the least interesting of the three major routes across County Limerick. It runs parallel to the Shannon estuary but mostly through flat alluvial land, without the compensation of having the waters alongside except for the last few miles into Glin.

Adare

Famously picturesque **ADARE** has cultivated nearly as many antiques shops as pubs. In peak season, it will more than likely be infested with tourists snapping the wayside cottages that sit in a neat row, their quaint deep-brown thatch hanging in low fringes. The cottages represent the nineteenth-century ideal of romanticized rusticity, as realized by the third Earl of Dunraven (1812–71), landlord and master of Adare Manor and an eternal improver of circumstances for his tenants. Given that Adare is now probably regarded as the prettiest (and, it must be added, prissiest) village in Ireland, it's hard to believe that before the earl's improvements it was one of the grottiest. The cottages today are pure upmarket thatch, with pricy restaurants and craft shops. The **tourist office** (March–Dec Mon–Fri 8.30am–7pm, Sat & Sun 9am–6pm; ☎061/396255) is in the main street alongside the **heritage centre** (June–Sept daily 9am–7pm; Oct–Dec & Feb–May Mon–Sat 9am–5pm).

Adare Manor House, to the north of the village, is a huge, near fanatical assembly of castellations and turrets in limestone, built by the earl to Gothic Revival designs in 1832. This castle has only recently passed into private hands as a grand hotel, the *Adare Manor* (☎061/396566), at over £130 a night – it costs even to walk into the grounds. The River Maigue flows by the estate a little further up, at the head of the village, and although an exciting-looking triumvirate of **medieval buildings** beckons, a golf course steers its course next to all of them, inhibiting any snooping around you might want to do. You're meant to declare your intentions at the clubhouse (entrance a little further up the road) but you could probably slip from ruin to ruin without being noticed. It may not be worth the effort anyhow, for the **Desmond Castle** – interesting to explore as it looks – is completely bricked up and deemed unsafe. The fifteenth-century Friary appears far better preserved, but it was extensively restored as late as the mid-nineteenth century. All of these are perhaps easiest viewed from the bridge.

Back in the village there are ecclesiastical sites, too, starting with an **Augustinian Priory** just by the bridge. Beautifully preserved, this still serves as the local Church of Ireland church, its interior as close as any to the old medieval model. The **Trinitarian Abbey**, halfway down the main street, was founded in 1230 for the Trinitarian Canons of the Order of the Redemption of Captives, and is the only house of this order in Ireland. Today, it's Adare's Catholic church, with one of its turrets at the back a deserted columbarium. If you're thinking of staying over in Adare there are numerous **B&Bs** in the village, including *Berkeley Lodge* (☎061/396857; ③); *Avona* (☎061/396323; ③) and *Church View House* (☎061/396371; ③), all situated on Station Road. You can get decent meals at *The Arches Restaurant*, Main Street, or for snacks try the café inside the tourist visitor centre. *Bill Chawke's* and *Collin's Bar* both have traditional sessions one evening a week all year round.

There is excellent **hostel** accommodation at *Trainor's Hostel* (☎069/68164; mid-Feb to Oct), five miles southwest of Adare in the pleasant village of **BALLINGARRY**. The village is also home to an upmarket restaurant of some renown, *The Mustard Seed* (☎069/68508; closed Feb), which serves imaginative Irish cuisine.

Rathkeale and Castle Matrix

About eight miles on from Adare along the N21, **RATHKEALE** was once an important Geraldine town, and the main source of interest here is their one-time stronghold, **Castle Matrix** (mid-May to mid-Sept daily 11am–5pm; £2). To get there, turn right at the south end of the exceptionally long main street, just after the bridge: the castle lies half a mile down the road, on the right. Castle Matrix is a fifteenth-century tower house built by the seventh Earl of Desmond, and would inevitably have met with the same ruinous fate as virtually all the other 427 tower houses that once existed in Limerick, or the 2700 that once stood throughout the country – but for the brilliant restoration work of current owner Seán O'Driscoll, an Irish-American military enthusiast. With his army expertise, he understood the design of the fortifications and realized that measurements needed to be within an inch for the battlements on the parapets to be effective (in contrast, the ornamental battlements at somewhere like Bunratty in County Clare wouldn't have lasted long in a fifteenth-century siege).

Tower houses flourished between the fifteenth and seventeenth centuries, especially in these southern counties. They provided a robust enough mini-fortress for the shift in the times; Anglo-Norman confidence was increasing, resulting in an expansion of settlements. The big Irish estates were being broken up owing to the fall of the old Gaelic chiefs, and more towns were cropping up, with land being cultivated in hitherto uninhabited areas. Tower houses took on a uniform plan, usually of four or five floors, the top floor being the living quarters, the bottom windowless and usually used for storage. Castle Matrix has a tiny chapel re-created on its top floor and a medieval bedroom on another floor. It's stocked with exciting *objets d'art*, including a jewel-encrusted nineteenth-century Gaelic harp made by Fall of Belfast; an ebony writing bureau imported by the Southwells from China and finally donated back to Matrix some years ago, now sitting in the Oriental Room; documents referring to the Wild Geese (Irish officers who fled to the Continent at the beginning of the seventeenth century); and the most remarkable item of all to return home – the original deed of the Southwells (the Earls of Desmond), which Seán O'Driscoll came across accidentally in London's Portobello Road.

The castle derived its name from the *matres*, a Celtic sanctuary, on which it stands. The scattering of destroyed cashels and raths in the surrounding area give substance to the idea of an ancient sanctuary here. An annexe of the castle offers luxury **B&B** (☎069/64284; ⑥). A slightly cheaper alternative in the village is *Rathkeale House Hotel* (☎069/63333; ⑥), which also does food, and there is quality B&B at *The Willows* (☎069/63157; ④), just along the road to the castle from the village.

Newcastle West

Between Rathkeale and Newcastle West a signpost points to **Ardagh**, the ring fort where the wonderful Ardagh Chalice was found in 1868 (it's now in the Dublin National Museum). The site here is unimpressive, however, and it's not worth dragging yourself off the main road.

NEWCASTLE WEST should be your last, if very brief, stop on your way out of Limerick, to look at the Desmond Banqueting Hall. The hall is on the main square and very little fuss is made of it; but it's part of a scattered and hidden complex of ruined buildings – a keep, a peel tower, a bastion and curtain wall. Even though this was once the principal seat of the Fitzgeralds, the town hasn't harnessed its history to its advantage. The hall is in a near perfect state of preservation, and ready for an inspired restoration. At present, apart from a marriage fireplace said to have been imported from Egypt, it's all bare. As we go to press, access is still being decided upon by Dúchas; ☎01/661 3111 for details). Again, there are several small **B&Bs** – try, for example, Mrs Kennedy on Bishop Street (☎069/62287; ③); you can also get food and rooms at the *Courtney Lodge Hotel* (☎069/62244; ⑤).

There's another excellently preserved but entirely deserted tower house, **Glenquin Castle**, signposted left several miles off the Newcastle–Abbeyfeale road by a petrol station (head for Killeady). It has very good views of the countryside, but the effort to get here is really only worthwhile if you have a car. If you have children in tow, you might visit **Springfield Castle Deer Centre** (summer daily 1–6pm) outside Dromcollogher, about ten miles south of Newcastle West. There are pets for children to handle, and a tractor trailer takes you on a tour past herds of deer, so tame they feed from your hand.

West of Limerick

The first sign of interest you'll spot is **Carrigogunnell Castle** – no more than a well-worn ruin, overgrown with shrubs and trees, but with striking views across the estuary's waist. It's probably not worth leaving the main road; catch sight of it as the road passes Clarina, from where the ruin cuts a dramatic appearance atop its rocky outcrop. Beyond here, a good mile off the N69 at Kilcornan, is the **Celtic Theme Park and Gardens** (March–Nov daily 9am–7pm; £3). Don't let the words "theme park" put you off – there's not a drop of moulded plastic in sight. The hour or so stroll through the park takes in a string of features associated with ancient Ireland – a stone circle, dolmen, holy well and twelfth-century church. While some are replicas, others, most notably the lake dwelling and the (unexcavated) ring fort, are original, and overall this is a very sensitive blending of ancient landscape with imitation. Back up by the tearoom, there's an attractive formal garden, with fine scented flowers, a tranquil lily pond and walkways between silver birch and blackthorns.

Back on the N69, the road passes a few more tower houses on the right and the **Currahchase Forest Park** (see p.251) on the left before reaching ASKEATON. Here, there's an Anglo-Norman **friary** next to the River Deel, just off the main road at its second entry to Askeaton from the east. The friary was founded by the fourth Earl of Desmond, Gerald the Poet, in 1389. It now seems particularly hidden away, and has one of the loveliest cloisters you'll come across and some excellent window tracery. From the dormitory above, you can pick out the towering remains of the **castle**, penned in towards the centre of the town. This is worth no more than a quick scout around; there's a large banqueting hall, very similar to the better example in Newcastle West, its vaulted ground-floor chambers remaining just within the walls. A very dodgy-looking fifteenth-century end tower stands upon a rock in the centre of what was once an island in the River Deel. The castle's present decay does little to suggest its one-time Anglo-Norman prominence, when it flourished in the hands of the Earls of Desmond, until their fall to the Earl of Essex during the sixteenth century.

FOYNES is a moderately busy seaport, with a **flying boat museum** (April–Oct daily 10am–6pm; £3) which celebrates the town's past as an aviation centre. In the late 1930s and early 1940s, Foynes, as Limerick's only seaport, was the terminus for a transatlantic flying-boat service. Moving on, the afforested hillsides that now appear mark a pleasant route along the estuary as far as Glin on the Limerick–Kerry border.

travel details

Trains

Limerick to: Cahir (Mon–Sat 2 daily; 1hr 15min); Carrick-on-Suir (Mon–Sat 2 daily; 2hr); Clonmel (Mon–Sat 2 daily; 1hr 35min); Dublin (8–13 daily; 2hr 20min); Rosslare Harbour (Mon–Sat 2 daily; 2hr 20min); Tipperary (Mon–Sat 2 daily; 50min).

Waterford to: Dublin (3–6 daily; 2hr 25min); Limerick (2 daily; 3hr).

Buses

Cahir to: Waterford (5–6 daily;1hr 15min).
Cashel to: Cahir (2–8 daily; 1hr 35min); Cork (3–4 daily; 1hr 35min–2hr); Mitchelstown (3–4 daily; 45min).

Limerick to: Cahir (5–6 daily; 1hr 10min); Cork (6 daily; 1hr 50min); Dublin (7–10 daily; 3hr 15min); Shannon Airport (frequent service; 45min); Tipperary (5–10 daily; 50min); Waterford (5–6 daily; 2hr 25min).

Nenagh to: Dublin (5–7 daily; 2hr 40min); Limerick (6–8 daily; 1hr 20min).

Roscrea to: Dublin (5–7 daily; 2hr 40min); Limerick (6–8 daily; 1hr).

Waterford to: Dublin (7–10 daily; 3hr 30min); Tramore (frequent service; 25min).

COUNTY CORK

Cork, Ireland's largest county, is the perfect place to ease yourself gently into the exhilarations of Ireland's west coast. Cork city, the south's self-proclaimed cultural capital manages to be at one and the same time a relaxed and a spirited place. There are no spectacular sights, but Cork is one of Ireland's most pleasurable and accessible cities. Always a port, and with an island at its core, Cork nestles well inland on the estuary of the River Lee, which sustains the city with that same clear, soothing atmosphere that characterizes most of the county, and in particular its coast and rivers. In the east of the county maritime history is still more richly distilled, in the small ports of Cobh, Youghal and – most of all – Kinsale, all suggestive of a prosperity that Ireland could have had were it not for the strangulation of its overseas trade by Britain. On the other side of this coin are the riches of the Anglo-Irish legacy, most in evidence at Bantry House with its outrageously sumptuous art treasures.

Every county of Ireland's wild west coast has its devotees, and Cork is certainly no exception. The place elicits strong reaction from locals and visitors alike, and its rivalry with neighbouring Kerry is legendary. Critics like to call the scenery of **West Cork** tame or mild – even genteel – since it can only occasionally match the sheer wild physicality of coasts further north. But this quality probably has as much to do with the people and the relative mildness of the climate – blessed by the continual influence of the Gulf Stream – as with landscape.

In the main the charms of the Cork countryside are those of a gently rural backwater, but as you head west along a fabulously indented coastline of hidden bays and coves to the **wild peninsulas** of the extreme southwest, or through the ravine of Gougane Barra high above **Glengarriff** and **Bantry Bay**, the soft contours of a comfortable and easy prettiness slip away to reveal beauty of a more elemental kind. There's not as much of this as you might find in, say, Kerry, but in the **Caha Mountains** careering north from Bantry Bay, the scintillating cliffs of **Mizen Head** or the seascapes of the **Sherkin** and **Clear Island**, teeming with birdlife, Cork has scenery as exciting and dramatic as you'll find anywhere.

Public transport around the county is fairly plentiful. **Bus Éireann** covers the whole of Cork except for the extreme west of Mizen Head and the Beara Peninsula. Major towns have daily connections – though there's only one bus a week along Sheep's Head and one linking Kenmare with Castletownbere. Small towns and villages off the main roads are served less frequently, so if you are relying on public transport it's worth taking details of times and days of services you are likely to want while in a major bus station. Ask about return fares – often they are as cheap as single tickets if used on certain days. On certain routes private buses provide the only transport: see

---

ACCOMMODATION PRICE CODES

Throughout this book, prices of hotels, guesthouses and B&Bs have been graded with the codes below, according to what you can expect to pay for a double room in high season. For more details on accommodation, see p. 29.

① Under £26	④ £40–55	⑦ £90–110
② £26–33	⑤ £55–70	⑧ £110–130
③ £33–40	⑥ £70–90	⑨ Over £130

"Travel Details" at the end of this chapter for details. The intricate landscape of West Cork, in particular, is best explored at a slow pace, making it ideal country for touring by **bike** or **hitching**. If you are travelling by car the N71 is the main coastal road, but it's much more rewarding to meander off along the minor roads through remoter areas, past sandy coves and small communities.

If you have a tent, you can **camp** almost anywhere along the coast if you ask permission first, though the Beara Peninsula and the Caha Mountains are very rocky. The few official campsites are listed in the text.

Cork City

Old **CORK** city – the second city of the Republic – is built on an island, the two channels of the River Lee embracing it either side while nineteenth-century suburbs sprawl up the surrounding hills. The river gives the city centre a compactness and sharp definition. It's a place of great charm, with a history of vigorous intellectual independence, and approached from rural Ireland, it has a surprisingly cosmopolitan feel to it.

Evidence of Cork's history as a great mercantile centre is everywhere, with grey stone quaysides, old warehouses and elegant and quirky bridges spanning the river. Many of the city's streets were at one time waterways: St Patrick's Street had quays for sailing ships, and on the pavement in Grand Parade you can still see moorings dating from the eighteenth century. Important port though Cork may be, however, it doesn't feel overridingly commercial, and the Lee is certainly not the river of an industrial town. The all-pervading presence of its waters reflects and seems to double any light, so that even on the cloudiest of days there is a balmy, translucent quality to the atmosphere which effects a calm on the visitor. Cork is a welcoming, friendly place. While it has the vibrancy to enliven and excite, the pace is always Irish and somehow the island breathes enough space for all temperaments.

Some history

Cork (*Corcaigh*, meaning "marshy place") had its origins in the seventh century when St Finbarr founded an abbey and school on the site where the impressive nineteenth-century Gothic St Finbarr's Cathedral stands today. A settlement grew up around the monastic foundation, overlooking a marshy swamp where the city centre now stands. In 820 the Vikings arrived, bringing their usual violence and destruction, and wrecked both abbey and town. They built a new settlement on one of the islands in the marshes and eventually integrated with the native Celts. The twelfth century saw the Norman invasion and Cork, like other ports, was taken in 1172. The new acquisition was fortified with massive stone walls, which survived Cromwell but were destroyed by Williamite forces at the Siege of Cork in 1690. From this time the city began to take on the shape recognizable today. Expansion saw the reclamation of marshes and the development of canals within the city, and waterborne **trade** brought increasing prosperity. Evidence of this wealth survives in the form of fine eighteenth-century bow-fronted houses and the ostentatious nineteenth-century church architecture decorating the city – sharp, grey and Gothic, much of it by the Pain brothers. Traces of the great dairy trade of that period can still be seen in the Shandon area.

CORK TELEPHONE NUMBERS

Around August 1999 telephone numbers in the 021 area will change; the prefix 4 will be added to Cork numbers beginning with 2, 3, 5, 8 or 9.

More recently, Cork saw much violence and suffered greatly during the Anglo-Irish and Civil wars: the city's part in **Republican** history is well documented in the local museum. The Black and Tans reigned here with particular terror, destroying much of the town by fire, and were responsible for the murder of Thomas MacCurtain, the mayor of Cork, in 1920. Cork's next mayor, Terence MacSwiney, was jailed as a Republican and died in Brixton prison after a hunger strike of 74 days. He was a popular hero, and his hunger strike remains one of the longest achieved in the history of the IRA. One of his colleagues in Cork prison, Joseph Murphy, achieved the longest fast on record, going 76 days without food.

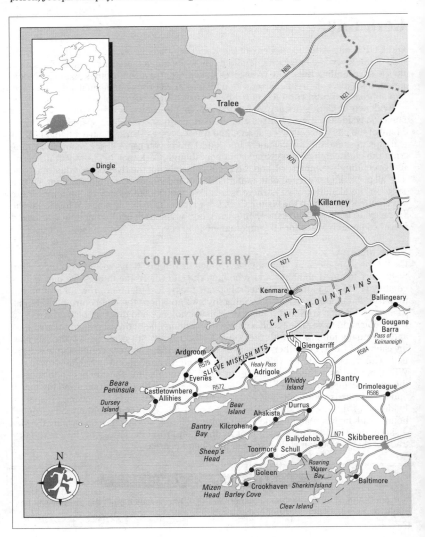

As part of the Republic, Cork has continued to develop – as a port, a university city and a cultural centre – and to assert its independence of Dublin.

Arrival and information

One of the joys of Cork is the fact that its scale is human: most of what it has to offer can be explored on foot. **Buses** to the suburbs and outlying towns and villages all go from the **Bus Éireann** station at Parnell Place alongside Merchant's Quay, and most of these also pick up from the more central St Patrick's Street. The Bus Éireann station

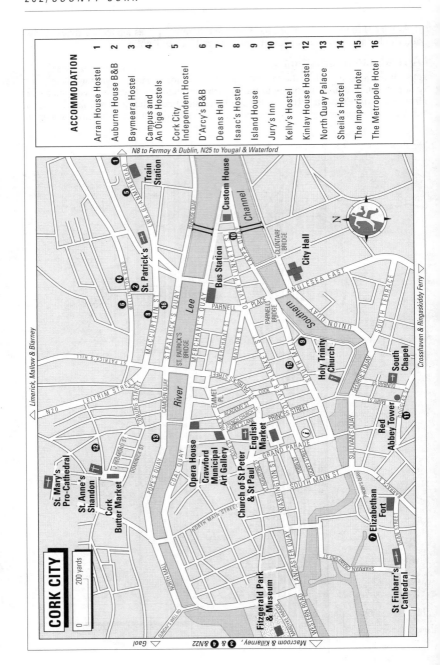

ACCOMMODATION

Arran House Hostel	1
Auburne House B&B	2
Baymeara Hostel	3
Campus and An Óige Hostels	4
Cork City Independent Hostel	5
D'Arcy's B&B	6
Deans Hall	7
Isaac's Hostel	8
Island House	9
Jury's Inn	10
Kelly's Hostel	11
Kinlay House Hostel	12
North Quay Palace	13
Sheila's Hostel	14
The Imperial Hotel	15
The Metropole Hotel	16

CORK CITY

0 — 200 yards

N8 to Fermoy & Dublin, N25 to Yougal & Waterford

Train Station

Custom House

Channel

City Hall

St. Patrick's

Bus Station

Lee

Clontarf Bridge

Anglesea East

Parnell

Oliver Plunkett Place

Parnell Bridge

Southern

Union Quay

South Terrace

Holy Trinity Church

South Chapel

Red Abbey Tower

River

Opera House

Crawford Municipal Art Gallery

Church of St Peter & St Paul

English Market

Princes Street

Grand Parade

South Main St

St. Mary's Pro-Cathedral

St. Anne's Shandon

Cork Butter Market

Elizabethan Fort

Fitzgerald Park & Museum

St Finbarr's Cathedral

Limerick, Mallow & Blarney

Crosshaven & Ringaskiddy Ferry

Macroom & Killarney, N22 & 8

Gaol

also operates an extensive nationwide bus service, while the **train station** is less than a mile out of the city centre on the Lower Glanmire Road. Irish Rail's travel centre is located at 65 Patrick St. **Private buses** operate from various central points, mostly along St Patrick's Street and from outside *Mulligan's*, Parnell Place. If you arrive by **ferry** you'll be at Ringaskiddy, some ten miles out, from where you can catch a connecting bus into the centre. Coming in by **plane** you can easily pick up a bus for the twenty-minute journey into town: a shuttle service from the airport operates every 45 minutes (April–Sept till 8.45pm; Oct–March Mon–Sat till 6.30pm, Sun till 3.30pm; £2.50 single, £3.50 return). A taxi to the airport will cost around £5, to the ferryport £10. If you're driving remember that, as in all the major cities, a disc parking system is in operation: discs can be bought from newsagents or the tourist office.

The **tourist office** on Grand Parade supplies the usual wide variety of information and can also book accommodation (July–Aug Mon–Sat 9am–6pm, Sun 10am–1pm; June & Sept Mon–Sat 9am–6pm; March–May & Oct Mon–Sat 9.15am–5.30pm; Nov–Feb Mon–Sat 9.15am–1pm & 2.15–5.30pm). Cork is a great city for **festivals**, the biggest of which are the **film festival** at the beginning of October and the **jazz festival** towards the end of October – for more on both see p.269. For information year round on theatre and music performances, ask at the tourist office or consult the *Cork Examiner* or *Cork's List*.

Accommodation

The few **hotels** in the city are at the top end of the market; the mid-range, however, is more than adequately covered by the numerous **B&Bs**, mainly concentrated near the university along Western Road, and at the opposite end of town on Lower Glanmire Road, near the train station. If you are planning your stay to coincide with one of the October festivals, advance booking is advisable, and prices tend to rise during this period. Cork also has plenty of good budget accommodation, including a number of **hostels** and a **campsite**.

Hotels

The Imperial Hotel, South Mall (☎ & fax 021/274040). Cork's oldest hotel. The foyer retains glimmers of the grand Victorian era in chandeliers and portraiture. Worth checking out their lower-rate offers out of season. ⑦.

The Metropole Hotel, MacCurtain St (☎021/508122). Pleasantly refurbished grand Victorian hotel; residents have full use of a leisure centre, including gym, pool, saunas and supervised creche facilities. If traffic noise bothers you, ask for a room not overlooking MacCurtain St. ⑦.

Guesthouses and B&Bs

Antoine House, Western Rd (☎021/273494). Regular B&B, all rooms en suite with satellite TV; private parking. ⑤.

Auburn House, 3 Garfield Terrace, Wellington Rd (☎021/508555). Beautifully kept B&B with TVs in all rooms, in a quiet location within ten minutes walk of city centre. ④.

The Blarney Stone, 1 Carriglee Terrace, Western Rd (☎021/270083). TVs in all rooms, off-street parking, no-smoking bedrooms. ③.

Clare D'Arcy, 7 Sydney Place, Wellington Rd (☎021/504658). Worth paying a little more to stay in this beautiful Georgian town house. ④.

Clon Ross, 85 Lower Glanmire Rd (☎021/502602). All rooms have TVs; it's also handy for the train station. ③.

Garinish House, Western Rd (☎021/275111). Good quality guesthouse offering an astonishing breakfast menu, including porridge with Irish whiskey and spiced grapefruit with cinnamon toast; jacuzzis in some rooms. Off-street parking. ⑤.

Kent House, 47 Lower Glanmire Rd (☎021/504260). A standard B&B, handy for the train station. No car parking. ③.

Number Forty Eight, 48 Lower Glanmire Rd (☎021/505790; ③). Comfortable, smart B&B; no parking.

Oakland, 51 Lower Glanmire Rd (☎021/500578). Regular B&B offering both standard and en-suite rooms. ③.

Seven North Mall, 7 North Mall (☎021/397191). Good quality guesthouse in eighteenth-century town house, centrally located beside the river. Excellent breakfasts; secure car park. ⑤.

Tara House, 52 Lower Glanmire Rd (☎021/500294). Regular B&B with standard and en-suite rooms; TVs throughout. ③.

Westbourne House, 2 Westbourne Villas, Western Rd (☎021/276153). Pleasant, traditional B&B about a mile from the centre; all rooms are en suite and non-smoking throughout; secure parking. ④.

Inns and self-catering apartments

Deans Hall, Crosses Green, nr St Finbarr's Cathedral (☎021/312623, fax 316523). Student accommodation let as self-catering apartments. Central, clean, well-equipped four–six-person apartments. Open from the end of June to mid-Sept. £60–75 per night.

North Quay Place, Pope's Quay, near Shandon (☎021/551300). Clean, comfortable and efficiently run, with full cooking facilities and TVs. Apartments accommodate six people. £70 per night; £230 per week.

Jurys Cork Inn, Anderson's Quay (☎021/276444). Smart accommodation, especially reasonable for families; rooms accommodate either three adults or two adults and two children. £55 per night.

Hostels

An Óige Hostel, 1–2 Redclyffe, Western Rd (☎021/543289). Newly refurbished hostel with mainly six-bedded rooms.

Aaran House Hostel, Lower Glanmire Rd (☎021/551566). Small town house near the train station with comfortable bunks, kitchen and bike lock-up.

Baymeara Hostel, Ashbrook, Dennehy's Cross (☎021/346565). Purpose-built apartment block offering comfortable budget accommodation, just under a mile from the centre, close to the N71 & N22; popular with groups.

Campus Hostel, 3 Woodland View, Western Rd (IHH; ☎021/343531). Tiny hostel that can feel a bit overcrowded; pick up a #8 bus from the station on Western Rd.

Cork City Independent Hostel, 100 Lower Glanmire Rd (☎021/509089). Handily situated about 100 yards from the train station. Friendly, rainbow-coloured hippie hostel.

Isaac's, 48 MacCurtain St (IHH; ☎021/508388). Certainly the plushest in town, but if you are intending to cook your own food, the kitchen facilities become pretty cramped during high season; inconvenient daytime lock-out of all dormitory accommodation, too. Bike rental; credit cards accepted.

Island House, Morrison's Quay (☎021/271716). Purpose-built apartment block in a central location. The rooms are comfortable, but their twins and doubles are more expensive than many B&Bs. Two to four-bedded dorm £10.50.

Kelly's Hostel, 25 Summerhill South, off Douglas St (☎021/315612). Small, friendly and colourful hostel. Cable TV dominates the common room. Laundry facilities. Dorm, twin and three-bedded rooms available.

Kinlay House, Shandon (IHH; ☎021/508966, fax 506927). Very clean and efficiently run USIT hostel, with laundry facilities. Price includes breakfast. Also singles and twin rooms. Bike rental available.

Sheila's Cork Tourist Hostel, Belgrave Place, Wellington Rd (IHH; ☎021/505562). A central, friendly and well-run hostel with good cooking facilities, a garden to the rear, breakfast, sauna, bike rental and email facilities.

Campsite

Bienvenue Caravan and Camping Park (☎021/312711). Near the airport – the Airport/Kinsale bus stops 600 yards from the site, or follow the signposts to Kinsale and airport, and then the signs from the airport gates. £5 per tent plus £1 per adult. The campsite may increase charges at festival times.

The City

Cork has no really spectacular sights, but it's a fine place to wander: around the quays, through the narrow lanes, into the markets, up to Shandon. The ambience and sense of place are enjoyable in themselves, and for those with a taste for it there's plenty of nineteenth-century Gothic church architecture punctuating the river banks, and evocative remnants of a great mercantile past. Exploration on foot is rewarding – the city's medieval core is embedded in its central narrow lanes, and the meshing of its history can be felt embodied in its buildings, reflected in the constant flow of the Lee. But don't go expecting to be astounded. Enjoying Cork city is to do with tuning in to the pace and life of the place.

The island

The **city centre** is essentially the island, with its quaysides, pretty bridges, alleyways and lanes, plus that segment to the north of the River Lee that has MacCurtain Street as its central thoroughfare, and the lanes leading up to Shandon. **St Patrick's Street** and **Grand Parade** form the modern commercial heart, with a healthy smattering of the modish amenities generally associated with much larger European cities. Not that you are ever engulfed by commercialism; aggressive multinationals barely dominate, and major chainstores exist alongside modest traditional businesses. It is in such immediate contrasts that the charms of the city lie. A hundred yards from the elegant shopfronts of St Patrick's Street you'll find **Coal Quay Market** in Cornmarket Street – a flea market, worth investigating if you are fascinated by the shabby side of a damp, rural life in its unchanged nineteenth-century setting. A minute's walk from Coal Quay Market down **Paul Street** brings still more variety in the bijou environs of **French Church Street** and **Carey's Lane**, busy with new restaurants, pavement cafés, artists' studios and period clothes shops.

The eastern, downstream, end of the island is the more clearly defined: many of its quays are still in use, and it's here that you best get a sense of the old port city. In the west the island peters out in a predominantly residential area. Heading in this direction, though, you can follow the signs off Western Road for **Fitzgerald Park**, home of the **Cork Public Museum** (June–Aug Mon–Sat 11am–1pm & 2.15–6pm; Sept–May Mon–Fri 11am–1pm & 2.15–5pm; Sun all year 3–5pm; free except Sun, 75p), about a mile out of the city centre, easily combined with a trip to Cork Gaol (see overleaf). Primarily a museum of Republican history, it has an excellent commentary on the part played by nationally significant local characters and events in the Republican movement. There are exhibits of local archeological and geological finds, too, and a section on the history of the dairy trade.

Shandon

North of the River Lee is the area known as **Shandon**, a sadly neglected reminder of Cork's eighteenth-century status as the most important port in Europe for dairy products. To get there head up John Redmond Street, or simply aim for the giant fish atop the church tower. The most striking survival is the **Cork Butter Exchange**, stout nineteenth-century Classical buildings recently given over to select craft workshops. The old **butter market** itself sits like a generously proportioned butter tub in a cobbled square, recently renovated to house the Firkin Crane Theatre. Despite the air of dereliction, this part of town is worth a visit for the pleasant Georgian church of **St Anne's Shandon** (1750), easily distinguishable from all over Cork city by its weather vane – an eleven-foot salmon. For £1 you can view the not particularly remarkable interior of St Anne's, and the old books. For a much more worthwhile £2 you can climb the tower (June–Aug Mon–Sat 10am–5pm; Sept–May Mon–Sat 10am–4pm), two of its sides finished in red sandstone, two in white limestone, for excellent views, and ring the famous bells – a good stock of sheet tunes is provided.

To the west of here is an area known as Sunday's Well, and **Cork City Gaol** (March–Oct daily 9.30am–6pm, Nov–Feb 10am–5pm; taped tours year round; £3). It's a good 25 minutes' walk from the city centre, up the hill from North Mall. A lively taped tour takes you through the prison, focusing on social history in a way that is both engaging and enlightening. It's occasionally threaded with characters of national importance, all vividly brought to life by a dramatic audiovisual finale. There's a pleasant walk from here to Fitzgerald Park: turn right as you leave the prison, left, right and then left down a flight of steps and over the Shaky Bridge.

The stark precision of nineteenth-century Gothic which is repeated time and again in the city's churches may not be to everyone's taste, but here it undeniably gives the city a rhythmic architectural cohesion. Both Pugin and Pain are very much in evidence, Pugin in the brilliant Revivalist essay of the Church of St Peter and St Paul on Friar Mathew Quay, with its handsome lantern spire, and in St Patrick's Church on Lower Glanmire Road. Best of all is William Burges' **St Finbarr's Cathedral** (built 1867–79), obsessively detailed, with its impressive French Gothic spire providing a grand silhouette on the southwesterly shoulder of the city.

Eating

Cork doesn't have a wide range of cuisines for you to choose from – the main influence is Mediterranean – but it does have a high standard of food on offer, with several cafés and restaurants serving dishes made from organic local produce, plenty of seafood and vegetarian options. Alongside the more conventional eating places, **The English Market** located between Grand Parade and Princes Street, with entrances off both, is a wonderful place to share in the city's enthusiasm for all things culinary. Here the cosmopolitan rubs shoulder with the decidedly unpretentious; stalls specializing in the finest olive oils and cheeses jostle for space among the rakes of tripe and bacon.

Cafés and budget places

Bia Beo, Thompson House, MacCurtain St. Breezy art gallery café serving inexpensive wholesome snacks and lunches.

The Bodega, Coal Quay. Cork's most talked about new venue, worth calling in for its wonderfully bold interior alone; Mediterranean-influenced menu. Open Mon–Sat 12.30–9.30pm.

The Farm Gate Café, upstairs in The English Market, Princes St. Great for affordable lunches and teas; listen to the pianist and watch the market below. Lots of Mediterranean salads, savoury tarts, and plenty of seafood. The emphasis is on using fresh, local produce, and, in line with tradition, they also serve tripe and drisheen (a kind of black pudding). Mon–Sat 8.30am–5.50pm.

Gables, Douglas St. Relaxed, friendly pub with unlikely menu featuring, for example, grilled polenta with roasted vegetables and Portuguese-style shark steaks.

The Gingerbread House, Paul St. Great café for soaking up the Paul Street scene. Tasty baguettes, tartlets, soups and coffees. Mon–Sat till 10pm, Sun till 6.30pm.

Gino's, Winthrop St. Good cheap pizzas and homemade ice cream.

Harlequin Café, 26 Paul St. Cheap and fairly wholesome café, though not all as homemade as its appearance might suggest. A nice spot to sit and watch the world drift past or read the café papers. Open 10am–6pm.

Kafka's, 7 Maylor St. Great veggie and non-veggie breakfasts, and a huge range of tasty baguettes, filled jacket potatoes and sandwiches. Mon–Sat 8am–6pm.

Café Mexicana, Carey's Lane. Enchiladas, tacos, tortillas, all from around £7, served in informal and welcoming atmosphere. Mon–Thurs & Sun noon–11pm, Fri & Sat noon–midnight.

The Other Side, South Main St. Offshoot of *The Quay Co-op*; cheap vegetarian café and gay meeting place. Mon–Sat 10am–6.30pm.

The Quay Co-op, 24 Sullivan's Quay. Delicious, large vegetarian and vegan meals, soups, puddings and teas, all in surroundings of wonderfully faded elegance. Self-service. Open Mon–Sat till 9pm.

Tribes, Tuckey St. Smoky coffee bar for trendy diehards. Over 30 strains of coffee, and many herbal teas. Till 4pm daily.

The Triskel Arts Centre, Tobin St, off South Main St. Homemade bread, soups and salads; hot vegetarian and non-vegetarian dishes from £4; tasty and good value. Mon 11am–3pm, Tues–Fri 10.30am–5.30pm, Sat 11am–5pm.

Restaurants

Bully's, 40 Paul St. Wine bar serving pizzas, fresh pasta and fish; popular with families; inexpensive–moderate. Mon–Sat noon–11.30pm & Sun 1–11pm.

Café Paradiso, 16 Lancaster Quay, Western Rd (☎021/277939). This relaxed, informal restaurant is generally thought to have the best vegetarian/vegan menu in town: gleefully high fat. Inexpensive lunches; expensive dinner menu. Tues–Sat 10.30am–10.30pm.

The Crawford Municipal Art Gallery Café, Emmet Place. The gallery's café is an affordable offshoot of the famous *Ballymaloe House* restaurant near Cloyne. Specializes in Mediterranean and traditional Irish cuisine. Mon–Sat 10am–5pm.

Food Fiction, upstairs in *The Gingerbread House* (☎021/276411). Relaxed restaurant serving fresh fish, meat and poultry, with a few vegetarian/pasta options. Moderate–expensive. Mon–Sat 6pm till late.

Isaac's Restaurant, MacCurtain St (☎021/503805). Deservedly popular restaurant. Light, delicious food with a good range of salads, fresh breads, cheeses, seafood and pasta. High emphasis on local and organic produce. Moderate–expensive. Mon–Sat 10am–10.30pm, Sun 6–9.30pm.

The Ivory Tower, The Exchange Buildings, 35 Princes St (☎021/274665). The place to go to treat yourself: adventurous menu specializing in wild and organic food. Exquisite. Three courses cost around £20–25. Thurs–Sun.

Jacques Restaurant, Phoenix St (☎021/277387). Top-notch, imaginative restaurant with excellent reputation, serving mouthwatering Mediterranean cuisine. Dinner is around £20. Lunch Mon–Fri; dinner Mon–Sat 6–10.30pm.

Paddy Garibaldi's, Carey's Lane. Friendly café-restaurant for burgers and pizzas. Daily noon–midnight.

Proby's Bistro, Proby's Quay, Crosses Green, nr St Finbarr's Cathedral (☎021/316531). Slightly formal bistro; eclectic menu with strong American and Mediterranean influences. Closed Sun lunchtime.

Strasbourg's Goose, 17–18 French Church St (☎021/279534). Young person's restaurant with casual, pavement café atmosphere. Set dinner menu around £10.

A Taste of Thailand, Bridge St (☎021/505404). Authentic Thai cuisine; early-bird three-course special around £10; licensed or BYO wine. Daily 6–11pm.

Valparaiso, 115 Oliver Plunkett St (☎021/275488). Huge range of dishes taken from a broad sweep of Spanish cuisine. Lunch menu includes inexpensive tapas; evening meals are expensive. Closed Sun lunchtime.

Pubs, nightlife and the arts

There are plenty of good watering holes in the city, and if all you want is a drink, you won't need a guide to find somewhere – though a couple of the city's older bars mentioned overleaf are worth seeking for their atmosphere. Many bars have **music**, traditional or otherwise, and the following list should give some good pointers on where to find the best of this. Cork also has a strong **club scene**; the major venues are listed below. As with any large city, venues and session nights change: pick up *Cork's List* for detailed what's-on information and look for fliers in *The Quay Co-op*, *The Other Side*, *The Phoenix* pub and in Comet Records, Washington Street. Wherever you end up, this is not a difficult town to enjoy yourself in.

Pubs and bars

An Bodhrán, 42 Oliver Plunkett St. Chance midweek sessions of traditional music in summer.

An Bróg, 78 Oliver Plunkett St. Popular young bar, with unplugged indie, rock, alternative folk.

An Siol Broin, MacCurtain St. A fairly mixed crowd with traditional music in the summer (Mon & Wed).

An Spailpín Fánach, 28 South Main St. Traditional Irish and cajun sessions (Sun–Wed).

The Bodega, Coat Quay. See "Cafés" on p.266.

The Corner House, Coburg St. Popular, young bar with a mixture of mainly cajun, bluegrass, folk and Irish music (Sun–Wed).

An Crúiscín Lan, Douglas St. Small bar with traditional music (Thurs) and blues (weekends).

The Donkey's Ears, Union Quay. Mainly reggae with leanings towards funky house and hip-hop. A good place to pick up club concessions.

Fred Zeppelin's, Parliament St. Live gig venue for indie, ska, hip-hop, hardcore; it has the touch of a bikers' hang-out, but attracts a mixed clientele.

Gable's, Douglas St. Handy for *Kelly's Hostel*, with occasional traditional music and singing.

Isaac Bells, St Patrick's Quay (behind the *Metropole Hotel*). Very popular, lively bar playing traditional Irish or folk and rock (midweek).

The Isobar, Little Hanover St, off Washington St. Large selection of Continental beers and comfy couches. A good place to settle in for the evening.

Loafers, 26 Douglas St. Friendly bar with pleasant beer garden, attracts a bohemian clientele; probably the most relaxed place for gays to drink in the city.

The Lobby, Union Quay. A great spot to catch live music year round. Traditional Irish sessions take place on Tuesdays, Wednesdays and Fridays. The upstairs bar has a concert every Saturday during summer – traditional, folk, world music – very much a place to *listen* rather than drink. Cover charge.

The Long Valley, Winthrop St. Something of a one-off and a locals' favourite; the place also does good substantial sandwiches.

The Mutton Lane Inn, Mutton Lane, off Patrick St. Convivial, old, traditional city-centre bar.

Nancy Spain's, Barrack St. Upbeat bar with plenty of live music – rock & indie bands – plus house and world music.

The Oyster Tavern, 4 Market Lane, off St Patrick's St. Old-fashioned atmosphere – all brass and polished wood.

The Phoenix, Union Quay. Traditional, blues and folk (Mon & Wed); the bar upstairs attracts a younger crowd into heavy metal.

The Torch, Douglas St. Intimate, traditional bar, and a gay-friendly place.

The Vineyard, Market Lane, off Patrick St. Continental-style café-bar also serving Italian food.

Clubs

Cork has a growing reputation for its club and dance scene, and it's well worth checking out *Cork's List* or calling into Comet Records, Washington Street, to find out what's happening. You might also tune into Radio Friendly (104.6FM) to get a taste of the scene. The Southern Soul and Disco Festival, held over the June bank holiday weekend, is increasingly popular, and it's worth looking out for anything promoted by Simply Délicieux.

The Annexe, Grand Parade. Indie music, plus occasional gigs; look for fliers around town. Tues–Sun.

City Limits, Coburg St. Mixed crowd at this fun and unpretentious club, with salsa, acid jazz, world music, disco; comedy from 9pm on Fridays and Saturdays followed by dancing till 2am – anything from Ska to Blondie, James Brown to Sinatra; Sunday there's a mellower mix.

Elroy's, behind Westimer, Sullivan's Quay. At the Friday & Saturday discos neat dress is the norm; till 2am. Also a live music venue.

Gorby's, above *Brannagan's*, 74 Oliver Plunkett St. This is a popular club, with indie, pop, rock and dance music.

The Half Moon Theatre, in the back of the Opera House (☎021/272680). Both theatre and club venue; early evening drama productions followed by bands midnight–2am.

The Metropole Hotel, MacCurtain St. A focal point for the jazz festival and worth checking out for gigs and DJs on Saturdays.

Sir Henry's, South Main St. Cork's top club and winner of Best Dance Club in Munster award. Reggae (Mon), funk, techno and dance music (Tues–Sun).

The Other Place, St Augustine St. Women-only disco first Friday of every month.

Zoë's, Caroline St, above the *Black Bushe*. Immensely popular club, particularly for the Tuesday MOR disco – a really sociable affair for gays and others – and for its Friday Fry Up, an excellent dance night. Open daily.

Art, theatre, film and festivals

The hub of artistic activity in Cork is the Triskel Arts Centre, found down the narrow and dingy Tobin Street, off South Main Street (☎021/272022). It has changing exhibitions of contemporary art, a film theatre, a continuous programme of performance art, poetry reading, contemporary music, and a very good café. It is also an excellent source of information about what's on – Triskel will know about any theatre or music performances in the city.

Considering the amount of painting and sculpture generated around the county, Cork city is poorly served in terms of the visual arts. **Fine art** has a high profile in cafés, restaurants and private houses, but good galleries are in short supply. Worth a visit, however, is the Crawford Municipal Gallery in Emmet Place (Mon–Sat 10am–5pm), which has a permanent collection of Irish and European painting and usually an interesting contemporary exhibition. The Cork Arts Society, 5 Father Matthew Quay, off South Mall, is a good commercial gallery, with exhibitions of contemporary works. The Blackcombe Galleries, 44A MacCurtain St (above the antiques shop), is a pleasant space, showing eighteen contemporary exhibitions per year.

The **Cork Opera House** (☎021/276357), in Emmet Place, offers a full programme of drama, concerts both classical and popular, ballet, opera, review and variety, though very rarely anything at all out of the mainstream. Classical concerts are also held at **Triskel**, the **School of Music**, on Union Quay, and the **City Hall**, Anglesea Street. The **Everyman Palace**, MacCurtain Street (☎021/501673), and **Cork Arts Theatre** **(CATs)**, in Knapps Square, off Camden Quay, both offer a range of local small-scale productions. **The Firkin Crane**, Shandon (☎021/507487)is the best place to catch **classical and contemporary dance**. Cork has a very popular **international jazz festival**, one of the last two weekends in October. With music bursting out of every doorway, you don't need to go and see the big names to enjoy yourself if you are short of cash. It's a great time to be in the city, though accommodation is scarce. There's also an important **film festival** at the beginning of October, with films screened at Triskel and the Opera House, while the excellent **art house cinema**, *Kino*, Washington Street (☎021/271571) screens films throughout the year. The International Choral Festival is held the first weekend in May, and there is a folk festival during September: ask at the tourist office for exact dates of all festivals.

Listings

Airlines Aer Lingus, 38 Patrick St (☎021/274331); Ryanair (☎021/313000); British Airways (☎1 800/626747).

Airport Information ☎021/313131.

Banks Branches of the Allied Irish Bank in Patrick St, North Main St, Bridge St and Western Rd.

Bike rental CycleScene, 396 Blarney St (☎021/301183); Kilgrews, 6 Kyle St (☎021/276255), or from the campsite; Aidann Quinlan, 2 Bandon Rd, Barrack St (☎021/313133); Irish Cycle Hire, at the train station (☎021/551430).

Bookshops Collins, Carey's Lane; Eason's, Patrick St; Keogh's Books, 6 MacCurtain St (old, rare and second-hand); Liam Russell, Oliver Plunkett St; Mercier Bookshop, 4 Bridge St; *The Other Side*, South Main St – gay bookshop and drop-in centre; Waterstones, Patrick St.

Bureau de change At the tourist office and at *Sheila's Hostel*.

Buses Bus Éireann station, Parnell Place, alongside Merchant's Quay (☎021/508188) for local and intercity buses. Several private bus companies also operate from Cork: see "Travel Details" at the end of this chapter.

Camping equipment The Tent Shop, Rutland St, off South Terrace, offers camping gear for sale or rent; Matthews, Academy St, for equipment and Gaz.

Car rental Car Rental Ireland, Monahan Rd (☎021/962277); Eurodollar Rent a Car, Cork airport (☎344884), city office: Carrigrohane Rd (☎021/344884); Great Island Car Rentals, 47 MacCurtain St (☎021/503536 or 811609).

Ferries to France operate from Ringaskiddy, about ten miles from Cork. Brittany Ferries, 42 Grand Parade (☎021/277801), sail to Roscoff (April–Oct one a week); Swansea–Cork Ferries, 52 South Mall (☎021/276000), operates a 10-hour crossing, four–six days a week according to season.

Gay information *Gay and Lesbian News*, Munster edition, available at *The Other Side* café, South Main St.

Hospital Cork University Hospital, Wilton Rd (☎021/546400).

Hurling and gaelic football For fixtures phone ☎021/385876 or 963311.

Internet access *Plaza 2000*, 65 North Main St (☎021/272344; *plaza@iica.net*); *Jumpin' Jack's Cellar Bar*, Sheres St (☎021/273000; *leevale@indigo.ie*); *Sheila's hostel* (*sheilas@iol.ie*).

Laundry MacCurtain St, next door to the Everyman Palace theatre, Mon–Sat from 9am to last wash at 8pm.

Music The Living Tradition, 40 MacCurtain St (☎021/502040), sells a great range of Irish and world music on CD and cassette, as well as sheet music and traditional instruments such as *bodhráns* and tin whistles. Comet Records, Washington St can provide the latest info on Cork's dance and club scene and also does ticket sales.

Pharmacy Phelan's Late Night Pharmacy, 9 Patrick St (☎021/272511); Denis O'Leary, 8 Grand Parade (☎021/274563).

Post Office Oliver Plunkett St and MacCurtain St.

Swimming pool Douglas Swimming Pool, Douglas Rd (☎021/293073).

Taxis Tele Cabs ☎021/505050 or 505533; Supercabs ☎021/500511.

Trains Iarnród Éireann's travel centre ☎021/506766 or 504888.

Travel agents USIT have two offices in Cork: at 10–11 Market Parade (☎021/270900), and UCC Student Travel, near The Boole Library, University College (☎021/273901).

East of Cork

East Cork has none of the scenic splendour of the west, but there are points of interest as you pass through, and a couple of spots that make a good day trip from Cork city if you don't have the time or means to venture further afield. A trip across the harbour to

Fota, with its wild animals and eighteenth-century Classicism, and **Cobh** with its fine watersports, will allow you to get back in the evening early enough to take advantage of Cork's nightlife. On the way further east to the quaint port of **Youghal** – with its colourful maritime history and scenic location – there are a string of places worth a brief stop, including **Midleton**, the home of Jameson whiskey, and some pleasant beaches at **Ballycotton** and **Garryvoe**.

Fota and Cobh

A visit to Fota House Wildlife Park and the pretty harbour town of Cobh can be managed in a day on a return train ticket from Cork. Going by train really is the best option, taking you across the mudflats of an estuary teeming with birdlife. Both are situated on islands in the mouth of Cork harbour. **Fota Wildlife Park** (April–Oct Mon–Sat 10am–6pm, Sun 11am–6pm; £3.50) is a small, pleasant park with apes, cheetahs, giraffes, red pandas and zebras, among others, all wandering about the landscaped eighteenth-century estate of Fota House.

The **house**, originally an eighteenth-century hunting lodge, but much enlarged in 1820, is no longer open to the public, though this situation may change. You can, however, visit the estate's **arboretum** (daily: April–Oct 10am–6pm; Nov–March 10am–5pm; free): one of the most important in Europe, with a great variety of rare and exotic flowering shrubs and trees.

Cobh

Rejoining the train from Fota takes you out to the pretty little town of **COBH**. Cobh (pronounced *Cove*) is held in a quaint cup of land with steep, narrow streets climbing the hill to the Pugin cathedral. One of the most enjoyable of these neo-Gothic monsters, it dominates the town, giving marvellous views out across the great curve of the bay to Spike Island. Thanks to its fine natural harbour, Cobh has long been an important port: it served as an assembly point for ships during the Napoleonic wars and was a major departure point for steamers carrying emigrants to America and convicts to Australia. The first-ever transatlantic steamer sailed from here in 1838, and the *Titanic* called in on her ill-fated voyage, too; a monument to the victims of the *Lusitania* disaster stands in Casement Square. Cobh's dramatic maritime history is retold at its excellent heritage centre, **The Queenstown Story** (daily 10am–6pm; £3.50). Today the port is still used by a substantial fishing fleet. From September to February, when it is awash with fishermen, the town's character changes completely.

First and foremost, though, Cobh is a holiday resort, itself an historic function. Ireland's first yacht club was established here in 1720, and from 1830 on the town was a popular health resort, imitative of English Regency resorts like Brighton, a style reflected in its architecture. The main square is flanked by brightly painted Victorian town houses, and the place has a robust cheerfulness – though none of the cosmopolitan flavour of harbours further west. It attracts Irish holidaying families and offers pitch and putt, tennis, swimming and a stony beach. The **International Sailing Centre** on

---

CORK COAST ROUTE

If you want to head west from Cobh along the coast, or you want to cut around twenty minutes' driving time off your return to Cork city, you can take a five-minute ferry to Glenbrook from Carrigaloe, a couple of miles north of Cobh as you head back up towards the N25. Cross River Ferries services start at 7.15am from Carrigaloe and run about every ten minutes till 12.20am. Car £3.50 return, £2.50 single; adult £1/60p; bikes carried free.

East Beach (☎021/811237) runs courses in sailing, canoeing and wind-surfing and also has accommodation available for long-term use. There's a **regatta** weekend in mid-August, and for enthusiasts, the third week in July sees the exciting **Ford Yacht Week** across the harbour in Crosshaven (alternate summers); best observation points are reckoned to be Ringabella, Fennel's Bay, Myrtleville or Roche's Point. Any other time in the summer you can at least take a **harbour boat trip** (Marine Transport Services, Atlantic Quay; ☎021/811485; £3.50).

Cobh **tourist office** (Mon–Fri 9.30am–5.30pm, Sat & Sun 11.30am–5.30pm; opens 2.30–5.30pm mid-Oct to Feb; ☎021/813301), housed in the old yacht club, in the town centre, has maps and local information – it also hosts art exhibitions in conjunction with The Crawford Municipal Gallery in Cork city. If you want to stay, **B&Bs** include *Atlantic*, 8 West Beach (☎021/811489; ③), *Ardeen*, 3 Harbour Hill (☎021/811803; ③); and *The New European*, 1 East Beach (☎021/811122; ④). Take the ferry west across the harbour to **CROSSHAVEN**, for smart hostel accommodation at *The Grand* (☎021/832270), overlooking Cork harbour, and particularly handy for the **Ringaskiddy ferries**.

Midleton to Garryvoe beach

The cheery market town of **MIDLETON**, about ten miles east of Cork, is best known for being the home of Jameson Irish whiskey. The **Jameson Heritage Centre** tour is a highly polished promotional affair, taking you through the distillery and culminating in a whiskey-tasting session (March–Oct daily 10am–6pm, last admission 4pm; Nov–Feb Mon–Fri tours at noon & 3pm only; £3.50). The best place to eat is *The Farm Gate*, Coolbawn (☎021/632771), a deli and restaurant selling and serving fresh local produce (lunches Mon–Sat, dinners Fri and Sat only). For accommodation, try the **hostel** *An Stór* (IHH; ☎021/633106), a newly converted mill.

Four miles to the south is the sleepy, historic village of **CLOYNE**. One of Ireland's earliest Christian foundations, the monastery of St Colman, was established here in the sixth century. In medieval times the village continued to be of religious importance with the establishment of the See of Cloyne, a diocese which extended well into County Limerick. Reminders of this era, though, are few. There's a fine tenth-century **round tower**, from whose top, 100ft up, there are superb views (key from Cathedral House; £1), and you can also visit **St Colman's Cathedral**, a large building of warm, mottled stone originally built in 1250 but disappointingly restored in the nineteenth century. Inside are the grand and grim seventeenth-century Fitzgerald of Imokelly tomb and the alabaster tomb of George Berkley, the famous philosopher who was bishop here from 1734 to 1753. An Egyptian tau cross and the St Anthony's cross on the cathedral doorway are faint traces of earlier Mediterranean influences. Off the Cloyne–Ballycotton Road, *Ballymaloe House* (☎021/652531; ⑨) is an exceptional **restaurant**, one of the most famous in Ireland; a meal here will cost you around £32. Accommodation is in a large seventeenth-century manor house set on a four-hundred acre farm.

Although the beaches on this stretch of coast are unspectacular and have nothing like the charm of the west, five miles on from Cloyne, **BALLYCOTTON** is a pleasant enough spot, with a little quayside, fine cliff walks for miles to the west, and a beach half a mile away. If you want to stay, there's fine guesthouse **accommodation** at *Spanish Point Restaurant* (☎ & fax 021/646177; ④; dinner £21). Bright and airy, it's in a terrific spot and has a beautiful conservatory–dining room overlooking Ballycotton Bay. *The Cliffstop Café* (June–Aug only Tues–Sun noon–8pm, till 9pm weekends) is worth the steep climb to the west of the village for good pizzas, seafood and salads, and views over the rock-island lighthouse. Not far away to the north are the holiday villages of Shanagarry and **GARRYVOE**. Garryvoe **beach** is very long and sandy, but it's beset by caravans advancing upon the shore and very busy during high season. To the east

> **CHANGES TO TELEPHONE NUMBERS**
>
> Around August 1999 numbers in the 021 Midleton area beginning with 6 will be prefixed with the number 4.

of here the bay is flat and of interest only to birdwatchers, its reed-infested estuary now a protected bird sanctuary. Here a river sidles its way, smooth and khaki, through the mudflats to the sea.

Youghal

YOUGHAL (pronounced *Yawl*) is an ancient port at the mouth of the River Blackwater, where the counties of Cork and Waterford meet. In a small way it combines the richness of the Blackwater towns with the prettiness of Kinsale and Cobh. A picturesque holiday town, Youghal has real character, with a colourful history and some fine architecture to remember it by.

Youghal's walls were first built by the Norman settlers who established the town, but those which stand today were erected by Edward I in 1275. From medieval times the town prospered as one of Ireland's leading ports, trading with the Continent – particularly France – and with England. Political disturbances and trade restrictions imposed on Irish ports by the English Crown, however, meant the town's growth began to slow in the mid-sixteenth century. It fell into the hands of the Earl of Desmond, and in 1579 the "Rebel" Earl (rebelling against Elizabeth I) sacked and burned the place. After Desmond's death, Youghal was part of the 40,000 acres granted to Walter Raleigh during the Munster Plantations, with which Elizabeth hoped to control Ireland. Raleigh, though, had little interest in Ireland, and spent most of his time composing poetry in an attempt to curry favour with the queen. In this he was abetted by Edmund Spenser, another local colonist, author of *The Faerie Queen*. Spenser proved to be capable of both great poetry and of barbarism in his dealings with the Irish: they eventually repaid him by burning down his castle, Kilcolman, near Buttevant. Raleigh himself spent little time in Youghal, selling his land to Richard Boyle, the "Great" Earl of Cork (and father of the scientist), who then greatly developed the town as he did all his newly acquired land.

When Cromwell reached New Ross in 1649, the English garrison at Youghal went over to the Parliamentarian side, and so the town escaped destruction. Nonetheless, the importance of the port continued to diminish through the seventeenth century. Still, the decline was only relative to its former stature, and there is enough fine eighteenth-century architecture to make it clear that a small but affluent class of merchants still prospered. Today Youghal is a quiet seaside resort, and the history preserved in its buildings continues to suggest prosperity earned through centuries of vigorous commerce, and offers an insight into the privileged lives of the early colonists.

The Town

Youghal's most famous landmark is the **clock tower**, which bridges the long, curvy main street: a superbly proportioned Georgian structure of warm, plum-coloured stone. A century ago it was used as a prison, more recently it served as a museum, but it's now closed indefinitely. Steps leading off the tower climb the steep hill through little lanes to the top of the town, where the walls and turrets of the old defences still define the shape of the compact harbour.

The most charming buildings lie, in the main, on the landward side of North Main Street and in the lanes that run behind it. On North Main Street itself the **Red House**, built in 1710, is a fine example of domestic architecture, clearly showing the Dutch influence of the original merchant owner. Here, too, are seventeenth-century almshouses, built by Richard Boyle to house Protestant widows. Lanes off to the west of this end of Main Street lead to the Elizabethan **Myrtle Grove**, known as "Raleigh's House", one of the oldest unfortified houses in Ireland but, sadly, no longer open to the public.

Nearby, you'll find the **Collegiate Church of St Mary's**, a large, simple, thirteenth-century building, one of the few of such age still in use in Ireland. The building has been greatly altered over the centuries, but still has interesting medieval tombs and effigies. Particularly notable are the thirteenth-century monuments in the south transept (entrance is by a little door to the left as you walk up towards the church, or by the main door when open). Wrecked when the town was sacked by Desmond's men in 1579, they were later restored by Boyle, with the addition of effigies in seventeenth-century costume. Heading out of town towards Waterford, you pass the ruins of North Abbey, a thirteenth-century Dominican priory of which little remains.

On the east side of North Main Street is **Tyntes Castle**, a fifteenth-century tower house that is now sadly dilapidated (and, by the look of it, rapidly deteriorating). Edmund Spenser's widow married Robert Tynte, who lived here. Lanes off this side of the street lead to the **quayside**. Here it's all very quaint: warehouse buildings warm with the patina of age surround the harbour; yucca palms decorate the walkways, and the cultivated fields of Waterford across the water look very near.

There is an interesting walking tour of the town (June–Aug Mon–Sat at 11am and 3pm; £2.50) which starts at an exhibition in the tourist office and lasts around ninety minutes. Signposted from here too is **Fox's Lane Museum** (July & Aug Mon–Sat 10am–1pm & 2–6pm, Sun 2–6pm; by arrangement through the tourist office at other times; £2), which displays with illuminating clarity and imagination a collection of domestic gadgetry – everything from sausage makers to petrol-fuelled irons and cucumber straighteners – all mapping the dogged march of progress from the nineteenth century.

Practicalities

The **tourist office** is on Market Square, just behind the harbour (June–Sept Mon–Fri & Sun 9.30am–6pm, Sat 9.30am–1pm & 2.15–6pm; Oct–May Mon–Fri 9.30am–1pm & 2–5.30pm; ☎024/92390). You'll find plenty of **B&Bs** along the main streets and around the quayside – try *Avonmore House* (☎024/92617; ④) or *Attracta*, (☎024/92062; ③), both on South Abbey or *Roseville* on New Catherine Street (☎024/92571; ③). There are plenty more out on the Cork Road, including *Shalamar* (☎024/93398; ②), about two miles out of town. Hotel accommodation is available at *The Devonshire Arms Hotel*, Pearse Square (☎024/92827; ⑥), and *Aherne's*, 163 North Main St (☎024/92424, fax 93633; ⑧), both in the centre of town. The latter is also renowned for its seafood restaurant (☎024/92424). The other hotel in the area is *The Hilltop Hotel* (☎024/92911; ⑤), a mile and a half along the road towards Cork. The International Busking Festival during the first weekend in August offers £3,000 prize money – and suddenly **camping space** is available everywhere. To the west of town, sandy (European Blue Flag) **beaches** stretch for miles.

There's no shortage of **places to eat** in Youghal. *The Coffee Pot*, North Main Street, just near the clock tower, serves good-value meals (till 7.30pm in summer), while *Merrick's* next door dishes up inexpensive home-cooked meals till 7pm daily. Also on this side of town, the bistro-style *Perfect Blend* serves moderately priced Irish, Italian and vegetarian dishes. For good bar food, try *The Devonshire Arms Hotel*, Pearse Square, and *The Walter Raleigh*, North Main Street, both at the west end of the town centre.

You'll find **music** of some sort in Youghal's bars most nights during the summer, and at the weekends throughout the year. *The Nook* on Main Street is the best bet for traditional music (Wed), and both *The Clock*, 56 South Main St, and *The Spinning Wheel*, Friar Street, have rock and pop bands. If you just want a quiet pint, head for the *Moby Dick* on the quays – Youghal was used as a location for the film of the same name, and inside you'll find memorabilia and photographs from the making of the film.

Inland Cork

Although most people head straight for the coast, **inland Cork**, aside from providing a quick route west, does have its merits, and, unless you yearn for the sea, it's just as beautiful. The main tourist attraction is the famous historic town of **Blarney**, close to the scenic Lee Valley; it makes a pleasurable stop on your way westwards or an easy day-trip from Cork city. Further inland, the **Boggeragh Mountains** and the route from Macroom to Bantry provide opportunities for gentle walking.

Blarney

BLARNEY is an easy six miles from Cork city; buses leave the bus station every half hour. The town itself functions chiefly as a tourist service centre – it is perhaps the only place in Ireland where you see not *Mná* and *Fir*, not Ladies and Gents, but "Rest Room". Naturally there are plenty of places to eat here: try *The Muskerry Arms* or the bar of *Christy's Hotel* for pub food. One surprise is the **Blarney Woollen Mills**, one of Blarney's original industries, now doing very nicely out of the castle's visitors. It has a couple of shops here, and the smaller of the two is one of the best places in Ireland for woolly bargains. Alongside is a tourist office (daily April–Sept 9am–7pm, Oct–March till 5pm), and you can **rent bikes** from McGrath Cycles, Stoneview (☎021/385658) for some easy and scenic cycling from Blarney up the Lee Valley.

If you can manage to divorce the **castle** (daily 9am–5.30pm; £3) from the whole "Blarney phenomenon", it actually is a fine stronghold, built in 1446 by Dermot McCarthy, King of Munster. The **Blarney Stone** has been kissed by visitors for over a hundred years, the legend being that to do so gives you the gift of eloquent and persuasive speech. The most famous story of how the legend came about tells of one McCarthy – King of Munster and Lord of Blarney – who, supposedly loyal to the colonizing Queen Elizabeth I, never actually got around to fulfilling any of the agreements between them, always sidetracking her emissaries with drinking, dancing and sweet talk. He was said to be able to talk "the noose off his head". In her frustration the queen is said to have eventually cried out "Blarney, Blarney, what he says he does not mean. It is the usual Blarney." And so the word entered the English language.

The stone itself is a four foot by one foot limestone block set in the battlements 83ft above the ground, so kissing it requires a head for heights. If you want to, you'll have to join the queue (it can take an hour) in the castle keep from which you can watch everyone else (one at a time) being dangled backwards by the shins over the battlements aided by two strong men. This also gives you time to consider whether or not you really want to join in. According to a less challenging legend, the stone is half of the Stone of Scone, given to Cormac McCarthy by Robert the Bruce in gratitude for the support of 4000 men at the Battle of Bannockburn (the rest is at Edinburgh Castle). Views from the top of the castle are superb.

In the castle grounds, **Rock Close** is a nineteenth-century folly, a rock garden supposedly built around druidic remains. It is a pity that myths, authentic or not, are such big business around here, because without the hype these ancient yews and oaks could create a potent atmosphere.

Macroom

The secondary roads west of Cork city run up the Lee Valley, through scenic countryside and a number of small villages. Chief of these is **MACROOM**, a focus for tourists and music enthusiasts heading for Killarney. It's on a main road and is a relatively easy hitch through the mountains. The **Boggeragh Mountains** to the north of the Lee Valley appear as high, rolling moorland, unspectacular compared with other ranges in Cork and Kerry but particularly rich in archeological remains: stone circles, standing stones, wedge tombs and ring forts. A leaflet, *Antiquities of the Boggeragh Mountains,* is available from the tourist office in Cork city – of great value in locating these sites. The Bantry road from Macroom is far quieter, leading into the mountains and one of the county's last remaining Gaeltacht regions. There's a small, friendly **hostel**, *Tigh Barra* (IHH; mid-March to Sept; ☎026/47016), which also offers camping, about a mile and a half west of the tiny village of **BALLINGEARY**; beyond here the road passes through the dramatic glacial valley of Gougane Barra and down to Bantry Bay (see p.287 and p.290).

Dunmanway

Alternatively, taking the road south of Cork city to Bandon and then west to **DUN-MANWAY** brings you to very promising country of deserted hills and lakes. Dunmanway is a plain country town, but just outside it the excellent **hostel**, *Shiplake House Mountain Hostel* (IHH; ☎ & fax 023/45750; closed Jan), is in a beautiful setting and also has gypsy caravans for couples and families (£12), **camping** and delicious vegetarian food. To find it take the Castle Road next to the *Market Diner* out of town, follow it for two and a half miles in the direction of Coolkelure (the road to Kealkill) and turn right at the hostel sign. Bus Éireann runs at least two daily buses from Cork to Dunmanway, and a bus from Dunmanway to Bantry and Glengarriff. A **private bus** runs a Dunmanway–Cork return trip at weekends; phone the hostel for details of times.

Kinsale

KINSALE has retained much of the flavour of its rich maritime history and has much in common with the formerly affluent ports of Youghal, Cork and Cobh. The eighteen-mile road from Cork city travels through gentle rolling farmland and alongside an estuary. This easy, meandering coast is a favourite for fishing and birdwatching, so alive with birdlife that it's rewarding even for the uninitiated. At Kinsale the harbour is broad, and cormorants and shags skim across its gentle waters. A tongue of land curls from the west into the centre of the harbour, protecting the town from harsh winds, and on this promontory are the ivy-clad ruins of James Fort, a ruddy castle built by the English James I.

With its pretty harbour, the opportunities it offers for watersports, and its reputation as the gourmet centre of the southwest, Kinsale is an extremely successful tourist town. For the most part development has been tasteful, though the pace of change is swift and a garish scar of pastel-coloured apartments disfiguring the hillside illustrates the threat commercialism poses to Kinsale's historic character. Still, despite the crowds and the cars, there is plenty of interest in the life, landscape and history to keep you here.

Some history

Originally a fishing town, Kinsale's sheltered harbour has made it a place of strategic importance in Irish, and English, history. The town received its first royal charter from Edward III in 1333, but it was of little importance up until the Battle of Kinsale in 1601, a disastrous defeat for the Irish which signalled the end of the Gaelic aristocracy as a power for the English to reckon with. A Spanish fleet stood in the bay ready to support the Irish cause against Elizabethan forces, but was unable to make useful contact with O'Neill and O'Donnell attacking from the north. So the battle was lost, and although resistance to English rule continued, six years later came "the flight of the Earls" – when the Irish nobility fled to the Continent, giving up the fight for their own lands.

CHANGES TO TELEPHONE NUMBERS

Around August 1999 numbers in the 021 Kinsale area beginning with 7 will be prefixed with the number 4.

It was also at Kinsale that **James II** landed with French support in an attempt to regain his throne in 1689, and it was later the port of his final departure from Ireland after the Battle of the Boyne. The town was an important naval base for the English Crown in the seventeenth and eighteenth centuries, and the sixteenth-century tower house in Cork Street – Desmond Castle – became known as "The French Prison" when it was used to hold as many as 600 French prisoners during the Napoleonic wars.

It was off the Old Head of Kinsale that the ocean liner, the **Lusitania**, en route to Liverpool from New York, was torpedoed by a German submarine in 1915, killing 1198 people. It remains a controversial incident: Germany claimed there was ammunition on board; the US said it contained only civilians. Whatever the truth, it has been seen as a catalyst for America's entry into World War I.

The Town

The town's history is recorded in the **museum** (irregular hours – check with the tourist office; £1), bang in the centre of town above the old market (1600) with its Dutch-style facade (1704). It's an intriguing jumble of stuff, including memorabilia from the *Lusitania* disaster; sixteenth-century royal charters and maps; local craftwork; personal effects of the eighteenth-century giant of Kinsale; and a variety of bizarre local inventions that never got further than the local museum. Here, too, is the musty old courtroom that had remained much the same from the eighteenth century up until 1915, when the inquest into the sinking of the *Lusitania* was held here and Kinsale suddenly became the focus of the world's press; after the inquest it was decided that the courtroom should be left as a memorial.

Desmond Castle (mid-April to mid-June Tues–Sun and bank holidays 10am–6pm; mid-June to early Oct daily 10am–6pm; £1.50; Heritage Card) offers little to see beyond its simple, sturdy structure, although the tour is worth taking since the guides are instructive and entertaining. Nearby **St Multose Church** has traces of a medieval structure, and in the church porch are the town stocks dating back to the eighteenth century.

Beyond the town's centre, situated on the hummocky fist of land that curls into Kinsale Harbour, **James Fort** (1601) is fun to clamber over, and during the summer you can take a ferry out to it from the *Trident Hotel* marina, a short walk west of town (every hour; 3min, £1 each way). Better preserved is **Charles' Fort** (1677), two miles out of town at Summercove (mid-April to mid-June & mid-Sept to mid-Oct Mon–Sat 9am–5pm, Sun 9.30am–5.30pm; mid-June to mid-Sept daily 9am–6pm; £2; Heritage Card). There's a very pleasant walk out here from Kinsale that takes you alongside the harbour: to find it, follow the minor coast road east for a quarter of a mile to *The Spaniards* pub at Scilly, and look out for a path down towards the sea. The outer walls of Charles' Fort, barely touched by weather or gunfire, seem pretty innocuous, but they conceal a formidable war machine. Within is an awesome system of barracks, ramparts and bastions, impressive testimony to the complexity and precision of seventeenth-century military science. The barracks were occupied until 1922, when the British left and handed the fort over to the Irish government. Today they remain largely intact, with only the barracks' missing roofs to give the place an eerily deserted feel.

Practicalities

The **tourist office** is next to the bus depot and cinema in the centre of town (March–Nov Mon–Sat 9am–1pm & 2.15–6pm, Sun 10am–1pm & 2.15–5.30pm; ☎021/772234); when it's closed, tourist information is readily available at *Peter Barry's*, opposite *The Spaniards* pub in Scilly, on the eastern coast road out of town. If you plan to **stay**, you're strongly advised to book ahead during July, August and the gourmet festival (see opposite). In the town centre, comfortable B&B is offered by *The Little Skillet*, 47 Main St (☎021/774202; ④) and *Pier House*, Pier Road (☎021/774475; ④), which also has balconies overlooking a pleasant garden. Other central options include *O'Donovan's*, Guardwell Street (☎021/772428; ③), *Ivy House*, Long Quay (☎021/774563; ④), *O'Farrell's*, 15 Main St (☎021/774169; ④), above a newsagent's, and *Seagull House*, a plain old-style B&B, next door to Desmond Castle, (☎021/772240; ③). Slightly more upmarket accommodation is available at *The Lighthouse* (☎021/772734; ⑤), a flurry of antique lace, a steep walk up the hill behind the museum. You'll also find quality guesthouse accommodation at *The Old Presbytery*, Cork Street (☎021/772027; ⑤), and *Long Quay House*, Long Quay (☎021/774563; ⑤), both fine Georgian buildings.

For **hostel** accommodation, a short walk from the town centre is *Dempsey's Hostel*, Eastern Road (IHH; ☎021/772124). A smarter budget option is *Castlepark Marina Centre* (☎021/774959; mid-March to Oct), less than a couple of miles west out of town: cross over the new bridge and take a sharp left, or take the ferry from the *Trident Hotel*

BLOW-INS AND ARTISTS

The potential of the beautiful, unspoilt and remote West Cork countryside was first widely perceived over twenty years ago, when the area was subject to a significant social upheaval with the immigration of large numbers of northern Europeans. "Blow-ins", as they're referred to, are people who have come to the area and have somehow managed to create an alternative lifestyle for themselves. Most of them are German, Belgian or Dutch and came here for a number of reasons: to escape political systems they abhorred at home; to distance themselves from nuclear issues; to escape pollution, overcrowding and stress; or to key into the perceived creative energies, and the romantic mysticism, generated by the west coast.

This influx of outsiders began in the 1960s at a time when there was plenty of money to be earned in the major cities of western Europe, and since then there has been a process of natural selection. Those who don't make a total commitment to the lifestyle no longer find it so easy to nip back to developed Europe, to earn swift cash with which to subsidize their romantic idyll. Consequently those who are still here are either survivors, or rich at home, too. Missing the irony, many visitors consider them an intrusion, making the experience somehow less "Irish", less authentic. In fact the presence of "blow-ins" is positively beneficial to the budget traveller. While they may have originally settled with a vision of living off organic farming, craftwork and home-grown entertainment, the harsh realities of subsistence have necessitated a real resourcefulness, one outcome of which has been the mushrooming of **independent hostels**. Many of these are tucked away in delightfully secret places the owner has discovered and now chooses to share with visitors, and they're often worth visiting purely for the setting or the very special personal atmosphere that's been created. Another spin-off from the "blow-in" phenomenon is the high incidence of **wholefood** shops in tiny towns; welcome indeed in an area where traditional grocery shops are poor at providing anything that doesn't come in a tin.

Finally, West Cork has attracted a large number of people who have come here to be artists, some of whom have succeeded. A local **arts centre** may be nothing more than a shed, but it can hold surprises, so look out for them. Some of the work is folksy and boring, but you may also stumble across exciting work of refreshing originality. What adds to these centres' appeal is the deeper understanding of the land they can offer: the best work has been inspired by, and so reflects, the colours and textures of the landscape.

(see p.277). Clean, comfortable and well run, with basic cooking facilities, it's in a beautiful spot looking out across the harbour to Kinsale, and also offers deep sea angling, scuba diving and harbour trips. There's a pub, *The Dock*, next door, and a lovely sandy beach two minutes' walk away where you can rent windsurfers, sailing dinghies and canoes at very reasonable prices (contact the Outdoor Education Centre in advance ☎021/772896). You can camp at *Dempsey's Hostel* or at Ballinspittle, seven miles southwest of Kinsale. Bike rental is available at C&B Cycles, Main Street.

Kinsale is a well-known **gourmet centre** – it even has a **gourmet festival** which starts the first Thursday in October (book well ahead) and has numerous expensive restaurants: one of the best is *The Blue Haven* in Pearse Street (☎021/772209), where there's also a less expensive menu in the bar. Pick up details of others from the tourist office. For more everyday food and drink, you'll find cheap daytime cafés around Market Square; for more stylish brunch and snacks try *Café Kokopelli*, Guardswell. Numerous pubs do **bar food**: on Pearse Street, *The White House* is one of the best, and *The 1601* is a reasonable alternative. *Café Palermo*, Pearse Street, is a pleasant Italian café with moderately priced pizza, pasta and heavily indulgent cakes. For **music** try *The Shanakee*, *The Lord Kinsale* or *The Tap Tavern* in the centre of town, or stroll out to *The Spaniards* pub in Scilly, a mile away. You can hear jazz at *Acton's Hotel* on Saturday evenings and Sunday lunchtimes, or for a quiet pint, head for *The Grey Hound*, a quaint old bar, the interior of which originally came from England.

The Seven Heads Peninsula

The stretch of coast from Timoleague to Clonakilty, known as the **Seven Heads Peninsula**, is a pretty, indented shoreline, good for walking and birdwatching. The spruce village of **TIMOLEAGUE** sits inland on the muddy estuary of the Ardigeen river, dominated by the extensive remains of a **Franciscan abbey** which was sacked in 1649. The much advertised **Castle Gardens** include a beautiful walled garden, but the ruins of Timoleague Castle itself are negligible and not worth the entrance fee. Timoleague is only a small place, but it boasts a handful of good bars, including *Charlie Madden's* and *The Mill House Bar*, both popular music venues, and *Dillon's* a cross between a French café and an Irish bar with a very reasonably priced menu (mid-March to late Oct, Mon–Sat 1–4pm, daily 6.30–9.30pm; no reservations). Nearby *Lettercollum House* guesthouse and **restaurant** serves exquisite food (dinner around £21) and offers good-quality accommodation (☎023/46251; ④). If you want to stay in the village itself, *Panorama B&B*, Chapel Hill (☎023/46248; ③), offers very comfortable accommodation and excellent views. There's also good **camping** around two miles out of Timoleague along the R600 towards Clonakilty at *Sexton's Camping* (☎023/46347).

At the broad mouth of the estuary, the village of **COURTMACSHERRY** is a safe, quiet family resort. It's certainly tranquil – when asked what happens here one local reckoned "the tide comes in and the tide goes out again". That's slightly exaggerated – if you're feeling rich you can go deep-sea angling or shark fishing (Courtmacsherry Sea Angling Centre; ☎023/46427), and horse riding can be arranged through the *Courtmacsherry Hotel* (☎023/46198; ⑥); in the evenings you may find a singsong round the piano at the *Lifeboat Inn* or *Anchor Bar*. If you're looking for B&B, *Travara Lodge* (☎023/46493; ④) is a good option, or you could head a few miles south to **BUTLERSTOWN** and *Sea Court* (June–Aug; ☎023/40151; ④), an eighteenth-century mansion, furnished with antiques.

Clonakilty

The busy little town of **CLONAKILTY**, birthplace of the Republican leader Michael Collins, has a growing reputation as a **traditional music centre**, thanks to the enthusiasm of local people. The traditional **Clonakilty Festival** is held in late June/early July and includes pub talent, debating contests and street entertainment.

There are plenty of excellent old **bars**: for music *De Barra's* on Pearse Street is probably the most popular place, with traditional or rock music more or less every night all year round. *MacEoin's*, MacCurtain Hill, is a venue for rock, folk or traditional on the weekend; *Shanley's* in Connolly Street has MOR pop and 1960s sessions (5–7 nights a week); and *An Teach Beag* (behind *O'Donovan's Hotel*) has traditional music every night during July and August, and at weekends throughout the year. *O'Donovan's Hotel* hosts live bands every night during July and August – anything from rock 'n' roll and ceilis to ballroom dancing. The hotel is also a good place to pick up what's-on information, and look out too for their gigantic 130-year-old polyphon – a kind of ancient jukebox, which still works. *Fiddler's Green*, Clarke Street, is always popular with a younger crowd, though there's rarely live music.

Pubs and music aside, the recently excavated Lisnagun Christian **ring fort** might appeal, especially if you have young children in tow. It's the only one in Ireland to be reconstructed on its original site, with defensive walls, a thatched central house, souterrains, replica weapons, utensils and clothing – all of which create a vivid picture of tenth-century life. Your ticket includes entrance to a small animal park nearby, where you can encounter fowl, rabbit and reindeer (June–Sept Mon–Fri 10am–5pm, Sat & Sun 11am–5pm; £2, children £1). Clonakilty also makes a good base from which to explore the crazily indented coastline roundabout, especially enjoyable by bike. Just over a mile north of town are the remains of the Templebryan **stone circle** – four of the original nine stones still stand, along with a central white quartzite pillar; to find it head out of town up MacCurtain Hill.

There's a **tourist office** in the town centre (June–Sept daily 10am–6pm, Tues–Fri closed 1–2pm; ☎023/33226). The town's numerous **B&Bs** include *Nordar*, Western Road (☎023/33655; ③), and the hospitable *Wytchwood*, off Emmet Square (☎023/33525; ③). At the east end of town are the very welcoming *Bay View*, Old Timoleague Road (☎023/33539; ③), and *Desert House* (☎023/33331; ③), or you could try *Aisling*, Clogheen Road (☎023/33491; ③). For upmarket accommodation, try the central *Strand House Guest House* (☎023/33498; ⑤) or *O'Donovan's Hotel* (☎ & fax 023/33250; ④), Pearse Street, which also serves meals till 9pm daily.

Smart, comfortable travel-lodge accommodation is available just off the N71 southwest of town at *Clonakilty Lodge* (☎023/34466; dorms £13.50, double £24.50pp). The comfortable, well-run *Clonakilty Old Brewery Hostel*, Old Brewery Lane (☎023/33525), has private rooms, good facilities for wheelchair users, and is in a central but quiet location off Emmet Square.

Camping is available a mere 500 yards' stagger from the pubs at *Desert House*, near the shore (☎023/33331; May–Sept); head east out of the village and turn right at the roundabout. For **bike rental** try MTM Cycles, Ashe Street (☎023/33584).

The town has several decent **places to eat**: for inexpensive breakfasts, lunches and takeaways check out *Russwurm's* deli, 38 Ashe St. *An Súgán*, Wolfe Tone Street, does good bar food. *Fionnuala's*, 30 Ashe St, is a cheap and cosy Italian restaurant, while the nearby *Druid's Table* offers its customers an imaginative menu of seafood, lamb and vegetarian dishes (dinner around £12; ☎023/33310).

West to Castletownshend

The coastline west of Clonakilty is a beautiful stretch of little bays and creeks, sandy coves and tidal loughs. There are tiny lagoons here and there, isolated along the shore from the main body of the sea, providing placid contrast to the furling white ocean spray. Each place has its own special charms – Rosscarbery, Glandore, Leap, Union Hall, Castletownshend. If you take the main N71 you're never far from these places, with easy access by a couple of miles' walk or a short hitch.

The broad bay at **ROSSCARBERY** has lost a great deal of its ethereal beauty since the building of the ugly, modern *Celtic Ross Hotel*. Still, their bar does serve excellent food. If you want to stay in more discreet surroundings, there's a family-run **hostel** and **B&B** about one mile from here, *Curraheen Lodge* (☎023/48498; B&B ②), and quiet camping too – to find it continue west, turn left opposite the pleasant *Courthouse Bar*, and then take the second lane on the left. Alternatively, you could stay two and a half miles away from Rosscarbery at *Castle Salem* (☎023/48381; ②), a seventeenth-century farmhouse in an extraordinary setting of deep green rolling fields; it's signposted off the N71 after about one mile. There's plenty of history too – the house adjoins a fifteenth-century castle, accessible via a doorway off the main stairs, and **William Penn**, founder of Pennsylvania, is known to have stayed here.

Heading on from Rosscarbery, take the minor R597 and look out for signs to the **Drombeg stone circle**. Dating from the Bronze Age, the seventeen stones that make up this circle are particularly impressive for their fine location – overlooking fields that fall to the sea. Nearby is a **fulacht fiadh** – a cooking site from the same era, where troughs of cold water would have been heated by hot stones thrown into them from a fire. Back on the R597, about a mile outside Glandore, the road passes the neat little *Meadow* **campsite** (☎028/33280), where there are laundry facilities and a wet weather room.

There's a fleeting outrageous glamour to **GLANDORE** with its turquoise-blue waters and deep green slopes, and there can be no better way to absorb the scene than with a plate of seafood and a cool drink from *Hayes* bar overlooking the bay. The somewhat dearer *Pier Head Bistro* at the foot of the hill also has a good reputation. Accommodation is thin on the ground, but *Bay View* is a pleasant **B&B** (☎028/33115; ②), or there's the *Marine Hotel* (☎028/33366; ⑤), both overlooking the water. The nearest **hostel** is *Maria's Schoolhouse* just outside Union Hall (IHH; ☎028/33002), a bright and cheery place, with comfy armchairs and big log fires; excellent – and expensive – vegetarian and non-vegetarian meals are readily available, and the hostel also organises **diving**, **canoeing** and **bike rental**. Just over a mile inland from Glandore, **LEAP**, a small village straddling the N71, is best known for *Connolly's* bar, arguably the best **live music venue** in West Cork, with a great range of bands year round: rock, traditional, bluegrass – just about anything that makes it out of Dublin will be on here. There are a couple of B&Bs in the village if you want to stay: *Highfield* (☎028/33273; ②) and *Riverside* (☎028/33577; ②).

Heading west towards Skibbereen, it's worth a quick detour to see **CASTLETOWNSHEND**. The village clings to a steep lane, a tree in the middle of the road sending what traffic there is gingerly either side, and ends abruptly at a tiny stone quay. It's an eerie, twee place, and appropriately enough was once the home of Edith Somerville of Somerville & Ross fame, authors of the *Irish R.M.* stories. Their graves are to be found in St Barrahane's churchyard.

Skibbereen and around

Cheerful **SKIBBEREEN**, smartly painted and set on the River Illen, is the main service and administrative centre for the south of West Cork. This traditional role is still remarkably alive: on Wednesdays the cattle market still operates, drawing crowds from the surrounding country, and every Friday afternoon there's the regular country market. For travellers, it's a good place to stock up or to stop over – there are plenty of supermarkets and liquor stores, a smattering of health-food shops and delis, and plenty of pubs. The West Cork Arts Centre on North Street (Mon–Sat 10am–6pm year round) is worth checking out. It hosts monthly exhibitions which can be first-rate, stages occasional music and dance performances, and has a reference and slide library through which you can locate local artists.

The **tourist office** (June–Aug Mon–Sat 9am–7pm, Sun 10am–1pm & 2.15–6pm; Sept–May Mon–Fri 9.15am–5.30pm; ☎028/21766) is also on North Street and will help with accommodation. For **B&Bs** *Ilenroy House* (☎028/22751; ⑤) and *The Ivanhoe* (☎028/21749; ④) are a couple of comfortable, central options, both in North Street, or you might try *Riverside* (☎028/33577; ③). *Maple Lodge* (☎028/21553; ②) is a comfortable family home set back from the road about one mile east out of town, while *Mont Bretia* (☎028/33663; ④), four miles out of town (phone for directions), is developing a reputation for relaxed accommodation, offering vegetarian food, breakfast till noon, free bike loans, and a gay- and lesbian-friendly environment. If you feel like splashing out, there's the *Liss Ard Lake Lodge* (☎028/22365; ⑨) on the road to Castletownshend. A masterpiece of understatement, it's a nineteenth-century house refurbished in a minimalist style. It's in a choice spot too, overlooking a glassy lake. Residents have access to the Liss Ard Experience (see below), and non-residents also can eat in the excellent restaurant (dinner around £33; closed Tues; Sat vegetarian only).

There's a good **hostel**, *The Russagh Mill Hostel*, a mile out on the Castletownshend Road, (☎028/22451; mid-March to Nov), a beautifully renovated mill house. Mick Murphy, the hostel manager, is happy to talk to visitors about his Everest climb in 1993, and leads hillwalking, canoeing or sail-boarding activities most days (£8–10 per day).

You can get **Bus Éireann** information from *O'Cahalales* in Bridge Street, and **rent bikes** from N.W. Roycroft and Son in Ilen Street (☎028/21235).

For good **pub food** make for *Annalaoi*, North Street, *Bernard's* (till 9pm) on Main Street, or *Eldon's Hotel* on Bridge Street. You can tuck into good budget meals at *The Stove* café, Main Street, and *O'Driscoll's,* further along (Mon–Sat till 11am, Sun till 10pm). Slightly more expensive is *Kalbo's Bistro*, North Street. As for bars, try *Baby Hannah's*, Bridge Street, a lively young place. For **music** there's *Sheehy's* on the square, or you might try *The Wine Vaults*, Bridge Street (Wed).

About a mile or so out along the Castletownshend road is the **Liss Ard Experience**, a New Age garden where the emphasis is very much on conservation (Mon–Fri 11am–6pm, guided tour 4.30pm; Sun 10am–1pm, guided tour 11am; £5). The original landscaped garden had been left unmanaged since 1924; consequently wild flora and fauna have found their own balance, and the area has been developed in such a way as to allow the natural order to hold sway. Discreet pathways lead to natural "chambers" of vegetation, the idea being to encourage secluded contemplation and a deeper awareness of the environment. The real highlight at Liss Ard, however, is the **Sky Garden**, the work of contemporary American artist James Turell. When finished, it will have five key "monuments": a pyramid, a crater, a mound, a sky walk and a grotto, which you will be led towards along narrow pathways. At the moment only the crater is finished: a huge elliptical grassy bowl with a stark stone slab at its centre for two people to lie on and view. Using light and landscape, the artist creates space and plays with our powers of sensory perception – the result is a profoundly powerful experience, awe inspiring in its stillness. Irreverent as it may sound, sunglasses are advisable on bright days, and in wet weather viewing is impossible.

Creagh Garden

Less than four miles southwest of Skibbereen along the Baltimore Road, the **Creagh Gardens** (March–Oct 10am–6pm; £3) offer a very different horticultural experience from that of Liss Ard, and are a delightful place to unwind. They are ostensibly fairly traditional – with woodland glades, lawns running down to the estuary and a Regency walled kitchen garden – but the late owner's desire to create a garden based on the richness of tone and colour found in Rousseau's jungle paintings was less conventional and is achieved here by a dense, textured build-up of lush vegetation and exotic palms. If you head back a little way up the road and take the turning on your right, you'll soon find **Lough Hyne** (pronounced *Ine*), a land-locked salt lake, linked to the ocean only by a very slender channel down which the receding tide returns to the sea. The lough, surrounded by hillsides dripping with lush, moist greenery, is a unique phenomenon, of great interest to marine biologists. From the head of the lake steep slopes, easily climbed, rise to panoramic views: eastwards along the coast to Kinsale; west across the length of the Mizen Peninsula; and out across to Sherkin and Clear islands.

Baltimore and the islands

The approach to Baltimore takes you through a landscape that is disarmingly low-key. Instead of some dramatic climax at this, the most southerly point of all Ireland, the land seems simply to be fading away: rocky terrain and scrawny vegetation accompany the windy, listless estuary, untidy with lumps of land that seem to have been tossed at random towards the sea. The whole ragged effect is as if the country is running out of substance; the landmass, already moth-bitten, is now fraying, too. But as the ocean comes into full view this tailing off is put into spectacular context: the whole weight of Ireland is behind you, while ahead are dots, wracks and scraps of islands, petering out across the great open expanse of water to Sherkin and Clear islands.

Baltimore

BALTIMORE, a delightful harbour village overlooked by a sixteenth-century O'Driscoll stronghold, is the last significant mainland settlement. Combining traditional fishing activities with tourism, it's also the departure point for ferries to Sherkin, Clear Island and Schull (see p.286): for most people this is the chief reason to come. During the last two weeks of July and the first weekend in August the yachting crowd descend en masse for the **regatta**: there are a few pricy restaurants to cater for them. If you're staying, there's **B&B** accommodation at *Island View* (☎028/20124; ②), *The Algiers Inn* (☎028/20145; ③) and *Channel View* (☎028/20440; ③), which overlooks the bay. *Bushe's* bar offers good accommodation with continental breakfast (☎028/20119; ②). For good

---

FERRIES

Baltimore–Sherkin Island (£4 return) June–Sept depart Baltimore daily 9am, 10.30am, noon, 2pm, 4pm, 5.30pm, 7pm & 8.30pm; returning from Sherkin roughly a quarter of an hour after these times. Oct–May 9am, 10.30am, 2pm & 5.30pm: ask at *Bushe's* bar or telephone ☎028/20125, eves ☎20218.

Schull–Sherkin (£4 single, £8 return, bikes free) Daily June & Sept depart Schull 1.45pm, depart Sherkin 5.30pm; July & Aug depart Schull 10.30am, 1.45pm, 4.15pm, depart Sherkin 11.30am, 3pm & 5.30pm; 1 hour; ☎28138.

Baltimore–Clear Island (£8 return) May depart Baltimore Mon–Fri 11am & 5.30pm, Sat 2.15pm, Sun 5pm, depart Clear Island Mon–Fri 9am & 4pm, Sat 9am, Sun 3pm; June & Sept depart Baltimore Mon–Sat 2.15pm & 7pm, Sun noon, 2.15pm, 5pm & 7pm, depart Clear Island Mon–Sat 9am & 6pm, Sun 11am, 1pm, 4pm & 6pm; July & Aug depart Baltimore Mon–Sat 11am, 2.15pm & 7pm, Sun noon, 2.15pm, 5pm & 7pm, depart Clear Island Mon–Sat 9am, noon & 6pm, Sun 11am, 1pm, 4pm & 6pm; Oct–April depart Baltimore Mon–Thurs 2.15pm, Fri 10.30am & 5.30pm, Sat 2.15pm, Sun 5pm, depart Clear Island Mon–Thurs & Sat 9am, Fri 9am & 4pm, Sun 3pm; 45min.

Baltimore–Schull (£6 single, bikes free) June to mid-Sept depart Baltimore 10am, 1.45pm & 4.40pm; depart Schull 11.30am, 3pm & 5.40pm; 45min; ☎028/39153.

Schull–Clear Island (£9 return, £6 single, bikes free) June & Sept daily depart Schull 2.30pm; depart Cape Clear 5.30pm; July & Aug depart Schull 10am, 2.30pm, 4.30pm; depart Clear Island 11am, 3.30pm & 5.30pm; 45 minutes; ☎028/28138.

quality guesthouse accommodation right by the harbour, book in at *Baltimore Bay* (☎028/20600; ⑤). *Rolf's* independent **hostel** is cheerful and friendly, a real favourite (IHH; book ahead in July and August; ☎028/20289; private rooms £11.50). Tasty **meals** are available in the *Café Art* alongside, while great seafood and steaks are available at *Casey's Cabin*, about a mile towards Skibbereen. The popular *Declan McCarthy's* bar by the harbour also serves seafood and hosts traditional, folk and ballad sessions several nights a week in summer; it also cashes cheques and **changes money**. More upmarket, the Australian-run *Customs House restaurant* (☎028/20200) specializes in seafood and organic produce and has an excellent reputation. As well as the scheduled Bus Éireann, there is a private service that operates from the harbour to Skibbereen around 10–10.30am – check the exact schedule locally.

Sherkin Island

Tiny **SHERKIN ISLAND** is a delightfully pretty place: the considerable remains of a fifteenth-century Franciscan friary nestle down by the quayside, and little fuchsia-spattered lanes lead across the island to fine sandy beaches in the west. There are the remains of an O'Driscoll stronghold, too, and the annual O'Driscoll clan gathering in June is a hectic five-day event spread between Sherkin, Clear Island and Baltimore. For a community of only some ninety people, the island has a great **pub scene**, with sessions at *The Jolly Roger* attracting crowds from the mainland. If there's a band booked and you are staying in Baltimore, there's usually a late-night ferry laid on to take everybody home.

The place can get busy with day-trippers at bank holidays and in July and August. If you want to stay you can get **B&B** at *Cuina* (☎028/20384; ②) and *Island House* (☎028/20314; ②) – both closed in winter. If these are full, it's worth asking at the pub for alternatives. The *Jolly Roger* does **bar food** during the summer: at other times you can buy supplies at the post office.

Clear Island

CLEAR ISLAND (*Oioeán Chléire*), also known as Cape Clear, offers rather more to do, but it would be worth visiting for the ferry trip alone, though it can be a topsy-turvy, stomach-churning ride. There's an important ornithology station here, and on the 45-minute ride out to the island, it's obvious that the place is paradise for **wildlife** enthusiasts. The bay is alive with seabirds – guillemots, cormorants, auks and storm petrels – and with luck you may see seals and, in warm weather, basking sharks. With even more luck you might find your boat raced by a playful dolphin or two, dodging around the bows and leaping out of the ocean to crash back down right alongside the ferry.

The hilly, rocky island seems to have been pinched in the middle where two inlets, North Harbour and South Harbour, almost meet. In the south, steep and inaccessible cliffs rise from the water; the North Harbour is perfectly sheltered. Roads climb up from here through hills covered in the coarse grass that seems to spread over everything, including old walls and houses long derelict. Sea pinks cling to rocky outcrops, and honeysuckle clambers wherever it can. The island's high points give spectacular views back across the archipelago to the mainland.

The **bird observatory** at North Harbour has been here since 1959 and has complete records going back to that time. When it was set up, by an amateur group, this station was a pioneer of the constant observation of seabirds, and its work has done much for the knowledge of migratory patterns. Clear Island is one of the most important places for seabirds in Ireland, including some genuine rarities – especially plentiful are storm petrels, shearwaters, black guillemots and choughs. There is **hostel**-style accommodation here (book in advance), available for ornithologists, too, but likely to be full in late spring and in September and October. If you are new to birdwatching, but fancy learning more, call in and see what's happening, though be warned that mid-summer is not the best time.

Clear Island is also an isolated remnant of the *Gaeltacht*, where Irish is still spoken by about 130 islanders. During the summer, Irish youngsters are sent here to practise the language. The island has a **festival** of drama, music, art and dance, *Féile Shamhna Chléire*, usually held on the bank holiday weekend in late October. **The Heritage Centre** (June–Aug daily 2.30–5.30pm; £1.50), a steep, well-signposted walk from North Harbour, is a tiny museum of the domestic, fishing and seafaring history of the island. The island prides itself on being the birthplace of St Kieran, who supposedly preceded St Patrick by thirty years, but the holy well and stone that are attributed to him stand in a sadly unromantic spot by the road at North Harbour. The best of Clear Island's historic ruins is **Dún an Óir** ("Fort of Gold"), an O'Driscoll fort, impressive on a high, narrow splinter of rock which is now an island at high tide – sadly inaccessible, though you can see it as you walk down the hill from the Heritage Centre, or from the 200ft cliffs to the south.

If you intend to stay, it makes sense during the summer to arrange accommodation before sailing. There are a number of **B&Bs**: try *Cluain Mara*, North Harbour (☎028/39153; ②), or *Fáilte*, Glen East, up by the lighthouse (☎028/39135; ②). The An Óige **hostel** at South Harbour (☎028/39198; March–Nov) offers canoeing, archery and snorkelling. **Camping** is available a short walk from the ferry (June–end Sept). The island has three pubs: two down by the North Harbour, *Cotters Bar* and *The Club*, where you may well find music in the summer months, and the other on the road to the South Harbour, *Ciaran Danny Mike's*. This last serves bar food and has a restaurant alongside. *Chistin Cléire* by the North Harbour is the island's one **café** (Easter–Oct). There's an excellent shop beside North Harbour, though bring your own Gaz if you're camping.

Mizen Head

The Mizen Head Peninsula is a beautiful, remote finger of land poking its way west, offering superb sandy beaches and cliff scenery, getting wilder the further west you go. It's an area rich in **archeological sites**, from Bronze Age wedge graves contemporary with the first copper mining of Mount Gabriel, through Iron Age and early Christian ring forts, down to medieval castles – pick up a copy of the leaflet *Antiquities of the Mizen Peninsula* from the tourist office in Cork city if you want to locate these sites. Great care should be taken at the Mizen cliffs, as the land ends abruptly and without warning.

The most spectacular scenery along this stretch of coast is at Mizen Head itself – sheer, vertiginous cliffs, with an offshore lighthouse linked by a little suspension bridge, and accessible if you visit the Mizen Vision **heritage centre** (mid-March to May & Oct daily 10.30am–5pm; June–Sept daily 10am–6pm; £2.50). Standing at this exhilarating spot it takes little effort to imagine the great number of ships that have been wrecked in Dunlough Bay to the north. A walk round to **Three Castles Head** brings in sight the curtain wall and two turrets of an O'Mahoney stronghold, one of twelve that were built along this peninsula in the fifteenth century. The setting makes this one truly spectacular. The whole of the peninsula's wild and empty northern coast, in fact, is one of sheer cliffs and stupendous views – an impossible route for hitching, but great for those with transport.

The south coast of the peninsula is more travelled, with small towns at Ballydehob, Schull and Crookhaven, and lovely sandy **beaches**. The best of these is the long and sandy strand at Barleycove, whose rolling breakers make it a favourite with **surfers**. Nearby is the busy little holiday resort of Crookhaven with a large caravan and camping park on the Goleen–Crookhaven road; unless you want the facilities, though, there is no real need to use this – there are plenty of remote spots where you can pitch a tent for free. At Goleen is the delightful upmarket **restaurant** and **B&B**, *Heron's Cove* (☎028/35225; ⑤), where if you don't want a full meal you can still enjoy chowder, cakes and creek life. Highland and Harbour offer **pony trekking** through this wild, beautiful countryside (☎028/35416). The only public transport along the peninsula is run by Bus Éireann as far as Goleen.

Ballydehob

BALLYDEHOB, a small town of gaily-coloured streets at the neck of the peninsula, was once known as the hippie capital of the west because it was said to have more "blow-ins" than locals. Heavily colonized in the 1960s, it still has traces of their influence, like health food and artists, and remains a liberal place compared to others of its size. For all this, it's a sleepy town with just a handful of craft and antique shops worth exploring and a large number of pubs. If you want to stay, *Dun an Oir* (☎028/37272; ③) is a pleasant option, and *The Old Crossing* (☎028/37148; ②) enjoys fantastic views of the surrounding countryside – follow the lane alongside *Levi's* bar to find it. There's a **campsite** just a couple of hundred yards down the Durrus Road, and a **laundry** in the centre of the town. *Annie's Restaurant* (☎028/37292; book for dinner, £21), Main Street, is renowned for its seafood, and the same people serve lunches during the day at *The Bookshop Café*. There are some interesting old **bars** – Julie and Nell run *Levi's*, a bar-grocery store (opposite *Annie's*), or try *O'Sullivan's*, a few doors up.

Ballydehob's nearest **beach** is three miles away at Audley Cove: a secluded pebbly cove, with lovely views of the islands.

Schull

SCHULL, as well as being the place to catch the ferry for Clear Island, Baltimore and Sherkin (see p.283), is perhaps the most obvious place to stay on the peninsula, an attractive seaside market town with plenty of cheery amenities aimed at holidaying families and the unpretentious yachting fraternity. Schull's sheltered, bulb-shaped harbour looks out over Carbery's Hundred Islands, while **Mount Gabriel** rises to 1339ft to the north, offering wonderful views. To make this walk from Schull (nine miles there and back) head up Gap Road past the convent and you'll find a clear track all the way. From the top you can continue around the north side of the mountain, to return through Rathcool and Glaun. The domes at the summit of Mount Gabriel are aircraft-tracking stations. As you walk, beware of unguarded mine shafts: this rough and rocky land was heavily mined for copper in the nineteenth century, and is still dotted with Cornish-style mining chimneys.

Schull is at its liveliest during its **sailing events**. The international sailing festival for children is usually held the second week in July, when the town is awash with nautical teenagers, and the yachting set proper swamp the town for the regatta held in Calves week (following the August bank holiday weekend, usually the first week of the month). At these times accommodation can be difficult, and phoning ahead is advisable.

PRACTICALITIES

A number of **B&Bs** can be found on Main Street: *O'Regan's*, (☎028/28334; ②), the extremely pleasant *Old Bank House* (☎028/28306; ③) and *Adele's* (☎028/28459; ①). Five minutes' walk from the village centre is *Schull's Backpackers' Lodge* (IHH; ☎ & fax 028/28681), an attractive wooden **hostel** surrounded by trees, where you can also **camp. Ferries** run from Schull to Baltimore, Sherkin and Clear Island (see p.283) and Karycraft (☎028/28138 or 28278) operates **cruises** around the Fastnet Rock (July & Aug Wed 7pm, June & Sept by arrangement; 2hr 30min; £10). If you fancy taking to the water yourself, Schull Watersports Centre, The Pier (☎028/28554), organizes **sea-**

angling trips, **dinghy rental**, **wind-surfing** and, for the experienced only, **diving**. For canoeing try Argonauts (☎027/70692), which also provides wet suits. **Horse riding** can be arranged with *The Colla House Hotel* on Colla Road (☎028/28105). **Bike rental** is available from Cotter's Yard, Main Street (☎028/28165).

As for **eating**, *Adele's Coffee Shop* in Main Street does excellent home-made cakes, soups, salads and fresh pasta and is also open in the evening. *The Courtyard*, Main Street, serves seafood and vegetarian meals and has a good deli selling fresh bread from its brick-built steam oven, local cheeses, oils and pickles. You can get superior fish and chips at *George's Grapevine*, Main Street, and **bar food** at *The Courtyard*, *The Galley Inn*, or the *Bunratty Inn*. Schull's pubs have **music** year round – look out for posters around town, or check out *The Courtyard*, *The Bunratty Inn*, *The Galley* or *Arundel's*. If you just want a relaxing pint, try *Hackett's*. The town also has a bank, and Fuschia Books (second-hand) is good for rainy afternoons.

Sheep's Head

The peninsula north of Mizen, **Sheep's Head**, has an ancient feel to it: barren land almost entirely devoid of people. There are only a couple of tiny villages here, and traffic is sparse – the sole weekly bus runs on Saturday – so don't try to hitch if you're going to need to return in a hurry. It's a changing landscape, where surges of harsh granite rise from sweet green fields, fuchsias and honeysuckle scramble over greystone walls, gorse and heather colour wild heathland, and at every twist of the road plantlife, rock and water fall together to describe some new magic ideal. Whichever way you head down to the Sheep's Head, the scenery is superb. The north coast looks down on the magnificent Bantry Bay, backed by the wild Caha Mountains and offers cyclists a wonderful descent towards Bantry. There are also fabulous panoramic views over County Cork, the Beara Peninsula, and County Kerry from the top of **Seefin**, Sheep's Head's highest hill (1136ft). All of this can now be enjoyed by walking the **Sheep's Head Way** a 55-mile circuit of the peninsula; it's relatively easy walking, clearly signposted, and marked on the Discovery Series OS map number 88.

DURRUS has a handful of pubs, shops and a small **tropical house** with free-flying butterflies, exotic insects and tropical plants (late April to mid-Sept; £2.50). If you want to stay, pleasant, central **B&B** accommodation is available at *Avoca House* (☎027/61511; ②), with good home-cooking alongside in the *Bistro Suzanne*. The *Long Boat Bar* serves inexpensive meals and the *Millrace House* (May to mid-Sept; ☎027/61333) is a pretty and intimate upmarket restaurant. *Dunbeacon* **campsite** (☎027/61246; wet-weather hut), is three miles down the Crookhaven Road, a relaxing, low-key affair. West towards Sheep's Head, minuscule **AHAKISTA** has a narrow slip of sandy beach backed by a showering of trees. *Arundel's* bar here is a quiet old place to stop off for tea and sandwiches, and there are snacks, too, at *The Ahakista Bar*, along with a gorgeous lush beer garden that runs down to the water's edge. For directions to the only place selling **basic provisions**, ask at either bar. One and a half miles beyond the bars is *Reenmore* **B&B** (☎027/67051; ③). At **KILCROHANE**, three and a half miles southeast of Ahakista, there's a post office, a bar serving sandwiches, and basic accommodation at *Carbery View Hostel* (☎027/67035). A summer **café** with erratic opening times can be found right at the end of the peninsula.

Bantry

The beauty of **BANTRY** is its setting at the head of ever-turbulent Bantry Bay, which stretches thirty miles from the town to the ocean. The deep, churning blue waters of the bay, backed by the dramatic heights of the Beara's Caha Mountains and cowering, usually, under a notoriously changeable sky, form as dramatic a backdrop as any in

Ireland. The town itself sits around a long square focused at the head of the bay, with a slaty Regency Gothic church and a statue of St Brendan staring out to sea. In the immediate surrounds are lush wooded slopes – a safe haven indulged between the ravages of the sea and the wilds of the rocky mountains, and the **Sheep's Head Way** starts here, passing through the grounds of Bantry House before heading west for the low hills of the Sheep's Head Peninsula. Bantry is a commercial harbour, fishing port and market town, where the traditional market is still held on the first Friday of every month. It's also a place of history and character. For centuries, **Bantry Bay** attracted attempts from abroad to overthrow English rule, the two most notable of which were in 1689 when a French fleet sailed up the bay to assist James II and Wolfe Tone's expedition a century later. Once inside its shelter, ships were protected from attack by the rugged mountains of the peninsulas on either side.

Arrival, information and accommodation

Bus Éireann **buses**, connecting with Cork, Skibbereen, Glengarriff, Killarney and the Mizen Head Peninsula, leave from outside *Murphy's Bar* (information inside), towards the harbour from the tourist office. Private buses leave from Wolfe Tone Square (usually just referred to as the The Square), outside the Old Courthouse. This building also houses the **tourist office** (May–Sept Mon–Sat 9.15am–5.30pm, July & Aug also Sun 10am–1pm & 2.15–6pm; ☎027/50229). **Bike rental** is available at Kramer's, Glengarriff Road (☎027/50278), and at *Bantry Independent Hostel*.

Finding somewhere to **stay** in Bantry should present few problems. **B&Bs** abound: try *Bay View House*, The Square (☎027/50403; ②) or *The Cosy Cabin*, Barrack Street (☎027/50687; ②), with accommodation above the bar. There are plenty of smart modern B&Bs out along the Glengarriff road – *Sunville* (☎027/50175; ③), *The Mill*, Newtown (☎027/50278; ③), or *Doire Liath* (☎027/50223; ③). If you feel like splashing out on a night or two of real luxury, you can enjoy bed and breakfast at the aristocratic **Bantry House** (☎027/50047; ⑧). Friendly, welcoming *Bantry Independent Hostel*, Bishop Lucey Place (IHH; ☎027/51050; mid-March to mid-Nov), is a short signposted walk from The Square. Budget accommodation is also available on The Square at *Harbour View Independent Hostel* (☎027/51140). The nearest **campsite** is at Ballylickey, four miles from Bantry along the Glengarriff Road: the *Eagle Point Caravan and Camping Park* (May–Sept; ☎027/50630) is a superbly situated site right on the edge of the bay; you can swim from their pebbly beach and there are excellent wild mountain walks roundabout. It's well worth calling in at Manning's Emporium nearby, an excellent deli with a huge range of Irish cheeses.

The Town

Bantry House (daily 9am–6pm, July & Aug closes 8pm most evenings; house and gardens £6; gardens only £2), nowadays provides an elegant vision of the rarefied life led by the Anglo-Irish aristocracy. Sumptuously decorated and packed with art treasures, it deserves some time. Much of the furniture is French Napoleonic, and there are Gobelin tapestries and Aubusson carpets; but what makes this house such a gem is the sheer variety of artefacts that have been collected, many of them during the second earl's European wanderings in the nineteenth century. The setting is superb: ordered landscaped gardens look down over the bay, calmly asserting the harmony of the aristocratic order, unruffled by the ruggedness of the surroundings. **The Bantry 1796 French Armada Exhibition Centre** (April–Oct daily 10am–6pm, other times by arrangement; £3; ☎027/51796), housed in one of the courtyards, gives a blow-by-blow account of Wolfe Tone's failed mission to try to overthrow the Protestant Anglo-Irish with help from the French. By the time Tone reached Bantry, Channel storms had already reduced the fleet from 43 ships to 16, and the remaining vessels spent six days in the bay unable to land, even though, as Tone said, "we were close enough to toss a biscuit on shore". After this failure they were forced to turn back. You can see artefacts recovered from the wreck of the frigate *La Surveillante*, scuttled on Whiddy Island in 1797 and excavated in 1982.

Another aspect of the past is remembered with relish by the ladies who run the **Bantry Museum**, behind the fire station on Wolfe Tone Square (June–Sept Tues & Thurs 10am–1pm, Wed & Fri 2–5.30pm; 50p). The museum is the collection of the local history society – domestic paraphernalia, old newspapers and everyday trivia of every sort – which the curators willingly demonstrate with an entertaining blend of history and gossip. The modern library, at the top of Bridge Street, was built in 1974 and, at first glance, looks like some sort of spaceship, though the design was in fact inspired by a prehistoric dolmen: as adventurous a piece of modern architecture as you'll find in the west of Ireland, it's let down by a white facade that already seems thoroughly tacky.

One final thing worth going out of your way to see is the fine, early Christian **Kilnaruane Pillar** Stone just out of town. Its worn carvings depict four men rowing, an apostle and the cross. Follow the main road south out of town and take the first turning on the left past *The Westlodge Hotel*: the stone is in a field 500 yards further on the right.

Eating, drinking and entertainment

One of the most popular **eating places** in Bantry is *Ó Síocháin*, in Bridge Street, a cheery café serving hearty lunches and seafood platters during the summer months till 9.30pm. The *5A* in Barrack Street is more of a hippie hang-out and similarly popular, serving soups, vege-burgers and delicious homemade cakes. Also in Bridge Street, *Claret's Bistro* is probably the most relaxing place to eat in town, with an interesting and inexpensive lunch menu, dinner around £22. *Peter's Restaurant*, New Street, looks deceptively like a greasy spoon, but in fact serves excellent fresh salmon salads along with the grills and fries (till 10.30pm, Sat & Sun till 12.30am). If you want **pub food**, a handful of places around The Square are good value, including *The Snug*, which serves superb food in generous quantities (till 8.30pm).

Regular **pubs** are plentiful: the *Anchor Bar* is a convivial place to start, with a good, friendly mix of locals and visitors, as is *The Clinic*, Main Street. Bantry is a small town, and entertainment is a matter of getting involved in whatever's going on. You're as likely to enjoy a handful of **rock music** or **ballad** sessions in the bars as anything else: try *The Bantry Bay* or *The Snug*; *Vickery's*, New Street, is rather low key, but with folk or traditional on a Monday night. For **discos** try *The Bantry Bay* (Fri & Sat) or *The Westlodge Hotel* (Sun) a couple of miles along the main road to Skibbereen. Finally, Bantry's **mussel festival** over the second weekend in May brings with it music, late bars and plenty of seafood.

BOWLING

One local sport worth looking out for is **bowling**, a West Cork game played around Bantry on Sundays. A 28oz iron ball is thrown along country roads, and the winner of the game is the person who moves the ball over a prescribed distance (usually two and a half miles) with the fewest throws. Undoubtedly a fair amount of betting goes on too. If you come across handfuls of grass that have been dropped along a lane at intervals, it generally means a game has been or is being played along that route – clumps of grass are used as markers.

Glengarriff and the mountains

Heading on from Bantry you're spoilt for choice: whichever way you travel, the scenery is magnificent. Heading **east**, the road to Dunmanway and its fine independent hostel (p.276) takes you through fabulous empty mountains, while the Pass of Keimaneigh further north leads through a steep, rocky ravine up to the *Ballingeary hostel* (p.276), **Gougane Barra** and a corrie lake, the source of the River Lee. An island on this lake was the site of St Finbarr's hermitage before he founded his monastery at Cork city downstream. The remains on the island are, however, eighteenth century. It's an area famous for its beauty, popular for day-trips, and there's a bar that does teas and sandwiches beside the lake. Gougane Barra also has a forest park with nature trails (£2).

Glengarriff

Cradled between the Caha Mountains and Bantry Bay, **GLENGARRIFF** is an oasis of greenery. South-facing and sheltered by rugged mountains, it has a peculiarly gentle climate; oak and holly woodlands hug the shoreline while occasional palms flourish in hotel gardens. This picturesque juxtaposition has been exploited since the nineteenth century, when sensitive Victorians became alerted to the beneficial effects of the uniquely mild atmosphere in this pocket of lushness. Unfortunately, recent exploitation has resulted in a barrage of billboarding; ads for gift shops and boat trips have destroyed virtually all of the village's former character. When a bus tour meets Glengarriff nowadays, it's difficult to say which is the victim.

Despite the commercialism, Glengarriff is a great place to stay if you want to explore some of Cork's and Kerry's most beautiful and wildest countryside. The surrounding mountains are wonderfully rugged; huge areas of barren rock show odd patches of scrawny, rough vegetation, and then the occasional seam of brilliant deciduous woods. There is a real exhilaration up here as you watch the constantly changing patterns of weather over the mountains and the bay, with squalls of rain and pools of sunlight bowling across the landscape. Pick up a leaflet of suggested walks at the **tourist office** (June–Aug Mon–Sat 10am–1pm & 2.15–6pm; ☎027/63084) in the main street. They will also help with accommodation. Comfortable **B&Bs** include *Conimar* (☎027/63405; ②), *Rockwood House* (☎027/63097; ③), and *River Lodge* (☎027/63043; ③), a rather more old-fashioned B&B, situated in a beautiful spot beside the river. For traditional hotel accommodation try *Casey's* (☎027/63010; ⑤) in the centre of the town. There are a few independent **hostels**: *Murphy's* (IHH; ☎027/63555) is central, well-run and cheerful, or if this is full, *O'Mahoney's* (☎027/63033) three minutes' walk from the centre on the road towards Bantry, is a rather more basic alternative. You can camp here, too, or at *O'Shea's* **campsite** (mid-March to mid-Oct; ☎027/63140), a beautiful little site, about a mile out of Glengarriff on the Castletownbere Road (R572). **Bike rental** is available at Jem Creations, Ladybird House.

Places to eat are limited. Your best bets are the bars at *Casey's Hotel* and *The Eccles Hotel* or the café at *Murphy's Hostel* (May–Sept daily 7.30am–6pm), which serves good-value wholesome lunches and snacks. Glengarriff's **bars** are very lively during July and August; there's usually music at *The Blue Loo*, *Bernard Harrington's* or *Johnny Barry's*.

Garinish Island

Walking down the street in Glengarriff you'll inevitably be hassled sooner or later by a stage-Irish boatman trying to sell you a ticket for **Garinish Island**. The island trip is quite something, although massively overpriced. In 1910, the owner of Garinish conceived a plan to turn his island – then bare rock – into a floating oasis of exotic plantlife. All the topsoil had to be imported and the resultant growth delicately nurtured for years. The end product is undeniably impressive: flowers and shrubs from all over the world flourish here, and through much of the year the place is ablaze with colour, in vibrant contrast to the desolate mountains of the Beara a stone's throw across the water. If you decide to take the ten-minute trip out there past basking seals, be warned that the price you pay the boatmen (£5) does not include admission to the island (July & Aug Mon–Sat 9.30am–6.30pm, Sun 11am–7pm; April–June & Sept Mon–Sat 10am–6.30pm, Sun 1–7pm; March & Oct Mon–Sat 10am–6.30pm; £2.50; Heritage Card).

The Beara Peninsula

The **Beara Peninsula**, barren and remote, seems to have an energy all of its own, bounding in great ribs of rock thirty miles out into the ocean. In good weather it can be outrageously beautiful, especially in the extreme west, but the weather is notoriously changeable and when the mists roll in and the wind rises there are precious few places to shelter from it all. It is a fine place for tough cycling and energetic hiking, though you need to be prepared: careful planning of routes, particularly the descent, is vital. Alternatively, you could try the Beara Way, a signposted, long-distance walk (125 miles) following old roads and tracks, stretching from Glengarriff west along the southern side of the peninsula to Dursey Island, along the north side to Kenmare and back down to Glengarriff (route guides available locally; OS 1:50,000 Discovery map 84). Everywhere along the peninsula you are accompanied by fine views of the mountains and the sea, and there are occasional sandy beaches on either side; take local advice before swimming, as currents can be treacherous.

In practical terms, there are just enough hostels and B&Bs to make lengthy exploration a viable proposition, but it's worth bearing in mind that a sparse population means there's little traffic of any sort – don't rely on being able to hitch back if you're in a hurry. If you're planning to **camp**, be aware that though there is no shortage of open land, a lot of it is very rocky. **Private buses** connect the Beara communities with Glengarriff, Bantry and Cork several days a week. See "Travel Details" at the end of the chapter. Bus Éireann connects Castletownbere with Kenmare.

Adrigole

The first settlement along the coast, about fifteen miles west of Glengarriff, is **ADRIGOLE**, a string of houses stretching over a couple of miles with no real centre. You are most likely to be here if you've walked along the **Beara Way** from Glengarriff. Just to the west of the junction for the Healy Pass is a shop and a pub; three miles to the east you'll find a couple of old-style **B&Bs**: *Bayview Farmhouse* (☎027/60026; ②) with standard rooms and lovely views of the sea, and the nearby *Beachmount* (☎027/60075; ②; March–Oct). There's good **camping** at the otherwise basic **hostel** (☎027/60228) – phone ahead to check they are open. It's all wild and wonderful walking country. **Hungry Hill** rises to 2251ft, a good climb rewarded by fabulous views, hidden lakes and waterfalls, while the steep road through the **Healy Pass** leads north to Lauragh, County Kerry, where there is an An Óige **hostel** at Glanmore Lake (Easter–Sept; ☎064/83181).

Castletownbere

Beara communities have always relied heavily on fishing; **CASTLETOWNBERE**, the peninsula's main town, is no exception. Set on Ireland's second largest natural harbour, it's periodically awash with Spanish and Portuguese sailors. To serve them there's a handful of cafés, well-stocked shops, a chip shop and some enjoyable pubs (see overleaf).

The town serves as a useful place to pick up provisions or rest up if you're travelling through the area. It's also the point of departure for **ferries** to Bere Island, which shelters the harbour: three–five ferries a day run during July and August, and by arrangement at other times (☎027/75009; car £15 return, foot £3). The **stone circle** a mile from town is worth seeing A coastal walk west from Castletownbere takes you to the ruins of **Dunboy Castle** (where an Irish and Spanish force was besieged and overcome by the

English in 1602) and **Puxley's Castle**, the eerie, dilapidated shell of a Victorian Gothic mansion. This was the home of the Puxley family, who made their money out of copper-mining; their story, and that of the mines, was used by Daphne du Maurier in her novel *Hungry Hill*. The castle itself was burnt down by the IRA in the 1920s, but its setting is idyllic: a placid inlet behind Castletownbere harbour fringed by rich woodlands, with stunning views of the wild mountains – expect to be charged £2 to enter the grounds.

There's a useful **tourist information** hut on the square (☎027/70054). If you want to stay in the town, there are several **B&Bs**: options at the west end of town include the pleasant *Old Presbytery* (☎027/70424; ④), hung with some interesting paintings by Allihies artists, and *Knockanroe* (☎027/70029; ②). *Murphy's* (☎027/70244; ①), Main Street (above the restaurant) offers decent budget B&B, and at the east end there's *Ár dTeachna* (☎027/70071; ②), a family home that also has inexpensive single rooms. You can **camp** at nearby *Beara Hostel* (☎027/70184), two miles west of Castletownbere on the road towards Allihies, a clean hostel with laundry facilities and bike rental. The alternative for campers is *Berehaven Camper Amenity Park* (☎027/70700), about one mile east of town, a well developed site for tents and camper vans. One of the best places to **eat** is *The Old Bakery*, West End (summer daily 9am–11pm; winter early closing), serving excellent home-cooked food, a welcome refuge on a rainy day with plenty of art books and board games to while away the time. You'll also hear music here on weekends in the summer. For more regular café fare try *Murphy's* and *Jack Patrick's* on Main Street, and *Cronin's*, West End. Seafood features prominently on the menu at *Niki's*, Main Street (Mon–Sat till 9.30pm, Sun till 9pm; 3 courses around £15), while the more upmarket *Old Cottage* (☎027/70430), about two miles east of town, enjoys a good reputation for seafood and Mediterranean dishes. Provisions are available at all hours from *MacCarthy's* shop-cum-bar – one of the nicest places to drink. For **music** in the summer, check out *Twomey's*, West End or *O'Donoghue's* on the square. There is a **laundry** on Main Street. **Bike rental** is available from the Supervalu supermarket. If you want to explore this coastline from the water, try **sea kayaking** with Beara Kayaks (☎027/70692).

Allihies and around

Moving on from Castletownbere you can head down to the remote, tiny villages at the end of the peninsula, a few houses, a shop and a pub being the typical set-up. This extreme of the peninsula saw some development in the nineteenth century when copper was mined, but little remains beyond the unguarded shafts; beware of these if you're walking. Signposted to the left off the road around five miles west of Castletownbere (then about another half a mile on) is the remote *Garranes Farmhouse Hostel* (☎027/73147), clinging to a beautiful, ravaged coastline. The **hostel** is next to the Buddhist Dzogchen Beara Retreat Centre, and hostellers are welcome to join meditation classes. Phoning ahead is advised since the hostel can be full of people on retreat at any time of the year. Note that the nearest shop is one mile away towards Allihies and stocks only basic provisions; the nearest pub is six miles away.

Tiny **ALLIHIES**, formerly a major mining centre, nowadays has simply four pubs, a shop, a sandy beach and a handful of places to stay. For **B&B** *Sea View House* (☎027/73004; ③) in the main street offers very comfortable rooms, as does *Sea Haven Lodge* (☎027/73225; ②) in a fabulous spot overlooking the beach. There are a couple of **hostels**: the comfy, central *Village Hostel* (IHH; ☎027/73107; April–Oct) is a delightful place and has a good bookshelf, but you'll need to book ahead in the summer; the An Óige hostel (☎027/73014; June–Sept) is about a mile from the centre and is rather more basic, though adequate nonetheless – and beautifully secluded – follow the **Beara Way** signs from the south end of the village if you're walking. You can **camp** by the beach – either rough or on a small site. Just about the only place to get a meal is *O'Neill's* bar, and there's folk music here (Wed) and in *The Oak* (Thurs).

Perhaps the quietest of the islands to be visited off West Cork is **DURSEY ISLAND**, situated at the very tip of the peninsula and fringed by high cliffs. Dursey's attractions include fabulous views, solitude and the thrill of taking a very dodgy-looking cable car across the narrow and treacherous sound. You can walk up its hills for endless views westward over the ocean, with three great lumps of rock in the foreground: the Cow, the Calf and the Bull. For a day-trip, you need to get to the very end of the R572 in the morning. The **cable car** has no regular schedule, but during July and August you can usually get to the island Monday to Saturday between 9am and 11am, 2.30pm and 5pm, and between 7pm and 8pm. Sunday times vary slightly. There is a **B&B** near the cable car station: *Windy Point House*, Garrish (☎027/73017; April–Oct; ②), which also serves tea and snacks in the summer. If you want to stop over you'll need to pitch a tent, as Dursey Island has just a few houses – which claim to be the most westerly habitation in Europe, and no pub or shop.

Heading along the northside of the Beara Peninsula towards Kenmare, the fine scenery continues, with peerless views of the Kerry mountains. About four miles west of Eyeries you can get simple **hostel** accommodation at Urhan Post Office (☎027/74005 or 74036). Phoning ahead is strongly advised, especially in July and August. There's nothing here but a shop, a pub, a little beach and fabulous views to enjoy. **EYERIES** itself is a brightly painted village with some pleasant pubs and the friendly little *Ard Na Mara* **hostel** (☎027/74271), a spacious bungalow in a beautiful spot overlooking the sea, where you can also **camp** – to find it walk around half a mile along the road east from the pubs and it's signposted off to the left. Phoning ahead is strongly advised. There is **B&B** in the village at *Coulagh Bay House* (☎027/74013; ②), high on the main road.

Four miles north of here, the small village of **ARDGROOM** also enjoys beautiful scenery, backed by the Slieve Miskish mountains and set beside a rushing river. It makes a very pleasant stop-over if you're walking the **Beara Way** or want to fish for brown trout in nearby Glenbeg Lake. **B&B** is available at *O'Brien's* (☎027/74019; ②) in the main street, and you can get bar food at *The Village Inn*.

travel details

Trains

Cork to: Cobh (8–19 daily; 25min); Dublin (6–9 daily, 3hr); Fota (8–19 daily; 15min); Rosslare Harbour (Mon–Sat 2 daily; 5hr 25min–9hr 17min).

Buses

Bantry to: Glengarriff and Castletownbere. Mon: Castletownbere 9.30am, calling at Glengarriff 10.10am, arrives Bantry 10.40am. Return from Bantry Mon noon, Glengarriff 12.30pm, arrives Castletownbere 1.10pm. Tues, Fri & Sat: Castletownbere 10.30am, calling at Glengarriff 11.20am, arrives Bantry 11.50am. Return same days from Bantry 3.45pm, Glengarriff 4.15pm, arrives Castletownbere 6.55pm. Schedule may change so phone for confirmation (☎027/70007).

Castletownbere to: Cork; O'Donoghue's Buses (☎027/70007). Depart Castletownbere Thurs only 7.30am, Glengarriff 8.10am, Bantry 8.30am, arrive Cork 10.15am. Return from Cork (Parnell Place) 6pm, Bantry 7.45pm, Glengarriff 8.25pm, arrive Castletownbere 9.15pm.

Harrington's Buses (027/74003). Depart Castletownbere Mon, Tues, Wed, Fri (& Sat in summer) at 8am to arrive in Cork 10.15am; Sun at 5pm to arrive in Cork 7.15pm. Services depart from Cork (Mulligan's, Parnell Place) Mon–Sat at 6pm, to arrive in Castletownbere at 8.30pm; Sun departure at 8pm.

Other private companies serving the Beara from Cork include Peter O'Sullivan (☎027/74168), whose buses run once every day except Thurs; phone for schedule as it can vary.

Castletownbere to: Kenmare (June 28–Aug 30 only Mon–Sat 2 daily; 1hr 20min).

Cork to: Cork airport (4–18 daily, 20min); Dublin (3–4 daily; 4hr 25min); Limerick (5–6 daily; 1hr 50min).

Ferries

Cork–Swansea (4–6 days a week according to season; 10hr).

Cork–Roscoff (1 per week; April–Oct only; 14 hr).

COUNTY KERRY

I f you've come to Ireland for the scenery, mountains, sea and the remoteness, you'll find them all in County Kerry: miles and miles of mountain-moorland where the heather and the bracken are broken only by the occasional lake; smooth hills whose fragrant, tussocky grass is covered with sea pinks, speedwells, thrift and red campion, and that fragment into jagged rocks as they reach the sea. The ocean looks enormous, and you can stand in the sunshine and watch a storm coming in for miles before you have to run for cover. The only catch is that a good part of the county is very much on the tourist trail.

The plus side of Kerry's long tradition of welcoming tourists is that it's very easy country to travel in, with plenty of accommodation and food in all price brackets. And, during the summer at least, transport is pretty good – though with some notable exceptions.

Broadly speaking, Kerry divides into four areas: the Dingle Peninsula; the Iveragh Peninsula, encircled by the Ring of Kerry, with Killarney in its hinterland; the Kenmare River, bordered to the north and south by the Iveragh and Beara peninsulas; and northern Kerry, from Tralee to the Shannon. Each section is quite distinct and has its partisans. By far the most visited area – indeed the most visited in the whole of Ireland – is **Killarney and the Ring of Kerry**. Deservedly famous for the beauty of the adjacent lakes and mountains, this region is, predictably, geared up for tourism, and the principal roads and sights are often overburdened with visitors. Luckily, however, the real wilds are never far away, and whether you head for the mountains or the sea you can soon lose yourself and feel remote from modern civilization. The **Dingle Peninsula** is on a smaller scale than Iveragh, but equally magical: peppered with monastic remains, it has a contemplative atmosphere that makes you understand why people talk about the mystic quality of the west. Around **Kenmare** things are different again, with a tamed feeling about the scenery; one half of the Beara Peninsula belongs to more cultivated, genteel County Cork. To the **north**, flat, fertile farming land makes for less exciting scenery, but in contrast to the rest of the county there are many signs of a long-established Anglo-Norman presence.

Killarney and around

Although **KILLARNEY** has been commercialized to saturation point and has little in the way of architectural interest, the real reason for coming here is without doubt the surrounding landscape. Its three spectacular **lakes**, Lough Leane (the Lower Lake),

---

ACCOMMODATION PRICE CODES

Throughout this book, prices of hotels, guesthouses and B&Bs have been graded with the codes below, according to what you can expect to pay for a double room in high season. For more details on accommodation, see p. 29.

① Under £26	④ £40–55	⑦ £90–110
② £26–33	⑤ £55–70	⑧ £110–130
③ £33–40	⑥ £70–90	⑨ Over £130

Muckross Lake (the Middle Lake) and the Upper Lake, are only the appetizer. Behind them loom **Macgillycuddy's Reeks**, which have a grandeur out of all proportion to their height: rarely exceeding 3000ft, they're still the highest mountains in Ireland. Much of this is contained within the huge **Killarney National Park**.

Arrival, information and accommodation

Killarney's train and bus **station** is pretty central, off East Avenue Road. Although there's plentiful accommodation of all sorts, the town gets very crowded in high season and it's worth calling the **tourist office**, on Beech Road (June & Sept Mon–Sat 9am–6pm, Sun 10am–6pm; July & Aug daily 9am–8pm; Oct–May Mon–Sat 9am–5pm; ☎064/31633) to make advance bookings. Even if you're not planning to bike round the Ring of Kerry, cycling is a great way of seeing Killarney's immediate surroundings, and makes good sense because local transport is almost non-existent. **Bike rental** is available at O'Callaghan Brothers, College Street, O'Neill's in Plunkett Street, and at several of the hostels. Banks and the post office can be found on New Street. Killarney's laundry is down a lane next to Dunnes Stores, New Street.

One thing the tourist office can't do is make specific recommendations of **B&Bs** – a shame since price and quality seem to vary a lot here. Reasonable central options include *Lisaden*, Countess Grove, off Countess Road (☎064/32006; ③), Arch House, East Avenue Road (☎064/32184; ③), and *Orchard*, Fleming's Lane, off High Street (☎064/31879; ②).

Over the last few years there has been a **hostel**-building epidemic, and there are now a staggering nine to choose from in and around Killarney. In Killarney itself, there's the *Súgán Kitchen Hostel* (IHO; ☎064/33104), Lewis Road, a few minutes' walk from the station, and the extrovert and noisy *Four Winds Hostel*, 43 New St (IHO; ☎064/33094; closed Jan), which has bikes for rent. The *Neptune Hostel* off New Street (IHH; ☎064/35255) is welcoming, manages to combine size and intimacy, provides masses of information and does discounts for most tours around the area. Along the same lines is the comfortable *Railway Hostel* near the Franciscan church (☎064/35299). *Atlas House* (☎064/36144), signposted off the Cork road about a mile from the station, is very large, clean, and efficiently run. *The Park Hostel* (IHH; ☎064/32119) is also up the hill off the Cork road. *Bunrower House Hostel* (IHH; ☎064/33914; March–Nov), is in a lovely spot near Ross Castle a mile from Killarney, where you can camp in a beautiful garden, though frustratingly you have to head back towards town to access the National Park from here. The An Óige hostel (☎064/31240) is three miles out along the Killorglin road at Aghadoe: set in beautiful countryside, it is worth considering as a base if you intend walking in the mountains. There is a free shuttle service to and from the bus and train station, and bike rental. Six miles out of town, the beautifully situated *Peacock Farm Hostel* at Muckross (☎064/33557; April–Sept) can arrange lifts from Killarney. There are three **campsites:** *Fleming's White Bridge* (☎064/31590) is just a mile east of Killarney – follow the N22 Cork road and turn right for Ballycasheen; *Flesk Muckross Caravan and Camping Park* (☎064/31704) is a mile from Killarney on the N71 Kenmare road, and handy for the Kerry Way and Muckross House; *White Villa Farm* (☎064/32456) is a small site about two miles east of town on the N22.

The Town

The town is essentially one main street and a couple of side roads, full of souvenir shops, cafés, pubs, restaurants and B&Bs. Pony traps and jaunting cars line up against walls while their weather-beaten owners talk visitors into extortionate trips through the surrounding country. It's all done with bags of charm, true to Killarney's long tradition of profitably hosting the visiting masses ever since its discovery as a resort in the mid-eighteenth century.

The town's Irish name (*Cill Áirne*, Church of the Sloe) doesn't imply a settlement of any great antiquity, and the Cromwellian Survey of 1654 found no town or village of that name. By 1756, however, a burgeoning **tourist trade**, soon fed by the growing Romantic attraction to lakes and mountains, had created Killarney: "A new street with a large commodious inn was designed to be built here, for the curiosities of the neighbouring lake have of late drawn great numbers of curious travellers to visit it," said a contemporary survey. The local landowner, Lord Kenmare, quickly spotted commercial opportunities and granted free leases for new inns and houses, building four major roads to connect his creation with the outside world.

That said, the town doesn't look particularly planned, and the only building of any distinction is the high Gothic Revival cathedral, built by Augustus Pugin in 1855. A particularly florid Victorian interpretation of medieval architecture, the **cathedral**

KILLARNEY'S FLORA AND FAUNA

It was the last Ice Age that formed the Killarney landscape. Glaciation has left its mark on the contorted limestone valleys of the Lower and Middle lakes, and the nearby Devil's Punch Bowl and Horses' Glen show other signs: huge rocks smoothed to sucked-sweet shapes, and improbably teetering boulders. The lower slopes of the mountains are covered with what is often virgin **forest**, a joy to see in a country that has cut down almost all its trees. Almost everything seems to thrive in the local combination of high rainfall and humidity, and in the woods you'll find a rich mix of trees dominated by oak, but with bilberry, woodrush and woodsorrel plus mosses, liverworts and lichens, sensitive organisms whose continued survival testifies to the clean air here.

As elsewhere in the west of Ireland, the Killarney area's **vegetation** includes a number of plants generally found in quite different parts of Europe. The famous arbutus, or strawberry tree – so called from its bright-red (and non-edible) fruit – for example, generally grows only in Mediterranean countries and Brittany. Some saxifrages and the greater butterwort, with its fleshy purple flowers and sickly green leaf rosettes, are otherwise found only in northwest Spain and Portugal.

inspires respect or derision, but is worth seeing either way. During the Famine, when building work ceased for five years, the covered area served as a hospital for victims of starvation and disease.

Eating, drinking and entertainment

Places to **eat and drink** are thick on the ground in Killarney. *The Green Onion Café*, Fleming's Lane, off High Street, is a lovely place for excellent budget sandwiches and lunches (till 5.30pm), and *The Celtic Cauldron* (☎064/36821) serves delicious Celtic dishes, including fresh galettes and stews. Ray wing salad is one of the more unusual dishes on offer at *Yer Man's* bar, next to *The Strawberry Tree*, Plunkett Street (till 9pm in summer), while more traditional, inexpensive hot meals, are served day and evening, at *Cronin's*, Lewis Road and at *Caragh*, New Street (☎064/31645), popular with families. The vegetarian dishes at *A Taste of Eden*, Bridewell Lane, opposite Dunnes Stores on New Street, (closed Mon) won't disappoint, nor will the delicious home-cooked lunches and dinners at *Bricín*, 26 High St (closes 5pm in winter).

Evening **entertainment** is everywhere as you walk along the streets: the widely publicized "traditional" Irish music can seem pretty spurious when you are surrounded by bus loads of other tourists, but it sounds great nonetheless. Good venues include *The Danny Man*, *Eviston House Hotel*, New Street (folk & ballads every night during the summer, weekends in winter), and *Buckley's* bar, College Street (traditional music 3–4 nights per week in winter, every night in summer). A great holiday atmosphere reigns in *The Grand*, Main Street, with ballads from 9.30pm and then a full traditional Irish band from 11.30pm to 1.30am. If you want to listen to unaccompanied singing, head for *Courtney's*, High Street, and you can hear blues (Sat year round) and a mix of traditional and MOR (summer midweek) at *Meara's*, High Street. *Yer Man's* is an atmospheric old bar with plenty of jazz (most nights July & Aug; winter spontaneous sessions) and occasional local theatre productions.

In May, July and October there's **racing** at Killarney's race course on Ross Road, which, like any Irish race meeting, is well worth a detour. The tourist office can give details of **gaelic football** matches; Killarney is a top team and feelings run high. The Rally of the Lakes brings hordes of motor fanatics to Killarney over the first weekend in May. Rally drivers roar along the roads around the lakes, so if you want to enjoy the mountains in peace, this is probably a weekend best avoided.

Knockreer Estate and Lough Leane

Oddly enough, given its origins as a tourist town, Killarney turns its back on the grand scenery to the west and south, hunching itself inwards so that you'd hardly guess at the delights that await you. But the gates of the old Kenmare Estate – now known as the **KNOCKREER ESTATE** – are just over the road from the cathedral, and a short walk through the grounds takes you to the banks of Lough Leane. The Browne family, Earls of Kenmare, were unusual among the Irish peerage in that they never renounced their Catholic faith. Given lands confiscated from the O'Donoghues in the seventeenth century, they were subject in the eighteenth century to the penal laws which decreed that every Catholic landowner had to divide his property among his male heirs. The Brownes' estate remained intact quite simply because there was only one son in each generation.

At **LOUGH LEANE**, the scenery is magnificent: tall wooded hills plunge into the water, with the mountain peaks rising behind to the highest, **Carrauntoohil** (3411ft). Ireland's last wild wolf was killed here in 1700, and when the weather's bad (as it often is) there's a satisfying similarity to early Romantic engravings. The main path through the Knockreer Estate leads to the restored fourteenth-century tower of Ross Castle, the last place in Munster to succumb to Cromwell's forces in 1652. The story is that General Ludlow, having learned of a tradition that **Ross Castle** would never be taken from land, brought prefabricated ships from Kenmare and sailed them up from Castlemaine, whereupon the defenders – whom nothing else had budged – immediately surrendered. Near the water you can make out copper workings, last used during the Napoleonic Wars and thought to date back four thousand years.

From Ross Castle you can **tour the lake** in large glassed-over boats like the bateaux-mouches that ply the Seine in Paris; but these don't make stops, and an alternative is to get a fisherman to take you out in a little craft with an outboard motor, or rent one yourself. This way, you can land on and explore the island of Inisfallen. (If you're navigating yourself, look for a limestone outcrop in the water. Inisfallen is the island to the left, about a mile out.)

Inisfallen

Of the thirty-odd small islands that dot Lough Leane, **INISFALLEN** is the biggest and the most enchanting. The monastery founded here in the seventh century was an important scholastic centre for a thousand years. Brian Boru, the eleventh-century High King and victor over the Vikings at Clontarf in 1014, was reputedly educated here, and the twelfth-century Annals of Inisfallen, now in Oxford's Bodleian Library, are an important source document for early Irish history. Wandering round the island is a delight: heavily wooded, it's also scattered with monastic buildings – nothing from the original seventh-century foundation, but there's a small Romanesque church and a ruined twelfth-century Augustinian priory. Eighteenth-century tourists were clearly awake to Inisfallen's charms: Lord Kenmare used to give parties for his influential friends here, and the gap in the wall of the Romanesque church is where he installed a bay window when the building was converted into a banqueting house. The picturesque ruin you see now is the result of further tinkering, around 1840.

Muckross Estate and the lakes

The road from Killarney to the **MUCKROSS ESTATE** passes through unlovely territory dominated by huge modern hotels, and though jaunting cars from the centre of Killarney will take you out to Muckross (cars are prohibited on the Muckross Estate), it's more fun to rent a bike. Take the earliest turning right into the park that's available, to escape the busy main road. The first place to head for is **Muckross Abbey**, not only for the ruin itself – one of the best preserved in Ireland, part Norman, part Gothic, though sadly despoiled by Cromwell's troops – but also for its calm, contemplative location, and the fact that it, like Ross Castle, hints at something predating Killarney's tourist history. Founded as a Franciscan institution by Macarthy Mor in the mid-fifteenth century, it was suppressed by Henry VIII; the friars returned again, but were finally driven out by Cromwell's army in 1652.

Back at the main road, signposts direct you to **Muckross House**, a solid, nineteenth-century neo-Elizabethan mansion designed by the Scottish architect William Burn. The **museum** here (daily 9am–6pm; £3.80), while no great shakes, has a section on Kerry folk life where craftspeople (blacksmiths, weavers, potters) demonstrate their trades – but only at peak times, and there's a **traditional working farm** too (£3.80, combined house, museum and farm £5.50). The excellent tea shop provides a good refuge from the rain, but the **gardens** – well known for their rhododendrons and azaleas – are the place to be when the weather is fine.

The estate gives access to well-trodden paths along the shores of the **Muckross Lake**, and it's here that you can see one of Killarney's celebrated beauty spots, the **Meeting of the Waters**. Actually a parting, but highly picturesque nonetheless, it has a profusion of indigenous and flowering subtropical plants – eucalyptus, magnolia, bamboo and an arbutus, or strawberry tree, on the left of the Old Weir Bridge. Close by is the massive shoulder of Torc Mountain, shrugging off the spectacular 60ft **Torc Waterfall**. There's a not terribly informative visitor centre by the car park for the waterfall; but the climb up the side of the mountain is worth doing, if only for the view across to Macgillycuddy's Reeks. On a good day, the Slieve Mish Mountains on the far side of Dingle Bay are visible.

About two miles south, the **Upper Lake** is beautiful, too, but still firmly on the tourist trail, with the main road running along one side up to **Ladies' View**, where many queue up to admire the scenery – which is, in fact, truly amazing, including the Gap of Dunloe and the wild and desolate Black Valley beyond the lake.

The Gap of Dunloe

Although the **Gap of Dunloe** – a narrow defile formed by glacial overflow that cuts the mountains in two – is one of Killarney's prime tourist attractions, it's possible to find a modicum of solitude if you're willing to use your legs. **Jaunting cars** continually run here from Killarney's centre, a fact which, as the jarveys tout loudly for business, you're not likely to miss. One version of the trip, combining jaunting cars with a bus ride, sets off from Killarney at 10.30am, transferring you to a pony and trap for the Gap itself, before returning to town at 5.15pm. Apart from being highly overpriced, this entails being stuck in the traffic jam of bored ponies pulling traps up the Gap. The other option is to walk, ignoring the offers of rides that will assail you for the first half-mile or so. If you peg out before the four miles are up, it's possible to haggle for a lift – the whole trip generally costs about £13 for the car, plus £13 per person for the pony.

Kate Kearney's Cottage, at the foot of the road leading up to the Gap – a confusion of shops and sweating horses – is the last place for food and water before Lord Brandon's Cottage (open June–Aug), seven miles away over the other side of the Black Valley. The best time to walk is late afternoon, when the jaunting cars have gone home and the light is at its most magical. The road – closed to motor traffic – winds its way up the desolate valley between high rock cliffs and waterfalls (Macgillycuddy's Reeks to your right, and to your left the Purple Mountain, so called because in late summer it's covered in purple heather), past a chain of icy loughs and tarns, up to the top, where you find yourself in what feels like one of the remotest places in the world: the **Black Valley**.

Named after its entire population perished during the potato famine, and now inhabited by a mere handful of families, the Black Valley makes you begin to feel that you've left mass tourism behind. The fact that it was the very last valley in Ireland to get electricity is some measure of its isolation, and there are no pubs or shops here. There is, however, a **hostel** run by An Óige (☎064/34712; March–Nov), where you can also get meals. Moving on, you can either carry on down to the Upper Lake or pick up the Kerry Way.

The Ring of Kerry

The 110-mile Ring of Kerry, which encircles the Iveragh Peninsula, can be driven around in a day, and most tourists view its spectacular scenery without ever leaving their bus or car. Consequently, anyone straying from the road or waiting until the buses

THE KERRY WAY

The **Kerry Way**, 133 miles long, is part of a long-distance footpath that goes through Macgillycuddy's Reeks then right around the Iveragh Peninsula through Glenbeigh, Cahersiveen, Waterville, Caherdaniel and Kenmare – a sort of walkers' Ring of Kerry. More than most of Ireland's long-distance footpaths, it's resonant of the culture, as well as the nature, of the area and consists largely of green roads, many of them old drovers' roads or "butter roads" (along which butter was transported) and routes between Kerry's ancient Christian settlements. Whichever section you choose to walk, you'll need the relevant 1:50,000 OS map – numbers 78 and 83 respectively.

The Kerry Way starts inauspiciously in **Killarney**, threads down through the Muckross Estate and alongside the Upper Lake – road walking, most of it – before heading up to meet the Black Valley (see above). From the Black Valley, it heads on towards **Cloghernoosh** via a stony path that becomes a green road. After the footbridge over the stream running out of Curraghmore Lake, there's a stretch of bridleway, and from here on you're among the peaks, with exhilarating views of Carrauntoohil to the north.

Next, the footpath follows the Lack Road, zigzagging up to a saddle point at the top, then skirting the side of **Lough Acoose** before reaching the Glencar Valley (and the first tourist accommodation since the Black Valley). No longer traversing really high ground, the rest of the way into Glenbeigh is less exciting, although the stretch on Seefin Mountain above Caragh Lake is still spectacular. From here the Way runs around the peninsula, is especially scenic between Waterville and Caherdaniel and eventually leads back to Killarney.

All the usual precautions need to be taken seriously in a region where gales blowing in off the Atlantic can make the weather change rapidly. Bring waterproofs, walking boots and food.

You should really fix up **accommodation** beforehand. There's an An Óige hostel in the **Black Valley** (see above), roughly eight hours' walk from Killarney; hitching isn't recommended, since the nearest road seeing any traffic is eight miles from the start of the valley. Next stop is the *Climbers' Inn*, offering both B&B and hostel accommodation, hidden among woodlands at **GLENCAR** (☎066/976 0101; ④; April–Oct); meals are available in the bar, decorated with a church pulpit, and there's a shop and advice on local walks and climbs; check they have hostel accommodation in advance if you don't want to end up paying for B&B. For accommodation in **GLENBEIGH** see opposite. Nine miles from Killarney, the *Mountain Rest Lodge* (☎064/44272), Carnahone, **BEAUFORT**, is close to the main approach to Carrauntoohil and there's **B&B** at *Inisfáil* (☎064/44404; ③) just near the *Beaufort Bar*. About one mile along the N72 west of the Beaufort turn-off there's camping at *Riverside Park*. If you do plan to scale Ireland's highest mountain, you should really get some local advice first. Try John Walsh at the *Climbers' Inn*, Glencar, or phone Eileen Daly of Killarney Mountaineering Club on ☎064/34677. Alternatively, pick up a copy of the excellent *Walk Guide: South West of Ireland* by Seán Ó Súilleabháin (pub. Gill and Macmillan), which details 47 walks in and around Kerry, including walks up Carrauntoohil.

knock off in the afternoon will be left to experience the long, slow twilights of the Atlantic seaboard in perfect seclusion. Part of the excitement of travelling round the Kerry coast comes from the clarity with which its physical outline stands out against the vast grey expanse of the Atlantic. Every gully, bay, channel and island is as distinct as it is on the map, giving a powerful sense of place amidst the isolation.

If you really are limited to a day's exploration of the wild coastal scenery, it could be worth heading for Dingle, the next peninsula north, instead: its intimacy of scale means you can see a lot more without having to rely upon buses or cars. **Cycling** the Ring itself takes three days (not counting any diversions), and a bike will let you get on to the largely deserted mountain roads; just be sure your machine has lots of gears, and you have plenty of energy – the combination of gradients and strong winds can be gruelling. **Buses** serve the entire circuit from late May to mid-Sept only (two daily); the rest of the year buses from Killarney only go as far as Cahersiveen (twice daily from July to mid-Sept, once daily at other times) – but during summer, flotillas of tourist buses ply the Ring. You can get details of tours from the tourist office and for an extra charge some companies will drop you off somewhere along the way and pick you up the next day. Hitching is unreliable; while you're likely to get a lift from anyone who passes, traffic simply may not exist away from the main roads.

Killorglin to Glenbeigh

By travelling the Ring of Kerry **anticlockwise**, you get a gradual introduction to the wild grandeur of the coastline scenery, with the Dingle Peninsula and the dim shapes of the Blasket Islands visible in the distance.

The first stop on the way out from Killarney is the pleasantly unexceptional hillside town of **KILLORGLIN**, whose main claim to fame is the **Puck Fair**, held over three days in mid-August, a bacchanalian event with a wild goat captured and enthroned, plenty of dancing and drinking, plus a cattle, sheep and horse fair. These rituals honour the wild goats which, stampeding through the town, warned residents of the approach of Cromwell's army. The fair's pagan origins date back to the Celtic festival of Lughnasa, three days of feasting and ritual sacrifices to celebrate the beginning of harvest. If you want to **stay**, try the *Laune Valley Farm Hostel* (☎066/976 1488), which has camping facilities and serves meals. For B&B there's *Riverside House* (☎066/976 1184; ③), Ballykissan Road, or the homely *Fáilte Towers*, Iveragh Road (☎066/976 1155; ②). The *Bianconi Inn*, Lower Bridge Street, does very good if pricy **bar food**; less expensive is *Bunker's*, Iveragh Road, or try the carvery lunches at the *Manor Inn*. Also recommended is the hugely popular *Nick's Restaurant* (☎066/976 1219; dinner £20). *The Old Forge Inn*, an atmospheric old bar on the steep main street, has traditional music from Mondays to Wednesdays and pop bands on other nights, while *Coffey's* bar does good traditional sessions on Thursdays. If you're feeling energetic, the Cappanalea Outdoor Education Centre (groups collected from Killorglin or Killarney by arrangement; ☎066/976 9244) organizes a wide range of adventure sports – turn left off the main street at the *Bianconi*, then follow the weather-beaten wooden signs.

Next comes **GLENBEIGH**, where almost everything is given over to tourism; despite plenty of accommodation, the town illustrates the disadvantages of sticking rigidly to the Ring – however, there are wonderful views all along the coastline and across to Dingle and a Blue Flag beach just a mile away. For **accommodation**, try the *Glenbeigh Hotel* (☎066/976 8333; ⑦), the *Village House* B&B (☎066/976 8128; ④), or the tiny *Horseshoe Hostel* (☎066/97 68606) at the end of the main street, catering for walkers and cyclists. *Sweeney's* and *The Towers* are a couple of lively bars; both serve good bar food, and the latter has a good deal of rock and traditional music at weekends. By taking the road up past **Caragh Lake**, you'll find some of Kerry's best mountain scenery, full of deep silences and the magical slanting light of the west. If you're on a

SOUTH KERRY AND THE FIANNA

Many legends of the **Fianna**, a band of warriors led by **Finn Mac Cool** who served the High King in the third century, are set in South Kerry. One of them tells of how, near Killarney, Niamh, a golden-haired beauty on a white horse, persuaded Finn's son Oisin to come away to her kingdom. Where the magical wave Tonn Toime roars between Inch and Rossbeigh, they galloped out across the sea to Tír na nÓg, the Land of Eternal Youth. After a blissful three hundred years, Oisin borrowed Niamh's magical horse to visit his homeland, with a warning not to dismount. Unable to find any of the Fianna in Kerry, he rode north to Dublin and found a band of puny men trying to shift a boulder. Leaning down to help, he broke a girth and landed on the ground a very old man. Before he died, St Patrick persuaded him to convert to Christianity.

relaxed budget and are looking for comparative luxury, you could stay at the *Glendalough House*, a mid-nineteenth-century country house on the shores of Caragh Lake (☎066/976 9156; ⑤). Alternatively, you could carry on up to the three small lakes of **Coomnacronia**, **Coomaglaslaw** and **Coomasaharn** (good trout fishing, but you'll need a licence).

The lack of trees that contributes to the feeling of austerity in this area was not an original feature of the landscape; Sir William Petty, Cromwell's surveyor general, had an iron mine at Blackstones and felled the forests to fuel a smelter.

Cahersiveen

At **Kells Bay** the road veers inland for **CAHERSIVEEN**, giving you an opportunity to take a detour. On the way you'll pass *Caitín Baiters* pub, beside which is the clean and bright *Kells Ring of Kerry Hostel* (☎066/77614). Any of the turnings right will lead eventually to the sea, past bright fuchsia hedges, with little or no traffic. "One wonders, in this place, why anyone is left in Dublin, or London, or Paris, when it would be better one would think, to live in a tent, or a hut, with this magnificent sea and sky, and to breathe this wonderful air, which is like wine in one's teeth," wrote J. M. Synge of the Kerry landscape; and here, for the first time, you begin to understand how the Ring inspires such hyperbole.

Cahersiveen (*Cathair Saidhbhín*; pronounced *Caher-sigh-veen*, stress on the last syllable) was said by Daniel O'Connell, its most famous son, to be the only town established in Ireland after the Act of Union. It is a long, narrow street of a town and the main shopping centre for the western part of the peninsula, giving itself over cheerfully to the tourist trade in summer. A laid-back, unremarkable place, it has more relaxed attitudes to shopping hours than anywhere else on the peninsula, and there are plenty of friendly bars, such as *The Anchor Bar* or *Mike Murt's*, both full of character. The latter also hosts music sessions during the summer, as does *Cráineen's* and *The Skelligs Rock*. As for **food**, you can get all-day breakfasts at *An Cupan* and bar food at *The Town House*. For good, though expensive, evening meals, try *O'Donoghue's* fish restaurant on the main street. Worth having a look at is the community-funded **Barracks Heritage Centre** (June–Sept Mon–Sat 10am–6pm, Sun 1–6pm; ☎066/72777; £3), which contains a concise history of the town and a gallery of paintings and sculptures by local artists. The **tourist office** is also in the Heritage Centre. Not far from here is the magnificent Daniel O'Connell Memorial Church (June–Sept daily 10am–7pm), highly unusual in that it is dedicated to a statesman rather than a saint, an indication of the high regard in which the liberator was held (for more on Daniel O'Connell see p.619). On Valentia Road you can get **B&B** at *Castleview* (☎066/72252; ②) or *San Antoine* (☎066/72521; ③). Another alternative is *Ocean View Farmhouse* (☎066/72261; ④) half a mile out of town on the road towards Waterville; and if you fancy galloping along a beach or

trekking through the countryside, try *The Final Furlong Farmhouse Accommodation and Riding Stables* (☎066/72810; ③), just over a mile out on the Glenbeigh road. There are two independent **hostels**, the cosy *Sive Hostel*, 15 East End (☎066/72717), with camping facilities, and laid-back *Mortimer's*, West Main Street (☎066/72338). It is possible to arrange trips to the **Skelligs** from Cahersiveen (see box on p.304).

REENARD POINT, three miles west of Cahersiveen, is the departure point for the ten-minute ferry crossing to **KNIGHTSTOWN** on Valentia Island (☎066/76141; cars return £4; cyclists return £3; last sailing from Reenard Point 10pm, last sailing from Knightstown 9.50pm). It's also a departure point for trips to the **Skelligs** (see box on p.305), and there's excellent, reasonably priced seafood here at *The Point Bar* – it's hugely popular, so you may well have to wait to be served. If you need **B&B**, *Sea Breeze* (☎066/72609; ③) has stunning views over the island.

Beyond Cahersiveen, the main road takes the bulk of the traffic inland again towards Waterville, giving you an opportunity to explore the quiet lanes that lead out to Valentia Island and the peninsula's end. **PORTMAGEE** nestles beside a small harbour, its handful of bars and coffee shops providing welcome refuge on a blustery day. The village's much-hyped Skellig Heritage Centre (May–Sept daily 10am–6pm; £3) provides information on Celtic monastic life, lighthouses and lighthouse-keeping, seabirds and aquatic life, but it's all too easy to see it as just another example of theme-park Ireland. The often single-track, and very steep, road south of here signposted the **Ring of Skellig**, affords spectacular views out to the Skelligs and Puffin Island, and eventually winds down to the tiny village of **BALLINSKELLIGS**. Monks from the Skellig Islands retreated to Ballinskelligs Abbey in the thirteenth century; today the area is largely Irish-speaking and is a focus of the Kerry *Gaeltacht*, drawing large numbers of schoolchildren and students of Irish in the summer. The village is tiny – there's a pretty basic An Óige **hostel** (☎066/79229; Easter–Sept) and shop, a similarly basic pub, which seems to be full at any time of the day or night, and a lovely sandy beach with fabulous views across Ballinskelligs Bay to the Kerry Mountains. Trips to the Skelligs can be arranged from here (see p.305).

Valentia Island

VALENTIA, an island now linked to the mainland by bridge, is Europe's most westerly harbour, and standing at Bray Head on the island's tip, there's nothing but ocean between you and Newfoundland, 1900 miles away. Valentia's significance is out of all proportion to its size: the first ever transatlantic telegraph cable was laid from here in 1857 – though permanent contact wasn't established until 1866 – and for years it had better communications with New York than with Dublin.

In contrast to the endless vistas west, the island itself is small, and consequently every scrap of land has been cultivated, forming a rolling patchwork of fields stitched with dry slate walls. Valentia's position in the Gulf Stream gives it a mild, balmy climate, and the abundance of fuchsias grown by the inhabitants in local hedgerows enhances its domesticated atmosphere. It's a homely, tame place to stay, though from July onwards the peace is disturbed by tourists.

Arrival and accommodation

Access by ferry is from Reenard Point (see above) to Knightstown, or via the Maurice O'Neill Bridge, Portmagee, at the south end of the island, thirteen miles from the main coast road and a difficult hitch. Once on the island, there's no public transport at all. Accommodation is at a premium during the summer season; **B&Bs** include homely *Walsh's* (☎066/76115; ②) and *Spring Acre* (☎066/76141; ②), both in Knightstown, and *Glenveen Heights*, Knightstown Road (☎066/76241; ③), about a mile away towards Chapeltown. The An Óige **hostel** has space for forty at the Coastguard Station in

Knightstown, though services are spartan (☎066/76141; June–Sept). The island's other hostel, the independent *Ring Lyne Hostel* (☎066/76103), lies midway between the bridge and Knightstown at Chapeltown.

The island

KNIGHTSTOWN is the focal village on the island and, facing Cahersiveen across the Portmagee Channel, affords fine panoramic views of the Kerry Mountains. A pretty harbour front with sprucely painted fishers cottages is dominated by the Victorian *Royal and Pier Hotel*; now rather dilapidated and something of a white elephant, it's currently being run as an independent hostel. Tolerating rather than encouraging tourists, Knightstown is deeply old-fashioned, and if there are more than three in your group, you could feel something of an intruder. About a thousand houses cluster around a slate church hidden within a dark rookery. The main street has a few well-stocked shops, a post office offering a good selection of Irish literature and free maps of the island, and a couple of bars. There's **bar food** at *The Boston Bar*, and *The Gallery Kitchen Restaurant* (☎066/76105) is a rather racy addition to this otherwise dour village, and its food has an excellent reputation.

From Knightstown, take the Kilmore Road down towards the lighthouse, where there's a fine view of Valentia's empty harbour, the Beginish Islands and tiny **Church Island**. This mere rock supports the ruins of an eighth-century cell, once inhabited by a solitary monk, a soulmate of the brotherhood on the nearby Skellig Islands, whose only company was the seabirds. On a clear day you can also make out the sheer cliffs of the Blasket Islands west of the Dingle Peninsula.

Continuing west, the foreshore is an imposing clutter of megalithic slabs hurled together by the waves, with deep, limpid pools left by the winter storms. A couple of miles further on, a cove, great for swimming, combines intimacy with the grandiose, sheltered by lush, deciduous woods, with the whole of Kerry as its scenic backdrop. This adjoins the incongruously exotic gardens (May–Oct daily 11am–5pm; £2.50) of **Glanleam House**, former seat of the local magnate, the Knight of Kerry.

The fervour with which locals urge you to visit the **Grotto**, at the north end of the island, is misplaced. A gaping slate cavern, it boasts a crude, municipal bath-blue statue of the Virgin (erected 1954) perched 200ft up, amidst monotonously dripping icy water. Nevertheless, this is the highest point on the island and a good walk for a clear day. But more exciting by far is the cliff scenery to the northwest, some of the most spectacular of the Kerry coast.

The Skellig Islands

From Valentia you get a tantalizing view across a broad strip of sea to the **Skellig Islands** (*Na Sceilig*), apparently no more than two massive rocks. **Little Skellig** is a bird sanctuary, home to 40,000 gannets, and landing isn't permitted, but you can visit Great Skellig, or Skellig Michael as it's also called, and climb up to the ancient monastic site at the summit.

There are several departure points for the Skelligs around the Kerry coast (see box opposite); the trips are not cheap at around £20 but, if the weather's good they make a fascinating and dramatic voyage. Once at sea, boats are followed by wheeling seagulls and, if you're lucky, puffins, too, from the nature reserve of Puffin Island, further north. You'll also pass the huge, jagged arch of rock that forms Little Skellig, where gannets with six-foot wingspans career overhead or make headlong dives into the sea for fish.

Skellig Michael looms sheer from the ocean, a gargantuan slaty mass with no visible route to the summit. From the tiny landing stage, however, you can see steps cut into the cliff face, formerly a treacherous monks' path. Nowadays there's also a broad path leading to Christ's Saddle, the only patch of green on this inhospitable island. From here, it narrows and leads on to the arched stone remains of **St Fionan's Abbey** (560 AD). Among the ruins are six complete beehive cells – drystone huts that have survived centuries of foul weather. The island is dedicated to St Michael, guardian against the powers of darkness and patron of high places, who helped St Patrick drive the last of the venomous serpents over the 700ft cliffs to perish in the sea. Contrasted with Valentia, it's a wild, cruel place, an awesome sanctuary of devotion, even if the monks didn't remain here all year round to feel the violence of the elements. The Viking invasion of the island in the ninth century lived long in folk memory, inspiring a Skellig monk to write:

Bitter and wild is the wind tonight
Tossing the tresses of the sea to white
On such a night as this I feel at ease
Fierce Northmen only course the quiet seas.

Waterville and around

WATERVILLE may be touristy, but it manages to avoid being tacky. Popular as a Victorian and Edwardian resort and angling centre, it still has an air of consequence that sits oddly with the wild Atlantic views. Its few bars and hotels aside, the town is chiefly notable as the best base on the Ring for exploring the coast and the mountainous country inland. If you want to stay, cheaper **B&Bs** include *Ashling House*, Main Street (☎066/74247; ③), and the friendly *Lake Rise*, Lake Road (☎066/74278; ②). *Peter's Place Hostel* (no phone), on the seafront at the south end of town, is small and cosy, and its jovial owner may rustle you up a meal, and you can also camp. Most of the bars and hotels do food, one of the best being *The Lobster Bar*, and for inexpensive home cooking, try the welcoming *An Corcán*, at the north end of the main street (till 10pm in summer).

From Waterville, it's a long haul by bike or on foot up to the **Coomakista Pass**, but the effort is well worth it for the breathtaking views over the mouth of the Kenmare River, all greys and blues, the three rocks called the Bull, the Cow and the Calf, and beyond them the Beara Peninsula – most spectacular when the weather's good; when it rains you can see the squalls being driven in across the ocean. However, you can't hope to avoid lots of other tourists here.

WATERVILLE IN LEGEND: NOAH'S CHILDREN IN IRELAND

Waterville and Ballinskelligs Bay form the setting for one of the more wayward Irish legends. When the biblical flood was imminent, so the story goes, Noah's son **Bith** and his daughter **Cessair** found that there was no room for them in the ark. So they and their retinue set sail for Ireland which, Cessair was advised, was uninhabited, free of monsters, reptiles and sin, and would therefore escape the flood. However, although 49 women survived to land along with Cessair in 2958 BC, only two men besides Bith made it. The three men divided the women between them, but when Bith and Ladra, the pilot, died, Fintan, the last man, was overwhelmed and, to his eternal shame, ran away – upon which Cessair, who loved him, died of sorrow.

Derrynane to Sneem

Tucked away on a little promontory of its own between the Ring of Kerry and the sea is **DERRYNANE** (pronounced *Derrynaan*), home of the family of Daniel O'Connell, the Catholic lawyer and politician who negotiated limited Catholic emancipation in 1829. You can visit his house down by the sea. Derrynane itself is a pleasant place, with wide, flat sand beaches, two miles of dunes, good swimming and rocks glistening black with mussels. Although fun in the daytime, like everywhere along this western seaboard it's most atmospheric at sunset, when the long twilight lingers; the Gaels believed that sunset and sunrise were points of transition (like stiles and gates) where it was possible to slip from the real world into the faerie one, and here you can see their point.

Derrynane House (April & Oct Tues–Sun 1–5pm; May–Sept Mon–Sat 9am–6pm, Sun 11am–7pm; Nov–March Sat & Sun 1–5pm; £2; Heritage Card), remodelled by Daniel O'Connell himself, is absolutely simple – a square slate tower and roughly elegant rooms with the slanting sea-light a constant presence. The O'Connells were an old Gaelic family who'd made their money trading and smuggling – the west of Ireland had a long tradition of trade with Europe in wine, spices and silks. Daniel O'Connell's uncle bequeathed him a fortune, giving him the financial independence necessary to devote himself to politics. Discrimination against Catholics was widespread and closely experienced by Daniel: another uncle was shot dead because he would not give up his fine horse, as the law demanded of Catholics.

The touristy *Scarriff Inn* (☎066/75132; ④), right on the N70 just east of the Beenarourke viewing point, is a focal point for the area and offers good bar food to the hordes of coach parties passing by. The steep lane down behind here leads to a couple of pleasant **B&Bs** with spectacular views: *Harbour View*, Farraniaragh (☎066/75292; April–Oct; ③) right on the Kerry Way, and down by the bay, *Skellig House* (☎066/75129; ②; Skellig trips available). From here you can pick your way east for around 2km along a Mass Path to *Bridie Keating's* pub, though it's advisable to arrange a lift back as it's a treacherous walk in the dark.

The little village of **CAHERDANIEL**, around three miles east of the *Scarriff Inn*, makes a very good base and there's excellent **hostel** accommodation right in the centre at the *Traveller's Rest Hostel* (☎066/75175). Most other accommodation is on the main road west: nearby is *O'Sullivan's* **B&B** (☎066/75124; ③); *Derrynane Bay House* (☎066/75404; ③) is about a mile from Caherdaniel, and the pleasant *Carrigbeg Hostel* (IHH; ☎066/75229) is about two miles away. For camping head a mile south of the village for *Wave Crest Caravan Park* (☎066/75188), a fabulous spot overlooking the sea. Caherdaniel has a small shop, petrol and a couple of lively **pubs**: *Freddy's* and *The Blind Piper* – in the latter you can get very good bar food and fine traditional music in the summer (Wed & Sat). The best restaurant in the area, *Loaves and Fishes* (Easter–Oct Tues–Sun; ☎066/75273; dinner £18–22), is clearly signposted off the main road through the village.

The immediate area has plenty of ancient forts and standing stones. On the way to Castlecove, there's a sign on the left for **Staigue Fort**; after two-and-a-half miles up a rough lane (part of the Kerry Way), you'll come to a very well-preserved ring fort, possibly created as early as 1000 BC, and probably a residence of the Kings of Munster. Back on the N70, as the road winds on towards Sneem past hedgerows blossoming with fuchsia and hydrangea, there's good **swimming** along the way, particularly at White Strand.

Spectacularly set against the mountains, **SNEEM** (*An tSnaidhm*), is dominated by the 2245ft Knockmoyle; but the village has lost something by selling out to tourism. Sneem's houses are washed in different colours – reputedly so that drunken residents can find their way home – and their picture-book prettiness juxtaposed against tourist shops and cafés has a touch of the surreal. Good local fishing is advertised by the salmon-shaped weathercock on the Protestant church. You'll probably want to push on to more interesting Kenmare, but if you do decide to **stay** here, you could try *Avonlea House* (☎064/45221; ③), *Woodvale House* (☎064/45181; ③) or *Rockville House* (☎064/45135; ②).

The approach to Kenmare along the estuary is unexciting, seemingly more in character with the Beara Peninsula opposite than with wild Iveragh, and you'll have a more scenic journey back to Killarney if you take the mountain road direct from Sneem. The two routes join up again at the spectacular **Moll's Gap**, north of Kenmare. If you want to stop over along the way, there's comfortable B&B – and plenty of advice on hill-walking – at *The Old School House*, Direendaragh, Blackwater (☎064/82913; ③), three miles off the main Sneem–Kenmare road.

Kenmare and around

With its unlikely shops – delicatessens, designer boutiques and arty second-hand clothes shops – **KENMARE** feels like a foreign enclave, and you're more likely to hear English or German tones here than Irish. Neatly organized on an X-plan (laid out by the first Marquess of Lansdowne in 1775), the town is pleasantly cosmopolitan: besides the resident foreigners, it's the natural crossing-over point for everyone travelling up from Cork.

Kenmare was founded by **Sir William Petty**, Cromwell's surveyor general, to serve his mining works beside the River Finnihy. Petty was extremely active in (and benefited greatly from) the dealings in confiscated properties that went on after the Cromwellian wars. Many soldiers were paid by the impecunious government in land, but not all of them wanted to settle in Ireland and so sold their land to dealers – such as Petty. His acquisition of land all over Ireland, including roughly a quarter of Kerry, was surely helped by his commission to survey the country on behalf of the government, when he investigated two-thirds of the Irish counties in the amazingly short period of fifteen months. Petty's other achievements were no less remarkable: a professor of medicine at Oxford at 27, he was also a professor of music and founder member of the Royal Society in London; an early statistician, economist and demographer; and politically astute enough to get yet more land and a knighthood out of Charles II, even though he had earlier served Cromwell faithfully. In Kerry, he laid the foundations of the mining and smelting industries, encouraged fishing, and founded the enormous Lansdowne estate which once surrounded the town; many of its buildings still remain today.

Evidence of a much more ancient settlement is the fifteen-stone **stone circle** just outside the centre of town on the banks of the river; go up by the right of the market house that faces the park, and past some estate houses. Then walk up the lane at the cul-de-sac sign, and a few yards after it meets another lane coming in from the left you'll find the circle, behind a high ditch.

Practicalities

The **tourist office** is on The Square (☎April–June & Sept to mid-Oct Mon–Sat 9.15am–1pm & 2.15–5.30pm; July & Aug Mon–Sat 9am–7pm, Sun 9.15am–1pm & 2.15–5.30pm; ☎064/41233). Kenmare's famous *Park Hotel*, at the top of Main Street (☎064/41200; ⑨) is phenomenally expensive, but worth investigating if only for a drink. There are plenty of **B&Bs**, both in and just outside town; check vacancies at the tourist office. Some that are worth a try are: *Sunville* on the Cork Road (☎064/41169; ②), the welcoming *Druid Cottage* (☎064/41803; ③) a mile out on the Sneem road, *Rose Cottage*, The Square (☎064/41330; ③), right in the centre of town, and *Bay View Farm* (☎064/41383; ③) on the Ring of Kerry Road at Templenoe, 6km away. Kenmare has an independent **hostel**, the *Fáilte* in Shelbourne Street (IHH; ☎064/42333).

Kenmare is an affluent tourist town and, while this means there's a good range of **places to eat**, prices – particularly for bar food – do tend to be more expensive than elsewhere. The *Bean and Leaf Café*, 4 Rock St, serves cheap tacos and tortillas. A couple of places in Henry Street serve good bar food: *The Purple Heather* and *The Wander Inn*. For inexpensive evening meals try *La Brasserie Bistro* or *The New Delight* vegetarian restaurant (☎064/42350), both in Henry Street. Moderately priced restaurants include *Mulcahy's Wine Bar*, Henry Street, and *Giuliano's* Italian restaurant, Main Street. Moving upmarket, *An Leath Phingin*, 35 Main St (☎064/41559), serves excellent Italian-Irish food. You'll hear traditional **music** at *The Wander Inn* (Tues & Wed) and *Foley's* (Mon, Wed, Thurs in summer), both in Henry Street. Also good bets for music are *The Square Pint*, The Square, and *Moeran's*, off the top of Main Street (Wed in summer); for music in a rather more refined and trendy setting, try *The Bean & Leaf Café* (traditional and folk Fri & Sun).

Bike rental is available from the Fáilte Hostel, *Finnegan's*, Henry Street, and White's on Killarney Road. If you want to see Kenmare from the water, Seafari River Cruises (☎064/83171) depart from the pier three times a day in high season.

The Beara Peninsula

Cross the river from Kenmare and you're on the **Beara Peninsula**, which Kerry shares with Cork. Beara has its followers, but after the wildness of the rest of Kerry, it can at first seem over-lush and polite, with more of the flavour of Cork. Even along the River Kenmare, though, the scenery is attractive enough and curiously, once you actually cross into County Cork, the Beara becomes far wilder (see p.291).

Turn right after the bridge, and the road runs through heavily wooded country alongside the Kenmare estuary, with a signpost to the left for **Inchiquin Lake** a few miles later. Following this, you soon quit the luxuriant vegetation as the bumpy road ascends rapidly to the lake, affording exhilarating views of the countryside left behind. A waterfall tumbles down from a second lake, and on the far side of Inchiquin Lake is **Uragh Wood**, one of the last surviving remnants of the ancient sessile oakwoods that once covered most of Ireland. The entire valley is packed with **plants**: large-flowered butterwort covers the meadows in spring, and you can find Irish spurge, saxifrage, arbutus and other flora specific to the southwest. At the lake itself, the surrounding hills seem to act as some kind of intensifier focused on a tiny stone circle by the side of the water – bringing to mind the theory that these prehistoric monuments indicate earth forces. There's salmon, sea trout and brown trout fishing in both lakes, but, as always, check the licence position before you start.

Lauragh

Following the main road for **LAURAGH**, you're still in the enormous estate once owned by Petty. The gardens at **Derreen House** (April–Sept daily 11am–6pm; £2.50), for a long time one of the Irish residences of Petty's descendant, the Marquess of Lansdowne, are open to the public and stocked with plants that clearly luxuriate in the mild sea climate, including such exotica as tree ferns and bamboo, plus rhododendrons and camellias. Yet despite its magnificence, it doesn't compare with the wild and windswept grassy uplands. Head westwards from Lauragh and you're soon over the border into Cork; south, the road climbs spectacularly above Glanmore Lake to the Healy Pass – again, the county border – giving amazing views in both directions. There's the fairly basic An Óige *Glanmore Lake* **hostel** here (☎064/83181; Easter–Sept).

Dingle Peninsula

In common with the rest of the far west, particularly the Irish-speaking areas, the **Dingle Peninsula** has almost fallen victim to its own romance. It's as if it has been telling stories about itself for so long that it has come to believe them: the remoteness and beauty, the hard life and poverty and – above all in the **Irish-speaking** or *Gaeltacht* areas – the language have all lent fuel to easy romanticizing, creating the modern chocolate-box, almost mythologized picture of the west. In Dingle's case, the myth is strengthened by its location on the extreme western seaboard of Europe, its numerous early Christian remains, the wealth of Irish literature created on the now uninhabited Blasket Islands – and the fact that *Ryan's Daughter* and parts of *Far and Away,* starring Tom Cruise, were filmed here. Concern about the peninsula's reputation for fey other-worldliness is such that the local paper has found it necessary to assure Irish visitors that there are such things as nightspots here.

But Dingle really scores with its **landscape** and **antiquities**. The former is spectacular, dominated by Beenoskee Mountain (2627ft), while west of Dingle town lies an Irish-speaking region, strongly resonant of its history. Dingle also has probably the greatest concentration of Celtic monastic, and older, **ruins** outside the Aran Islands. Ring forts, beehive huts, oratories and stone crosses are more prevalent here than almost anywhere else in Ireland (a useful map of the local antiquities can be had from Dingle tourist office); and the vigour of the Christian culture that set out from here to evangelize and educate the rest of Europe is almost palpable.

HORSE-DRAWN CARAVAN HOLIDAYS ON THE DINGLE PENINSULA

The ultimate Irish tourism cliché it may be, but a horse-drawn caravan holiday is a great way to unwind and to absorb the breathtaking beauty of the Dingle Peninsula. What's more, you're likely to have a very sociable time, the caravan's theatricality provoking plenty of conversation. You can also expect to develop a strong relationship with your horse – one way or another.

Slattery's Travel, 1 Russell St, Tralee (☎066/712 1722; freephone from the UK ☎0800/515900 for brochure) rent out caravans for three-day weekends (£150, low season only) and week-long breaks (£250 low season, £550 high season); additional costs include £7 per night stopover fee, £4 per day insurance and £10 per week horsefeed. Slattery's will tell you no previous experience of handling horses is necessary, but it certainly helps – as do height and brute strength. Before setting off, however, friendly stable-workers take you through the basics of catching, harnessing, driving, watering and feeding your horse. Slattery's also supply a map of the peninsula with a range of routes and stopover sites; most sites are fields alongside pubs, so you can have a drink beneath the stars and still keep an eye on the children.

Caravans have one double bed, a small single, and a couple of extra fold-down bunks – with bedding. In theory there's room for five people, though in fact any more than three adults may well find it a bit cramped, and if there are more of you, it's a good idea to have a small tent. The caravans also come equipped with a small stove and cooking utensils.

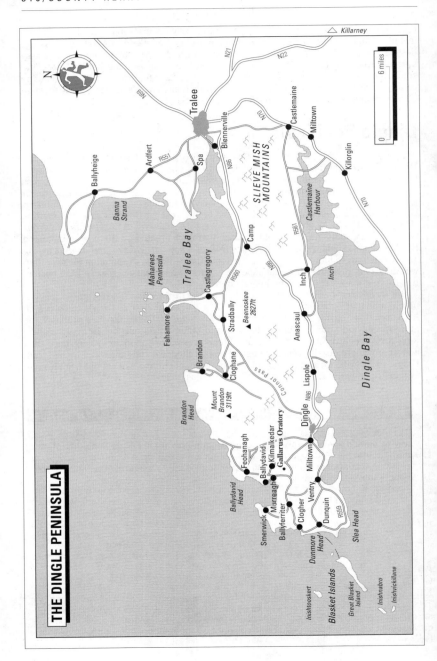

THE DINGLE PENINSULA

△ Killarney

N

N21

N22

N69

Tralee

Blennerville

Castlemaine

Milltown

N20

SLIEVE MISH
MOUNTAINS

R551

Ballyheige

Ardfert

Spa

N86

Killorglin

Banna
Strand

Camp

N70

Castlemaine
Harbour

R561

Tralee Bay

Maharees
Peninsula

Castlegregory

R560

Inch

N86

Inch

Fahamore

Stradbally

Beenoskee
2627ft

Anascaul

Dingle Bay

Brandon

Cloghane

Connor Pass

Lispole

Brandon
Head

Mount
Brandon
3119ft

N86

Dingle

Feohanagh

Ballydavid

Kilmalkedar

Gallarus Oratory

Milltown

Ballydavid
Head

Murreagh

Ventry

Smerwick

Ballyferriter

Clogher

Dunquin

R559

Dunmore
Head

Slea Head

Inishtooskert

Blasket Islands

Great Blasket
Island

Inishnabro

Inishvickillane

0   6 miles

On a fine day it can be exhilarating, with views out as far as the monastic settlement on Great Skellig, off the Iveragh Peninsula; but it's more exciting still in the rain, when the cloud shifts down over the land and you find yourself in a white mist through which the dim shapes of oratories and beehive huts loom mysteriously.

Inch and Anascaul

Though most of the peninsula's delights are to the west of Dingle town, there are a few notable stopping points on your way to Dingle town from the east. First of these is *The Phoenix Organic Vegetarian Restaurant & Farmhouse Accommodation* (☎066/976 6284), three miles west of **Castlemaine** village on the Killarney–Dingle road, providing hostel accommodation with a difference: rooms are decorated with furnishings from Bali, India and Egypt and the restaurant's menu strikes a similarly exotic note. You can also camp here. There's a break in the shoreline at **INCH**, where a long, narrow sandbar pushes out into Dingle Bay. In the eighteenth century, the beach was used by wreckers who, on stormy nights, would tie a lantern to a horse's head and leave the horse grazing; mariners mistaking the bobbing light for another ship steered their vessels aground on the strand. There's B&B **accommodation** about a mile east of here at *Waterside B&B* (☎066/915 8129; ②). For hostel accommodation, as you head west take a sharp right after *Foley's* pub; after about three miles turn right for the *Bog View Hostel*, situated mid-way between Camp and Anascaul (IHH; ☎066/915 8125; May–Sept). Back in Inch, you can hear lively traditional music sessions at *Foley's* pub (Sat year round, summer Wed).

Soon the road turns inland towards **ANASCAUL** (*Abhainn an Scáil*), a single street of brightly painted houses, pleasant enough but with a curiously safe, inland feel considering the proximity of the wild Atlantic coast. Two pubs here have famous associations: the magician Dan Foley's shocking-pink bar, familiar from a host of postcards, and the *South Pole Inn*, so named by local man Tom Crean, a veteran of Scott's Antarctic expedition. There are several **B&Bs**: *The AnchorHouse* (☎066/915 7382; ③) and *Brackluin House* (☎066/915 7145; ②), both centrally located, and slightly further out on the road to Dingle, *Four Winds* (☎066/915 7168; ③). In addition there's a **hostel**, *Fuchsia Lodge* (☎066/915 7150), about two miles east of the village, where it is also possible to camp. For good inexpensive vegetarian and seafood meals, make for the quaint *Country Kitchen* restaurant on the road into the village. Heading northwards, along a string of increasingly rough tracks, you'll reach Anascaul Lake, overshadowed by the scree slopes of Stradbally Mountain: a secret-seeming place, with plenty of wilder country beyond.

Dingle town

DINGLE (*An Daingean*) doesn't offer a huge amount to see, but the town is a pleasant place to stay, devoted to fishing and tourism, and certainly makes the best base for exploring the peninsula. Though crammed with pubs, little restaurants and B&Bs, Dingle somehow never feels too crowded, and even if you don't like the way the place has geared itself up for tourism, you'll be glad when the weather's bad – which it often is – that there are plenty of places to hole up. The town services the tiny communities west of here, so if you are heading on it makes good sense to stock up on supplies.

Arrival and accommodation

Getting to Dingle is easy. From late June to September, a **bus** leaves from outside Killarney's train station twice daily; there's a more frequent year-round service from Tralee (see "Travel Details" at the end of the chapter). For getting around the town and surrounding countryside, buses leave Dingle for Dunquin on Mondays and Thursdays only (three daily year round), and during the summer months they depart Mon–Sat twice daily and go via Slea Head. **Bikes** can be rented from Moriarty's in Main Street, which has mountain bikes, useful on the punishing Conor Pass, and Paddy's in Dykegate Street. There are a number of ways of getting out onto the water: The Dingle Angling Centre behind the tourist office, offers harbour trips (£6), sea angling (£12) and yachting (£12; to the Blaskets £40) – a thrilling way to see the coast. If you want a less expensive visit to the Blaskets but don't have transport, *The Mountain Man*, Strand Street (☎066/915 2400) runs a minibus out to the ferry at Dunquin (£5, summer only).

The **tourist office** in Strand Street (March–June, Sept & Oct Mon–Sat 10am–1pm & 2.15-6pm; July & Aug Mon–Sat 9am–7pm, Sun 10am–6pm; closed Nov–Feb; ☎066/915 1188) has an accommodation service. For standard old-fashioned hotel comfort, try *Benners Hotel* on Main Street (☎066/915 1638; ⑧).

There's no shortage of **B&Bs**, though book ahead in July and August. At the top of Main Street try *Boland's* (☎066/915 1426; ③) or *Devane's* (☎066/915 1193; ③); on Dykegate Street there's *Connor's* (☎066/915 1598; ④); *Greenmount Guesthouse*, Upper John Street (☎066/915 1414; ⑤) offers comfort and fabulous views, and *Doyle's* excellent restaurant (see below) also takes guests (☎066/915 1174; ⑤; March–Nov). Dingle now has at least seven **hostels**, one of the best being *Ballintaggart House*, Racecourse Road (IHH; ☎066/915 1454), one mile east of Dingle, boasting huge roaring fires, plenty of space and wonderful views. It also offers camping and operates a regular free pick-up service from town. More central are the cheerful and welcoming *Grapevine*, Dykegate Street (☎066/915 1434), *An Caladh Spainneach*, Strand Street (☎066/915 2160), and *Lovett's Hostel* (☎066/915 1903), opposite the Esso garage. The *Rainbow Hostel* is about a mile west out of town (☎066/915 1044), with camping, bike rental and free pick-ups from town. If these are all full, you could try the *Seacrest Hostel* in Lispole, a few miles east, overlooking cliffs and beach (IHH; ☎ & fax 066/915 1390; March–Oct), with a shop and camping space.

The Town

Essentially just a few streets by the side of Dingle Bay, the town has a hugely impressive natural **harbour** where the boats come in and **Fungi the dolphin** likes to play; half-tame Fungi is one of Dingle's main tourist attractions. It may sound silly, but there are people who talk of their meetings with this solitary, 663lb maritime mammal in the terms of a religious conversion, and others travel hundreds of miles just to see him (enquire at the tourist office about boats, or walk down to the coast via the lane alongside the *Skellig Hotel* – Fungi often comes in this far).

The solidity of the town's colour-washed houses suggests this was a place of some consequence, and Dingle was indeed Kerry's leading port in the fourteenth and fifteenth centuries. It later became a centre for smuggling, and at one stage during the eighteenth century (when the revenue from smuggling was at its height) even minted its own coinage. Contemporary reports describe the stone houses with balconies and oval windows, imparting a Spanish feel to the town. In the nineteenth century, Dingle was the focus of a uniquely successful attempt to woo the Kerry Catholics from their faith, when in 1831 the Protestant curate T. Goodman began preaching in Irish, establishing schools on the peninsula and building houses as inducements for converts; these still stand at the edge of town.

Eating, drinking and entertainment

Dingle's top **restaurants** serve excellent fresh seafood, landed just a few hundred yards away. *Doyle's Seafood* in John Street (☎066/915 1174; evenings only) is the best-known restaurant locally and pioneered haute cuisine in Dingle. The often miraculous dishes are expensive, but worth it. *The Global Village*, Main Street, serves huge breakfasts and inexpensive meals all day, while *Tig Lise*, Bridge Street does inexpensive sandwiches and lunches, and is open into the evening. Try *Greaney's* nearby for cheap lunches and dinners. *Adams*, Main Street, serves excellent bar food, or you might try

Máire de Barra's on Strand Street. Pizzas feature prominently on the menu at *The Oven Doors*, Gray's Lane, and for vegetarians there's *Sméara Dubha*, The Wood, on the western edge of town (☎066/915 1465; summer daily 6–9pm). For daytime, and for getting away from the weather if it rains, there's no better place than the excellent bookshop-café, *An Cafe Liteartha*, Dykegate Lane. You can browse through the shelves (politics and local-interest sections are especially good), tuck into home baking and soups, read the papers and listen to conversation in Irish and English. Dingle's **internet café** is *The Dingle Web* on Lower Main Street (email *Web@Dingleweb*).

Life in the evenings is centred on Dingle's many **pubs**, which between them offer **traditional music** sessions on just about any night you choose. *Dick Mac's*, opposite the church on Green Street, *An Droichead Beag* at the bottom of Main Street, and *O'Flaherty's* in Bridge Street are good places to start, with music most nights or advice on where to find it somewhere else. *Máire de Barra's* has traditional or folk just about every night in summer, and there's occasional small-scale theatre at *McCarthy's*, Upper Main Street. **Special events** here include the compulsive Dingle Races in early August, the Dingle Regatta later in the month and *Féile na Mara* in September, when the entire fleet sails out in procession to the mouth of the harbour to be blessed by the bishop; see the tourist office for details.

Ventry and ancient monuments

The first village of interest west of Dingle is tiny **VENTRY** (*Ceann Trá*), once the main port of the peninsula and another fine natural harbour: a wide curve of sandy beach supporting just a few houses, shops and a pub. Beyond it looms the enormous, gnarled shoulder of **Mount Eagle**, dropping almost sheer to the sea with only a precarious ledge for the road. It's in these inhospitable surroundings on the stretch out to Slea Head that the main concentration of **ancient monuments** can be found. What follows here can only be an introduction to the major sites; the minor ones alone could take weeks to explore. A good local **map**, such as the one available at the tourist office, is essential, while several excellent guides to the peninsula exist for real enthusiasts (available at bookshops in Dingle town).

First off there's the spectacular **Dún Beag** (dating from the eighth or ninth century AD), a scramble down from the road towards the ocean about four miles out from Ventry (entry £1). A promontory fort, its defences include four earthen rings, with an underground escape route, or souterrain, by the main entrance. It's a magical location, overlooking the open sea and the Iveragh Peninsula, the drama of its setting only increased by the fact that some of the building has fallen off into the sea.

Between Dún Beag and **Slea Head**, the hillside above the road is studded with stone beehive huts, cave dwellings, souterrains, forts, churches, standing stones and crosses – over five hundred in all. The beehive huts can be deceptive – they were still being built and used for storing farm tools and produce until the late nineteenth century, so not all of them are as old as they look. But once you're standing among genuinely ancient buildings like the signposted **Fahan group** (entry £1) and looking south over a landscape that's remained essentially unchanged for centuries, the Iveragh Peninsula and the two Skellig Islands (see p.304) in the distance (if not hidden by clouds), you get a strong sense of past lives, with their unimaginable hopes and aspirations. If you're travelling with children, they may enjoy **The Enchanted Forest** (daily summer 11am–6pm; £2.50) just past the shrine at Slea Head, "a merry, magical, miniature fairyland where bears and dolls celebrate the seasons"; there's a café downstairs serving bear-shaped scones. If you want to stay in Ventry there are a couple of **B&Bs** up the lane past the Post Office: *Ceann Trá Heights* (☎066/915 9866; ③) and *The Plough* (☎066/915 9727; ③). The only place you are likely to get a **meal** is *The Ventry Inn* – and even there only in July and August.

The Blasket Islands

At Slea Head, the view opens up to include the desolate, splintered masses of the **Blasket Islands** (*Na Blascaodaí*), officially uninhabited since 1953, though there are still summer communities on the islands. The weather in Blasket Sound can be treacherous – two of the Armada's ships were shattered to matchwood when they came bowling round the Head in September 1588 – but inhospitable as they seem, the islands were once the home of thriving communities. The astonishing body of **Irish literature** that emerged from these tiny islands (Maurice O'Sullivan's *Twenty Years A-Growing*, Peig Sayers's *Peig* and Tomas O'Crohan's *Island Cross-Talk*) gives a vivid picture of the life of the islanders which, although remote, was anything but unsophisticated. Ironically, these literary works describe life among people who could neither read nor write; but their oral tradition emerges as far from primitive. Locals are less than enamoured of the ugly interpretive centre, **Ionad an Bhlascaoíd Mhoír**, at Dunquin (daily Easter–June & Sept–Oct 10am–6pm; July & Aug 10am–7pm; £2.50), but nevertheless the material it holds on the lives and literature of the islanders is very interesting, and there's a good café for lunch too.

In the summer, boats bound for **Great Blasket** (*An Blascaod Mór*) leave the pier just south of Dunquin every half hour between 9.30am and 5pm for around £10 return (May–Sept in good weather; ☎066/915 6455 or 915 6422). Whether or not you choose to stay over, Great Blasket's delights are simple ones: sitting on the beaches and staring out to sea, tramping the many footpaths that crisscross the island, or trying to spot a seal. If you want to swim be careful as currents are very strong – and the water will be icy. The only way to stay is to camp, and you'll need to be prepared – take food (there's no shop), water carriers for the well, and bags to carry refuse home. Good cheap dinners are available at the island café (noon–5pm). It's advisable to check the longterm weather forecast with the boatmen in advance, as it's possible to be stranded for days if the weather breaks.

There's an An Óige **hostel** on the mainland a little further on at **DUNQUIN** (*Dún Chaoin*), with plenty of beds (☎066/915 6121). Meals are available at the hostel but there is no shop in Dunquin. *Kruger's* pub (☎066/915 6121; ②) is the hub of local activity, with food in summer, traditional music, and B&B. Across from here the new *An Portán* restaurant (☎066/915 6212; ③) enjoys a good reputation and also offers B&B. The best place for daytime eating is the *Dunquin Pottery Café*, with a spectacular view out across the Blaskets and, behind, a mass of mountain laced with a network of stone dykes. *Tig Áine* (☎066/915 6214), further on at An Ghráig, is good for seafood and salads.

Ballyferriter and Ballydavid

A couple of miles further round the headland, largely Irish-speaking **BALLYFERRITER** (*Baile an Fheirtearaigh*) can be bleak out of season, but in summer there are several cafés, plus a museum in the old schoolhouse, **Músaem Chorca Dhuibhne** (June–Sept daily 10am–5.30pm; £1.50). *Tig an Tobair* (May–Sept 12.30–3pm & 6.30–9.30pm; closed Mon) is the best restaurant. Alternatively, *Tigh Pheig* serves good **bar food.** The little northward lanes will lead you to impressive 500ft hilltop walling at Sybil Head and the Three Sisters rock (with the Norman ruins of Castle Sybil, built within an older promontory fort); or to Smerwick Harbour and **Dún an Óir**. In September 1580 at Dún an Óir (the Golden Fort), a band of Italian, Spanish, English and Irish supporters of the rebellion in Munster, backed by papal funds in support of Catholic Ireland against Protestant England, were defeated by the English. The rebels were massacred – men, women and children – as a warning to others; the poet Edmund Spenser participated in the indiscriminate slaughter.

In Ballyferriter, the *Dun an Oir Golf Hotel* (☎066/915 6133; ⑦) offers comfortable rooms and a swimming pool; there are also a few **B&Bs** – try *An Speice*, Ballyferriter West (☎066/915 6254; ③). There's also a **hostel**, *An Cat Dubh* (The Black Cat), outside Ballyferriter on the road to Dunquin (☎066/915 6286; May–Oct), which has a grocery shop attached.

At the other end of Smerwick Harbour lies **BALLYDAVID** (*Baile na nGall*), backed by the mass of Mount Brandon and within easy reach of the cliffs at Ballydavid Head. **Brandon Creek** (signposted "Cuas"), just east of Ballydavid Head, is one of a number of contenders for St Brendan's sixth-century departure point, when he sailed off to discover the Islands of Paradise in the Western Ocean and, arguably, America. If you wish to stay the comfortable *Tigh an Phóist* **hostel** (IHH; ☎066/915 5109; April–Oct), which rents out bikes and has a shop, is beside Carraig church, two miles from Ballydavid village, and there's **music** and **dancing** sessions in *Teach Siamsa* nearby (Wed & Fri). **B&B** at *Ard na Carraige* (☎066/915 5295; ③), about a mile away from Ballydavid, between Murreagh and Feahanach, comes recommended, or there's *Caife na Mara*, Glaise Bheag (☎066/915 5162; ③), midway between Ballydavid and Feahanach.

Riasc, the Gallarus Oratory and Kilmalkedar

A short way out of Ballyferriter – keep left on the main road, turn right over the bridge by a petrol pump, then right again – is the monastic site of **Riasc**. Recent excavation has revealed walls and foundations a few feet high, and the ruins evoke the early Christian monastery, dating from the tenth century.

The single most impressive early Christian monument on the Dingle Peninsula, however, is the **Gallarus Oratory**, a little further east. The most perfectly preserved of around twenty such oratories in Ireland, it looks almost too good to be true, though apparently it hasn't undergone any great restoration programmes. Though the oratory can't be dated with any great certainty, it's thought to have been built between the ninth and twelfth centuries (Christian architectural activity dates from the late sixth or early seventh century, but it wasn't until the ninth century that churches began to be built of stone rather than wood), and to represent a transition between the round beehive huts elsewhere on the peninsula and the later rectangular churches. The problem with this construction (and the reason why so many similar buildings have fallen down) is that the long sides tend to cave in – if you look carefully at the Gallarus Oratory, you can see it's beginning to happen here, too.

The next architectural stage can be seen a mile to the north in the rectangular church at **KILMALKEDAR**. Its nave dates from the mid-twelfth century, and the corbelled stone roof was a direct improvement on the structure at Gallarus. The site marks the beginning of the Saint's Road, dedicated to **St Brendan**, patron saint of Kerry, which leads to the top of Mount Brandon – the route taken by pilgrims to St Brendan's shrine. If you want to follow this tough but historically resonant route up the mountainside, it's marked on the Ordnance Survey map. Alternatively, there's a good route from the east beginning at the townland of Faha, between Cloghane and Brandon; Seán ó Súilleabháin's *South West Walks* is recommended if you want to follow this route.

The Conor Pass and The Maharees Peninsula

The interior of the Dingle Peninsula is dominated by two **mountains**, Mount Brandon and Stradbally Mountain, separated by the steep **Conor Pass**. This mountainous terrain is excellent walking country; not only are there countless relics of the Celtic church and earlier to explore, but the area is dotted by a series of lakes that give the tussocky landscape some focus. There's a **hostel** at the foot of the pass on the northern side, the *Conor Pass Hostel* (IHH; ☎066/713 9179; mid-March to Nov) in

STRADBALLY. You'll find good sandy beaches for swimming at Stradbally and **CASTLEGREGORY**, where *Fitzgerald's Euro Hostel* (☎066/713 9133) is a friendly place, well situated over a pub and shop, and with private rooms; or try *Lynch's Hostel* (☎066/713 9128). For home-cooked food, there's *O'Riordan's Café* on the Conor Pass road from Tralee (R559/560), just before the turning for Castlegregory. The **Maharees Peninsula** stretches north from here, an exposed spit of land fringed by long sandy beaches, affording plenty of opportunities for surfing, wind-surfing, canoeing and water-skiing, all of which can be arranged through the Castlegregory Visitor Information Centre in Strand Street (☎066/713 9422). **CLOGHANE**, eight miles west of here, is a tiny village lodged beneath Mount Brandon and flanked by lovely beaches. There's good bar food in the pubs, and you can stay at *O'Connor's* (☎066/713 8113; ③).

Tralee and around

TRALEE (*Trá Lí*) has had quite a facelift of late, and chief among its new attractions is the excellent **Kerry County Museum** in the Ashe Memorial Hall (daily: mid-March to July; Sept & Oct 10am–6pm; August 10am–7pm; Nov & Dec 2–5pm; £5.50), which uses interactive media and lifesize models in tracing Irish history back to 5000 BC. Other attractions include the **Tralee–Blennerville Steam Railway** (daily May–Oct; £2.50), which is part of the famous Tralee–Dingle line (1891–1953), and the largest working windmill in Ireland and Britain, the **Blennerville Windmill** (daily April–Oct 10am–6pm), which has its own exhibition, craft workshops and the usual tourist trinkets.

Tralee is a point of orientation rather than somewhere to stay. The helpful **tourist office** (July & Aug Mon–Sat 9am–7pm, Sun 9am–6pm; May, June & Sept Mon–Sat 9am–6pm; Oct–April Tues–Sat 9am–1pm & 2–5pm; ☎066/712 1288) is in the Ashe Memorial Hall. Tralee has innumerable **B&Bs**, among them *Denton* (☎066/712 7637; ②) and *Ardroe House* (☎066/712 6050; ③), both on Oakpark Road in the centre. There's no shortage of **hostels** either: try the friendly and cosy *Lisnagree Hostel* (☎066/712 7133), out towards the general hospital, or *Finnegan's Hostel* on Denny Street near the tourist office (IHH; ☎066/712 7610), which also rents out bikes. *Atlas House*, Castle Street (☎066/712 0722), a large modern hostel, also offers bike rental. If you want to **camp**, *Woodland Park*, Dingle Road (☎066/712 1235) is a short walk from the centre of town. You can **rent bikes**, including mountain bikes, from Tralee Gas Supplies in Strand Street, part of the Raleigh rent-a-bike scheme (though if you're headed for Dingle, it's a tough ride over the Conor Pass).

Finding a cheap place to **eat** in Tralee isn't a problem – the town is full of them. *Roots*, on Boherboy, serves terrific organic vegetarian lunches, which you can also take away. *Brat's Place*, Milk Market Lane, also does very good, inexpensive vegetarian food. *Finnegan's* restaurant at 17 Denny St (☎066/712 7610) combines good food and a great atmosphere, with dinner for around £15, or you might try the *Swedish Bistro*, McCowan's Lane, off Castle Street (☎066/712 1711). There are plenty of **pubs**, too; for **traditional music** try *McDaide's*, Castle Street (every night, year round), *Baily's Corner*, Ashe Street (Tues), *Sean Og's* on Bridge Street or *Kirby's Brogue Inn* on Rock Street (every night in summer). If you just want a pleasant old bar try *Jack's Pub* on the Square.

The **Folk Theatre of Ireland** has its home at the Siamsa Tíre Theatre beside the tourist office (☎066/712 3055), though their excellent performances don't draw the same crowds as the Rose of Tralee International Festival. Held in the last week of August, with much accompanying merriment, this is a beauty contest in which women, including foreigners who can demonstrate some credible Irish connection, compete for the dubious honour of being Rose of Tralee; details are available from the Festival Office in Lower Castle Street (☎066/712 1322).

Ardfert and Banna Strand

More worthy of your time than anything in Tralee itself is the ruined thirteenth-century cathedral at **ARDFERT**, five miles to the northwest. In a landscape littered with ruined ring forts, castles and churches, Ardfert was the site of a monastery founded by St Brendan in the seventh century, and later became the centre of the Anglo-Norman church in Kerry. As well as some interesting monastic remains, there's a **Franciscan friary** and two smaller fifteenth-century churches.

It's also worth taking the road out to **BANNA STRAND** for the spectacular view over Tralee Bay, and its association with Sir Roger Casement, to whom there's a monument. In April 1916, on the eve of the Easter Uprising, Casement was captured by local police as he attempted to land at Banna Strand from a German submarine. He was tried and executed for high treason in 1916, and his body was returned from England to Ireland in 1965 to be reinterred with full military honours (for more on Casement see p.521). If you're driving, you can carry on round the cliffs of **Kerry Head** for more great vistas – south over Tralee Bay, north across the mouth of the Shannon.

Castleisland and Crag Cave

If getting to Limerick in a hurry is your main preoccupation, the faster route (the N21) runs east inland via Newcastle West. On this road **CASTLEISLAND** offers shops, and places to stop for a drink or a bite to eat. Nearby **Crag Cave** (daily June–Aug 10am–7pm; March–May & Sept–Nov 10am–6pm; £3) is an impressive limestone cave system extending a couple of miles underground. If you're passing, the thirty-minute guided tour is enjoyable, with plenty of weirdly sculpted stalactites and stalagmites to keep you amused.

North Kerry

This coastal road aside, **North Kerry** is unexciting – undulating farmland rolling up to the Shannon. The main road from Tralee heads up through **LISTOWEL**, a workaday Irish town that does, however, have a degree of literary distinction, boasting a number of fine writers and in June playing host to a week-long festival of literary workshops and meetings. Arguably, the town's most famous writer is John B. Keane, especially known for his *Man of the Triple Name*, an amusing account of North Kerry matchmaking during the 1930's and 1940's. The time when Listowel – and surrounding places as far away as Tarbert and Ballybunion – really come to life, however, is for the annual **Listowel races**, in the third week of September, when farming people from far and wide, their harvest in, take time off to eat, drink and lose money on the horses. Further information can be had from the **tourist office** (May–Sept Mon–Sat 10am–1pm & 2–6pm; Oct–April Mon–Fri 9.30am–1pm & 2–6pm; ☎068/22590). There's plenty of **accommodation** here, ranging from the comfort of the *Listowel Arms* (☎068/21500; ⑧) to simpler B&Bs such as *The North County House*, 67 Church St. (☎068/21238; ④), or *Fairhill*, Cahirdown on the Tarbert Road (☎068/21561; ②) and *Ashford Lodge*, Tarbert Road (☎068/21280; ③).

From Listowel the main road continues to **TARBERT** on the Shannon estuary, and from there trails the river inland (through County Limerick) towards Limerick and Shannon Airport. There's a **hostel**, *The Ferry House*, on the Square (☎068/36555). Immediately north of the town, the **car ferry** across the estuary provides a useful short cut into County Clare; there's no other river crossing west of Limerick (April–Sept Mon–Sat 7.30am–9.30pm, Sun 9.30am–9.30pm; Oct–March Mon–Sat 7.30am–7.30pm, Sun 10am–7.30pm; sailings on the half-hour, return from Killimer on the hour; car £7 single, £10 return; foot passenger/cyclist £2 single, £3 return; ☎065/53124).

Turning westwards at Listowel, **BALLYBUNION** lies about ten miles away on the coast at the mouth of the Shannon. It does have a kind of charm – it's the sort of sleepy resort that most people remember with a mixture of affection and horror from childhood holidays, and there are good sandy beaches – but unless you're beguiled by nostalgia you're unlikely to want to stay long. If you do, in addition to the complement of cheerful tat, pubs and amusement arcades, there are two golf courses, the caves under the cliffs and the seaweed baths to occupy you. One of the cliff caves, the **Seven Sisters cave**, is named after the seven daughters of a local chieftain, who tried to elope with seven Norsemen he was holding prisoner. When the plan was discovered, their father had them thrown through the roof of the cave.

Perhaps the town's most intriguing feature is its **seaweed baths**. In Ballybunion, great store is set by the restorative powers of seaweed: in the past, local people would take to the sea at the end of the summer, to ease joints aching from the exertions of the harvest, and there are two bathing houses – dating back to the 1920s – perched above Ladies' Strand. Collins' and Dalys' seaweed baths both consist of a series of private bathrooms, supplied with hot salt water from a constantly stoked boiler and seaweed gathered from the Black Rocks beyond the headland each morning. After your soothing, slithery soak you can take a tray of restorative tea and apple tart onto the beach.

B&Bs in this holiday resort tend to be expensive (and full) in summer. A couple worth trying are *Invergordon*, Cliff Road (☎068/27246; ②), and *Doon House*, Doon Road (☎068/27411; ④), but you'll save a long walk around the "No Vacancy" signs by checking out possibilities first at the **tourist office**, which operates in season out of a mobile caravan: check at the local post office for details of its whereabouts. Cheap accommodation is available in Ballybunion at *O'Flaherty's Hostel*, East End (☎068/27684), or if you seek somewhere quieter visit **BALLYHEIGUE**, further down the coast, where there's **camping** at *Casey's Caravan & Camping Park* (☎066/713 3195).

If you've time to spare on your onward journey, you can allow yourself to be beguiled by the flatlands of the **Shannon estuary**, whose quiet plains are bathed in the oblique light of the west and dotted with monasteries and castles. The ruined fifteenth-century **Carrigafoyle Castle** rises miraculously from the water, joined to the land by a causeway; close by, a road separates two sheets of water, the land it's built on long since submerged.

travel details

Trains

Killarney to: Cork (3–5 daily; 2hr); Dublin (3–5 daily; 4hr); Tralee (3–7 daily; 35min).

Buses

Killarney to: Tralee (5–14 daily; 35min).

Tralee to: Cork (1–7 daily; 1hr 40min–2hr 30min); Dingle (summer 5–9 daily, winter 3–5 daily; 1hr 15min); Limerick (4–6 daily; 2hr).

COUNTY CLARE

P hysically, County Clare is clearly defined, with Galway Bay and the Shannon estuary to the north and south, massive Lough Derg forming its eastern boundary, and the Atlantic to the west. Strangely, although plenty of people visit, the county is sometimes glossed over by travellers as simply land between the magnificent scenery of Kerry and Galway. It's true that it doesn't have the scenic splendour of either of these, and for many, the north of the county is too bleak to be attractive. Nonetheless, Clare has a subtle flavour that, once tasted, can be addictive.

Clare has earned itself two epithets: "the banner county" and "the singing county". It was called "the banner county" originally because of the part played by its men in the battle of Ramilles and more recently because of its courageous political history, particularly in the fight for Catholic emancipation. The second epithet reflects the strong musical traditions that are still very much alive in the county and constitute a major reason for coming here. Throughout the summer you will find sessions in pubs and in *teach cheoils* (pronounced *chuck key 'ole*), the latter more sober entertainments, with tea and brown bread rather than stout for refreshment, and very fine musicians too. To find out what's going on, pick up a copy of the *Shannon Region Traditional Irish Music Pubs* leaflet from any tourist office or check out *The Clare Champion*, and, above all, ask around. Pub sessions very often start late in the evening, so don't give up on a bar just because it's half nine and still nothing is happening. A great session can seemingly spring from nowhere, and is liable to prove a wholly memorable experience. Don't underestimate the popularity and excitement of Clare's festivals either. If you have yet to experience "the craic", you are sure to find it here.

Both Clare's titles, "the banner county" and "the singing county" – the strong and the gentle – suggest something of the character of the place and are echoed in the contrasts of the landscape. The **Burren** heights in the north are startlingly stark and barren, while **Ennis**, the county's capital, is surrounded by low, rolling farmland. Fabulous cliff scenery stretches for miles round Clare's southern extreme at Loop Head and is spectacularly sheer at the **Cliffs of Moher**, further north. In between are small seaside towns and villages and wonderful sandy beaches, most dramatic at **Lahinch** – famous for surf. In the east, **Lough Derg** offers panoramic views across to the mountains of Tipperary from the slopes of the Slieve Bernagh and Slieve Aughtie mountains, and also affords opportunities for watersports.

This varied countryside holds plenty of specialist interest. The Burren is a major attraction for geology and botany enthusiasts, and is also rich in ring forts, dolmens and

<table>
<tr><td colspan="3">

ACCOMMODATION PRICE CODES

</td></tr>
<tr><td colspan="3">Throughout this book, prices of hotels, guesthouses and B&Bs have been graded with the codes below, according to what you can expect to pay for a double room in high season. For more details on accommodation, see p. 29.</td></tr>
<tr><td>① Under £26</td><td>④ £40–55</td><td>⑦ £90–110</td></tr>
<tr><td>② £26–33</td><td>⑤ £55–70</td><td>⑧ £110–130</td></tr>
<tr><td>③ £33–40</td><td>⑥ £70–90</td><td>⑨ Over £130</td></tr>
</table>

SHANNON AIRPORT

Arriving at Shannon International Airport – where Irish coffee was invented to placate stranded passengers – you're most likely to want to head for **Limerick**, barely fifteen miles away, where you can get bus and train connections to just about anywhere in the country. **Ennis**, a similar distance, is also easily accessible and a pleasant place to stop over if you plan to spend some time in County Clare or want to break your journey before you head north. Alternatively, both **Quin and Bunratty** are worth considering as overnight options. From the ariport Bus Éireann **buses** (☎061/313333) run around nine services daily to Bunratty (20 min; £2.10), around sixteen daily to Limerick (45min; £3.50) and around fifteen daily to Ennis (45 min; £3.50). There are no buses direct to Quin. A **taxi** (☎061/471538) to Limerick, Ennis or Quin will cost about £15, to Bunratty about £8. If you just want to find a bed for the night, you could stay at one of the **B&Bs** in Shannon town, all around a five-minute drive from the airport. Try *Mrs Lohan*, 35 Tullyglass Crescent (☎061/364268; ③), *Mrs O'Meara's*, 20 Coill Mhara (☎061/364602; ②), or *Avalon*, 11 Balleycaseymore Hill (☎061/362032; ②).

The airport **tourist office** (daily: May–Oct 6.30am–7pm; Nov–April 6.30am–5.30pm; ☎061/471664) is extremely helpful and will book accommodation for you for the usual charge. There's a Bus Éireann and Irish Rail information point (April–Oct) right next to the tourist office, and an **airport information desk**, open to serve all flights – if there's no one there, pick up the phone and dial 0. For Aer Lingus enquiries call ☎061/471666. The **airport bank** is open daily from 6am until 5.30pm, though it sometimes closes early if there are no flights.

cairns in the north. The legacy of later communities is found throughout the county, in the thickly sprinkled medieval monastic remains and the tower houses of the O'Brien and MacNamara clans.

Ennis

A bustling market town and the commercial capital of County Clare, **ENNIS** has a pleasantly inconsequential air. Its handful of central lanes lace together a nineteenth-century cathedral, a stout monument to Daniel O'Connell and a medieval friary. You could probably walk from one side of Ennis to the other in half an hour, and you can certainly see all it has to offer in a single afternoon – but it's worth staying longer for the plentiful traditional music, and it makes an excellent base from which to explore the church ruins and tower houses dotted about the surrounding countryside.

Arrival, information and accommodation

There are direct bus connections between Ennis and **Shannon Airport** (see above), which is thirteen miles away in the south of the county and is the major airport on the west coast, with flights to Dublin, the UK, Europe and the US. The **bus** and the **train** **stations** sit alongside one another, a ten-minute walk from the town centre.

The very helpful **tourist office** is less than two miles out along the Limerick Road (mid-May to Sept daily 9am–6pm; April to mid-May & Oct Mon–Sat 9am–5.45pm; Nov–March Mon–Fri 9.30am–5.15pm; ☎065/682 8366). For a small town, Ennis has a good range of **accommodation**. *The Abbey Tourist Hostel*, Harmony Row (IHH; ☎065/682 2620) enjoys a prime location, just across the river from the Friary, while *The Clare Hostel*, The Cornmarket (☎065/682 9370; £12.50) is a luxurious budget alternative, though there is no hostellers' kitchen. Ennis has no shortage of B&B accommodation: *Avonlea*, Francis Street (☎065/682 1632; ②) is a pleasant option, a short

walk to the town centre. Other good possibilities include *Cloneen*, Clon Road
(☎065/682 9681; ②) and *Derrynane House*, O'Connell Square (☎065/682 8464; ③).
There are several good hotels too, including the pleasantly conservative *Old Ground
Hotel*, O'Connell St (☎065/682 8127; ⑨), and *The Queen's Hotel* (☎065/682 8963; ⑦),
Abbey Street. A little further out is *The West County Inn* (☎065/682 3000; ⑦), a comfortable modern hotel with a leisure centre and a very nice pool. If these are full, the
tourist office can direct you to many more. For alternative tourist information, including what's on around town, head for Upstairs, Downstairs (daily 9am–9pm), a gift shop
on O'Connell Square.

The Town

The finest monument in town, **Ennis Friary**, lies right in the historic centre
(guide/information service daily late May to late Sept 9.30am–6.30pm; at other times
phone ☎065/682 9100; £1; Heritage Card). It was established by the O'Briens, Kings of
Thomond, in 1242, but most of the existing building dates from the fourteenth century.
At that time, it had 350 friars and over 600 pupils and was considered the finest educational institution in Ireland for the clergy and upper classes. In parts it remains striking: graceful lancet windows fill the east end of the chancel, while adjacent convent
buildings include cloister ruins and a stoutly barrel-vaulted chapter house. There is
good sculpture, too: look out for the small square carving on the jamb of the arch
between the nave and transept, which shows a half-length figure of Christ with his
hands bound; the relief of Saint Francis with cross-staff and stigmata at the east end of
the nave; and the carved corbels beneath the south tower showing the Virgin and Child
and an archbishop. The real sculptural highlight, however, is the fifteenth-century
MacMahon tomb (now incorporated in the Creagh Tomb), embellished with fine
alabaster carvings of the Passion.

Despite the beauty of the friary, Ennis today seems more proud of its later history,
as capital of the unyielding "banner county" and a bastion of Nationalism. A monument
to **Daniel O'Connell** solidly dominates the old, narrow streets that meet in O'Connell
Square. In 1828, County Clare returned O'Connell to Westminster by such a huge
majority that he had to be allowed to take his seat, despite the fact that he was a
Catholic, which should have barred him at the time; he went on to force through parliament the Catholic Emancipation Act. It was in Ennis, too, that **Parnell** made his
famous speech advocating the boycott in the land agitations of the late nineteenth century. **De Valera** was TD for the county from 1917 to 1959 (and Taoiseach for much of
that time) and is remembered in a memorial outside the courthouse, and in the **De
Valera Library Museum** on Harmony Row (Mon & Thurs 11am–5.30pm; Tues, Wed
& Fri 11am–8pm; free), a small, local museum covering a history of national importance. Exhibits include an interesting collection of letters and telegrams: from Daniel
O'Connell seeking support in the forthcoming election; from De Valera while in prison
expecting to be executed; from the Black and Tans threatening retribution for the kid-
napping of two constables, and so on. The museum also houses a collection of weapons
used by the Royal Irish Constabulary and the IRA, and hosts changing exhibitions by
modern Irish artists.

As for other things to search out, Ennis's **cathedral**, a nineteenth-century building
with a sharp spire, stands icy and grey at the far end of O'Connell Street, somewhat at
odds with the friendly atmosphere of the town. More interesting is to wander the
ancient lanes that run from O'Connell Street to the **old market place**, where a
Saturday vegetable and livestock market is held. You could also follow the river a short
way up from Woodquay to the newly renovated mill chase.

Eating, drinking and entertainment

There are a handful of **places to eat** in Ennis. If you're on a tight budget, *The Sherwood Inn* (daily till 6pm, Thurs & Fri till 9pm) in the Ennis Shopping Centre, Francis Street, is probably the best place for a hearty breakfast or lunch. You can get takeaway pizzas from *Numero Uno*, Barrack Street, and imaginative vegetarian and non-vegetarian meals at *An Goile Mór*, Salthouse Lane, off Parnell Street. *The Food Emporium*, Francis Street, stocks a superb selection of Irish and European cheeses, salamis and prepared meats, and also has a small coffee and sandwich bar where you can sample from the range. A number of pubs offer decent bar food, such as *Brogan's* (till 7pm) or *The Derrynane* in O'Connell Street. For general provisions, tardis-like Dunne's Store's small O'Connell Street shop-front opens into a huge supermarket.

Ennis has two music festivals, the **Fleadh Nua**, which takes place over the last weekend in May, and the **Guinness Traditional Music Festival**, a fabulous event, which is usually held over the second weekend in November and draws top musicians. The town, in fact, is particularly well served any time of the year. Perhaps the best place to start is Cois na hAbhna, a centre for local traditional music enthusiasts, located less than half a mile out on the Gort Road. Throughout the summer they have Oíche Ceili evenings of song and dance (most Saturdays), and year round there are informal traditional music sessions (Thurs; all welcome) and set dancing (Wed, £1.50). Sessions organized by Cois na hAbhna also move around the county, so it's worth watching out for them in smaller towns roundabout.

For such a small town, Ennis itself has a surprising number of **bars** with traditional, cajun and rock sessions. For **traditional music** try *Brogan's*, 24 O'Connell St (summer Mon & Tues); *Fawl's Railway Bar*, 69 O'Connell St (Fri); *Micky Kerin's*, Lifford, a short walk along Newbridge Road (summer Fri); *May Kearney's*, Lifford (daily except Tues), which has a beer garden to the rear; *P.J. Kelly's* in Carmody Street (Sat & Sun); *Cruise's*, Abbey Street (Sun lunchtime and every night, year round); *Ciaran's*, Francis Street (all year round Thurs–Sun plus Mon in summer); and *Lucas's*, Parnell Street, a great little bar with traditional music in the old bar (Fri, plus Sat in summer). Two of the liveliest young bars are *Brandon's*, O'Connell Street, and *Brannagan's*, Mill Road (off the bottom of Parnell Street), both of which have a good rock, folk and cajun mix. *El Paso's*, Parnell Street, is a huge, Western-themed bar with contemporary pop and folk (every night in summer), and *Alexander Knox*, Abbey Street, attracts a young crowd with contemporary pop and rock (Mon, Wed, Thurs, Fri year round). For **clubs**, try *Central Park* above *Brannagan's*, (Thurs, Fri, Sat), *The Sanctuary* (behind *Cruise's*, daily) or *The Bordwalk*, behind *Brandon's* (rock, world, cajun mix).

Around Ennis

Ennis sits in a low-lying strip of land that runs from a deep inlet of the Shannon River right up to South Galway. To the east of the town lie lush fields edged by white-grey walls and clumps of wild flowers: pinks, purples and yellows of willow herb and ragwort, the strong white horns of bindweed, and even the occasional orchid. Further out, the land breaks into little lakes and rivers before becoming gently hilly to meet the Slieve Bernagh Mountains. This gentle farmland makes for easy cycling, and your trip can be punctuated by village pubs and plenty of church ruins and castles. It is worth bearing in mind that the N18 Galway–Limerick road is horribly busy, a nightmare for cyclists as drivers adopt motorway attitudes on what is in fact quite a narrow road.

Quin, Knappogue and Craggaunowen

One of the most pleasant rides east of Ennis is to **Quin Abbey**, the area's best-preserved Franciscan friary, founded in 1433. The main church building is graceful, its slender tower rising clear over the high, open archway between chancel and nave and making a distinct outline against the green of the surrounding pastures. Climb up a floor to the first storey and you can look down on the abbey's complete cloister with its arches and buttresses. For all the uplifting beauty of the tower, the abbey seems to have been built on a human scale, to function as a place in which to live and worship rather than to impress and dominate.

On the other hand, the massy walls of **Knappogue Castle** emanate an awesome sense of power. Leave Quin and continue two miles south on the L31 to reach this huge sixteenth-century tower house (May–Oct, daily 9.30am–5.30pm; £2.75). It was originally built by the Macnamaras, but they lost it to Cromwell, who then used it as his HQ – thereby, no doubt, saving it from the major damage he inflicted elsewhere. At the Restoration, the Macnamaras managed to regain ownership of the castle and hung on to it until 1800. It's been beautifully restored, and inside are boldly carved sixteenth-century oak fireplaces and stout oak furniture. At odds with the overall flavour of Knappogue, the nineteenth-century domestic additions are furnished as if eighteenth-century rooms, beautifully appointed with Irish Chippendale furniture and Waterford crystal. The main body of the castle is used for medieval banquets.

The village makes a very peaceful stopover if you are coming to or from Shannon Airport. *Nonnie's Village Inn* (☎065/682 5929; ②) offers pleasant **B&B** over the bar and there are several others within the village as you head towards Limerick: *Abbeyside House* (☎065/682 5681; ②), offering inexpensive standard accommodation, and just past the Post Office, the more modern *Rooska House* (☎065/682 5661; ②). You can get bar meals at *The Abbey Tavern*, a smoky, locals' haunt (midday and evenings till 9pm), or dinner in the more formal surroundings of *The Árdsolus Restaurant*, just next door.

The Craggaunowen Project

The second left turning, two miles south of Knappogue, brings you to the **Craggaunowen Project**, situated on the edge of a reedy lake under a wooded hillside (mid-March to October bank holiday, daily 9.30am–6pm; £4). This is based around another fortified tower house, the ground floor of which houses a collection of sixteenth-century European wood carvings. The project itself aims to re-create a sense of Ireland's ancient history, with reconstructions of earlier forms of homes and farmsteads; a ring fort and a *crannóg*, or artificial island, for example. Young workers experiment with old craft techniques, using replicas of wooden lathes, kilns and other traditional devices, and double up as guides if asked.

The most adventurous and certainly the most famous of the working replicas here is Tim Severin's **Brendan**, a leather-hulled boat in which he and four crew successfully sailed across the Atlantic in 1976, to prove that the legend of St Brendan could be true. St Brendan's story – he was supposedly the first European to reach America – is recorded in a ninth-century manuscript, and the design of the *Brendan* is based on its descriptions, along with the features of curraghs still used off Ireland's west coast. The result is a remarkable vessel of oak-tanned oxhides stretched over an ashwood frame. Craggaunowen also has an actual **Iron Age road**, excavated at Corlea Bog, County Longford and moved to this site. Made of large oak planks placed across runners of birch or alder, it must have formed part of an important route across difficult bog. For refreshment, there's also a nice **tea shop** here, serving delicious homemade cakes.

Eight miles beyond Craggaunowen, the village of **CRATLOE** is renowned for its oak-wooded hills overlooking the Shannon and Fergus estuaries and is a particularly lovely spot for walking.

Bunratty

Bunratty Castle (daily 9.30am to last admission 4.15pm; Folk Park June–Aug until 7pm; £5) stands on what was once an island on the north bank of the Shannon, now handily situated on the N18 Limerick–Ennis Road. The Vikings of Limerick recognized the site's strategic importance for protecting trade, and so they fortified it – you can still see the moat. The first castle on the site was built by Normans, but they lost control and, in 1460, the Macnamaras built the castle that stands today. It's exceptionally impressive: the fine rectangular keep has been perfectly restored and now houses a large collection of furniture, tapestries, paintings and ornate carvings from all over Europe, spanning the fourteenth to the seventeenth centuries. In the castle grounds stands **Bunratty Folk Park** (£3.70), a complete reconstruction of a nineteenth-century village. Although extremely touristy, both castle and folk village are well worth taking time over, and you can break up your visit in the excellent tearoom or the pub within the Folk Park. The nearby *Durty Nelly's* is a favourite tourist bar, regularly overrun by bus parties, and *Kathleen's Irish Pub*, in *The Bunratty Castle Hotel* (☎061/364116; ⑤), serves excellent bar food, though again coach parties can mean a long wait to be served. Follow the Lower Road, which runs between Bunratty Castle and *Durty Nelly's*, for *Bunratty Caravan and Camping Park* (☎061/369190), a serviceable site, or for one of numerous good quality **B&Bs** – *Bunratty Villa* (☎061/369241; ④) is a handy ten-minute walk from the castle; further along are *Ashgrove House* (☎061/369332; ③), *Innisfree* (☎061/369773; ②), *Bunratty Heights* (☎061/369324; ③), and, about a mile from the castle, the friendly *Castleside* (☎061/369390; ②).

Dysert O'Dea

Alternative routes from Ennis can take you north through low-lying country fretted with rush-bordered lakes, their banks dotted with O'Brien strongholds. Seven miles north is **Dysert O'Dea**, the site of the ancient monastic foundation of St Tola (d. 737) and the scene of an important battle in 1318 when the O'Briens defeated the de Clares of Bunratty, thus preventing the Anglo-Norman takeover of Clare. To get there, take the Ennistymon Road out of Ennis, then after two miles take the right fork for Corofin and it's up a road to the left. At the site you can wander around the remains of a twelfth- to thirteenth-century Romanesque church with a richly carved south doorway and carvings of grotesque animal heads and human faces. Of particular interest is the twelfth-century White Cross of Tola, with carvings of Christ and a bishop in high relief, Daniel in the lion's den, as well as intricate patterning. The **O'Dea Castle** nearby houses a museum (May–Sept daily 10am–6pm; £2.50) and archeology centre. Travelling north of Dysert O'Dea, you'll come across an abundance of little lakes, offering good fishing.

Lough Derg

The west bank of **Lough Derg** is a seam of beautiful countryside set between bald, boggy mountains and the great expanse of the lake. It forms the county's eastern boundary and, isolated by the empty heights of the Slieve Bernagh and the Slieve Aughtie mountains, has a different character from the rest of Clare. The waterway's wealth of fish and bird life, and the quaint villages on either shore, have long made Lough Derg popular with a wealthy Lough-cruising set, whose exclusive brand of tourism means villages are fairly conservative and well kept. The hunting, shooting and fishing crowds are well catered for and tend to dominate the character of local pubs; but there are also pockets renowned for their traditional music sessions, attracting predominantly local crowds, and there are excellent – and inexpensive – opportunites for watersports.

The main road north varies the scene, at times clinging to the lakeshore, at others gaining higher ground and panoramic views over the lough, its islands and the mountains of Tipperary. It connects the historic, picturesque towns of Portumna in County Galway, at the head of the Lough, and Killaloe at its southerly tip, and laces together a handful of choice little villages.

Access to the area is via Limerick or Portumna. Bus Éireann runs at least one bus (Mon–Sat) from Limerick to Killaloe, Tuamgraney, Scarriff and Mountshannon. For timetable information, phone Limerick ☎061/313333. You could try **hitching** or **cycling**, though hitching isn't such a good idea in the Slieve Bernagh and Slieve Aughtie mountains to the west where roads are empty. This isn't ideal cycling country either, as the roads are deceptively steep and unsheltered. However, if you are keen to cycle, you can arrange bike rental through Killaloe tourist office.

Killaloe

At **KILLALOE**, the Shannon narrows again after the Lough for the final stretch of this great river's journey to the sea. An old stone bridge still spans the waters at this traditional crossing point. The old part of Killaloe centres on **St Flannan's Cathedral**, and the narrow lanes that run up the steep slopes to the west suggest the town's ancient origins. The cathedral itself is a plain thirteenth-century building, impressive in its solid simplicity, with a low square tower and straight, strong buttresses. Just inside the entrance is a heavily decorated Romanesque doorway from an earlier church, and alongside it the huge **Thorgrim Stone**, unique in its ogham and runic inscriptions (ogham is a form of the Latin alphabet associated with early Christianity; the runic forms are Scandinavian in origin), which is probably the memorial of a Viking convert. In the churchyard the stout Romanesque **St Flannan's Oratory** dates from the twelfth century and is complete with barrel-vaulted roof. Well signposted just over a mile north of town on the western shore of Lough Derg stands the earthern fort **Beal Boru**, possibly the site of Brian Boru's palace "Kincora", which was either here or in Killaloe itself. The best way to spend your time in Killaloe, though, is to get out onto the water; see below for details of cruises and boat rental.

Practicalities

The **tourist office**, in Lock House on The Bridge (May to mid-Sept daily 10am–6pm; ☎061/376866), is very helpful with accommodation. If you want to stay, you could opt for one of the central **B&Bs**, such as *Kincora House*, Church Street (☎061/376149; ④), a lovely old town house with old-world furnishings or *Lyon's B&B* (☎061/376652; ②), just next door. Slightly further out is *Canters Lodge*, Cloonfadda (☎065/682 4285; ③) or for something more luxurious, check in at *The Lakeside Hotel* (☎061/376122; ⑦). If you want to camp beside the lake, head for *Lough Derg Holiday Park* (☎061/376329; May–Sept), just three miles north of Killaloe along the Scarriff Road.

For lough **cruises** or dinghy rental call R&B Marine Services Ltd (☎061/376364); for boats with outboard engines call in at Whelan's Foodstore (☎061/376159). You can rent out wind-surfers, canoes, wetsuits and dinghies from The University of Limerick Activity Centre (☎061/376622), situated two miles out along the Scarriff Road.

You'll find a few pubs serving decent **food** over on the Tipperary side of the bridge. Try *Molly's*, also a venue for traditional music, or the somewhat pricier *Gooser's*. The *Simply Delicious* café nearby is just that, serving very cheap meals (Mon–Sat till around

---

THE EAST CLARE WAY

The East Clare Way is a recently mapped long-distance walking route through a less touristed – but for some tastes no less scenic – part of the county. It passes through a green and rugged corner of Clare, taking in rivers, lakes, woodlands and boglands. It's a circular walk and the latter stages can be broken up with boat trips out onto Lough Derg from Mountshannon, or, in fine weather, swimming from the lakeshore (ask locally about currents). The route begins at Killaloe and goes through Broadford, O'Callaghan's Mills, Tulla, Feakle, Flagmount, Mountshannon and Ogonnelloe. The longest stage is Flagmount to Whitegate – some 21 miles.

Accommodation: B&Bs at Killaloe, Tulla, Feakle, Mountshannon and Ogonnelloe; these are small communities, so it makes sense to book accommodation in advance.

Access: There is a limited bus service from Limerick to Killaloe and Scarriff. A bus service operates Saturdays only from Limerick to Mountshannon, Whitegate, Broadford and O'Callaghan's Mills; buses to Tulla run on Wednesdays.

Overall distance: 180km/112 miles.

Highest Point: Cragnamurragh, 527m/1729ft.

Maps and guides: *East Clare Map Guide*, available from the tourist office in Ennis; OS map Nos. 58, 65, 1:50,000 (1.25 inches to 1 mile).

9pm, Sun till 6pm). Over on the County Clare side of the bridge, *Crotty's Courtyard Bar*, Bridge Street, has a fabulous collection of old signs, a cheery beer-yard, and serves bar food till 10pm in summer. Round in Church Street, *The Dalcassian* also serves bar meals. Most pubs have some kind of **music** at weekends during the summer – usually a traditional/country mix. Try *The Seanachaoí* or *Crotty's Courtyard Bar*, both in Bridge Street. For traditional set dancing head for *The Anchor Inn* (Wed). In **Ogonnelloe**, two and half miles north of Killaloe, life at *The Piper's Inn* (☎061/376885; B&B; ②) revolves around traditional music with sessions most nights during the summer, and a host of festivals during the course of the year, including *Feíle*, the first weekend in July, given over to traditional music, and the Uílleann Piper's Festival– from which the bar takes its name – the second weekend in November. The village is also on the East Clare Way.

The West Bank

The villages along the scenic road north are all very small. Wealthy tourists into hunting, shooting and fishing tend to stay in fancy hotels, and amenities for other visitors are sparse. That said, it's still very beautiful countryside, especially the lakeside area up as far as Mountshannon. Traditional music here is very much alive, and there are some excellent opportunities to get out onto the water.

SCARRIFF is a little farming town set high up in rough, open country overlooking the lough. It's a handy place to pick up provisions. There's a Bank of Ireland here and a couple of pubs serving bar food, *McNamara's* and *Ryan's*. The latter also has traditional music (Fri, summer). **FEAKLE**, about six miles to the west, is another small village, but has a far busier social calendar; there are excellent **traditional sessions** throughout the year in *Pepper's* bar, *Lena's* and *Shorts'* bar. Feakle also holds an International Traditional Music Festival (usually the second weekend in August) and a Traditional Singing Festival over the May bank holiday. **Accommodation** can be problematic; unless you bring a tent and ask at a farm your choices are limited to the comfortable *Kilcronan B&B*, Moynoe (☎061/921561; ③), about a mile out towards Mountshannon, *The Smyth Village Hotel* (☎061/924000; ⑥) or *Laccaroe House* (☎061/924150; ②), about a mile away.

Around nine miles southwest of Feakle sits the similarly quiet village of **TULLA**. You are most likely to be here if you are walking the East Clare Way, or if you want to sample some of the excellent traditional music to be had in *Torpey's* bar (Sun, year round). Tulla also hosts a long weekend festival of traditional music over the first weekend in October known as The Humour of Tulla Festival (details on ☎065/683 5130). Accommodation is limited to a few **B&Bs**: *Cragville* (☎065/683 5110; ②) in the village, *Castle Lodge* (☎065/683 5231; ②), one mile away, and the welcoming *Toonagh House* (☎065/683 5316; ②), two and half miles away.

The best spot to stay right by the lake, Killaloe and Portumna aside, is **MOUNTSHANNON**, about five miles north of Scarriff. It's among the prettiest of the villages and has a couple of cosy pubs and some good **places to eat**. Good bar food and sometimes traditional music in the summer are to be had at *Cois na hAbhna*, while meals are served all day at *An Cupán Caifé* (☎061/927275), a relaxed, small bistro with a cosy atmosphere. Places to stay include the central *Mountshannon Hotel* (☎061/927162; ⑤), and slightly further out, *Derg Lodge* (☎061/927180; ②) and *Oak House* (☎061/927185; ②), which has its own private beach. **Watersports** enthusiasts will find reasonably-priced canoeing, wind-surfing, sailing and motor boat rental at the nearby *Lakeside Watersport Caravan and Camping Park* (☎061/927225). From Mountshannon, you can also take a boat to **Holy Island** (☎065/921615), the site of the ruins of a monastic settlement dating from the seventh to the thirteenth centuries.

Southwest Clare

The southwest of the county has glorious sandy beaches, stunning cliff scenery and a couple of popular family holiday resorts. Inland doesn't look so promising. Southwest from Ennis the country flattens out and becomes scrubby and barren: bog, marsh, the odd bit of cotton grass here, the occasional lump of thistles there, with only sporadic pockets of cultivated land. The bald flank of Slievecallan is to the north and the outline of the Kerry hills to the south across the Shannon.

Kilrush and Scattery Island

The best reason to stop in **KILRUSH** is for a trip across the broad Shannon estuary to Scattery Island (see opposite). The town itself hosts traditional **Horse Fairs** in June, October and November, but the character of the place is changing. What was a muddy, tidal harbour is now a fine marina, the main thrust of the town's bid for the upmarket tourist trade, and in the market square, a statue of the Maid of Éireann (see box opposite) looks resolutely down the broad main street to the quayside where it's all happening. The old market house and town hall is now a **heritage centre** (June–Aug, Mon–Sat 10am–6pm, Sun noon–4pm; £2), for the most part a stand-and-read display telling the eighteenth- and nineteenth-century economic and social history of the town. In Toler Street, just off the main street, the spacious **St Senan's Catholic church** is worth looking in for the Harry Clarke stained glass windows.

The **tourist office** is in the town hall in the main square (late May–Aug Mon–Sat 10am–1pm & 2–6pm; Sun noon–4pm; ☎065/905 1577). There's no shortage of **B&Bs** in the town centre. Recommended are *Crotty's* (☎065/905 2470; ③) on the square and Mrs M. O'Mahony's friendly establishment, *Ferry Lodge*, Cappa Road (☎065/905 1291; ②). *Katie O'Conner's Hostel*, Frances Street (☎065/905 1133; ②) is a decent place, while superior hostel accommodation is available at *Kilrush Creek Lodge and Adventure Centre*, Cappa Road, just beside the marina (☎065/905 2595, dorms £13; B&B ②). They have an adventure centre alongside where you can get out onto the water kayaking, canoeing, sailing or wind-surfing. Though primarily for caravans, *Aylevarroo Caravan* *and Camping Park*(☎065/905 1102; May to early Sept), also caters for campers – you'll find it on the N67 Killimer Road, less than two miles from Kilrush. The town has two **banks**, Allied Irish Bank and Bank of Ireland, both on Frances Street. Bus Éireann information for **buses** to Ennis and around the coast throughout the year, and to Galway and Cork during the summer, is available from the tourist office. You can rent out **bikes** and get camping Gaz from Gleesons, Henry Street.

Access to Scattery Island is by small boat (£4.50), and trips are restricted by tides. Enquire at the **Scattery Island Centre** down by the marina (June–Sept daily 9am–6pm; ☎065/905 2139), where an exhibition recounts Scattery's monastic history. For trips to the island at other times, and for details of dolphin-watching trips, phone ☎065/905 1327 or 905 2031. Alternatively, Atlantic Adventures can take you deep sea angling, and that can mean shark fishing (☎065/905 2133).

Kilrush has a handful of decent **places to eat**. In Henry Street, just off the square, *Ryan's Deli* serves burgers, pizza and tacos, and good **pub food** is available at *Kelly's* and *The Haven Arms*, both on Henry Street. For coffee, cakes and sandwiches there's *The Quayside* on Frances Street. For evening meals, try *Kelly's* mid-range restaurant, above the bar, probably the best alternative to the fast-food outlets around the square. Kilrush is a quiet town, but *Crotty's* is a great old bar, with traditional sessions every night during the summer. *O'Looney's*, John Street just off the square, has rock music (Fri) and folk (Sat). Other spots for traditional music include *The Percy French Bar*, Moore Street (summer Wed, Fri & Sun), and *The Way Inn*, Vaudeleur Street (Sun year round).

Scattery Island

SCATTERY ISLAND was last inhabited in the late 1970s, and as you land, you'll notice that the quay before you is dotted with overgrown derelict cottages. Walking up the lanes, spongy with moss and bracken, you disturb the burrows the island is riddled with, and rabbits pop out madly all over the place. St Senan founded a **monastery** here in the sixth century, and at one time there were seven monastic settlements. The community suffered greatly from Viking raids, but there are still the remains of several churches dating from between the ninth and the fifteenth centuries.

Wherever you wander on Scattery, you feel as though you're stepping back into a timeless past, a mythical world protected by its isolation in the Shannon estuary. But Scattery's most impressive feature has to be the **round tower**, perfect in form, the stone made a warm mustardy yellow by the lichen that covers it. Unusually for a round tower, the doorway here is at ground level, as opposed to the more typical high-up entrances reached by a ladder that could be withdrawn to make the tower impregnable.

Killimer

If you have children in tow, it's well worth calling at Fortfield Farm, **KILLIMER**, just a mile before the ferry terminal (see p.330) if you're travelling from Kilrush. It's a small **farm zoo** (May–Sept Mon–Sat 10am–6pm, Sun 2–6pm; £2, children £1, family £6) with llamas, red deer, pot-bellied pigs, numerous breeds of rabbits and other domesticated

---

THE FERRY TO KERRY

If you're **cycling or driving on to Kerry**, you can cut out many miles and the mental congestion of Limerick city by heading for Killimer, five miles from Kilrush, and taking the **car ferry** to Tarbert (April–Oct Mon–Sat 7am–9pm, Sun 9am–9pm; Nov–March Mon–Sat 7am–7pm, Sun 10am–7pm; sailings every 60min on the hour from Killimer, return from Tarbert on the half-hour; £7 single car, £10 return; pedestrians/cyclists £2, £3 return; ☎065/905 3124).

---

rare animals. It's run by a friendly crowd who encourage children to handle the animals. The farm also does **B&B** (☎065/905 1457; ②); if you are staying there, access to the zoo is free.

Kilkee and around

KILKEE, over on the Atlantic coast, is a small, busy, seaside holiday town with all the amenities you'd expect: cheap cafés, restaurants, amusements and nightlife. Popular with the bucket-and-spade brigade, the town comes as a healthy piece of normality if the offbeat romanticism of the west coast has become too much. The westerly tip of the town's magnificent golden beach, set in dramatic cliff scenery, meets an apron of laminated rock strata known as the Duggerna Rocks, which protects it from the ravages of the Atlantic. Here, when the tide is out, deep, clear pollock holes form, filled with colourful marine life.

The area is a favourite for scuba diving and snorkelling, but even without equipment, exploration is rewarding. There are exhilarating walks for miles along the cliffs both to the north and, more spectacularly, to the south round **Loop Head**, where you can walk for sixteen miles along the cliff's edge past stack rocks, puffing holes (where the sea spouts up through crevices in the rock) and the natural Bridges of Ross. The other good way to see this peninsula is by **bike**; you can rent them from Brian Melican (☎065/905 6622), next door to the hostel.

In the little church at **MONEEN**, near Kilbaha at the tip of the peninsula, you'll find a nineteenth-century curiosity known as **The Little Arc**. In penal times, Catholics were forced to be both ingenious and secret in the practice of their faith. Here they were not allowed to worship on land, and so built a little hut on wheels which was kept on the beach and wheeled down below the high-water mark between tides, beyond the legal grasp of the local Protestant landowner. The priest would then say Mass in it while the congregation knelt around it on the beach. If you want to break your explorations of Loop Head, there are a couple of pubs at the tiny village of Cross, but better by far is the unspoilt fishing village of **CARRIGAHOLT**, which has a slither of beach beside the quays, a ruined castle overlooking the harbour and some very welcoming pubs (*The Long Dock* does good pub food). It's also an excellent area for **dolphin spotting**; for trips out, phone Dolphin Watch (☎065/905 8156; 2hr boat trip, £10, advance booking essential).

Practicalities

The **tourist office** in The Square (late May–Aug daily 10am–1pm & 2–6pm; ☎065/905 6112) is very helpful with accommodation; Kilkee is a popular resort and often booked out in August. *Kincora* (☎065/905 6107; ③) and *Bay View* (☎065/905 6058; ③), both in O'Connell Street, are good bets for **B&B**. Alternatively, you could try *Purtill's Guesthouse*, O'Curry Street, a solid, newly refurbished place (☎065/905 6771; ④), or

Dunearn House, West End (☎065/905 6545; ③). The cheapest decent accommodation is at *Kilkee Hostel*, O'Curry Street (IHH; ☎065/905 6209; Feb–Nov), a friendly, family-run **hostel** right in the centre of town. If you need to **camp**, try *Cunningham's Holiday Park* (☎065/905 6430; Easter weekend & late-April to mid-Sept), reached as you approach town from Kilrush by taking the first left after the petrol station.

The **Bank** of Ireland and the Allied Irish Bank are in O'Curry Street. As for **sport**, the choice is pitch and putt at the west end, golf at the new eighteen-hole championship golf course (☎065/905 6048), scuba diving (Kilkee Diving and Watersports Centre ☎065/905 6707), pony trekking (☎065/905 6635), or Waterworld, at the north end of the beach, which has slides and pools, gushers and geysers and is great for kids. In fine weather there can be few better places to swim than in the safe waters of the Blue Flag beach. The beach is also an ideal place for sheltered wind-surfing; lessons and board rental are available. **Bus Éireann services**, departing from outside *Kett's* pub just along the Lahinch Road, link Kilkee with Ennis and other towns along the coast.

Lodged in among the bars and chippies you'll find a handful of good **places to eat**, including *The Strand Restaurant* (☎065/905 6177) on the seafront, a popular spot for seafood (evening menu around £15); on O'Curry Street, *Purtill's*, which dishes up pasta, steaks and pizzas, and *The Pantry*, which does café-style home baking. On the same street, you'll get good bar food at *Myles' Creek* and at *Ketts* in Erin Street. Kilkee has no shortage of **pubs**. *O'Mara's*, O'Curry Street, is a great old bar, with traditional, folk and singalongs and a lively local crowd. *Fitzpatrick's*, Chapel Street, also has traditional music sessions. A younger crowd frequent *Myles' Creek* (rock and pop five nights a week in summer, weekends in winter) and *The Strand*, on the seafront, a regular bar with a mix of ballads, traditional, blues and rock music. Finally, *The Greyhound* in O'Curry Street is arguably the cutest bar in Clare; closed for over forty years, it's just been reopened, had the dust blown away and a fresh fire laid.

Miltown Malbay and Spanish Point

The coastline north of Kilkee is one of fine cliffs and sandy beaches, though not all of them are accessible. The Victorian resort of **MILTOWN MALBAY**, eighteen miles north of Kilkee and situated some way inland, comes alive for the Willie Clancy Summer School, held here usually the first or second week in July, when it's packed with traditional music enthusiasts from all over the world. *Clancy's* and *Queeley's* bars are likely to be lively any time during the summer. For **B&B**, try *The Station House* (☎065/708 4008; ②), Lahinch Road. Equally good are *An Gleann* (☎065/708 4281; ③) and *Malone's* (☎065/708 4246; ②), both on Ennis Road. Two and a half miles away you'll find an excellent sandy swimming beach at **SPANISH POINT**, so called because it was here that survivors from wrecked Armada ships swam ashore, only to be executed by the High Sheriff of Clare. It's a holiday spot for nuns, and appropriately enough has a very quiet campsite, *Lahiff's Caravan and Camping Park* (☎065/708 4006; May–Sept). Other places to stay include *Atlantic Star* (☎065/708 4782; ③), a spacious, modern B&B just across from the golf course on the main N67, and a couple of new hotels: *Armada Hotel* (☎065/708 4110; ⑥) and the less expensive *Bellbridge House Hotel* (☎065/708 4038; ⑤).

To the east of Spanish Point, **Slieve Callan** rises beside the main road to Ennis. Taking this road you pass Knocknalassa, where there's an impressive wedge-shaped gallery grave, known as Diarmuid and Gráinne's Bed (after the Irish version of the Tristan and Isolde story). It's quite tricky to find: five miles along the road from Miltown Malbay you will pass a house with a thatched little barn alongside; the grave is about half a mile further east from here, tucked out of sight behind a hummocky rise to the left of the road. Follow the cows – it's worth seeing.

Lahinch and Ennistymon

LAHINCH, eight miles north of Spanish Point, is a busy family holiday resort with a fabulous broad sandy beach. Families aside, Lahinch attracts golfers and surfers, a weird hybrid well served by the town. To get a round at Lahinch **golf** course you will need to book well ahead (☎065/708 1003); **surfing** is there for the taking. You can hear good **music** in the bars, especially in the summer months.

B&B accommodation is available at *Seafield Lodge* (☎065/708 1594; ③) and *Mulcarr House* (☎065/708 1123; ③), both close to the centre on Ennistymon Road. Slightly further out, but offering wonderful views of the bay are *Le Bord De Mer*, Cregg (☎065/708 1454; ③) and *Nazira*, School Road (☎065/708 1362; ③). The resort has several traditional **hotels**: *The Aberdeen Arms* (☎065/708 1100; ⑦), *The Claremont Hotel* (☎065/708 1007; ⑥) and *The Atlantic* (☎065/708 1049; ⑥), all on Main Street. At the other end of the scale, *Lahinch Hostel* (IHH; ☎065/708 1040), next door to the church, is a decent budget option, with laundry facilities and bike rental. You can **camp** at *Lahinch Camping and Caravan Park* (☎065/708 1424; May–Sept), an orderly family site that has a laundry for service washes, bike rental and a wet-weather shelter. The mighty meals served in the bar of *The Shamrock Hotel*, Main Street, will satisfy post-surf hunger. Other bars good for food include the seafront *O'Looney's* and nearby *The Spinnaker Bar*, both frequented by a lively young crowd. If all you want is a quiet pint, head for *The Nineteenth Bar*, Main Street. For seafood, good vegetarian options and fine views head for *The Barrtrá* (☎065/708 1280; dinner around £20), signposted off the road two miles south of Lahinch. A good bar for traditional **music** is *Galvin's*, Church Street.

About two miles east of Lahinch, the old market town of **ENNISTYMON**, with its low shop-fronts, pretty nineteenth-century Gothic church and great old bars tucked away in the most unlikely of places, has a life, albeit a leisurely one, regardless of tourism. Its people enjoy **traditional music** and ballads in the bars year round. Try *The Archway Bar, Phil's Bar, Daly's Bar, Eugene's* or *Cooley's House*, all on Main Street. The church at the end of Main Street has been converted into a *teach cheoil* (ceili house) where you can catch evenings of traditional music. The town's Traditional Singing Festival is held over the June bank holiday weekend. Ennistymon's setting is surprisingly green; nip down behind the *Archway Bar* and the **Cascades Walk** takes you a short way alongside the River Cullenagh as it rushes over slabs of rock through the heart of the little town. Ennistymon's eighteenth-century church stands on a hill above the town, from where you can see the blue river snaking its way out of the woods and beyond to the sea at Liscannor.

Reasonably central **B&Bs** include the welcoming *Station House*, in Ennis Road (☎065/707 1149; ③), and *The Matchmakers' Rest* (☎065/707 1385; ②), Main Street.

The Burren

The Burren (*Boireann*, or "rocky land") is a huge plateau of limestone and shale that covers over a hundred square miles of northwest Clare, a highland shaped by a series of cliffs, terraces and expanses of limestone pavement, with little to punctuate the view. Bleak and grey, the northern reaches of the Burren can come as a shock to anyone associating Ireland with all things lush and verdant. It's an extraordinary landscape of stark rock, fading lower green fields, and above all the sky and the ocean. Its cliffs and terraces lurch towards the sea like huge steps of wind-pocked pumice. Bone white in sunshine, in the rain the rock becomes darkened and metallic, the cliffs and canyons blurred by mists. A harsh place, barely capable of sustaining human habitation, it was aptly summed up in the words of Cromwell's surveyor Ludlow: "savage land, yielding

GEOLOGY AND FAUNA

The Burren has an austerity of almost mythical dimensions, suggesting ancient privations. The pavementing that stretches before you is a floor of grey rock, split by long parallel grooves known as grykes. Throughout the Burren, rainwater seeps through the highly porous rock and gouges away at the many underground potholes, caves and tunnels. The only visible **river** is the Caher at Fanore, but there are a multitude of underground waterways, and there are **lakes**, known as turloughs, that are peculiar to this landscape; they appear only after heavy rainfall, when the underground systems fill up, and vanish once again after a few dry days.

The panorama is bleak, but close up, **wild flowers** burst from the grooves in specks and splashes of brilliant colour. A botanist's delight and enigma, the Burren supports an astounding variety of **flora**, with Arctic, Alpine and Mediterranean plants growing alongside each other. The best time to see the flowers is late spring, when the strong blue, five-petalled spring gentians flourish. Here, too, are mountain avens, various saxifrages and maidenhair fern. Later in summer, the magenta bloody cranesbill and a fantastic variety of orchids (considered rare elsewhere) bloom: bee orchids, fly orchids and the lesser butterfly. More common flowers look stunning by sheer force of quantity: bright yellow birdsfoot trefoil and hoary rockrose, and milkwort. Obviously flowers must not be picked.

Nobody knows exactly how these plants came to be here, nor why they remain. It has been suggested that some of the Mediterranean flowers have been here since Ireland had a far hotter climate, but how they survived is a source of speculation: it may be the peculiar conditions of moist warm air coming in from the sea, the Gulf Stream ensuring a mild, frostless climate, and very effective drainage through the porous limestone. It's also thought that the bare rock absorbs heat all summer and stores it, so that the Burren land is appreciably warmer in wintertime than areas of a different geology. There's more on the Burren's geology in the **Burren Display Centre** in Kilfenora and at the Whitehorn Visitor Centre, Ballyvaughan.

neither water enough to drown a man, nor a tree to hang him, nor soil enough to bury". There are no sweet rolling fields here, but stick with it and its fascination emerges – cruel and barren as it is, there's a raw beauty about the place with its exceptional combination of light, rock and water.

In recent centuries, the Burren has supported a sparse population, living, like most of the west of Ireland, in harsh poverty. It was to this land, west of the Shannon, that Cromwell drove the dispossessed Irish Catholics after his campaign of terror. Few could survive for long in such country. The area's lack of appeal to centuries of speculators and colonizers greedy to cream the fat off Ireland's lusher pastures has meant that evidence of many of the Burren's earlier inhabitants has remained. The place has over sixty **Stone Age** (3000–2000 BC) burial monuments, the most common types being wedge-shaped tombs, cairns and dolmens; over four hundred Iron Age **ring forts** (500 BC–500 AD), which were defensive dwellings; and numerous Christian churches, **monasteries**, round towers and high crosses.

You can get to the area by taking a Bus Éireann connection from stations at Galway or Limerick. There's a direct **bus** service from Limerick and Galway to Doolin and in summer at least one bus a day from Limerick passes through Ennistymon and Lisdoonvarna, and at least one a day connects Galway with Lisdoonvarna. The **West Clare Shuttle** (☎091/581618) runs a Doolin–Galway door-to-door service during the summer, taking in Fanore, Lisdoonvarna, and anywhere else on route, and picking up at all hostels. To see the Burren's archeological and ecclesiastical sites, it's best to go by car or bike (bike rental is available in the main centres of Doolin, Lisdoonvarna, Ballyvaughan, Corofin and Kinvarra, over in County Galway); to get to know its landscape and flowers, go on foot. For either of these, the excellent Tim Robinson **map**, *The*

Burren, (available in tourist offices, good bookshops or directly from him at Roundstone, County Galway) is usefully detailed and will make finding sites easy, though it does not show contours. For walking, the Ordnance Survey map number 51 (1:50,000) is ideal – and also covers the Aran Islands. There are two north–south routes across the Burren that are of particular **archeological interest**; these run from Bell Harbour to Killinaboy and from Ballyvaughan to Leamaneh. If you're doing a lot of walking, a compass is a good idea as there's a shortage of easy landmarks. You're allowed to walk more or less where you want, though do be aware that there are a large number of bulls in the fields. A good start might be to follow the Burren Way (see box below for more details).

Liscannor and the Cliffs of Moher

Once a tiny village, **LISCANNOR** has been swept along by the tide of development that surges around Ireland's west coast. Still, as a base for exploring Clare's most famous tourist spot, the Cliffs of Moher, it makes a good alternative to the busier tourist centre of Doolin. Soon visitors will be able to explore the Aran Islands from here – a catamaran service is due to start up shortly. The village has a few nice bars, a caravan site which accepts tents, a supermarket and a post office. The area is famous for **Liscannor Flag**, a durable stone used for paving, cladding, fireplaces and, traditionally, the roofs of dwellings. If it's raining, Liscannor Stone, St Brigid's Well (on the road as you go out of the village towards the Cliffs of Moher) is a useful diversion: an audiovisual display tells the story of the stone, and its shop is worth visiting for its dazzling display of exotic crystals and fossils.

    Accommodation is mostly at the cheaper end of the scale and includes *The Village Hostel* (IHH; ☎065/708 1385), located right next to the bars, and a number of B&Bs: *Cahilly Lodge* (☎065/708 1749; ②), *The Anchor Inn* (☎065/708 1548; ②), *Cois na Mara* (☎065/708 1527; ②), the modern, spacious *Sea Haven* (☎065/708 1385; ③) and

---

THE BURREN WAY

Although the Burren Way is marked on maps as starting at Liscannor, this first stretch is currently closed and walkers now have to start at the Cliffs of Moher. From here, the path runs parallel to the coast a little way inland, affording spectacular views across to the Aran Islands and, on a fine day, the mountains of Connemara. It descends to Doolin and then picks up a gradual ascent past Ballynalacken Castle and on across open fields around the shoulder of Slieve Elva. There are no really steep climbs and as the path descends to the Caher River, a valley of classic Burren scenery opens up all around, with stark grey limestone hills and barely a tree in sight. At this point there is the tantalizing option of wandering two and a half miles down the valley to stop over in Fanore, from where you have access to other great walks. The Burren Way follows the quiet road southeast through the valley, round past medieval Newtown Castle and down to the silvery shoreline of Ballyvaughan Bay. It's a gentle walk from here into Ballyvaughan, accompanied by fine views across the great expanse of Galway Bay.

Access: It is possible to take the bus from Ennis to the Cliffs of Moher and from Ballyvaughan to Galway, Lisdoonvarna and Doolin.

Accommodation: There are numerous B&Bs and hostels in Doolin, a few B&Bs and a fine little cottage hostel at Fanore, B&B and budget accommodation at Ballyvaughan.

Total: 22 miles.

Highest point: Slieve Elva (flank) 300m/980ft.

Maps and guides: The Ordnance Survey Map No. 51 (1:50,000) is quite sufficient; *The Burren Way Map and Guide* is available in tourist offices.

Seamount (☎065/708 1367; ③). At the opposite end of the scale, *The Liscannor Bay Hotel* (☎065/708 1186; ⑦), despite its off-putting entrance, offers comfortable rooms, some with wonderful views across the bay to Lahinch. A good place to eat is the cheerful *Mermaid Restaurant* (☎065/708 1076). The sandy stretches south towards Lahinch, near the mouth of the river, are unsafe due to quicksand.

Circling north round the Burren from Liscannor, you arrive almost immediately at the **Cliffs of Moher**. At their highest, they reach 660ft above the Atlantic, and standing on the headlands that jut over the sheer, ravaged cliffs with their great bands of shale and sandstone, you can feel the huge destructive power of the waves. At points, the battering of the water has left jagged stack rocks standing, continually lashed by white spume. Erosion is constant; during a storm some years ago a section of the cliff fell, taking a picnic table with it. The cliffs have to be seen – ideally on a summer evening, when the setting sun is full on them – but be prepared for the oppressively commercial **visitor centre**, where readily changed money and travellers' cheques are quickly spent on coffee, cakes and souvenirs. Be prepared, too, for the professional Irish "characters", ready to sell you any baloney you're willing to buy, and the swarms of tourists newly armed with piercing tin whistles. Do see the cliffs, though – you can soon walk away from the crowds in either direction, after checking there are no bulls in the field to the north. The cliffs actually stretch for five miles, from Hag's Head, just west of Liscannor, to a point beyond **O'Brien's Tower** – a superfluous viewing point with telescope – some four miles south of Doolin.

Doolin

The village of **DOOLIN** itself – marked as "Fisherstreet" on some maps – is for many the music mecca of the "singing county", and in fact of Ireland's west. By the time you get here, you'll no doubt already have met a good few traditional music enthusiasts on their way from across northern Europe, and there are extra buses laid on to bring them here. This said, it is not necessarily the best place for top traditional sessions – these tend to move around – but you are guaranteed to find some kind of merriment in each of Doolin's three pubs every night throughout the summer – though while the music will be fine, the "pub experience" might pall, as you can find yourself either sitting amidst an audience rapt in reverential silence, awed at just being there, or overwhelmed by huge swathes of tourists.

Without the music, Doolin would be a rather forlorn and desolate place, lodged as it is beside a treacherous sandy beach at the tail end of the coast that climaxes with the Cliffs of Moher. Bold shelves of limestone pavement step into the sea by the pier, from which a **ferry** now runs to **Inisheer** and **Inishmore** (☎065/707 4455; mid-April to late Sept 1–8 daily; single £7.50 & £10, return £15 & £20 respectively) and to **Inishmaan** (mid-May to Aug 1 daily; single £8, return £18). If you want more than a couple of hours on the islands – and this is a very good idea – then day trips are only really feasible to Inisheer. It is possible to sail from Doolin to all three islands and then on to Galway or return to Doolin (£20; bikes £2). See p.359 for more on the Aran Islands.

Music may be Doolin's *raison d'être*, but the village is now ruthlessly geared to providing accommodation for as many visitors as it's possible to squeeze into the place's three pubs. For **B&B**, *Seacrest* (☎065/707 4458; ②), towards the pier, has wild, blustery views of the coast, or try *Atlantic View* (☎065/707 4189; ②). There are several smart new B&Bs behind *O'Connor's* pub: *Fisherman's Rest* (☎065/707 4673; ②), *Cuckoo's Nest* (☎065/707 4774; ②) and *Lane Lodge* (☎065/707 4747; ②). Other good options include *Riverfield House* (☎065/707 4113; ②), *Doolin House* (☎065/707 4259; ④),*The Horseshoe* (☎065/707 4006; ③), *O'Connor's* (☎065/707 4314; ②), and just near the *Aille River Hostel* (see overleaf), two good budget options: *The Blue Dolphin* (☎065/707 4692; ①) and *Doolin Cottage* (☎065/707 4762; ①).

Despite their number, the **hostels** do get packed in July and August, so ringing ahead is essential (if they're full, try the ones in Liscannor or Lisdoonvarna, both five miles away, or Fanore, ten miles north). Doolin's hostels include *The Rainbow Hostel* (IHH; ☎065/707 4415), which also has camping space; the friendly, laid-back *Aille River Hostel* (IHH; ☎065/707 4260; early March to early Nov); or *Paddy's Doolin Holiday Hostel* and *Fisherstreet Hostel* (IHH; ☎065/707 4006), with tennis court, laundry facilities and bike rental; and *Flanagan's Village Hostel* (☎065/707 4564), a new family-run hostel with excellent facilities and great views, five minutes' walk north out of the village. There's **camping** down by the pier at *Nagle's* (☎065/707 4458; May to late Sept) – a great spot to absorb the drama of the landscape – and near the *Aille River Hostel* at *Riverside Camping* (☎065/707 4314; April–Sept).

You'll find no shortage of **places to eat**. All of the pubs do good-value bar meals. You can get good vegetarian meals at *The Doolin Café* and fish dishes at *The Lazy Lobster* (☎065/707 4390). More expensive and highly recommended are *Bruach Na haille* (☎065/707 4120), next door to *McGann's* pub, and *Cullinan's Guesthouse Restaurant* (☎065/707 4183), not far from *McDermott's* pub.

Fanore to Bell Harbour

North of Doolin, the coast remains spectacular but bleak and empty. The first place to stop is **FANORE**. A number of excellent Burren walks are easily accessible from here, the best of which is the magnificent walk up to the Caherdoonfergus ring fort and the heights of Dobhach Bhrainin and Gleninagh – a round walk of nine and a half miles. If you decide to use Fanore as a base, you'll find pleasant B&B at *Monica's* (☎065/707 6141; ②) or cosy hostel **accommodation** at *Bridge Hostel* (☎065/707 6134; March to end Oct), which also does camping and evening meals; it only has eighteen beds, so in July and August it's best to ring ahead. **Horse riding** is available at The Burren Riding Centre (☎065/707 6140).

Beyond, the scenic coast road to Black Head and Ballyvaughan is well worth taking. Beautifully poised between Galway Bay and the Burren, **BALLYVAUGHAN** is an attractive village with a quay of neat grey blocks. Its significance as a trading centre has dwindled into tourism, but it makes a calm haven from which to explore the Burren hills, and it's also the northerly limit of the Burren Way (see p. 334). At the **Whitethorn Visitor Centre**, on the Galway road east out of the village, Burren Exposure (☎065/707 7277; £3.50) shows a 35-minute audiovisual display on the geology, history and flora of the Burren. It gives a good overview and the aerial photographs of ring forts are particularly interesting. Further along this road (about 1.5 miles from the village centre), a signposted lane leads to the tranquil and sandy Bishop's Quarter beach. The **tourist office** (mid-May to Oct daily 9am–8.30pm; ☎065/707 7105), in the village centre, can advise on accommodation. **B&Bs** in the centre of the village include: *Gentian Villa* (☎065/707 7042; ②), the luxurious and welcoming *Ballyvaughan Lodge* (☎065/707 7292; ④) and *Bellevue* (☎065/707 7004; ①). A short walk beyond *Monk's* pub will take you to *Oceanville* (☎065/707 7051; ②) and *McGann's* (☎065/707 7294; ②). For a secluded Burren location try *Merrijig Farmhouse* (☎065/707 7120; ③), three miles inland; head out along the Lisdoonvarna road and take the right fork towards Lismacsheedy Cliff Fort; it's on the right after about a mile and a half.

Whitethorn Restaurant & Crafts (☎065/707 7044; closed winter) is worth visiting just for its style and setting. *Monk's* bar does good seafood and the **bar meals** at *Hyland's Hotel* cater for hearty appetites. You can get tea and snacks at *An Féar Gorta Tearooms* in an attractive setting down by the quays. **Traditional music** is played most nights during the summer at *Monk's* bar, while *O'Brien's* has rock, pop and MOR contemporary cover bands. *Greene's* is ideal for a civilized pint.

From Ballyvaughan, interesting routes strike south through the heart of the Burren. Within three miles of Ballyvaughan lie **Newtown Castle** and the **Aillwee Caves**, both signposted off the Lisdoonvarna Road. Although the newly restored sixteenth-century Newtown Castle is nothing more than a fortified tower house, the guided tour is interesting, telling of the medieval law and bardic schools of the surrounding area. The mile-long Newtown Castle Trail takes one and a half hours and covers folklore, botany and history (Easter–Oct daily 10am–6pm; £2; castle and trail £3.50). The well-lit tour through the two-million-year-old Aillwee Caves (mid-March to early Nov daily 10am–5.30pm, July & Aug till 6.30pm; £4.25) will take you past amazing caverns of stalagmites and stalactites and spectacular rock formations.

All along this coast, east of Ballyvaughan, where the Burren borders Galway Bay, short stretches of well-tended farmland reach from the foot of the hills to the shoreline, and water glints through gaps in the high stone walls, while way over Galway Bay the muted cobalt mountains of Connemara lie hazy in the distance. There's a wealth of **birdlife** along these shores: cormorants, guillemots, terns, herons, grebes, fulmars, mallards, teals and swans, as well as sea-otters and seals. Heading towards Galway on the coast road, you pass through **BELL HARBOUR** (*Beulaclugga*), at the southern tip of Muckinish Bay, where the road towards Killinaboy sets off, soon passing the placid **Corcomroe Abbey** signposted on your left. A twelfth-century Cistercian foundation, its considerable remains are beautifully set in a secluded valley.

NEW QUAY, around seven miles east of Ballyvaughan, signposted off the main Galway road, is famous for *Linnane's* seafood bar – in fact there is little else there. It's an unpretentious, cosy bar serving delicious seafood year round and is renowned for its traditional music sessions.

Lisdoonvarna and the heart of the Burren

"**LISDOONVARNA** – for the crack and the women": the radio ad sets the tone for what the spa town of Lisdoonvarna's famous month-long **matchmaking festival** has become. Traditionally, after the harvest, farmers come down from the hills to spend their hard-earned cash and look for a wife in a September festival of singing, dancing and drinking. Today, tradition wears a sad and sleazy face: it's a hugely promoted festival, and the bars – in particular *The Hydro*, *The Matchmakers Arms* of *The Imperial Hotel* and *The King Thomond* – heave with middle-aged money-spinners and the bewildered and lonely, nervously cracking dirty jokes, drinking, singing and leering at any women brave enough to venture in. Between the crooning balladeers and the fortune-tellers' caravans the place bubbles with decades of repression and disappointment – a sad, archaic curiosity, fascinating in its own way.

There is, however, another side to Lisdoonvarna, best enjoyed in spring and early summer, since the place serves as one of the handiest spots from which to explore the Burren. It remains a popular **spa town**, too: the spring waters here contain magnesia, iodine and iron, and reputedly have restorative qualities. The town's principal sulphur spring is in the Spa Wells Health Centre (daily 10am–6pm; ☎065/707 4023), where you can take the waters in the pumphouse, or have a sulphur bath, a sauna, a shower or a massage. Generally full of elderly holiday-makers, the centre offers an invigorating afternoon for weary cyclists and walkers. The whirlwind tour of **The Burren Smokehouse** (daily 9am–7pm; ☎065/707 4432), right in the centre of town, will fill you in on all there is to know about traditional methods of smoking fish: frankly, there's not much to it, but it's worth taking for the banter and the sliver of smoked salmon thrown in to tempt you to buy more.

If you're staying, recommended **B&Bs** are *Joseph's*, Main Street (☎065/707 4076; ②) and *Ballinsheen House* (☎065/707 4806; ③). The town's pleasant hostel, *The Burren Hostel & Kincora House*, is located right in the centre (IHH; ☎065/707 4300); it's advisable to book in advance for the month of September. When it comes to **eating**, plenty of pubs serve food; especially good is *The Roadside Tavern* (till 8.30pm). All of the pubs have music most nights during July and August, some of it pretty mixed, but good starting points include *The Roadside Tavern* and *The Royal Spa*. **Bike rental** is available at Burke's.

If you're heading north, the Ballyvaughan road leads you through a brief area of dank forestry and out onto the **corkscrew hill**, a famous winding descent with fabulous views between grey hills to the broad expanse of Galway Bay – a visual treat and an especially exhilarating release for cyclists after the long steady climb.

Kilfenora

The tiny village of **KILFENORA**, about four miles south of Lisdoonvarna, is a great spot for **traditional music** and is renowned for its year-round music pubs: *Linnane's*, *Vaughan's* and *Nagle's*. Kilfenora's music festival, held over the October bank holiday weekend, is a wonderful and strictly traditional event. The village is also home to the much-publicized **Burren Display Centre** (daily: March–May & Oct 10am–5pm; June–Sept 9.30am–6pm; £2.50). The centre explains clearly the basic geography and geology of the Burren with the aid of a landscape model and a film. The tearoom makes a good refreshment stop.

Next door stands **Kilfenora Cathedral**, certainly worth a visit for its high crosses, the finest of which is the **twelfth-century Doorty Cross**, showing three bishops and what is probably Christ's entry into Jerusalem, with beautiful Celtic patterning. Nearby in the churchyard are remains of two other twelfth-century high crosses, one near the northwest corner, one opposite the church door. Wander through the gateway behind the church and you'll see a fourth cross, with a decorated Crucifixion, in the field to the west. The cathedral itself was built in 1190 and altered in the fifteenth century. It has a roofless chancel with a finely carved triple-light east window and two effigies of bishops, possibly fourteenth century.

For **B&B**, try *Mrs Murphy's*, Main Street (☎065/708 8040; ②). If you want to **camp** in the village ask at Dermot Hogan's shop; the site is the very public patch of green opposite (no showers). Alternatively, you can stay at *The Cottage Hostel*, Lissylisheen, four and a half miles away, a small, charming place with very limited facilities run by an organic gardening enthusiast (no phone; camping also available); ask locally for directions.

Leamaneh Castle and Carran

Heading east from Kilfenora you pass **Leamaneh Castle**, a fifteenth-century O'Brien stronghold, adjoining which is a four-storey building with mullioned and transomed windows (c.1640). The area north of here is littered with ancient remains. Take the Ballyvaughan road north at Leamaneh Castle and you will pass the **Poulnabrone Dolmen**, the most famous of the Burren's portal dolmens, dating from 2500 BC. It's a marvellous place at dusk, when the fading light turns the surrounding fields of stone a vibrant lilac. Alternatively, continue east from Leamaneh Castle and take the left turn north just before Killinaboy. The lane rises steeply through hazel hedgerows and brings you up to a limestone plateau. You will pass two signposted wedge tombs on your left and, after another mile or so, come to **Caher Commaun**, a ninth-century triple ring fort. You may have to pay a small fee to walk across the farmer's field. From here, you can wend your way north through a tangle of roads to minuscule **CARRAN**. The hamlet's prime feature is a turlough: in summer it appears as a meadow, in winter a lake. Overlooking the turlough are *Clare's Rock*, a brand new **hostel** (☎065/708 9129), and *Croide na boirne* bar and restaurant (☎065/708 9109), which serves probably the only Burren-themed bar food in the world. Look out for their speciality, *burren mionáin*, organically-reared kid. From Carran the road north leads down to Bealaclugga (Bell Harbour) and nearby Corcomroe (see p.337).

Killinaboy and Corofin

Follow the road east from Leamaneh Castle and you'll reach **KILLINABOY**, where a ruined eleventh- to fourteenth-century church has a striking Sheila na gig over the doorway – a carving of a naked woman with grotesquely exaggerated genitalia (sheila means "femininity", and gig "breast") which was probably some kind of fertility symbol. They're more usually found above castle doorways, and it may be that its siting here was intended as a warning against the sins of the flesh. There are a handful of pleasant **B&Bs** in the area: try *Cottage View* (☎065/683 7662; ③) or *Fergus View* (☎065/683 7606; ③).

From Killinaboy the road winds down into the more substantial village of **COROFIN**, consisting of a handful of houses and a string of cheerful pubs. It makes an excellent base from which to explore the Burren or to enjoy fishing in the abundance of little lakes hereabouts. Lough Inchiquin is particularly scenic and, if you are driving, a detour around the lake and up Clifden Hill affords spectacular views. The village is also home to the **Clare Heritage Centre** (April–Oct daily 10am–6pm; Nov–March Mon–Fri 9am–5pm; ☎065/683 7955), which portrays the traumatic period of Irish history between 1800 and 1860 and fills in the horrors that the Bunratty Folk Park omits: famine, disease, emigration and the issue of land tenure. It also has a genealogy service for those with origins in the county and holds details of over half a million people, McMahon, Macnamara, Moloney and O'Brien being the most common names. If you want to research your roots in detail, write to the centre a few months before your trip and find out as much as possible before you visit (names, dates, marriages, deaths, location, occupation, parish etc). An initial search costs around £40–60, a full one £100–150. Alternatively, the new library here is freely available: a morning spent poring over records will probably convince you just why it's worth paying a trained genealogist to do it for you.

You can stay here at the friendly, family-run *Corofin Village Hostel* (IHH; ☎065/683 7683), with its pleasant **campsite**. Traditional music is dished up with tea and brown bread in summer at the village's pleasantly relaxed *teach cheoil* (music house) in the main street, and there is also bound to be **music** on in one of the pubs most nights during the summer. *Bofey Quinn's* does excellent **bar food** – try their Corofin Smokies, a kind of smoked fish and potato hot pot. For something more upmarket, head for *The Gairdín Restaurant*, Market Street (☎065/683 7425) whose menu offers guinea fowl, veal, and quail. **Bikes** can be rented from the hostel, **boats** from Burke's shop.

travel details

Trains

Ennis to: Dublin (1–2 daily; 3hr 5min), Limerick (1–2 daily; 50min).

Buses

Doolin to: Galway (summer 2–4 daily; 1hr 35min).

Ennis to: Doolin (summer 2–3 daily; 1hr 20min); Galway (summer 2–4 daily; 1hr 35min); Kilkee (summer 2–3 daily; 1hr 10min); Lahinch (summer 2–3 daily; 45min); Limerick (summer 9–17 daily); Lisdoonvarna (summer 1–2 daily; 1hr 15min); Shannon Airport (11–17 daily; 45min).

Limerick to: Doolin (1–3 daily summer; 1hr 40min–2hr 20min); Ennis (6–9 daily; 1hr); Killaloe (Mon–Sat 1 daily); Shannon (16 daily; 45min).

GALWAY, MAYO AND ROSCOMMON

Galway, Mayo and Roscommon mark a distinct change in the west of Ireland scene. Coming from the south, County Galway may at first seem a continuation of what has gone before in Clare and Kerry. And Galway city is in some ways the west coast town par excellence – an exceptionally enjoyable, free-spirited sort of place, and a gathering point for young travellers. But once you get beyond the city things start to change. The landscape is dramatically harsher and far less populous, and there are fewer visitors, too.

Lough Corrib, which divides Galway in two, delineates another dramatic split in the landscape of the county, this time between east and west, inland and coast. To the east of the lake lies tame, fertile land which people have farmed for centuries, while to the west lies **Connemara**, a magnificently wild terrain of wind and rock and water. The **Aran Islands**, in the mouth of Galway Bay, resemble Connemara both in their elemental beauty and in their culture; the Galway *Gaeltacht* – areas where Irish is still spoken – comprises the islands, Iar-Chonnacht and some scattered communities in north Connemara and Joyce country. While it can't compete with the rest of the county, **east Galway**'s medieval monastic sites are well worth taking in as you pass through. Again, **Galway city** straddles the divide. A bridging point both physically and culturally, it's a fishing port, an historic city and now the focus of an energetic social and artistic scene.

If you carry on up the coast you'll enter **County Mayo**, where the landscape softens somewhat but is still relatively free of tourists. The pilgrimage centre of **Knock** and the attractions of historic towns like **Westport** aside, it's the coast which is once again the main draw. Physically, it's as exciting and rugged as any in the Republic, and far less exploited, though the downside is that facilities for travellers are relatively thin on the ground. An exception is **Achill**, the largest Irish offshore island and popular holiday resort, which provides both some of the most spectacular cliffs in the country and caters well for travellers. **County Roscommon** is entirely landlocked and less visited still. There are few real excitements, and the land is for the most part flat and low lying; nevertheless, the fine detail of this landscape, scattered with small lakes and large houses, has a slow charm. There are places that merit a look as you pass through, and in the extreme north, around **Lough Key**, there's some very attractive scenery indeed.

ACCOMMODATION PRICE CODES

Throughout this book, prices of hotels, guesthouses and B&Bs have been graded with the codes below, according to what you can expect to pay for a double room in high season. For more details on accommodation, see p. 29.

① Under £26	④ £40–55	⑦ £90–110
② £26–33	⑤ £55–70	⑧ £110–130
③ £33–40	⑥ £70–90	⑨ Over £130

COUNTY GALWAY

County Galway splits into clearly identifiable areas, each with strong distinctive characteristics. **Galway city** is the great social magnet of the region, a lively place to visit any time of the year. **Connemara** – a term loosely applied to encompass the west of the county – has the best of the scenery, with vast open expanses of bog, exhilarating mountains and superb white-sand beaches. Equally appealing, the **Aran Islands** combine raw landscape with some of the most exciting pre-Christian sites in Europe – and considerable legends. The east of the county is far less compelling; flat and less inspiring, it nonetheless does hold medieval ruins of interest. The area around south Galway Bay, nestling between the **Burren** and the water, at times has some of the tantalizing mercurial quality of north Clare.

Galway city

The city of **GALWAY**, folk capital of the west, has a vibrancy and hedonism that make it unique. People come here with energies primed for enjoyment – the drink, the music, the "crack" – and it can be a difficult place to leave. University College Galway guarantees a high proportion of young people in term time, maintained in summer by the attractions of the city's festivals. This youthful **energy** is an important part of Galway's identity. Galway has become a playground for disaffected Dubliners, and folksy young Europeans return each year with an almost religious devotion. The city commands a vigorous loyalty: try criticizing the place and you're liable to find yourself in a fight.

As is the case with many other Irish cities, Galway is experiencing a surge of economic **growth**. Constant renovation is in progress in the small and crowded city centre, and during the summer it has the energy of a boom town, with an expanding number of shops and restaurants to cater for the increase in fashionable visitors and students. The downside of this is the huge amount of property development galloping ahead in the city centre, threatening to knock all character out of the place, though, for the time being at least, Galway retains its human scale.

Prosperity allows a vigorous independence from Dublin, mirrored in the artistic dynamism of the city. It's a focus for the traditional **music** of Galway and Clare – Galway's status as an old fishing town on the mythical west coast adding a certain potency – and there's strong interest in drama. The new theatre here reflects a renewed sense of civic and artistic optimism. At no time is the energy of Galway more evident than during its **festivals**, especially the Galway Arts Festival during the last two weeks in July, when practitioners of theatre, music, poetry and the visual arts create a rich cultural jamboree. It's a great time to be in the city, but be prepared for a squeeze on accommodation. The festival is swiftly followed by the **Galway Races** (the week before the Irish bank holiday – which usually makes it the first week in August), when accommodation is again at a premium. At the end of September, the Galway Oyster Festival completes the annual round.

Some history

Galway originated as a crossing point on the River Corrib, giving an access to Connemara denied further north by the lough. It was seized by the **Norman** family of De Burgos in the thirteenth century and developed as a strong Anglo-Norman colony, ruled by an oligarchy of fourteen families. They maintained control despite continual attacks by the bellicose Connacht clans, the most ferocious of which were the O'Flaherties. To the O'Flahertie motto "Fortuna Favet Fortibus" (Fortune Favours the

Downpatrick
Head
Ballycastle
Killala
Bay
Killala
Ballina
Crossmolina
Lough
Conn
Pontoon
Lough
Cullin
Foxford
Swinford
Charlestown
Castlebar
Knock
Lough Gara
Boyle
FOREST
PARK
Lough Key
Keadew
Leitrim
Carrick-on-Shannon
Frenchpark
Elphin
R O S C O M M O N
Ballyhaunis
River Suck
Castlerea
Tulsk
Strokestown
Claremorris
Lough
Cara
Ballymoe
Ballinrobe
Dunmore
Roscommon
Lanesborough
M A Y O
Cong
Lough
Corrib
Headford
Tuam
Mount
Bellew
Athleague
Ballyforan
Lough
Ree
Athlone
Oughterard
G A L W A Y
Spiddle Salthill
Barna
Galway
Athenry
Bullaun
Aughrim
Ballinasloe
Clarinbridge
Loughrea
Doorus
Kinvora
Thoor
Ballylee
Portumna
Birr
Gort
Kilmacduagh
River Shannon
SLIEVE AUGHTY MOUNTAINS
Sligo
Castlebar
Ennis
Longford
N16
N59
N7
N4
N5
N17
N60
N84
N5
N61
R368
N4
N63
N56
N6
R355
R356
N62
R353
N18
N66

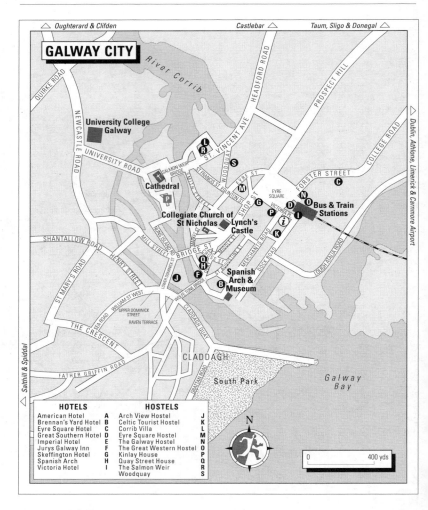

GALWAY CITY

HOTELS		HOSTELS	
American Hotel	**A**	Arch View Hostel	**J**
Brennan's Yard Hotel	**B**	Celtic Tourist Hostel	**K**
Eyre Square Hotel	**C**	Corrib Villa	**L**
Great Southern Hotel	**D**	Eyre Square Hostel	**M**
Imperial Hotel	**E**	The Galway Hostel	**N**
Jurys Galway Inn	**F**	The Great Western Hostel	**O**
Skeffington Hotel	**G**	Kinlay House	**P**
Spanish Arch	**H**	Quay Street House	**Q**
Victoria Hotel	**I**	The Salmon Weir	**R**
		Woodquay	**S**

Strong), the citizens of Galway responded with a plea inscribed over the long-vanished city gates: "From the fury of the O'Flaherties, good Lord deliver us."

Galway was granted a charter and **city status** in 1484 by Richard III and was proudly loyal to the English Crown for the next two hundred years. During this time the city prospered, developing a flourishing trade with the Continent, especially Spain. However, its loyalty to the monarch ensured that when Cromwellian forces arrived in 1652 the place was besieged without mercy for ninety days. It was Cromwell who coined the originally derisory term "the fourteen tribes of Galway"; this didn't worry the Irish, who returned the disdain by proudly adopting the name as a title. The city went into a decline from the mid-seventeenth century onwards and only recently started to revive.

The history of the **Claddagh**, a fishing village that existed long before Galway was founded alongside it, is quite distinct from that of the city proper. An Irish-speaking village of thatched cottages, the Claddagh was fiercely independent, having its own laws, customs and chief, and it remained a proud, close-knit community long after the cottages had gone. Boat-building skills are still passed down through generations, though of course this work has massively declined, and the old vessels known as Galway hookers are now used more by boating enthusiasts than for fishing. It is from here that the famous **Claddagh ring** originates, worn by Irish people all over the world. It shows two hands clasping a heart surmounted by a crown and represents love, friendship and respect. It's worn with the heart pointing towards the fingertip when betrothed, the other way when married.

Arrival, information and accommodation

You're almost bound to arrive in Galway at **Eyre Square**, also known as the J.F. Kennedy Memorial Park. The **Bus Éireann** and train **stations** are off the south side of the square, while the **tourist office** (May Mon–Sat 9am–5.45pm; June Mon–Sat 9am–6.45pm; July–Aug daily 8.30am–7.45pm; Sept–April Mon–Fri 9am–5.45pm, Sat 9am–12.45pm; ☎091/563081) is just off the southern corner at the junction of Victoria Place and Merchant's Road. It runs walking tours of the city which depart daily at 11.30am and cost £3.50 (☎091/794435). If you arrive by plane you can catch a bus from **Carnmore Airport** into the city centre at 1.25pm (Mon–Sat); a bus from Galway bus station to the airport departs at 12.50pm (Mon–Sat). The journey costs around £2.25 each way. A taxi to the airport costs around £7 with Corrib Taxis (☎091/564444).

Accommodation

Accommodation is plentiful in Galway. **B&Bs** are concentrated in the centre and eastern side of town, with an abundance of smart options along Father Griffin Road – about eight minutes' walk from Eyre Square. The tourist office will make your booking for a £1 fee – not a bad idea at peak times. There are also a large number of **hostels** in Galway, but they get very full during festival time and throughout August – ring ahead, arrive early or, best of all, book ahead. We would advise ignoring the touts at the station, and only using the hostels which are either listed here or are approved by the tourist office. The range of **hotels** is rather limited and most are expensive, though a few budget options have opened lately.

You can **camp** at *Ballyloughane Caravan Park* on Dublin Road (☎091/55338; May–Sept) and at several in Salthill, the pleasantest being *Hunter's Silver Strand Caravan and Camping Park*, about four miles west on the coast road (☎091/92452 or 92040; Easter–Sept).

Hotels

American Hotel, Eyre Square (☎091/561300). Adequate hotel in the centre of town. ⑤.

Ardilaun House Hotel, Taylor's Hill (☎091/521433). Between Galway and Salthill, an excellent hotel with first-rate leisure facilities and restaurant. ⑦.

Brennans Yard Hotel, Lower Merchants Rd (☎091/568166). Not far from the Spanish Arch, this hotel boasts fine rooms in a tastefully converted warehouse. ⑦.

Corrib Great Southern Hotel, Dublin Rd, Renmore (☎091/755281). Large modern hotel complex overlooking Galway Bay with crèche facilities in summer. ⑨.

Eyre Square Hotel, Forster St, off Eyre Square (☎091/569633). New hotel just off Eyre Square with first-rate service and facilities. ⑥.

Great Southern Hotel, Eyre Square (☎091/564041). Rambling Victorian establishment, taking up one side of the square, with a rooftop pool and spacious rooms. ⑨.

Hotel Ibis, Headford Rd (☎091/771166). Modern hotel with excellent flat room rates; £49.50 for a room that sleeps two adults and two children. ④.

Imperial Hotel, Eyre Square (☎091/563033). Not the best-value hotel in town, but the location is ideal. ⑤.

Jameson's Hotel, Upper Salthill (☎091/528666) A value-for-money hotel with a fine restaurant and good wheelchair access. ⑥.

Jurys Galway Inn, Quay St (☎091/566444). A friendly modern hotel with family rooms. Breakfast not included. ③.

Skeffington Arms Hotel, Eyre Square (☎091/563173). An attractive cheaper alternative to the *Great Southern*, with a popular bar. ⑥.

Spanish Arch, Quay St, (☎091/569191). A hotel right in the heart of the action with individually designed, period-themed rooms, though those facing onto the street can be noisy. ⑧.

Victoria Hotel, Eyre Square (☎091/567433). Almost opposite the tourist office, this elegant new hotel is probably the best option around Eyre Square. ⑥.

B&Bs

Corrib Haven, 107 Upper Newcastle Rd (☎091/524171). Clean and friendly house; all rooms non-smoking. ③.

Crookhaven, 96 Father Griffin Rd (☎091/589019). Fine place with en-suite rooms and TVs. ②.

Inishmore, 109 Father Griffin Rd (☎091/582639). A little pricier than most places in this area, though still good value. ③.

Joan Sullivan's, 46 Prospect Hill (☎091/566324). A friendly option just off Eyre Square. ③.

Petra, 201 Laurel Park, Newcastle Rd (☎091/521844). Family-friendly modern house with good parking. ③.

St Martin's, 2 Nuns Island Rd (☎091/568286). The owners could not be more obliging and the location is ideal with the house backing onto the Corrib River. Highly recommended. ③.

The Swallow, 98 Father Griffin Rd (☎091/589073). Family-friendly B&B with fine rooms and decent breakfasts. ③.

Villa Maruea, 94 Father Griffin Rd (☎091/589033). Value-for-money B&B with parking. ③.

Villa Nova, 40 Newcastle Rd (☎091/524849). Quiet bungalow off the main road with good parking. ③.

Hostels

Arch View Hostel, 1 Upper Dominick St (☎091/586661). Has seen better days, though the atmosphere is good and it's close to the excellent *Roisin Dubh* bar.

Celtic Tourist Hostel, Queen St (IHO; ☎091/566606). Around the corner from the tourist office, this hostel has few frills but it does have a large kitchen and often has beds when all the other hostels are full.

Corrib Villa, 4 Waterside (IHH; ☎091/562892). Large old-style hostel that's making efforts at refurbishment.

Eyre Square Hostel, Eyre St (☎091/568432). Basically okay hostel, though it's a little cramped.

Galway Hostel, Frenchville Lane, Eyre Square (IHH; ☎091/566959). Opposite the station. A good, friendly budget option, with twin and 4-bedded rooms available.

Great Western House, Frenchville Lane, Eyre Square (IHH; ☎091/561139). Also opposite the station, a very smart, comfortable hostel, with disabled access. Four-bedded, twin, double and family rooms available, plus laundry, bike shed, TV rooms, sauna. Takes credit cards. No curfew.

Kinlay House, Merchants Rd, Eyre Square, opposite the tourist office (IHH; ☎091/565244). Purpose-built hostel, with double rooms available; clean and efficiently run. Price includes continental breakfast, bed linen and towel. No curfew.

Mary Ryan's, 4 Beechmont Rd, Highfield Park (☎091/523303). Very popular small hostel a little way from the centre. Mostly small 2- or 3-bedded rooms. Take #2 bus from Eyre Square to Taylor's Hill Convent, cross the road and walk up the lane into the estate; it's to your right. Summer only.

Quay Street House, 10 Quay St (IHH; ☎091/568644). A pleasant place; light and airy rooms – also 4-bedded and twin/double – well-equipped kitchen and laundry. Price includes bed linen. Credit-card bookings accepted.

The Salmon Weir Hostel, St Vincent's Ave, Woodquay (☎091/561133 or 522653). A small, friendly, comfortable hostel with laundry facilities and a bike shed.

Woodquay Hostel, 23–24 Woodquay (☎091/562618). A little cramped, though near to town.

The City

Galway's centre is defined by the **River Corrib**. Issuing from the lough, it thunders under the Salmon Weir Bridge and wraps itself round the full body of the city, meeting the lively **Shop and Quay streets** areas at Wolfe Tone Bridge, where it flows into the bay. The quaint old shops and bars that give Galway its villagey appeal are being squeezed on all sides by ugly postmodern facades and bone-headed business development; the area around the bridge has to be one of the most architecturally abused spots in Ireland. Still, Galway is a robust city and somehow its charm pulls through. Over the bridge is the Claddagh, and about a mile and a half west of that is **Salthill**, Galway's commercial seaside town. The **CLADDAGH** now appears as a small area of modest housing, strangely flanked by a crusting of luxury apartments, but it's worth getting to know for some of its excellent bars and cheap eats. From any of the bridges you can wander beside the pleasant walkways of river and canals, checking out the industrial archeology, watching salmon make their way upstream, anglers fly-fishing in the centre of the city and cormorants diving for eels, while gawky herons splash through watery suburban back gardens. At the harbour, a walk out around the stone pier places the city in its impressive setting, with a level coastline stretching to the west and the eerie Burren hills washed and etched in half-tones across the bay.

   Eyre Square is an almost inevitable starting point. This small park, set in the middle of a traffic interchange, is one of the places to which everyone seems to gravitate, the other being the Shop and Quay streets area. It's used as a performance space during festivals, and outdoor sessions can start up here at any time, the relaxed atmosphere lending itself to improvisation. Visually, though, the place is a mess. A sentimental statue of the writer Pádraic Ó Conaire, a seventeenth-century doorway, a couple of cannon from the Crimean War and a clutter of disused flagpoles all detract from what should form the focus of the square: Eamonn O'Donnell's splendid sculpture, whose arcs of rusted metal and gushing white fountains evoke the sails of the Galway hookers and the city's nautical history. The distinctive **town houses** of the merchant class – remnants of which are lightly littered around the city – also hark back to the prosperity of maritime Galway and its sense of civic dignity, with their finely carved doorways, windows and stone slabs bearing armorial carving. The **Browne doorway** in Eyre Square is one such monument, a bay window and doorway with the coats of arms of the Browne and Lynch families, dated 1627. Before you leave the square, it's worth calling into the **Eyre Square Centre**, as the building of this shopping mall in the late 1980s revealed impressive sections of medieval city walls, and these are now preserved within the new complex.

   Just about the finest medieval town house in Ireland is **Lynch's Castle** in Shop Street (leading off from the southwest of the square), now housing the Allied Irish Bank. The Lynchs were Galway's most prominent family for three hundred years. A local story relates that in 1493 James Lynch Fitzstephen, mayor of the town, found his own son guilty of the jealous murder of a Spanish visitor, and that such was the popularity of the lad that no one in the town would take on the job of hangman – so the boy's father did it himself. The house, dating from the fifteenth century, has a smooth stone facade decorated with carved panels, medieval gargoyles and a lion devouring another animal. Step inside for a detailed history of the building and its heraldry. The similarly styled **Lynch's Window** is on Market Street (further down Shop Street and to the right) just outside the **Collegiate Church of St Nicholas**. The largest medieval church in Ireland, it was built in 1320 and enlarged in the next two centuries. The building – dedicated to St Nicholas of Myra, patron saint of sailors – is also decorated with finely chiselled carvings and gargoyles. Continuing south along Market Street, and turning off into Bowling Green Lane, you'll come across the house that **Nora Barnacle**, wife of James Joyce, lived in. It's now been converted into a small museum (Mon–Sat; £1) and contains, among other Joycean memorabilia, copies of the couples' letters.

For arguably the best sense of medieval Galway make your way through the punters and the pints up to the top floor of **Busker Browne's Bar**, Cross Street (a short walk south from Nora Barnacle's house). The upper room was the meeting place of the tribes of Galway, and the building has served as a barracks and a Dominican convent.

Down by the harbour stands the **Spanish Arch**; more evocative in name than in reality, it's a sixteenth-century structure that was used to protect galleons unloading wine and rum. Behind it is a fine piece of medieval wall, and next door is the uninspiring **Galway Museum** (daily May–Sept 10am–1pm & 2.15–5.15pm), where the only things of real interest are old photographs of the Claddagh and a few examples of sixteenth- and seventeenth-century stone carving from around the city.

From the Spanish Arch you can take a pleasant walk north along a riverside path and across the Salmon Weir Bridge to the **Cathedral of Our Lady Assumed into Heaven and St Nicholas**. Commissioned about thirty years ago and in hideous contrast to the Collegiate College, its copper dome seeps green stains down ugly limestone walls. Inside, the horrors continue in a senseless jumble of stone, mahogany and Connemara marble. It's so remarkably awful that it demands attention, and viewed from a distance its sheer bulk does achieve a grandeur of sorts. Nearby, across the bridge, the clean lines of the Neoclassical courthouse are now mirrored in the municipal theatre opposite – an assured symbol of contemporary Galway's civic pride, and surprisingly conservative for a post-colonial nation.

On the road behind the cathedral is **University College Galway**, a mock-Tudor imitation of an Oxbridge college, which was opened in 1849 at a time when the majority of people in Connacht were starving. The university has the dubious distinction of having conferred an honorary degree on Ronald Reagan. More importantly, it is now UNESCO's base for an archive of spoken material in all Celtic languages, and summer courses for foreign students are held annually in July and August.

The river

If you want to get out onto the water, at nearby **Woodquay** (cross the Salmon Weir bridge at the cathedral, turn left and walk a little way along Waterside Street) you can either rent a rowing boat (May–Sept) or take the Lough Corrib river cruise (year round 2.30pm & 4.30pm; £5), which goes five miles up the river through flat countryside punctuated by derelict castles, out into the open expanse of the lough.

Salthill and the beaches

Beyond the Claddagh lies **SALTHILL**, Galway's seaside resort, complete with amusement arcades, discos, seasonal cafés and a fairground – as well as scores more hotels and B&Bs. Salthill's **tourist office** is on the front (June Mon–Sat 9am–6pm, July & Aug daily 9am–8.15pm; ☎563081 ext 48/49). The huge **Leisureland** amusement complex is used as a venue for big concerts and also has a swimming pool (summer daily 8am–10pm). **Lower Salthill** has a long promenade with a series of unspectacular but safe and sandy beaches. Even on a hot summer's day it's never so busy as to be oppressive, and its great asset is the view over a glittering expanse of water to the Burren. West of here, **Upper Salthill** is a mess of a suburb that sits around its golf course, despoiled by huge billboards and caravan parks.

Probably the nicest of the sandy beaches immediately west of Galway City is the small one at **Silver Strand**, nestling beneath a grassy headland about three miles out of the centre. Here, in a small inlet backed by a copse, is also the area's pleasantest **campsite**, signposted *Hunters* (see p.345). *The Twelve Pins* pub, around a mile west of the site, is renowned for seafood. Galway's other special beach is **Ballyloughrun**, east of the city; this, too, has a campsite alongside and can be reached by taking the public footpath along by the railway line, or by either the Renmore or the Merlyn Park bus from the station.

Eating, drinking and entertainment

You'll find a good range of food on offer in Galway – from hot dogs to cajun and Thai – with some particulary upmarket Continental **restaurants** and great seafood. For day-time eating, there are plenty of cafés and bars offering good-value meals and snacks.

If the "crack" has eluded you so far on your travels, Galway is where you're going to find it. The **bars** are the social lungs of this town, and even the most abstemious travellers are going to find themselves sucked in. **Traditional music** is performed in many of them; some of it will be depressingly over-amplified, but you can hit a great session on any day of the week and at almost any time of the day during the summer months. The bars of Shop and Quay streets are especially good, as are those over the bridge around Dominick Street. You can't really go far wrong; those listed on p.351 are popular in the main with a young crowd, but there are plenty more well worth exploring. Look out for *The Edge*, Galway's free listings magazine, and the *Galway Advertiser* (out Thurs).

There are numerous **clubs** and **discos** in Galway and Salthill – the latter easy enough to walk back from, though not advisable if you are on your own. As ever, clubs change frequently; to find out what's on look out for flyers round town, and for concessions being handed out in bars. Note, too, that clubs can stop serving at 1.30am, and generally wind down at around 2am. The **gay scene** moves around, so call the information line (see "Listings", p.353) for up-to-the-minute information, and look out, too, for Liberation posters. Gay clubbing usually happens on Sundays.

Cafés

A plethora of new cafés has appeared recently in the centre of Galway. Those listed here are chosen for their atmosphere as well as for their food.

Apostasy, Dominick St. A great alternative to the numerous pubs in the area, with backgammon and chess and walls decorated with quotations from Yeats, Beckett and Joyce.

Cobblestone Café, off Cross Street. Continental-style café with tablecloths and fresh flowers. Try the excellent soups.

The Hungry Grass, Cross St. Wholesome sandwiches amid the hustle and bustle.

Java-Art of Coffee, Abbeygate St. Good coffee, great music and late hours makes this a perfect place to hang out, especially after late-night dancing.

Café du Journal, Quay St. Squeeze through a blur of smoke for a caffeine-heads' nirvana. Numerous blends served: Italian, Spanish and cajun. Also does omelettes, croissants and desserts; newspapers to read. Till 10.30pm.

The Latin Quarter, Quay St. Laid-back café serving possibly the best salads in town.

Left Bank Café, Dominick St. Good sandwiches at reasonable prices.

Mocha Beans, Cross St. Roasted coffee and home-baked pastries.

Restaurants

The Brasserie, Middle St (☎091/561610). Pizza, tacos and ribs. Mon–Sat 12.30–10pm.

The Bridge Mills Restaurant, O'Brien's Bridge (☎091/566231). Relaxed licensed restaurant and coffee shop in beautifully restored mill, complete with working mill wheel. Homemade cakes, chowders, sandwiches and lunches (£5); evening menu £8–15. Organic produce; vegetarian dishes always available. Till 10.30pm in summer.

Busker Browne's Bar, Cross St. Original rough medieval stonework, pitched Gothic roof and floor upon floor of alcoves for comfy eating and drinking (see "Bars and music" opposite). Bar serves salads and open sandwiches – crab, salmon and oysters. Till 7pm.

Branagan's, Upper Abbeygate St. Restaurant with varied menu, popular with groups.

An Chistin, West William St. Popular with students for its cheap all-day breakfasts.

Couch Potatas, Upper Abbeygate St. Or 101 ways to serve a potato, with all manner of sauces and stuffings – and a good selection for vegetarians.

Da Tong Noodle House, Middle St. One of the few authentic noodle houses in Ireland, this is a real treat. Apart from the noodles there are also some excellent soups.

Doc's Diner, New Dock St. Cheap all-day breakfasts.

Eddie Rocket's, Eglinton St. American diner, offering hot dogs, chicken wings, shakes and burgers. Very vinyl. Handy for late-night munchies. Till 3am.

Fat Freddy's, Quay St. Great atmosphere, great pizzas; one of the cheapest places to get an evening meal.

Food For Thought, in the tourist office and also in Lower Abbeygate St. Cheap wholefood and vegetarian snacks, light meals and something that sounds like a misnomer, the "healthy Irish breakfast".

Galway Bakery Company, 7 Williamsgate St. Coffee shop and restaurant serving good-value breakfasts, lunches and dinners. Till 10pm.

Get Stuffed Olive, St Anthony's Place, Woodquay. Tucked away down a small alley off Woodquay, this café-restaurant is well worth searching out for its great atmosphere, high-quality vegetarian food and service.

The Home Plate, Mary St. Café serving tasty pitta, pasta, Thai meals, and a clutch of vegetarian options. Around £3.50–4.50. Mon–Sat till 8pm.

Hooker Jimmy's, Spanish Arch (☎091/568351). If you want value-for-money seafood then this is definitely the place.

Java's, 17 Upper Abbeygate St. Excellent coffee shop serving a dozen blends, plus scones, salads, croissants. Daily till 4am. Also see "Bars and music" opposite.

The Kebab House, 4 Dominick St. Takeaway offering delicious, sizeable helpings. Daily noon–3am.

Kirwans Lane, Creative Cuisine, Kirwans Lane, off Cross Street. Good service and food in a chic two-storey modern interior. Main courses around £15; no children under 7.

Le Wine Bar, Spanish Arch (☎091/561114). Authentic French wine bar and charcuterie. Wines from small vineyards sold by the glass or bottle; affordable light meals from an imaginative menu – where else in Ireland could you savour sea urchin soup or smoked eels on toast? Food till 11pm daily, wine till later.

Macken's, The Cornstore, Middle St. Self-service café: an excellent spot for a multitude of breakfasts, lunches and afternoon teas.

McDonagh's Seafood Bar, 22 Quay St (☎091/565001). A must for seafood; nip in for a thick and creamy chowder, or stay for a full meal – nobody minds what you order, you get the feeling that someone actually wants to feed you. Also excellent English-style fish and chips. Daily till 12.30am.

MacSwiggans, Eyre St. Good lunchtime pub grub for around £5; and a lively, popular young hangout in the evenings.

Nimmo's, Long Walk, Spanish Arch (☎091/563565). An imaginative Continental menu with plenty of seafood and organic produce (lunch around £5; eves from £15). Closed Mon eve.

Pierre's, 8 Quay St (☎091/566066). A haven away from the bedlam that can be Quay Street, this restaurant has a relaxed atmosphere and fine food. Does an excellent pre-theatre menu for £7.95.

The Round Table, 6 High St. Dishes up huge traditional lunches around midday – roasts, pies and gravy etc, in a wholly unpretentious setting. £3.50–4.50.

Sev'nth Heaven, Courthouse Lane, Quay St (☎091/563838). Popular restaurant/bar serving cajun, Tex-Mex, Italian and vegetarian food. Delicious 3-course lunch £5. Daily noon–midnight. Regular late-night blues, country and folk music 3–4 nights a week.

Strawberry Fields, Cross St. Gum-pink diner for the sweet-toothed – waffles and homemade ice cream; locals reckon their Salthill outfit is even better.

Tulsi, Buttermilk Walk, Middle Abbey St (☎091/564831). The city's best Indian with excellent vegetarian food.

Bars and music

An Púcán, Forster St. Popular with boozy, tub-thumping tourists. Can be fun.

An Tobar, Mainguard St. Small non-smoking bar, good for relaxing in.

Aras na Gael, 45 Dominick St. Irish traditional music and folk theatre run and frequented by Irish-speaking enthusiasts. Admission is usually free, though during the summer it has special programmes costing £3.

The Blue Note, Sea Rd. Highly laid-back and groovy bar: acid and mainstream jazz.

Brennans, New Dock St. A no-nonsense drinkers' bar.

Busker Browne's Bar, Cross St. Frighteningly popular. Traditional Irish music three nights a week during summer; jazz on a Sunday lunchtime.

Calico Jack's, Sea Rd. Another great place for traditional Irish sessions.

Cooke's, *Thatch Pub*, Cooke's Corner. Traditional pub with great pints.

The Crane, Sea Rd. Busy bar with great traditional sessions.

Java's, 17 Upper Abbeygate St. Mellow jazz fusion, folk and traditional. Till 4am; £1 cover charge.

The King's Head, Shop St. Diddle and stomping, traditional music. Lunchtime comedy and theatre.

Le Graal, Dominick St. A bistro-brasserie with fun, upbeat atmosphere, popular with Galway's gay community.

The Long Walk, Spanish Arch. A lively wine bar near the river, often with live music.

Mick Taylors, Dominick St. Traditional bar – and values. You might catch the occasional session.

Monroe's, Dominick St. Good for live bands: rock, blues, cajun, washboards – more or less anything that can pass for rhythm. Seven nights a week plus Sun lunchtime.

Neachtains, 17 Cross St. The jewel in the Galway pub crown. Unlike other older pubs it has resisted the temptation to remove its traditional interior of small rooms and snugs to maximize profits. If with a group, get there early, commandeer a snug and sit tight till last orders.

O'Ché's, Francis St. Wine bar and café with occasional live performances.

O'Riada's, High St/Cross St. A newly-converted pub with unusual decor, frequented by an eclectic crowd.

The Quays, Quay St. Traditional bar; not the greatest spot to drink all night, but worth calling in for a heritage pint early evening. Usually heaving by 9.30pm. Live music.

Roísín Dubh, 9 Upper Dominick St. Lively bar with folk, traditional, cajun or world music nightly.

Sally Long's, 33 Upper Abbeygate St. Bikers' pub – rock, metal. Live bands Fri & Sat. Worth a look for Last Supper mural of rock heroes.

The Snug, Shop St. Worth checking out at weekends for its traditional music.

Clubs and discos

Benley's, Prospect Hill. Pub until midnight, disco afterwards; if you're in before 11pm you won't pay an admission charge.

The Castle, Salthill. Dance music, house and hip-hop; ravey atmosphere.

Central Park, Upper Abbeygate St. Bit of a cattle market; commercial dance and chart music.

GPO, Eglinton St. One of Galway's best. Young, trendy crowd; acid jazz, funk, ska and soul – all highly danceable – plus live bands. Look out for the Fri night **comedy club**, *The Funny Baie* – acts from 9pm; your £4 entrance sees you through to the club later.

Oasis, Salthill. Techno club.

Vagabond's, Salthill. Popular, busy but relaxed, studenty club with two dance floors. Soul, blues, reggae (Thurs); grunge (Fri); dance music and more grunge downstairs (Sat); indie bands (Sun).

Warwick Hotel, Salthill. Older studenty venue – upper 20s. No dress hang-ups. Danceable, offbeat soul.

Wicked Fish, Church Lane. Trance and hard house on Weds.

The arts

Galway is experiencing a real growth in artistic activity, and it's at its most vibrant during **The Galway Arts Festival** (last two weeks in July; check with the tourist office for details of the Festival Box Office location). There's plenty to detain you year round too: Galway's the home of the versatile **Druid Theatre Company** (☎091/568617), in Chapel Lane, off Quay Street; a relatively young company, it produces six new plays a year – many of them new Irish works – and undertakes extensive tours. If you're lucky enough to be in Galway city when they're on, book a ticket in advance, as they play to packed houses.

Look out, too, for **The Punchbag Theatre Company**, based in the city down by the quays (☎091/565422), committed to performing new Irish plays along with the classics and hosting touring companies, live bands, readings and comedy. **An Taibhdhearc na Gaillimhe** in Middle Street (☎091/562024) is an Irish-language theatre that puts on an annual summer show of traditional singing, music and drama. The **Galway Arts Centre**, Nun's Island, off Mill Street, is used as a performance space for dance, theatre and music; for bookings, information and visual arts exhibitions call in at 47 Dominick St (☎091/565886). It's also a good place to find out what's going on in the arts locally. Another venue worth checking out is Galway's new municipal theatre.

There are a couple of **commercial art galleries**, too: The Bridge Mills Gallery, O'Brien's Bridge, and The Kenny Gallery, Middle Street. One of the most exciting recent developments in Galway is the **Design Concourse Ireland** (☎091/566016), down a lane off Cross Street, just near *Busker Browne's*. Housed in a beautifully restored medieval town house, it's a permanent exhibition centre promoting quality manufacture and design – mainly domestic – from both the Republic and the North. There's a quiet library café where you can examine the portfolios of the designers on show. Dating from the sixteenth and seventeenth centuries, the building once housed a theatre owned by Humanity Dick (see p.370), and it is said that Wolfe Tone performed here.

Galway is now home to the **Irish Film Board**, and the city's film festival is a part of the Arts Festival; however, during the rest of the year cinema is pretty unappealing.

Listings

Airport Carnmore Airport (flight enquiries ☎091/55569); Aer Árann at Connemara Regional Airport, Inverin (☎091/593034).

Bike rental Europa Bicycles, Earls Island (☎091/563355) opposite the cathedral; £3 a day, £5 for 24 hours, £30 deposit; Rent-a-bike-Ireland from *Great Western Hostel*, Frenchman's Lane (☎091/561139).

Bookshops Charlie Byrne's, The Cornstore, 4 Middle St (☎091/561766), is a good second-hand bookshop (July & Aug Sun till 7pm); Eason's, Shop St, is a major general bookshop with foreign newspapers; Hawkins House, Churchyard Lane, includes comprehensive feminist and Irish-language sections; Needful Things, Cathedral Buildings, Middle St (☎091/565882), has sci-fi, horror, fantasy and cult writers.

Buses Bus Éireann (enquiries ☎091/562000) runs 5–8 buses to Dublin daily (3hr 45min) from as little as £6 single, £8 return – check in advance for special deals. Bikes are carried subject to space – £5 extra each journey. CityLink (☎091/564163 or 564164 & 01/626 6888) also runs a Galway–Dublin service from £5 return. Feda O'Donnell Coaches (☎091/761656 or 075/48114) operates services to Sligo, Donegal and Letterkenny. Nestor Travel (☎091/797144 & 01/832 0094) runs services to Dublin and Dublin Airport from £5 return – depending on the times you travel, bikes are free.

Camping equipment Great Outdoors, Eglinton St (☎091/562869); Radar Stores, Mainguard St (☎091/568810).

Gay and lesbian line (☎091/566134); lesbians Wed 8–10pm; gay men Tues & Thurs 8–10pm.

Horse riding Clonboo Riding School, Clonboo Cross, Corrundulla (near Annaghdown; ☎091/591362).

Hospital University College Hospital, Newcastle Rd (casualty ☎091/563081).

Laundry The Launderette, Sea Rd (Mon–Sat 9am–6pm); Old Malte Laundrette, Old Malte Arcade, High St (Mon–Sat 8.30am–6pm), does service wash only.

Left luggage *Quay Street House Hostel,* 10 Quay St, 50p per bag, or at the station for £1.

Library Galway County Library, Hynes Building, St Augustine St.

Market For more than just fruit and vegetables, try the Sat market around St Nicholas's Church; stalls sell everything from handmade cheeses to sculptured bog oak. There's also a junk and antiques market beneath the medieval walls inside the Eyre Square Centre (Fri & Sat).

Music Mulligan, 5 Middle St (☎091/564961). Traditional, world music, reggae, country, folk and blues on tape, vinyl and CD.

Parking Free in front of the cathedral; elsewhere, buy a disc from a newsagent (20p per hr).

Police, Mill St (☎091/563161).

Sailing Galway Sailing Club, Rinville, Oranmore, five miles from the city (☎091/594527).

Taxi MGM (☎091/757888). Taxi ranks at Eyre Square and Victoria Place.

Train Enquiries ☎091/561444 or 564222. Galway–Dublin (4 daily) from £13 single, from £19 return; Galway–Killarney (2–3 daily) £19 single.

Travel agents USIT, at the New Science Building on the university campus (Mon–Fri 10am–5pm; ☎091/524601), is the best agent for youth and student travel; Corrib Travel, in the centre of town in Cathedral Building, Lower Abbeygate St (☎091/563879 or 568318), deals with Slattery's, Supabus, student flights and youth fares.

Wind-surfing At Rusheen Bay (☎091/557486 or 525295).

East Galway

East Galway cannot rival the spectacular landscapes of west Galway or County Clare, nor their romantic isolation. Nonetheless, to hurry through east Galway without seeing what the place does have to offer would be a mistake. A lot of the land here is low lying and easily cultivable, attributes which made it attractive to earlier settlers. They've left not only a network of roads and villages, but also a wealth of historic remains, particularly medieval monastic sites. The east of the county has nothing like the strong culture of the west, but towards the south, the musical traditions of County Clare wash over the county boundaries and form an important part of the region's culture. And while the landscape is never exciting, some of it is very pleasant, notably the lakesides of **Lough Derg** at **Portumna** and the delightful southern shore of **Galway Bay**, which becomes particularly special where the heights of the Burren of County Clare become a part of the scene.

In contrast to Connemara, transport in east Galway is easy. Galway–Dublin **trains** call at Athenry and Ballinasloe (for train information phone Athenry ☎091/544020 or Ballinasloe ☎0905/42105), and there are Bus Éireann services to surrounding towns. North Galway Club runs a Dublin–Galway bus that picks up in Tuam, Athlone and Ballinasloe. **Hitching** is relatively easy, too, since the area is well served by busy main roads. There is plenty of accommodation throughout the area, in the form of B&Bs and independent and An Óige hostels.

Galway Bay and the south

The countryside in the south of the county, around the southern shores of Galway Bay and on towards Clare, is some of the prettiest in Galway, and was greatly loved by Yeats, Lady Gregory and others associated with the Gaelic League. The main N18 road round the bay from the city is a busy one, passing through the villages of Galway's "**oyster country**" – Oranmore, Clarinbridge and Kilcolgan (where the main road leaves the water to head south towards Ennis) – and bringing plenty of visitors, particularly during the **Oyster Festival** over the second weekend in September. The most famous of the oyster pubs are *Paddy Burke's Oyster Tavern* at **CLARINBRIDGE** and *Moran's of the Weir*, in a beautiful waterside setting at **KILCOLGAN**. Two miles south of Kilcolgan, off the Kinvarra Road, stands **Drumacoo Church**, a fine stone building dating back to around 1200, with a Regency Gothic chapel of iron alongside, rusting and derelict.

Kinvarra and Doorus

Set in the southeasterly inlet of Galway Bay, the charming little quayside village of **KINVARRA** is something of a satellite playground for Galway city. Down at the tranquil harbour-side, with its smattering of pubs and restaurants, swans drift across the water to Dunguaire Castle. The **castle** (May–Sept daily 10am–4.30pm; £2.75) was built in 1520 and is a particularly good example of a **tower house**. These tower houses or "castles" were in fact fortified houses, very much a fashion for wealthy landowners from 1450 to 1650, and found in their greatest concentration in East Clare, East Limerick and South Galway. If you've not yet been in one, this is a good one to visit, as the guide delivers a vigorous interpretation of both local history and the political importance of the old building.

Back in the main street, locals are not quite sure what to make of a new landmark: *The Merriman Inn and Restaurant* (☎091/638222; ⑥), a massive thatched affair (thatch from Turkey, thatchers from England), with tasteful interiors, a comfortable restaurant and a Design Ireland shop. All in all, Kinvarra's a lively spot and, if you have transport, there's enough variety in the area to warrant a reasonable stay between the rigours of Burren-walking and Galway city-life. The informative *Kinvarra: A Ramblers Map and Guide*, by Anne Korff and Jeff O'Connell, is worth buying if you intend to explore the immediate countryside and is available in local shops and at Dunguaire Castle.

For location, *Cois Cuain* **B&B** (☎091/637119; ②), down by the quays, is hard to beat. Also recommended is *Collins* (☎091/638168; ③), a comfortable house set back off the road, a short walk out of the village towards Ballyvaughan, and, down a road to the left just past here, you'll find *Muileann House* (☎091/637593; ③). *Johnston's Hostel*, Main Street, (☎091/37164; ②; June–Aug) also caters for campers. Bikes can be rented from McMahon's filling station.

Good **places to eat** include *The Café on the Quay*, serving seafood, salads and sandwiches. *The Pier Head Bar and Restaurant* is similarly appealing and has a good reputation locally, while *The Merriman Inn* serves bar food till 10pm in summer and also has a formal restaurant. Kinvarra's **bars** are worthy of exploration: *The Auld Plaid Shawl* is a good starting point, with a mixed clientele; *Winkles* can be great fun, especially if you join in the set dancing on a Friday night; *Tully's* is a charming place for a civilized pint; and *The Pier Head* is a lively spot which frequently has music. Kinvarra's early spring **festival**, the *Fleadh na gCuach* (the cuckoo fleadh), is held over the May bank holiday weekend, while the *Crumniú na mBád* takes place usually over the second weekend in August and involves, along with singing and dancing, the racing of Galway's traditional fishing vessels (Galway hookers).

Doorus

In addition to all its other attractions, this part of South Galway is closely associated with the poetry of the literary revival group of Yeats, Lady Gregory, AE and Douglas Hyde; it was in what is now the An Óige hostel in **DOORUS** (out on the peninsula northwest of Kinvarra) that the idea of a national theatre was first discussed – later to become the Abbey Theatre in Dublin. The hostel was then the home of Count Florimond de Basterot, who entertained and encouraged the group (and also the likes of Guy de Maupassant and Paul Bourget). Given the political implications of the Irish literary revival, it's perhaps ironic that Count Florimond's cash came from French estates which his fleeing aristocratic ancestors had somehow hung on to, despite the Revolution.

Doorus is on a small peninsula of the same name that was an island until the eighteenth century. The village has only a pub and a shop, and you can stay at the welcoming **An Óige hostel** (☎091/37512). You can also camp down by the beach – ask at the farm. One of the best **B&Bs** is *Burren Farm View* (☎091/637142; ②) with great views of the Burren hills. The gentle waters to the south are pleasant, tidal backwaters that contrast sharply with the wide sweep of Traught Blue Flag beach to the north, which is stony but safe for swimming and surfing – there's a lifeguard on duty in summer. The beach at Parkmore, to the northeast, however, is dangerous. Along this coast, mussels are free for the picking – ask a local for the good spots. You can walk the coastline from Doorus down to Aughinish or back to Kinvarra, or cycle out to the Martello tower at Finavarra and around the inlet of Muckinish Bay towards Bell Harbour.

Coole Park and Kilmacduagh

Back on the Ennis Road, two miles to the north of Gort, you'll find **Coole Park** (mid-June to end Aug daily 9.30am–6.30pm; mid-April to mid-June & Sept Tues–Sun 10am–5pm; £2; Heritage Card), the old demesne of the house of Lady Gregory, much visited by Yeats, and the subject of some of his most famous poetry. All that remains of the house itself are some crumbling walls and a stable yard, but the grounds and the lake are now a particularly beautiful forest park. Sadly, its **autograph tree**, bearing the graffiti of George Bernard Shaw, Sean O'Casey, Augustus John and others, has been railed off to stop the less famous getting in on the act. A pleasant tearoom has been opened by the stables. A mile and a half northeast of Coole, **Thoor Ballylee** (Easter–Sept daily 10am–6pm; £2.50) is signposted off the N18. This is a sixteenth-century tower house which Yeats bought in 1916, renovated and made his home off and on over the next ten years. A short film tells the story of his life, rare and first editions are on show and readings of his verse are relayed into the spartan rooms of the tower – all best enjoyed if you can avoid clashing with a bus party. Alongside is a very cosy tearoom.

Four miles southwest of Gort, just off the Corofin Road, lie the remains of **Kilmacduagh**, a monastic settlement founded by St Colman Mac Duagh around 632. The sheer quantity of buildings – dating from the eleventh to the thirteenth centuries – is more impressive than any particular architectural detail: a cathedral, four churches, the Glebe House and a round tower 115ft high, all on one site. And the setting, against the shimmering, distant Burren slopes, lends something magical to the ancient grey stone.

Portumna

PORTUMNA, on the north shore of Lough Derg, is a traditional market town and Shannon crossing point, happy to be cashing in on the upmarket tourism that drifts its way on the lough cruisers, yet still retaining a friendly and unpretentious character. Close to the shore stands the ruin of **Portumna Priory**, for the most part a fifteenth-century Dominican building, though its delicately arched cloisters are built around the remains of a much earlier Cistercian foundation. Nearby **Portumna Castle** (Mon–Sat 9.30am–6.30pm; £1), a fine, early seventeenth-century mansion with Jacobean gables (something of a rarity in Ireland), is currently undergoing renovation. Nobody minds if you take a look via the fields to the rear. The castle's estate is a wildlife sanctuary with a large herd of fallow deer.

There's a **tourist office** (June–Sept daily 9am–9pm; 0509/41644) at the entrance to the grounds of the castle and you'll find several good **B&Bs** in the centre: try Mrs Ryan's *Auvergne Lodge*, Dominick Street (☎0509/41138; ②), Mrs Finlay's *Cnoc Rua*, St Brendan's Road (☎0509/41197; ③) or the Dolan's *Shannon Villa*, Bridge Road (0509/41269; ③). It's easy **camping** country, too – just ask a farmer – and in the summer there are **public showers** down by the lough jetty (July and Aug only). Swimming is relatively safe in the lake, but not in the river. For **bike rental** and repairs, Tony Cunningham's on Dominick Street (☎0509/41070) is the place to go. The Bank of Ireland is on Clonfert Avenue, and the post office is on Abbey Street. There's also a **laundry** – Frank's in Brendan Street.

There are two very friendly places to **eat**, both in the main street: *Peter's Restaurant*, a fast-food place that will rustle up whatever you fancy, and *Clonwyn House*, which does traditional cooked meals any day any time. Although small, Portumna has an astounding 21 **pubs**, and there's no shortage of ballad sessions. The *Corner House* offers regular nights hosted by owner John Horan, and you can catch a traditional ceili at *Clonwyn House* on Sunday nights, when the old folk come in to do their set dancing.

Clonfert Cathedral

About four miles north stands **Clonfert Cathedral**, on the site where a Benedictine monastery was founded around 560 by St Brendan. In subsequent centuries the monastery was pillaged, but towards the end of the twelfth century the church was rebuilt and dedicated to St Brendan. There's a superb Romanesque doorway made up of six arches, each a perfect semicircle and richly carved with heavily stylized plants and animals. The capitals are Romanesque cubes carved with crazy, bold animal heads. The Bishop's Palace beyond the cathedral – now derelict as a result of an accidental fire – was the home of Sir Oswald Mosley after his release from prison in 1949.

Athenry

Chances are you'll see **ATHENRY**, midway between Galway and Ballinasloe, if at all, from a train. The place is more renowned for the song *The Fields of Athenry* – which you're unlikely to have got this far without hearing – than as a tourist centre. Still, if you've time to kill between connections, it's worth nipping out of the station to take a look at its remains of Anglo-Norman power – so much a feature of east Galway and so conspicuously absent further west. The town was founded by the de Berminghams, and large portions of its Norman town walls have survived, along with a tower gate, five flanking towers and a market cross. On the edge of town stands a bold thirteenth-century **castle**, again built by the de Berminghams; its stout, three-storey keep is still impressively intact, though the castle is closed to the public. If you're looking for **B&B**, try *Mrs MacDonagh's*, Ballygurrane South (☎091/844579; ②).

Loughrea

LOUGHREA, on the main road to Ballinasloe, is like Portumna (see opposite) in that it's a lakeside market town. But it's much smaller, and tiny Lough Rea can't compare with the beauty of Lough Derg for a setting. In the thirteenth century, Richard de Burgo founded a **Carmelite monastery** here, and it still stands in an excellent state of preservation. The town also has a late nineteenth-century **cathedral**, whose interior demonstrates the development of the modern Dublin School of Stained Glass – an acquired taste. Much earlier religious art is on display next door in the **Loughrea Museum** (by appointment only; ☎091/841212). This small museum includes episcopal vestments and carved crucifixes from the seventeenth century, beautifully simple silver and gold chalices from as early as 1500, penal crosses and a few rare woodcarvings from the twelfth and thirteenth centuries. The Kilcorban *Virgin and Child* is the earliest of only three such carvings that have been found in Ireland.

In a field two miles to the north of Loughrea, near Bullaun, stands the **Turoe Stone**. A superb, rounded pillar-stone, this is decorated with the bold swirls of Celtic La Tène art, a style found more typically in Brittany. The finest of its kind in Ireland, it dates from the third or second century BC and was probably a phallic fertility stone, used in pagan rituals. If you decide to stay, you'll find a couple of fine **B&Bs**: Mrs Pauline Burke's *Four Seasons*, Athenry Road (☎091/541414; ③), and Mrs Rose Plower's *La Riasc*, Clostoken (☎091/841069; ③), three miles out of town on the Dublin–Galway Road. Loughrea also has a fine established hotel, *O'Dea's*, Bride Street (☎091/841611; ⑤), while probably the best place to eat in the area is the *Meadow Court Restaurant*, with main courses at £13 (☎091/841051).

Aughrim and Kilconnell Friary

Tiny **AUGHRIM**, on the road just short of Ballinasloe, makes a good base from which to explore some of the ecclesiastical remains of the area. In 1691, Aughrim was the scene of a key battle in the Williamite Wars in which the Irish and French forces were defeated. The Battle of Aughrim Interpretive Centre (Easter–Oct daily 10am–6pm) explains the battle's significance and places the Williamite Wars in the context of seventeeth-century European power struggles. *Hynes* **hostel** (☎0905/73734) also does camping and is attached to the local pub, which has music at weekends during the summer. It's advisable to book ahead in July and August and also during Ballinasloe's horse fair (see overleaf). The other reason for stopping here is to visit the excellent *Old Schoolhouse Restaurant*, on the other side of the Dublin Road from the village, its adventurous menu featuring such delicacies as tournedos of ostrich with a shallot confit and port and dry plum juice (£13.85).

Four miles to the northwest lie the very beautiful remains of **Kilconnell Friary**, a Franciscan foundation built near the site of the sixth-century church of St Conall, which gives the place its name. The friary held out successfully against Cromwellian attack in 1651. The ruins are extensive, with additions to the early fourteenth-century building showing that there was increased monastic activity in the later Middle Ages. There's a very pretty arcaded cloister, and in the north wall of the nave are two splendid canopied wall-tombs.

Ballinasloe

Galway's eastern boundary is one of water: Lough Derg, the Shannon and the River Suck. The tourist-geared villages are again catering mainly for the fishing fraternity, but there is enough of historic interest to warrant leisurely exploration. **BALLINASLOE** is the main town in east Galway. Important as a crossing point of the River Suck since

1124 when Turlough O'Conor, King of Connacht, built a castle here, the remains that can be seen today date mainly from the fourteenth century. You're only really likely to be here if you've come for the famous **horse fair**, which starts on the first weekend in October and lasts for eight days. The largest of the ancient fairs left in the country, drawing horse dealers from all over Ireland and England, it gives a fascinating glimpse of a way of life that is slowly disappearing. The bartering is very much a game, though a serious one. Generally, both parties know the value of the horse in question but enjoy the bartering ritual anyway, with its possibilities of outdoing an opponent. The logic seems to be that if you're not up to the bartering, you don't deserve the right price for the animal. This system of exchange is threatened by EU regulations which insist that animals be sold by weight, a sorry demise for an ancient tradition.

If you intend to visit the fair, you'll have to book accommodation well in advance. The **tourist office**, part of Keller Travel, Main Street (July–Aug Mon–Sat 10am–6pm; ☎0905/42131), can give more information on accommodation around the region and make bookings. The main **hotel** in town is *Hayden's* in Dunlo Street which is good value though breakfast is not included in the price (☎0905/42347; ④); for **B&B** try Angela Lyons' *Nephin*, Portumna Road, Kellygrove (☎0905/42685; ③). **Bike rental** is available from P. Clarke & Sons, Dunlo Street (☎0905/42417).

The countryside to the south of Ballinasloe makes a dull setting for a fine piece of ecclesiastical architecture, well worth taking in if you're staying in the area or heading south towards Portumna and Lough Derg. From the R357 road five miles south of town, **Clontuskert Abbey** looks impressive in this open countryside, like some iron-grey battleship adrift on the flat and muddy approaches to the Suck. The church is the only sizeable remnant of the abbey complex, with a perpendicular west door of 1471, carved with figures of the saints.

The east shore of Lough Corrib

The east shore of Lough Corrib provides a gentle route between County Mayo and Galway city, less dramatic than the Connemara roads. The lake shore and the many rivers are popular with fishermen (for trout and salmon in summer, pike in winter), and visitors with no taste for field sports have a number of medieval ruins to admire.

Two miles north of Headford, virtually on the border of County Mayo, is **Ross Errilly** (or "Ross Abbey"), the biggest and best-preserved Franciscan abbey in Ireland. It was founded in the mid-fourteenth century, but the bulk of the buildings belong to the fifteenth – the Franciscan Order's greatest period of expansion. The church buildings themselves are impressive, with a battlemented slender tower (typical of Franciscan abbeys) and well-preserved windows, and there's a wonderful tiny cloister, but it's the adjacent domestic buildings and the picture they give of the everyday life of the order that are perhaps the most interesting. Stand in the cloister with your back to the church and you'll see the refectory ahead and to the right, with the reader's window-side desk up in the far northeast corner. Straight ahead is a second cloister (this one without arcading) and behind that the bakehouse. To the northwest of this second courtyard lies the kitchen, where you can see a water-tank used for holding fish and an oven which reaches into the little mill-room to the rear.

Five miles south of Headford, a detour off the main road leads you right down to the lough shore and the ruined Franciscan friary of **Annaghdown** – far less impressive than Ross Errilly – and a nearby Norman castle. It was at this site, after all his voyaging and preaching, that St Brendan finally died, nursed by his sister, who was head of Annaghdown nunnery. The road loops back to rejoin the main Galway Road. Seventeenth-century *Gregg Castle* at Corandulla (☎091/591434; ⑥) is an unusual B&B: a place of beautiful faded splendour. Everything is geared towards relaxation (with breakfast till noon) and conviviality: the owners are garrulous traditional musicians and enjoy evenings with guests around the log fire in the Great Hall. Self-catering is also available. Another quality option in the area, with wonderful views over Lough Corrib, is the welcoming *Balindiff Bay Lodge*, Luimnagh, Corrundulla (☎091/791195; ③).

Tuam and around

Northeast County Galway is served chiefly by the small market town of **TUAM** (pronounced *choom*). There's little here to detain you, but should you wish to sniff out the scant remnants of the town's former importance, have a look inside the Church of Ireland **cathedral** on Galway Road. It's primarily a nineteenth-century building, but survivals from the twelfth-century chancel include a magnificent Romanesque arch, showing strong signs of Scandinavian influence, and the accompanying east window. The shaft of an ornamented high cross is set in the wall near the west door. It's a great shame that so little remains of medieval Tuam; a monastery was founded here in the sixth century by St Iarlath, a disciple of St Enda of Inishmore, and in the medieval period Tuam became not only an archiepiscopal seat but also the power centre of the O'Conors of Connacht. The high cross in the town square dates from the twelfth century: it's highly decorated but actually a bit of a patchwork, as the head and the shaft don't really belong together. The **tourist office** is in the Mill Museum (July–Aug Mon–Sat 10am–6pm; ☎093/25486) and can book **accommodation**. Should you need to stop over, the *Imperial Hotel* (☎093/24188; ④), in the central square, offers rooms and food. There's no shortage of **B&Bs**: try *Gabrielle Hurst*, Dublin Road (☎093/25934; ③) or Mrs O'Connor's *Kilmore House*, Galway Road, Kilmore (☎093/28118; ③), half a mile out of town.

Dunmore and Knockmoy abbeys

Yet more medieval ruins are dotted roundabout: if you're heading through Dunmore in the northeast of the county, there's **Dunmore Abbey**, an Augustinian priory of 1425, and just to the west of the town, a Norman castle built by the de Berminghams. Alternatively, seven miles south of Tuam off the N63 Galway–Roscommon road, **Knockmoy Abbey** is a Cistercian foundation of 1190 – though the central tower is probably a fifteenth-century addition. The most remarkable feature of the abbey is on the north wall of the chancel, where you'll see one of Ireland's few surviving medieval frescoes. Extremely faint (only the black outlines retain their original colour), it depicts the legend of the Three Dead Kings and the Three Live Kings. Under the dead kings an inscription reads "We have been as you are, you shall be as we are"; the live kings are out hawking. Underneath this is a picture of Christ holding his hand up in blessing and a barely visible angel with scales.

The Aran Islands

The **Aran Islands – Inishmore**, **Inishmaan** and **Inisheer** – lying about thirty miles out across the mouth of Galway Bay, have exerted a fascination over visitors for over a hundred years. Their geology creates one of the most distinctive landscapes in Ireland, the limestone pavement giving the islands a stark character akin to the Burren of County Clare. This spectacular setting contains a wealth of pre-Christian and early Christian remains and some of the finest archeological sites in Europe. And it's not only works in stone that have survived out here: the islands are Irish-speaking, and up until the early part of this century a primitive way of life persisted, a result of the isolation enforced by the Atlantic.

The most detailed **map** of the islands is produced by Tim Robinson of Roundstone, available on Inishmore and at bookshops and tourist offices in the Galway and Clare area. In fact the Aran Islands are quite easy to explore and the map isn't essential for

TRANSPORT TO THE ARAN ISLANDS

Several ferry companies operate between Galway and the Aran Islands. As with any of the ferry services to islands on the west coast, it's a good idea to check on the times of return journeys with the skipper, especially if you are going to Inishmaan or Inisheer as services can be unreliable – during winter, you're at the mercy of the weather, and there's a chance you'll get cut off from the mainland. If you are planning on travelling between the islands check the schedule closely as doing so can be more complicated and time-consuming than you might at first imagine. If you intend to drive to **Rossaveel** (signposted *Ros an Mhil*) and pick up a ferry from there, bear in mind you will be charged £2–3 per day, £10–15 per week respectively to park a car or van.

Island Ferries, Victoria Place, Eyre Square (☎091/568903; in the evenings ☎091/561767 or 572273). A return, Galway to Inishmore, costs around £15; sailings are at 10.30am (summer only), 11.30am, 1.30pm and 6.30pm. Boats to Inisheer or Inishmaan cost around £18 return and sail at 10.30am and 6.30pm. The ferry company runs a bus to Rossaveel (leaving one hour and fifteen minutes before the sailing) which costs £4, though if you have a bike it's worth noting that often the bus cannot carry them and there is a £2 charge to carry bikes on the ferry itself. B&Bs can be booked free of charge and package deals are available. Round trips taking in all three islands are also negotiable.

O'Brien Shipping, tourist office, Galway (☎091/567283 or 567676), operates from Galway to Inishmore (1 daily year round), to Inishmaan and Inisheer (4 days weekly). Fare £12 return; to all three islands by arrangement. Student reductions of £2–4; bikes free.

Doolin Ferry Co (☎065/74455; evenings ☎065/74189) sails mid-April to end Sept from Doolin (County Clare) to Inisheer (1–6 daily) and to Inishmore (2 daily). Return prices are Doolin–Inisheer £15, Doolin–Inishmore £20, Doolin–Inishmaan £18 (phone confirmation is strongly advised). A trip to all three islands, returning to Doolin or going on to Galway, costs £20. Bikes £2 return.

Aer Árann (☎091/593034) are based at the airstrip at Inverin, west beyond Spiddal. They offer **flights** to all three of the islands: at least three flights daily throughout the year and during the summer months a non-stop shuttle service seven days a week. A connecting bus from Galway city meets all flights. The return fare is £35, students £29, bookable at the Aer Árann desk in the tourist office, where it is also worth asking about **fly/sail** deals. It is not possible to take a bicycle on the plane. Island airport numbers are: Inishmore ☎099/61109 or 61131; Inishmaan ☎099/73020; Inisheer ☎099/75039.

finding the major sites. It is, however, of great value to those interested in detailed archeology and in Irish placenames. Although it's possible to do a **day-trip** from Galway to Inishmore, and from Doolin (County Clare) to Inisheer, you really need two full days to see the main sites of Inishmore alone, and an overnight stay on Inisheer adds a priceless dimension to a visit. As for Inishmaan, staying the night is the only way to experience its bewitching silence – and to be guaranteed a return journey. For more detailed information on transport to the islands see box above.

Some history

The Aran Islands abound with evidence of their **early inhabitants**: the earliest ring forts possibly date from the Iron Age (c.400 BC–500 AD), though recent research suggests that some of the larger structures may be even earlier, perhaps Late Bronze Age (c.700 BC). The next group of people to figure are the **Christians**, who came here to study at the foundation of St Enda in the fifth century and went on to found Iona, Clonmacnois and Kilmacduagh. However, the earliest surviving ecclesiastical remains date from the eighth century.

As Galway's trade grew, so the strategic importance of the islands increased, and in **medieval** times control of them was disputed by the O'Flahertjes of Connacht and the O'Briens of Munster, the latter generally maintaining the upper hand. In 1565, Queen Elizabeth resolved the dispute by granting the islands to an Englishman on condition he kept soldiers there to guarantee the Crown's interests. In the mid-seventeenth century the islands lost their political usefulness; the Cromwellian soldiers garrisoned there simply transferred to the new regime after the Restoration and became absorbed into the islands' traditional way of life.

After the decline of English interest and influence, the islands fell into poverty, aggravated in the nineteenth century by rack-renting. That rents should be levied on this barren rock suggests a cruel avarice and, not surprisingly, Aranmen were active in the **Land League** agitations: acts of defiance included walking the landlord's cattle blindfold over the Dún Aengus cliff edge. Despite this link with the general political movement on the mainland and the islands' use as a refuge for Nationalists during the War of Independence, it is their isolation that has allowed the continuation of a unique and ancient culture and that has rendered the islands so alluring to outsiders in the twentieth century.

THE GAELIC REVIVAL

With the burgeoning fascination for all things Gaelic from the 1890s onwards, the Aran Islands, along with the Blaskets, became the subject of great sociological and linguistic enquiry, the most famous of their literary visitors being J.M. Synge. His writings brought the islands to the attention of other intellectuals involved in the **Gaelic Revival**, and the notion of a surviving community of pure Gaels provided fuel for the Nationalist movement. Ironically, this notion may have been misconceived. The distinct physical type found on Aran – the dark skin, large brow and Roman nose – is, some argue, the legacy of the Cromwellian soldiers who were left on the islands.

In 1934, Robert Flaherty made his classic documentary *Man of Aran*, which recorded the ancient and disappearing culture he found here. (The film can be seen during the summer in Halla Rónáin, Kilronan.) While the **folklore and traditions** recorded in the film have obviously declined, *currachs* – light wood-framed boats covered formerly with hide, now with tar-coated canvas – are still used for fishing and for getting ashore on the smaller islands when the ferry can't pull in, and you may even witness, as in the film, a man fishing with a simple line off the edge of a 200ft cliff. Fishing and farming are still very much a way of life on Inishmaan, while tourism is the major earner on Inishmore and Inisheer. This means that, though their purpose will change, knowledge of these customs will not vanish, and tourism may even help ensure the language survives, as Irish provides the islanders with a curtain of privacy against the visitors.

Inishmore (Inis Mór)

Although there's some truth behind the attitude that does down **Inishmore** as the most tourist-oriented and least "authentic" of the Aran Islands, its wealth of dramatic ancient sites overrides such considerations. Increased numbers of minibuses and bicycles can make the main road west along the island pretty hectic in high season, and it's worth taking the low road along the north shore if you want to escape the crowds.

It's a long strip of an island, a great tilted plateau of limestone, with a scattering of **villages** along the sheltered northerly coast. The land slants up to the southern edge, where tremendous **cliffs** rip along the entire length of the island. Walking anywhere on this high southern side, you can see the geological affinity with the Burren of County Clare, and visualize the time when these islands were part of a barrier enclosing what is now Galway Bay. As far as the eye can see is a tremendous patterning of stone, some of it the bare formation of the land (the pavementing of grey rock split in bold parallel grooves), some the form of dry-stone walls that might be contemporary,

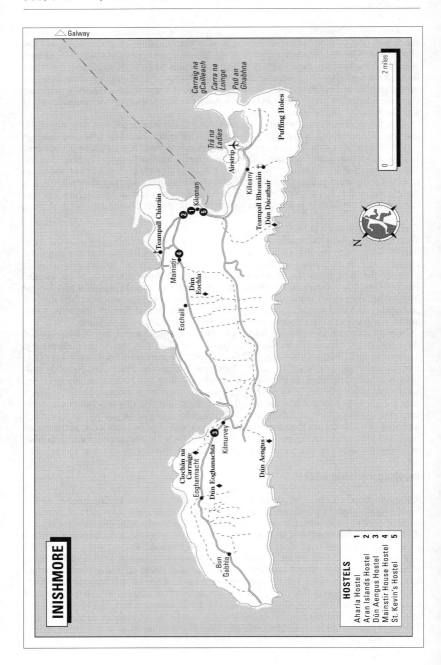

INISHMORE

△ Galway

Carraig na
gCailleach
Carra na
Loinge
Poll an
Ghabhna

Trá na
Ladies

Puffing Holes

Airstrip

Killeany

Teampall Bheanáin
Dún Dúcathair

Teampall Chiaráin

Kilronan

2 1
5

Mainistir

4

Dún
Eochla

Eochaill

Dún Aengus

Kilmurvey

3

Clochán na
Carraige

Eoghannacht

Dún Eoghanachta

Bun
Gabhla

N

0   2 miles

HOSTELS

Aharla Hostel   **1**
Aran Islands Hostel   **2**
Dún Aengus Hostel   **3**
Mainstir House Hostel   **4**
St. Kevin's Hostel   **5**

or might be pre-Christian. The textures blur so that it's impossible to make sense of planes and distances, the only certainties being the stark outline of the cliffs' edges and the constant pounding of the waves below. Across the water stand in contrast the Connemara mountains, coloured pink and golden and slatey blue in the evening sun. Up the bay is Galway, now an insignificant speck, and around to the southeast, appearing as just a silvery ridge, are the Cliffs of Moher.

Getting around and accommodation

The best way to **get about** Inishmore is by a combination of cycling and walking. You can rent bikes from Aran Bicycle Hire, beside the pier in Kilronan, where the ferry docks, Costello's Bike Hire (☎099/61241; May–Oct), opposite the *American Bar* further up the lane, or Mullin & Burke, next to the *Aran Islands Hostel*. The latter will deliver bikes free of charge to B&Bs on the island. **Pony buggies** will take you on a round tour for about £20 for a group of four, and **minibuses** ply the length of the island constantly. If you have limited time you can take the public minibus up the island through the villages that stretch over seven miles to the west – Mainistir, Eochaill, Kilmurvey, Eoghannacht and Bún Gabhla – and walk back from any point. The bus leaves Kilronan grocery shop, up behind the hostel, every two hours between 9am and 5pm (£2 single). The village of Killeany, a mile and a half to the south of Kilronan, has to be either walked or cycled to.

If you're looking for **places to stay** there are six **hostels** on Inishmore, three of which are in Kilronan. The best of these is probably *Aran Islands Hostel*, Kilronan (☎099/61255; April–Oct). It is very near the pier, handy if you want to spend the night in the pub below, noisy if you don't. Away from the hub of Kilronan, one of the most tranquil spots to stay is the excellent hostel in Kilmurvey, *Dún Aengus Hostel* (☎099/61318), a converted country house, ideally located. On the road to Kilmurvey is the *Mainistir House Hostel* at Mainistir (☎099/61169), which does excellent evening buffets (£7) and breakfasts of porridge and freshly baked scones, included in the price. Doubles are available for £23.

B&Bs can be booked through the **tourist office** (June to mid-Sept daily 10am–6pm), a couple of minutes' walk from the pier in Kilronan, although there will be a small service charge. Try Mrs Gill, *Ard Éinne*, Killeany (☎099/61126; ③), *St Brendans House*, Kilronan (☎099/61149; ③), or *Bayview Guesthouse* (☎099/61260; ③) on the water's edge near the harbour. *Dormer House*, Kilronan (☎099/61125; ③), is a good central option. Towards Kilmurvey the best place to stay is Conneely's *Beach View House* (☎099/61141; ③), overlooking one of the island's idyllic beaches, or *Oatquarter House* (☎099/61328; ②), which is excellent value and run by a friendly Irish-speaking family. If you have a taste for kitsch then you'll enjoy staying at the *Man of Aran Cottages* (☎099/61301; ④), specifically built for the filming of *The Man of Aran* according to what the film-makers thought traditional Irish cottages should look like.

There is a basic **campsite** (no showers) an easy walk from Kilronan: take the lane heading west out of the village and turn right in front of *Joe Watty's* pub. Better equipped are *Inishmór Camp Site* (☎099/61185) in Mainistir or the campsite at the *Dún Aengus Hostel* (☎099/61318) in Kilmurvey. Alternatively, it's just about possible to pitch a tent down by the idyllic beach at Kilmurvey, a lovely sweep of white sand looking out over to the Connemara mountain range; anywhere else is either bare rock or a treasured piece of cultivated land: finding the owner and asking permission is absolutely essential.

There is a large Spar **supermarket** in Kilronan and a second shop by *Joe Watty's* bar. The village has a **post office**, with a public phone (and cardphone) outside, and the Bank of Ireland opens here Wednesdays (10.15am–12.30pm & 1.30–3pm), plus additional Thursdays in July and August. You can also **change money** at the tourist office, the post office and Carraig Donn, a craft shop selling hand-knitted Aran sweaters by the pier at Kilronan (April–Oct daily) – this last will also advance cash on credit cards. Should the weather break, Snámara Crafts has a good selection of Irish books.

The island

Inishmore's villages are strung along the main road that runs the length of the northern shore, the hub of activity being **KILRONAN**, where the ferry lands. There are some great sandy **beaches**: the one at **KILMURVEY** (four miles west of Kilronan) is safe and sheltered, with fabulous views of the Connemara mountains, or you could take the main road to its eastern extreme and then walk north to get to the safe beaches from Carraig na gCailleach, through Carra na Loinge, down to Poll an Ghabhna. Tucked closer to **KILLEANY**, three quarters of a mile to the south, is Cockle Strand, safe for swimming; little over a mile further on, near the airstrip, is Tra na Ladies, which looks nice but where you can get caught by tides or sinking sand. You can **walk** just about anywhere so long as it doesn't look like someone's garden, but be careful when walking on the south of the island in poor visibility, as the cliffs are sheer and sudden.

DÚN AENGUS AND THE FORTS

The most spectacular of Aran's prehistoric sites is Inishmore's fort of **Dún Aengus** (signposted from Kilmurvey, three-quarters of a mile), a massive semicircular ring fort of three concentric enclosures lodged on the edge of cliffs that plunge 300ft into the Atlantic. The inner citadel is a 20ft-high, 18ft-wide solid construction of precise blocks of grey stone, their symmetry echoing the almost geometric regularity of the land's limestone pavementing and the bands of rock that form the cliffs. Standing on the ramparts you can see clearly the *chevaux-de-frise* outside the middle wall, a field bristling with lurching rocks like jagged teeth, designed to slow down any attack.

The place is tremendously evocative, and it's easy to understand how superstitions have survived on the islands long after their disappearance on the mainland. Visible west of the cliffs of Inishmore under certain meteorological conditions is the outline of what looks like a mountainous island. This is a mirage, a mythical island called *Hy Brasil* that features in ancient Aran stories as the island of the blessed, visited by saints and heroes. Until the sixteenth century *Hy Brasil* was actually marked on maps.

Dún Eoghanachta is a huge drum of a fort, a perfect circle of stone settled in a lonely field with the Connemara mountains as a scenic backdrop. Its walls are 16ft thick, and inner steps give access to the parapets. Inside are the foundations of the ancient drystone huts known as *clocháns*. The stronghold is accessible by tiny lanes from Dún Aengus if you've a detailed map; otherwise retrace your steps to Kilmurvey and follow the road west for just over a mile, where it's (poorly) signposted off to the left.

Dún Dúcathair (the Black Fort) is especially worth visiting for its dramatic location. It's a promontory fort, and what remains is a massive stone wall straddling an evershrinking headland precariously placed between cliffs. The eastern gateway fell into the sea early in the last century, leaving the entrance a perilous twelve inches from the sheer drop. Inside are the curved remains of four *clocháns*. It's about a two-mile walk from Kilronan – head south out of the village for three-quarters of a mile, take a turning to the right (signposted to "Cliff House") and follow the lane to the cliffs. If on a bike be warned: the lane becomes extremely rocky, making cycling impossible. Once at the cliff edge you can see the fort on the second promontory to your left.

The **dating** of these forts is tricky: Dún Aengus and Dún Dúcathair have long been considered to date from the first century BC, though recent excavations of the middle enclosure have found pottery fragments from the Late Bronze Age, suggesting a much earlier date of 700 BC. Dún Eoghanachta and **Dún Eochla** (just south off the road to the west of Mainistir) could have been constructed at any time between the first and seventh centuries AD, or possibly earlier. The massive buttresses of Dún Eochla are nineteenth-century additions, but the forts have generally been kept in exceptional condition.

CHURCH SITES AND CLOCHÁNS

From the fifth century onwards, the Aran Islands were a centre of monastic learning, the most important of the eremitic settlements being that of St Enda (Eanna). At the **seven churches**, just east of **EOGHANNACHT**, there are ancient slabs commemorating seven Romans who died here, testifying to the far-reaching influence of Aran's monastic teaching. The site is in fact that of two churches and several domestic buildings, dating from the eighth to the thirteenth centuries. Here **St Brendan's grave** is adorned by an early cross with interlaced patterns and, on the west side, part of a Crucifixion carving. There are also parts of three high crosses, possibly eleventh century, and in the southeast corner of the graveyard, alongside the slabs of the Romans, lie several ninth-century slabs incised with crosses and inscriptions.

The most interesting of the ecclesiastical sites on Inishmore, however, is **Teampall Chiaráin**. Take the low road from **MAINISTIR** (opposite *Joe Watty's* pub), follow the lane parallel to the shoreline, and you'll come to it, a simple twelfth-century church on an old monastic site. Alongside is **St Kieran's Well**, a long U-shaped spring backed by huge blocks of plant-covered stone. It's very pagan-looking – such wells often held sacred significance in pre-Christian times, and were adopted and renamed with the arrival of Christianity. Similarly, some of the tall stones that stand around the site look pre-Christian, even though they have crosses inscribed on them. The one by the east gable has a hole in it that may have held part of a sundial, and nowadays people sometimes pass handkerchiefs through it for luck.

Teampall Bheanáin, on the hill behind Killeany, is a pre-Romanesque oratory dating from around the sixth or seventh century, dedicated to St Benen. It's distinguished by its very steep gable ends and its unusual north–south orientation. In all probability, it used to form part of the great early monastic site that existed at Killeany.

The finest of Aran's *clocháns* is **Clochán na Carraige**, just north of Kilmurvey. This 19ft-long dry-stone hut has a corbelled roof whose arrangement is probably an early Christian design. There are fifty lesser examples of such huts on Inishmore.

Eating, drinking and entertainment

Not surprisingly, **seafood** is the great speciality on the island. *Dún Aonghasa* in Kilronan (☎099/61104; Easter–Oct) has probably the most varied menu and is good value for anything from light snacks to full meals (main course £13). *Dormer House* in Kilronan offers an extensive and reasonable menu, with seafood and steak a speciality. And there are a couple of self-service places in Kilronan: *An tSean chéibh* (lunch from £5, dinner from £7) and *Aran Fisherman* (lunches from £4.50). Kilronan also has a fast-food restaurant (summer daily until 10pm, later if there is a ceili on). *Joe Watty's* bar is good for soups and stews (summer until 8pm), and *Pota Stair* in the Heritage Centre serves homemade soups and cakes. Non-residents are welcome for evening meals, too, at *Mainistir House Hostel* (£7, see p.363). You can punctuate your cycling or walking with lunch, tea or snacks at *Man of Aran Cottages* in Kilmurvey, used as a set in the eponymous film (June–Sept daily 11.30am–7.45pm), though it is a little expensive.

The film, made in 1934, is shown during the summer in the community centre, Halla Rónáin Kilronan (3pm, 5.30pm & 8pm; £2.50). The Aran Heritage Centre, *Ionad Árann*, (April–Oct daily 10am–7pm; £2) offers a rather more sober introduction to the island's history, geography and geology.

The **pub** beneath the hostel in Kilronan is convivial enough, but it's still a good idea to wander away from here to sample some of the island's other bars: *The American Bar*, *Joe Watty's* further west, *John Dirrane's* at the top of the road as it slopes down to the beach at Kilmurvey, or *Tigh Fitz* bar in Killeany. In addition to this there are **ceilis** in Kilronan parish hall (June–Sept Fri, Sat & Sun; winter Sat; £3) and a **disco** on Thursday nights.

Inishmaan (Inis Meáin)

Inishmaan, or middle island, is the least visited of the three Aran Islands. Locals go about their lives seemingly oblivious to the trickle of tourists who come over, mostly on day trips from Inishmore. After Inishmore, you're immediately struck by how much greener Inishmaan is. Brambles and ferns shoot from walls, and bindweed clings to the limestone terraces. Here the stone walls are a warm brown and seem almost to glow with yellow moss. They're remarkably high – up to six feet – and form a stone maze that chequers off tiny fields of lush grass and clover. Yet despite this verdancy, the island still feels dour and desolate. Farming here is at subsistence level; farm buildings and cottages are grubby and dull, and soggy thatches sag over low doorways. The only sudden splashes of colour are from tiny cultivated gardens – the bright reds, pinks and oranges of geraniums, gladioli and carnations. The island is shaped something like an oyster shell. It rises in clear levels from the soft dunes of the north, through stages of flat naked rock, up to minuscule green pastures, then again up a craggy band of limestone (along which sit the main villages of the island), eventually levelling out on higher ground to meet the crinkled blowhole-pitted southerly edge. Inishmaan is the least visited, least touched by tourism of the three islands, though it has had visitors since the turn of the century. J.M. Synge stayed here for four summers from 1898, recording the life and language of the people. His play *Riders to the Sea* – which influenced Lorca's *Blood Wedding* – is set here, and his book *The Aran Islands* provides a fascinating insight into the way of life he found. **Synge's Chair**, a sheltered place on the westerly cliffs overlooking St Gregory's Sound, was his favourite contemplative spot. Traces of the **culture** he discovered remain. Some of the women still wear traditional brightly coloured shawls; Irish is the main language, though English is understood; and the islanders get on with what they've always done: farming and fishing. There's no hostility to visitors, but tourism isn't the islanders' concern. If you want to be impressed or entertained, you'll have to look elsewhere.

Forts and churches

One of the most impressive of the Aran forts is Inishmaan's **Dún Conchúir**, loosely dated between the first and seventh centuries AD. Its massive oval wall is almost intact and commands great views of the island, being built on the side of a limestone valley. (In myth, Conchúir was the brother of Aengus of the Firbolg.) To the east, the smaller **Dún Fearbhaí** stands above the village of Baile an Mhothair and looks out over the little eighth-century **Cill Cheannannach** by the shore. If you have visited the Hugh Lane Gallery (see p.87) and been impressed by the stained glass windows on display there then you will adore the windows in the modern church on the island from the same workshop of Harry Clarke. Some find his rich purples and turquoise too much but these windows are a real delight, especially since each depicts a scene from the island among the Christian iconography.

Practicalities

Inishmaan's indifference to tourism means that amenities for visitors are minimal. The three **shops** in the main street of the central village have limited provisions: tinned foods, bread and milk. The **pub** is central, too, serving snacks throughout the day during July and August (till 7.30pm); lunches (£4) and evening meals (around £15) are avail-

---

FERRIES

Before getting off the ferry on Inishmaan, check with the ferrymen when exactly they will pick you up for your return trip and which pier they will be arriving at (there are two).

able at *An Dún*, a seasonal café and restaurant just below Dún Conchúir (summer only; ☎099/73068). The island's other restaurant is beside *Ó'Congaile's B&B* (☎099/73085; ②) which is along the road from the pier. There are few other going commercial concerns on the island: Cniotáil Inis Meáin, the knitwear factory, produces beautifully simple designs in alpaca, linen and wool; it's home, too, to the **museum**, a fascinating photographic archive of island history, largely documented in Irish, and there's a pleasant tearoom. **B&Bs** are cheaper than on the mainland, though if you have an evening meal it may nearly double the price. If you arrive on spec, ask at the pub for some information; the phone number is ☎099/73003. If you want to book ahead, try *Mrs A. Faherty* (☎099/73012; ②) or *Máire Bu Uí Mhaolchiaráin* near the church (☎099/73016; ②), which also offers free camping (campers' breakfast £2.50) and guided walks. Also recommended is *Ard Álainn* (☎099/73027; ②), the owner of which cooks possibly the most filling breakfast of any B&B in Ireland and has bikes for rent near the pier. Other advanced-booking accommodation information is available on ☎099/73010. Most farmers will let you **camp**, but remember to ask them – all land belongs to somebody here; it's also worth making sure that the knitwear factory is out of ear-shot before pitching your tent. There is no chemist or doctor on the island, and **emergencies** are dealt with by a nurse (☎099/73005). A **public phone** is located outside the post office and in the pub, and the Bank of Ireland operates on the second Tuesday of every month.

Inisheer (Inis Oírr)

Inisheer, at just under two miles across, is the smallest of the Aran Islands. Tourism has a key role here; Inisheer doesn't have the archeological wealth of Inishmore, or the wild solitude of Inishmaan, but regular day-trip ferry services from Doolin bring a constant, if small, flow of visitors. This service also makes for a handy route from County Clare to Connemara. Of course tourism threatens the very stuff of its attraction – the purity of traditions and a romantic isolation – but for the moment Inisheer retains its old character, and for some it's a favourite place.

A great plug of rock dominates the island, its rough, pale-grey stone dripping with greenery. At the top the fifteenth-century **O'Brien's castle** stands inside an ancient ring fort. Set around it are low fields, a small community of pubs and houses, and windswept sand dunes. Half buried in sand just south of the beach is the ancient **church of St Kevin**; still in use in the last century, it is now used only to commemorate him as the patron saint of the island every June 14.

Practicalities

The **tourist office** (June–Sept daily 10am–7pm), in a hut by the pier, will give you a map and a list of **B&Bs**; you may want to try *Uí Chongaile's*, Lioseinee, West Village (☎099/75025; ②). If you need any other information about the island you can also contact Inisheer Island Co-operative (☎099/75008). You should have little trouble finding accommodation unless you arrive in the first weekend of August or at Whit weekend, which are usually booked up well ahead. The *Bru Radharc na Mara* **hostel** (IHH; ☎099/75024) is comfortable, with meals available. The only **camping** is on the official site, open May to Sept.

There are a handful of places to get cooked **food** on Inisheer: *Radharc na Mara* (June–Sept until 9pm) does breakfasts and lunches (£3–4) and evening meals (£7–8), and the *Óstán Inis Oírr* (*Hotel Inisheer*; ☎099/75020; Easter to mid-Sept) does bar meals for non-residents, from 9am to 9pm, with evening meals from £10. *Fisherman's Cottage* restaurant (☎099/75073; May–Sept) uses organic produce, catches its own seafood and caters well for vegetarians (lunches around £5, dinner including wine £17). Both the hotel bar, *Tigh Ruairí*, and *Tigh Ned* bar have **music** any time of the week during the summer. There is no bank on the island, but the hotel has a bureau de change.

Connemara

Dominated by two mountain ranges, **Connemara** is exceptionally beautiful. The **Twelve Bens** and **Maam Turks** glower over vast open areas of bog wilderness, while to the southwest the land breaks up into myriad tiny islands linked by causeways, slipping out into the ocean. The whole area has superb beaches, huge sweeps of opalescent white sand washed by clear blue water. Chance upon good weather here and you feel you've hit paradise; even on the hottest of days the beaches are never crowded.

This is country you visit for its scenery rather than its history. There is little evidence of medieval power in Connemara, either ecclesiastical or secular, beyond a few castles along the shore of Lough Corrib and the occasional one further west. The great exception is the profusion of **monastic remains** dotted over the little islands off the west coast. Mainland settlements up until the nineteenth century were widely scattered, and the area has always been sparsely populated, due to the poverty of the land. There's never been much to attract marauders or colonizers, and any incursions have involved a battle against the terrain as much as against the people. It's easy to see how such a land would remain under the control of clans like the O'Flaherties for centuries, while gentler landscapes bowed to the pressure of foreign rule. In the famine years the area suffered some of the worst of the misery, and a thinly peopled land was depopulated further as people chose to escape starvation by emigration.

Continued economic deprivation and isolation have meant that an ancient rural way of life has continued for far longer here, so Connemara is still Irish-speaking, the largest of the *Gaeltacht* areas. A *Gaeltacht* summer school is held in **Spiddal**, and **Casla** (Costelloe) is the home of *Raidió na Gaeltachta* radio station (556m. MW, broadcasting 8am–7.30pm). English is spoken too, however, and the only difficulty for the visitor is that the signs on the roads, and on some buses, are often in Irish only.

For all its beauty, the dramatic mountain landscape of west Galway is surprisingly undeveloped in terms of tourism, owing in part to the infamous Irish weather and in part to the fact that walking has not been the popular recreation in Ireland that it is in other, more urbanized European countries. If you're in search of solitude, you won't have to go far to find it.

Practicalities

Bus Éireann services link all villages on major routes between Galway, Oughterard, Roundstone, Clifden and Cong. They are reliable, although infrequent, often with only one service daily, occasionally even less frequently. Timetables can be picked up in Galway bus station (☎091/562000).

Hostels and **B&Bs** are both in reasonably good supply throughout Connemara, and you can **camp** more or less anywhere, but bear in mind that a lot of the area is bog and therefore very wet. Away from towns and villages, you may have trouble getting hold of water. Gaz canisters are available in Galway city, at Keogh's in Oughterard, Michael Ferron's in Roundstone, Peter Veldon's in Letterfrack, and in Clifden at The Twelve Bens, Stanley's and Miller's. Bord Fáilte-approved **campsites** are listed in the text.

If you intend to go **walking** bear in mind that the mountains here are potentially **dangerous**. There is no organized mountain-rescue service such as you get in European countries that are more developed for mountain sports. The Ordnance Survey 1:126,720 maps are based on surveying done in 1837 and are inaccurate, especially above 1000ft. If you are doing any serious walking, it is worth getting either the *Connemara Map and Guide Booklet* or *The Mountains of Connemara*, a map and guide to eighteen walks, including the Western Way. Both are produced by Folding Landscapes of Roundstone, Connemara, County Galway, and can be obtained in tourist offices in the west of Ireland or by post. **Bike rental** is available at Clifden, Galway, Roundstone and at several hostels (mentioned in the text).

Most of Connemara's more beautiful **beaches** are safe for swimming, including Clifden, Lettergesh, Dog's Bay, Gurteen Bay, Renvyle, Ardmore, Mannin Bay, Aillebrack, Omey, Letterfrack and Spiddal. It is, however, a very varied coast, so if in doubt, ask about safety locally.

Finally, being the *Gaeltacht*, the area's **signposts** are often in Irish, as are names on buses (even Galway is sometimes *Gaillimh*); where common these are added in parentheses in the course of the guide. Variations in the Irish spellings are common – sometimes the "An" is omitted.

Iar-Chonnacht

Draw a large triangle between Maam Cross, Rossaveel and Galway and you've defined the area known as **Iar-Chonnacht**, an open and bleak moorland of bog. Occasional white-splotched boulders lie naked on the peat that stretches to the skyline; any grass that survives is coarse and wind-bitten, and, but for small pockets of forestation, the bog has no trees. It's difficult, wet walking country, but numerous lanes and *boreens* lead to tiny loughs set in the granite hollows of the hills – good for fishing for brown trout, sea trout or salmon. The moorland reaches its highest point near Lough Lettercraffoe on the **Rossaveel–Oughterard Road**, giving fine views down onto **Lough Corrib**, whose green and wooded shores are a vivid foil to the barren west.

To Oughterard and around

If you're heading for the dramatic **walking country** of the mountains, or if you plan to base yourself at Clifden, the road to take from Galway is the N59 through Oughterard. It makes the easiest hitch and most pleasant cycle ride from Galway, avoiding the boring strip development down to Spiddal and taking you instead along the shore of island-flecked **Lough Corrib**, past crumbling ruins. These include the main sixteenth-century O'Flaherty fortress of **Aughnanure Castle**, two miles south of Oughterard (mid June to mid-Sept daily 9.30am–6.30pm; £2). A six-storey tower house standing on a rock island surrounded by a fast-flowing stream, Aughnanure was one of the strongest fortresses in the country at the time of Cromwell's blockade of Galway during 1652–54.

OUGHTERARD itself is a small town serving fishing-based tourism, from where you can rent boats on the lough or take a trip to the uninhabited island of **Inchagoill** (boat trip around £8; you can either book at the tourist office or call ☎091/552644); it's a magical place, with a couple of evocative ruined churches: St Patrick's and the twelfth-century *Teampall na Naomh* (Church of the Saints), which has interesting carvings and a superb Romanesque doorway. Approached from the east, Oughterard can beguile you into thinking that Connemara is going to be a populated, thriving, developed place, but arriving from the west, it seems a lush, green oasis, the beech trees that line the banks of the river sumptuous and luxuriant after the barren wilds of the bog.

The town's **tourist office** is on Main Street (April–Sept daily 9am–6pm; Oct–March Mon–Fri 9am–5.30pm; ☎091/552808). If you want to stop over, there is no shortage of **B&Bs**: in town, try the *Jolly Lodger*, Bridge Street (☎091/552682; ②) or a few minutes walk from town, *River Walk House* (☎091/552788; ③). Also on the river bank is Deirdre Forde's *Camillaun* (☎091/552678; ③), though it is probably best to stay in one of the fine houses outside the town to enjoy the impressive countryside. The best of these include the elegant *Waterfall Lodge* (☎091/552168; ③), which has private fishing in the grounds and does good child reductions; just over a mile out of town in Portacarron on the lake shore is *Lakeland Country House* (091/552121; ③). There are two fine **hotels** in the area: the *Corrib House* (☎091/552329; ⑤) and the excellent *Currarevagh House* (☎091/552312; ⑥) on the Lough Corrib shore. Of the two **hostels** in town the better is the non-smoking *Canrawer House Hostel* (☎091/552388). *Lough Corrib Hostel* in Camp Street (☎091/552866) also has camping and bike and canoe rental.

The best place for lunch in town is O'*Fatharta's* on Main Street, while for an evening meal it might be worth trying the excellent new **restaurant** beside River Run Lodge (☎091/552697), with main courses from £10; to get there follow Camp Street to the end, turn left over the bridge and the restaurant is on the right.

Oughterard is the starting point of the **Western Way** (approximately 31 miles), which follows the lough shore northwest, heads through the Maam Turks a couple of miles north of Maum and winds up in Leenane. Alternatively, if you want a quick route north, there's a ferry (£8 return; same number as for boat trips above) to Cong in County Mayo twice daily during summer.

The main N59 road then takes you through the hamlets of **MAAM CROSS** (*Crois Mám*), where there's a craft shop, petrol station and a pub which serves rather uninspiring **food** all day, and **RECESS**, where all you will find is *Joyce's* bar and shop. Five miles further west, close in under the rugged peaks of the Twelve Bens, is *Ben Lettery An Óige* hostel, *Binn Leitrí* Ballinafad (☎095/51136), a cosy haven run by friendly wardens, with a well-stocked shop; its location makes it one of the best spots from which to strike off into the mountains. The nearby castle of **Ballynahinch** was once the home of the land-owning Martin family and is now a hotel with a bar – and food – open to non-residents (☎095/31006; ⑨). On Ballynahinch lake are the remains of an old O'Flahertie castle, known as Martin's Prison after the use it was put to by Ballynahinch's most famous son, Dick Martin – aka **Humanity Dick** (1754–1834). The story behind the name is that Richard Martin, originally dubbed "Hairtrigger Dick" because of his duelling prowess, spent his adult life campaigning for animal rights, and any tenant he caught causing suffering to animals was thrown into jail in the castle. Dick was known to have fought duels on behalf of threatened animals, and when asked why he did so replied: "Sir, an ox cannot hold a pistol." More constructively, he pushed various acts through parliament protecting farm animals from maltreatment and was instrumental in founding the RSPCA.

West around the coast

The **coast road** is the alternative route west from Galway, passing through the *Gaeltacht* villages of Barna (*Bearna*, "Gap") and **SPIDDAL** (*An Spidéal*, "The hospital"). The Spiddal Craft Centre is a collection of workshops showing high-quality sculpture, ceramics, weaving and jewellery. Spiddal itself can be surprisingly lively for such a tiny, drive-through town. You can catch good sessions in the pubs here; try *Tigh Hughes* or, if you are passing through on a hot day, the beer garden in *An Crúiscán Lán* makes a good place to slake your thirst. Camping is available at *Spiddal Caravan and Camping Park* (*Parc Saoire an Spidéal*); it's off the main road and is well signposted. The *Bridge House Hotel* (☎091/553118; ⑤) is a good upmarket option and there are **B&Bs** aplenty; if you value friendly service and fine food then head straight for *Ardmór Country House* (☎091/553145; ③) where Vera Feeney will take great care of you; other fine places include *Tuar Beag* (☎091/553422; ③), *Ard Aobhinn* (☎091/553179; ③) and Maura Conneely's *Caladh Gearr Thatch Cottage* (☎091/593124; ③), three miles out of Spiddal on the road towards Inervin. Travellers looking for budget accommodation here are **strongly** advised to check with the tourist office in Clifden or Galway before booking in at independent hostels in the area. The nearest hostel is the An Óige *Indreabhán*, at nearby Inverin (☎091/593154), which is not as bad as its drab facade would suggest; it has a huge kitchen and many smaller rooms with washbasins.

Beyond **ROSSAVEEL** (*Ros an Mhil*), another departure point for the Aran Islands, the land breaks up into little chains of low-lying islands, linked to one another by natural causeways. These islets, more gentle than the main body of Connemara, make a perfect place to get lost: meandering around the inlets and gullies you experience a happy disorientation.

CARRAROE (*An Cheathrú Rua* "The red coloured area") has a strangely suburban feel to it, but the boulder-strewn coast looks across to the Aran Islands, and the beach is made up of tiny fragments of coralline seaweed. *Réalt na Maidne* (☎091/595193; ③) offers a bar, a restaurant and **B&B**; if this is busy try the modern *Carraroe House* (☎091/595188; ③). Near Rosmuc, a speck of a hamlet, is the cottage of the Republican and poet **Pádraig Pearse** (mid-June to mid-Sept daily 9.30am–6.30pm; £1; Heritage Card), who signed the 1916 proclamation and was subsequently executed. The cottage is where he wrote short stories, plays and *O'Donovan's Funeral Oration*, and although there is little of real interest inside, its tranquil setting makes it worth a visit. At Carna you can wander out onto Mweenish Island and look out to St Mac Dara's Island, where the remains of a monastery still stand. Such was the former reverence for the saint that fishermen would dip their sails three times when passing the island. A three-day festival, *Féile Mhic Dara*, is still held in July in Carna. Five miles north of Carna on the R340 is a pretty campsite at Gowla Cashel (☎095/31208).

Roundstone

The next place of interest along the coast is **ROUNDSTONE** (*Cloch na Rón*), a fishing village at the foot of the Errisbeg Mountain. Curving its back to the Atlantic, the quaint stone harbour looks across its sheltered waters to the magnificent Twelve Bens of Connemara. Fishing is the main source of income, along with an unobtrusive tourism that makes the most of the unique prettiness of the setting and the glorious beach at Gurteen Bay, one and a quarter miles away to the west. A huge sweep of white sand with lucid blue water, this is really very seductive. There's a **campsite**, the *Gurteen Caravan Site* beside the beach (☎095/35882; March–Sept), with laundry facilities, a shop and a tennis court. An Industrial Development Authority complex is discreetly tucked away to the west of Roundstone, where you can wander around the various studios and see *bodhráns* being made, buy flutes, whistles and harps, and visit pottery workshops.

It's an easy couple of hours' walk from Roundstone up to the top of **Errisbeg** – follow the fuchsia-flooded lane up the side of *O'Dowd's* bar and then the track ahead. The views are panoramic: the frilly coast of isthmuses and islets runs out to the south, while the plain of bog to the north is vast and open, punctuated only by the irregular glinting surfaces of dozens of little lakes, like sinister jellied eyes on the stark face of the landscape. It's through this wilderness that the **bog road** runs, the source of such superstition that some local people will not travel along it at night. Around the turn of the century, two old women, who lived in the road's only dwelling, robbed and murdered a traveller who'd taken refuge with them, and the road is considered to be haunted. From Errisbeg the view across the bog to the Connemara mountain ranges is tremendous. To the west, extensive beaches of white sand scoop their way north – Gurteen, Dog's Bay, Ballyconneely, Bunowen and the coral strand of Mannin Bay – each one echoing the beauty of the last.

Several places do **B&B** – try Patricia Keane, *Heather Glen* (☎095/35837; ③); Mrs C. Lowry, *St Josephs* (☎095/35865; ③); or the friendly *Wits End* (☎095/35951; ②). If you don't want to stay in the village itself and feel like splashing out, there are two exceptional **hotels** near the village of Cashel, about a fifteen-minute drive away towards Clifden. The first of these is *Zetland House Hotel* (☎095/31111; ⑧), which also has a fine restaurant, but, if you want true style, then follow in the footsteps of Charles de Gaulle and indulge yourself at the *Cashel House Hotel* (☎095/31001; ⑨), set in award-winning grounds and surely one of the finest places to stay in the country.

If you want to **eat** or drink while in the village, try *O'Dowd's* which, as well as having a wonderful atmosphere, does fine bar food and has an excellent restaurant attached serving mostly seafood (main courses £7–15). *Vaughan's House Hotel* (☎095/35864; ⑥)

also serves filling bar food and is also a good place to stay. You can buy Camping Gaz bottles and **rent bikes** from Michael Ferron's shop. **Pony trekking** is available at Derrada West Pony Trekking Centre, Toombeola, Roundstone (☎095/31022). Popular bars are *Connolly's Vaughan's Lounge* in the *Roundstone House Hotel* and *The Hilltop* bar, which has music every night (traditional on Fri & Sat) during the summer.

Clifden

Because of the dramatic grandeur of the Connemara mountains and the romantic pull of Galway, you expect **CLIFDEN** (*Clochán*, "the stepping stones") – known as the capital of Connemara – to be something special. In fact it's a very small place with only two significant streets. Its great asset is its position, perched high above the deep sides of the boulder-strewn estuary of the River Owenglin. The circling jumble of the Twelve Bens provides a magnificent scenic backdrop, and the broad streets seem consciously to open out, to take in the fresh air of the mountains and the Atlantic. Gimlet spires of matching nineteenth-century churches pierce the sky, giving Clifden a sharp, distinctive skyline.

Clifden seems to be trying hard to cultivate the cosmopolitan atmosphere of Galway. Lots of European tourists come here, but, aiming to serve all tastes, the town somehow misses the mark. Bars have loud disco music blaring out onto the streets – exactly the kind of thing most Gaelophile Europeans have come to get away from. It attracts a fair number of young Dubliners, too, revving up the life of this otherwise quiet, rural town. The place is at its most interesting when it's busy being Irish: during the annual **Connemara Pony Show**, for example, on the third Thursday in August (entrance £3). This is for the sale and judging of Connemara ponies, tough, hardy animals that are well suited to a harsh bog and mountain existence, yet renowned for their docile temperament. There's also a community festival in the last week of September.

Arrival and accommodation

Clifden is an obvious base if you're hostelling or camping, despite its limitations, and even though the Connemara mountains *look* magnificent from here, they're not at all accessible without transport of one kind or another. Bus Éireann **buses** leave from Market Street, with three buses to Galway daily in the summer and one a day for the rest of the year; Michael Nee Coaches (☎095/51082) also operates a daily service to Galway. The **tourist office** is in Market Street (July–Aug Mon–Sat 9am–6pm, Sun 10am–5pm; mid-May to end June and early Sept to mid-Sept Mon–Sat 10am–6pm; ☎095/21163).

There's plenty of hotel and B&B **accommodation** in the centre of Clifden, though everything can be very busy in July and August. The best hotel in the area is the *Ardagh* (☎095/21384; ⑦), Ballyconneely Road, its relaxed ambience created by candles and scented burners. Other fine hotels include the large modern *Station House Hotel* (☎095/21699; ⑤) on the coast road from Ballyconneely and *Foyle's*, Main Street (☎095/21801; ⑥). The best value B&B in the area is probably *Winnowing Hill*, Ballyconneely Road (☎095/21281; ②). Also recommended is Maureen Kelly's *Failte*, Ardbear, off Ballyconneely Road (☎095/21159; ③), which does good family reductions, as does the excellent *Hylands Bay View*, Westport Road (☎095/21286; ③). A couple of central pubs offer rather more upmarket rooms: *Barry's* on Main Street (☎095/21287; ⑤) or *Alcock & Brown* (☎095/21206; ⑤). At the other end of the scale there are several **hostels** in the centre of town. *The Clifden Town Hostel*, Market Street (IHH; ☎095/21076) is by far the best hostel, tastefully decorated with prints by the artist Paul Henry and other well-known Irish artists. Family rooms are available from

£10. *Leo's* on the Beach Road (IHH; ☎095/21429) is a friendly place with cosy turf fires and private rooms; what it lacks in luxury it makes up for in atmosphere. It also has the best campsite for miles. Built on a pier, *Ard-Ri Bayview Hostel* (☎095/21866) is friendly and clean.

There are plenty of places for **bike rental**: try John Mannion, Bridge Street (☎095/21160; they also stock Gaz). Clifden's **laundry** is in Main Square. **Pony trekking** is organized at Errislannan Manor (☎095/21134; closed Sun; £15 per hour), about a mile beyond the Alcock and Brown Memorial, south of Clifden on the L102. **Wind-surfing** is available at the boat club, Coast Road. **Dinghy sailing** can be arranged through Clifden Boat Club (☎095/21711; £120 for a week course) – the setting is superb. The Island House, Market Street (☎095/21379), organizes **guided walks** (4–5hr; around £10–20), focusing on the archeology and natural history of Connemara, an excellent way to explore the countryside, especially if you're travelling alone or don't have your own transport.

Eating and drinking

As for **food and drink**, there's no problem getting provisions in Clifden, and the town's two main streets harbour plenty of places to eat. For coffee and home-baked cakes, try either *Walsh's Bakery*, Market Street, or *My Tea Shop* on Main Street. *E.J. King's* pub does cheap soups and salads or for seafood try *Mitchells*. The friendly, upmarket *Crannmer Restaurant* (☎095/21174; from 6pm) is tucked away off Church Hill. Seafood is their speciality, and if you can't afford a full meal (£13–30), you're welcome to enjoy a starter or a dessert along with the fine views from the terrace. For good vegetarian dishes try *Fogarty's* or *O'Grady's*.

There are plenty of decent **bars** in Clifden, and several places where you'll find music: for traditional sounds, try *Tom King's*, *Lowry's* or *Barry's Hotel* during the summer, *Mannion's* or *Griffin's* at any time of year. Loud and lively *E.J. King's* on The Square is the likeliest spot for rock and roll and modern folk.

Around Clifden

Clifden offers easy access to some beautiful scenery. To get to the **Twelve Bens** (see p.375) you will need to cycle, hitch or skilfully manipulate the bus service. For more spontaneous walking, take the westward **coast road** out of Clifden (past *Leo's* hostel) to a fine, sandy beach and a path that follows the shore of Clifden Bay. The shell of a nineteenth-century Gothic castellated mansion that you pass on the way was the home of John D'Arcy, who founded the town. Running north from beside the hostels, the **sky road** takes you to more desolate countryside and the long thin inlet of Streamstown Bay. Stick to the road and you'll eventually come down to the little village of Claddaghaduff, where at low tide you can walk across to **Omey Island**. There are excellent beaches here. In the bay three miles north is the little village of **CLEGGAN**, where most people go simply to get the ferry to Inishbofin. However, the village is attractive in itself and may be a better place to stay than the overcrowded Clifden. There are plenty of B&Bs, usually a little cheaper than in Clifden – try *Harbour House* (☎095/44702; ②) or a mile out of town, not far from the beach, is *Cnoc Breac* (☎095/44688; ③).

To the immediate south of Clifden, there's equally pleasant country. A 14ft aeroplane wing carved in limestone sticks out of the bog four miles from Clifden on the **Ballyconneely Road**, as a melodramatic memorial to the landing of **Alcock and Brown** at the end of their pioneering non-stop transatlantic flight in June 1919. Beyond this is the coral strand of Mannin Bay, excellent for swimming, as is that at Doonlonghan.

Inishbofin

The island of **INISHBOFIN** is a mellow, balmy place, quite different from the main-land. It's more fertile, with sheltered sandy beaches, and there's a general softness to its contours. The only jagged features are the cliffs to the west (the *stags*), a fine van-tage point for viewing seals basking on the shore. Even the high, heathery moorland soon gently descends to the placid **Lough Boffin**, rimmed with rustling water iris and bullrushes. The lough is the scene of the island's most durable **myth**, a story that explains how it got its name. Several versions of the tale exist, but the basic elements are constant. For eons the island lay shrouded in mist under the spell of an enchant-ment, but one day two lost fishermen came upon it and lit a fire by the shore, thus breaking the spell. As the mist cleared, they saw an old woman driving a white cow along the strand. She hit it with a stick and was instantly turned to rock. Taking her for a witch, the men hit her and they too immediately turned to rock: *Inis Bó Finne* means "Island of the White Cow".

The known **history** of the island starts in the seventh century, when St Colman arrived here from Iona after a quarrel with Rome over the method of calculating the date of Easter. No remains exist of the monastery he founded, but ruins of a thirteenth-century church stand on the original site in a sheltered vale beside the lake in the east. Later the island was taken over by the O'Flaherties, and then Grace O'Malley is sup-posed to have fortified the place for her fleet. Coming into the island's long protected harbour you'll see the remains of a sixteenth-century castle, low on the hummocky ter-rain. It was taken and strengthened yet further by Cromwell, who used Inishbofin – and other west coast islands – as a kind of concentration camp for clerics. The most chill-ing reminder of his barbarity is the rock visible in the harbour at low tide. Known as **Bishop's Rock**, it was here that Cromwell chained one unfortunate ecclesiastic, then let his troops watch the tide come slowly in and drown him.

Practicalities

Both *Day's Bofin House* (☎095/45809; ④) and *Doonmore Hotel* (☎095/45804; ④) have restaurants open to non-residents, and also serve good **bar food** (Easter–Sept). If you want to book **B&B**, try *Regina King* (☎095/45833; ③), or *Lena Schofield* (☎095/45812; ②). The *Inishbofin Island Hostel* (IHH; ☎095/45855; April–Sept) is an extremely friend-ly and well run place; private rooms are available for £18. *Miko's* **pub** is very friendly and has **music sessions** any time of the week during the summer season and at week-ends in winter. There's an island shop, with the usual limitations on supplies, and *Miko's* pub will change travellers' cheques.

You can **camp** on any of the open common land. A particularly good spot is at the east end of the island at Rusheen beach, from where you're treated to the glorious sight of the Connemara mountains lurching into the sea. The only places that are dangerous for swim-ming are at Tra Geall, just beneath Doonmore, opposite the island of Inishark in the west.

TRANSPORT TO INISHBOFIN

You can visit Inishbofin on a day-trip from Clifden, even without a car. Take the bus to **CLEGGAN** (summer Tues & Fri 8am, returning 7.50pm; check with driver). A private bus leaves the square at 11am daily in summer. **Ferry** tickets are available at King's store, Cleggan, Inishbofin Ferry Office on Market Street, Clifden or Clifden tourist information office for sailings on *The Island Discovery* (£12 return; April–Sept), departing Cleggan 11.30am & 6.45pm, with an extra sailing at 10 am and 2pm during July & Aug; departing Inishbofin April–Sept 9.30am & 5pm, July & Aug an extra 1pm sailing. In winter there's a boat approximately once a week (☎095/44642).

The Connemara National Park

The **Connemara National Park** typifies the scenic splendour of west Galway. Its chief functions are to promote the area's natural beauty while conserving this area of bog, heath and granite mountains. The park includes part of the famous **Twelve Bens** range – Benbaun, Bencullagh, Benbrack and Muckanaght – all of which are for experienced walkers only. Less threatening are the spectacular Polldark River gorge and Glanmore Valley, and the multifaceted granite Diamond Hill – though problems of soil erosion here have led the park to discourage a walk to the top: ask at the visitor centre for the current state of play.

The park's **visitor centre** (May–Sept daily 9.30am–6pm; £2; Heritage Card), near Letterfrack, is an excellent source of information on the fauna, flora and geology of the area; there's an exhibition on ten thousand years of Connemara, which takes in peatland and the changing landscape. It's also the focus for the bogland conservation work that's going on in the area, and the herbarium here is worth looking at if you're interested in botany. The staff can suggest safe hiking routes of varying length and difficulty, and you can leave details of your own route and intended time of return – an invaluable service in this potentially hazardous landscape. The centre has kitchen facilities available for walkers, an indoor "picnic" area and a new tearoom. In July and August a botanist leads a guided walk of about two and a half hours, currently leaving at 10.30am on Monday, Wednesday and Friday, though it's wise to ring and check the schedule. As well as offering facilities to outsiders, the centre is doing much to raise local awareness of the value of the area as a tourist amenity – particularly important in view of the current threat of goldmining in the area.

Letterfrack

LETTERFRACK itself is an orderly nineteenth-century Quaker village in a rugged setting. The village is tiny, but there's good food (especially wholefood and cheeses), and occasionally music, at *Veldon's* and discos in *The Bard's Den* (Fri & Sat). There's also a post office, phone, shop and bureau de change and the lovely rambling independent *Old Monastery* hostel (IHH; ☎ & fax 095/41132) with camping, bike rental and great food; breakfasts of baked scones and porridge are included in the price, while dinners are available for £6. It makes a perfect base for walking in the national park. Bog Week (the weekend leading up to the first Monday in June) and Sea Week (the weekend leading up to the last Monday in October) see Letterfrack at its liveliest, when a heady mix of conservationists and musicians descend upon the place for field trips, conferences and sessions.

Two miles east of here, the towers of **Kylemore Abbey** sit in a rhododendron-filled hollow against lush deciduous slopes. Its white castellated outline, perfectly reflected in the reed-punctured lake, has made it the subject of many a postcard: Kylemore is in fact a nineteenth-century neo-Gothic building. It's home to Irish Benedictine nuns and houses a girls' boarding school, but the library and entrance hall are freely accessible, and there's an exhibition telling the history of Kylemore (Easter–Oct daily 10am–6pm; £1.50). A stroll through the woods leads to the Gothic church, a small-scale copy of Norwich Cathedral built in 1868. The abbey also has a major heritage shop and restaurant. **Renvyle House**, some eight miles northwest of Kylemore Abbey, is of immense interest in Irish literary and political history. At one time it was visited by the great Edwardian comic twosome Somerville and Ross, authors of *Stories of an Irish R.M.*, but the house's most famous owner was Oliver St John Gogarty, the distinguished surgeon, writer and wit. An associate of the Gaelic League, he attended the literary evenings of Yeats, Moore and AE (George Russell), and is immortalized as "stately plump Buck Mulligan" in Joyce's *Ulysses*. *Renvyle House* is now a hotel (☎095/43511 or 43444; ⑨; June–Sept) offering facilities such as horse riding, wind-surfing and a swimming pool to non-residents. About a mile west of the hotel lies a ruined O'Flahertie **castle**, superbly positioned overlooking the sea. On Derryniver Bay, one mile west of Renvyle is the Ocean's Alive Aquarium and Visitor's centre (☎095/43473; £3), featuring a reconstructed traditional cottage, a mini farm and a short coastal walk where you can examine old fishing boats. The coast road to the east offers magnificent scenery, a great route for the **hostel** at Killary Harbour, if you are cycling, and some lovely beaches.

Killary Harbour and around

Inland, the N59 route to **KILLARY HARBOUR** is faster and similarly beautiful. The lightly wooded shore around Ballinakill Harbour provides a brief luxuriant interlude before the landscape of wild bog and granite reasserts itself with ever increasing austerity. The An Óige **hostel** at Killary (☎095/43417; March–Sept), where Wittgenstein finished writing his *Philosophical Investigations* in 1948, has a deeply ponderous setting at the mouth of Ireland's only fjord, a cold dark tongue of water which cuts eight miles into the barren mountains. The hostel is five miles of extremely difficult hitching off the N59, so be prepared to walk. There's a shop at the hostel open evenings; otherwise you have to go to Lettergesh shop and post office. From the hostel walk south, past the adventure centre (see below), then take the right turn before the crest of the hill, and keep on for about one and a quarter miles; the shop is the first big house on the left, with a phone box outside. There are good sandy beaches in the vicinity.

The Little Killary Adventure Centre, Salruck, Renvyle (☎095/43411), runs courses in mountain walking, climbing, sailing, canoeing, sailboarding, archery and orienteering. Courses are generally booked well in advance, though it is often possible to join a course for part of a week or weekend. Further north, **LEENANE** is most famous as a location for shooting *The Field*, stills from the film hang on the walls of *Gaynor's Bar*. It's also a finishing (or starting) point for the Western Way. Leenane Cultural Centre (April–Sept; £2) explores the history of wool, with spinning and weaving demonstrations and a collection of various sheep outside – if you've an interest, it's very enjoyable, and there's a good tea shop, too. For **B&B**, Mrs Hamilton's *Bayview House* (☎095/42240; ③), Mrs Hoult's *Hillcrest House*, Clifden Road (☎095/42244; ③) or Mrs Roberts' *Sancta Maria* (☎095/42250; ②), while a little more expensive is the superb *Killary Lodge Country Home* (☎095/42276; ⑤), an old hunting and fishing lodge down by the harbour. If you're heading towards Cong in County Mayo (p.393), the desolate road takes you through Maum and on past *Cornamona Hostel* on the shores of Lough Corrib (IHH; ☎092/48002; April–Oct), just nine miles from Cong.

COUNTY MAYO

Often seen as simply a passage between scenic Galway and literary Yeats country, **Mayo** is little visited – though it's hard to see why. Like Galway to the south and Sligo to the north, it has a landscape of high cliffs, lonely mountains and bright fuchsia hedges; in the wild, boggy area to the northwest are the vestiges of a *Gaeltacht*; and on Lough Conn there's some of the best fishing in Ireland. The Georgian town of **Westport**, an elegantly urban playground for travellers needing a break from the dazzling lights and landscapes of the wild west, is the only place that's really on the international tourist trail. **Achill Island**, the biggest of the Irish offshore islands and a traditional Irish family holiday resort, has an oddly fly-blown air that won't suit everyone. Some of the most exciting country, however, is the little-travelled northwest. The new interpretive centre at **Ceide** holds the key to understanding a landscape that's hardly changed for millennia. The area is easily accessible: the railway will take you right out to Westport, and there's an international airport at **Knock** (with cheap flights designed for pilgrims to the shrine of the Virgin Mary). Furthermore the whole of the county is magical cycling country. Mayo is bound to become busier, but for the moment it remains wonderfully empty.

The Barony of Murrisk and Clare Island

If you're travelling by road, you'll probably enter Mayo from Galway, via the spectacular scenery of **Killary Harbour**, part of the lobe of land between the Galway border and Westport that's known as the **Barony of Murrisk**. This is country as rugged and remote as anything you'll find in the west, and two ranges of hills, the Mweelrea Mountains and the Sheefry Hills, provide terrain for energetic walking, mountaineering, riding, fishing and canoeing.

Delphi and Louisburgh

The road due north from Killary threads along a narrow valley which opens up, briefly, for a famous salmon and sea-trout lough-fishery with the unlikely name of **DELPHI** (in the local pronunciation, *Delph-eye*). The story behind the name involves the first Marquess of Sligo, whose seat, misleadingly, was at Westport. The flamboyant Marquess, a friend of Lord Byron, was caught in the sway of romantic Hellenism and in 1811 set sail for Greece to search for antiquities. He swam the Hellespont with Byron and rode with him overland to Corinth; but when he got to Delphi, he suffered a bout of homesickness, finding that it reminded him of nothing so much as his fishery at home in County Mayo. After numerous adventures, and some pillaging of ancient sites, the Marquess returned home to reminisce. Nowadays, there's an **adventure centre** at Delphi (☎095/42307), offering supervised instruction in anything from wind-surfing and canoeing to abseiling and mountaineering. More important for people of a more sedentary disposition, there's also a **hostel** and a comfortable, glassed-in coffeeshop where you can sit and gaze out as the cloud creeps down the slopes of Mweelrea and Ben Gorm. **Pony trekking** is based at the *Drumindoo Stud* (☎098/66195). Luxurious **accommodation**, excellent cuisine, plus a taste of the area's history, can be had at the *Delphi Lodge* (☎095/42211; ⑧; Jan–Oct), an 1830s sporting lodge by the lake, built for the Marquess of Sligo in a surprisingly austere, and predictably Hellenistic, style.

Take the right turn at the southern end of the lough, and the road climbs high into the **Sheefry Hills**, giving some of the best access for walking. A mile past the village of **DRUMMIN**, three-quarters of a mile up a track, is one of the best places to **stay** in these parts: the *Derryann* vegetarian B&B (☎098/26885; ③). Housed in a stone-built cottage, it offers an amazing range of breakfasts for veggie sybarites (or anyone else who's had one Irish breakfast too many): mushroom and pine-nut crêpes, eggs Florentine, French toast with maple syrup – but no evening meals, although they will produce snacks or sandwiches; the **pub** in the village does a limited range of pub food.

North of Delphi, the road runs alongside sombre **Doo Lough**, also known as the Black Lake, and over desolate moorland before reaching **LOUISBURGH** (*Lewis-burg*). This is one of the few instances where a town this side of the Atlantic has been named after one on the other: it was renamed after Henry Browne, uncle of the first Marquess of Sligo, had taken part in the capture of Louisburgh, Nova Scotia, in 1758. Louisburgh is essentially little more than a crossroads, but its planned buildings give it an incongruous air of importance, and it's a pleasant enough place to stay. The Granuaile Centre (June–Aug Mon–Sat 10am–7.30pm; £2) details the exploits of Grace O'Malley, the pirate queen (see p.382), and has an audio-visual display and local tourist information. There is also an exhibition on the Great Famine, as this area suffered heavily from 1845–49: there's a harrowing tale about the march of six hundred starving locals in 1849 to Delphi Lodge to beg, unsuccessfully, for famine relief; many of them, weak and ill clothed, died on the return journey amid the uncompromising scenery of Doo Lough. This event is commemorated annually in the Great Famine Walk (enquire at the centre for details).

Louisburgh makes a good base for exploring the sandy **beaches** that run along the north coast as far as Murrisk Abbey. One of the best places for food is *Durkan's* in Chapel Street, while there are any number of excellent B&Bs around the area; try the excellent, family-friendly *Sringfield House* (☎098/66289; ③) or two miles out of town is the modern *Three Arches* (☎098/66484; ③) which also has good family rates. Just outside Louisburgh, at **OLD HEAD** (on the Westport Road), there's a **campsite** with showers and laundry (☎098/66021; June–Aug). Old Head has a good **beach**, though little can compare with the nearby **Silver Strand** beach, claimed grandiosely in the local tourist leaflets to be second only to Florida's Key West; it is, incidentally, the site of a mass Famine burial. You can reach it by turning southwest at the crossroads just outside Louisburgh on the Killary Road along lanes that pick their way through rolling country rich in megalithic monuments, with a clear view out to Clare Island, Inishmore and the smaller islets; it has a couple of **B&Bs** – *Silver Strand House* (☎098/68730; ③) is homely and comfortable and offers evening meals of local seafood.

Clare Island

Follow the road from Louisburgh west along the strand to the land's tip, and you reach **Roonagh Quay**, where a boat leaves three times a day for **CLARE ISLAND**. (The bus from Westport runs at least twice a day and will drop you two miles away in Louisburgh.) The crossing takes 25 minutes; boats leave Roonagh at 11.00 am, 2.15pm and 6pm. The most reliable place to get information about the ferry is at the *Bay View Hotel* (☎098/26307); fares are £10 return. Although it's tiny – only fifteen or so square miles – Clare Island rises to a height of 1522ft in a massive shoulder of land that dominates everything around. There's not much here besides the hills, some ruins and some unfrequented sandy beaches, but there's plenty of walking, and you can go pony trekking, or water-ski, sailboard or fish.

The island is famed above all as the stronghold of Grace O'Malley (see p.382). Her massive castle is at the eastern end of the island; also at the eastern end of the island, she – or a close relative – is buried in a tomb on the north side of the ruined thirteenth-century Cistercian abbey halfway along the south coast of the island.

You can **stay** overnight on Clare Island, at the *Bay View Hotel* (☎098/26307; ④), which also organizes local watersports and operates the ferry.

Croagh Patrick and Murrisk Abbey

The land between Louisburgh and Westport is dominated by the strange, perfectly conical silhouette of **Croagh** (pronounced *Croak*) **Patrick**, which at 2513ft is by far the highest mountain in the immediate area. The sandy beaches of the shore peter out at Bertra Strand, just short of Murrisk and the ruins of **Murrisk Abbey**, a house of Augustinian canons set up on the shore of Clew Bay by the O'Malley family in 1457, less than a hundred years before Henry VIII's dissolution of the monasteries.

ST PATRICK AND THE SNAKE

In 441, **St Patrick** spent the forty days of Lent on Croagh Patrick in prayer and fasting, and it's from here that he is supposed to have sent the reptiles of Ireland crawling to their doom. Just to the south of the summit is the **precipice of Lugnanarrib**, where he stood, ringing his bell, then repeatedly hurled it over the edge, each time taking with it a stream of toads, snakes and other creepy-crawlies. Luckily he didn't have to go down to the bottom to get his bell back – helpful spirits did the job for him. There's a pilgrimage to the top of Croagh Patrick, which is carried out by some 60,000 people, some of them in bare feet, every year on the last Sunday of July.

Looking out over the hummocky islets of the bay, the abbey is the best starting point if you want to climb the mountain. On the landward side, a little saint's head carved in the wall peers glumly up the slope – it's a very tough **climb**. Still, there's a surprise when you get to the top. The summit isn't conical, as it looks from the bottom, but forms a flat plateau, with a little chapel and a breathtaking view: on a good day you can see right from the Twelve Bens in the south to the mountains of Achill Island in the north, the Nephin Begs east of the island and on to the Slieve League in Donegal.

At the foot of the mountain on the shore side of the road is the national monument to *an nGórta Mór* (the Great Famine); the bronze sculpture, by John Behan, is of a coffin ship headed for America, its rigging made up of the skeletons of the starving and is particularly evocative when lit up at night. If you want to stay in the area try *Ceann Cúrsa B&B*, Pier Road (☎098/64864; ②), which has family rooms and does good vegetarian breakfasts.

A fine place to stop for **refreshments** after a climb, barefoot or not, up the mountain is *Glosh House*, a restaurant overlooking the sea and specializing in seafood and vegetarian dishes. It also does Irish breakfasts and sustaining afternoon teas.

Westport

"The islands in the bay which was of gold colour, look like so many dolphins and whales basking there," wrote the English novelist W.M. Thackeray on a visit to Westport in 1842. Set in a picturesque eighteenth-century landscape on the shores of Clew Bay, **WESTPORT** is a comfortable, relaxed town, still recognizably Georgian – it was planned by the architects Richard Castle and James Wyatt – with a leafy mall, octagonal square, a canalized river and one of Ireland's great stately homes, Westport House. For the past ten years, it has capitalized on its fine architecture and busy urban buzz to offer visitors some elegant town living in the midst of the wild scenery of the remote west. During summer, the place is tremendously lively, with Irish, British, French and German visitors returning annually to resample its charms, and a couple of excellent festivals.

In its heyday the town was extremely prosperous, fattened by the trade in linen and cotton cloth and yarn. However, like many places throughout Ireland, Westport was hit hard by the Act of Union of 1801. Although local landowners like the first Marquess of Sligo supported the Act in the belief that it would be of economic benefit, the reverse was in fact true: Irish hand looms were no competition for the new spinning jennies in Britain's industrial towns, the national linen and cotton industries declined, and Westport's economy was ruined. Mass unemployment forced a choice between reverting to subsistence farming or starting a new life in America.

Its quiet Georgian beauties and its lively modern streetlife apart, the reason Westport is on the tourist trail nowadays is **Westport House** (Mon–Sat 10.30am–6.30pm, Sun 2–6pm; house £6, zoo £3.50, both £8), a mile or so out of town towards Clew Bay. Built on the site of one of the castles of the sixteenth-century pirate queen Grace O'Malley (a direct ancestor of the current owner; see p.382), Westport House was beautifully designed in 1730 by the ubiquitous Richard Castle, with later additions by Thomas Ivory and James Wyatt. This was one of the first Irish houses opened to the public – and it's had a go at any and every way of making money. There's a zoo park in the grounds and horse-drawn caravans for rental, while the dungeons (which belong to an earlier house) have everything from a trace-your-ancestor service to ghostly sound-effects; the loos are billed, with some welcome self-irony, "Westport House Toilet Centre". On the plus side, though, the delicate response of the house to its luminous surroundings of land, light and water is undimmed and wonderful if you can ignore the commerce – and feel like shelling out the swingeing admission fee.

Inside the house there's a *Holy Family* by Rubens, a violin which used to belong to J.M. Synge and, on the first floor, a room with lovely Chinese wallpapers dating from 1780. A lot of the mahogany in the house was brought back from Jamaica by the first marquess, who was instrumental in freeing slaves during his time as governor there. On the walls of the staircase, a series of paintings of local views by James Arthur O'Connor, commissioned by the second marquess in 1818 and 1819, shows an idyllic nineteenth-century landscape, an overweeningly romantic version of the dramatic scenery at Delphi; bustling activity as sailing boats are unloaded at Westport Quay. This was wishful thinking – Westport in the 1810s was already overshadowed by the changes in the relationship with England, and by 1825 was finished as an industrial centre.

Further out on The Quay, the Clew Bay Heritage Centre (Mon–Fri 10am–6pm, Sat–Sun 2–6pm; £1) – an engaging but chaotic jumble of old coins, agricultural implements, typewriters, ration books and other detritus – fails to live up to its grandiose title.

Information and accommodation

The **tourist office** in the Mall (April–Sept Mon–Sat 9am–6pm, open Sun during July and August; Oct–March Mon–Fri 9am–5.15pm; ☎098/25711) can also help with accommodation. Although you may be put off by the olde-worlde pretensions of the *Olde Railway Hotel* (☎098/25166; ⑨), its abundance of Victorian artefacts and its location opposite the canalized river on the leafy Mall, make it the top choice of hotels in the town; there are three mid-range **hotels**, the *Grand Central* (☎098/25027; ⑤), the *Knockranny House Hotel* (☎098/28600; ⑦), though the best option of the three is the friendly *Clew Bay Hotel* (☎098/28088; ⑥). There are also dozens of **B&Bs**: try Mrs Sheridan at *Altamont House*, Ballinrobe Road (☎098/25266; ③), *Annagh House* (☎098/25557; ③), half a mile out of town on the Leenane Road, or *Cedar Lodge*, Kings Hill (☎098/25417; ③). Vegetarians or those wanting an alternative from the standard B&B should try *Boheh Lough*, Liscarney (☎098/21797; ②), which is a fine farmhouse serving vegetarian food and has a treatment room for holistic massage. Out at The Quay, the *Helm* **bar** has rooms (☎098/26194; ②); make sure to ask for one facing the bay. A terrace of newly built **self-catering cottages** on the quayside blends in very effectively with the eighteenth-century architecture around it (☎098/25511).

For cheap accommodation, you've a choice of one An Óige and three independent **hostels**. The newest and most central is the fine, independent *Old Mill Hostel* (IHH; ☎098/27045, fax 21745), converted from part of an eighteenth-century complex of mills and warehouses it's on James Street, up from the Octagon. The large *Club Atlantic* is affiliated with both An Óige and the IHH and is very well run and maintained (mid-March to Oct; ☎098/26644, fax 26241); it's opposite the train station on Altamont Street and very close to Fair Green, where buses stop. If these two are full you can try either the roughly stone-built *Granary* (☎098/25903), past *Ryan's Hotel* on Quay Road, just before the road forks, or the cramped *Slí na hÓige* (☎098/26459) on the Fair Green. If you want to pitch a **tent**, *Parklands Caravan and Camping Park* (☎098/27766; May–Aug) is on the Westport Estate; there's more camping further out at Old Head.

Eating

There is a surprising variety of places to eat in Westport at all ends of the market. *The Lemon Peel* just off the Octagon (☎098/26929), has deservedly gained a good reputation locally, serving fine main courses such as medallion of lamb. Two restaurants with similar menus are *Torinos*, through the arch on Bridge Street, serving pasta and pizza dishes (last seating is early at 9.45pm) and *Sol Rios* also on Bridge Street opposite *Matt Molloys* pub. Popular locally is *O'Malleys* on Bridge Street, while at the other side of town is the *Asgard* (☎098/25319) which has a delicious bar menu. The *Continental Café and Healthfood Shop*, High Street (☎098/26679), offers a different interpretation of healthy food: fried eggs (free range), baked beans (organic) and frankfurters (unspecified) in an old-fashioned New Age environment (open until 6pm), while almost opposite is *Bernies Café* where you can get an all-day breakfast for £3.75. If you're self-catering, you can find some excellent local produce, much of it organic, at the **Thursday market** at the Octagon.

Festivals, nightlife and entertainment

Westport is fast developing a real cosmopolitan feel and attracting artistic types from Ireland and beyond. The main focus for this is the **Arts Festival** at the end of September while new public art studios have opened up in the redeveloped area of The Quay by the entrance to Westport House. In the centre, the best **music pubs** are on Bridge Street, where *The West* is hugely popular (arrive early and stay put) and *Matt Molloy's Bar*, owned by the eponymous flautist of The Chieftains, features occasional musical celebrities. The *Castle Court Hotel* features dancing on both a Friday and Saturday night, while on a Wednesday it holds a cabaret and céilí. The *Towers* pub, overlooking Clew Bay has traditional music most nights. If you want to enjoy a quiet drink then *Conway's* on Bridge Street is the place to go.

Daytime activities, sightseeing apart, are plentiful. If you're lucky with the weather the best **beaches** are at Bertra, six miles out on the Louisburgh Road, and Mulrany, eighteen miles away on the Achill Road. **Cycling** from Westport is rewarding, if strenuous – there are hills in almost all directions except towards Newport: bike rental is from J.P. Breheny & Sons, Castlebar Street (☎098/25020). **Walking** in the nearby Sheefry Hills or Dartry Mountains can be spectacular – pick up Paul Simms and Tony Wyatt's *Northwest Walks* at the tourist office or in any of the local bookshops. **Horse riding**, which will let you get right off the road, is available half a mile out of town on the Castlebar Road at the Drummindoo Equitation Centre (☎098/25616) and also at Westport House. The **sea angling** in Clew Bay is magnificent, and there are also good opportunities for salmon and trout fishing in nearby lakes and rivers – details from the Sea Angling Centre in town. **Sailing** in sheltered waters can be arranged through the Mayo Sailing Club in Rosmoney – good facilities and teaching for newcomers.

Newport

The road north out of Westport, bordered by bright fuchsia hedges, follows the shore of Clew Bay to **NEWPORT**, a neat, trim little eighteenth-century town unashamedly devoted to tourism and a serviceable base for both the sea and the Nephin Beg Mountains. Newport's main boast is that one of Grace Kelly's ancestors once lived in nearby Drimurla. It's also a centre for sea angling; if you go in the evening to the swanky *Newport House Hotel*, you'll see massive sea trout – caught by guests earlier in the day – laid out for the less energetic to admire.

About two miles outside Newport and signposted off the road to Achill is **Burrishoole Abbey**, a Dominican priory in a peaceful setting, lapped by the waters of the bay – at high tide you have to hop across a stepping stone to get in. Founded in the fifteenth century by Richard Burke – second husband of the pirate queen Grace O'Malley and unfortunately nicknamed "Iron Dick" – who spent the last years of his life here. The abbey has some cloisters still surviving and stands as a symbol of the spread of religious life under the "more Irish than the Irish" Normans. Another mile or so along the Achill Road, the turning labelled "Carrickanowley Castle" brings you to **Rockfleet Castle**, a perfect fifteenth- or sixteenth-century tower house that stands with its feet in a quiet outlet of Clew Bay – you'll get your feet wet stepping up to the door at high tide. An English attack on it was quelled by Grace O'Malley, who subsequently lived here.

GRACE O'MALLEY: THE PIRATE QUEEN

There came to me also a most famous feminine sea captain called Granny Ny Mally and offered her services unto me, wheresoever I would command her, with three galleys and 200 fighting men, either in Scotland or in Ireland. She brought with her her husband, for she was as well by sea as by land well more than Mrs Mate with him.... This was a notorious woman in all the coasts of Ireland.

Sir Henry Sidney, Lord Deputy of Ireland, 1577

Grace O'Malley, or Gráinne Ní Mháille (c.1530–1600; often corrupted to **Granuaile**), was the daughter of Owen O'Malley, chief of the west coast islands. Through fearless and none-too-scrupulous warfare and piracy, she made herself queen of the Clew Bay area when he died. She effectively controlled the vigorous trade between Galway and the Continent, as well as running a lucrative business importing Scottish mercenaries for chieftains' wars against Elizabeth I and their cattle-rustling and plundering. She earned her place in Irish legend by being one of the few Irish chiefs to stand up to the English.

In 1575, she visited the St Lawrences of Howth Castle near Dublin (see p.96), expecting to be made welcome in the Irish fashion. When, instead, she was told that the family was eating and that she would have to wait, she responded by abducting the family's heir. When she met Elizabeth I in London in 1593, she insisted on being treated as her regal equal. However, always a canny tactician, Grace switched sides when she realized she couldn't beat the English, and her son was created first Viscount Mayo. Continually mentioned in sixteenth-century dispatches, her exploits included dissolving her Celtic secular marriage to her second husband, Sir Richard Burke of Mayo, by slamming the castle door in his face and then stealing all his castles. At a time when the old Gaelic world was crumbling around her, Grace ensured the continuation of her own dynasty and something of the old culture.

The **tourist office** is on Main Street (☎098/41822) and is open weekdays from June to September. If you want to **stay** in Newport, there's the upmarket *Newport House Hotel* (☎098/41222; ⑧) or for B&B try *De Bille House*, a handsome stone building on the main street (☎098/41195; ③), which also runs a pleasant coffee shop; its generously sized rooms are a good option for families. The house is named after a Danish sea-captain who was shipwrecked en route for the Danish West Indian Isles in 1782; he and his crew were rescued, but subsequently died of a fever. You can still see the house in which he was nursed in the back yard. There's **self-catering** accommodation at Loch Morchan at Kilbride, just outside Newport (☎098/41221). **Eating** can be a problem after 9pm: good, basic food is available from *De Bille House Cafe* on the main street or *The Black Oak Inn* across the bridge. **Drinking** itself is best done at *Cowley's Singing Lounge* or at the *Angler's Rest*, which also does traditional music and good food.

Five miles away, high among the powerful outlines of the Nephin Beg Mountains – take the Achill Road and follow the signs – is the An Óige **hostel**, *Traenlaur Lodge* at Lough Feeagh (☎096/13272; Easter–Sept), a hefty climb but well worth it to stay in an unparalleled location at the head of this upland lake – and a perfect base for **walking** in the area (see p.386 for details of the long-distance Bangor Trail). For **horse riding** and pony trekking the contact is ☎098/36126; permits for **fishing** are available from the *Newport House Hotel*.

The road northwest towards Achill runs, for the most part, too far inland for the glories of Clew Bay to be visible; but it's always worth making detours down the lanes that lead to the water's edge.

Achill Island

More than with most places in the west, you need good weather for **ACHILL ISLAND**. Although it's the part of County Mayo most developed for tourism, this means no more than a few hotels, B&Bs and hostels, and if it rains there's simply nothing to do but pack up and head for Westport or Sligo. Because of a government tax allowance scheme Achill has been blighted by a plethora of tourist developments many of which are modern "cottages" that take no account of traditional architecture or landscape. Against this, however, there's the magnificence of the mountains and cliffs, and in good weather, Achill can be magical, especially for campers who can live at the water's edge. The island's sandy beaches never seem overcrowded, although they attract plenty of (mostly Irish) tourists in high summer. Inland, the bogs and mountains are dotted with ancient relics – standing stones, stone circles and dolmens. The largest of the Irish islands (although it's connected to the mainland by a road bridge), Achill was Irish-speaking until very recently. Tourism here seems to have had an almost entirely beneficial effect, economically at least: before its arrival, islanders subsisted to a very great extent on remittances sent home by emigrant relatives.

Achill Sound

The bridge that crosses to the island will bring you first to **ACHILL SOUND**. There's a small **tourist office**, on the mainland side at *Alice's Harbour Inn* (July & Aug Mon–Sat 10am–6pm; ☎098/45384), and a number of souvenir shops. These can be discouraging, but it's best to ignore them – they're in no way typical of what's to come. More useful are a post office and **bike rental** over the bridge at *Óstán gob A'choire*, aka *Achill Sound Hotel* (☎098/45245; ③). Before you cross the bridge over Achill Sound, opposite the Garda Station, you'll find the *Station House Hostel* (☎098/45187), with good rooms, two kitchens and an open fire. Achill Sound really isn't the best base for exploring the island, but if you decide to go no further, it's worth pressing on a few hundred yards for an excellent independent **hostel**, the *Wild Haven* (☎098/45392), which does offer the comforts of warm duvets and an open fire. Nearby, there's a little café, *An Bolg Lán*, that serves good home baking and sandwiches.

The island

A combination of walking and cycling is the most pleasurable way to get to know Achill, although the island can be fairly strenuous going (hitching is a viable alternative, especially in season when the island is full of visitors).

The road that encircles the island has now been signposted as the "Atlantic drive". After a left turn, you'll follow a narrow inlet of the sea for three miles, before coming to **KILDOWNET**, where the well-preserved tower of the fifteenth-century **Carrickdaunet Castle**, once owned by the redoubtable Grace O'Malley, gazes out at the mainland (keys from the house next door). There are also the ruins of a twelfth-century church. As you round the corner of the island, the view of the ocean opens up, and the massive shoulder of **Minaun**, Achill's third highest mountain, appears.

Keel and Dooagh

At **KEEL**, there's a wonderful two-mile sandy **beach**, which ends at the twin village of Dooagh. At the Keel end of the strand are the fantastic Cathedral Rocks, eroded into a series of caves and pillars by the wind and water. They are backed by **Minaun**, at 1532ft another mountain worth climbing for the view. A turning off the road into Keel will take you close up to the summit.

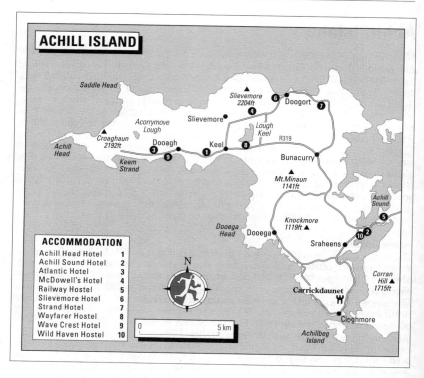

ACHILL ISLAND

Saddle Head

Slievemore
2204ft 6 Doogort 7

Acorrymove
Lough Slievemore 4

Lough
Keel R319

Croaghaun
2192ft Dooagh 3 Keel 1 8

Achill
Head 9

Keem
Strand Bunacurry

Mt.Minaun
1141ft

Achill
Sound

Dooega
Head Dooega Knockmore
1119ft 5

Sraheens 10 2

Corran
Hill
1715ft

Carrickdaunet

Cloghmore

Achillbeg
Island

N

0   5 km

ACCOMMODATION

Achill Head Hotel	1
Achill Sound Hotel	2
Atlantic Hotel	3
McDowell's Hotel	4
Railway Hostel	5
Slievemore Hotel	6
Strand Hotel	7
Wayfarer Hostel	8
Wave Crest Hotel	9
Wild Haven Hostel	10

West along the strand at **DOOAGH**, one road leads on over the side of the Croaghaun to the golden sands and, on a good day, sparkling turquoise waters of **Keem Strand**. Often deserted, it's a rewarding place to make for, with its impressive views over Clew Bay, but if you're on a bike, be warned: it's tough going (and the sheer drop on the seaward side is vertigo inducing). A turning off the Keem Road will take you up to **Acorrymore Lough** – surrounded by scree slopes, and now dammed to supply water locally. It's a bleak, rather than poetic, spot and is the best ascent of **Croghaun**, the island's second highest mountain and just a whisker lower than Slievemore at 2195ft – its seaward side boasts spectacularly high cliffs, the island's highest. This is decidedly tough hill-walking country, so you need to be reasonably experienced even to think of attempting it. Once at the top, however, you're rewarded with a magnificent view of the Belmullet Peninsula and the scattered islands, while mountains rise spectacularly in the southeast.

If you want to **stay**, at Keel there's the *Wayfarer Hostel*, which is right on the strand (IHH; ☎098/43266, fax 47253; mid-March to mid-Oct), though it does lack communal facilities. The **campsite** (☎098/43211; June–Sept) is also on the strand. Dooagh's *Achill Head Hotel* (☎098/43108; ⑤) has a nightclub and could make a more lively base. There is also a fine B&B in Dooagh, the *West Coast House* (☎098/43317; ③). The best places for eating and drinking are in Dooagh; here the *Beehive* is a relaxed crafts and coffee shop, and you can get fresh or the culinary star of the area – indeed, the island – is *The Boley House* (6–9pm; ☎098/43147), with modest home cooking using super-fresh ingredients (signposted from the eastern end of the village). You can rent **bikes** at O'Malley's Island Sports in Dooagh (☎098/43125); for **music**, try the nearby *Village Inn* or *The Mihaun*.

Dugort

DUGORT, decidedly less fly-blown than Keel or Dooagh, though without their magnificent open views of the Atlantic, may make a more comfortable base. Follow the signs for the Deserted Village, and take the Atlantic Drive for Dugort. Half a mile out of Keel, a signposted footpath leads to a mini megalithic tomb set in the hillside where the gorse meets the heather – well worth the climb, if only for the view. A couple of miles further on, some ruined buildings and scattered gravestones are all that's left of a village known simply as **The Settlement**. It was founded in 1834 by a Protestant vicar, the Reverend E. Nangle, who bought up sixty percent of the island and built schools and a printing press in an ultimately unsuccessful effort to evangelize the islanders. Towering to the north is **Slievemore**, Achill's highest mountain at 2205ft – a massive pile of quartzite and mica. Here on its southern slopes stands a **dolmen** with a stone circle at each end and a *booley* village of huts formerly used during summer pasturing – a reminder of a much newer, but equally extinct, transhumant way of life. At the foot of Slievemore, on the seaward side, are the **Seal Caves**, burrowing way back under the mountain; you can visit them by boat from the tiny pier at Dugort.

If you want to get away from the seaside holiday atmosphere, you can **stay** on the southern slopes of the mountain at *McDowell's Hotel* (☎098/43148; ④; April–Sept), which does excellent food, including vegetarian, and runs frequent traditional music sessions, or, closer to Dugort, at the *Slievemore Hotel* (☎098/43224; ④). In Dugort itself you can stay in comfort at *Gray's Guest House* (☎098/43244; ③). Two miles east of the village, *Atoka House*, at Valley Crossroads, is a comfortable **B&B** (☎098/47229; ②) with a good restaurant attached. A few hundred yards away and signposted is the *Valley House Hostel* (☎098/47204; April–Nov), a handsome, crumbling edifice that was once home to the woman whose story is told in J.M. Synge's *The Playboy of the Western World* – her rejected suitor burned down a barn and tossed her onto the flames. The place now has four-bed rooms and the luxury of a bar in the courtyard behind the house. Dugort has two **campsites**: the *Seal Caves Caravan and Camping Park* (☎098/43262; April–Sept) and *Lavele's Golden Strand Caravan and Camping Park* (☎098/47232; April–Sept).

The flatlands between Achill and Belmullet are currently being reafforested with thick conifer plantations, but are less than exciting.

North Mayo

Predominantly bogland, **north Mayo** – and especially the northwest – is an area that can seem forbidding in bad weather, but when the sun shines and suffuses everything in a hazy glow, you can forgive all. The most interesting sights are the **Céide Fields**, where prehistoric field patterns have been uncovered beneath nearly seven feet of bog, offering a startling view of the unchanging nature of human habitation here over five millennia; and the historically resonant town of **Killala**, scene of the 1798 French invasion.

Bangor, the walking trail and Erris

About 25 miles north from Achill, **BANGOR (or sometimes Bangor Ennis)** is pleasant enough, although its landlocked location makes it less exciting than the seaside places nearby.

Bangor marks the start of a spectacular 22-mile hike, the **Bangor Trail**, an ancient route that runs southeast through the **Nephin Beg Mountains** to Newport. As R.L. Praeger, who walked the route in 1937 wrote: "Where else even in Ireland will you find this hundred square miles which is homeless and roadless – nothing but brown heather rising as far as you can see... into high bare hills breaking down here and there in rocky scarps, with the Atlantic winds singing along their slopes?"

It is indeed lonely country, with the legacy of the Famine everywhere visible, but the desolation of the landscape can be exhilarating. A couple of fine guides to the route are available: *County Mayo, The Bangor Trail* (£6) by Joe MacDermott, or the locally produced *Bangor Trail* by Uinsíonn MacGrath and Theresa ní Ghearraigh, which is available in most newsagents in the area.

Belmullet and the peninsula

Heading on from Bangor along the R313 through bleak uninhabited bogland you'll come to **BELMULLET** (*Béal an Mhuirthead*, "mouth of the Mullet"), a functional little village, its streets perpetually mired from the mud of the bogs. Like most Irish towns, it's a planned settlement, founded as late as 1825 by the local landlord, William Carter, to "create a home market for produce that did not previously exist nearer than thirty miles by land". Its success was such that it eclipsed the older landlord village of Binghamstown (*An Geata Mór*), on the peninsula, which was deserted by the late nineteenth century. The attraction of the place lies not so much in its physical charms as in a kind of unpretentious unhurriedness – life goes on, shops stay open until late, and the sun arches slowly toward the horizon over the wide western sea.

There is a small **tourist office** on the left side of the main street as you enter the town (☎097/81500). You can **stay** in the *Western Strands Hotel* (☎097/81096; ④), which has basic rooms, and there are numerous B&Bs; for value try *Mill House* in American Street (☎097/81181; ②) or *Drom Caoin* (☎097/81195; ③), popular with anglers. There are plenty of bars and fast-food joints, so take your pick; the liveliest **bar** is probably the one at the *Western Strands*, where you'll also get a good cheap dinner. *Leneghan's*, next to the hotel, has *comhaltas* (traditional music) sessions on the third Friday of the month; so does the *Anchor Bar*, which serves local seafood.

A flat slab of land that seems tacked on to the mainland almost as an afterthought, **Belmullet Peninsula** is sparsely populated, but the houses are scattered in the characteristically Irish way (town-dwelling, as well as Ireland's town-planning, was largely an Anglo-Irish invention). Along with this pattern of habitation, you'll also see field-systems not much different from the Stone Age ones uncovered at Céide (see opposite).

The seaward side of the peninsula is raked by Atlantic winds to the extent that almost no vegetation can survive. The landward side, overlooking Blacksod Bay, at the southern tip of the peninsula, is much more sheltered and has some good **beaches**, notably at Elly Bay halfway down. To the east and north the land rises; although the cliffs are not hugely spectacular, there's some rewarding walking. The peninsula is one of the locations where the legendary Children of Lír (see p.186) were condemned to spend their last three hundred years; they are buried, according to legend, on Inishglora, a tiny island off the west coast. The peninsula is rich in historical remains, too: there are promontory **forts** at Doonamo, Doonaneanir and Portnafrankach. The one at Doonamo, on an impressive clifftop site, encloses three *clocháns* and a circular fort. Under the waters of Blacksod Bay lies **La Rata**, the largest of three Spanish Armada galleons that sank in 1588.

In calm weather, Matthew and Josephine Geraghty run boat trips out to the islands of **Inis Gé** (Inishkea North and South) for £10 return (☎097/85741) from Belmullet; Millicent Sweeney at Blacksod is an alternative (☎097/85662 or evenings ☎097/85774). You can arrange **riding** at the Durham Riding Centre near Blacksod (☎097/85811).

Northeast along the coast to Downpatrick Head

East of Belmullet, the country becomes much wilder: surveyed by the ice-polished shapes of the mountains, it's rough, boggy terrain where many of the remoter villages are still Irish-speaking.

Heading out of Belmullet, towards Ballycastle, you'll see a signpost for the village of **POLLATOMISH** (*Poll an Tómais*, "Thomas' Hole"), a delightful little place deep in fjord-like country, with a handful of houses and two pubs. If you intend to stay in this area then by far and away the best place is the superb independent hostel at *Kilcommon Lodge* (☎097/84621). The dorm rooms are excellent and there is a reading room, heated by a turf fire with tables with individual reading lamps. *McGrath's* bar can be fun and it has set dancing on Wednesday nights.

From here single-track roads lead up to Benwee Head; at almost 820ft, this massive cliff has great views of the Donegal cliffs to the northeast and the **Stags of Broadhaven**, a series of seven 300ft rocks, which stand a mile and a half off the coast. **PORTACLOY**, where there's a deply indented bay edged with golden sand, makes a good starting point for walking on the headland; there's a B&B high up on the hill facing the headland. The **Hackett and Turpin** factory shop is on the road to Rinroe Point at Ceathrú Thaidgh (Carrowteige), the other obvious setting-off point for Benwee Head and an unlikely – not to be missed – outpost of the fashion industry. Here local women work on six hand looms to produce designer knitwear in linen, silk and wool at amazingly low prices. The road descends through intricate interlockings of land and sea to golden beaches and the tiny harbour at Rinroe itself.

Further east, near Porturlin, the waves have carved the rocks into weird, contorted shapes, including the **Arches**, a 30ft opening in the cliff which the brave – or foolhardy – attempt to row through in good weather at low tide.

At **Downpatrick Head**, there are some puffing holes that send up tall plumes of water in rough weather, and a detached stack of rock with a fort perched on it; a plaque commemorates those who were killed in the aftermath of the 1798 uprisings. There's a profusion of rare birds and grand views over to Céide Fields and the wild country to the west, eastwards to the Sligo mountains and north across the wide, empty sea.

Céide Fields

In terms of understanding the landscape, the most important site on this stretch of coast is the prehistoric farm that covers some 24 square miles of boggy moorland between Belderrig and Ballycastle. Although signposted from the road, the Belderrig site offers little enlightenment to the untrained eye: for that, carry on another five miles to the main site at **Céide Fields** – pronounced "cajun" without the *n* – (mid-March to May & Oct daily 10am–5pm; June–Sept daily 9.30am–6.30pm; Nov daily 10am–4.30pm; £2.50). As Seamus Heaney's poem *Belderg* observes:

> *They just kept turning up*
> *and were thought of as foreign*
> *one-eyed and benign, they lie about his house*
> *quernstones out of a bog*

Under nearly seven feet of blanket bog, archeologists have unearthed the stone walls of a Neolithic farm system and apparently solved the riddle of how the builders of the great megalithic tombs that run across the northern part of Ireland lived. They were, it seems, farming people who joined the original fishers and hunters of Ireland around 5000 years ago and seem to have lived in harmony with them, and each other: the pattern of settlement is dispersed and shows no defensive features. The fields run longitudinally with the slope of the land and appear to have been used for pasture – as in contemporary Ireland, where the largest single contribution to the national economy still comes from grass-raised livestock.

The faint marks left by these ancient farmers don't look like much to the untrained eye, and the Céide Fields centre is, inevitably, heavy on interpretation. The building itself is impressively conceived, the pyramidal shape not at odds with the landscape. The interior is a combination of sandstone, oak and glass and in the middle, stretching towards the apex of the pyramid is a huge piece of bog pine. The centre includes an exhibition, a viewing platform an audiovisual theatre (with a romantically voice-overed show giving some of the area's geological background) and an excellent café. The entrance fee also includes a guided tour, usually by one of the archeological workers on the dig.

Ballycastle

The coastal road from the Céide Fields to Ballycastle is as spectacular as any on Ireland's west coast. **BALLYCASTLE**, just east of the Céide Fields, in the wide valley of the River Ballinglen, is a tranquil village of just one broad, sloping street, with good swimming beaches.

THE FRENCH INVASION

On August 22, 1798, three warships flying British colours anchored at Kilcummin, near Killala. The Protestant Bishop Stock, relieved that they were apparently English and not the rumoured French invasion fleet, sent his two sons and the port surveyor to pay their respects. They were immediately taken prisoner; the **invasion** had begun. After a brief resistance, Killala yielded to the French, and at sunset that evening a French soldier climbed to the top of the Bishop's Palace and replaced the British flag with a green flag with a harp in the centre, bearing the words *Erin go Bragh* (Ireland for Ever).

Wolfe Tone, the inspirational leader of the United Irishmen, had been working since his exile from Ireland in 1794 to secure foreign aid for his planned insurrection against the British. However, by the time the first French expedition of 1100 men under General Humbert had reached Killala, rebellion had already been all but crushed. Not only was there a military mismatch between the French professional soldiers and the few poorly armed Irish novices who joined them, but there were also ideological clashes. The French had expected that liberation from British rule would appeal to Catholics and Protestants alike, and were further confused to find the Irish volunteers greeting them in the name of the Blessed Virgin and apparently having no idea of the significance of the French Revolution.

The rest of the story is sadly predictable. With some heroic fighting, the Franco-Irish army took Killala, Ballina and Castlebar, but on September 8, near the village of Ballinamuck in County Longford, seriously depleted in both numbers and weapons, it was defeated by the united armies of Lord Cornwallis and General Lake. The French were taken prisoner and returned to France; the Irish rebels were hanged. At Rath Lackan, there's a statue to the first French soldier who fell in the 1798 struggle, as well as a wide bay with golden sands looking over to the Sligo mountains.

A month later, sailing with another French force from Brest, Wolfe Tone was himself captured – along with the French fleet – off the coast of Donegal. He was subsequently court-martialled and condemned to death. Despite his insistence that he should be treated with military honour, and therefore shot, he was sentenced to hang. Before that could be carried out, he cut his throat with a pocketknife and died after seven days of agony. He came to personify the tradition of both revolutionary violence and religious tolerance (he was a Protestant) in the cause of an independent Ireland.

The events of 1798 led directly to the Act of Union with Britain three years later, while the land agitation that spread throughout the country laid the foundations for land reform, Catholic emancipation and, eventually, the long process that led to Irish independence.

The **tourist office**, which will be able to offer detailed advice on walking nearby, is based just below the church (Mon–Sat 10.30am–5pm, Sun 1–4pm; closed for long lunches). There are a handful of relaxed **bars** – try the tiny *Lavell's* or *Barlett's* pub. The best restaurant around is *Doonfeeny House* (☎096/43092) which does a five-course meal for £20, while for accommodation try *The Hawthorns* (☎096/43148; ③) a ten-minute drive from Ballycastle.

Killala and around

KILLALA, (*Cill Ala*, "Ala's Church") overlooking Killala Bay as the coast curves back round towards Ballina, is a must, both for the magnificent local scenery and for its historical connections. Scene of one of the most significant events in Irish history – the unsuccessful French invasion organized by Wolfe Tone in 1798 (see opposite) – it's a pleasantly run-down seaside town, so small it's difficult to believe it's a bishopric, with lovely wild sea coasts and some good roads for cycling. As far as sights go, the highlights are an attractive quayside and a fine round tower, but it's the historic atmosphere that's the real attraction here. Killala's a convivial place with a disproportionate number of **pubs** – *An Gránuaile* and *The Village Inn* are two of the most traditional. Music is available at *The Anchor Bar*, as is local seafood. There's a tea shop down on the strand with fine views out to sea. A mile or so north there's a good, sheltered, sandy beach for swimming at Ross Point (signposted from the Ballycastle Road).

If you want to **stay**, there are a few **B&Bs**. Nearest to the centre is *Kevin Munnelly's farmhouse* (☎096/32331; ③), half a mile out on Crossmolina Road. Further out is Mrs Carey's *Rathoma House* (☎096/32035; ③), four miles out of town, while *O'Hara's Beach View House* (☎096/32023; ③) is three miles out towards the beach. The **tourist office** (June–Sept 10am–5pm; ☎096/32166) is in the community centre next door. Most local newsagents sell Bishop Stock's *Narrative* of the events of 1798 – a surprisingly sympathetic account of the uprising.

Ballina to Castlebar

The interior of County Mayo can't match the splendour of its sea coasts, and unless you're keen on fishing or walking, you're unlikely to spend much time here. Like all of Ireland's less touristed areas, however, it has a charm of its own if you stick with it. A region of rough moorland – the foothills of the Nephin Beg and Ox ranges – it's strewn with lakes, giving way in the east to flatter, more fertile country. It's dotted, too, with market towns, each with its own distinctive architecture and character.

The road from Killala to Ballina runs through flat farm country. The minor road that runs closer to the Moy estuary is more interesting, with two abbeys on the estuary, **Moyne** and **Rosserk**, both of them founded in the fifteenth century. Rosserk, with a tower at the water's edge, is the bigger and more poetic of the two – and considered the best Franciscan building in the country – but both have good cloisters. Look out for the sixteenth-century graffiti on the wall at Moyne; the place was burned down by Sir Richard Bingham, the English governor of Connacht, in 1590.

Ballina

The busy town of **BALLINA**, clustered around two graceful bridges on the River Moy, makes a good place to stock up on provisions and information. The elegant Victorian and Edwardian pub- and shop-fronts testify to a long history of vigorous trading, and this tradition continues in the rebuilding and energetic business activity that's evident everywhere. Stock up on smoked salmon at Clarke's Salmon Smokery on O'Rahilly Street, which also displays an impressive range of fresh, whole fish in its windows. Keehane's in Arran Street is a reasonable bookshop.

The **tourist office** (April–Sept Mon–Sat 10am–1pm & 2–5.45pm; ☎096/70848) is between the bridges on the side of the river away from town. If you want to **stay** and indulge in some real splendour, with a touch of Gothic-horror excess, try *Belleek Castle* (☎096/22400; ⑧). Take Pearse Street eastward from the centre, and follow the signs; a left turn will bring you through an imposing stone gateway and to a long drive through dark forest to a neo-Jacobean mansion in forbidding grey stone. For more affordable accommodation the *Bartra House Hotel* (☎096/22200; ⑤) is a cheerful and friendly place; while the excellent *Salmon Weir Hostel* (IHH; ☎096/71903), built on the site of an old timber and grain mill on the banks of the River Moy, is an imaginative piece of industrial rehab – the car park is graced with a series of Firoic columns. The best of the many B&Bs are *Whitestream House* (☎096/21582; ③), on the Foxford Road, or four miles out of town, *Jordan's Red River Lodge* (☎096/22841; ③).

When **eating**, make sure you try the famous Moy salmon. The *River Bar Inn*, on the right bank of the Moy, a little downriver from town, does good seafood. *The Broken Jug*(☎096/72379) – named after John Banville's play – a roomy bar and restaurant at the top of Pearse Street, offers a fine selection of carvery meals from about £4. The *Old Bond Store Restaurant and Crafts Shop* in Dillon Terrace, another refurbishment, makes a good stop for daytime meals.

Crossmolina and Lough Conn

Five or so miles southwest, relaxed, raffish **CROSSMOLINA**, at the top of Lough Conn, has a place to stay that's a sight in itself. Not far south on the lakeshore, *Enniscoe House* (☎096/31112; ⑥), a Georgian mansion that does B&B, is a good example of easygoing Georgian attitudes to architecture. Originally built in the mid-eighteenth century as a three-storey house, it was extended in the 1790s (and damaged in 1798 when the French army marched down the back avenue) to include a grand facade overlooking Lough Conn. The result inside is two completely different structures whose floor levels and room sizes don't correspond at all. The **North Mayo Family History Research and Heritage Centre** is nearby where visitors can trace their north Mayo ancestors and browse around the heritage centre which has mainly agricultural artefacts, with demonstrations of traditional crafts (year round Mon–Fri 9am–4pm plus weekends June–Sept 2–6pm).

There is a **tourist office** in town (May–Oct Mon–Fri 10am–1.30pm & 2–5pm, Sat 10.30am–1pm & 2–4.30pm; no phone). The *Dolphin Hotel* (☎096/31270; ③) makes for a comfortable run-down alternative to the *Enniscoe*, or for B&B try *Lake View House* (☎096/31296; ③). You can get good daytime **meals** in the *Tea Room*, and there are plenty of **bars**, most with **music** a couple of nights during the week – *McMorrow's* has traditional sessions on Friday nights, and also sells fishing tackle for anglers bound for the nearby lough.

The main attraction of **Lough Conn** is for fishermen: the lake itself is rich in trout, and the River Moy is a delight to salmon anglers. If this is your thing then the place to stay would be the marvellously eccentric *Mount Falcon Castle* (☎096/21172; ⑧), run by the indomitable Constance Aldridge a few miles out of Ballina, which has its own fishing. If you're staying elsewhere you'll need to check the position on licences locally. However, the area has plenty of scenic and historical interest to sustain non-anglers. The moorland hills that border the lake are good for gentle **walking**; for a taste of the Nephin Beg wilderness and some more demanding hikes (see p.382) head south from Crossmolina down the west side of the lough and take a right at Lahardaun. The lakesides themselves are scattered with abbeys, castles and megaliths, as well as some hidden sandy beaches.

Pontoon and Foxford

Continuing south along the R315 for Foxford, through rough, peaty terrain strewn with boulders, you reach **PONTOON**, on the neck of land that separates Lough Conn from Lough Cullin. The village is a good base for exploring both the lakes' shores and the foothills of the Nephin Beg Mountains to the northwest and the Ox Mountains to the northeast. For **accommodation**, try *Healy's Hotel* (☎094/56443; ⑤), a no-nonsense anglers' **hotel** and former coaching inn on the lakeside, where the restaurant specializes in home-cooked Irish food using local produce.

FOXFORD, a couple of miles east, is a trim village in the lee of the Ox Mountains which owed its late nineteenth-century survival to the **Foxford Woollen Mill** (April–Oct Mon–Sat 10am–5.30pm & Sun noon–5.30pm; £3.00; includes tour of present-day factory), which now has an elaborate audiovisual presentation to tell its story. There's a gift shop and, upstairs, a pleasant tea shop; rooms are let to local artists and craftspeople. After the 1840s Famine, the potato crop failed again in the 1870s, resulting in evictions and abject poverty for the people of the town and the peat-cutting districts around. Most families led a precarious existence, relying on their own potato crop and, in the absence of significant cash employment in Foxford, the meagre earnings the men were able to bring back from summers working on big farms in Scotland. Such conditions led to demands for land reform – the Land League was founded in 1879 by Michael Davitt, also the bringer of trade unionism to Ireland, whose cottage at **STRADE**, between Foxford and Castlebar, you can also visit (Tues–Sat 2–6pm; 50p). The mill at Foxford was founded in 1890 by a far-sighted nun called Marrough Bernard, who called it Providence. At a time when more professionally run mills were failing – so unused were her workers to ideas of productivity that she had to bribe them with cash prizes – the success of the mill could certainly be called providential. Its profits were used to fund schools and a diverse range of cultural activities, of which one, the Foxford Mill brass band, still survives.

The **tourist office**, in one of the mill buildings (Mon–Sat 11am–5pm, Sun noon–6pm; ☎094/56488), has useful details of walking and fishing in the area; the North Mayo Angling Advice Centre, where you can buy licences, is also in the town. There are a few **B&Bs** in Foxford – try *Mrs M. Gannon* on Providence Road (☎094/56101; ②), but on the whole, you're probably better off among the scenic beauties of Pontoon. *Hennigan's* pub has traditional music and ballad nights.

Castlebar and around

CASTLEBAR, although it's the county town of Mayo, offers little reason to hang around. The tree-bordered green is attractive, and the main street has all the facilities you might need conveniently gathered together, but since the demise of the annual rock festival there seems to be little going on. Historically, it's notable for a Franco-Irish victory in 1798, at which General Humbert's army routed a stronger force commanded by General Lake – the event has gone down in history as the "Castlebar Races" because of the speed of the British retreat. The **tourist office** (Mon–Sat 9.30am–6pm; ☎094/21207) is in the Old Linen Hall – which was the venue for a celebratory dinner after the rout of the British in 1798 – and, with information about the whole of north Mayo, is more than usually useful if you're planning an extended stay; it's particularly strong on walking. In the same building is the Linen Hall Arts Centre, which puts on sometimes imaginative shows (including plenty for children); and, if your body is crying out for cappuccinos, you can buy them in the attached café.

Should you need to **stay**, you'll find no shortage of accommodation. There's the swanky *Breaffy House* (☎094/22033; ⑦), a Victorian pile out on the Claremont Road, with hideous modern extensions; or back in town, the friendly and comfortable *Daly's Hotel* (☎094/21961; ⑥), which is ideally situated on the green. **B&Bs** are mainly concentrated on the Westport Road, where you could try *Nephin House* (☎094/23840; ③) or *Millhill House* (☎094/24279; ③), both of which allow children to stay for half price. In the centre of town, in Thomas Street, is a fine **hostel**, *Hughes House* (IHH; ☎094/23877, fax 23877; June–Sept).

There's a fine fish **restaurant** on Chapel Street, *An Carraig* (☎094/26159), or try the new *Cox's* restaurant on Linenhall Street (☎094/26611), which serves good traditional cuisine and has proved very popular. *Café Rouge* in New Antrim Street does a good range of home cooking for daytime eating (10am–6pm). For pub food there's the excellent *Flannelly's* behind the train station, while filling lunches are served at *Daly's Hotel* (see overleaf). *McCarthy's Bar* in Main Street has snugs and **traditional music**. *Johnnie McHale's*, opposite the *Welcome Inn* in Upper Chapel Street, is a great old Castlebar music pub, as is the *Irish House* in Thomas Street. *Moran's*, off the green in Spencer Street, has music on Thursday nights.

Seven miles south of Castlebar on the Ballinrobe Road (N84) is **Ballintubber Abbey**. Founded in 1216 by Cathal O'Connor, King of Connacht, it is claimed to be the oldest church in Ireland to have been in continual use. Leaflets on the church are freely available and there is an informative, if rather dated, video showing the local community performing its annual passion play and following pilgrims along **Tóchar Phádraig**, the 22-mile pilgrim route to Croagh Patrick, which starts at the abbey.

Southeast of Ballintubber Abbey, on the shores of Lough Carra, you can explore the **Doon Archeological Nature Peninsula** (10am–6pm June–Sept; £3). With things to see from standing stones to Norman castles, and a Famine grave, the place opens up the complex human history of this seemingly little-populated area.

About five miles southeast along the N60, **Balla**, a single wide street of pastel-coloured houses, has a short round tower, off the main square, that may be a twelfth-century "fake". The hamlet of **Mayo**, lost in a maze of unsignposted lanes, has only an abrupt right-angle bend in the road to mark the ghostly presence of the Augustinian abbey that gave the place enough importance to make it the county town.

Knock to Cong

East Mayo is dominated by the devotional shrine at Knock, easier to visit since the opening of an international **airport** at nearby Charlestown in 1986. However, if you're not a believer or religious kitsch isn't a strong enough draw, you're best off heading south to the more engaging and historically rich town of Cong.

Knock

Ever since an apparition of the Virgin Mary, accompanied by St Joseph and St John, was seen on the gable of the parish church of **KNOCK** in 1879, it has been a place of pilgrimage. As a passer-by in Ireland, it's surprisingly easy to forget the all-pervasive influence of the Catholic Church, but at Knock you're brought slap up against it. Whatever you may believe about the possible authenticity of the apparitions, Knock rates for Catholics, along with Lourdes in France and Fatima in Portugal, as one of the leading modern miraculous confirmations of their faith. A massive and ugly church with a capacity of twenty thousand was opened nearby in 1976, and the pope visited the shrine in 1979.

When Monsignor Horan, a local priest, first hatched the plan for the new airport it seemed a crazy and profligate idea, and there were years of bitter controversy over this apparent waste of public funds. In fact it has proved remarkably successful, and as well as bringing in pilgrims to see the shrine, the airport has had the effect of opening up the northwest of Ireland for travellers – to the extent that Mayo is in reach of London for weekend breaks, and house prices in the county are booming as wealthy inhabitants of southeast England buy their second homes. The Lourdes–Knock run is also used by fishers from the southwest of France to reach west Ireland's lake fisheries.

The **airport** (situated three miles from Charlestown at the junction of the N17 and N5) is open from 9am to 6pm daily, serving many UK airports including Luton, Stansted and Coventry. An Aer Lingus shuttle service to Dublin connects with major international flights. There's a **tourist office** in the airport, open to greet arriving flights (winter closed Tues & Thurs; ☎094/67247), and another in Knock itself (May–Sept daily 10am–6pm; ☎094/88193); ask them for details of transport – most of the time you seem to have to rely on taxis to Charlestown (a major crossroads where you can pick up buses and there are a number of B&Bs) or Knock.

As a **place**, Knock is nothing much to look at but if you are interested in religion or the Marian phenomenon in Irish life it can prove fascinating. The best place to start is the **Museum of Folk Life** (May–Oct daily 10am–7pm; £1.50), which contains artefacts relating to the apparition and the miracles associated with it. The scene of the apparitions has been glassed in to form a **chapel**, and pilgrims can be seen there praying at all hours. As you might expect, there is no shortage of kitsch plastic religious souvenirs on sale. If you need a place to **stay**, there's no problem finding somewhere. There are a couple of hotels, such as the *Belmont* (☎094/88122; ⑥) or the *Knock International Hotel* on Main Street (☎094/88466; ⑦), and numerous B&Bs: try Mrs McGrath's *Bridge House* (☎094/88205; ③), Airport Road, which does excellent family deals, Mrs Carney's *Burren*, Kiltimagh Road (☎094/88362; ③) or *Mervue*, overlooking the shrine (☎094/88127; ②).

Ballinrobe to Cong

BALLINROBE is probably worth visiting only if you're here in the third week of July, for the **Ballinrobe Races**. This is Irish racing as you've imagined it, with a great atmosphere at a picturesque and compact course; there's excellent viewing and it's all very relaxed and amateur. For accommodation, there are a couple of **B&Bs** – book early for race week – try Mrs Anne Mahon's *Riverside House* in the Cornmarket (☎092/41674; ③).

South of Ballinrobe, on the R334 around Neale, is clustered a sequence of monuments, ancient and not-so-ancient. They range from a series of stone circles, nearer Cong, to a cross and another of the mysterious monuments that abound in Ireland, a massive stone-stepped **pyramid**, with an almost indecipherable inscription, including the name George Browne and some worn Roman numerals, dating it somewhere in the eighteenth century. The Brownes are the family who occupy Westport House; but the reason for the pyramid remains obscure.

Cong and around

CONG lies on the narrow spit of land that divides Lough Mask from Lough Corrib at the point where the dramatically mountainous country of Connemara to the west gives way to the flat and fertile farmland that makes up the east of County Mayo. A picture-book pretty village that caters for plenty of tourists, it's also the site of the ruined **Cong Abbey**, which was founded in 1128 for the Augustinians by Turlough O'Connor, King of Ireland (though it's probably built on a seventh-century monastic site). The doorways represent the transition between the quite different styles of Romanesque and Gothic. The cloisters look just a little bit too good to be true: they were partially rebuilt in 1860. At its height, Cong Abbey had a population of some 3000, and the practicalities of feeding such multitudes can be glimpsed in the remains of the refectory and kitchen by the river, where a fishing house over the water contains a fish trap beneath the floor. The **Cross of Cong**, a twelfth-century ornamented Celtic cross originally made in County Roscommon for the abbey, gives an indication of the wealth and status of the foundation – it's now on show at the National Museum in Dublin. From the abbey there's a pleasant wander through woods down to the river and the lough, although this runs through the grounds of the local big house, **Ashford Castle**, now a luxury hotel (see below), which charges for admission to its lands (£2).

It's also worth taking a look at the **canal**. In the 1840s attempts were made, as a famine relief project, to dig a canal between Lough Corrib and Lough Mask. The river that links the two, though you can get to it at various points, including the Pigeon Hole, a mile or so north of Cong, runs underground through porous limestone for most of its length. This might have been an indication of what would happen to the canal: the porosity of the rock meant that the water just drained away, and Cong is left with a dry canal, complete with locks.

The town is obsessed with *The Quiet Man*, a film that much of the rest of the world may have forgotten but which, shot here in 1956 and starring John Wayne and Maureen O'Hara, is well remembered here. It's a highly romanticized portrayal of Ireland and is in many ways an expression of the emigrants' notion of Ireland and Irishness.

Practicalities

The **tourist office** in Abbey Street (May–Sept daily 10am–6pm; ☎092/46542) has many books and leaflets about the area most of which concentrate, predictably, on *The Quiet Man*; in fact guided tours leave the office for the locations used in the film. Undoubtedly the swishest place to **stay** – Ronald Reagan did – is *Ashford Castle,* which stands at the point where the river meets Lough Corrib, and has been converted into a luxury hotel (☎092/46003; ⑨). Although its history goes back to the thirteenth century, what you see now is essentially a Victorian castellated reconstruction. Two spruce hotels offer comfortable rooms: pastel green *Danagher's* (☎092/46494; ④), by the abbey, and terracotta red *Ryan's*, on the main street (☎092/46243; ⑤). Among the numerous **B&Bs**, half a mile from the village in Drumshiel is Mrs Coakley's *Hazel Grove* (☎092/46060; ③) or in the same area O'Connor's *Dolmen House* (☎092/46466; ③). *The Quiet Man* **hostel** (IHH; ☎092/46089, fax 46448; May–Sept) is centrally located on Abbey Street, while the *Cong Hostel* is one mile outside Cong itself in Lisloughery (same phone number). Both hostels rent out **bikes**, as does O'Connor's Garage on Main Street. There's more hostel accommodation and **camping** seven miles to the east in **Cross** (IHH; ☎092/46203). You can pitch your tent for nothing on the island of Incháojl (one of literally hundreds). The *Corrib Queen* does a tour from *Ashford Castle* pier, taking in Oughterard, on the Galway shore of the lough (☎092/46029; return £10). The island is the site of two early Christian churches as well as the Stone of Lugha, the tombstone of St Patrick's nephew, which bears the earliest Christian inscriptions in Ireland.

For **eating** in Cong, the place to treat yourself is *Echoes* (☎092/46059), with plenty of fish dishes, and lots of organic vegetables and herbs. The hotels do good bar food, and the *Quiet Man Coffee Shop* is a friendly place with good home baking.

Loughmask House

Loughmask House (not open to the public), on the shores of Lough Mask a couple of miles due north of Cong, was the home of the notorious **Charles Boycott**, a retired captain of the British army and land agent to Lord Erne. His behaviour towards the tenant farmers during the Land League unrest of the 1880s – particularly acute in Mayo, where the League originated and many of the "congested areas" were located – made him one of the victims of Parnell's "moral Coventry" policy, subsequently known as "boycotting". As Parnell himself put it in a meeting in Ennis in 1880:

You must show what you think of him on the roadside when you meet him, you must show him in the streets of the town, you must show him at the shop counter . . . even in the house of worship, by leaving him severely alone, by putting him into a sort of moral Coventry, by isolating him from the rest of his kind as if he were a leper of old, you must show him your detestation of the crime he has committed.

COUNTY ROSCOMMON

Roscommon has the unjust reputation of being the most boring county in Ireland. A long sliver of land running from south to north, it's the only county in Connacht without any sea coast, though it is bounded for almost its entire western border by the upper reaches of the Shannon. Although most of the county is either bog or good grassland pasture, the **Curlew Mountains** on the Sligo and Leitrim border rise high and wild. Chances are you'll be approaching the county from the south, which is not its best aspect: the most worthwhile places are **Boyle**, in the far north, for its access to the Curlew Mountains, and **Strokestown** in the east, with its remarkable Georgian mansion and Famine Museum.

Roscommon town

More or less in the centre of the county, there's nothing much to **ROSCOMMON**, but it's an oddly pleasant town to spend time and soak up the atmosphere. Its solid tone is set by heavy stone buildings – among them the Bank of Ireland, once the courthouse, and the **county jail**, now housing a collection of shops, its serrated top giving the town a characteristic silhouette, identifiable for miles around. The jail was the scene of all public hangings in the county and used to have a woman executioner called Lady Betty, whose own sentence for murder was revoked on condition that she did her gruesome job for free.

Roscommon boasts two impressive ruins: on the Boyle road out of town, the enormous and well-preserved **Roscommon Castle** was built by the Normans in 1269, burnt down by the Irish four years later and rebuilt in 1280. Remodelling clearly continued for some time – there are some incongruously refined windows among the massive walls. The other ruin, in the lower part of the town, is the **abbey**. Roscommon takes its name from a Celtic saint, St Coman, who was the first bishop here and under whom the see became well known as a seat of learning, having close ties with the more famous abbey at Clonmacnois in County Offaly. The priory ruin, however, is Dominican, dating from 1253. Amazingly enough, despite the religious persecution that followed the Reformation and the Plantations, the Dominicans managed to hang on well into the nineteenth century, the last two incumbents, parish priests of Fuerty and Athleague, dying in 1830 and 1872 respectively.

The church in the centre of town houses a slightly higgledy-piggledy **museum** of local history (mid-June to mid-Aug daily 10am–5.30pm; free), the kind of place that museologists are beginning to regard as an endangered species. The building's striking Star of David window was put there by its nineteenth-century Welsh builders in honour of their patron saint.

Practicalities

The **tourist office** is in Harrison Hall in Market Square (May–Sept daily 10am–6pm; ☎0903/26342), which houses the museum. For **accommodation** in Roscommon, there's the central *Royal Hotel* on Castle Street (☎0903/26317; ④), one of those fine, upstanding inns that still exist in rural Irish towns: comfortable and good fun, with plenty of locals in the bar. Otherwise, you've a sprinkling of B&Bs to choose between. These include Mrs O'Grady's *The Villa* (☎0903/26048; ③) and Mrs Campbell's *Westway*, on the Galway Road (☎0903/26927; ②), or, if you have children, the best option is Mrs Carthy's *Hillcrest House* one mile out of town on Racecourse Road (☎0903/25201; ③). *Gleeson's* is a restaurant and B&B (☎0903/26954; ③) situated in what used to be the manse of the Presbyterian church opposite the old courthouse. For **eating**, the restaurant side of

Gleeson's (8am–9pm) does everything from breakfast to dinner, with delicious home baking; you can sit outside in good weather. There's also a reasonable Chinese, the *China Palace*, a little further down the hill on Main Street, above the *Lyons Den* bar.

Strokestown

In the east of the county, on the N5 from Longford, **STROKESTOWN** is a gem of a planned town whose reason for existence is Strokestown Park House, once the centre of the second biggest estate in Roscommon after Rockingham. The enormously wide main street – reputedly the result of an ambition on the part of an early owner to have the widest street in Europe – ends abruptly in a castellated wall with three Gothic arches, behind which lies Strokestown Park House.

The **St John's Heritage Centre** (May–Sept Tues–Fri 9.30am–1pm & 2–3.30pm, Sat & Sun 2–6pm; £2) is located in the elegant St John's church, designed in 1819 in imitation of a medieval chapter house by the fashionable English architect John Nash (who never visited Ireland). There's material on the Ireland of the Heroes, with a focus on the Rathcroghan monuments (see p.398) and the epic *Tain Bo Chúailgne*, but check what's currently on show before you pay up.

Accommodation is thin on the ground in Strokestown. Try B&B at the *Percy French* (☎078/33300; ③), *Martin's* (☎078/33247; ②) or with Mrs Cox, two miles out of town at *Church View House* (☎078/33047; ②).

Strokestown Park House

Strokestown Park House (April–Oct 11am–5.30pm) is a graceful Georgian residence designed by Richard Castle on a plan – a central block with two side wings linked by curved arms – whose adaptability as a sort of glorified farmhouse ensures that it turns up again and again throughout Ireland. Sold by the family of the original owners to the local garage in 1979, the house has never gone through an auction and therefore retains everything from furniture to papers relating to the Famine and 1930s school exercise books.

The **house** (£3) makes a good place to get to grips with the Anglo-Irish tradition. Its story is a fairly typical one. Originally a massive 27,000 acres, the estate was granted to one Nicholas Mahon in reward for his support of the House of Stuart during the English Civil War. The original building, finished around 1696, was fortified but not particularly grand; only one room of it survives, the stillroom in the cellar. As the family became richer and more secure, it made more grandiose additions, and the current house dates essentially from the 1730s, with some early nineteenth-century alterations. In the mid-nineteenth century Major Denis Mahon, who was a particularly nasty piece of work, is believed to have been one of the first landowners to charter less-than-seaworthy vessels (the notorious **coffin ships**) to take evicted tenants to America during the Famine. His activities were reported and censured in contemporary newspapers both in Ireland and abroad. In 1847 he was shot dead on his own estate.

To give a measure of the interconnectedness of Anglo-Irish society even in comparatively recent times, the lady who sold the house to the garage, the redoubtable Mrs Olive Hales Pakenham-Mahon, married the heir to the Rockingham Estate in 1914, thus uniting the two biggest estates in Roscommon, though the land empire set up by this dynastic marriage ceased to exist very soon afterwards, as did the marriage: the Rockingham heir was killed at the front in the first few days of fighting of World War I. Also in the house, in one of the upstairs bedrooms, is a painting of horses and stooks of corn by Woodbrook's Phoebe Kirkwood (see p.401).

The interior of the house gives off a feeling of very comfortable living, but not extraordinary opulence; there's a relaxed living room, and a spacious library and dining room, while upstairs you can see the old schoolroom, complete with desks, blackboard and school-books. One of its really extraordinary features is a gallery that runs the length of the kitchen, allowing the lady of the house to watch what was happening there without having to venture in; on Monday mornings she would drop the week's menu down from above.

The **Irish Famine Museum** (£3) in the stableyards of the Strokestown Estate provides a provocative interpretation of the house and its history and explores wider issues of Famine migration, emigration and oppression in a historical context, aiming, in particular, to break the traumatic silence that surrounds the subject. In 1945, a century after the terrible events, the Irish Folklore Commission noted:

I am sorry that this is such a meagre account of what was a dreadful period; but there seems to be very little information or interest left in the minds of the old people about that time. Indeed, it seems there was a sort of conspiracy of silence on the part of their mothers and fathers about it all.

Informed by a sense of outrage at the attitudes, on the part of the British government and landlords, that allowed this terrible disaster to happen, the exhibition follows the harrowing story of the Famine, juxtaposing it with images of Ascendancy luxury and of present-day famine and emigration. In 1841, Ireland was the most densely populated country in Europe, with a vigorous trading and commercial life. The exhibition shows the tragic results of over-reliance on the potato, which had been introduced into the country in the early eighteenth century; by the 1840s, it was the staple diet of the population. Blight arrived in Ireland in October 1845. In a letter to the British Secretary of the Treasury, a contemporary eyewitness surveyed the devastation:

On the 27th of last month I passed from Cork to Dublin and this doomed plant bloomed in all the luxuriance of abundant harvest. Returning on the third instant I beheld with sorrow one wide waste of putrefying vegetation. In many places the wretched people were seated on the fences of their decaying gardens, wringing their hands and wailing bitterly the destruction that has left them foodless.

The exhibition traces the poverty and hard-heartedness of the Whig government's laissezfaire economic response to the crisis. Its callousness in the face of human suffering on a massive scale – as well as its attitude to Irish ways of life – is indicated by Trevelyan's response, as the famine deepened:

The great evil with which we have to contend is not the physical evil of famine but the moral evil of the selfish, perverse and turbulent character of the [Irish] people.

The government resolved to make no official intervention to hinder the operation of private enterprise: relief food imports were stopped. Between 1841 and 1851, about 1.4 million Irish people died and another 1.4 million people emigrated – figures almost entirely attributable to the Famine.

The house and museum – plus a walled garden (£2.50) with a spectacular herbaceous border – are geared for group visits, but it can still be a thought-provoking experience, particularly if you arrive between busloads.

West from Strokestown

Heading west from Strokestown, there are a number of historical attractions that may divert you on your way to Mayo, including an extensive ancient Irish settlement near Tulsk, and Clonalis House, at Castlerea, the home of one of Ireland's oldest Gaelic families.

Elphin

The trim village of **ELPHIN**, about four miles northwest of Strokestown, has been the seat of a bishopric for 1500 years, ever since St Patrick founded a church on this spot. The **cathedral**, rather unconvincingly restored in part in 1982, contains the tombs both of early bishops and of members of the Goldsmith family – Oliver's birthplace is disputed between here and Pallas in County Longford, which has been doing its best to cash in on the Goldsmith connection (see p.192). Even his famous poem *The Deserted Village* may describe County Roscommon rather than County Longford (and the English claim it's about the *English* enclosures); at any rate, he went to school here.

Tulsk and Rathcroghan

> *Paganism has been destroyed though it was splendid and far flung . . . their old cities are deserts without worship.*
>
> *Oengus the Culdee, early Christian poet*

Centred roughly on the village of **TULSK** on the main N5 is a collection of some seventy megalithic monuments that mark one of the great centres of ancient Ireland, plus more than eighty ring forts. Unlike the monuments of, say, County Sligo, they're unmarked and largely unexcavated – most of them are no more to look at than grassy shapes in the fields – and access is generally free and unrestricted. According to legend, the most important of them, the long-barrow of Rathcroghan itself, was built by Eochard Fedleach, King of Connacht and father of Medb – who herself took power by killing her pregnant sister Clothro, who had inherited the title from their father.

In the absence of signposting, the area's monuments are difficult to identify, even using the detailed map in *The Heritage Guide to Rathcroghan* (available from tourist offices; £1.95). **Rathcroghan** – or Cruachan – itself lies just beyond the first crossroads on the N5 northwest of Tulsk and is signposted. It's a ring-barrow, traditionally the inauguration place of the kings of Connacht; close by are a cluster of standing stones, cairns and ring-barrows with legendary associations with Medb.

For the rest, it's probably best to rely on inspired guesswork when moving among these unexcavated monuments, knowing that, in this ancient landscape, anything you identify is likely to be at least as old as you think.

Frenchpark

Carrying on along the N5, you'll come to **FRENCHPARK** and the **Douglas Hyde Interpretive Centre** (*Gairdin an Craoibhin*, "Garden of the Little Branch") (May–Sept

---

MEDB AND EARTH MAGIC

Medb's prodigious appetite for men – she was reported to have thirty lovers a day, "each man in another man's shadow" – reflects her non-historical career as a spiritual symbol: her name links her with the sanskrit *madhu*, a sort of demon, and with Shakespeare's Queen Mab, Queen of the Fairies. She's now enjoying a renaissance in a reincarnation as Gaia, the spirit of earth.

Clothro's unborn child, in one of the gruesome details beloved of those legends, was cut from her womb with a sword and himself grew up to become a warrior. Medb took as a lover the great Cuchulainn of the epic poem *Tain Bo Cúailgne*.

Tues–Fri 2–5pm, Sat & Sun 2–6pm; donation suggested), housed in an old Church of Ireland church. Hyde (1860–1949), one of the founders of the Gaelic League in 1893 and the leading exponent of the importance of the Irish language and culture in the Nationalist movement, was – like his approximate contemporaries, the poet W.B. Yeats and the playwright J.M. Synge – of Anglo-Irish background. The son of the rector of Tibohine, he was sent home from boarding school when he contracted measles, and was brought up here among Irish-speakers, and later did much to record the rich vernacular tradition, as well as writing in the language – he collaborated with Lady Gregory on a number of Irish-language plays, many of which he published under the pen name An Craoibhin Aoibhinn, "delightful little branch", from which the centre gets its name. Hyde's aim was to unite all classes in an Irish Ireland, through the Irish language; but such political naivety was bound to end in disappointment. His unhappiness with the Gaelic League's espousal of revolutionary violence led him to resign from it; eventually, however, he returned to political life when he served as the first president of Ireland. With the founding in Dublin of popular new Irish-speaking primary schools in recent years, there is some sign that Hyde's legacy, which had sometimes seemed a conservative and retrograde form of nationalism, may still be of importance. Hyde is buried in the graveyard of this simple church.

Castlerea

CASTLEREA in the west, Roscommon's third most important town after Roscommon and Boyle, is an unprepossessing place, and the only real reason for going there is to visit **Clonalis House** (June to mid-Sept Tues–Sun 11am–5.00pm; £3.50), just outside the town to the west. Clonalis is the ancestral home of the O'Conor clan, which claims to be Europe's oldest family; it is, in fact, one of the few ancient Gaelic families – the O'Conors were traditional Kings of Connacht and last High Kings of Ireland, and can trace their family back to one Feredach the Just in 75 AD – although an even more fanciful family tree preserved in the house goes back to the fifteenth century BC. If you're expecting the house itself to be ancient, however, you're in for a disappointment – it's a Victorian pile, even if an engagingly Italianate one, of 1878. Unlike most noble Irish families, the O'Conors always remained Catholic and, although their royal past allowed them to hang on to some of their ancestral lands, they weren't in a position to flaunt their wealth – much of it derived from astute marriages to rich heiresses – until the late nineteenth century.

The house, still very much lived in, is a fascinating jumble of furniture, paintings – many of them portraits charting the family's colourful history at home and abroad – and mementos. There's a modest chapel displaying a penal chalice, which unscrews into three parts to make it easy to hide. The manuscript room contains the oldest surviving judgement under the ancient Irish Brehon law system, as well as a number of letters from Douglas Hyde (see above). Pride of place, however, goes to the harp of the blind harpist Turlough O'Carolan (1670–1738; see p.423), who numbered the then O'Conor Don among his patrons.

The house aside, there's no need to linger in Castlerea apart perhaps to visit *Hell's Kitchen*, an antiques-packed pub on the main street on the corner of the Boyle Road, describing itself as "the only national museum with a licence".

Boyle

It's disparagingly said that County Roscommon doesn't have any towns. It does, and **BOYLE**, although not the county town, is a fine, upstanding example. It's not a place marked out by particular charm or beauty, but there's enough here to keep you entertained for a one-night stopover, if you're not hurrying to cross the Curlew Mountains into Sligo. Boyle grew up around the greatest estate in County Roscommon, **Rockingham**, and although what remained of the estate was disbanded long ago and the house – in what is now the Lough Key Forest Park – was burned down in 1957, the town is still marked by their ghostly presence.

In Boyle itself, the most charismatic building is the Cistercian monastery, **Boyle Abbey** (June to mid-Sept daily 9.30am–6.30pm; out of season, keys available from Abbey House, next door; £1; Heritage Card), consecrated in 1220 and one of the early results of the arrival of foreign monastic orders in Ireland during the medieval pan-European upsurge in spiritual life. In 1142 a group of monks sent to Ireland by the redoubtable Cistercian abbot St Bernard of Clairvaux, at the instigation of St Malachy, established the great abbey of Mellifont in County Louth. Clonmacnois, the important Celtic monastery on the banks of the Shannon in County Offaly, was quickly abandoned, and within twenty years monks from Mellifont had settled at a site beside the River Boyle here at *Mainistir na Buaille*.

The abbey is small and compact, in very pale stone, well enough preserved to let you see how the monks must have lived. You still go in through the gatehouse (a sixteenth- or seventeenth-century addition), and there's a wonderful twelfth-century church. During the sixty-odd years it took to build the place, the Gothic style arrived in the west of Ireland; in a remarkably playful relaxation of their famous austerity, the Cistercian monks allowed themselves to build Romanesque arches down one side, and the new Gothic down the other. Look out, too, for the fantastically ornate (at least, for Cistercians) column capitals.

Boyle's big house may be gone, but the earlier residence of the King family, **King House** (May–Sept daily 10am–6pm; April & Oct Sat & Sun only; £3), in the centre of town, has recently been restored and opened to the public with a range of high-tech exhibitions. An imposing stone mansion built around 1730, King House, with its pleasure grounds across the river, was home to the family for fifty years before they moved to Rockingham, and it represents the heyday of what was aptly known as the Ascendancy. The original Sir John King, a Staffordshire man, had been granted his land for "reducing the Irish to obedience", achieved in part through violent subjugation and by the enforcement of the notorious anti-Catholic Penal Laws. For the King family, establishing themselves in Ireland was a process of determined and successful social climbing: inheriting a baronetcy in 1755, by 1768 Edward King had ensured his elevation to Earl of Kingston.

One section of the exhibition deals with the Famine and recounts a familiar story: Robert King, Viscount Lordon, although not an absentee landlord, did – like many other landlords, after the removal of the corn tariffs flooded the Irish market with cheap grain – find it economic to evict his tenants, transport them to America and use the land for cattle grazing. Other accounts detail the Kings' colourful family history – an eighteenth-century crime of passion and a very public nineteenth-century divorce – and there's a section on the house's use as a base from 1775 for the Connacht Rangers. This details their service to the British Army in such conflicts as the Crimean and Boer wars and World War I, culminating in their mutiny at Jullandar in the Punjab in 1920 in protest at the atrocities being perpetrated by the Black and Tans back home in Ireland. Boyle's civic art collection, with some interesting modern pieces, is housed on the ground floor of the building, and there's a pleasant coffee shop, much frequented by locals at lunchtime.

At the other end of town, down the driveway that leads from beside the bridge, **Frybrook House** (June–Sept Tues–Sun 2–6pm; £3.00; B&B ④; ☎079/62170) offers a view of more modest eighteenth-century living – as well as a great place to **stay**. Built around 1752, the house belonged to Henry Fry, an English Quaker (the family may be related to the Cadbury Frys of confectionery fame), who came to Boyle at the invitation of the Earl of Kingston to establish a weaving community in the town. The house has been extensively restored and, although only three pieces of the original furniture remain, it has been sympathetically decorated with items from the same period and there are some fine paintings.

Practicalities

The **tourist office** is at the entrance to King House in Patrick Street (May–Sept 10am–5pm; ☎079/62145), near the bridge; as well as the usual services, it can give you details of the Boyle Arts Festival, well worth catching for its ambitious programme of concerts, theatre, poetry readings, lectures and exhibitions if you're in town in late July/early August. You can also get information from the Úna Bhán Tourism Cooperative also in the grounds of King House (☎079/63033). *Abbey House* is a pleasant place to **stay**, wedged between the rushing river and the abbey (☎079/62385; ②; Feb–Nov); if this doesn't suit try *Forest Park House*, Carrick Road (☎079/62227; ③), particularly welcoming to families, while four miles out of town in Doon is the fine *Hillside House* (☎079/66075; ③). The 250-year-old *Royal* (☎079/62016; ⑥) is a solid country inn where the river rushes by your window. A little outside the town at Knockvicar is *Riversdale House* (see below for details).

You can **rent bikes** (this makes a good starting point for touring the lakelands of northern and southern Sligo) from Brendan Sheerin, on Main Street. **Horse riding** is available at the Curlew Trekking Centre (☎079/62764). Places to **eat** are thin on the ground: the restaurant at the *Royal* serves indifferent food at extraordinarily high prices, but has a good coffee shop for daytime eating; and there's a useful Chinese restaurant, *Chung's*, by the bridge. *Bia Beo* ("living food") in the shopping arcade on Bridge Street does fine evening meals, while the best lunches are served at *An Craoibhín* in the Crescent, also an excellent pub. For really good food, plus accommodation, head out on the Sligo Road to *Cromleach Lodge* (☎071/65155; ⑨), up in the Curlew Mountains.

Lough Key Forest Park and Woodbrook

The road west out of Boyle towards the **Lough Key Forest Park**, part of the old Rockingham Estate, leads through the gate of the grounds, itself a Gothic fancy, and past a castellated lodge. The park has been thoroughly and relentlessly amenitized, with a hideous wood-and-glass restaurant at the side of the lake and masses of tarmacked car-parking on the former site of the great house. The latter was designed, in an elegant if fanciful Classical style, by the English architect John Nash, who was also responsible for the Classical mansions in London's Regent's Park. Yet the stable block, church, icehouse and temple – the graces of an eighteenth-century estate – as well as the spine-chilling subterranean passages used to keep the servants out of sight, give an impression of what it must have been like. With boats for rental and plenty of ring forts to explore, it's a pleasant enough place to spend a sunny day.

You can gaze out, too, at the islands on the lake; in a disused castle on one of them W.B. Yeats planned, after his Innisfree days, to base an Irish cult devoted to the occult principles of Theosophy and the Order of the Golden Dawn – the idea was to aid the Nationalist cause by trapping the hidden forces of the land. The **circuit** of the lake is well worth doing, particularly the west side, where the road rises to give you a panoramic view. A possible stop on the way is B&B **accommodation** at *Riversdale House* (☎079/67012; ④), where the River Boyle flows out of the lough – a compact Georgian lodge on a working farm that was once home to Maureen O'Sullivan – where you can also have dinner (£12).

A little further out of Boyle on the Carrick-on-Shannon Road, **Woodbrook** is another old Anglo-Irish house. It's not open to the public, and the reason for mentioning it is that it's the subject of a remarkable book, *Woodbrook*, written by an Englishman, David Thompson, who worked there for most of the 1930s as tutor to the Kirkwood family's two young daughters, one of whom – Phoebe – was a well-known painter. Sometimes naive, sometimes sentimental, it's strong in its evocation of place and in its documentation of the passing of Anglo-Irish culture.

The very north of the county, hilly terrain where farmland gives way to the moors and lakes of the **Arigna Mountains**, is a good introduction to the more spectacular landscape over the county border in Sligo. You can break your journey in the twin villages of **Ballyfarnon** and **Keadue** and, outside Keadue by the ruins of the sixth-century **Killoran Abbey**, visit the grave of the famous blind harpist Turlough O'Carolan (see p.423).

travel details

Trains

Galway to: Athenry (4 daily; 15min); Athlone (4 daily; 1hr); Dublin (4 daily; 2hr 30min–3hr); Portarlington (3 daily; 2hr).

Westport to: Castlebar (3 daily; 14min); Castlerea (3 daily; 1hr 10min); Dublin (3 daily; 3hr 30min); Roscommon (3 daily; 1hr 30min).

Buses

Galway to: Clifden (2–5 daily; 1hr 45min–2hr 20min); Cork (5 daily; 4hr); Doolin (3 daily; 1hr 30min); Dublin (5–8 daily; 3hr 30min); Letterkenny (2 daily); Limerick (9 daily; 2hr).

SLIGO AND LEITRIM

Counties Sligo and Leitrim pair up well, offering a luscious and gentle scenery that contrasts with the wilder streaks of Donegal and Mayo, yet equally far removed from the dullness of Longford and Cavan to the east. Leitrim, one of the most neglected counties in the country, is an area of lakelets and low mounds, and presents a singularly withdrawn face to the outside world. Sligo, also underrated, is the more enticing of the two, containing the beautiful mountains of Benbulben and Knocknarea and the enchanting Gill and Glencar loughs, as well as an array of standing stones and other megalithic monuments as dramatic as any in Ireland. Much of the terrain is gently undulating farm land, allowing long cross-country views to the higher outcrops in the county's far corners: the Ox Mountains range to the west, the Bricklieve to the south and the Dartry to the north. At Streedagh and Mullaghmore you'll find some of the country's finest beaches.

COUNTY SLIGO

Sligo has the greatest concentration of megalithic monuments in Ireland, as well as some of the wildest and most remote country. Especially poetic testaments to the ancient fusion of landscape and human presence are the extensive Neolithic cemetery at **Carrowmore**, to the south of Sligo town, and the large prehistoric village at **Carrowkeel**, on top of the Bricklieve Mountains. The pimple on top of Knocknarea is an unexcavated burial mound known locally as Maeve's Lump: legend has it that Queen Medb – Sligo's guardian spirit – is buried there, standing upright and still facing her enemies. The wealth and variety of legends covering the terrain of Sligo and Leitrim have no rival, and the modern literary associations are no less strong, as this landscape and its culture inspired the great Irish poet **W.B. Yeats**. His poetry is saturated with the atmosphere of Sligo, and his presence still makes itself felt: above all, at places such as the island of **Innisfree** on Lough Gill and **Lissadell House**, north of Sligo.

Sligo town

With a population of 16,000, **SLIGO** is, after Derry, the biggest town in the northwest of Ireland and a real focal point for the surrounding area. This engaging place, overshadowed by the presence of the Knocknarea and Benbulben mountains, manages to

△ *Donegal Town*

DONEGAL

Bundoran

Tullaghan

Kinlough

R281

Lower Lough Erne

A32

Lough Melvin

FERMANAGH

Glenade

Rossinver

Gleniff
Horseshoe

MOUNTAINS

Glenade Lough

Kiltyclogher

R282 R283 R281

Enniskillen

Glencar Lough

N16

Manorhamilton

N16

A4

LWOOD
ST

Parke's Castle

Blacklion

Innisfree

Dromahair

R280

Dowra

IRON
MOUNTAINS

Drumkeeran

CAVAN

Riverstown

Heapstown Cairn

Castlebaldwin

*Lough
Allen*

R207

Slieve Anierin
▲ *1922 ft*

*Lough
Arrow*

Drumshanbo

R208

Ballinamore

Ballinafad

Lough Key

*Lough
Scur*

R209

Keshcarrigan

Fenagh

R204

LEITRIM

Cootehall

Leitrim

R280

R209

LOUGH KEY
FOREST PARK

N4

Carrick-on-Shannon

R202

Carrigallen

Boyle

Jamestown

Drumsna

Mohill

R201

N61

R202

Lough Rinn

N4

Dromod

Roosky

LONGFORD

MON

▽ *Roscommon*

▽ *Longford & Dublin*

be relaxed and busy at the same time, with a fair dash of the Irish New Age spirit that suffuses much of the country. If you've been too long in the wildernesses, you can soak up something of a city atmosphere; the annual Yeats summer school in August, the arts festival in May and the choral festival in November are indications of Sligo's vitality.

The first recorded mention of Sligo dates from 807 AD, when the town was sacked by the Vikings, and by the thirteenth century it had become the gateway between Connacht and Ulster, with a castle (since destroyed) on what is now Castle Street. The Middle Ages was a period of sporadic violence, most notably between the Anglo-Norman Maurice Fitzgerald and the O'Connells. Thanks to its strong defences, Sligo was the last of the western garrisons to surrender to Williamite forces after the Battle of the Boyne.

The town suffered during the Great Famine, when its population fell by a third through death and emigration, but by the end of the last century things had picked up to the extent that it was described in guidebooks as "a progressive and busy centre". The upswing has continued to the present day, and in summer the streets are always crowded with visitors – but if you have a chance to look at the photos of old Sligo hanging in the County Museum on Stephen Street, you'll appreciate how remarkably constant the look of the town has been. The tightly packed and narrow back streets make it feel a little like Latin Quarter Paris, with grocery stores and bars on the street corners open late into the evening. Apart from the Dominican Abbey there's not much left in the way of sites that recall the town's long history, but the old-fashioned market town atmosphere and the atmospheric old pubs make it an ideal base for exploring the surrounding countryside and sights. Lough Gill, Drumcliffe, the megalithic dolmens of Knocknarea and the beaches at Strandhill are all within five miles radius of town; Lissadell, Benbulben and Glencar Lough are within ten.

Arrival, information and accommodation

The **bus** and **train** station is handily placed on the western edge of town in easy walking distance of almost everything. Feda O'Donnell Coaches (☎075/48114) stop off in Sligo en route to Galway and Donegal (2–3 buses daily). For journeys north, the bus departs from outside *Connolly's* pub, Wine Street, for journeys south, from outside *Matt Lyon's*, Wine Street. Sligo airport (☎071/68280) is out at Strandhill; a taxi into town costs around £10. Sligo's **tourist office**, on Temple Street (July & Aug Mon–Sat 9am–8pm, Sun 10am–2pm; Sept–June Mon–Fri 9am–5pm; ☎071/61201), is the headquarters for Sligo, Leitrim, Monaghan, Cavan and Donegal. They offer car rental, money exchange and an accommodation booking service. To find out what's happening in town get hold of a copy of the weekly *Sligo Champion*, which lists music in pubs and other entertainment, or *Art West* for monthly arts listings covering Mayo and Sligo.

If you're staying in Sligo town itself you'll find a good range of **accommodation** on offer and certainly no shortage of **B&Bs**. Try the hospitable *Renaté House*, 9 Upper John St (☎098/62014; ②) or *Ross Brian House*, 1 Hanley Terrace (☎071/62186; ②), a small traditional establishment next to the tourist office. Numerous good B&Bs are to be found on the fairly central Pearse Road, among them *St Anne's* (☎071/43188; ③), which has a swimming pool, and *Pearse Lodge* (☎071/61090; ③), a smart place with en-suite facilities and TVs in all rooms. You'll find plenty more out on Strandhill Road, viable if you have a car. There are also several **hostels** in the centre of town: *The White House Hostel*, Markiewicz Road (IHH; ☎071/45160), *The Yeats County Hostel*, Lord Edward Street (☎071/46876) and *The Eden Hill Hostel* on Pearse Road (IHH; ☎071/44113), offering a range of facilities, including laundry, bike rental and camping, though the beds – and bedrooms – have seen better days. Finally, *Harbour House*, Finisklin Road (☎071/71547) is a comfortable new hostel. The only real drawback is its location – three quarters of a mile from town, and not a very pleasant walk. *Gateway*

Caravan and Camping Park, Ballinode (☎071/45618), is three quarters of a mile from the centre of town along the N16 Belfast Road. For something more upmarket, book into the pleasant, modern *Sligo Park Hotel* on Pearse Road (☎071/60291; ⑦) or for really luxurious living, head out of town to *Glebe House* or *Markree Castle*, a few miles south at Collooney (see p. 418).

You can get details of minibus and walking **tours** in the area from the tourist office. For **boats** on the river and out onto Lough Gill – one of the very best ways to spend time here – contact Peter Henry at *The Blue Lagoon*, Riverside (☎071/42530), or see p.410 for information on the Wild Rose Waterbus.

The Town

The thirteenth-century Dominican **Friary**, known locally as the Abbey, (mid-June to mid-Sept daily 9.30am–6.30pm; £1.50) has had a chequered history, having been destroyed a couple of times by both accident and design since its foundation. Its life as a religious foundation came to an end in 1641, when the whole town was sacked during the Ulster rebellion. These days, the abbey makes a good place to have a picnic as its walls still stand, and the chancel and high altar, with fine carvings, are in a good state of preservation. However, if you are here off season you won't be missing much if you just take a look through the gates.

The **Sligo County Museum** and **Yeats Memorial Museum** on Stephen Street (Mon–Sat 10am–noon & 2–4.50pm) occupy only two rooms, but are full of fascinating old photos of Sligo as well as some more unusual items, including a sequence of excellent nineteenth-century sketches of the monastic ruins on Inishmurray and a double-weight hundred-year-old firkin of bog butter. Memorabilia in the Yeats museum include photographs of and commentary on his funeral, lots of letters and photos of the man himself and the Nobel Prize medal awarded him in 1923. Before you head out, read a section of the long article on Michael Coleman, one of Ireland's most famous fiddle players. At the beginning of the century, Fritz Kreisler, one of the greatest of classical violinists, wrote that even he could not attempt the kind of music Michael Coleman played, even if he practised for a thousand years.

Just down the road, at Douglas Hyde Bridge, the Yeats Society Building (☎071/42693) is the headquarters of the **Yeats Society** and venue for August's Yeats International Summer School. It has become something of an academic institution, attracting scholars from all over the world, and of late has also gained something of a reputation for controversy. At Keohane's bookshop, a few minutes' walk away in Castle Street, you can also pick up as much of Yeats's poetry as you can carry.

For a taste of the northwest's energetic arts scene, head for **The Model Arts Centre** (daily 11am–5pm) on The Mall, housed in an imposing nineteenth-century stone building. It's home to The Niland Collection, which includes paintings and pencil drawings by Jack Yeats, brother of the poet. His work has a strong local flavour, and his later works such as *The Graveyard Wall* and *The Sea and the Lighthouse* are especially potent evocations of the life and atmosphere of the area. If you're going to be heading north into Donegal, look out for Paul Henry's *Early Morning in Donegal Lough*, which will give you a taste of things to come. Also worth more than a passing glance are the paintings by George Russell, better known as AE, the mystical poet and a contemporary of W.B. Yeats. The centre also has a busy annual schedule including three **festivals**: the *Scríobh* literary festival in September, an Early Music festival in October and a contemporary music festival in November.

Another place of great interest is an old butcher's shop turned **sculpture studio**, Michael Quirke's on Wine Street. A butcher for 31 years, Michael Quirke began in the 1980s to sculpt the figures of Irish mythology in windfallen wood. Every feature of these small carvings bears the mark of his encyclopedic knowledge of every legend or myth ever dreamed up about Ireland – if you get a chance to listen to him, it could well be one of the most inspiring moments of your stay. So far his work isn't too expensive (£40–50), but it's getting increasingly popular. You can get high-quality Irish art and crafts, including particularly interesting jewellery and ceramics, at The Cat and The Moon, 4 Castle St. For souvenirs of a more traditional kind, Dooney's in O'Connell Street sells excellent Irish tweed and knitwear at well below Dublin prices. If you have children in tow, **Woodville Farm** (June Sat & Sun 2–5pm; July & August daily 2–5pm; adults £2.50, children £1.50), about a mile out of town on the Sligo road, is a useful diversion, with sheep, lambs, free-range hens, peacocks, pigs and a woodland nature trail.

Eating, drinking and nightlife

One of Sligo's more stylish places to eat is *Café Cairo*, Rockwood Parade, offering an imaginative menu with good vegetarian options. *Bistro Bianconi*, opposite *Hargadon's* in O'Connell Street, is a pleasant Italian **restaurant** with an elegant decor to match its upmarket aspirations, while a varied menu of burgers, fish and Mexican dishes is on offer at *The Loft Restaurant*, above *M.J.Carr's*, Lord Edward Street.

Every pub in Sligo seems to serve a **bar lunch**, and with so much competition the food is great value. *M.J.Carr's* serves good-value bar snacks till 9pm and does a popular midday carvery lunch; *The Ark Bar*, High Street, serves delicious bar meals; *Fiddler's Creek*, Rockwood Parade, and *The Journeyman*, Grattan Street, also come highly recommended. Away from the pubs, there are plenty of inexpensive options, including a couple of pleasant **cafés** from which to watch the world drift by. Try *The Winding Stair Bookshop and Café*, Wine Street, which serves excellent homemade soups and sandwiches, or *Crazy Jane's*, a cheerful riverside café on nearby Rockwood Parade. You can get **picnic supplies** from *Kate's Kitchen* at 24 Market St or from *Cosgrove's*, a delicatessen on Market Square and something of a tourist attraction in itself, with its nineteenth-century interior and craft shop attached.

When it comes to **pubs**, Sligo does well. *Hargadon's* on O'Connell Street is one of the most enjoyable places to drink and talk. An exclusively male establishment until about fifteen years ago, it's a fine old pub, with dark recesses and shut-off rooms, and shelves of nineteenth-century earthenware stout jugs. Note the little swivel windows at the far end of the serving bar, where the whiskey could be slipped through with little fuss by either drinker or landlord. *Shoot the Crows*, Castle Street, is a lively bar for an interesting pint, just opposite the Lady of Erin statue. For **traditional music**, the two best regular spots are *T.D.s* on Adelaide Street and *The Leitrim Bar*, across the river on The Mall; both have something happening most nights throughout the year. *MacLynn's* on Old Market Street is cosy and usually crowded; there's an open fire in the bar and it too has a great deal of traditional folk music throughout the year. Check the *Sligo Champion* for details of other pubs with live music. *The Clarence Hotel* on Wine Street has a live band (Fri & Sat) and also has a dance floor. *The Weir* on The Mall, hosts rock and indie bands most weekends, and *Beezies*, Tobergal Lane, off Rockwood Parade, attracts a young crowd with a mix of karaoke, rock and dance music. The big **nightclub** in town is *Toff's* at the Embassy Rooms, John F. Kennedy Parade (Thurs–Sun) and *Equinox* on Teeling Street also has discos (Wed & Fri–Sun 11pm–1.30am).

The **Hawk's Well Theatre** (☎071/61518) on Temple Street is home to both amateur and professional drama in Sligo, and also shows musicals and classical music concerts, particularly during the Yeats International Summer School (Aug) and the Sligo Arts Festival (May). It's also worth checking to see what's on at The Factory Theatre, Lower Gill Street (☎071/70431), home to the movement-based Blue Raincoats Theatre Group, who have recently been gaining some attention nationally.

Lough Gill

The 24-mile circuit of **Lough Gill**, a broad lake with luscious woodland covering the small hills that rise off its indented banks, makes a great day-trip by bike from Sligo – or you could break the journey midway in Dromahair and allow yourself more time to explore. There are also plenty of shorter walks, and this is one of the most enjoyable ways to spend time around Sligo. To walk to the lake set off from Bridge Street along Riverside on the south bank of the Garavogue, until you come after about a mile to Doorly Park. Follow the path through the park alongside the river until it rejoins the road, which leads eventually to a lakeside jetty where you can take a waterbus out to Parke's Castle (see p.410); sadly the walk goes no further, but from here the entire length of Lough Gill is spread out before you.

If you have transport, the northern shore is much the more interesting and is reached from town by taking The Mall past the hospital, turning onto the R286 at the garage and then following signposts for the Hazelwood Estate on the right. A left turn off the road leading into the estate grounds will bring you after half a mile to Half Moon Bay, where there's a picnic site and a pleasant lakeside walk. Wooden sculptures by

---

THE LEGENDS OF LOUGH GILL

A place of such natural beauty inevitably features in legend: Lough Gill's story tells of a warrior called Romra who had a daughter named Gille ("beauty" in Irish). One day Gille was seen bathing by Omra, a friend of Romra. Omra was captivated by the girl, and she wasn't altogether indifferent to him; but when Romra got to hear about it, a fight ensued in which Omra was killed and Romra received wounds from which he later died. Grief-stricken, Gille drowned herself, and from the tears of her doubly grief-stricken nursemaid Lough Gill(e) was formed. According to another tale, the silver bell from the Dominican Abbey in Sligo lies at the bottom of the lake. Only those free from sin can hear its pealing.

---

various artists are ranged in the woods around – the most stunning is a set piece of chariot and horses, set in its own artificial dell.

Back on the R286, a left turn soon after the road forks for the "Lough Gill Loop" will take you up to the Deerpark Forest, where a magnificent megalithic court tomb surveys the wild country. Ten minutes of walking on an unpaved road brings you to the top of Cashelgal Mountain, where you'll find both the tomb and unparalleled views of the surrounding country.

At the Leitrim end of the lake, the road begins to skirt the shore on its approach to **Parke's Castle** (March 14–17 & Oct daily 10am–5pm; April 11–end May Tues–Sun 10am–5pm; June–Sept daily 9.30am–6.30pm; £2; Heritage Card), a romantic-looking seventeenth-century fortress only yards from the water. The castle, built by one Robert Parke in the 1620s, is an evocative example of an early planter building and of the talents displayed by the Office of Public Works for conjuring heritage sites out of virtually nothing. The foundations discovered in the courtyard of the present castle are thought to be those of the moated tower-house of the Irish chieftain Brian O'Rourke, prince of Breffni. In 1588, O'Rourke sheltered a Spaniard from the wrecked Armada; arraigned for high treason, he was executed at Tyburn in 1591. It seems that Parke used the simplest (and cheapest) method of making a home for himself, by utilizing the outer walls of O'Rourke's castle (and probably completing the demolition of the tower in the process). The reconstruction is clearly a fairly creative one, but it works well as a focus for the surrounding topography. The entrance ticket also admits you to the audiovisual show, which, as a quick introduction to the area's built environment, is also worth seeing.

You can visit Parke's Castle by **boat** from Sligo. The Wild Rose Waterbus (☎071/64266) operates between Doorly Park, a mile and a half walk from town along the shore of the lake, and Parke's Castle (June–Aug daily; April, May, Sept Sun only; depart Doorly Park 2.30pm, returning at 5.30pm; £6). A bus shuttle service from Sligo to Doorly Park is available and there are also trips out on the lake from Parke's Castle. The same company runs **boat trips to Innisfree** from Parke's Castle (July & Aug 12.30pm, 3.30pm and 6.30pm; £4).

From the Leitrim end of the lough, the signposted Manorhamilton road leads to the modern, uninspiring **Newtown Manor church**; but the journey, a steep climb through the high wild moorland behind the lake, is exhilarating. The main road around the lake winds on through lush woodland to Dromahair, Co. Leitrim, where, at the end of a short walk on the other side of the rushing River Bonet, lies **Creevelea Friary** (see p.426).

Continuing from Dromahair, the road climbs to offer breathtaking views of the mountains opposite. A signposted lane shortly after the Sligo county sign will lead you down to the lakeside where you can gaze out at Yeats's tiny "Lake Isle of Innisfree" and breathe in the tranquillity:

I will arise and go now, and go to Innisfree
And a small cabin build there, of clay and wattles made
Nine bean-rows will I have there, and a hive for the honey-bee,
And live alone in the bee-loud glade.

And I shall have some peace there, for peace comes dropping slow,
Dropping from the veils of the morning to where the cricket sings;
There midnight's all a glimmer, and noon a purple glow,
And evening full of the linnet's wings.

I will arise and go now, for always night and day
I hear lake water lapping with low sounds by the shore
While I stand on the roadway, or on the pavements grey,
I hear it in the deep heart's core.

Inismor, Innisfree's sister island, was the site of the medieval school of poets to the O'Rourke's; unfortunately, the priceless library of manuscripts was destroyed by fire. Continuing back towards Sligo, the road winds gently through woods with occasional views of the lough. At **Dooney Rock**, a brief stroll through woodlands brings you to a secluded shore where you can view the island opposite and consider swimming over.

The south road back into Sligo passes **Cairns Hill Forest Park**. From the car park a path leads to the top of Cairns Hill, with a view across to a second cairn on the peak of Belvoir Hill. These are reckoned to be the tombs of Romra and Omra, though another legend makes them out to be the breasts of a monstrous hag, with Lough Gill as her navel.

North of Sligo town

Leaving Sligo along the coast to the north, almost immediately there's the option of a short detour to **ROSSES POINT** (bus #473), via the promontory that forms the north side of Sligo Bay. This (or Strandhill, see p.415) is the place to go for a day at the **beach**, a perfect picture-postcard scene, with the streaks of Coney and Oyster islands guarding the entrance to the bay and the distinctive beauty of Knocknarea and Benbulben standing behind. A sea marker called the Metal Man marks the deepest part of the channel for Sligo-bound boats; placed there in 1822, it was called by Yeats the "Rosses Point man who never told a lie". The tip of the headland, Deadman's Point took its name from a sailor who was buried at sea here with a loaf of bread thoughtfully provided by his comrades – they weren't sure whether he was really dead but wanted to despatch him quickly so they could make port before the tide turned. There are a few hotels, including the imposing *Yeats Country Hotel* (☎071/77211; ⑨), which looks out across the Atlantic, and lots of **B&Bs**, too: try *Oyster View* (☎071/77201; ②), pleasantly situated overlooking the bay, or the inexpensive *Allesley* (☎071/43781; ②). For seafood, head for *The Moorings Restaurant* (☎071/77112).

Drumcliff, Benbulben and Glencar Lough

Sticking to the main N15 road out of Sligo you'll bypass this small peninsula, reaching water again at **DRUMCLIFF** (bus #480 from Sligo), an early monastic site probably better known as the last resting place of **W.B. Yeats**. His grave is in the grounds of an austere nineteenth-century Protestant church, within sight of the nearby Benbulben Mountain, as the poet wished. The grave of W.B. and his wife, George, has a simple headstone bearing the epitaph from Yeats's last poem:

Cast a cold eye
On life, on death.
Horseman, pass by!

In 575, St Columba founded a **monastery** here, and you can still see the remnants of a round tower to the left of the road and a tenth-century high cross – the only one in the county – on the right. The east face of the cross has carvings of Adam and Eve, Cain killing Abel and Daniel in the lion's den; the west face shows scenes from the New Testament, including the Presentation in the Temple and the Crucifixion. Local excavations have turned up a wealth of Iron and Bronze Age remains, too. If you're feeling peckish, there's a good teashop, with home baking, next to the church (closed in winter) – a welcome refuge on a rainy day. For something more substantial, there's good bar food at *The Yeats Tavern*, about a hundred yards further on.

At 1730ft, **Benbulben** is one of the most dramatic mountains in the country, and its profile changes constantly as you round it. According to the Fionn Mac Cumhaill legend, it was here that Diarmuid, the ill-fated young warrior, was killed by the wild boar, its bristles puncturing his heel – his one vulnerable point. Access to the slopes is easy, but you need to take care as there are a lot of dangerous clefts into which the unsuspecting walker can all too easily plunge – especially as it's invariably shrouded in mist.

Just to the east of Drumcliff is **Glencar Lough**, squeezed between Benbulben and the range of hills known as the Sleeping Warrior, a secluded lakelet with good salmon and trout fishing, if you're lucky. Follow the road round the northern edge of the lake passing the recently reopened barium mine sheds on the left, until you see the "Waterfall" signpost. From the nearby car park a path leads up to the 50ft-high waterfall, especially impressive after heavy rain. There are more waterfalls, visible from the road, in the upper reaches of the valley, although none is quite as romantic as this one. For even better mountain walking continue along the road to the eastern end of the lake, where a track rises steeply northwards to the Swiss Valley, a deep rift in the mountain crowned with silver fir. To reach Glencar Lough from Sligo, a distance of about ten miles, take the Manorhamilton bus, ask to be dropped off at the junction for the lake and walk the remaining two miles.

Cooldrumman and Lissadell House

Beyond Drumcliff, the first left turn off the main road (signposted "Lissadell") runs to Carney village, to the north of which is an area known as Cooldrumman, where the **Battle of the Book** took place. This battle followed the refusal of St Columba to hand over a psalm book copied from the original owned by St Finian of Moville, in defiance of the High King, who ruled that just as a calf belongs to its cow so every copy belongs to the owner of the book from which it is made. Columba won the battle at a cost of 3000 lives; repenting the bloodshed he had caused, he then went into exile on the Scottish island of Iona.

In Carney a signpost to the left indicates the way to **Lissadell House** (June to mid-Sept Mon–Sat 10.30am–12.30pm & 2–4.30pm; £3), an austere nineteenth-century Greek Revival mansion, whose popularity is mainly due to its Yeats associations. This was the home of the Gore-Booth family, which produced several generations of artists, travellers and fighters for Irish freedom. During the Famine, Sir Robert Gore-Booth, who built Lissadell, mortgaged the place to feed the local people and doled out rations from the hall. His grand-daughters, Eva Gore-Booth and Constance Markiewicz, were friends of Yeats and took part in the 1916 Rising. Constance was condemned to death by the British for her participation but was pardoned and went on to become the first British female MP and then Minister of Labour in the Dáil's first cabinet.

Inside, the house seems in many ways like the archetype of the decaying Anglo-Irish home: despite the fact that the Gore-Booths still live there, the place hasn't been decorated since 1908, and problems with a leaking roof mean that a valuable Italian Baroque tapestry hangs in the hall festooned with strips of tea-bag paper, intended to hold it together until better times. The roof's now been fixed, however, and the house, bathed in Sligo's luminous marine light, still has an intimacy that makes it easy to imagine how it looked when Yeats used to visit in 1894:

> *Light of evening Lissadell*
> *Great windows, open to the south,*
> *Two girls in silk kimonos, both*
> *Beautiful, one a gazelle*
>
> From *In Memory of Eva Gore-Booth and Constance Markiewicz*

During that year, Yeats was in the throes of his unrequited love for Maude Gonne, and much of his time at Lissadell was spent confessing his problems to the gazelle-like Eva, to whom he also briefly considered declaring his love.

It was not only Constance and Eva who espoused radical ideas; their brother, Jocelyn, was drummed out of his club in Sligo for his practical encouragement of the early co-operative movement. He was also one of the first landlords to start selling off land to tenants, retaining no more than 3000 acres of the original 31,000 to run a thriving market garden.

Among the more eccentric decorative features of the interior are a series of elongated mural portraits of Jocelyn and family retainers and a self-portrait in the dining room, all by Constance's husband Count Casimir Markiewicz. They came into being only because bad weather kept the count from shooting during Christmas 1908. One of the rooms has Constance's name scratched on a window, and a photograph shows her playing Joan of Arc in her husband's theatre company: an appropriate role for a woman whose life was soon to turn so completely to politics and propaganda.

The house went through a difficult period after World War II, when the family lost control of the estate to the government: Sligo newspapers were keenly aware of the irony of the Gore-Booth sisters, nieces of Constance – one of the founders of the Irish Free State – being pursued by the police as they protested against the state's inept administration of the property. The experience has left the family with a distrust of government intervention, even in the form of funding, and although plans for restoration are afoot, Lissadell is likely to retain its air of elegant decay for some time.

Walks around Lissadell: Ellen's Pub

The area around Lissadell has some lovely walks and reputedly the warmest patch of sea on the Sligo coast. Also worth seeking out is *Ellen's Pub* at Ballyconnell, whose cottage-home atmosphere draws people from miles around. Ceilis are sometimes held in the back room, and on Fridays, Saturdays and Sundays from June to September, musicians gather here to belt out tunes on fiddles, accordions and banjos. There's a relaxed attitude to the licensing laws, so relaxed in fact that the pub was closed down for a while in 1986. To find it, follow the road past the turning for the Lissadell Estate, bear right away from Maugherow church, turn left at the pub/grocery store at the crossroads and then take the second right – it's another mile straight on. Hitching is easy, because everyone will assume you're headed for *Ellen's*.

Raghly Point to Mullaghmore

A couple of miles to the west of Lissadell is **RAGHLY**, a small harbour with a lonely pier and raised beach from where there are spectacular views of the bay and surrounding mountains. On the way there you'll pass Ardtermon Castle (closed to the public), the seventeenth-century fortified manor house once occupied by Francis

Gore-Booth, an ancestor of the Lissadell Gore-Booths. Ten years ago the place was more or less a ruin, but since then it has been well restored by its German industrialist owner – although, in the absence of documentation of the house's original appearance, the resulting garish yellow is rather more Scottish Baronial than Irish.

The next stop along the coast is sandy **Streedagh Strand** (seven buses daily from Sligo to Grange), most easily accessible by taking the main road to Grange (see below) and following the signposts from there, as roads on the Raghly Peninsula are hard to disentangle. The beach itself is a fantastic stretch of sand, superb for long walks or horse riding by the waves (there are several stables in the district), and when the tide is at its lowest you can walk round to the caves at the southern end to do some fossil collecting. At the very north end of the beach is Carraig na Spáinneach (Spaniards' Rock), where three ships of the Spanish Armada foundered. There are numerous anonymous burial stones nearby, said to mark the mass graves of some 1100 sailors who either drowned or were butchered by the British and the locals. There's **B&B** at *Shaddan Lodge* right by the strand (☎071/63350; ③), offering a wholefood menu and various alternative healing therapies.

Grange, Moneygold and Cliffony

At **GRANGE** itself there's not much apart from an old boys' bar off to the right, over the bridge, and the Sligo Crystal factory; there's a factory shop where you can buy the fantastically ornate cut glass at reduced prices. However, if you venture inland past the pub, you'll get a changing perspective of Benbulben as you approach the Gleniff Horseshoe, a scenic road that runs along a glen on the flank of the Dartry range and gives easy access to the top of Benbulben.

MONEYGOLD, a short way beyond Grange, offers basic accommodation at the *Karuna Flame Hostel* (☎071/63337; bike rental; ring ahead, as the property was up for sale at the time of writing), and you can also try organically produced cheeses and sample local fish and shellfish. **CLIFFONY**, a couple of miles on again towards Bundoran, is remarkable for the Creevykeel Court Tomb (just past the village by the roadside), one of the most extensive Neolithic sites in the country, comprising two roofless tombs within a stone court. The graves, which were originally enclosed in a barrow, probably date from between 3500 and 3000 BC, and it's easy to see in this ancient evidence of human presence a reflection of a power in the landscape that has gone on working ever since, right down to the poetry of Yeats and beyond. Among the **B&Bs** scattered around the area are *Dervogilla House*, Creevykeel, Mullaghmore Road (☎071/66300; ②) and, just outside Cliffony, Hans and Gaby Weiland's farm cottages (☎071/66399; £150–170 per week for four people) where the Weilands grow vegetables organically, and make delicious cheese, sourdough bread and cheesecake. You can also stay four miles away at the inexpensive *Gleniff Horseshoe*, Gortnadrung (☎071/66302; ②).

The Mullaghmore Peninsula

Mullaghmore headland may not have the sense of wild isolation of the other promontories north of Sligo town but it has a charm of its own and, unlike the remoter areas, offers a choice of accommodation and eating places, albeit a limited one. By now the coast is facing north, not west, bringing the Donegal mountains into view, and Benbulben and the Dartry range are a constant presence behind you. A left turn at the Cliffony crossroads takes you onto it, past **Classiebawn Castle** (closed to the public), a construction worthy of Disneyland built by Lord Palmerston; it became the home of Lord Mountbatten shortly before he was killed by the IRA in 1979, when his boat was blown up in the bay.

MULLAGHMORE itself is a fine place with a peaceful skiff-filled harbour and an excellent, safe sandy beach. It's an exhilarating spot any time of the year, but take care not to walk on the rocky shelves of Mullaghmore Head at the end of the village; the crashing waves here can be very dangerous. If you're wondering what all the nuns are doing in Mullaghmore, it's because the village has a convent holiday home at which they can relax after the rigours of their parishes. Non-ecclesiastical travellers can camp in the sand dunes, as long as they're inconspicuous. **B&Bs** are thin on the ground, but *Seacrest* (☎071/66468; ③) is beautifully appointed and has a wonderful location over-looking the beach. A reasonable alternative is *Seawood* (☎071/76671; ②), situated in a quiet spot behind a small copse; to find it look out for a signpost off to the left before you enter the village. Heading more upmarket, there are a couple of comfortable hotels: *Pier Head House* (☎071/66171; ⑥) and *The Beach Hotel* (☎071/66103; ⑥), which has a gym and swimming pool. As you would expect, during the summer, seafood is available in the bars and restaurants of both hotels, and at *Eithna's Seafood Restaurant* (☎071/66407).

Inishmurray Island

The island of **INISHMURRAY**, about four miles offshore, has been deserted since the 1950s, but the trip out to it is noteworthy because of its ruined sixth-century monastery, an oratory – which the islanders used as a school – and the early Christian gravestones that are some of the best preserved in the country. The crossing takes an hour and a half, and you can spend several hours on the island. Trips are dependent on the weather and the number of people wanting to go; book in advance (☎071/66124)

West of Sligo town

The major sites of interest directly west of Sligo – off the Strandhill road or R292 – are the ancient remains at the **Carrowmore Megalithic Cemetery** and, on top of Knocknarea Mountain, **Medb's Cairn**. Both make for easy day-trips from town. The main road south and then westward from Sligo (the N59), flanked by the thrilling out-lines of the Ox Mountains and the uninspiring coastline of western Sligo county, is scarcely an enthralling route, yet a few things crop up on the way to Mayo that are worth a mention – if you're not in a hurry, take the road running parallel to and nearer the coast.

Strandhill

STRANDHILL, four miles west of Sligo (bus #472), is swiftly becoming something of a city suburb, but does have a wonderful beach and has the dramatic Knocknarea mountain as an ever-present backdrop. As you head out there, a right turn off the road will lead you down to Sligo Bay, where concrete markers delineate a low-tide crossing to **Coney Island**. New York's Coney Island is said to have been named after this one by a homesick sea captain from Rosses Point, the headland opposite. Visitors can enjoy plenty of good birdwatching and tranquil sandy beaches and find refreshment in the island's only pub.

At Strandhill itself there's a fabulous, wild beach, with huge breakers rolling in from the Atlantic, a great favourite with **surfers**. The Sligo Open Surfing Championship is usually held here during the first weekend in August, and you can rent boards locally. It's unsafe for bathing unless you're a strong swimmer, but there is an exhilarating walk southwest around the headland to the quieter Cullenamore strand where you can take a dip: follow the coast until you are walking back around into a broad bay with Knocknarea Mountain in full view. The bay is home to a colony of two hundred seals, so your chances of spotting one are good. As the dunes fall to lower fields you can pick your way back towards Strandhill around the back of the golf course (the walk takes a leisurely one and a half hours). Alternatively, stroll towards Sligo airport over to the east of Strandhill surf beach for the thrilling sight of small Aer Lingus planes coming in over the top of Medb's Cairn. At the end of the airstrip stands the tenth-century Killaspugbone Church (access across the beach), where St Patrick allegedly tripped on the threshold and lost his tooth. A beautiful casket in which the sacred tooth was enshrined – the Fiacal Pádraig – is now in the National Museum in Dublin, but the whereabouts of the tooth is a mystery. The old Strandhill village was sited here until the drifting sand forced the villagers to move a few centuries ago.

Today, Strandhill sprawls over the best part of a mile from the main Sligo Road, with its handful of bars and hotels, down to the beach. If you want to stay, there's an abundance of **B&Bs** to choose from, including *Burma Lodge* (☎071/68233; ③), Burma Road, and *Knocknarea House*, Shore Road (☎071/68313; ②), both a short walk to the sea. If you're having to count your pennies, the new *Knocknarea Hostel* (☎071/68777) is a respectable budget option. A more upmarket choice is the pleasant family-run *Ocean View Hotel* (☎071/68115; ⑥), at the top end of town. Down beside the sea, the cosy fireside of *The Strand* pub is the ideal place to satisfy a well-earned appetite with delicious homemade soup and bar meals. Their **restaurant** next door serves an imaginative range of seafood and vegetarian dishes (☎071/68641). Other alternatives are *The Shell Café* on the seafront or the restaurant and bar at the *Ocean View Hotel*.

Strandhill is pretty lively during the summer: there is **music** every night in *The Strand* pub (folk, traditional and ballads), and *The Venue*, on the main Sligo Road, also has its fair share of live music.

Carrowmore Megalithic Cemetery and Medb's Cairn

A left turn off the R292 west of Sligo takes you to a field studded with 45 megalithic dolmens, standing stones and stone circles: the Carrowmore Megalithic Cemetery (May–Sept daily 9.30am–6.30pm; £1.50; Heritage Card). The oldest of the tombs predates Newgrange by some 700 years (and there's an unconfirmed dating of one of the tombs that suggests it may be 500 years older) – and though more than half the stones have disappeared, this is still the second-largest megalithic standing stone site in Europe after Carnac in Brittany. You can opt for the reasonably informative slide show and exhibition, but there's nothing to stop you wandering around to look at the monuments without paying the entrance fee. It's an intoxicating meander, under the eye of the big mother cairn of them all – Medb's Cairn, on top of Knocknarea. The easiest ascent of the mountain is along the path that meets the R292 as it skirts its southern flank (the western slopes are too difficult). The 60ft cairn on the summit is said to be the tomb of Queen Medb of Connaught, but as she was killed elsewhere it's unlikely that she's buried here; experts reckon that the 40,000 tons of rock were put here by Neolithic farmers – but it has yet to be excavated to find out why. There's a custom of taking a stone away with you which is resulting in a shrinkage of the cairn; the authorities are trying to promote an alternative tradition that says if you take a stone with you from the bottom of the mountain and put it on top of the cairn, your wish will come true...

If you want to go horse riding, the Sligo Riding Centre is right opposite the site (☎071/61353). It's a smart establishment with a bar where you can watch through a plate-glass window as nattily dressed girls put their nags through their paces in the riding school as you while the time away over a Guinness to endless country and western music.

Ballysadare and Aughris

Situated at the head of a beautiful bay with striking views back to Knocknarea and Benbulben, **BALLYSADARE**, five miles south of Sligo on the N59, has the remnants of a seventh-century monastery and a pre-Romanesque church, neither really worth making a detour for.

THE OX MOUNTAINS

Just after Skreen comes the turn-off for the Ladies' Brae Scenic Route, one of only two trails across the vast **Ox Mountains** (Sliabh Ghamh, stony mountain) into south Sligo. Following the course of a tumbling stream between forests of fir, the road ends not far from Coolany, a one-street village with accommodation at *The Mountain Inn* (④). Nearby is the Hungry Rock: these harsh surroundings were the scene of many deaths during the Famine of 1845–49. **Walking** in the more remote regions of the mountains, where all you'll see are sheep and the odd turf-cutter, can be rewarding; take care, as the bogs can be treacherous. Much of the Ox range consists of surprisingly undramatic heathery slopes and flat boggy upland, but the second route across the mountains – starting with a left turning off the road just before Easky (see below) – takes you up through the gorgeous setting of **Easky Lough** and then down a dramatic descent of the southwestern face of the range into the area surrounding Tobercurry (see p.420).

About ten miles further west and just after Skreen, you can take the turning south for the route through the Ox Mountains (see above), or take the lane north down to the coast and the tranquil harbourside village of **AUGHRIS**, home to an early monastic site and a promontory fort. In the fields you can see remains of *booleys*, the temporary shelters built by the old nomadic herdsmen who brought their flocks to graze in these remote coastal areas. There are several good beaches nearby and the little beach at Aughris is safe for swimming. The cliffs west of the pier are good for birdwatching and dolphin-spotting. If you want to get out onto the water, boat trips to Inishmurray are available, as are angling trips, including evening mackerel fishing (☎071/66000). You can feast on delicious seafood during the summer months at *Maggie's Beach Bar & Restaurant*, an eighteenth-century thatched shebeen down by the pier and a venue for traditional music. **Accommodation** is in short supply: *The Beach Bar* does **B&B** (☎071/66703; ②) and also has a caravan and **camping** site. Alternatively, you can stay three miles away at *Ave Maria Farmhouse,* Corkamore, Templeboy (☎071/66674; ②). Back near the beach, self-catering accommodation is available at *The Water's Edge* (☎096/49255), which boasts unparalleled views across to Knocknarea and Benbulben, and up to the Ox Mountains.

Dromore West and Easky

At **DROMORE WEST**, the Culkins Emigration Museum (June–Sept Mon–Sat 10am–5pm, Sun 1–5pm; £2) fills in some of the story behind the deserted buildings that litter the landscape hereabouts. The museum building once housed the Shipping and Emigration Agency run by the local draper, Daniel Culkin, which helped many local people onto the bitter road to a better life. The agency, founded in the nineteenth century, functioned right up to the 1930s.

Originally a monastic settlement, **EASKY**, about five miles northwest of Dromore West along the coast road, was a vital link in the anti-Napoleon coastal defensive chain, as two nearby Martello towers attest. With its fine reputation for consistent waves, Easky has become something of a **surfers' paradise**; in the summer months the shore fills up with surfers' campervans. It hosts the Surfing Association's Tiki Cold Water Classic over the last weekend in September and the national surfing championships have also been held here. You'll find the Easky Surf and Information Centre (☎096/49020) in the middle of the village. At the mouth of the salmon-rich Easky river stand the ruins of the fifteenth-century Rosalee Castle, which many of the locals are convinced is cursed (key from Mrs Mary Morrissey, above Clerk's shop). A few years back it was all set to be renovated with government money, and a committee was set up to steer the village into a new tourist-fed prosperity. Suddenly the chairman of the committee dropped dead, then the secretary drowned, and finally, before the project was hastily disbanded, the treasurer choked on a steakbone and was rushed to hospital. Maybe this is why the village signs read GOD BLESS YOU as you leave.

The village has a range of **accommodation**. Budget options include the *Barr Na Dtonn* (☎096/49376), a well-equipped new **hostel** in the village centre, and various **B&Bs**, among them the central *Atlantic 'n' Riverside* (☎096/49001; ③), which also does camping *Cuan Gearr*, Killeenduff (☎096/49189; ②), about a mile and a half out of the village and the grander *Old Rectory* (☎096/49181; ④), back in the village, which also serves dinner.

Easky has a lively pub scene: *McGowan's* has good **traditional music** and set dancing; try *The Poitín House* for all manner of sessions and singalongs; you might catch a ballad in *The Lobster Pot*, and you can expect pop bands and karaoke in *The Fisherman's Weir*. **Eating** options are a bit limited; you might try the pubs for snacks and there is always *The Split Rock* chip shop.

A mile south of the village, beside the road, is the extraordinary **Split Rock** – a glacial erratic, ten feet high, that's said to have been thrown here by Fionn Mac Cumhaill from the top of the Ox Mountains. Legend also has it that the rock will close on anyone who dares to go through the split three times. The beach path north offers a magical walk with huge numbers of fossils all along the shoreline.

Enniscrone

ENNISCRONE, on the east side of Killala Bay and the western boundary of County Sligo, is a popular, rather ramshackle, seaside resort for the Irish, with caravan sites hidden away in the sand dunes, and an exceptionally good golf course. There's a sweeping three-mile crescent of sandy beach with Victorian bath-houses, built to exploit the health-giving properties of seaweed and hot seawater. The seaweed bathing tradition continues at the wonderful Kilcullen's Bath House (☎096/36238; May–Oct daily 11am–9pm; July & Aug daily 10am–10pm; Nov–May weekends noon–8pm), a strapping Edwardian establishment where for under a tenner you can experience the slightly strange sensation of lying in fronds of slimy seaweed in an enormous glazed porcelain bath of iodine-rich brown water before finishing off with a cold water rinse. It is extremely popular, and there is a pleasant tearoom alongside where you can wait for your soak.

One other thing you can't fail to notice in Enniscrone is a powerful metal sculpture of a black pig in someone's front garden on the main street (the mythical Black Pig was chased across Donegal Bay and came ashore at Enniscrone). It was supposedly commissioned by the council, then appropriated by the house's owner when the unprepossessing final result was rejected.

The town is not short of **B&Bs**: try *Central House* on Main Street (☎096/36234; ③) or one of the several good options down Pier Road, such as *Enniscrone Lodge* (☎096/36181; ③) or *Gowan Brae* (☎096/36396; ③).You can eat at *The Castle Arms Hotel*, Main Street and get home baking and confectionery at *D.D.'s Pastry Case*, Pier Road.

South Sligo

The sight worth stopping for in the village of **COLLOONEY**, five miles south of Sligo where the N4 and N17 separate, is the **Teeling Monument** at the northern entrance to the village, built to commemorate Bartholomew Teeling, hero of the Battle of Carricknagat. The battle was fought nearby during the rebellion of 1798, when a combined Franco-Irish force – on its way from Killala in County Mayo, where the French had landed (see p.388), to Ballinamuck in County Longford – was held up by a single strategically placed English gun. Teeling charged up the hill and shot the gunner dead, turning the tide of the engagement. After their defeat at Ballinamuck the French were treated as prisoners of war, but five hundred Irish troops were massacred. Irish-born Teeling, who was an officer in the French army, was later hanged in Dublin. The monument links Teeling and his fallen comrades with subsequent generations of Irish freedom fighters.

Close to Collooney is the battlemented **Markree Castle**, originally seventeenth century but with grandiose Victorian extensions, which is still the home of the Coopers – who used to be Sligo's most powerful Anglo-Irish family. It's set in impressive parklands and is now open as a **hotel** (☎071/67800; ⑧); the place also houses an excellent, though expensive, **restaurant**, or you can just wander in for a drink and a taste of the old high life. Comfort and gastronomic delights at a more affordable level are on offer at *Glebe House* (☎071/67787; ④), just outside Collooney on the other side of town. A "restaurant with rooms" rather than a guesthouse (6.30–9.30pm for dinner; also open to non-residents), it's a fairly austere building filled with an assortment of heavy, Victorian-and-later furniture – the point is not so much the surroundings as the food and the freshness of the ingredients, many of which are grown in the garden outside.

Heapstown Cairn and Lough Arrow

The more appealing route south from here, to Lough Arrow, involves a turn off the N4 at Drumfin along the road that goes through the geriatric village of Riverstown. Several miles on, standing by the roadside behind a modern bungalow, is Heapstown Cairn, a Neolithic passage tomb as large as Medb's Cairn and traditionally the last resting place of Aillil, brother of King Niall of Tara. A lot of the cairn stones have been plundered for building material, but even in its diminished state the cairn remains impressive, best appreciated by climbing it and taking in the view from the top. What's most fascinating about the view is the relationship with the surrounding landscape: the cairn takes a perfect central position in relation to the nearby circle of hills, many with cairns on their peaks.

One option from here is to go down the eastern shore of Lough Arrow, whose blue waters are set with ringlets of isles and whose banks are dotted with ancient landmarks, many of them unmarked on the map. When the sun is shining there are few spots to beat it, especially if you can take a rowing boat onto the tranquil lake – keep your eye out for boats lying by the banks and then ask at a nearby house; or try Lough Arrow Boats (☎071/65491), which rents out fibreglass boats. The road round the southern edge of the lake goes through **BALLINAFAD**, at the back door of the Bricklieve Mountains. The road into Ballinafad from the Curlew Mountains of Roscommon gives the most stupendous view in the whole of Sligo, right up to Benbulben – it's worth backtracking up the hill to get it. Ballinafad Castle (left off the road at the top of the village) is a sixteenth-century building remarkable only because its huge circular towers and squat walls are of thirteenth-century design. If the charms of the area tempt you to stay to watch the luminous twilight descend on the lake, you've a choice between the *Rock View Hotel* (☎079/66073; ④), a down-to-earth angler's hotel halfway down the lough (much further than the signs indicate) – the owners will give plenty of advice on trout-fishing in Lough Arrow's limpid waters – and the swankier *Cromleach Lodge Country House* (☎071/65155; ⑨), which is close to the northern end of the water. Further north, outside **RIVERSTOWN**, you can stay in a graceful eighteenth-century Big House, *Coopershill* (☎071/65108; ⑦), belonging to a branch of the Coopers of Markree.

Carrowkeel and Keshcorran

The other route southwards from the Heapstown Cairn takes you along the top of Lough Allen to meet the N4. Cross at Castlebaldwin and climb the road that forks left behind McDermot's Pub for the Bronze Age **Carrowkeel Cemetery** – you can drive all the way up, on unmetalled roads, or walk: either way, watched over by cairns and (signposted) tumuli, the panorama is marvellous, with the whole of County Sligo spread out beneath you. Comprising fourteen cairns, a few dolmens and some fifty-odd pieces of stone foundations, the site is the most important cairn colony west of Sliabh Na Caillighe in northwest Meath. Several cruciform **passage graves** set in the cairns are still roofed, the smaller ones with great lintel stones, the larger with corbelled vaults. You can actually enter Cairn K, one of the roofed tombs: cruciform in shape, with its dry stone roof intact, it's been compared to Newgrange in County Westmeath (see p.166). Here, however, it's lit by the sun on the year's longest day.

Also of interest in the area are the **caves** on the hill of Keshcorran, the cairn-topped summit that faces Carrowkeel to the west, which you can get to by rejoining the main road across the mountains, then turning left down the hill, taking every descending turning until you reach a major road where the pub *The Traveller's Rest* stands. Take a right here towards Kesh, and beyond the *Foxes Pub* and grocery store, a fingerpost points right – after a couple of hundred yards you'll spot the line of caves cut into the forehead of the mountain. The caves have no depth at all, but the feeling of isolation is immense at this spot. According to legend, this was one of the places where the lovers Diarmuid and Gráinne lived when they fled the anger of Fionn Mac Cumhaill, and it was here that the baby Cormac Mac Airt, later to be the greatest of all the High Kings who ruled at Tara, was reared by wolves. On the last Sunday in July, in a reflection of ancient pagan rituals, locals still gather by the caves for sessions of prayer.

Ballymote

If, instead of taking the Lough Arrow route from Collooney, you follow the N17 south-west, you could make a diversion along the R293 to the small market town of **BALLY-MOTE**. Its fourteenth-century castle, built by Richard de Burgo (the "Red Earl of Ulster"), was once the strongest in Connacht but has associations with major defeats – it was O'Donnell's before he lost at the Battle of Kinsale, and it was James II's posses-sion before he lost at the Boyne. The place has an important and ancient literary con-nection: it was here, in about 1400, that the Book of Ballymote was compiled, giving the key to the geometrical *ogham* letters that are formed on many standing stones of the fourth and fifth centuries – the name comes from the townland of Ogham, outside near-by Tobercurry, which has plenty of examples of them. Ballymote makes a good centre for both angling and rath-spotting – the low, undramatic countryside all around is cov-ered in ancient ring forts.

For moderately-priced **accommodation** you could try *The Millhouse* (☎071/83449; ③), a very pleasant B&B, or *The Castle Hotel* (☎071/83342; ④), a reasonable alterna-tive. The most stylish B&B in the vicinity, however, is at *Temple House* (☎071/83329; ⑥; April–Nov), three miles from here on the shores of the lake. Founded by the Knights Templar and expanded in 1560, this is one of the grandest and earliest Anglo-Irish houses ever built in Ireland – the bulk of the house was grandly refurbished in 1864 – on a 950-acre estate, with 97 rooms, five of which are for B&B guests, and they do a good dinner for £20. To get there take the left fork off the Collooney end of town; the house is near the N17 to Tobercurry. *The Stone Park Restaurant* (☎071/83372), behind *Corran's*, is probably the best place to **eat** in town and the village sports a cou-ple of nice old bars, including *Hayden's* which occasionally has open sessions.

Tobercurry

The district around **TOBERCURRY** – and south Sligo in general – has a reputation for traditional music: Michael Coleman, the greatest of Irish fiddle players, came from here, and it's also where The Chieftains had their roots. Tobercurry itself is a spruce market town, but you are not likely to want to stay around; its most scenic attraction is the lovely Lough Talt, around four miles away.

Although the town is usually devoid of tourists, **tourist information** is available in *Killoran's Traditional Restaurant*, Teeling Street – don't miss out on the famous fresh salmon from the River Moy. In the second week of July the town has a music week, featuring short courses in music and Irish dancing. When it comes to **accommodation**, there are several guesthouses and B&B's to choose from. *The Ox Mountain Lodge*, Teeling Street (☎071/85007; ②) is pleasant and good value, and also has a café attached (till 7pm), or you could try *Cawley's* in Emmet Street (☎071/85025; ④). If you're keen to do some fishing on Lough Talt, you can rent out rods from Carrick's sport and fishing tackle shop, a few doors down from *Killoran's*.

Gurteen and the far south

Follow the R294 ten miles or so southeast and you'll reach **GURTEEN**, once another thriving centre for traditional music, now a place with something of the scent of a ghost town. Yet some of the finest musicians in the country still live up in the hills, and from time to time they might come down to strike up a tune. *Teach Murray* has a session on Mondays; *Róisin Dubh* has spontaneous music-making throughout the year, and a regular session every Tuesday, and also hosts a festival, usually over the last weekend in August.

Lough Gara, tucked away in the southernmost pocket of the county, is not as appealing as the map suggests it might be, having a very undramatic surrounding shoreline. **Moygara Castle**, signposted near the lake, is similarly anticlimactic, with just one of its original four towers left intact.

COUNTY LEITRIM

The Leitrim scenery is more distinctive than it's normally given credit for – the mountains and glens, of the north in particular, have a rugged, wide-open appeal and some great walking, although the county can't compete with Sligo for historical interest. Leitrim stretches fifty miles from County Longford to its slim two-mile coastline at Tullaghan and is neatly split into north and south sections by the vast interruption of Lough Allen, the first lake on the River Shannon. The southern half is dominated by the presence of the Shannon, and the lake-peppered terrain to the east of the river, with its characteristic drumlins, or hillocks, also merits exploration. The mountains of the northern section are grouped around Manorhamilton, and it shares its most beautiful features – Glencar and Lough Gill – with Sligo (see p.409 and p.412).

Carrick-on-Shannon

The small county town of **CARRICK-ON-SHANNON**, beautifully positioned on a wide stretch of the Shannon just below Lough Key, is a major **boating** centre, and its marina is full of pleasure boats and Shannon cruisers. It also makes a good base from which to cycle round the southern loop of Leitrim or to investigate Lough Key and Lough Boderg in Roscommon, and there's good coarse fishing to be had.

The town has good bus and train connections. **Buses** to Athlone, Boyle, Sligo, Mullingar and Dublin leave from in front of *Coffey's Pastry Case* in Bridge Street. The **train station**, ten minutes out by foot to the southwest, is on the main Dublin–Sligo line, with three trains a day in each direction (☎078/20036).

Carrick's *raison d'être* as a tourist centre has recently received a boost with the reopening of the Ballyconnell–Ballinamore Canal in the summer of 1994. The canal provides the final link in the **Shannon-Erne Waterway**, 239 navigable miles taking in stretches of still-water canal, canalized river and a sequence of lakes (see the map "The Canal System" on p.128), and ending up in Belleek in County Fermanagh. A latecomer to the canal-building boom that swept the country in the eighteenth and nineteenth centuries, the waterway was completed in 1860, and was used for only nine years before being made redundant by Ireland's growing rail network.

The single piece of historical interest the town itself has to offer is the minuscule **Costello Chapel**, at the top end of Bridge Street. Billed as the second smallest chapel in the world, it was built in 1877 by the fanatically devout businessman Edward Costello as a memorial to his wife, who died young that year. The couple's lead coffins, protected by thick slabs of glass, lie in two sunken spaces on each side of the tiny, beautifully-tiled aisle. Also worth a call is Cyril Cullen's pebbledashed Georgian house and factory shop, Summerhill, on the road to St Patrick's Hospital, where he sells porcelain figures and his own distinctive knitwear designs – he breeds his own Jacob sheep for their wool.

Practicalities

Carrick's **tourist office** (May, June & Sept Mon–Sat 9am–5pm; July–Aug Mon, Tues, Thurs–Sat 9am–8pm, Wed 9am–6pm, Sun 10am–5pm; ☎078/20170) is on the quay on the Leitrim side of the river. Recommended **B&Bs** are: *Aisling* (March–Oct ☎078/20131; ②) and *Hillside Lodge* (☎078/21143; ②), located in quiet, central St Mary's Close; and back on Main Street, *The Four Seasons* (☎078/21333; ②). In a rather grander setting, B&B is also on offer at *Hollywell* (☎078/21124; ⑥), Liberty Hill, a short walk from the centre of town. Carrick also has a hostel, *The Town Clock Hostel* (IHH; ☎078/20068; June–Sept), at the junction of Main Street and Bridge Street – phone ahead in high season, as it's fairly small. Rooms at *The Bush Hotel*, Main St (☎078/20014; ⑥) vary considerably, but the best of these are very comfortable.

   Carrick has **pubs** to suit most tastes within a short walk down Bridge Street: starting at the top opposite the clock tower is *Flynn's*, an animated bar with lively conversation; just below here is *Armstrong's*, where the silence is golden; a few paces further down is *Burke's Bar*, a fairly conservative place for a pint, and *The Oarsman*, a newly antiquated bar with live music from 10pm on Fridays and Sundays – generally a mix of pop and traditional. Across the road from here *The Anchorage Bar* appeals to a young crowd, with a live band on Thursday nights covering anything from Oasis to The Hills of Donegal. Zigzag back across the road from here and you will reach *Cryan's*, which has traditional sessions (Tues, Thurs, Sat & Sun) and bluegrass on Fridays.

   You can get reasonably priced lunches and evening meals at the immensely popular *Cryan's* or *The Oarsman*. Away from the bars, a couple of other places serve **food** during the day: try *Coffey's Pastry Case* for light lunches and snacks or the coffeeshop of *The Bush Hotel* for roasts.

   Michael Lynch's, on the Roscommon side of the river, has **fishing boats** for rental, and there are numerous companies that rent out **Shannon cruisers** (two- to ten-berth) by the week, for example Emerald Star Line (☎078/20234). The locks on the Shannon-Erne Waterway – there are sixteen of them in all – are operated electronically with a swipe-card, so you don't need to be an expert to use the canal. For shorter excursions, Moon River organizes trips up the river leaving from the bridge (daily 2.30pm & 4.30pm; 1 hour 30 mins; £5). Another starting point for the waterway is at Ballinamore (see p.425), where you can also rent boats. Rental of **bikes** and fishing tackle is available at Geraghty's on Main Street. If you want to email home, there's a small cybercafé at the back of Gartlan's newsagency, Bridge Street.

South of Carrick: Jamestown to Roosky

As with most of Leitrim, there's little of dramatic interest in the area south of Carrick, but if you're passing through, there are a couple of places where you could at least slow down a bit and enjoy the leisurely pace of life around the Shannon.

Jamestown and Drumsna

The village of **JAMESTOWN**, off the N4 Dublin road, is a town dating from James I's plantation of Leitrim in 1622 – its main road passes through a gate in the old estate walls. The Georgian houses and the wooded river banks create a peaceful atmosphere of planned eighteenth-century living. Jamestown makes a good centre for fishing: Shannonside Lodge, right in the centre, has information on angling, maps and guides. If you want to stay, try *Weir Veiw* (☎078/24726; ②). Jamestown has a couple of nice pubs too; you can hear traditional music on a Friday night at *The Arch Bar*. It's worth calling into *Tig Bríd*, a combined craftshop and restaurant, selling quality pottery and knitwear and serving homemade soups and casseroles.

At nearby **DRUMSNA**, excavations in the summer of 1989 unearthed huge stretches of a Stone Age wall – one of the oldest artificial structures in the world. It's been estimated that it would have taken a labour force of 30,000 men ten years to build its full length. The village itself is a single street of neat houses leading down to the river. A plaque on the wall of *Taylor's Lounge* claims that Anthony Trollope began his novel *The MacDermots of Ballycloran* here in 1848. The MacDermots were great Catholic landowners during the eighteenth century, then were ruined by the anti-Catholic Penal Laws.

Mohill and Carrigallen

To the east lies **MOHILL**, a trim, busy village reached by turning off the main road south of Carrick at Drumsna or Dromod. A sculpture on the main street commemorates its most famous son – **Turlough O'Carolan** (1670–1738), the blind harpist and composer. The last of the court bards, he lived by travelling round the chieftains' households playing his new compositions. He was also reputed to have been as great with the whiskey bottle as he was on the harp; it's said that on his deathbed he asked for a cup of the stuff, and finding that he hadn't the strength to drink it, touched the cup with his lip, saying that two old mates shouldn't part without a kiss. Mohill was the site of an abbey founded in the sixth century by St Manachan, but today its associations are entirely secular: it's a coarse fishing centre, with fifteen different choices of lake and river in a five-mile radius. For information on fishing, ring ☎078/31071.

The executive-home style advertising graphics and squeaky-clean restoration of the **Lough Rynn Estate** (mid-May to mid-Sept daily 10am–7pm; £1) near Mohill may strike you as slightly smarmy, but don't be put off; the place offers a rare opportunity to get to grips with a way of life that's currently out of favour with historians and punters alike: the heyday of the property-owning aristocratic elite of high Victorian Ireland. The house stands on a handsome site on the shores of Lough Rynne, and was first acquired by one Nathaniel Clements, a successful Dublin banker and politician, in 1750. The Clements dynasty, Earls of Sligo, built the original Rynn Castle – an exact copy of a house in Ingestry, Staffordshire – in 1833, and in 1878 extended it to the Scottish Baronial pile you see now. By this time the house was the centre of an estate that encompassed a massive 90,000 acres, and the grounds include 1840s' farm buildings, the estate office – a picturesque building by the architect Digby Wyatt, who was also responsible for the Senate Chambers in Leinster House, Dublin – a pretty summerhouse, as well as the ruins of a seventeenth-century castle and a dolmen.

The area around Mohill, rich rolling pastureland crisscrossed by hedged lanes, makes good cycling country. Further east, the terrain becomes rougher and less interesting, but **CARRIGALLEN** is a pleasant enough eighteenth-century town, with excellent fishing all around. It's at a point in Carrigallen parish that the three provinces of Ulster, Leinster and Connacht meet, though nothing about the modest demeanour of the town suggests it. If you want to stay – and perhaps only keen anglers will – *Hartes Hotel* in the main street (☎049/39737; ④) is a good bet.

In Mohill itself, you can get B&B **accommodation** on a grand scale at the nineteenth-century stone-built *Glebe House*, set in beautiful parklands a couple of miles out of town on the Ballinamore Road (☎078/31086; ⑤). At a more mundane level there's *The Traveller's Rest* guesthouse in the village (☎078/31174; ④) and the very comfortable *Ballymore House* (☎078/31278; ③), which also does evening meals. *Fitzpatrick's* pub has sessions on a Tuesday night.

Roosky

Apart from its location – either side of the N4 – **ROOSKY**, about seven miles south of Mohill, is an otherwise pleasant riverside village catering for holidaying anglers. If you want to stay, there's B&B at *Shannonville* (☎078/38184; ②), a smart new house set squarely back off the main road, or you might try the brand new *Shannon Key West Hotel*, a smart and imposing building overlooking the bridge(☎078/38800; ⑥). As for places to eat, you can tuck into pizza and pasta at *Gino's* Italian restaurant, while bar food and country and western are on offer at *The Weir Lodge*. You can hear a variety of live music at *Reynold's* bar and *The Crews*, across the bridge, throughout the summer.

North of Carrick

A couple of miles north of Carrick lies the county's namesake, **LEITRIM** village. It's a tiny one-street place with a lovely canalside setting – best appreciated from the pub on the bank. Though its name translates as "the back of the old cow's arse", Drumshanbo, four miles north from Leitrim, would make a decent alternative base.

Drumshanbo

DRUMSHANBO, poised at the southern tip of the beautiful Lough Allen, is a neat, cheerful place with an air of briskness. The Sliabh an Iarainn visitor centre (April–Oct Mon–Sat 10am–6pm, Sun 2–6pm; £1.50) gives some interesting background on local life, including the use of the sweathouse, a sort of sauna, and the tradition of coal and iron mining, especially out towards Arigna. The last of the mines in the area closed in 1990.

In July, the village holds the Joe Mooney Summer School, a week of traditional music classes and set dancing. You need to be experienced to join the music classes, but there is set dancing for novices and plenty of sessions in the bars – details from the **tourist office**, based at *Mrs Mooney's* **B&B** on the corner of the High Street and the Carrick Road (☎078/41013; ①). Other places to stay include *Paddy Mac's* pub and guesthouse (☎078/41128; ②), High Street, and *Fraoch Bán* (☎078/41260; ③), a smart new B&B half a mile out on the Dowra road, with lovely views over the lake. You can **camp** for free in a field a little way down the Carrick road, near the heated swimming pool complex, or at Moorlands Equestrian Centre (☎078/41500) at the southernmost tip of Lough Allen. **Meals** are served all day at *The Allendale Restaurant*, Convent Avenue. There are a handful of bars where you might find **music** during the summer: *Conway's*, at the head of the Manorhamilton road, is a cosy favourite, with sessions on Thursdays; other bars worth checking out are *Paddy Mac's*, *The Mountain Tavern*, and *Monica's*.

Music aside, Drumshambo's finest asset is its proximity to Lough Allen and Slieve Anierin. By car the scenery is not particularly dramatic, but there is plenty of enjoyable walking, cycling and pony trekking. The Leitrim Way from here to Dowra (signposted *Slí Liatroma*, ten miles) affords expansive views across the lake to Corrie Mountain for almost the whole way. You can **rent a bike** from Moran's on Convent Avenue; a circuit of the lake via Dowra and Drumkeeran is around 25 miles. **Horse riding** is available at Moorlands Equestrian Centre (☎078/41500), and fishermen are well served too. Lough Allen is noted as having the best pike fishing in Europe, and **boats** can be hired from Lough Allen Angling Services (☎078/41648).

Towards Ballinamore

The best move from Drumshanbo is to take the R208 southeast and then head east along the R209 into the array of lakes that attracts most of Leitrim's tourism. This route makes a pleasant trip on a bike, as many of the lanes skirt the shores as they wind between the hills. Two of these hills have legendary names – Sheemore and Sheebeag (the hill of big fairies and the hill of the little fairies; there's a well-known Irish set dance by the same name). As with all such enchanted hills, this pair is supposed to open up on *Samhain* (Hallowe'en), when the fairy folk roam the land.

Sheemore lies before Keshcarrigan on the south side of Lough Scur; unfortunately it's not signposted, so you might have to question a few of the locals for directions. Topped by a cairn and a St Patrick's Cross, the hill commands the best view across Leitrim; the cairn is believed locally to be Fionn Mac Cumhaill's (Finn McCool's) grave. On your way again along the south of Lough Scur you'll pass a dolmen by the roadside before reaching **Sheebeag**, which has a gorse-covered cairn but is less exciting than its bigger brother. To get there follow the road straight on rather than turning left into Keshcarrigan, and take a sharp right up the hill and continue for a mile or so.

KESHCARRIGAN is one of the places that has been revitalized by the reopening of the Shannon-Erne Waterway. You can stay at *Canal View House* (☎078/42056; ④), an imposing bungalow overlooking the waterway; it also runs a fairly sophisticated restaurant (open to non-residents, dinner £15). For excellent, large portions of hearty food make for *Gertie's Bar*, an amiably relaxed, child-friendly place, decorated with a chaotic mix of ancient beer ads and road signs, and a venue for traditional sessions during the summer. *McKeown's* bar has traditional music on Friday nights, and a good restaurant alongside. About four miles east, **FENAGH** has the ruins of a monastery and two churches founded in the seventh century by St Caillain. The key for the ruins is kept in the first house as you turn off the road for *Kealadaville Rectory* (☎078/44089; ②), a beautiful Georgian house in a superb location overlooking Fenagh Lough, just a hundred yards up the Mohill road. You can hear live music at both of the village's pubs at weekends during the summer.

Ballinamore

It's not far north from Fenagh to **BALLINAMORE**, a wide-streeted former coaching town, which has a heritage-folk museum in the library building, once the courthouse, halfway down its main street. Highlight of the dull and chaotic collection is the "authentic detachable shirt collar worn by executed 1916 patriot Seán MacDiarmada" – and if you don't believe it, there's a photograph of the man to prove it. The library also houses the Leitrim Genealogical Centre. Today, Ballinamore acts as a centre for angling in Leitrim's lakes, and for boating on the Shannon-Erne Waterway (see p.428). Canal barges can be rented from Riverside Barge Holidays (☎078/44122), canoes from Thomas Parkes (☎078/44860). Alternatively, you could take a two-hour river cruise (☎078/44079; £6). For **tourist information**, call in at Smyth's Gift Shop, at the top end of town. You can get cheap **accommodation** at the fine *Ballinamore Holiday Hostel* (☎078/44955), located above *Smyth's Restaurant*. One of the nicest **B&Bs** is *Ardnum Lodge* (☎078/44278; ②), on the road towards Fenagh; *Town View* (☎078/44464; ②), on the same road, caters largely for anglers and also does evening meals, while *Mrs Gormley's* (☎078/44082; ②), Main Street, is plain and unpretentious. A notch up in price, *McAllister Hotel* (☎078/44068; ⑤) is central and newly refurbished. Probably the best **place to eat** is the cheerful *Smyth's Restaurant*, Main Street, a good spot for tasty homemade food. During the summer you can hear music in one of the town's nineteen bars; *Reynold's* has traditional music on a Thursday, *Prior's* has rock bands on a Wednesday.

North Leitrim

The North Leitrim Glens offer some breathtaking scenery: rugged mountains fall to ribbon lakes, and the area is quiet and as yet undiscovered. Focal point of the mountainous area north of Lough Allen is **MANORHAMILTON**, lying in the saddle of five valleys. The town was founded on top of a strategic plateau by Sir Frederick Hamilton, a Scots colonist, during the seventeenth century; his castle was destroyed in the 1650s, but the ruins can still be visited. Today it's a handsome crossroads town, with a sense of self-importance underlined by the sturdiness of its architecture, and makes a good base for walking and potholing in the surrounding hills, on both sides of the border. Chief among local sights is the well-preserved megalithic tomb at Cashel Bir, on the slopes of Benbo. The remains of Hamilton's seventeenth-century Plantation castle stand on the edge of town, and here The Manorhamilton Heritage Centre (Tues–Sat 11am–6pm, Sun 2–7pm) tells its bloody and violent history in an audiovisual display; the coffee shop alongside makes a pleasant refreshment stop. For advice on walking, potholing, caving, fishing and hang-gliding, as well as other local pursuits, go to the Glens Centre, housed in the old Methodist church in the centre of town (10am–6pm daily during summer; ☎072/55833).

Manorhamilton has a handful of **B&Bs**, including the welcoming *Cill Chiaráin* (☎072/56135; ②) and *Laurel Lodge* (☎072/55018; ②). *Maguire's Bar* (☎072/56053; ③) is more appealing inside than the exterior would suggest and also serves hearty bar lunches. Sturdy **bar meals** can be had from *The Granary*, Main Street, which advertises itself as a bistro and coffee shop, but is actually a straightforward bar. *Maguire's* serves similarly hearty bar lunches – the salmon is excellent. *The Market Bar* has music on Thursday nights, and if you're in town on a summer Wednesday, you may catch *Siamsa Samhraidh*, a music-hall version of traditional Irish entertainment, at the Glens Centre. For a quiet pint there's no better place than *Gilbride's*, Main Street, a lovely old family-run bar.

The R280 south of Manorhamilton leads to the pretty village of **DROMAHAIR**; if you have transport it makes an excellent base from which to enjoy the rugged valleys and the peerless Lough Gill and its environs. A short walk from the centre lies **Creevelea Friary**, its ruined east window turned away from the harsh outlines of the mountains and towards the friendly valley below. This Franciscan friary, founded in 1508, was the last to be built in Ireland before Henry VIII's dissolution of the monasteries. It still has some fine sculptures in the cloister arcade: look out for St Francis with the stigmata, and another of him preaching to the birds from a pulpit.

If you want to **stay** in the centre, head for *St Anne's* (☎071/64096; ②) or *Stanfords* (☎071/64140; ②), a quaint creeper-clad little pub with quiet rooms. Light **meals** are served in the bar of the latter and a set dinner in the restaurant will cost around £13. Alternatively, *Beech Cottage and Equestrian Centre*, situated about two and a half miles out of the village on the road to Parke's Castle, offers delightful B&B in a beautiful eighteenth-century house (☎071/64808; ③); they have self-catering accommodation too in the old converted stables, and offer riding lessons .

Kiltyclogher

About ten miles northeast of Manorhamilton, **KILTYCLOGHER**, although trim and pretty has nothing to detain you after you've seen the Seán MacDiarmada statue. You can also visit the three-room cottage where MacDiarmada, executed in Dublin in 1916 for his part in the uprising, was born. It is kept up as a kind of national shrine, a short way out of town and signposted off the Manorhamilton Road. There's good bar food at *Meehan's*, which also does inexpensive B&B (☎072/54179; ②). *The Leitrim Lakes Hostel* (☎072/54044) is a large, well-run affair, often used by groups. Heading south, less than a mile from the village, the road passes a well-preserved gallery grave, dated between 2000 and 1500 BC, on a tranquil windblown site among the heather-covered slopes of Thur Mountain, overlooking a tiny lough; it's known locally as Prince Connell's Grave.

Rossinver to Tullaghan

North from Kiltyclogher and just outside **ROSSINVER**, at the southern end of Lough Melvin, there's a cool, leafy walk along a river that cascades through its valley in a series of waterfalls – a good outing for the baking hot days that happen sometimes even in the west of Ireland. Immediately outside the village on the Garrison road, Eden Plants (☎072/54122) is one of the growing band of Irish producers of organic herbs and vegetables, and is open to visitors (Tues–Sun 2–6pm). The route on up to Kinlough, much less scenically spectacular than the country to the west, runs along the eight-mile western shore of **Lough Melvin**. The ruin of **McClancy's Castle** stands on an islet a few yards from the northern end of the lake. It was here that eight survivors from the three Spanish galleons wrecked off Streedagh Point finally found refuge.

KINLOUGH, near the tip of the lake, is a wholly unpretentious village and has a surprisingly interesting little folk museum at the Manorhamilton end. Part of the museum is the old *McCurran's Bar* (key from the grocery store across the road), where a half-bottle of Guinness stands fermenting on the wooden bar counter. There's another more conventional room to the museum, with folk and historical knick-knacks crammed into every available space, including a newspaper cutting showing De Valera on his way to the Dáil for the first session of the new Irish Free State. Among the **places to stay**, *Bluerock*, on the Dartry Road (☎072/41610; ③) is recommended. *The Courthouse Restaurant* also does accommodation (☎072/42391; ②). When it comes to eating, try *The Speckled Trout* bar and restaurant in the centre of the village; it also hosts traditional music on a Sunday.

A few miles away, **TULLAGHAN**, Leitrim's only outlet to the sea, boasts a ninth- or tenth-century high cross, standing forlornly askew on a hummock by the roadside – all in all, a rather dreary resort on a dreary strip of coast.

travel details

Trains
Sligo to: Ballymote (3–4 daily; 20min); Boyle (3–4 daily; 40min); Carrick-on-Shannon (3–4 daily; 50min); Collooney (3–4 daily; 10min); Dublin (3–4 daily; 3hr 20min).

Buses
Sligo to: Belfast (1–3 daily; 4hr); Galway (3–7 daily; 2hr 30min).

CAVAN AND MONAGHAN

Cavan and Monaghan sit side by side as if one were a physical imprint of the other – Monaghan all small hills, Cavan all small lakes. County Monaghan is renowned for being drumlin country – rashes of rounded hills that diminish as you head west into Cavan where the land breaks up into a crazy pattern of tiny lakes. Both landscapes have their charms, both their practical difficulties. If you're walking or cycling in either county, a compass can be very useful; although the terrain isn't inaccessible or dangerous, you should be aware that there's such a network of winding, crisscrossed roads – the minor ones often riddled with potholes – that you can very easily get lost. In Monaghan, the drumlin hills all look similar, while the myriad lakes of Cavan enforce constant twists and turns. The lakes, however, now offer a more leisurely means of travel; since the reopening in 1994 of an old canal system, you can sail through Cavan along the Shannon-Erne Waterway.

Like County Donegal, Cavan and Monaghan share the peculiar identity of being historically part of **Ulster** yet included in the Republic since Partition in 1921. Not surprisingly, Cavan and Monaghan people (Protestant and Catholic) still share a strong affinity with their northern neighbours. As border counties, they have also sheltered Republican activity during "The Troubles", and, despite the peace process, the communities are still largely polarized along staunchly held political lines.

Although the border has sharpened political and social definitions, there is a sense in which it has also sheltered both of these counties. You'll probably be struck by the old-fashioned feel of the countryside: while slow, rural ways are as prevalent in other Irish counties, the sharp contrast with the industrialization and development over the border makes them more striking here. Uncertainty about the future has left an unhurried rural ordinariness that constitutes much of these counties' appeal. They are not gaily painted for tourists, nor visibly quaint, and there's a dour Scottish severity in many of the villages, particularly in Monaghan – clear evidence of the Ulster planters. But as you explore, you'll find both counties have an understated and quiet charm.

COUNTY CAVAN

Long neglected by most holiday-makers, **County Cavan** is slowly becoming more popular, thanks to the major redevelopment of the old **Ballinamore-Ballyconnell Canal**, linking the mighty Shannon waterway, which serves all four provinces of the country – ending up in the southwest and boasting some great lakes – and the **Lough Erne** lake

---

ACCOMMODATION PRICE CODES

Throughout this book, prices of hotels, guesthouses and B&Bs have been graded with the codes below, according to what you can expect to pay for a double room in high season. For more details on accommodation, see p. 29.

① Under £26	④ £40–55	⑦ £90–110
② £26–33	⑤ £55–70	⑧ £110–130
③ £33–40	⑥ £70–90	⑨ Over £130

system, which flows to the northwest. The project extended the original canal and renamed it the **Shannon-Erne Waterway** (see "The Canal System" map on p128), weaving together streams, rivers and lakes through 39 miles of wild, unspoilt countryside, free of cities and major industries. It is now possible to sail the length of the Shannon, then along the new canal, through the Erne system to Belleek, County Fermanagh, a total of 239 miles.

In former times, the region was even more water-ridden, boggy and forested than it is today. This complex of lake and bog was extremely difficult for foreign invaders to penetrate and control, and also made the land less desirable. Only the most durable relics have survived. The county is renowned for its **fishing**, and a conservative tourism is growing which neither scars the land nor disturbs the peace. Forest parks have been developed to give fishers access to the heart of the lake complex. Everywhere, the stillness is profound. If you want to enjoy this largely untouched part of the country by bicycle, you could follow the recently opened Kingfisher Cycle Trail, a long-distance cycle path (200 miles), linking Cavan with Fermanagh and Leitrim in the north and west, and Clones, County Monaghan to the east.

Some history

Evidence of Neolithic peoples from as early as 6000 years ago are scattered about the region in the form of **court cairn tombs**, but they're hard to find unless you know what you're looking for. Similarly invisible are the lakes' *crannógs* – artificial islands built as early as the Stone Age, but more typically developed as secure settlements from the first century AD and now melted back into the general landscape, indistinguishable from natural islands. The **Celts** had their principal pagan shrine at **Magh Sleacht** near present-day Ballyconnell. Several Celtic stone idols bearing bold representations of the human head have been found in the lake areas of Cavan and Fermanagh, particularly potent pagan symbols. Some of them were found in circumstances suggesting that they were deliberately hidden in more recent times to deny them their power, a sign of their continuing folkloric importance. Sadly, though, none of these idols can be seen in their original setting; most now form part of the collections of The National Museum in Dublin and the Fermanagh County Museum at Enniskillen. Replicas of them are on display at Cavan County Museum, Ballyjamesduff.

When **St Patrick** established his seat at Armagh, he also set up a monastery at Kilnavert. Rather than crudely asserting a new dogma, the proselytizing Christians allowed pagan and folkloric traditions to continue, mingling them with the new creed. The filtering through of the new faith was fairly rapid; but more brutal invaders found the area far harder to penetrate. The network of lakes and waterways proved difficult to negotiate, and foreign invaders arrived with neither knowledge of the terrain nor the apparatus needed for conquest. The **O'Reilly** family, who dominated Cavan from the beginning of recorded history to the seventeenth century, continually blocked Anglo-Norman attempts to take control, and this explains the lack of Norman developments in the region.

Despite Elizabeth I's attempts to divide and rule by creating the **County of Cavan** (more a piece of propaganda than a sign of real political strength) and playing one Irish barony off against another, it was only after the failure of the Irish cause at the Battle of Kinsale that Cavan received the stamp of foreign invaders. Ancient Gaelic ways were crushed by the Jacobite plantation, and the county was divided up between English and Scottish settlers. Every parish was to have a Protestant church, and the new town of Virginia was built in memory of Elizabeth. As usual, the best land was given to the English and Scottish newcomers, leaving the Irish population to face poverty and the loss of religious freedom.

The rebellion of 1641 was a direct result, and **Owen Roe O'Neill**, the Ulster Confederate leader based at Cavan, played an important part, defeating the British General Munro at Benburb to the north of the county in 1646. However, O'Neill failed to follow his victory through, and the Irish Confederates were eventually defeated. After O'Neill's death in 1649, Cromwell quickly took control of Cavan and the resulting confiscation of land and property from the Irish guaranteed the Protestant domination of the county.

Until Partition, Cavan's subsequent history was much in line with the rest of Ulster. In the eighteenth and nineteenth centuries the linen and woollen industries ensured a measure of economic growth – though Cavan was always one of the poorer parts of the province because of the difficulties of the land; and the Famine of 1845–49 brought large-scale emigration. At **Partition**, Cavan was included in the Republic, thus retaining its Irishness; but it shared the fate of Monaghan and Donegal in being torn from its historic and cultural Ulster identity.

Cavan town and Lough Oughter

CAVAN town grew up around an abbey, but nothing remains of this beyond its memory and an eighteenth-century tower beside the burial place of Owen Roe O'Neill. The town is quite subdued, with only two main streets: Main Street is the principal artery of shops and bars, while Farnham Street has an older character with some very nice stone Georgian houses, a Classical courthouse of warm sandstone and a huge Catholic cathedral, built in the 1940s, that surprisingly succeeds in confirming status and a sense of place without being overbearing.

The **tourist office** on Farnham Street (all year Mon–Fri 9am–5pm, Sat 9am–1pm; ☎049/433 1942) will direct you to the town's highlights: The Lifeforce Mill, Mill Road, a renovated nineteenth-century flour mill (May–Sept; £3.50) and Cavan Crystal Glass, Dublin Road (☎049/433 1800, tours by arrangement). For **B&B**, try *Oakdene*, 29 Cathedral Rd (☎049/433 1698; ③) or *McCaul's Guesthouse*, 10 Bridge St (☎049/433 1327; ③). The welcoming *Lisnamandra Farmhouse*, four and a half miles out of Cavan towards Crossdoney, is good value, especially for single travellers (☎049/433 7196; ③). *The Farnham Arms Hotel* on Main Street (☎049/433 2577; ⑥) provides pleasant and comfortable accommodation, and their bar and restaurant is open to non-residents. Beyond this, eating options are limited to **bar food** at the loud and popular *Blackhorse Inn*, Main Street (till 9pm), and *Louis Blessings*, tucked away behind a grocery store in the same street, also a good place for a drink and a lively spot at weekends. Excellent, hearty bar meals are also served at *The Imperial Hotel* from midday through till 8pm. There's no shortage of viable watering holes: *An Cruiscín Lán*, 82 Main St, draws a young crowd with live pop/rock/MOR on Thursdays, while *An Sibín* at 86 Town Hall St, is similarly lively with a DJ on Thursday nights, traditional Irish on Wednesdays. There's a laundry on Dublin Road. You can **rent bikes** from On Yer Bike, Abbeyset Buildings, Farnham Street. Cavan is very much the transport centre of the county, and Bus Eireann (☎049/433 1353) connects it with all major towns in the Republic and the North. Wharton's private **buses** (☎049/433 7114) also operates a daily service to Dublin, leaving from outside the *Lakeland Hotel*.

Lough Oughter

A major focus of scenic interest in County Cavan is the complex of tiny lakes which riddle the north of the county. They're known collectively as Lough Oughter and form part of Upper Lough Erne. The land here is so fretted with water that its very fabric seems to be disintegrating. Contours are provided by very low, unassuming hills while the waters are edged with reeds, spindly silver birch and alder. Everything is on a small scale, but the landscape has a subtle attraction nonetheless, and the roads making their way through the labyrinthine network of lakes are quiet and empty. It makes little sense to head for a particular point in Lough Oughter – it's hard to tell when you've got there anyway – and the best plan is probably just to enjoy the gentle confusion.

The nicest of the little towns serving visitors, especially those interested in fishing, are Cavan town itself and, a few miles north, Belturbet. In between, there's also the pretty village of **BUTLERSBRIDGE**, with a popular bar, *The Derragarra Inn* – touristy but serving good food throughout the day (10.30am–10.30pm). **BELTURBET** itself sits prettily on a hill beside the River Erne and is an angling and boating resort with a marina and cruiser station. River trips to Upper Lough Erne are run by Turbet Tours (☎049/952 2360; June–Sept). For **B&B**, try *Mrs R. Hughes*, 8 Church St (☎049/952 2358; ②), up behind the library, off the main road.

Heading round the lough there are a few sights of interest. Just south of Milltown, you'll find **Drumlane Church and Round Tower**. A monastery was founded here by St M'Aodhog in the sixth century, and Augustinians from Kells took the place over in medieval times. The church itself is plain and roofless, but its setting beside a lake, and its size in such an intimate landscape, are impressive. The earliest parts of the building are thirteenth century, but it was substantially altered in the fifteenth century, the period from which the carved heads outside the doorways and windows date. The round tower is eleventh century and of good, clean stonework.

Continuing south through **Killeshandra** round the west side of Lough Oughter, bear right at the Arvagh signpost, then first right – it's difficult to reach without transport – to **Mrs Faris's Pighouse Collection**, a quasi-**folk museum** at Corr House, Cornafean (ring ☎049/433 7248; £2). It's a huge accumulation of miscellaneous remnants of the past; three huge barns are full of dusty junk, only a small part of which, the section on domestic utensils and furniture, has so far been catalogued and labelled – the rest you rummage through and interpret for yourself. There's a vast and fascinating range of stuff which includes (for example) a fine collection of embroidered eighteenth-century waistcoats, Victorian and Edwardian evening gowns, samples of old lace and a huge collection of porcelain cheese dishes. The Protestant cathedral of **KILMORE**, on the R198 three miles southwest of Cavan town, is a modern structure of little interest. However, set in the wall is an impressive Romanesque doorway, removed here from a monastery that stood on Trinity Island, three miles to the west in Lough Oughter. Its deep, chunky carving is superbly intricate and repays detailed attention. Follow the narrow road that runs north from here to the hamlet of Garthrotten, and you can enter *Killykeen Forest Park*, a self-catering complex with accommodation in wooden chalets (☎049/433 2541). There is open access to woodland walks and fishing, and horse riding is available. Here Clough Oughter is a thirteenth-century circular tower built on a *crannóg*, the best of its kind in Ireland.

Ballyjamesduff

BALLYJAMESDUFF, eleven miles south of Cavan town, just off the N3, is the location for the new **Cavan County Museum** (June–Sept Tues–Sat 10am–5pm & Sun 2–6pm; Oct–May closed Sun; £2). The small collection includes replicas of Celtic stone idols dating from the second century BC to the second century AD. Among the exhibits from the medieval period there's the Lough Errol dugout boat (900 AD) and a couple of impressive sheila na gigs. Surprisingly, the history of Cavan's emigrants yields Sioux girdles and headdresses, and there's extensive coverage of the GAA footballing history of the county.

West Cavan

To the northwest of Milltown and Killeshandra, west Cavan sticks out like a handle, tracing the line of the border. It's quite different from the rest of the county – wilder and higher, with peat-covered hills, granite boulders and mountain streams. In this inhospitable bleakness, it has more in common with the wilds of Donegal than the more intimate Cavan lakeland.

About six miles from Belturbet is **BALLYCONNELL,** two miles west of which is the county's one independent **hostel**, *Sandville House Hostel* (☎049/952 6297; March–Nov). Housed in a converted barn alongside a large Georgian house, it's a tranquil spot, and there are bikes for rent and space for tents. **B&Bs** in the area include *An Crannog*, Cranaghan (☎049/952 6545; ③) and *Rossdean*, Daisyhill (☎049/952 6358; ③).

Right up in the northwestern corner of the county, the Cavan Way is a signposted walk of seventeen miles that takes you through rugged terrain from **DOWRA** to **BLACKLION**, where it meets the southwestern end of the Ulster Way. Small maps of the route can be picked up in tourist offices. From the heights above Blacklion there are spectacular views over Lough MacNean and the Fermanagh lakeland, to the Sligo and Leitrim mountains in the west, and on a clear day to the heights of south Donegal. Along the route, The Shannon Pot is the source of Ireland's mightiest river – the Shannon – and figures heavily in Irish myth, though it's little visited.

Dowra and Blacklion themselves are tiny and remote: the former high on the young Shannon before it fills Lough Allen, the first of many lakes, the latter a border crossing point. Both have very limited facilities indeed. Their B&Bs are almost certain to have space, though it's best to phone ahead and check. In Blacklion there's *Lough Macneann House* (☎072/53022; ④), in Main Street; dinner in their award-winning bistro costs around £16. In Dowra, a tiny place with just a few bars and a grocery shop, *The Hi Way Inn* (☎078/43025; ①) is the only option.

COUNTY MONAGHAN

Monaghan's countryside is first and foremost drumlin country. Drumlins are softly rounded mounds of land left by retreating glaciers at the end of the last Ice Age, and the exceptional number of these small hills packed together in County Monaghan serves as a very good example of what textbooks call "basket of eggs" topography – a reference to the land's appearance from on high; at ground level the soil is poor and the land is broken up into small units which are difficult and uneconomic to farm. The drumlins are grass-covered, and light hedgerows stitch their way across them, marking out the fields. Initially it's a charming scene, but it soon becomes repetitive: the pathways between drumlins are pretty enough, but once you're round or over one small hill the next is much the same. Little lakes provide occasional relief and are excellent for fishing, but they're nothing like as numerous as in Cavan.

The feel of this landscape has been captured in the poetry and prose of Patrick Kavanagh, rated by many as Ireland's finest poet after Yeats. He was born in Inishkeen in the south of the county, and his writing evokes the poor quality of peasant life – and also something of the monotony of the rural landscape.

Particularly in the north of the county, the terrain has led to an insane crisscrossing of lanes: a compass is a good idea, as is an up-to-date map. It makes for delightful walking if you're not in too much of a hurry: in these hilly areas you can wander undisturbed for miles along the labyrinth of ancient tracks and lanes – though it is advisable to avoid the border. If you know what to look for you can seek out the sites of court tombs, forts and cairns from the Bronze Age. Many of them, thanks to the underdevelopment of the land, have remained virtually untouched. The best megalithic sites in the region are the Lisnadarragh wedge tomb, Dún Dubh, at Tiravera, and the Tullyrain triple ring fort near Shantonagh.

But most of Monaghan's towns and villages have very clear origins in the seventeenth and eighteenth centuries. The influence of Scottish planters and English colonists is obvious in the number of planters' Gothic and Presbyterian churches, and in the planned towns and the landscaped estates developed around conveniently picturesque lakes. Stark, stern architecture reflects the character of the hard-working and hard-driving settlers who came here determined to extract prosperity from farming, and from the linen industries which they introduced. Probably the most extreme examples of such discipline are the dour, austere stone cottages of Glaslough, cold and orderly in the north of the county. Like Cavan, Monaghan's cultural identity is deeply rooted in Ulster history.

Monaghan town

You're most likely to find yourself in **MONAGHAN** town while on your way to somewhere else, but the actual fabric of the place is quite interesting as you pass through. Monaghan town epitomizes what makes this county very definitely Ulster and yet quite distinct from Cavan. The planning of seventeenth-century settlers, the prosperity of the eighteenth-century linen industry (largely the achievement of Scots Presbyterians) and the subsequent wealth and status of the town in the following century are all very much in evidence.

The Town

Three central squares are linked by a chain of lanes, a layout not, in fact, altogether typical of plantation towns. At the centre is the **Diamond** – the name given to all these Ulster "squares" – in the middle of which stands a grandiose Victorian drinking fountain, the kind of memorial strongly reminiscent of any nineteenth-century industrial British city, yet strangely out of place in rural Ireland. When it was placed here, the earlier seventeenth-century Scottish settlers' cross, with its multifaceted sundial, was shifted a short distance along Dublin Street to Old Cross Square, where it still stands.

Alongside the Diamond is **Church Square**. Here a classical courthouse, a solid Victorian bank and hotel and a very pretty Regency Gothic church, large and spacious, stand together, conferring a strong sense of civic dignity. The town's former importance as a British garrison town is quite clear, and a large obelisk commemorates a colonel killed in the Crimean War. Everything about the place suggests a conscious attempt at permanency, buildings placed with a view to posterity; even the rounded corners of the most mundane buildings and their boldly arched entries – both features unique to Monaghan – suggest strength and pride.

Beyond Church Square, at the top of Market Street, is a pretty, arched **Market House** built in 1792, a solid, graceful building of well-cut limestone, with finely detailed decoration of carved oak leaves and oak apples. In the opposite direction, Dublin Street leads down to **Old Cross Square**. At number ten stands the birthplace of Monaghan's most famous son, **Charles Gavan Duffy** – a Nationalist who was instrumental in the founding of the Irish Tenant League. He was also the co-founder, along with Thomas Davis, of *The Nation*, a paper which was to disseminate politically sensitive ideas. Beyond, high on a hill out of town, **St Macartan's Catholic Cathedral** commands views over the whole town and surrounding countryside. Completed in 1892, it's a Gothic Revival building of hard grey sandstone, with a tall spire and a spacious interior, complete with an impressive hammer-beam roof. As you stand on the steps looking out over the surrounding land you get a real feeling of its era – it's a most successful nineteenth-century statement of religious liberation and pride.

As well as being a busy commercial and administrative centre, Monaghan looks after the county's vigorous and sometimes violent history at the **Monaghan County Museum** on Hill Street (Tues–Sat 11am–1pm & 2–5pm; free). This fine building houses a permanent collection of archeological material, prehistoric antiquities, examples of traditional local crafts, domestic utensils and paintings, prints and watercolours from the late eighteenth century to the present day. The museum's most prized artefact is the **Cross of Clogher**, a processional cross dating from around 1400. Contemporary art exhibitions are also held here. The **Heritage Centre**, Broad Road (Mon, Tues, Thurs & Fri 10am–noon & 2.30–4.30pm; Sat & Sun 2.30–4.30pm; £1), tells the story of the religious order of St Louis, with an intelligent display meticulously put together by one of the sisters; you're guided through it with a cassette recording.

Practicalities

The **tourist office** is in Market House in Market Street (end March to June & Sept–Dec Mon–Fri 9am–1pm & 2–5pm, Sat 9am–1pm; July and August Mon–Sat 9am–6pm, Sun 10am–2pm; ☎047/81122). There are several decent **B&Bs**, including *Ardail House*, 7 Cathedral View, just opposite Macartan's Cathedral (☎047/71311; ②), a pleasant and unpretentious option; *Ashleigh House*, 37 Dublin St (☎047/81227; ③), and *The Cedars*, Clones Road (☎047/82783; ③; closed Dec). If you are looking for a hotel, the *Westenra Arms* on The Diamond (☎047/81517; ⑥) is traditional and central, while *The Hillgrove Hotel*, Old Armagh Road, near the cathedral (☎047/81288; ⑥) has comfortable well-appointed rooms.

As for **places to eat**, you'll get decent bar food at *McConnon's Olde Cross Inn*, Olde Cross Square, and at *Andy's*, 12 Market St. One of the best spots for budget home-cooked lunches is *Flannery's* coffee shop above Super Valu, Church Square, and for burgers and chips, try *Mo's Bar*, Dublin Street. There is a limited choice of places to eat during the evenings: one of the best is award-winning *Andy's Restaurant* (dinner around £13); the menu at *Mediterraneo*, 58 Dublin St, includes plenty of Italian dishes and vegetarian options; alternatively you could try the carvery of *The Hillgrove Hotel* (roasts and grills from around £7 till 10pm), or the extensive and varied menu of the hotel restaurant (dinner £17–25). Fast food to eat in or take away is available at *Tommie's Restaurant*, 7 Glaslough St.

You won't have to go far to hear **music** in the evenings. In Dublin Street, *McKenna's* has blues bands and occasional folk and rock; *The Shamrock Bar* has country and rock bands (Sat & Sun), and there are flocks of would-be Eagles in *Mo's Bar* (Fri, Sat, Sun). *McConnon's Olde Cross Inn* is a good spot for a quiet pint; on the Diamond, *The Squealing Pig* has an MOR band on a Tuesday; for traditional music try *Kavanagh's*, Park Street, just across from the tourist office. The local Friday and Saturday night discos are held at *The Hillgrove Hotel*. There are some very active local theatre groups: check out The Garage Theatre (☎047/81597) to find out what's on. There's an international jazz festival over the first weekend in September, usually starting on the Thursday night.

Bus Éireann (☎047/82377) links Monagahan with all major towns in the Republic and with Armagh, Belfast, Derry, Omagh and Strabane in the North. McConnon's (☎047/82020) operates a private daily bus service to Dublin, picking up in Church Square.

Around the county

There are just a few reasons for pushing northeast of Monaghan to the eerie, chill-grey village of **GLASLOUGH**, and the best of these is *Castle Leslie* (☎047/88109; ⑨), a gormenghastian aristocratic pile, crammed with antiques. Book in and you leave the twentieth century behind: there are no phones, TVs, or room service, just wonderfully relaxed hospitality and a sense of fading splendour. Previous guests have included Yeats, George Moore and Winston Churchill. If an overnight stay is beyond your budget, you can sample some of the atmosphere if you book in for dinner (Sat only, around £24). Back in the village, *The Olde Bar* is a tiny place, similarly seemingly unchanged for decades, open Thursdays and Saturdays only. **B&B** accommodation is available at the *Greystone Equestrian Centre* (☎047/88100; ④), a large Victorian house on the *Castle Leslie* estate. The menu at the popular *Hunting Lodge Restaurant* (☎047/88100; dinner £18.50) alongside includes plenty of fresh local produce, including salmon, steak and lamb.

Castleblaney

Unless you're heading for Glaslough or the North, there are two main routes out of Monaghan: west to the pleasant town of Clones or south to Carrickmacross. On the latter route you'll pass first through **CASTLEBLANEY**, whose two proud broad streets hinge upon a fine Georgian courthouse at what was once the market square. Castleblaney was built by English colonists to serve the needs of a large estate, beautifully situated beside Monaghan's largest lake, Lough Muckno, and this is still the town's finest asset. When the English picked their spot they knew what they were about: it's a particularly attractive demesne of mixed woodlands and gentle slopes beside placid waters. The estate is now a forest park, with clearly signposted walks around beautiful grounds; access is just behind the courthouse. On the whole, the Lough Muckno Leisure Park attracts families and anglers in search of peace and quiet, but it's also home to an independent **hostel**, *The Lough Muckno Adventure Centre and Holiday Hostel* (☎042/974 6356), where you can hire canoes, sailing dinghies and windsurfers. It's advisable to ring ahead as the hostel caters mainly for groups. There's more water-based excitement to be had at Castleblaney Waterski Club (☎042/974 0752), and plenty of coarse angling available at Lough Muckno and in the series of small lakes roundabout. **B&Bs** include *Hillview*, just outside town (☎042/974 6217; ②), and the spacious and comfortable *Palm Grove Lodge*, Lough Egish, two miles out on the Shercock Road (☎042/974 5170; ②). The best **place to eat** is *The Hope Castle Bar and Restaurant* (☎042/974 9450), within the grounds of the forest park, beautifully situated overlooking the lake. It also has the lion's share of nightlife around here, with bands six nights a week during the summer months – mainly country, though there's an occasional foray into the realms of world music. If you just want a pint, try *McAree's*, just down the hill from *The Hope Castle* entrance.

Carrickmacross

CARRICKMACROSS is the county's second most important town, boosted in the nineteenth century by a prosperous lace-making industry. Still, it's a rather modest place with just one broad main street: a planter's Gothic church stands at one end, and a fine mid-nineteenth century courthouse at the other. In between, lies a bustling array of pubs, shops and Georgian houses, and today's lacemakers have their tiny showcase in the nineteenth-century market buildings at the lower end of the main street. Just outside town, landscaped parkland of sumptuous oaks and beeches surrounds **Lough Fea**. Further out, some three miles down the Kingscourt Road, is the **Dún a Rí Forest**

Park with more good wooded walks. The massive *Nuremore Hotel* is very expensive (☎042/966 1438; ⑨), but there are plenty of **B&Bs** near the centre of Carrickmacross, up the Derry Road past the Texaco filling station: try *Cloughvalley House* (☎042/966 1246; ②), *Nocdale*, 9 Ard Rois Ave, Cloughvalley (☎042/966 1608), or *Eureka* at 27 Ard Rois Ave (☎042/966 2009; ①), a friendly, low-key B&B.

Iniskeen

INISKEEN, to the east of Carrickmacross, is the birthplace of **Patrick Kavanagh**. There's a small plaque bearing some of his verse in the village, and the house he lived in is well signposted – but you can't go in and it's an entirely uninteresting building. Kavanagh is buried in the graveyard of St Mary's church. The church is also home to the **Patrick Kavanagh Rural and Literary Resource Centre** (Mon–Fri 11am–5pm; Sat, Sun and bank holidays 2–7pm; ☎042/78560; £2), which has displays on Kavanagh and his work as well as local history. In a more distant past, Inishkeen was the site of a sixth-century monastic centre: scant remains of the abbey and a round tower survive. The **Folk Museum** (by arrangement only, ☎042/78102) deals with local history, folklife and the old Great Northern Railway.

Clones

Heading west from Monaghan, **CLONES** (pronounced *Clo-nez*) is a busy, friendly market town, barely half a mile from the border. Situated on top of a hill, its streets give a good perspective over the surrounding countryside. The town – as it appears today – dates from 1601 when the English took it over and started to develop it. It's very obviously an Ulster town, with large Presbyterian and Methodist churches to rival the usual Catholic and Church of Ireland offerings. The solemn and impressive **St Tiernach's Church** (Church of Ireland) gives out onto the fine Diamond, and there is some evidence of eighteenth-century prosperity in the town's handful of Georgian houses. There are also traces of Clones' earlier identity, the most impressive being the weathered, deeply carved **high cross** which stands in the Diamond. Depicted on it are Adam and Eve, Abraham's near sacrifice of Isaac, Daniel in the lion's den and, on the north side, the Adoration of the Magi, the miracle at Cana and the miracle of the loaves and fishes. Though worn, there's still a strong impression of the richness of the carving. In the sixth century St Tiernach founded a monastery at Clones. It became an Augustinian **abbey** in the twelfth century, and the tumbled-down traces of this can be seen in Abbey Street, along with those of a round tower. Just on the edge of town is an ancient rath (an enclosure used as a dwelling) of three concentric earthworks.

Nowadays, the town's chief claim to fame is as the home of Barry McGuigan, the former world-champion boxer, and there are plenty of photos of him in *The Lennard Arms Hotel*, which also does **B&B** (☎047/51075; ③); *Creighton's* in Fermanagh Street (☎047/51284; ④) is the other hotel option if you're looking for somewhere to stay. *The Round Tower Bar* in Cara Street serves good bar food, as does *Cúil Darrach* on the Diamond, where there is also a restaurant alongside. **Ulster Canal Stores** provides information and has exhibitions on the area's history, including lace-making and the old Erne–Belfast Canal. The town is a good point from which to get onto **The Kingfisher Cycle Trail** (see p.601); you can rent bikes at Snipe Cycle Hire, Ulster Canal Stores.

Just east of Clones is the **Tyrone Guthrie Foundation** at Annamakering, **NEWBLISS**. Commemorating the famous Shakespearian director, the oversubscribed centre offers a retreat and workspace to writers, artists and composers from all over the world. You can stay in the grandeur of *Glynch House* (☎047/54045; ④), an eighteenth-century mansion just outside Newbliss.

travel details

Buses

Cavan town to: Belfast (1–4 daily; 2hr–4hr 50min); Dublin (4–9 daily; 1hr 40min).

Monaghan town to: Belfast (2–5 daily; 2hr–3hr 30min); Dublin (5–8 daily; 2hr).

COUNTY DONEGAL

ew would disagree with the assertion that County Donegal has the richest scenery in the whole country. Second only in size to County Cork, it has a spectacular 200-mile coastline – an intoxicating run of headlands, promontories and peninsulas – rising to the highest sea-cliffs in Europe at Slieve League. Inland is a terrain of glens, rivers and bogland hills, of which the best-known parts are the Glencolmcille Peninsula and around Ardara and Glenties in the southern part of the county. The Glencolmcille area attracts more visitors than any other, yet the landscape of northern Donegal is, if anything, even more satisfying, especially the Rosguill and Inishowen peninsulas and the interior region – sometimes called the Donegal Highlands – around Errigal Mountain, Lough Beagh and Lough Gartan. Other noteworthy areas are the Rosses and Bloody Foreland, which are reminiscent of the more barren stretches of Connemara and make up the strongest *Gaeltacht*, or Irish-speaking, districts in the county.

The county's original name was *Tír Chonaill*, which translates as "the land of Conal", one of the twelve sons of Niall of the Nine Hostages. Subsequent to the **Flight of the Earls** in the early seventeenth century, the English changed the name to that of their main garrison *Dún na nGall* ("the fort of the foreigner") which has a certain irony, because Donegal always eluded the grip of English power, mainly owing to its wild and untillable terrain. At the time of Partition in 1922, the Protestant leader **Carson** let the county remain with the Republic, reasoning that its Catholic population would probably have voted the county and the whole of the North back into the Republic at a later stage. Hence the peculiarity of its being the most northerly piece of the island, yet belonging to the Republic, to which it's attached by just a thread of land.

Bundoran and around

It's hard to avoid disappointment, if **BUNDORAN** is your first sight of Donegal. This popular, though tacky, seaside resort offers no indication of the pleasures which lie beyond. It does have three miles of Blue Flag beaches, packed with holiday-makers in summer, but the town itself provides pretty grim fare. The tiny River Doran separates the more genteel **West End** from the **East End** and its rather down-at-heel Main Street, filled with pubs, B&Bs, eating places, and a headland dominated by a golf course.

Unless you're fond of golf, Bundoran's chief attraction is a lovely golden-sand beach known as **Tullan Strand**, a bracing stroll along the coastal promenade from the northern end of the town beach. The walk takes in rock formations known as the **Fairy**

ACCOMMODATION PRICE CODES

Throughout this book, prices of hotels, guesthouses and B&Bs have been graded with the codes below, according to what you can expect to pay for a double room in high season. For more details on accommodation, see p. 29.

① Under £26	④ £40–55	⑦ £90–110
② £26–33	⑤ £55–70	⑧ £110–130
③ £33–40	⑥ £70–90	⑨ Over £130

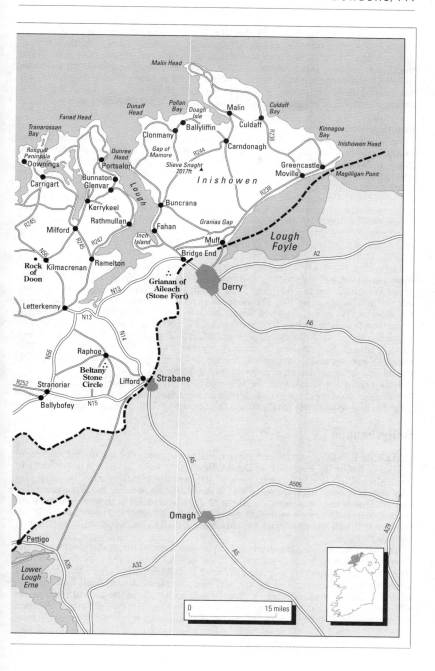

Bridge and the **Puffing Hole**, with the Atlantic thundering below and appetizing views across to the much more rewarding Glencolmcille Peninsula. Along with the beach at Rossnowlagh, Tullan Strand is reckoned among the most exciting surfing spots in the world and, in 1997, Bundoran hosted the European Championships here. Far safer waters for swimming are to be found at **Waterworld** (Easter week, April–May & Sept Sat & Sun 11am–7pm; June–Aug daily; £4.50), located on the seafront near the river's mouth, a complex of heated pools with wave machine, water slides and seaweed baths.

Practicalities

There's no longer a tourist office here, but you should have no trouble finding **accommodation**. The cheapest place to stay in Bundoran is the *Homefield Holiday Hostel*, Bayview Avenue (☎072/41288), an activity centre and language school often full of hearty young groups; to get to it, cross the bridge into the West End and turn left at the church shortly afterwards. B&Bs are plentiful and several in the West End have wonderful views of Donegal Bay: *Avondale*, Bay View Terrace (☎072/41091; ③); *Conway House*, almost next door (☎072/41220; ②; March–Sept); and *Bayview Guesthouse*, Main Street (☎072/41296; ③). Best-known of the numerous hotels is the huge old *Great Northern* (☎072/41204; ⑧), dominating the golf course right on the headland. Among other options are the popular *Allingham Arms* (☎072/41075; ⑥) and the *Holyrood Hotel* (☎072/41100; ⑥) on either side of the bridge.

For **eating**, the *Angler's Restaurant* provides a reasonably priced three-course meal. More upmarket, but still not too expensive, is the *Fitzgerald Hotel*, just over the bridge in the West End, and the *Whistling Oyster*, on the main street, serving varied seafood dinners in a bar-room setting. The *Imperial Hotel* in the West End serves good value bar lunches. There are plenty of simple cafés like the *Kitchen Bake*, in a converted chapel on the main street, for excellent cakes, coffee and snacks. Most **pubs** in Bundoran are pretty ordinary and permanently crowded with northern holiday-makers in high season. For sessions in summer, try *The Chasin' Bull* on Main Street. The *Planet Earth* complex on Central Avenue hosts incredibly popular **discos** with coachloads arriving from all over the county and beyond.

Bike rental is available from the Hire and Sell Centre, East End (☎072/41526) and for fabulous pony-trekking over sandhills and beaches, contact the Stracomer Silver Strand riding school (☎072/41288), just out of town on Tullan Strand Road.

Ballyshannon

BALLYSHANNON, four miles further north at the mouth of the River Erne, more genuinely marks the beginning of County Donegal. It was the site of a major battle in 1591 when Hugh Roe O'Donnell drove off the besieging English army. Nowadays its hilly streets become most animated during the **Music Festival** on the first weekend in August. One of the most popular festivals of traditional music in Ireland, it attracts big names, such as Donegal's own Altan along with a multitude of unknown talents. If you want a room, you'll need to book well in advance, though space can often be found on someone's floor.

The town stands a few hundred yards upstream from a ford, at the point where the river's fresh waters begin to mingle with the ocean. Most of the interest lies up the steep northern slope and is easily combined in a single, straightforward stroll. The main arteries here form a wishbone, and near the top of the left-hand branch, signposted to the left, stands St Anne's Church, built on the site of the ancient royal palace of Mullaghanshee. The church's graveyard is the final resting place of the poet **William Allingham** (1824–89). His grave, to the left of the church, is marked by a simple marble slab, inscribed with the word "poet". Allingham was born in Ballyshannon and, like

T.S. Eliot, began work in a bank (the town's Allied Irish Bank has a bust of the poet and preserves the words scratched by him on a windowpane).

His first volume of verse, *Poems* (1850) is very light, though characterized by an exceptional sonorous and lilting quality, and contains his best-known work *The Fairies* ("*Up the airy mountain, down the rushy glen, we dare not go a'hunting for fear of little men...*"). His verse attracted the attention of the pre-Raphaelites, and another work, *Day and Night Songs*, was illustrated by Rossetti and Millais. Later, however, he focused on more weighty matters, in particular his homeland. Edited by his wife, the illustrator Helen Paterson, his posthumous *Diary* recounts his friendships with literary contemporaries, most notably Tennyson.

From the graveyard there's a marvellous view over the town. Down at the quay you can see the backs of the tall, old warehouses lined along the river bank, their basement walls dripping with seaweed, and also the ancient isle of **Inis Saimer** just out in the river. There's only a wooden summerhouse on the island now, but it claims to have sheltered the first colonists of Ireland, around 3500 BC, offering safety from the ferocious beasts that would have roamed the forests on the mainland. A recently excavated ancient Greek coin has provided evidence of the site's antiquity. The water here teems with fish, and you'll find anglers still trying to bag them well into the night.

Practicalities

Although there is no tourist office at present, there are plans to build one in the Market Square. For **B&Bs** around town try *Mullac Na Si*, Bishop Street (☎072/52702; ③), *Carrickboy House* (☎072/51278; ③), across the roundabout in East Port, or *Channel View* (☎072/51713; ③), a little way down the road to Abbey Assaroe; others are mostly further along here or out on the Bundoran road. **Hotel** accommodation includes the refurbished *Dorrian's Imperial* (☎072/51147; ⑥), on Main Street, on the way to the churchyard. The small, but welcoming *Duffy's Hostel*, a couple of hundred yards up the Donegal Road (☎072/51535; March–Oct) has its own second-hand bookshop and camping facilities.

There are several reasonably priced **restaurants** for daytime eating, including *Cúchulainn's* on Castle Street, with its healthy portions of fast food, and the popular upstairs coffee rooms at *Grimes Kitchen Bake* on Main Street, where you can get marvellous fresh cakes and pastries. In the evening, check out *Embers Restaurant*, above *Paddy's Bar*, on Castle Street for seafood, pasta and vegetarian dishes, or try *Shannon's Corner Bistro*, at the top of Main Street, for reasonably-priced French-style cuisine. For something more exotic, head across the bridge for Mexican specialities at *El Gringo*. The best **pubs** in town are *Seán Óg's*, with traditional **music** every Wednesday night and rock on Saturday, the modern *Dicey Reilly's* opposite, *The Thatch* pub on Bishop Street, with thatched roof and cottage-kitchen interior and traditional music most nights, and the *Old Distillery*, on the bridge opposite the bus station. Most pubs have music on Sundays and you'll find folk at the *Corner Bar*. *Dino's* nightclub in the *Assaroe Hotel*, Main Street, is the hub of **disco** life.

As well as its August music **festival**, Ballyshannon has a number of other festivities worth investigating. An amateur **drama festival** of mainly Irish plays is held during the week of March 17 (St Patrick's Day), the **Allingham Arts Festival for Writers** takes place over a weekend at the end of November, while the town's traditional **harvest fair** celebrations around the middle of September draw crowds from the surrounding countryside. The rest of the time you can fill your evenings at the two-screen Abbey **cinema** in the Community Arts Centre, at the north end of town by the Donegal Road. At **Ballintra**, four miles along the Donegal Road, there's **horse racing** in the open fields on the first Monday in August.

Abbey Assaroe and Creevy

Back on the road, a left turn by *The Thatch* pub at the top of the hill takes you along the Rossnowlagh road, where a second signposted left turn leads to the scant remains of **Abbey Assaroe**, founded by the Cistercians in 1184. Past the abbey and round to the left, you'll come to a restored **mill** beside a bubbling stream. This makes a pretty picture of millrace and rotating cog wheels, and there's an **interpretive centre**, The Watermills (☎072/51580), explaining the restoration project and the role of the Cistercians in medieval Ireland. The log gate next to the old bridge takes you onto the stream's bank and leads to two artificial **caves**. One is a small grotto known as the Catsby; the other – now around 90ft deep – is said to have once reached all the way under the abbey and run for two miles towards Rossnowlagh. The grotto was once a site for Masses, which had to be held in secret during the enforcement of the penal laws in the eighteenth century – and you'll find in the Rossnowlagh museum the carved stone known as the Monk's Head that once sat above the entrance. A couple of hundred yards upstream are *Eas Aedha Ruadh*, the falls of the chieftain Red Hugh, who reputedly drowned here.

A few yards up the lane from the mill and over a stone stile next to a bungalow a little track runs down to the shore of the **bay**. St Patrick is said to have once stepped ashore here, and today there are several rusted metal crosses perched on small stony outcrops and a tree covered in assorted weather-beaten thanksgiving mementos. The natural **well** here is said to have sprung up at the spot where the saint's foot touched the shore and its waters, when present, have supposed curative powers.

Back on the Rossnowlagh road, two miles on, a turning leads to the tiny seaside hamlet of **Creevy**. It's a tranquil, though lonely spot and a memorial on the pier sadly records the death of three local fishermen in 1988, testament to the sometime ferocity of the waters in the bay.

Rossnowlagh

Appropriately named **ROSSNOWLAGH** ("The Heavenly Cove") lies on the coast away from the main Donegal Road, with a magnificent expanse of beach raked by Atlantic surf, and to the south, good cliffs for walking. It has a surfing club beside the *Sand House Hotel*, which is unfortunately private, but one of the many surfing buffs will probably be able to help you out with equipment, or at least advise where else to get your hands on it.

The **Franciscan Friary** nearby houses a captivating one-room museum (daily 10am–6pm), run by the Donegal Historical Society and crammed with Stone Age flints, Bronze Age dagger blades, penal crosses, pistols and other local miscellany. This includes a lovely set of *uilleann* pipes with green felt bag and very handsome regulators, a fiddle that belonged to the great piper Turlough MacSuibhne and a seventeenth-century Flemish painting on glass (*The Christ of Pity*) used as a devotion plate. If you decide to stay, there's cliff-top **B&B** at *Ard-na-Mara House* (☎072/51141; ④) and nearby, the splendidly situated *Smugglers Creek* inn does excellent food and has music at weekends. A mile north of Rossnowlagh towards Ballintra lies **Glasbolie Fort**, a huge earthen rampart 20ft high and nearly 900ft round, said to have been the burial place of a sixth-century High King of Ireland.

Donegal town

DONEGAL town is not the most exciting of places, but it is making an effort. It's not even the county capital (which is Letterkenny), and the lasting impression is one of traffic jammed around the busy triangular **Diamond** at the centre, the old market place. A surprising number of tourists visit the town, but the only real reason to stay long is to explore the surrounding countryside, especially the **Blue Stack Mountains** which rise at the northern end of **Lough Eske**.

Arrival, information and accommodation

Buses stop outside the *Abbey Hotel* on the Diamond, with timetables displayed in the helpful and information-packed **tourist office** on the Quay (July & Aug daily 9am–8pm; Easter–June & Sept Mon–Sat 9am–5pm; ☎073/21148). One advantage of staying in Donegal is that you've plenty of choice of accommodation. There are literally dozens of B&Bs scattered around the town, but many of them are very small, so to avoid a lot of walking it's simplest to call at the tourist office. Some **B&Bs** to try if you arrive out of hours are the *Atlantic Guesthouse* on Main Street (☎073/21187; ③), *Drumcliffe House* on Coast Road (☎073/21200; ③) and *Castle View House* (☎073/22100; ②) and *Riverside House* (☎073/21083; ②) both on Waterloo Place across the river from the castle. For something more upmarket, try the comfortable *Abbey Hotel* (☎073/21014; ⑥) on the Diamond, and if you really want to push the boat out, book in at *St Ernan's House* (☎073/21065; ⑨), built by Wellington's nephew in 1836 and situated on its own private island, signposted a few hundred yards up the Sligo road.

There are three **hostels**: *Cliffview* (☎073/21684), a short walk along Coast Road in the direction of Killybegs; half a mile futher on, the popular *Donegal Town Independent Hostel* (☎073/22805), which has camping and a jovial atmosphere; and the secluded, but often busy, An Oige *Ball Hill Hostel*, about three miles out in a former coastguard station on the north side of Donegal Bay (☎073/21174; Easter–Sept), which also offers camping facilities. On the way here you'll pass Ashleigh Riding Stables (☎073/21097) where you can arrange **horse riding**.

Bikes can be rented from the Bike Shop, Waterloo Place (☎073/22515) and from O'Doherty's on Main Street (☎073/21119) which also sells **fishing permits** and rents out **tackle**. The owner is a mine of information on the region, including the best angling spots and hiking routes. The Apollo **laundry** (Mon-Sat Easter–Sept 9am–6pm) is on Upper Main Street just past the cathedral or there's Dermo's (same hours) in the Millcourt Shopping Arcade on the Diamond. If you need **provisions**, there are a couple of well-stocked supermarkets – Foodmarket on the Diamond and Super Valu up the Sligo road – and also Simple Simon's natural foods, also on the Diamond.

The Town

Donegal takes its name from *Dún na nGall*, and the original "fort of the foreigners" was thought to have been built on the banks of the River Eske by invading Vikings. There's no doubt, however, that the first Red Hugh O'Donnell, king of Tír Chonaill, had a Norman-style tower house, known as **O'Donnell's Castle**, constructed on its site in the fifteenth century. When the English defeated the second Red Hugh in 1603, Sir Basil Brooke was given command of the town and it was he who rebuilt and extended the old castle, retaining the lower parts of the original tower, which had been razed to the ground by Red Hugh to prevent its capture. This well-restored example of Jacobean architecture sits on Tirconaill Street by the Diamond (daily May–Oct 9.30am–5.45pm; £2). It's a fine marriage of strong defence and domestic grace – note the mullioned windows, arches, ten gables and no fewer than fourteen fireplaces, over the grandest of which are carved the escutcheons of Brooke and his wife's family, the Leicesters. Brooke topped the tower with a Barbizon turret and added the mansion on the left, with the kitchens and bakery on the ground floor and living quarters on the floor above. Brooke was highly prolific in Donegal and was responsible for the overall design of the town.

On the stone bridge by the castle on the Killybegs road is a plaque commemorating the town's most famous author, the Rev Dr John Boyce, better known by his pseudonym "Paul Peppergrass". After ministering for some years in the county, he travelled to America in 1845, concerned for the spiritual welfare of the newly-arrived Irish emigrants. Though largely forgotten now, his most popular work was *Shandy Maguire*, a novel describing the tribulations incurred by the Irish Catholics in defence of their faith. Later dramatized, it became a major success on the American stage.

In the Diamond stands an obelisk in memory of the compilers of the famed **Annals of the Four Masters**. The *Annals* were compiled in Donegal Abbey, on the coast close to Bundoran, and were a systematic attempt to collect all known Irish documents into a history of the land beginning in 2958 BC and ending at the time of writing, 1616 AD. The first entry dates back forty years before the Flood and relates a visit of Noah's granddaughter to Ireland. Around the Diamond there's good shopping, especially the Four Masters bookshop and Magee's department store.

Down at the **quay** an anchor is on display, retrieved from the sea near Mountcharles in the 1850s and traditionally believed to have belonged to the French frigate *Romaine,* a member of the fleet transporting French troops to support Wolfe Tone's rebellion in 1798. On the left bank of the River Eske, not far from here, stand the few ruined remains of a **Franciscan friary**, built in 1474 by the first Red Hugh and his wife Nuala O'Brien of Munster. It was occupied by the English in 1601 and seriously damaged by the besieging O'Donnell army, being finally abandoned after the Flight of the Earls. On the opposite side a woodland path known as the **Bank Walk** runs out alongside the bay with a pleasant view towards its many sandy islets and stony shoreline.

The County Donegal Railway, which ran from Derry to Ballyshannon, closed in 1959, but its history is told at the **Donegal Railway Heritage Centre** at the Old Station House, Tirconaill Street (June–Sept Mon–Sat 10am–5.30pm, Sun 2–5pm; Oct–May Mon–Fri 10am–4pm; £1). Here you'll find a model of the old railway and lovingly restored railcars and carriages from the steam age.

Food, drink and entertainment

Eating places are plentiful, though it's the pubs as ever that seem to offer most choice. Alternatives include steaks, salmon and pizzas at *The Harbour*, opposite the tourist office, or fish from Killybegs at the *Errigal Restaurant* on Main Street. If all you want is a cheap hearty meal make for the nearby *Atlantic Restaurant* or the *Deli-bar.* The restaurant in Magee's store on the Diamond serves light lunches, or the *Abbey Hotel* will feed you rather more substantially.

Donegal has a lively **music** scene and its summer **festival**, held in early July, is one of the biggest in the county. Many of the town's **pubs** offer traditional entertainment year round and Thursday's *Donegal Democrat* provides local listings. The *Olde Castle* bar, next to the castle, has an excellent restaurant, plus high-quality music and dancing till 2am most nights. Lively *McGroarty's*, a few doors down, has a Thursday night traditional session and other music at weekends, while the nearby *Central Hotel* is the place for home-grown country and western. Others are mainly out on Main Street: the *Coach House* has nightly sessions; the *Star Bar* is a lively place with sing-songs and live acts, the *National* has more traditional music in the lounge at weekends, and best of all is *The Schooner*, just past the cathedral, with a nautical interior, an original nineteenth-century bar and music almost every night. In Laghy, three miles south on the Sligo Road, *Carlin's* pub has old-time dancing on Tuesday and Irish nights in summer. If all you want is a quiet pint, try *Tirconaill*, opposite the Ulster Bank on the Diamond. *Club N*, on Main Street, holds regular **discos**, but the most popular are on Sundays in the *Abbey Hotel* (10.30pm–2am; sometimes also on Fri in summer).

If you're after souvenirs, or simply a way to fill a wet afternoon, then it might be worth heading out to the **Craft Village**, three-quarters of a mile from town on the Sligo road. The workshops are leased to professional craftworkers whom you can see in action, including an *uilleann* pipe-maker.

Around Donegal

Southeast of Donegal town, the corner of the county tucked into a fold in the border is replete with little lakes well stocked for fishing; the largest of these, and a place of pilgrimage, is Lough Derg. Less than five miles upriver from town is another spot of gentle natural beauty, Lough Eske; from here you can walk into the wilds of the Blue Stack Mountains, which rise to the north.

Lough Derg

In the middle of **Lough Derg** (Red Lake) is a rocky islet known as **Station Island** or, more popularly, St Patrick's Purgatory, which has long served as a retreat for Catholics needing rigour and solitude to recharge their faith. Today it still thrives as a strong centre for pilgrimage (especially from June to Aug), and the island cannot be visited for any other reason – though some casual travellers and non-believers do get some sort of stimulation out of passing through this ancient ceremony. Participants in the three-day retreats (£18) go without sleep or food (bar black tea and toast) and walk barefoot over rocks, praying at stations of the cross, though the one-day retreats (£11) are less austere. Despite the exigencies, it seems particularly popular with Irish students studying for exams – or waiting for the results. Northern Irish poet Seamus Heaney's book, *Station Island*, contains a number of poems dealing with the mystique surrounding this ritual. If you're interested in participating, contact the Prior (☎072/81518). The island is approached via the R233 from Pettigo, or a bus from Ballyshannon or Enniskillen will drop you in the village, six miles away. There's a small interpretive centre, explaining the island's background (March–Oct 9am–5pm; £2) in Pettigo itself and a remarkable number of pubs for such a small village, suggesting spiritual nourishment of a rather different kind.

Lough Eske

Lough Eske (Lake of the Fish) is no longer a particularly great fishing spot, though it is known as a place to catch char, a tasty nine-inch-long species of the salmon family. They lurk in the depths at the centre of the lake, moving out to the shallower edges around late October where they can easily be fished using worms. The sandy banks of the River Eske are also known for freshwater oysters – some of which are reputed to contain pearls – but they're a protected species so it's illegal to take them. The ruins of an O'Donnell tower, once a prison, stand on one of the small islands. At the southern end of the lough stands *Harvey's Point* (☎073/22208; ⑤), a hotel owned by a Swiss millionaire with fine accommodation and one of the best **restaurants** in the county (lunch £12.50, dinner £25). There's also high-quality **B&B** at *Ardnamona* (☎073/22650; ⑥), set in glorious lough-side gardens.

The most enjoyable way to get to this area of soft beauty is to take the minor road which runs north of the river, signposted "Lough Eske Drive", half a mile out of Donegal town on the Killybegs road. This leads to a forgotten, forested estate, once belonging to the Brooke family, but now owned by the Forestry Commission. Circling the lake clockwise from here, you'll pass the western gate of the estate and then a farmyard: a hundred yards or so further on look out for a gap in the hedge on the left, where you'll find hidden a massive cauldron nearly six feet high and six feet round. This is a **Famine**

Pot, manufactured in Britain and shipped over to Ireland by English landlords. It would be filled with Indian maize (a substitute porridge) and placed in a field where local people would come during the Famine and fill their own smaller pots to take home.

The Blue Stack Mountains

Carrying on along the western shore, you'll reach the point where the river flows in at the lough's northern tip. Nearby, a dirt road runs off to the left to take you into the **Blue Stack Mountains**. At the top of the pathway that leads on from the track, there are superb views over the lough and nearby the very fine Doonan waterfall. From here you can join the **Ulster Way**, which passes Lough Belshade (*Bél Seád*, "lake with the jewel mouth". If you're intending to tramp around the mountain range, it's best to keep to the skirts of the hills, for there are many marshy patches on lower ground and be prepared for misty pockets during bad weather. For walks in this area and in the rest of the county, a copy of David Herman's excellent *Hill Walkers' Donegal* is well worth acquiring from either the Four Masters bookshop or the tourist office in Donegal town both of which also sell Ordnance Survey maps of the area.

The southern coastline

The most appealing route from Donegal town is the one which follows the shore of the bay all the way west to Glencolmcille. The first turning off this road will lead you down to **Holmes beach** and the *Ball Hill* hostel (see under Donegal town, p.444). The first sizeable settlement you come to is **MOUNTCHARLES**, spread over a hillside. Near the top of the hill stands a bright green pump commemorating the birth nearby of the poet and *seanachie* (storyteller) Seamus MacManus. The village is a sea-angling centre and boats can be rented from Michael O'Byrne (☎073/35257).

FROSSES (*na Frosa* – "the showers"), a mile or so inland off the road between Mountcharles and Inver, is a pleasant, crossroads hamlet that has occasional ceilis on Sunday nights in the village hall (dancing begins at 10pm), while *Breslins* bar hosts traditional sessions on Saturdays. The cemetery here contains the graves of the poet Seamus MacManus and his wife, the very underrated poet, Ethna Carberry. Along with Alice Milligan, she edited the important nationalist literary paper *Shan Van Vocht* (*sean-bean bocht* – "the poor old woman") at the end of the last century.

The secluded seaside village of **INVER** with its small strand, just a few hundred yards off the road, is a tranquil spot and affords good views over Inver Bay. The *Rising Tide* pub is good for a drink (or to hear traditional music on Sat & Sun) and has a ceiling in the shape of the hull of a boat and stone shelves for the spirit bottles. It was also the birthplace of Thomas Nesbitt, inventor of the harpoon gun.

Dunkineely and Bruckless

At **DUNKINEELY** there's the *Blue Moon* **hostel** (☎073/37284), with space for camping, and Wednesday night traditional sessions in the *Central Bar*. Another deviation left from the main road takes you first past *Castlemurray House Hotel* (☎073/37002; ⑤), noted for its French gourmet **meals** (dinner around £20, though you'll need to book ahead) and comfortable, though chintzy accommodation, then down a long, narrow promontory to **St John's Point**, where a crumbling castle stands at the tip. As you head out, there are great views over Donegal Bay, especially back towards the narrow entry of Killybegs bay, with **Rotten Island** at its mouth. The waters off the Point are reckoned to offer the best diving in Ireland. If you decide to stay, there's the strategically-positioned *Harbour Lights* **B&B** (☎073/37291; ③).

A little further on, approaching **BRUCKLESS**, you'll spot a magical little lagoon staked out with poles for rearing mussels. Look out for an "Oysters Handknits" sign at the top of a track that will lead you down to a dwelling where you can buy locally-caught oysters as well as handknitted garments. On the other side of the lagoon you can see an eighteenth-century Georgian house, *Bruckless House* (☎073/37071; ⑤), which now offers stylish **B&B**. There's also an excellent **hostel** in Bruckless, *Gallagher's Farm Hostel*, Darney (☎073/37057), with camping. Also here is *Deane's Open Farm* (☎073/37160) offering **riding** lessons, trekking and a pitch and putt course.

Killybegs

Moving on from Bruckless and sticking to the coast road, you'll round Killybegs Bay and arrive in the most successful fishing port in the country, **KILLYBEGS**, where tons of top-quality fish are hauled onto the quaysides daily. This marks the halfway point from Donegal town to Glencolmcille and also the point where the scenery changes dramatically for the better. The mile-long approach road around the bay would be idyllic were it not for a fishmeal processing plant interrupting the view. Killybegs itself is perched on a slope above the harbour, its gleaming whitewashed buildings huddled around narrow cramped streets. The town is well served by shops and banks and in summer buzzes with traffic, mostly heading down to the quay, where you can purchase fish after watching the fleet come in during the early evening. A huge international **sea angling festival** takes place here in the second half of July but you can go sea angling any time with one of six boats that go out daily – the Harbour Store (☎073/31569) has details and sells all manner of fishing gear. Picturesque though Killybegs is, it isn't exactly overflowing with interest, and most of the pubs are aimed squarely at working fishermen, though students from the local Tourism College liven the place up in term-time.

If you're staying, it's worth visiting the church at the top of the hill for a glimpse of the sixteenth-century **tombstone** of **Niall Mór MacSweeney**, covered in Celtic carvings and contained in a glass case to the left of the church door. The stone was removed from his grave at Ballysaggart Friary on St John's Point. The MacSweeneys were one of Donegal's ruling families prior to the Flight of the Earls and Niall Mór was head of the clan. The cross standing on the hillock behind the church is an ugly specimen that stands to remind one of ugly times – the penal days.

Practicalities

Accommodation possibilities include the refurbished *Bay View Hotel* (☎073/31950; ⑦), overlooking the harbour, and there are rooms in a number of pubs, including *Cope House*, Main Street (☎073/31834; ⑥), and the *Pier Bar* (☎073/31386; ③). The former also has a popular Chinese restaurant. Most of the **B&Bs** are a mile or two out of town on Fintra Road, heading west towards Kilcar.

Melly's Café, by the harbour, is a local institution and the best place for cheap snacks and fast **food**, though the nearby *Galley* restaurant is a pleasant alternative. Otherwise, there are lunches in the pubs, including fresh seafood in the *Harbour Bar*, or for something slightly more upmarket, try the brasserie at the *Bay View Hotel*.

As for evening entertainment, regular **traditional sessions** are held at the *Sail Inn*, led by its landlord, the fiddler Martin McGinley, and at the *Harbour Bar*. You can also hear sessions on Wednesday nights at the *Pier Bar*. *Cope House* offers a mixture of musical styles and *The Chocolate Factory* is the place for **discos** and **live bands**.

McGeehan's **buses** (☎075/46150) leave from outside the *Pier Bar* for Ardara and Dublin: enquire at Hegarty's grocery shop by the bus stop.

Kilcar to Slieve League

A couple of miles west of Killybegs, signposts point the way to the Blue Flag **Fintragh Beach**. Further on, the road to Kilcar passes *Kitty Kelly's Restaurant*, open in summer for especially good Irish cuisine, before dividing just after the *Blue Haven Restaurant* (Irish dancing on Thurs). For the scenic route, take the road to the left, a narrow switchback ride along the coastline with stupendous views over the ocean, especially from **Muckross Head**, and the looming presence of the hills and mountains to your right. Pleasant **KILCAR** is a centre for the Donegal tweed industry and there are several small factories open to visitors. The village comes alive during its **sea angling festival** at the beginning of August, followed shortly afterwards by a raucous **street festival**. There are five bars, including one of Donegal's finest, the *Piper's Rest,* a session pub with traditional music most nights in summer and regularly at weekends. You can sample the oysters here or the seafood and French cuisine at the *Village Restaurant* (summer evenings) across the road. For more physically taxing activities, boats can be rented from Adrian Molloy (☎073/38377) or Jim Malone (☎073/38316) while Paddy Clarke (☎073/38211) offers guided game angling and hill walking. McGeehan's **buses** leave from outside *John Joe's* bar at 7.40am for Letterkenny and Dublin via Killybegs and Ardara, and for Glencolmcille at 6.40pm.

CLIMBING SLIEVE LEAGUE

There are two routes up to the ridge of **Slieve League** (*sliabh leic*, "grey mountain", or *leica*, "flagstone mountain"): a less-used back route following the homemade fingerpost pointing to Baile Mór just before Teelin, and the road route that follows the signs out of the village to Bunglass (*bunglas*, "end of the cliff"), round sharp bends and up steep inclines where all you can see is your car bonnet. Bunglass turns out to be exactly what it says, the end of the grass way above a sheer drop. These claim to be the highest marine cliffs in Europe, and standing here that seems all too likely. The sea moves so far below that the waves appear silent, and the near 2000ft high face glows with mineral deposits in tones of amber, white and red. They say that on a clear day it is possible to see one-third of the whole of Ireland from the summit. A **sightseeing tour** of the cliffs from the waters below is organized from Teelin (weather permitting) by *Smith Campbell* (☎073/39079).

Both routes up are walkable and very enjoyable, though it's a great deal easier to drive: the less popular back route looks up continually to the ridge and is known as the One Man's Path; the frontal approach swings you up and round in a spectacular way to one of the most thrilling cliff scenes in the world, the **Amharc Mór**, from which the views are staggering.

If you want to make a full day of it, you can follow One Man's Path, which leads on to Old Man's Path (simply because it's a few inches wider), over the crest of the mountain and down the heather-tufted western slope. The paths are accurately named: in places they are only a few feet wide, and in wet or windy weather they can be *extremely hazardous*. On a fine day, though, it's a wonderful – if terrifying – traverse. Then make your way across towards the verdant headland village of **MALINBEG**, where there's a sublime crescent-shaped golden strand enclosed by a tight rocky inlet. *Malinmore Adventure Centre* (☎073/30123) organizes **diving** here (from £75 for three dives over two days) and provides other activities, including canoeing and hill-walking. Malinbeg itself is a village of white bungalows, with the land around ordered into long narrow strips. On the cliff edge a ruined Martello tower faces **Rathlin O'Birne Island**, three miles offshore, a place with many folklore associations. There are occasional boats across, but nothing to see beyond some early Christian stone relics and a ruined coastguard station.

Beyond Malinbeg it's relatively easy to extend your walk through Malinmore – where the large *Glencolmcille Hotel* (☎073/3003; ⑤) serves food – and on to Glencolmcille. The whole distance from Teelin can be comfortably completed in six hours.

If you want to stay in Kilcar, there's **B&B** at *Kilcar Lodge*, Main Street (☎073/38243; ③; April–Oct) or nearby on the coast road to Carrick at *Hillcrest* (☎073/38243; ③) and *Dún Ulún House* (☎073/38137; ②), which also offers **hostel** accommodation. Alternatively, a little further on is *Derrylahan* (☎073/38079), run by Shaun McCloskey, one of the friendliest hostels in the country – a shorter approach involves taking the right-hand of three options just outside the village and following the lane over the hill, though Shaun will pick you up from Kilcar or *The Rock* near Carrick. This is an ideal base for exploring the beautiful countryside around **CARRICK**, especially Teelin Bay and the awesome Slieve League cliffs to the west. In the pretty village of Carrick itself the friendly and atmospheric *Slieve League* **pub** is a must and there are sessions here, at *Enright's* and the *Central* bars. There are **bikes** for rental at Boyle's on Main Street (☎073/39195) and, back on the Coast Road, Little Acorn Farm (☎073/39386) offers **riding and trekking**.

The road to **TEELIN** (*tigh linn*, "house of the flowing tide") follows the west bank of the River Owenee, whose rapids and pools are good for fishing – licences are available from *Teelin Sea Angling Club* (☎073/39079). Like most of the peninsula, the village is Irish-speaking and rich in folklore, which has been recorded over the last half-century by Seán Ó'hEochaidh, Donegal's great folklorist. The *Rusty Mackerel* pub is a welcome find, easily spotted by its garish colour and mural painting of one of its old fisherman regulars, and you can **stay** in the village at *Sea Crest* (☎073/39108; ③).

Glencolmcille and around

As it approaches **GLENCOLMCILLE** (the Glen of St Columbcille) the road traverses desolate moorland, dominated by oily-black turf banks amidst patches of heather and grass where not even sheep seem able to subsist. After this, the rich beauty of the Glen (as it's invariably known) comes as a welcome surprise. Settlement in the area dates back to the Stone Age as testified by the enormous number of megalithic remains scattered around the countryside, especially court cairns and standing stones. There's evidence too of the Celtic era, in the form of earth and stone works. Traditionally, **St Columba** founded a monastery here in the sixth century and some of the standing stones, known as the *Turas Cholmcille*, were adapted for Christian usage by the inscription of a cross. Every Columba's Day (June 9) at midnight, the locals commence a barefoot circuit of the fifteen *Turas*, including Columba's Chapel, chair, bed, wishing stone and Holy Well, finishing up with mass at 3am in the village church. (Columba and Columbcille/Colmcille are the same person – the latter is the name by which he was known after his conversion, and means "the dove of the church").

In more recent times, widespread emigration left the Glencolmcille area a typical example of rural decay. In 1951, however, a new and energetic curate, Father James McDyer, was appointed and instigated immediate efforts to revitalize the community, while retaining and strengthening its culture. Electricity arrived in the village and road improvements reduced its isolation and allowed new collective enterprises in knitting and agriculture to thrive, simultaneously increasing the area's accessibility to tourism. Thankfully, these developments have not lessened the village's innate attraction. The buildings in Cashel, the village centre, are painted in radiant colours – the village church is lavender, there's a whitewashed semi-detached estate for the newly married, one old pub is a submarine yellow and another a Mediterranean sky-blue.

One of McDyer's major initiatives stands in Doonalt down by the beach – the **Folk Village Museum and Heritage Centre** (Easter–Oct Mon–Sat 10am–6pm, Sun noon–6pm; £1.50; hourly tours), a clustered *clachan* of replica thatched cottages, each equipped with the particular furniture and artefacts of the era it represents. A new reception building introduces you to the area's history and cultural heritage, including a reputed visit by Charles Stewart ("Bonnie Prince Charlie") There's free access to the **National School** replica, which has a display of informative photographs and research projects, and a section on the American painter Rockwell Kent, who painted marvellous treatments of the area's landscapes. At **Sheebeen** house, you can try a taster of seaweed wine and other concoctions such as honey, fuchsia and elderberry (most much better than they sound) and then buy a bottle. There's also a tea house and craft shop.

From behind the hostel (see below), **cliff walks** steer off around the south side of the bay above a series of jagged drops. Rising from the opposite side of the valley mouth, the promontory of **Glen Head** is surmounted by a Martello tower. On the way out you pass the ruins of **St Columbcille's Church**, with its "resting slab" where St Columba would have lain down exhausted from prayer. North across this headland you can climb and descend again to the forgotten little cove of **Port** a few miles away, a village deserted since the 1940s. Absolutely nothing happens here – although Dylan Thomas once stayed in the next valley at Glenlough, renting a cottage for several weeks and then disappearing early one morning without paying.

Practicalities

The **tourist office** (daily June–Aug 10am–6pm; ☎073/30116) is in the *Lace House* craft shop on the main street. **B&B** accommodation is available at *Brackendale*, (☎073/30038; ②) and *Corner House* (☎073/30021; ③; April–Sept), both in Cashel. You can catch the sunset at the beautifully positioned *Dooey Hostel* (☎073/30130) set high above the fine shingle strand at the mouth of the valley which offers **camping** too. If walking, keep on the village road as far as the Folk Village, and then take a path up to the left: in wet weather the longer route, by road, may be easier. The tea house at the Folk Village does cheapish **food**, though the most popular place for lunch is *An Bradán Feasa*, part of the Foras Cultúir Uladh complex (see p.452). Another option is the *Lace House Restaurant* above the shop, with freshly baked bread and evening meals. The **bars** here are often quiet during the week, though tend to come alive at weekends and during the **fiddle festival** at the beginning of August. The July folk festival was revived in 1998, based at the *Glencolmcille Hotel*, and may continue, if successful.

On the way down the main street to the Folk Village is Foras Cultúir Uladh, the Ulster Cultural Centre. There's a traditional **music** archive here, regular exhibitions and Tapeis Gael, a group of local artists with an innovative approach to tapestry design. The centre also hosts the many **courses** run by Oideas Gael (☎073/30248), including courses in Irish language, painting, *bodhrán* playing, archeology, hill-walking and tapestry.

Maghera to Crohy Head

Leaving Glencolmcille you can either retrace your steps along the coast or take the road through the heart of the peninsula towards Ardara. This travels through the dramatic **Glengesh Pass** (*gleann géis*, "glen of the swans"), spiralling down into wild but fertile valley land. Just before reaching Ardara, a road to the left runs along the northern edge of the peninsula for five and a half miles to **MAGHERA**, with narrow **Loughros Beg Bay** on one side and steep mountains rising from the road on the other. A mile before Maghera you'll pass the transfixing **Assarancagh Waterfall** and there's a hardy six-mile waymarked walk uphill from here to the Glengesh Pass. Maghera itself is an enchantingly remote place, dwarfed by the backdrop of hills and glens and fronted by an expansive and deserted strand that extends westwards to a rocky promontory riddled with caves. One of the largest of these is said to have concealed a hundred people fleeing Cromwell's troops, but their light was spotted from across the strand and all were massacred except a lucky individual who hid on a high shelf. Most of the caves are accessible only at low tide and a torch is essential. Beware the tides, however, for even experienced divers have been swept away by the powerful currents. Behind the village, a tiny road, unsuitable for large vehicles, runs up to the Granny Pass, an alternative route to and from Glencolmcille.

Ardara

Traditionally a centre for weaving and knitwear, the bustling little town of **ARDARA** has recently acquired heritage town status. The European grant which accompanied this award has been used to transform the old Law Courts by the bridge into a **Heritage Centre** (☎075/41262; Easter–Oct daily 10am–6pm; voluntary donation). Inside there's a fascinating exhibition on the history of hand-weaving, Aran knitwear and lots of intriguing photographs and equipment, but the real treat is watching the weaver plying away at his loom and supplying his own anecdotes about the industry. There's **tourist information** in the reception area and the friendly staff can answer most questions about the town.

Unsurprisingly. Ardara is one of the best places to buy **Aran sweaters**, sometimes at half the price you'll find further south. Molloy's Tweed Factory, a mile or so out of the southern end of town, is the biggest outlet, but Kennedy's, at the top of the hill, is handier (its owner is also a mine of local tourist information), and all the stores are well stocked with hand-loomed knitwear and tweeds. Elsewhere, the Catholic church west of the Diamond has a striking stained glass window, *Christ among the Doctors*, by the Modernist-inspired **Evie Hone**, one of the most influential Irish artists this century. Up the top of the hill, by the Methodist church car park, stands a house once occupied by Jimmy O'Rourke, a notable storyteller and fiddler on whom the Disney film *Darby O'Gill and the Little People* was based.

The grand old *Nesbitt Arms Hotel*, named after the town's former landlords, is undergoing major refurbishment at the time of writing, but there are plenty of **accommodation** alternatives. A mile out of town off the Donegal road is the stylish, seventeenth century *Woodhill House* (☎075/41112; ⑤), set in its own extensive grounds. Central **B&B** is available at *Laburnum House* on the Diamond (☎075/41146; ②), *Brae House*, Front Street (☎075/41296; ③), and *Homeward Bound*, Glenties Road (☎075/41246; ③; March–Oct), or, for sea views, try *Greenhaven* (☎075/41129; ③) or *Bay View Country House* (☎075/41145; ③) both up the Portnoo Road. There is a small **hostel** on the Diamond too, the *Drumbaron Hostel* (☎075/41200). **Bike rental** is available from Don Byrne south of town (☎075/41156), and he also does **camping**.

The best place to **eat** is *Woodhill House* whose restaurant offers an innovative menu, changed daily and well worth the £20 or so it costs. It's worth a visit even if you're not hungry as there's a bar, often with music. *Nancy's*, just across the bridge, has good value bar meals and snacks and light meals are available at the Heritage Centre restaurant and *Charlie's West End Café*.

Ardara's L-shaped main street is crammed with **pubs**. For a quiet drink, try the ancient *Pádraig MacGiola Dé*, to the west or the renovated *Corner House* bar. For a livelier time, you shouldn't miss *Peter Oliver's*, with music in the front bar (June–Sept nightly) and traditional dancing at the back every Saturday (from 10.30pm or later). *Nancy's*, a cosy 200-year-old pub run by the same family for seven generations, is also excellent, with something happening most nights during the summer. A McGeehan's **bus** leaves for Dublin from outside the post office daily at 8.30am.

Glenties

Set at the foot of two glens, **GLENTIES** lies six miles east of Ardara on the N56; a tidy village of plantation grandeur, reflected in its elegant neoclassical courthouse, old lodge and *Highlands Hotel*. It also sports one of the largest **discos** in the northwest, the

Limelight (adult discos Saturday nights), at the north end of town, and a host of bars on the main street. Another community attraction is a beautiful modern **church** at the Ardara end of town, designed by the Derry architect Liam McCormack; the vast sloping roof reaches down to six feet from the ground, and the rainwater drips off the thousand or so tiles into picturesque pools of water.

Opposite the church, the **St Conall's Museum and Heritage Centre** (June–Sept Mon–Fri 11am–1pm & 2.30–5pm, Sat & Sun 2.30–6pm; £1) houses items from all periods, including an interesting set of pleas submitted to the courts during the Famine and an Edison phonograph that plays *It's a Long Way to Tipperary*. The town's most famous son was **Patrick MacGill** (1890–1963) who was sold by his parents at a hiring fair for servants. He escaped and fled to Scotland, working as a farm-labourer and a navvy, while at the same time writing poems and attempting to hawk them around. He was lucky to attract patronage and ended up working on the *Daily Express,* was wounded in France fighting for the British in World War II, then returned to Ireland before marrying the American author Margaret Gibbons and emigrating to the USA. His best-known work is the semi-autobiographical *Children of the Dead End* which brilliantly recounts the wayward lives of migrant navvies, while *The Rat Pit* parallels this in its tale of young Irish women forced into prostitution. A huge **summer school** is held in his honour annually in mid-August, drawing hundreds of people to its exhibitions, seminars and literary debates.

Accommodation in town includes the family-run *Highlands Hotel* (☎075/51111; ④), on Main Street, and, among several B&B choices, *Lisdanar*, Mill Road (☎075/51800; ③; March–Oct), *Claradon*, less than a mile out on Glen Road (☎075/51113; ③) or *Oakdale Farmhouse* (☎075/51262; ③; March–Nov) a mile away in Derries. Next to the museum is the comfortable *Campbell's Holiday Hostel* (☎075/51491; March–Oct). **Eating** out options are limited, but the excellent *Highlands Hotel,* very much the centre of town life, with weekend discos and a small art gallery displaying the works of its landlord, John Boyle, offers a wide range of food – the gargantuan lunches are exceptional value. Alternatives on the main street include *Nighthawk* for pizzas and, for snacks, the *Central Café* and *Jim's Cafe* outside which stop *McGeehan's* **buses** en route to Letterkenny and Glencolmcille.

Although there's little in the way of entertainment, there are plenty of places to **drink** – *Wee Joe's Bar* and *McMonagle's Riverside Bar* are both good. If you want **traditional music**, *Paddy's Bar* has Wednesday night sessions and there's the **fiddlers' weekend** at the beginning of October, otherwise head for the *Glen Inn*, three miles out on the Ballybofey Road, beautifully situated by the river at the foot of the Blue Stacks; there are sessions on the last Saturday of the month at 9.30pm. **Fishing** equipment and advice are available at McDevitt's Tackle Shop.

Dawros Head

To the immediate north of Ardara, the **Dawros Head Peninsula** is much tamer than Glencolmcille, with many tiny lakes, dotting a quilt of low hills. The terrain of purple heather, fields, streams and short glens makes a varied package for the enthusiastic walker. The first turning to Rosbeg takes you past the **Sheskinmore Nature Reserve**, home to geese of the Barnacle and Greenland White-footed varieties. The flat sandy coastal plain and patches of short grass are popular too with choughs in late summer and hunted by hen harriers and merlins in winter. **ROSBEG** itself is an isolated village, straggling beside a series of rock-strewn coves, and you can **camp** among the dunes at **Tramore Beach** (☎075/51491). It's even lonelier out at **Dawros Head**, but at least there's the welcoming bar at the *Dawros Bay Hotel* to provide succour. In contrast, the caravan and camping sites of Portnoo and Narin, on the peninsula's northern coast, are densely populated with Northern Irish tourists.

Approaching Narin from Ardara, to the right, just before the pastel-shaded Kilclooney church, is the **Kilclooney Dolmen**, probably the best-preserved portal stones in the country. The capstone is over thirteen feet long and is reckoned to date from around 3500 BC. Continuing onwards, the most worthwhile sight on the peninsula is **Doon Fort**, which occupies an entire oval-shaped islet in the middle of Lough Doon. To get there turn left at the Rosbeg/Tramore Beach signpost a kilometre before Narin, then head right up the lane just after the school. A few hundred yards later you'll see a sign for boat rental leading down to a farmhouse where you can rent a rowing boat to take you across for a few pounds. The idyllic setting, rarely disturbed by visitors, makes the hassle worth it: although its walls are crumbling, the fort has been untouched for over two thousand years. The walls stand 15ft high and 12ft thick – their inner passages were used in the 1950s for storing poteen. Two other lakes nearby, **Lough Birrog** and **Lough Kiltoorish**, also have ruined castles, both built by later Irish chieftains, the O'Boyles. Their stones, however, have mostly been carted away for house building.

NARIN and **PORTNOO** offer the majority of facilities on the peninsula and the spearheaded two-and-a-half-mile-long **Narin Strand** is a wonderful beach, safe for bathing. At low tide you can walk out to **Iniskeel Island** where St Conal founded a monastery in the sixth century. This has long since disappeared, but there are the ruins of two twelfth-century churches with some cross-inscribed slabs. The villages host a **seafood festival** each June where you can participate in oyster-opening contests and all the bars offer seafood specials.

If you want to **stay** on the peninsula, *Carnaween House* in Narin (☎075/45122; ②) and *Thalassa* in Portnoo (☎075/45151; ③) offer good B&B; or you could rent a caravan at *Dunmore Caravan and Camping Park*, by the beach in Narin (☎075/45121; £60–150 a week). The *Lake House Hotel* in Portnoo (☎075/45123; ④) offers a great deal more comfort.

Gweebarra Bay, Dooey Point, Doocharhy and Fintown

The routes north from Ardara and Glenties converge at the village of Maas. The road then twists along the edge of **Gweebarra Bay** before one last turn suddenly brings you to the broad iron bridge spanning the estuary. Until the first bridge was built in 1890 rarely a year passed by without someone being drowned attempting to ford the river, sometimes home-workers bringing wool back from Glenties.

Across the bridge and west of Lettermacaward, a signposted scenic route tours the **Dooey Point headland**, a scenically interesting little detour if you have time at hand. The northern shore, on Trawenagh Bay, is the more gratifying, with a fine stretch of beach backed by sand dunes. Classic thatched cottages are the main characteristics. On the southern side is **Cor Strand**, fertile ground for mussels and clams, with a handy bar nearby.

Alternatively, a minor road to the east from Lettermacaward follows the Gweebarra five miles inland to **DOOCHARRY**, a tiny place with just a couple of pubs and a grocery, but leading to some of the most dramatic scenery in the county. From here you can head further upstream northeast along a narrow and tortuous lane past **Slieve Snaght**, through the **Glendowan Mountains** and skirting the southern edge of the **Glenveagh National Park** to **Gartan Lough** and **Churchill** (see p.463). The desolate, though beautiful countryside bears little sign of human impact and you'll be lucky to see any life beyond the odd sheep or fluttering bird. Another road heads five miles southeast from Doocharry through rugged, rock-strewn moorland, streaked by turf banks, to **FINTOWN**. This is a simple roadside village set at the foot of towering mountains in the Finn River valley where the river broadens to form an elongated strip of lake. Once again, the setting has a mythical colouring – it was here that Fergoman was attacked by wild boars and cried out so piteously that his sister was driven to distraction and dived into the lake, where she drowned. Running beside the lake for a mile or so is the **Fintown Railway** (☎075/46280; daily June–Sept 11am–5pm), a recently restored stretch of narrow-gauge track along which an original railcar runs. There's little else in the village apart from the bar whimsically named *Finnian's Rainbow* and roads head back to Glenties and off eastwards to Letterkenny or Ballybofey.

The Crohy Head Peninsula

The southern approach to **Crohy Head** curls round the headland's central mountains, looking down to a rocky shelf of coastline from which plumes of spray rise like geysers. As you come round the headland to the final leg, you'll firstly see the three-storey An Óige **hostel** (☎075/21950; Easter–Sept), then the domed outline of **Arranmore Island** comes into view, lying close to the Rosses coast. The hillside below the road can be dangerous at points because of a remarkable landslip known as the *tholla brista* (broken earth), but this, and the great sea stack known as *an bríste* (the breeches), make the headland an even more dramatic experience for the walker.

The one-pub fishing village of **MAGHERY** lies at the foot of the north side of the headland. Its most unusual feature is the tall wall that runs by the abandoned mansion house at the far side of the short strand: called the Famine Wall, this windbreak was built by the villagers for the landlord, who devised the task so that he could pay them a wage as famine relief.

The Rosses

The **Rosses**, a vast expanse of rock-strewn land and stony soil, is one of the last strong *Gaeltacht* areas. Dotted with over 120 tiny lakes, the crumpled terrain stretches from Dungloe in the south to Crolly in the north, but the forbidding nature of much of the landscape meant most settlements could only survive near the sea, so following the shoreline route around the Rosses is far more rewarding than the more direct road north.

Dungloe

An Clochán Liath is the name you'll see on signposts as you approach **DUNGLOE**, referring to the grey-coloured stepping stones which were once used to cross the town's river. The modern Anglicized version comes from *Dún an Ghleo*, meaning "noisy fort", a name you might consider apposite as you stroll down its bustling main street. For most of the year, there's little to detain you except entertainment in the pubs. In late July, however, the Mary From Dungloe festival, a local, more wholesome variation of the Miss World contest provides a good pretext for general festivities and late-night drinking. There's no antiquity behind the festival's origins or name – it dates from only 1968 and the title comes from a hit single by the Emmet Spiceland Band. The excellent local band Goats Don't Shave has its own satirical take on the festival in the song *Mary, Mary*.

Dungloe is also synonymous with the rejuvenating work of **Paddy 'the Cope' Gallagher** (1871–1966), who envisaged the salvation of these then poor communities through co-operative ventures, in particular, by reducing their dependency on gombeen men (moneylenders). Oddly enough, the enterprise's practical origins lay in Paddy's discovery that the price of manure was reduced when purchased by societies. As a result, he founded the Templecrone Co-operative Agricultural Society (the "Cope") in 1906 and its main branch still stands proudly on Dungloe's main street with branches throughout the Rosses. Copies of his entertaining autobiography, *My Story*, are available in a local edition from the supermarket.

The **tourist office** (June–Aug Mon–Sat 10am–6pm; ☎075/21297) is just off Main Street, to the left as you go downhill towards the bridge. At other times, a very useful information service is provided by the Ireland's Alive office on Gweedore Road (Mon–Sat 10am–6pm, also May–Aug Sun 10am–6pm; ☎075/22299), which also organizes activity breaks and excursions. There's a handy **laundry** next door too (Tues–Fri 9am–1pm and 2–6pm). Swish **accommodation** is provided by *Ostan Na Rossan*, Mill Road (☎075/21088; ⑦), with its own leisure centre and pool. On the same road are the **B&Bs** *Roninnis House*, (☎075/21094; ③; April–Sept) and *Sea View* (☎075/21353; March–Nov) and, in the centre, the *Midway Guesthouse*, Main Street (☎075/21251; ③), which also has a bar and provides meals. *Greene's Independent Holiday Hostel* (☎075/21021) on Carnmore Road is a modern building with **camping** in its grounds. The popular *Coffee Dock* serves excellent value lunches and other **eating** choices include *Doherty's Restaurant*, a good low-priced grill, and the *Riverside Bistro* for more upmarket, though reasonably priced, fare. The *Tirconnaill* **bar** at the top end of the street is a genuine old-timers' bar with not a note of music interfering; the *Atlantic Bar* has rock music (every Sat) and traditional sounds (Fri & Sun). *Beedy's Bar* has sessions in summer and there's assorted entertainment in the *Bayview Lounge* at weekends. The *Central Bar*, in the middle of Main Street, is open during summer only, after more than twenty years in which nothing seems to have been touched – a fascinating old place. **Fishing** tackle and permits for local fisheries are available from Bonner's, Main Street.

Burtonport

Passing the smoking funnels of a kelp factory, the coastal route heads off in the direction of **BURTONPORT** (signposted **Ailt an Chorráin**, "curved ravine"), half a mile off the main road and the embarkation point for Arranmore Island or, if you can find someone to take you out, for other smaller islands. In the late eighteenth century, the English attempted to establish **Rutland Island** as a major trading centre and, consequently, this area became the first English-speaking district in the whole of Donegal. During the 1798 rebellion James Napper Tandy landed on the island with French troops, but became somewhat inebriated during his stay and had to be carried back on board. More recent English connections have included the Screamers, a post-hippie commune with a belief in primal therapy and sexual liberation whose leaders departed some years ago for Colombia, and the Silver Sisters, a trio of apparently demure Victorian-dressed ladies who fled the village once it became clear that the disciplined life they espoused had more to do with sado-masochistic activities than moral fibre.

Apart from busy activity at the harbour, the village has little to say for itself, but if you want to stay, *Mrs McGinley*, down by the pier, does year-round **B&B** (☎075/42047; ②) and, nearby, there's *Campbell's Pier House* (☎075/42017; ③). For **eating**, *The Lobster Pot* specializes in seafood and the *Harbour* provides bar meals. Otherwise you'll have to make do with pies and fish and chips. There's little nightlife here, though the *Skipper Tavern* offers occasional traditional music. There are plenty of **fish** in the nearby waters and you can rent a boat from Burtonport Sea Angling and Boating Centre (☎075/42077).

Arranmore Island

The twenty-minute boat trip to **Arranmore Island** passes through the straits between the nearest cluster of islands (Rutland, Inishfree, Inishcoo and Eighter), and then across a free expanse of water to the main village, **LEABGARROW**. Arranmore Island Ferry Service (all year Mon–Fri 5–8 sailings, Sun 3–7, £6 return, car plus driver £18; ☎075/20532) operates a **car ferry**. The An Óige hostel has closed, but there is

accommodation at the *Glen Hotel* (☎075/20505; ③), and *Bonner's* (☎075/20532; ②) by the pier. The island's permanent population of around 800 people is almost entirely concentrated along the eastern and southern coastline. The high centre ground of bogland and lakes reaches a greater altitude than anywhere else in the Rosses and it's well worth hiking a few hundred yards upland for great views back to Burtonport.

A circuit of the whole island will only take three hours and the terrain isn't especially taxing. Much of it consists of blustery clifftop views of the Atlantic, but there are a few intriguing spots to investigate or ponder on. The island's greatest tragedy occurred off the very southeastern tip during the stormy night of November 9, 1935 when a sailing ship carrying returning islanders ran aground on the rocks. Nineteen people died, including seven from the same family – the eighth member on board, Patrick Gallagher, was the only survivor. Many ships have foundered in the choppy seas hereabouts, but, in 1983, the lone American yachtsman, Wayne Dickinson, landed on the island's west coast after 147 days at sea in the smallest boat ever to cross the Atlantic. In the cliffs below St Crone's Church on the southern shore is **Uaimh an Áir** (the "cave of slaughter") where seventy hiding islanders were massacred in the seventeenth century by a certain Captain Conyngham, an action which lay somewhat outside his remit from Charles I to rid the Rosses of "rogues and rapparees". Two islanders took revenge by killing the Captain in Dunfanaghy. Uninhabited **Green Island**, at the southwestern tip, is now a **bird sanctuary** and rare species have been spotted elsewhere on the island, including the Snowy Owl in 1993. The most dramatic of the several **beaches** is at the northwestern end of the island, on the way to the lighthouse and approached by a set of steps down the side of a perpetually crumbling cliff.

Facilities on Arranmore are limited, but the half dozen **pubs** are blessed with a 24-hour fishing port licence which is helpful, as there is little nightlife apart from *Boyle's* nightclub, though *Pally's* bar has regular entertainments. A few of the pubs have small shops attached and you can eat at *Bonner's* café or, more expensively, the *Glen Hotel,* while *Phil Ban's* bar serves snacks all day. **Association football** is the sport here and Arranmore is the only Irish island to have a team playing in a mainland competitive league.

Upper Rosses and Crolly

The road up through the Rosses to Gweedore cuts through a wild and crazed terrain of granite boulders and stunted vegetation. **Cruit Island**, a couple of miles north of Burtonport and accessible by bridge, has beautiful beaches and a cluster of thatched cottages available for rental (☎071/77197; £160–550 per week). A little further along the coast at **KINCASSLAGH** is the *Viking Hotel* (☎075/43295; ④), owned by Irish singing star **Daniel O'Donnell**. Another local-born Irish hero is **Packie Bonner**, the goalkeeper who saved a penalty in the 1990 World Cup Finals. Not far away is **CARRICK-FINN**, which boasts a fine strand and **Donegal Airport** (daily flights to Dublin; ☎075/48232). About a mile further on, in **ANNAGRY**, *Jack's* pub serves fine food, and, if you wish to spend a little more, *Dannie Minnie's* restaurant in the centre of the village offers superb cuisine. There's **B&B** in the village at *Bayview House* (☎075/48175; ③; April–Oct) and the Rosses Trekking Centre (☎075/48152) can arrange pony trekking around the local countryside. The local festival takes place here at the end of May. A short detour to the north leads to **RANN NA FEIRSTE**, a village with an astonishing Irish literary heritage. The oral tradition has always been strong in the Rosses, but its writers only came to prominence once the school system was improved earlier this century. Foremost among them were three brothers from Rann na Feirste's **Clann Mhic Grianna**: Séamus Ó'Grianna, the author of 27 books and a popular choice for recent school Leaving Certificate examinations; Seosamh Mac Grianna, whose most famous works are *An Droma Mór* and his autobiography, *Mo Bhealach Féin*; and, Séan Bán Mac Grianna, the youngest and the poet of the family.

In the townland of Meenaleck, just before Crolly, look out for a sign pointing to **Leo's Tavern**. The proprietors, Leo and Baba Brennan, were both well-known on the dance-band circuit in the fifties and sixties, but other family members have achieved greater fame. Three of their children are members of the group Clannad and another is the singer/musician Enya; often you'll find one or other serving behind the bar. The *Tavern* is hugely popular with tourists and the nightly music sessions are often adapted to suit their tastes. Their are regular traditional sessions too at nearby *Tessie's* bar.

If you take the main road from Dungloe to Crolly, look out for the small signs to your left marked "**Kerrytown Shrine**". In January, 1939, some residents of this townland four miles south of Annagry claimed to have witnessed an apparition of the Virgin Mary on a rock and, once the newspapers had reported the story, large crowds began to gather nightly for prayer meetings. Pilgrimages arrived from all over the country and continue to this day, especially on August 15, the Feast of Assumption. A couple of miles further north on the N56 is **LOUGHANURE**, pleasantly set beside the lough from which it takes its name. The local Anglers Club (✆075/48689) has **boats** for rent (£6 per day) and fishing permits (£6 per day; £12 per season) and further information is available in the village shop. The thatched *Casad na Tsúgáin* is a popular bar/restaurant with sessions in summer.

CROLLY (signposted *Croichsli*) marks the end of the Rosses and the beginning of neighbouring Gweedore. The large *Teach Phaidi Oig* pub has bar food, caravan, camping and laundry facilities and traditional music (Tues & Thurs in summer). For **B&B**, try *Leachrann House* (✆075/32194; ③); failing that, the postmistress in Crolly is a mine of information on accommodation in the area. However, far the most exciting option is to take the narrow road on the right-hand side, just after the bridge, leading up into the Derryveagh Mountains (see p.462). This passes lovely **Lough Keel** and its deserted village before reaching its highest point by an abandoned school and swinging sharply right to return to Dungloe. If you head straight on instead, you'll arrive at the most wonderfully situated **hostel**, *Screag an Iolair* (✆075/48593; April–Oct; at other times ring ahead), with cosy rooms, open fires, traditional music and lots of advice on walking. Nestling in beautiful semi-wild gardens on the side of **Cnoc na Farragh** mountain, *Screag an Iolair* (which means "eagle's nest") provides magnificent views of mountains, lakes, distant Arranmore Island and spectacular sunsets are almost a nightly occurrence. Hostellers regularly return here for the warmth of the welcome and the congenial atmosphere.

Gweedore and Tory Island

Like its southern neighbour, the Rosses, the interior of the **Gweedore** district is largely desolate and forbidding country and settlements again cling to the shoreline. To the southwest lie the villages of Bunbeg, Middletown and Derrybeg, their cottages sprinkled across a blanket of gorse and mountain grasses. It's a dispiriting kind of landscape and the ruggedness intensifies as it continues up the coast and round the **Bloody Foreland** to Gortahork and Falcarragh in the Cloghaneely district. Yet surprisingly, there has been significant house building across the area and it's said to be the most densely populated rural area in Europe.

BUNBEG has a gorgeous little harbour, packed with smallish trawlers, half a mile from the village along an enchanting rollicking road. There's now a regular year-round **ferry** service to Tory Island (see overleaf), and it's possible to negotiate a boat trip from the pier to other, mainly uninhabited, offshore islands such as Inishinny, Inishmaine, Inishirrer, Umfin, Inishfree, Owey and Gola. The **beach** further up the coast is approached by taking any track off to the left from the road running north out of the village. For accommodation, there's the luxurious *Ostan Gweedore* (✆075/31177; ⑧), or *Brookvale House* (✆075/31149; ⑥), also pretty comfortable. At Bunbeg Harbour, there's cosy **B&B** at *The Haven* (☎075/31014; ②) and *Tir na nOg* self-catering apartments (☎075/31232; £18 per double room) are a less expensive accommodation option. You can **eat** extremely well at *Mooney's Restaurant* or down by the harbour at *Bunbeg House*, while *Sergeant Pepper's* is a good place for kebabs and pizzas. The most popular bar in Bunbeg is *Teach Húdaí Beag*, which hosts a famous Monday night traditional session, sometimes involving members of Altan. Both the *Ostan Gweedore* and *Seaview (Radharc na Mara)* hotels hold regular weekend **discos**. Summer **Irish language** courses are run by *An Chrannóg*, Derrybeg (☎075/32188) and also at *Teach Jack,* on the coast road, (☎075/31173; ②), which also offers courses in music and dancing and has a restaurant and accommodation.

At Glassagh, about four miles after Derrybeg, the road climbs abruptly to the **Bloody Foreland**, a grim, stony, almost barren zone, crisscrossed by stone walls, and so called because of the red hue acquired by its heather from the light of the setting sun. The road turns eastwards at Knockfola, hugging the side of the mountain, with the bogland and its hard-worked turf banks stretching below towards the Atlantic. You should be able to spot the distinctive shape of Tory Island far out to sea and, at **MAGHEROARTY**, five miles east of Derrybeg, a road runs down to the pier, where you can pick up the ferry to the island. There's the *Teac Coil* pub and a grocery store nearby – handy if you're waiting for a boat.

Tory Island

With its ruggedly indented shores pounded day and night by the ocean, **TORY ISLAND**, though only eight miles from the mainland, is notorious for its inaccessibility. You can but marvel that anyone should want to inhabit this isolated speck of land and struggle for survival against the ferocity of the elements. Yet despite the odds, the Tory islanders are thriving, a situation no one could have predicted after the events of 1974 threatened to curtail abruptly thousands of years of settlement. During that winter the harshest of storms battered Tory for over eight weeks, severing communications and preventing helicopters from landing. When it finally abated, two dozen families applied for mainland housing, ten of them eventually moving to Falcarragh and, as it later transpired, Donegal County Council drew up a full-scale evacuation plan. As in Glencolmcille (see p.451) the arrival of a new priest, Father Diarmuid Ó Péicín, stimulated a transformation. He came on a day-trip in 1980, but ended up staying for four years as the island's pastor. Conditions were poor and the islanders dispirited. Essential amenities such as a water supply, proper sanitation and reliable electricity were lacking. There was no ferry service and, even if there had been, the harbour was unfit to receive it. Rallying the islanders, the pastor began to

---

FERRIES TO TORY

Ferries to Tory are operated by Turasmara Teo (☎075/31320), whose offices are at the harbour crossroads in **Bunbeg**. From October to May there's usually a daily sailing leaving Bunbeg at 9am and returning from Tory soon after its arrival. There are also additional sailings as follows: June daily from **Magheroarty** at 11.30am and 5pm; July–August daily from Magheroarty at 11.30am, 1.30pm and 5pm, and on Wednesdays only from **Portnablagh** (near Dunfanaghy) at 2pm. The company also runs a number of coastal cruises in July and August calling at the island. Note that departure times may be affected by both the tides and the weather, so always call ahead to check. Whatever the weather, be prepared for sudden changes and for an overnight stay, if necessary.

lobby every possible target, securing support from such disparate characters as the US Senator, Tip O'Neill, and Ian Paisley. The campaign attracted media attention and, despite Ó Péicín's replacement, conditions gradually began to improve with the eventual support of the embarrassed state and the financial assistance of an American philanthropist. Nowadays, around 120 people live permanently on the island and 25 children attend the local junior school, a happy sign of the island's revival; older children spend term-times in Falcarragh.

Tory's inaccessibility has long reinforced its remoteness, ensuring the retention of a powerful culture which has almost vanished from the mainland, referred to by islanders as "the country". Only two and a half miles long and less than a mile wide, its openness to the elements means little can grow here, and what does, has to be protected from the salty winds behind stone walls. The Irish-speaking islanders have a deep respect for Tory and its landscape, both as inspiration for their musicians, storytellers and artists, and as powerful sources of myth and legend. Tory was the stronghold of the Fomorians, who raided the mainland from their island base (the island's name is possibly derived from *toiridhe*, robber or pirate) and most notable of their number was the cyclops **Balor of the Evil Eye** (the Celtic god of darkness). Intriguingly, the local legend places his eye at the back of his head. The ruins of Balor's Fort lie on the east coast. There's also said to be a crater in the very heart of the island that none of the locals will approach after dark, for fear of incurring the god's wrath. In the sixth century, **St Colmcille** was helped to land on Tory by a member of the Duggan family. In return, the saint made him King of the island – the line has been unbroken ever since and you're more than likely to meet the present King, Patsy Dan Rodgers. Some monastic relics from St Columba's time remain on Tory, the most unusual of which – now the island's emblem – is the **Tau Cross**. Its T-cross shape is of Egyptian origin, and is one of only two such monuments in the whole of Ireland. It has now been relocated and set in concrete on Camusmore Pier in West Town. There are other mutilated stone crosses and some carved stones lying around, several by the remains of the round tower. Another superstition focuses on the **wishing stone** in the centre of the island, three circuits of which will supposedly lead to your wish being granted. It was utilized to defeat invaders by wrecking their ships – the British gunboat *Wasp*, sent to collect taxes, was caught in a sudden storm that killed all but six of its crew. The islanders have never paid tax since.

Fishing is still the staple trade, but some of the men supplement this a little through **painting**, a development which originated in a chance encounter between the English painter Derek Hill and one of the fishermen, **James Dixon**, in 1968. Dixon (now dead) had never lifted a brush before the day he told Hill that he could do a better job of painting the Tory scenery, but he went on to become the most famous of the island's school of **primitive painters** – Glebe House has a remarkable painting by him; see "Lough Gartan" (p.463). You can view their work and, more than likely, meet the artists at the **James Dixon Gallery**, the originator's former home, a little way to the east of the harbour.

Tory has two villages, East Town and West Town, and you'll find most of the amenities in the latter. There's a couple of shops and the *Caife an Chreagáin* serves hearty snacks and meals. Alternatively, there's the restaurant at the *Ostan Thoraigh* which provides comfortable **accommodation** (☎074/35920; ⑤), has one of the only two bars, and organizes a range of summer events, including traditional music, *sean nós*, painting and birdwatching weekends. For **B&B** there's *Graceanne Duffy* (☎074/35136; ②) in East Town or there's the basic, but very welcoming **hostel**, *Radharc na Mhara Hostel* (☎074/65145; April–Sept) in West Town. The **Social Club** is one of the hubs of island life, with a bar and regular traditional music and dancing.

The Derryveagh Mountains and Letterkenny

The central area of north Donegal rivals any of the best parts of the Donegal coastline and, if you're travelling northwards from the south of the county, is a fine alternative to Bloody Foreland in northwest Donegal.

Heading east on the N56 from Gweedore, the imposing and starkly beautiful mass of **Errigal Mountain** becomes increasingly prominent. From a distance the mountain appears to be snow-covered, but as you skirt the northern shore of Lough Nacung it becomes apparent that the white colouration has geological, rather than meteorological, causes. The minor R251 leads to **DUNLEWY**, where an An Óige **hostel** (☎075/31180) sits by the lough at the foot of the mountain. Here too, in the former *Dunlewy Hotel*, is the independent *Lakeside Hostel* (☎075/32133). Quite often the area is shrouded in mist, but on a clear day the beauty of Errigal is unsurpassable, its silvery slopes resembling Hokusai's images of Mount Fuji. A hike up to the top is a must and there's a waymarked trail from the road up the southeast ridge. The climb to the summit is well worth it for the staggering views: virtually all of Donegal, and most of Ulster, is visible and you could easily spend several hours just sitting and absorbing the contrasts provided by coastline, loughs and mountains. Back down in the village, there's a post office, shop and *McGeady's* bar. The lane next to the *Lakeside Hostel* leads to **Ionad Cois Locha/Dunlewy Lakeside Centre** (Easter–Oct Mon–Sat 10.30am–6pm, Sun 11am–7pm; tour £2.50, boat trip £2.70), an impressive visitor centre on the lough shore. There's an excellent restaurant here and a book-cum-craft shop, with maps of the area on sale. It's very child-friendly outside with a small farmyard 'zoo', adventure playground and pony rides on offer. For adults the highlight is the re-creation of the home of the notable local weaver, Manus Ferry, and the boat trip around the lough is a pleasure for all ages. It's worth keeping a look out for details of the centre's weekly concerts during the summer as it manages to attract some major names.

Glenveagh National Park

According to legend, the **Poisoned Glen** is where the cyclops Balor of the Evil Eye was slain by Lugh, poisoning the ground on which his single orb fell. There are many other explanations for the origins of its name, from the darkly conspiratorial (the glen's waters were polluted to kill English soldiers) to the simply botanical (poisonous Irish spurge used to grow here).To reach the glen, head a little way further east on the R251 and take the signposted lane leading downhill to the right. Just below the ruined church at the eastern end of Lough Nacung turn off to the left and follow the track over the old bridge. The path dwindles away and you should follow the left bank of the river deep into the gorge until it turns sharply left. Cross the water here and climb up towards a granite crest. From here walk beside the small stream through a gully and finally you'll emerge on a ridge. It's not an easy tramp, for a lot of the ground is marshy, but the views are fantastic, with the River Glenveagh flowing into Lough Beagh down below. You're now in the **Glenveagh National Park** and may well see deer hereabouts. If you don't want to retrace your tracks and are prepared for a longer hike, you have a number of options. Experienced hill-walkers will probably be tempted by the sight of **Slieve Snaght**, the highest point in the Park, off to the west. Alternatively, if you head downhill to the southeast, the Glendowan road at the bottom leads eastwards to **Lough Gartan** (see opposite) and westward to **Doocharry** (see p.455). If you take this towards Gartan for a short distance, an old disused vehicle track to the left will lead you down the barrel of the glen alongside the river to Lough Glenveagh. It's vital to follow all the basic rules of hill-walking (see p.41) and essential to keep to the designated roads and paths during winter deer-culling season (Sept–Feb) or you run the risk of being shot.

The less arduous approach to Glenveagh is to follow the R251 alongside the mountains until it curves to meet the lough's northern tip. A little further on is the official entrance to the **National Park** (10am–6.30pm: Easter weekend and mid–April to Sept daily; Oct Mon–Thurs, Sat & Sun; £2; Heritage Card). The visitor centre complex has detailed and interactive displays on the area's ecology and geology and there's also a reasonably-priced restaurant. Free minibuses ply between here and **Glenveagh Castle** (same hours; £2), built on a small promontory for George Adair in 1870. Adair was the creator of the estate which now forms much of the park and though you might admire the end-product it's impossible to condone the means by which it was achieved. Though some land was obtained through purchase, Adair despicably evicted 244 tenants during the bitterly cold April of 1861 – the **Derryveagh Evictions** – forcing many into the workhouse and others to emigrate to Australia. A second look at the castle might now suggest other reasons why its owner desired to occupy such a fortified construction. The surrounding rhododendron-filled gardens were very much the work of Adair's wife, Cornelia, who also introduced the herds of red deer to the estate. The steep ascent to the viewpoint behind the gardens is more than worthwhile for the wonderful views down to the castle and along the lough deep into the glen.

Lough Gartan

The environs of **Lough Gartan** are one of the supreme beauties of Ireland. **St Columba** was born into a royal family here in 521 AD; his father was from the house of Niall of the Nine Hostages and his mother belonged to the House of Leinster. If you walk over from Glenveagh you'll pass his birthplace – take the first road right at the first house you see at the end of the mountain track, and you'll come to a colossal cross marking the spot; the site is also signposted by road. Close by is a slab locally known as the **Flagstone of Loneliness**, on which Columba used to sleep, thereby endowing the stone with the miraculous power to cure the sorrows of those who also lie upon it. During times of mass emigration, people used to come here the night before departure in the hope of ridding themselves of homesickness. Archeologically, it's actually part of a Bronze Age gallery tomb and has over fifty cup marks cut into its surface.

Going back to the track leading downhill will bring you to a main country road, where a left turn leads to the remains of a church known as the **Little Oratory of St Colmcille**. It's an enchanting ruin, no larger than a modern living room, with a floor of old stone slabs with grass growing up through the cracks. A holy well is here too and nearby the Natal Stone, where the baby Columba first opened his eyes; to this day pregnant women visit the slab to pray for a safe delivery.

Glebe House

Glebe House (Easter week & mid-May to Sept daily except Fri 11am–6.30pm; £2; Heritage Card) is a gorgeous Regency building set in beautiful gardens on the northwest shore of the lake. Richly decorated both inside and out, it owes its fame to the time of its tenure by the artist Derek Hill, though it's now run by the Office of Public Works. The converted stables house some of his **paintings** and are used for visiting exhibitions while the rooms of the house itself feature a rich collection of paintings and sketches, including works by Kokoschka, Yeats, Renoir, Braque, Picasso and Degas. The study is decked out in original William Morris wallpaper, and there are Chinese tapestries in the morning room. The kitchen has various paintings by the Tory Island group of primitive painters (see p.461), most remarkably James Dixon's impression of Tory from the sea. It's well worth buying the guidebook and taking the tour.

Heritage centre and outdoor pursuits

Moving on round the northeast of the lake, in the direction of Churchhill, a right turn immediately after crossing the bridge will take you down to the modern **Colmcille Heritage Centre** (Easter week & May–Sept Mon–Sat 10.30am–6.30pm, Sun 1–6.30pm; £1.50), on the opposite shore from Glebe. The exhibition space is devoted to Columba's life and the spread of the Celtic Church throughout Europe. If you have no interest in ecclesiastical history, there are other intriguing items, including very beautiful stained glass windows of biblical scenes by Ciaran O'Conner and Ditty Kummer and a step-by-step illustration of vellum illumination and calligraphy. The road to the heritage centre continues a little further on to the **Gartan Outdoor Education Centre** (☎074/37032), which runs a range of outdoor activities in the locality and on the Donegal coast, including courses in mountain skills and leadership and sea kayaking (prices start at £80 for a mountain skills weekend). Continuing east from here towards Letterkenny, you ascend from the northern shore to **Churchhill**, with superb cross-country views as far north as the peninsulas.

The Rock of Doon and Kilmacrennan

Lying a few miles northeast of Gartan, **The Rock of Doon** and **Doon Well** are signposted off the R255 shortly after the village of Termon on the way to Kilmacrennan. Following the directions will lead you to a rural cul-de-sac right next to the well. A path from here ascends to a large bushy outcrop that is the Rock of Doon. From 1200 to 1603 this was the spot where the O'Donnell kings were crowned standing above a huge gathering of their followers. The inauguration stone on the summit is said to bear the imprint of the first Tír Chonaill king, a mark into which every successor had to place his foot as his final confirmation.

Doon, an ancient pagan healing **well**, is still a place of pilgrimage, marked out by a bush weighed down with personal effects left behind by the sick, hoping for a cure. You're meant to take off your shoes as you approach and be well intentioned before taking the water. You'll probably pick up a story or two of dramatic conversion and miracles effected by the water, which is sent to Irish emigrés all over the world.

KILMACRENNAN is a sweet-looking inland village on the road southeast to Letterkenny. *Lurgyvale Thatched Cottage* (daily Easter–Sept 10am–7pm; £1) is a restored nineteenth-century dwelling with furniture to match. There's a small exhibition of farm implements here, a handy tearoom and traditional sessions every Thursday. The *Village Tavern* has reasonably priced pub grub.

Letterkenny

LETTERKENNY is the largest town in Donegal and, indeed, the only one with a population in excess of ten thousand. It has been the county's commercial focus ever since Derry was partitioned into the North and has undergone massive redevelopment in recent years with a refurbished town centre, huge new shopping malls and a growing industrial sprawl beyond its boundaries. Letterkenny's boast is that it is the main place for entertainment in the northwest and there certainly is an ebullient bustle about the place. Although it sits at the mouth of Lough Swilly, there's no water in sight, and the main visual element is the file of shop windows down the main street. The most notable sight is the huge nineteenth-century **St Eunan's Cathedral**, with its intricate stone-roped ceiling, flying buttresses and gaelicized Stations of the Cross. The only other place of interest in town is the **Donegal County Museum** (all year Tues–Fri 11am–12.30pm and 1–4.30pm, Sat 1–4.30pm), housed in part of the old Letterkenny workhouse. Temporary exhibitions occupy the downstairs area while upstairs is a typical display of artefacts from megalithic to more recent times, including the keys and lock of the old Lifford jail, and an account of the old Donegal County Railway which ran to and from Letterkenny. If you're heading west on the R250 Fintown road, look out for the restored **Newmills Corn and Flax Mills** (daily June–Sept 10am–6.30pm; £2; Heritage Card), in a pleasant setting by the River Swilly and, naturally, powered by its waters. The mill only closed in 1982 and much of the old machinery is still present.

The amenable **tourist office** (July–Aug Mon–Fri 9am–1pm & 2–8pm, Sat 10am–2pm, Sun 9am–1pm & 2–5pm; Sept–June Mon–Fri 9am–1pm & 2–5pm; ☎074/21160) is a mile out of town on the Derry Road. There are plenty of **B&Bs** in the area, but just a few in the centre, including the *Gleneany Guesthouse*, Port Road (☎074/26088; ⑤); *Oakland*, Oaklands Park (☎074/25529; ②); and *Willow House*, Kilmacrennan Road (☎074/21871; ③). The central *Gallagher's Hotel*, on Upper Main Street (☎074/22066; ⑦), is the pick of the more expensive places to stay. A good alternative is *Castlegrove House* (☎074/51118; ⑧), out of town on the Ramelton road, offering luxury accommodation and a restaurant with prices to match.

There are three **hostels**: *Rosemount*, 3 Rosemount Terrace, in a terraced house at the back of Upper Main Street (☎074/26284; June–Sept); *The Manse*, High Road (☎074/25238); and *Port*, Port Road (☎074/26288).

As you'd expect, there are plenty of places to eat here. Meals are available at *Pat's On The Square*, 9 Market Square, an excellent family-run **restaurant** specializing in appetizing homemade pasta and ice cream, freshly ground coffee and desserts to die for; or if you want to go more upmarket, try *The Boxtree*, Pearse Road, or *Nero's* on Port Road. Close to the heart of town, you'll find good **pub lunches** at *McGinley's* on Lower Main Street. *Bakersville*, on Church Lane on the way up to the cathedral, is a good coffee shop, using all wholefood ingredients, or try *The Granary*, Academy Court, for homemade bread and healthy snacks. The best coffee in town is to be had at *Café Rio* opposite the library. The *Yellow Pepper* bistro, on Upper Main Street, offers probably the widest choice for vegetarians. There's a multitude of fast-food joints, too, and the *O'Boyce Snack Bar,* down by the roundabout at the Derry side of town is handy if you're whiling away time between buses.

There are enough **bars** here to defeat even the hardiest pub-crawler and a fair few offer Irish music, too. *McCarry's*, at the corner of the High Road, has music most nights, while the *Downtown Lounge*, on Main Street, has regular Wednesday sessions; both *McGinley's* and the *Cottage Bar* are popular with students. On Market Square, *The Brewery*, with its striking brass interior, is very popular and has music nightly, including the odd session. Letterkenny also has five **nightclubs**, of which *The Golden Grill* and *Pulse*, both on Port Road, are currently the most popular, attracting up-and-coming and well-established DJs. The *Clanree Hotel*, about a mile out on the main Derry road, also boasts a nightclub and holds occasional *comhaltas* evenings.

There's a four-screen **cinema** nearby, a **bowling centre** out on Ramelton Road and **bikes** for rental from Church Street Cycles (☎074/26204). Letterkenny also hosts two festivals: the Donegal International Car Rally in June; and a major folk festival in mid-August. Finally, there's a **bureau de change** (daily 11am–6pm), plenty of **banks**, and a **post office** on Main Street.

Raphoe and the Beltany stone circle

The gently rolling countryside to the southeast of Letterkenny is probably the least visited of any area in the county. A glance at a map shows a roughly triangular area, delineated by the major roads linking Letterkenny, Ballybofey and Strabane. Almost at its centre is the small town of **RAPHOE**, set trimly around one of the largest Diamonds in the county. Once an important ecclesiastical centre,the town has had its own **cathedral**, dedicated to St Ernan, since the ninth century, but the present plain Gothic cathedral church dates merely from 1702. Transfixed in the inner wall is a stone block with some peculiar and indecipherable carvings and there's a very impressive and resonant wooden baptismal chapel. The former Bishop's Palace lies in ruins to the rear.

The major reason for visiting the area, however, lies two miles to the south – **Beltany stone circle**. To get there follow the signs from the south of the Diamond and eventually you'll arrive at the entrance to a farm. The circle is a quarter of a mile up the bridle path to the right, over a stile and across a field full of sheep. This is one of the best-preserved circles in the country, consisting of approximately sixty stones, varying in height between one and four feet. It's easy to comprehend one of the reasons for its construction as there's a marvellous panoramic view of the local valleys and the distant mountains. The town itself makes a pleasant overnight stop, though there's little in the way of **accommodation**, choices being limited to the grandly-fronted *Central Hotel* on the Diamond (☎074/45126; ⑤), which has a restaurant, or there's B&B provided by *Mrs Chambers*, Strabane Road (☎074/45410; ③; April–Nov). There are quite a few pubs – *Tirconnail House* serves a good pint – and, surprisingly, one of the biggest **clubs** in the county, *Frankie's* with very popular discos. There's **riding** available nearby at the *Greenacres Lodge Equestrian Complex*, Rooskey Upper, Convoy (☎074/47451).

From Cloghaneely to Fanad Head

North of the Gweedore district and Glenveagh National Park, Donegal's northern coastline contains some of the most spectacular scenery in the whole country where the battle between the elements is often startlingly apparent. Overshadowed at first by the bleak beauty of Muckish Mountain to the south, the main road from Gortahork in the Cloghaneely area to Milford passes through verdant countryside as it meanders around the deep bays and inlets and alongside the glorious and often deserted beaches which punctuate the shoreline. The coast itself is dominated by three contrasting peninsulas: Horn Head with its rugged, sea-battered cliffs; Rosguill, almost circumscribed by the marvellous Atlantic Drive; and the more sedate Fanad for lonely walks and tremendous views across Lough Swilly to Inishowen.

Gortahork and Falcarragh

The first town you'll come across in the Cloghaneely area to the east of the Bloody Foreland is nondescript **GORTAHORK**, though the village and neighbouring area are good for Irish music. *Teac Billie* is an old men's drinking place with Tuesday night sessions, while the Irish College – up to the right after you pass *Whorskey's* on the left – has ceilis every night throughout July and August. There are sessions too on Thursdays at *Teach Ruari*, a mile away in Beltany. The bar in *Ostan Loch Altan* (☎074/35267; ⑤) has snack lunches and a reasonably priced Sunday carvery lunch and there's **B&B** at *Ard Aine* (☎074/35398; ②), a mile out of town in Cashel.

FALCARRAGH is more interesting and better supplied with pubs, shops and other amenities. In the village, there's B&B at *Ferndale* (☎074/65506; ③; April–Sept), while hostel accommodation is available at the *Shamrock Lodge* independent **hostel** (☎074/35859; mid-Jan to mid-Dec), over the *Shamrock Pub*. Alternatively, try the large and recently refurbished *Ballyconnell House Hostel* (☎074/35363), set in 500 acres of woodland, which was built in the mid-seventeenth century and once belonged to one of the great landlords of the area, Sir John Olphert; to get there, take the coast road from the village crossroads, and the gateposts of the estate are beside the main road where it bears left. There are a few **eating** places in the village: *John's Café*, at the Gortahork end of town or the upstairs restaurant at the *Gweedore* are the best options and the latter has **music** of varying kinds most nights in July and August. The *Shamrock Pub* and *The Loft* also have live music and the *Errigal* runs Friday **discos**.

Great Skellig, Co. Kerry

Southwest Dingle Peninsula near Dunbeg

Surfer off the south coast of Cork

Poulnabrone Dolmen, Co. Clare

Irish music session, Doolin, Co. Clare

Errigal Mountain, Co. Donegal

Dunluce Castle, Co. Antrim

Bantry House, Co. Cork

Lake scenery near Killarney

White Island, Co. Fermanagh

Crown Liquor Saloon, Belfast

Samson and *Goliath*, Belfast

Giant's Causeway, Co. Antrim

Flax loom, Ulster American Folk Park

Falcarragh **beach** is reached by following the coast road for a few miles – eventually the dunes will appear behind a car park. This is one of the more beautiful strands on this northwest coast, but a strong undercurrent makes it unsafe for bathing.

Leaving Falcarragh, the road south to Glenveagh passes through **Muckish Gap**. The slate-grey mass of **Muckish** ("pig's back") **Mountain** dominates the view all the way from Falcarragh and the hillsides are pitted with old workings where quartzite sand was extracted for the manufacture of optical glass. It's a relatively easy climb from the roadside shrine at the Gap up a grassy ridge to the summit and, on a clear day from here, the entire coastline from the Bloody Foreland, with distant Tory, to Malin Head is splendidly visible. Heading east out of Falcarragh, the road to Dunfanaghy opens up a significantly milder landscape, with the green grass now beginning to outstrip the ruggedness, and the odd reed-fringed lake with swans by the roadway.

Horn Head and around

The small resort of **DUNFANAGHY**, seven miles from Falcarragh, is the gateway to the Horn Head Peninsula. It's an aristocratically self-conscious plantation town, whose strongly Presbyterian atmosphere contrasts vividly with settlements to the west or south. On the outskirts of town is the impressive **Workhouse** (March–Oct Mon–Fri 10am–5pm, Sat & Sun noon–5pm; £2), sympathetically restored as a local history and community centre. It was originally built in 1845 on the eve of the Great Famine and at first had only five inmates, but by 1847, as the Famine intensified, over six hundred people were crowded inside. The Famine story is recounted in admirable detail and style, through the tale of one local inmate, 'Wee' Hannah Herrity, who lived until 1926. The centre hosts occasional innovative world and traditional music sessions and displays work by local artists or you can simply sit, sup and chat in the coffee shop. Next door the former fever hospital houses *The Gallery*, where you can admire more artwork and consider purchases from a range of crafts.

For accommodation, there are two **hotels**, *Arnold's* (☎074/36208; ⑥), which also has a riding stables, and *Carrig Rua* (☎074/36133; ⑦); both also offer food. There are plenty of B&Bs, including *Rushvale* (☎074/36404; ②) and *The Whins* (☎074/36481; ③). For somewhere cheaper, the excellent *Corcreggan Mill Hostel* (☎074/36409) is a mile or so out towards Falcarragh and also has private rooms in a converted railway carriage and camping.

As for **places to eat**, there's a fast-food outlet, *Josie's*, *Danny Collins* pub offering soups and pricy but delicious seafood, and the upmarket *Danaa's* (☎074/36150), serving lobster and turbot dishes from £20. *McGilloways Oyster Bar* is light and airy, enhanced by the Derry artist John McCandless's tremendous portraits of musicians and literati, from Sinead O'Connor to Brendan Behan. There's occasional live music here, too (from traditional to blues), and sessions also at *Michael's Bar* up the street. *Dan Devine's* is lively and cosy with friendly bar staff and a nightclub, *Roonies*, attached.

Horn Head is magnificent, a 600ft rock face scored by ledges on which perch countless guillemots and gulls. Puffins are also returning in significant numbers. The best view of the cliffs, sea-stacks and caves is from the water, but the cliff road is vertiginous enough in places to give you a good look down the sheer sides. To get there take the slip road at the Falcarragh end of Dunfanaghy village; it descends to skirt the side of a beautiful inlet before rising steeply to go round the east side of the head. A spectacular vista of headlands opens up to the east – Rosguill, Fanad and Inishowen – but none can match the drama of Horn Head's **cliffs**, their tops clad in a thin cover of purplish heather. Alternatively, you can walk from Horn Head bridge across the dunes to **Tramore Beach** and then follow the sheep track north, passing two small blow-holes called the Two Pistols and then a much larger one, **McSwyne's Gun**, so called because of the power of the sonic boom produced by the explosion of compressed air from the cavern. Erosion has occurred over the years, however, and you'll be lucky to hear anything. Continuing onwards, you'll come to Pollaguill Bay and the beach. The next wondrous site is the 70ft high **Marble Arch**, cut by the sea through the base of Trawbreaga Head, and soon Horn Head itself becomes visible as you ascend the next headland. The walk as far as here takes around three hours and you can either complete the whole circuit of the peninsula or head back by road to Falcarragh.

Moving east again from Dunfanaghy, the road follows the side of **Sheephaven Bay**; signposted turn-offs run to the popular holiday spots Portnablagh and Marble Hill Strand. From the former you can catch the Wednesday **ferry** to Tory Island (see p.460). A little further east, Marble Hill Strand is a vast sweep of sand and is also the location for the *Shandon Hotel and Leisure Centre* (☎074/36137; ⑦), equipped with pool, tennis courts and pitch and putt. Overlooking the strand, Marble Hill House, was once owned by **Hugh Law**, TD for Donegal in the first Irish Parliament of 1922, who entertained all manner of celebrities here, including W.B. and Jack Yeats. Nearby **Ards Forest Park** occupies the former demesne of the Capuchin Friary of Ard Mhuire and a mile-long avenue alongside Lough Lilly takes you into its centre where there are fine walks through the woodland.

The Creeslough area

The sleepy village of **CREESLOUGH** stands on a slope commanding gorgeous views across the head of Sheephaven Bay. Partway down its main street is a church designed by Liam McCormack, its whitewashed whorl and back-sloping table roof reflecting the thickly set **Muckish Mountain** nearby. You can see the mountain from within the church – it's usually swathed in mist, or what's known locally as the Donegal *smir*. There are pubs and grocery stores in the village, but little to detain you for long.

The coastal road northwards onto the Rosguill Peninsula offers a couple of worthwhile diversions. To the left, just before Lackagh Bridge, **Doe Castle** (presently undergoing further restoration) has been superbly reconstructed. The tall central keep, standing within a *bawn* and rock-cut fosse, was the original fortress of **McSwyney Doe**, whose grave slab is now fixed to its wall, and the base for the O'Dohertys' raids on Derry in 1608. The carving on the stone is faint, but its intricacy makes it historically important; the seven-speared fleur-de-lis at the top represents the close family connections with Scotland, while other carvings show a fox, cow, dolphin and eagle, as well as Celtic tracery. A walk around the battlements affords a view of the southernmost corner of **Sheephaven Bay**; when the tide is out the whole peaceful expanse looks like a desert, with only a slim channel of water gliding through the sandbanks. If the castle gate is padlocked, a key is kept in the cottage fifty yards back down the approach road where you can also buy a guide (£1.60).

Lackagh Bridge is an even better viewpoint, the curving silty shoreline lying downstream and a ginger-brown picture of rushes and heather reaching deep into the hills. Immediately after the bridge there's a turn-off to **GLEN** (two miles), a roundabout way to Carrigart that's worth taking for the scenery and the opportunity to drop in at the *Olde Glen Bar*. This is a low-ceilinged place, smoky and atmospheric, with music at weekends and other nights too. If solitude is what you want, this is a good area to explore: apart from Lough Glen, there are several other lakelets in the district, all enclosed in a silent, rocky landscape.

The Rosguill Peninsula

CARRIGART is the back-door entrance to the extremely beautiful and very manageable **Rosguill Peninsula**. It's a beguiling village, whose **bars** define the essence of the place: *P. Logue's,* at the west end of town, is a welcoming sort of hideaway.

Accommodation is available in the village at *Hol-Tel Carrigart* (☎074/55114; ⑥) and *Sheephaven Lodge* (☎074/55685; ③), both open between April and September. There are plenty of stores for stocking up on provisions or you can **eat** economically at *Weavers Restaurant*. The only **bank** on the peninsula is in Carrigart (July–Aug Mon–Fri 10am–noon; Sept–June Mon–Tues & Thurs–Fri 10am–noon).

The route onto the peninsula starts by the side of the church; follow this road for a little, then fork left, and you'll pass the rabbit-infested dunes at the back of a fantastic and usually deserted beach. The three-mile strand runs in a scimitar's curve all the way back round to the bottom of **Sheephaven Bay** – it's a marvellous four-hour walk to Doe Castle, though when the tide comes in, you could have to do a mile or so of the journey on the lanes.

Downings and Trá Na Rosann

At the top of the strand is **DOWNINGS**, a small and sprightly holiday centre, patronized mainly by Northern Irish tourists, with caravan sites hogging the rear end of the beach and holiday chalets creeping up the hillside behind the village. The one **pub** you should be sure to head for is *Downings Bar*, uphill at the far end of the village, a welcoming place with an open fire, lots of *craic* and music at weekends. The *Beach Hotel* has occasional summer sessions too. The most luxurious place to **stay** is the *Hotel Rosapenna* (☎074/55301; ⑦; March–Oct), next to its own eighteen-hole golf course. Alternatively, there's the *Beach Hotel* (☎074/55303; ④; April–Oct), or there are a couple of B&Bs: *Baymont* (☎074/55395; ③; April–Aug) and *An Crossóg* (☎074/55498; ③; May–Sept). You can **camp** at *Casey's Caravan Park* (☎074/55301).

The main street runs on round the west side of the headland to become the panoramic **Atlantic Drive**, first passing by the harbour slip-road. Just before the pier is McNutt's tweed shop with a *Coffee Shop* (10am–6pm) attached offering superb home baking. The drive itself completely circuits the headland and also makes a stupendous eight-mile walk. The range of views encompasses the essence of Donegal – rugged landscapes in constant tussle with the Atlantic Ocean. About halfway round, a turning leads to **Melmore Head** where you'll find the Alpine-style An Óige **hostel** at Trá Na Rosann beach (☎074/55374), perfectly placed at the northeastern corner of the headland. A quicker way to get here is to take the right hand fork on the way to Downings and it's quite easy to **hitch** to the hostel, as everyone knows where you're heading. South of the Melmore Head road you'll pass the congenial *Singing Pub* (traditional music Sat), sited on a turning up to the left. Opposite this turning and down to the right is **Mevagh Church** graveyard. It has an early Christian cross and an intriguing slab into which some cup-like cavities have been carved. And there's one gravestone that cannot but bring an appreciative smile: *Pat MacBride 1910–86, Shoemaker and Philosopher.*

The Fanad Peninsula

The road from Carrigart to the **Fanad Peninsula** passes close to Mulroy Bay before arriving in **MILFORD**, a village with amenities but little attraction. From here, the road up the western side of the peninsula leads to **KERRYKEEL**, passing, on the way, the *Mulroy Ballroom*, one of the few remaining sixties showband ballrooms (ceilis Wed night June–Aug). The *Rockhill Caravan Park* (☎074/50012), opposite the ballroom, provides the only basic **accommodation** in the place. The *Village Inn* at the northern end of the village has a somewhat expensive but wide-ranging menu and *Mr Ed's* serves huge portions of fish and chips. *McGettigan's* Bar has almost nightly entertainment in summer.

From Kerrykeel the road north runs along the water's edge up to **TAMNEY** where there's **B&B** at *Avalon House* (☎074/59031; ③; April–Sept). Further on, the landscape flattens and the ubiquitous "Fanad fences" begin to appear, scything across the countryside and deterring adventurous walking. A left turn at the *Fanad Lodge* bar will take you past the large **Ballyhiernan Strand** through hillocks and boulder-strewn terrain to **BALLYWHORISKEY** where a restored pre-Famine cottage houses a small heritage centre (open 2pm daily), with **boats** for rent. From here you can return to the main road to Fanad Head (see opposite).

Ramelton

The road crawling up the **east** side of Fanad is a much more interesting approach to the Head. It starts at **RAMELTON**, a quaint and sedate little town which sits attractively on the eastern bank of the broad black flow of the salmon-rich River Leannan. The town has heritage status because of its many Georgian houses and there are some fine stone warehouses on the bank side, some of which have been converted for other uses, such as *Fish House*, now a gallery and tearoom. The old Meeting House in Back Lane houses the **Donegal Genealogical Centre**, a must for anyone seeking to verify their local ancestry. *Mirabeau* is a popular **restaurant**, serving steaks and seafood, while the *House on the Brae* coffee shop dispenses home baking. For entertainment, try the *Bridge Bar* (Wed & Fri–Sun), where you can hear R&B, jazz or rock. If you're only passing through, *Sweeney's Tavern,* dating back to 1795, is the nicest refuge for a restful drink. If you decide to stay, there's fine **B&B** at *Ardeen* (☎074/51243; ③; April–Oct).

Rathmullan

The next stop north, **RATHMULLAN** is a pretty place with its long row of multi-coloured houses facing Lough Swilly. The beach here is classed among the cleanest in Europe – note the Blue Flag at the pier where **boats** can be rented from Malcolm Bowden (☎074/58282). In 1587 **Red Hugh O'Donnell** was lured onto a British merchant ship here, on the pretext of a merry drink, and ended up in Dublin jail for six years; and in 1607 it was a departure point for the **Flight of the Earls**, the event that marked the end of the Gaelic nation. **Rathmullan Heritage Centre** (Easter to mid-Sept Mon–Sat 10am–6pm, Sun noon–6pm; ☎074/58229; £1) recounts this event and provides a host of information on local accommodation and leisure activities. In October, 1798 the French frigate *Hoche*, with Wolfe Tone on board, was intercepted in the Lough nearby and Tone was captured and taken to Dublin for trial.

The view across to Fahan on the Inishowen Peninsula is enticing (a small ferryboat operates in summer), but otherwise the only thing to delay your passing through is **Rathmullan Friary**, one of the better-preserved historical ruins in Donegal. The original part of it was built by Rory MacSweeney in 1508 and then presented to the Carmelites. George Bingham plundered it in 1595 and used it as a barracks, and in 1618 it was further adapted as a castle residence by Bishop Knox. Only the chancel area continued to serve as a church until its eventual abandonment in 1814. Today you can see traces of Gothic doorways and narrow window apertures.

On the way into Rathmullan, there's very good **eating** to be had at the *Water's Edge Restaurant* while gourmets and oenophiles are also catered for by *An Bonnán Bui* on Pier Road. The comfortably old-fashioned *Pier Hotel* (☎074/58178; ④; April–Sept) serves excellent fresh salmon for a fraction of what you'd pay at swanky *Rathmullan House* (☎074/58188; ⑨; March–Oct), nearby. You can savour the Lough Foyle view and your pint in the friendly *Beachcomber* **bar**. *Fort Royal Hotel* (☎074/58100; ⑧; April–Sept) offers the only other **accommodation** in the village and, for a cheaper option, you'll need to head to Saltpans, three miles north, where *Carriglough House* (☎074/58197; ②; March–Nov) provides B&B. The *Pier Hotel* has ceilis on Thursday nights in summer.

Towards Portsalon

Two miles north of Rathmullan, on the coast road, a signpost to the left indicates a little track that leads towards the tenth-century **Drumhallach cross slab**; only four and a half feet in height, it has delightful carvings of two figures sitting on the arms of the cross sucking away at their thumbs. This curiosity is linked by local folklore with Fionn Mac Cumhaill, who one day burned his thumb while tending to the salmon of knowledge, and immediately stuck it in his mouth – thereafter doing the same whenever he needed to be wise. The lower figures on this front face are harder to make out but are meant to represent bishops.

Back on the main route, the road climbs to give great views across to **Dunree Head** and the **Urris** range of mountains on the Inishowen Peninsula. About seven miles north of Rathmullan is *Bunnaton Hostel* (☎074/50122), housed in an old coastguard station with pleasant views of a small cove with a rocky beach. The hostel can provide details of the great walks nearby, both beside the lough and inland through the Irish-speaking **Glenvar** valley to Kerrykeel on the western side of the peninsula. Further on the road towards Portsalon is the *Knockalla Caravan and Camping Park* (☎074/53213).

Continuing north, the road rises until you're running along the clifftop approach to **Saldanha Head**. Here you'll witness the most spectacular views on the entire peninsula, looking across to Inishowen and down onto the three-mile stretch of golden sand at Ballymastocker Bay. The tiny village of **PORTSALON**, on the other side of the strand, was once a great holidaying spot, but there's little sign of this now apart from a courtyard full of holiday chalets. The highlight is *Rita's Pier Stores* by the tiny harbour, with its 1950s decor, wooden bar counter and shelves for sweets and bottled drinks. For **B&B** try the award-winning *Croaghross Cottage* (☎074/59548; ④; March–Sept) which also serves excellent dinners. The Portsalon **golf** course must have one of the most picturesque settings in the country.

Fanad Head

Though some stretches are forested, most of the five-mile route north from Portsalon to Fanad Head is through humpy and barren land, with clusters of granite pushing through marshy ground. By the roadside there's a **Holy Well**, decked out with a crazier than usual collection of mementos. Before reaching the Head, there is one other curiosity worth taking in – the rock formation known as the **Seven Arches**, created by the constant erosive battering of the waters. To get there, follow the signpost on the right of the road, then take the path down to the new house, and finally cross the fields to the rocky strand.

Returning to the main road, you'll find that it leads straight on to **Fanad Head**, where it reaches a dramatically placed cliff-edge lighthouse and its namesake public house, the *Lighthouse Tavern*. The road from here runs on down to the low rocky coast, and a pebble beach.

The Inishowen Peninsula

The **Inishowen Peninsula** is perhaps the great overlooked treasure of the Irish landscape (and certainly has the longest signposted scenic drive – the "Inishowen 100"). Few tourists come here, perhaps because of its proximity to the North. Yet, if you do visit, you'll discover a diverse and visually exciting terrain, where the views usually encompass the waters of the loughs or the Atlantic waves. Virtually every aspect of the landscape is superb – the beaches (especially Fahan, Tullagh and Pollan), the towering headland bluffs (Malin, Inishowen, Dunaff and Dunree) and the central mountain range, with **Slieve Snaght** (*sliabh sneachta*, the "mountain of the snows") at the centre of it all. The peninsula derives its name from **Eoghán**, who was made First Lord of the island by his father Niall, High King of Ireland. Phases of the peninsula's history before and after Eoghán have left a legacy of fine antiquities, from the **Grianán of Aileach** to a host of beautiful early Christian crosses (Cloncha, Mura, Carrowmore and Cooley).

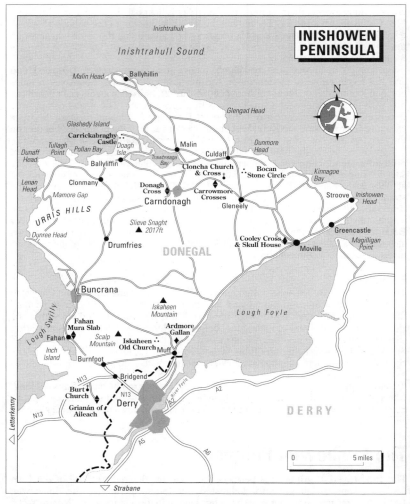

Western Inishowen

The approach to the most stimulating of all the Inishowen sights, the ancient fort known as the **Grianán of Aileach**, is by the Liam McCormack-designed **Burt Church**, near Bridgend on the N13 Letterkenny–Derry road. This is probably the most beautiful new church in all Ireland, and like other McCormack designs in Donegal, its structure is evocative of the mystical landmark nearby. The seating is set concentrically, under a whitewashed ceiling that sweeps up into a vortex to allow sunlight to beam down directly upon the altar; the allusions in every detail to Neolithic sepulchral architecture (especially Newgrange) are fascinating and very atmospheric.

The origins of the Grianán of Aileach (a mile up the hill from the church) date back to 1700 BC and is thought to be linked to the Tuatha de Danann, pre-Celtic invaders. It was sufficiently significant to be included by Ptolemy, the Alexandrian geographer, in his second century AD map of the world, and was the base of various northern Irish chieftains. Here in 450 AD St Patrick is said to have baptized Eoghán, the founder of the O'Neill clan who ruled the kingdom of Aileach for more than 500 years. In the twelfth century the fort was sacked by Murtagh O'Brian, King of Thomond, in retribution for a raid on Clare, with the result that a large amount of its stone got carried away. Today's impressive building was largely reconstructed in the late nineteenth century and is the only remaining terraced fort in Ireland. It's enclosed by three earthen banks, but its most stunning asset is the view across the primordial jumble of mountains and hills far away to the west and the loughs to each side of Inishowen immediately to the north. You can discover more about the fort at the **visitor centre** (daily: June–Aug 10am–6pm, Sept–May noon–6pm; £2), back on the main road towards Letterkenny, which also contains a superb, innovative **restaurant** (☎077/68512; open until 10pm), serving Lough Neagh eels and wild boar.

Inch Island, Fahan and Buncrana

The lane on the opposite side of the N13 to the Burt Church leads to western Inishowen (or you can head east to Bridgend and turn onto the R238). Whichever you choose, a couple of miles past Burnfoot is a signposted turning to **INCH ISLAND**, connected to the mainland by a causeway. This was once a strategic O'Doherty base, guarding Lough Swilly and the clan heartlands, and has a ruined castle to boot. If you have time for a detour, there are great views of the lough and the Inishowen coastline from the pier, while wetland habitats to the west of the island attract vast colonies of Whooper and Bewick swans and other waterfowl. Inch Island Stables (☎077/60335) organizes **riding** holidays around the Inishowen 100. The beach at **FAHAN**, next stop on the mainland, is delightful, as are its monastic ruins. The first abbot was St Mura (one of six saints in the one family), and what remains today from his time is the **St Mura cross slab**, a spellbinding example of early Christian stone decoration. Long-stemmed Latin crosses are carved on both faces with typical Celtic interlacing. There's said to be a rare Greek inscription on the edge, but it's hard to locate. *Restaurant St John's,* as you enter the village, offers local seafood specialities, but expect to pay from £20, while the *Railway Tavern* has a regular Friday night ceili.

BUNCRANA, a few miles north, is the largest town on the peninsula and its high street is a long cavalcade of shops and bars, many with names saluting one or other of the local clans – McLaughlin, Hegarty, O'Doherty, Grant, McGonagle. The town is packed out during the summer, for this is the Derry people's unrivalled seaside resort. To escape the crowds, take the left turn that runs down to the pier at the north end of the main street and you'll reach the coastal path to **Stragill Strand**, a beautiful and isolated stretch of golden sand. The view across **Lough Swilly** here is delightful, as if the waters were those of a large mountain lake.

Buncrana might have no end of amusement arcades, but when it comes to accommodation, there are surprisingly few places to stay. Rooms are in especially short supply during the mid-July music **festival** and the seasonal **tourist office** (June–August; ☎077/62600) on the front should be able to help. For **B&Bs**; try *Ross na Ri*, Old Road (☎077/61271; ②; March–Oct), or *Kincora*, Cahir O'Doherty Avenue (☎077/61174; ②). There are a couple of **hotels**: the *Lake of Shadows*, Grianan Park (☎077/61902; ⑤) overlooking the lough; and, the recently redeveloped *Inishowen Gateway*, Railway Road (☎077/61144; ⑦).

For **eats** in Buncrana, there's *McDaid's Café*, for home-bakes, or the *Ubiquitous*, also on Main Street, for more substantial fare. Here too *Dorrians* is also a good bet for lunch. Buncrana is jam-packed with **pubs**; if you're looking for a plain and unpretentious bar try *Roddens* or the *Drift Inn*. More upbeat venues include *O'Flaherty's*, which often has traditional music, and the new *Millennium* music bar. However, at the weekends, car and coach loads of northerners pour over the border to dance into the small hours at **clubs** such as *Liberty's* and *Club Sands* in the Inishowen *Gateway Hotel*.

Dunree to Doagh Isle

Perched on a headland overlooking the mouth of Lough Swilly, just past the tiny village from which it takes its name, **Fort Dunree** began life as a Martello tower and was then enlarged into a fortress. It now has a museum of predictable military memorabilia (June–Sept Mon–Sat 10am–6pm, Sun 1–6pm; £2), though the audiovisual display at least provides an insight into the fort's former use. North out of the village the road climbs steeply past a scattering of weather-beaten thatched cottages before crossing a small bridge close to the **Gap of Mamore** (*madhm mór*, "the great mountain pass"), which seems like a chunk bitten out of the Urris Mountains. From here the road spirals steeply downwards, each bend providing an ever wider and more spectacular view of the flat foreground to Dunaff Head. The mile-long **Tullagh Strand**, to the east of Dunaff Head, is a safe bathing beach, with *Tullagh Bay Camping and Caravan Park* just behind it (☎077/76289 or 76138). *The Rusty Nail*, by the roadside, has music at weekends and offers good-value bar food and Sunday lunch. The road from here works its way inland between the mountains to **CLONMANY**, a village of predominantly cream-coloured terraced houses, a few grocery shops and several bars. The backdrop of mountains on all sides shields it from any thought of an outside world.

The holiday village of **BALLYLIFFIN** makes an earthy contrast, with a hotel at each end, popular **discos** at *JD's* (Sat and Sun) and several **B&B**s. Try *Castlelawn House* (☎077/76600; ②), or *Rossaor House* (☎077/76498; ④). Apart from golf – the Glashedy course here is reckoned to be one of the toughest in Ireland (☎077/67119) – the other main draw here is the folk song and ballad **festival** held on the last weekend in March. If you want to explore the area, **bikes** can be rented from McEleney's Cycles (☎077/76541) on the road to Clonmany. The minor road heading north leads to the entrancing **Pollan Strand**, at the northern tip of which stands the ruin of **Carrickabraghy Castle**, an O'Doherty defence built in the sixteenth century. Weathered by centuries of spray and sea salt, the stones of the tower show colours ranging from the darkest hues through oranges and reds to golden yellows. The strand itself has wonderfully wild breakers, which unfortunately make it dangerous to swim.

The castle sits on the western side of **Doagh Isle**, another former island, linked to the mainland through centuries of silt accumulation. which you can drive onto by a road a couple of miles east of Ballyliffin. You can't miss the turning, as there's a female mannequin in a pirate hat and, a little further on, a similar male on a bike towing an old 2CV. These announce the way to the **Doagh Visitors Centre** (daily Easter–Sept 10am–5pm; £2.50), one man's intriguing attempt to tell the Famine story. You'll discover a re-created farm cottage (including a remarkably small 'kitchen' bed), the fairy house home of Fergus McArt, and more mannequins in various symbolic tableaux. Head out further east for **Trawbreaga Bay** (*trá bréige*, "the treacherous strand"), an exquisite piece of coastline. The mouth of the bay is bewitching – if you walk onto the beach here you'll find the sea has fashioned the rocks into myriad shapes and colours.

Carndonagh

Just before you turn into **CARNDONAGH**, coming from the Ballyliffin direction, there's a church on the corner against whose wall is the elegantly shaped and decorated seventh-century **Donagh Cross** (*domhnach,* commonly "Sunday", but also "church founded by St Patrick"), with two diminutive pillar stones to its right and left. The pillar stones show figures with rather large heads, while the cross depicts evil little characters jumping out of its Celtic interlacing – all of which harks back to the

Druidic religion. A few other decorated stones stand by the entrance. The buildings of Carndonagh town are stacked up the hillside, near the crown of which stands the omniscient Catholic church. Most of the activity here occurs in the environs of the Diamond and this is the place to stock up on supplies. On the corner of Chapel Street is the **Inishowen Tourist Office** (June–Aug Mon–Fri 9.30am–7pm, Sat 10am–6pm, Sun noon–6pm; Sept–May Mon–Fri 9.30am–5.30pm; ☎077/74933) whose friendly staff can supply you with any information on the peninsula you need. The town **museum**, in the basement of the Wesleyan church, near the base of the hill as you come from the Ballyliffin direction (July & Aug Mon–Sat 1–5pm), has many intriguing folk items. For **accommodation**, try *Radharc na Coille*, Tiernaleague, left off Church Street then on for a mile (☎077/74471; ②), or *Ashdale Farmhouse* (☎077/74017; ③; April–Oct), half a mile out on the Malin road. For **food**, there's the restaurant at *Trawbreaga House* on the Diamond, while on Malin Road, *The Quiet Lady* has extremely good-value lunches and *The Corncrake*'s evening specials are popular enough to warrant booking ahead (☎077/74534). *The Sportsman's Inn*, on the Diamond, does stews and salads and has traditional music most nights throughout the year. *Bradley's*, on Bridge Street, is an old-time sing-song bar. *Tul-na-ri*, out on the Culdaff road, attracts the crowds to its weekend **discos**. Carndonagh has a **street festival** in the third week of July but it's not one of the more lively ones. **Bikes** can be rented from Bikes and Toys (☎077/74084), three miles out of town on the Ballyliffin road, but they'll deliver to anywhere on the peninsula.

East of Carndonagh: the ancient sites

Not far to the east of Carndonagh are a neighbouring set of historical remains – the Carrowmore high crosses, the Cloncha cross, the Bocan stone circle and the Temple of Deen. To get to the **Carrowmore high crosses**, take the Moville direction out of Carndonagh for four miles, then turn right forty yards after the signposted turning for Culdaff: the two plain crosses are eighty yards up the lane, one on each side, the northern cross undecorated, while its partner has a figure, supposedly of Christ. These and a few meagre building stones are all that remain of the ancient monastery of St Chonas, husband of Dareaca, a sister of St Patrick. For the **Cloncha cross and church**, return to the Culdaff turning and follow it for a couple of miles until you see a bungalow with a garden hedge of small firs – the site is up a path alongside. This was once the most important monastic foundation in Inishowen, a status reflected in the beautiful designs carved on the cross's stem. Inside the ruined sixteenth-century church are a few more carved stones, the outstanding piece being a tenth-century tombstone.

For the other two sites, continue onwards towards Culdaff, turn right at the church and then first left – the **Bocan stone circle** is through the first field gate on the left. Only seven of the original stones still stand, among a residue of fallen ones; they were all placed here at least 3000 years ago. There's a fine view of the surrounding ring of hills and it's believed that the stones were deliberately aligned on an east–west axis between Slieve Snaght and Jura. On the other side of the main road from the circle is a gallery tomb known as the **Temple of Deen** (go a little further along towards Moville and take a right up as far as the wire barrier – you'll spot it from there). It's nothing special, but it's possible that what is exposed today is only the central chamber of an immense cairn. Unfortunately, there has been no archeological investigation of either this or the stone circle. **CULDAFF** is the nearest base for all of these places, a cosy village set around an ancient stone bridge. There's a major sea angling festival here at the end of July and, in October, a cultural weekend commemorates the seventeenth-century actor, Charles Macklin. However, for the rest of the year, it's *McGrory's* bar which is the centre of attention. It may be hard to credit, considering its isolated location, but the *Back Room* here is one of the best venues in Ireland for live music and the bar is decorated with numerous pictures of the stars who've appeared to prove it. You can stay here too (☎077/79104; ②), and at *Cee Cliff House* (☎077/79159; ③) or *Culdaff House* (☎077/79103; ②; March–Oct). Summer **trips** to Inishtrahull Island (see below) leave from the pier (☎077/70605).

Malin and Malin Head

Four miles north of Carndonagh, and approached via a ten-arched bridge, is **MALIN** village, tucked picturesquely into the side of Trawbreaga Bay. A planter settlement with a charming grassy Diamond, it has two pubs, *McClean's* and *McGonnigle's*, as well as the *Malin Hotel* which hosts a variety of entertainments. A little way north of Malin a signpost shows the way to **Five Fingers Strand**, across the bay from Doagh Isle – it's worth the diversion for the ferocity of the breakers on the beach and the long walks on its sands. Following the "Inishowen 100" signs will next lead you around Knockamany Bens, from which there are tremendous views of the strand and, occasionally at low tide, of the wreck of the *Twilight* which sank in 1889 en route to Newfoundland.

Malin Head, the northernmost extremity of Ireland, might not be as stupendously over-the-top as other Donegal headlands but is nevertheless excellent for windy and winding coastal walks. The headland's tip is marked by **Bamba's Crown**, a ruined signal tower, built in 1805. The words "S.S.Eire" (*Saor Stát*, "Free State") are written below the tower. Five miles out is the now-deserted **Inishtrahull Island**, though boats from the pier will take you there in summer. Some say this translates as the "Island of Yonder Strand", though others claim its meaning derives from a legendary murder – "Island of the Bloody Strand" or even "Shore Grave". Whatever the case, the island is composed of the oldest rock in Ireland, 2000 million years' old Lewisian gneiss. The western path from the Crown heads out to **Hells Hole**, a 250ft chasm in the cliffs, which roars with the onrushing tide. The headland is an ornithologist's dream; choughs, with their glossy black plumage and red legs and bill, inhabit the cliffs and the rasping cry of the rare corncrake can be heard in the fields. Past the *Seaview Tavern* to the east, a path leads to the **Wee House of Malin**, a hermit's cell in the nearby cliff, once the home of St Muirdealach, where there's a "wishing-chair". **B&B** places in the village include *Barracin* (☎077/70184; ②; Easter–Oct) and *High View* (☎077/70283; ②), both overlooking the Atlantic. There are a couple of excellent **hostels** here too. The *Malin Head Hostel* (☎077/70309; open all year, but advance booking necessary Nov–March), just past the post office on the way into the village, is well-equipped and the owner is a mine of information on the area. Alternatively, *Sandrock Holiday Hostel* (☎077/70289), at Port Ronan Pier – fork left at the *Crossroads Inn* – has sea views and bikes for rent. The best place to **eat** is *The Cottage* (June–Sept Mon–Sat 11am–6.30pm, Sun 1.30–6.30pm; March–May Sun 1.30–6.30pm), a restored thatched cottage near Bamba's Crown. Apart from the fine tearoom, with salmon available in season, there's **tourist information** here and traditional sessions in summer. Both the *Seaview Tavern* and the *Bree Inn* serve meals and have music on Saturdays, while *Farren's* bar is a cosy place to sit and chat to the locals.

Eastern Inishowen

Though still attractive country, the eastern coastline of Inishowen holds less interest than the west. Its proximity to Derry means that it is substantially busier, especially at the weekends when the city's clubbers hit the area's nightclubs. Nevertheless, it's still possible to find isolated spots, especially to the west of Inishowen Head, and, if you need company, there are pleasant places all over the area.

Muff and around

The tiny village of **MUFF**, just a few minutes' drive north of the border, is not quite as moribund as it may at first appear. *Carmans Inn* has Irish music on a Wednesday and another place to try is *The Flough*, a traditional Irish cottage with sessions and dancing to match. There's a lively festival here on the first weekend in August and Lenamore Stables (☎077/84022) offers **riding** and **trekking** in the vicinity and beyond.

The countryside immediately around Muff is scattered with several interesting remains. Uphill from Muff in **Iskaheen**, and opposite St Patrick's Church, a plaque in the wall of the ruined church in the graveyard marks the burial place of Eoghán, son of Niall of the Nine Hostages. Of greater antiquity is the Bronze Age **Ardmore Gallan** stone, a striking monument, heavily carved with symbolic forms. There are forty small cup-dents and a large vertical valley down the middle of one face. To get to it, take a left off the Moville Road about half a mile out of Muff, then up the lane at the side of the red-doored house; follow the road straight up, and turn right to the farmyard at the end – the stone is in the far side of the field in front of the yard.

Also to be recommended is the fourteen-mile trip across the mountains through **Gráinne's Gap** and on to Buncrana on the western side of the peninsula (see p.473). There are fantastic views back down onto the Foyle estuary from the gap, and the inland scenery is all trickling burns, heathery boggy slopes lined with turf banks, and rocky granite outcrops.

Moville and around

Set on a gentle hillock beside the Foyle, **MOVILLE** is an agreeable seaside resort and was once a port of call for transatlantic liners, though there's little activity in today's compact harbour. It's handy for a rocky shoreline walk that you can pursue as far as Greencastle without too much difficulty, although at a few points you'll have to walk circumspectly across the bottom of a few private gardens. The village rarely stirs itself to offer anything more than the odd tingle of excitement, except during the late September **Foyle Oyster Festival**, a cross-border event with buckets of entertainment and the chance to devour shellfish galore. There are plenty of places to **stay**. *McNamara's Hotel* (☎077/82564; ⑤) is the grandest and has *Club Max!* attached. For B&B try *Mrs McGroarty's*, Main Street (☎077/82091; ②; April–Oct) or *Iona House*, Gulladuff Road (☎077/82173; ②). The *Moville Holiday Hostel*, Malin Road (☎077/82378) also has a campsite and rents out bikes. *Rosatos*, nearer town on the same road, is the best place for a **meal**, while there are traditional sessions at *Rudden's Bar and Grocery* on Fridays. *The Prospect Bar* down on the front by the gaudily blue-painted Temperance Hall has music at weekends. A livelier time is to be had at the *Hair of the Dog* pub by the pier, which promises varied music every night.

The most notable historical remains in the district are the **Cooley Cross** and **Skull House**, approached by taking the left turn just before the petrol station on the way into Moville. Follow the turn-off up the steep hill for about a mile, always bearing right and you'll discover an ancient Celtic wheel-cross, guarding the entrance to a walled grave-yard. There are very few examples of this kind of cross with the pierced ringhole in its head – the hole was once a pagan device used to clinch serious treaties, the hands of the opposing parties being joined in amity through it. The Skull House, in the graveyard, is in the form of the beehive huts of early monks and it was once possibly an oratory before becoming an ossuary. However, any bones stored here have long since vanished.

Greencastle to Kinnagoe Bay

The harbour village of **GREENCASTLE** has a pleasant view across to the extensive golden sands of Magilligan Strand on the British side of Lough Foyle. At dusk you'll see the area across the water begin to sparkle with lights like a ship at sea – these are the lights of the prison camp, just hidden behind the dunes. A highlight of village life is the regular visits by cruise ships, though, next to the harbour, in the old coastguard station, the **Maritime Museum** (daily June–Sept 10am–6pm; £2) recalls maritime travel from a bygone era. Amongst the range of maritime memorabilia, pride of place goes to a nineteenth-century rocket cart used to fire flares to aid survivors of wrecked ships. By the road to Stroove (see below) are the ruins of a fourteenth-century **Richard de Burgo** castle, built on a rocky knoll to allow the Anglo-Normans to guard the narrowest part of the lough. However, it was briefly captured in 1316 by Edward Bruce of Scotland who had himself crowned King of Ireland. The castle was retaken shortly afterwards and remained in De Burgo's hands until 1333 when his grandson William, the Brown Earl, was murdered and Anglo-Norman control of the North-West ended. Later the castle fell into the hands of the O'Dohertys, but it was badly damaged by an attack by their rival Calvagh O'Donnell. Though there were subsequent attempts at renovation, by 1700 the castle was a complete ruin and has remained so ever since. Nearby is **Greencastle Fort**, a lookout post built during the Napoleonic Wars which unsurprisingly affords good views across the estuary, though nowadays it houses a bar and restaurant with **B&B** (☎077/81426; ⑤). You can also stay right next door to De Burgo's ruin in the *Castle Inn* (☎077/81426; ③), which also has a restaurant and traditional sessions on Fridays, and at *Brooklyn Cottage* (☎077/81087; ③; March–Oct). As you'd expect, seafood is available in abundance and, in addition to the restaurants above, the place to try it is *Kealy's*, reckoned to be one of the best in Donegal.

At **STROOVE** (pronounced *Shroove*), the scenery jumps into a more exciting gear, with lovely clambering walks along its coastline to the lighthouse. There you'll have to return to the road to reach the small beach, from where doughtier walkers can resume the clamber as far as the cliffs of the awesome **Inishowen Head**. An easier way to the Head is simply to follow the road until it turns left, where you go straight on up the hill; a car can make it up the first couple of miles, but after that you run the risk of getting stuck in a rut. From the Head, it's a beautiful but tiring walk to isolated **Kinnagoe Bay**, one of the most secluded sandy beaches around, tucked between the rocky walls of headland against which the waves throw spray as delicate as lace. The alternative route here entails going back to the main road and following it to the right turn by the thatched cottage in Stroove – this will take you along the narrowest of roads over the headland and through two beautiful glens. A plaque by the roadside at Kinnagoe records the sinking of *La Trinidad Valencera* during the Spanish Armada and other ships around the coast. Forty of its crew died in the water and most of the remaining three hundred survivors were killed outside Derry by an English army. The wreckage was recovered and is on display at Foyle College in Derry. *Kinnagoe Bay House* (☎077/81280; ③; April–Oct) is a fine place to **stay** with wonderful views of the Bay. Back in Stroove, the *Drunken Duck Seafood Bar* (☎077/81362), offering good **food** and fantastic views, is well worth a visit.

travel details

BUSES

Annagry to: Dublin via Gweedore, Dunfanaghy & Letterkenny (7am daily, 3pm Mon, Thurs, Fri & Sun 10.50am Friday). Return from Dublin, Parnell Square to Annagry (5.45pm Mon–Sat, 9.30am Mon & Sat, 12.30pm & 4.30pm Fri, 12.30pm & 8.30pm Sun).

Buncrana to: Carndonagh (2–3 daily except Sun; 50min), Derry (3–18 daily; 35min).

Crolly to: Galway City, via Dunfanaghy, Letterkenny, Donegal town, Bundoran and Sligo (7.20am & 2.45pm Mon–Sat, 10.20am Fri, 7.20am & 1.50pm Sun; 5–6hr). Return from Galway Cathedral (10am & 4pm Mon–Sat, 1.30pm & 5.30pm Fri, 8pm Sun).

Donegal to: Ballybofey (7 daily; 30min); Ballyshannon (8 daily; 20min); Bundoran (8 daily; 35min); Derry (7 daily; 1hr 25min–1hr 50min); Dublin (4 daily; 4hr); Enniskillen (4 daily; 1hr 10min); Galway (3 daily; 4hr 25min); Glencolmcille (1 daily at 6.15pm and, additionally, 10.30am in summer); Killybegs (4 daily; 45min); Letterkenny (6 daily; 1hr); Sligo (8 daily; 1hr 5min–1hr 45min); Strabane (3 daily; 1hr 40min); Westport (1 daily; 4hr 10min).

Downings to: Letterkenny (10.45am daily).

Dunfanaghy to: Derry (4 daily; 1hr 45min); Letterkenny (4 daily; 1hr 45min).

Dungloe to: Annagry (2 daily; 30min); Burtonport (2 daily; 10min); Derry via Falcarragh and Letterkenny (1–2 daily except Sun; 5hr 25min); Dublin via Glenties, Ardara, Donegal & Enniskillen (7.45am daily, noon Mon, Fri–Sat and 3pm Sun). Return from the *Royal Dublin Hotel*, O'Connell Street, Dublin (6pm daily; 2pm Fri–Mon, 4.30pm Fri only & 10am Mon only); Belfast via Letterkenny & Derry (7.15am Mon–Sat, 4.30pm Sun; 4hr 30min). Return from Belfast (5.30pm) from Derry (7.15pm Mon–Sat & 9.15pm, 10.50pm Sun).

Glencolmcille (departures from *Biddy's Bar*) to: Dublin via Donegal town (Mon–Thurs & Sat 7.20am); Letterkenny (July–Sept 11.40am Mon, Fri–Sat).

Killybegs to: Glencolmcille (2–3 daily; 45min); Glenties (2–4 daily; 45min); Malinmore (1 Sat; 1 hr); Portnoo (2 daily; 1hr 10min).

Letterkenny to: Derry (10 Mon–Sat; 1hr); Dublin (4 daily; 4hr); Fanad (2 daily; 1hr 45min); Moville via Buncrana, Clonmany & Carndonagh (9.30am Mon–Fri, 5.40pm Mon–Sat; 1hr 50min); Rosguill Peninsula (6pm daily); Strabane (5 daily; 55min).

Malin Head to: Derry (1–4 Mon–Sat; 1hr 40min).

Stroove to: Derry via Moville (7 Mon–Sat; 1hr 10min).

THE NORTH

On May 22, 1998, the people of Northern Ireland turned out in unprecedented numbers to vote on what had become known as the Good Friday agreement. When the results were declared the following day (significantly, the bicentenary of the 1798 rebellion), 71.12 per cent had voted in favour of the settlement. Interpretations differed, but most analysts agreed that a majority of both Nationalist/Republican and, more remarkably, Unionist/Loyalist communities had given their support. Simultaneously, electors in the Republic overwhelmingly endorsed the agreement, thus mandating their government to renounce the Irish constitutional claim to the Six Counties. This bilateral ratification was an undoubted triumph for all the agreement's signatories, but, much more momentously, only one possible conclusion could be drawn from the results of the referenda – after almost thirty years of the Troubles the people of Northern Ireland had unequivocally expressed their desire for peace.

A month later, the North returned to the polls to vote for candidates to the new **Assembly**, a key element of the accord, and the first organization to have, albeit limited, legislative and executive authority over the province since the Stormont Parliament was dissolved in 1972. Again, Nationalists and Republicans demonstrated their support and the pro-agreement Unionist/Loyalist coalition just scraped enough seats to ensure that the Assembly's operation would not be scuppered by the increasingly vociferous Unionist opposition led by Ian Paisley and Robert McCartney. David Trimble, leader of the Ulster Unionists, and Seamus Mallon of the Socialist and Democratic Labour Party were appointed First and Deputy Minister respectively. However, while the talking continued, dissident Republican hardliners attempted to expose the fragility of the settlement by more traditional means. A series of town centre bombings during the first half of 1998 culminated in the explosion of a massive car bomb in the centre of Omagh later that year on August 15, killing 29 people. It was the worst single atrocity in the whole history of the Troubles and drew outraged condemnation from all sides. Both British and Irish governments announced their intention to strengthen anti-terrorist legislation and frantic efforts were made to deter any Loyalist reprisal and save the peace process. In the event, however, there were no reprisals. In fact, the bombing produced quite the opposite outcome. Two weeks later, the Real IRA declared a cease-fire. The announcement helped to reduce the tension surrounding the first face-to-face meeting in September between Gerry Adams and David Trimble. Shortly afterwards, two of the chief negotiators in the Good Friday Agreement, David Trimble and John Hume, leader of the nationalist SDLP, were awarded the Nobel peace prize.

These developments are undoubtedly great strides forward. However at the time of writing, key questions remain unanswered. The IRA's cease-fire has been maintained, but decommissioning of its weaponry is seen by many as a fundamental step towards a lasting peace. Profound divisions in the Unionist camp and the continued controversy over the rights of the Orangemen to march through Catholic areas are indicative of the precariousness of Unionist support for the agreement. Nevertheless, whatever the outcome, there is no doubt that the political landscape of Northern Ireland has been irrevocably transformed and the mood of cautious optimism which first surfaced during the IRA's 1994–1996 cease-fire is prevailing once more. There's considerable hope of a resurgence of economic growth and, crucially, there's been a small, yet significant, fragmentation of the old loyalties, exemplified by the support for the Women's Coalition during the Assembly elections.

Much of the Northern Irish countryside is intensely beautiful and thankfully unspoilt. Yet, despite its obvious appeal and the promotional efforts of the Tourist Board, the number of visitors has declined since the heady days of 1995 when inquisitive tourists, especially from the Republic and Britain, flocked to discover the delights of this neglected corner. Many are still deterred by the uncertainties of the political situation and the decline in the punt's value against sterling has enhanced the Republic's alternative attractions. As a result, the tourist industry's growth rate has decelerated, though facilities continue to improve and many new hotels, hostels and restaurants have opened in the last couple of years. Despite this, accommodation can still be scarce during peak periods and festivals, especially in Belfast and Derry and the traditional Northern holiday resorts of Portrush and Portstewart on the north coast and Newcastle in County Down.

Most of Northern Ireland's major attractions lie at its fringes. To the north, are the green **Glens of Antrim** and a coastline as scenic as anywhere in Ireland, with, as its centrepiece, the bizarre black basalt geometry of the **Giant's Causeway**. In the south-east, **County Down** offers the contrasting beauties of the serene **Strangford Lough** and the brooding mass of the **Mourne Mountains**. To the west, the inland counties of **Tyrone** and **Fermanagh** are dotted with megalithic remains and ruined Plantation castles and, while the former's main attraction is the wild and desolate Sperrin mountain range, Fermanagh has **Lough Erne**, a fabulous place for watersports, fishing and exploring island monastic remains. Elsewhere, near **Lough Neagh**, lie the planned towns of the merchant companies, entrusted with the resettlement of this region in the seventeenth century, and rolling countryside almost unsullied, but for lingering military installations, like **South Armagh**. However, to get to grips with the history of the north, a visit to its cities is essential: **Belfast**, with its grand public buildings, was built on the profits of Victorian industry; **Derry** has shed the security barriers and barbed wire that shrouded its medieval walled town; and the cathedral town of **Armagh**, set on seven hills, is where St Patrick established Christianity in Ireland. The **Ulster Way**, which loops around Northern Ireland for 500 miles, takes in many of these scenic highlights. Unfortunately, the efficiency of its maintenance and signposting varies from county to county – so check with the local tourist offices before setting out.

BELFAST

The capital, BELFAST, is by some way the largest city in Northern Ireland. More than a third of the province's population live within the Belfast conurbation and, consequently, there's a pace and bustle about the place that you'll find almost nowhere else in Northern Ireland. In appearance it closely resembles Liverpool, Glasgow or any other industrial port across the water, and, similarly, its largely defunct docklands are undergoing massive redevelopment. Though the city centre is still characterized by numerous elegant Victorian buildings, there's been an enormous transformation here, too, and the streets leading northwards from the hub of Belfast life, Donegall Square, are packed with chain stores and new shopping precincts. Yet it is not simply the city's appearance that is changing. Nowhere is the optimism engendered by the peace process more obvious than Belfast at night. Most evenings, the city's bars, clubs and restaurants, especially around the Golden Mile, are crammed to overflowing and new venues seem to spring up almost daily. It's almost as though a generation deprived of nightlife by the Troubles has decided to stage a permanent party while it has the chance. Belfast is thriving culturally too. As the tension diminishes, visiting artistes and performers are returning in large numbers and there's been a significant resurgence of homegrown talent. Music, theatre and the visual arts are all flourishing and traditional Irish culture is the subject of rapid rediscovery.

Belfast is a place for getting out and about and there's plenty here to experience. This need not take more than a couple of days, though Belfast is also an easy base from which to visit virtually anywhere else in the North. In the centre, concentrate on the glories that the industrial revolution brought: **grandiose buildings** and magnificent Victorian **pubs**. To the south are the lively and influential **Queen's University** and the extensive collections of the **Ulster Museum**, set in the grounds of the **Botanic Gardens**. A climb up **Cave Hill**, to the north, rewards you with marvellous views of the city spread out around the curve of the natural harbour, **Belfast Lough**. Security measures in the city have been considerably relaxed and many of the barriers and controls have been removed. However, the iron blockade known as the **Peace Line** still bisects the Catholic and Protestant communities of **West Belfast**, a grim physical reminder of the city's and country's sectarian divisions.

Some history

Belfast began its life as a cluster of forts built to guard a ford across the River Farset, which nowadays runs underground beneath the High Street. The Farset and Lagan rivers form a valley that marks a geological boundary between the basaltic plateau of Antrim and the slaty hills of Down: the softer red Triassic sandstones from which their courses were eroded are responsible for the bright red colour of Belfast's brickwork.

Belfast developed slowly at first and, indeed, its history as a city does not really begin until the seventeenth century. A Norman castle was built here in 1177, but its influence was always limited, and within a hundred years or so control over the Lagan Valley had reverted firmly to the Irish, under the O'Neills of Clandeboye who had their stronghold to the south in the Castlereagh Hills. Theirs was the traditional Irish pastoral community, their livestock and families spread between the hills and valley plain. Then, in 1604, Sir Arthur Chichester, a Devonshire knight whose son was to be the first Earl of Donegall, was "planted" in the area by James I, and shortly afterwards the tiny settlement was granted a charter creating a corporate borough. By the restoration era of 1660 the town was still no more than 150 houses in five or six streets, and Carrickfergus at the mouth of the lough held the monopoly on trade.

The eighteenth and nineteenth centuries

By the end of the seventeenth century, things were looking up. French Huguenots fleeing persecution brought skills which rapidly improved the fortunes of the local linen industry which, in turn, attracted new workers and wealth. In 1708, the town was almost entirely destroyed by fire, but it was only a temporary setback: throughout the **eighteenth century** the cloth trade and shipbuilding expanded tremendously, and the population increased tenfold in a hundred years. It was a city noted for its liberalism – in 1784 Protestants gave generously to help build a Catholic church and, in 1791, three Presbyterian Ulstermen formed the society of **United Irishmen**, a gathering embracing Catholics and Protestants on the basis of common Irish nationality. Belfast was the centre of this movement, and thirty Presbyterian ministers in all were accused of taking part in the 1798 rebellion – six were hanged.

Despite the movement's Belfast origins, the rebellion in the North was in fact an almost complete failure, and the forces of reaction backed by the wealthy landlords quickly and ruthlessly stamped it down. Within two generations most Protestants had abandoned the Nationalist cause, and Belfast as a sectarian town was born. In the **nineteenth century**, Presbyterian ministers like the Reverend Henry Cooke and Hugh (Roaring) Hanna began openly to attack the Catholic Church, and the **sectarian divide** became wider and increasingly violent. In 1835, several people were sabred to death in Sandy Row, and sporadic outbreaks of violence have continued from that day on. Meanwhile, the nineteenth century saw vigorous commercial and industrial expansion. In 1888, Queen Victoria granted Belfast city status; the city fathers' gratitude to her is stamped on buildings throughout the centre. By this time the population had risen to 208,000 and, with the continued improvement in both the linen and shipbuilding industries, the population exceeded even that of Dublin by the end of the century.

The twentieth century

Although **Partition** and the creation of Northern Ireland with Belfast as its capital inevitably boosted the city's status, decline has been fairly constant over recent years. Bombing in World War II destroyed much of the city, and in the past ten years great tracts of West Belfast have been pulled down in a belated attempt to improve living conditions. Outside the centre, this is a very modern-looking place. Nowadays the city is struggling very hard for **revitalization**, and billions of pounds are being poured in from Britain and the European Union, in the hope that economic growth might help to bring about a more hopeful future. The linen industry, which had almost completely disappeared, is undergoing a modest revival in high-fashion clothing, and shipbuilding is also surfacing again after reaching rock bottom.

Arrival, information and transport

Belfast is served by two airports. Most international **flights** and those from London Heathrow arrive at **Belfast International Airport** in Aldergrove, nineteen miles west of the city (airport buses to Europa bus station run Mon–Sat every 30min 6.40am–10.50pm, Sun every hour 7.10am–10.50pm; £4.10; a taxi costs around £20). Other flights arrive at **Belfast City Airport**, three miles northeast of the city (Citybus #21 runs to City Hall in the centre Mon–Sat 6.55am–8pm every 20–30min, Sun hourly from 9.35am; 90p; trains run every half hour to Central Station from Sydenham Halt – a short walk from the airport terminal; a taxi costs around £5).

Ferries arrive at various dockside terminii. The ninety-minute Seacat Stranraer catamaran and summer-only Isle of Man–Belfast service run by Isle of Man Steam Packet Company both use Donegall Quay. A taxi from here to the city centre should cost between £2 and £3, but, if you're unburdened by luggage, the centre is only a fifteen-

BELFAST TELEPHONE CODE

The **current** Belfast code is ☎01232. However, new telephone codes will be introduced throughout Northern Ireland from June 1, 1999 although it will still be possible to use the old codes until April 22, 2000. The new codes will prefix the existing subscriber number regardless of where you are calling from; calls from outside Northern Ireland will require the 028 prefix in addition. The **new code** for Belfast will be ☎ (028) 90 – thus (01232) 147893 will become (028) 90 147893.

minute walk away. Stena high-speed ferry services from Stranraer dock at Ballast Quay – a taxi from here will cost around £4. Norse Irish Ferries arrive from Liverpool even further north on West Bank Road – expect to pay a taxi fare of at least £5. Finally, P&O ferry services from Cairnryan dock at Larne, twenty miles north, connected by Ulsterbus to the Laganside Buscentre and by train with Yorkgate and Central Stations.

All **trains** arrive at **Central Station** on East Bridge Street, a little way east of the centre. From here you can hop on a connecting service to Great Victoria Street Station in the centre, or Botanic or City Hospital rail stations if you're staying in the university area. Alternatively, the **Centrelink** bus runs every fifteen minutes on a circular route from and to Central Station, via Donegall Square and the Europa and Laganside Bus Stations.

Long-distance **buses** arrive either at the **Europa** bus station, in Glengall Street behind the *Europa Hotel* (services to Armagh, Tyrone, Derry, Fermanagh and west Down, as well as for the Republic and for the airports and cross-Channel ferry terminals), or **Laganside Buscentre** in Queen's Square (serves Antrim, east Down and east Derry). Both of these are extremely central and well served by Citybus services.

Information

Tourist information is available from the **tourist information centre**, 59 North St (July–Aug Mon–Fri 9am–6.30pm, Sat 9am–5.15pm, Sun noon–4pm; Sept–June Mon–Sat 9.30am–5.15pm; ☎246609), which has the usual supply of brochures and maps and an accommodation booking service (£1 in Belfast area, £2 elsewhere; also credit card bookings – ring ☎0800/404050). There's also a 24-hour touch-screen outside the office – a lifesaver if you find yourself bedless late at night. In the summer, a supplementary tourist information booth can be found on Donegall Square North (Mon–Wed 9.30am–5pm, Thurs & Fri 9.30am–8pm, Sat 9.30am–4pm). Both airports also have tourist offices – Belfast International (daily 24 hours); Belfast City (Sun–Fri 5.30am–10pm, Sat 5.30am–9pm). **Bord Fáilte**, supplying tourist information for the Republic, is located at 53 Castle St (☎327888). For a guide to entertainment in the city, consult the fortnightly listings freesheet, *That's Entertainment*, available at the tourist office, pubs, clubs and record shops, the *Belfast Telegraph* evening newspaper or the tourist board's own monthly freebie, *Artslink*.

City transport

Although you can easily walk around the centre, distances to some of the outlying attractions are considerable, and a number of the places to stay are also a little way out. Fortunately, the excellent Citybus provides frequent services to almost every conceivable Belfast destination, while the blue and white long-distance Ulsterbuses serve some of the sights on the city's fringes. Almost all local **buses** set off from or pass through Donegall Square, right at the city centre, or the streets immediately around; you can pick up the map which outlines the main services from the tourist office or the Citybus

Crumlin & Belfast Int. Airport △   Larne, Belfast Castle, Cave Hill & Zoo △

BELFAST

Dunmore Park

ARDOYNE

0   1 mile

N

Brookfield Mill

FLAX STREET

WOODVALE ROAD

CRUMLIN ROAD

ANTRIM ROAD

Mater Hospital

Crumlin Road Gaol

CLIFTON STREET

SHANKILL

SPRINGMARTIN

SHANKILL ROAD

DONEGALL ST

Belfast Cathedral

NORTH ST

ROYAL AVE

FALLS

Conway Mill

SPRINGFIELD ROAD

DIVIS ST

Divis Flats

CASTLE ST AVE

HIGH ST

FALLS ROAD

St. Peter's Cathedral

Royal Victoria Hospital

BALLYMURPHY

City Hall

GROSVENER ROAD

Bus Station & International Airport Terminal

WESTLINK

GT. VICTORIA S

B.B.C.

ORMEAU AVE

DUBLIN ROAD

WHITEROCK ROAD

FALLS ROAD

DONEGALL   ROAD

Arts Theatre

Gallery

Botanic Rail Station

City Cemetery

Falls Park

TURF LODGE

Queen's Film Theatre

Queen's University

Botanic Gardens

GLEN ROAD

MOTORWAY M1

Milltown Cemetery

UNIVERSITY ROAD

STRANMILLS ROAD

Ulster Museum

STRANMILLS EMBANKMENT

see inset for accommodation

ANDERSONSTOWN

ANDERSONSTOWN ROAD

LISBURN ROAD

ADELAIDE PARK

MALONE ROAD

Lyric Theatre

King's Bridge

Governor's Bridge

Casement Park

STRANMILLS ROAD

Belfast Boat Club

△ Lisburn

△ Derry & Dublin

LISBURN

King's Hall

FINAGHY

MALONE

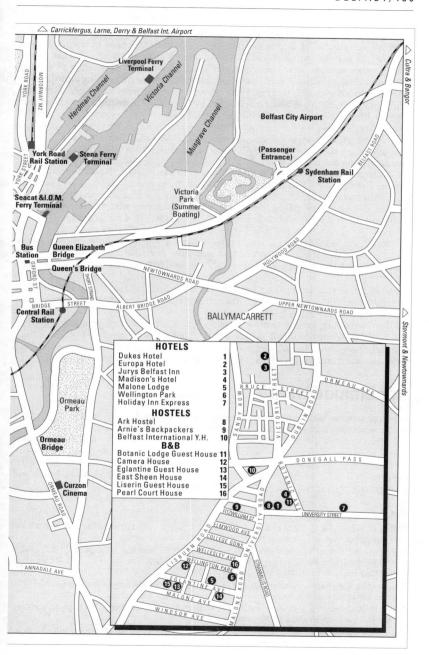

△ Carrickfergus, Larne, Derry & Belfast Int. Airport

▷ Cultra & Bangor

Herdman Channel

Victoria Channel

Liverpool Ferry Terminal

MOTORWAY M2

YORK ROAD

Musgrave Channel

Belfast City Airport

York Road Rail Station

Stena Ferry Terminal

(Passenger Entrance)

Sydenham Rail Station

Seacat &I.O.M. Ferry Terminal

YORK STREET

Victoria Park (Summer Boating)

HOLYWOOD ROAD

BELFAST ROAD

▷ Stormont & Newtownards

Bus Station

Queen Elizabeth Bridge

OXFORD ST

Queen's Bridge

SHORT STRAND

NEWTOWNARDS ROAD

UPPER NEWTOWNARDS ROAD

BRIDGE STREET

Central Rail Station

ALBERT BRIDGE ROAD

BALLYMACARRETT

Ormeau Park

Ormeau Bridge

ORMEAU ROAD

Curzon Cinema

HOTELS

Dukes Hotel	1
Europa Hotel	2
Jurys Belfast Inn	3
Madison's Hotel	4
Malone Lodge	5
Wellington Park	6
Holiday Inn Express	7

HOSTELS

Ark Hostel	8
Arnie's Backpackers	9
Belfast International Y.H.	10

B&B

Botanic Lodge Guest House	11
Camera House	12
Eglantine Guest House	13
East Sheen House	14
Liserin Guest House	15
Pearl Court House	16

SANDY ROW

BRUCE STREET

VICTORIA STREET

ORMEAU AVE

DUBLIN ROAD

DONEGALL PASS

BOTANIC AVE

FITZWILLIAM ST

UNIVERSITY STREET

LISBURN ROAD

ELMWOOD AVE

COLLEGE GDNS

WELLESLEY AVE

WELLINGTON PARK

SHAFTESBURY ROAD

UNIVERSITY ROAD

ANNADALE AVE

EGLANTINE AVE

MALONE AVE

MALONE ROAD

WINDSOR AVE

kiosk in Donegall Square West (Mon–Fri 8am–5.30pm; bus information on ☎246485). Fares are determined by a zone system; the city centre is covered by the Inner Zone and fares for journeys within it cost 50p; most other journeys cost 90p. You can pay on board – make sure you have enough small change – but if you're intending to visit any of the suburban attractions, you'll save time and a little money if you buy a **multi-journey** ticket in advance (£2.70 for four journeys, from newsagents and other shops city-wide). You push the ticket into a machine (or get the driver to do it) to cancel one journey each time you travel – two people can use the same ticket as long as it is cancelled twice. Ulsterbus also serves the routes from the city centre to the outer suburbs, and Citystoppers provides an additional service on the Falls and Lisburn roads (#523–538); late-night buses run from Shaftesbury Square along five routes on Friday and Saturday (midnight, 1am & 2am; £2.50).

Citybus also runs a couple of **guided tours** of Belfast which can save time and shoe leather. The City Tour (Weds and Sat; 1pm) lasts three and a half hours and includes the architectural highlights, while more recent history, including visits to both West and East Belfast, is covered by the two-and-a-half-hour Living History Tour (Thurs and Sun; 1pm). Both leave from Castle Place and cost £8 (☎458484 for details).

Taxis, based at the main rank in Donegall Square East and other points throughout the city, charge a minimum £2, which rapidly starts to increase on the meter if you're going any distance. Or you can phone a **minicab** (try Blue Star Cabs ☎243118 or 230022), a good idea late at night as passing taxis tend to be en route to passenger pick-ups. There are also black taxis based at the revitalized Smithfield area of Castle Street. Normally, these cabs travel along set routes into West Belfast, picking up and dropping passengers anywhere along the way, while similar cabs servicing Protestant areas leave from North Street, slightly further north.

If you're **driving**, you need to be careful about where you park your car: there are still a few city-centre **control zones** (clearly marked with black-and-yellow signs), although these are being phased out throughout the North. You'll find plenty of car parks, however, and pay-and-display parking operates in many of the streets.

Accommodation

Although tourism has waned since the years following the 1994 cease-fire, the number of places offering accommodation has increased, especially at the top end of the range, reflecting continued optimism in the city's future. However, there's still a relative dearth of budget places and it's worth ringing ahead at peak times.

Much of the city's accommodation is concentrated south of the centre in the university area on Botanic Avenue, Eglantine Avenue and the Malone Road. Many hotels and guesthouses offer significant reductions for weekend breaks.

Hotels

Dukes Hotel, 65 University St (☎236666, fax 237177). Smart, modern redevelopment with a small gym and sauna, popular bars and a restaurant serving Glenarm salmon. ⑦.

Europa Hotel, Great Victoria St (☎327000, fax 327800). Often bombed in the past, this city centre hotel near the Opera House has now been grandly refurbished. The bar, with its huge windows overlooking the city's main drag, is a poseur's paradise. ⑨.

Holiday Inn Express, 106 University St (☎311909, fax 311910). The newest hotel in Belfast – with Internet and email facilities. ④.

Jurys Belfast Inn, Fisherwick Place, Great Victoria St (☎533500, fax 533511). A gargantuan, newly-developed branch of the Dublin chain. ⑥.

Madison's Hotel, 59–63 Botanic Ave (☎330040, fax 328007). A plush, new, economically-priced hotel with large rooms and a popular bar/nightclub. ④.

Malone Lodge Hotel, 60 Eglantine Ave (☎382409, fax 382706). Friendly hotel near Queen's, with off-street parking and a notable restaurant. ⑦.

Wellington Park Hotel, 21 Malone Rd (☎381111, fax 665410). Recently redeveloped business travellers' hotel in the university area, with a bar probably best known as a cruising ground for singles. ⑧.

Bed and breakfast

Botanic Lodge, 87 Botanic Ave (☎327682). Long-standing, family-run B&B. ③.

Camera Guest House, 44 Wellington Park (☎660026). Very luxurious and elegantly decorated townhouse. ⑤.

Eglantine Guest House, 21 Eglantine Ave (☎667585). Small, family-run establishment. ③.

East Sheen, 81 Eglantine Ave (☎667149). A popular choice. ③.

Liserin Guest House, 17 Eglantine Ave (☎660769). Well-equipped, homely B&B. ③.

Pearl Court House, 11 Malone Rd (☎666145). Large house with some family and triple rooms. ④.

Roseleigh Guest House, 19 Rosetta Park (☎644414). Deluxe accommodation in a quiet area at the bottom of the Ormeau Road. ④.

Hostels and student accommodation

The Ark, 18 University St (IHH; ☎329626). Latest addition to the budget scene; clean, well-equipped and welcoming, with 24 beds and three private rooms.

Arnie's Backpackers, 63 Fitzwilliam St (IHH/IHO; ☎242867). Independent, friendly hostel; 22 beds in five-dorm rooms; laundry and cooking facilities.

Belfast International Youth Hostel, 22–32 Donegall Rd (☎315435). Recently built 124-bed hostel (with some double rooms) near the Protestant Sandy Row enclave; all-year-round 24-hour staffing; no self-catering, but has restaurant. Booking ahead is advisable. From £10.

YWCA, Queen Mary's Hall, 70 Fitzwilliam St (☎240439). Old-fashioned hostel accommodating both sexes, but usually fully booked by students during term time; sixteen rooms, including some doubles; open all year except Christmas and Easter. £15.

The City

The physical core of Belfast is undoubtedly **Donegall Square**: in the centre stands the City Hall, and from the sides of the square, buses and taxis depart for every part of the city. The main shopping area lies a stone's throw north and the main areas for entertainment and accommodation are immediately south. Most of the grand old Victorian buildings which characterize the city are in the north and east, towards the river. Further out, **North Belfast** boasts Cave Hill, with its castle and zoo, while **South Belfast** is home to the "Golden Mile", leading down to the university, Botanic Gardens and Ulster Museum. The River Lagan flows from Belfast Lough along the eastern side of the city centre and offers riverside walks. The riverside is also the focus for the most radical development in the last few years, the Laganside. Further **east**, across the river beyond the great cranes of Harland & Wolff, lies suburbia and very little of interest apart from Stormont Castle, the former Northern Irish parliament and home to the new Assembly. Working-class **West Belfast**, by contrast, seems almost a separate city in its own right, divided from the rest by the speeding traffic of the Westlink motorway.

The city centre

Belfast's centre is fairly compact and easy to wander around. The heart of the old city can be found in the narrow atmospheric lanes of the former commercial district, the Entries, about five minutes' walk northeast of Donegall Square. On a grander scale,

many of Belfast's most handsome buildings, evidence of the city's transformation during the industrial revolution, are concentrated further north and east, between St Anne's Cathedral and the River Lagan. Right by the river you'll find the Lagan Weir and a little further south, the huge new Laganside development, currently focused on the Waterfront Hall.

Donegall Square

City Hall dominates Donegall Square and the entire centre of Belfast. Completed in 1906, it's a smug-looking building of bright white Portland stone, quadrangular and squat, and with its turrets, saucer domes, scrolls and pinnacle pots, is representative of all the styles absorbed by the British Empire. In front of the building stands the imposing statue of Queen Victoria, the apotheosis of imperialism, her maternal gaze unerringly cast across the rooftops towards the Protestant Shankill area. At her feet, sculpted in bronze, stand proud figures representing the City Fathers' world-view: a young scholar, his mother with spinning spool, and father with mallet and boat – learning, linen and liners, the alliterative bedrock of Belfast's heritage.

The City Hall offers the only opportunity to be shown around one of Belfast's many Neoclassical buildings; guided **tours** last 45 minutes (July–Sept Mon–Fri 10.30am, 11.30am & 2.30pm, Sat 2.30pm; Oct–June Mon–Tues & Thurs–Sat 2.30pm, Wed 11.30am; free) and access is through a security entrance at the rear, opposite Linenhall Street. Inside, the **main dome**, with its unreachable whispering gallery, arches 173ft above you. Modelled on St Paul's Cathedral in London, the dome is adorned around its rim with zodiac signs, both painted and in stained glass windows. The marbled **entrance hall** itself is palatial, with staircase pillars, colonnades and bronze and marble statues. Two of the statues portray Frederick Robert Chichester, Earl of Belfast (1827–53): the first, upright and stern, stands on the principal landing, while the other, Frederick embraced by his mother on his deathbed, has been hauled out of the rain into the Octagon entrance porch. Also on the principal landing is a **mural**, executed in 1951 by John Luke and celebrating Belfast's now mostly defunct traditional industries – ropemaking, shipbuilding, weaving and spinning. Oddly though, the central position in the picture is occupied by the Town Crier, a cryptic reference perhaps to Belfast having the oldest continuously published newspaper in the world – *The Newsletter*, founded in 1737. The tour also takes in the **robing room**, where the trick is to ask to try on one of the civic cloaks for a snapshot. The building's highlight is the oak-decorated **council chamber** with its hand-carved wainscotting and councillors' pews as well as a visitors' gallery (open only on the first of the month). When councillors meet, it's often stormy, but, in their absence, it's a very urbane scene with a backdrop of portraits of British royalty and aristocracy. The seating arrangement puts the majority Unionists on the far side, with the rest of the parties on the near side, while the ever-present press sit in between as a kind of firebreak.

At the northwest corner of Donegall Square stands Belfast's oldest library, the **Linenhall Library** (Mon–Wed & Fri 9.30am–5.30pm, Thurs 9.30am–8.30pm, Sat 9.30am–4pm), established in 1788. The Irish literature collection occupies much of the first floor, and a grand curving staircase sweeps upwards to the second where language and reference books are shelved, as well as what is known as the "Political Collection", a unique accumulation of over 80,000 publications dealing with every aspect of Northern Irish political life since 1966 – a range of literature that encompasses every election poster printed since then, as well as documents ranging from party political ephemera, doctoral theses sent in from all over the world, to prison letters smuggled out of Long Kesh. This radical approach is not a new departure for the Linenhall: one of the institution's librarians was Thomas Russell, executed in Downpatrick in 1803 for inciting rebellion in sympathy with Robert Emmett's 1798 uprising down south. The library also contains probably the best collection of early

Belfast printed books in the country and has a small selection on display, including *Paddy's Resource*, from 1796, an early collection of Irish patriotic songs.

The Linenhall is an independent institution and visitors are free to examine its collection (tours daily except Sat): there is a computerized catalogue on the first floor, use of which is free, though a donation is welcome. The library also boasts excellent facilities for tracing family trees, stocks all the daily newspapers and has a good tearoom.

Between the back of the City Hall and the BBC, on Alfred Street, look out for the turrets of the strange and wonderful Catholic **St Malachy's Church** (1844), the finest Victorian building in Belfast. The interior resembles nothing so much as an inverted wedding cake, and the fan-vaulted ceiling is modelled on that of Henry VII's chapel in Westminster Abbey. Other elaborate features are the canopied pulpit and carved marble altar both dating from a 1926 restoration.

The commercial district

The streets northwards from Donegall Square lead you into downtown Belfast. The main shopping street, **Donegall Place**, continues into **Royal Avenue** and houses familiar chain-store names. Castle Place, off Donegall Place, was once the hub of Victorian Belfast, and the grand old department stores here, in creams, pinks and browns, have only recently been transformed into a plethora of voguish shops, though, happily, only the ground floors have been converted, leaving the lofty grandeur of the stories above undisturbed. New structures, too, have risen swiftly, but they at least tend to reflect the rhythm and sheer bulk of their nineteenth-century forebears. Much of this zone is pedestrianized (though buses go through), and nearly every conceivable shopping need can be supplied in this relatively small area.

The pedestrianized **Cornmarket**, marked by a cap-hooded red bandstand, is where the various cults gather on Saturdays: skinheads, punks, mods and drunks, though most prevalent are the religious ranters. This spot – or near enough to it – is where Henry Joy McCracken was hanged, after leading the Antrim rebels in the ill-fated (and in the North almost farcically unsuccessful) 1798 rebellion.

Nearby, along Ann Street, and off down any left or right turning, you're among the narrow alleyways known as the **Entries**. You'll stumble across some great old saloon **bars** down here, like *The Morning Star* in Pottinger's Entry, with its large frosted windows and Parisian café-like counter; *The Globe* in Joy's Entry; and *White's Tavern* in Winecellar Entry (off High Street), the oldest pub in the city. **Crown Entry** was where the "Society of United Irishmen" was born; its was led by the Protestant triumvirate of Wolfe Tone, McCracken and Samuel Nielson. Nielson also printed his own newspaper in this area, the *Northern Star*. Heavily influenced by the French revolutionary ideals of liberty, equality and fraternity, the newspaper's inflammatory material led to him being hounded out of town.

Across the High Street, to the north, a similar set of Entries used to run through to Waring Street, but were destroyed by bombing in World War II. Still, this end of the **High Street**, with the River Farset running underground, is the oldest part of the city, its atmosphere in places redolent of the eighteenth century. On Waring Street itself stands the **War Memorial Building**, containing a small exhibition (Mon–Fri 10am–4.30pm; free) commemorating the role of Northern Ireland in World War II. At the rear is the **Royal Ulster Rifles Museum** (Mon–Fri 10am–12.30pm & 2–4pm), with the usual array of insignia, uniforms and weaponry, and Billy, a rather despondent-looking regimental dog, stuffed in 1901. At the docks end of the High Street stands the **Prince Albert Memorial Clock Tower**, built in 1867–69 and wilting slightly off the perpendicular as a result of its construction upon gradually sinking wooden piles. It's a strange memorial, especially as Prince Albert never had anything to do with Belfast, but it's a handy landmark.

The Custom House and the Lagan Lookout

North of the Albert Memorial you'll come across a series of grand edifices inspired by the same civic vanity as that behind the design of the City Hall. The restored **Custom House**, on Donegall Quay, is a Corinthian-style, E-shaped edifice designed between 1854 and 1857 by Charles Lanyon who was responsible for several of the city's finest buildings. Unfortunately, it's not open to the public, leaving you unable to verify rumours of fantastic art masterpieces stored in its basements – though it is known that Anthony Trollope, the nineteenth-century novelist (and not-so-well-known inventor of the pillar box), once worked here as a surveyor's clerk.

Just beyond the Custom House on Donegall Quay is the ambitious **Laganside** development project. The most obvious changes to the city's skyline can be seen further south along Oxford Street, the site of a new concert venue, the two-thousand-seater **Waterfront Hall**, a housing development, and a *Hilton* hotel. Future plans include the construction of the gargantuan Odyssey leisure complex. The first component of the project to be completed was the Lagan Weir, designed to protect the city against flooding. Millions of pounds have been pumped into dredging the river to maintain water levels and revive the much depleted fish population – successfully it seems: there was salmon fishing on the weir's inauguration day.

You can find out more about the weir project at the **Lagan Lookout** (April–Sept Mon–Fri 11am–5pm, Sat noon–5pm, Sun 2–5pm; Oct–March Tues–Fri 11am–3.30pm, Sat 1–4.30pm, Sun 2–4.30pm; £1.50), a raised circular visitor centre on the riverfront. It also explores the river's crucial role in the successful development of the city as a centre for industries as diverse as linen, tobacco, ropemaking and shipbuilding – a glance across the Lagan to the Harland & Wolff shipyard confirms that the last-named still survives. Windows all round the centre match Belfast landmarks to explanations of their significance, interwoven with fascinating potted histories of local characters. If the sea air's twitching your nostrils, head further north towards the Seacat terminal where you'll find the restored **Harbour Office** and nearby **Sinclair Seamen's Church** (Sun services 11.30am & 7pm; visiting Wed 2–4.30pm) on Corporation Square. The latter is yet another Lanyon design, but it's the contents that are most intriguing. Sailors must have felt truly at home among the cornucopia of maritime equipment – an old-fashioned wooden wheel, the bell from *HMS Hood*, assorted navigation lights and a ship's prow for a pulpit.

To St Anne's Cathedral

Walking back from Donegall Quay towards the cathedral past the Albert Clock and up Victoria Street, you'll soon hit Waring Street and another of Charles Lanyon's designs, the **Belfast Banking Company** building of 1845, now the Northern Bank. Originally containing eighteenth-century Assembly Rooms, the building was transformed by Lanyon into a palazzo-style remodelling of Barry's Reform Club in London. On the same street, you'll also come across the **Ulster Bank** (1860), an indulgent Italianate building of rich yellow sandstone, fronted by a spate of fluted pillars and, up on the parapet, decorated Grecian urns flanking an allegorical representation of war maidens. The building is surrounded by intricate wrought-iron railings and a few reassembled stubby, but quaint, Victorian street lamps.

Off to the right, by the junction of Donegall and Talbot Streets, sits the most monolithic of all these grand buildings, the **Protestant Cathedral of St Anne**, a neo-Romanesque basilica started in 1899. Entrance is via the huge west door and immediately to the right is an intricately designed representation of the Creation on the baptistry ceiling, consisting of 150,000 tiny pieces of glass. Most significant, however, is its only tomb marked by a simple slab on the floor of the nave and containing the body of **Lord Edward Henry Carson** (1854–1935). His is a name that Ulster has never forgotten: the bodily symbol of Partition, he's seen either as the hero who saved Ulster or the villain who sabotaged the country's independence. A Dubliner of Scots– Presbyterian background, Carson took the decision in 1910 to accept the leadership of the opposition to Home Rule, which in effect inextricably allied him to the Ulster Unionist resistance movement, an association which is about the only thing for which he is remembered. Yet his personality and integrity went far deeper than this. He abhorred religious intolerance, and behind the exterior of a zealous crusader was a man who sincerely believed that Ireland couldn't prosper without Britain and only wished that a federalist answer could have involved a united Ireland. Nonetheless, this was the same man who, as a brilliant orator at the bar, and in the role he loved the most, brought about the humiliating destruction of Oscar Wilde at his trial in 1895.

Clifton House

As it continues north, Donegall Street becomes Clifton Street, which takes its name from **Clifton House** (built 1771–74). Better known as the "Poor House", or the "Charitable Institute for the Aged and Infirm", it's in handsome Georgian style, of pedimented brick with an octagonal-based stone spire at its rear and symmetrically projecting wings to its sides. This is one of the simpler but more effective buildings that Belfast has to offer, yet was designed by an amateur architect and local paper merchant, Robert Joy, uncle of the hapless Henry Joy McCracken. The Institute was built at a time of much poverty and unrest, brought about by the Donegalls' eviction of tenants when their leases started running out – the very same Donegalls whose name is tagged to so many of Belfast's streets. A little further along is the **Clifton Street Graveyard** which contains the graves of Robert Joy and Mary Anne McCracken, Henry Joy's sister, along with several United Irishmen, including Dr William Drennan, reputed to have been the originator of the phrase "Emerald Isle".

East Belfast

The Lagan Lookout (see overleaf) is a good position from which to view the world's second and third largest cranes, *Goliath* and *Samson*, across the river in **East Belfast**'s Harland & Wolff shipyard. This is the city's proudest international asset: the ill-fated *Titanic* was built here, and the **shipyard** is nowadays said to possess the largest dry dock in the world – over 600 yards long and 100 yards wide. Unfortunately, the area is very security-conscious, as its workforce has always been predominantly Protestant, and access is impossible without making a formal application.

In fact, there's virtually no reason to cross the river into **East Belfast** at all. **Van Morrison** fans might get a thrill from seeking out his birthplace at 125 Hyndford St and the many streets that feature in his songs (Cyprus Avenue, Castlereagh Road) and you might like to stroll around the area's two pleasant **parks**.

Four miles east of the city, off the Newtownards Road, is **Stormont** (#16 or #17 bus from Donegall Square), the home of the Northern Ireland Parliament until the introduction of direct rule in 1972, and now housing the new Assembly, elected in June 1998. You can't visit the house itself, which is occupied by civil servants, but it's an impressive sight, a great white neoclassical mansion crowning a rise in the middle of a park at the end of a magnificent long, straight drive. You can wander freely in the **grounds**, a popular place for a walk. Also here, though obviously not open to the public, is **Stormont Castle**, the office of the Northern Ireland Secretary.

South Belfast

The university area occupies part of the stretch of **South Belfast** known as "The Golden Mile", starting at the Opera House on Great Victoria Street and continuing past the university, up into the Lisburn, Malone and Stranmillis roads. You're likely to spend much of your time here, since it's littered with eating places, pubs and bars, B&Bs and guesthouses. Dozens of restaurants have sprung up here in the last few years, the gourmet explosion said to have been triggered by the refurbishment of the grandiose, turn-of-the-century **Grand Opera House** in 1980.

The Golden Mile

Among the welter of attractions on the Golden Mile is one of the greatest of Victorian **gin palaces**, the *Crown Liquor Saloon*, now a National Trust property but still open for drinking. The saloon has a glittering tiled exterior – amber, carmine, rouge, yellow, green, blue and smoke-grey – resembling a spa baths more than a serious drinking institution. The rich, High Victorian stucco work continues inside, too: the scrolled ceiling, patterned floor and the golden-yellow and rosy-red hues led John Betjeman to describe it as his "many coloured cavern". Once armed with drinks, and if it's not too crowded, grab a snug and shut the door. It's like sitting in a railway carriage compartment, with snatches of conversation floating over from the neighbouring snugs. There's no let-up in decoration here either, what with the painted mirrors, the oak panelling sporting flourishes of frieze-work (like the heraldic beasts guarding each snug entry) and the mounted gun-metal plates provided for striking matches. The push-button bell activates an indicator on a board above the bar, though it's just as much of an experience to order at the bar from the white-aproned and black-bow-tied staff – the bar counter is a gorgeous S-curve of tile work, with exotically carved timber dividing screens.

The **Golden Mile** itself buzzes with activity in the evening, even on a weekday, as long as it's in term time. As a rule, the cheaper restaurants are at the city end of Great Victoria Street, with the more expensive ones up the Stranmillis Road or in and around the skirts of the BBC in Bedford Street. There's a plethora of accommodation, too, in amongst the grid pattern of the broad, tree-lined streets surrounding the university campus, much of it in the old three-storey Victorian houses.

Sandy Row

Before heading straight into the university quarter, sidestep off Great Victoria Street into **Sandy Row**, which runs parallel. A strong working-class Protestant quarter with the tribal pavement painting to prove it, it's one of the most glaring examples of Belfast's divided worlds, wildly different from the Golden Mile's cosmopolitan sophistication, yet only yards away. In Blythe Street and Donegall Road, off to the west, are some of the murals which characterize these sectarian areas (see "Belfast Murals", p.500). Sandy Row used to be the main road south, and although hard to credit today, it was once a picturesque stretch of whitewashed cottages.

The university area

Back on the Golden Mile, just past the southern end of Sandy Row, stand three churches (Moravian, Crescent and Methodist), whose distinctive steeples frame the entrance into the **university quarter**. It's a highly characteristic area; many of the terraces leading up to the university buildings represent the final flowering of Georgian architecture in Belfast. The **Upper Crescent** is a magnificent curved neoclassical terrace, built around 1845 but sadly neglected since, and now used mainly for office space. The **Lower Crescent**, perversely, is straight.

Queen's University, however, is the architectural centrepiece, flanked by the most satisfying example of a Georgian terrace in Belfast, University Square, where the red brickwork mostly remains intact, with the exception of a few bay windows added by Victorians. The terrace now houses various faculty buildings. The Italianate **Union Theological College**, nearby on College Park, was temporarily the site of the Northern Ireland Parliament until Stormont was built in 1932. Both this and

University College itself are Lanyon designs, the latter built in 1849 as a mock-Tudor remodelling of Magdalen College, Oxford. Across the road from here is the Students' Union, a white 1960s design. A little further south down University Road, the university **bookshop** is especially good for Irish history and politics and, oddly enough, for its collection of Beat poetry.

Botanic Gardens and Ulster Museum

Just below the university are the popular **Botanic Gardens**, first opened in 1827, and well cushioned from the noise of surrounding traffic. Within the gardens is the **Palm House** (April–Sept Mon–Fri 10am–noon & 1–5pm, Sat & Sun 2–5pm; Oct–March closes 4pm; free), a hothouse predating the famous one at Kew Gardens in London, but very similar in style, with a white-painted framework of curvilinear ironwork and glass. It was the first of its kind in the world, another success for Lanyon who worked in tandem on this project with the Dublin ironfounder Richard Turner. The nearby **Tropical Ravine** (same hours) is a classic example of Victorian light entertainment – a hundred-year-old sunken glen chock-full of "vegetable wonders" extracted from far-flung jungles and replanted for the delight of the visiting Belfast public.

Also in the Botanic Gardens you'll find the **Ulster Museum** (Mon–Fri 10am–5pm, Sat 1–5pm, Sun 2–5pm; free but admission charged to special exhibitions; buses #69, #70 & #71), resited here in 1929 and expanded in 1972 with a concrete extension that subtly matches the original Portland stone. You'll need a fair bit of stamina to get round the museum, since it's a monster of a collection covering over 2000 square feet. Displays run from a dinosaur show through reproductions of early Irish Christian jewellery to the history of the post office in Ireland, water wheels and steam engines, local archeological finds, Irish wildlife, rocks, fossils and minerals. The latest gallery houses the fascinating **Early Ireland** exhibition, tracing the development of the prehistoric population. Among the many explanatory displays you'll find the earliest remains yet discovered (eel bones and burnt waterlily seeds), some remarkable gold lunulae and a couple of polished stone axes dug up on nearby Malone Road. Interesting though this is, the museum's undoubted showpiece is the **Girona exhibition**, treasures from the Spanish Armada ships which foundered off the Giant's Causeway in 1588, salvaged by divers in the 1960s.

The various **art collections** on the top floor are excellent for modern work by Barbara Hepworth and Francis Bacon and, best of all, the range of Irish artists represented – Louis le Brocquy, Paul Henry, Belfast's own most acclaimed painter, Sir John Lavery, and contemporary sculptors like Jill Crowley and Christopher Keeney.

Further south: the river and Giant's Ring

Beyond the university area lie the glades of middle-class suburbia – an area that is singularly uninteresting. However, a ten- to fifteen-minute stroll south down Stranmillis Road (*struthán milis*, "sweet stream"), turning left into Lockview Road, will take you back to the river and to the start of the **Lagan Towpath**, where the *Cutter's Wharf* draws thirsty crowds for Sunday lunch and jazz. From here follow the signs to the Lagan Meadows. The newly tarmacked towpath can be tramped for about eight miles south to Lisburn, passing old locks and lock-houses, rapids, woodland and marshes. The waterway opened in the late 1790s, ready to carry the newly discovered coal from Lough Neagh, but its utility declined with the advent of the railway in 1839. Today, it's been harnessed as part of the Ulster Way, for rambling and canoeing enthusiasts. Travelling further south under the ring road, you'll pass by **Malone House** (Mon–Sat 10am–4.30pm; free). It's well worth climbing up the hill for the views of the surrounding area and to see the house itself, an almost pristine white bow-fronted late-Georgian mansion, built for William Wallace Legge, a prominent local merchant. The house was rebuilt by Belfast Council following a devastating fire in 1976 and is now mainly used as a conference centre, though you can visit the Higgin Gallery which hosts regular art exhibitions and there's a fine restaurant here too. A little further along the towpath, you'll find the internationally renowned **Mary Peters Track**, part of the Malone Playing Fields, which is just off the Upper Malone Road. Set in what amounts to a natural amphitheatre, with the Castlereagh Hills in the distance, the track, established by Olympic gold medallist Mary Peters, is on the European Grand Prix Athletics Circuit.

Alternatively, if you leave the towpath at Shaw's Bridge, the ring road crossing, it's a mile-long signposted walk along country lanes to the **Giant's Ring**. This colossal, 200 yard-wide earthwork is thought to be a burial ground or meeting place. You wouldn't be far wrong in thinking that its inwardly sloping wall would make an excellent speed-track circuit, for in the eighteenth century it was used for horse racing – six circuits making a two-mile race, with the punters jostling for position on the rampart's top. Most captivating of all is the huge dolmen at the central hub of this cartwheel structure. As a single megalithic remain, it is immediately more impressive than even the great structures of the Irish High Kings at Tara, though here there's little information concerning its origins and usage. The ground chosen for the site, high above the surrounding lowlands (probably once marshy lake), is impressive; there's a powerful feeling that the great dramas and decision-making of the ancient northeast must have been played out here. If you want to do the walk in just one direction, Ulsterbus #22 passes below the site three times a day.

North Belfast

North Belfast's attractions amount to no more than a castle and the city's zoo, both out on the Antrim Road and conveniently next door to one another on the slopes of Cave Hill. In truth, though, it's **Cave Hill** itself that should be your real target. Several paths lead up from the castle estate to the hill's summit – a rocky outcrop known as "Napoleon's Nose" – which affords an unsurpassable strategic overview of the whole city and lough. From here you can't help but appreciate the accuracy of the poet Craig Raine's aerial description of the city in his *Flying to Belfast*: like "a radio set with its back ripped off". Cave Hill was once awash with Iron Age forts, for there was flint (for weapon-making) in the chalk under the basalt hill-coverings. In 1795, Wolfe Tone, Henry Joy McCracken and other leaders of the United Irishmen stood on the top of Cave Hill and pledged "never to desist in our efforts until we have subverted the authority of England over our country and asserted our Independence".

Belfast Castle and its wooded estate are open to the public (all year Mon–Sat 9am–10.30pm; Sun 9am–6pm). The Castle was restored and refurbished in 1990 but, sadly, is virtually empty of Victorian period accoutrements, though the cellars have been redesigned in an attempt to re-create a typical Victorian Belfast narrow street and contain a bar and restaurant. It stands on the former deer park of the Third Marquis of Donegall, whose wish it was for the sandstone castle to be built here to the designs of Lanyon and his associates, in 1870. Consequently, the exterior is in the familiar Scottish Baronial style, inspired in part by the reconstruction of Balmoral Castle in Aberdeenshire in 1853: six-storey tower, a series of crow-stepped gables and conically peak-capped turrets. The most striking feature of all, however, is the serpentine Italianate stairway that leads down from the principal reception room to the garden terrace below. Upstairs a modest **visitor centre** (daily 9am–6pm; free) is best visited for a look through its remote-control camera on the roof.

Belfast Zoo

Adjoining Belfast Castle is the Bellevue Estate, the old pleasure gardens laid out by the Belfast Street Tramway Company, but functioning since 1934 as **Belfast Zoo** (April–Sept daily 10am–5pm; Oct–March 10am–3.30pm, Fri closed 2.30pm; £4.90;

buses #8, #9, #10, #45–51). After a fifteen-year renovation programme and an investment of £10 million the zoo is looking less like an animal prison. Set in well-landscaped parkland stretching up towards Cave Hill, the zoo is an island of spider monkeys, Malayan tapirs, penguins and sea lions, and a free flight aviary, where rare species have room to breed.

West Belfast

Like many other cities, Belfast's population expanded dramatically during the nineteenth century as people flocked from the countryside to work in the booming new flax and linen industries. Many of these migrants were crammed into jerry-built housing in the grids of streets which still today define **West Belfast**. Conditions were deplorable and did nothing to ease tensions between Catholic and Protestant residents. There were numerous sectarian riots – the worst was in 1886, during the reading of the Home Rule Bill, when 32 people died and over 370 were injured – leading to the almost inevitable creation of two separate neighbourhoods. In 1968 and 1969, this division was pushed to its limit when sectarian mobs and gunmen evicted over eight thousand families from their homes in the city, mainly in Catholic West Belfast. The RUC called for government assistance and British troops arrived on the streets on August 15, 1969 and a month later the makeshift barrier dividing the Catholic Falls from the Protestant

---

BELFAST MURALS

As much of a marker of an area's allegiances as painted kerbstones or fluttering flags, the **murals** of Northern Ireland are among some of the most startling sights in the country. This ephemeral art form characterizes the struggles of the last few decades. New murals are painted over old ones or the houses which they adorn are demolished. Consequently, some of the slogans and murals mentioned here may have vanished by the time of your visit.

For most of this century, mural-painting in Northern Ireland has been a predominantly **Loyalist** activity. The first mural appeared in East Belfast in 1908 and, like many of its successors, celebrated King Billy's victory at the Battle of the Boyne. Loyalist murals have tended to use imagery symbolic of power, such as the clenched scarlet fist, known as the Red Hand of Ulster (Newtownards Road and elsewhere), or flags, shields and other heraldic icons. However, the Loyalist response to the Troubles translated into what is now the most common form of painting, the militaristic mural. If King Billy appears at all, it is often with a guard of balaclava-clad, weapon-toting paramilitaries, accompanied by a threatening slogan. Inspired by the desire for "no surrender" and preservation of the status quo, Loyalist mural painting is certainly less dynamic and diverse than its Republican counterpart. A typical example, on the Shankill Road, is of two masked gunman kneeling in front of the furled flags of England and Scotland, with a bronze shield between them, the Red Hand at its centre, surrounded by the words "UVF for God and Ulster". Despite the Loyalist cease-fire there has been no diminution in the production of militaristic images, although in recent years cartoons have been added to the repertoire. A classic example is on Martin Street, off Templemore Avenue in East Belfast – a huge British bulldog in the uniform of a marching band carries a pair of Unionist flags. Another famous example, now removed, had an aggressive Spike the dog grabbing Jerry the cat by the scruff of his Celtic football shirt.

The greatest concentration of Loyalist murals is to be found on and around the Shankill Road, especially the Shankill Estate, to the right, and Percy Place, off Dover Street, to the left; nearby Crumlin Road has its fair share too. Other areas are Sandy Row and Donegall Pass in South Belfast, and Newtownards Road, Martin Street and Severn Street in East Belfast.

Shankill had become a full-scale reinforced "peace line". British intervention may have averted a civil war, but failed to prevent an escalation in sectarian conflict. Indeed, the army soon came to be viewed as an occupying force and a legitimate target for a reviving IRA. In return, Loyalist paramilitaries sought to wreak revenge for Republican violence, often through indiscriminate acts of aggression. Over the next 25 years, West Belfast remained the major battleground of the Troubles.

Today, however, West Belfast is an undoubtedly safe area for the stranger to stroll around. There's little of architectural note among the principally residential streets and most of the "sights" are associated with the area's troubled past. Much of the old terraced housing has been replaced in recent years by rows of modern Housing Executive homes, but it's impossible to miss examples of the partisan **mural paintings** which decorate walls and gable ends in both Catholic and Protestant areas (see box below).

The busy **Westlink motorway** separates West Belfast from the rest of the city. At the height of the Troubles, the various overhead bridges and roundabouts were used by the police and army as virtual border crossings to control access to and from the area.

The Falls

Two routes lead into the heart of the **Falls** area: one along Grosvenor Road, the other through Divis Street. The latter is the more infamous and is also the route that carries the main injection of black taxi-cab traffic into the area (see "City transport", p.487).

Republican murals were at first limited to simple sloganeering or demarcation of territory – the most well-known example is the long-standing "you are now entering free Derry" in the Bogside (see p.539). As with much else in Republican politics, however, the 1981 hunger strikes had a significant influence. Murals in support of the ten hunger strikers abounded and the (usually smiling) face of Bobby Sands remains an enduring image. He's there on the Falls Road, sporting a v-necked sweater, accompanied by the quotation "Everyone Republican or otherwise has his/her own part to play". Murals soon became a fundamental part of the Republican propaganda campaign and an expression of the community's current cultural and political concerns, though militaristic images have never really dominated Republican as much as Loyalist murals. Prominent themes have been resistance to British rule and the call for the withdrawal of troops.

A striking crop of Republican murals can be found at the top of Whiterock Road in the Ballymurphy estate. Several of these were the work of Gerry Kelly who has been responsible for many of the best Republican murals. Redevelopment of the estate offered convenient new canvases for muralists on the fresh brickwork of the houses' gable ends. Of Kelly's murals, one of the most impressive is a 40ft wide by 16ft high piece on the release of prisoners (carried out with the help of painter Spud Murphy). It depicts a prisoner in the foreground standing out against an image of Long Kesh, with two female prisoners on either side and the symbol of **Saoirse** (freedom) to the left. To get there, turn right off the Falls Road up Whiterock Road, passing alongside the City Cemetery wall. Once over the brow of the hill, take the next right into Ballymurphy Road, heading towards Springhill Avenue.

More recently, however, Republican muralists have turned increasingly to Irish legends and history as their sources of inspiration. Just off the Falls Road is the striking mural commemorating the 150th anniversary of the Famine, depicting a crush of anxious women and men waiting for a boat to carry them to salvation in the New World. Near the Cultúrlann MacAdam Ó Fiaich centre, 216 Falls Rd, is the Children of Lir mural, an astonishingly colourful image of the mythical offspring forced to wander the earth in the form of swans for 900 years before they could regain their human form.

Other main areas where you can find Republican murals are on the Falls Road itself, Beechmount Avenue, Donegall Road, Shaw's Road and Lenadoon Avenue in West Belfast, and New Lodge Road and Ardoyne in North Belfast.

The taxis assemble in ranks at the end of Castle Street, in the Smithfield area; the drivers, incidentally, are said to be Republican ex-prisoners.

Smithfield itself used to have a large covered bazaar that has now been replaced by **Smithfield Retail Market** – actually a set of small shop units rather than a traditional open-air market. The area has undergone major redevelopment through the building of the massive Castlecourt shopping centre, though there is a reminder of its old character in Gresham Street, home to several bookshops and junk shops.

THE FALLS ROAD

Moving on, you enter the **Falls Road** proper, which continues for a further two miles out past Milltown Cemetery (see below) and into Andersonstown. Most of the interest is concentrated in the area you've now entered – the **Lower Falls**. While most of the land to your left consists of the recently built red-brick terraced housing estates, the right-hand side of the road is more of a hotchpotch and features some of the local landmarks: the bright blue swimming baths, a new railing-secured shopping plaza, the DSS (the Department of Social Security, known as "the Brew" a corruption of "bureau") cooped up in an awning of chicken wire, a weary-looking Victorian library and a Worshippers of Peace convent.

By now, you'll have noticed the walls of iron sheeting which block the ends of the streets to the right. This is the "**Peace Line**" and living directly behind is the Protestant working class of the Shankill. Down Conway Street (by the DSS), stands the old Conway Mill, revitalized by a concerted community effort, spearheaded by local activist Father Des Wilson. Inside you can buy the wares of the few small businesses that operate from here.

Further on, you'll pass the red-brick buildings of the **Royal Victoria Hospital**, at the junction with Grosvenor Road. Since the Troubles began, the Royal, as it's known locally, has received international acclaim for its ability to cope with the consequences. Just beyond the Royal in a disused Presbyterian church, at 216 Falls Rd, is the **Cultúrlann MacAdam Ó Fiaich**, a cultural centre for Irish speakers, housing a bookshop, café, school and theatre. The Irish language is thriving in Catholic areas of Belfast and throughout the North; the first Irish-speaking primary school is over twenty years old, and the first secondary school was opened in 1991. A year earlier, the Ultach Trust was set up, a group that aims to broaden the appeal of Irish among Unionists. Although you are unlikely to hear any Irish being spoken on the streets or in most pubs, the language has a growing presence in the city.

The **Springfield** area to the northwest is the focus for a massive new £80 million campus jointly run by the University of Ulster and the Belfast Institute, geared towards offering a second educational chance to the local population.

MILLTOWN CEMETERY

Follow the Falls Road on for another mile and it'll lead to **Milltown Cemetery**, the main Republican burial ground in Belfast, lying peacefully opposite a fortified RUC station. Enter through the stone arch and you're immediately surrounded by a numbing array of Celtic and Roman crosses. If you're in search of the Republican plots, continue directly on from the entrance for about a hundred yards, then veer right, heading towards a corrugated warehouse shed just outside the perimeter of the cemetery. Along the way are two plots, marked off by a low green border fence. The nearer one holds a large memorial tablet listing the Republican casualties in the various uprisings from 1798 to the present day. The far plot contains a modern granite-block sculpture, and also the graves of Bobby Sands, Mairead Farrell, Seán Savage and others. Once you start to look, it's not difficult to spot the graves of many other victims of the Troubles, a devastatingly long list of (usually young) men and women. The M1 motorway lies below, at the bottom of the burial park: it was onto this stretch of road in 1988 that Michael Stone, a solo Loyalist attacker, was pursued after he'd opened fire and hurled grenades at mourners at the funeral of Seán Savage, one of the IRA members (along with Mairead Farrell and Danny McCann) killed by the SAS in Gibraltar.

Shankill

The Protestant population of West Belfast lives in the area between the Shankill and Crumlin Roads. As with the Falls, there's little here of especial interest, apart from an array of Loyalist murals and street names familiar from news bulletins. Along the **Crumlin Road**, in particular, are a number of evocative sites symbolizing the worst years of the Troubles. From the Westway you'll pass between the courthouse and the notorious Crumlin Road jail, with their underground connecting tunnel. Nearby is the bizarre sight of a completely fortified bookie's, standing in grim isolation in the centre of a patch of wasteland. Further along is an army encampment, set back from the road, with a tentacled iron sheeting corridor and lookout post. Despite many obvious signs of redevelopment and renovation – the most apparent being the new leisure centre – the area is in decline, its population shrinking in inverse proportion to the Catholic population the other side of the Peace Line. Yet Shankill (*sean cill*, "the old church") does have a rich history, though you'll have to travel almost out of town to learn more about it. A two-mile journey on bus #63 from Wellington Place will convey you to the end of Glencairn Road and a further ten-minute stroll down here will take you to **Fernhill House: The People's Museum** (all year Mon–Sat 10am–4pm, Sun 1–4pm; £2), a re-created 1930's Shankill house. Here you'll find displays on the history of the Shankill district, with particular focuses on the 1886 Home Rule crisis and both World Wars. Fortunately, there's a café here to restore your spirits for the return trek.

Cafés and restaurants

Eating out is one of young Belfast's favourite evening pastimes and an astonishing number of fashionable cafés and chic restaurants have sprung up around the city centre during the last few years. Although there's an emphasis on modern Irish and European cuisine, with French and Italian especially popular, you'll find a smattering of Indian and Chinese restaurants too. Standards are generally high and often exceptionally good value for money. The choice is limited for vegetarians, and there's a real dearth of wholefood restaurants, but many more restaurants now include vegetarian dishes on their menu.

There are plenty of places for daytime eating in the centre and along the Golden Mile, from the new cafés to traditional pubs (many of the latter serve excellent lunches, see below); most of the city's well-established restaurants are south of the centre from the Golden Mile outwards.

Cafés

Bewley's, Donegall Arcade. Welcoming branch of the much-loved Dublin coffee house.

Bonne Bouche, 19 Fountain St. At this breakfast place, you'll be stuffed with a massive Ulster fry for around £3.

Bonnie's Museum Café, 11a Stranmillis Rd (☎664714). Opposite the Ulster Museum, a café with an interesting, cheapish menu in the artist Willie Conor's former studio. Good for brunch.

Bookfinders, 47 University Rd (☎328269). Second-hand bookshop with a café at the back serving healthy lunches.

Café Renoir, 5 Queen St. Unpretentious self-service café with excellent and oversized wholefood dishes and baguettes.

Café Vincents, 78 Botanic Ave (☎242020). Known to all as *Vincents*, this place does excellent breakfasts and value-for-money high teas. Open from early 'til late.

Equinox, 32 Howard St. One of the new bloom of café society hang-outs, at the back of Equinox interiors shop. As you'd expect, it looks good with food to match.

Mogwai, 45 University Rd. Belfast's first all-night café, part-owned by local music star David Holmes who personally selects the café's sounds.

Queen's Espresso, 17 Botanic Ave. Good coffee and all sorts of snacks, from toasted sandwiches to tasty salads.

Revelations – The Internet Café, 27 Shaftesbury Square (☎320337; email: *www.revelations.co.uk*). Friendly "surfing" café with diligent and helpful staff and DTP facilities.

Roscoff Café, 27–29 Fountain Place. More affordable branch of *Roscoff* (see below), with a modernist interior, gourmet coffees and, best of all, the Mediterranean breads.

Students' Union Cafeteria, second and third floors of the Union building. Adequate and cheap. Open lunchtimes only.

The Upper Crust, 15 Lombard St. Serves homemade pies and bakes, and is guaranteed to be packed with shoppers and office workers at lunchtime.

Restaurants

Ashoka, 363 Lisburn Rd (☎660362). Excellent Indian restaurant. Expect to pay around £10–15 a head.

Bananas, 4 Clarence St (☎339999). Bright and breezy with – for Belfast – a fair-sized vegetarian menu.

Beatrice Kennedy, 44 University Rd (☎202290). Ever-changing and innovative menu at around £17 per head.

Café Society, 3 Donegall Square East (☎439525). The downstairs bistro serves inexpensive meals all day, while from the upstairs restaurant you can feast on more substantial modern and imaginative cuisine and watch the Belfast whirl below.

Chez Delbart, also known as *Frogities*, 10 Bradbury Place, off Great Victoria St (☎238020). Vast quantities at unbeatable prices, though you often have to queue.

Deane's, 38 Howard St (☎560000). Former Helen's Bay stalwart, now in swankier city centre premises with an excellent brasserie and astonishingly good modern Irish cuisine in the restaurant.

Friar's Bush, 159 Stranmillis Rd (☎669824). A bit of a walk, but worth it for the excellent reasonably-priced four-course meals, with wild venison or turbot specials.

La Belle Epoque, 61 Dublin Rd (☎323244). Fancy, expensive French restaurant.

Maggie May's, 45 Botanic Ave. Huge portions with lots of veggie choices. Be prepared to queue and bring your own wine.

The Manhattan, 23 Bradbury Place (☎233131). Cajun specials with live music upstairs.

Nick's Warehouse, 35 Hill St (☎439690). Chic, pricy restaurant upstairs and an atmospheric wine bar and cheaper menu downstairs.

Planet Harvey's, 95 Great Victoria St (☎233433). Popular, brightly-lit American-style place with pizzas, tacos and ribs.

Rajput, 461 Lisburn Rd (☎662168). Further out, but handy to B&Bs. A good reasonably-priced Indian restaurant and takeaway.

Roscoff, Lesley House, Shaftesbury Square (☎331532). Thought by some to be the best restaurant in Ireland, serving local produce in a modern French style. Dinners from around £30 plus wine. Booking essential.

Saints and Scholars, 3 University St (☎325137). Stylish, upmarket restaurant with extravagant specialities, such as wok-roasted monkfish, and prices to match.

Speranza, 16 Shaftesbury Square (☎230213). Massively popular Italian restaurant with a three-course menu for under £10; expect to queue.

Sun Kee, 38 Donegall Pass (☎312016). No-frills decor, but superb adventurous Chinese restaurant.

Villa Italia, 39 University Rd (☎328365). Queues outside are the best indicator of the quality of this cheapo Italian's menu.

Pubs, nightlife and entertainment

Until fairly recently, Belfast used to operate as a city under curfew, and unless you were a native, it was difficult to track down just where the best pubs, clubs and music were to be found. Now new bars have appeared and the club scene is booming. Overall, the city centre is far more open and vibrant at night, although Sundays can be quiet with many bars closing early or remaining shut all day. To tap into the pulse of the city, your best bet is to wander down the **Golden Mile**, where you'll find an abundance of pubs and clubs to choose from. For the latest information on what's going on in the city, the fortnightly listings freesheet *That's Entertainment* is essential.

As always in Ireland, the **pubs** are the heart of the city. The liveliest are on Great Victoria Street or around the university, and if you start drinking at the *Crown* you can manage a substantial pub crawl without moving more than about 100 yards from where you started.

The best Belfast entertainment is **music** in the pubs. The range on offer covers excellent traditional and folk, blues, country, jazz and indie music, and the number of visiting international artistes has increased dramatically. The local scene is thriving too and, despite the absence of any real music industry infrastructure, there are always good up-and-coming bands playing in the city, just waiting to get noticed. Classical music concerts, however, are thin on the ground and almost entirely performed in the Ulster Hall and Waterfront Hall; opera fans are catered for at the appositely-named Grand Opera House.

Belfast's **club scene** is buzzing; rave is big, so are celebrity DJs. Check *That"s Entertainment* for who's on when; you'll find most clubs run different sounds on different nights. Clubs are scattered fairly evenly around the city centre; students – not surprisingly – tend to dominate those closest to the university area.

Most of the **theatres** and **cinemas** are concentrated in the south of the city; although the choice for both is relatively limited, there is enough of a range to please most tastes. Recently, the city has seen a rapid expansion in the number of **art galleries**, and there's now an interesting selection to choose from, showing the best of modern and contemporary Irish art.

Drinking: pubs and bars

The Beaten Docket, 48 Great Victoria St, opposite *The Crown*. Fashion-conscious youngsters pack both floors. Very loud music.

Bob Cratchits, 38 Lisburn Rd at the corner of Camden St, near the university. Another trendy crowd.

The Botanic Inn, 23 Malone Rd, opposite the "Egg". Perhaps inevitably, known as the "Bot". Again almost entirely students, and plenty of atmosphere. Bands every Sunday night – open until midnight.

The Crown Liquor Saloon, 46 Great Victoria St, opposite the *Europa Hotel*. The most famous and spectacular pub in Belfast with a clientele that thinks itself intellectual (there's no music). Good repertoire of Ulster food – champ, colcannon etc – and also Strangford oysters in season, usually gone by early afternoon.

The Eglantine Inn, 32 Malone Rd. Known to the students who pack it out as the "Egg". Very crowded, with a disco bar upstairs for the smart casual set.

The Empire, 42 Botanic Ave, just up from the station. Cellar bar in a former church with a boisterous beer-hall atmosphere. Good-value food and bands from Thursday to Saturday.

Flanagan's, 19 Amelia St, above the *Crown's* side entrance. Sedate, cosy alternative to the packed bar below. Daily except Sun.

Lavery's Gin Palace, 14 Bradbury Place. Snazzy outside but a regular pub within, with a student and local crowd and discos on the top floor almost every night.

Morning Star, 17 Pottinger's Entry. Fine old-fashioned bar, busy in the day, quiet at night. Other good bars in the Entries include *The Globe* (Joy's Entry), *White's Tavern* (Winecellar Entry) and the *Kitchen Bar* (16 Victoria Square). The last-named offers great lunches – stews, fries and pizza on a soda bread base – and weekend sessions.

Morrison's Spirit Grocers, 21 Bedford St, city centre. Another retro pub; go mid-afternoon to sip fruit vodkas and marvel at the hand-painted faux nicotine ceiling.

Robinson's, 38 Great Victoria St. Theme bar spread over four floors and overshadowed by the *Crown* next door. Packed at lunchtimes with local workers taking advantage of the cheap menus. Music most nights.

Students' Union, University Rd. Basement bar and first-floor "speakeasy" with lots of heavy student drinking, but good-natured and cheap. You're really meant to be a student to drink here, but no one seems to mind if you're not.

Music: pubs and bars

The Bridge Tavern, 33 Queen St (☎231271). Live bands on Friday and Saturday nights.

Café Boulevard, Botanic Ave (☎319422). Regular Wednesday night jazz sessions.

The Duke of York, 11 Commercial Court (☎241062), off Donegal St. Music most nights with bands on Saturdays.

The Elms, 36 University Rd (☎322181). Student hang-out with live music/disco on Thursdays to Saturdays.

Errigle Inn, 320 Ormeau Rd (☎641410). Live music on Thursday to Sunday nights.

The Front Page, 108 Donegall St, upstairs from *McElhatton's* (☎324924). Packed with journalists from the nearby *Belfast Telegraph* and *Irish News* during the day; there's live music Wednesday to Sunday.

Ivanhoe Inn, Saintfield Rd (☎812240). One of the city's few regular jazz venues.

Katy Daly's, Ormeau Ave. Singers most evenings and regular club nights.

Kelly's Cellars, 30 Bank St (☎324835). According to legend a frequent meeting place for the United Irishmen behind the doomed 1798 rebellion – Henry Joy McCracken hid under the bar counter from British soldiers. Good lunches (thumping portions of homemade Irish stew and steak pie). Folk music on Thursday nights and Saturday afternoons, blues on Saturday nights.

The Liverpool, 44 Donegall Quay (☎324796), virtually opposite the Seacat terminal. Small, two-roomed place with a pool table. Friendly and handy if you're waiting for the boat. Traditional sessions on Sunday evenings and some Saturdays.

Maddens, 74 Smithfield (☎244114). Wonderful, unpretentious, atmospheric pub. Lots of locals drinking in two large rooms, one upstairs, one downstairs. Serves cheap stew and soup and there are excellent traditional sessions (Mon, Wed & Sat afternoons and evenings). Sometimes there are as many as twenty musicians, with music going on upstairs and downstairs at the same time.

Pat's Bar, 20 Prince's Dock St (☎744524), in the north of the city by the docks, off York Rd, most easily reached by taxi. Recently renovated in traditional style, with a choice of two bars (one large, one small) and open fires. Sessions irregular but great when they happen.

The Rotterdam, 54 Pilot St (☎746021). Reopened dockland institution with bands most nights, leaning towards blues and new country.

Other music venues

King's Hall, Balmoral (☎665225). The biggest pop and rock gigs are staged here.

Students' Union, University Rd. Officially you must show a student pass or get a Queen's student to sign you in, though pleading may work. A folk evening is held in the upstairs bar on Thursdays. There's a riotous atmosphere and it's great fun: plenty of mock ceili swinging goes on because nobody there seems to know how to do it properly.

Ulster Hall, Bedford St (☎323900). Most of the city's classical music performances are given by the Ulster Orchestra; the hall is also used for big rock and pop concerts.

Waterfront Hall, Lanyon Place, Laganside (☎334455). Hosts classical music and ballet, mainstream jazz and occasional big names from the moribund world of MOR pop and rock.

Whitla Hall, Queen's University (☎245133). Stages some professional and amateur classical concerts.

Clubs and discos

Crescent Bar, Sandy Row (☎320911). In the heartland of the working-class Protestant area; very popular with students. Different DJs on each night, (Wed–Sat).

The Factory, Virgin Cinema Centre, Dublin Rd (☎233555). Seventies retro on Friday, house on Saturday.

Kaos, *Renshaw's Hotel*, 75 University St (☎333366). Student discos Thursday & Sunday, retro and house Friday to Saturday.

The Limelight, 17 Ormeau Ave. A serious dance club with various club nights and sporadic indie gigs.

The Loft, Dempseys International, 43–45 Dublin Rd (☎234000). Club nights on Saturdays, but Sunday's "Live in the Loft" is the one to head for.

Madison's, 59–63 Botanic Ave (☎320966). Be seen, but wear the right threads.

Manhattan, Bradbury Place (☎233131). Every night except Sunday on three floors, a good light show and very popular but sneered at by hardcore ravers.

M–Club, *The Manhattan*, 23 Bradbury Place (☎233131). Different themes Wednesday to Saturday.

The Network Club, 11a Lower North St (☎238226). Saturday night DJs are a major draw.

Shine, Mandela Hall, Queen's Student Union (☎324803). Saturday student bash to deep house and funky techno.

Thompson's Garage, 3 Pattersons Place, Arthur St (☎323762). Once a garage owned by aviation freak Harry Ferguson – an addiction commemorated with a mural of an aeroplane in mid-flight; it now hosts a variety of club nights, "Sanctuary of Sound" on Saturday being the big draw.

Theatre

Arts Theatre, Botanic Ave (☎316900). Mostly mainstream stuff – often children's specials.

Empire Bar, Botanic Ave (☎328110). Transforms into the **Comedy Club** on Tuesday nights with satire and killing Northern wit that will reveal more about Belfast than a volume of history. Queue early to avoid disappointment; the slaughter starts at 9pm. If you can't get in, then try the up-and-coming **Murphy's Laughter Lounge** in The Laughter Loft, Great Victoria St (☎247447) on Thursday nights from 10pm.

Grand Opera House, Great Victoria St (☎241919). Belfast's most prestigious venue, showing many of London's West End productions and regular operatic performances.

Group Theatre, Bedford St (☎323900). Tends to be used mainly by local drama companies.

Lyric Theatre, further out on Ridgeway St (☎381081). The *Lyric* takes on more serious contemporary drama, and gave actor Liam Neeson an early platform.

Old Museum Arts Centre, College Square North (☎233332). The place to go for experimental or fringe productions.

Cinema

Mainstream cinemas showing the usual general-release movies include: the monster ten-screen Virgin on the Dublin Rd (☎0541/555176), the Movie House, Yorkgate on York St (☎755000), the Curzon on Ormeau Rd (☎641373) and the Strand, Hollywood Rd (☎673500).

Queen's Film Theatre, 7 University Square Mews off Botanic Ave (☎244857). Two screens showing art-house movies and late-night shows at exceptionally good prices.

Art galleries

Eakin Gallery, 237 Lisburn Rd (☎668522). A family-run terraced house gallery, which highlights Belfast's star painters.

Fenderesky Gallery, Crescent Arts Centre, University Rd (☎242338). Presents important Irish moderns – Barrie Cooke, Patrick Hall, Felim Egan.

One Oxford Street (☎310400). Down by the new Laganside development, the gallery shows young, mostly Northern talents.

Ormeau Baths Gallery, Ormeau Ave (☎321402). Set in what was once public baths, this is the hippest venue on the arts scene, with four exhibition spaces spread over two floors. Hosts exhibitions of contemporary Irish and international artists' work.

Ulster Museum, Stranmillis Rd (☎381251). Has a wide-ranging collection of international – Francis Bacon and Henry Moore – and national art – Colin Middleton, Willie Conor, Basil Blackshaw and Paul Henry. Conor's old studio across the road is now *Bonnie's Café*.

Waterfront Hall, Lanyon Place, Laganside (☎334455). Regular displays for viewing while waiting for the show to commence.

Listings

Airlines Aer Lingus, 46 Castle St (☎0645/737747); British Airways and British Airways Express (☎0345/222111); British Midland, Suite 2, Fountain Centre (☎0345/554554); Jersey European (☎01392/360777).

Airports Belfast International Airport (☎01849/422888); Belfast City Airport (☎457745).

Banks Most of the major UK banks are allied to the following Northern Irish ones (see also "Basics", p.18), all of which have city-centre branches: Bank of Ireland, 54 Donegall Place (☎234334); Northern Bank, Donegall Square West (☎245277); Ulster Bank Ltd, 47 Donegall Place (☎244112). Remember that British cash cards will work in their machines.

Bike rental McConvey Cycles, 467 Ormeau Rd (☎491163) & Unit 10, Pottinger's Entry (☎330322); Bike-It, 4 Belmont Rd (☎471141); Recycle, 1–5 Albert Square (☎313113).

Bookshops Bookfinders at 47 University Rd has second-hand books; there's also the University Bookshop on University Rd, Waterstones on Royal Ave, Dillons on Fountain St and branches of Easons on Ann St and Botanic Ave. For antiquarian books try Dublin Roma Ryan's Books and Prints, Dublin Rd.

Buses Citybus enquiries ☎246485; Ulsterbus ☎333000 for long-distance information. There's also a touch-screen information service at the Great Victoria Street station with full timetables and information on places to visit and accommodation throughout Northern Ireland.

Car rental Avis, Belfast International Airport (☎01849/422333) and Belfast City Airport (☎452017); there are many other big names at the airports; or try Dan Dooley, Belfast International Airport (☎01849/452522).

Exchange As well as banks try Thomas Cook, 11 Donegall Place (☎550030); the Tourist Information Centre, 59 North St (☎246609); and the post offices at Castle Place, Donegall Square and Shaftesbury Square.

Ferries Seacat, Donegall Quay (☎0345/523523); Stena Line, Ballast Quay (☎747747); Isle of Man Steam Packet Co, Donegall Quay (☎351009); Norse Irish Ferries, West Bank Rd (☎779090); P&O, Larne Harbour (☎0990/980777).

Festivals Belfast International Festival at Queens (two to three weeks in Nov) claims to be Britain's second biggest arts festival after Edinburgh. Others are Belfast Folk Festival (ten days in Sept); Orange Day on July 12 (and marching season from Easter onwards); Royal Ulster Academy Annual Exhibition (Ulster Museum, three weeks in Oct); Belfast Literary Festival (a week in April) and West Belfast Féile an Phobdil (one week at the start of Aug), a film, theatre, music and dance festival – originally a Republican event, it increasingly includes Unionist voices.

Football Internationals are played at Windsor Park, near the Lisburn Rd (buses #58 and #59 to Lower Windsor Ave). Belfast League clubs include Crusaders (Seaview, off Shore Rd, buses #7–11); Glentoran (The Oval, Redcliffe Parade, buses #16, #20, #21, #24 down the Newtownards Rd to Dee St); Cliftonville (Solitude, Cliftonville Rd).

Gaelic football Matches are played most weekends at Roger Casement Park, Andersonstown Rd (buses #14, #15, #90).

Gay The gay scene in Belfast is small and there's much travel back and forth to Dublin. The main city venues are *The Crow's Nest*, 26 Skipper St (☎325491), which caters for the older crowd, with quizzes, sing-songs or discos; and *The Parliament Bar*, 2 Dunbar St (☎234520), which has events Thurs–Sun, and is especially popular on Sat, with dancing to house on table-tops. On Mon night there's classical music with food, chess and backgammon. The gay helplines are Lesbian Line on ☎236668 (Thurs 7.30–10pm) and Mensline on ☎322023 (Mon–Wed 7.30–10pm).

Golf Nearest links to the city centre are at Ormeau Park (☎641069), weekday fees £12.00, weekends £14.50.

Hospitals Belfast City Hospital, Lisburn Rd (☎329241); Royal Victoria Hospital, Grosvenor Rd (☎240503). ☎999 for emergency service.

Hurling Matches are played most weekends at Roger Casement Park, Andersonstown Rd (buses #14, #15, #90). The Ulster Hurling final is held in July.

Laundry Duds 'n' Suds, 37 Botanic Ave (☎243956).

Left luggage Despite the reduced level of security, there is still, unfortunately, no official place where you can leave your luggage.

Lost property Musgrave police station, Ann St (☎650222 ext 26049).

Markets The St George's Casual Retail Market (also known as the Variety Market) in May St (Tues & Fri mornings) is the liveliest: the Friday food and variety-market is by far the more popular with about 200 traders taking part; on Tues it's more of a fleamarket-type affair, selling new and second-hand clothes and a variety of junk. The Smithfield Retail Market, at the back of the new Castlecourt development on West St/Winetavern St, is also pretty good; it operates from about 30 shop units and sells new and second-hand goods and clothes. For **antiques**, try the Sat market at Alexander The Grate, Donegall Pass.

Motoring organizations AA, 108 Great Victoria St (☎0990/500600; 24-hr rescue ☎0800/887766); RAC, 14 Wellington Place (☎232640; 24-hr rescue ☎828282).

Police ☎ 999 for emergency service. Main city-centre police station is in North Queen St.

Post office General Post Office, Castle Place (Mon–Sat 9am–5.30pm).

Rugby Top-class games are played by the Malone Club at Malone Park, off Woodstock Rd (buses #33 and #34) and by Collegians at Deramore Park, Malone Rd, (buses #70 and #71).

Tennis Belfast Indoor Tennis Arena, Ormeau Embankment (☎458024).

Trains For information call Central Station (☎899411).

Travel agents USIT, Fountain Centre (☎324073); Thomas Cook, 11 Donegall Place (☎550030).

travel details

TRAINS

Belfast to: Bangor (37 daily; 35min); Coleraine (9 daily; 2hr); Derry (7 daily; 2hr 40min); Dublin (8 daily; 2hr 10min); Dundalk (6 daily; 1hr 20min); Larne Harbour (15 daily; 55min); Lisburn (22 daily; 30min); Newry (8 daily; 1hr); Portadown (20 daily; 1hr 10min).

BUSES

Belfast (Europa) to: Armagh (11 daily; 1hr); Bangor* (4 daily; 40min); Cavan (2 daily; 2hr 30min); Comber* (4 daily; 45min); Cork, connecting with Bus Éireann (1 daily; 10hr 5min); change at Cahir for Waterford (10hr), at Roscrea for Limerick (9hr) or at Athlone for Mullingar (6hr 40min); Derry (6 daily; 1hr 40min); Donaghadee* (3 daily; 1hr); Downpatrick (every 30min daily: 1hr); Dublin (7 daily; 2hr 55min); Dungannon (15 daily; 50min); Enniskillen (9 daily; 2hr 35min); Galway, connecting with Bus Éireann (1 daily; 7hr 5min); Kilkeel (14 daily; 2hr); Lisburn (35 daily; 30min); Monaghan (7 daily; 1hr 50min); Newcastle (22 daily; 1hr 20min); Newry (every

30min; 1hr 15min); Newtownards* (12 daily; 35min); Omagh (7 daily; 2hr) Portaferry* (4 daily; 1hr 15min); Portadown (11–14 daily; 50min); Sligo (3 daily; 4hr); *indicates more frequent service from Laganside.

Belfast (Laganside) to: Antrim (every 15min; 40min); Ballycastle (8 daily; 1hr 40min–3hr 10min); Ballymena (20 daily; 55min–1hr 20min); Bangor (every 30min; 35min); Carnlough (8 daily; 1hr 40min–2hr 15min); Carrickfergus (25 daily; 25min) Coleraine (9 daily; 1hr 40min–2hr 30min); Comber (20 daily; 30min); Cookstown (9 daily; 1hr 30min–2hr 15min); Cushendall/Cushendun (3 daily via Larne; 2hr 45min/3hr; 4 daily via Ballymena; 2hr 35min/2hr 45min); Holywood (every 30min; 20min); Killyleagh (8 daily; 1hr); Larne (7 daily; 55min); Magherafelt (13 daily; 1hr 45min); Newtownards (every 20min; 35min); Portaferry (20 daily; 1hr 25min–1hr 50min); Portrush (11 daily; 2–3hr).

Belfast (Wellington Place) to: Lisburn (every 20min; 30min).

ANTRIM AND DERRY

Much of the coastline of counties **Antrim** and **Derry** is as spectacular as anything you'll find in Ireland and, consequently, unlike other parts of the North, it has always attracted an abundance of tourists. On fine days, the Mull of Kintyre and the islands of Islay and Jura are clearly visible, and much of the predominantly Protestant population derives originally from Scotland.

County Antrim's major attractions are the nine **Glens of Antrim** in the northeast corner, green fertile fingers probing inland from high cliffs, almost immediately followed by the weird geometry of the **Giant's Causeway**. Along this part of the coast the **Ulster Way** offers great opportunities for short walks and long hikes, and passes some wonderful deserted beaches. As you follow the coast road (A2) further west, you'll come to two of the North's great seaside resorts, **Portrush** and, across the border in County Derry, **Portstewart**, attractive holiday spots with sandy beaches and waves perfect for surfing. Modern **Derry city** sprawls around the old steep, walled town and spills over the banks of the River Foyle. A border town, with a substantial Catholic majority, it was traditionally the starting-point for emigrants from Donegal and around on their journey to the Americas. Derry is a more alternative city than Belfast and its forward-looking council has encouraged the arts with great success.

If you're not driving, **transport** around the coastline can be a problem. **Buses** are infrequent, although there are summer specials to the various sights. **Hitchhiking**, though, is easy enough hereabouts or you can take the **train** which cuts a less interesting **inland** route through bland farming country. Trains from Belfast run to both Larne and Portstewart, but the rest of the stops along the way to Derry are at some fairly grim inland towns: **Antrim**, **Ballymena** and **Coleraine**. The other route inland is the A6 road from Antrim to Derry, passing through and near some of the Plantation towns, the most impressive being **Moneymore**, and ascending steeply through the northeastern fringe of the Sperrins by means of the **Glenshane Pass**.

If transport is somewhat scarce, then at least finding **accommodation** is usually easy. There are some fine hotels and plenty of unpretentious, reasonably-priced B&Bs where you're generally assured of a friendly welcome and a cup of tea. Hostels are growing in number and improving in quality and there's a fair smattering of campsites. Keep in mind, though, that this is where Northerners also holiday, so accommodation may be hard to come by in July and August and at festival times.

ACCOMMODATION PRICE CODES

Throughout this book, prices of hotels, guesthouses and B&Bs have been graded with the codes below, according to what you can expect to pay for a double room in high season. For more details on accommodation, see p. 29.

① Under £26	④ £40–55	⑦ £90–110
② £26–33	⑤ £55–70	⑧ £110–130
③ £33–40	⑥ £70–90	⑨ Over £130

ANTRIM AND DERRY TELEPHONE CODES

New telephone codes will be introduced throughout Northern Ireland from June 1, 1999 although it will still be possible to use the old codes until April 22, 2000. The new codes will prefix the existing subscriber number regardless of where you are calling from; calls from outside Northern Ireland will require the 028 prefix in addition – thus Larne ☎01574/223456 will become ☎(028) 28 223456. The Antrim and Derry codes will change as follows:

ANTRIM
Antrim ☎01849 to ☎ (028) 94
Ballycastle ☎012657 to ☎ (028) 207
Martinstown ☎012667 to ☎ (028) 217
Ballymena ☎01266 (plus five-digit number) to ☎ (028) 256
Ballymena ☎01266 (plus six-digit number) to ☎ (028) 25
Ballymoney ☎012656 to ☎ (028) 276
Larne ☎01574 to ☎ (028) 28
Kilrea ☎012665 to ☎ (028) 295
Ballyclare ☎01960 to ☎ (028) 93

Lisburn ☎01846 to ☎ (028) 92
DERRY
Coleraine ☎01265 (plus five-digit number) to ☎ (028) 703
Coleraine ☎01265 (plus six-digit number) to ☎ (028) 70
Derry ☎01504 to ☎ (028) 71
Limavady ☎015047 to ☎ (028) 777
Magherafelt ☎01648 (plus five-digit number) to ☎ (028) 796
Magherafelt ☎01648 (plus six-digit number) to ☎ (028) 79

North from Belfast

The coastal strip from Belfast to Larne is largely unprepossessing countryside, although there are a few spots to detain you as you head towards the Antrim glens further north.

Carrickfergus

Heading past Belfast's northern suburbs, the A2 skirts the edge of Belfast Lough before reaching **CARRICKFERGUS**, an unremarkable seaside town whose seafront is dominated by its only real point of interest, **Carrickfergus Castle** (April–Sept Mon–Sat 10am–6pm, Sun 2–6pm; Oct–March Mon–Sat 10am–4pm, Sun 2–4pm; £2.70), one of the earliest and largest of Irish castles. Built on a rocky promontory above the harbour around 1180 by the Anglo-Norman invader John de Courcy (and in continuous use until 1928), it reflects the defensive history of this entire region. In 1315, it endured a year's siege before falling to the combined forces of Robert and Edward Bruce, after which it was retaken and held by the English for most of the next three centuries. In 1760, the castle was overwhelmed by a French force and hurriedly recaptured; and, in 1778, the American privateer, John Paul Jones, fought a successful battle with the British vessel *HMS Drake*, America's first naval victory. The story is that Belfast citizens – most of the Protestants were sympathetic to the American Revolution – rushed out to cheer the victors. The castle has now been restored and is peopled with alarming life-size figures plucked from various moments of its history – including King John in the garderobe. You can buy a joint ticket (£4.85) for the castle and a trip on the **Knight Ride** (April–Sept Mon–Sat 10am–6pm, Sun noon–6pm; Oct–March same days till 5pm; £2.70), a short walk away in the Heritage Plaza on Antrim Street (also the tourist office, see p.514). A monorail journey in a huge Norman helmet through Carrickfergus history from 581 AD when noble Fergus was shipwrecked on a rock

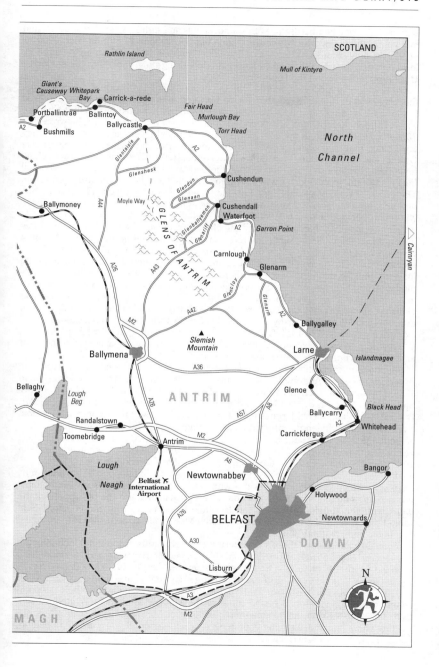

(*carrick*), the ride bombards you with sound, smells and sights. A smell of another kind hits you at the **Gasworks Museum** (June–Aug Sun 2–5pm; £1.50), on Irish Quarter South, the only complete Victorian coal-fired gasworks in Ireland, lovingly-restored by local enthusiasts, which helped to power the town's lighting, including the surviving **Big Lamp** at the end of the High Street.

Otherwise, Carrickfergus and its environs claim plenty of **literary associations**, though not all of them are tangible: the Restoration dramatist William Congreve lived in the castle as a young child – his father was a soldier; Jonathan Swift's first sinecure was at Kilroot, just outside Carrickfergus, where, between 1694 and 1696, he wrote *The Tale of a Tub*. ICI bought the land and levelled the thatched cottage in the 1960s; they have since moved on, and the only commemoration to the writer is the **Swift Art Gallery** on the same site. Poet **Louis MacNeice** (1907–63) spent a miserable childhood here; he says sourly of the town: "The Scotch Quarter was a line of residential houses/But the Irish Quarter was a slum for the blind and halt" (*Carrickfergus*, 1937). The Protestant son of a local Home Rule cleric, he was equally repelled by Orange bigotry and the complacency found in the Republic. Although he was educated in England, where he became associated with the Auden-led left-wing poets of the 1930s, his upbringing indelibly tinged his poetry and character. In *Valediction* (1934), he explores his ambiguous feelings towards his roots: "I can say Ireland is hooey... But I cannot deny my past to which myself is wed/ The woven figure cannot undo its thread." The rectory on North Road – from which his mother was committed to an asylum – no longer stands. Instead the MacNeice Fold on the same spot offers sheltered accommodation and a plaque on its walls proclaims the connection. In the town centre overlooking Market Place, the **Church of St Nicholas** (the patron saint of mariners and children; open mornings only), where MacNeice's father ministered, was built by John de Courcy in 1205 – like many of the castles and historic buildings hereabouts – but extensively reworked in 1614. Some interesting features set it apart: a leper's window, a "skew", or crooked aisle, symbolizing Christ's head on the cross falling to the right and, in the porch, a Williamite bomb fired in 1689.

Still, none of these claims to fame is as tenuous as that of the connection with the American president Andrew Jackson, whose parents emigrated from Carrickfergus in 1765. The **Andrew Jackson Centre** (June–Sept Mon–Fri 10am–1pm & 2–6pm, Sat & Sun 2–6pm; April, May & Oct Mon–Fri 10am–1pm & 2–4pm, Sat & Sun 2–4pm; £1.20), two miles north of Carrickfergus on the Larne Road, isn't even their home, but a reconstruction of an eighteenth-century thatched cottage, with a little museum. Next door is something a little more substantial: the **US Rangers' Centre** (same hours and ticket) celebrates the formation of the first Battalions of this American Commando force in 1942 from US troops based in the North and trained at Carrickfergus.

One reason to give Carrickfergus a little more time might be the **annual fair**, *Lughnasa*, which is tackily medieval – with wrestlers, archers, minstrels and people dressed up as monks – but great fun nonetheless. It's held at the end of July; check the dates with the **tourist office** at the Heritage Plaza on Antrim Street (April–Sept Mon–Fri 9am–6pm, Sat 10am–6pm; Oct–March Mon–Fri 9am–5pm; also July & August Sun noon–6pm; ☎01960/366455).

If you do want **to stay**, there's a scattering of hotels and B&Bs around, including the *Dobbins Inn Hotel*, 6 High St (☎01960/351905; ⑤), and B&B at *Tramway House*, 95 Irish Quarter South (☎01960/355639; ②), or *Seaview*, 33 Larne Rd (☎01960/363170; ②; April–Oct). This is also **golf** and **fishing** country. Carrickfergus Golf Club (☎01960/363713), on North Road west of the town centre, is an eighteen-hole parkland course with great views to Scotland and over the Mourne Mountains. Whitehead Golf Club (☎01960/353792), half a mile north of town at McCrea's Brae, also offers distracting views and a challenging course over varied terrain. If you want to go fishing, you can rent boats at Carrickfergus or fish off the rocks and piers along the coast.

Whitehead and Islandmagee

The small coastal village of **WHITEHEAD**, three miles further up the coast, marks the entry point to the narrow peninsula of Islandmagee. There's little to detain you here, apart from a bracing stroll along the promenade or onto the Blackhead path and its clifftop views of the Down coast to the south. However, the village provides a base for visiting the **Railway Preservation Society of Ireland** at the end of Castleview Road. There's a collection of steam locomotives for viewing and riding (July & August, Sun pm) and the Society runs a number of summer excursions from Belfast Central to Portrush and Whitehead to Derry (☎01960/35367 for details).

Seven miles long and two wide, **ISLANDMAGEE** is a predominantly rural strip of land with the blatant exception of the Ballylumford power station at its northern tip. In the seventeenth century, the "island" was held by the Bissett family in return for an annual payment of goshawks, which breed on the cliffs. The most notable of these cliffs are the **Gobbins**, halfway along the eastern seaboard, and once much visited, though the paths and bridges constructed to guide tourists have long since fallen into disrepair and the cliffs are remembered more for a notorious incident in 1641 when the local inhabitants were hurled into the sea by soldiers from the Carrickfergus garrison. You can approach the cliffs via a gate on Gobbins Road, but much of the path around the cliffs is now decidedly unsafe.

Further north lies the tiny harbour village of **Portmuck**, named after the apparently pig-shaped island it faces (*muc* being Irish for "pig"), and a sandy beach at **Brown's Bay**, where there's a caravan park that allows camping (☎01960/382497). At **Ballylumford**, at the tip of the peninsula, you can catch a ferry across the water to Larne (hourly 7.30am–5.30pm; 60p), and on the road to Mill Bay, sitting incongruously in the front garden of a house, spot the 4000-year old Ballylumford Dolmen, known locally as the "Druid's Altar". There are few bars on the peninsula, but one, the *Mill Bay Inn*, in Mill Bay, holds regular traditional sessions on Wednesday nights and offers **B&B** (☎01960/382436; ④).

Ballycarry and Glenoe

Back on the A2, **BALLYCARRY**, just off the main road, is the site of the remains of the first Presbyterian church ever to be built in Ireland, **Templecorran**, with a memorial to its first minister, ordained in 1613. The **church**'s graveyard contains the tombs of some of the supporters of the 1798 rebellion, including that of James Burns, whose cryptic gravestone can only be deciphered using the following key: the numbers 1, 2, 3 and 4 represent the vowels "a", "e", "i" and "o" respectively, and 5 and 6 the letter "w". Another United Irishman, James Orr – better known as the Bard of Ballycarry, Ulster's answer to Robbie Burns – is also buried here, and some ringing verses in dialect are carved into his tombstone. There's also a grand Masonic memorial of 1831, which bears a patriotic poem about Ireland: "Erin, loved land! From age to age, Be thou more great, more famed and free". The author might not have been impressed by one of the village house's huge and colourful gable-end mural of William of Orange astride a prancing horse.

Five miles along the back road from Ballycarry nestles the picturesque village of **GLENOE**, visited for its pretty waterfall and for Maud's Ice Cream Factory (all year Mon–Fri 9am–4pm), where you can discover the intricacies of the production process and in the factory's café sample such flavoursome varieties as Pooh Bear and Guinness.

Larne

Seven or so miles north of Ballycarry, the A2 enters **LARNE**, the last town of any size for a considerable distance on the coastal route. Until fairly recently, Larne was the main port of entry for visitors to Northern Ireland, but nowadays, though it's still a freight centre, only the P&O ferries from Cairnryan call here. Though the town's seaside position is impressive and its main street bustles with shoppers most of the week, it is, in reality, a rather drab and conservative place, with little of inherent attraction. Larne's **history** is inextricably linked to its convenience as a landing stage. Norse pirates used Larne Lough as a base in the tenth and eleventh centuries; Edward Bruce, brother of Robert, landed here in 1315 with a force of 6000 men in his attempt to urge the Irish to overthrow the English; and in 1914, the Ulster Volunteers, opposed to the Irish Home Rule Bill, landed German arms here. Some 140 tons, consisting of an astonishing 35,000 rifles and five million rounds, were unloaded one April night and rapidly distributed to supporters throughout Ulster by a waiting motorcade of several hundred vehicles. Such was the racket that local residents believed an invading army had arrived. History apart, though, Larne is not a place to hang around in. The only real landmark is the **round tower**, at the entrance to the port, and even that's an 1888 reproduction – a memorial to James Chaine MP, the driving force behind the development of Larne's sea routes to Scotland and the Americas. The other sight is the ruined sixteenth-century **Olderfleet Castle**, which cowers amid the industrial wasteland of the harbour.

The coast around Larne, stretching from Garron Point in the north to Black Head in the south, is of great **geological** interest, with examples of just about every rock formation and period, from the earth's original crust to raised beaches and glacial deposits. At **Curran Point**, just south of the harbour, flint bands, frequently found in the chalk of this coast, provided useful material for Stone Age people, and many arrowheads and other artefacts have been found. Three-quarters of a mile out on the Antrim Coast Road, north of Larne, beyond Waterloo Cottages, stands a large monument to the engineer of this road, William Bald, and his stalwart workers, who blasted their way through, over and round this route in the 1830s. Here, at low tide, bands of fossil-rich Lias clay are exposed – even dinosaur remains have been discovered – and beneath the black basalt boulders, the mollusc shell, *Gryphea*, known locally as the Devil's Toenail, is common. Check at the Larne tourist office for geological tours and their useful guidebook to the rock formations of this part of the coast.

AMANDA M'KITTRICK ROS

In contrast to Larne's lack of vigour is the work of the town's best-known author. **Amanda Malvina Fitzalan Anna Margaret McLelland M'Kittrick Ros** – her signature gives some indication of the embroidery of her prose style – has gone down in history as the world's worst novelist. Born in 1860 in Ballynahinch, twenty miles south of Belfast, she was a true child of the Victorian era. She came to Larne as a schoolteacher and married the station master, Andrew Ros. On their tenth wedding anniversary he gave her a present that generations of fans must be grateful for – the publication of her first fantastical alliterative work, *Irene Iddlesleigh* – and a stream of feverish hyperbole followed. Take, for instance, a passage from *Helen Huddleston* about her heroine:

> *She had a swell staff of sweet-faced helpers, swathed in stratagem, whose members and garments glowed with the lust of the loose, sparked with the tears of the tortured, shone with the sunlight of bribery, dimpled with the diamonds of distrust, slashed with sapphires of scandal and rubies wrested from the dainty persons of the pure...*

Mark Twain and Aldous Huxley swooped on her work with delight and formed appreciative societies, reading circles and dining clubs dedicated to her "unintentional enormities". She became a cult figure, never, it seems, realizing what inspired such devotion. "My works", she said, "are all expressly my own – pleasingly peculiar – not a borrowed stroke in one of them." Quite. She also wrote excruciating verse.

Practicalities

If you want to stay, the **tourist office** (July & Aug Mon–Wed & Sat 9am–5pm, Thurs–Fri 9am–6.30pm; Easter–June & Sept Mon–Sat 9am–5pm; Oct–March Mon–Fri 9am–5pm; ☎01574/260088), in Narrow Gauge Road, will book B&B **accommodation** for you, and there is plenty to choose from. Close to the ferry terminal is the *Manor Guest House*, 23 Olderfleet Rd (☎01574/273305; ②); for more luxury, try the upmarket Victorian *Magheramorne House Hotel* (☎01574/279444; ⑤), just south of town on the A2. There's a campsite at Curran Caravan Park, 131 Curran Rd, near the harbour (☎01574/260088), but you are better off at Carnfunnock Country Park on the way to Ballygally (see below). **Ferry information** is available on ☎0990/980980; see p.5 for more details of the crossing. For **bus** information dial ☎01574/272345.

The Glens of Antrim and Rathlin Island

Northwest of Larne lie the nine **Glens of Antrim**, cutting back from the sea to wild country behind. It's a curious landscape, with enormous contrasts between the neat seaside villages and the rough moorland above, and its well-defined topography gives first-time visitors the strange sensation that they know it already.

Despite their proximity to the Scottish coast, the Glens were extremely isolated until the completion of the coast road. As a consequence, they were also one of the last places in Northern Ireland where Irish was spoken. **Transport** is still a problem here and the only service to run from one end of this coast to the other is the daily Belfast–Portrush Ulsterbus express (☎01232/333000 for times), or if you've time, you can dawdle along on a series of local buses; check the times with local tourist offices. **Hitching** is generally fine, but don't expect lifts to take you very far. **Cycling** is heady but strenuous, and don't rely on being able to rent a bike: one of the few places that has some is the Ardclinis Activity Centre (☎012667/71340) in Cushendall. One alternative means of getting about is **pony trekking**, which can be a delight in good weather. The main centre is at **Ballycastle**, at the northern extremity of the glen-fractured coast; see p.521.

Ballygally and Glenarm

The impressiveness of the road builders' achievement becomes apparent the moment you leave Larne's dull suburbs. The view broadens out to take in the open sea and, beyond it, the low outline of the Scottish coast. **Carnfunnock Country Park** (daily June–Sept dawn–8pm; Oct–May dawn–dusk; car £2) is a good walking stop with a maze in the shape of Northern Ireland, a walled garden, a time garden with a collction of sundials ranging from the simple to the arcane, and a nine-hole golf course. You can also camp here (☎01574/260088; April–Sept). The first settlement you come to is **BALLYGALLY**, with a wide, wild bay and a sandy beach embraced by hills. There's something about the sobriety of the architecture that makes it look more like Scotland, an impression heightened by the crow-stepped gables of **Ballygally Castle**, built by seventeenth-century planters. You can call in here for a drink – it's now a hotel (☎01574/583212; ⑥) with, they tell you, a ghost in the dungeon bar – although the building is more impressive from the outside.

The southernmost of the glens, **Glenarm**, is headed by a village of the same name, which grew up around a hunting lodge built by Randal MacDonnell after Dunluce Castle, further up the coast, was abandoned. Glenarm became the major seat of the Earls of Antrim, something that might lead you to expect that **Glenarm Castle** would be worth seeing, but major rebuilding in the eighteenth and nineteenth centuries have left it an architectural mishmash of conflicting styles.

GLENARM village itself, though, is a delight and very much a taste of what's to follow, with a narrow main street of colour-washed buildings broadening out as it approaches an imposing gateway, the old estate entrance, which now provides access to the glen itself. The lower part of the glen is blighted with Forest Service conifers, but carry on and you reach National Trust land, and far better walking. Back in the village, you'll find a couple of cosy bars, a coffee shop and a salmon processing plant on the outskirts with a shop where you can inspect the wares. There's a **tourist office** here in the Community Hall (Tues 9am–3pm, Wed noon–3pm, Thurs & Fri 9am–noon; ☎01574/841087) and a smattering of places to **stay**, including *Margaret's House*, 10 Altmore St (☎01574/841307; ②), and *Nine Glens*, 18 Tobermore St (☎01574/841590; ②).

Carnlough and Waterfoot

Shortly after leaving Glenarm, you'll pass through the hamlet of **STRAIDKILLY,** the "sliding village", so named because of the houses' moving about an inch annually towards the sea. Rounding the next bay, you'll arrive at **CARNLOUGH**, standing at the opposite side of the next bay north of Glenarm, at the head of **Glencloy** – the "glen of hedges". The village's most striking feature is the sturdy, white limestone architecture: until the 1960s, Carnlough's way of life was linked to its limestone quarries. The shining white stone buildings in the centre of the village were constructed by the Marquess and Marchioness of Londonderry in 1854. Over the main road there's a solid stone bridge that once carried the railway bringing material down to the harbour which itself has an impressive breakwater, clock tower and courthouse of limestone. A mile north of the village, in a cottage garden on the Ballymena road, there's an idiosyncratic alfresco "scrap museum", consisting of an astonishing range of cleaned up *objets trouvés*, ranging from Roman coins to tin baths.

The **tourist office** inside McKillop's souvenir and ice cream shop on Harbour Road (shop hours; ☎01574/885236) can solve any problem, accommodation or otherwise. Almost next door, the solid *Londonderry Arms Hotel* (☎01574/885255; ⑥), once owned by Winston Churchill, is a comfortable **place to stay**; you can sample the smoked salmon fished in Glenarm, or just go for a drink and admire the bizarre collection of mementos of the 1960s steeplechaser, Arkle. For cheaper B&B, try *Harbour View*, 50 Harbour Rd (☎01574/885335; ②), *Bethany House*, 5 Bay Rd (☎01574/885667; ②), or the rooms above the *Bridge Inn* in Bridge Street (☎01574/885669; ③). If you're **camping**, the *Bay View Caravan Park* (☎01574/885685) and *Ruby Hill Caravan Park* (☎01574/885692), both on Largy Road, have spaces for tents. *Black's Pub*, on Harbour Road, is the place to head for **music**, with sessions most nights. This is also a good place to attack the **Ulster Way**, with walks up behind the village to forests and waterfalls along the Carnlough River – check at the tourist office for maps and an update on the state of the paths first.

From Carnlough the road skirts round a gaunt shoulder of land and on to **WATERFOOT**, a short strip of houses with a couple of bars that comes to life in the evenings. There's also **B&B** at *The Bay*, 201 Garron Rd (☎012667/71858; ②), and *Lurig View*, 4 Lurig View (☎012667/71618; ②). Waterfoot is the scene of the *Feis na nGleann*, one of the great competitive Irish sporting and cultural festivals, held in July.

It's **Glenariff**, though, Waterfoot's glen, that is the real attraction. Wide, lush and flat-bottomed, it's abruptly cut off by the sea, while a few miles up the glen is the **Glenariff Forest Park** (car £3; pedestrians £1.50) which has a **campsite** (☎012667/58232; contact the head forester in advance) and a number of waymarked trails. Opt for the Waterfall Trail to see a spectacular series of **waterfalls** skirted by a timber walkway, first built one hundred years ago. However, you'll pass *Altnagowna*, the highest waterfall of all, as you travel up the Glenariff road from Waterfoot and you can see some of the others by turning left at the *Manor Lodge* sign and stopping at the restaurant.

Between Waterfoot and **Red Bay** pier, where boats can be rented by the hour (☎012667/71331), there's a series of **caves** with an odd history. The so-called "school cave" was where lessons were conducted for the children of Red Bay in the eighteenth century, a practice made necessary by the oppressive penal laws that outlawed Catholic education. One such pupil was Dr James McDonnell, founder of the Belfast Medical School. The largest of the caves, "Nanny's Cave", 40ft long, was the home of the redoubtable distiller of illicit poteen, Ann Murray, who died, aged 100, in 1847.

Cushendall and around

CUSHENDALL lies at the head of three of the nine Glens of Antrim, a delightfully understated village, its charming colour-washed buildings grouped together on a spectacular shore. The red sandstone **tower** at the main crossroads was built in 1809 by one Francis Turnly, an official of the East India Company, as "a place of confinement for idlers and rioters". Now it's owned by the art terrorist pop band, the KLF. Down the road on Mill Street, sharing premises with the Glens of Antrim Historical Society, is Cushendall's **tourist office** (July & Aug Mon–Sat 10am–1pm & 3–7.30pm, Sun 2–4.30pm; Sept–June Tues–Fri 10am–1pm & 3–5pm; ☎012667/71180), where you can check for details of **dancing and traditional music** in local pubs: *McCollam's*, known to all as *Johnny Joe's*, also on Mill Street, is not to be missed, sessions usually taking place on Friday and Sunday. Cushendall itself comes alive during the Heart of the Glens festival in the middle of August. **Eating** options are limited to *Gillan's* friendly café during the day, while *Harry's Restaurant* and the *Half Door* offer good evening menus.

Cushendall is probably the best base for exploring the Glens of Antrim, and accordingly it's well provided with **accommodation**. For B&B, try *Tros-ben-villa*, 8 Coast Rd (☎012667/71130; ③), or the welcoming *Cullentra House*, 16 Cloghs Rd (☎012667/71762; ②), a mile outside town off the Cushendun road, with its wonderful views. There's a YHANI **youth hostel** on Layde Road (☎012667/71344; open March–Dec 23; Jan & Feb advance bookings only), but it's a fair step and a steep one if you're backpacking, so hitch a ride – leave town by Shore Street, go left at the fork, and look out for the youth hostel sign on the wall. The Glenville Caravan Park (☎012667/71520) is further up the road, and the municipal **campsite** stands on the hill to the north of the town (☎012667/71699). You can **rent bikes** from the hostel or from the Ardclinis Activity Centre, 11 High St (☎012667/71340), which also arranges all manner of outdoor pursuits. **Fishing** licences are available from O'Neill's Country Sports, Mill Street.

Layde Old Church and Ossian's Grave

Beyond Cushendall, the land rises sharply and the main road swings away from the coast, which is good news for **walkers**. A cliff-top path, running northwards from the beach, takes you to the ruins of the **Layde Old Church**, originally dating from the thirteenth century, and chief burial place of the MacDonnells. The local historical society has published a catalogue of the gravestones here, an interesting read in itself, but more so if you have Glens ancestry.

The other trip from Cushendall is to **Ossian's Grave**, on the main road to Cushendun. There's a double fake involved here. The legendary son of Fionn Mac Cumhaill was the supposed author of the popular Ossianic cycle of poems, though these were in fact largely fabricated by James Macpherson in the 1760s. The poems inspired the early Romantic movement, particularly in Germany, where Goethe quoted Ossian at length in *The Sorrows of Young Werther*. However, the tomb doesn't actually have anything to do with either legendary or poetic incarnation as it's really a Neolithic court grave. All the same, standing in a sloping field above the valley, with views to

Glendun, Glenaan and, in the distance, Scotland, it oozes spirit– as good a place as any to reflect on the shaky origins of the first Celtic literary revival.

Beyond the grave runs **Glenaan**, one of the smallest of the glens, soon petering out to little more than a dip of red reeds and black seams of peat between two hills of heather and cotton grass.

Cushendun to Fair Head

The once fashionable resort of **CUSHENDUN** is an architectural oddity, almost entirely designed, between 1912 and 1925, by the stylish architect of Portmeirion in Wales, Clough Williams-Ellis. However, it has nothing of the twee Italianate style used famously as the setting for *The Prisoner* TV serial. Built to a commission from Ronald McNeill, the first (and last) Lord Cushendun, and his Cornish wife, Maud, Cushendun's houses are of rugged, rough-cast whitewash with slate roofs – a Cornish style which clearly weathers the Atlantic storms as efficiently here as in Cornwall. The town was home to Agnes Nesta Shakespeare Higginson (1870–1951), who crafted folksy, sentimental ballads under the far more apposite adopted name, **Moira O'Neill**. Very popular in her day, now she's better known as the mother of Mary Nesta Skrine (d. 1996), who went one better than her mother and wrote under two pen names, Molly Keane and M.J. Farrell. *Good Behaviour*, written in her eighties after a thirty-year silence, is a piercingly witty novel of family life in the Big House tradition.

All of Cushendun is National Trust property, and it shows. It's a tiny and well-tended place where tourists – and everyone else – seem peculiarly out of place; but there is a **National Trust Information Office** (July & Aug daily 12.30–6pm; Easter–June & Sept Sat & Sun 12.30–6pm; ☎012667/61506) in the main street and some **places to stay** and for **B&B**: the popular *Sleepy Hollow*, 107 Knocknacarry Rd (☎012667/61513; ③), and, out towards Torr Head, *Drumkeerin* (☎012667/61554; ③) and *The Villa* (☎012667/61252; ③). The council caravan park, 14 Glendun Rd (☎012667/61254), has space for **camping**.

The main road north from Cushendun runs inland, traversing some impressively rough moorland, but, if you take it, you'll be missing some of the best of the northern coastline. Edged with fuchsia and honeysuckle, the coastal road switchbacks violently above the sea to **Torr Head**, the closest point on the Irish mainland to the Mull of Kintyre; Protestants would row across these thirteen miles to attend church on the Scottish mainland. You can also pick up the signposted **Ulster Way** around here, although it swings inland immediately after Cushendun, joining the coast again at Murlough Bay. If you're keen to linger, there's farmhouse **B&B** at *Torr Brae*, 77 Torr Rd (☎012657/69625; ③).

That said, people will tell you that the **Ballypatrick Forest Park** (daily 10am–sunset; car £2.50), on the main road, is worth seeing. It's not, unless you're thrilled by the idea of a one-way driving route past things like fjords and even prehistoric cairns marked out like a fairground ghost train. **Camping** is allowed in the park, but check with the Head Forester (☎012657/62301) before turning up, and at the nearby *Watertop Open Farm* (☎012657/62576), a working farm with pony trekking and fishing available. Just past both of these is **Loughareema**, the "vanishing lake", so termed because of its ability to drain away completely in hot weather.

Murlough Bay and Fair Head

Murlough Bay is probably – perhaps because of the absence of a main road – the most spectacular of all the bays along the northern coast. From the rugged cliff tops, the hillside curves down to the sea in a series of wildflower meadows that soften an otherwise harsh landscape. As much as anywhere else on the Irish coastline this is a place for just spending time and drinking it all in.

SIR ROGER CASEMENT

A stone cross in the second Murlough Bay car park commemorates **Sir Roger Casement**, who was, extraordinarily, both a successful administrator for the British and later a martyr for the Nationalist cause. Born in Dublin, he moved to Antrim following the death of his parents, to live with his guardian and, initially at least, espoused the Loyalist views that characterized his Anglo-Irish upbringing. His brilliant diplomatic career included a stint in the Belgian Congo, where he fearlessly exposed all manner of colonial exploitation, and Peru, which he called the "Devil's Paradise of the Amazon". He was knighted in 1911, but, influenced by his foreign experiences, on his return to Ireland became increasingly involved with the Sinn Féin movement. Believing that World War I offered Ireland the opportunity of achieving independence from Britain, he negotiated military aid from Germany and arranged for a shipment of arms to be landed at Banna Strand on the Kerry coast. His plans were discovered and he was captured before the crucial 1916 Easter Rising and tried.

Seemingly set on martyrdom, at his trial he asserted: "I committed high treason with my eyes open – and for a cause I love above all else. I must some day pay the penalty – I do not mind if I have helped Ireland." However, aside from treason, Casement's homosexuality played a part in his fate. His diaries – the notorious "black diaries", supposedly recording his sexual exploits – were confiscated by the British government after his arrest and circulated unofficially. Their contents were said to be so damning that the chance of a reprieve was out of the question, despite campaigning behind the scenes by Conan Doyle, George Bernard Shaw and others, and he was hanged in Pentonville Prison, London. More than eighty years later, debate still rages over the authenticity of Casement's diaries and whether they were a British fabrication designed to sully Casement's reputation as a champion of the colonially oppressed. Whatever the case, it's more likely that Casement's sexuality compounded his treachery in the eyes of the British establishment and made it determined to exact revenge on one of its own. A further twist to the tale has come with the release of once-secret MI5 papers in which Casement admits the futility of the uprising, once Germany had refused to send troops in support, but that he would be branded a coward and traitor to the Irish cause if he did not complete his part in the plan.

The last headland before Ballycastle is **Fair Head**, whose massive 600ft-cliffs offer a really spectacular view across the North Channel to the Scottish islands – Islay, the Paps of Jura and, beyond them, the Mull of Kintyre – a proximity which helps to unravel the confusion of land ownership between Ireland and Scotland. Rathlin Island (see p.523) was hotly contested right up to the seventeenth century, while the MacDonnells owned land both here and on Kintyre (itself considered dangerous enough to English interests to be settled, or "planted", with people from elsewhere in Scotland during the seventeenth century, just as Ireland was). **Lough na Cranagh**, one of three lakes in the hinterland behind the cliffs, has an oval island that is actually a *crannóg*, a lake dwelling, encircled by a parapet wall.

Ballycastle

The lively market town and port of **BALLYCASTLE** sits at the mouth of the two northernmost Antrim glens, Glenshesk and Glentaisie and makes a pleasant base for exploring the Causeway Coast or the glens themselves, especially if you find yourself passing through at the time of the cross-community Northern Lights Festival in May, the *Fleadh Amhrán agus Rince* three-day music and dance **festival** in June, or the **Ould Lammas Fair** held on the last Monday and Tuesday in August. This last event is more than just a tourist promotion: Ireland's oldest fair, it dates from 1606 when the MacDonnells first obtained a charter, and has sheep and pony sales as well as the obligatory stalls and shops. You may be able to find the edible seaweed, dulse, and "yellow man", the tooth–breaking yellow toffee (so hard, you break it with a hammer), delicacies that feature in a sentimental song that originates locally:

Did you treat your Mary Ann
To dulse and yellow man
At the Ould Lammas Fair in Ballycastle–O?

The town still has a solid, prosperous feel about it that derives from the efforts of an enlightened mid-eighteenth-century landowner, Colonel Hugh Boyd, who developed it as an industrial centre, providing coal and iron ore mines, a tannery, brewery, soap, bleach, salt and glass works. Ballycastle's prosperity, though, really depended on its coal mines; lignite was mined at Ballintoy, on the coast a few miles further west, an enterprise which came to an abrupt end in the eighteenth century when the entire deposit caught fire, burning on for several years. More recently, the harbour area has been redeveloped to cater for the ferry to Campbeltown on the Mull of Kintyre (see "Basics", p.5, for more details), though, fortunately, Morton's fresh fish shop has been left intact. Boats leave from here also to Rathlin Island (see opposite).

At the seafront there's a memorial to Guglielmo Marconi, the inventor of the wireless, who in 1898 made his first successful transmission between Ballycastle and Rathlin. From the seafront, Quay Road leads gradually uphill past houses and shops to the Diamond, the town's focus. Up the steeper Castle Street hill the town's tiny **museum** (daily June–Sept noon–6pm; free) occupies the old eighteenth-century courthouse. Temporary exhibitions are hosted upstairs, while, downstairs in the former cells, there's a small and somewhat poignant collection of artefacts produced by the pre-World War I Irish Home Industries Shop. Pride of place goes to the Glentaisie banner for the first *Feis na nGleann* in 1904. A little way out, on the main road to Cushendall, are the ruins of **Bonamargy Friary**, founded by the dominant MacQuillan family around 1500. One family member, Julia, insisted on being buried in the main walkway, so that she might be humbled by the stepping feet of others even in death. A number of the rival MacDonnell family are also buried here, including the hero of Dunluce Castle, Sorley Boy MacDonnell, and his son Randal, first Earl of Antrim (see p.528). An indication of the strength of the Irish language in these parts is that the tomb of the second earl, who died in 1682, is inscribed in Irish as well as the usual English and Latin: the Irish inscription reads "Every seventh year a calamity befalls the Irish" and "Now that the Marquis has departed, it will occur every year". The **Margy river**, on which Bonamargy Friary stands, is associated with one of the great tragic stories of Irish legend, that of the Children of Lir (see p.186), whose jealous stepmother turned them into swans and forced them to spend 300 years on the Sea of Moyle (the narrow channel between Ireland and the Scottish coast). Also on this shore is **Carraig Uisneach**, the rock on which the mythical Deirdre of the Sorrows, her lover Naoise, and his brothers, the sons of Uisneach, are said by some to have come ashore after their long exile in Scotland (also see p.525).

Practicalities

If you're going to **stay** in Ballycastle, the **tourist office** in Sheskburn House on Mary Street (July & Aug Mon–Fri 9.30am–7pm, Sat 10am–6pm, Sun 2–6pm; Oct–June Mon–Fri 9.30am–5pm; also Sat 10am–4pm Easter–June & Sept; ☎012657/62024) can point you in the right direction. If your budget is generous, the *Marine Hotel*, at the bottom of Quay Road on the waterfront (☎012657/62222; ⑤), is very comfortable. Otherwise try one of the many **B&Bs** at the harbour end of Quay Road – *Glenluce* at no. 42 (☎012657/62914; ③) or *Fragrens Guest House* at no. 34 (☎012657/62168; ③). No. 62, the last house on the left, incorporates the independent *Castle Hostel* (☎012657/62337) while round the corner on North Street is *Ballycastle Backpackers* (☎012657/63612).

There are also several **caravan sites** which take tents, but the most pleasant is six miles out of town at *Watertop Open Farm* (see p.520).

The usual range of fast **food** and tea shops can be found around town: *Donnelly's Coffee Shop* on Ann Street is excellent, and there are good bar lunches at nearby *McCarroll's* and at the *Marine Hotel*, which also has live music on Sundays and hosts *Legends* nightclub for entertainment of the karaoke kind. *Wysner's*, 16 Ann St, has an adventurous and inexpensive menu and is next door to the famous butcher of the same name. You'll find Ballycastle's **pubs** surprisingly lively – *McCarroll's* has traditional music on Saturdays; the *House of McDonnell*, on the main street, is young and lively with music on Fridays; even better is the bar at the *Antrim Arms*, next door, with a magnificent range of whiskeys; the *Central Bar* has sessions on Wednesdays and the *Boyd Arms* on Fridays; down on the seafront, the friendly *Angler's Arms* is a great place to end the evening.

There's **pony trekking** on offer in Ballycastle, too, at the Loughareema Trekking Centre (☎012657/62576), on the Ballyvennaght Road.

Rathlin Island

Northern Ireland's last remaining inhabited offshore island, **Rathlin Island**, is five miles from the mainland and just twelve miles from the Mull of Kintyre in Scotland. **Boats** make the fifty-minute trip from Ballycastle harbour four times daily between June and September (call Caledonian MacBrayne ☎012657/69299) when fares are £7.60 return. Outside these months both fares and services are reduced but, in winter, the wreck-filled waters in the race can become too treacherous for the boat to sail at all or make the return trip, so it's worth making sure in advance that you find a bed on the island, as accommodation is strictly limited.

Shaped like a truncated figure seven, Rathlin is an impressive, rugged island, with a coastline consisting almost entirely of cliffs and a lighthouse at each tip. As the island's width is nowhere more than a mile across, the sea dominates the landscape and its salty winds discourage the growth of vegetation – wind turbines harness this energy source for electricity generation. The presence of dry-stone walls and numerous ruined cottages indicates a time when the population was far larger than the hundred or so current inhabitants concentrated around Church Bay. A stroll around the island will reveal relics of far greater antiquity. Halfway to the West lighthouse, there's the site of a stone-age axe factory, and, to its north, earthworks known as Doonmore (*dún mór*, "big fort"). In the early Christian period the island was a haven for monks, who've left evidence of their presence in the form of a sweathouse (a kind of primitive sauna) at Knockans, back towards Church Bay. In 795 AD Rathlin was the first place in Ireland to be raided by the Vikings. Subsequent times saw three bloody massacres, one by the Scots and two by the English. In 1575, the mainland MacDonnells sent their women, children and old people to Rathlin for safety from the English, but that didn't stop the invading fleet, under the Earl of Essex (whose soldiers included Sir Francis Drake), from slaughtering the entire population. Later, in 1642, the MacDonnells were again butchered by their Scottish enemies, the Campbells; Rathlin was deserted for many years afterwards. You can discover more about the island's history in the **Boathouse**, down by the harbour (daily in summer; £0.50), recently converted to house a heritage centre.

The island's cliffs make superb **birdwatching** country, particularly **Bull Point**, on the western tip, part of a large RSPB nature reserve. The viewpoint at the West lighthouse (April–Aug) provides wonderful views of Northern Ireland's largest colony of seabirds – a minibus plies between here and Church Bay in summer. The foot of the cliff is riddled with caves, many of them accessible by boat only in the calmest of weather, and many also filled with detritus from wrecked ships, brought to the surface by storms. **Bruce's Cave**, on the northeast point of the island, below the lighthouse, is a cavern in the black basalt where, in 1306, so the story goes, the despondent Robert the Bruce retreated after being defeated by the English at Perth. Seeing a spider determinedly trying to spin a web persuaded him not to give up, so he returned to Scotland and defeated the English at Bannockburn. You can **rent a boat** to see the cave (see below), but only in calm weather.

Practicalities

There's not much in the way of **accommodation** on Rathlin and booking ahead is always advisable. There's B&B by the harbour at the *Rathlin Guest House* (☎012657/63917; ②; March–Sept), while ten miuntes' walk to the south, overlooking Mill Bay is the newly-opened *Soerneog View Hostel* (☎012567/63954). Alternatively, *Richard Branson's Activity Centre* (☎012657/63915) does hostel-style accommodation. **Campers** can pitch their tents for free on the East side of Church Bay. Life on the island is simple and uncomplicated, but not entirely basic: you'll find bar-restaurant, *McCuaig's*, and a couple of shops. Rathlin is a good place for fishing, and you can **rent a boat** (☎012657/63933 or 63935) or get Tom Cecil (☎012657/63915) to take you scuba diving around one of the many wrecks offshore. Rathlin's two major events are the week-long **festival** in mid-July, with everything from ceilis to model yacht-racing, and the **regatta** on the last weekend in August.

The north Antrim coast and northeast Derry

The north coast of Antrim, west of Ballycastle, is dominated by Northern Ireland's most famous tourist attraction, the strange formation of basalt columns at the mythical **Giant's Causeway**. However, on the way, around the town of **Ballintoy**, there are several attractions to divert you, not least the precarious rope bridge to **Carrick-a-rede Island**. Beyond the Causeway, you can sample some whiskey at **Bushmills** and visit the imposing and well-preserved remains of **Dunluce Castle**, the stronghold of the local MacDonnell clan.

The coastline west of Dunluce is another major holiday spot, the twin resorts of **Portrush** and **Portstewart** filled with tourists in July and August and students the rest of the year. Inland, lies the dull manufacturing town of **Coleraine**, which you're only likely to visit en route to the coast.

To Ballintoy and Dunseverick Castle

Heading west from Ballycastle to Ballintoy, there are a couple of places on the way that are worth stopping off at. The first of these, **Kinbane Castle**, is a decaying sixteenth-century fortification on a long white headland, built by Colla Dubh, brother of the redoubtable Sorley Boy MacDonnell. The pathway is slippery and badly eroded, but it's worth climbing up to the castle to inspect these Irish defences against the English.

Drawing level with **Carrick-a-rede Island**, not far outside Ballintoy, you'll see the **rope bridge**. Strung 80ft above the sea, the rope-connected planks lead to a commercial salmon fishery on the southeast side of Carrick-a-rede (the name means "rock in the road": the island stands in the path of migrating salmon) – but its main function seems to be to scare tourists, something it does very successfully. Walking its 60ft length, as the bridge leaps and bucks under you, is enough to induce giggles and screams from the hardiest of people. The bridge is up from May to September, when the salmon fishing season ends; there's a car park – always open (£2) – and a café (April–Aug daily 10am–6pm). You can camp here too for a maximum of one night at the National Trust's *Larrybane Campsite* (☎012657/62178).

BALLINTOY itself has a dramatic harbour, much-loved by artists, with a dark, rock-strewn strand contrasting oddly with the neat pale-stone breakwater. It's lively with boats in the summer, and visitors pack the café, *Roark's Kitchen*, but in winter it's bleak and exposed. The little white church that stands at the top of the harbour road was a replacement for the one where local Protestants took refuge from Catholics in 1641, before being rescued by the Earl of Antrim. A landlord of Ballintoy in the eighteenth century, Downing Fullerton, founded Downing College in Cambridge; the staircase and oak panelling were removed from the castle at Ballintoy when it was demolished and taken there. In good weather you can rent boats for fishing and trips along the coast. **Sheep Island**, the bizarre rocky column standing just offshore, is home to a colony of cormorants. In the summer, **boat trips** run out from Ballintoy, past Sheep Island, to Carrick-a-rede (£1). If you're tempted to **stay** in the village, try the refurbished *Fullerton Arms*, 22 Main St (℡012657/69613; ④), or *Ballintoy House*, 9 Main St (℡012657/62317; ②). Hostel accommodation is also available at the brand new and extremely comfortable *Sheep Island View Hostel*, 42a Main St (℡012657/69391), which has space for tents and rents out bikes.

Continuing up the coast, **Whitepark Bay** is a delight, a mile-long sweep of white sand with a YHANI **youth hostel** (open all year; ℡012657/31745), which will organize pony trekking, canoeing, pub trips and parties and is the sort of place where you arrive for one night and stay several. A footpath from Ballintoy leads past here to **PORT-BRADDAN**, a tiny hamlet of multicoloured houses, next to one of which is St Gobban's, a slate-roofed little church which, at twelve feet by six and a half is, supposedly, the smallest church in Ireland. Needless to say, there are other contenders and indeed the ruins of an even smaller one, St Lasseragh's, stand on the cliff above.

Dunseverick Castle

From here the coast path leads round a headland, through a spectacular hole in the rock and then, by degrees, up to the cliffs of **Benbane Head**. The road and path almost converge at **Dunseverick Castle**, now no more than the ruins of a sixteenth-century gatehouse. This was once capital of the old kingdom of Dalriada, which spread over north Antrim and Scotland, and the terminus of one of the five great roads that led from Tara, the ancient capital of Ireland. Its location, naturally enough, made it one of the main departure points for the great Irish colonization of Scotland that took place from the fifth century onwards, and the castle was stormed by the Danes in the ninth and tenth centuries. Dunseverick also features in one of the great Irish love stories, the ninth-century *Longas mac n-Usnig* or "The fate of the children of Uisneach". Deirdre, the betrothed of King Conor, falls in love with his bodyguard, Naoise. Together with Naoise's two brothers, the sons of Uisneach, they flee to Scotland. Fergus, one of Conor's soldiers, believes the king has forgiven them and persuades them to return home. Landing at Dunseverick (or, some say, Ballycastle), they take the high road to Conor's court at Armagh, but the king kills the brothers and seizes Deirdre, who dashes her head against a stone and dies. And Fergus, outraged, destroys Conor's palace (though not, apparently, the king himself). Down in postcard-picturesque Dunseverick harbour, there's a tiny **museum** (June–Aug Mon–Sat 10am–4pm), focusing on objects salvaged locally and elsewhere, including lumps of coal from the *Titanic*.

The Giant's Causeway

Ever since 1693, when the Royal Geographical Society first publicized it as one of the great wonders of the natural world, the **Giant's Causeway** has been a major tourist attraction. The highly romanticized pictures of the polygonal basalt rock formations by the Dubliner Susanna Drury, which circulated throughout Europe in the eighteenth century, did much to popularize the Causeway: two of them are on show in the Ulster Museum in Belfast, and copies are in the visitor centre at the site. Not everyone was impressed, though. William Thackeray ("I've travelled a hundred and fifty miles to see *that*?") especially disliked the tourist promotion of the Causeway, claiming in 1842 that "the traveller no sooner issues from the inn by a back door which he is informed will lead him straight to the causeway, than the guides pounce upon him". Although the

---

FIONN MAC CUMHAILL: THE CAUSEWAY LEGENDS

According to the romantic version of the legend, the Causeway is the everyday story of a love affair between giants. The Ulster warrior, Fionn Mac Cumhaill (Finn McCool), became infatuated with a female giant who lived on the island of Staffa, off the Scottish coast (where the Causeway resurfaces), and built the great highway to bring his lady love to his side. This tale is recounted, alongside the scientific account, in the visitor centre's exhibition – with some fanciful embellishments, such as an estimate of Fionn's height calculated on the basis of a large shoe-shaped stone that's known as his boot. A more robust version has Fionn involved in a row with a Scottish giant. He built the Causeway to go over to Scotland for a punch-up, but on seeing the size of the other giant, lost his nerve and fled home. Safe in Ireland, he had his wife tuck him up in an outsize cot– when the Scots giant arrived in pursuit he saw the size of Fionn's "baby" and in turn took fright and fled, never to be heard of again.

Causeway is probably less overtly money-making than it used to be, it still attracts hundreds of thousands of visitors annually, filling the architecturally incongruous visitor centre (see below) and the minibus which scurries back and forth. However, even in high season, it's easy to escape the crowds by taking to the cliffs.

For sheer otherworldliness, the Causeway can't be beaten. Made up of an estimated 37,000 black basalt columns, each a polygon – hexagons by far the most common, pentagons second, and sometimes figures with as many as ten sides – it's the result of a massive subterranean explosion, some sixty million years ago, that stretched from the Causeway to Rathlin and beyond to Islay, Staffa (where it was responsible for the formation of Fingal's Cave) and Mull in Scotland. A huge mass of molten basalt was spewed out onto the surface, which, on cooling, solidified into what are, essentially, crystals. Though the process was simple, it's difficult, when confronted with the impressive regular geometry of the columns, to believe that their production was entirely natural. The Irish folk versions of their creation (see above) are certainly more appealing.

Undoubtedly, the best way to **approach** the Giant's Causeway is along the cliffs, preferably on a wet and blustery day when you're scared you'll lose your footing along the muddy way. The waymarked **North Antrim Cliff Path**, cut into the cliff side alongside the black geometric configurations, runs all along this stretch of coast. **Public transport** to and from the Causeway is well organized in summer: the "open topper" **bus** runs in July and August five times daily between Coleraine (where the stop is opposite the train station) and the Causeway, stopping at Portstewart, Portrush, Portballintrae and Bushmills; you can flag it down anywhere along the way. If you're travelling by **train** from Belfast, the line ends at Portrush, from where you can catch either the open topper or the regular #172 to Ballycastle; for more details phone ☎012657/43334. If you want to **stay** close to the Causeway there's the *Causeway Hotel* (☎012657/31226; ⑥) near the visitor centre or the *Carnside Guesthouse*, 23 Causeway Rd (☎012657/31337; ③), which has superb views.

Visiting the Causeway

The Causeway's **visitor centre** (July & Aug daily 10am–7pm, April–June & Sept–Oct Mon–Sun 10am–6pm; Nov–Mar Mon–Fri 10am–4.30pm, Sat–Sun 10am–5pm; parking £3) has a Tourist Information Centre (☎012657/31855), bureau de change, craft shop, coffee shop and audiovisual displays, but it's not a place to linger unless you're very cold or very wet – the real excitement is outside. There's a paying exhibition (£1) that doesn't tell you a great deal; its single interesting exhibit is one of the **trams** from the tramway that used to run until 1949 between the train station in Portrush and the Causeway. Opened in 1883, it was the first hydroelectric tramway in Europe, its power generated by the River Bush. The tramway wasn't built simply for the tourists: it was thought that the area would be developed for iron mining, and the tram-owner, William Traill, planned to make his fortune. There was some concern over the possible dangers of using hydro-electricity, and Traill sought to allay fears by dropping his trousers and sitting on the live rail – it was only later that he admitted that he'd suffered a severe shock.

Resist the temptation to follow the crowds along the path straight down to the sea and the famous hexagonal blocks (and dodge the minibus that runs every 15min; £1 return); instead take a better route that's a round trip of roughly two miles. Follow the cinder path up behind the visitor centre and round the edge of promontories – among them **Weir's Snout** – from which you can gasp at the Causeway, and watch the eider and gannets wheeling across from Ailsa Craig, thirty miles away in Scotland. If you're here in autumn and in luck, you may sight the Aurora Borealis bouncing in the sky northwards. A flight of 162 steps takes you down to sea level and a junction in the path, leading further along to the 40ft basalt columns, known as the **Organ Pipes**. Many of the formations have names invented for them by the guides who so plagued Thackeray and his contemporaries – the Harp, for example – but at least one, **Chimney Point**, has an appearance so bizarre that it persuaded a ship of the Spanish Armada to think it was Dunluce Castle, a couple of miles further west, where they might get help from the MacDonnells: instead, the *Girona* was wrecked.

Before you reach Chimney Point, **Port-na-Spánaigh** is the place where the ship foundered in September 1588. The treasure it was carrying was recovered by divers in 1968, and some of the items are on show in the Ulster Museum in Belfast. Sadly, extensive cliff erosion prevents any further exploration and prohibitive costs are likely to deter future reparation.

Tucked into the coastline, inaccessible from land, are some spectacular caves: Portcoon Cave, 450ft long and 40ft high; Leckilroy Cave, which you can't go into; and Runkerry Cave, an amazing 700ft long and 60ft high. Your best option, if you want to explore, is to persuade a fisherman in Portballintrae (see p.528) or Dunseverick Harbour to take you – £40 is considered a persuasive sum.

If the weather is inclement, you can warm yourself up by playing with the whipping tops and skipping ropes in the museum of the Williams-Ellis designed **Causeway School** (daily July & Aug 11am–5pm; £2), next to the centre car park, or sit at an ink-splotched desk in the re-created 1920's classroom.

Bushmills and Dunluce Castle

The next stop on the main road beyond the Causeway is **BUSHMILLS**, whose fore-most attraction is the **Old Bushmills Distillery**, on the outskirts of town. Whiskey has been distilled here legally since 1608, making it the oldest licit distillery in the world, and it's well worth making the **tour** (April–Oct Mon–Sat 9.30am–5.30pm, Sun noon–5.30pm, last tour 4pm; Nov–March Mon–Fri tours at 10am, 11am, noon, 1.30pm, 2.30pm & 3.30pm; £3). Bushmills whiskey is distilled three times, once more than Scotch; but perhaps the biggest surprise is just how unsubtle a business the industrial manufacture of alcohol is, despite all the lore that surrounds it. The distillery is a massive factory where an extraordinary range of (mostly unpleasant) smells assail your nostrils, making it difficult to imagine that the end product really does delight the taste buds. All the same, at the end of the tour you're offered a tot of the hard stuff. The best bet is the unblended malt, representative of what goes on in Bushmills itself, as the grain whiskey that goes into the blend is almost all dis-tilled in Cork; alternatively ask for a tot of Coleraine whiskey, only a tiny amount of which is still produced. They also serve hot toddies, which may be more in order in winter. To find the distillery follow the signs from the cenotaph in the centre of town – it's barely a quarter of a mile.

Practicalities

Accommodation is mostly out of town: *Ahimsa*, at 243 Whitepark Rd (☎012657/31383; ②), with an organic garden and good vegetarian meals, offers inexpensive accommodation in a modernized traditional cottage. Just about the only cheap place in Bushmills itself is *Ardeevin*, 145 Main St (☎012657/31661; ③), on the road out to the distillery. The very best rooms in town are at the *Bushmills Inn*, 25 Main St (☎012657/32339; ⑦), a former coaching **inn** with cottage-style interior complete with secret room and peat fires. Also attached is the excellent *Barony Restaurant*, with an à la carte menu and meals for around £15 – you should at least pop in for a drink in the gaslit bar while waiting for the bus (which stops outside). There's more luxury at *Killen's*, 28 Ballyclough Rd (☎012657/41536; ③), a converted nineteenth–century schoolhouse four miles out of town off the Coleraine Road; it's well equipped with swimming pool, sauna and solarium and a **restaurant** with excellent local produce.

A detour of a mile westwards along the minor coast road from Bushmills will take you to **PORTBALLINTRAE**, a decorous little place with **accommodation** at the friendly *Bayview Hotel* (☎012657/31453; ⑤), 2 Bayhead Rd, or nearby *Bayhead House* (☎012657/31441; ③). There's **camping** at the caravan park on Ballaghmore Avenue (☎012567/31478) and good **fishing** from the tiny harbour.

Dunluce Castle

The main road rejoins the coast, a couple of miles further east. Here you'll see the most impressive ruin on this entire coastline – sixteenth-century **Dunluce Castle** (April–Sept Mon–Sat 10am–7pm; Oct–March Mon–Sat 10am–4pm; also Sun April–June 2–7pm & July–Aug 11am–7pm; £1.50). Perched on a fine headland, high above a cave, it looks as if it only needs a roof to be perfectly habitable once again. Its history is inextricably linked to that of its original owner, **Sorley Boy MacDonnell**, whose clan, the so-called "Lords of the Isles", ruled northeastern Ulster from this base. English incursions into the area culminated in 1584 with Sir John Perrott laying siege to Dunluce, forcing Sorley Boy ("Yellow Charles" in Irish) to leave the castle. But as soon as Perrott departed, leaving a garrison in charge, Sorley Boy hauled his men up the cliff in baskets and recaptured the castle, later repairing the damage with the proceeds of the salvaged wreckage of the *Girona* and arming the fort with three of its cannons. Having made his point, Sorley Boy agreed a peace with the English, and his son, Randal, was created Viscount Dunluce and Earl of Antrim by James I. In 1639, Dunluce Castle paid the penalty for its precarious, if impregnable, position when the kitchen, complete with cooks and dinner, fell off the cliff during a storm. Shortly afterwards, the MacDonnells moved to more comfortable lodgings at Glenarm, and Dunluce was left empty.

However, it remains an extraordinary place. The MacDonnells' Scottish connections – Sorley Boy's son continued to own land in Kintyre – are evident in the gatehouse's turrets and crow-step gables and the tapering chimneys of the seventeenth-century Great Hall. There's a strange touch of luxury in the loggia that, oddly, faces away from the sun.

A spectacular scramble, particularly in wild weather, takes you down to the **cave** below the castle which pierces right through the promontory, with an opening directly under the gatehouse.

Portrush

PORTRUSH, on the Ramore Peninsula, has sandy beaches backed by dunes, running both east and west, and everything you'd expect from a seaside resort, including summer drama in the Town Hall and plenty of amusements for children. Many students from the University of Ulster at Coleraine live here, and make it a considerably livelier place than you might expect, even out of season. The **beach** is long and sandy, ending, towards eastern Dunluce, at the **White Rocks**, where the weather has carved the soft limestone cliffs into strange shapes, most famously the so-called "Cathedral Cave", 180ft from end to end. On a different level, Portrush offers a range of activities and entertainments for children and wet afternoons. There's the all-weather **Waterworld**, by the harbour, with water flumes, slides, sauna, jacuzzis, aquarium and restaurant, **Fantasy Island** indoor adventure playground, on the promenade, and **Barry's Fairground** just behind the seafront. The controversially expensive **Dunluce Centre**, 10 Sandhill Drive (Easter week 10am–8pm; April–June Mon–Fri noon–5pm, Sat & Sun noon–6pm; July & Aug daily 10.30am–7.30pm; Sept daily noon–5pm; Oct Sat & Sun noon–5pm; £5 combined ticket) houses the tourist office (see below), a viewing tower and a variety of interactive and cinematic experiences. The former bath-house for the well-heeled patrons of the *Northern Counties Hotel* on the seafront is now the **Portrush Countryside Centre** (June–Sept Wed–Mon noon–8pm; free), with an indoor sea-creature-filled rock pool, local natural history displays and staff who will happily name your rock samples or flower specimens. There is rewarding **surfing** here off West Strand and White Rocks. You can rent boards and gear at one of the surf shops in Portrush or further along the coast in Portstewart, but first check the safety of the waves (☎01265/824596). Safety considerations are seemingly jettisoned during the annual **raft race** at the end of May when participants race each other across the harbour on homemade rafts. The main sporting attraction, though, is the **Royal Portrush Golf Club** (☎01265/822311), which in 1993, hosted the British Amateur Championships. The North's premiere club, it boasts one nine-hole and two eighteen-hole courses, though in fact most of the coast seems to be covered in greens and putters – eighty in all – whose vistas offer a welcome distraction from your handicap. Demand is high in the summer, especially in good weather, and it's wise to book ahead. A detailed list of green fees, course lengths and standard scratch scores is available from the tourist office.

Practicalities

The very friendly and efficient **tourist office** (mid-June to Sept daily 9am–8pm, April to mid-June Mon–Fri 9am–5pm, Sat & Sun noon–5pm; March & Oct Sat & Sun noon–5pm; ☎01265/823333) is in the Dunluce Centre, on Sandhill Road, south of the town centre.

Accommodation ranges from the *Eglinton Hotel*, near the station, at 49 Eglinton St (☎01265/822371; ⑤), to dozens of **B&Bs**, most of them very friendly and welcoming. Try, for example, *Glenkeen Guest House*, 59 Coleraine Rd (☎01265/822279; ③), which has won tourist board awards, or the excellent *Harbour House*, 36 Kerr St (☎01265/822130; ④). *Macools* independent **hostel** (☎01265/824845) is nearby on Causeway View Terrace. For superb farmhouse B&B, there's the award-winning *Maddybenny Farmhouse* (☎01265/823394; ④), out of town on Loguestown Road; the breakfasts are sumptuous and there's an attached riding school. **Campsites** abound in the area – though most of them are actually fairly unattractive caravan parks that take tents; closest are the *Margoth Caravan Park*, 126 Dunluce Rd (☎01265/822531), and the municipal *Carrick Dhu Caravan Park*, 12 Ballyreagh Rd (☎01265/823712). Note that rooms fill up quickly in high season and also during the North West 200 motorcycle road races in May and major golf championships in July.

The *Ramore Restaurant* (☎01265/824313; at least £25 a head; expensive wine) serves good **food**, while its wine bar offers a less pricy menu, or try the excellent *Don Giovanni's*, 9 Causeway St; otherwise there are plenty of cheap cafés and takeaways. **Nightlife** is quite a serious business here. *Lush!* on Bushmills Road (☎01265/823539) attracts major DJs and, consequently, groovers from all over the North. Then there are regular discos at *Kelly's Hotel* and *Burberry's* at the *Magherabuoy House Hotel*, out of town on Magherabuoy Road, which also has a decent modern restaurant. The town has no end of convivial pubs – the nicest **bar** in town is the *Harbour Inn* – but if you're hoping to hear traditional music your best option is to go to Ballycastle and the *House of McDonnell* pub.

Portstewart and beyond

Across the county border in Derry **PORTSTEWART**, like Portrush, is full of Victorian boarding houses. Of the two, Portstewart is decidedly quieter and has always had more airs and graces: the train station is said to have been built a mile out of town to stop the hoi polloi from coming. In terms of sheer location, though, Portstewart wins hands down. Just west of the town is **Portstewart Strand**, a long sand beach firm enough to drive on – which the locals delight in doing – with some of the best **surfing** in the country. It's a grand place too, if you hit fine weather and feel like getting out your bucket and spade. The best way to take the sea air is the bracing **cliffside walk** which runs between the beach and the town, passing battlements and an imposing Gothic mansion, now a Dominican College.

The **tourist office** (July & Aug Mon–Sat 10am–4pm; ☎01265/832286), in the Town Hall, can help with **accommodation** bookings if you have any problems – there's less choice here than in Portrush. **B&Bs** are mostly along the promenade or nearby. Hotel accommodation is available at the *Edgewater Hotel*, 88 Strand Rd (☎01265/83314; ⑦), which has breathtaking views from its lounge bar. There's also a good independent **hostel**, *Causeway Coast*, at 4 Victoria Terrace (☎01265/833789) and a municipal **caravan park**, *Juniper Hill*, at 70 Ballyreagh Rd (☎01265/832023). *Morelli's*, on the promenade, is justly famous for its ice cream, and also serves snacks and Italian **food** in *Nero's* next door. In the evenings, *Nero's* **nightclub**, part of *Nelly's Complex* on Coleraine Road, is the place for late-nighters, and has a pleasant pub attached. The Flowerfield **Arts Centre**, 103 Coleraine Rd (☎01265/833959), runs a variety of courses and stages occasional exhibitions.

Coleraine

COLERAINE is the county's second largest town after Derry, a lively enough manufacturing and shopping centre during the day, but a depressingly empty, pedestrianized wasteland at night. Most of the interesting action here takes place down by the river, where there are pleasant walks and a thriving marina, and at the University of Ulster campus, with its excellent Riverside Theatre.

The helpful **tourist office** on Railway Road by the station (July & Aug Mon–Sat 9am–6pm; Sept–June Mon–Sat 9am–5pm; ☎01265/44723) will attempt to convince you of the town's attractions and there's a mildly diverting "Historical Trail" to follow. In summer, it's worth enquiring at the tourist office about the environmental **walks** regularly conducted in the area. **B&Bs** are mostly out of town; try *Beardiville Lodge*, 9 Ballyhome Rd (☎01265/31816; ③), off the road to Bushmills or *Rockmount* (☎01265/42914), four miles southwest at 241 Windyhill Rd. The University of Ulster campus provides cheap rooms during the summer vacation (☎01265/44141 ext 4567; ③).

Just a mile south of Coleraine, on the eastern bank of the river, **Mountsandel** is a 200ft mound, apparently the earliest-known dwelling place in Ireland, though the discoveries in Boora Bog in County Offaly must run a fairly close second. The post-holes and hearths of the wooden houses that once stood here have been dated at around 7000 BC.

The northwest Derry coast and Limavady

West of the Bann estuary, the remaining northern coastline of County Derry sees relatively few visitors, but makes a pleasant detour. There are marvellous beaches here all the way from **Castlerock** to **Magilligan Point** and stunning views from the cliffside **Mussenden Temple** and around **Binevanagh** mountain. Inland, **Limavady** retains a few relics of Georgian times.

Castlerock and Mussenden Temple

Five or so miles from Coleraine, at the Castlerock crossroad, is **Hezlett House** (noon–5pm; July & Aug Wed–Mon; April–June & Sept Sat & Sun; £1.80), built in 1690 and restored after a fire in 1986. The house is a fine example of cruck-truss construction, an early method of prefabricated building using wooden frames, filled with clay and rubble, common in England, but enough of a rarity here to warrant preservation by the National Trust. The last owner of the house is buried in the graveyard at Downhill, where his gravestone quaintly bears both his own version of the spelling of his name and that of his father, a Mr Hazlett.

Lying almost a mile south, the small resort of **CASTLEROCK** has a long strand reaching eastwards to the Barmouth, where the River Bann's estuary draws flocks of migratory birds and watchers. Unless you're a surfer, there's not much else to tempt you, apart from the cosy *Castlerock Bar* (known locally as *Love's*).

Two miles west along the A2, a pair of huge ornate Pompeian gates mark the entry to **Downhill Palace** and **Mussenden Temple** (noon–6pm: July & Aug daily; April–June & Sept Sat & Sun; free; grounds open all year). Both were built in the 1780's by Frederick Augustus Hervey, Anglican Bishop of Derry and fourth Earl of Bristol. The Palace lies in ruins and was last occupied by US troops, billeted there during World War II. Lower down, the Temple clings precariously to the eroding cliff edge (restoration work was in progress at the time of writing). The classic domed rotunda was apparently modelled on the Roman temple of Vespa and was built by the Bishop in honour of his cousin Mrs Frideswide Mussenden, who died aged 22 before it was completed. It was subsequently used as a summer library. Later, with characteristic generosity and a fairly startling lack of prejudice, Hervey allowed a weekly Mass to be celebrated in the Temple as there was no local Catholic Church. The inscription on the temple frieze translates, rather smugly as: "It is agreeable to watch, from land, someone else involved in a great struggle while winds whip up the waves out at sea." The Bishop was also an enthusiastic grand traveller, after whom all the *Hotel Bristols* throughout Europe are named. He was an art collector and a great sportsman, once organizing a pre-prandial race along the strand between Anglican and Presbyterian clergy. His other constructions include a folly, in the grounds of the Palace, and the Bishop's Road, which runs from Downhill and across Binevanagh Mountain on its way to Limavady.

There's **camping** in nearby Downhill Forest (☎01265/848728), across the road from Mussenden Temple, and, in **DOWNHILL** village itself, the excellent and spacious *Downhill Hostel* (☎01265/849077) overlooks the strand.

Magilligan Strand and Point to Limavady

Beyond Downhill the road hugs the cliffs, while the seven-mile stretch of beach curves around to **MAGILLIGAN POINT**, passing further **camping** opportunities at the *Benone Tourist Complex* (☎015047/50555). The road to the point runs across the dunes, skirting the edge of an open prison, once an army base and later an internment camp, before reaching the end of the peninsula. Here, at the narrow entrance to Lough Foyle, stands a Martello tower, dating from the Napoleonic Wars, with walls more than nine feet thick. There's the *Point Bar*, too (open Summer only), where you can enquire about the ferry for foot-passengers and cyclists across the water in Inishowen. One of Ireland's most famous harpers, Dennis O'Hempsey, was from the Magilligan townland and attended the last great Belfast harp festival of 1792 where he played the *Londonderry Air*.

From the peninsula the road cuts south alongside the foot of Mount Binevanagh before reaching **BELLARENA**. The land around the mountain is now a conservation park, dedicated to the preservation of birds of prey, in particular, falcons and kestrels. In the village itself lies Bellarena House, an old plantation mansion, dating back in parts to the seventeenth century. This was once the home of Sir John Heygate, a minor novelist now long out-of-print, who achieved some notoriety when he travelled with his more famous Fascist-sympathizing colleague, Henry Williamson (author of *Tarka the Otter*) to pay homage to Adolf Hitler in the 1930's. Unfortunately, the house is no longer open to the public, but is visible from the common ground banks of the River Roe.

LIMAVADY was once a major settlement, its old site lying two miles further south down the valley of the River Roe. The town was refounded as Newtown Limavady in the early 1600s by Thomas Phillips, speaker of the Irish House of Commons, and promptly spent the next three hundred and fifty years or so in relative obscurity. However, in recent years, Limavady has undergone major economic expansion and most roads to the centre now pass through industrial estates. Although the town's population has consequently increased, there's still relatively little to do or see here. The six-arch bridge spanning the river was built in 1700 and Main Street which runs down from it is still recognizably Georgian. Number 51 was once the home of Jane Ross who noted down the *Londonderry Air* ("Danny Boy") from a travelling fiddler in 1851. Limavady's only other recent claim to fame is as the birthplace of William Massey, Prime Minister of New Zealand from 1912 to 1925. **Tourist information** is available from the council offices at 7 Connell St (July & Aug Mon–Fri 9am–5.45pm; Sept–June Mon–Fri 9am–5pm; also Easter–Sept Sat 9.30am–5.30pm; ☎015047/22226). There are some lively bars in the centre of town, including the atmospheric *Owens*, and a few **B&B** options, such as the *Alexander Arms*, 34 Main St (☎015047/62660; ③). At **Drenagh**, just outside Limavady, *Streeve Hill* (☎015047/66563; ⑥), a Palladian-fronted house dating from 1730, offers superb accommodation and gourmet meals.

The **Roe Valley Country Park**, a couple of miles south of Limavady, preserves Northern Ireland's first hydroelectric power station, opened in 1896, with much of the original equipment intact, as well as a small weaving museum and a visitor centre (daily: June–Aug 10am–8pm; Sept–May 10am–5pm).

Derry city

DERRY lies at the foot of Lough Foyle, immediately before the border. It's a crossroads city in more ways than one; roads from all cardinal points arrive here, but it was also a major point of emigration from the eighteenth century onwards, an exodus which reached tumultuous proportions during the Great Famine. Derry is the fourth largest town in Ireland and the second biggest in the North, but it has a markedly different atmosphere to Belfast, being two-thirds Catholic. Within Ireland, Derry is highly regarded for both its characteristically caustic humour – best caught in the busier bars and at the football matches at the Brandywell – and its musical pedigree, having produced names as diverse as Dana, Phil Coulter, The Undertones, and many less famous. This last claim to recognition is misleading, though – Derry may produce musicians, but its own music scene is largely inaccessible to outsiders.

Approached from the east in winter twilight or under a strong summer sun, the city presents a beguiling picture, with the spread of the **River Foyle** and the rise of the city's two hillsides, terraced with pastel-shaded houses from which rise the hueless stone spires of the ever-present Church Orders. This scenic appeal apart, at first sight Derry might appear to offer little cause to linger longer, for all the richness of its history. Yet there are several real attractions, mostly enclosed within the seventeenth-century **walls**, themselves the most significant reminder of the city's past. And four miles or so out of the centre, across the border on the Letterkenny Road, is the unmissable **Grianán of Aileach** (see p.472), a stone fort and the oldest habitation left standing in Ireland.

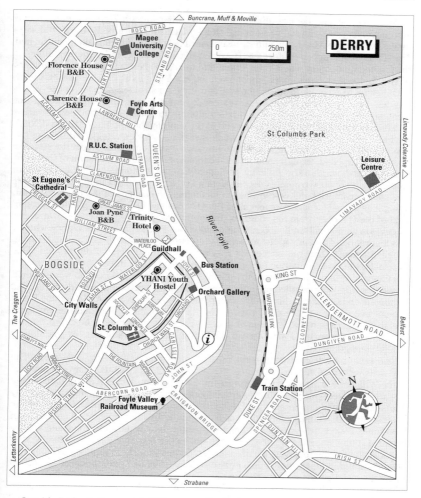

Outside Ireland, the name of Derry recalls the Troubles of recent years and savage events like the Bloody Sunday massacre. Under no circumstances be deterred, for, unlike Belfast, the cutting edge of violence had receded considerably here even before the cease-fires, and the city is still imbued with a real sense of optimism. Perhaps the greatest vote of confidence in Derry's future is from the big retail chains, such as Marks & Spencer and Sainsbury's, which have built their first outlets in the city.

Some history

Derry's original name was *Daire Calgaigh* ("oakwood of Calgach"), a warrior who led the Caledonians at the battle of the Grampians. Some time after St Columba founded a monastery here in 546 AD, the spot was renamed *Doire Cholmcille*. The monastic settlement must have been relatively unimportant for, although Vikings settled around Loughs Foyle and Swilly, only one actual attack was made on *Doire*. By the twelfth century, however, the Mac Lochlainn dynasty, based in Inishowen, had taken control and a small township began to develop. However, decline had set in by the beginning of the fourteenth century when it was granted to the Anglo-Norman de Burgos, builders of the fortress at Greencastle, Inishowen (see p.477). By 1500, the power of the O'Dohertys had spread from Inishowen and they constructed a tower house which was later to be absorbed into the seventeenth-century walls. In 1566, Elizabeth I of England sent a small task force in a failed attempt to pacify such troublesome Irish chieftains as Shane O'Neill, but at the end of the century the uprising of Hugh O'Neill, Earl of Tyrone, provoked another English invasion. *Doire's* strategic position on the River Foyle was quickly appreciated and the town was soon captured and the resident population expelled, though an accidental explosion led to the evacuation of the garrison soon afterwards. The military presence was not restored until 1600 when an English army of 4000 troops under Sir Henry Docwra landed at Culmore Point. *Doire* was soon recaptured and Docwra began fortifying the remains of the medieval town, using it as a base for incursions against the O'Neills and O'Donnells, gaining the support of the O'Dohertys in his ventures. When the war ended in 1603, the town began to develop as a small trading centre and *Doire* became anglicized as **Derry** when it was incorporated as a city in the following year. However, in 1608, Sir Cahir O'Doherty rebelled against Docwra's successor, Pawlett, and burnt Derry to the ground. This destruction made the city ripe for the "plantation" of English and Scottish **settlers** and the financial assistance of the wealthy businessmen of the City of London was obtained to achieve this. A new walled city was constructed and renamed Londonderry in 1613 in honour of its backers, the Twelve Companies of the Corporation of London. Today the entrance routes to the city bear the two different names reflecting the changing sectarian majority on the city council. Indeed, the place has come to be called "Stroke City" – a reference to the tactful placating of both traditions by naming it Londonderry/Derry.

The **seventeenth century** was the most dramatic phase of the city's evolution. The city walls withstood successive sieges, the last of which (in 1688–89) played a key part in the Williamite army's final victory over the Catholic King James II at the Battle of the Boyne – the Derrymen's obduracy crucially delaying the plans of James and his ally Louis XIV. James's accession had seen the introduction of a policy of replacing Protestants with Catholics in leading positions in the Irish administration and army. In December 1688, a new garrison attempted to enter the city, but was prevented when a group of young apprentices seized the keys and locked the city's gates. Eventually, after negotiation, an all-Protestant garrison under Governor Robert Lundy was admitted. Over the following few months the city's resident population of two thousand swelled to thirty thousand as people from the surrounding area took refuge from Jacobite forces advancing into Ulster. Fearing that resistance against the Jacobite army was futile, Lundy left – his effigy is still burnt each December by Protestants. Around seven thousand Protestants died during the fifteen-week **siege** (the longest in British history) that followed, the survivors being reduced to eating dogs, cats and rats. The suffering and heroism of those weeks still have the immediacy of recent history in the minds of Derry's citizens, who commemorate the siege through the skeleton on the city coat of arms, and the lyrical tag "maiden city", a reference to its unbreached walls.

After the siege, many Derry people emigrated to America to avoid the harsh English laws, and some of their descendants, such as Daniel Boone, achieved fame there. George Farquhar (b. 1678), a Derryman who chose to stay, achieved fame as a playwright. Derry's heyday as a **seaport** came in the nineteenth century, a period in which industries such as linen production also flourished. It was a Derry weaver, William Scott, who established the world's first industrialized shirt manufacturers, cutting the shirts in Derry and sending them to the cottage women of Donegal for stitching. After **Partition**, the North–South dividing line lay right at Derry's back door, and the consequent tariffs reduced much of its traditional trade.

CIVIL RIGHTS

Though Derry remained relatively peaceful, its politics were among the North's most blatantly discriminatory, with the substantial Catholic majority denied its civil rights by gerrymandering geared towards ensuring the Protestant minority's control of all important local institutions. On October 5, 1968, a 2000-strong **civil rights march** demanding equality of employment and housing, and other political rights, and led by a Protestant, Ivan Cooper, and a Catholic, John Hume, the current SDLP leader, set off on a route through the walled city. Confronted by the batons of the Protestant police force and the B Specials, rioting spilled over into the Bogside and over eighty people were injured. The clash is seen by many as the catalyst for the modern phase of the Troubles: faith in the impartiality of the Royal Ulster Constabulary was destroyed once and for all, and the IRA was reborn a year or so later.

The Protestant Apprentice Boys' March, in August 1969, was a further step. The notorious "Battle of the Bogside" ensued when the RUC attempted to storm the area (from where stones were being thrown at the march) which for several days afterwards lay in a state of siege. The Irish prime minister, Jack Lynch, moved units of the army to the border and set up field hospitals for injured Bogsiders. In the mounting tension that ensued, British troops were for the first time widely deployed in the North, and many of the demands of the civil rights movement were forced on Stormont from Westminster. Then, on January 30, 1972, came **Bloody Sunday**. Thirteen people were shot dead when British paratroopers (who subsequently claimed that they had been shot at first) opened fire on another unarmed civil rights march.

These days, the city is controlled by the Social Democratic and Labour Party, which attempts to be scrupulously non-sectarian. In this they seem to have been successful (at least in Northern Irish terms), and they also pursue an enlightened arts policy which has succeeded in making this a lively and unexpectedly entertaining place to visit. The city's fabric has also undergone dramatic changes with the construction of huge new developments such as the Foyleside, Quayside and Richmond shopping centres.

Arrival, information and accommodation

Northern Ireland Railways runs about seven **trains** a day from Belfast to Derry (information on ☎01504/342228), and there are also frequent **buses** from all parts of the North and the Republic; Ulsterbus (☎01504/262261) serves all the main Northern Ireland destinations and Dublin, at frequencies ranging between five daily to Dublin and eleven most days to Strabane; Bus Éireann operates a good network, connecting Derry to such as Galway and Dublin; and Lough Swilly Bus Services (☎01504/262017) and North West Busways (☎077/82619) run buses from across the border in north Donegal. Good roads enter the city from all directions, making it very straightforward to **hitch**. You can also **fly**: Jersey European, British Airways and Gill Airways operate from a range of UK departure points to the revamped City of Derry Airport (☎01504/810784), seven miles out on the A2 road. A regular bus service runs from the Ulsterbus station, Foyle Street, and from the railway station to the Airport. The AIRporter coach service also connects Derry with Belfast International Airport (☎01504/269996). **Black taxis** run from Foyle Street and most operate in a similar way to those in Belfast, functioning like minibuses to ferry the Catholic community to and from their housing estates. For a regular taxi, call Auto-Cabs (☎01504/345100) or Quick Cabs (☎01504/260515).

The **tourist office** is situated in a spanking new building at 44 Foyle St (July–Sept Mon–Fri 9am–7pm, Sat 10am–6pm, Sun 10am–5pm; Oct–June Mon–Thurs 9am–5.15pm, Fri 9am–5pm; also Easter–June Sat 10am–5pm; ☎01504/267284) and also houses a **Bord Fáilte** office (all year Mon–Fri 9am–5pm; ☎01504/369501) and a **bureau de change**. Grab a free pocket guidebook for up-to-date information. The Catholic *Derry Journal* (Tues & Fri) is good for entertainment listings.

Top-of-the-range accommodation in Derry includes *The Trinity Hotel*, 22–24 Strand Rd (☎01504/271271; ⑦); and, on the Waterside, *Everglades*, Prehen Road (☎346722; ⑦), and the *Waterfoot Hotel*, 14 Clooney Rd (☎01504/345500; ⑥). **B&Bs** are fairly thin on the ground in the centre, but you could try the following: *Clarence House*, 15 Northland Rd (☎01504/265342; ④); *Florence House*, 16 Northland Rd (☎01504/268093; ②); and *Joan Pyne*, 36 Great James St (off Strand Road; ☎01504/269691; ②). There's a 150-bed YHANI **hostel** in the city centre, *Oakgrove Manor*, 4–6 Magazine St (☎01504/372273), which does a generous and cheap Ulster fry, **rents bikes** and acts as an unofficial tourist information centre. There's also the *Independent Hostel* at 29 Aberfoyle Terrace (☎01504/370011), a mile down Strand Road. **Rooms** are also seasonably available at the university to the north of the centre (mid-June to mid-September; Mon–Fri ☎01504/371371; £14.10).

The City

Since the removal of the security blanket of metal barricades and barbed wire following the cease-fire, it has once again been possible to walk the entire circuit of Derry's city walls. One of the best preserved defences in Europe, a mile in length and never higher than a two-storey house, the walls are reinforced by bulwarks and bastions and a parapeted earth rampart as wide as any thoroughfare. Within their circuit, the original medieval street pattern has remained, with four **gateways** (Shipquay, Butcher, Bishop and Ferryquay) surviving from the original construction, albeit in slightly revised form.

You're more than likely to make your approach from the Guildhall Square, once the old quay. The neo-gothic ecclesiastical appearance of the **Guildhall** (Mon–Fri 9am–5pm; guided tours ☎01504/377335) itself belies its true function as the headquarters of the City Council. Inside, the city's history is depicted in a series of stained glass windows. Most of the city's cannon are lined up opposite here, between the Shipquay and Magazine gates, their noses peering out above the ramparts. A reconstruction of the medieval **O'Doherty Tower** (10am–5pm; July & Aug Mon–Sat; Sept–June Tues–Sat; £3.25) is home to a prize-winning **museum** telling the city's history over the past four centuries. Tableaux and audiovisual displays supplement traditional museum exhibits in this determinedly non-sectarian gallop through time – and, as far as possible, you're supplied with the facts and left to make up your own mind. The upper gallery houses artefacts from the Spanish Armada wrecks, while the basement occupies tunnels and cellars dating back to the siege. The **Harbour Museum** (Mon–Fri 10am–1pm, 2–5pm; free) recounts Derry's maritime history and contains a replica of the thirty-foot curragh in which St Columba sailed to Iona in 563 AD.

Turning left at Shipquay Gate into **Bank Place**, you follow the promenade as it doglegs round at Water Bastion, where the River Foyle once lapped the walls at high tide. On to Newgate Bastion and Ferryquay Gate, you can look across the river to the prosperous and largely Protestant Waterside. Several sculptures have been placed at strategic points on the walls by the English artist Antony Gormley, their gaping eye sockets looking out in diametrically opposite directions from a single body – a frank comment on the city's ideological split. Aesthetics aside, the figures provide welcome visual relief against the office buildings that swamp the immediate view.

DERRY CITY WALLS

BOGSIDE

Free Derry Wall ●

Long Tower Church

Bloody Sunday ● Memorial

Butcher's Gunner's Gate Bastion

Coward's Bastion

Magazine Gate

Guildhall

Shipquay Gate

Bus Station

Water Bastion

UNION HALL STREET

BANK PLACE

Steps

Hangman's Bastion

Tower Museum

Derry Craft Village

Orchard Gallery

MAGAZINE ST

SHIPQUAY STREET

YHANI Youth Hostel

Castle Gate

CASTLE STREET

NEWMARKET STREET

Epicure's

Richmond Shopping Centre

Newgate Bastion

Steps

LINEN HALL ST

BUTCHER ST

THE DIAMOND

FERRYQUAY STREET

MAGAZINE ST

Orange Order Memorial Hall

Calgach Centre

PUMP STREET

USIT Office

Ferryquay Gate

The Playhouse

ARTILLERY ST

SOCIETY STREET

LONDON STREET

BISHOP STREET WITHIN

Ferry Bastion

Royal Bastion

GRAND PARADE

PALACE STREET

St Augustine's Church ✝

R.U.C. & British Army Fort

Courthouse

Verbal Arts Centre

St Columb's Cathedral ✝

New Gate

Double Bastion

PATHWAY

Bishop's Gate

THE FOUNTAIN AREA

Church Bastion

PATHWAY

N

0   40 yds

Just off steeply sloping Shipquay Street as you penetrate towards the heart of the old city is **Derry Craft Village** (Mon–Sat 9.30am–5.30pm), an Inner City Trust project in a purpose-built traditional stone village complex, with shops, restaurants and a craft shop representing a range of traditional skills. Though now largely well-established, like the rest of the city, the shops here have been affected by the falling value of the punt against the pound, with shoppers flocking across the border to Donegal, and there are a few vacant lots. But it's still well worth a visit and the elegant *Boston Tea Party* coffee shop is a good place to sit and take it all in.

A right turn at the Diamond will take you down Butcher Street to Derry's latest attraction, **The Fifth Province** (shows Mon–Fri 11am and 2.30pm; £3), in the Calgach Genealogy Centre, a multimedia "journey" through Ireland's heritage. The trip begins in a stone chamber "Departure Lounge" where the actor Richard Harris provides a video introduction to the history of Derry. Next it's off to the module and a trip into space to meet Calgach, founder of ancient Derry, who regales you with tales from the past. Finally, your senses are bombarded with a panoply of images celebrating Irish culture.

Near the city walls on London Street (from the Diamond walk down Ferryquay Street, then turn right), **The Verbal Arts Centre** is a unique project aimed at sustaining and promoting forms of communication and entertainment once central to Irish culture: legend, folklore, *seán nos* – a nasalized and unaccompanied narrative singing – and storytelling performed by a *seanachie* (storyteller). The centre commissions works from writers, hosts poetry readings and storytelling and has its own resident *seanachie*. It also visits schools and community centres and has a determinedly non-sectarian ethos, influenced by its understanding of the importance of the oral tradition in all cultures. Every year at the beginning of April, it promotes an international storytelling **festival**; and there are also plenty of events year-round, so drop in and check out what's on the programme.

St Columb's Cathedral, the Fountain area

The Church of Ireland **St Columb's Cathedral** (April–Oct Mon–Sat 9am–5pm; Nov–Mar 10am–4pm; closed all year 1–2pm; £1 donation) was built in 1633 in a style later called Planter's Gothic and was the first post-Reformation cathedral to be constructed in the British Isles. Displayed in the entrance porch is a cannon shell catapulted in during the siege by the besieging army, to which was attached their terms of surrender. The cathedral was used as a battery during the siege, its **tower** serving as a lookout post; today it provides the best view of the old city. The present spire dates from the late Georgian period, its lead-covered wooden predecessor having been stripped to fashion bullets and cannon shot. Inside, an open-timbered roof rests on sixteen stone corbels carved with figures of past bishops; hanging above the nave, French flags captured in the siege, and others brought back from various military expeditions, serve to make the interior a forceful reminder of British Imperialism. Other things to look out for are the finely sculpted reredos behind the altar, the eighteenth-century bishop's throne and the window panels showing scenes as diverse as the relief of the city on August 12, 1689 and St Columba's mission to Britain. In the **chapter house museum** (50p) are more relics of the siege, plus the grand kidney-shaped desk of Bishop Berkeley (who only visited Derry once) and mementos of Cecil Frances (1818–95), wife of Bishop Alexander and composer of the famous hymns *Once in royal David's city* and *There is a green hill far away*.

By Bishop Gate stands the **courthouse**, built of white sandstone from Dungiven in crude Greek Revival style. The gate itself was remodelled for the first centenary of the siege and reopened in 1789. Immediately outside the walls here is the **Fountain** area, named after the freshwater source that once supplied the city, though there are few remnants of any antiquity here apart from the immediately visible remaining tower of the old Derry jail, jammed up against the grim modern houses. The Fountain area is a housing estate that sticks into the Catholic west bank like a sore thumb, with a single road entrance close to the Craigavon Bridge. It's of interest solely for its Union Jack kerb paintings and huge wall murals which read as direct responses to the more famous Catholic "Free Derry" mural in the next valley. Until recently, the Fountain area had the **oldest mural** in the north. Painted in the early part of this century by Bobby Jackson, it showed the Siege of Derry and the Battle of the Boyne, and was repainted every year. In the 1970s, when the area was redeveloped, the wall was painstakingly dismantled, moved, reassembled and repainted, but it finally disintegrated in 1994. A replica was painted in 1995 on a special Bobby Jackson memorial wall. Other Loyalist murals are to be found in Fountain and in Bond Street in the Waterside.

The Bogside

Back on the walls, and continuing west, you reach the Double Bastion where the Roaring Meg cannon sits. During the siege it was said that "the noise of the discharge was more terrifying than were the contents of the charge dangerous to the enemy". In the valley below is the **Bogside**, where, at the start of the Troubles, young Catholics were caught up in an advancing disarray of army and police, who replied to bricks and petrol bombs with tear gas, rubber bullets and careering Saracen armoured cars. The area at the foot of the escarpment has been redeveloped in the form of a dual carriageway, a new estate of tenement flats and empty concrete precincts. But clinging to the opposite hillside is a classic urban landscape, with turn-of-the-century terraces of stucco facades, blue tile roofs and red chimney stacks.

Most eye-catching in this panorama is an isolated wall bearing the slogan "You are now entering Free Derry". The **Free Derry Mural** was originally painted by local man John "Caker" Casey in the aftermath of the attack by Loyalists on a civil rights march in 1968. Since then the signature of the Nationalist camp in Derry has become almost a community notice board, marking events as disparate as Derry's win in the All-Ireland Gaelic Football Final in 1993 and the release of Republican prisoners. A nearby wall carries another well-known mural, with a message to the British Army, *Slán Abhaile* ("goodbye/safe home"), that you'll see displayed in many other Catholic areas in the North.

For the first two years of the Troubles, the territory beyond the mural was the notorious "no go area", the undisputed preserve of the IRA. This autonomy lasted until 1972, when "Operation Motorman" was launched; the IRA men who had been in the area were warned, though, and got across the border before the invasion took place. Further across to the right of the wall stands the memorial pillar to the thirteen Catholic civilians killed (another died later of his wounds) on **Bloody Sunday** (January 30 1972) by British paratroopers. The soldiers immediately claimed they were fired upon, an assertion that was later disproved, though some witnesses have come forward to report seeing IRA men there with their guns. The bitter memory of the subsequent Widgery Commission's failure to declare anyone responsible for the deaths has festered in Catholic Derry and maintained pressure on successive governments to reopen investigations. A new inquiry was finally announced in spring 1998. To the right of this area once stood the Rossville flats, by far the most infamous part of the Bogside – Derry's equivalent of the Belfast Divis. Further up the Westland Road, which runs up by the *Bogside Inn* – a former IRA stronghold, where the gunmen would set their revolvers on the bar while drinking – is a busy mural grouping the silhouetted faces of Bobby Sands, Che Guevara and Lenin.

Near the Royal Bastion, a more recent slogan comes into view, "No Sectarian Marches", symmetrically printed out on the panels of a balcony of flats just down the hill. This Bastion was constructed between 1826 and 1828 and used to be topped by a nine-foot high statue of Rev George Walker, the defender of Derry (to quote the still legible inscription) "against an arbitrary and bigoted monarch". The statue was blown up in 1973 and the surrounding area remains a significant flashpoint every August 12 when the Apprentice Boys march in Walker's and their predecessors' memory (see box on p.500).

Railway Centre

To the southeast of the walled city, the **Foyle Valley Railway Centre** on Foyle Road by Craigavon Bridge (all year Tues–Sat 10am–5pm; free) is more interesting than it might sound and has train rides (£2.50) at weekends. The highlight is a short trip up the Foyle Valley on a steam train, but there are also plenty of old engines and models, plus extensive displays on the history of railways in the area, a sad tale of decline enthusiastically explained.

Eating, drinking and entertainment

Although **eating** out in the city has improved dramatically over recent years, you still won't be put out by a bewildering choice. The best food is to be found in the suburbs at *Schooner's*, 59 Victoria Rd (☎01504/311500) in the Waterside, or *Brown's* (☎01504/45180) at 1 Bond Hill. *Piemonte Pizzeria* (☎01504/266828) on Clarendon Street is the best pizza place in town, while *India House*, 51 Carlisle Rd (☎01504/260532), is an excellent Indian with main courses around £7. Nearby, at 45a, is the best Italian, *La Sosta* (☎01504/374817). For seafood and an especially good chowder, head out to *Reggie's*, 165 Strand Rd (☎01504/262050). *The Galley*, 12a Shipquay St, is a good daytime choice with good pizzas and home baking. Otherwise, try bustling and good-value *Anne's Hot Bread Shop,* 8 William St, open until 2am Mon–Sat, or the very sociable *Leprechaun* on the Strand. As ever, you can also get lunch in many of the pubs: *Badgers Place*, in Orchard Street, has recently won awards, but the *Metro* in Bank Place, the *Linenhall* in Linenhall Street and the *Monico Lounge* opposite the main post office are also worth checking out. In the Waterside, *Brendan's Diner*, 164 Spencer Rd, is renowned for its sit-down fast food.

Bars and music

What Derry lacks in restaurants, it makes up for, inevitably, in the **pubs**. For drinking and talk, the student set congregates at the *College*, *The Strand Tavern* and *Andy Cole's*, all grouped at the bottom of the Rock Road, and of course in the campus bar in Magee College grounds, where beer is cheapest. Other congenial and conversational places are *The Clarendon Bar*, 44 Strand Rd, *The Anchor Bar*, 38 Ferryquay St, *Badgers Place*, 18 Orchard St for an older clientele and *Mullins* on Sackville Street. The swish *Porters Bar* in *The Tower Hotel* on Strand Road is the place to sit, spot and be spotted. Out past Magee College on the Culmore Road is *Da Vinci's*, one of Derry's newer pubs with a restaurant and nightclub.

Traditional music in the city is not as exciting as it once was: the venues that remain are mostly grouped in and around **Waterloo Street**, just outside the northern section of the walls, a mainly Catholic working-class area. The *Dungloe Bar* claims to be the most regular music-making place here, with traditional sessions on Friday and Saturday. Other sessions take place at the *Rocking Chair Pub* and the *Gweedore Bar*, which has a function room upstairs with good music and dancing. It often stays open until 1am and is connected to *Peadar O'Donnell's* next door, a retro pub, which does set dancing. Elsewhere, the *Casbah Club* in Hennessy's, Strand Road, has regular rock and blues, *J&J McGinley's*, on Foyle Street, offers live music six nights a week, and *Sandinos,* around the corner in Water Street, has a mixed bag, including jazz. The *Phoenix Bar*, on Park Avenue in the Rosemount area, has traditional music on Tuesday evenings, as does the *Pilot's Row Centre* (7.30–9.30pm), which also offers classes in Irish dancing, music and language. The *Bogside Inn* on Westland Road has music on Thursday evenings. Bear in mind, though, that the city is highly politicized, and if a hat comes round, you're advised to contribute without asking questions.

For livelier **nightlife**, head for Shipquay Street, where the *Gluepot* and *Townsman* pubs and the cavernous *Squire's* nightclub all attract a young crowd. Also worth checking out is the *Carraig*, at 113–121 Strand Rd, or the *Delacroix*, on Buncrana Road, where the dancing is more traditional and there's a Wednesday night comedy club. Another popular thing to do on Friday and Saturday nights is to cross the border, to nightclubs at Letterkenny, Redcastle and the White Strand, Buncrana.

Arts and other entertainment

Classical music thrives in the city through the Londonderry Arts Association (☎01504/264481), with around a dozen concerts a year held in the Great Hall of Magee University College. Orchestral concerts by the Ulster Orchestra are held much less regularly in the Great Hall of the Guildhall. The Playhouse on Artillery Street is a good venue for art, dance, music and drama, while The Rialto in Market Street offers a broad range of populist entertainment; however, **theatre** in Derry since the early 1980s is still associated, despite its current inactivity, with the polemical, and hugely controversial, Field Day Theatre Company, whose principal members have included, at one time or another, the poet Seamus Heaney (see p.544), the academic Seamus Deane, the actor Stephen Rea and the playwright Brian Friel. **Film** buffs are catered for by the seven-screen Strand cinema and the Foyle Film Club at the Orchard cinema.

The **visual arts** are also attracting a lot of international attention, thanks largely to the highly innovative contemporary art programming of the Orchard Gallery in Orchard Street; a visit there is a must – and watch out for the exhibitions it sometimes arranges in the Foyle Arts Centre, off Lawrence Hill, or at other venues around the city. The Heritage Library, on Bishop Street, occasionally has local artists' work on display.

Several **arts festivals** take place at regular times throughout the year (see "Listings" below). In addition, **Halloween** is traditionally an excuse for riotous celebration, with fireworks, fancy dress and partying in the streets. The tourist information office will have further details of all events.

Listings

Airlines British Airways (to and from Aberdeen, Glasgow, Liverpool, Manchester, Amsterdam, Brussels & Frankfurt; ☎0345/222111); Jersey European Airways (to and from Belfast, Blackpool, Bristol, Exeter, Guernsey, Isle of Man, Jersey, Leeds, London Gatwick, ☎01504/457200).

Banks Principally situated on Guildhall Square, Shipquay St and Waterloo Place.

Bike rental and repairs Rental at *Oak Grove Manor*, 4-6 Magazine St (☎01504/372273) and Eakin Bros Ltd, Maydown (☎860601); repairs at Bee's Cycles, 4 Waterloo St (☎01504/372155) and Beragh Hill Cycles, 21 Beragh Hill Rd (☎01504/358400).

Bookshop Bookworm, 18 Bishop St, is one of the best bookshops in the country, with superbly comprehensive coverage of contemporary and historical Irish works and a café too.

Car rental Avis, City of Derry Airport (☎01504/811708); Desmond Motors, 173 Strand Rd (☎01504/360420).

Coach tour Foyle Civic Tour – one-hour tour of the city (July & Aug Tues 2pm from Foyle St bus station; ☎01504/262261; £3)

Exchange Available from all banks; the Tourist Information Centre; Thomas Cook, Quayside Centre (☎267284); branches of NW Money Exchange at 68 Strand Rd (☎01504/367710) and in the Richmond Centre (☎01504/260636); *Oak Grove Manor Youth Hostel*, 4–6 Magazine St (☎01504/372273).

Festivals Celtic Spring Festival (March – three weeks of various events, including drama and Irish language festivals); Foyle Film Festival (late April – one of the most prestigious in Ireland); International Jazz and Blues Festival (late May); Two Cathedrals Festival (October – classical music); Halloween Carnival (a week of mayhem with a huge firework display on October 31).

Hospital Accident and emergency department, Altnagelvin Hospital, Belfast Rd (☎01504/345171); contact this number also for **dental** emergencies after working hours or at weekends.

Laundry Foyle Dry Cleaners, 147 Spencer Rd; Duds 'n' Suds, 141 Strand Rd.

Library The Central Library, Foyle St, has a good selection on Irish studies and local history.

Market Bottom of William St – stalls most days, but busiest every Sat.

Newspapers The Catholic *Derry Journal* (Tues & Fri) has a good run-through of what's on in the city; the Protestant local paper is the *Londonderry Sentinel* (Wed).

Police Main Police Station, Strand Rd (☎01504/367337).

Post office Custom House Street (☎01504/362563; Mon 8.30am–5.30pm, Tues–Fri 9am–5pm, Sat 9am–12.30pm).

Travel agents USIT, 33 Ferryquay St (☎01504/371888); Thomas Cook, Unit 7, Quayside Centre (☎374174); Co-op Travelcare, 10 Strand Rd (☎01504/261514).

Walking tours McNamara's Tours (☎01504/265536); guided tours of historic Derry, £1 per person.

Southern Derry

South of the A6, the Derry–Antrim road, the landscape settles down into a pattern more familiar to the Republic: fertile farming land, rising to the **Sperrin Mountains**, punctuated by small planned towns. The pattern in the North is subtly different, though, because the grants of land here were not made to individuals but to various London guilds or companies. Consequently, there isn't the strange, late-flowering feudalism that you see in the Republic, with its repeated archetype of big house and surrounding town, but rather entirely **planned towns**, such as **Magherafelt** and **Moneymore**, often built on green-field sites selected by professionals, who specialized in doing just that. The huge expanse of Ireland's biggest lake, **Lough Neagh**, laps against the county's southeastern corner and here too is one of the must-see sites of the entire North, **Bellaghy Bawn**.

The road to Dungiven

Seven or so miles east from Derry, a turning leads to **Ness Wood Country Park**, a pleasant place to stop and stroll through a mixture of natural and imported woodland. The centepiece is **Shaun's Leap waterfall**, the highest in the North, whose waters cascade into a small glen below a thirty-foot wide chasm, across which the outlaw, Shaun Crossan, is said to have leaped to evade capture. The waterfall featured in the Mills and Boon guide to the *Most Romantic Places in Britain* and, although the scene is undoubtedly picturesque, you might reckon the authors need to get out more in the evenings.

DUNGIVEN, ten miles further on, is a fairly unremarkable town, though it does harbour one or two ruins of interest. Originally an O'Cahan stronghold, Dungiven was given to the Skinners' Company to settle in the seventeenth century. The remains of the O'Cahan fortifications are incorporated into the ruined nineteenth-century **castle**, whose battlemented outline gives Dungiven a particular flavour when approached from the south. This was the scene of the 1971 attempt to set up an independent Northern Ireland parliament.

Dungiven Priory, signposted down a footpath a little way out of the town towards Antrim, gives a taste of the pioneering life of the early plantation settlers, and of the continuity of tradition. No more than a ruin, the Augustinian priory stands on an imposing, defensible site on a bluff above the river. Founded in 1100 by the O'Cahans, it belongs to the first wave of European monastic orders which arrived in Ireland to supplant the Celtic Church. The church contains the tomb of Cooey na Gall O'Cahan, who died in

1385, rated as the finest medieval tomb in Northern Ireland: beneath the effigy are six bare-legged warriors in kilts, presumably denoting Scotsmen, who represent the O'Cahan chieftain's foreign mercenaries, from whom he derived his nickname, na Gall, or "of the foreigners". At some point, the O'Cahans added a defensive tower to the west end of the church, and later – when Dungiven was granted to the Skinners' Company, in the person of Sir Edward Doddington – this was enlarged to become a two-and-a-half storeyed defensive manor house. There's an evocative artist's impression on the site of what that building looked like.

Although the church hasn't been used since 1711, Dungiven Priory remains a religious site of sorts. The tree knotted with rags – handkerchiefs, torn off bits of summer dresses, socks – stands over a deeply hollowed stone, originally used by the monks for milling grain, and now an object of pilgrimage for people seeking cures for physical illness. There's little to tempt you to stay, although if you fancy a night in a converted stone mill, try *The Flax Mill* (☎015047/42655), an independent **hostel** three miles north of town and signposted off the Limavady Road.

The ruined **Banagher Old Church**, a couple of miles southwest of Dungiven, was founded in the twelfth century by St Muiredach O'Heney, who is buried in the well-preserved mortuary house built on a sandhill in the churchyard. The ruins themselves are sedately impressive and the walks around the nearby Banagher Glen nature reserve equally so (daily June–Sept 9am–9pm).

Plantation towns

South of Dungiven, well into the Sperrin Mountains, are more of the **plantation towns** of the London companies, most of them characteristically planned around a central diamond. **DRAPERSTOWN**, is essentially a junction, with well-mannered houses facing each other in a very grand street design. The **Plantation of Ulster Visitor Centre** on the High Street (daily 11am–5pm, but Oct–Easter Sun 1–5pm; £2.50), as its name suggests, recounts the story in more detail, using multimedia technology. At **UPPERLANDS**, ten miles north beyond Maghera, you can get some idea of the impact of the new eighteenth-century technology on the area at the **Middle House Museum**, a private textile museum owned by the Clark family. In 1740, Jackson Clark dammed the river to provide power and installed linen-finishing machinery here. If you want to look around, phone William Clark & Sons (☎01648/42214) in advance to arrange a guided tour (Mon–Thurs). *Ardtara Country House* nearby (☎01648/44490; ⑦) offers a taste of Victorian elegance (and roast racks of Sperrin lamb).

Heading south, **MAGHERAFELT**, granted to the Salters' Company by James I, has another wide, sloping main street and an increasingly successful Arts Festival in March. The town makes a reasonable base for exploring Lough Neagh and the Bellaghy area (see overleaf) with **accommodation** at *Laurel Villa*, 60 Church St (☎01648/3228; ④), which also organizes heritage and angling breaks, plenty of food choices, and a pleasant old-time bar in *Mary's* on the Market Place. The real gem, though, is **MONEYMORE**, about five miles further south, built by the Drapers and reconstructed by them in 1817: graceful pedimented buildings face each other across a wide main street topped by an Orange Hall (plenty of red, white and blue kerbstones here). It was the first town in the North to have piped water – amazingly, as early as 1615. Just outside Moneymore, **Springhill** (2–6pm: July & Aug daily except Thurs; April–June & Sept Sat & Sun; £2.50) is a typical example of the fortified manor houses built by the early planters. Dating from the late seventeenth century, it's a lovely bit of sober whitewashed architecture, housing a good costume collection and a delightfully overgrown garden. You can **camp** in the farmyard here (☎016487/48210).

Lough Neagh and Bellaghy

East of Magherafelt and Moneymore, are the fish-filled waters of the biggest lake in Ireland, **Lough Neagh**. Tributaries flow from every point of the compass: the **Lower Bann**, which drains the lake and runs north to Lough Beg (finally reaching the sea north of Coleraine), contains some huge trout, including the rare *dollaghan*, the Lough Neagh trout (best fishing mid-July to Oct). Similar to salmon – which are also common – they grow by 3lb every year and can be caught by spinning, worming and fly fishing. In fact the Ballinderry Black and the Bann Olive are famous flies derived from this region.

To fish in the lough or the river, all anglers require a Fisheries Conservation Board Rod Licence (call Lough Neagh Tourism; ☎01849/481312); however, while this entitles you to carry a rod it doesn't mean that you can fish unless you have a permit from the owner or you're in free water. The angling clubs which control much of the water let day tickets at reasonable rates. For details of licences and permits ask at local tackle shops, the nearest being Heuston's Sport, Main Street, Castledawson (☎01648/68282) and Hamilton's Sport, Burn Road, Cookstown (see p.596; ☎016487/66541).

BELLAGHY, just east of Lough Beg, like many of the plantation settlements in the area, has a history which reflects the divisions between communities. Indeed, no less than two of the ten 1981 Hunger Strikers (see p.626), cousins Francis Hughes and Thomas McElwee, came from the village, and Orange Parades have been a regular flashpoint. The village is neatly laid out around a T-junction and, if you wander south, past the whitewashed terraces on Castle Street, you'll come to one of the best examples

---

SEAMUS HEANEY

There was a sunlit absence.
The helmeted pump in the yard
heated its iron,
water honeyed

in the slung bucket
and the sun stood
like a griddle cooling
against the wall
of each long afternoon.

(From *Mossbawn: 1. Sunlight*)

It's impossible to conceive of a contemporary poet, Irish or otherwise, whose works are more evocative of time and place than **Seamus Heaney**. He was born, the eldest of nine children, on the family farm of Mossbawn (itself the title of two poems in his fourth collection *North*), in the townland of Tamniarn, near Bellaghy, on April 13, 1939. Heaney's family background, his Catholic upbringing and his study of Irish at school imbued him with a strong sense of being Irish in a state which considered itself British, a paradox which would form a major motif in his work during the 1970s. While at Queen's, he was further influenced by the literature he discovered in Belfast's Linenhall library, especially the works of John Hewitt, the Antrim-born "Poet of the Glens", and the English "naturalist" poet, Ted Hughes where he found an "association of sounds in print that connected with the world below". The rural Monaghan setting of Patrick Kavanagh's poetry further echoed his own experience and vision.

Heaney's first poem, *Tractors* was published in the *Belfast Evening Telegraph* in 1962, and his first significant collection, *Death of a Naturalist*, followed in 1966 and was immeof a surviving plantation castle, **Bellaghy Bawn** (April–Sept Mon–Sat 10am–6pm, Sun 2–6pm; Oct–March closes 5pm; £2), constructed in 1622 by the Vintners' Company. Most of its fortifications were lost in 1641, but it still retains an impressive circular flanker tower. Now owned by the Department of the Environment, the Bawn has been sensitively restored and was opened to the public in July 1996. Inside you'll find fascinating interpretive displays explaining the 7000-year-old history of the settlements in this area, the Vintners' construction of the village – today's houses still occupy the same original allocated plots of land – and the diverse ecology of the Lough Beg wetland area. The real treasure here, however, is the dedication of much of the Bawn's space to a most notable local man, **Seamus Heaney**, one of the twentieth-century's greatest living poets, who was born and brought up nearby (see box below). Heaney himself is the star of a unique and atmospheric video, "A Sense of Place", in which he recounts the influence of his upbringing, local character and landmarks on his poetry. His father, for instance, rented grazing rights on the strand at Lough Beg and, in *Ancestral Photograph*, he recalls helping to herd the cattle that grazed there down Castle Street on their way to market. Prints of other poems are displayed on the walls of various rooms and the Bawn's library contains the ultimate collection of his works, including first drafts and extremely limited editions. The building's helpful curators are extremely knowledgeable and there's a small café here too.

You can see the shimmering Lough Beg from the windows of the flanker tower and a stroll down to the lake is well worthwhile. In summer, the lake's waters recede and Church Island becomes accessible from the strand. Besides a walled graveyard, there

---

diately recognized for its earthiness and command of diverse metrical forms. While lecturing at Queen's, his career expanded into journalism and television and he became increasingly involved in the Civil Rights movement. His response to the Troubles saw him seeking for "images and symbols adequate to our predicament" and he began to see poetry as a mode of resistance, but, eventually, the violence so disturbed him that he moved with his family to County Wicklow. Ian Paisley's *Protestant Telegraph* bade farewell to "the well-known papist propagandist" on his return to his "spiritual home in the popish republic". While his seventies collections *North* and *Field Work* received mixed receptions – some saw the strong influence of Robert Lowell on the former – Heaney found himself turning increasingly to his Irish heritage as a source of inspiration, particularly the long medieval poem *Buile Suibhne (The Madness of Sweeney)*, publishing his own *Sweeney Astray* collection in 1983. The following year's *Station Island* drew upon his experiences as a participant in St Patrick's Purgatory (see p.447.

The hunger strikes of the early 1980s brought a new urgency to Northern politics and a revival of Heaney's polemicism. Prompted by the staging in Derry in 1980 of Brian Friel's play, *Translations*, which showed English surveyors travelling through eighteenth-century Ireland anglicizing all the place names, Heaney co-founded the **Field Day Theatre Company** with Friel, his old friend and fellow-academic Seamus Deane, the actor Stephen Rea and others. While the group's theatrical activities were themselves controversial, it was their publications which engendered the most antipathy. Their pamphlets were criticized as attempts to over-intellectualize the Troubles and the 1991 *Field Day Anthology of Irish Writing* was decried for its under-representation of work by women writers, although a new edition was recently brought out in which this was rectified.

Heaney's reputation, however, has remained largely unsullied, maintained not merely by the sheer literary strength of his work and its ready accessibility, but by his undoubted "presence" and a lack of pomposity, notwithstanding his nickname, "Famous Seamus". In 1995, his abilities were more widely recognized by the award of the Nobel Prize for Literature.

are the ruins of a medieval church, said to have been founded centuries before by the ubiquitous St Patrick, with a tower and spire added by the eccentric Frederick Augustus Hervey, Anglican Bishop of Derry and fourth Earl of Bristol, in 1788 (see p.531) to improve his view from Ballyscullion House on the mainland nearby. He commissioned Lanyon to build a huge replacement for the original, with, apparently, 365 windows, but died abroad before ever moving in. You can view the ruins, if you rent one of the *Lough Beg Coach Houses* (☎01648/386235; £200–380 per week) which offer good **self-catering accommodation** and run coarse fishing and birdwatching weekends. The village's only **B&B** is at tiny, though comfortable *Bawn Lodge*, 10 Castle St (☎01648/386241), while the sole **restaurant** is at *McKenna's Bar*. Five buses run daily to Bellaghy from Magherafelt and seven from Ballymena.

South Antrim: Ballymena to Belfast

South Antrim is unlikely travelling country, being largely rolling and unexciting farmland, with places whose names are familiar because you've heard them so often on the news: Ballymena, Antrim and Lisburn. Still, you're likely to see something of most of these towns as the train from Belfast passes through them on the way to the northern coast.

Ballymena and Gracehill

BALLYMENA (pronounced *Ballamena*, unless you're a BBC newsreader) is a fine, upstanding, predominantly Protestant town that could have been transplanted straight from the Scottish lowlands. Indeed, most of its plantation settlers came from the southwest of Scotland, and the Ballymena accent still retains traces of Scottish lowlands speech. Like many Northern Irish towns, its prosperity derived from the linen trade, while the alleged tightfistedness of its residents earned it the sobriquet of the "Aberdeen of Ireland". The town's Saturday market is a lively affair and its streets are often thronged with shoppers and crammed nose to tail with traffic, but significant redevelopment has left little surviving from the pre-Victorian era. In the summer, there's a **tourist office** at 13–15 Bridge St (☎01266/653663), otherwise it's a trek out to the Council Offices, 80 Galgorm Rd (Mon–Fri 9am–5pm; ☎01266/44111). A mile and a half west of Ballymena is **GRACEHILL**, a reminder of the curious mixture of religious oppression and tolerance that has characterized Northern Ireland's history: at the same time as Ireland's Catholics were suffering heavy penalties, the country was welcoming dissenting Protestant groups, among them the Moravians (the United Brethren), who founded a model settlement at Gracehill in 1746. The elegant square survives, with separate buildings for men and women, whose main trade was making lace and clocks. Segregated in life, the sexes remained divided in death, and in the graveyard you can walk down the long path that separates the graves of the men from those of the women. For miles around Ballymena the landscape is dominated by one of Antrim's most mystical reference points, **SLEMISH MOUNTAIN**, best approached from the village of Buckna, eight miles or so east. This extinct volcano is said to be the place where St Patrick herded swine as a slave boy after being captured and brought to Ireland, and, consequently, is a place of pilgrimage on March 17, though others claim his writings indicate the place of his captivity was Killala, County Mayo. Whatever, the mountain's a steep climb of about 700 feet from the car park to the summit, but the views are well worth the effort; to the north, you'll see the ruins of Skerry Church, the ancient burial place of the O'Neills of Clandeboye.

Antrim

ANTRIM, by way of contrast, is a largely undistinguished town, and, although its population has trebled since the 1970s, it doesn't feel especially fecund with possibilities. If you've time to kill, there's a tenth-century **round tower** in Steeple Park, a mile out of town, indicating the site of an important monastery that flourished between the sixth and twelfth centuries; and a pretty, if unremarkable, eighteenth-century cottage, Pogue's Entry, the preserved childhood home of Alexander Irvine, author of *My Lady of the Chimney Corner* recalling his boyhood years before the famine; the tiny, neighbouring **tourist office** (all year Mon–Sat 9.30am–6pm; ☎01849/465156) will let you in. If you pop through the Castle Gate at the Market Square, you'll find yourself in the pleasant gardens of the old Antrim Castle. The building itself was totally destroyed by fire in 1922, but the carriage house and stables now house the **Clotworthy Art Centre**, worth checking for its galleries of work by local artists and occasional international exhibitions. **Belfast International Airport** is just four miles south of Antrim, but luckily this doesn't mean that you have to stick around – the transport links to Belfast are much better than to Antrim. There's camping at *Sixmilewater Marina & Caravan Park* (☎01849/464131; May–Sept) on the shore of Lough Neagh and daily cruises on the waters.

Lisburn

LISBURN, eight miles from Belfast, is the administrative centre of Northern Ireland's second largest local authority and its busy, pedestrianized shopping streets and packed car parks, indicate a recent commercial success perhaps unknown in its days as an important linen town. After the revocation of the Edict of Nantes in 1685, which removed French and Dutch Huguenots' freedom of worship, large numbers of them were persuaded to come to Ulster, where they founded the linen trade. Bleach greens were set up along the banks of the River Lagan; the first of them started in 1626 at Lambeg, a mile downstream from Lisburn. The place has given its name to the big drums which appear in the Orange marches, deriving from the military drums of Prince William's army. Lisburn's one major attraction is the **Irish Linen Centre and Museum** (April–Sept Mon–Sat 9.30am–5.30pm, Sun 2–5.30pm; Oct–March Mon–Sat 9.30am–5pm; Linen Centre £2.75; museum free), situated in the eighteenth-century assembly rooms in the Market Square. A permanent exhibition, "Flax to Fabric", recounts the industry's history and you can watch weavers plying away in the purpose-built hand-loom workshop. The museum typically collects items and artefacts of essentially local interest. The building's modern attachment contains the **tourist office** (April–Sept Mon–Sat 9.30am–5.30pm, Sun 2–5.30pm; Oct–March Mon–Sat 9.30am–5pm; ☎01846/660038), a café and shops, and there are often art displays and lunchtime recitals. There's been a Tuesday market in the town since 1627, but little architecturally survived a catastrophic fire in 1707. The seventeenth-century cathedral opposite the Linen Centre was rebuilt as a result and, in its churchyard, you'll find a number of Huguenot graves. However, nowadays, the fourteen-screen **Omniplex** cinema on Governor's Road tends to be a more popular draw. Lastly, standing a mile from Lisburn in the village of Hilden, the **Hilden Brewery** (Mon–Sat 10am–4.30pm; £2) is one of only two real ale breweries in Ireland (the other is Whitewater in Kilkeel, Co Down), established in 1981 in the courtyard of a former linen baron's mansion. A visit is an olfactory treat; the whiff of malted barley and hops leaving you eager to slake your thirst with a taste of the amber-coloured ale or the dark, malty Special Reserve. You can lunch here, too, in the attached *Tap Room Restaurant*.

THE MAZE

The political prison of **Long Kesh** (or the Maze), which lies to the south of Lisburn and is clearly visible from the main M1 motorway, incorporates the notorious H-blocks which were the focus of the 1981 **hunger strikes**, in which Republican inmates demanded the reinstatement of political status. The prison, erected on an old airfield soon after the Troubles began, housed hundreds of activists, Loyalist and Republican, interned without trial by the British government. Originally all inmates – convicted prisoners as well as internees – had special category status (a kind of POW status), in accordance with the Emergency Powers legislation under which they had been convicted, but when the British government phased out internment in late 1975, special status went with it. From March 1, 1976, the prison was in the peculiar position of housing the last of these special category prisoners as well as – in the H-blocks – those convicted after this cut-off date, who were now classified, and treated, as ordinary criminals.

The IRA campaign for the reinstatement of status began in 1976 when Kevin Nugent, in refusing to wear prison clothes, initiated what became known as the "blanket protest" (quite simply, draping a blanket around himself instead of wearing prison clothes). By 1978, this had escalated into the famous "dirty protest", in which Republican prisoners refused to undertake ordinary prison duties such as emptying chamber pots, resorting instead to smearing the cells with their own excrement in order to get rid of it. In 1981, a concerted hunger strike led to the deaths of ten men, including Bobby Sands, provisional commander of the IRA men inside the prison, who had, significantly, been elected MP for Fermanagh–South Tyrone six weeks into his fast (Sands popularized the Republican slogan, *Tiocfaidh ar lá*, "our day will come"). None of this succeeded in budging the government, which steadfastly refused to back down in the face of what it believed was nothing more than moral blackmail. The motivation for the hunger strikes was made manifestly clear in a piece of contemporary graffiti that appeared in Republican areas:

I'll wear no convict's uniform
Nor meekly serve my time
That England might brand Ireland's fight
Eight hundred years of crime.

Since the hunger strike, the Maze has regularly returned to the headlines, most notably in early 1998 when the LVF leader, Billy Wright, was shot dead in the prison by the INLA, an action which led to retaliation killings across the North, including the murder of a pair of Catholic and Protestant friends in Poyntzpass. The almost universal disgust that this act provoked was, undoubtedly, a central factor in the resolution of the peace settlement talks in April 1998.

travel details

TRAINS

Antrim to: Belfast (10 daily; 1hr 10min).

Coleraine to: Belfast (10 daily, 2hr); Portrush (7 daily; 15min).

Derry to: Ballymena (7 daily; 1hr 20min); Belfast (7 daily; 2hr 40min); Coleraine (7 daily; 40min).

BUSES

Ballycastle to: Ballymena (9 daily; 50min); Belfast (3 daily; 1hr 50min); Coleraine (4 daily; 1hr); Cushendun/Cushendall (1 daily in term-time; 40/50min); Giant's Causeway (6 daily; 35min); Larne via Cushendall (2 daily; 1hr 45min); Portrush (5 daily; 1hr).

Coleraine to: Limavady (12 daily; 1hr); Portrush/Portstewart (daily every 30–60min; 17/30min).

Derry to: Belfast (daily hourly; 2hr); Buncrana (10–16 daily; 40min); Coleraine (6 daily; 1hr); Cork

(1 daily; 10hr 30min); Derry Airport (6 daily; 20min); Donegal (3 daily; 1hr 30min); Dublin (5 daily; 4hr 15min); Dunfanaghy (4 daily; 50min–1hr 45min); Dungloe (3–4 daily; 4hr 30min); Letterkenny/Sligo/Galway (3 daily); Limavady (15 daily; 50min); Limerick (1 daily; 9hr); Malin Head (2–4 Mon–Sat; 1hr 30min); Monaghan (2 daily; 2hr 5min); Moville (4 daily; 50min); Stroove (3 daily; 1hr 10min); Waterford (1 daily; 10hr 30min).

Dungiven to: Derry (daily hourly; 30min–1hr); Limavady (7 daily; 45min).

DOWN AND ARMAGH

Counties **Down** and **Armagh** occupy the southeastern corner of Northern Ireland, between Belfast and the border. It's a region where all too many of the place-names are familiar from the news, and certainly the border areas, especially south Armagh, have borne more than their share of the Troubles. But it's also very attractive country, especially around the coast, and you're never far away from associations with **St Patrick**, who sailed into Strangford Lough to make his final Irish landfall in Down, founded his first bishopric at Armagh, and is buried at either Downpatrick or Armagh, depending on whose claim you choose.

Heading south from Belfast, the glowering **Mourne Mountains** increasingly dominate the panorama, and it's in this direction that most of the attractions lie. If you simply take the main roads in and out of Belfast – the A1 for Newry and the border or the M1 motorway west – you'll come across very little to stop for: it's in the rural areas, the mountains and coast, that the charm of this region lies. Probably the best option is to head east from Belfast around the Down shore, through the **Ards Peninsula** or along the banks of **Strangford Lough**, towards **Newcastle**, the best base for excursions on foot into the Mourne Mountains. Along the way there are plenty of little beaches, early Christian sites, defensive tower houses and fine mansions to visit. Immediately outside Belfast in this direction are the **Ulster Folk and Transport Museum**, one of the best in the North, and the blowsy suburban resort of **Bangor**. Beyond the Mournes a fine coast road curves around to **Carlingford Lough** and the border.

Inland there's less of interest, certainly in County Down. **Armagh city**, though, is well worth some of your time for its ancient associations, cathedrals and fine Georgian streets. South Armagh has some startlingly attractive country, especially around **Slieve Gullion**.

COUNTY DOWN

The coast and the Mourne Mountains at the southern extremity are the major attractions of County Down. The big towns in the north, **Newtownards** and **Bangor**, are much less appealing, but beyond them the A2 road clings to the coast for much of the way down the Ards Peninsula and, via the Strangford Ferry, all the way to Newry. Other routes follow the shores of Strangford Lough towards **Downpatrick** and its

---

ACCOMMODATION PRICE CODES

Throughout this book, prices of hotels, guesthouses and B&Bs have been graded with the codes below, according to what you can expect to pay for a double room in high season. For more details on accommodation, see p. 29.

① Under £26	④ £40–55	⑦ £90–110
② £26–33	⑤ £55–70	⑧ £110–130
③ £33–40	⑥ £70–90	⑨ Over £130

associations with the arrival of St Patrick. There are numerous small resorts around the coast, but **Newcastle** is the biggest, and in some ways the most enjoyable. It's also the ideal place to start your exploration of the mountains.

East of Belfast

Heading east into County Down from Belfast, you've a choice of two routes: the A2, which heads up to Bangor or the A20 directly east to Newtownards, at the head of Strangford Lough, on the way to which you'll pass **Stormont** (p.496) four miles from the city centre.

Following the A20, the single interesting sight as you near Newtownards is **Scrabo Tower** (Easter & June–Sept Sat–Thurs 11am–6.30pm; free), whose looming presence dominates the surrounding area. The tower protrudes from the top of a rocky, gorse-strewn hump of a hill (a long-extinct volcano), but getting to it after you've spotted it is quite a circuit – follow the signs to **Scrabo Country Park** and you'll arrive in the car park just below. The hill itself is pitted with quarries used to extract Scrabo stone, employed for all manner of local building including Grey Abbey (see p.558). Up close the tower looks like a monstrous rocket in its launcher, hewn out of rough black volcanic rock. It was built in 1857 as a memorial to the third Marquess of Londonderry, General Charles William Stewart-Vane, in gratitude for his efforts on behalf of his tenants during the Great Famine. The spot was originally a Bronze Age burial cairn, probably the resting place of one of the grand chieftains of the area, and there's evidence of a huge hill fort here too. It's now very popular with sightseers, who come mostly for the wonderful views across Strangford Lough and the healthy, blustery weather that often curls around the side of the hill. The woodland immediately behind is a country park open to the public (April–Sept Mon–Fri 9am–5pm, Sat 10am–4pm, Sun 2–6pm; Oct–March Mon–Fri 9am–5pm; free); in contrast to the tamed, prosperous countryside round about, Scrabo is the only piece of ground for miles around to feel at all wild.

Newtownards

Scrabo Tower looks down on **NEWTOWNARDS**, a place strong on manufacture but unexciting for the traveller. Despite its name, it's an old town, founded in 1244, though there's little evidence of this beyond the ruined Dominican priory just off Castle Street. The Scrabo stone market house (1765), now the town hall and arts centre, lords it over a large square filled on Saturdays by market activity. The **tourist**

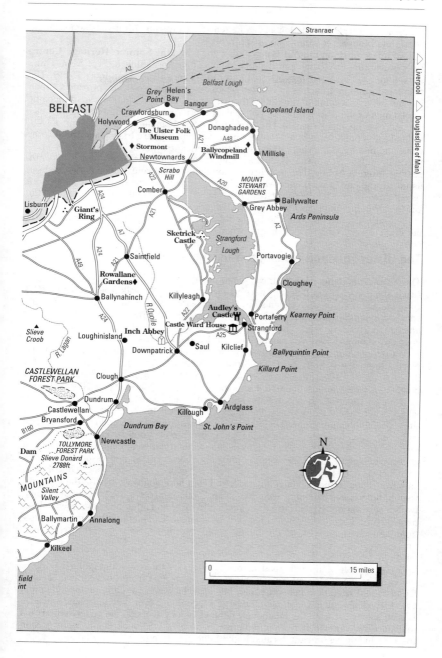

Stranraer

Liverpool ▷

Douglas(Isle of Man) ▷

Belfast Lough

Copeland Island

BELFAST

Grey Point Helen's Bay

Crawfordsburn

Bangor

Holywood

Donaghadee

The Ulster Folk Museum

A48

◆ **Stormont**

Ballycopeland Windmill

Millisle

Newtownards

Scrabo Hill

A21

MOUNT STEWART GARDENS

A20

Comber

Lisburn

Giant's Ring

A24

A7

Sketrick Castle

Strangford Lough

Saintfield

Ballywalter

Grey Abbey

Ards Peninsula

A2

Portavogie

Rowallane Gardens ◆

A49

Ballynahinch

R. Quoile

Killyleagh

Cloughey

Slieve Croob

Inch Abbey

Loughinisland

Audley's Castle

Castle Ward House

Portaferry

Strangford

Kearney Point

Downpatrick

Saul

Kilclief

A25

Ballyquintin Point

R. Lagan

Killard Point

CASTLEWELLAN FOREST PARK

Clough

Ardglass

Dundrum

Killough

St. John's Point

Castlewellan

Bryansford

Dundrum Bay

B180

Newcastle

Dam

TOLLYMORE FOREST PARK

Slieve Donard 2788ft ▲

MOUNTAINS

Silent Valley

N

Ballymartin

Annalong

Kilkeel

field int

0 ——————— 15 miles

office is near the bus station at 31 Regent St (July–Aug Mon–Sat 9am–5.30pm; Sept–June Mon–Sat 9.30am–5pm; ☎01247/826846).

Two miles north on the A21 Bangor road you'll find the **Somme Heritage Centre** (July–Aug Mon–Fri 10am–5pm, Sat–Sun noon–5pm; April–June & Sept Mon–Thurs 9am–4pm, Sat–Sun noon–4pm; Oct–March Mon–Thurs 10am–4pm; tours £3.50). The re-created frontline trenches are staffed by guides in battledress who provide a sobering and moving account of the role of the Irish and Ulster Divisions in the futile battle – 5500 men of the 36th (Ulster) Division alone were reported dead, wounded or missing. Across the main road is **The Ark** (Mon–Sat 10am–6pm, Sun 2–6pm; £2.30), Ireland's first public rare breeds farm, where you can compare Irish Moiled and Kerry cattle and marvel at the sheer ugliness of the Vietnamese pot-bellied pig.

A mile out of Newtownards on the Millisle road stand the ruins of the fifteenth-century **Movilla Abbey**; it's a largely disappointing site, but some ancient grave slabs in its north wall hint at what once was here. In the cemetery next door there's the more recent grave of James Francis, a Greyabbey man who fought in the Irish Brigade on the Union side in the American Civil War. The Brigade suffered heavy casualties during two of the War's bloodiest actions, the Battle of Cold Harbour and the Siege of Petersburg, but Francis survived both and later returned to Newtownards, dying there in 1921.

The Ulster Folk and Transport Museum

The A2 towards Bangor is both more scenic and more interesting, and still within easy reach of a day-trip from Belfast. There's a lovely fifteen-mile walk from **HOLYWOOD** (pronounced *Hollywood*) to Helen's Bay (see opposite), along a mildly indented estuary coast with some beautiful silvery sand beaches, especially the small crescent-shaped ones at Helen's Bay itself. The train line runs between the path and the road, with a couple of stations where you can pick up services on towards Bangor.

At Cultra station you can alight for the one of the most fascinating museums in the North, the **Ulster Folk and Transport Museum** (April–June & Sept Mon–Fri 9.30am–5pm, Sat 10.30am–6pm, Sun noon–6pm; July–Aug Mon–Sat 10.30am–6pm, Sun noon–6pm; Oct–March Mon–Fri 9.30am–4pm, Sat & Sun 12.30–4.30pm; £4) – Ulsterbus #1 from the Laganside Buscentre also stops here. The main site is an open-air museum village where about thirty typical buildings from all over the North, some dating from the eighteenth century, have been taken from their original sites and rebuilt complete with authentic furnishings, including an entire street from Dromore and Belfast terraces. Conceptually, you can walk from one part of Northern Ireland to another, amid appropriate scenes. Traditional farms have also been created and assorted livestock roam between the buildings. The starting point is a gallery on Ulster's social history and an introduction to the buildings themselves. From here you walk around the grounds, visiting the various buildings, including a small village street with church and rectory, two schools, various typical farm dwellings, and a forge and other buildings used in light manufacture. Each of these is "inhabited" by a member of staff, garbed in period costume and informative about the building and its origins. Such historical realism is impressive, though sometimes a little disquieting: the Kilmore Church graveyard contains real tombstones donated by family members.

On the far side of the main road, across a bridge, are the **transport galleries**, where the exhibits include every conceivable form of transport from horse-drawn carts to lifeboats and a vertical take-off plane, but especially veteran cars, motorcycles and trams. You'll also meet *Old Maeve*, the largest locomotive ever built in Ireland and a De Lorean sports car from the infamously defunct factory. Outside the galleries there's a miniature railway which runs on summer Saturdays, and back in the main section there's a handy **restaurant**, located in the Education Centre.

Helen's Bay

If you're not walking, **HELEN'S BAY** is signposted a mile off the A2, or it's another stop on the Belfast–Bangor train line. It's a rather twee but restful little place, with a red-painted Scots Baronial-style station. Down at the bay itself, a walking path leads east to **Grey Point Fort** (April–Sept Wed–Mon 2–5pm; Oct–March Sun 2–5pm; free), positioned to command the mouth of Belfast Lough, along with its sister fort at Kilroot on the other side. The fort has what you'd expect by way of quarters and stores, as well as an impressive battery of gun emplacements, ready to challenge the shipping that entered the lough during the two world wars. In the event, the two six-inch breech-loading guns were never fired except in practice (local residents had to be warned to open their windows and doors to prevent blast damage), but for one occasion in World War II, when a merchant ship failed to respond to the signal "heave to or be sunk" and received a warning shot across its bows. The guns were sold for scrap in 1957 when the Coast Artillery was disbanded. After the fort was opened to the public in 1987 an identical six-inch gun was relocated here from the prison on Spike Island in Cork harbour. The Battery Observation Post and Fire Command Post are today staffed by dressed-up mannequins, like stills taken from a war movie – though they're now staring straight into a growth of trees that have sprung up to obscure the view. There's also a selection of photos showing the original guns and their positions; but it's really as a viewpoint with an atmosphere of military history, rather than the other way round, that the fort is worth visiting nowadays. If you want to stay, there's a classy **B&B**, *Carrig-Gorm*, 27 Bridge Rd (☎01247/853680; ⑤).

Crawfordsburn Country Park

The whole short stretch of coast from Helen's Bay, including the fort, is actually part of the **Crawfordsburn Country Park** (Easter–Oct 9am–8pm; Nov–Easter 9am–4.45pm), an estate handed down from the Scottish Presbyterian Crawford family, then acquired by Lord Dufferin (whose mother Helen gave her name to the bay) and now in public hands. Its glens and dells are replete with beeches, cypresses, exotic conifers, cedars, the usual burst of rhododendrons and also a Californian Giant Redwood. But the park's best features are the wildflower meadow and the woodland planted with native species. Perhaps the most scenic walk (well marked by green arrows) is to follow the pathway back from Grey Point to the top of the bay's beaches and turn inland by the trickle of Crawford's Burn. This will take you up through the best of the woodland, under a fine – and still used – nineteenth-century rail viaduct, and up to a waterfall at the head of the glen. The **Park Centre** (daily: April–Sept 10am–6pm; Oct–March 10am–5pm) has a restaurant and an incredible amount of information on local ecology and wildlife. **Helen's Tower**, which can be seen from a considerable distance, was built by Lord Dufferin in the nineteenth century to honour his mother, and as a famine relief project.

　　CRAWFORDSBURN village is on one of Ireland's most ancient highways, a track that ran from Holywood to Bangor Abbey (now the B20), and has a nice but twee (like many things in this part of the world) early seventeenth-century **pub**, *The Old Inn* (☎01247/853255; ⑦), which claims to be Ireland's oldest.

Bangor

BANGOR probably takes its name from its curving bay set between a pair of symmetrical headlands (*beanna chor* – "curved peaks") and its sheltered position made it ideal for exploitation as a holiday resort. The town has been hugely popular with Belfast people since the railway came in the 1860s, but today it's as much a suburb of Belfast as a holiday spot. It still possesses a tawdry charm, stuck in a 1960s time warp with all the appropriate bucket-and-spade paraphernalia – giant swan boats to paddle around a mini-lake, amusement arcades – and the presence of a semi-resident mobile Christian centre to discourage excess. There's also a 500-berth marina which makes Bangor a good place for stocking up on provisions or exploring the coast, while for the land-based the town is well equipped as a stop-off point for dinner and a stroll along the prom.

Bangor's period of greatest historical significance was almost entirely associated with its abbey, founded by St Comgall in 586 AD, from which missionaries set forth to convert pagan Europe. Though the abbey remained powerful for eight hundred years, there's not a trace of the building and the only vestige of its fame now lies in the Ambrosian Library in Milan. This is the *Antiphonarium Benchorense*, one of the oldest known ecclesiastical manuscripts, consisting of collects, anthems and some religious poems. You can view a facsimile of it in the **North Down Heritage Centre** (Tues–Sat 10.30am–4.30pm, Sun 2–4.30pm; July–Aug open daily to 5.30pm; free), tucked away at the back of the town hall. Other displays trace the rise of the Ward family (see Castle Ward p.564) who were largely responsible for the town's development and built Bangor Castle (now the town hall). There's also a fascinating collection of Eastern *objets d'art* collected by a locally born diplomat, Sir John Jordan, and a collection of archeological discoveries featuring the Ballycroghan swords, a wonderful pair of Bronze Age weapons, dating from 500 AD.

The only building of any antiquity in the town is the seventeenth-century **Old Custom House and Tower** on the seafront, now occupied by the **tourist office** (July–Aug Mon–Fri 9am–7pm, Sat 10am–7pm, Sun noon–6pm; Sept–June Mon–Fri 9am–5pm, Sat 10am–4pm; plus June & Sept Sun 1–5pm; ☎01247/270069). As expected, there are dozens of places to **stay** here. The two most luxurious **hotels** are on Quay Street – the *Marine Court* (☎01247/451100; ⑨) and the *Royal* (☎01247/271866; ⑦) – but you'll find plenty of cheaper **B&Bs** on Queen's Parade, Princetown and Seacliff roads. The nearest **camping** is at Donaghadee, six miles south along the coast. Most of the **restaurants** are dotted along the seafront or up nearby sidestreets. *Café Brazilia*, on Bridge Street, serves eleven varieties of espresso plus an imaginative and cheap menu; further along the esplanade and up Gray's Hill, *Knuttel's Restaurant* – named after and decked out in paintings by the owner himself – offers a good value four-course dinner. Other relatively inexpensive restaurants are the *Marine Court Hotel*, the *Canteen* on High Street and the *Back Street Café* on Queen's Parade. But the best food hereabouts is a few miles south in **Clandeboye** at *Shanks* in the *Blackwood Golf Club* (lunches Tues–Fri & Sun, dinners Tues–Sat; ☎01247/853313), with a menu in the pesto/sun-dried tomato line and a decor styled by Terence Conran.

Most of the **pubs** here opt for discos or balladeers with a beatbox, but you'll find regular traditional **music** sessions at *Calico Jacks*, Quay Street (Sun lunch and evening) and the *Jenny Watts,* High Street (Tues & Sun nights) which also has a Sunday lunchtime jazz session. There are regular **boat trips** (☎01247/455321) from the harbour to various destinations, such as the Copeland Islands, and for deep-sea fishing (rods and tackle supplied).

The Ards Peninsula

The **Ards Peninsula** stretches out an arm to enclose the waters of Strangford Lough, with only the narrowest of openings to the sea in the south. The eastern seaboard coast south of Bangor is far from the most attractive hereabouts, but, if you have the time for a detour, there are still some pleasant spots.

Donaghadee

East of Bangor's sprawling suburbs, the first place of any size is **DONAGHADEE**, a small market town whose origins lie in its proximity to the Scottish coast – on a clear day, it's easy to see Galloway across the water, if you climb up the little hill to **The Moat**, the remains of a nineteenth-century folly. From the 1600s until the middle of the nineteenth century, ferries ran from here to Portpatrick, the shortest sea-crossing available. Various notables arrived in Ireland by this route, including, in 1818, John Keats on his walking tour of the British Isles. He was reputedly so depressed by the poverty he saw on his way to Belfast and the mockery attracted by his fancy London clothes, that he soon returned to Scotland. *Grace Neill's Inn*, on the High Street, dates back to 1611 and claims to have put up Peter the Great of Russia, during his European tour. Donaghadee's decline began when the ferry service was transferred to Larne in 1849. Nowadays, apart from watching the dulse-gatherers at low tide or fishing activity at the harbour, there's little going on here and the town's only other claim to fame is that its lighthouse received a lick of paint from Brendan Behan when he was employed after the war by the Commission for Irish Lights. More enticing is the possibility of visiting the three **Copeland Islands**, uninhabited since the 1940s and a mile or so offshore. The middle one, Cross Island, is now a bird sanctuary run by the RSPB, who arrange cruises to it (☎01232/491547); Nelson's Boats in Donaghadee run regular trips to the other two (☎01247/883403).

There are several small **B&B**s around town, including *The Deans*, Northfield Road (☎01247/882204; ③) and *Herdstown House* (☎01247/883773; ②), a listed farmhouse on Hogstown Road. **Camping** is available at *Donaghadee Caravan Park* (☎01247/882369; April–Oct) on Millisle Road. *Big Alfie's Café*, on the High Street, serves huge, cheap lunches, while the bistro in *Grace Neill's* next door offers a popular upmarket option for **meals**.

Millisle to Kearney

Unless you're a caravan devotee, you'll want to give the villages of **Millisle** and **Ballywalter**, further down the coast, a complete miss – each is swamped by half a dozen sites.

Just about the only piece of interest around here is the late eighteenth-century **Ballycopeland Windmill** (April–Sept Tues–Sat 10am–7pm, Sun 2–7pm; £1), a mile west of Millisle. This claims to be the only windmill in working order in Ireland, though it hasn't ground grain on a regular basis since 1915. An electrical model in the miller's house demonstrates its functions. If you leave the A2 in Ballyhalbert and stick to the coast road, you'll pass **Burr Point**, the most easterly place in Ireland, before reaching **Portavogie**, a fishing port famous for its catches of giant prawns, which can be bought ready peeled in the village. From here the coast road curves inland, taking you around Cloghy Bay and past **Kirkistown Castle**, a tower house built in 1622 by one of the Savage family, the Anglo-Norman landlords of the peninsula – unfortunately, it's on private land, so you can't inspect the remains from a closer viewpoint. The next stop, **Kearney**, is a charming village, consisting almost entirely of whitewashed cottages and now mostly owned by the National Trust. You can walk from here to Kearney Point, an often blustery stroll with panoramic views across the Irish Sea. Instead of heading directly to Portaferry from here, choosing the road around Ballyquintin Point will take you past the entrance lane to **St Cowey's Wells**, where the faithful optimist is spoilt for choice – there's a drinking well, a wishing well and a well for bathing sore eyes. Look out for the rock nearby – the indentations are supposed to mark the places where the saint's hands and feet rested as he prayed.

Strangford Lough

Ancient annals say **Strangford Lough** was formed around 1650 BC by the sea sweeping in over the lands of Brena. This created a beautiful, calm inlet, the archipelago-like pieces of land along its inner arm fringed with brown and yellow bladderwrack and tangleweed, and tenanted by a rich gathering of bird life during the warmer months and vast flocks of geese and waders in the winter. It's an attractive haven for small boats and yachts, and several picturesque halts for the land-bound make the road along the lough's western bank the most interesting route leading south from Belfast.

The eastern shore

The eastern edge of Strangford Lough is not as indented as its opposite shore but betters it in having a major road (the continuation of the A20) that runs close to the water virtually all the way down. Also the scenery is delightful, and there are two places to stop off en route to Portaferry – the Mount Stewart Gardens and Grey Abbey.

Mount Stewart

The National Trust-owned **Mount Stewart House and Gardens** (April–Sept Mon–Sat 10.30am–6pm, Sun noon–5.30pm; Oct–March Sat 10.30am–6pm & Sun noon–5.30pm; £3.30 for house and gardens; £2.70 gardens; April–Sept Wed gardens free), the former family home of the Londonderry family, lie five miles southeast of Newtownards (take Ulsterbus #9 or #10 from Belfast Laganside Buscentre). The 98 acres of **gardens** were laid out by Lady Londonderry, wife of the seventh marquess, in the 1920s and a thorough job she made of it: among others, there are Spanish and Italian gardens, a Space Garden and the Shamrock Garden (with a topiary harp and an appropriately-leaved Red Hand of Ulster). The trees and shrubs here are no more than sixty to seventy years old, but they've grown at such a remarkable rate that they look twice that. The principal reason for this is the unusually warm and humid microclimate: the gardens catch the east coast sun, causing a heavy overnight dew, and the Gulf Stream washes the shores only a stone's throw away – despite the northerly latitude, conditions here rival those of Cornwall and Devon.

Although the gardens are the highlight, the **house** is also worth viewing. The family was a leading member of the Protestant Ascendancy and its members included Lord Castlereagh, who was Foreign Secretary under Pitt the Younger and is best remembered for guiding the Act of Union into operation. Among the splendid (and occasionally eccentric) furniture inside is a set of 22 Empire chairs used by the delegates to the Congress of Vienna in 1815, who included the Duke of Wellington and Talleyrand; the chairs were a gift to the Castlereagh's brother Lord Stewart, another high-ranking diplomat of the time. The Continental connection is flaunted further in bedrooms named after various historically important cities: Rome, St Petersburg, Madrid, Moscow and Sebastopol (from the time of the Crimean War). The house contains a number of paintings, particularly portraits of Castlereagh's political contemporaries, but the most notable and largest is *Hambletonian* (1799) by George Stubbs, showing the celebrated thoroughbred being rubbed down after a victory at Newmarket. A little to the east of the house, the octagonal **Temple of the Winds** is a remodelling of Athen's Tower of Andronicus Cyrrhestes by James "Athenian" Stuart (1713–88), one of the pioneers of Neoclassical architecture. The temple is set on a promontory overlooking Strangford Lough, making it a great place for birdwatching.

Grey Abbey

A couple of miles on the shore road, **Grey Abbey** (April–Sept Tues–Sat 10am–7pm, Sun 2–7pm; Oct–March Tues–Sat 10am–1pm & 2–4pm, Sun 2–4pm; £1; Ulsterbus #10) lies slightly to the east of the village which later developed around it. The abbey was founded in 1193 by Affreca, daughter of Godred, King of Man, and wife of John de Courcy, as a thanksgiving for having made a safe sea-crossing during a storm. Typical of the Cistercian order, of which Mellifont was the mother house in Ireland, the abbey sits in once remote parkland beside a rivulet, which would have been a source of fresh water and fish –

self-reliance was crucial to Cistercianism. Even today, that setting is barely disturbed, and reason in itself to visit, with a substantial set of ruins to complete the picture.

Following the standard design of Cistercian abbeys, it has a church at one end and the living and working quarters of the monks ranged around a cloister, a plain structure overall without distracting embellishments. Grey Abbey is unusual for Ireland, though, in showing early Gothic features at a time when late Romanesque work was still common here. Among the best-preserved remains are the **west door**, much of whose carved decoration can still be made out, and the fine lancet windows in the east end. Another unusual feature is that the church is a simple hall, with no aisles. Outside the church there's a re-created "physick garden" and the notes on display help you to imagine the elongated cloister when it was overshadowed on three sides by the chapter house, dormitories and refectory, which are now no more than stumps.

Nearby **B&Bs** are *Brimar*, 4 Cardy Rd (☎012477/88681; ⑤), *Woodview Farm*, 8 Ballywater Rd (☎012477/88242; ②), and, out towards Kircubbin, *Mervue*, 28 Portaferry Rd (☎012477/88619; ③).

Portaferry

PORTAFERRY, at the mouth of the lough, is the home of the **Exploris** (April–Sept Mon–Fri 10am–5pm, Sat 11am–6pm, Sun 1–6pm; Oct–March closes 5pm; £3.25), an aquarium with a touch tank for the brave to stroke a stingray and an open sea tank where you can view the odd roaming shark. But the main attraction is the marvellous **sunset** looking across the "Narrows" to Strangford, a view enhanced by a ten-minute climb to the stump of the old windmill just behind the town. In July the **Galway Hookers Regatta** livens the place up – the traditional boats sail round from Galway to be welcomed by the Portaferry Yacht Club, and every pub has virtually 24-hour music sessions.

Information is available from the office in The Stables, Castle Street (Easter–June & Sept Mon–Sat 10am–5pm, Sun 2–6pm; July & Aug Mon–Sat 10am–5.30pm, Sun 2–6pm; ☎012477/29882) next to the ruined tower house. If you're looking for somewhere to **stay**, the *Portaferry Hotel*, 10 The Strand (☎012477/28231; ⑥), is relatively luxurious and has a decent restaurant; or try the brilliantly designed *The Narrows*, 8 Shore Rd (☎012477/28148; ⑥), where every room has a stupendous view across the lough. There's super food here too and all manner of special craft and activity weekends on offer. For good-value B&B try *The Adairs*, 22 The Square (☎012477/28412; ②). The town also has a YHANI-affiliated **youth hostel** called *Barholm*, 11 The Strand (☎012477/29598). The nearest **campsite** is *Tara Caravan Park*, Ballyquintin Road (☎012477/28459), three miles southeast, by a long, sandy beach. As for **food**, the *Cornstore* bistro on Castle Street has a reasonably priced menu and the *Castle Restaurant* across the road offers ample portions; for coffee and good cakes try the *Harlequin*, *The Shambles* next door or *Cuisine du Sol* on The Square. The **pubs** are good at just about any time of year, with run-of-the-mill sessions at *The Fiddler's Green* most nights; better music is at the *Saltwalter Brigg*, six miles out of Portaferry towards Kircubbin, on Fridays. **Ferries** leave regularly (every 30min or so; single 80p on foot, £4 per car; return £1.30/£6.40) for the five-minute ride across the lips of the lough to Strangford.

The western shore

Leaving Scrabo Tower on the A22, you'll pick up signs for **COMBER** – famous for its potatoes and for the eighty-seater **Tudor Cinema**. Built by B-movie addict Noel Spence, it's meticulously furnished to re-create the atmosphere of old-time movie going, with red-velvet seating, gold braid, footlights etc. Essentially a place for Noel and his friends to go and watch their favourite shlock movies, you can expect American favourites such as *The Blob*, *Attack of the Fifty-Foot Woman* or that tigerskin-bikini special, *The Wild Women of*

Wonga. Some nights, the viewing is themed; on Sherlock Holmes evenings, for example, the audience dresses in deerstalker and pipe, and the muttering of "Elementary, my dear Watson" nearly drowns the soundtrack. Sadly a burglary in 1994 robbed Noel Spence of his vintage movie poster collection, which included the Penny Black of posters, the original bill for *War of the Worlds*. The cinema (22 Drumhirt Rd; ☎01247/878589) is open three nights a week; admission is free, but donations very welcome.

A short distance beyond Comber, at Downpatrick, there's a turning to **Castle Espie Wildfowl and Wetland Centre** on your left (March–Oct Mon–Sat 10.30am–5pm, Sun 11.30am–6pm; Nov–Feb Mon–Sat 11.30am–4pm, Sun 11.30am–5pm; £3), where admission earnings are ploughed back into conserving the wetlands area for the 7000 birds that visit it, and the resident population of waterfowl. The centre also has a coffee shop and art gallery. Immediately beyond Castle Espie, you'll see the excellent *Old Schoolhouse Restaurant* by the roadside, unmistakable with a fire engine lodged in its front garden; there's a fair-priced Sunday lunch (otherwise Tues–Sat 7–10.30pm; ☎01238/541182). From here, you can wind along the very edge of the lough, on a series of minor roads.

Travelling this scenic route is enjoyable in itself, but there are a couple of spots worth making for. First of them is **Mahee Island**, named for St Mochaoi, supposedly the first abbot of the island, and reached via a twisting lane and several causeways. Heading past the crumbling remains of Mahee Castle at the entrance to the island, and over the final causeway, you come to the Celtic **Nendrum Monastic Site** (April–Sept Tues–Sat 10am–1pm & 1.30–7pm, Sun 2–7pm; visitor centre 75p), a few hundred yards further on. It's a marvellously isolated spot, surrounded by drumlins and the lough's waterways. Annals and excavations indicate that a sizeable community lived here from the seventh century onwards, but the remaining ruins probably date from the twelfth century at the very earliest. It was clearly a substantial establishment, with church, round tower, school and living quarters all housed in a *cashel* of three concentric wards. Today, the inner wall shelters the ruined church, and a reconstructed sundial uses some of the original remnants. There's an illuminating reconstruction map at the site and a helpful visitor centre.

Back on the road along the lough, follow the signs to Ardmillan, Killinchy (*Balloo House* here is an excellent restaurant, with a garden), and then Whiterock for **Sketrick Island** (which itself is not signposted). As with Mahee Island, there's a castle to guard the entrance, now no more than a shattered reminder. *Daft Eddy's Pub and Restaurant*, behind the castle, offers bar snacks as well as a more elaborate restaurant menu. An equally daft competition known as the **Hen Island race** takes place here in October, when craft constructed from oil drums and crates are ridden and paddled between Sketrick and the nearby Hen Island.

The tiny coves and inlets at the feet of little drumlins continue as far as Killyleagh, almost any of them worth exploring. The best way to do this would be to **rent a sailing boat** for a day or more, which you can do at Sketrick marina (☎01238/541400).

Killyleagh

Approaching **KILLYLEAGH**, what looks like a huge sandcastle comes into view, a sight wholly out of character with the area. The oldest inhabited castle in Ireland, it was erected by John de Courcy in the late twelfth century, but was rebuilt by the Hamilton family in 1648 and again in 1850 to give it the Bavarian schloss appearance it has today. It's still a private house, and when viewed close up it's much more gaunt, with a squat mixture of crenellations, turrets and cones. The stone outside the castle gates commemorates the town's most famous son, Hans Sloane (1660–1753), physician to King George II and founder of both the British Museum and Kew Gardens – London's Sloane Square is named after him. The gatehouse towers themselves have been adapted for holiday letting (☎01396/828261; £200–350 per week). A little way back down the hill *The Dufferin Arms* coaching inn (☎01396/828229; ⑤) offers extremely comfortable **B&B** and organises a wide range of activity breaks.

The Lecale region

Jutting into the southern reach of Strangford Lough, the **Lecale Peninsula** is above all St Patrick's country. Ireland's patron saint was originally a Roman Briton, first carried off as a youth from somewhere near Carlisle in northern England by Irish raiders. He spent six years in slavery in Ireland before escaping home again and, at the age of thirty, decided to return to Ireland as a bishop, to spread Christianity. Christianity had already reached Ireland a while earlier, probably through traders and other slaves, and, indeed, St Patrick was not in fact the first bishop of Ireland, but he remains easily the most famous. He arrived in Ireland this second time, according to his biographer Muirchú (also his erstwhile captor, converted), on the shores of the Lecale region, and his first Irish sermon was preached at Saul in 432. Today the region commemorates the association with sites at Struell Wells and Saul, as well as at Downpatrick town itself. The **Lecale Trail** is a thirty-mile tour of the peninsula starting in front of the Down County Museum in Downpatrick (further information and trail maps can be obtained from the tourist office); if you've had enough of St Patrick and his seeming connection with nearly every landmark, alternative ways of exploring the peninsula are the nature rambles and horse-riding trails also available in Downpatrick (see overleaf).

Downpatrick and around

DOWNPATRICK, the county capital, comes to life during race meetings, but, at other times it seems depressed and rather lethargic, as if awaiting the invigorating kiss of economic revival. On the other hand its history is a rich and well-preserved one, with the major sites conveniently concentrated at one end of town, around the **Hill of Down**. This was once a rise of great strategic worth, fought over long before the arrival of St Patrick made it famous. A Celtic fort of mammoth proportions was built here and was called first *Arús Cealtchair*, then later *Dún Cealtchair* (Celtchar's fort). Celtchar was one of the Red Branch Knights, a friend of the then King of Ulster, Conor MacNessa, and, according to the *Book of the Dun Cow*, "an angry terrific hideous man with a long nose, huge ears, apple eyes, and coarse dark-grey hair". The *Dún* part of the fort's name went on to become the name of the county, as well as the town.

By the time the Norman knight **John de Courcy** made his mark here in the late twelfth century, a settlement was well established. Pushing north out of Leinster, and defeating Rory MacDonlevy, King of Ulster, de Courcy dispossessed the Augustinian canons who occupied the Hill of Down to establish his own Benedictine abbey. He flaunted as much pomp as he could to mark the occasion, and one of his festive tricks was to import what were supposedly the disinterred bodies of Saint Brigid and Saint Columba to join St Patrick, who was (supposedly) buried here. One of the earliest accounts of Patrick's life asserts that he's buried in a church near the sea; and since a later account admits that "where his bones are no man knows", Downpatrick's claim seems as good as any.

The site of the three graves is meant to be just to the left of the tower entrance and is marked today by a rough granite boulder, put there around 1900 to cover the huge hole created by earlier pilgrims searching for the saints' bones. The cathedral built by de Courcy was destroyed in the fourteenth century, and a new abbey erected in the early sixteenth century was even more short-lived. Today's **Cathedral** (daily 9am–5pm) dates basically from the early part of this century, though it incorporates many aspects of earlier incarnations. Its most unique feature is the private box-pews, characteristic of the Regency period and the only ones remaining in use in Ireland.

Leaving the cathedral and retracing your steps a little down English Street, which is crowded with Georgian buildings, you come to the eighteenth-century jail, now home to the **Down County Museum** and the **St Patrick Heritage Centre** (June–Aug Mon–Fri 11am–5pm, Sat & Sun 2–5pm; Sept–May closed Sun & Mon; free). The heritage centre occupies the gatehouse and has a range of displays telling the St Patrick story, principally through words taken from his autobiographical *Confessions* (the short video also provides a handy summary of what the rest of the peninsula has on offer by way of relics of the saint). The three-storey Georgian **Governor's House** in the centre of the walled courtyard, includes a local history gallery, which has regular exhibitions. The cell block at the back of the enclosure once held the United Irishman Thomas Russell, who had already survived the 1798 uprising but was found guilty of complicity in Robert Emmett's rebellion and was duly hanged in 1803 from a sill outside the main gate of the jail.

Turn downhill between the jail and the barricaded courthouse and you come to the **Mound of Down**, a smaller prominence half submerged in undergrowth. It's in fact 60ft high and inside its outer ditch is a horseshoe central mound of rich grass. Once a rath, or round hill-fort, it was considerably altered and enlarged to create a Norman motte and bailey fortification, with a *bretasche* (a wooden archery tower) at the centre. Its view of the Hill of Down clearly displays the attractions the hill had for its earliest settlers; it's believed by some to be the site of the palace of the Kings of Ulster.

At the rear of the market car park the **Downpatrick Railway Museum** (June to mid-Sept Mon–Fri 11am–1pm; £1), offers tours of the restored station and workshops and occasional weekend train rides (details ☎01396/617517).

Practicalities

The **tourist office** is at 74 Market St (mid-June to Sept Mon–Sat 9am–6pm, Sun 2–6pm; Oct to mid-June Mon–Fri 9am–5pm, Sat 9am–1pm & 2–5pm; ☎01396/612233). The best and most central of the B&Bs is *Hillside*, 62 Scotch St (☎01396/613134; ②); others include *Hillcrest*, 157 Strangford Rd (☎01396/612583; ②), and *Havine Farm*, 51 Ballydonnell Rd (☎01396/851242; ②); the upmarket option is the *Abbey Lodge Hotel* (☎01396/614511; ⑤), out on the Belfast road. If you're **camping**, your best bet is to go to Castle Ward Park (see p.564), six miles away on the A25 to Strangford.

The *Abbey Lodge Hotel* does a three-course Sunday lunch for around £12, and bar food on weekdays. The *Hootenanny Bar* and *McGivern's Restaurant*, in a mid-eighteenth century coach house on Irish Street, offer good food. You can get vast phenomenal breakfasts and vast Sunday brunches at *Harry Afrika's* on Market Street – a diner popular with students; while the *Arts Centre Café,* in the refurbished old town hall on Irish Street, definitely does the best lunches and imaginative snacks. Good **pub lunches** are easy to find: try *Brendan's Pub* on Market Street, or nearby *Rea's* pub, which has a big open fire, or the *De Courcy Arms* on Church Street, a popular **music** venue. There may be occasional performances in the excellent **Down Arts Centre**, which has an art gallery and performance space. A good coffee shop in the centre is *Oakley Fayre*, 52 Market St, with the usual home-baked pastries.

Out of town, off the A25 Strangford road, the **Quoile Countryside Centre** (April–Sept daily 11am–5pm; Oct–March Sat & Sun 1–5pm; free) focuses attention on the natural habitats created by the building of a tidal barrier to prevent local flooding and organizes **nature rambles**, seal watches in Strangford Lough, dawn chorus walks on Quoile River, and even butterfly trips. *Tullymurray Equestrian Centre* on Ballyduggan Road takes **trail rides** to the local big houses – Tollymore, Castlewellan and Castle Ward – or along the coast with beach rides to Newcastle and Tyrella (Mon–Sat; £10 per hour; ☎01396/811880).

Inch Abbey

Over to the other side of the Quoile Marsh from Downpatrick lie the remains of the Cistercian **Inch Abbey** (April–Sept Tues–Sat 10am–7pm; Oct–March Sat 10am–4pm, Sun 2–4pm; 75p). The exquisite setting is temptingly visible from the town, but the river's intervention makes the only access a mile out along the Belfast Road, taking the left turn down Inch Abbey Road just before the *Abbey Lodge Hotel* and another sign-posted left turn shortly afterwards. The site was once an island, and its early church was replaced by de Courcy with the Cistercian abbey, whose monks were shipped over from Furness Abbey in Lancashire with the intention of establishing a strong English centre of influence. Little of it is now left standing – it was burnt in 1404 and monastic life was completely over by the mid-sixteenth century. Still, its setting, among small glacial drumlins and woodland, is picturesque; and strolling up the valley sides is a very pleasant way to pass time.

On the trail of St Patrick

About four miles west of Inch Abbey (take the B2 to Annacloy and then the first turning on the left), **Loughinisland** is probably the most worthwhile of all the sites in the area associated with St Patrick, and indeed one of the most idyllic spots in County Down. It comprises a reed-fringed lake contained by ten or so little drumlin hills, one of which forms an island in the lake. Here, across a short causeway, are the ruins of three small churches, set next door to each other. The most interesting of the churches is the smallest one, **MacCartan's Chapel** (1636), which has an entrance door no taller than four or five feet. The larger northern church was used by both Catholics and Protestants until they quarrelled on a wet Sunday around 1720 over which camp should remain outside during the service. The Protestants left and built their church at Seaforde instead.

The next St Patrick landmark is at **SAUL**, a couple of miles out of Downpatrick and off the Strangford Road. St Patrick is said to have landed nearby, sailing up the tiny River Slaney, and it was here that he first preached, immediately converting Dichu, the lord of this territory. Dichu gave Patrick a barn as his first base (Saul in Irish is *Sabhal*, meaning "barn") and the saint frequently returned here to rest from his travelling missions – legend has it that he died here in 461. Today a memorial chapel and round tower in the Celtic Revival style, built of pristine silver-grey granite in 1932 to commemorate the 1500th anniversary of the Saint's arrival, is open daily to visitors. Two cross-carved stones from between the eighth and twelfth centuries still stand in the graveyard, though there's not a trace of the medieval monastery built here by Saint Malachy in the twelfth century.

A short distance further south, between Saul and Raholp, **St Patrick's Shrine** sits atop Slieve Patrick, a tract of hillside much like a slalom ski-slope, with the stations of the cross marking a pathway up. This huge Mourne granite statue, clad at the base with bronze panels depicting Patrick's life, was erected in the same year as Saul church. The summit is no more than a twenty-minute climb and offers a commanding view of the county, a vista of the endless little bumps of this drumlin-filled territory.

At **RAHOLP** itself is the ruined church of **St Tassach**, named for the bishop from whom the dying Patrick received the sacrament. Tassach was given Raholp by Patrick as a reward for crafting a case for Christ's crozier, the *Bachall Isú*, one of Ireland's chief relics until its destruction in 1538. The ruins here were mainly restored in 1915 from the rubble that lay around, but their material is thought to date from the eleventh century. If you're eager for the complete St Patrick experience, it's a mile from the Slaney Inn car park in Raholp to the spot on the lough shore where he is believed to have first landed: head towards Strangford, then left down Myra Road; cross the main Strangford road and turn left at the first fork; at the bottom of the hill take the track on the right to the shore.

The easiest way to find the last St Patrick site, **Struell Wells**, is to return to Downpatrick. Take the Ardglass Road, turn left just past the hospital, then right down a narrow track into a secluded rock-faced valley and you'll come to **the wells**. The waters here, believed to be the wells referred to in early accounts of Patrick's mission, have been attributed with healing powers for centuries. In 1744 Walter Harris described the scene: "vast throngs of rich and poor resort on Midsummer Eve and the Friday before Lammas, some in the hopes of obtaining health, and others to perform penance". Mass is still said here on midsummer night, and people bring containers to carry the water home with them; but if you're not looking for health or penance, there's still the joy of spotting one of the tiny gems of Irish landscape beauty – a hideaway rocky dell with an abundance of yellow-flowering whin, its underground stream rechannelled to run through the wells' purpose-built bath houses.

Strangford and the Lecale coast

If you're coming by ferry to Lecale from the tip of the Ards Peninsula, and following the A2 round the coast, you'll arrive at tiny **STRANGFORD** village, directly opposite Portaferry. The earlier name of this inlet was Lough Cuan, but it was renamed Strangfiord by the Vikings over one thousand years ago because of the eight-knot current in the narrows. Its small harbour makes a pleasant setting for watching the to and fro of the ferry boats, and the *Lobster Pot*, on the front, has a welcome pub garden and middle-of-the-range prices for evening meals. The only **places to stay** are *Strangford Cottage,* 41 Castle St (☎01396/881208; ⑦), a listed Georgian terraced house, and the recently opened rooms at *The Cuan* (☎01396/881222; ⑥), on the square, a friendly bar with tasty food in its restaurant. There's **camping** at *Strangford Caravan Park*, Shore Road (☎01396/881888). Just on the far side of Strangford is a sixteenth-century **tower house** which can be viewed if you visit Mr Seed at 39 Castle St for the key and – if you are lucky – an informative chat.

Immediately around Strangford are a few houses and castles worth visiting, the first of them on the road back towards Downpatrick. **Castle Ward** (open 1–6pm: Easter; April & Sept–Oct Sat–Sun; May–Aug Fri–Wed; house £2.60; grounds £3.50 per car) is Ireland's Glyndebourne: every June three weeks of opera enliven the house and grounds, and *bon viveurs* flock with picnic hampers, starched napkins and candlesticks (for information call ☎01232/661090). The house, which was the eighteenth-century residence of Bernard and Anne Ward, later Lord and Lady Bangor, is now owned by the National Trust. It's a positively schizophrenic building, thanks to the opposed tastes of its creators (they later split up): one half (Bernard's) is in the Classical Palladian style, the other (Anne's) neo-Gothic, a split carried through into the design and decor of the rooms inside. Outside there are pleasant gardens (daily dawn–dusk) and preserved farm buildings. There's also a sixteenth-century tower house (Old Castle Ward) inside the grounds; the fifteenth-century **Audley's Castle** just outside on the lough shore, with superb view across the lough – though there's a better example of a tower house just south of Strangford (see opposite); and the Strangford **Lough Wildlife Centre** house in a restored barn (April–June & Sept Sat & Sun 2–6pm; July–Aug daily except Thurs 2–6pm). If you want to stay, you can **camp** in the grounds (☎01396/881680). On your way back to the main coast road, **Audleystown Cairn** is marked across the fields to the right – though access isn't easy as it's in a field which usually seems full of bullocks.

South along the Ardglass Road

A signposted turning one mile south of Strangford directs you to the **Cloghy Rocks** observation point. The rocks themselves are twenty yards or so out in the lough and, for most of the day look decidedly inconsequential, but, at low tide, you can spot basking seals. They're well camouflaged against the seaweed, so a pair of binoculars would be handy.

Further on, **Kilclief Castle** (April–Sept Tues–Sat 10am–7pm, Sun 2–7pm; 75p) is a well-preserved fifteenth-century tower house. One of Ireland's earliest tower houses, this was originally the home of John Cely, Bishop of Down – until he was unfrocked and thrown out for living with a married woman.

The next stop is **St Patrick's Well**, set on a wonderful rocky shore between Ballyhornan and Chapeltown. You can get to within a few hundred yards of the well by road, but the best approach is to start from Ballyhornan – where you'll see a narrow strip of water separating the village from Guns Island, still used for grazing and accessible at low tide – and follow the foreshore path for about a mile. The well is easily spotted – it looks rather like a sheep dip with concrete walls, but with a crucifix at its head. Its holy water has turned into something closer to stagnant consommé than an ever-youthful source of new life.

Half a mile or so before you reach Ardglass, the ruin of fifteenth-century **Ardtole Church** is well signposted just a few hundred yards off the road. It's set on the spur of a hill, which gives it a fine perspective out to sea and back across the undulating flat of Lecale. Once dedicated to Saint Nicholas, patron saint of sailors, this church was used by English fishermen until a quarrel broke out with the Irish around 1650. The story goes that the fishermen tied a sleeping Irish chief to the ground by his long hair so that he couldn't get up when he awoke. Tradition has it that Swift derived the similar episode in *Gulliver's Travels* from this tale, and certainly the Ardtole region runs amok with tiny drumlins – very much like the description of the Lilliputian mountains.

Ardglass

ARDGLASS is set on the side of a lovely natural inlet. Its domestic buildings, rising steeply from the harbour (*ard glas* in Irish means "the green height"), are interspersed with seven fortified mansions, towers and turrets. These date from a vigorous English revival in the sixteenth century, when a trading company first arrived to found a colony here. The best preserved of the fortifications, and the only one open for visits, is **Jordan's Castle**, next door to the *Anchor* pub on the Low Road (July–Aug Tues–Sat 10am–7pm, Sun 2–7pm; 75p). The most elegant and highly developed of all the Down tower houses, this has recently been renovated – all whitewashed walls and massive ceiling beams – and has regular exhibitions on local history. The tall, crenellated building with white plaster trimming up on the hill was once **King's Castle**; its nineteenth-century renovation is obvious, as is modern work to turn it into a nursery. The lone ornamental-looking turret on the hilltop is **Isabella's Tower**, a nineteenth-century folly created by Aubrey de Vere Beauclerc as a gazebo for his invalid daughter.

In the nineteenth century, Ardglass was the most thriving **fishing** port in the North; and even today, as well as the prawns, herrings and whitefish brought in by the fishing fleet, there's very good rod fishing to be had off the end of the pier for codling, pollack and coalfish. Even the *Spar* supermarket on the quay is wonderfully stocked with a fantastic range of seafood (scallops, monkfish, oysters, salmon etc), enough in itself to entice a quick shopping visit. It's also sometimes possible to buy direct from fishing boats or from the cannery on the quay. The old inn, the *Commercial*, on the main street has a well – still in use; it's covered over with glass on the lounge floor. You can **eat** well at *Aldo's* popular Italian **restaurant**, 7 Castle Place, which serves evening meals (Thurs–Sun 5–10pm) and Sunday lunch. **Campers** are catered for at *Coney Island Caravan Park* (☎01396/841448) and there's **B&B** at *Burford Lodge*, 30 Quay St (☎01396/841141; ②) and *The Cottage* (☎01396/841080; ②), next door to *Aldo's*.

From Killough to Clough

KILLOUGH, a few miles on, is an unworldly village stretching around a much larger harbour than Ardglass, but now silted up. The A2 passes through Killough's main street: a fine avenue of sycamores with a string of picturesque cottage terraces at its southern end, making an unlikely major thoroughfare. It was the Wards of Castleward who built the harbour in the eighteenth century, and there's still a direct road running inland, virtually in a straight line, from Killough to Castleward.

From the southern end of Killough you can head out to **St John's Point** – much favoured by birdwatchers – on which lie the ruins of one of the North's best examples of a pre-Romanesque church. It's an enjoyable two-and-a-half-mile walk. The tiny west door of the tenth-century church has the distinctive sloping sides, narrowing as the doorway rises, that were a common feature of these early churches. Also still apparent are the *antae*, enclosures created by the extension of the west and east walls to give extra support to the roof. Excavations in 1977 showed up graves that extended under these walls, indicating that an even earlier church existed from the early Christian period, probably made of wood. There's a black-and-gold-striped lighthouse on the nail of the point.

From Killough, the A2 passes long, sandy beaches at Minerstown and Tyrella Strand – the latter ruined by hot dog stands and cars parking (£1.20) on the beach – before reaching **CLOUGH**, a crossroads village between Downpatrick and Newcastle. Tucked behind the petrol station at the northern end of the village is a Norman motte and bailey earthwork castle, as pristinely preserved as a carpet of fresh grass, though marred by the remains of a thirteenth-century stone keep stuck in the middle. Despite its low-lying position the site has surprisingly good views across Dundrum Bay inlet towards the Mournes and back over to Slieve Croob in central Down. It's worth taking a short detour north at Clough on the A24 to the **Seaforde Tropical Butterfly House** (April–Sept Mon–Sat 10am–5pm, Sun 1–6pm; £2; including gardens, £3.50). There's a flight area swarming with hundreds of giant, vividly coloured butterflies, quails running underfoot and a ferocious collection of large and fast-moving insects and reptiles, fortunately kept in glass cases. Best of all, though, is the overgrown walled garden, whose maze leads to a rose-covered pavilion that shelters a statue of the goddess Diana. Nearby, *Drumgooland House* on Dunnanew Road (☎01396/811956; ③) does a great **B&B** and offers riding or fishing in their own lake.

Dundrum

Although it's not officially in the Lecale region, whose inland ending is at Clough, just a few miles down the road at **DUNDRUM** you'll find some quite spectacular ruins of a large Norman **castle** (April–Oct Tues–Sat 10am–7pm, Sun 2–7pm; 75p). The town lies beside a hammer-headed tidal bay, with the ruins sitting dramatically above, a steep fifteen-minute walk uphill from the village. The castle has a central circular donjon (with a fine spiral stairway in its walls), a fortified gateway and drum towers, all set upon a motte and bailey. In its time it was described as the most impenetrable fortress in the land, yet it was captured on several occasions and partly dismantled by Cromwell's soldiers in 1652. Some say it was a de Courcy fortress, designed for the Knights Templar; but the circular keep, a rarity in Ireland, is unlike the other fortresses de Courcy built to defend the stretch of coast from Carlingford right up to Carrickfergus. De Courcy's successor, de Lacy, is a more likely candidate – his Welsh connections tie in with the castle's similarity to the one at Pembroke, Wales. Dundrum's **B&B** is *Mourneview House*, 16 Main St (☎013967/51457; ②). There are also two semi-detached National Trust properties, *Murlough Cottages* on the shore of Dundrum Bay, which can be rented by the week and sleep four people (☎01238/510721). Obviously, these get booked up well in advance, but you may be lucky out of season. Both the *Bay Inn* and the *Murlough Tavern* serve good meals and snacks.

Newcastle and the Mourne Mountains

Newcastle, with its lovely stretch of sandy beach, is the biggest seaside resort in Down – packed with trippers from Belfast on Bank Holidays and summer weekends – and, with Slieve Donard rising behind the town, it's by far the best base if you want to do any serious walking or climbing in the **Mourne Mountains**. On busy days the main drag can feel like nothing more than a soulless strip of amusement arcades, fast-food outlets and tacky souvenir stores, but when the trippers have gone the town's more sedate qualities can be appreciated.

The Mournes are a relatively youthful set of granite mountains, which explains why their comparatively unweathered peaks and flanks are so rugged, forming steep sides, moraines and occasional sheer cliffs. Closer up, these give sharp, jagged outlines; but from a distance they appear much gentler, like a sleeping herd of buffalo. The wilder topography lies mostly in the east, below Newcastle, although the fine cliff of **Eagle Mountain** (2083ft), to the southwest, is wonderful if you can afford the time and effort to get there, and the tamer land above Rostrevor has views down into **Carlingford Lough** that can rival any in Ireland.

In summer at least (winters can be surprisingly harsh) there are plenty of straightforward hikes in the Mournes that require no special equipment, with obvious tracks to many of the more scenic parts. For further information, and maps, go to the Newcastle tourist office or to the youth hostel there (see below). There are also, of course, more serious climbs: **climbing courses** in the Mournes are run by the Northern Ireland Mountain Centre in Newcastle (☎013967/22158), but they must be booked at least two weeks in advance (contact The Sports Council for Northern Ireland, House of Sport, Upper Malone Road, Belfast; ☎01232/381222).

Newcastle

NEWCASTLE isn't exactly exciting, but it's well equipped to send you walking, pony trekking, or fishing on the river and it has **Royal County Down** golf course (☎013967/23314), with a reputation as one of the top ten links courses worldwide. For the inevitable rainy day there are indoor alternatives at the Newcastle Centre and Tropicana Complex on the promenade (summer only), with swimming pools, water slides and playgrounds. Out on Dundrum Road **Route 66 US Automobile Museum** (Easter–Sept daily 10.30am–6pm; Oct–Easter Sat & Sun 2–6pm; £2.50), has all the great American cars – Thunderbirds, Cadillacs, Mustangs – and a wondrous collection of jukeboxes. Behind the Newcastle Centre a plaque celebrates one of the first powered flights in Ireland, undertaken in 1910 by Harry Ferguson to win a £100 prize – he was later to become famous through the success of the Massey Ferguson tractor.

The very helpful **tourist information office** is at 10–14 Central Promenade (Mon–Sat 10am–5pm, Sun 2–6pm; ☎013967/22222). There's a wide choice of **places to stay**; the best of the more upmarket **hotels** is the *Slieve Donard Hotel* on Downs Road (☎013967/23681; ⑦), but the *Brook Cottage Hotel*, 58 Bryansford Rd (☎013967/22204; ⑤), might be more fun at half the price. Cheaper central B&Bs include the refurbished *Glenada Holiday Centre*, 29 South Promenade (☎013967/22402; ⑤), *Fountainville House*, 103 Central Promenade (☎013967/25074; ②), and *Castlebridge House*, 2 Central Promenade (☎013967/23209; ②). The only YHANI **youth hostel** in this region is in a terraced house on the seafront at 30 Downs Rd, near the bus station (☎013967/22133). The best **camping** is out at one of the nearby forest parks (see p.568).

Mario's Italian Restaurant on the front is the best place for evening **meals** and Sunday lunches, unless you go out of town towards Castlewellan (take the A50) and to

WALKS IN THE MOURNES

There's little to see in Newcastle itself, but the mountains offer some beautiful walks close to the town, and, for more serious walking, plenty of good hiking routes throughout the range. Before you set off it's worth visiting the **Mourne Countryside Centre**, 91 Central Promenade (Mon–Fri 9am–5pm; plus June–Aug Sat–Sun 9am–4pm; ☎013967/26493) for information on walks, access and ecology.

The climb up **Slieve Donard**, just south of Newcastle, is the obvious first choice. Although at 2796ft it's the highest peak in the Mournes – and in all Ulster – the ascent is a relatively easy one on a well-marked trail that ends at the massive hermit cell on the summit; from here the views across the whole mountain landscape are quite spectacular.

For more gentle local walking, there are several pleasant **parks**, created from the estates of old houses. The nearest is **Donard Park** on the slopes of Slieve Donard. There's a good meander along the River Glen from the town centre to the park, and if you keep following this path uphill you'll emerge on the other side and eventually come to the Saddle, a col between the two mountains of Slieve Donard and Slieve Commedagh. If you want to carry on further into the mountains from here, a good route is via **Trassey Burn** towards the **Hare's Gap**, where minerals have seeped through the rock to form precious and semi-precious stones – topaz, beryl, smoky quartz and emeralds – in the cavities of the **Diamond rocks** (hidden behind an obvious boulder stone on the mountainside). Around this point in spring, you might get the chance to hear the song of the Ring Ouzel, a bird which migrates from Africa to breed in these upland areas.

Two miles inland from Newcastle, along the Bryansford Road, **Tollymore Forest Park** (daily 10am–sunset; cars £3.50) is considerably bigger and better equipped than Donard, and has a **campsite** (call the ranger on ☎013967/22428). The park creeps up the northern side of the Mournes, and its picturesque trails wind through woodland and beside the river. You enter the park by one of two ornate Gothic folly gates – there are more follies in Bryansford nearby – and there's an **information centre** and café in an elaborate stone barn. **Castlewellan Forest Park** (same hours; cars £3.50) is also inland about five miles further north, outside the elegant market town of Castlewellan. The estate lies in the foothills of the Mournes, and from the highest point in the forest, Slievenaslat, you get panoramic views over the mountain range. A wonderful **arboretum**, dating originally from 1740 but much expanded since, is its outstanding feature: the sheltered south-facing slopes of its hills, between the Mournes and the Slieve Croob range, allow exotic species to flourish. There's trout fishing in its main lake and coarse fishing in the smaller lakes; there's also a café in the 1720 Queen Anne-style farmstead and courtyards, near the main entrance. *Hillyard House* (☎013967/70141; from £15), at the park entrance, offers hostel-style accommodation and arranges outdoor pursuits. You can **camp** in the park here, too (call the forest officer on ☎013967/78664). Inside the park, **Dolly's Brae** (one of the westernmost hills) is often remembered at Loyalist celebrations as the site of one of the greatest victories against Catholic uprisings.

If you are planning on more serious hiking in the Mournes, heights worth chasing include **Slieve Binnian**, beyond the Hare's Gap, and reached through the Brandy Pad passes by the Blue Lough and Lough Binnian; **Slieve Commedagh**, with its Inca-looking pillars of granite; and **Slieve Bearnagh**, up to the right of the Hare's Gap. Also, try and cross the ridge from **Slieve Meelmore** to **Slieve Muck**, the "pig mountain", descending to the shores of Lough Shannagh, where there's a beach at either end – useful for a dip, though the water's freezing. In the panorama beyond the Hare's Gap, the places not to miss are the eastern slopes of the **Cove Mountain** and **Slieve Lamagan**. If you're sticking to the roads, all you can really do is circle the outside of the range, though there is one road through the middle, from Hilltown to Kilkeel.

the luxurious, but rather characterless, *Burrendale Hotel and Country Club*. The *Donard Hotel* on Main Street also does reasonable lunches. The *Pavillion* on Downs Road does everything from snacks to steaks, while the *Percy French*, also on Downs Road, offers reasonable à la carte. Otherwise there are plenty of cafés and chip shops scattered among the amusement arcades.

Out of town, three miles away, in **BRYANSFORD** village, opposite *Tollymore Forest Park*, is the award-winning *Briers Country House*, 39 Middle Tollymore Rd (☎013967/24347; ⑤), with a popular restaurant. There are also eleven **caravan and camping sites** around the town – ask at the tourist information office. Nearby **riding schools** include Woodlodge Riding Centre (☎013967/78947) beside the park (see opposite) and, for the more experienced, Mourne Trail Riding Centre, 96 Castlewellan Rd (☎013967/24351).

The western slopes of the Mournes

The landward side of the Mourne Mountains is a patchwork of fields divided by dry-stone walls: attractive, especially in the morning light, but with nothing of pressing interest. **HILLTOWN** has a main street extraordinarily well provided with pubs – supposedly because it was once a smugglers' hideaway, where the spoils would be divided – and it's still a crossroads where numerous roads meet. There's a pretty parish church which was founded in 1776, a Georgian market house opposite and a fortnightly market; but most of the time it's quiet as a ghost town. Little over a mile from Hilltown on the Newcastle Road is the handsome **Goward dolmen**, known locally as "Pat Kearney's big stone". It's well signposted off the road, though the last quarter mile of track is severely potholed.

Drumena Cashel, two miles southwest of Castlewellan on the A25, is one of the better-preserved ring forts, or defended homesteads, in the area. It has a T-shaped underground chamber intended to give shelter from the Vikings – though this is only twelve yards long and seems better suited to its peacetime function of providing cold storage for food. The stone foundations of a few circular beehive huts (known as *clocháns*) also remain. The puzzling aspect of the *cashel* is its position below the summit of the hill: possibly a compromise between the needs of defence and those of comfort, so there would be some shelter from the harsh winds that curl through the area.

The Mourne coast

The A2 south along the coast from Newcastle is a beautiful drive, trailing the shore around the edge of the mountains and taking you past the chasm known as Maggie's Leap, after a local woman who jumped to avoid the attentions of an unwanted suitor, and over the Bloody Bridge, reputedly so called because of a nearby massacre during the 1641 rebellion. Further along the way, the fishing harbour towns of **Annalong** and **Kilkeel** are the best bases for **walking** or exploring the mountains.

Annalong and around

The small fishing harbour of **ANNALONG** – its name in Irish is *Áth na Long*, or "the ford of the ships" – is a pleasantly relaxed seaside town during the summer, with a stony beach and Slieve Binnion providing a grandiloquent backdrop. In the harbour, pleasure craft are tied up alongside the fishing boats and small trawlers – the whiff of their herring catches sometimes permeates the whole town.

A path from the campsite just off the main road gives immediate access to an early nineteenth-century **cornmill**, still in working order and open for visits (Feb–Nov

Tues–Sat 11am–5pm; £1.30), and to a herb garden down by the walled harbour and the beach. The village itself goes about its maritime work in its narrow streets much as it always has done, and it comes as a surprise in this out-of-the-way part of the North to find the grey harbour walls adorned with the familiar ritualized Protestant graffiti – Ulster 1690, UVF and a Union Jack flag.

There are a number of small **B&Bs** here, including *Sycamores*, 52 Majors Hill (☎013967/68279; ③) and *Kamara*, 106a Kilkeel Rd (☎013967/68072; ②), along with luxurious country house accommodation at *Glassdrumman Lodge*, 85 Mill Rd (☎013967/68451; ⑧). The municipal *Marine Park* **camping/caravan site** (☎013967/68736) by the harbour is a dreary place, landscaped in the shape of a shamrock. There's little in the way of places to eat, but right on the harbour, the *Harbour Inn* serves adequate lunches and evening **meals**, while the *Halfway House* north out of town on the A2 does pub food.

Inland a mile or so from Annalong, signposts point to the **Silent Valley** (daily: Easter–Sept 10am–6.30pm; Oct–Easter 10am–4.30pm; car £3, pedestrians £1.50); here you'll find Belfast and County Down's reservoir, a huge thirty-year engineering project, completed in 1933. There's a car park by the lower reservoir bound by the Mourne Wall, a sturdy 22-mile-long granite boundary to the catchment area that joins the summits of fifteen mountains along its route. The views out to Slieve Binnian and Ben Crom, behind it to the west, are worth the effort of the Viewpoint Walk (starts at the car park). Less energetic, but still superb, is the half-mile Sally Lough stroll (or you can take the shuttle bus; £1.10) up to the dam at Ben Crom; again the views are spectacular.

Kilkeel and Ballymartin

Continuing south, there's a good small beach just outside the hamlet of Ballymartin. Further on, **KILKEEL** – "the church of the narrows" – is a much grander version of Annalong, remarkable mainly for the even heftier stench of fish from the canneries on the harbour; the town is home to nearly a hundred trawlers. The biggest excitements here are the fish auctions that take place on the quayside when the fishing boats come home, and the annual summer **harbour festival**. Bang next to the harbour stands the brand new **Nautilus Centre** which contains a small exhibition on the fishing industry, a fish shop (if you're subsequently tempted), a gift shop, café and conference centre.

The ruined "narrows" church, built in the fourteenth century, stands in the centre of Kilkeel in a ring fort. Kilkeel is a prosperous, predominantly Protestant place, but behind the village on the banks of its river memories of less happy days remain – small grave markers identify where the inmates of Kilkeel workhouse are buried. One of those buried here is the infamous **William Hare**, who murdered sixteen people in the space of a year in Edinburgh. Hare owned a lodging house and, when an old lodger died owing rent, he and his accomplice William Burke decided to sell the body to a medical school. The £7.10 they were paid spurred them on to greater efforts; however, eventually their enthusiasm raised the neighbours' suspicions and their profitable venture came to an end. Hare turned king's evidence and got his freedom, while Burke was hanged. Deciding to lie low, Hare came to Kilkeel and soon landed in the workhouse; his identity was only revealed to the locals when a Dr Reid, former medical student from Edinburgh, recognized him.

There's a small **tourist office** in Kilkeel at 6 Newcastle St (Mon–Sat 9am–5.30pm; ☎016937/62525), which can help find **places to stay** in town and in Ballymartin. In Kilkeel there are a couple of hotels – *Cranfield House*, 57 Cranfield Rd (☎016937/62327; ⑥), and *Kilmorey Arms*, 41 Greencastle St (☎016937/62220; ④), both of which serve food – and numerous B&Bs, the pick of which are *Morne Abbey*, 16 Greencastle Rd (☎016937/62426; ③), *Homesyde*, 7 Shandon Drive (☎016937/62676; ②), or *Heath Hall*, 160 Moyad Rd (☎016937/62612; ③).

BALLYMARTIN has small B&Bs such as *Sharon Farm House*, 6 Ballykeel Rd (☎06937/62521; ②) and the award-winning *Wyncrest*, 30 Main Rd (☎016937/63012; ④), with delicious home cooking. If you're **camping** take your pick of one of the seven campsites hereabouts – the best along Cranfield Point, a flat grassy piece of land jutting out at the entrance to Carlingford Lough. Try *Sandilands Caravan Park* on Cranfield Road (☎016937/63634) or *Chestnutt Caravan Park*, next to the beach on Grange Road (☎016937/62653).

Restaurants in Kilkeel are thin on the ground, but *The Fisherman* (☎016937/62130) has an extensive, but pricy, fish menu, while *Jacob Hall's*, at the other end of the price scale, does tasty fish and chips.

Carlingford Lough

The eastern shore of Carlingford Lough bordering the Mournes offers some wonderful views back to the mountains and across the lough. Driving round to Warrenpoint, though, the villages become increasingly politicized as you get nearer the border, where IRA slogans alternate with Union Jacks.

Greencastle Fort

Guarding the mouth of the lough, **Greencastle Fort** (April–Sept Tues–Sat 10am–7pm, Sun 2–7pm; 75p) sits in brooding isolation about four miles southwest of Kilkeel, and its views alone are worth a diversion. The fort is a comparatively well-preserved Anglo-Norman edifice, with a unique rock ditch, built in the same year (1261) as Carlingford Castle on the southern side of the lough. After succumbing to several attacks from the local Magennis clan, and falling to Edward Bruce in 1316, it collapsed into complete ruin after the Cromwellian invasion and now only guards the farm across the road. It's hard to imagine the fort's great fireplaces providing a counterblast to the buffeting winds that sweep across from the lough– you can feel their full force by climbing up the corner turrets to the top storey, where you can look down on the sandy beach below and enjoy tremendous views of the lough.

North to Rostrevor

If you take the main road inland from Kilkeel (cutting behind Greencastle Fort), four or five miles out of Kilkeel a signpost points to the **Kilfeaghan dolmen**, a mile inland then a short walk through a couple of fields and kissing gates. Its capstone is enormous and could only have arrived here during the retreat of the glacial drift.

Further up the lough, **ROSTREVOR** sits at the point where the bay waters dramatically begin to narrow towards Newry – and where the population and political climate turn more in favour of the Catholic communities of County Armagh and those of the ever-nearing border. It's a charming and sleepy village of Victorian terraces and friendly pubs, meandering up the lower slopes of **Slieve Martin**. There are a few tiny **B&Bs** in town but it's worth travelling out of Rostrevor to *Forestbrook House* on Forest Road (☎016937/38105; ③) – a vaguely French chateau-style B&B. **Camping** is available at *Kilbroney Park*, Shore Road (☎016937/38134), where you can hike up the hill to the thirty-ton Cloughmore ("big stone") for views across the lough to the Cooley Mountains over the border; geologists reckon the stone is a remnant of the Ice Age, but locals prefer a more spectacular story involving Fionn Mac Cumhaill. Huge inexpensive steaks are popular at the *Top of the Town* (known as *Annie O's*) in Church Street and there are other eating options at the *Cloughmoor Inn* and *Corner House* pubs. The newly refurbished *Glenside Bar* is a grand place for a pint. The **Fiddler's Green Festival** in July or August is a big, enjoyable event, attracting folk musicians from across Europe.

Warrenpoint

WARRENPOINT is equally picturesque, with a colourful esplanade of seafront housing and a spacious central square. It's a much more traditional seaside resort than Rostrevor and has been attracting visitors since the early 1800s, when an enterprising local man advertised warm baths for the "gentry, nobility and public". The **tourist office** (Mon–Fri 9am–5pm, plus weekends in summer; ☎016937/52256) is in the Town Hall on Church Street. There are handy **boat trips** across to Omeath on the opposite side of Carlingford Lough, leaving from just in front of the *Marine Tavern* (June–Sept 1–6pm, tides permitting; £2 return).

You shouldn't have any trouble finding accommodation, except during the Maiden of the Mournes festival in August, a local version of the Rose of Tralee (see p.316). **B&Bs** include the *Lough View*, 10 Osborne Promenade (☎016937/73067; ③), and two in the hills above town – friendly *Fern Hill House*, 90 Clonallon Rd (☎016937/72677; ③) and *Mariann's*, 18 Upper Dromore Rd (☎016937/52085; ②), with panoramic views.

You can dine at *Aylesforte House* on the outskirts towards Newry; or for cheaper **eating** try *Diamond's*, on the main square, with a choice of low-priced specials. Wholesome food is also available at two pubs: *Bennett's*, on Church Street, and *Jack Ryan's*, The Square. There's also cosy **drinking** at *Molly McCabes*, on Duke Street, uphill from the square, where the old boys gather to drink bottled stout only – it can accommodate twelve people at the most. There's regular **ceili** dancing in St Peter's Gaelic Hall, and **traditional sessions** and discos in the *Forresters' Hall* on the seafront. *The Duke of Mourne*, Duke Street, and *Shenanigan's* by the harbour have sessions most nights in summer. Showband fans are catered for at the *Crown Hotel*. The **disco** activity is at *Club Cheri* on the front and *Mingles* above the Crown. In the daytime you can **rent bikes** at East Coast Adventure Centre (☎016937/74006), which is based in a kiosk on the seafront; they will also set you up with jet skies, wind-surfing boards, canoes and all the information on local sports you could want. For **horse riding** try Annett's Equestrian Centre, Rath Road (☎016937/72976).

Less than a mile from Warrenpoint along the Newry Road is the **Narrow Water Castle**. The original was built in 1212 by Hugh de Lacy to guard against access to Newry via the river, but this was burnt down during the 1641 rebellion and the ruins here are of a building erected some twenty years later. In this serene setting, it's hard to imagine that sixteen British soldiers were blown up here by the IRA, on the same day that Lord Mountbatten was killed in Mullughmore Bay in 1979. There are very slight remains of the earlier castle nearby, and on the other side of the road an avenue leads up to **New Narrow Water Castle** (a private residence but can be viewed on request; 75p). A couple of miles to the north is the **Burren Heritage Centre** (April–Sept Tues–Sat 10am–6pm, Sun 2–6pm; Oct–March Mon–Fri 10am–5pm; £1), a small interpretive museum which traces the locality's development from prehistoric times.

Newry

Although **NEWRY**, astride the border of Down and Armagh, is this area's most important commercial centre, it's the least attractive proposition for a visit. Traditionally, it was the place for people from the Republic to come and shop; on market day (Thurs) you'll still find traffic at a standstill. The town here was founded by Cistercian monks in 1144, but for most of its history has been a garrison, guarding the borders of Ulster at the narrow point between the mountains known as the Gap of the North. There's no trace at all of the bitterly contested early fortresses; rather what you see dates mostly from the eighteenth and nineteenth centuries, when a canal to Lough Neagh (cut in 1742, the first in the British Isles) brought the produce of the inland towns to the markets of Newry. This business has long gone, however, and Newry is probably better known from the news: the town and its immediate surroundings were repeatedly bombed by the IRA in the 1970s, and the area is still sometimes a hive of helicopter and police activity. Given its central position you're highly likely to pass through Newry, and it does make a possible base for exploring Slieve Gullion and the south Armagh district, but you're unlikely to be tempted to stay.

One thing you'll notice as you wander around is that there seem to be dozens of lawyers practising here, with whole streets full of their offices. Perhaps the most interesting building in town, however, is the **Catholic Cathedral** on Hill Street, in the pedestrian precinct. Despite an unpromising granite exterior, the rich mosaic pattern along its walls gives a Byzantine feel to the interior, which also has a striking vaulted ceiling of decorative sweeping plaster arcs and vivid stained-glass windows. Nearby, there's a strange bronze totem pole by sculptor Paddy McElroy which depicts, in tortured relief, scenes from Newry's past. Not far away, the **Town Hall** is remarkable mainly because it's built on a bridge over the Clanrye river – it's half in Down, half in Armagh. Inside, the **Newry Museum** (Tues & Thurs–Fri 9am–5pm; free) displays a variety of exhibits, including Nelson's table from *HMS Victory*, and local historical information. The **Newry and Mourne Arts Centre**, next door at 1a Bank Parade, hosts exhibitions of local artists' work, plays and all types of music in the auditorium.

Newry's **tourist office** is in the town hall too (June–Sept Mon–Fri 9am–8pm, Sat 10am–4pm; Oct–May Mon–Fri 9am–1pm & 2–5pm; ☎01693/68877). If you want to **stay**, the *Mourne Country Hotel*, 52 Belfast Rd (☎01693/67922; ⑤), is luxurious but characterless, or there's the brand new *Canal Court Hotel*, Merchants Quay (☎01693/251234; ⑦), equipped with a gym and sauna. Alternatively, there are a fair number of **B&Bs**, including *Hillside*, 1 Rock Rd (☎01693/65484; ③); and *Millvale House*, 8 Millvale Rd (☎01693/63789; ③). The best **food** is at the *Brass Monkey* bar on Sandy Street, opposite the courthouse, with Kilkeel fish and local produce; there's little in the way of **nightlife**, but you could try *Nan Rice's* on Frances Street for traditional sessions, or like the locals head for the *Forresterrs' Hall* in Warrenpoint, or the *Independent Club* en route on the A2.

Southwest of Belfast: Hillsborough to Banbridge

Heading west from Belfast, the M1 motorway offers very rapid access to Armagh and Tyrone, while the A1 cuts south towards Newry. On the former route there's little to stop for until you're in County Armagh; on the latter the historic village of **HILLSBOROUGH**, just a mile off the main road, merits a quick detour. The main street has a chintzy, Middle English ambience, reinforced by a sprinkling of tea and antique shops. You get the best of Hillsborough by following a route that starts from the **war memorial** and heads up the magnificent approach to the rather spooky parish church. Bear right here for the main entrance to Hillsborough's elegant but ruined **fort** (April–Sept Mon–Sat 10am–7pm, Sun 2–7pm; Oct–March Tues–Sat 10am–4pm, Sun 2–4pm; free), constructed by Colonel Arthur Hill (after whom the village is named) in 1650 and remodelled in the eighteenth century as a fun palace. Beyond this a deciduous forest opens up, curving around a lake stocked with brown and rainbow trout. Footpaths meander through the trees in all directions – a circuit of the lake takes around an hour. Exiting via the car park, a driveway brings you out near the *White Gables Hotel* (☎01846/682755; ⑧), beyond which you'll notice a statue on a raised column, master of all it beholds – the third Marquis of Downshire, erstwhile owner of the estate.

A right turn at the end of the drive brings you back into town, with **Hillsborough Castle** on your left. Frankly, the ornate gates are the best part and even these were transferred from Richhill in 1936. The mansion itself dates from 1797 and from 1925 to 1973 was the residence of the Governor of Northern Ireland. Since then it's been used mainly to house visiting diplomats, although headlines were hit when the Anglo-Irish Agreement was signed here in 1985. More recently, Tony Blair stayed here during the April 1997 peace settlement talks.

By this time you'll be in need of **refreshment**, for which the *Plough Inn* on the square is recommended. A little further down, the *Hillside Inn*, built in 1777, serves more substantial fare in a Victorian-style dining room. Best of all, however, is the *Red Fox* tea shop at the bottom of the hill, through an arch and behind a boutique of the same name. When you've finished here, you'll be back where you began, at the war memorial. From here a regular Ulsterbus service runs to Newry and Belfast. However, if you want to stay there's **camping** three miles away at *Lakeside View*, 71 Magheraconluce Rd, Annahilt (☎01846/682098) and a number of small **B&Bs** scattered around.

Banbridge and around

Follow the A1 south from Hillsborough and you'll pass through **BANBRIDGE** on the River Bann. A trim, mainly Protestant town, with a growing Catholic population, Banbridge was a major linen centre and also a stop on the old coach route to the Mourne Mountains. However, the steep hill – now the main street – to the south of the river presented problems to the horse-drawn mail coaches. A threat to bypass the town was enough to initiate drastic action – and the result is the town's best-known feature. In 1834 the wide main street was divided into three with an underpass, known to locals as "the cut", carved out in the middle to lower the hill, and the Downshire Bridge was built over the gap. The town's most famous offspring is Captain Crozier, pioneer of the Northwest Passage (the passage by sea from the Atlantic to the Pacific along the north coast of America), who was born in 1796 in a house on Church Square. The house now overlooks the Crozier Memorial, on which four polar bears gaze at the captain, who in turn gazes to the northwest.

Banbridge Gateway Tourist Information Centre, a couple of miles out of town at 200 Newry Rd (July–Aug Mon–Sat 9am–7pm; Sept–June Mon–Sat 10am–5pm; plus Easter–Oct Sun 2–6pm; ☎018206/23322), is the departure point for the Linen Homelands Tour (May–Sept Wed 10am; £10). This explains the development of the manufacturing process by whizzing you around the district via visits to a flax farmer's scutching mill, a local linen factory and the Irish Linen Centre and Museum in Lisburn (see p.547).

THE BRONTË HOMELAND DRIVE

The start of the **Brontë Homeland Drive** is best approached by taking the A50 from Banbridge southeast to Moneyslane and thence to Ballroney. If you've followed the signs correctly, you should end up at the Drumballyroney **interpretive centre** (March–Oct Tues–Fri 11am–5pm, Sat & Sun 2–6pm; £1), a minuscule place with a mock schoolroom. The drive itself is justified by a rather tenuous link – the Brontës in question are not the famous sisters or even Branwell, but father Patrick Brontë and his parents. Nor is there any evidence that the literary daughters ever visited Ireland, though there is a story that one of the uncles took his shillelagh and headed to England to sort out a reviewer critical of *Jane Eyre*. It's more the story of local boy made good – Patrick obviously dragged himself up by his bootlaces, working in the linen works by day and reading the classics by night. With help from a local rector, he got a place to read theology at Cambridge. In 1806 he came back to preach his first sermon at Drumballyroney Church, but eventually moved to Yorkshire where he married Maria Branwell and had his six children – all of whom he outlived. Little remains of Patrick's birthplace at Emdale – a few feet of stone wall. And several of the other sights are specious: Knockiveagh, a hilltop stopping point, seems to be on the signposted route mainly to give you a chance to get your bearings. But if the drive doesn't yield nuggets of literary history, it does offer a route – however difficult to follow – through lovely hillocky countryside that you might not otherwise explore.

Should you want to stay the best **B&B** in the district is four miles away at *Mount Pleasant,* 38 Banbridge Rd (☎01762/831522; ②) just beyond Ilford. This vast castellated Georgian linen house sits on a grassy knoll with a fine view, and has bedrooms the size of tennis courts. There's little nightlife in Banbridge, though occasional club nights at the *Coach*, Church Square (☎018206/62195) draw the crowds. Banbridge's proximity to the Bann offers numerous **angling** opportunities and advice, equipment and licences are available from James Coburn & Son, 32 Scarva St (☎018206/62207).

The area around Banbridge contains a number of sites of varied antiquity and importance. **Lisnagade Fort**, three miles west on the Scarva road, is an impressive circular earthwork, consisting of three massive ditch-separated banks. The diameter of the inner circle is a good thirty metres, but, though bronze artefacts have been recovered from the site, little is known about its occupants. A little more is understood about the **Loughbrickland Crannog**, three miles southwest of Banbridge near the village of the same name (take the A1 then B3 Milltown road). Constructed sometime around 500 AD it was inhabited in the seventeenth century by the Magennis family, who had vacated a castle that's thought to have been located on the lough shore. Lastly, and most notably, the **Legannany Dolmen** is worth a considerable detour. Its direction is signposted at the A50/B7 crossroads (nine miles southeast of Banbridge) and at the village of Leitrim, north of Castlewellan. Whichever your approach, you'll find yourself on narrow humped lanes, gradually ascending the southern edge of the Slieve Croob range, and feeling increasingly distant from modern realities. You may also experience a sense of *déjà vu* too when you arrive at the site, for the dolmen is a popular choice of guidebook and tourist board photographers, but there's no doubting the impressiveness of the structure, looking for all the world like a giant stone tripod.

COUNTY ARMAGH

Recent history has hardly heightened **County Armagh**'s appeal for tourists. The villages of **South Armagh** – a predominantly Catholic area – are the heartland of violent Republicanism, so much so, in fact, that it has often been referred to as "Bandit Country" or "The Killing Fields", even by locals. On the other side of the sectarian divide, the name of **Portadown** has become synonymous with recalcitrant Unionism thanks to the stand-off between the authorities and the Orange Order at Drumcree church. Yet the county does warrant exploration, for it has some luscious landscapes and a history as rich as any county in Ireland: **Armagh city** has strong associations with St Patrick and early Christianity, while the sedately rural areas harbour some sites that are redolent of the island's legendary past, notably **Navan Fort** and **Slieve Gullion**.

ARMAGH TELEPHONE CODES

New telephone codes will be introduced throughout Northern Ireland from June 1, 1999 although it will still be possible to use the old codes until April 22, 2000. The new codes will prefix the existing subscriber number regardless of where you are calling from; calls from outside Northern Ireland will require the 028 prefix in addition – thus Portadown ☎01762/303456 will become ☎(028) 38 303456. The four Armagh codes will change as follows:

Newry ☎01693 (plus five-figure digit) to ☎ (028) 302

Newry ☎01693 (plus six-figure digit) to ☎ (028) 30

Armagh ☎01861 to ☎ (028) 37

Portadown ☎01762 to ☎ (028) 38

North Armagh

Below **Lough Neagh**, the north of County Armagh is dominated by the developed industrial strip containing the almost connected towns of **Lurgan**, **Craigavon** and **Portadown**. There is little in this urban hinterland to attract you – and, indeed, Portadown's reputation as the most bigoted town in the North is in itself deterrent enough.

Outside the towns, however, there are a number of points of interest. The **Lough Neagh Discovery Centre** (April–Sept daily 10am–7pm; Oct–March Wed–Sun 10am–5pm), best approached from junction 10 of the M1, is to be found on Oxford Island, which is in fact a small peninsula jutting out into the lough. The woodlands and shoreline swamps draw a multitude of waterfowl and other birds, which can be viewed from various hides, while inside the centre you can learn more about the lough, its management and ornithology (and have some fun in the Ecolab games room). You can explore more a little to the east at **Kinnego Bay**, where there's a marina, boat trips, specialist powerboat and sailing courses, a **campsite** and accommodation available in *Waterside House* **hostel** (details of all activities ☎01762/32573).

Further on to the west, Junction 13 is the access point for **Peatlands Park** (open daily 9am–dusk), where the visitor centre (Easter–Sept Sat & Sun 2–6pm, plus

---

THE ORANGE ORDER AND THE MARCHING TRADITION

Ireland's oldest political grouping, **The Grand Orange Lodge of Ireland**, was founded in September, 1795, following the so-called **Battle of the Diamond**, which took place in Dan Winter's farm near **Loughgall**. The skirmish involved the Peep O'Day boys (Protestants) and the Defenders (Catholics) and was the culmination of a long-running dispute about control of the local linen trade. The Defenders attacked an inn, unaware that inside the Peep O'Day boys were armed and waiting. A dozen Defenders were killed, and in the glow of victory their opponents formed the Orange Order.

The first Orange Lodge march in celebration of the 1690 **Battle of the Boyne** took place in 1796 and they've been happening ever since. The Boyne is the Loyalist totem, even though the actual battle at Aughter which ended Jacobite rule did not take place until the following year, and William of Orange is their icon, despite the fact that his campaign was supported by the pope and most of the Catholic rulers of Europe and that William himself had a noted reputation for religious tolerance. For Protestant Ulster the Boyne came to represent a victory that enshrined Protestant supremacy and liberties, and the Orange Order became the bedrock of Protestant hegemony. Between 1921 and 1969, for example, 51 of the 54 ministers appointed to the Stormont government were members of the Orange Order and, at its peak, so was two-thirds of the Protestant male population of the North. In the 1990s, however, it became clear that the Orangemen's march to the beat of the Lambeg drum was falling increasingly out of step with the political realities of Northern Ireland. What may well come to be seen as the turning point in its fortunes arrived during the **summer of 1998**.

For several years the **Drumcree** church parade on the July Sunday before the "Glorious Twelfth" had been the focus for the Orange Order's assertion of their political identity, their march down the Catholic Garvaghy Road in Portadown constituting a massive statement of the permanency of their power in Northern Ireland. Opposed to the peace settlement and the formation of the new Assembly, the Order made Drumcree its rallying cry, and was provoked to even greater stridency when the march was banned by the **Parades Commission**, a body that was formed to limit the fractiousness (and cost) of marches by controlling or even stopping them. The Order expected a massive security operation preventing their march, but failed to anticipate the subsequent Protestant violence which

June–Aug Mon–Fri 2–6pm) can tell you everything you ever wanted to know about peat. A narrow gauge railway (£1) runs for a mile along part of the track once used to transport extracted peat by the previous owners, the Irish Peat Development Company.

The roach-filled upper section of the River Bann, south of Portadown, is the place for coarse anglers to head, and another watery attraction is the **Newry Canal**, which flows into the river through a natural trough in the landscape, running through fourteen locks on the way. One of these features the restored **Moneypenny's Lockhouse** (Easter–Sept Sat–Sun 2–5pm; free), named after the family who kept the lock for 85 years – it's a two mile stroll along the towpath from Shillingford Quay in Portadown.

Armagh city and around

ARMAGH's small size disappoints some people, and certainly the city doesn't immediately present a greatly exciting prospect – but, rich in history at least, Armagh and its surroundings have plenty to keep you occupied for a day or two. The city offers cathedrals, museums and a planetarium set in handsome Georgian streets, while the ancient site of once-grand Navan Fort and two stately homes, Ardress and the Argory, are features of the excellent cycling country hereabouts. Armagh has been the site of the Catholic primacy of all Ireland since St Patrick established his church here (it's also the seat of the

swept across the country, fuelled by Orange rhetoric and catalysed by the Loyalist Volunteer Force. Every day saw petrol bombings, vehicle hijacks, Catholic areas besieged and, hardest for the patriotic Orangemen to stomach, attacks on the RUC and troops. Early in the morning of Sunday, July 12, 1998 a petrol bomb was thrown into a Catholic family's house on a largely Protestant estate in **Ballymoney**, County Antrim, killing three young brothers. The reaction of some Orange Lodge members, who seemed more concerned about maintaining their "traditional right to march" than with condemning the murder of innocent children, outraged people of both communities and exacerbated the divisions in the Order. Its chaplain called for Drumcree to be abandoned and many Orangemen resigned. The RUC raided the protesters' camp and found weapons and explosives; the Church of Ireland banned the protest from its grounds, forcing the abandonment of Drumcree. The death of a policeman wounded by a blast bomb at Portadown further diminished the Orange Order's standing.

Though Loyalist marches have tended to be the flashpoints for major disturbances, it shouldn't be forgotten that the **marching tradition** is common to both communities. Around three thousand marches take place each year and, although the vast number are Loyalist parades, a significant number are Nationalist. These include the **St Patrick's Day marches** of the Ancient Order of Hibernians and the Irish National Foresters and commemorative parades and wreath-laying ceremonies by Sinn Féin and other Republican bodies on Easter Monday and various anniversaries. **The Loyalist marching season** begins in March and culminates in celebration of the **Battle of the Boyne** on **July 12**, although the **Apprentice Boys** have traditionally marched around the walls of Derry on August 12. Most of the Loyalist marches are uncontentious – small church parades, or commemorations of the Somme – but it can't be denied that some of them are something other than a vibrant expression of cultural identity. Marching can be a means by which one community asserts its dominance over the other, selecting routes which deliberately pass through Nationalist areas, for instance, or deliberately playing sectarian tunes and making provocative gestures – such as the raising of five fingers on Belfast's **Lower Ormeau Road** (where five Catholics were shot dead in 1992) or the gratuitously offensive stamping dance performed by marchers in **Portadown** (where a young Catholic was kicked to death in 1998). Drumcree was a profoundly politicized gathering, and the events of 1998 will be recorded as a crucial episode in the modern political history of Ireland.

ARMAGH

Belfast & Portadown

Tandrangee (A51)

Ballynahone River

DRUMADD ROAD

TOWER HILL

COLLEGE HILL

VICTORIA ROAD

BARRACK HILL

Leisure Centre

Newry (A28)

Observatory

Eartharium

Planetarium

Clonhugh Guesthouse

Regimental Museum

County Museum

THE MALL EAST

The Mall

THE MALL WEST

Bus Terminus

BARRACK ST

Armagh Gaol

NEWRY ROAD

Telephone Exchange

Community Centre

R.U.C. Station

SCOTCH ST

LINENHALL STS

DOBBIN ST

War Memorial

Court House

De-Averell Guesthouse

Charlemont Arms Hotel

COLLEGE ST

RUSSELL ST

ENGLISH ST

THE MALL SOUTH

St. Patrick's Trian

Cathedral (C.I.)

THOMAS ST

FRIARY ROAD

Palace Stables Heritage Centre & Palace Demesne

Drumshill Hotel

MOY ROAD

RAILWAY STREET

LONSDALE ROAD

Dungannon

Cathedral (R.C.)

Padua Guesthouse

Desart House

Shambles Market

EDWARD STREET

DAWSON STREET

ABBEY ST

CATHEDRAL CLOSE

ENGLISH ST

VICARS HILL

CASTLE ST

CHAPEL LANE

Queen's University Youth Hostel

Robinson's Library

CALLAN ST

CULDEE DRIVE

NAVAN ST

IRISH ST

CATHEDRAL ROAD

CONVENT ROAD

WINDMILL HILL

NURSERY ROAD

CULDEE DRIVE

NAVAN ROAD

KILLYLEA ROAD

Callan River

N

0   100 yds

CALLAN BRIDGE ROAD

Navan Centre, Enniskillen & West (A28)

Protestant Church of Ireland Archbishop of Armagh) and has rather ambitiously adopted the title the "Irish Rome" for itself – like Rome, it's positioned among seven small hills.

Some history

Armagh (*Ard Macha*, "Macha's height") was named after **Queen Macha**, wife of Nevry, who is said to have arrived in Ireland 608 years after the biblical flood. She built a fortress on the main hill where the Church of Ireland now stands and is supposed to be buried somewhere in the hillside. The claim that Armagh is one of the oldest settlements in Ireland is supported by the city's position on one of the most ancient roads in the land, the Moyry Pass, which once stretched from the extreme south of Ireland, through Tara, to the north. In about 300 BC, the centre of power shifted westward across the River Callan to where another queen (of the same name, Macha) built the legendary **Navan Fort**.

After nearly seven hundred years, the ruling dynasty at Navan was defeated by the Collas brothers, and the new rulers re-established their main base back on the hill of Armagh. A hundred years later, in 445 AD, **St Patrick** declared the hill the site of his primacy and first bishopric and built his cathedral here (having first converted the local chieftain, Daire, a descendant of the Collas brothers). Other churches grew up around the cathedral, and Armagh became *the* great centre of learning during the Dark Ages, the period when Ireland was known as the "Isle of Saints and Scholars". Armagh strongly challenges Downpatrick's claim to be the burial place of St Patrick; they argue that since the relics of Patrick's book, bell and staff are here, his body must be, too (though the burial site is not identified). The settlement developed around three distinct districts (*Trians*), their boundaries still reflected today by English, Irish and Scottish Streets.

Between the ninth and the eleventh centuries, the city was repeatedly pillaged by the **Vikings**, mainly from the Norse settlements at Lough Neagh. The Irish king who claimed final victory over the Norsemen, **Brian Boru**, was killed in the process, at the Battle of Clontarf in 1014, and was buried in Armagh cathedral. The arrival of the Normans in the twelfth century saw the city become a constant battleground as the O'Neills sought to maintain their control. Despite this, Armagh's ecclesiastical power did not waver until the Reformation. Further local conflict ensued and it was not until the end of the Williamite wars that peace finally broke out. The arrival of Richard Robinson as Archbishop in 1765 saw a final flourish of building, much of which survives today, despite the encroachment of recent supermarket developments. Modern Armagh is a predominantly Catholic city, strong on Gaelic sports, and, although physically it has borne up well to the Troubles (certainly in comparison to Newry and Derry), it has not avoided them.

The city

The best way to find your bearings is to walk up the steps of **St Patrick's Roman Catholic Cathedral**, built on a hillside just northwest of the Shambles Market. The view of the town from here is impressive and you should be able to identify most of the key sites spread out below. The cathedral's foundation stone was laid in 1840, but completion was delayed by the Famine and a subsequent lack of funding. Whilst the pope and local nobility chipped in, money was obtained from public collections and raffles – one prize of a grandfather clock has still not been claimed. On the outside the cathedral first appears little different to many of its nineteenth-century Gothic Revival contemporaries. But it is impressively large and airy, and inside, as befits the seat of the cardinal archbishop, every inch of wall glistens with mosaics, in colours ranging from marine- and sky-blue to terracotta pinks and oranges. Other striking pieces include the white-granite "pincer-claw" tabernacle holder, reflected in a highly polished marble floor, and a statue of the

Crucifixion which suggests (deliberately or otherwise) the old city's division into *Trians*. This cathedral city is known for its choral music, and the annual Charles Wood Summer School (check with the tourist office for dates) is worth catching.

Heading south along Dawson Street you'll soon reach Cathedral Close and **St Patrick's Church of Ireland Cathedral** (April–Oct 10am–5pm; Nov–March closes 4pm; tours June–Aug Mon–Sat 11.30am & 2.30pm). This lays claim to the summit of the principal hillock, Drum Saileach, where St Patrick founded his first church in 445 AD. It commands a distinctive Armagh view across to the other hills and down over the clutter of gable walls and pitched roofing on its own slopes. A series of churches subsequently occupied the site and, although the core of the present one is medieval, a nineteenth-century restoration coated the thirteenth-century outer walls in a sandstone plaster of which Thackeray remarked, "It is as neat and trim as a lady's dressing room". Many of the ancient decorations were removed, leaving the spartan interior you see today. Just as you enter from the highly distinctive timber porch, you'll see a few remnants of an eleventh-century Celtic cross and a startling statue of Thomas Molyneux. Inside, high up, you should be able to sight the medieval carved heads of men, women and monsters. One other unusual feature is the tilt of the chancel, a medieval building practice meant to represent the slumping head of the dying Christ. The **chapter house** has a small collection of stone statues (mostly gathered from elsewhere), the most noticeable of which are the Stone Age Tandragee Idol and a sheila-na-gig with an ass's ears.

Just down the hill from the cathedral, the **public library** (known locally as Robinson's), (Mon–Fri 9am–1pm & 2–4pm; free but donations welcomed), has a first edition of *Gulliver's Travels*, annotated by Swift himself, and an early edition of Raleigh's *History of the World* (1614), among many other rare tomes, as well as a collection of etchings, including some by Hogarth. The library was founded in 1771 by Archbishop Richard Robinson, who was described as converting Armagh "from mud to stone" and is responsible for almost all the older buildings in Armagh – the nearby infirmary was one of his too, though it's now occupied by the University.

Cathedral Close leads downhill to the main shopping area, where an entry leads into the narrow winding lane of **McCrum's Court**. The *Hole in the Wall* antique shop here occupies the site of the old town jail and the similarly-named rock-walled pub is well worth a visit. Walking back and a little way north up English Street you'll come to **St Patrick's Trian Centre**, an ambitious complex containing the tourist office and two separate exhibitions. The first of these, peopled with figures representing the Land of Lilliput and Jonathan Swift's connection with Armagh, occupies the former Presbyterian Meeting House, which was partly constructed from the ruined abbey of St Peter and St Paul – Swift is reputed to have commented that the masons were "chipping the popery out of the stones." The second installation, "The Armagh Story", is a multimedia account of both the town's growth and the nature of belief (both April–Sept Mon–Sat 10am–7pm, Sun 1–7pm; Oct–March Mon–Sat closes 5pm, Sun 2–5pm; £2.20 each, £3.30 both).

The Mall

Russell Street leads down to **The Mall**, an elegant tree-lined promenade fringed to the east by two terraces of handsome Georgian houses designed by the Armagh-born architect Francis Johnston, who worked primarily for Archbishop Robinson. He was also responsible for many of Dublin's best Georgian buildings and you'll encounter more examples of his work around town, including the classical courthouse at The Mall's northern end. Significantly, the former jail occupies the opposite position. In its late eighteenth-century heyday The Mall was once a racecourse; nowadays there's nothing more athletic than the occasional jogger and Sunday cricket matches.

A former schoolhouse on the east side of The Mall houses the **County Museum** (Mon–Fri 10am–5pm; Sat 10am–1pm & 2–5pm; free), an old-style museum with all the usual local miscellany on display, including an alarmingly vivid collection of stuffed wildlife, plus a little art gallery tucked away on the first floor. Here there are twenty or so mystical pastels, oils and cartoon sketches by the Irish turn-of-the-century poet **George Russell**, a much-neglected companion to Yeats who acquired the alias AE as a result of a Dublin newspaper misprinting a letter he had signed "Aeons". The local artist J.B. Vallely is also represented with a superb oil showing five musicians enjoying a session – he currently runs the town's Armagh Pipers' Club. Elsewhere, a display devoted to railway history recounts the story of Ireland's worst railway disaster when two passenger trains collided outside Armagh in 1889, killing 89 people, many of whom are buried in the nearby St Mark's churchyard. Further north along The Mall, built from the leftovers of the Courthouse, is the **Royal Irish Fusiliers Museum** (Mon–Fri 10am–12.30pm & 1.30–4pm; £1.50). It's pretty much as you'd expect: tons of weaponry, uniforms, medallions and regimental silverware.

The Observatory, Planetarium and Eartharium

College Hill, the road that leaves The Mall by the Fusiliers museum, will take you to the **Observatory** (dome open April–Sept Mon–Fri 9.30am–4.30pm) and a ten-inch telescope, and the **Planetarium** (Mon–Fri 10am–4.45pm, Sat–Sun 1.15–4.45pm; £1; star theatre shows Mon–Fri 3pm, Sat–Sun 2pm & 3pm; £3.75). The Observatory is an ancient one – it celebrated its second centenary in 1990 – but it's still at the forefront of astronomical research. The Planetarium was built much more recently, in 1968, and its best feature are the **star theatre** shows where you whizz through the universe from the safety of a reclinable seat. It also has solar system galleries, various antique astronomical instruments from the earliest days of the Observatory, as well as high-tech equipment to show you the latest pictures from NASA's space telescope. There's also the **Eartharium** which – rather chillingly – allows you to zoom in on Belfast or Armagh using spy satellite pictures, or to predict the weather.

Armagh Friary

The ruins of **Armagh Friary**, founded by the Franciscans in 1263, lie within easy walking distance of the city centre, just off Friary Road by the entrance to the grounds of the Archbishop's Palace, now the District Council offices. The ruins are those of the church alone, and the site is an unfortunate example of how atmosphere can be destroyed when a major road runs alongside. The focus now is the **Palace Stables Heritage Centre** (April–Sept Mon–Sat 10am–5.30pm, Sun 10am–6pm; Oct–March Mon–Sat 10am–5pm, Sun 2–5pm; £3), where tableaux of life-sized figures depict July 23, 1776, the day on which Archbishop Robinson entertained agricultural entrepreneur Arthur Young – you're guided around by living history interpreters garbed in contemporary costumes. From here you move into the main part of the palace, which dates from around 1770, though the final storey was added in 1825, and was inhabited by subsequent archbishops until 1975 when the private Primate's Chapel next door was deconsecrated. In the grounds there's a well-preserved ice house, a curious tunnel by which servants accessed the basement kitchens, a stimulating sensory garden (opened in 1996) and, somewhat incongruously, the municipal dog pound.

Practicalities

The **tourist office** is in St Patrick's Trian Centre on English Street (Mon–Sat 9am–5pm, Sun 2–5pm; ☎01861/521800). *De-Averell Guest House*, 47 English St (☎01861/511213; ⑥), offers central, comfortable **accommodation** and has an innovative basement restaurant, while the nearby *Charlemont Arms Hotel*, 63 English St (☎01861/522028; ④) is also noted for its menus; half a mile north of town on the Moy

---

ROAD BOWLS

The sport of **road bowls** is popular in Holland and Germany and was once played throughout Ireland, but is now limited mainly to Cork and Armagh, where it's also known as "road bullets". The game's principle is simple: a pair of rival contestants each propel a 28oz solid iron ball along a course of country roads (usually about two and a half miles long), the winner being the player who reaches the finishing line with the fewest number of throws. In practice, it's a complicated business. The Armagh roads twist and turn, up and down, and bowlers are assisted by a team of camp followers, including managers and road guides who advise on the most advantageous spots to aim and the force of the throw. Traditionally, a male sport, it's become increasingly popular with women who've held their own championship since 1981. Roads around Armagh where you're likely to catch sight of the game include Napper Road, Blackwater Town Road, Rock Road, Tassa Road, Keady Road, Newtonhamilton Road and Madden Road, usually on Sunday afternoons. The most reliable information on coming games is probably in local pubs. The "World Championship" takes place in Armagh in May and there's even a specialist book on the subject – Brian Toal's *Road Bowling in Ireland*.

Road is *Drumsill Hotel* (☎01861/522009; ⑦). **B&Bs** are scarce, but they include two on Cathedral Road – *Desart* at no. 99 (☎01861/522387; ②) and *Padua House* at no. 63 (☎01861/522039; ①) – plus *Dean's Hill*, College Hill (☎01861/524923; ⑤). There's a fine new YHANI **hostel** (☎01861/511800), superbly situated near the cathedral at 39 Abbey St. The nearest **camping** is *Gosford Forest Park*, seven miles along the A28 near Markethill (☎01861/551277), with fine facilities set in wooded grounds around a castle.

Many of the **pubs** will serve bar food at lunchtime, but **eating** in the evening can be more problematic. Pick of the pubs with food is the lively *Calvert's Tavern*, 3 Scotch St. *Harry Hoots*, 143 Railway St, also has an excellent restaurant (with discos at the weekends); or you can always get a reasonably priced full meal at the *Drumsill Hotel*. An excellent place with healthy food is *Jodies*, upstairs at 37 Scotch St. *Hester's Place* on English Street and *The Wheel and Lantern*, in the remnants of *Lennox's* department store on Market Street, both serve good-value lunches. The best places for coffee and snacks are *The Archway*, 5 Hartford Place, through an arch off the east side of The Mall, and the *Pilgrim's Table* in the St Patrick's Trian Centre.

The most atmospheric pub for a pint is the *Hole in the Wall Bar* in McCrum's Court. The top end of English Street is a good area to pub crawl in search of **music**; weekends are best but many places have sing-songs (Tues & Thurs). The *Northern Bar*, 100 Railway St, is the place for blues and rock. For **nightclubs**, your options are limited – locals head to nearby Keady, Moy or across the border to Castleblaney – but try *The Met* complex on Moy Road. Armagh has a number of events during the year, but the biggest concentration occurs during the May **Apple Blossom** festival when their are daily events, blues and dance festivals and the World Road Bowling Championship (see box above).

Navan Fort

For nearly seven hundred years **Navan Fort** (open access; free) was the great seat of northern power, rivalling Tara in the south. It was here that the Kings of Ulster ruled and Queen Macha built her palace on the earthworks' summit. It's a site of deeply mystical significance, but one also of enormous archeological significance. The court of the **Knights of the Red Branch**, Ireland's most prestigious order of chivalry, was based here too. The knights, like those of the Round Table, are historical figures, entirely subsumed into legend, their greatest champion being the legendary defender of Ulster, **Cúchulainn**. The stories of these warriors' deeds are recited and sung in what's now known as the *Ulster Cycle*. Their dynasty was finally vanquished in 332 AD, when three brothers (the Collas), in a conquest known as the Black Pig's Dyke, destroyed Navan Fort, razing it to the ground and leaving only the earthen mounds you see today. The defeated Red Branch Knights were driven eastwards into Down and Antrim, but their glories withered away soon afterwards.

The best approach to the fort (two miles west of Armagh on the A28; bus #73) is to visit the new interpretive centre first. The **Navan Centre**, cut into the land near the site (April–June & Sept Mon–Sat 10am–6pm, Sun 11am–6pm; July–Aug Mon–Sat 10am–7pm, Sun 11am–7pm; Oct–March Mon–Fri 10am–5pm, Sat 11am–5pm, Sun noon–5pm; last entry 75min before closure; £3.95), is a circular grass-covered mound supported inside by columns, replicating the real fort as it's thought to have been structured. The seventy-minute tour, which deposits you at the doors leading to the fort proper, begins with an excellent talk on the history and archeology of the site, with fascinating asides – a Barbary ape skull, for example, implies trade links with North Africa. You then move onto an audiovisual show that replays four key myths associated with this ancient fort, including that of Cúchulainn, the hound of Ulster, and the *Taín Bó Cuailngè* (Cattle Raid of Cooley).

When you reach the fort, you find an earthen mound which gives a commanding view but no hint of its past. Excavation of the mound took place over a ten-year period (1961–71) and revealed a peculiar structure, apparently unique in the Celtic world. Archeologists reckon that around 100 BC the buildings that had existed since the Neolithic period were cleared, and a huge structure 108ft in diameter was constructed. An outer wall of timber surrounded five concentric rings of large posts, 275 in all, with a massive post at the very centre. This was then filled with limestone boulders – and set on fire, creating a mountain of ash that was then covered with sods of clay to make a high mound. It is anybody's guess what the purpose of the structure was – possibly a temple, or maybe a monumental funeral pyre.

The site area is defined by a massive bank with a defensive ditch. Nearby you can visit for free other ancient archeological structures: a second fort, the earliest known artificial lake in Ireland and a large natural lake which has yielded incredible treasures.

Loughgall, Ardress House and the Argory

LOUGHGALL, an estate village about five miles north of Armagh along the B27 in the middle of apple orchard country, beautiful in the spring, is worth visiting mainly for its **Orange Museum**. It was just northeast of Loughgall at Diamond Hill that the Battle of the Diamond took place in 1795 and led to the foundation of the first Protestant Orange Order (see box p.576). Today the little village, like many others in Armagh's rural north, is a strongly Protestant enclave. The tiny museum is sandwiched between two terraced houses at the northern end of the main street (key door with Mrs Vallary) and includes such Orange paraphernalia as sashes, flags and the banner from the Dolly Brae victory, the first Orange Order warrant signed on a Catholic after the Battle of the Diamond, and a couple of UVF armbands. Nowadays the village is deceptively quiet – in 1988, however, it was the scene of a British army ambush in which eight IRA men died. The main street is lined with antique shops, and there's a nice teahouse parlour, *Emily's Cottage*; the *Famous Grouse*, two miles out on Ballyhagan Road (☎01868/891778), is rather livelier, with the best restaurant for miles and regular live music. There's B&B **accommodation** at *Greenhall Country House*, 123 Cloveneden Rd (☎01868/784218; ②).

A further five miles or so north, and only a few miles apart, are two National Trust properties worth visiting if you've more than a day in the area. **Ardress House** (open 2–6pm: Easter; April–May & Sept Sat–Sun; June–Aug daily except Tues; £2.30) is a seventeenth-century manor house with ornate plasterwork by Michael Stapleton, a good collection of paintings, a sizeable working farmyard and wooded grounds. **The Argory** (same hours; £2.50), a fine neoclassical building dating back to 1824, which contains its original furniture and a fabulous cabinet barrel organ, is still lit by an original 1906 acetylene gas plant in the stable yard.

South Armagh

The **South Armagh** countryside is amongst the most attractive in the North, yet many visitors are deterred from coming here by the area's notoriety. Proximity to the border and a predominantly Catholic population have resulted in this being a nucleus of resistance to British rule, and evidence of military occupation is everywhere – from the hilltop surveillance posts to the constant whirring blades of helicopters monitoring the ground from above. Since the first ceasef-ire, however, many of the border controls and barriers have been removed, and South Armagh has remained a safe and remarkably welcoming place for tourists.

The Ring of Gullion

Most of South Armagh's attractions are concentrated in and around the area known as the **Ring of Gullion**, a naturally formed ring-dyke of low-lying hills which encircles (and predates) the mountain at its core. People have lived here for more than six thousand years and left a rich heritage of remains and monuments. On the Ring's western fringe is **The Dorsey Enclosure**, two huge earthen banks and ditch ramparts, dating from the Iron Age, running for a mile either side of the old route to Navan Fort. Elsewhere are numerous dolmens and cairns, Christian relics and monuments from the Plantation era.

Slieve Gullion (*sliabh gCuilinn*, "the mountain of Culainn"), which dominates the southeast corner of Armagh, is one of the most mysteriously beautiful mountains in the country. A store of romantic legends is attached to it, especially concerning **Cúchulainn**, who took his name here after slaying the hound (*Cú*) of the blacksmith, Culainn. Due south at Glendhu is where he single-handedly halted the army of Queen Medb of Connaught, who was intent on capturing the great bull of Cooley. **Fionn Mac Cumhaill**, who founded the *Fianna*, a mythical national militia whose adventures are told in the *Fenian Cycle*, also appears in stories here.

A scenic way to approach the mountain is from the north, passing the turning to **BESSBROOK**, a nineteenth-century model village developed by a Quaker linen entrepreneur; the Cadbury family's Bourneville estate in Birmingham followed a very similar layout. Just outside the village stands **Derrymore House** (May–Aug Thurs–Sat 2–5pm; £1.80), an eighteenth-century thatched manor house built for Isaac Corry, Chancellor of the Exchequer of the last Irish Parliament before the Act of Union, which was drafted in his drawing room here. After **CAMLOUGH** ("crooked lake"), where the Tricolour flutters, turn off the main road to go down by the eastern slopes of Camlough Mountain and you'll see the beautiful lake, set like a jewel within its green banks. A little further on, between Camlough Mountain and Slieve Gullion, are the **Killeavy churches** (*Cill Shléibhe* – "Church of the Mountain"). Two churches of different periods share the same gable wall: the west church is pre-Romanesque and one of the most important survivors of its kind in the country; the other, larger church dates from the thirteenth century. A granite slab marks the grave of St Bline, the founder of a fifth-century nunnery sited here – there's a holy well dedicated to her a little further up the slopes of Slieve Gullion, which pilgrims visit on her feast day (the Sunday nearest July 6).

The official, tarmacked entrance up into Slieve Gullion is on the mountain's afforested southern face, after you've passed through the village of Killeavy. Here there's a small forest park (daily Easter–Sept 10am–dusk; car £2.50), fronted by the new **Courtyard Centre** (Mon–Fri 9am–6pm, plus Easter–Sept Sat & Sun noon–6pm), where there are self-catering apartments (☎01693/848084; £150–200 per week) and, possibly, a hostel opening shortly. From the Centre it's an eight-mile winding drive up to the summit (or you can follow a walking trail), where there's a couple of megalithic cairns. Fionn Mac Cumhaill was bewitched here by Miluchra and local superstition holds that bathing in the small lake here will turn your hair white; another tale states that under certain conditions a visitor to the site will be given the power to foresee everything that will happen that day. Various vertiginous viewpoints offer spectacular views over the Ring of Gullion and the surrounding countryside for miles around.

Jonesborough and around

JONESBOROUGH, east of the mountain, is the venue each Sunday for a vast open-air **market** (11am–5pm), drawing traders and customers from both sides of the border. The range of goods on offer is equally enormous and it's well worth experiencing. The excellent *Flurrybridge Inn* serves food Thursday to Sunday and holds occasional sessions.

Two miles south of Jonesborough is the **Pillar Stone of Kilnasaggart**, a beautifully inscribed monument dating from 700 AD, marking the site of an early Christian cemetery. Several small crosses are marked within circles on its back face, and the defaced markings on its edges are possibly *ogham* writing. It's surrounded by several other tiny stones with similar cross markings, all held within a pentagonal enclosure three fields away from the roadside, behind a farmhouse. Less than a mile west of here, on the other side of the train line, you should be able to see **Moyry Castle** on the hill. It's a timid affair and not really worth even this slight detour, but among its interesting features are several musket loopholes. It was built by Lord Mountjoy, Queen Elizabeth I's deputy, in 1601 as the defence for the Gap to the North.

Forkhill and Mullach Ban

You might expect **FORKHILL** to lie in an elevated position, but this tiny village derives its name from the Irish *foirceal* ("trough") and nestles in the southwestern foothills of Slieve Gullion. It's a simple, quiet and remote-looking place though dominated by the massive army encampment stacked upon the crown of an overlooking hill. The village is strong on traditional culture: O'Neill's *Welcome Inn* has a storyteller, John Campbell, and sessions most Tuesday nights and other music at the weekends; there's weekend music too at *The Forge*. A two-day festival of *sean nós* (unaccompanied singing) takes place over the first weekend in October here and at neighbouring **MULLACH BAN** further north, where *O'Hanlons' Bridge House* also has regular sessions and the innovative *Thí Chulainn* cultural activities centre (☎01693/888828) is dedicated to the promotion of the area's culture and literary heritage.

If you want to **stay** in Forkhill, there are a couple of B&Bs: *Lakeview*, 34 Church Rd (☎01693/888382; ③) and *Green Vale*, 141 Longfield Rd (☎01693/888314; ②), which also offers **pony trekking**. In Mullach Ban there's *Lar Na Tuaithe*, 89 Maphoner Rd (☎01693/888897; ③).

Passing through Mullach Ban, you get back to the main Newry–Crossmaglen Road, where, a little up the road in **Glassdrummond**, there's *Hearty's Folk Cottage* (Sun 2–7pm), where you can admire the arts and crafts collections and enjoy excellent afternoon teas to the accompaniment of traditional music.

Crossmaglen and Creggan

In the far southwestern corner of Armagh, **CROSSMAGLEN** has reputedly the largest market square in Ireland, the scene of a fortnightly Friday market. Face south and its impossible to ignore the huge RUC/British army barracks here with its outcrops of aerials, cameras and sangars (small pillbox-like fortifications). During the Troubles the town's reputation for armed struggle against the British was fearsome and, in truth, it has been a cauldron of activity ever since Partition. Indeed, had the 1924 Boundary Commission's proposals been fully implemented, the town and surrounding countryside would have been transferred to Dublin rule rather than staying just inside the North. All this said, on arrival you'll find the pubs much friendlier than might have been expected and you're hardly likely to brush up against any trouble. Traditional music sessions are abundant and the square comes vividly alive during the horse-trading fairs in September. *Chums* bar has reasonably-priced lunches and the *Cartwheel*, also on the square, is a popular alternative. Should you want to stay there's **B&B** at *Murtagh's Bar*, 13 North St (☎01693/861378; ②) and out of town at *Lima Country House*, 16 Drumalt Rd, Silverbridge (☎01693/861944; ②). A new and extremely helpful **tourist office** (Mon–Fri 9am–5pm, extended to 6pm and weekends in summer; ☎01693/868900) is in Ó Fiaich House on the square.

A couple of miles east of Crossmaglen on the B30 is **CREGGAN** and its **Poets' Graveyard**, so named because three eighteenth-century Gaelic poets are buried here: **Art Mac Cooey, Patrick Mac Aliondain** and **Seamus Mór Mac Murphy** (also an outlaw of some notoriety). The inscription on Mac Cooey's stone is taken from his most famous poem, *Úr-Chill an Chreagáin* – "That with the fragrant Gaels of Creggan I will be put in clay under the sod".

travel details

TRAINS

Bangor to: Belfast (every 30min; 30min); Lisburn (every 30min; 1hr 10min); Lurgan (hourly; 1hr 35min); Newry (6 daily; 1hr 45min); Portadown (hourly; 1hr 45min).

Newry to: Belfast (8 daily; 1hr); Dublin (6 daily; 1hr 10min); Dundalk (6 daily; 15min).

BUSES

Armagh to: Belfast (10 daily; 1–2hr); Benburb (1 daily; 25min); Caledon via Navan Fort (5–8 daily; 20min); Castleblaney (5 daily; 1hr); Cork (1 daily; 9hr); Dublin (6 daily; 2hr 45min); Enniskillen (1 daily, July–Aug; 1hr 50min); Galway (1 daily; 5hr 55min); Keady (11 daily; 30min); Loughgall (5 daily; 15min); Markethill (8 daily; 20min); Monaghan (10 daily; 30–45min); Newry (6 daily; 1hr 10min); Portadown (26 daily; 30min); Portrush (1 daily; 2hr 20min).

Downpatrick to: Ballyhornan via Ardglass (9 daily; 40min); Belfast (hourly; 45min–1hr); Newcastle (13 daily; 35–40min); Newry (4 daily; 1hr); Strangford (7 daily; 25min).

Newcastle to: Banbridge (2 daily; 55min); Belfast (24 daily; 1hr 20min); Bryanford (5 daily; 10min); Castlewellan (28 daily; 10min); Downpatrick (18 daily; 35–40min); Kilkeel (17 daily; 40min); Newry (4 daily via Hilltown; 35min; 9 daily via Kilkeel; 40min).

Newry to: Crossmaglen (6 daily; 50min); Downpatrick (4 daily; 1hr); Dublin via Dundalk (7 daily; 2hr); Kilkeel (12 daily; 55min); Rostrevor (21 daily; 30min); Warrenpoint (25 daily; 20min).

Newtownards to: Bangor (every 30min; 20min); Belfast (every 20min; 35min); Comber (hourly; 15min); Millisle via Donaghadee (hourly; 35min); Portaferry (17 daily; 50min–1hr 15min).

TYRONE AND FERMANAGH

N eighbouring Tyrone and Fermanagh, which form the bulk of inland Northern Ireland, are both predominantly rural counties, and the only towns of any size are at the eastern and western fringes of the region. The chief scenic attractions of County Tyrone are to be found in the wild and desolate **Sperrin Mountains** in the north, an area that's patchily covered by the local bus network, so you really need your own transport to explore it. Even in the southern lowlands, the scattered castles, archeological sites and heritage centres are sometimes difficult to reach without a car or bike, though an exception is the excellent **Ulster American Folk Park**, close to the county town, **Omagh**.

In contrast to Tyrone, **County Fermanagh** attracts plenty of visitors – chiefly for the watersports and fishing that are widely available. At its core is the great **Lough Erne**, a huge lake complex dotted with islands and surrounded by richly beautiful countryside. Its county town of **Enniskillen** evinces a strong sense of history, while the remnants of the medieval past – along with those of the seventeenth and eighteenth centuries – are found all over the region, on islands and mainland alike. As in Tyrone, sights of interest are dispersed, and buses mostly serve only the main routes; but the key to enjoying Fermanagh is to get out onto the water – and this is easy enough from Enniskillen and a number of the villages that rest on the lakes' shores.

COUNTY TYRONE

Stretching from the shores of the vast Lough Neagh in the east to the border of the Republic and Donegal in the west, County Tyrone lies bang in the middle of Northern Ireland. Its northeastern limits are high in the desolate and beautiful **Sperrin Mountains**, and in the south it reaches near the lakes of County Fermanagh. It's a large and mainly featureless county, and if you are here at all the chances are you're heading elsewhere. The towns of Tyrone are not much of a draw; **Omagh** is the county's capital and is agreeable enough but with little to warrant a stop. **Cookstown** and **Dungannon** in the east, and **Strabane** on the border with Donegal, are similarly places to pass through, with minimal points of interest scattered around. It's first and foremost farming country, with little evidence of industrialization apart from the starchily neat planters' villages that grew up with the linen

---

ACCOMMODATION PRICE CODES

Throughout this book, prices of hotels, guesthouses and B&Bs have been graded with the codes below, according to what you can expect to pay for a double room in high season. For more details on accommodation, see p.29.

① Under £26	④ £40–55	⑦ £90–110
② £26–33	⑤ £55–70	⑧ £110–130
③ £33–40	⑥ £70–90	⑨ Over £130

industry. Perhaps the nearest the county's settlements get to being picturesque are the villages to the north and northwest of Omagh: Castlederg, Newtownstewart, Sion Mills and the tiny hamlets of the Sperrins.

The Sperrin range also offers the major scenic attractions; it's rich in **wildlife** and is an excellent target for determined, lonesome walking. For this, the place to head is **Gortin**, a village on the **Ulster Way** footpath and the only easily accessible overnight stop in the area. Tyrone also has no shortage of archeological remains, the most remarkable being the **Beaghmore Stone Circles**, in the southeast of the Sperrins. There's little to detain the visitor in the way of sights around the county beyond the historic connections between Ulster and the US. Of these, the **Ulster American Folk Park** near Omagh is by far the best. The only **local transport** in the region is Ulsterbus, which is reliable along main routes and not as infrequent as you might expect in such a rural area. Nonetheless, if this is your only way of getting around, it makes sense to pick up a timetable in a major bus station before you head off into the country. However, so scattered are the attractions of this largely empty county that you're likely to see little of the most interesting parts without a car or a bike. The one exception, of course, is in the Sperrins, where **hiking** is the best way to get around.

Some history

County Tyrone was the land of the **O'Neills**, who ruled Ulster from their seats in Omagh, Dungannon and Cookstown and claimed descent back to the legendary sons of "Niall of the Nine Hostages". Isolated geographically by bog, lake and mountain, Ulster was a key centre for Gaelic resistance to English rule. When Conn O'Neill received the English title Earl of Tyrone in the mid-sixteenth century, he held to the Gaelic Brehon Laws of inheritance and chose his youngest son, Shane the Proud, as successor, though the English favoured Matthew, his eldest son. After years of bitter feuding Matthew died in battle in 1558, and his son Hugh was taken to England to be educated. Meanwhile, Shane, elected The O'Neill and determined to extend his kingdom, attacked his neighbours and was promptly called to London to face Elizabeth I. The two cultures met in mutual incomprehension: the Queen sat surrounded by perfumed courtiers in silks and velvets, while O'Neill in saffron tunic and Irish mantle stood flanked by his wolfhounds and followers. He refused "to writhe his mouth in clattering English" or attend Protestant services. After six months he returned home and continued to pursue his aims. Finally he was murdered by the MacDonnells and his head sent to Dublin as a mark of their loyalty to the Crown.

It was Shane's nephew, **Hugh O'Neill**, who witnessed the final demise of Gaelic power in Ulster. In 1585, suitably anglicized, Hugh returned from England to Dungannon as the second Earl of Tyrone. Soon, however, he began to "go native". English spies carried tales to London and he was proclaimed a traitor. For five years he fought off English armies, but in 1601 Gaelic forces were defeated by Lord Mountjoy at the crucial battle of Kinsale. O'Neill signed the Treaty of Mellifont (1603), which bade him adopt English laws, language and dress and give up his clan title and his land. Ulster was divided into six counties and English rule was enforced. In 1607, he led the **Flight of the Earls** out of Ireland with a retinue of Gaelic chiefs and their followers. It was the end of the old Gaelic chiefdoms and customs. Most of the *file* (bards) – respected members of every noble family and clan historians – left with their patrons. The flight ended at the Church of St Pietro in Rome. Hugh O'Neill stayed on in Rome, where romantic legend has it that he died of sadness. He is buried in St Pietro before the high altar.

With the leaders of resistance gone, the subsequent plantation of Ulster under James I (1603–25) established the hegemony of the Crown, giving control of Tyrone to the Protestant immigrants from England and Scotland. This was certainly not the end of Gaelic insurrection, and it was again from this part of Ulster that the next serious threat to English control came. The **Great Rebellion of 1641** began in Tyrone with Phelim O'Neill's capture of Dungannon and Charlemont. The rising spread throughout the country as Catholics all over Ireland joined together to claim their religious and civic rights. The rebellion was inevitably accompanied by considerable brutality, but horror stories grew to such an extent that settlers came to believe there was a concerted plan to butcher the entire Protestant population, and the alleged scale of the violence gave Cromwell his justification for the massacre at Drogheda ten years later. Ulster remained in the hands of the planters, and it was they who introduced linen manufacture in the eighteenth century – the county's only experience of industry until more recent times.

The first significant **emigration** from Ireland to America was that of Ulster men and women in the early eighteenth century, many of whom were of Scottish Protestant origin. Of all the immigrant communities, it was the Irish who most quickly – and profoundly – made their mark: the three first-generation American presidents were all of Ulster stock, and a further nine presidents could trace their roots here. Sit in any bar in Tyrone long enough and someone will tell you with pride that these men and women emigrated because they had ambition and vision, and that they were not, unlike later emigrants, forced out by famine and eviction.

Omagh and around

On the afternoon of Saturday, August 15, 1998 a 500-pound car bomb, planted by a dissident Republican group calling itself the Real IRA, exploded on Market Street in the centre of Tyrone's largest town, **OMAGH**. In the ensuing carnage 26 people were killed (a further three were to die later) and more than 200 were injured. It was the worst single atrocity in the history of the Troubles and drew outrage and condemnation from every quarter. Indeed, unprecedentedly, Sinn Féin's President, Gerry Adams, denounced the bombing "without any equivocation whatsoever". Politicians moved frantically to save the peace process and prevent any Loyalist reprisals while the Irish and British governments announced their intentions to reinforce anti-terrorist legislation. Such efforts, however, offered scant consolation to the people of Omagh, a town more integrated and harmonious than most in Northern Ireland, and now unified in its grief.

Much of the eastern part of Omagh's main street was devastated by the bombing and, at the time of writing, it is not clear how long the reconstruction process will take. The area uphill to the west, originally thought to be the bombers' target on the basis of their misleading warning, remains unscathed and contains two adjacent buildings which would grace any town – the fine classical courthouse and the irregular twin spires of the Sacred Heart Catholic Church.

The **tourist office** is right in the centre of town at 1 Market St (July & Aug Mon–Fri 9am–5.30pm; Sept–June Mon–Fri 9am–5pm; also Easter–Sept Sat 9am–1pm & 1.30–5pm; ☎01662/247831). You'll need transport to see most of the region it promotes and **car rental** is available from Johnson King Motors, 82 Derry Rd (☎01662/242788). The **Ulsterbus** depot (☎01662/242711) is just across the river in Mountjoy Road (north off the High Street) and you can rent **bikes** from Conway Cycles (☎01662/246195) on Old Market Place.

The *Royal Arms Hotel* on High Street (☎01662/243262; ⑥) offers top-notch **accommodation** and probably has the best food in the area. Alternatively, *Silverbirch Hotel* on Gortin Road (☎01662/242520; ⑤) is relatively luxurious. The nearest **B&B** is *Ardmore*, 12 Tamlaght Rd (☎01662/243381; ②), up the left fork in front of the Sacred Heart and along the second turning on your right. Also near the centre is *Bridies*, 1 Georgian Villas, Hospital Road (☎01662/245254; ②) – go down the main street away from the courthouse and turning to the right across the river. For Sperrin views try *Rylands* (☎01662/247318; ②), a comfortable farmhouse B&B on Loughmuck Road, a mile out of town off the A32 Enniskillen road. The nearest **hostel** is *Glenhordial*

(☎01662/241973), two and a half miles north, signposted off the B48 (the hostel managers will pick you up from Omagh bus station). However, if you're hiking the Sperrins, a better bet might be to base yourself in Gortin (see p.595).

The town is a good place to stop for **food**, particularly during the daytime. The *Pink Elephant* in the High Street is a local favourite, serving breakfast and lunches in huge helpings; almost as popular are the nearby *Carlton Coffee Lounge*, a little further down the hill, and the *Bridge Restaurant*, round the corner on Bridge Street. The *Royal Arms Hotel* serves excellent pub grub at midday and evening meals of a similarly high standard in its restaurant. *Molly Sweeney's* on Gortin Road has an excellent fish menu and *Grant's* on George Street offers a bistro menu or snacks in the wine bar.

Just outside town on the B4 Carrickmore Road is the Dún Úladh Cultural Heritage Centre of Ulster (☎01662/242777), the provincial branch of Comhaltas Ceoltori Éireann, the national organization promoting Irish traditional culture. There's all manner of events running here, including a traditional session on Saturday nights. However, musically, this is showband country and most of the pubs and hotels have live **music** at weekends: you can usually find something happening at *McElroy's* on Castle Street or the *Silverbirch Hotel*, and traditionalists may be satisfied by occasional sessions at *Sally O'Brien's* on John Street or *Bogan's* near the tourist office. Saturday night discos at the *Royal Arms Hotel* are also a major draw.

The Ulster American Folk Park

The most successful of Northern Ireland's American heritage projects, the **Ulster American Folk Park** (Easter–Sept Mon–Sat 11am–6.30pm; Sun 11.30am–7pm; Oct–Easter Mon–Fri 10.30am–5pm; £3.50), is only three miles north of Omagh in Camphill, a short hop on one of the regular Strabane-bound buses. In the eighteenth and nineteenth centuries thousands of people left Ireland to establish new lives in North America, a steady flow of emigrants which became a torrent during the Famine years. An indoor **gallery** provides detailed information on the causes and patterns of migration, but the real attractions lie outside in the park itself, where original buildings have been transplanted or replicas constructed to provide a sense of **Ulster life** in the past. The disparity in living conditions is represented by a typical pre-Famine single-room cabin from the Sperrins which you'll pass on your way to the Mellon Homestead, a significantly more substantial dwelling from which the local Mellon family migrated in 1818. There's an austere Presbyterian meeting house and the squat Tullyallen Mass House, a Catholic chapel dating from 1768. A re-created Ulster street, including the impressively authentic Reilly's Spirit Grocers from Newtownbutler, leads to the *Union*, a full-size brig reconstructed to demonstrate the gruelling conditions endured during the voyage across the Atlantic. An American street leads to edifices constructed by the **Pennsylvanian settlers**, including a multipurpose log barn and massive six-roomed log farmhouse. There are plenty of other buildings and you'll meet costumed guides and craftworkers ready to explain their activities and answer questions, augmenting the folk park's attention to authenticity.

The complex also houses the **Centre for Emigration Studies** (Mon–Fri 9.30am–4.30pm), a major reference and research library, containing an enormous variety of material, such as emigrants' letters, passenger lists and contemporary newspaper articles.

The folk park makes a good afternoon out from Omagh and a fine day-trip if combined with the Ulster History Park (see p.595). Bring your own picnic though, as the restaurant is basic, or cross the road for more substantial fare at the *Mellon Country Inn* where they can also provide you with walking routes and maps for the nearby Ulster Way, which enters the scenic Gortin area to the northeast.

Northwest Tyrone

The northwestern part of Tyrone is seldom visited by tourists yet has some of the county's most attractive towns and countryside. The fastest route through the area – and the only feasible one if you're hitching – is the A5 via Newtownstewart, Sion Mills and Strabane to Derry or Letterkenny. A quieter alternative is the route via Castlederg along minor country roads to Castlefinn, County Donegal.

Castlederg

The friendly market village of **CASTLEDERG** sits around a spruced-up square beside the River Derg, across whose waters lie the ruins of a plantation castle, built in 1619 and destroyed by Sir Phelim O'Neill during the 1641 Rebellion. Modern Castlederg retains something of its traditional flavour as a staging post for travellers and a watering hole for pilgrims on their way to St Patrick's Purgatory on Lough Derg (see p.447). The town's bars and cafés make this a good place to stop for refuelling; and the **Castlederg Visitor Centre** on the Lower Strabane Road (April–Oct Tues–Fri 11am–4pm, Sat 11.30am–4pm, Sun 2–5pm; ☎016626/70794) will give you lots of information on local sites of interest. Davy Crockett's family came from the Castlederg area and the visitor centre contains a small model of the Alamo Fort where the celebrated frontiersman made his last stand. One mile north of the village – off the Lurganboy Road and close to each other – two large megalithic tombs stand as memorials to the area's pre-Christian past. Todd's Den is a cairn with a portal stone, but more impressive is the Druid's Altar – a chambered grave with two portal stones and capstones, one inscribed with *ogham* runes. **Accommodation** in the town itself is limited to the *Derg Arms*, 43 Main St (☎016626/71644; ②); a few miles west off the Killeter road, *Ardmourne House and Stables*, 36 Corgary Rd (☎016626/70291; ②) offers comfortable B&B with **riding** and **trekking** too. Surprisingly, the evenings can often be quite lively here, with various musical entertainments, from sing-a-longs to discos, at bars such as the *Castle Inn* and *Gallen's*.

Newtownstewart

The quicker route north from Omagh passes through rich farmland to **NEWTOWN-STEWART** which, surprisingly for its size, boasts remnants of two **castles**. In the main street a gable wall is all that remains of the Stewart castle burned down on the orders of James II; squatting in isolation on a hill to the southwest are the ruins of the fourteenth-century Harry Avery's castle, another O'Neill stronghold. But Newtownstewart's real draw is the gem of a **museum** that's housed in the tiny **tourist office** (summer Tues–Fri 11am–4pm, Sat 11.30am–5pm, Sun 2–5pm; ☎016626/62414; £1) a couple of hundred yards down the Omagh road. Local historian Billy Dunbar, a walking encyclopedia, donated his collection of vintage packaging, man traps, stereoscopes and war memorabilia to the museum when he could no longer navigate from one end of his house to the other. Highlights include a Bordalous (a mini-chamberpot named after a French priest renowned for his over-long sermons), and a threepenny bit engraved with the Lord's Prayer. Next door is *Aunt Jane's* welcoming café, and there's **B&B** accommodation in the Baronscourt Forest area, south on the B64 to Drumquin, at *Hunting Lodge* (☎016626/61679; ④), a converted nineteenth-century schoolhouse. In town itself there's **camping** at the municipal *Harrigan Caravan Park* (☎016626/62414), just over the Strule River on the north side of Newtownstewart, but you need to arrive before 5pm.

Sion Mills

The linen industry of the eighteenth century made a big impact in Tyrone, as it did all over Ulster, but its traces are mostly faint ones – such as the disued mills along the Ballinderry River near Cookstown. **SION MILLS**, a planned linen village just two miles south of Strabane, is the obvious exception. The quaint village, which belies the gruesome conditions of nineteenth-century factory work, is designated a conservation area, though the Herdman's linen works still operates, amidst security fences and cameras. You can skirt around it on foot and down to the Mourne River, where there's good fishing. The **tourist office** at Sion Mills (summer Mon–Thurs 9am–5pm; ☎016626/58027) is geared towards the motoring traveller but can direct you to a **B&B** – otherwise *Bide-a-Wee* (☎016626/59571; ③) on the main Omagh–Strabane Road (A5) is friendly and has a swimming pool.

Strabane and around

Present-day **STRABANE** is pretty grim and often traffic-congested. As a small Catholic enclave surrounded by largely Protestant-owned farmland and sitting right on the border it has suffered more than most from the Troubles. Economic depression was a consequence and at one time the town had the highest unemployment rate in the country. In the eighteenth century, however, Strabane was an important printing and publishing centre. John Dunlap emigrated from here and went on to print the broadsheets of the American Declaration of Independence in 1776, as well as the *Pennsylvanian Packet*, America's first daily paper. All that is left in Strabane of these times is the cute, bow-windowed frontage of **Gray's Printing Shop**, 49 Main St, which is now owned by the National Trust; there's a small printing **museum** upstairs (April–Sept Mon–Wed, Fri & Sat 2–5.30pm; £1.80) with a selection of old presses and an audiovisual show on print history. Sadly the shop's interior has been ripped out to provide maximum space for cards, completely destroying the scale and atmosphere the place must have once had.

One of Strabane's most famous sons was Brian O'Nolan (better known as the novelist **Flann O'Brien** and the *Irish Times* columnist Miles Na Gopaleen), who was born in 1911 into an Irish-speaking household at 15 Bowling Green. Another, less entertaining, individual to have his roots in the area is the American president **Woodrow Wilson**. Head east of Strabane two miles down the Plumbridge Road and you'll find the President Woodrow Wilson ancestral home in the village of **DERGALT** (open any reasonable hour; ☎01504/883735; £1). The president's father, who was a printer in Strabane, lived in this small, traditional farmer's cottage. Stuffed with furniture and effects belonging to the family, it's now a target for American tourists, who dutifully meander through the hallowed rooms.

If you really can't avoid an overnight stay in Strabane, the **tourist office**, in a glass pagoda on Abercorn Square (April–Oct Mon–Thurs 9am–5.30pm, Fri & Sat 9am–4.30pm; ☎01504/883735), will help with finding accommodation; or try the central **B&B** *Bowling Green House*, 6 Bowling Green (☎01504/884787; ②). There's a good atmospheric pub called *Felix's* that's alleged to have the best pint for miles, while the *Fir Trees Lodge* on Melmont Road does decent **meals**.

The Sperrins

The impressive, undulating Sperrin Mountains form the northeastern limits of County Tyrone. Wild, empty and beautiful, they reach 2240ft at their highest, yet the smooth and gradually curving slopes give them a deceptively low appearance. The covering of bog and heather adds to this effect, suggesting nothing more than high, open

---

WALKING THE SPERRINS

The forty-mile-wide range of the Sperrin Mountains offers good long-distance walking, without necessarily involving steep inclines. You can ramble wherever you like, but remember that – despite appearances – these are high mountains, and changeable weather makes them potentially dangerous. A map and compass are essential for serious walking. For those not equipped for the high ground, the **Glenelly** and **Owenkillen** river valleys run through the heart of this stunning countryside from Plumbridge and Gortin respectively (see below) and are particularly enjoyable for cyclists.

The official **Ulster Way** takes an arduous 34-mile route – the steepish Glenelly Trail – from Dungiven up over Glenshane Mountain to Goles Forest. From Gortin a second stage of the Way leads to the Ulster American Folk Park, a ten-mile trek. Parts of both sections of the Way are on road, however, and along some stretches signposts have disappeared or, worse, point in the wrong direction. You can pick up a guide to the Ulster Way in tourist offices (see Basics, p.22) or from the Sports Council of Northern Ireland (☎01232/381222), but your best bet is to ask locals about the state of the Way. For less strenuous walks the Northern Ireland Tourist Board has produced routes for fourteen mini-ways – the longest of which is thirteen miles.

---

moorland. For all this, views from the summits are panoramic, and the evenness of texture can make these mountains sumptuous when bathed in evening light. Once in the mountains, it's impossible not to catch sight of the **wildlife**. Sparrowhawks and kestrels hover above, and you might see buzzards or the far rarer hen harrier. They're attracted by rich prey in a landscape mostly undisturbed by development – the mountains teem with assorted rodents, rabbits, badgers and even the Irish hare. One threat to this delicately balanced ecosystem has been the rediscovery of gold in the mountains. Their future is in the balance, but for the moment at least, the Sperrins offer a wilderness to be enjoyed.

For local sheep-farming communities, however, the underpopulation of the Sperrins is a real problem, and their traditional way of life is now slowly dying. The sparseness of the population and the lack of focal centres make it difficult for an outsider to key into this culture. For the same reason, hitching isn't easy, and walkers should bear in mind that there's a shortage of places to buy food, so thinking ahead is essential. Rely only on large villages for provisions of any sort; hamlets often have nothing.

The **Sperrin Centre** (Easter–Oct Mon–Fri 11am–6pm, Sat 11.30am–6pm, Sun 2–7pm; £1.90) lies between Cranagh and Sperrin, nine miles east of Plumbridge (see below), and enables you to explore the area's environmental and cultural issues without getting your feet wet. The video games and audiovisuals of this welcoming interpretive centre are quite a surprise – particularly the holographic storyteller and the quaint 3-D slideshows – and they also organize gold-panning expeditions. Its pleasant tearoom is also one of the few places outside Belfast and Derry where you'll get a real cup of coffee, or even an espresso. The centre is tricky to get to without transport, though buses do run here from Plumbridge, and the Sperrin Sprinter (July–Aug Tues–Thurs) also passes nearby.

Plumbridge and Gortin

If you're tackling the Sperrins to the north of Omagh, there are really only two places that'll offer you any amenities at all. And even these are comatose for much of the year.

The first, **PLUMBRIDGE**, sits clustered on the banks of the Glenelly River. Apocryphally, it gets its name from the building of the village bridge: the engineer in charge didn't have a plumb line and so, from his scaffolding, spat in the water, using his phlegm to take the perpendicular. There's little here beyond a few bars, a couple of shops and *Pinkerton's Café*, and the liveliest times are probably during the annual Glenelly sheepdog trials in August. However, you might encounter the odd optimistic gold panner, convinced that the river's waters hold the key to their fortune.

Nearby **GORTIN**, three and a half miles south, is a long one-street village with a surprising number of pubs, one of which, the *Badoney Tavern*, offers evening **meals**. The Ulster Way passes through here, though the signposting which should connect it with Goles Forest is at the moment incomplete and stops at Craignaddy (984ft), two and a half miles north. However, the signposted Way does continue to the south of Gortin through the forest park, with its little loughs and wild deer, before swinging west to low farmland and the Ulster American Folk Park (see p.591). The only central **accommodation** is the *Gortin Outdoor Centre* **hostel** (☎01662/648083; July–Sept), fifty yards south of the village crossroads. For **camping** head for the *Gortin Glen Caravan Park* (☎016626/48108), three miles south on the Omagh road (3 buses daily); the site also has self-catering cottages. Smaller, but far more attractive, is the Gortin Glen Forest Park campsite opposite (☎016626/48217), a good place to stay if you're contemplating some hill-walking. A little way further on is the **Ulster History Park** (April–Sept Mon–Sat 10.30am–6.30pm, Sun 11.30am–7pm; Oct–March Mon–Fri 10.30am–5pm; last admission 90min before closing; £3.25), with full-scale reconstructions of buildings in Ireland from 7000 BC up to the seventeenth century. Inside there are videos and displays that serve to distract in bad weather, but far more rewarding is the interactive tour on which a guide talks you round such authentic traditional dwellings as a stinking deerskin-covered teepee, shows you how to chip flint, explains ancient symbols and answers questions expertly, no matter how daft. The rath, *crannóg* and medieval castle are particularly interesting, and the latest addition is a seventeenth-century Plantation settlement.

Three and a half miles east of Gortin (on the B46 Creggan Road) is the tiny village of **Rouskey**, with the ruins of a "sweat lodge", an early form of sauna. After the steam treatment, the luckless invalid was plunged into the icy stream nearby. Widespread use of sweat lodges died out after the Famine years, possibly because the experience of typhoid that accompanied the Famine dealt a severe blow to people's confidence in traditional medicinal treatments, but some were still functioning up to the 1920s. Also in the village is *Teach Ceoil* (☎016227/71551), a restored stone barn worth investigating for its regular ceili evenings.

Prehistoric remains and the Beaghmore Stone Circles

County Tyrone is peppered with archeological remains: there are more than a thousand standing stones in the Sperrins alone and the county as a whole has numerous chambered graves. The **Lough Macrory** area, just east of Mountfield on the A505 (Omagh–Cookstown Road), is particularly rich in dolmens and megaliths, though many of these are hard to find and of specialist interest only.

The uninitiated will get most out of the Bronze Age **Beaghmore Stone Circles**, in the southeast of the Sperrins; from Gortin take the B46 east onto the A505, and from here they are well signposted, just three and a half miles north off the main road. If you are coming from the opposite direction, they are also signposted all the way from Cookstown. Although most of the stones on this lonely site are no more than three feet high, the complexity of the ritual they suggest is impressive: there are seven stone circles, ten stone rows and a dozen round cairns (burial mounds, some containing cremated human remains). All of the circles stand in pairs, except for one, which is filled with over 800 upright stones, known as Dragon's Teeth. The alignments correlate to movements of sun, moon and stars. Two of the rows point to sunrise at the summer solstice; another may point to moonrise at the same period.

Just off the A505, roughly halfway between Omagh and Cookstown, **An Creagán Visitor Centre** (April–Sept daily 11am–6.30pm; Oct–March Mon–Fri 11am–4.30pm; £2) is modelled on the many cairns that surround it – 44 in a five-mile radius. Circular and built from local stone, the centre stands on the land of one of the last native speakers in the district, Peadar Joe Haughey, who died in the 1950s. Staff in the centre speak Irish, and the place is actually more a cultural centre than a museum, with locals coming along to the traditional music sessions, dancing, storytelling and singing events. But An Creagán also explores the rare raised bog terrain around, with interpretive displays and signposted rambling and cycling routes over the countryside (bikes can be rented at the Centre). The farmers driven to these bogs in the eighteenth century made huge efforts to reclaim the soil; there are limekilns from which they treated the reclaimed land, and you can still see the potato ridges. These grassed-over Copney spade ridges – a form of cultivation that maximized production – point back to the devastating Famine of 1845–49 and the farmers' desperate attempts to survive. You can organize self-catering **accommodation** here (☎016627/61112; £220–330 per week) in the traditional *clochán* settlement, with open turf fires supplemented, fortunately, by central heating.

Cookstown, Lough Neagh, Dungannon and around

The only places in the east of the county that could be described as anything more than villages are Cookstown and Dungannon. A planned planters' town, **COOKSTOWN** boasts the longest main street in Ireland, seemingly blessed by eternal roadworks, and the site of an extensive Saturday market. The **tourist office** is at 48 Molesworth St (July & Aug Mon, Wed, Fri & Sat 9am–5pm, Tues & Thurs 9am–6pm; Easter–June & Sept Mon–Fri 9am–5pm, Sat 10am–4pm; ☎016487/66727); the pick of the local **accommodation** is the very plush *Tullylagan Country House Hotel* (☎016487/65100; ⑦) set in thirty acres of grounds in Sandholes, four miles south of the town.

The **Wellbrook Beetling Mill**, three and a half miles west of Cookstown off the A505, is a National Trust-owned eighteenth-century water-powered linen mill (April–June & Sept Sat & Sun 2–6pm; July–Aug Wed–Mon 2–6pm; £1.80). "Beetling" was the final stage of production whereby linen was given a sheen and smoothness by hammering with heavy wooden "beetles". Though it ceased operation in 1961, the mill is excellently preserved, and all the engines still work. For more monumental interest, two miles south of Cookstown on the B520 is **Tullaghoge Fort**, the erstwhile headquarters of the O'Hagans, chief justices of Ireland, who undertook the coronations of the O'Neill kings from the twelfth to the seventeenth century. From the road it appears to be simply a copse of beech and Scots pine on the top of a very gentle hill, but in fact these are very clear earthworks of the early Christian period – a circular outer bank with an inner oval enclosure. It was in Tullaghoge forest that O'Neill tribesmen hid after the Flight of the Earls.

It seems even the legendary Fionn Mac Cumhaill was unimpressed by east Tyrone's low-lying terrain. Legend has it that he took a massive lump of land from Ulster and hurled it across the Irish Sea. It landed and became the Isle of Man, and the hole it left behind became **Lough Neagh** (pronounced *nay*). The lough's shores form the county's huge eastern boundary and provide excellent fishing and plenty of bird-life, but, beyond this, both land and lake are almost featureless. Small settlements house eel fishermen, whose catches go to the Toome Eel Fishery at Toomebridge (at the northern tip of the lake), the largest eel fishery in Europe. Slight relief is to be found at **ARDBOE**, ten miles east of Cookstown, where there's a tenth-century High Cross. The elements have eroded the various biblical scenes carved onto the sandstone almost beyond recognition, but its exceptional size – 18ft high – is impressive. The cross stands in the grounds of an early monastery associated with St Colman, but the ruined church nearby dates from the seventeenth century and is of little interest. On a humid day, you'll also not fail to be impressed by the swarms of black Lough Neagh flies, a particularly pointless insect which, lacking a mouth, is born merely to copulate and die.

Mountjoy Castle lurks behind a farm eight miles south of here near Washing Bay. Built in 1602 as part of the English campaign against Hugh O'Neill, it was strategically important, but, sadly, the setting is disappointing.

If you pass through **COALISLAND** on the way to Dungannon, check out the town's **Cornmill Heritage Centre** on Lineside (Mon–Fri 10am–5pm; £1.50), a melange of artefacts and exhibits from the area's industrial past, particularly coal-mining, and photographs of local luminaries (including Dennis Taylor, the former world snooker champion). The mill itself ground to a halt in 1978 after providing employment for more than seventy years. The town's a relatively sleepy place, but becomes more animated during the annual international music festival in July.

DUNGANNON, about ten miles south of Cookstown, is a dreary town with no trace of its illustrious past as the hilltop seat of the O'Neills, from which they ruled Ulster for over five centuries. Outside town, on the A45 Coalisland Road, is the **Tyrone Crystal** factory (tours all year Mon–Fri 9.30am–3.30pm plus April–Oct Sat 9.30am–3.30pm; £2) where you can see demonstrations of glass-blowing and hand-cutting. If you are tempted to stay in the area, there's excellent **B&B** and home cooking in the Georgian *Grange Lodge*, 7 Grange Rd (☎01868/784212; ⑤) and surprisingly good lakeside **camping** in *Dungannon Park* on Moy Road (☎01868/727327). At **DONAGHMORE**, three miles northwest, there's another high cross dating from the tenth century in front of the parish church, though whoever reassembled this in the nineteenth century clearly botched the job as there's an obvious join halfway down the shaft.

If you're heading onwards from Dungannon towards Armagh, the picturesque village of **BENBURB** merits a detour. The tiny cottages in Main Street were once apple-peeling sheds and the parish church, dating from 1618, is one of the oldest still in regular use in Ireland. This stands next to the gates of a **Servite Priory** – the monastic order of Servants of the Virgin, founded in Florence in 1233, but which did not establish itself here in Ireland until 1948. Its grounds offer a pleasant stroll, but far better are the walks along the Blackwater River in **Benburb Valley Park** (daily 10am–dusk), where, perched on a rock one hundred feet or so above the water, are the substantial remains of a **castle** built by Viscount Powerscourt in 1615. A mile south of the village in the canal-side hamlet of Milltown is the **Benburb Valley Heritage Centre** (Easter–Sept Tues–Sat 10am–5pm, Sun 2–7pm; £2), housed in a nineteenth-century weaving factory and containing a range of old linen-making machinery and a model of the Battle of Benburb, where a Scottish army suffered catastrophic losses in an encounter with Owen Roe O'Neill in 1646. There's a teashop and a **hostel** here too (☎0181615/49752; April–Sept).

The Clogher Valley

Ten miles or so west of Benburb, the Blackwater River forms the **Clogher Valley**, a twenty-mile stretch running from the somewhat run-down market town of Aughnacloy (near the Monaghan border) to Fivemiletown, and encompassing the villages of Ballygawley, Augher and Clogher. There's nothing here of special interest, but the pleasantly rolling countryside is sufficient in itself to justify a diversion.

Three miles east of **BALLYGAWLEY**, to the north of Aughnacloy, is the **Grant Ancestral Homestead**, signposted off the A4 road to Dungannon (April–Sept Mon–Sat noon–5pm, Sun 2–6pm; £1). The land here was once a smallholding farmed by the maternal ancestors of the eighteenth US President, Ulysses S. Grant (1822–85), whose life and exploits during the American Civil War are depicted in the Visitor Centre. A tiny two-roomed cottage has been restored and refurnished in typical nineteenth-century style, while the surrounding working farm displays agricultural implements from the same period and is stocked with traditional breeds. A similar distance to the west of the village, signposted to the north, is a hill known as **Errigal Keerogue**, where there is an unfinished high cross and a ruined fifteenth-century church dedicated to St Ciaran.

At one time a railway connected the valley's villages and at **AUGHER** you can sample home-baking in the old station, which now houses *Rosamund's Coffee Shop*. The village makes much of its connection with the writer **William Carleton** (1794–1869), whose most notable novel was *Black Prophet*, a sombre tale of the Famine years. A summer school celebrates his life and work each August. The cottage where the author was born is a mile south in Springtown (signposted from Augher) and is part of the longer of two Carleton Trails which start and finish at Clogher. A couple of miles northwest of Augher lies **Knockmany Forest**, where a cairn on the top of a steep wooded hill protects a Bronze Age passage tomb, said to be the resting place of Ainé, the mother-goddess with whom Fionn MacCumhaill was infatuated. The stones in the tomb are inscribed with complex swirling patterns, but you can merely peer at them from a distance through a locked grille. If you want to stay in Augher, the only accommodation is **B&B** at *Beech Lodge*, 43 Glenhoy Rd (☎016625/48106; ③).

CLOGHER, further west, is a little more lively, its main street climbing gently upwards to its eighteenth-century Church of Ireland cathedral. The village lays claim to the oldest bishopric in Ireland – its first bishop was St MacCartan, a disciple of St Patrick – but there is evidence of the place's earlier significance. In the park behind the cathedral is a recently excavated Iron Age hillfort, thought to be the seat of the old kings of Oriel. Inside the church is "the golden stone", dating from the ninth century, and a gallery of portraits of former bishops bearing expressions of appropriate solemnity. Several bars on the main street provide **meals** and you can also dine in the evenings at *Corick House*, 20 Corick Rd (☎01662/548216; ⑤), which offers the best **B&B** in the area. Alternatively, there's *River Furey House*, 24 Monaghan Rd (☎01662/548843; ②), set on a working farm half a mile south on the B83, or **camping** at the *Clogher Valley Country Caravan Park* (☎016625/48932; March–Oct) in Fardross Forest, a mile west on the A4.

The **Clogher Valley Scenic Route** is ideally accessed from **FIVEMILETOWN**, seven miles west, though the lack of signposts at certain crucial junctions means it's best tackled with an Ordnance Survey map. The complete circuit runs for around 25 miles in a loop either side of the A4, but the southerly section is easily the more enjoyable and takes you into the most isolated part of the county outside the Sperrins. Head south from the crossroads in Fivemiletown, and once you've picked up the first sign, you'll find yourself on narrow woodland lanes gradually ascending towards Slieve Beagh. It's more than likely that sheep will be your only company unless you encounter the odd hiker on the Ulster Way, which you'll traverse as the route enters moorland. The whole valley can be surveyed from the car park viewpoint before you descend into Fardross Forest. The only other site of note is a few miles onwards. Look out to your left for a bizarre, three-tiered hilltop tower known as **Brackenridge's Folly**, named after George Brackenridge, who had the tower constructed as his mausoleum, compelling the squirearchy who had looked down on him during his lifetime to look up to him once he was dead. Fivemiletown has a couple of hotels on the main street and several B&Bs in the area, including *Al-Di-Gwynn Lodge*, 103 Clabby Rd (☎013655/21298; ③) and *Church View* (☎013655/22059). There's also **camping** at *Round Lake Caravan Park* (☎01868/767259), half a mile north off the Fintona road.

COUNTY FERMANAGH

Fermanagh is justly famous for the intense beauty of its lakes. Virtually wherever you look, the landscape is dominated by their waters which, along with numerous rivers, constitute more than a third of the county's area. Though there are many attractive smaller loughs, it's the two inter-connected Lough Ernes which draw the most visitors – Lower Lough Erne in the northwest and Upper Lough Erne in the southeast. Surrounding hills are wooded with oak, ash and beech, producing a scene of fresh, verdant greens in spring and rich and rusty colours in autumn. The water's rippling surface reflects whatever light there is, mirroring the palest of skies through to the ruddiest of magenta sunsets. It's a breathtaking landscape, where land and water complement one another in a fine, stately harmony.

The **Lower Lough** in winter has the character of an inland sea, dangerous waves making even the locals wary of sailing. Fabulous vistas reach across to the mostly uninhabited shores of richly wooded islands, on which are scattered early Christian ruins and evidence of earlier pagan cultures. The **Upper Lough** is quieter and less spectacular. The waterway here is a delightful muddle of little inlets and islands, where waters are shallower and shorelines reedy. Fields have shocks of bristly marsh-grasses; definitions between land and water are blurred.

The county town of **Enniskillen** sits at the point where the Upper and Lower loughs meet. Long a strategic bridging point, it has more amenities than the rest of Fermanagh put together and, consequently, is a good base for exploring the region. With your own transport you can easily access Fermanagh's impressive series of planters' castles, while the county's two stately houses, **Florence Court** and **Castle Coole**, are both open to the public.

There are plenty of opportunities for watersports, and the less energetic can get out onto the lakes by renting a boat or taking one of the lough cruises. Walkers will find the countryside to be mostly gentle hills and woods, which rise to small mountains in the south and west of the county, made accessible by the Ulster Way. For cyclists, there are well-surfaced, empty roads (though routes around the Upper Lough are harder to negotiate, with little lanes often leading to nowhere but some empty reed-infested shore). Public transport is limited to Ulsterbus; although reliable enough, only the main routes from Enniskillen are served with any frequency. If you look like a foreign tourist, then hitching along main roads is possible during the summer months, though never easy: County Fermanagh is as friendly as anywhere in the North, but people tend to be cautious because of the border.

Some history

The region's early history was dictated by the intricacies of the Lough Erne waterways, once even more confused and forested than today. Recorded history begins with the

---

FERMANAGH TELEPHONE CODES

New telephone codes will be introduced throughout Northern Ireland from June 1, 1999 although it will still be possible to use the old codes until April 22, 2000. The new codes will prefix the existing subscriber number regardless of where you are calling from; calls from outside Northern Ireland will require the 028 prefix in addition – thus Enniskillen ☎01365/313456 will become ☎(028) 66 31345. The three Fermanagh codes will change as follows:

Enniskillen ☎01365 to ☎(028) 66   **Lisnaskea** ☎013657 to ☎(028) 677
Kesh ☎013656 to ☎(028) 686

early Christians, who slowly permeated Celtic culture and established religious foundations. They appreciated the seclusion of the lakes, and ruins of medieval monasteries remain. Centres of ecclesiastical power and learning were dotted on islands in the lough, and it is likely they were visited by pilgrims on their way to St Patrick's Purgatory, the shrine on Lough Derg. More brutal invaders found the lough complex difficult to infiltrate. Neither Vikings nor Normans ever managed to control the region, and throughout the medieval and Tudor periods, the English similarly failed to subdue it. The surrounding land was unruly and hard to govern even for the Irish. The Maguires, who ruled the west of the kingdom of Oriel (Fermanagh, Monaghan, south Tyrone and Louth) from 1250 until 1600, were originally based at Lisnaskea, but the cattle raids of neighbouring chiefs forced them to move to Enniskillen in the early fifteenth century. The town was to become strategically crucial as the determination of the English to dominate Ireland increased during the sixteenth century. As the crossing point through the waterways it was one of only three land routes into Ulster available to the invaders, the others being over the river near Ballyshannon and the Moyry Pass between Dundalk and Newry. So Enniskillen and the Maguire castle became the focus of Irish resistance to the Tudors. It was taken in 1594, although shortly afterwards retaken by the Maguires. However, after its recapture in 1607, the planters arrived.

The usurpers were obliged to build a ring of castles around the lough in order to maintain control of their domain: Crom, Portora, Tully, Castle Archdale, Crevenish and Caldwell. Most importantly of all, the old Maguire castle at Enniskillen was enlarged and fortified. Given sizeable grants from the English Crown, the planters of Enniskillen built an Established church, a fort and a royal school, turning the place into a British colonial town. It became a Loyalist stronghold, which successfully defended itself against the Irish during the Great Rebellion of 1641 and against an attack by James's troops in 1689. The Loyalists of Enniskillen formed a regiment that William of Orange chose as his personal guard at the Boyne. In the late eighteenth century, Enniskillen proved to be of key military importance, with the threat of a French invasion through the northwest of Ireland. By now the town had two royal regiments – a unique phenomenon.

At Partition, Fermanagh became a part of the state of Northern Ireland, despite its predominantly Catholic population and despite this majority's cultural affinities with Cavan in the Republic, with whom it shares the tail end of the Lough Erne complex. In 1921, the county returned a Nationalist majority in local government elections, an undesirable state of affairs for the British. The abolition of proportional representation in 1922, and the gerrymandering which followed, ensured the subsequent Loyalist majority. With a history of such blatant injustices, a large Catholic population and a lengthy border with the Republic, Fermanagh is a nucleus of Nationalist activity and today has strong Sinn Féin sympathies. It was Fermanagh and South Tyrone that in April 1981 returned Bobby Sands as MP to Westminster. At the time of the election Sands was serving a fourteen-year prison sentence for possession of weapons and was leading a hunger strike for political status for IRA prisoners. His death from starvation after 66 days made him one of the most famous IRA heroes.

Enniskillen and around

A pleasant, conservative little town of around 11,000 people, **ENNISKILLEN** sits on an island like an ornamental buckle, two narrow ribbons of water passing each side, connecting the Lower and Upper lough complexes. The strategic strength of this position has long been recognized – indeed, the town takes its name from *Innis Ceithleann*, "the island of Kathleen", wife of Balor (see p.461) who sought refuge here after a defeat in battle. Later the island became a Maguire stronghold before William Cole, a planter from Cornwall, was appointed governor in 1607. The town played a major role in the rebellion of 1641 and the Williamite wars, the latter leading to the formation of its two famous regiments, the Inniskilling Dragoons and the Royal Inniskilling Fusiliers, which played a significant role in the victory at the Battle of the Boyne. However, the name Enniskillen is still associated primarily with of one of the most devastating atrocities of the Troubles. On Remembrance Day 1987 an IRA bomb killed 11 and injured 61 people as they gathered to commemorate the dead of the two world wars. In a town of only 10,500, the murders profoundly affected the lives of every citizen, and you can't spend a day here without becoming conscious of the shadow cast by the outrage.

Arrival, information and accommodation

The **tourist office** is situated next to the bus station on Wellington Road, a block south of the High Street (July & Aug Mon–Fri 9am–6.30pm; Sept–June Mon–Fri 9am–5.30pm; also Easter–Sept Sat 10am–6pm, Sun 11am–5pm; ☎01365/323110). You can get **fishing licences and permits** here or book a place on one of the summer guided **tours** of the town or Lough Erne. The Round "O" jetty for lough cruises is sign-posted off the Derrygonnelly Road to the northwest of town – see p.604 for more boat rental details. Enniskillen is on the 192-mile Kingfisher Cycling Trail which skirts around the loughs and runs through Cavan and Leitrim (☎01365/327205 for details); for **bike rental**, try the Lakeland Canoe Centre on Castle Island (☎01365/324250; £9 per day) – free ferries leave (8am–midnight) from the Lakeland Forum leisure centre just behind the tourist office. Lochside Garages, Tempo Road (☎01365/324366), and County Cars, 4 Irvinestown Rd (☎01365/322727), are two **car rental** outlets. The post office on Main Street will change money and there are plenty of banks too. From Enniskillen's **bus station** (☎01365/322633), next to the tourist office, you can get buses to Belfast, Dublin, Dungannon, Sligo, Derry, Omagh, and local services.

Accommodation

The tourist office has comprehensive accommodation lists and will book a room for a small fee. You could try the conveniently central, family-run *Railway Hotel*, 34 Forthill St (☎01365/322408; ⑤), or the *Killyhevlin Hotel* (☎01365/323481; ⑥) on the Dublin Road (this becomes the N3 once over the border). There's plenty of **B&B** options – pick of the bunch is *Mountview*, 61 Irvinestown Rd (☎01365/323147; ④), with TVs in all the rooms and a snooker room; or try *Lackaboy Farmhouse*, Tempo Road (☎01365/322488; ②), or *Rossole House*, 85 Sligo Rd (☎01365/323462; ③). If you're driving, there

---

FISHING IN FERMANAGH

There are countless opportunities for angling in Fermanagh, with the two Lough Ernes, Upper and Lower Lough Macnean, Lough Melvin, thirty smaller lakes and numerous rivers. A good move is to get a copy of *Fishing in Fermanagh* from the tourist office in Enniskillen, which can also tell you of any temporary restrictions and allow you to secure particular waters in advance. Most of the waters of Lough Erne are suitable for coarse fishing and you can obtain a rod licence for this from tackle shops or the tourist office; if you're fishing for salmon or trout you'll need a game licence too. Note that a game licence must be held if you're fishing from a boat on Lower Lough Erne. There are signs at vir-tually all the designated fisheries providing information on the fish available and whether you'll need a permit from the water's owner. As you'd expect, there are plenty of angling boats for rent and several tackle shops, including Enniskillen's Home, Field and Stream, Church Street (☎01365/322114), and Mullin's Pet and Shooting Supplies, Sligo Road (☎01365/324975).

are two country houses to sample: *Killyreagh* (☎01365/387221; ④), a couple of miles southeast of town on the A4 in Tamlaght, and a Gothic fantasy, *Tempo Manor* (☎01365/541450; ⑦) in Tempo, about six miles northeast on the B80. The nearest **hostel** is run by YHANI at Castle Archdale ten miles north on the B82 (see p.606). There's a handy **campsite** at the Lakeland Canoe Centre (☎01365/324250) on Castle Island just offshore of Enniskillen. All the others are well out of town: *Blaney Caravan and Camping Park* (☎01365/641634), eight miles to the northwest, off the A46, directly behind the Blaney service station, is a beautifully situated and well-equipped site.

The town

The waterways loop their way around the core of the town, the glassy surface imbuing Enniskillen with a pervasive sense of calm and reflecting the mini-turrets of **Enniskillen Castle**. Rebuilt by William Cole, the castle stands on the site of the old Maguire castle damaged by siege in 1594, next to the island's westerly bridges. Cole's additions show obvious Scottish characteristics in the turrets corbelled out from the angles of the main wall. It houses the **Watergate History and Heritage Centre** (all year Mon 2–5pm, Tues–Fri 10am–5pm; plus May–Sept Sat 2–5pm and July–Aug Sun 2–5pm; £2, includes museum below) archeological displays in the arcaded barracks and, in the keep, **The Regimental Museum of the Royal Inniskilling Fusiliers** (same times), a proud and polished display of the uniforms, flags and paraphernalia of the town's historic regiments.

Much of Enniskillen's character comes from a wealth based on the care of a colonial presence. Evidence of British influence is widespread: on a hill to the west the stately **Portora Royal School** overlooks the town, discreetly reminding one of the continued elitism in the social order. It was founded by Charles I in 1626, though the present building dates from 1777; old boys include Oscar Wilde – the pride of the school, until his trial for homosexuality – and Samuel Beckett. Over on a hill to the east, **Cole's Monument**, a statue commemorating one of Wellington's generals, keeps an eye on the town from Forthill Park; catch the park keeper and pay 60p to ascend to the viewing gallery (daily May–Sept 2–6pm). Immediately below is the war memorial, scene of the 1987 bombing. The centre invites strolling: the main street undulates gently, lined with confident Victorian and Edwardian town houses, thriving shops and smart pub fronts. This street changes its name five times between the bridges at either end, running from Ann Street to East Bridge Street: lanes fall to either side down towards the water, and clustered together are three fine church buildings, Church of Ireland, Catholic and Methodist.

On Down Street, just off the High Street, the **Buttermarket** is a craft and design centre with a range of artisans working on site. The original buildings date from 1835, and you'll find displays of art, music and drama, as well as craftwork and design. You can buy direct from the craft workers or from the shop attached to *Rebecca's* excellent coffee shop. For something less sedate, Thursday's street **market** on Forthill Street is worth a trip.

Castle Coole, Tamlagh and Brookeborough

Evidence of how the richest of the colonists lived is found about a mile from the town centre at **Castle Coole**, the eighteenth-century lakeside home of the Earls of Belmore (April & Sept Sat & Sun 1–6pm; May–Aug Fri–Wed 1–6pm; last tour starts at 5.15pm; £2.80; grounds open all year, £2 per car). A perfect Palladian-fronted building of silver Portland stone, with elegant Regency furnishings and recently restored interior of exquisite plasterwork, the castle sits in a beautiful landscaped garden, exemplifying cultivated naturalness, part of a huge 700-acre estate. It can be approached either from the Dublin Road (signposted just opposite the Ardhowen Theatre) or across the golf course from the Castlecoole Road. A couple of miles further down the A4, at Tamlagh, is the **Old Barn Family Museum** (Mon–Sat 11am–10pm), an astonishing collection of old books, swords, bottles and various curios hoarded over the 250 years. One other specialist collection hereabouts is Robert Coalter's **Cycle Museum** (April–Sept Mon–Sat 11am–8pm; £1.50) in the village of **BROOKEBOROUGH**, another seven miles east. There's more than sixty vintage cycles on display here, including post office and butcher's boys bikes and a real old treasure from the 1870s with levers instead of pedals.

Eating, drinking and entertainment

Enniskillen has a handful of good cheap places to **eat**. Currently everybody's favourite is *Franco's* (Mon–Sat from noon till 11.30pm, Sun 5–10pm; ☎01365/324424) in Queen Elizabeth Road; it has delicious pizza, pasta, seafood and satay. Around the corner, on Water Street, is *Kamal Mahal* (☎01365/325045), which does great Indian vegetarian dishes. *Peppercorn,* on Townhall Street by the post office, serves large lunches and good coffee. A lot of the bars along the main street also do decent pub food, particularly *Mulligan's* on Darling Street, and, on Townhall Street, the *Vintage* and *Pat's Bar* – above which the *Melvin House Restaurant* offers lunches, grills and dinners. The restaurant at the *Ardhowen Theatre*, a mile out of town on the Dublin Road (Mon–Sat 11am–3.30pm; ☎01365/325440), is worth visiting for its waterside setting (you can also enjoy the view from an excellent bar), should you be hungry after a traipse around Castle Coole.

Enniskillen is also well served for **cafés**, many of which do excellent inexpensive meals. Most imaginative is the *Barbizon* on East Bridge Street, with felafels, houmous and salads on the menu. *Leslie's*, also on the main street, offers good ice cream, and *Johnston's* coffee lounge further down is worth a try, too, for its fresh-baked pastries and breads.

There's no shortage of cheerful **pubs**, and bar extensions until 1am are commonplace in summer. **Country music** is big here, and bands play at *The Crow's Nest* in the main street most nights, on Fridays and Sundays at *Mulligans* on Darling Street, and on Saturdays and Sundays at the *Three Way Inn*, Sligo Road, which also has line dancing on Fridays. For **traditional music** try the *Bush* (Mon), the *Railway Hotel*, Forthill Street (Sun), or, on the main street, *Blakes of the Hollo*, a traditional Victorian bar with original fittings, a fine pint and a chatty crowd. At the west end of town, the *Tippler's Brook* is the place for a quiet drink or to play cards with local farmers in town for the night. As ever, **discos** are in the hotels, in particular Forthill Street's *Fort Lodge Hotel* on Saturday nights, which occasionally has local bands too, and *McCartney's Inn*, Belmore Street. The *Vintage*, on the main street, is a trendy disco bar with video jukebox and live rock and pop music at weekends.

The hub of Enniskillen's **arts scene** is the *Ardhowen Theatre* (see above), which has a year-round programme of top-quality drama, film and ballet, and hosts a great range of music events – traditional Irish, jazz, opera, country, classical – as well as productions by local community groups and stages an annual theatre festival in March. Check with the tourist office for dates of the Fermanagh *feis* in March – lots of traditional music, dancing, drama and crafts – and the *Fleadh* in June.

Lough Erne

Lough Erne has had a profound effect on the history of Fermanagh. The earliest people to settle in the region lived on and around the two lakes; many of the islands here are in fact *crannógs* (early Celtic artificial islands). The lough's myriad connecting waterways were impenetrable to outsiders, protecting the settlers from invaders and creating an enduring cultural isolation. Evidence from stone carving suggests that Christianity was accepted far more slowly here than elsewhere: several pagan idols have been found on Christian sites, and the early Christian remains to be found on the islands show the strong influence of pagan culture. Here Christian carving has something of the stark symmetry and vacancy of expression found in pagan statues. Particularly suggestive of earlier cults is the persistence of the human head motif in stone carving – in pagan times a symbol of divinity and the most important of religious symbols.

White Island and **Devenish Island**, the most popular of the Erne's ancient sites are on the **Lower Lough**, as is **Boa Island** in the far north, which is linked to the mainland by a bridge at each end. The **Upper Lough** is less rewarding, but has interesting spots which repay a leisurely dawdle. Whichever you choose, the easiest way to reach them is on one of the **cruises** or **ferries** listed in the box below. Aside from cruising the waterways and visiting the islands, there are a number of minor attractions around the loughs that are worth dropping into during your stay. Perhaps the most impressive are the early seventeenth-century planters' castles scattered around the shoreline.

Devenish Island and Monea and Tully castles

If you don't have transport of your own, the easiest place to visit from Enniskillen is **Devenish Island**, in the south of the Lower Lough. A monastic settlement was founded here by St Molaise in the sixth century and became so important during the early Christian period that it had 1500 novices attached. Though plundered by Vikings in the ninth century and again in the twelfth, it continued to be an important religious centre

---

LOUGH ERNE FERRIES AND CRUISES

To Devenish Island Devenish Island Ferry Service operates a continual service to Devenish from Trory Point, three miles north of Enniskillen (April–Sept Tues–Sat 10am–7pm, Sun 2–7pm; £2.25, includes entrance fee to tower and museum). It's advisable to check times with the tourist office before setting out as sometimes poor weather can delay or cancel departures.

To White Island A boat from Castle Archdale Country Park marina (☎013656/21333) runs to White Island on the hour (July & Aug daily 11am–6pm; Easter–June & Sept Sat & Sun; £3).

Lough Erne cruises The *MV Kestrel* operated by Erne Tours (☎01365/322882) runs from the Round "O" jetty (see p.601) and sails around the Lower Lough, calling at Devenish Island (May & June Sun 2.30pm; July & Aug daily 10.30am, 2.15pm & 4.15pm; Sept Tues, Sat & Sun 2.30pm; morning cruises £4, afternoons £5) with additional evening cruises via the Upper Lough (July–Aug Tues, Thurs, Sun 7.15pm; £5). A recent arrival is the Inishcruiser which sails from the Inishclare restaurant complex at Killadeas (☎013656/28552). Finally, a "Viking longship" cruises the Upper Lough daily in summer from the Share Holiday Village at Smith's Strand, signposted off the Lisnaskea–Derrylin Road (April–June & Sept Sat & Sun; July–Aug daily except Tues & Thurs; 3pm; £4; ☎013657/22122).

Renting your own boat is another possibility and there are a number of operators. Most offer open rowing boats, with or without outboard, though some have larger 20ft boats available. Prices range accordingly from £4 per hour to £60 for a full day, depending on the operator. The tourist information centre produces a list of rental companies and another, if you fancy something grander, of cruisers available for weekly rent (though prices in high season range from £565 for smaller boats to £1450 for 8-berth specials). Unless you're going out on a small lake you should always let the boat owner know where you're going and ask to borrow navigation charts – Lough Erne can be dangerous, especially outside the summer months.

up until the plantations. It's a delightful setting, not far from the lough shore, and the ruins are considerable, spanning the entire medieval period. Most impressive are the sturdy oratory and perfect round tower, both from the twelfth century; St Molaise's church, a century older; and the ruined Augustinian priory, a fifteenth-century reconstruction of an earlier abbey. The priory has a fine Gothic sacristy door decorated with birds and vines; to the south is one of Ireland's finest high crosses, with highly complex, delicate carving. Other treasures found here – such as an early eleventh-century book shrine, the Soiscel Molaise – are now kept in the National Museum in Dublin.

Monea Castle (free access at all times), seven miles northwest of Enniskillen off the B81, is a particularly fine ruin of a planters' castle in a beautiful setting at the end of a beech-lined lane. Built around 1618, it bears the signs of Scottish influence in its design, with similar features to the reworked Maguire castle in Enniskillen. It was destroyed by fire in the Great Rebellion of 1641 and by Jacobite armies in 1689, and was eventually abandoned in 1750 after another fire. Five miles further north, beyond Derrygonnelly, the fortified house and bawn of restored **Tully Castle** (April–Sept Tues–Sat 10am–7pm, Sun 2–7pm; £1), itself burned by the Maguires in 1641, sits down by the lough shore. Further to the west, there are tremendous views of the lough and surrounds from **Lough Navar Forest** (daily 10am–dusk; car £2.50).

Castle Caldwell forest and Belleek

The forest of **Castle Caldwell**, on the A47, near the western extremity of Lower Lough Erne, is formed by two narrow promontories which make it a natural breeding site for waterfowl such as the common scoter (a species of duck) and a habitat of rarities such as the hen harrier, peregrine falcon and pine marten. However, its seventeenth-century castle has long since fallen into dilapidation and the surrounding estate is now a commercial, state-owned forest of spruce, pine and larch. At the entrance look out for the giant stone fiddle in front of the gate lodge, the sobering memorial to Denis McCabe, a local musician who in 1770 tumbled from the Caldwells' barge while drunk, and drowned.

The **Fiddle Stone Festival** is held in McCabe's memory every June in lively **BELLEEK**, a couple of miles further on. Its other main attraction is the famous **Belleek Pottery** (July–Aug Mon–Fri 9am–8pm, Sat 10am–8pm, Sun 11am–8pm; rest of year Mon–Fri 9am–5.30pm, Sat 1–5.30pm, Sun 2–6pm, but closed weekends Nov–Feb; tours every 20min; free), which offers interesting tours of the works and a chance to buy the rather fussy products. On Main Street, you'll find **Fermanagh Crystal** (Mon–Sat 10am–5pm), where you watch the creation of glassware and even, funds permitting, commission your own piece. Across the river on the main A46 Enniskillen Road, in the Erne Gateway, is the **ExplorErne Centre** (Easter–Oct daily 10am–6pm; £1), an interpretive centre that offers what's basically a day out on Lough Erne for landlubbers. A giant video wall screens an explanation of how the lake was formed and how it moulded the lives of lakeside dwellers over the centuries. **Tourist information** is also available in the Erne Gateway (same hours as ExplorErne Centre; ☎01365/658866). If you want **to stay**, there's fine accommodation at *Hotel Carlton* (☎013656/58282; ⑤) at the end of Main Street, and B&B further up the road in *Moohan's Fiddlestone* pub (☎013656/58008; ③). The village has a couple of cafés and *Rooney's* provides excellent bar meals. There are several places you can rent boats; for rowing call Carlton Cottages (☎01365/658181).

Killadeas, Irvinestown and Castle Archdale

In **KILLADEAS** churchyard, seven miles north of Enniskillen on the eastern side of the lough (take the B82), stands the **Bishop's Stone**, carved some time between the ninth and eleventh centuries. It's one of the most striking examples of the appearance of pre-Christian images in early Christian culture, having a startled pagan-style face on one side and a bishop with bell and crozier on the other. There are other interesting carved stones in the graveyard, too, including two cross slabs and a rounded pillar, possibly a pagan phallic stone. If you want to get out onto the water, Manor House Marine (☎013656/28100) rents out **motor boats** from £45.

The only site of any interest in **IRVINESTOWN**, a few miles northeast and inland, is Dr Patrick Delany's church built in 1734, though the clock tower and pinnacled battlements are all that remain. Jonathan Swift played an unlikely cupid to the rector, introducing him to court favourite and London society hostess, Mary Granville. They married and Delany later became Dean of Down; while she left a revealing record of eighteenth-century Anglo-Irish society and gossip, gathered during their visits to the Big Houses. If you want to stay in Irvinestown, there are a few **B&Bs** around the village, including *Lettermoney House* on the Enniskillen–Omagh Road (☎01365/388347; ②), or *Len-Aire*, Kesh Road (☎013656/21627; ②). Just outside town there's accommodation and **equestrian** activities in the splendidly situated *Necarne Castle* (☎013656/21656; ④); to get there take the road behind the town centre clock and turn right at its end.

To immerse yourself thoroughly in the beauty of the lough scenery, you could hardly do better than stay in the YHANI **hostel** set in the **Castle Archdale** forest park (☎013656/28118; March–Oct), near Lisnarick, about five miles west of Irvinestown. If you're relying on public transport, the Pettigo bus (4 daily) will drop you a mile away at the park entrance; otherwise take one of the buses from Enniskillen to Kesh (4 daily) to Lisnarick and walk or hitch. The hostel is a perfect place for getting out to the lough and is a stone's throw from a large caravan park and **campsite** (☎013656/21333), which has a small supermarket and a fast-food outlet in high season. The ferry to White Island (see below) leaves from nearby, and you can also **rent boats** and **bikes** here in July and August. And, if you fancy exploring the area on **horseback**, *Drumhoney Riding Stables* (☎013656/21892) is handily adjacent too.

White Island

Mounted on the wall of a ruined abbey, the seven early Christian carvings of **White Island** look eerily pagan. Found earlier this century, they are thought to be caryatids – columns in human form – from a monastic church of the ninth to eleventh centuries. The most disconcerting statue is the lewd female figure known as a *sheila na gig*, with bulging cheeks, a big grin, open legs and arms pointing to her genitals. This could be a female fertility figure, a warning to monks of the sins of the flesh, or an expression of the demoniacal power of women, designed to ward off evil. (In the epic *Taín Bó Cuailngè*, Cúchulainn was stopped by an army of 150 women led by their female chieftain Scannlach. Their only weapon was their display of nakedness, from which the boy Cúchulainn had to avert his face.) Less equivocal figures continue left to right: a seated Christ figure holding the Gospels on his knees; a hooded figure with bell and crozier, possibly St Anthony; David carrying a shepherd's staff, his hand towards his mouth showing his role as author and singer; Christ the Warrior holding two griffins by the scruff of their necks; and another Christ figure with a fringe of curly hair wearing a brooch on his left shoulder and carrying a sword and shield – here he is the King of Glory at his Second Coming. There is an unfinished seventh stone and, on the far right, a carved head with a downturned mouth which is probably later than the other statues. The church of White Island also contains eleventh-century gravestones; the large earthworks round the outside date from an earlier monastery.

Boa Island and Kesh

One of the most evocative of the carvings of Lough Erne is the double-faced Janus figure of **Boa Island**, at the northern end of the Lower Lough – barely an island at all these days, as it's connected to the mainland by bridges. The place to look out for is Caldragh cemetery, signposted off the A47, about a mile west of Lusty Beg Island. Follow the signs down a lane and the graveyard is through a gate to your left.

This ancient Christian burial ground of broken moss-covered tombstones, shaded by low, encircling hazel trees, has an almost druidic setting. Here you'll find the **Janus figure**, an idol of yellow stone with very bold symmetrical features. It has the phallus on one side, and a belt and crossed limbs on the other. The figure was probably an invocation of fertility and a depiction of a god-hero – the belt being a reference to the bearing of weapons. Alongside it stands the smaller "Lusty Man", so called since it was moved here from nearby Lustymore Island. This idol has only one eye fully carved, which may be to indicate blindness – Cúchulainn had a number of encounters with war goddesses, divine hags described as blind in the left eye. Across on Lusty Beg Island just off Boa, luxury log cabins with saunas (☎013656/32032; £140–280 a weekend for 2/3 twin bedrooms), B&B in the guesthouse (④) canoeing, gentle walks and a restaurant make this quiet island a popular weekend retreat for Enniskillen people. A free car ferry will take you across; dial ☎0 from the telephone on the pier.

The nearest village, **KESH**, four and a half miles to the east, is a possible overnight stop, having some cheapish **B&B** accommodation. Try *Rosscah Lodge*, 11 Crevenish Rd (☎013656/31001; ③) or *Roscolban House*, Enniskillen Road (☎013656/31096; ②). If you've transport there's also the option of staying in the *Ardess Craft Centre* (☎013656/31267; ④), housed in a fine Georgian rectory, which offers day and residential courses in various crafts, (from £25 per day); take the Enniskillen Road out of Kesh, turn left just before the police barracks, take a hard right, then follow the road for one and a half miles. There's also dormitory accommodation at the *Willow Pattern Complex* on Crevenish Road (☎013656/31012; from £5).

The chief recommendation of Kesh itself is its position on the lough. You can rent **motor boats** here from Mr R.A. Graham, Manville House (☎013656/31668; £25 a day; £60 if he comes too and shows you the best trout spots), or *Erinona Boats*, Boa Island Bridge (☎013656/32328; £40 per day). *Drumrush Watersports*, Boa Island Road (☎013656/31578) offers everything from jetski rent to banana boat rides. If you want to combine **camping** and **watersports** it makes sense to stay at the *Lakeland Caravan Park*, Boa Island Road (☎013656/31025), which offers wind-surfing, canoeing and water-skiing. Alternatively, there's *Loaneden Caravan Park* at Muckross Bay (☎013656/31603) or in *Clonelly Forest* (☎013656/31253), three miles north. **Bikes** can be rented from Cycle-ops, 31 Mantlin Rd (☎013656/31850).

Upper Lough Erne and Lisnaskea

Upper Lough Erne holds nothing like the interest of the Lower Lough, nor the scenic splendour, although it does have the best-preserved of the planters' castles nearby. The most you're really likely to do around the lough is disturb the anglers or get lost among its crazy causeways and waterways – fun on a boat, but frustrating on dry land. Should you be tempted to venture further into the maze of reeds and water, a "Viking longship" runs **cruises** (see p.604) from the *Share Holiday Centre* (☎013657/22122) at Smith's Strand, signposted off the Lisnaskea–Derrylin Road, where they also offer water-based activity holidays with facilities for disabled travellers, and B&B, self-catering chalets and a campsite. The National Trust **Crom Estate** (April–Sept Mon–Sat 10am–6pm Sun noon–6pm; car £3), three miles southwest of Newtownbutler on the eastern shore of the lough, has the largest surviving area of oak woodland in Northern Ireland, home to rare species such as the purple hairstreak and wood white butterflies. There's a café and interpretive centre here, and you can rent **rowing boats** too. Unfortunately, the modern Crom Castle is in private occupation and not open to the public, though you can visit the ruins of the old castle. The estate has renovated courtyard **cottages**

(☎013657/38118; £185–435 per week for 2–6 people). If you have transport, the elegantly chiselled **gravestones** on Galoon Island, with their reliefs of skull and cross-
bones, hourglass and coffin, are worth a detour. *Ports House*, right by the waterside at
Ports, not far from Newtownbutler, offers **B&B** (☎013657/38528; ③).

Almost five miles north of Newtownbutler, **Castle Balfour** at **LISNASKEA** was built
for Sir James Balfour, a Scottish planter, in the early seventeenth century and shows
strong Scottish characteristics in the turrets and parapets, high-pitched gables and tall
chimneys. Lisnaskea itself is one of Fermanagh's few towns – and a small one at that.
Its tiny nineteenth-century Cornmarket yard has an early Christian carved cross
depicting Adam and Eve beneath a tree, and the library up the road towards
Enniskillen contains a diminutive but interesting **folk museum** (Mon–Tues & Fri
10am–5.30pm, Wed 10am–7.30pm, Sat 10am–1pm), with displays on local Gaelic traditions and festivals, including plenty of detail on the making of poteen. There's a **campsite** within two miles of Lisnaskea at Mullynascarthy (☎013657/21040).

Western Fermanagh

The stretch of countryside on the western edge of the county offers some good walking opportunities, particularly in the hills to the south. **The Ulster Way**, which runs
northwest from the Upper Lough or east towards Tyrone, makes the riches of the terrain easily accessible.

The west also has two attractions that are well worth seeking out. The magnificent eighteenth-century **Florence Court**, about eight miles southwest of Enniskillen, is the most
assured achievement of the colonists, built 150 years after the initial defensive planters'
castles; and, if you have transport, a visit to the house can be combined with an hour or so
at the **Marble Arch Caves** – the finest cave-system in Northern Ireland. To get to the

---

THE ULSTER WAY

From Marble Arch Caves the **Ulster Way** heads past Lower and Upper Lough Macnean
before you thread your way through the bog and granite heights of the Cuilcagh Mountains to
Ballintempo Forest, where there are fabulous views over the loughs. The Way then continues north, through the Lough Navar Forest, a well-groomed conifer plantation with tarmacked roads and shorter trails. Although a great deal of fir plantation walking is dark
and frustrating, this forest does, at points, provide some of the most spectacular views in
Fermanagh, looking over Lower Lough Erne and the mountains of Tyrone, Donegal,
Leitrim and Sligo. The Lough Navar Forest also sustains a small herd of red deer, as well
as wild goats, foxes, badgers, hares and red squirrels.

Accommodation along the Way is limited. There are a half a dozen B&Bs near
BELCOO, two and a half miles west from the trail's ascent to the Ballintempo Forest: try
Bella Vista, Cottage Drive (☎01365/386469; ③), or *Corralea Forest Lodge*, Corralea
(☎01365/386325; ③). There are a campsite and holiday cottages (£55 per cottage per night)
in the *Tir Navar Holiday Village* (☎01365/641673) in Lough Navar Forest, five miles northwest of Derrygonnelly, off the A46. A bit further away from the route of the Way, west near
the border at **GARRISON** (take the minor road from Derrygonnelly), the *Lough Melvin
Holiday Centre* (☎013656/58142; prior arrangement essential) offers caving, canoeing,
windsurfing and hill-walking – prices from £5 per half-day, £55 per weekend. The centre has
hostel accommodation and camping, though you should ring ahead to check on space if
you want to stop here.

Before setting out, it's well worth obtaining a copy of the *The Ulster Way: Southwest
Section* from the tourist office in Enniskillen. This describes in detail the five connected
trails constituting the Way's route through the county.

house from Enniskillen follow the A4 Sligo Road for three miles, branching off on the A32 Swanlinbar Road and taking the signposted right turn four miles further on. The Swanlinbar-bound bus passes this last junction, whence it's a mile's walk. From here to the caves head a further five miles west. Walkers can reach them along the **Ulster Way**, which runs four miles south from the A4 near Belcoo and past Lower Lough Macnean.

Florence Court

The magnificent three-storey mansion of **Florence Court** (April & Sept Sat & Sun 1–6pm; May–Aug Wed–Mon 1–6pm; £2.80; grounds and forest park open all year 10am–dusk; £2 per car), completed around 1775, was commissioned by John Cole, one of the Earls of Enniskillen, and named after his wife. The house is notable for its recently restored rococo plasterwork and rare Irish furnishings; the dining-room is especially lavish, its ceiling hosting a cloud of cherubs with eagles flying out of a duck-egg blue sky. You can stay in the pretty *Rose Cottage* in the Florence Court walled garden, well equipped and with two double bedrooms (☎01365/348249; £185–430 per week). There's award-winning **accommodation** nearby at *Tullyhona House*, 59 Marble Arch Rd (☎01365/348452; ③), whose **restaurant** offers hearty home cooking; booking is essential.

The Marble Arch Caves

Fermanagh's caves are renowned, and while some are for experts only, the most spectacular system of all – the **Marble Arch Caves** – is accessible to anyone. A **tour** of the system lasts around an hour and a quarter, beginning with a boat journey along a subterranean river, then on through brilliantly lit chambers, calcite-walled and dripping with stalactites and fragile mineral veils. Tours of the caves are sometimes booked out by parties, so it makes sense to ring ahead to check that your journey there will not be wasted (daily: Easter–June & Sept 10am–4.30pm; July & Aug 10am–5pm; £5; ☎01365/348855); in a steady Irish downpour the caves can be flooded, so check weather reports. You'll need to wear sturdy walking shoes and bring warm clothing as the temperature can drop significantly. Whichever way you approach the caves, you'll travel along the **Marlbank Scenic Loop** with tremendous views of Lower Lough Macnean, and on either side you'll see limestone-flagged fields, much like those of the Burren in County Clare. It was 50,000 years of gentle water seepage through the limestone that deposited the calcite for the amazing stalactite growths in the caves below.

travel details

BUSES

Enniskillen to: Armagh (1 daily; 1hr 45min); Ballyshannon (1 daily; 1hr 25min); Belfast (6 daily, 2 daily in summer; 2hr 35min); Belleek (2 Tues, Thurs & Sat, 1 Sun; 1hr 5min); Bundoran (1 daily; 1hr 35min); Dublin (3 daily; 3hr 45min); Irvinestown (8 daily; 45 min); Lisnarick (4 daily; 35min); Monaghan (2 daily; 1hr 10min); Omagh (7 daily; 1hr 20min); Pettigo (4 daily; 1hr).

Cookstown to: Coalisland (9 daily; 30min).

Dungannon to Coalisland (21 daily; 20min); Cookstown (10 daily; 45min).

Omagh to: Athlone (1 daily; 4hr); Cahir (1 daily; 7hr); Castlederg (5 daily; 50min); Clogher (2 daily; 40min); Cookstown (1 daily; 1hr 10min); Cork (1 daily; 9hr); Derry (12 daily; 1hr 45min); Dungannon (2 daily; 1hr 30min); Gortin (3 daily; 35min); Portrush (summer, 1 daily; 2hr 15min); Strabane (12 daily; 1hr).

Strabane to: Castlederg (7 daily; 30min); Derry (19 daily; 50min); Dublin (4 daily; 4hr 40min); Enniskillen (1 daily; 3hr); Monaghan (4 daily; 2hr 5min); Omagh (4 daily; 1hr 5min).

THE
CONTEXTS

THE HISTORICAL FRAMEWORK

An understanding of Ireland's history is essential in order to make sense of its troubled present. In these few pages, we cannot do more than provide a brief outline of that history, in the hope that it will serve as a starting point for further reading and discussion.

EARLIEST INHABITANTS

During the last Ice Age, when most of the country was covered by an ice-cap, low sea-levels meant that Ireland was attached to Britain, and Britain to the European continent. As the climate warmed (from about 13,000 BC), and the ice gradually retreated, sea-levels rose and the broad land connection between Ireland and Britain began to recede to one or more narrow land bridges. The first human inhabitants arrived over these routes, probably from Scotland, some time after 8000 BC. By about 7000 BC the land bridges were submerged and Ireland geographically isolated, while Britain remained connected to continental Europe for much longer.

The first inhabitants, **Mesolithic** (middle Stone Age) hunter-gatherers, found a densely forested land that could only be penetrated easily along its waterways, and, for the most part, they seem to have lived close to the sea, rivers and lakes (flint work from the period has been found in Antrim, Down, Louth and Dublin). Their way of life continued undisturbed until, from

about 3500 BC, **Neolithic** (late Stone Age) farmers began arriving by sea, probably from Britain. With skills in animal and crop husbandry, weaving and pottery, the new arrivals used their stone axes to clear large tracts of forest for cultivation. The hunter-gatherer and agricultural economies were, however, complimentary, and it is thought the two peoples co-existed for many centuries before the older way of life was gradually assimilated by the new.

The Neolithic people were the creators of Ireland's **megalithic remains**. There are more than 1200 such burial sites scattered throughout the country, with the greatest concentrations in the north and west. Such sites are also found all along the Atlantic seaboard of Europe, from Spain to Scandinavia – a sign of Ireland's ancestral and cultural links with the rest of Europe at this time and, in particular, with the peoples of Britain and Brittany.

The most dramatic and well-known megalithic remains in Ireland are the great **passage graves** at Knowth and Newgrange in County Meath, with their elaborate spiral engravings, cut into the stone entirely without the use of metal tools. It is thought that the function of these tombs was not purely religious or ceremonial; they were also territorial markers, which at times of population pressure staked a communal claim to the surrounding lands. Little is known of the people themselves, although their civilization was long-lasting, with thousands of years separating the earliest and the latest megalithic constructions. Only rarely have skeletons been found in the graves (in most cases only the cremated remains of bones are discovered), but what few there have been seem to indicate a short, dark, hairy race with a life expectancy of little more than 35 years.

Around 2000 BC the use of bronze spread to Ireland, though it is uncertain whether this was the result of the commercial contacts of the existing population or the migration of a new people. The next significant technological development, generally associated with the arrival of the Celts, was the introduction of iron around 700 BC.

THE CELTS

The **Celts** were an Indo-European group called Keltoi by the Greeks and Galli by the Romans, who spread south from central Europe into Italy and Spain and west through France and Britain.

By 500 BC, Celtic language and culture were dominant in Ireland, but there is no evidence of any large-scale invasion or social upheaval. It is probably more accurate to think of their arrival as a gradual and relatively peaceful process that took place over hundreds of years.

Their settlements took the form of ring forts (or raths), and they divided the island into about one hundred small **kingdoms** or *Tuatha*, each with its own king. The *Tuatha* were grouped into the Five Fifths or provinces, which were Ulster (*Ulaid*), Meath (*Midhe*), Leinster (*Laigin*), Munster (*Muma*) and Connacht (which retains its Irish spelling). In theory, the High King (*Ard Rígh*) ruled over all from his throne on the Hill of Tara – a place long associated with mysterious power – although only rarely did any one figure of sufficient strength emerge to lay undisputed claim to that title.

It is hard to separate the truth about the Celts from the stories they told of themselves. Theirs was an oral culture in which the immortality to be gained from being the hero of an epic tale was highly prized. With an enthusiasm for war little short of bloodthirsty, they celebrated battles decided by the single combat of great champions, guided and aided by the unpredictable whims of the gods. They also appropriated the religion and beliefs already current in Ireland and, although they had nothing to do with their building, megalithic sites continued to have great symbolic significance for them.

The two greatest heroes of the epics, **Cúchulainn** and **Fionn Mac Cumhaill** (Finn McCool), have been tentatively identified as warrior champions of the second and third centuries, transformed by legend into semi-divinities in much the same way as King Arthur was in England.

THE COMING OF CHRISTIANITY

The **Christianization** of Ireland began as early as the fourth century AD, well before the arrival of St Patrick (whose existence is now the subject of some controversy). Vestiges did survive of the previous religion of the Celts, but after the collapse of the Roman Empire, Ireland assumed a position at the very forefront of European Christianity. (Also around this time the people of Ireland took the name Goidil – Gaels – for themselves from the Welsh Gwyddyl.)

In the sixth century, the early Christian leaders successfully adapted established church organization to suit the scattered and tribal nature of Gaelic society by setting up monastic foundations. The country became a haven for religious orders, the only sources of learning at this time. The sheer impassibility of the landscape supported monastic development, and many of the great Irish monasteries, such as St Enda's on the Aran Islands, Clonmacnois in County Offaly and Clonard in County Meath, date from this period. **Ogham**, the Celtic line-based writing system seen on standing stones, was rapidly supplanted by the religious scholars, who introduced Latin. The first – and best-known – of their richly illuminated Latin manuscripts, the **Book of Kells**, can be seen in the Library of Trinity College, Dublin.

The traditional view of these times as "Dark Ages" of terror and chaos throughout Europe is not supported by events in Ireland. Although intertribal warfare was constant, the country enjoyed relative cultural and religious stability. Alongside this, well-established diplomatic and trading contact along the Atlantic seaboard encouraged the development of a strong missionary impulse in Irish Christianity. Between 500 and 800 the Irish church spread the gospel widely across the Continent. The most prominent of the many missionaries was St Columba, who founded monasteries in France, Switzerland, Germany and Austria, and at Bobbio in Italy – where he died in 615.

INVASION: VIKINGS AND NORMANS

From 795, Ireland was increasingly plagued by destructive **Viking raids**, in which many of the great monasteries were plundered and burned (though many more were destroyed as a result of indigenous intertribal warfare in the eighth and ninth centuries). The instability of the period led to the development of the **round towers**, which were used as lookout posts and places of sanctuary – and which characterize early Irish architecture. The Viking raids culminated in a full-scale invasion in 914 and the subsequent founding of walled cities, usually at the mouths of rivers, such as Dublin, Wexford, Waterford, Youghal, Cork, Bantry and Limerick. The decisive defeat of the Danes by the High King Brian Boru at the Battle of Clontarf in 1014 at least spared Ireland from becoming a Viking colony. However, the death of Brian Boru at the battle, and the subsequent divisions among his followers, meant that his victory was never consolidated by the formation of a strong unified kingdom. The Vikings that remained soon merged fully into the native Irish population.

From the time of the Norman conquest onwards, the kings of England coveted Ireland. The first of the **Anglo-Normans** to cross over to Ireland was a freelance adventurer, Richard FitzGilbert de Clare, more usually known as **Strongbow**. He came in 1169 at the invitation of Dermot MacMurrough, the exiled king of Leinster, who sought help to regain his throne. Henry II of England, however, was concerned that Strongbow might establish a threatening power base and therefore went personally to Ireland as overlord. He had earlier secured papal support and authorization over all powers – native, Norse and Norman – from, as chance would have it, the only English pope in history, Adrian IV.

In 1172, Pope Alexander III reaffirmed Henry II's lordship. This seemed to open the prospect of Anglo-Norman rule in which Gaelic tribal kingdoms would be reshaped into a feudal system on the English model, but the Irish resisted so effectively that royal authority outside the "English Pale" (an area surrounding Dublin) was little more than nominal.

THE STATUTES OF KILKENNY

By the fourteenth century, the Anglo-Norman settlers had integrated with the native Irish population to such an extent that the Crown, eager to regain control, sought to drive a permanent wedge between the natives and the colonists with the introduction of The **Statutes of Kilkenny** (1366). This legislation prohibited intermarriage with the Irish, forbade the Irish from entering walled cities, and made the adoption of Irish names, dress, customs or speech illegal. Despite these measures, Gaelic influence continued to grow until, by the end of the fifteenth century, the "Pale" had been reduced to just a narrow strip of land around the capital.

THE TUDORS AND THE STUARTS

The continued isolation of Irish politics from English and Continental influence during the fifteenth century, and England's preoccupation with the Wars of the Roses, helped Ireland's most powerful Anglo-Norman family – the **FitzGeralds** of Kildare – to establish and consolidate control of the east and southeast of the country. For the most part, their growing authority was left unchallenged by the early Tudor monarchy, whose policy towards Ireland was based mainly on considerations of economy – it was cheaper to accept Kildare's rule than establish an English deputy who would need expensive military backing – and security – Irish discontent with English rule should not be allowed to take forms which might be exploited by England's foreign enemies.

THE REFORMATION

Henry VIII was able to retain his attitude of expedient caution until his break with Rome introduced several new factors. The clergy began to preach rebellion against the schismatical king, while Henry was able to reward his supporters with the spoils from the dissolution of religious houses. Convinced that his family's power was under threat, Kildare's son, Lord Offaly ("Silken Thomas"), staged an insurrection in the summer of 1534. Aid from the pope – who for the first time was seen as a potential supporter of opposition to England – was hoped for, but never came. Henry, inevitably, reacted forcibly and exchanged his policy of prudence for one of aggression. War dragged on until 1540, by which time Kildare and his supporters, their power all but crushed, were forced to submit to the Crown.

The Dublin parliament enacted legislation accepting Henry's **Act of Supremacy**, which made the king head of the Church. At least three distinct factions emerged in Ireland: the "Old English", who were loyal to the king but denied him spiritual primacy; the independent-minded and staunchly Catholic Gaelic Irish; and the new Protestants, many of whom had benefited materially by acquiring Church property. (At this stage, those "recusants" who refused to swear the oath acknowledging Henry as head of the Church were not yet subject to discrimination.) In an attempt to bind the chiefs and nobles of Ireland more closely to its authority, the Crown forced them to surrender their lands, only to return them again with the reduced status of landlords. Central to Henry's policy was the wish to rule Ireland cheaply, with least risk of foreign intervention, through Irish-born "deputies" whose loyalty was assured. But such loyalty could not be counted on, and after Henry's death the authority of the English Crown was again challenged.

ELIZABETH I AND JAMES I

During the reign of **Queen Elizabeth I** (1558–1603), a growing number of adventurers, mainly younger sons of the aristocracy, arrived from Protestant England to pillage Ireland. For the first time, the supposed moral imperative to turn the Gaelic Irish away from the papacy was used as an excuse to invade and dispossess. This justification for the suppression of Irish culture, religion and language was to be the trademark of English occupation of Ireland for many years to come.

Elizabeth's aim was to establish an English colony. This policy of **plantation** had been started, albeit unsuccessfully, some thirty years earlier during the reign of Mary I, when Laois – renamed "Queen's County" – and Offaly – "King's County" – were confiscated from their native Irish owners and given into the possession of loyal Old English. Elizabeth's first attempt, in the 1570s, to "plant" northeast Ulster, which was then the most Gaelic area of the country, failed miserably. But the colonization process, when eventually completed, was the principal instrument in subjugating the entire country.

At least three major Irish **rebellions** were prompted by Elizabeth's policies. Two of these, led by the Desmonds of Munster, were easily put down; the Desmond lands were confiscated and given to English settlers. The third, last, and most serious was in Ulster, and was led by **Hugh O'Neill**. O'Neill, originally a protegé of the English court (see p.589), participated in crushing the revolt of the Desmonds, and had long been groomed to become chief of Ulster. He'd always imagined the role to be that of an autonomous Gaelic chieftain; he turned against his queen in 1595 when he began to appreciate the extent to which he would be the pawn of English Protestantism. His forces won a major victory over the English at the Battle of the Yellow Ford in 1598, but were defeated at **Kinsale** in December 1601 after failing to link up effectively with the Spanish reinforcements who had arrived there.

The Tudor conquest of Ireland was completed when O'Neill signed the **Treaty of Mellifont** in 1603, ignorant of the death of Elizabeth just a few days before. Half a million acres of land were confiscated from the native Irish, including all the estates of O'Neill and O'Donnell. English plans to redistribute the land supposedly included generous endowments to the "natives". However, an abortive and unplanned insurrec-

tion was enough to frighten them into abandoning any such idea, and English and Scottish "planters" – many of whom were ex-soldiers – were brought over to be ensconced in fortified "bawns". Chiefs such as O'Neill were still nominally landlords but, unable to accept the loss of their ancient authority, and living under constant suspicion that they were plotting against the Crown, many chose instead to leave their country as exiles. Their mass departure to continental Europe in 1607 became known as the **Flight of the Earls**.

It was at this time that the character of Ulster began to change. James VI of Scotland had just become **James I** of England, and he encouraged many Scots to emigrate the short distance to Ulster where so much newly confiscated land awaited them. There was a great deal of bitterness on the part of the dispossessed native people, and little intermarriage with the planters, so that the whole country, and above all Ulster, became divided along Catholic and Protestant lines.

CHARLES I AND THE ENGLISH CIVIL WAR

The widespread belief in England and Ireland that James's successor, **Charles I**, harboured pro-Catholic sympathies was one of the spurs for the armed rebellion in Ulster in 1641. Terrifying stories circulated in England of the torture and murder of Protestant planters, and the rebels' (bogus) claim that they were acting with Charles's blessing did much to provoke the **English Civil War**. The origins of the current situation in the six northeast counties of Ulster can in many respects be traced to the policy and events of this period.

During the Civil War, the "Old English" in Ireland allied with the native Irish in the **Confederation of Kilkenny**, supporting the Royalist cause in the hope of bringing about the restoration of Catholicism. It was an uneasy alliance, characterized by inadequate leadership and personal rivalries, in which the Irish felt they had nothing to lose in pursuit of liberty, whereas the Old English lived in fear of a Protestant invasion should the forces of **Oliver Cromwell** achieve victory. The war did indeed end with the establishment of Cromwell's Protectorate and the execution of the king; and the conquest of Ireland became Cromwell's most immediate priority.

CROMWELL AND THE ACT OF SETTLEMENT

Cromwell's ruthless campaign in Ireland remains a source of great bitterness to this day. He arrived in Dublin with 12,000 men of the New Model Army in August 1649, and was soon joined by another force under General Ireton. **Drogheda** was stormed in September, and thousands, including civilians and children, were slaughtered. Cromwell continued south and quickly took Wexford and New Ross, whereupon the towns of Cork, Youghal and Kinsale in the southeast (all in the hands of Royalists) swiftly capitulated. Although Waterford held out for several months, it was not long before Cromwell's forces had overrun the entire country and broken the backbone of resistance.

By the time the struggle was over, almost two years on, one-quarter of the Catholic population was dead and those found wandering the country orphaned or dispossessed were sold into slavery in the West Indies. The **Act of Settlement** drawn up in 1652 confiscated land from the native Irish on a massive scale. All "transplantable persons" were ordered to move west of the River Shannon by May 1, 1654, on pain of death; in the famous phrase, it was a matter of indifference whether they went "to Hell or to Connacht". The mass exodus continued for months, with many of the old and sick dying on the journey. Cromwell's soldiers were paid off with gifts of appropriated land, and, remaining as settlers, constituted a permanent reminder of English injustice.

KING BILLY AND KING JAMES

Irish hopes were raised once more by the **Restoration** of Charles II in 1660. He had regained the English throne, however, only after lengthy negotiations with the Protestant parliamentarians of London and Dublin, and was in no position to give expression to any Catholic sympathies which he may have held.

Things changed only when Charles's brother James II succeeded him in 1685. He appointed a Catholic viceroy in Ireland and actually got as far as repealing the Act of Settlement. Had this had time to take effect, the land confiscated by Cromwell would have been returned to its former (Catholic) owners. However, the Whigs and the Tories in England united to invite the Protestant William of Orange to take the throne. James fled and was soon raising an army in Ireland. He was successful until 1689, when he came to lay siege to the city of Derry in Ulster; young trade apprentices, known thereafter as the **Apprentice Boys**, shut the gates of the city in the face of James's troops – an event still celebrated today during the annual marching season.

However, arguably the most significant victory of Protestant over Catholic was on July 12, 1690, when William's army defeated that of James at the **Battle of the Boyne**. The repeal of the Act of Settlement was therefore never implemented – but the very idea that the Catholics still had claims to their old property which they might one day be able to reassert became established in the Protestant consciousness. As William's victory was consolidated, measures were taken to ensure irreversible Protestant control of the country.

THE PENAL LAWS TO THE ACT OF UNION

In 1641, 59 percent of the land in Ireland was owned by Catholics. In 1688, the figure was 22 percent, and by 1703 it was 14 percent. The Protestant population, about one-tenth of the total, lived in fear of an uprising by the vast majority of dispossessed and embittered Catholics. In order to keep the native Catholics in a position of powerlessness, a number of acts were passed, collectively known as the **penal laws**. Not only were Catholics forbidden to vote or join the army or navy, but it became illegal to educate a child in the Catholic faith; they could not teach, open their own schools or send their children to be educated abroad. Catholics could neither buy land nor inherit it, other than by the equal division of estates between all sons. There were vast rewards for turning Protestant; a male convert was entitled to all his brothers' inheritance, a female to her husband's property. Irish language, music and literature were banned, as was the saying of the Mass. The intention was to crush the identity of the Irish people through the suppression of their culture. However, clandestine "hedge schools" developed where outlawed Catholic teachers taught Irish language and music; Mass was said in secret, often at night in the open countryside, and although the erosion of the culture had begun, for the time being it remained strong (it wasn't until the devastating effects of the Famine that the culture went into serious decline).

GRATTAN'S PARLIAMENT

The next turning point in Irish history came in the late eighteenth century, when the increasingly prosperous merchant class ceased to identify its own interests exclusively with those of the British Crown. The British, in their turn, were forced to realize that the best guarantee of stability was the country's economic strength. This was an age of bourgeois revolution, and the events of the **American War of Independence** attracted much attention in Ireland. As early as 1771, Benjamin Franklin was in Dublin suggesting future transatlantic co-operation. Although the rebellion of the American colonies threatened Irish commercial interests, opposition to the war did not mean opposition to the American cause. Thus far, the bulk of Irish emigrants to the American colonies had been Ulster Presbyterians, Catholic emigration being subject to legal restrictions, and the Protestants of Ireland felt a deep sympathy with Washington's campaign. The demand for "no taxation without representation" struck an emotional chord with the parliamentarians of Henry Grattan's Patriot Party – although Ireland was not taxed directly by the British parliament, the Irish Protestants felt, increasingly, that their interests were not properly represented in the politics and policies of the British Isles as a whole.

Protestants and Catholics in Ireland made common cause to the extent that Grattan declared "the Irish Protestant could never be free till the Irish Catholic had ceased to be a slave". Its resources stretched to the limit by war, the British government was sufficiently intimidated by the thought of Irish rebellion to be in the mood for concessions. The land stipulations of the penal laws were repealed in 1778, and in 1782, **Grattan's Parliament** achieved what was felt at the time to be constitutional independence for Ireland, beyond the interference of the London parliament, although still subject to the veto of the king. In the **Renunciation Act** of 1783, the British parliament declared that the executive and judicial independence of Ireland should be "established and ascertained forever, and... at no time hereafter be questioned or questionable".

As it turned out, the independence of the Dublin parliament lasted for just eighteen years, and even those were long on dissent and short on achievement. Economic measures certainly benefited the merchants, but such issues as the extension of voting rights to Catholics – despite Grattan's personal support – were barely addressed. A major reason for its failure was the influence of the **French Revolution** in 1789.

WOLFE TONE AND THE UNITED IRISHMEN

In the 1770s, the threat of French invasion, coupled with the obvious inadequacy of the British force stationed in the country, had led to the formation throughout Ireland of bands of **Volunteers**. These were exclusively Protestant groups, at their strongest in Ulster and particularly Belfast, which rapidly acquired a political significance way beyond their role as a sort of Home Guard.

The French Revolution transformed French invasion, for Irish Nationalists of all persuasions, from a menace to be feared to a prospective means of national liberation. **United Irishmen**, led by Wolfe Tone and built on the foundations of the Protestant Volunteers but attracting, if anything, more support from Catholics, rallied to the call of Liberty, Equality and Fraternity. Tone himself was a Protestant barrister, who saw equal rights for Protestants and Catholics in Ireland as the only route to independence from England. The United Irishmen were originally disposed towards non-violence, but for Tone the possibility of French aid was too appealing to resist. The British, and the majority of Ulster Protestants, were by contrast so alarmed by tales of the bloodshed in France that they too prepared for war; it was at this juncture that the Protestant Orange Society, later the Orange Order, was established (1795). Although influenced by revolutionary ideas from France, its main aim was to maintain Protestant power (for more on the Order, see p.576).

The uprising came in **1798** (see pp.206 & 388); disorganized fighting broke out in different parts of the island well before the French fleet – and Tone himself – arrived, and the scattered rebels were swiftly and bloodily suppressed. Tone was sentenced to be hanged, but committed suicide by cutting his own throat before his execution. The limited advances Henry Grattan had won for Catholics were withdrawn as a result of the rebellion.

THE ACT OF UNION

The destiny of Ireland during the period following the uprising was largely subject to the whim of political factions in England, ever ready to make an emotional cause célèbre of the latest developments. The rebellion of 1798 provoked Prime Minister William Pitt into support for the complete legislative union of Britain and Ireland and the dissolution of the Dublin parliament. Pitt argued that this offered the most hopeful road towards Catholic emancipation while also ensuring the perpetuation of the Protestant Ascendancy. In 1801, the **Act of Union** came into force, abolishing the 500-year-old Irish parliament and making Ireland part of the United Kingdom.

All hopes of independence seemed crushed. Ireland itself housed an utterly divided people, a minority Protestant ruling class and a politically powerless Catholic majority. Robert Emmet, a romantic figure in Irish history, inspired by Wolfe Tone, made one last stand for independence, and attempted a rising in 1803. His followers, however, were small in number and disorganized. The rising failed, and Emmet was executed.

DANIEL O'CONNELL

The quest for Catholic emancipation by peaceful constitutional means was the life's work of **Daniel O'Connell** (1775–1847), the lawyer who became known as "The Liberator" and whom Gladstone called "the greatest popular leader the world has ever seen". He founded the Catholic Association in 1823, which attracted a mass following in Ireland with its campaign for full political rights for Catholics. O'Connell himself was elected to the British House of Commons as the member for Ennis, County Clare in 1828. As a Catholic, he was forbidden to take his seat in Westminster; but the moral force of his victory was such that a change in the law had to be conceded. Royal assent was given to the **Catholic Emancipation Bill** on April 13, 1829, granting voting rights to some Catholics. Stringent property qualifications, however, ensured that the Catholic vote remained a small one.

At the height of his success, O'Connell's popularity was phenomenal. He was elected Lord Mayor of (Protestant) Dublin for the year of 1841, and two years later embarked on an ambitious campaign for the **repeal of the Union** with England. O'Connell addressed a series of vast "monster meetings" throughout Ireland; according to the conservative estimate of *The Times*, over a million people – one-eighth of the Irish population – attended the meeting symbolically held at the Hill of Tara.

The climax of O'Connell's campaign was to be a meeting at Clontarf (where Brian Boru had defeated the Danes in the eleventh century) on October 8, 1843. All Ireland was poised and waiting, conscious of the sympathy that O'Connell's profoundly peaceful movement had won from around the world. The pacifism which had led him to say that "no political change is worth the shedding of a single drop of human blood", and his determination always to act within the law, were, however, exploited by the British. One day before the Clontarf meeting it was declared to be an illegal gathering and O'Connell, remarkably, obliged by calling it off. The crowds which had already gathered, and the population at large, were baffled that O'Connell backed down from direct confrontation. His moment passed and the stage was left to those who, having seen pacifism fail to secure independence, believed that armed struggle would prove the only way forward. The **Young Ireland movement**, once aligned with O'Connell, attempted an armed uprising in 1848, but by then there was little chance of mass support. The country was already undergoing a national disaster.

THE FAMINE

The failure of the Irish potato crop from 1845 to 1849 plunged the island into appalling **famine**. Elsewhere in Europe, the blight was a resolvable problem but Irish subsistence farmers were utterly dependent on the crop. No disease affected grain, cattle, dairy produce or corn and throughout the disaster Irish produce that could have fed the hungry continued to be exported overseas. Millions were kept alive by charitable soup kitchens, and some individual landlords were supportive to their tenants; for millions more, the only choice lay between starvation and escape.

Between 1841 and 1851, census returns suggest that 1.4 million people died in Ireland and 1.4 million emigrated to the United States and elsewhere – though the exact numbers in each case were probably higher. Many emigrants were too ill to survive the journey on what became known as "coffin ships", some drowned when overcrowded ships sank, and still more died on arrival in the United States, Canada, Britain, Australia and New Zealand.

One consequence of **mass emigration** was the creation of large Irish communities abroad, which henceforth added an international dimension to the struggle for Irish independence. Financial support from the Irish overseas became crucial to such Nationalist organizations as the Irish Republican Brotherhood, also known as the **Fenians**. Their attempted uprising in 1867 was little short of a fiasco, but they nonetheless retained a loyal following both in the States and in England (where a number of bombings were carried out in their name).

The legacy of the Famine was such that the long-standing bitterness instilled by the English connection now deepened to a new level of emotional intensity. Resentment focused on the failure of the British government to intervene, and more specifically on the **absentee English landlords** who had continued to profit while remaining indifferent to the suffering of their tenants. Such landlords had little or no contact with the realities of life on their estates; rents were far higher than most tenants could pay, and evictions became widespread.

PARNELL AND THE HOME RULE

The second half of the nineteenth century was characterized by a complex interplay of political and economic factors which contributed towards the exacerbation of religious differences. The most important of these was the struggle for land and for the rights of tenants. A coherent Nationalist movement with modest aims began to emerge, operating within British parliamentary democracy.

Charles Stewart Parnell (1846–91; see p.117), a Protestant who was elected to Westminster in 1875 and became leader of the **Home Rule Party** two years later, was the tenants' champion. He insisted that only a parliament meeting in Dublin could be responsive to the needs of the people and, to that end, consistently disrupted the business of the British House of Commons.

Parnell also organized the Irish peasantry in defiance of particularly offensive landlords, adding a new word to the English language when the first such target was a Captain Boycott.

A breakthrough seemed to be approaching when Parnell won the support of the Prime Minister, Gladstone, but the **Phoenix Park** murders in Dublin in 1882 (see p.91) again hardened English opinion against the Irish. Three Home Rule Bills were defeated in the space of ten years; instead the Prevention of Crimes Act (temporarily) abolished trial by jury and increased police powers. The transparent honesty of Parnell's denials of complicity in the murders for a while served to boost his career, but public opinion finally swung against him in 1890, when he was cited in the divorce case of his colleague Captain O'Shea.

The attitude of many Irish Protestants to the agitation for Home Rule was summed up by the equation "Home Rule = Rome Rule"; such a threat was enough to unite the Anglican (broadly speaking, conservative gentry) and Presbyterian (liberal tradesmen) communities. These were certainly the people who were doing best from a modest boom in Ireland's economic fortunes, with Ulster, and specifically Belfast, having been the main beneficiary when the Industrial Revolution finally arrived in the country. Large-scale **industrialization**, in export industries such as shipbuilding, linen manufacture and engineering, gave the region an additional dependence on the British connection, while the fact that these industries were firmly under Protestant ownership increased social tensions.

The end of the nineteenth century saw a burst of activity aimed at the revival of interest in all aspects of Irish culture and identity. Ostensibly non-political organizations such as the **Gaelic League** and the Gaelic Athletic Association were founded to promote Irish language, music and traditional sports, and these inevitably tended to attract the support of politically minded Nationalists. As well as those who sought to encourage the use of Irish, a body of writers, with W.B. Yeats in the forefront, embarked on an attempt to create a national literature in English.

In 1898, Arthur Griffith, a printer in Dublin, founded a newspaper called the *United Irishman*, in which he expounded the philosophy of **Sinn Féin**, meaning "We, Ourselves". His was a non-violent and essentially capitalist vision, arguing that the Irish MPs should simply abandon Westminster and set up their own parliament in Dublin, where, with or without the permission of the British, they would be able to govern Ireland by virtue of their unassailable moral authority. Such political freedom was a prerequisite for Ireland to achieve significant economic development. Sinn Féin incorporated itself into a political party in 1905. Meanwhile, socialist analyses of the situation in Ireland were appearing in the *Workers' Republic*, the newspaper of **James Connolly's** Irish Socialist Republican Party, pointing out that Ireland's frail prosperity rested on a basis of malnutrition, bad housing and social deprivation.

REACTION AND COUNTER-REACTION

In reaction to the declared intentions of Asquith's Liberal government in Britain in 1911 to see through the passage of yet another (exceptionally tame) Home Rule Bill, the Protestants of Ulster mobilized themselves under the leadership of **Sir Edward Carson**. A Dublin barrister who at first glance had little in common with the people of Ulster, a region he barely knew, his one great aim was to preserve the Union, in the face of the "nefarious conspiracy" hatched by the British government itself. To that end he declared that, should the Home Rule Bill become law, the Unionists would defy it and set up their own parliament. In preparation for that eventuality, they organized their own militia, the **Ulster Volunteers**.

James Connolly, who had spent the years from 1903 to 1910 in disillusionment in the United States, found himself on less fertile ground when he tried to convert the workers of Belfast to socialism. He was impressed, however, by the example of the Ulster Volunteers, and the brutal police suppression of a protracted and bitter strike in Dublin, organized by James Larkin's Irish Transport Workers Union, gave him the opportunity to form the **Irish Citizen Army**. Other militant Republicans had also resolved to create an armed force in the south to parallel the Ulster Volunteers, and almost simultaneously, in November 1913, the **Irish Volunteers** came into being. The Gaelic League and Gaelic Athletic Association acted as prime recruiting places and provided such leaders as Pádraig Pearse. The movement should not, however, be seen in strictly sectarian terms; at least two of its most prominent leaders were Ulster Protestant.

REBELLION AND THE CIVIL WAR

The British parliament eventually passed the **Home Rule Bill** of 1912, and for a while the conditions appeared to exist for Ireland to erupt into civil war. Before this could happen, however, the outbreak of World War I dramatically altered the situation. An immediate consequence of war was that implementation of the Bill was indefinitely postponed.

For the majority of the Irish Volunteers, the primary aim of their movement was to safeguard the postwar introduction of Home Rule. Not simply to that end, but also out of loyalty to the British Crown, many of them joined the British Army. Some, however, led by Eoin MacNeill, in part supported the British war effort but were reluctant to commit too much of their strength towards defending Britain without a pledge of concrete rewards. These in turn fell under the domination of a small and secret militant faction, the revived **Irish Republican Brotherhood** (after 1916 they became the Irish Republican Army, or IRA), to whom "England's difficulty was Ireland's opportunity". They made tentative overtures for German support (and even contemplated installing a German prince as King of Ireland) but went ahead with preparations for armed insurrection regardless of whether or not they received foreign aid – indeed all but regardless of the virtual certainty of defeat.

THE EASTER RISING

The outbreak of fighting on the streets of Dublin on Easter Monday in 1916 was expected by neither the English nor the Irish Army, and was a source of bemusement to the Dubliners themselves. Republican forces swiftly took over a number of key buildings, although they missed an easy opportunity to capture the Castle itself.

The leaders of the Rising made their base in the General Post Office in O'Connell Street, and it was from there that Pádraig Pearse emerged to read the "Proclamation from The Provisional Government of the Irish Republic to the People of Ireland":

> Ireland, through us, summons her children to the flag and strikes for her freedom... The Irish Republic is entitled to, and hereby claims, the allegiance of every Irishman and Irishwoman. The Republic guarantees religious and civil liberty, equal rights and equal opportunities to all its citizens... cherishing all the children of the nation equally, and oblivious of the differences carefully fostered by an alien Government, which have divided a minority from the majority in the past.

To these fine democratic sentiments Pearse in particular added a quasi-mystical emphasis on the necessity for blood sacrifice; although potential allies such as Eoin MacNeill declined to join them with so little prospect of success, these were men prepared to give their lives as inspiration to others.

So weak was the rebel position that they only held out five days; at the time of their surrender they were even less popular with the mass of the nation than when they began, as a result of the terrible physical damage Dublin had suffered.

And yet, as the leaders of the Rising were systematically and unceremoniously executed by the British – the wounded James Connolly was shot tied to a chair – sympathy did indeed grow for the Republicans and their cause. In the words of Yeats's *Easter 1916*:

> ... changed, changed utterly:
> A terrible beauty is born.

WAR WITH BRITAIN

When the British government felt able once again to turn to Irish affairs, it found a dramatically altered situation. Sinn Féin won a resounding victory in the elections of 1918 and refused to take its seats at Westminster. Instead the newly elected MPs met in Dublin as the *Dáil Éireann* (Assembly of Ireland) and declared independence. Leadership passed to Eamonn de Valera, the sole surviving leader of the Easter Rising, whose sentence of death had been commuted. Michael Collins, the Minister of Finance in the new government and its most effective military organizer, began mobilizing the IRA for war. In January 1919, the killing of two members of the Royal Irish Constabulary (RIC), the main instrument of British power in Ireland, marked the beginning of the hostilities, which were to last for two and a half years.

The RIC experienced severe difficulties in recruiting sufficient new members (other than from Ulster). Newly demobilized British soldiers were therefore brought over from England, and by virtue of their distinctive uniforms became known as the **Black and Tans**. The Irish Republicans, fighting on home territory, were well able to hold their own in guerrilla fighting across the country, while the Black and Tans acquired an infamous reputation which endures.

The **Government of Ireland Act** of 1920 created separate parliaments for "Northern Ireland" (Derry, Antrim, Fermanagh, Down, Tyrone and Armagh) and "Southern Ireland" (the 26 counties of the present-day Republic), to remain under the nominal authority of the British Crown. Elections were held for the two bodies in 1921, but the members elected to the Southern Parliament constituted themselves instead as the **Dáil Éireann**, with De Valera as their president. With the Protestants of Ulster still firmly pledged to the Union, and the fighting at a stalemate, a negotiated settlement seemed the only way out. A truce was called in July 1921 and De Valera sent emissaries to London, including Arthur Griffith and Michael Collins, to negotiate a treaty. Lloyd George persuaded them to agree to peace terms based on the partition of the island along the terms of the Government of Ireland Act. The 26 southern counties would become not a republic but an independent nation within the British Commonwealth – the Irish Free State. The northern border, Lloyd George suggested, would be so small as to preclude the North from being a viable entity, thus bringing about eventual unity. The alternative to the treaty was, he said, "immediate and terrible war".

CIVIL WAR

The **Anglo-Irish Treaty** was signed in London on December 6, 1921, and hailed by Lloyd George as "one of the greatest days in the history of the British Empire". A provisional government was formed in Ireland in January 1922, pending elections. The link with Britain had been broken at last – but not completely or cleanly enough for a militant minority in Ireland. During the negotiations, Griffith and Collins in London and De Valera in Dublin had failed to agree a clear line on an acceptable outcome. On the negotiator's return, De Valera rejected the treaty as it veered too far from the Republican ideal. He resigned from office and left the Dáil; by July he and his military supporters had plunged Ireland into a squalid and economically devastating **civil war**.

Men who had been fighting alongside each other the year before were now pitched into a bitter conflict: the "Free Staters" who supported the treaty against the Republicans who could not. In the North, the understandably alarmed Protestant community created the Ulster Special Constabulary, including the "**B Specials**" drawn from Carson's Ulster Volunteers, ostensibly to control the rioting which persistently broke out in response to events south of the border.

De Valera and his supporters were eventually forced to capitulate in May 1923; as he put it, "military victory must be allowed to rest for the moment with those who have destroyed the Republic".

THE IRISH FREE STATE

With the death of Michael Collins and Arthur Griffith during the civil war, the leadership of the Irish Free State fell to William T. Cosgrave, and finally in the summer of 1923 the new government got on with the business of building Ireland as an independent nation. A civil service was set up, along with a police force and the hydroelectric scheme on the River Shannon, which was to lead to the establishment of the ESB (Electricity Supply Board).

Meanwhile Eamonn de Valera, still an important political force, abandoned Sinn Féin's post-civil war policy of boycotting the Dáil to form his own political party in 1926. This took the explicitly mythological name of **Fianna Fáil** (Soldiers of Destiny) and was victorious in the 1932 general election. Under de Valera other state bodies were set up, including Coras Iompair Éireann (road and rail transport), Aer Lingus (air transport) and Bord na Mona (peat production). In 1933, the rival **Fine Gael** (Tribes of Gaels) party was founded.

The recession of the 1930s was made considerably worse for Ireland by the **Economic War**. De Valera had withheld repayments to England of loans made to tenants to buy their holdings; the British responded by imposing heavy duties on Irish goods.

In 1938, a new **constitution** came into effect, which finally declared Ireland's complete independence by renouncing British sovereignty. The Free State, under the new name of **Éire**, was to be governed by a two-chamber parliament (the Dáil and the Seanad), with a president (the Uachtarán), and a prime minister (the Taoiseach).

Ireland remained officially neutral during World War II, although considerable informal help was given to the Allies. De Valera, on the other hand, was the only government leader in the world to offer his commiserations – to a Nazi German minister in Dublin – on the suicide of Adolf Hitler.

THE REPUBLIC

It took the Republic (which finally came into being in 1949) twenty years to recover from the economic stagnation brought on by the war. Vast numbers of people, disproportionately drawn from among the young and talented, moved across to fill Britain's labour shortage. Not until a break was made with the past, with the accession to the premiership in 1959 of the vigorous

and expansionist **Sean Lemass**, was a sufficient level of prosperity achieved to slow down the process of chronic emigration. Foreign enterprises began investing heavily in Ireland, unemployment fell by a third, and the way was paved for the country's successful application to join the European Economic Community in 1972. The immediate benefits were enjoyed by those employed in agriculture (twenty percent of the working population), although Irish fishing waters had now to be shared with other EEC members.

Ireland's and Britain's membership of the **EEC** did not, however, bring the Republic and Northern Ireland closer together. Their membership was made official on January 22, 1972; eight days later came Bloody Sunday (see p.625), and on February 2 the British Embassy in Dublin was destroyed by an angry mob.

The international recession hit Ireland very severely in the 1980s. Emigration rocketed once again and unemployment remained consistently high. Referendums on abortion in 1983 and divorce in 1986 (both remained illegal) reflected the Catholic Church's considerable influence.

CHARLES HAUGHEY

The 1987 general election, fought principally on the issues of taxation and unemployment, resulted in accession to power of the Fianna Fáil party, led by the resilient and wily **Charles Haughey**. In the summer of 1989, Mr Haughey called another election with the intention of increasing his majority. The result, however, was a Fianna Fáil/Progressive Democrat alliance, in which Haughey's hold on power always seemed tenuous.

The presidential election of 1991 yielded a surprise result when the feminist lawyer **Mary Robinson**, an independent candidate supported by Labour and Workers' parties, was elected. Some in Haughey's party (and outside) accused the Taoiseach of sabotaging the campaign of his own party's candidate, Brian Lenihan (an old rival), but whatever the causes of her success, there can be no doubt that the president breathed new life into the office and into Irish politics in general: as a woman, and as a representative of causes outside the old two-party stalemate. In particular, her election gave hope to many that a new era of greater integrity and **liberalism** in politics, and perhaps some easing of positions on the intractable problems of the North, was about to dawn.

Early in 1992, Charles Haughey, whose government was weighed down by constant (and later to be proven) allegations of financial mismanagement and even corruption, resigned. The final straw came when Sean Doherty, speaker of the Seanad and a former minister under Haughey, claimed that he personally had delivered tapes of tapped phone calls, made by journalists unfriendly to Fianna Fáil, to Mr Haughey in 1982. Although Haughey denied any knowledge of such tapes, the threat of his coalition falling apart finally forced him to resign.

FROM ALBERT REYNOLDS TO BERTIE AHERN

The new prime minister, **Albert Reynolds**, took over the leadership of a seemingly exhausted Fianna Fáil party. His downfall, however, less than three years later, was due to a moral issue – as so often in Irish politics. Reynolds' years as prime minister were plagued by scandal and the powerful influence of the Church in public and political life. An early case was that of the fourteen-year-old rape victim whom the Irish High Court at first refused to allow to go to Britain to seek an abortion. In May 1992 came the dramatic confessions of an American woman, former lover of Dr Eamonn Casey, the Bishop of Galway, who had apparently been using church funds to bring up his teenage son. Then, in 1993, it emerged that warrants from Belfast for the extradition of the paedophile priest Father Brendan Smyth had been ignored for several months. The government – under pressure from the Church – continued to cover up the scandal, but in November 1994, after questions in the Dáil, the prime minister's part in the affair came to light and he was forced to resign. It didn't help that at the same time a 68-year-old priest, Liam Cosgrave, died in a Dublin gay sauna club; this spate of clerical scandals caused disarray among Irish Catholics and would appear to have irrevocably undermined the Church's authority on moral issues.

Since 1994, there has been a series of coalition governments. The current one is Fianna Fáil-led, under their new leader **Bertie Ahern**. Ahern's term in office has been dogged with damaging **financial scandals**, involving leading figures in his party, notably Charles Haughey and foreign minister, Ray Burke. Haughey was found guilty in 1997 of taking a "gift" of £1.3 million from top Irish businessman, Ben Dunne.

Shortly afterwards, Burke resigned when it was revealed he had received £30,000 from a company wanting to develop land in his constituency. One positive outcome of these scandals has been the passing of an Ethics in Public Office Act – evidence that Ireland is developing into something approaching a mature democracy.

The presidential election in October 1997 saw another woman, **Mary McAleese**, elected to the post. Her politics, however, differ fundamentally from her predecessor's. Born in Belfast, President McAleese's politics are Nationalist and influenced by her strongly-held Catholic beliefs (she is ardently pro-life). However, it was the greenness of her Nationalism not her social conservatism that caused concern for some southerners during her election campaign. There were fears that she might alienate Ulster Unionists at a delicate time in the peace process (she had once described Northern Ireland as "the archetypal police state"). Other critics worried that her campaigning zeal, most in evidence in her role as Vice-Chancellor of Queen's University, Belfast, would be inappropriate for the apolitical position of president. These fears, however, have not been realized.

One of the most significant developments in Irish society in the nineties has been the staggering growth of the country's GDP, earning it the epithet "Celtic Tiger", an allusion to the tiger economies of South East Asia. The reasons for this impressive performance are manifold, but are chiefly due to the granting of generous tax concessions to multinationals, economic support from Europe and a young, highly educated workforce. However, there are doubts over the sustainability of this growth. The main criticism of the economy is that growth is concentrated in five high-tech sectors, owned by multinationals, attracted to Ireland by generous tax concessions. Indigenous industries, on the other hand, are showing no real growth in comparison. This has resulted in a high-growth multinational and a sluggish indigenous sector sitting uncomfortably side by side. There are also concerns that only certain sectors of society are benefiting from the recent wealth-creation and that social inequalities are growing.

NORTHERN IRELAND FROM 1921

On June 22, 1921, the new political entity of Northern Ireland came into existence with the opening of the **Northern Irish Parliament** in

Belfast's City Hall. In order to understand the present situation in the North it is necessary to grasp the political background to this development. Since the settlements of the seventeenth century, the Protestant descendants of the settlers had been concentrated in the northern part of the island; they rarely intermarried with the local people or assimilated into the native culture, feeling both superior to and threatened by the Catholics, who formed the vast majority of the population of Ireland as a whole. The economically dominant group in the northern counties was essentially Protestant, and when an industrial base developed in this part of the island, the prosperity of the region was inextricably tied to the trading power of Britain. In negotiating for their exclusion from the new Irish state, Carson and the Unionist Council decided to accept just six counties of Ulster out of a possible nine, because only in this way could a safe Protestant majority be guaranteed. Thus Westminster gave political power into the hands of those whose pro-British sympathies were certain.

The Unionists were not slow to exploit their supremacy: a Protestant police force and military were set up, and "gerrymandering" (the redrawing of boundary lines in order to control the outcome of elections) was commonplace, so securing Protestant control even in areas with Catholic majorities. Thus Derry City, with a two-thirds Catholic majority, returned a two-thirds Protestant council. Nothing was done to rectify the situation for several decades. The Catholic community was to benefit from the British welfare state, but they were discriminated against in innumerable ways, most notoriously in jobs and also in housing, an area controlled by Protestant local authorities.

CIVIL RIGHTS

In 1967, inspired by the civil rights movement in America, the Northern Irish **Civil Rights Movement** was born, a nonsectarian organization demanding equality of rights for all. Massively supported by the Catholic community, the campaign led to huge protest marches, some of which were viciously attacked by Loyalist mobs. The **RUC** (Royal Ulster Constabulary) rarely intervened, and when they did take action, it was generally not to protect the Catholics. The Apprentice Boys' march of 1969 proved to be the flashpoint. This triumphal procession, commemorating the city's siege in 1689 (see p.534), annually passes through Derry's Catholic areas. The 1969 march provoked rioting that ended in the Catholic community barricading themselves in and Jack Lynch, the Irish prime minister, mobilizing Irish troops and setting up field hospitals on the border.

On August 14, British troops were sent to Derry to protect the besieged minority, and at first they were welcomed by the Catholics, who were relieved to see the troops pushing back the RUC and B Specials. Belief in the neutrality of the British army did not last long, however. Escalating violence between the two communities across the North forced the army into a more interventionist role, but confusion arose as to whether **Stormont** (the Northern Parliament) or Westminster was giving the orders. Before long the army was acting not as a protective force but as a retaliatory one, and it was clear that retaliation against the Catholics was far harsher than measures taken against the Protestants. With the Catholics again vulnerable, the resurgent IRA quickly assumed the role of defenders of the ghetto areas of Derry and Belfast. Within a few months the **Provisional IRA**, now stronger than the less militant Official wing of the organization, had launched an intensive bombing and shooting campaign across the North.

At the request of Brian Faulkner, prime minister of Northern Ireland, **internment without trial** was introduced in 1971, a measure which was used as an indiscriminate weapon against the minority population. Then, on Sunday, January 30, 1972, thirteen unarmed civil rights demonstrators were shot dead by British paratroopers in Derry, an event that shocked the world and was to become known as **Bloody Sunday**. The Irish government declared February 2 a national day of mourning; on the same day an angry crowd in Dublin burned down the British Embassy. Stormont was suspended and direct rule from Westminster imposed.

POWER SHARING AND ITS AFTERMATH

In 1973 a conference was held at **Sunningdale** between representatives of the British and Irish governments and both sections of the community in Northern Ireland, a meeting that led to the creation of a power-sharing executive representing both Unionists and Nationalists. An elected executive took office in November 1973, but in May of the next year the United Ulster Unionist Council responded by organizing a massive strike which, enforced by the road-blocks of the UDA (Ulster Defence Association), crippled the power stations and other essential services run by a strongly Unionist workforce. In the same week as the strike, three car bombs planted by the UDA exploded in Dublin, without warning, at rush hour – 33 people were killed, the highest death toll since 1969. By the end of the month, the Sunningdale executive – the first ever to have Catholic representation – was disbanded, and direct rule from Westminster has continued to the present day.

Almost immediately a **bombing campaign** was launched in Britain by the IRA, aimed at destabilizing the government by provoking public revulsion. Twenty-one people were killed in a pub bombing in Birmingham in 1974, and in the same month seven people died in simultaneous pub bombings in Woolwich and **Guildford**. The British response was to introduce the **Prevention of Terrorism Act**, permitting lengthy detention without charge. Four people were arrested for the Guildford bombings and convicted on the basis of confessions which even at the time were thought by many people to be unreliable. After fifteen years of imprisonment, all four were released when the judiciary finally conceded, with no hint of regret for the injustice, that they were indeed innocent. Six Irish people were given life sentences for the Birmingham attack, and their convictions, too, were finally overthrown in 1991.

In 1976 Special Category Status was abolished for future prisoners in Northern Ireland (previously those arrested for offences connected with what had become known as the Troubles enjoyed the status of political prisoners), and when Republican prisoners refused to wear prison uniforms in accordance with their change in status, prisoners were locked naked in their cells in Long Kesh – the beginning of the famous "**blanket protest**" (see p.548). In 1978 Britain was found guilty by the European Court of Human Rights of "inhuman and degrading treatment" of Republican prisoners. Soon afterwards in Northern Ireland the "dirty protest" began in Long Kesh and Armagh women's prison, with Republican prisoners forcing the issue of political status by refusing to wear criminal uniform or slop out their cells. In late 1980 a **hunger strike** for the same demands was called off when one of the strikers was close to death. The following March, a hunger strike was begun by **Bobby Sands**, who on April 11 was elected as MP for Fermanagh and South Tyrone. By the day of his election, nine other Republicans had joined the hunger strike. All ten died, an outcome that brought widespread condemnation of British intransigence.

THE ANGLO-IRISH AGREEMENT AND THE DOWNING STREET DECLARATION

The year 1982 saw the British government make a timid attempt to break the impasse, introducing the **Northern Ireland Assembly**, a power-sharing body with some legislative but no executive powers. It was boycotted by the Nationalists, and survived only until 1985, by which time the final stages had been reached in the negotiations over the **Anglo-Irish Agreement**. Largely drafted by John Hume, the leader of the moderate Nationalist SDLP, and signed in 1986, it instituted official co-operation between Dublin and Westminster on security and other issues, and strengthened the consultative part played by Dublin in Northern affairs. Unfortunately, the Agreement was weakened by the non-participation of the Ulster Unionists, who had not been involved in its preparation, in the processes it inaugurated.

The next major step in addressing the stalemate in the North came with the **Downing Street Declaration** of December 1993. Brokered courageously, once again, by John Hume, and issued jointly by the Irish and British premiers, Albert Reynolds and John Major, it signalled a new readiness for dialogue with all sides involved in the Troubles – including Sinn Féin and the IRA. Previously, the Republican movement had been "psychopaths, godfathers, crypto-fascists", and worse; now, in a remarkable volte-face, they were people who could be reasoned with. They were repeatedly assured of their place at a negotiating table if they embraced the Downing Street Declaration and if the violence stopped.

The Irish government's ban on broadcast of interviews with, or direct statements by, representatives of Sinn Féin, the IRA and other organizations associated with militant Nationalism or militant Loyalism fell due for renewal just a month after the Downing Street Declaration. This ban, which provided the inspiration for a similar, though less restrictive, prohibition in Britain, had been consistently opposed by civil liberties organizations and media professionals, and the government had it under review for months before the Downing Street Declaration. In a rare example of liberal leadership to Britain, the Irish government decided not to renew the ban, and was subsequently followed by the British government.

THE CEASEFIRE, THE PEACE PROCESS AND THE GOOD FRIDAY AGREEMENT

In July 1994, a Sinn Féin conference rejected the Downing Street Declaration, but continued political bargaining by Albert Reynolds and lobbying by Irish-American groups eventually persuaded the party of the virtues of participation in a nationalist coalition. On August 31, 1994, the IRA declared a "complete cessation" of military activities. Loyalist paramilitaries announced their own **cease-fire** two months later.

After further negotiation, in February 1995, the London and Dublin governments produced a framework document which attempted to satisfy some of the Republicans' constitutional demands, including provision for an all-Ireland authority with far-reaching executive powers.

Major's precondition that the IRA should commence decommissioning its weaponry before Sinn Féin be allowed to participate in the all-party talks proved a huge stumbling block. Seen by Republicans as a demand for the IRA's unconditional surrender, the deadlock was not broken until the establishment of an international commission in November 1995 to advise on the decommissioning process. Chaired by the US senator George Mitchell, it recommended that talks should go ahead in tandem with the handing over of weapons. Crucially, the report detailed six conditions for participation in such talks. Known as the **Mitchell Principles**, these included an overriding commitment to peaceful and democratic principles and all-party consensus and acceptance of the outcome of the political process. However, in the absence of any weaponry being yielded, and bowing to Unionist pressure, the British Government unilaterally announced its intention to hold elections in May 1997 for participation in the all-party talks which would commence in June if the IRA maintained its cease-fire.

The patience of Republicans, however, was being severely tested by what they saw as British intransigence. Sinn Féin's insistence on the whole of the Irish people's right to national

self-determination meant that it could not accept the principle of majority consent in Northern Ireland. The IRA's cease-fire was itself essentially fragile and its threats of a return to violence if the political process did not achieve its desired ends became reality with the explosion on February 9, 1996 of a massive **bomb** near London's **Canary Wharf**, killing two people, injuring many more and causing several hundred million pounds of damage to buildings.

Many feared this was the end of the process, but support for political change in Northern Ireland remained powerful and vociferous. The key players remained active, not least the SDLP leader, John Hume, who saw negotiation in the absence of Sinn Féin as redundant and resumed contact with Gerry Adams, seeking a restoration of the IRA's cease-fire. This call was reiterated by **Bill Clinton** whose support for the peace process had become much greater than a simple desire to target the Irish-American vote. Adams was permitted entry to the United States and the White House became a vital intermediary, risking the displeasure of its traditional ally. Signs that the political stalemate might be over came with the election of new parties and leaders in both Britain and the Republic. Elected by an enormous majority, the first Labour Prime Minister for eighteen years, **Tony Blair**, made clear his commitment to the Northern Ireland peace process in his visit to Belfast less than two weeks after his election in May 1997. **Mo Mowlam** was his inspired choice as Northern Ireland Secretary. As the first woman to hold the post, her bluff no-nonsense "matey" approach was to undermine significantly the suspicions of many involved in the peace process. The following month, Bertie Ahern's Fianna Fáil won the Republic's General Election. **Ahern**, along with Foreign Secretary **Dick Spring**, was to play a major role in subsequent events, not least in becoming the first Taoiseach to meet the leader of the Ulster Unionists. It was his securing of the trust of David Trimble which was to have huge significance in later events.

The elections for the **all-party talks** took place at the end of May 1997. Sinn Féin had obtained a large enough vote to participate, but could not do so because of the IRA's refusal to return to a state of cease-fire. However, intense lobbying within Republican circles resulted in the IRA's announcement of "an unequivocal restoration of the cease-fire of August 1994" on

July 19, 1997. Though Sinn Féin was now actively engaged and **Gerry Adams** was to make a historic visit to **Downing Street**, at Blair's invitation, on December 9, 1997, little demonstrable progress was made until the following year. Violation of the principles set out by George Mitchell, who had been appointed chair of the talks, led to representatives of the Loyalist paramilitaries and, later, Sinn Féin being suspended. Moreover, the INLA's assassination of the LVF's leader, **Billy Wright**, in the Maze prison just before Christmas 1997 threatened a full-scale return to the violence of the past. The IRA's and Loyalist groups' cease-fires seemed increasingly precarious, especially once dissident Loyalists embarked on a spree of random sectarian attacks. In March 1998, two close friends were shot dead in the Railway Bar in **Poyntzpass**, County Armagh, a village regarded as one of the friendliest and most integrated in Northern Ireland. That one of the pair was Catholic and the other Protestant enhanced the general outrage at the killings and the increasing pointlessness of violence as a solution to the Troubles. Blair seized the impetus by declaring that the all-party talks had to reach a compromise by April 9, 1998 or the process was finished for the foreseeable future.

As the deadline loomed nearer, the chances of a successful conclusion seemed to recede and the day and night of April 9 saw a frenzy of activity and frantic negotiation. Finally, a settlement was achieved and the agreement, known as the **Good Friday Agreement**, was signed on April 10, 1998. It was, without doubt, the most significant development in the political history of Northern Ireland. The agreement committed its signatories "to partnership, equality and mutual respect as the basis of relationships within Northern Ireland" and reaffirmed the participants' dedication "to exclusively democratic and peaceful means of resolving differences on political issues". The principle of "consent" lay at the agreement's core. Hugely significant in securing Unionist and Loyalist support, this categorically stated that both governments would respect the legitimacy of the wishes of the majority of the people of Northern Ireland, whether that be to remain part of the United Kingdom or, at some later date, to become part of a united Ireland. In reinforcement, the two governments also agreed to make legal changes – the British Government to repeal the

Government of Ireland Act 1920 asserting the sovereignty of the United Kingdom's Parliament over Ireland, and the Irish to hold a referendum on Articles Two and Three of its constitution, claiming territorial sovereignty over the North.

Further provisions included the establishment of a 108-member **Assembly**, elected by proportional representation to ensure the rights of Nationalists, and with a twelve-strong executive committee of ministers appointed on a cross-community basis. The Assembly would have legislative and executive authority over six departments previously run by the British government's Northern Ireland Ministers. An intergovernmental Council of the Isles was also to be established, with membership from the Assembly, Dáil, Commons and the new devolved Welsh and Scottish assemblies. The signatories also committed themselves to the incorporation of the European Convention of Human Rights into Northern Ireland law and the establishment of a new Northern Ireland Human Rights Commission. Apart from the consent principle, the most controversial aspects of the agreement dealt with the accelerated release of political prisoners (an issue that divided the Ulster Unionist Party) and the establishment of an independent commission to review the RUC and the future of policing in the North. In addition, the agreement's signatories "reaffirmed their commitment to the total disarmament of all paramilitary organization". However, at the time of writing, the issue of the **decommissioning** of terrorist weaponry has yet to be resolved. As yet, no arms have been handed over and Unionists continue to argue with vehemence that this should debar Sinn Féin from membership of the Assembly's executive.

On May 22, 1998, the people of Northern Ireland took part in a **referendum** on the agreement while, simultaneously, the people of the Republic voted on the proposal to amend the Irish constitution. There were strong divisions within the Unionist camp with both Ian Paisley's DUP and Bob McCartney's UKU urging opposition to any potential loosening of the bonds with the United Kingdom. The turnout in the North was an unprecedented 81 per cent, of whom 71.12 per cent supported the settlement, enough to suggest that Trimble had been backed by a majority of Unionist voters. Though the Republic's turn-out was lower, a massive 94.4 per cent ratified the deal. In the consequent assembly elections in June, enough pro-agreement Ulster Unionists and Progressive Unionists were returned to guarantee Trimble a working majority over dissident Unionist parties, while the SDLP and Sinn Féin both received handsome support. For the first time since 1972, Northern Ireland had its own form of government and, for the first time ever, one that largely represented the composition of the electorate. **David Trimble** was elected its **First Minister** and the SDLP's **Seamus Mallon** his **deputy**.

The first test for the new political order in Northern Ireland came in July 1998, the traditional climax of the Orange Order's marching season. Since 1995, the Orangemen's march on the Sunday before the "Glorious 12th" from Drumcree Church to its lodge in Portadown, County Armagh, via the predominantly Nationalist Garvaghy Road, had become a focus for the assertion of traditional Unionist rights and identity. The **July 1998 parade** took on extra significance in the light of the peace agreement and the asserted intention of many dissident Unionists to embody the spirit of their opposition in the march. However, when the march was banned by the Parades Commission, Orangemen reacted by employing a strategy of brinkmanship, calling Unionists and Loyalists from all over Northern Ireland to assemble at Portadown, knowing full well that the RUC and army had already set up blockades to prevent them marching down the road. Mass demonstrations at the barricades inspired an astonishing wave of violence throughout Northern Ireland. There were numerous attacks on Catholics and their property and, much to the horror of more conservative Unionists, on members of the RUC itself. A tragic event in County Antrim led to many Orangemen abandoning their protest. Early in the morning of July 12, the home of Chrissie Quinn, a Catholic woman living on the mainly Protestant Carmany estate in Ballymoney, County Antrim, was fire-bombed. In the resulting conflagration, three of her four young sons were burned to death. Condemnation of this outrage brought to the boil divisions within the Orange Order which had already been simmering over the tactics employed at Drumcree. Rev. William Bingham, the Order's County Chaplain for Armagh, called

for the demonstrations to be abandoned, asserting that "a fifteen minute walk down Garvaghy Road would be ... in the shadow of the coffins of three little boys who wouldn't even know what the Orange Order is about". David Trimble, who had played an important role in previous Drumcree confrontations, stated simply that "no road is worth these lives". The Church of Ireland refused the Order permission to camp on its land and the demonstration gradually fizzled out, leaving residual questions about the continued relevance of the Orange Order to the new Northern Ireland.

Many hoped that the **tragic deaths** of the **Quinn children** in Ballymoney would be the last politically motivated killings in Northern Ireland, but this illusion was shattered by events on Saturday, August 15 1998 in the County Tyrone town of **Omagh**. A dissident Republican group calling itself the Real IRA had embarked upon a campaign of town centre bombings to express its opposition to the Accord and jeopardise continued Republican involvement in the peace process. Misleading telephone warnings led the RUC to evacuate people to the very area where a bomb had been planted and 29 people were killed and hundreds injured when the device exploded. It was the worst single atrocity in the entire thirty years of conflict in Northern Ireland. Politicians acted frantically to deter a Loyalist backlash, but were aided by an unprecedented statement by Gerry Adams who, visiting Omagh, declared his unequivocal condemnation of the bombing. Both Irish and British governments announced their intention to strengthen existing legislation against terrorism and, two weeks later the Real IRA declared a cease-fire.

As we go to press, all Loyalist and Republican paramilitary cease-fires are still in place, with the exception of the tiny Continuity IRA. The Real IRA's announcement helped to ease the tension surrounding the historic first **face-to-face meeting** between David Trimble and Gerry Adams at the beginning of September 1998. They may have stopped short of shaking hands, but their very contact demonstrates just how much progress has been made towards a lasting settlement. The international community's recognition of this came in October 1998 with the award of the **Nobel peace prize** to Trimble and John Hume.

ENVIRONMENT AND WILDLIFE

Ireland conjures up images of a romantic wild territory unscarred by human activity – a somewhat rosy picture, but with more than a little truth to it. Genuine wilderness may be scarce, but centuries of economic deprivation have ensured that most of Ireland is a rural landscape in which the only intervention has come from generations of farmers.

The topography of Ireland is fairly homogenous: there are few high mountain ranges and most of the centre of the country is covered by a flat boggy plain. And with only four degrees of latitude from north to south, it lacks extremes of weather, the enveloping Atlantic Ocean producing a mild, damp climate. Summers are rarely hot, winters rarely cold, and in parts of the west it rains on two days out of every three.

In these conditions you'd expect to find broad-leaved woodland, but intensive pressure on the landscape during the centuries leading up to the Great Famine of 1845–49 denuded the country of its original tree cover. It has been replaced mostly by a patchwork of small grass fields divided by wild untidy hedgerows – long lines of trees acting as refuges for the former woodland community of plants and animals. (In common with many islands, Ireland has a limited number of animal species – there are no snakes, no moles and no woodpeckers, for instance.) The small population in Ireland today means that over much of the country the inten-

sity of land use is lower than in many other European countries. Mixed farms are still more common than specialized intensive units. Visitor numbers in the countryside are still small, and it is possible to find long sandy beaches that are completely deserted even in summer.

Natural habitats such as peat bogs, dunes and wetlands still survive here, having all but disappeared elsewhere under the relentless pace of modern development. However, the pressures are growing. The great midland bogs are being rapidly stripped for fuel; mountainsides are disappearing under blankets of exotic conifers; shoals of dead fish are becoming all too frequent a sight in Irish waterways; and rapid housing developments threaten some of Ireland's most valuable habitats, most notably in coastal regions.

BOGS

Ten thousand years ago, when glaciers and ice sheets had stripped the soil from the Burren and retreated to the north, their melting ice left central Ireland covered by shallow lakes. As time went by, the lakeside vegetation grew, died and partly decomposed, in a cycle which changed these lakes to fens, and then the fens to bogs. Bogs – or peatland – now cover around one sixth of Ireland's total landmass, a proportion in Europe topped only by Finland. It is now recognized internationally that bogs provide habitats of great ecological value. However, although considerable progress has been made in their conservation, the Irish government has only conserved 61 percent of its proposed target area, a mere six percent of the original peatland surveyed.

The bogs are a remarkable legacy, not only in terms of biodiversity, but also as a living repository of cultural history. The bog is a great natural preservative, and along with providing botanists with a calendar of plant history over the past 9000 years, it has bequeathed a great deal to archeologists – dug-out canoes, gold and silver artefacts, shoes, amber beads and, of course, bodies in extraordinarily good condition. Bog pools were revered during the Bronze Age, and votive offerings such as weapons and ornaments were placed there. Iron Age wooden pathways (*tochair*) for crossing the bogs have also been discovered.

The exploitation of the boglands has been going on for centuries. Dried peat sods have always been used for fuel; the top layer of matted vegetation was once used to insulate thatched roofs; and preserved timbers dug from the bog – some of them 5000 years old – provided stout beams for lintels. The lime-rich marl below the peat was used to fertilize the land. In World War I sphagnum moss from the bogs was used for wound dressings, and extract of the carnivorous sundew was a traditional remedy for warts. Bogs occupy a unique place in folk history, too, and the annual ritual of "saving the turf" is well represented in stories, poetry and song, carrying with it traditions as strong as any other form of harvest.

Bogs fall into three main categories: blanket bog, raised bog and fen. Found in both low-lying and mountainous areas, **blanket bogs** are characterized by a layer of peat between six and twenty feet thick covering large areas of land. They support a range of plantlife, most notably black bog rush, purple moor grass, sphagnum mosses and milkwort. For the finest example of relatively undamaged blanket bog, head for the Slieve Bloom Mountains, straddling counties Laois and Offaly; the two mountain roads that divide the range rise to 1300ft, with wonderful views in every direction. You'll also find good examples in the dramatic landscapes of Connemara, Mayo and Donegal, with their huge expanses of wild, treeless and exposed countryside.

Somewhat smaller, and favoured by commercial operators, **raised bogs** are found in the central lowlands, domed in shape, with an average peat layer of 23ft, though they can develop to nearly twice that. You'll find a range of plantlife, including bog cotton, sphagnum moss, sundew, ling heather, cranberry and cladonia lichen. To see a raised bog of international importance, go to Mongan Bog in County Offaly.

Fens are found in waterlogged areas and lakesides and are different from blanket and raised bogs in that the layer of peat is only about two metres deep. The plantlife found in fens is quite different from that found in bogs, largely because here the water source is mineral-rich; you can expect to find fen rush, bog bean, saw sedge, pond weed, marsh marigold and flag iris, as well as various orchids, particularly marsh helleborine and the marsh orchid. A fine example of a fen is Pollardstown Fen, two miles northeast of Newbridge, Co. Kildare. For an excellent introduction to Irish bogs, drop into nearby **Peatland World**, in Lullymore (see p.127).

WOODLANDS

At one time Ireland was covered in oakwoods. This great forest canopy also included elm and alder, and holly grew beneath the tall trees. The first major clearances of woodlands were in the late Stone Age (5000 years ago), but vast areas of forest survived well into the medieval period. However, by the eighteenth century, felling for housing, shipping and smelting had become so extensive that wood actually had to be imported. Today, only six percent of Ireland is woodland (the lowest percentage of any European country), and afforestation in recent decades has tended to be coniferous, causing immense damage to natural habitats. As a result, **indigenous oak forests** are extremely rare, though good examples can still be seen at Glengarriff and in the National Parks at Killarney and Glenveagh. Throughout the country, strong westerly winds keep the treeline low (from about 490ft in the west to 1150ft in the east), and small trees growing diagonally towards the east as if swept by one almighty blast are a common sight in exposed areas, particularly in the west. The limited range of flowers found in forests include foxgloves, violets and primroses – this last growing in abundance, and flowering from March to May. Luckily, numerous hedgerows go some way to compensate for this shortfall in woodland habitat and here lichens, flowering plants, ferns and woody climbers thrive. The eastern midland counties consist largely of developed farming land. However, for all the trim maintenance of the stud farms and estates, the lanes burst with frothy white cow parsley in late spring, bright yellow cowslips are common in the meadows, and the ever-abundant hawthorn and the delicate spiky blackthorn form blossom-filled hedgerows in spring.

MOUNTAINS

Though renowned for the beauty of its wild mountainous regions, by European standards Ireland's mountains are actually fairly small. The mountains of the **Iveragh Peninsula**, Co. Kerry, form one of Ireland's most spectacular ranges, and yet here **Carrauntoohil**, Ireland's highest peak, is only 3414ft. In the valleys of Kerry's national park you'll see holly, rowan and the strawberry tree, while common on the mountainsides are various heathers, forming a beautiful purple cloak when in bloom in September.

The Maam Turk Mountains of Connemara have a somewhat colder climate and the plantlife is sparser; St Dabeoc's heath is a common sight and wild London Pride proliferates in the west of the region. River valleys in the **Mourne Mountains** support hazel, birch and holly, and above 860ft, ling and bell heather are widespread, crowberry and woolly fringe moss less so. Lower boggy hills and heaths support yellow gorse, most splendidly in Co. Wexford; the county is a blaze of colour from March though to June, and the air is laden with the gorse's heady scent of vanilla.

Mountainous regions also provide rocky crags and cliffs for **birds of prey**. The little-visited **Sperrin Mountains** in Co. Tyrone are noted for buzzards, hen harriers and sparrowhawks, and both here and in the Mourne Mountains you can see peregrine falcons and kestrels. In the uplands of the **Wicklow Mountains**, hen harriers are easily sighted, and other species include ouzel and red grouse, typical of heather-clad moorland. Although you'll no longer see golden eagles in the wild mountains of Cork, you can still catch sight of merlins and sparrowhawks. Wild goats can occasionally be spotted on remote hillsides, though have been known to explore Mayo villages.

THE COASTS

With over 2000 miles of **coast**, most of it undeveloped, and hundreds of **islands**, there is plenty of variety along the Irish coast. The wild coasts of the north and west have the most dramatic scenic appeal.

Co. Kerry and the peninsulas of West Cork benefit from a damp climate which, because of the Gulf Stream, is far warmer than elsewhere in the country. Consequently it's here that you'll find Ireland's limited number of fairly **exotic plant species**, including palm trees, the Mediterranean strawberry tree, (or arbutus) and very rare Lusitanian plants including Irish spurge and St Patrick's Cabbage, the latter found nowhere else in Europe.

The west coast cliffs also shelter large colonies of **birds**. Razorbills, guillemots, kittiwakes, shags and seven different types of gulls are among the commonest species. Ireland's largest colony of razorbill can be found on the spectacular cliffs of **Horn Head**, Co. Donegal, while **Kerry's islands** are among the best spots for observing puffins, gannets, manx

shearwaters and storm petrels. The best time to see breeding seabirds is in early summer (May and June), but later in the year you can watch large flocks on the move by positioning yourself on a prominent headland.

Clear Island, off the West Cork coast, is the site of an important observatory, from which the patterns of migratory birds are recorded. You'll see huge numbers of manx shearwaters here, as well as gannets, fulmars and kittiwakes. Other good spots for birdwatching include the spectacular Antrim coast and the Wexford Sloblands, the wintering ground for around 10,000 Greenland Whitefronted Geese.

The remoteness of the islands off the west coast make them havens for **marine life**: grey seals breed on island beaches and in caves during autumn months, while herds of common seals can be seen basking on sandbanks in numerous locations along the west coast. Nocturnal animals, such as otters, often venture out during the daytime, hunting for food among rocks and pools.

Patient sea-watching from a western headland may also be rewarded with a school of **dolphins** or porpoises, or the occasional **whale** feeding in the rich inshore waters. Whales might also be seen off the east coast of the Ards Peninsula, and if you're lucky you may even see basking sharks.

Extensive **sand dunes** are a common feature in some counties, notably Donegal, Mayo and Kerry. In summer, these are clothed in a profusion of wild flowers such as the yellow bird's foot trefoil and pink sea bindweed. Prickly-leafed sea holly, sea pansy and kidney vetch are common, and the exotic-looking bee orchid is one of the rarities sometimes found in the dunes. The absence of tree cover means few breeding birds, but **cuckoos** are a special feature of Irish sand dunes, as they exploit the nests of the ubiquitous meadow pipits. The chough, a comparatively rare crow, breeds extensively on the south and west coasts and can be seen in large flocks feeding in sand dunes. The low sandy coasts of the northwest, particularly where they adjoin small lakes or marshes, are populated by dunlin and lapwing.

Ireland's low coasts, especially on the east and south, are punctuated by **estuaries**, some with vast, lonely mudflats. Despite their bare appearance, below the surface they harbour countless shellfish and other burrowing ani-

USEFUL ADDRESSES

ENFO, 17 St Andrew St, Dublin 2
(☎01/679 3144).
Invaluable resource centre for information on
environmental issues and campaign groups
in the Republic; personal visits welcome, and
a wealth of literature available.

Northern Irish Tourist Board,
59 North St, Belfast (☎01232/246609;
☎0281 9024 6609 from April 2000).
Detailed information on birdwatching in
Northern Ireland.

mals, attracting feeding **waders** and wildfowl. From October to April, the estuaries are alive with the calls of curlews, redshanks, godwits, widgeon, teal and shoveler. Virtually all the pale-bellied brent geese to be seen in Europe are on Irish estuaries. There are also large numbers at Strangford Lough in the northeast, arriving from Arctic Canada in late August.

LAKELANDS

Travellers in the midlands and west of Ireland will encounter numerous small **lakes** and reed-fringed **marshes**. High rainfall and poor drainage ensure plentiful surface water, especially in winter, and breeding **water birds** are extremely common as a result. Every waterway has its resident pair of swans, moorhens and herons. Wetlands of international importance include Lough Neagh, which supports a dozen species of duck, large numbers of Bewick's and whooper swans, terns and grebes, and the Shannon Callows near Clonmacnois, where, in late summer, you can hear corncrakes as they search for mates. For Ireland's biggest corncrake population you will need to travel to Inishowen, and Malin Head in particular.

THE BURREN

The limestone karst region of the **Burren** in Co. Clare is a landscape of unique ecological importance. From a distance, its virtually treeless slopes appear completely barren, but the long cracks and grooves in the limestone support and shelter an astonishing array of both **alpine and arctic plants**: hart's tongue and maidenhair ferns grow well, and the profusion of wild flowers includes the blue spring gentian and mountain avens, saxifrages and a number of orchid species; the best times to vists are spring and early summer. For more on the geology and flora of the Burren, see box on p.333.

ARCHITECTURE

BEGINNINGS

The most tangible legacy left by the inhabitants of prehistoric Ireland are the numerous stone tombs, found throughout the country. The earliest of these date from the Neolithic period (3700–2000 BC) and the simplest form is the **dolmen**. Resembling a tripod, this is usually formed by several standing stones supporting one or two capstones, the largest of which can be as much as 20ft long. While these simply marked a grave, the **court-cairn** was more complex, consisting of a rectangular burial chamber, again built with large stones, and covered by a mound of earth. Conceptually similar, though most advanced of all, however, are the **passage-graves**, of which the best-known examples are clustered near Drogheda, in the valley of the River Boyne, at Newgrange, Howth and Dowth. As the name suggests, a passage from the edge of the mound provides access to one or two burial chambers. The **Newgrange** grave is positioned inside a circle of standing stones; its 280 ft diameter mound is almost 35ft high and the passage is 60ft long. The burial chamber's roof shows its builders' grasp of the technique of corbelling where layers of flat stones are placed on top of each other, each layer projecting gradually outwards below the next. Most striking here, however, is that an opening in the stonework was created to allow sunlight to penetrate the tomb on the winter solstice, December 21, the shortest day of the year, evidence of a society sophisticated in its understanding of the calendar.

The **Bronze Age** (2000–500 BC) saw further tomb-building, though the constructions were generally smaller. Most tombs surviving from this period were plain compartments of stone, though some more elaborate chambers were covered by a wedge-shaped mound. Domestic structures are thought to have been constructed of wood and daub and the most significant development, circular fortified enclosures built on hilltops, came towards the end of the period. However, the finest examples of these **hillforts** date from the **Iron Age**. The huge fortress of **Dún Aengus** on the Aran Island of Inishmore sits spectacularly on the cliff-top, while, the partially restored **Grianán of Aileach**, near Derry, affords staggering views down to Inishowen and for miles around in all directions. There is evidence of many other smaller ring forts, built of stone or earth, which were probably fortified dwellings. The Iron Age also saw the building of **crannógs**, artificial islands, set in defensive isolation in the middle of lakes.

EARLY CHRISTIAN AND MEDIEVAL PERIOD

Christianity arrived in Ireland in the fifth century and, consequently, most of the architectural remains from this period until medieval times are **ecclesiastical**. Ireland was divided into bishoprics which resulted in a system of scattered monasteries. Most buildings were constructed of wood and daub and none, whether religious or domestic, has survived. The stone churches you now see when visiting early monastic sites were constructed during a later era. However, among the ruins of **St Fionan's Abbey** on the rocky crag of Skellig Michael off the Kerry coast is a group of six dry-stone beehive huts, built according to the corbel technique. **Stone churches** began to be built in the ninth century, and an exceptional example dating from this time is **Gallarus Oratory** on the Dingle Peninsula, which represents a transition from the round beehive shape to the later rectangular church. The remains of **round towers** are often found on early monastic sites. These slender, stone, tapering structures, sometimes more than 100ft high, are a specifically Irish phenomenon. The entrance is usually several feet above ground level and it was once believed that this signified a defensive purpose. However, it now seems that they were used as bell-towers and the doorway's elevation was purely for structural purposes. One of the best-preserved towers is part of the St Molaise monastic complex on **Devenish Island** in Lower Lough Erne, near Enniskillen, Co. Fermanagh.

Increasing contact with England and continental Europe saw the introduction of the highly decorative **Romanesque** style to Irish ecclesiastical architecture from the twelfth century onwards. Built between 1127 and 1134, the beautiful, twin-towered **Cormac's Chapel** in Cashel, Co. Tipperary, is the earliest and best surviving example, though much smaller in scale than its European counterparts. Gradually, the simple box style of church architecture began to be superseded by the **basilica** style, characterized by a nave, side aisles and a round apse at the eastern end. Often, church doorways and chancel arches were decorated with intricate sculpture using traditional Celtic motifs, such as interlacing and animal patterns, seen to tremendous effect in the wonderful six-arched doorway of **Clonfert Cathedral**, Co. Galway.

Further changes resulted from the arrival of monastic orders, such as the Cistercians, Dominicans and Benedictines. They favoured large cruciform churches and their settlements, typified by the Cistercian **Boyle Abbey**, Co. Roscommon, were very European in their layout of a cloister surrounded by church, chapter house and domestic buildings.

Much of Ireland was under **Norman** subjugation by the end of the twelfth century and the invaders constructed fortifications to protect their new domains. The earliest of these were earthworks surmounted by wooden forts. However, soon more substantial **stone castles**, distinguished by a massive keep, began to be constructed, such as those at **Carrickfergus**, Co. Antrim, and **Trim**, Co. Meath. The fifteenth-century castle at **Cahir** in Co. Tipperary, surrounded by high enclosing walls and defended by eight towers, is the most impressive of the surviving feudal strongholds.

Simultaneously, the Anglo-Normans, as they came to be known, introduced **Gothic** architecture to Ireland. The huge new **cathedrals**, constructed in the main towns, were characterized by the use of high-pointed arches and clustered columns. Dublin's two thirteenth-century cathedrals, **St Patrick's** and **Christchurch**, are among the finest examples of this innovation.

Later Anglo-Norman fortifications tended to be smaller in size, typified by the **tower hous-**es which began to be constructed during the fifteenth century and continued to be built over the next two hundred years. There are the remains of hundreds of these rectangular, fortified multistorey residences across the island, several in relatively close proximity and varying states of ruin around **Strangford Lough**, Co. Down. In the west, two such houses have been restored and are open to the public – elaborate **Bunratty Castle**, Co. Clare, and the sixteenth-century **Dunguaire Castle**, Co. Galway.

THE SEVENTEENTH AND EIGHTEENTH CENTURIES

Few purely domestic residences constructed before the **seventeenth century** have survived. One such, **Rothe House** in Kilkenny, built in 1594, is a unique example of an Irish merchant's home from the prosperous Tudor period and is now open as a museum. Most domestic buildings from this period show some evidence of fortification, reflecting a turbulent time in Irish history. The first **unfortified mansion** is claimed to be **Beaulieu House**, Co. Louth, built in the 1660s following Cromwell's departure. A red-brick, hipped-roof dwelling, it closely follows the **Dutch style** popular in contemporary England. This century also saw the first **thatched cottages**, constructed of clay, whitewashed both inside and out, and consisting of merely one or two rooms poorly illuminated by small windows. Though these may have suited the damp Irish climate, the humble conditions reflected the continuation of a repressively feudal social system in which the rights of the landlord held sway.

Classical buildings began to appear in Ireland in the late-seventeenth century, the finest example of this period being the **Royal Hospital at Kilmainham**, Dublin, built between 1680 and 1687. It was designed by Sir William Robinson who used as his model Les Invalides in Paris, the home for retired soldiers. The building's core is an arcaded courtyard around which are ranged a great hall and chapel on one side and living quarters on the other three. During the 1980s, the now derelict building was fully restored at a cost of £20 million and reopened in 1991 as the Irish Museum of Modern Art.

The following century witnessed massive developments in public and private building. The Irish ruling class, known sometimes as the Protestant Ascendancy, drew its prosperity in part from lands granted or acquired during the 1600s and consolidated its position on them through the construction of mansions. The presence of an Irish Parliament in Dublin, though still subject to Westminster, gave the city a new confidence, and evidence of its consequent wealth is present in the many fine public buildings and elegant squares that still exist today. The Ascendancy's dominance was reinforced through the enactment of the repressive penal laws which prevented Catholics from holding public office, owning property or practising their religion. As a result, hardly a Catholic church was constructed during this period, though a notable survivor is the South Parish Church in Cork, built in 1766.

The architectural style favoured by the Ascendancy was influenced by the work and publications of the sixteenth-century Italian architect, Andrea Palladio. Equally popular in England, **Palladian** designs first appeared in Ireland in the 1720s and the largest and most palatial Palladian country house is **Castletown** in Co. Kildare, completed in 1732 and designed by Alessandro Galilei and Sir Edward Lovett Pearce. Elsewhere, the Palladian style was utilized in the construction of simpler houses built as much for utility as for ostentation, such as **Hazelwood**, Co. Sligo, and **Ledwithstown**, Co. Longford. Pearce was also responsible for the design of the great **Parliament House** (now the Bank of Ireland) in Dublin's College Green, constructed between 1729 and 1739. It is the earliest large-scale Palladian public building in all Ireland or England, and the model, a century later, for the British Museum in London. Another notable architect of the period was the German, Richard Castle, responsible for **Leinster House** (1745), commissioned as a town house for the dukes of Leinster, and now the seat of the Dáil.

Towards the end of the eighteenth century, **neoclassicism** became the prevailing architectural style, taking ancient Greece and Rome as even more direct influences than its predecessor. A refined neoclassical creation is the **Casino at Marino**, just northeast of Dublin, designed during the 1760s by Sir William Chambers as a country house for Lord Charlemont. **Castle Coole**, near Enniskillen, Co. Fermanagh, was designed by James Wyatt and is unarguably the best neoclassical house in Ireland. The house is now owned by the British National Trust and has been lavishly, if controversially, restored – the new colour scheme involves a shade that the pre-

vious owner, who still lives there, calls "Germolene pink".

The great architect of this period was undoubtedly **James Gandon** (1743–1823) who designed some of the most important public buildings in Dublin, including the **Custom House** and the **Four Courts**, both dating from the 1780s. Each building has an impressive columned riverside facade, topped by a magnificent dome.

Sadly, however, much of Ireland's Georgian architecture has vanished. As late as the 1950s, Dublin was still one of the most perfectly intact eighteenth-century cities in Europe, but much has since been lost (for more on this see opposite). Irish independence and the subsequent civil war led to a decline in the fortunes of the **Anglo-Irish Ascendancy**, resulting in the sale of many estates and **Big Houses**. Many of the houses themselves still lie in ruins following their destruction by a people who had long been repressed by a political system completely identified with their erstwhile owners. In recent years, however, there has been something approaching a *rapprochement* and the Anglo-Irish heritage is beginning to be seen as something inherently Irish. A good example of this change is **Strokestown Park House**, Co. Roscommon, an outstanding Palladian dwelling which has been meticulously restored by a local garage business and is now open to the public.

THE NINETEENTH CENTURY

Although the the Act of Union (1801) dissolved Ireland's independent government and diminished localized power and prosperity, architecture continued to flourish throughout the nineteenth century. Indeed the expansion in numbers of Irish-born members of the profession led to the establishment of the **Royal Institute of the Architects of Ireland** in 1839. At the same time, many English architects continued to be commissioned.

Perhaps feeling further isolated from their English contemporaries after Dublin ceased to be a centre of power, the Anglo-Irish Ascendancy embarked on a spate of building during the first few decades. Neoclassicism remained the predominant style, exemplified by such buildings as the **General Post Office** in Dublin's O'Connell Street, designed by Francis Johnston and completed in 1818, and William Morrison's **Carlow Courthouse**, dating from 1828.

The nineteenth century was also notable for the revival of the Gothic style, the catalyst for which was Catholic emancipation in 1829, leading to the construction of numerous **new churches**, influenced by the French style of slender towers and pointed spires surrounded by smaller pinnacles. Examples include **St Finbarr's Cathedral** in Cork and **St Colman's Cathedral**, Cobh, both begun in the 1860s. The similarly aged **Ashford Castle**, Co. Mayo, demonstrates the adaptation of the Gothic style to domestic architecture. Elsewhere, there are many examples of the architectural eclecticism which characterized the nineteenth century. **St Mary's Pro-Cathedral** in Dublin, started in 1814, shows a marked **Greek Revival** influence, a style more often associated with large-scale public building. **Tudor** and **Oriental** styles were also popular and it was almost as though architects saw the rapid development of the **railway system** as an opportunity to test the limits of their imagination in the design of station buildings.

Towards the end of the century, the **Celtic revival**, associated with the Gaelic literary movement, had a limited impact on architectural design, most noticeably in church-building. The favoured style was Hiberno-Romanesque and examples of its influence are visible in the design of the **Honan Chapel**, University College Cork, and **Spiddal Church**, Co. Galway.

THE PRESENT

A history of Ireland's twentieth-century architecture is as much about what has been lost as about what was built. Any post-colonial country necessarily inherits a complicated relation to its past, and buildings are one of the most tangible reminders of past eras. After Independence in 1922, the country entered a state of dormancy, from which it has only begun to emerge in the last three decades. The great public buildings of the colonizer continued to function as intended under the new order. Country house architecture fared badly with only a few hundred period houses left intact (see p.636), and Dublin's elaborate Georgian squares and domestic architecture have been vandalized as much by central government as by the property developers. The eminent English architectural historian Sir John Summerson was employed by the Electricity Supply Board in the 1960s to justify the demolition of a range of Georgian houses on Fitzwilliam Square, Dublin. Sir John said he believed that the interjection of some modern buildings would greatly relieve the monotony of red brick!

This is not to say that nothing notable was built between 1922 and 1960. The dominant influence during this period was **Art Deco**. While a restrained use of the style was invoked to good effect in the construction of institutions such as hospitals, it barely disguised their sombre debt to the workhouses of the mid-nineteenth century. As in the development of the visual arts, **modernism** reached Ireland relatively late in the twentieth century. Indeed, the first significant modern construction was the **Dublin Airport terminal**, designed by Desmond Fitzgerald, in 1940. One of the first postwar constructions to express this modernity with comfort was the **Busáras** station in Store Street, Dublin, which was designed in 1953 by Michael Scott, later to become one of the leading exponents of modern architecture in Ireland. The bus station contains a theatre, a sign of a bygone era's benevolence.

The economic boom of the 1960s and 1970s saw considerable expansion in architecture, though the demands of industry paid little heed to the heritage of the past. Systematic and effective legislation preserving buildings and monuments presupposes a buoyant economy and a sort of uncomplicated approach to the past which had not developed. Innately conservative Irish society had yet to discover any meaningful understanding of the importance of preservation and the rapid changes to the urban landscapes of Dublin and other cities took place without hindrance of debate or planning. For instance, it was only in the 1970s that **factory builders** began to consider the impact of such construction on the aesthetic nature of the local environment. Carroll's cigarette factory in Dundalk, designed by Ronald Tallon, is a worthy example of attractive development.

Similar modernist trends became visible in **school building**, such as Birr School by Peter and Mary Doyle, 1980, which applied new designs to accommodate contemporary educational theory. The most significant work in **ecclesiastical architecture** has been undertaken by Liam McCormick from Derry, whose style is marked by a consideration of the natural landmarks which overshadow his projects. Fine examples of his church designs are to be found in the Donegal villages of Burt, Creeslough and Glenties.

The recession of the 1980s reduced building activity and increasing world-wide awareness of environmental issues stimulated debate among architects about the cultivation of a new Irish architecture. Greater concerns for context and progressive town planning came to dominate new architectural theory. Postwar barbarism gradually became subsumed by desires to maintain the remnants of the country's built heritage and considerable state funding was provided for the restoration of buildings such as the **Custom House**, **Dublin Castle**, the **Casino at Marino** and the **Royal Hospital**, Kilmainham which was converted into the Irish Museum of Modern Art.

The grim public housing style of the 1960s, deck-access low- and high-rise blocks, was abandoned in favour of schemes such as **City Quay**, Dublin, and **Share Housing** in Cork. These 1980s developments paid far greater attention to street pattern and context and set the template for future designs. Similarly, private housing has undergone radical changes, though the virtual absence of planning regulations has resulted in a blight of **bungalow construction** which mars the landscape all the way from Kerry to Donegal.

Sadly, Dublin's cityscape is also marred by far too many examples of retarded modernist building. One of the worst examples of this trend is the Civic Offices at Wood Quay. Commonly known as the "bunkers", these offensive structures are doubly horrible in that they were constructed on the most important early Viking archeological site in Europe before it was fully excavated. In contrast, an especially fine example of the juxtaposition of old and modern buildings can be seen at New Square in Trinity College, Dublin.

During the 1990s, Ireland has been the beneficiary of considerable funding, resulting from its membership of the European Union. At the same time, tax incentives have encouraged private investment in the redevelopment of run-down areas in the major urban centres and towns. As a direct consequence, the country has witnessed a building boom of a magnitude similar to the accelerated urban expansion of the eighteenth century. The most significant changes have again taken place in the city centres, most notably in the construction of massive new shopping centres and in adaptations of Ireland's industrial and commercial past. Redevelopment of the semi-derelict **Temple Bar** area of Dublin was the subject of a competition. Revitalized as Dublin's answer to Paris's Left Bank or London's Covent Garden, the streets have been cobbled and pedestrianized, public sculptures installed, and a host of cultural institutions and fashionable bars and shops occupy the restored or newly-constructed premises. The gains are there for all to see, but the downside is that Dublin's appearance is edging nearer and nearer to that of any other European city.

Much state funding has also been directed towards tourism. Virtually every town now seems to have its own heritage or interpretive centre, no matter the level of justification. While existing buildings are, for the most part, converted to accommodate these attractions, several new buildings have been constructed. The Office of Public Works is at the forefront of this trend. Several large-scale interpretive centres have already been completed by them, including **Dunquin**, Co. Kerry, and **Ceíde Fields**, Co. Mayo and others have been developed through Heritage funding, such as **Ardara**, Co. Donegal. The marketing of the past in the service of economic recovery has touched every country town. Fake timber shopfronts abound, creating an illusory but gentler version of the past, which has more to do with cultural stereotypes than with the grim realities of the subsistence of the majority of Irish people in the last century.

Finally, in complete contrast, Ireland is currently in the grip of a **property pricing boom** comparable to the worst excesses of London in the 1980s. The cost of housing in Dublin and the most popular tourist and holiday home areas has risen to levels that prohibit all but the wealthiest from purchase. Though prices in the North remain relatively low, certain areas there too have seen a dramatic escalation. While homelessness has become a way of life for some in the Republic, there have been significant changes in the landscape, especially resulting from an apparently ever-broadening commuting range. Ugly new housing developments have sprung up around towns even as far as eighty or ninety miles from Dublin, and, if you drive around, the whole country can sometimes seem like one constant road-widening or resurfacing scheme. Coming to terms with these changes will be a major challenge for Ireland in the twenty-first century.

THE ART OF IRELAND

Irish art has long been overshadowed by the island's literature and, to some extent, its music. For the lay majority, Irish art is generally associated with the products of a Celtic culture in the centuries preceding and following the arrival of Christianity, and few, if pressed, are able to name a single Irish artist of the modern period. There is, however, a significant body of modern Irish work that deserves broader recognition.

THE STONE, BRONZE AND IRON AGES

The oldest art works in Ireland available to us can be found in the Stone Age tombs of the Boyne Valley, especially the passage-grave at **Newgrange** (see "Architecture", p.634). The stones and slabs of this 5000 year-old burial chamber are adorned with basic, but impressive whorls, zigzags and geometric forms whose purpose has long since been lost to us. The site has also yielded stone balls and beads as well as the remains of some rudimentary pottery.

Other decorative work on stone has survived from the **Bronze Age** (2000–500 BC), an epoch more notable for some startling work in goldsmithery. The National Museum of Ireland in Dublin houses a stunning collection of artefacts and jewellery, including a variety of lunulae (crescent-shaped collars of beaten gold), earrings and torques (twisted gold necklaces and armbands). One of the finest examples is the **Gleninsheen**

Gorget, an elaborate gold neck ornament with roundel fastenings, dating from around 800 BC.

The subsequent **Iron Age** witnessed continuing developments. There are a number of fine examples of figurative stone carving scattered around the country. Among the most notable are the **Janus statue**, two conjoined and grotesque figures carved back to back, in Calgach Cemetery on Boa Island, Co. Fermanagh, and the **Tandragee Idol**, now in the Church of Ireland Cathedral, Armagh city. Linear designs of flowing tendrils, typical of the La Tène style of Celtic art found in continental Europe, are visible on a number of surviving works, including the well-known **Turoe stone** in Co. Galway (see p.357). The National Museum holds several good examples of this style, including the **Somerset box lid** (also from Galway) and the so-called **Petrie Crown** gold collar, part of a hoard unearthed in 1896 in Broighter, Co. Derry, which also included a wonderful miniature sailing boat complete with oars.

EARLY CHRISTIAN ART

In Ireland, the early Christian era (432–1170 AD) is often described as the **Golden Age**. Irish society remained unscathed by the turmoil in the centuries following the fall of the Roman Empire and its society based on small tribal units was not disturbed radically by the advent of Christianity. Indeed, artists and craftworkers retained a privileged status, continuing to develop skills in metalwork and other areas. The period attained its zenith with the production of justifiably famous illuminated manuscripts such as the **Book of Kells**, but other wonderful artefacts have also survived from this era and a visit to the magnificent **High Crosses** will take you to some of the most beautiful parts of the country.

ILLUMINATED MANUSCRIPTS

The first of the surviving manuscripts is an early seventh-century book of psalms known as **the Cathach** (pronounced Kohok), now housed in the library of the Royal Irish Academy in Dublin. Only the initial letter of each paragraph of Latin text is decorated and such illustration consists of scrolls and animals in a limited range of colours. These motifs set the style for the greater books that followed.

The first of the truly magnificent illuminated texts is the **Book of Durrow**, dating from around 675 AD, and displayed alongside the

Book of Kells in the Old Library in Trinity College, Dublin. The *Book of Durrow* was produced by the monastery of the same name in Co. Offaly and consists of a copy of the four gospels. Though the artist's palette was limited to red, yellow and green, the three major stylistic components of spirals, animals and interlacing bands, typical of the great books, are plainly evident. These bands, like the dots which surround some of the initial letters in the *Cathach*, suggest a stylistic link with Coptic or other Middle Eastern sources. The *Book* is also notable for its full-page illustrations (called carpet pages) devoted entirely to ornamentation or a depiction of the saint whose gospel follows.

Other books were produced during the next hundred and fifty years. Two others displayed in Trinity College are the **Book of Armagh**, commissioned in 807 by Torbach, Bishop of Armagh, and the **Book of Dimma**, typical of a smaller pocket format designed to be carried around. Similar illuminated manuscripts, such as the *Lindisfarne Gospels*, can be found in museums and libraries abroad, reflecting the travels of many of the monks of the period. St Columba, for example, spread the Gospels and founded monasteries around Britain and Europe.

However, it was in the **Book of Kells** that this art form found its highest expression in Ireland. Again a copy of the Gospels in Latin, this glorious manuscript is a perfect synthesis of all the motifs and styles – both imported or developed locally – used in earlier books. Its origins are obscure and some suggest that it was produced by monks from Iona, St Columba's first Scottish base. Created around 800 AD, it takes its name from the Columban monastery at Kells, Co. Meath, where it was kept for centuries until it was transferred to Trinity in 1654 for protection during the Cromwellian wars. Mere words cannot convey the beauty of the book's illustrations, from the vividly ornamental geometric and floral patterns to the human and animal forms gracing the page margins. It is no wonder at all that the *Book of Kells* is easily Ireland's most popular visitor attraction and queueing for a view is an essential part of a trip to the island.

METALWORK AND JEWELLERY

The decorative style of the illuminated manuscripts is reflected in the best of the period's metalwork, including two impressive chalices. The first is part of the eighth- or ninth-century **Derrynaflan Hoard**, discovered in Co. Tipperary in 1980, while the second, a century older, was found at **Ardagh**. Both chalices are roughly eight inches high and similar in shape, with a rounded cup and a conical base, though the elaborately engraved Ardagh chalice is technically more refined than its plainer predecessor. However, for evidence that secular art also flourished during this period, look no further than the eighth-century bronze **Tara Brooch**, found on the seashore near Bettystown, Co. Louth, in 1850. Covered with gold and decorated with amber, glass and fine metalwork, intricate designs on both its sides bear close similarities to patterns in the *Book of Kells*. Both chalices and the brooch are on view in the National Museum.

The development of metalwork over the following centuries showed the increasing influence of Romanesque and Viking styles. While the latter is apparent in numerous examples of brooches and other jewellery, the former is best exemplified by the magnificent **Cross of Cong**. The Cross was made around 1123 in order to contain and protect a chip from the True Cross, presented by Pope Calixtus II to the King of Connacht, Turlough O'Connor. It is made of oak, encased in gilt bronze, copper and silver, and the arms are decorated with fine gold filigree. There is a central bronze boss into which is set a polished crystal.

HIGH CROSSES AND SHEILA-NA-GIGS

The Cross of Cong predated by several centuries another great, but also relatively short-lived, genre of Irish art, the **high crosses**. An early simple, but gloriously executed example is the seventh-century **Donagh Cross**, near Carndonagh, Co. Donegal. The interlaced design of the head of the cross is typical of many and, while each face is decorated, the east face depicts a number of biblical scenes, including the crucifixion. A pair of more elaborate crosses is to be found at **Ahenny**, Co. Tipperary. Here the arms of each cross are joined by a circle, a form which served as a prototype for subsequent sculptures.

The best of the later scriptural crosses can be ranked amongst Ireland's finest artistic achievements. One such is the **Cross of Moone**, Co. Kildare. Although its setting is less picturesque than others, there is an instant appeal about this long, narrowly proportioned cross with its almost naive flat figures depicting biblical scenes.

Other more striking examples are to be found at the beautiful locations of **Clonmacnois**, Co. Offaly, and at **Monasterboice**, Co. Louth. The former's Great Cross unusually includes a secular scene, while, at Monasterboice, the graphic biblical scenes of Muiredach's cross have survived a thousand years of Ireland's inclement climate. Elsewhere, various examples can be seen in **Kells**, Co. Meath, and at **Donaghmore** and **Ardboe** in Co. Tyrone. Sadly, many crosses were carved from local sandstone and their carvings have not withstood the elements, but the granite **Castledermot Crosses**, in Co. Kildare, have fared better than many.

Crosses continued to be carved in stone right up to the twelfth century, although there were significant changes in style. For instance, the White Cross of Tola at **Dysert O'Dea**, Co. Clare, where large figures in relief of Christ and a bishop have replaced flatter charactered biblical panels. The arms of this cross are not joined by a circle.

Evidence that Irish Christianity retained some idiosyncrasies is provided by the stone sculptured **sheila-na-gigs** found on some early church decorations and in castle walls (see p.190). A pair of these pagan fertility symbols are exhibited in the National Museum, but to see one in situ, a visit to **White Island** in Lower Lough Erne, Co. Fermanagh, is essential (see p.606). The figures are undeniably female, but what is also indisputable is the sheer provocative lewdness of their representation. The White Island figure grins lasciviously, her cheeks bulging, legs wide open and arms pointing towards her genitalia.

NORMAN AND MEDIEVAL ART

Until the dissolution of the monasteries in the sixteenth century, virtually all Irish art was religious in context and content and the church was the principal patron. Following the Norman invasion in the twelfth century, the earliest stone figure carvings were of bishops, such as those still visible in the Norman cathedrals of **St Patrick** and **Christ Church** in Dublin. Not to be outdone, some Norman knights also had effigies carved of themselves: that of Strongbow in Christ Church was reckoned to be one of the best until it was destroyed by the collapse of a wall and replaced by an anonymous earl.

The most notable achievement of this period was probably the refinement of stonecarving techniques and there are numerous surviving examples. The fifteenth-century cloister carvings at the important Cistercian monastery of **Jerpoint**, near Thomastown, Co. Kilkenny, were the work of the nearby Callan carvers, who were also responsible for the tomb of Piers Fitz Oge Butler in **Kilcooly Abbey**, Co. Tipperary. New stones were used by the craftworkers and a startling example from the sixteenth century is the beautiful black marble effigies of Piers Butler and Lady Margaret Fitzgerald, his countess, in **St Canice's Cathedral**, Kilkenny.

Fortunately, examples of the woodcarver's art have survived too. The earliest is thought to be the thirteenth-century **Kilcorban Madonna and Child**, displayed in the Loughrea Museum, Co. Galway, while, in Dublin, the National Museum has the **St Molaise of Inishmurray** and **God the Father** from Fethard, Co. Tipperary. St Mary's Cathedral in Limerick has the only set of misericords in the country – black oak choir seats, carved with various animals, both fabulous and real, in bold relief. Limerick's Catholic cathedral, **St John's**, is worth visiting for its fifteenth-century mitre and carved crosier and mitre, thought to be the finest religious artefacts of the Middle Ages in Ireland.

Protective shrines or casings in metalwork have survived from the first millennium, and some of these were reworked in medieval style. **The Cathach Shrine**, for example, has work dating from about 1050, but the most impressive panels are possibly fifteenth century. This, the **Breac Maodhóg** and the **Domhnach Airgid** shrines can all be seen in the National Museum. Each is lavishly decorated with bronze or silver gilt illustrations of the Crucifixion, the saints or other religious themes.

SEVENTEENTH- TO NINETEENTH-CENTURY ART

Following the models of England and continental Europe, guilds of urban craftworkers began to form during the later medieval period. A new "professionalism" produced significant technical advances in the decorative arts of goldsmithery, plasterwork, silver, glass and furniture, and some guilds, such as the Goldsmiths' Company, had acquired power in their own right. The visual arts were stimulated by the desire of the new Anglo-Irish ruling class to display images of itself and many such works were commissioned from painters and sculptors. Easel-based portrait painting thus became the dominant mode and a "painters' guild" was formed in 1670. Later prominent members included **Garrett Morphey**, noted for his portraits of the martyred Oliver Plunkett, and **James Latham**, probably the first Irish artist of major ability. Latham had studied at Antwerp, and the depth of perception displayed in his work, especially his portrait of the philosopher Bishop George Berkeley, influenced Irish art for decades.

Drawing Schools were founded in Dublin around 1740 and many artists, such as **Robert Healy**, were trained in charcoal and chalk techniques. Both his and the pastelist **Hugh Hamilton's** work can be seen in the National Gallery, while the latter was to become a distinguished painter in the Neoclassical style, which became popular later in the century. The greatest stimulus to the visual arts, however, came from **Edmund Burke's** theory of aesthetics, described in *A Philosophical Enquiry into the Origins of our Ideas of The Sublime and Beautiful*, published in 1756. Two major painters of the period, **George Barret** and **James Barry** were protégés of Burke and attempted to embody his aesthetic principles in their work. Influenced by such ideas as the excitement of pain or danger (the sublime) or love (the beautiful), the subject-matter of Irish painting broadened to include historical and some landscape work, often with classical and mythological allusions. Barry later became Professor of Painting at the Royal Academy, London, a position he held from 1782 until he was sacked in 1795 following an altercation with colleagues. Two paintings in the National Gallery, his *Self Portrait* and *Adam and Eve*, are typical of his style.

Another influential artist of the period was **Nathaniel Hone**, the first painter of note in a family which would much later produce other major artists. He was noted for his portraits of children and miniatures, but his most famous work, *The Conjurer*, now in the National Gallery, Dublin, was a satire on Sir Joshua Reynolds' attempts to emulate the Old Masters. Unsurprisingly, it was rejected for exhibition by the Royal Academy in London in 1775 and Hone defiantly held his own one-man show instead.

George Barret adopted Burke's principles to his landscapes and these paintings, together with **Robert Carver's**, were often characteristically romantic. However, a later Classical school developed, deriving much from the Frenchman Claude Lorraine, and including landscapists such as **Thomas Roberts** and **William Ashford**. Paintings of this genre typically featured a green and brown foreground, green middle-distance and often, further back, a Gothic-style ruin set against a lighter, blue background. Topography, too, gradually became an important concern and its finest proponent was **James Malton**, a former draughtsman in the architect James Gandon's practice. His series of line drawings, *Views of Dublin*, drawn in 1790–91, include some marvellous aspects of contemporary Irish architecture.

Classical and rococo styles were also seen in the applied arts in the eighteenth century, particularly in stucco work. Dublin's **Powerscourt Townhouse**, recently restored as an imaginatively designed shopping centre, has a magnificent ceiling by **Michael Stapleton** (also responsible for the plasterwork at Trinity) and a staircase by **James McCullagh** and **Michael Reynolds**, which have been decorated with motifs of urns, scrolls and heads. The rich Baroque ceiling of the **Chapel** in the Rotunda Maternity Hospital by **Bartholomew Cramillion** is unlike anything else in the country. Life-size figures by the Swiss-Italian **Francini brothers**, the foremost contemporary stuccoists, and detailed birds and musical instruments by Robert West decorate **Newman House** at 85/86 St Stephen's Green. The extraordinary beauty of these make it all the more poignant that heartless town "planners" and "developers" have allowed the wanton destruction or neglect of many equally fine interiors in Ireland's principal city.

The eighteenth century was also noted for heavy, deep-cut glasswork and for high-quality silverware, some of which, such as three-legged sugar bowls, were made in characteristically Irish shapes. Sculpture in classical and Neoclassical styles can be seen on a number of buildings such as the **Custom House**, the **City Hall** and the **Casino in Marino**, Dublin.

During the early years of the nineteenth century, following the 1801 Act of Union, many artists emigrated to London. Those who remained formed new organizations aimed at consolidating art in Ireland. The leading body was the Royal Hibernian Academy, established in 1823, and directly modelled on its London equivalent, holding annual exhibitions and seeking to stimulate debate on the direction and concerns of painting.

Nineteenth-century Irish art is dominated by the landscapists, led by **James Arthur O'Connor**. Though he was partially influenced by seventeenth-century Dutch works, the persistence of classical and romantic styles is visible in his *Homeward Bound* and **Edwin Hayes'** seascape *The Emigrant Ship*. The landscape tradition was further developed by **George Chinnery**, **William Sadler**, **Cecilia Campbell** and **Henry O'Neill** working in a variety of media – watercolour, gouache and oil. **George Petrie**, a distinguished archeologist who was for some time attached to the Irish Ordnance Survey, also produced many topographical illustrations for travel books, a popular publishing genre of the time.

Portrait painting continued, though occasionally it followed the Victorian English trend for cloying sentimentality, as in **Richard Rothwell's** *The Young Mother's Pastime*. Beginning as a pencil portraitist, Cork-born **Daniel Maclise** went on to produce historical frescoes, such as *The Meeting of Wellington and Blücher* and *The Death of Nelson*, both of which are displayed in the House of Lords' Royal Gallery; he also illustrated works by Dickens and Tennyson. His contemporary, **William Mulready** from Ennis, also studied at the Royal Academy and had an equally significant impact on English art through his studies *Barber's Shop* and *Boys Fishing*. **Francis Danby** was also notable for his large historical and biblical paintings, characterized by the romanticism still popular among Irish painters.

John Henry Foley, **John Lawlor** and **Samuel Ferris Lynn** collaborated with British sculptors to produce the Albert Memorial in London. Foley was also noted for his classical-style busts, but his major works were the commissions he received for **public monuments**; several examples of his work still stand in Dublin, such as the memorials to Oliver Goldsmith and Edmund Burke in College Green, and to Daniel O'Connell in O'Connell Street. There is some fine stucco work from this time, too, such as that in the hall of Ballyfin House, Co. Laois, by **Richard Morrison**.

IMPRESSIONISM AND THE TWENTIETH CENTURY

Developments in European art markedly influenced Irish painting from the late nineteenth century onwards. The landscapes of **Nathaniel Hone**, the great-grandnephew of his namesake, and early paintings of **Walter Osborne** were inspired by the rustic realism of Jules Bastien-Lepage, though Osborne became one of many native artists stimulated by Impressionism, its influence visible in such works as *Tea in the Garden*. His *St Patrick's Close* depicted the griminess of working-class Dublin. Postimpressionism had a powerful impact on the work of **Roderic O'Conor**, and his *Field of Corn* in the Ulster Museum, Belfast, is reminiscent of Cezanne and perhaps Van Gogh.

Other notable artists of the period include **William Orpen**, a precociously talented draughtsman who began training at the Dublin Metropolitan School of Art at the age of eleven. Later, as a young instructor at the school, he painted some marvellous coastal scenes with figures near Howth, but he is better-known for his sketches and paintings at the front during World War I and at the subsequent Paris Peace Conference, where he was official painter. His portraits are worth seeing simply for their vitality and feeling for character. Similarly adept was **John Lavery**, many of whose works are displayed in the Ulster Museum in his home-town, Belfast. In his early career, he too was influenced by Bastien-Lepage. Lavery studied in Glasgow, London and Paris and became a significant portraitist, especially during the 1920s when he painted many of the leading contemporary Irish political figures, including Carson and Collins.

Most prominent among artists of this period were **Jack Butler Yeats** and **Paul Henry**. Son of a successful portraitist and brother of the poet W.B. Yeats, Jack Yeats is probably the best-known Irish twentieth-century painter, though he worked originally as an illustrator, sketching horses for *Paddock Life* magazine and drawing the first cartoon strip version of Sherlock Holmes, *Chubblock Homes*, for *Comic Cuts*. Like his father, he was a fine portraitist although he later developed a highly personal Expressionist style, marked by extremely vivid colour and loose brush technique. Yeats' subjects were Celtic mythology and everyday Irish life, yet though he undoubtedly contributed to the upsurge of nationalist sentiment in the arts, following Irish independence, his influence on Irish art was largely osmotic, for he took no pupils and was never seen at work. Paul Henry studied first at his native Belfast School of Art before continuing his education in Paris. Like Yeats, he was originally an illustrator, working with high competence through the medium of charcoal. His early paintings were heavily influenced by Millet and, while living on Achill Island, Co. Mayo, he produced a number of works on Irish country life in which Millet's characteristic "peasant" poses were apparent. Later, Henry fell under the spell of Whistler and studied at his new Paris studio. Returning to Dublin he became active in the local arts world and, along with his wife, Grace Mitchell Henry, and a number of other painters, including Yeats, formed the **Society of Dublin Painters** in 1920. He had already developed his own characteristic style which remained hardly altered for the rest of his life and it is for his Connemara landscapes that he is most remembered. Using a palette of matt blues and greys, his paintings commonly consist of a few elements, natural or man-made, set in bold composition against a cloud-filled sky. *Lakeside Cottages* (c. 1930) is a typical example. In the 1920s, some of Henry's works were reproduced as posters and were also used in tourist literature and government publications. Such was the demand for similar pictures, that Henry's subsequent work almost sank to the level of romantic caricature.

In contrast to postimpressionism, abstract art was relatively late in arriving in Ireland. Some artists, such as **Seán Keating**, **Maurice MacGonigal** and **Sean O'Sullivan**, continued to work in the landscape tradition. Other young Irish artists travelled abroad to absorb the advances of Cubism and Futurism; the most influential on their return were **Mainie Jellett** and **Evie Hone** who had both trained under André Lhote and Albert Gleizes in Paris. Interestingly, early modernism's masculinist avant garde was given little credence in Ireland, leaving space for women like Jellett and Hone to be the main proponents of Irish modernism. Evie Hone was best known as a distinguished member of An Túr Gloine, a school for stained glass, founded by the painter Sarah Purser, and her best works include windows in the chapel at Eton College in England and the CIE headquar-

ters in O'Connell Street, Dublin. In 1943, along with fellow abstract artists Louis Le Brocquy and Norah McGuinness, Hone and Jellett, founded the **Irish Exhibition of Living Art** as an alternative showcase for modernist work rejected by the compilers of the Royal Hibernian Academy's annual exhibitions.

Postwar Ireland saw major advances in sculpture. **Clíona Cussen**, **Hilary Heron** and **Oisín Kelly** pioneered the use of new casting techniques and developed the concept of an Irish vernacular sculpture. Kelly's *Children of Lir*, inspired by the Celtic legend, stands in Parnell Square, one of a number of public monuments placed around the capital by the Dublin Corporation. Sculptors of achievement have included **Michael Bulfin**, **John Behan**, **Edward Delaney**, **Conor Fallon** and **John Burke**. More recently, sculptors such as **Christopher Keaney** and **Jill Crowley** have produced remarkable figures, the latter wittily caricaturing Irish men.

The influence of the Exhibition of Living Art developed during the 1950s, serving as a focus for the works of artists like **Barrie Cooke**, **Cecil King**, **Nano Reid** and **Camille Souter**, while the landscape tradition was maintained by **Patrick Collins** and **Tony O'Malley**. Le Brocquy's contorted human shapes dominated abstract art and an idiosyncratic school of primitive artists developed on **Tory Island** (see p.461) off the coast of Donegal. Partly as a result of government funding, the visual arts have flourished in Ireland since the 1970s, and, in more recent years, in the North. In the 1980s, Living Art opened its doors to video and performance artists, exhibiting the works of **Aileen MacKeough**, **Nigel Rolfe**, **Eilis O'Connell** and a host of others. A strong new expressionist movement has emerged from the Independent Artists group, represented by **Michael Kane**, **Patrick Hall**, **Brian Maguire**, **Patrick Graham**, **Eithne Jordan**, **Michael Mulcahy** and **Michael Cullen**.

Along with increased support, there has been a steady expansion in the number of exhibition spaces. In Dublin, the Irish Museum of Modern Art, opened in 1991, and the Douglas Hyde Gallery, in Trinity College, both offer opportunities for new experimentalism. There's a host of commercial galleries here too, such as the Kerlin and Green on Red, ensuring that a steady stream of contemporary Irish art is always on show, and around the country there are numerous local art centres and galleries such as the Triskel, Cork, and the Model Art Centre, Sligo. In Northern Ireland, the Orchard Gallery in Derry has a long history of top-quality exhibitions, and the Ormeau Baths Gallery in Belfast regularly presents an equally strong contemporary Northern Irish programme. Names to watch out for include John Carson, Brian Connolly, Rita Duffy, Philip Napler and Louise Walsh. Animated debates in the pages of *Circa* (published in both Dublin and Belfast) testify to the continued revitalization of the Irish arts.

Additionally, recent years have seen major developments in contemporary applied arts and design, especially in such fields as jewellery, glass, furniture and ceramics. In the Republic, such work has been supported by a government agency, the Craft Council of Ireland. The two capitals are the best locations for viewing, though there are plenty of others dotted around the island. In Dublin, there is the **Crafts Council gallery** in the Powerscourt Townhouse and several outlets in **Temple Bar**, including DESIGNyard, while in Belfast, work can be viewed in the **Craftworks gallery** in Bedford Street.

THE IRISH
IN FILM

The current international profile of film-making in Ireland is higher than it has ever been before. Owing to financial incentives for foreign filmmakers the level of activity in the country has soared since 1993. Increased government funding for indigenous filmmakers has spawned a thriving film community, catapulted onto the world stage over recent years thanks largely to the activities and successes of directors Neil Jordan and Jim Sheridan.

The Irish have always been conscious of the stereotypical images of Irishness in foreign, particularly American, pictures: the country a pastoral idyll, its people a good-humoured mix of priests and nuns, fiery redheads and hard-drinking and -fighting men. More recently, however, films made in and about Ireland have started to explore broader themes, reflecting the changing state of Irish society and giving the world a very different image of Irishness: urban, diverse and outward-looking.

The films below are listed in chronological order, each title followed by the director and year of release.

Knocknagow (Fred O'Donovan, 1917).
Set in the post-Famine years of the 1840s, this sprawling landlord/tenant silent drama, produced by the largely Nationalist Film Company of Ireland is effectively a call to arms and was considered propagandist by the British authorities.

Willie Reilly and his Colleen Bawn
(John McDonagh, 1920).
Political drama set in the 1740s in which the rights of the landowning classes are upheld regardless of religion. Protestant squire's daughter Helen and Catholic gentleman Willie Reilly fall in love; rival suitor and anti-Catholic bigot Sir Whitecroft attempts to use the Penal Laws to dispossess Reilly, burning down his house in the process. Sympathetic Protestants come to the beleagured Willie's assistance and ultimately justice prevails.

Irish Destiny (George Dewhurst,1926).
The first fictionalized film about the War of Independence and the civil war, with plenty of horrific detail including footage of the burning of Cork city and the Custom House, and the brutality of the Black and Tans. The film was banned by the British Board of Censors in 1926, but was received enthusiastically in Ireland and America.

Mother Machree (John Ford, 1928).
Silent movie made for the Irish-American market in which an impoverished Irish immigrant is forced to surrender her son for adoption and devote her energies to raising the child of her own employer, only to find both son and daughter fall in love in adult life.

Man of Aran (Robert O'Flaherty, 1934).
Landmark documentary about life on the Aran Islands. Long criticized as portraying the islanders' primitive struggle against the elements in an overly romanticized, epic form that runs contrary to its documentary status, it nonetheless remains a thrilling film.

The Quiet Man (John Ford, 1952).
US film included here because it represents the pinnacle of Hollywood "Oirishness". This romantic comedy stars John Wayne as the prize fighter who has hung up his gloves and returned to the auld sod from the States, and focuses on his courtship of the feisty Maureen O'Hara and the hostility he encounters from her pugilist brother.

Shake Hands With The Devil
(Michael Anderson, 1959).
The first international production to be made at Ardmore Studios in Bray, Co. Wicklow. Melodrama starring James Cagney in which an IRA man develops a taste for violence as an end in itself.

Saoirse? ("Freedom?" George Morrison, 1961).
Documentary account of the emergence of the

modern Irish state, focusing on events from 1918 to the civil war.

Ryan's Daughter (David Lean, 1970).
Set amid the gorgeous scenery of the Dingle Peninsula, the adulterous affair between a British officer (Christopher Jones) and the local schoolteacher's wife (Sarah Miles) is common knowledge by the time a boatload of IRA guns arrive to be intercepted by British forces; the year is 1916. The locals set upon Miles, believing her to be responsible for the treachery. For all this, a rather lacklustre film.

Down the Corner (Joe Comerford, 1974).
The first urban working-class film shot in Ireland by an Irish director, the action centres around the escapades of five adolescent boys. Their surrounding adult world is characterized by alcoholism, unemployment and memories of the 1916 Rising.

Withdrawal (Joe Comerford, 1974).
Film dealing with mental illness and drug addiction in an uncharacteristically raw manner.

On a Paving Stone Mounted
(Thaddeus O'Sullivan, 1978).
A tale of the lives of Irish emigrants in London, significant not just for its subject matter, but also for the improvisational scope given to its actors. The film deploys a mix of drama and documentary styles and presents a dislocated collage of memory and experience.

Our Boys (Cathal Black, 1981).
Iconoclastic milestone in Irish film history which combined documentary and drama to highlight the inequities of Irish Christian Brothers' schools. "The Brothers" were notorious for their insensitivity and the outbursts of savage brutishness which they inflicted on pupils. It was deemed so subversive that RTE, one of the film's backers, refused to broadcast it for the best part of a decade after its release.

Angel
(Neil Jordan, 1982/ US title "Danny Boy").
Fine revenge thriller set in Northern Ireland, in which a saxophonist pursues the murderer of a mute girl and is thus drawn into a world of violence.

Cal (Pat O'Connor, 1984).
Fatalistic love story set in the context of the Troubles in Northern Ireland. Cal, an IRA volunteer, seeks redemption for his part in the murder of a policeman from the dead man's widow. Love

blooms all too briefly and their relationship is destroyed when the past catches up with them.

Eat the Peach (Peter Ormrod, 1986).
Droll and quirky movie in which protagonists Arthur and Vinnie set out to build a motorcycle wall-of-death to relieve the unrelenting tedium of their bleak and desolate bogland home.

Reefer and the Model (Joe Comerford, 1987).
Highly enjoyable thriller in which an ex-prostitute heroin user, now pregnant, and an ex-IRA man meet up and rampage through Connemara, rob a mobile bank and effect a getaway of sorts.

My Left Foot (Jim Sheridan, 1989).
A fine and touching film based on Christy Brown's best-selling autobiography. Brown, almost entirely paralyzed by cerebral palsy, except for his left foot, retells the story of his courageous battle with disability.

December Bride (Thaddeus O'Sullivan, 1990).
Family drama set at the turn of the century, beautifully shot on location at Strangford Lough. Central to the film is one pregnant woman's refusal to marry at the behest of the local minister, and her growing understanding of the sacrifices that must be made for the sake of future generations. The film was commended at the 1990 European Film Awards for its rich and varied portrayal of Northern Protestants.

The Field (Jim Sheridan, 1990).
Sentimentalized story about one man's fight to keep the field he's created and tended over the years. A crude allegory of landownership and the dignity of toil.

The Commitments (Alan Parker, 1991).
One of the most popular film treatments of working class Dublin. Adapted from Roddy Doyle's novel, the film follows the rise of the eponymous soul band and is chiefly enjoyable for its rather obvious comedy and R&B/soul classics.

Hear My Song (Peter Chelsom, 1991).
Engaging light comedy in which Liverpool nightclub manager Micky O'Neill hopes to revive his fortunes by luring legendary tenor Josef Locke to perform in his ailing club. However, O'Neill has underrated the complexities of Locke's past and things do not run smoothly.

The Crying Game (Neil Jordan, 1992).
Excellent thriller in which an IRA man becomes haunted by his part in the death of a British hostage and subsequently develops an intimate relationship with the dead man's lover. However,

things are not that simple, and this gripping film comes to an unexpected ironic conclusion.

Into the West (Mike Newell, 1992).
Clichéd but nonetheless charming contemporary working of the Tír na nÓg myth – the quest for the Land of Eternal Youth. The film focuses on the horseback adventures of two young boys and their father's struggle to accept the death of their mother. The film fuses gritty Dublin realism with the magical landscape of the west.

In The Name of The Father
(Jim Sheridan, 1993).
Based on the true story of the Guildford Four who were wrongfully imprisoned for the 1974 IRA Guildford pub bombing in which five people died. The film focuses on the imprisonment of Gerry Conlon and his father Guiseppe, and the attempt to clear the family name. Although marred by historical inaccuracies and a ludicrous final courtroom scene, this remains a powerful drama, thanks chiefly to the towering performance of Daniel Day Lewis as Gerry.

Korea (Cathal Black, 1994).
Set in the border country of the 1950s. An adolescent boy's romance forces his father to confront a changing world and put local enmities dating back to the civil war behind him.

A Man of No Importance
(Suri Krishnamma, 1995).
Light movie in which gay bus conductor Alfie Byrne, played by a delightful Albert Finney, attempts to loosen up the travelling public in a repressive Dublin of the 1960s. Action revolves around his efforts to stage a production of Wilde's *Salome* in a church hall.

Circle of Friends (Pat O'Connor, 1995).
Light, chocolate-box tale of young romance and betrayal in 50s Ireland. This adaptation of a Maeve Binchy novel remains cosy and warm-hearted throughout.

Guiltrip (Gerard Stembridge, 1995).
Adultery, impotence and frustration drive squaddie Liam, an army corporal, to extremes in this tense small town drama.

Nothing Personal
(Thaddeus O'Sullivan, 1995).
Action-packed Troubles movie in which innocent individuals are caught up in the terrorists' war. Criticized as having pro-Republican sympathies, the film can be credited with some honest scrutiny of the motivations and inner tensions of

Loyalist organizations. As the film comes to its awful conclusion, the inevitability that violence begets violence is made horribly clear, and so too is the message that this is a war in which everyone loses.

The Run of the Country (Peter Yates, 1995).
The quiet, forgotten border country is the setting for this adolescent rite of passage, the drama centring around a cross-border romance and an unwanted pregnancy. Fine scenery and pale shadows of IRA activity provide a modicum of local colour.

The Boy From Mercury (Martin Duffy, 1996).
Slight, amusing film about a boy's obsession with science fiction, in particular Flash Gordon movies. The young James Cronin pulls through the trials of boyhood with the help of his wide-eyed imagination and the outer-space fantasies of the local cinema.

Michael Collins (Neil Jordan, 1996).
Hugely important biopic in which Republican leader Collins, played by Liam Neeson, is portrayed as an heroic figure in the struggle against imperial Britain. The film includes a powerful dramatization of the 1916 Easter Rising and, although it skirts over the details of the Treaty negotiations of 1921, follows Collins through the founding of the Free State to the civil war and his assassination.

Some Mother's Son (Terry George, 1996).
Enthralling and moving film about the 1981 Irish hunger strikers in the Maze prison, focusing on the effect of their endeavour on two mothers of differing political beliefs. Despite occasional lapses into sentimentality, this is a convincing evocation of those times and includes superb performances by Fionnula Flanagan and Helen Mirren.

The Van (Stephen Frears, 1996).
Based on Roddy Doyle's novel, this Dublin working-class comedy revolves around protagonist Bimbo's attempt to launch a chip van business in time for Ireland's World Cup games.

The Boxer
(Jim Sheridan, 1997/ US title "Hell's Kitchen").
Circles of violence explored as ex-con boxer returns to his Republican community to discover the continuing demands of sectarianism are as restricting as life inside. A very convincing portrayal of the men of violence's stranglehold on a community.

The General (John Boorman, 1998).
Based on the true-life story of a notorious Dublin art thief. The "general" becomes fatally caught up in the complexities of the political underworld when the UVF prove the only organization capable of buying his haul. A magnificent performance by Brendan Gleeson in the central role.

The Butcher Boy (Neil Jordan, 1998).
Powerful dark comedy set in small-town Ireland in which a young boy's failure to cope with the dysfunctional society in which he finds himself leads to violence. From the Patrick McCabe novel of the same name.

MUSIC

Ireland and music are as inseparable as fish and chips. Traditional music may form the well-known cultural backbone, but there is also an important, though often ignored, body of classical composition. And artistes such as Van Morrison, Thin Lizzy, U2 and Sinéad O'Connor have ensured Ireland's prominence in the world gazetteer of rock.

TRADITIONAL MUSIC

Kept alive by a combination of historical, political and cultural forces, Irish traditional music remains one of the richest musical cultures in the Western world. In Ireland itself, the growing interest in traditional music is further evidence of a national maturity that allows Irish people to be more relaxed about aspects of their traditional culture. Consequently, traditional music is neither seen as backward, rural and something shameful, nor is it a stick of cultural purity for fending off the twentieth century. Long after much traditional music in the industrialized West has ceased to exist in any meaningful way, Irish music continues to refashion itself, not as introverted, stagnant, and nationalistic, but as an evolving and progressive part of a common, universal folk tradition.

Most of the instrumental music the visitor will hear in Ireland is **dance music**, originally played in kitchens, barns and at crossroads, usually to mark an occasion, such as a wedding or a wake. The melody of any dance tune is but bare bones to a traditional musician; it's dependent on performance for flesh, blood and soul. Through ornamentation, decoration and embellishments the performer breathes life into the music and this controlled extemporization allows the player to re-create a tune with each performance.

SEAN NÓS AND THE VOCAL TRADITION

Songs in the Irish language are at the heart of Irish music and the most important belong to a tradition known as **sean nós** (literally "in the old style"). An unaccompanied singing style of great beauty and complexity, it is thought to derive in part from the bardic tradition which died out in the seventeenth century with the demise of the old Gaelic order. Hugely demanding for both singer and listener, it requires the skill of the former to vary the interpretation of each verse by means of subtle changes in tempo, ornamentation, timbre and stress, while the latter needs to possess the knowledge and discrimination to appreciate fully the singer's efforts. To the untutored ear it can easily "sound all the same", with its slightly nasal tone and unemotional manner of performance, but perseverance will lead to great rewards. Liam Ó Maonlai of Hothouse Flowers is an accomplished *sean nós* singer, but the one to catch is the marvellous **Iarla O'Lionáird** who also works with the roots-dance fusion outfit Afro-Celt Sound System.

THE SESSION: MUSIC AND CRACK

Travellers to Ireland will most likely come across traditional music in a pub setting and these quasi-impromptu musical get-togethers are known as "**sessions**". These are the life-blood of traditional music, accompanied by the associated notion of **craic** (or crack) whereby music, conversation and drink combine to produce an evening of fun. A session is not strictly a performance, but more of a dynamic of entertainer and listener – a group of people enjoying the *craic* together. Summer is a good time for sessions, particularly in the west of Ireland, and a few enquiries locally will point you to the best.

The instrumental repertoire mainly consists of dance tunes, but there is also a group of instrumental pieces known as **Fonn Mall** – "slow airs" – played without accompaniment and usually to hushed attention. Most are laments or the melodies of songs, some so old that the words have been lost. The *uilleann* pipes (see box overleaf) are particularly well suited to the performance of airs, as their plaintive tone and ability to produce complex ornamentation cleanly allows them to approach the style of *sean nós* singers (see opposite).

Playing in groups or with accompaniment is a prominent feature of traditional music performance today. One of the most exciting exponents of this style is the band **De Dannan**, which in its heyday featured three women singers who went on to have solo careers in commercial rock: **Mary Black, Dolores Keane**, and **Maura O'Connell**. Ireland's best-known traditional band, **The Chieftains**, carry on the virtuoso tradition, too. This group was the spearhead of the 1960s' revival of Irish traditional music, which itself was largely due to the efforts of the group's founder, composer and arranger, **Seán Ó Riada**. Living in the *Gaeltacht* (Irish-speaking area) of Cuil Aodha, renowned for its singers and passionate devotion to music, Ó Riada hit on the idea of ensemble music-making using traditional instruments like the pipes, fiddle and whistle. It was a brilliantly obvious innovation and, over the past three decades, The Chieftains have developed the concept of ensemble playing to the point where it has become universally accepted and adopted. In addition, Ó Riada brought his genius for interpretation to bear on choral, liturgical and orchestral music.

A relatively recent newcomer to the ensemble scene is **Sharon Shannon**. Playing furiously energetic dance music, Shannon is a mesmerizing accordion player who can also turn her hand to the fiddle and spent some time with The Waterboys before forming her own band. Her first solo album mixed well-known and much-played tunes like *The Silver Spire* and *O'Keefes* with Cajun, Swedish, and new material in traditional style. Her profile was further enhanced by her involvement with the *Woman's Heart* album combining with Maura O'Connell, Frances and Mary Black, Dolores Keane and Eleanor McEvoy to produce one of the most successful traditional albums of all time, while her more recent albums, *Out the Gap* and *Each Little Thing,* are less traditional but exude the ebullience that has become her trademark. Donegal-based **Altan** derive their energy from a twin fiddle attack led by **Mairead Ní Mhaonaigh** and **Ciaran Tourish**, while their earlier recordings feature the exquisite flute playing of the late **Frankie Kennedy** – all can be appreciated on the *First Ten Years* compilation. Northern band **Deanta** consist of five women and one man and their album *Ready for the Storm* has been hugely popular, while **Nomos** have gone from strength to strength since the release of *I Won't be Afraid Any More.* Other prominent new bands include **Lunasa**, whose eponymous debut album sparkles with the pipe playing of Belfastman John MacSherry, **Beginish** and **Danú** who have both recently released debut albums, the American-influenced **Solas** and the appropriately fast and furious **Dervish**.

FOLK MEETS TRADITIONAL

Singing **folk songs** to instrumental accompaniment became enormously popular in Ireland in the 1960s with the triumphal return from America of **The Clancy Brothers**. The Clancys had taken New York's Carnegie Hall and the networked *Ed Sullivan Show* by storm, and they were welcomed home to Ireland as conquering heroes. Their heady blend of rousing ballads accompanied by guitar, harmonica, and five-string banjo revitalized a genre of folk song that had all but vanished. Hundreds of sound-alike ballad groups sprang up, decked out in a motley selection of ganseys – The Clancys' hallmark was the Aran sweater. Before the ballad group fashion petered out, it had laid the foundations for a revival of interest in popular folk singing that endures to this day. Still going strong is another great group of this era, **The Dubliners**. With an uncompromisingly urban image, in contrast to the rather twee Oirishness of The Clancys, their work was often bawdy and their ribald spirit was captured in the most popular song of this era, *Seven Drunken Nights* (although the Dubliners only recorded five of them). Earthiness may have been part of the reason why their true musical accomplishment was never fully appreciated for, as well as fielding two unique singers, **Luke Kelly** (who died in 1984) and **Ronnie Drew**, they boasted two fine instrumentalists, banjoist **Barney McKenna** and fiddler **John Sheehan**. In many ways they helped lay the groundwork for the fusion of the traditional/ballad genre explored by bands such as **Sweeney's Men**, **The Johnstons**, **The Bothy Band** and, most influential of all, **Planxty**.

Planxty was formed from the musicians recording Christy Moore's *Prosperous* album and the evolution of traditional music can be traced through the band members' post-Planxty recordings. The band consisted of **Liam O'Flynn**, **Donal Lunny**, **Andy Irvine** and **Christy Moore** and their self-titled first album mixed traditional, modern folk and ballad singing through harmonies backed by O'Flynn's superlative pipe playing. They recorded three albums before their split and these are available on the 1976 album *The Planxty Collection*. The band reformed again in 1978, adding the former Bothy Band and currently Chieftain's flautist, **Matt Molloy**, to their ranks. Their best work in this period is *The Woman I Loved So Well* but the band split finally when Lunny and Moore moved on to stretch the traditional genre even further with the formation of Moving Hearts.

Moving Hearts radically attempted to fuse traditional and rock music and almost succeeded. Consisting of two pipers, saxophone, bass and lead guitars, electric bouzouki, drums and percussion, their gigs were memorable feasts of exciting music, seeming simultaneously familiar and new. Too large to survive financially, the band sadly folded in 1984. Since then there have been a few reunions which have played to crowds of fans old and new. Released after their break-up, their 1985 album *The Storm* is a landmark in its pioneering use of rock and jazz idioms to redefine the harmonic and rhythmic foundations of Irish music.

Moore has since moved on to become possibly Ireland's best loved folk musician recording a number of highly successful and acclaimed albums. In his first recordings, such as the album *Prosperous*, he was overtly polit-

---

INSTRUMENTS AND PLAYERS

We've included mention of the best instrumentalists on the Irish music scene in this round-up of traditional instruments. If you get the chance to see any of them at the festivals, don't miss it.

The harp

There are references to harp playing in Ireland from as early as the eighth century. Indeed, in Irish legend the harp is credited with magical powers and it was adopted as the island's symbol in the seventeenth century (and somewhat later by Guinness). As court musicians to the Gaelic aristocracy, the old Irish harpers were a musical élite and had a close acquaintance with the court music of Baroque Europe. The couple of hundred surviving tunes by the greatest of eighteenth-century harpers, O'Carolan, clearly reflect his regard for the Italian composer Corelli.

Their harp was metal-stringed and played with the fingernails. Today's harpists play (with their fingertips) a chromatic, gut-string version, which one of its best exponents, **Maire Ni Chathaisaigh**, describes as "neo-Irish". Maire has been notably successful in adapting dance music for the instrument, drawing on her knowledge and love of the piping tradition as inspiration.

Be warned that there is also a bland, anodyne type of twee Irish music played on a gut-strung instrument, often as accompaniment to ersatz medieval banquets held at tourist locations around the country. About as traditional as green beer, it should be given a wide berth.

Uilleann pipes

"Seven years learning, seven years practising, and seven years playing" is reputedly what it takes to master the *uilleann* (pronounced *illun*) pipes. Perhaps the world's most technically sophisticated bagpipe, it is highly temperamental and difficult to master. The melody is played on a nine-holed chanter with a two-octave range blown by the air from a bag squeezed under the left arm, itself fed by a bellows squeezed under the right elbow. As well as the usual set of drones, the *uilleann* pipes are marked by their possession of a set of regulators, which can be switched on and off to provide chords. In the hands of a master they can provide a sensitive backing for slow airs and an excitingly rhythmic springboard for dance music.

The pipes arrived in Ireland in the early eighteenth century and reached their present form in the 1890s. Taken up by members of the gentry, who became known as "gentlemen pipers", they were also beloved of the Irish tinkers or travellers, and two different styles evolved: the restrained and delicate parlour style exemplified by the late **Seamus Ennis**, and the traveller style which, designed as it was to coax money from the pockets of visitors to country fairs, is highly ornamented and often showy.

Some of the most acclaimed musicians of recent years have been pipers: Seamus Ennis, **Willie Clancy**, and travellers **Johnny** and **Felix Doran**, all alas now dead. Today **Liam O'Flynn** is regarded as one of the country's foremost practitioners and has pushed forward the possibilities for piping through his association with classical composer **Shaun Davey** and with the band Planxty. Other contemporary pipers include **Finbar Furey** and **Davy Spillane**, who learned much of his technique from travelling pipers.

ical in the style of Woody Guthrie or the early Bob Dylan. This commitment is also evident in his recordings with Moving Hearts, such as his protest against state repression *No Time For Love* and, in the mid-1980s album *The Time has Come*, his song *Section 31* which criticizes the Republic's media censorship of Sinn Féin. Though Moore has become less politically engaged, his popularity has been maintained through stunning live performances, including regular mainstays such as *Lisdoonvarna* and *Ride On*. Finally, in 1996, after years of singing others' songs, he released a self-penned album *Graffiti Tongue*. However, in 1998 he announced his retirement after a period of ill-health.

Moore's brother Barry records under the name **Luka Bloom** (a combination of Suzanne Vega's song and the protagonist of *Ulysses*). Early on he backed his brother who recorded some of Bloom's work, most notably *The City of Chicago*. With a reputation himself for magnificent live performances he has also made some fine albums including *Turf* and *Salty Heaven*.

Of the other musicians recording crossover trad and folk in the sixties, **Paul Brady** con-

The bodhrán

The *bodhrán* (pronounced *bore-run*) is an instrument much in evidence at traditional sessions and a relatively recent addition to the dance music line-up. It is not universally welcome, partly because it looks like an easy way into playing – and it isn't. The great piper Seamus Ennis, when asked how a *bodhrán* should be played, replied "with a penknife". The *bodhrán* is a frame drum usually made of goatskin and originally associated with "wren boys" or mummers who went out revelling and playing music on Wrens Day (Dec 26). It looks like a large tambourine without jingles and can be played with a small wooden stick or with the back of the hand.

When played well by the likes of famed Galway musician **Johnny "Ringo" MacDonagh**, **Donal Lunny**, **Mel Mercier**, or **Tommy Hayes**, the *bodhrán* sounds wonderful, a sympathetic support to the running rhythms of traditional music. Since it was introduced into mainstream traditional music in the 1960s by the great innovator Seán Ó Riada, it has come on by leaps and bounds, and new techniques are constantly being invented. Many traditional ensembles now regard it as *de rigueur*.

Flutes and whistles

It's the wooden flute of a simple type that is used in Irish music, played mostly in a fairly low register with a quiet and confidential tone which means that it's not heard at its best in pub sessions. Played solo by such musicians as **Matt Malloy** or **Desi Wilson**, its clear flow of notes displays a gentler side to the rushing melodies of jigs and reels.

While anyone can get a note, though not necessarily the right one, out of its little cousin the tin whistle, it can take a long time to develop an embouchure capable of producing a beautiful flute tone, and so piper Finbar Furey has introduced the low whistle, which takes the place of the flute when there is no proper flute player around. In the right hands, those of **Paddy Moloney**, **Packie Byrne** or **Mary Bergin**, for example, the whistle itself is no mean instrument, but it's also suitable for the beginner. If you're interested, make sure you get a D-whistle, as most Irish music is in this key.

Fiddles

The fiddle is popular all over Ireland, and each area has its own particular characteristics: Donegal breeds fiddlers with a smooth melodic approach but lively bowing techniques, whereas the Sligo style, exemplified in the playing of the great Michael Coleman, is more elaborate and flamboyant. Coleman's 1920s recordings in America still wield an incredible influence on contemporary fiddling. Currently worth catching are **Martin Hayes** or the semi-legendary **Tommy Peoples**.

The bouzouki

At first sight it might seem odd to include the bouzouki on a list of traditional Irish instruments. Nevertheless, its light but piercing tone makes it eminently suitable both for melodies and providing a restrained chordal backing within an ensemble, and since its introduction to the island by Johnny Moynihan, in the late 1960s, and subsequent popularization by Donal Lunny, it has taken firm root. In the process it has lost much of its original Greek form, and with its flat back the Irish bouzouki is really closer to a member of the mandolin family. Along with other string instruments like the guitar and banjo, which provide supporting harmonies in a "folky" idiom, bouzoukis crop up at sessions all over the country, and some of the best accompanists are bouzouki players.

tinues to produce music of an exceptional standard. From Strabane in County Tyrone, Brady became involved in the Dublin folk renaissance while studying there in the 1960s. His first recordings were made with the Johnstons with whom he made seven albums before leaving for London and New York, returning in 1974 to join Planxty for a short time. In 1976 he teamed up with Planxty member Andy Irvine and the album they produced, with its unique and sensitive interpretations of songs like *Arthur McBride* and *The Lakes of Pontchartrain*, make it one of the finest albums in the traditional canon. His work in the late seventies was of an equally high standard culminating in arguably his best solo album, *Welcome Here Kind Stranger*, in 1978. The 1980s saw Brady move away from his traditional roots through *Hard Station* (1981) which included the passionate exposé of anti-Irish racism, *Nothing but the Same Old Story*. Subsequent albums have further highlighted his tremendous songwriting talents – he's been recorded by Tina Turner and Eric Clapton among many others and the best way of sampling these is his compilation *Songs and Crazy Dreams*.

Contemporary bands striving for new ways to express the tradition are the excellent **Kila**, whose second album *Tóg é go Bog é* ("Take it easy"), mixes traditional singing with African rhythms, the superb **Afro-Celt Sound System**, **Anam**, who draw on a rich variety of musical influences from jazz and blues, and **Anúna**, a vocal group spanning classical, folk, traditional and contemporary. The borderlands of traditional and rock are being explored by **Four Men and a Dog** and **Goats Don't Shave**, while **The Saw Doctors** owe a great deal to the showbands of the 1960s (see p.651). **Clannad**'s blend of atmospherics has brought the group huge international success.

Any examination of Irish traditional music must include a reference to **The Pogues**. Originally known as Pogue Mahone ("kiss my arse" in Irish), this London Irish band emerged in the early 1980s playing a chaotic set of "Oirish" standards and rebel songs. Iconoclasts to the core, they brought a punk energy to the Irish ballad. They were also blessed with one of the finest Irish songwriters of recent years, **Shane McGowan**. His songs captured the casualties and condition of Irish exile in London and, said fan and producer Elvis Costello, "saved folk from the folkies". Certainly they helped bring a new audience, and a new generation of musicians, back to look at its roots. McGowan now records with his own band The Popes.

ROCK, POP AND WHATEVER YOU WILL

Naturally, Ireland's rock scene has always borne close similarities to Britain's. Physical proximity, the permeation of British mass-media, especially radio and the influential rock press, and British stars' use of Dublin as a tax haven have all facilitated a musical currency between the two. What happens in London, Liverpool or Manchester tends to be mirrored in Belfast and Dublin and, occasionally, vice versa. However, there are two significant exceptions. First, apart from mavericks like Richard Thompson, British rock and pop bear little indication of any traditional folk origins, whereas Irish rock culture is steeped in it – a hardly surprising conclusion considering the number of Irish musicians who learn a traditional instrument and its associated tunes at an early age. Secondly, the overwhelmingly mono-cultural nature of Irish society means that important components of the British scene – reggae, ragga, bhangra, black dance and soul music in its many variations – are rarely experienced first-hand or develop from cultural traditions. Two Tone, for instance, could never have happened in Dublin, just as a host of Clannad clones is never likely to appear in Coventry. Nevertheless, the country's rock heritage is a rich one and, for every dozen bands trying to be the new Radiohead, there's always something happening in the pubs and clubs of Dublin, Belfast and Derry.

SHOWBANDS AND BEAT

For most of the 1960s and the following decade, live music was dominated by that peculiarly Irish phenomenon, the **showband**. These groups of neatly-coiffed, shiny-suited cover-version merchants toured the country, playing their selections in vast ballrooms (barely a few of which survive today). Enthusiasm tended to supersede talent, but their regimentation did provide a training ground for future stars such as Rory Gallagher and Eric Bell (Thin Lizzy's first guitarist).

TWENTY ESSENTIAL IRISH ROCK ALBUMS

A House *I Am the Greatest* (1991;Setanta UK).

Paul Brady *Hard Station* (1981; Mercury UK).

Mary Coughlan *Under the Influence* (1987; WEA UK).

The Divine Comedy *Casanova* (1996; Setanta UK; Red Ink US).

The Fat Lady Sings *John Son* (1993; East West UK).

The Framesdc *Fitzcarraldo* (1996; ZTT UK; WEA/Elektra US).

Gavin Friday *Shag Tobacco* (1995; Island UK).

Hothouse Flowers *People* (1988; London UK; Polygram US).

Microdisney *The Clock Comes Down the Stairs* (1985; Rev-Ola UK).

Van Morrison *It's Too Late to Stop Now* (1974; Warner UK; A&M US).

Moving Hearts *Moving Hearts* (1981; WEA UK).

The Pogues *Rum, Sodomy and the Lash* (1984; Stiff UK).

Sinéad O'Connor *I Do Not Want What I Haven't Got* (1991; Ensign UK; Chrysalis US).

The Stars of Heaven *Sacred Heart Hotel* (1986; Rough Trade UK).

Taste *On the Boards* (1970; Polydor UK).

Them *Angry Young Them* (1965; Decca UK).

Thin Lizzy *Jailbreak* (1976; Vertigo UK; Polygram US).

Pierce Turner *The Compilation* (1998; Beggars Banquet UK).

The Undertones *The Undertones* (1979; Sire UK; Ryko US).

U2 *The Joshua Tree* (1987; Island UK; Polygram US).

The showbands' dominance was undermined by the arrival of **beat music**, conveyed by radio and, like Liverpool, by sailors bringing American R&B records to the ports of Dublin and Belfast. By the mid-1960s Dublin was awash with beat groups, the majority of whom are long- (and perhaps best-) forgotten, though you can hear examples of the recordings of The Greenbeats, The Movement, Purple Pussycat and a horde of others on the Sequel collection *Ireland's Beat Groups: 1964–69*. The most successful group was **Bluesville**, led by Ian Whitcomb, an American studying at Trinity College, which had a USA top ten hit with *You Turn Me On*. Meanwhile, in Belfast, George Ivan Morrison had got together with guitarist Billy Harrison to form **Them**. **Van Morrison** had toured with another Belfast band, The Monarchs, since 1959, when he was only 14, but Them's successes with *Baby, Please Don't Go* (the B-side was the wonderful *Gloria*) and *Here Comes the Night* established musical credentials which he has never relinquished. Dissatisfied with his management, constant personnel changes and the quality of the band's first two albums, Morrison left and moved to the USA. After disastrous experiences with the Bang label, he signed with Warner Brothers; his first two albums with them achieved astonishing critical, if not entirely commercial, success and estab-

lished the hallmarks of his style. The marvellously atmospheric *Astral Weeks* was recorded in only two days, consisting of apparent improvisation by an adept band adroitly working around Van's range of vocal stylings and poetic lyrics. *Moondance* followed two years later, in 1970, revealing his ability to construct compact songs characterized by a sense of relaxation, though driven by extremely tight instrumentation. Since then Morrison has released numerous albums, of late almost annually, but while none has attained the excellence of the early pair, he remains the consummate professional and a tremendous experience live.

Morrison's love of the blues was shared by the Donegal-born guitarist **Rory Gallagher**. Extracting himself from the showband scene, Gallagher was first successful as leader of the progressive blues band **Taste** where he developed a reputation for his powerful rolling guitar licks. Taste split acrimoniously in 1970, citing the then popular "musical differences" and Gallagher launched a creditable solo career, using a variety of bassists and drummers, notable for his range of checked shirts and the intensity of his live performances (captured semi-successfully on *Irish Tour* and *Live! in Europe*). His later career was bedevilled by health problems and, sadly, he died in 1995.

THE SEVENTIES

Ireland dabbled with psychedelia and for a time the music scene was dominated by bands such as Granny's Intentions, Dr Strangely Strange and Eire Apparent. However, it was **Skid Row**'s more straight-out-the-barrel rock which was to have a lasting impact. The original band featured the bassist **Brush Shiels** (still playing regularly in Dublin), an astonishingly young Belfast lad, **Gary Moore**, on guitar and, for a while, **Phil Lynott** as singer. Skid Row released two progressive albums in the early 1970s, after which Moore left – he later played with a variety of other bands running the gamut of rock to heavy metal before establishing himself as a major solo performer.

Phil Lynott, however, formed **Thin Lizzy**, the first Irish band to crack the world market which led to Lynott becoming the first black Irish superstar. Initial success came with a reworking of the traditional *Whiskey in the Jar* in 1973. Then followed a series of albums, dominated by Lynott's romantic lyrics and a characteristic twin lead guitar sound. The 1976 album *Jailbreak* retains its initial impact, even if the macho posturing of its biggest hit, *The Boys are Back in Town*, jangles raucously in an era of more considered sensibilities. Lynott later produced a couple of fine, though sadly overlooked, solo albums (*Solo in Soho* is the better), before dying from kidney and liver failure in 1986.

Elsewhere, two more folk-oriented bands enjoyed a modicum of popularity in the early 1970s. The acoustic duo **Tír Na nÓg** supported virtually everybody and made a couple of whimsical albums for Chrysalis. Meanwhile, **Horslips** were almost single-handedly responsible for Celtic Rock. Retrospectively, their Irish legend-based concept albums such as *The Tain* (1973) and *The Book of Invasions* (1976) seem clumsily contrived in context and obscure in content – as many such albums were – but their use of traditional instruments in a rock setting was of durable influence and they blazed a trail for later bands to follow, such as **Moving Hearts** (see p.652), **In Tua Nua** and **Lick the Tins**.

There may have been fewer Irish dinosaurs to be declared extinct, but the advent of punk and new wave in the second half of the 1970s reinvigorated the home scene. However, the initial success of **The Boomtown Rats**, led by **Bob Geldof**, relied on their ability to produce powerful three-minute pop songs such as *Rat Trap* (1978) and *I Don't Like Mondays* (1979). For a while the Dublin scene thrived through bands such as **The Radiators from Space** (featuring later Pogues guitarist Philip Chevron), **The Virgin Prunes**, **The Blades** and a very young bunch of hopefuls called **The Hype**. Perhaps the greater successes, however, were in the North. **Stiff Little Fingers** first came to notice in 1978 with their astonishingly powerful debut single *Suspect Device*, a song whose driving beat struggled to contain an equally powerful lyric of political discontent. Meanwhile, **The Undertones** had been formed in Derry in 1974, but failed to achieve any success until the BBC Radio One disc jockey Jon Peel adopted their *Teenage Kicks* as a virtual personal anthem. Four albums of finely-crafted perceptive songs followed, mixing in perfect harmony the **O'Neill Brothers** songs of adolescent yearning, **Feargal Sharkey's** idiosyncratic tremolo voice and a pumping beat. After their split in 1983 Sharkey had a couple of hit singles while Damien and John O'Neill formed **That Petrol Emotion** whose initial releases were marked by powerful political sentiments questioning the continued British presence in Ireland.

U2 TO THE CORRS

The Hype, having changed their name to **U2**, went on to become the biggest rock band in the world. Listening to their first album *Boy* (1980), it's just about possible to understand the reason. Then, as now, U2's ability to try their hand at a range of styles is very much apparent, even if the original efforts lacked their subsequent polish and grasp of studio technique. Nevertheless, the key elements have remained the same: a tight rhythm bedrock of **Adam Clayton** (bass) and **Larry Mullen** (drums) setting the framework for **Dave Evans**'s innovative chordal guitar stylings and **Bono**'s soaring voice. Their anthems proved ideal American stadium fodder and the video of *Under a Blood Red Sky* (1983) brought them an even wider audience. 1987's *The Joshua Tree*, however, was their major breakthrough, despite the bleakness of songs such as *Where the Streets Have No Name* and *I Still Haven't Found What I'm Looking For*. The album even spawned a notable group of Dublin parodists, **The Joshua**

Trio, featuring one of the future author's of *Father Ted*. The release of subsequent U2 albums and their associated tours have become major international events and Bono has become Ireland's greatest living love-hate figure, derided for his occasional pomposity (such as his on-stage telephone calls to political leaders), but revered for his undeniable care for his country (such as his appearance at Ash's 1998 peace settlement gig with the politicians David Trimble and John Hume).

Following U2's ascent to glory, Dublin's bars and clubs were awash with agents and talent scouts trying to sign "the next big thing". Most of the recordings of these bands have sunk without trace and few now recall Aslan, Cactus World News, Cry Before Dawn or Light a Big Fire. A couple are worth noting – the country-tinged **Stars of Heaven**, who sadly split before the talent displayed in their debut *Sacred Heart Hotel* could evolve further, and the continued efforts of **Gavin Friday** (first with the Virgin Prunes and later solo) to gain the audience he deserves for his original confection of the baroque and bizarre. A significantly successful signing, however, was the then shaven-headed young singer, **Sinéad O'Connor**, first with her Prince-written single *Nothing Compares 2 U* and later with the album *I Do Not Want What I Haven't Got* (1990). Yet it was her outspoken public pronouncements on Ireland, abortion and papal power which brought her even greater attention. Oppressed by her fame, she left Ireland and moved to London to rear her children and study, only returning to recording in the last few years.

Every musical genre seems to be represented in the Ireland of the 1990s. There are plenty of solo singers ploughing their lonely furrows. Apart from Paul Brady and Christy Moore (see p.652), the currently popular include **Sinéad Lohan**, **Kieran Goss**, **Nick Kelly** (formerly leader of the excellent *The Fat Lady Sings*) and two from the North, **Andy White** and **Brian Kennedy** who also works regularly with Van Morrison. Also worth seeking out are the sporadically-released albums by **Pierce Turner** (quirky avant-garde meets Irish sensibility) and the blues and jazz of the smoky-voiced **Mary Coughlan**. For a while, **The Cranberries** were a major force and it seemed as though the film *The Commitments* would sire a host of spin-off bands – only one, Glenn Hansard's **The**

Framesdc had any lasting impact, though since have disbanded. Other bands to enjoy success have included **Hothouse Flowers** (led by Liam O'Maonlai), **The Frank and Walters**, **A House**, **An Emotional Fish**, **Something Happens**, **the Sultans of Ping FC** and two notable results from the break-up of the wonderfully angry 1980s band **Microdisney** – the raw psychopathy of Cathal Coughlan's **Fatima Mansions** and the Beach Boys' inspired work of **The High Llamas**, led by Sean O'Hagan. Mention must also be made of the traditional-inspired soft rock of Donegal's **Clannad** and the more ambient, but exceedingly popular, doodles of their fellow family member **Enya**. The Enniskillen band **Celtus** is currently exploring a similar vein. There's a thriving dance scene in Ireland, too, and the most innovative work is probably being produced by **David Holmes** from Belfast.

Currently of note from the North are the youthful trio **Ash** from Downpatrick – their album *1977* showed precocious polish – and the one-man band, **Neil Hannon**, better-known as **The Divine Comedy**, whose recordings such as *Casanova* (1995) evoke the sharp-suited romance of a James Bond movie. The three-piece **Therapy?** have gained some success while the Belfast band **Watercress** and Derry's **Cuckoo** are both worth looking out for. Similarly, in the Republic, bands with significant potential include several trios (**Pelvis**, **Marbles**, **Blink**), the country-inspired **Great Western Squares**, **Picture House**, **Mexican Pets**, **Chicks** (the next Kenickie), **Juniper** and everybody's tip for mega-stardom, **Junkster**. Ireland's only rock paper, the superb *Hot Press*, is the place to look for information.

However, apart from the old favourites (Moore, Morrison, etc.) the favourite Irish artistes of the moment, naturally, come from the more mainstream areas. The teen market is catered for by the boy-band **Boyzone** and the girl-band **B*witched**, while the middle-aged have, of course, their darling **Daniel O'Donnell**, the homely Donegal singer of standards, C&W and gospel. Lastly, tapping the sensitivities of *Rumours*-period Fleetwood Mac, albeit with a strong Irish traditional influence, are the family foursome, **The Corrs** (three sisters, one brother), whose bright good looks and anodyne, but catchy, songs have already guaranteed them healthy bank accounts for years to come.

CLASSICAL MUSIC

As in the visual arts, Ireland has a strong classical music tradition, though it's little-known outside the island. The dominant instrument of early music was the **harp**, though we know little of how it was played since no written record has survived. However, more than two hundred works by the poet, harpist and composer **Turlough O'Carolan** (1670–1738) have survived. His work, together with the performances of the participants at the 1792 **Belfast Harp Festival**, transcribed and published by **Edward Bunting**, were the prime sources of the airs which have formed a major component of Irish music since that time.

During the eighteenth century, Dublin became an important musical centre and attracted many European composers, including **Handel**, who staged the premiere of the *Messiah* in the capital in 1742. The first native classical composer of note was **John Field** (1782–1837), who, as a child prodigy, was apprenticed to Clementi to demonstrate pianos. He taught in Europe for several years and produced a significant body of keyboard work, especially his *19 Nocturnes* which considerably influenced Chopin and other Romantics.

Another precocious child was **Michael Balfe** (1808–70), who made his debut as a violinist at the age of nine, though he had already begun composing two years earlier. During the 1820s, he studied under Rossini and became converted to the opera form. Numerous compositions followed and his *The Bohemian Girl* was a success of the time. From 1846, he was conductor of the London Italian Opera. Similarly popular were the operas of Waterford man **Vincent Wallace** (1813–65), particularly *Maritana* and *Lurina*. This Irish operatic tradition was continued by **Victor Herbert** (1859–1924), a cellist who played in the orchestras of Joseph Strauss before emigrating to the USA to join the New York Metropolitan Opera Company. His forte was the comic opera and he became popular for songs such as *Sweet Mystery of Life* before settling down to pen more serious work. Most prolific in this period, however, was **Charles Villiers Stanford** (1852–1924), who was organist at Trinity College, Cambridge. After a stint teaching at the Royal College of Music he became Professor of Music at Cambridge and taught

numerous young British composers of the era. In his own right he adapted Tennyson's poetry to choral settings, wrote a number of operas and religious pieces. His origins are reflected by his *Irish Symphony* and *Six Irish Rhapsodies*.

In the first half of the twentieth century, **Hamilton Harty** (1880–1941), from Hillsborough, Co. Down, attained a degree of fame through his conducting of the Hallé Orchestra from 1920 to 1933 and revived Handel's popularity through his arrangements of the *Fireworks* and *Water Music* suites. However, his own work, including an *Irish Symphony* utilizing the strains and melodies of traditional songs, is less well known. **A.J. Potter** (1918–80), the son of a blind Belfast piano-tuner, was Professor of Composition at the Royal Irish Academy of Music for almost twenty years and his own eclectic style influenced many of his students. Other notable figures have included the popular conductor **Brian Boydell** (b. 1917) whose works for orchestra and string quartet are influenced by Bartok and Hindesmith, and **Gerard Victory** (1921–1995), who became well-known via his work with the RTE Symphony Orchestra from 1967 onwards. Head of Music at the RTE for some of the same time was **John Kinsella** (b.1932) until he resigned in 1988 to devote himself to full-time composition, subsequently producing a number of influential works. **Seóirse Bodley** (b.1933) has written five full symphonies and numerous other works revealing influences ranging from the European avant-garde to traditional song. **Gerald Barry** (b.1952) studied composition under Stockhausen and has had many works commissioned by the BBC, additionally penning operas for the ICA and Channel 4. The flautist **John Buckley** (b.1951) has produced a range of works for solo instruments and various ensembles. Intriguingly, the latest generation of composers producing influential work includes a significant number of **young women**, including Elaine Agnew, Rhona Clarke, Siobhan Cleary and Deirdre Gribbin – a trend which bodes well for the future.

Finally, the more popular end of the home market has come to be dominated recently by composers experimenting with adaptations and reformulations of Irish traditional music. Notable exponents include **Patrick Cassidy**, **Michael Alcorn** and **Shaun Davey**. While

Michael Ó Súilleabháin's recordings in this genre, such as *The Dolphin's Way* and *Flowing*, have attained considerable success. However, without any doubt, the most famous (or notori- ous, depending on your viewpoint) is **Bill Whelan**, responsible for the *Riverdance* phenomenon and a huge increase in the sale of dancing shoes.

IRISH LITERATURE

Samuel Beckett, in an interesting turn of phrase, maintained that Irish writers had been "buggered into existence by the English army and the Roman pope". Oscar Wilde sighed to Yeats that "we Irish have done nothing, but we are the greatest talkers since the Greeks". Despite recurrent attempts to keep them separate, politics, religion and literature in Ireland have always been inextricably linked, sometimes in a futile effort to escape from each other. And the suppression of the Irish language did give rise to a fresh and vital use of colloquial English that managed to retain the musical rhythms of the dying tongue. But it's a more complex story than that, and any outline of Ireland's vast canon of very different literatures has to go back a long way.

THE GAELS

Irish writing first appeared in the fifth century AD when monastic settlers brought Classical culture into contact with a Gaelic civilization that had a long and sophisticated oral tradition. Faced with the resistance of the pagan bards, the newcomers set about incorporating the Celtic sagas into the comparatively young system of Christian belief. These ancient tales told of war and famine, madness and love, death and magical rebirth – story sequences from deep in the folk memory. One of the earliest of these, the *Taín Bó Cuailngè*, deals with a rumpus between **Cúchulainn**, a prototypical Celtic superman, and the mighty Queen Medb, over the theft of a prize bull.

Later Irish artists made much of the early tales, sometimes with less than proper reverence; in Beckett's novel *Murphy*, for instance, a character attempts suicide by banging his head repeatedly against the buttocks of the statue of Cúchulainn, which still adorns the lobby of Dublin's GPO. New versions still appear from time to time, Seamus Heaney's translation of the mythical wanderings of the mad king *Sweeney Astray* being particularly brilliant.

Fairy tales from this Celtic era reveal a world of witches, imps and banshees, all jollying around in a Manichaean struggle with the forces of love, wisdom and goodness – which,

refreshingly, do not always triumph. Check out Kevin Danaher's *Folk Tales of the Irish Countryside* for full-blooded retellings.

In the eighth century **Fionn Mac Cumhaill** toppled Cúchulainn from the top of the folk hero charts, and stories of his exploits with his posse, the Fianna, began to appear. Fionn was a more disturbing and sophisticated figure, and his antics can be read in various modern translations.

A LITERATURE OF RESISTANCE

The first of many incursions from England took place in the twelfth century, when gangs of Norman adventurers invaded at the invitation of an Irish king. But it wasn't until five centuries later that the English presence found its way into the literature, when the excesses of English rule began finally to provoke an early literature of resistance.

The high point of this Irish-language tradition is the long poem from 1773 by **Eibhlín Dhubh Ní Chonaill** (1748–1800), *Caoineadh Airt Uí Laoghaire* (in English, *A Lament for Art O'Leary*). A traditional *caoineadh* or lament infused with a new political awareness, it deals with the execution of the poet's lover, who had refused to sell his prized white horse to the local redcoat and was therefore hunted down and killed. Even in translation it has a sparse and chilling beauty.

Other marvellous laments include the anonymous *Donal Óg*, Lady Gregory's translation of which was included with cheeky but effective licence in the 1985 John Huston film of Joyce's short story, *The Dead*. But the early written tradition wasn't all tears, and some pieces harked back to a pre-Christian earthiness. One such text from the later Irish-language era is **Brian Merriman**'s satirical *aisling* (vision poem), *Cúirt an Mheán Oíche* (*The Midnight Court*), a trenchant attack on the sexual inadequacy of the Irish male. One translation which preserves the raunch of the original is by Frank O'Connor, in *Kings, Lords and Commons*.

Despite persecution the Irish language persisted well into the last century, and Séan Ó Tuama and Thomas Kinsella's book of translations, *An Duanaire: Poems of the Dispossessed*, records the voices of those marginalized by foreign rule and famine. But thanks to the ineptitude of successive Irish governments, the Irish language is now in an advanced state of decay, with people having to be subsidized to remain in the *Gaeltachts* (Irish-speaking areas). Despite occasional revivals, contemporary Irish-language literature has been almost completely wiped out. Urban Irish schoolchildren are forced into reading **Peig Sayers** (1873–1958), a miserable native of the Blaskets whose sentences usually start with "God between us and all harm" or "Ah sure, life, what can you do?" Arguably the finest of modern Irish-language writers is **Pádraig Ó Conaire** (1883–1928), whose statue stands in Eyre Square, Galway. His *Scothscéalta* reads like Maupassant, capturing the stark cruelty of the Irish landscape and the petty malices of rural life. But unless you want to know about turf cutting, hill farming and getting up at five in the morning to milk your one mangy cow, recent Irish-language literature is generally unrewarding.

THE START OF THE LITERARY TRADITION

Between the 1690s and the 1720s the hated penal laws were passed, denying Catholics rights to property, education, political activity and religious practice. British misrule created widespread poverty which devastated the countryside and ravaged the population. It's in this period that **Anglo-Irish literature** began.

One of the most prominent of the early pamphleteers and agitators was **John Toland** (1670–1722), whom the authorities gave the dubious distinction of being the first Irish writer to have his work publicly burned. But the first big-league player arrived in the angry little shape of **Jonathan Swift** (1667–1745), Dean of St Patrick's Cathedral, Dublin. Swift was a cantankerous but basically compassionate man who used his pen to expose viciousness, hypocrisy and corruption whenever he saw it, which in eighteenth-century Dublin was pretty often. In one of his 75 pamphlets he proposed that the children of the poor should be cooked to feed the rich, thereby getting rid of poverty and increasing affluence. His masterpiece is *Gulliver's Travels* (1726), a satire as terrifying now as it ever was. Following a life of unrequited love he died a bitter man, and in his will he left an endowment to build Dublin's first lunatic asylum, adding in a pithy codicil that if he'd had enough money he would have arranged for a 20ft-high wall to be built around the entire island. He is buried in the vault of St Patrick's, where, as his epitaph says, "Savage indignation can rend his heart no more".

The other great satirist of the eighteenth century was **Laurence Sterne** (1713–1768). A tremendous wit with more mad whimsy than venom, his greatest work *Tristram Shandy* was once memorably described as "the greatest shaggy dog story in the language".

The elegant prose of **Edmund Burke** (1729–97) – graduate of Trinity College, philosopher, journalist and MP – argued for order in all things, decrying the French Revolution for its destruction of humanity's basic need for faith. He is a complex and difficult figure, and his ideas are claimed in Ireland both by the civil-liberties-trampling Right and by elements of the progressive Left.

1780–1880: THE CELTIC REVIVAL

Towards the end of the eighteenth century, a Europe-wide vogue for all things Celtic prompted a renaissance in Irish music and literature. This period also saw the birth of that misty, ineffable Celtic spirit, which was to influence Yeats a century later. A couple of important books appeared, including **Joseph Cooper Walker**'s *Historical Memoirs of the Irish Bards* (1786) and **Edward Bunting**'s *General Collection of Irish Music* (1796).

Dublin at the time of the Act of Union with Britain (1801) had long been a truly European city, frequently visited by French, German and Italian composers. Indeed, Handel's *Messiah* was first performed in Dublin's Fishamble Street. One Irish composer and writer who thrived under the European influence was the harpist **Turlough O'Carolan** (1670–1738), who met and traded riffs with the Italian composer Geminiani.

At the turn of the century a series of Irish harp festivals began, their purpose being to recover the rapidly disappearing ancient music. With their evocation of the bardic tradition they became a focus not just for nifty fingerwork but for political agitation. The harpers continued into the nineteenth century until **Thomas Moore** (1779–1852) finally stole many of their traditional airs, wrote words for them, published them as *Moore's Irish Melodies* and made a lot of money.

The concomitant literary revival entailed a resurrection of the Irish language too, and although few went so far as to learn it, it became a vague symbol of an heroic literary past that implied a fundamentally Nationalist world view. **John Mitchell**'s Fenian movement, provoked by Britain's callous response to the Famine, was at least as influenced by the Celtic Revival as it was by the new revolutionary ideas being imported all the time from Europe. Particularly in their impact on Yeats, the Fenians were to provide a bridge between the heroic past and the demands of modernism. One of their supporters, **James Clarence Mangan** (1803–49), inaugurated in *My Dark Rosaleen* the image of suffering Ireland as a brutalized woman, awaiting defence by a heroic man. In a country where visual and literary imagery of the Virgin Mary is ubiquitous, the symbolism escaped nobody.

THE NINETEENTH-CENTURY NOVEL

The unease generated among the aristocracy by the growth of Irish Nationalism and the Fenian Rebellion of 1848 found expression in novels showing the peasantry plotting away in their cottages against their masters up in the mansion – the "Big House" sub-genre of Anglo-Irish writing, represented by such writers as **Lady Morgan** (1775–1859). Typically, such a book will involve an evil-smelling Irish hoodlum inheriting the mansion and either turning it into a barn or burning it to the ground. *Castle Rackrent* by **Maria Edgeworth** (1776–1849) is one of the few good Big House novels, its craftily resourceful narrator telling the story of the great family's demise with a subtle glee.

The Irish fought back, appropriating the well-made novel for themselves. **Gerald Griffin** (1803–40), **John Banim** (1798–1842), **William Carleton** (1794–1869) and **Charles Lever** (1806–72) emerged as the voice of the new middle class, protesting at the stereotyping of the Irish as savages, and demanding political and economic rights.

This period also sees the entry of the Anglo-Irish into the crisis that would haunt them until their complete demise in the 1920s, as they struggled between the specifically "Anglo" and "Irish" sides of their identity. This kind of angst can be found running throughout the work of **Sir Samuel Ferguson** (1810–86), **Standish O'Grady** (1846–1928), and **Douglas Hyde** (1860–1949), the founder of the Gaelic League (1893) who went on to become Ireland's first president in 1937.

The writing of **E.O. Sommerville** (1858–1949) and (**Violet) Martin Ross**

(1861–1915) – cousins and increasingly impoverished daughters of the Ascendancy – is typical of nineteenth-century Anglo-Irish confusion. Their work, such as *Some Recollections and Further Experiences of an Irish R.M.* (1899) and the powerful novel *The Real Charlotte* (1894), is imbued with a genuine love of Ireland and the ways of the Irish peasantry, yet occasionally there's a chilling sense of things not being quite right. Previously marginalized in the tradition, the peasants now seem to keep intruding, sneaking into the upstairs rooms, interrupting their betters, conspiring behind the bushes in the well-kept gardens. And we see them, in ominous prophecy of things to come, wielding ploughshares and scythes which slowly begin, in the grey light of Galway which the two genteel old ladies capture so well, to look like weapons.

Meanwhile **Bram Stoker** (1847–1912) was busily writing his way into the history books with a novel that would enter modern popular culture in all its forms, from the movies to the comic book. *Dracula* is a wonderful novel, more of a psychological Gothic thriller than a schlock horror bloodbath, and its concerns – the nature of the soul versus the bestial allure of the body, for instance – are curiously Irish. But even this had its political implications. With its pseudo-folkloric style and its pitting of the noble peasants against the aristocratic monster debauching away in his castle, its symbolism is inescapably revolutionary and romantic.

THE STORY OF THE STAGE IRISHMAN

It's one of the delicious twists of fate which seem to beset Irish literary history that the country's most important early dramatist only took up writing by mistake. One evening a young Derry actor named **George Farquhar** was playing a bit part in the duel scene of Dryden's *Indian Emperor* at the Dublin *Smock Alley* theatre when, in a moment of tragic enthusiasm, he accidentally stabbed a fellow actor, almost killing him. Understandably shaken, Farquhar gave up the stage for good and went off to London to write plays instead.

Farquhar (1677–1707) is often credited, if that is the word, with the invention of the stage Irishman, the descendants of whom can still be seen on many of the programmes euphemistically referred to as "situation comedies" on British television. Effusive in his own way, but basically sly, stupid and violent, this stock character stumbled through the dramas of **Steele** (1672–1729), **Chaigneau** (1709–81), **Goldsmith** (1728–74) and **Sheridan** (1751–1816), tugging his forelock, bumping into the furniture and going "bejayzus" at every available moment. In fact Irish stereotypes had existed in the British tradition for many centuries before these dramatists had at least the good sense to make some money out of them. The stage Irishman was brought to his ultimate idiocy by **Dion Boucicault** (1820–90), whose leprechaunic characters seemed to have staggered straight out of the Big House novel and onto the London stage. Boucicault, however, has undergone something of a revival in recent years, with a few clever critics arguing that his unstable and unpredictable dramas were subversive attacks against the version of colonial reality imposed upon Ireland in the nineteenth century.

Boucicault's chum, **George Bernard Shaw** (1856–1950), turned out to be the kind of stage Irishman the English couldn't patronize out of existence. A radical socialist and feminist, he championed all kinds of cranky causes and some very admirable ones, and lived long enough to be a founder member of CND. His cerebral and often polemical plays – of which *Saint Joan* is perhaps the best – have remained a mainstay of theatre repertoire.

Yet even Shaw paled in comparison to the ultimate king of the one-line put-down, **Oscar Wilde** (1856–1900). After a brilliant career at Oxford – during which he lost both his virginity and his Irish accent – Wilde went on to set literary London alight, creating the smiling resentment that would finally destroy him. In *The Picture of Dorian Gray* he expanded on the Gothic tradition of Stoker and Sheridan Le Fanu (1814–73) to explore the fundamental duality of the romantic hero. But it was in his satirical plays, particularly *The Importance of Being Earnest*, that he was at his most acerbic. A brilliant and gentle man, he poured scorn on his critics, openly espoused home rule for Ireland and lived with consummate style until the debacle of his affair with Lord Alfred Douglas. This self-obsessed bimbo persuaded Wilde into a foolish libel action against his thuggish father, the Marquess of Queensbury, which Wilde lost. Immediately afterwards he was arrested for homosexuality, publicly disgraced and privately condemned by his many fair-weather friends.

He served two years in prison where he wrote his finest works, *The Ballad of Reading Gaol* and *De Profundis*. In early 1900 Ireland's greatest, and saddest, comedian died alone and distraught in Paris. "I will never live into the new century", he declared. "The English would just not allow it."

IRISH MODERNISM: POETRY AND DRAMA

Shortly before Wilde's death, the myth of the fallen hero had entered the vocabulary of Irish literature with the demise of Charles Stuart Parnell, Protestant hero of the Irish Nationalist community. Savaged from the pulpit and the editorial page for his adulterous involvement with Kitty O'Shea, Parnell had resigned in disgrace, defended by only a few lonely voices in the literary world. He died shortly afterwards, and Irish constitutional politics died with him.

The changed atmosphere of Irish life is caught in the work of **J.M. Synge** (1871–1909) and **George Moore** (1852–1933), who wrestled to accommodate a tradition they now saw rapidly slipping into the hands of the priests. Synge's *The Playboy of the Western World*, with its parricidal hero, is the last and perhaps the most brilliant attempt at a fundamentally English view of Irish peasant life, and was greeted by riots when it opened at The Abbey. His friend George Moore identified Catholicism as a life-denying and authoritarian creed, and his extraordinary volume *The Untilled Field* in many ways anticipates much later writers.

Meanwhile the separatist Sinn Féin party made great advances, and in 1916, led by the poet **Pádraig Pearse** (1879–1916) and **James Connolly** (1868–1916), an important socialist figure and powerful writer, there was an armed insurrection in Dublin. It was crushed savagely. Connolly and all the other leaders were court-martialled and shot, thereby becoming heroes overnight, and leading Yeats to observe that everything had been "changed utterly" and that "a terrible beauty" had been born.

William Butler Yeats (1865–1939) is one of the most written-about but most elusive characters in Irish literature. A Protestant aristocrat who argued for Irish independence, he helped found the world's first national theatre, The Abbey, before the nation even existed. He wrote early lyrical ballads about gossamer fairies and stunning sunsets until, stricken with desire for the beautiful Maude Gonne, he began reaming out some of the century's greatest works of unrequited love. Much of the work of his middle period lambasts the Dublin middle class for its money-grabbing complacency — *September 1913* is well worth a read if white-lipped rage is your thing. The late period is more problematic, producing a series of spare, lucid but complex meditations on the artist's task, but also some dodgy marching songs for the fascist Blueshirt movement.

Until the 1920s Yeats kept up a friendship with **Sean O'Casey** (1884–1964), who was that rarest of things, a working-class Irish writer. The Dublin slums in which he was born were later immortalized in his trilogy, *Shadow of a Gunman, Juno and the Paycock* and *The Plough and the Stars*. As with Synge, O'Casey's first nights were occasions for rioting and were usually attended by more policemen than punters. Indeed one night, in one of the more unusual moments in Irish literary history, Yeats had to lead the coppers' charge into the stalls to break up the fracas. Later he harangued the audience, screeching that the very fact they had broken up his play meant that O'Casey was a genius, and that "this was his apotheosis". O'Casey's journal records that while he smiled nervously and twiddled his thumbs backstage he couldn't wait to get home so that he could look up the word "apotheosis" in the dictionary. He is currently the subject of a misplaced revisionism which condemns his plays as sentimental and preachy.

IRISH MODERNISM: FICTION

As the tide of history turned towards Nationalism and Republicanism, and Yeats wondered glumly whether the tradition would die with the aristocracy, one of the seminal figures of literary modernism was emerging in Dublin. While still a student at the new University College — established in 1908 as a college for Catholic middle-class youth along lines suggested by Cardinal John Henry Newman — **James Joyce** (1882–1941) set himself against the world of politics and religion, and announced that he would become, in his own phrase, "a high priest of art". His subsequent career was to be the epitome of obsessive dedication.

Dubliners, his first book, continued where George Moore had left off, evoking the city as a deathly place, its citizens quietly atrophying in a state of emotional paralysis. *A Portrait of the Artist as a Young Man* is largely autobiographical and deals with Stephen Dedalus's decision to leave Ireland, criticizing the country as a priest-ridden and superstitious dump. After ten years of trying to get it published, Joyce finally had the bad luck to get it printed in 1916, the year of the Easter Rising. Perhaps understandably, lack of patriotism was not fashionable. Joyce was condemned by just about everyone who mattered and quite a few people who didn't.

His next novel, *Ulysses*, came out in 1922, another flashpoint in Irish history, as the new Irish government turned its guns on its former supporters. Modelled on Homer's *Odyssey*, the book follows Stephen Dedalus and Leopold Bloom through one day and one night of Dublin life, recording their experiences with a relish and precision that repulsed the critics, including Virginia Woolf and D.H. Lawrence. The book was widely banned and its self-exiled author was condemned as a pornographer. *Ulysses* is a kaleidoscope of narrative techniques; Joyce's last work, the vast *Finnegans Wake*, is the only true polyglot novel, a bewitching — and often impenetrable — stew of languages, representing the history of the world as dreamed by its hero, Humphrey Chimpden Earwicker (alias "Here Comes Everybody", "Haveth Childers Everywhere" etc). Critics of different persuasions see it as either the pinnacle of literary modernism or the greatest folly in the history of the novel.

The other great Irish modernist, **Samuel Beckett** (1906–89), emigrated to Paris and became Joyce's secretary in 1932. One writer has remarked that while Joyce tried to include everything in his work Beckett tried to leave everything out, and that's a pretty good summary. Beckett is bleak, pared down, exploring the fundamental paradox of the futility of speech and yet its absolute necessity. A modernist in his devotion to verbal precision, Beckett is on the other hand a dominant figure in what has been termed the postmodern "literature of exhaustion". As he said shortly before his death — "I have never been on my way anywhere, but simply on my way." Despite his reputation for terseness, Beckett was a prolific writer — the best places to start are the trilogy of novels (*Molloy, Malone Dies* and *The Unnamable*), and the play *Waiting for Godot*.

The absurdity of **Flann O'Brien** (1912–66) goes a little easier on the desperation. His comic vision of Purgatory, *The Third Policeman*, includes the famous molecular theory, which proposes that excessive riding of a bicycle can lead to the mixing of the molecules of rider and machine – hence a character who is half-man, half-bike. O'Brien's other great book, *At Swim-Two-Birds*, is a weird mélange of mythology and pastiche that plays around with the notion that fictional characters might have a life independent of their creators. Under one of his several pseudonyms, Myles Na Gopaleen (Myles of the Little Horses), he wrote a daily column for the *Irish Times* for many years, and his hilarious journalism is collected in *The Best of Myles* and *Myles Away from Dublin*.

Traditional fiction continued, of course – for instance, **Brinsley MacNamara** (1890–1963) devastatingly portrayed small-town life in *The Valley of the Squinting Windows*. But many writers had moved away from social observation and into a kind of modernist fantasy that had its roots way back in the Celtic twilight. **James Stephens** (1882–1950), a writer with an unjustly insignificant international reputation, used absurdity as a route to high lyricism. His *The Crock of Gold* is a profoundly moving fantasy on the Irish mythological tradition, part fairy story and part post-Joycean satire – in a sense, a precursor of "Magic Realism".

POSTWAR LITERATURE

Ireland in the late 1940s and 1950s suffered severe economic recession and another wave of emigration began. Added to this, the people had in 1937 passed a constitution – still operational today – which enshrined the Catholic Church's teachings in the laws of the land. Intolerance and xenophobia were bolstered by an economic war against Britain and a campaign of state censorship which was truly Stalinist in its vigour. Books which had never been read were snipped, shredded and scorched by committees of pious civil servants.

No history of postwar Irish literature would be complete without at least a mention of *The Bell*, a highly influential but now defunct literary magazine. In its two runs, between 1940 and 1948 and 1950 and 1954, it was a forum for writers like **Frank O'Connor** (1903–66), **Seán Ó Faoláin** (1900–91) and **Liam O'Flaherty** (1897–1984), all of whom were veterans of the independence war, and all of whom became outstanding short-story writers. They chronicled the raging betrayal they felt at state censorship and social intolerance – O'Connor's *Guests of the Nation* is perhaps the most eloquent epitaph for Ireland's revolutionary generation, a terrifying tale of the execution of two British soldiers by the IRA that influenced Brendan Behan's *The Hostage* enormously. *The Bell* also opened its pages to writers like **Peadar O'Donnell** (1893–1985), a radical socialist who, only six months before he died, publicly burned his honorary degree from the National University of Ireland on the occasion of a similar honour being conferred on Ronald Reagan.

In an infamous speech President Eamonn de Valera envisaged a new rural Ireland full of "comely maidens dancing at the crossroads and the laughter of athletic youths". But writers such as **Denis Devlin** (1908–59), **Francis Stuart** (1902–90), **Mary Lavin** (b. 1912) and **Brian Moore** (b. 1921) took up the fight for truth against propaganda. Their youths and maidens didn't dance. They were too busy packing their bags, or wandering in bewilderment across the desolate pages of an Ireland that had failed to live up to its possibilities. In their poetry **Austin Clarke** (1896–1974) and **Thomas Kinsella** (b. 1928) mourned the passing of hope into despair and fragmentation.

Patrick Kavanagh (1906–67) was an exception to all the rules. His poetry is almost entirely parochial, celebrating what he called "the spirit-shocking wonder of a black slanting Ulster hill", and his contemplative celebrations of the ordinary made him perhaps Ireland's best-loved poet. But as time went on, the harshness of reality began to press in on his work. His long poem *The Great Hunger* portrays rural Ireland – the same Ireland he had formerly extolled – as physically barren, with the blasted landscape an incisive metaphor for sexual repression. Its publication was widely condemned and the writer was even questioned by the police, an event he discussed with customary venom in his own shortlived journal, *Kavanagh's Weekly*.

The forces of reaction were again about to wage war on Irish literature. O'Casey's anti-clerical play *The Drums of Father Ned* was produced in Dublin in 1955 and received aggressive reviews. Three years later there was a proposal to revive it for the new Dublin Theatre Festival. The Catholic Archbishop of Dublin, John Charles

McQuaid, insisted that the plans be dropped, and when the trade unions stepped into the fray on his behalf, he succeeded. The year before, the young director Alan Simpson had been arrested and his entire cast threatened with imprisonment for indecency following the first night in Dublin of Tennessee Williams's play *The Rose Tattoo*. The important novelist **John McGahern** (b. 1935) lost his teaching job in a Catholic school in 1966 following the publication of his second book, *The Dark*, which was immediately banned. It's a marvellous novel, dealing tenderly with adolescence and clerical celibacy.

A more celebrated literary victim – in this case a self-destructive one – was **Brendan Behan**, who died in 1964, only six years after the publication of his first book, *Borstal Boy*. He spent the last years of his life as a minor celebrity, reciting his books into tape recorders in Dublin pubs, drunk and surrounded by equally drunk admirers, some of whom sobered up for long enough to try and save him from becoming the victim of his own myth.

CONTEMPORARY WRITING

It was only in the 1970s that the post-revolutionary climate of repression began to lift, and a sophisticated and largely progressive generation began having their works published. **Seamus Heaney** (b.1939) is the leading light of an unofficial group of Northern Irish poets who combine a sophistication of technique with a self-conscious political commitment. In 1995 Heaney became Ireland's fourth Nobel literary laureate (after Yeats, Shaw and Beckett), and if his latest work doesn't have quite the same fire as the early collections (such as *Death of a Naturalist*, *North* and *Station Island*), he continues to explore the classic Yeatsian dilemma between commitment and aloofness in compelling ways. Heaney's poetical-cum-critical deliberations on his racial and literary lineage also earned him a place as personal advisor to President Mary Robinson.

John Banville (b.1945) is another writer who prefers to remain at a tangent to the national identity, taking Ireland (when he writes of it at all) as the means rather than the end of his artistic vision. His first book, *Long Lankin*, appeared in 1970, a precocious debut that has been followed by a string of extraordinarily inventive novels, the most recent being *The Untouchable*, a fictional treatment of the life of

Anthony Blunt, and a superb exploration of treachery and deception.

The Irish Writers' Co-op produced novelists such as **Desmond Hogan** (b.1951), **Ronan Sheehan** (b.1953) and **Neil Jordan** (b.1951), the last of whom has gone on to major international success as a film director (see "The Irish in Film", pp.646–649). Jordan's work (much like Banville's), is located firmly within the counter-tradition of the novel coming out of Joyce, which in its turn owed something to the fantastic narratives of the sagas and to the rejection of the traditional novel form – what Joyce saw as its built-in British view of the world. The 1970s also saw the establishment of courageous publishing companies founded by writers, including Peter Fallon's Gallery, Dermot Bolger's Raven Arts Press, and Steve McDonogh's Brandon.

At the end of the decade **Paul Durcan** (b.1944) emerged as the inheritor of Kavanagh's mantle. He is a quirkily witty and profoundly religious poet, whose work encompasses social issues such as IRA bombings and Ireland's prohibition, until recently, of divorce and continuing ban on abortion, but always addresses them in personal terms.

Other important poets include **Padraic Fiacc** (b.1924), **Richard Murphy** (b.1927), **Michael Hartnett** (b.1934), **Brendan Kennelly** (b.1936), and **Derek Mahon** (b.1941). **Michael Longley** (b.1939) seems doomed always to be cited as the husband of the major revisionist critic Edna Longley, although his poetry is innovative and striking. Two poets having close relations with the US, **Paul Muldoon** (b.1951), born in Mayo but now living in New York, and **John Montague** (b.1929), born in Brooklyn of Irish parents but brought up in Tyrone, explore the relations between different poetic traditions on the island. **Christopher Nolan** (b.1965), a severely disabled writer, has proved to be an amazing talent, employing a rich language reminiscent of Dylan Thomas. His first book of poetry, *Damburst of Dreams*, received great acclaim, and he later won the Whitbread Prize for his autobiographical novel *Under the Eye of the Clock*.

Perhaps the most exciting contemporary verse is being written by women writers who, in the absence of civic or political opportunities, have turned to poetry to express their experiences of modern Ireland. Up and down the country poetry groups and workshops turn out collections that deal with the realities of being an Irish daughter, wife or mother. In this they receive support from established poets such as **Eiléan Ní Chuilleanáin** (b.1942), **Eavan Boland** (b.1944), and **Medbh McGuckian** (b.1950). Boland, especially, has explored the complexities of modern Irish female experience in particularly enabling ways. McGuckian's poetry is tremendously imaginative, and in *Selected Poems* (1997) she creates ephemeral worlds where language is fluid, meaning forever shifting.

Drama has undergone a resurgence too, with Galway's Druid Theatre putting on ground-breaking reinterpretations of Irish classics under the guidance of its brilliant director Garry Hynes. Roddy Doyle and Paul Mercier's Passion Machine theatre company offers plays about urban working-class experience in the manner of Stephen Berkoff or John Godber. Rough Magic is another young company whose work is political and challenging, if more international in scope.

Without doubt, the most successful theatre company and cultural initiative on the island in recent times has been **Field Day**, a Northern-based team founded by Seamus Deane (b.1940), Tom Paulin (b.1949), Brian Friel (b.1929), Seamus Heaney and actor Stephen Rea. As well as being established poets, Deane and Paulin are also insightful critics who from their locations in England and the US continue to do battle with all comers over the rights to Irish literary history. Friel, who turned from short-story writing to the theatre in the 1960s, provided Field Day with their greatest successes, in particular his play about the suppression of the Irish language, *Translations* (1980). However, after giving his hugely popular work, *Dancing at Lughnasa* (1990), to Dublin's Abbey Theatre, he left the group.

In addition to producing plays the company published an excellent series of short cultural and critical essays, perhaps attempting to revive the radical pamphleteering culture of the early eighteenth century. Their most ambitious project was the commissioning and publication in 1991 of the *Field Day Anthology of Irish Writing*, a massive three-volume attempt to encapsulate some of the grandeur of the country's literary heritage. The project ran into trouble, however, when it was seen that women were grossly under-represented at both editorial and authorial levels. In response to such criticism a "girls-only" fourth volume has been promised, and it is already haunted by accusations of tokenism.

Any list of Ireland's innovative theatre writers must include **Tom Murphy** (b.1936) and **Thomas Kilroy** (b.1934), but in the opinion of many the most important dramatist to emerge in the last few decades is **Frank McGuinness** (b.1953). His play *Observe the Sons of Ulster Marching Towards the Somme*, staged in Dublin as talks began on the Anglo-Irish agreement, focuses on the participation of a group of Northern Loyalists in the battle of the Somme. Its imagery exploits the symbolism of the whole Irish tradition, permitting a range of readings, in which the Somme represents the current situation in the North, or the battlefield of the Boyne, or the slaughters of the early sagas. It was his 1987 piece, *Carthaginians*, a play set in his native Derry, which thrust him into the major league of Irish writers. The play found a vocabulary in which to explore ancient Irish themes — the nature of political allegiance, death and resurrection, the relationship between Britain, Ireland and the North, sexuality, religion — in a way that seems to sum up the whole tradition while simultaneously threatening to demolish it. Never afraid to articulate the unfashionable, he asks questions of nationalism in a manner that demands attention: his *Someone to Watch Over Me* (1992) starts out appealing to our readiness to accept crude national stereotypes, but ultimately becomes, among other things, a homage to the English literary tradition. McGuinness's work provides, if not some hope of unifying the various strands of Ireland's long cultural histories, at least the imperative to understand what divides them; in this act of enquiry lies great humanity.

The Irish stage has produced a handful of interesting dramatists in recent years: **Sebastian Barry** (b.1955) takes figures from his recent ancestry and weaves plays from their unique junction with history — the finest example of which is *The Steward of Christendom* (1995), a piece of staggering poetic intensity. The plays of **Alex Johnstone** and **Conor McPherson** (b.1971) are set in contemporary Ireland; McPherson's work in particular has met with considerable critical acclaim: in *This Lime Tree Bower* he brings pace and pathos — at times with acute hilarity — to stories of provincial life; his most recent play, *The Weir*, confirms his reputation as a compelling dramatist. Belfast writer **Gary Mitchell** has produced some fine work, most notably *In a Little World* *of Our Own* and *As the Beast Sleeps*, the latter a play which centres around a group of Loyalist militants trying to come to terms with the encroaching cease-fire. Arguably the most successful dramatist to be writing plays in an Irish context right now is in fact English: **Martin McDonagh**, the Jack Charlton of contemporary Irish theatre, sets his work in an Irish west coast of the imagination, managing to both exploit and explode its associated myths. Heavily reminiscent of Synge, he deploys the traditional themes of murder, ignorance, familial hatred and isolation with swift, dark humour. McDonagh is a gifted storyteller, and *The Beauty Queen of Leenane*, *The Cripple of Inishmaan* and *The Lonesome West* have all proved immensely popular.

It is perhaps in the novel and in autobiography that the richest seam of contemporary Irish literature is to be discovered. Over the past decade or so, writers like Colin Bateman, Hugo Hamilton, Anne Enright, Eoin McNamee, Ferdia McAnna, Ronan Bennett, Michael O'Loughlin, Glen Patterson and Robert MacLiam Wilson have begun to turn the accepted version of Irish literary tradition on its head. **Dermot Bolger** (b.1959), as well as being a gifted poet and playwright, has produced hard-hitting yet lyrical novels of contemporary Dublin. **Colm Toibín** (b.1955) has written two deceptively understated novels of Irish experience at home and abroad in *The South* (1990) and *The Heather Blazing* (1992); in *The Story of the Night*, set in Argentina at the time of the Generals, he achieves a novel of breathtaking poise. *The Butcher Boy* (1992) by **Patrick McCabe** (b.1955) won numerous awards as well as being shortlisted for the prestigious Booker Prize, and the grisly comedy of that novel reappeared in even grimmer form in *The Dead School* (1995); in his latest novel, *Breakfast on Pluto*, McCabe's mordant humour shifts its focus to a violent, seedy London underworld. Younger writers such as **Joseph O'Connor** (b.1963) and **Emma Donoghue** (b.1969) are typical inasmuch as they work in a number of genres besides the novel. Their writing responds to the new Ireland of sex and drugs and rock 'n' roll in which they grew up, with Donoghue producing in her debut novel *Stir-fry* (1994) perhaps the first happy lesbian love story in Irish fiction.

Without doubt, the most successful of the new generation of novelists has been **Roddy Doyle** (b.1958), a writer who, along with Bolger and others, disdains the critical title of "Northside realist" (referring to the North Side of the River Liffey where most of their work is set). The first two novels of The Barrytown Trilogy, *The Commitments* (1987) and *The Snapper* (1990), have been made into successful films, and after just missing out with the third, *The Van* (1991), Doyle snapped up the Booker Prize in 1993 for *Paddy Clarke Ha Ha Ha*. In his most recent novel, *The Woman Who Walked Into Doors*, Doyle tackles the darker theme of domestic violence. Doyle's fiction makes deceptively easy reading, while the enormous sales figures for his books must compensate somewhat for the criticism that he merely reproduces modern urban variations on the stage Irishman.

This young generation of novelists of the 1980s and '90s gave short shrift to the hackneyed themes of the traditional canon: the Catholic Church, the love of the land, the repression of sexuality. Irish novels and short stories began to anatomize social change rather than conservatism, revealing an Ireland populated by women as well as men, Protestants as well as Catholics, fervent atheists as well as true believers, gays as well as straights, people who feel British as well as people who feel Irish, and writers for whom Ireland is no longer a necessary subject. It is interesting then that after such a great loosening of the soil, there emerged in the 1990s a couple of writers who returned to explore these themes via personal memoir, and in so doing found that their experiences of repression, denial and acute poverty struck a deep resonance in the consciousness of an older generation. **Nuala O'Faolain**'s *Are You Somebody?*, an autobiography which deftly portrays the desolate marginalization of women, and **Frank McCourt**'s *Angela's Ashes*, an extraordinary book showing the degradation and poverty of an entire class of Irish people, were both enormously popular, and perhaps cathartic, in an Ireland moving to publically come to terms with huge areas of deprivation in its immediate past. Less emotively, but no less successfully, in the North, too, childhood has proved fertile ground for novelists. **Seamus Deane**'s semi-autobiographical *Reading in the Dark* stands as a powerful, myth-spectred work, a child's world full of half-gleaned tales of superstition, political reprisals and fear, and **Ciaran Carson**'s *The Star Factory* delivers a Belfast ringing bright with poetic imagery, fresh and full of life. The nineties have seen some novels of great inventiveness too: Ciaran Carson's *Last Night's Fun* is an astonishing book conjuring up the spontaneous magic of the world of traditional music; **Philip Casey**'s first novel *The Fabulists* is a fine love story, skilfully understated, and **Ann**

Haverty's *One Day As a Tiger* is a delightfully mischievous tale drawing us in to consider the emotional and romantic possibilities of life in an age of genetic engineering. With such a wealth and diversity of literature pouring out of Ireland at the moment, it's difficult to imagine how the future might unfold.

BOOKS

Most of the books listed below are in print and in paperback – those that are out of print (o/p) should be easy to track down in second-hand bookshops. Publishers follow each title; first the UK publisher, then the US. Only one publisher is listed if the UK and US publishers are the same. Where books are published in only one of these countries, UK or US follows the publisher's name.

HISTORY AND POLITICS

John Ardagh, *Ireland and the Irish: Portrait of a Changing Society* (Penguin). Comprehensive and lively, this is an excellent anatomy of Irish society and its efforts to come to terms with the modern world.

Jonathan Bardon, *A History of Ulster* (Blackstaff; Dufour). A comprehensive account from early settlements to the current Troubles.

Brian Barton, *A Pocket History of Ulster* (O'Brien). Accessible account of Northern Irish politics from the years prior to Partition to the present day.

J.C. Beckett, *The Making of Modern Ireland 1603–1923* (Faber; Trafalgar o/p). Concise and elegant, this is probably the best introduction to the complexities of Irish history.

David Beresford, *Ten Men Dead* (Grafton; Atlantic Monthly). Revelatory account of the 1981 hunger strike, using the prison correspondence as its basic material; a powerful refutation of the demonologies of the British press.

Terence Brown, *Ireland: A Social and Cultural History 1922–1985* (Fontana; Cornell University Press). Brilliantly perceptive survey of writers' responses to the dog's breakfast made of post-revolutionary Ireland by its leaders.

Max Caulfield, *The Easter Rebellion* (Gill & Macmillan; Roberts Rinehart). Recently revised account of the events of 1916, originally published in 1963.

Michael Collins, *In His Own Words* (Gill & Macmillan UK). A collection of extracts from the revolutionary's writings and speeches.

S.J. Connolly (ed.), *The Oxford Companion to Irish History* (OUP). Recently-published massive introduction to almost every aspect of Irish history.

Tim Pat Coogan, *The Troubles: Ireland's Ordeal 1969–1995 and the Search for Peace* (Hutchinson; Roberts Rinehart). The former *Irish Press* editor's popular-history writing has many followers and his *The IRA* (Fontana UK) is a contemporary classic. His earlier books on two icons of modern Ireland, *Michael Collins* (Arrow; Roberts Rinehart) and *De Valera: Long Fellow, Long Shadow* (Arrow; Harper), are essential reading.

Peter Berresford Ellis, *Hell or Connaught* (Blackstaff; Dufour o/p) and *The Boyne Water* (o/p). Vivid popular histories of Cromwell's rampage and the pivotal Battle of the Boyne.

Michael Farrell, *Arming the Protestants: The Formation of the Ulster Special Constabulary and the Royal Ulster Constabulary, 1920–1927* (Pluto o/p; Longwood o/p). Farrell is a fine journalist and veteran of Northern Ireland's civil rights campaigns. In *Northern Ireland: The Orange State* (Pluto UK) he argues, as the title implies, from a Republican standpoint; it's an occasionally tendentious but extremely persuasive political account of the development of Northern Ireland.

Garret FitzGerald, *All in a Life* (Gill & Macmillan UK). The first former Taoiseach to write his memoirs has produced an extraordinary book, characteristically frank, and full of detail on the working of government.

David Fitzpatrick, *Oceans of Consolation: Personal Accounts of Migration to Australia.* (Cork University Press; Cornell University Press). Using over a hundred unedited letters largely written around the 1850s and '60s, this book brings to life the experiences of loss and longing of Irish emigrants to Australia.

R.F. Foster, *Modern Ireland 1600–1972* (Penguin). Superb and provocative new book, generally reckoned to be unrivalled in its scholarship and acuity, although it has been criticized for what some feel to be an excessive sympathy towards the Anglo-Irish. Not recommended for beginners.

Kathleen Hughes and Ann Hamlin, *The Modern Traveller to the Early Irish Church* (Four Courts Press UK). The remains of monastic settlements are found all over Ireland and this revised edition enhances the visitor's appreciation by reconstructing the daily religious and secular life of Ireland in the Early Christian Period; also includes a detailed list of recommended sites.

Gemma Hussey, *Ireland Today: Anatomy of a Changing State* (Penguin o/p). A well-regarded and invaluable source of information on Ireland's changing identity by this ex-government minister.

Robert Kee, *The Green Flag* (Penguin; 3 vols). Scrupulous history of Irish Nationalism from the first plantations to the creation of the Free State. Masterful as narrative and as analysis.

Dáire Keogh and Nicholas Furlong (eds.), *The Women of 1798* (Four Courts Press UK). Women are often "hidden" in Irish history and this collection of essays reasserts the vital role many played in the 1798 Rebellion, from Matilda Tone (wife of Wolfe) who redefined the role of woman as patriot, to the Belfast revolutionary Mary Anne McCracken.

Christine Kinealy, *This Great Calamity* (Gill & MacMillan; Roberts Rinehart). Unravels fact from fiction through systematic analysis of primary source material related to the Great Famine.

F.S.L. Lyons, *Ireland Since the Famine* (Fontana UK). The most complete overview of recent Irish history; either iconoclastic or revisionist, depending on your point of view.

T.W. Moody and F.X. Martin (eds.), *The Course of Irish History* (Mercier; Roberts Rinehart). Highly readable collection of essays on many aspects of Irish history.

R.J. Scally, *The End of the Hidden Ireland: Rebellion, Famine and Emigration* (OUP). History revealing the strategies deployed by one particular Roscommon peasant community in their struggle to avoid eviction and emigration; this book also details their exploitation by Irish Catholic middlemen.

David Sharrock & Mark Prendergast, *Man of War, Man of Peace? The Unauthorised Biography of Gerry Adams* (Pan UK). Lengthy, detailed account of the Sinn Féin leader's rise to prominence.

Margaret Ward, *Hannah Sheehy Skeffington: A Life* (Cork University Press UK). Fascinating, scholarly biography of a militant suffragist; co-founder of the Irish Women's Franchise League in 1908, Skeffington was one of the most important political activists of her day.

Cecil Woodham Smith, *The Great Hunger: Ireland 1845–1849* (Penguin). The classic history of the Famine, superseded by recent research, but still a superb and harrowing narrative.

A.T.Q. Stewart, *The Narrow Ground* (Gregg Revivals; Ashgate o/p). A Unionist overview of the history of the North from 1609 to the 1960s, providing an essential background to the current situation.

Peter Taylor, *Provos: The IRA and Sinn Féin* (Bloomsbury), published in USA as *Behind the Mask* (TV Books). Study of the historical development of the Provisional IRA, including fascinating interviews with IRA members.

Kevin Toolis, *Rebel Hearts: Journeys within the IRA's Soul* (Picador; St Martin's Press). Highly acclaimed and topical account of what makes the IRA tick by this journalist and screenwriter.

GAELIC TALES

Kevin Danaher, *Folk Tales of the Irish Countryside* (Mercier; Irish Books & Media). The best volume on fairy and folk tales, recorded with a civil servant's meticulousness and a novelist's literary style.

Myles Dillon (ed), *Irish Sagas* (Mercier; Irish-American Book Co.). An excellent examination of Cúchulainn, Fionn Mac Cumhaill etc, in literary and socio-psychological terms.

Seamus Heaney, *Buile Suibhne*; in English, *Sweeney Astray* (Faber; Noonday). A modern reworking of the ancient Irish saga of the mad king Sweeney.

Pádraig Ó Conaire, *Finest Stories* (Poolbeg o/p; Dufour o/p). Ó Conaire's dispassionate eye roams over the cruelties of peasant life.

Tomás Ó Criomhtháin, (sometimes Thomas O'Crohan), *An tOileánach*; in English, *The Islandman* (OUP UK). Similar to Ó Conaire but non-fiction and, if possible, even more raw.

Seán Ó Tuama and Thomas Kinsella, *An Duanaire: Poems of the Dispossessed* (Dolmen; University of Pennsylvania, o/p). Excellent translations of stark Irish-language poems on famine and death. See also Kinsella's translation of one of the earliest sagas, the *Táin Bó Cúailnge* (OUP UK).

Peig Sayers, *An Old Woman's Reflections* (OUP UK). Unfortunately, Sayers' complacent acceptance of her own powerlessness is still held up as an example to Irish schoolchildren. Still, in spite of itself, a frightening insight into the eradication of the Irish language through emigration, poverty and political failure. A funny deconstruction of the Sayers style is Flann O'Brien's *An Beál Bocht*; in English, *The Poor Mouth* (Grafton; Dalkey Archive).

William Butler Yeats (ed.), *Fairy and Folk Tales of Ireland* (Colin Smythe; Simon & Schuster). Yeats gets all misty eyed about an Ireland that never existed.

FICTION

Peter Ackroyd, *The Last Testament of Oscar Wilde* (Penguin UK). Witty re-creation of the life of the tragic, abused artist in exile; a superb parody and an absolute must for anyone so familiar with Wilde's epigrams, they wish he'd written more.

John Banville, *The Newton Letter* (Minerva; David R. Godine); *The Book of Evidence* (Picador; Warner); *Ghosts* (Mandarin; Vintage); *Athena* (Picador; Vintage); *The Untouchable* (Picador; Vintage). Five novels from first-rate Irish novelist, including his 1989, Booker Prize nomination, *The Book of Evidence*, a sleazy tale of a weird Dublin murder. His most recent work, *The Untouchable*, is a superb fiction based on the life of Anthony Blunt, full of deception and treachery.

Leland Bardwell, *The House* (Brandon Books o/p; Longwood o/p); *There We Have Been* (Attic; InBook o/p); *The White Beach, New and Selected Poems 1960–88* (Salmon UK). Quirky, bleak prose, often dealing with domestic violence, male cruelty, drink and poverty; but funny too, in a black way.

Sebastian Barry, *The Whereabouts of Eneas McNulty* (Picador; Vintage). Tremendously moving, tragic account of one of Barry's ancestors who fought for the British in both World War I and II, and the life he then had to lead as a consequence.

Colin Bateman, *Cycle of Violence*; *Divorcing Jack*; *Of Wee Sweetie Mice and Men*; and *Empire State* (all Harper Collins; Arcade). Sparkling and increasingly fast-paced tales of violence and men in crisis by one of the North's most successful novelists.

Samuel Beckett, *More Pricks Than Kicks* (Calder UK); *Molloy*, *Malone Dies* and *The Unnamable* (Calder; Grove). Beckett's early short stories, grotesque tales set around the eccentric character of Belacqua Shuah, were followed by his wonderful and increasingly bleak trilogy of breakdown and glum humour.

Brendan Behan, *Borstal Boy* (Arrow UK). Behan's gutsy *roman à clef* about his early life in the IRA and in jail.

Dermot Bolger, *The Journey Home* (Penguin UK). Dublin unforgettably imagined as both heaven and hell. *A Second Life* (Penguin UK) is an assured novel about a man who, miraculously given a second chance at life, sets out to find out the truth about his adoption. *Father's Music* (Flamingo UK). Dublin's criminal underworld is the setting for this psychological thriller.

Elizabeth Bowen, *The Death of the Heart* (Penguin; Vintage). Finely tuned tale of the anguish of unrequited love; generally rated as the masterpiece of this obliquely stylish writer.

Clare Boylan, *Home Rule* (Abacus UK); *Room For a Single Lady* (Abacus UK); *Holy Pictures* (Abacus UK) and *Nail on the Head* (Penguin o/p; Viking o/p). A rising star of contemporary Irish fiction, her *Room for a Single Lady* features 1950s Dublin and a cast of eccentric lodgers.

Philip Casey, *The Fabulists* (Lilliput; Serif). Deftly woven tale of love and storytelling; a fine first novel.

Seamus Deane *Reading in the Dark* (Vintage). A turbulent semi-autobiographical tale set in Derry in the 1950s and 60s, full of ghosts, fear and political enmities.

J.P. Donleavy, *The Ginger Man* (Penguin; Atlantic Monthly). Outlandish exploits of a consummate bounder; semi-autobiographical; banned in Ireland for some time.

Emma Donoghue, *Stir-fry* (Penguin; Harper). Well-wrought love story from young Irish lesbian writer. *Hood* (Penguin; Alyson). Painful and at times funny story about overcoming bereavement.

Roddy Doyle, *Paddy Clarke Ha Ha Ha* (Minerva; Penguin). Hilarious and deeply moving novel of Dublin family strife that won the Booker Prize in 1993. The earlier trilogy, *The Commitments* (Minerva; Vintage), *The Snapper* (Minerva; Penguin), *The Van* (Minerva; Penguin), lighter and funnier, made Doyle's reputation. In *The Woman Who Walked Into Doors* (Minerva;

Penguin) Doyle shifts to the darker theme of domestic violence.

Maria Edgeworth, *Castle Rackrent* (Penguin; OUP). Best of the "Big House" books, in which Edgeworth displays a subversively subtle sympathy with her peasant narrator. Would have shocked her fellow aristos if they'd been able to figure it out.

Anne Enright, *The Portable Virgin* (Minerva; Butterworth-Heinemann o/p). Highly original stories of life on the outside. *The Wig My Father Wore* (Mandarin UK). A tale of sex, death and reproduction.

Oliver Goldsmith, *The Vicar of Wakefield* (Penguin; OUP). An affecting celebration of simple virtue.

Hugo Hamilton, *The Love Test* (Faber UK). Irish-German novelist's thriller set on both sides of the Berlin Wall, before and after its fall, combines excitement with a tender portrait of a disintegrating marriage. *Dublin Where the Palm Trees Grow* (Faber UK) is a fine collection of stories set with equal assurance in Berlin and middle-class Dublin.

Anne Haverty, *One Day as a Tiger* (Vintage; Ecco). Delightful, arcadian tale of love and genetic engineering twists as the betrayals set in. A sentimental journey for our times.

Dermot Healy, *A Goat's Song* (Harvill Press; Harcourt Brace). Dark and deep novel which convincingly weaves a study of obsessive love into a fresh view of the Northern conflict.

Aidan Higgins, *Asylum and Other Stories* (Calder; Riverrun o/p); *Langrishe, Go Down* (Minerva; Riverrun); *Lions of the Grunewald* (Minerva UK). The most European of Irish writers, whose later works play with language in a mordantly humorous and deeply personal way.

Desmond Hogan, *The Ikon Maker* (Faber UK). Impressive, impressionistic first novel from one of Ireland's most lyrical prose writers, about angst-ridden adolescence in the 1970s, before Ireland was hip. *A Farewell to Prague* (Faber UK) is an intense, episodic, autobiographical novel that wanders lonely through the new Europe.

Neil Jordan, *Night in Tunisia* (Vintage; Random House o/p). Film director Jordan first made his name with this impressive collection, which prefigures treatments and themes of his films. His most recent novel, *Sunrise with Sea Monster* (Vintage UK), is a delicate, powerful study in

love and betrayal set in neutral Ireland during World War II. *The Past* (Vintage UK) deals with the troubled early years of the Irish Free State.

James Joyce, *Dubliners; Portrait of the Artist as a Young Man; Ulysses* (all Penguin; Vintage); *Finnegans Wake* (Penguin). No novel written in English this century can match the linguistic verve of *Ulysses*, Joyce's monumental evocation of 24 hours in the life of Dublin. From the time of its completion until shortly before his death – a period of sixteen years – he laboured at *Finnegans Wake*, a dream-language recapitulation of the cycles of world history. Though indigestible as a whole, it contains passages of incomparable lyricism and wit – try the "Anna Livia Plurabelle" section, and you could be hooked.

Molly Keane, *Good Behaviour* (Sphere; Knopf o/p). Highly successful comic reworking of the "Big House" novel.

Benedict Kiely, *God's Own Country: Selected Stories 1963–1993* (Minerva UK). A good introduction to the quirky fiction of a veteran novelist and travel writer.

Mary Lavin, *In a Café* (Town House UK). New collection of previously published stories by one of the great short-story writers, in the Chekhov tradition. Earlier books include *The House on Clewe Street* (Virago o/p; Viking, o/p) and *Stories* (Constable; Viking o/p).

Hugh Leonard, *Parnell and the Englishwoman* (Deutsch UK). Fictional biography focusing on Parnell's affair with Kitty O'Shea.

Bernard MacLaverty, *Cal* (Vintage; Norton); *Lamb* (Penguin; Norton). Both novels of love beset by crisis; the first deals with an unwilling IRA man and the widow of one of his victims. *Lamb* is the disturbing tale of a Christian Brother who absconds from a borstal with a young boy. *Grace Notes* (Vintage; Norton). Finely crafted novel about grief, love and creativity.

Eugene McCabe, *Death and Nightingales* (Minerva UK o/p). Powerfully relevant novel of love, land and violence, set in late-nineteenth-century Ireland.

Patrick McCabe, *The Butcher Boy* (Picador; Dell); *The Dead School* (Pan; Delta). Scary, disturbing, but funny tales of Irish small-town life. *Breakfast on Pluto* (Picador; Harper Collins). Camp and macabre satire in which McCabe's protagonist takes his cross-dressing from his sleepy parochial home to a sleazy London underworld.

John McGahern, *The Dark* (Faber; Viking o/p); *The Barracks* (Faber UK); *Amongst Women* (Faber; Penguin); *Collected Stories* (Faber; Vintage). *The Barracks* is classic McGahern; stark, murderous and not a spare adjective in sight. *Amongst Women* is an excellent tale of an old Republican and the oppression of rural and family life.

Eoin McNamee, *Resurrection Man* (Picador). A darkly poetic and gripping tale of sectarian killings and the minds of the perpetrators, loosely based upon the Shankill Butchers.

Deirdre Madden, *Hidden Symptoms* (Faber, o/p in US); *The Birds of the Innocent Wood* (Faber); *Remembering Light and Stone* (Faber); and *Nothing is Black* (Faber UK). Evocatively grim novels of life in the North.

Aidan Mathews, *Lipstick on the Host* (Minerva; Harcourt Brace). Delicate stories of breathtaking skill.

Francis Molloy, *No Mate For The Magpie* (Virago o/p; Persea). Written wholly in dialect, this is the moving tale of a working class northern woman who finds herself demonstrating outside the American Embassy in Dublin.

Brian Moore, *The Lonely Passion of Judith Hearne* (Grafton; McClelland & Stewart). Moore's early novels are rooted in the landscape of his native Belfast; this was his first, a poignant tale of emotional blight and the possibilities of late redemption by love. The somewhat Cartlandesque *The Magician's Wife* (Bloomsbury; EP Dutton) is a tale of pernickety sexual repression at the court of Napoleon III.

Mary Morrissy, *A Lazy Eye* (Vintage; Simon & Schuster o/p); *Mother of Pearl* (Cape; Scribner). Impressive stories and a novel by rising star in the new generation of writers.

Christopher Nolan, *Under the Eye of the Clock* (Weidenfeld, o/p; St Martin's, o/p). Extraordinary and explosive fiction debut; largely autobiographical story of a handicapped boy's celebration of the power of language.

Edna O'Brien, *The Country Girls* (Penguin; NAL); *Down by the River* (Phoenix; Plume). *The Country Girls* is a sensitively wrought novel from a top-class writer sometimes accused, unjustly, of wavering too much towards Mills and Boon. In *Down by the River*, incest and bigotry in parochial Ireland is dealt with head-on and delivered with brutal poetry.

Flann O'Brien, *The Third Policeman* (Grafton; NAL). O'Brien's masterpiece of the ominously absurd and fiendishly humorous. *At Swim-Two-Birds* (Penguin o/p; Plume) is a complicated and hilarious blend of Gaelic fable and surrealism; essential reading. Also see "Memoirs and Journalism", p.678, under Myles na Gopaleen.

Frank O'Connor, *Guests of the Nation* (Irish Books & Media US). The best Irish political fiction this century.

Joseph O'Connor, *True Believers* (Flamingo; Trafalgar o/p); *Cowboys and Indians* (Fontana; Trafalgar o/p). *Desperadoes* (Flamingo UK); *The Salesman* (Secker and Warburg UK). The first two titles deal with life on the peripheries in London and Dublin: love and loss, madness and redemption. *Desperadoes* is a love story ranging from 1950s' Dublin to modern Nicaragua, while *The Salesman* is a pacy revenge thriller in which a man hunts the thief who has left his daughter in a coma.

Peadar O'Donnell, *Islanders* (Mercier o/p; Dufour o/p). Evocative, mesmerizing prose from important Republican figure.

Julia O'Faolain, *No Country for Young Men* (Penguin o/p; Carroll & Graf). Spanning four generations, this ambitious novel traces the personal repercussions of the civil war.

Seán Ó Faoláin, *Bird Alone* (Oxford University Press o/p); *Collected Stories* (Constable; Little Brown o/p). A master of the short-story form and the juiciness of rural dialect.

Liam O'Flaherty, *The Pedlar's Revenge and Other Stories* (Wolfhound; Irish American); *The Informer* (Wolfhound; Harcourt Brace). Best of the postwar generation of former IRA men turned writers.

Kate O'Riordan, *Involved* (Flamingo UK). A young Dublin woman's struggle to understand the passions at the root of Northern Irish republicanism.

Glenn Patterson, *Burning Your Own* (Minerva UK). Distinctive young Northern writer gives Protestant child's-eye view of late 1960s' Northern Ireland just about to explode. *Fat Lad* (Minerva UK). A man gives up a promising career to return to Belfast; an uncompromising yet positive portrayal of the city.

E.O. Somerville and (Violet) Martin Ross, *The Irish R.M.* (Abacus o/p; Little, Brown o/p). Hilarious tales in which the locals always outwit the resident magistrate. *Some Experiences of an Irish R.M.* (Dent UK). The needle pushes the begorra factor a little too heavily here and there, but Somerville and Ross write with witty flair and their tales are very significant for what they unwittingly reveal about a dying class.

James Stephens, *The Crock of Gold* (Gill & MacMillan; Dover); *The Charwoman's Daughter* (Gill & Macmillan o/p; North Books o/p); *The Demi-Gods* (Butler o/p). Three fabulous masterpieces from the country's most underrated genius.

Laurence Sterne, *The Life and Opinion of Tristram Shandy*, and *A Sentimental Journey Through France and Italy* (both Everyman; OUP; Viking). Essential reading from an eighteenth-century comic genius.

Bram Stoker, *Dracula* (Penguin; OUP; Koneman). Stoker woke up after a nightmare brought on by a hefty lobster supper, and proceeded to write his way into the nightmares of the twentieth century.

Francis Stuart, *Black List Section H* (Lilliput; Penguin). Once a protégé of Yeats, Stuart has consistently maintained a stance of opposition, in his life and his art. *Black List Section H*, his masterpiece, depicts the life of an Irishman in wartime Germany.

Eamon Sweeney, *Waiting for the Healer* (Picador UK). A single father's bleak descent into drink handled with wry humour.

Jonathan Swift, *Gulliver's Travels* (Penguin; OUP); *The Tale of a Tub and Other Stories* (Oxford University Press). Acerbic satire from the only writer in the English language with as sharp a pen as Voltaire.

Colm Tóibín, *The South* (Picador; Penguin); *The Heather Blazing* (Picador; Penguin); *The Story of the Night* (Picador; Henry Holt). In *The South* a woman turns her back on Ireland for Spain and returns thirty years later to resolve her life, and to die. A powerfully understated novel, *The Heather Blazing* explores themes of personal and political loss, while his *Story of the Night* is a haunting love story set in Argentina at the time of the Generals.

William Trevor, *Collected Stories* (Penguin). Five of Trevor's short-story collections in one volume, revealing more about Ireland than many a turgid sociological thesis. Often desperately moving, these stories confirm Trevor as one of the true giants of Irish fiction. *Two Lives* (Penguin), including *Reading Turgenev*, a sensitive account of an unhappy marriage, was shortlisted for the 1991 Booker Prize.

Oscar Wilde, *The Picture of Dorian Gray* (Penguin; Everyman). Wilde's exploration of moral schizophrenia. A debauched socialite maintains his youthful good looks, while his portrait in the attic slowly disintegrates into a vision of evil.

Robert McLiam Wilson, *Ripley Bogle* (Minerva; Arcade). Very funny first novel in which the irrepressible and precocious down and out Bogle tells his tale in wonderfully extravagant tones. *Eureka Street* (Secker and Warburg; Arcade). Acerbic, irreverent humour in both pre- and post-cease-fire Belfast.

POETRY AND DRAMA

Samuel Beckett, *Collected Shorter Plays* and *Waiting for Godot* (Faber; Grove). Bleak hilarity from the laureate of the void. All essential for swanning around Dublin coffee shops.

Brendan Behan, *The Complete Plays* (Eyre Methuen; Grove). Flashes of brilliance from a writer destroyed by alcoholism. His *The Quare Fellow* takes up where Wilde's *Ballad of Reading Gaol* leaves off.

Eavan Boland, *The Journey* (Carcanet UK o/p); *Selected Poems* (Carcanet UK) and *Outside History* (Carcanet; Norton). Thoughtful, spare and elegant verse from one of Ireland's most significant poets.

Pat Boran, *The Unwound Clock* (Dedalus UK). Wry, insightful poems of contemporary Irish life.

Austin Clarke, *Selected Poems* (Lilliput; Penguin). Clarke's tender work evokes the same stark grandeur as the paintings of Jack Yeats.

Patrick Crotty (ed.), *Modern Irish Poetry: An Anthology* (Blackstaff; Dufour). This anthology covers a broad range of poetry from 1922 onwards, includes Gaelic and English translations of a number of poems, and provides highly accessible introductions to both the period and the individual poets represented.

Denis Devlin, *Collected Poems* (Wake-Forest US). Pre-eminent Irish poet of the 1930s, owing allegiance to a European modern tradition rather than the prevailing Yeatsian.

Paul Durcan, *A Snail in My Prime* (Harvill; Penguin); *O Westport in the Light of Asia Minor* (Harvill UK); *The Berlin Wall Café* (Harvill UK). Ireland's most popular and readable poet. *Berlin Wall* is a lament for a broken marriage, recounted with agonizing honesty, dignity and, ultimately, forgiveness.

Peter Fallon, *News of the World* (Gallery; Wake-Forest). Reflections on a reassuring landscape, the present consciously linked to the past, punctuated by the petty rivalries and discrete madnesses of country life.

Padraic Fiacc, *Missa Terribilis* (Blackstaff UK o/p). Fiacc's work is informed by the political and social tribalisms of Northern Ireland, and explores personal relationships in these contexts.

Oliver Goldsmith, *She Stoops to Conquer* (Pocket Books; Dover). Sparky dialogue, with a more English sheen than Farquhar.

Seamus Heaney, *Death of a Naturalist* (Faber); *Station Island, Seeing Things* and *Opened Ground: Poems 1966–96* (Faber; Farrar Straus & Giroux). The most important Irish poet since Yeats. His poems are immediate and passionate, even when dealing with intellectual problems and radical social divisions. *The Redress of Poetry* (Faber; Farrar Straus & Giroux) is an example of his energetic prose, consisting of the lectures he gave while Professor of Poetry at Oxford from 1989 to 1994. The title of *Spirit Level* (Faber; Noonday), winner of the 1997 Whitbread Prize, alludes to the delicate balances of private and political life following the cease-fire; cool, reassuring poetry with its own quiet music. *Opened Ground* is a massive new collection selected from all his previous published work.

Patrick Kavanagh, *The Complete Poems* (Goldsmith Press UK). Joyfully mystic exploration of the rural countryside and the lives of its inhabitants by Ireland's most popular poet. See also his autobiographical novel, *Tarry Flynn* (Penguin UK).

Brendan Kennelly, *Cromwell* (Bloodaxe; Dufour). Speculative meditation on the role of the conqueror in Irish history. *Poetry My Arse* (Bloodaxe; Dufour) is an epic poem which "sinks its teeth into the pants of poetry itself".

Thomas Kinsella, *Collected Poems: 1956–1994* (OUP). See also his translations

from the Irish (see p671, with Seán Ó Tuama) and his first-rate anthology *The New Oxford Book of Irish Verse* (Oxford University Press).

Shane MacGowan, *Poguetry* (Faber UK o/p). Powerful and pungent lyrics by the former Pogues' bardperson. Not for Yeats fans.

Louis MacNeice, *Collected Poems* (Faber UK) or *Selected Poems* (Wake-Forest US). Good chum of Auden, Spender and the rest of the "1930s' generation", Carrickfergus-born MacNeice achieves a fruitier texture and an even more detached tone.

Derek Mahon, *Selected Poems* (Penguin UK); *The Hudson Letter* (Gallery UK). One of the more considerable Irish poets, a Northern contemporary of Heaney. See also his *Penguin Book of Contemporary Irish Poetry* (ed. with Peter Fallon). *The Yellow Book* (Gallery; Wake-Forest). Musky, sensuous verse belies Mahon's *fin de siècle* disenchantment. Terrific.

Medbh McGuckian, *Venus in the Rain* (Gallery; Dufour); *Selected Poems* (Gallery UK). Trawling the subconscious for their imagery, McGuckian's sensuous and elusive poems are highly demanding and equally rewarding.

Paula Meehan, *The Man who was Marked by Winter* (Gallery o/p; Eastern Washington University); *Pillow Talk* (Gallery UK o/p). Memorable work, often concerned with women's lives, issues of family, gender and sexuality.

John Montague, *Collected Poems* (Gallery; Wake-Forest). Terse poetry concerned with history, community and social decay. See also his anthology, *The Book of Irish Verse* (Faber; Bristol).

Paul Muldoon, *New Selected Poems* (Faber UK). Muldoon's own selection of his more accessible, witty and inventive poetry taken from work spanning thirty years.

Eileán Ní Chuilleanáin, *The Rose Geranium* (Gallery UK); *The Brazen Serpent* (Gallery; Wake-Forest). Manages to carve something new, purposeful and whole from the iconography and language of religion; quietly impressive.

Nuala Ní Dhomhnaill, *Selected Poems* (Raven Arts Press; New Island) is in Irish and English. Haunting translations of her modern erotic verse by the fine poet Michael Hartnett are included in *Raven Introductions 3* (Colin Smythe UK) and in Frank Ormsby's anthology (see overleaf).

Sean O'Casey, *Three Plays* (Papermac; St Martin's). Contains his powerful Dublin trilogy, *Juno and the Paycock*, *Shadow of a Gunman* and *The Plough and the Stars*, set against the backdrop of the civil war.

Frank Ormsby (ed.), *The Long Embrace: Twentieth Century Irish Love Poems* (Blackstaff UK o/p). Excellent anthology with major chunks from the work of almost every important twentieth-century Irish poet from Yeats to the present day. *A Rage To Order* (ed.) (Blackstaff UK); impressive anthology of poetry born of the Troubles. Horror, pain, anger and pity somehow all wrestled into some sense of form; an absorbing book. See also his *Poets from the North of Ireland* anthology (Blackstaff; Dufour).

Tom Paulin, *Fivemiletown; The Strange Museum; Walking a Line; Selected Poems 1972–90* (all Faber). Often called "dry" both in praise and accusation, Paulin's work reverberates with thoughtful political commitment and a sophisticated irony.

John Millington Synge, *The Complete Plays* (Eyre Methuen; Vintage). Lots of begorras and mavourneens and other dialogue kindly invented for the Irish peasantry by Synge; but *The Playboy of the Western World* is a brilliant and unique work, greeted in Dublin by riots, threats and moral outrage.

Oscar Wilde, *The Complete Works of Oscar Wilde* (HarperCollins). His drama is characterized by bittersweet satire, subversive one-liners and profound existentialist philosophy all masquerading as well-made, drawing-room farce. In his poem, *The Ballad of Reading Gaol* (Phoenix; Dover), the great comedian achieves his greatest success, in tragedy.

William Butler Yeats, *The Poems* (Pan; Scribner). They're all here, poems of rhapsody, love, revolution and eventual rage at a disconnected and failed Ireland "fumbling in the greasy till."

BIOGRAPHY AND CRITICISM

A.M. Brady and Brian Cleeve (eds.), *Biographical Dictionary of Irish Writers* (Lilliput o/p; St Martin's Press o/p). Succinct entries on all the greats, better used as a magical mystery tour through the lost byways of Irish literature.

Anthony Cronin, *Samuel Beckett: The Last Modernist* (Flamingo; Harper Collins). Accessible, anecdotal biography, good on the Irish background. *No Laughing Matter: The Life and Times of Flann O'Brien* (Fromm US). Witty and insightful biography, and particularly interesting on 1950s Dublin.

Seamus Deane, *Short History of Irish Literature* (Hutchinson o/p; University of Notre Dame Press o/p). Deane brings a poet's sensitivity to a massive and sometimes unwieldy tradition, with skill and a profound sense of sociopolitical context. See also his shorter analysis of modern writing in *Irish Writers* (Eason UK).

Richard Ellmann, *James Joyce* (OUP US); *Oscar Wilde* (Penguin o/p; Vintage). Ellman's *Joyce* is a major literary work in itself, a massive and brilliant book. His *Oscar Wilde* is at least its equal, an eloquent corrective to the image of Wilde as an intellectual mayfly.

Roy Foster, *W.B. Yeats – A Life – The Apprentice Mage,* Volume One of two volumes (Oxford UP). This is a superb biography – dispassionate, scholarly, and bound to augment your understanding of, though not necessarily your feelings for, the great man.

Michael Holroyd, *Bernard Shaw: A Biography* (Vintage; Random House). Unfairly slammed by the critics, this is actually a pretty successful stab at understanding one of the most difficult and complex authors of the whole Anglo-Irish canon.

Declan Kiberd, *Inventing Ireland* (Vintage; Harvard University Press). A massively scrupulous assessment of modern Irish literature from Yeats to Friel, set against a background of flux and turmoil.

James Knowlson, *Damned to Fame: The Life Of Samuel Beckett* (Bloomsbury; Touchstone). Stunning biography: thorough, balanced and scholarly.

Brenda Maddox, *Nora: A Biography of Nora Joyce* (Minerva; Fawcett). Eminently readable story of the funny, irreverent and formidable Nora Barnacle and her life with James Joyce – an interesting complement to Ellmann's Joyce biography.

Ulick O'Connor, *Brendan Behan* (Abacus UK). Moving account of the dramatist's life.

Robert Welch (ed.), *Oxford Companion to Irish Literature* (OUP). This encyclopedic tour through who's who and what they've written fills a long-standing need.

MEMOIRS AND JOURNALISM

Ciaran Carson *The Star Factory* (Granta; Arcade). Magical account of growing up in 50s and 60s Belfast; Carson has a poetic ingenuity reminiscent of Dylan Thomas.

Liam Fay, *Beyond Belief* (Hot Press UK). Hilarious, irreverent look at the state of religion in Ireland.

Myles na Gopaleen, (aka Flann O'Brien), *The Best of Myles* (Grafton UK). Priceless extracts from a daily humorous newspaper column by O'Brien's alter ego.

Frank McCourt, *Angela's Ashes* (Flamingo; Simon & Schuster). Stunning memoir of a Limerick childhood; a tale of bleak, desperate poverty, laced with astonishing moments of humour and a deep respect for the lives led.

Nuala O'Faolain, *Are You Somebody?* (Sceptre; New Island Books). Despite a life rich in ideas and experience, this memoir reveals an Ireland that until recently treated women with, at best, indifference. Neat sketches of literary Dublin in the 1950s, puncturing one or two cosy myths along the way.

Colm Tóibín, *The Sign of the Cross: Travels in Catholic Europe* (Cape; Vintage Departures). Novelist Tóibín uses his journalistic skills to find the old-time religion in Ireland and elsewhere. *Bad Blood* (Vintage UK) is a perceptive account of a journey along the line that divides Northern Ireland from the rest of the island.

John Waters, *Jiving at the Crossroads* (Blackstaff; Dufour o/p). Curiously engaging autobiography which traces a fascination with Fianna Fáil politics through the formative years of a western youth in the 1970s and 1980s.

ART AND MUSIC

Bruce Arnold, *Irish Art: A Concise History* (Thames & Hudson UK). Updated edition provides a fuller account of Irish modernism.

Breandán Breathnach, *Folk Music and Dances of Ireland* (Ossian UK). All the diddley-eye you could want, and in one volume.

Ciaran Carson *The Pocket Guide to Irish Traditional Music* (Appletree Press UK). Useful introduction to the world or traditional music, while *Last Night's Fun* (Pimlico; North Point Press) is a wonderful evocation of the elusive pleasures of traditional music sessions.

Tony Clayton-Lea & Richard Taylor, *Irish Rock* (Gill & MacMillan UK). Popular account of the growth of the Irish music scene, particularly good on the punk and new wave years.

Brian Fallon, *Irish Art 1830–1900* (Appletree Press UK). The development of art in Ireland and its reflection of questions of national identity and culture.

Thomas Moore, *Moore's Irish Melodies;* (Ossian; Captain Fiddle). Various editions of the prettied-up tunes Moore stole from the harpers, along with lyrics of mind-numbingly perfect rhythm. Moore is an important historical figure, who expressed the Nationalism of the emerging middle class and brought revolution into the parlour.

Nuala O'Connor, *Bringing It All Back Home* (BBC UK). Detailed account of the history of traditional Irish music written to accompany a 1991 BBC TV series.

George Petrie, *The Complete Collection of Irish Music* (Llanerch UK). One of the most important cultural documents in Irish history.

Mark J. Prendergast, *Irish Rock: Roots, Personalities and Directions* (O'Brien Press UK). Dated, but still the best in-depth account of the development of Irish rock music.

LANDSCAPE AND TOPOGRAPHY

Aalen, Whelan and Stout, (eds), *Atlas of the Irish Rural Landscape* (Cork University Press UK). Wholly absorbing collection of essays, maps and illustrations revealing and analysing the changing landscape of Ireland; a must for all concerned with its history and future.

Deirdre Flanagan & Lawrence Flanagan, *Irish Place Names* (Gill & MacMillan UK). Expertly researched account of the origins of virtually everywhere on the island – a dipper's delight.

Tim Robinson, *The Stones of Aran: Pilgrimage* (Penguin; Viking o/p). Treats the largest of the Aran Islands to a scrutiny of Proustian detail. *The Stones of Aran: Labyrinth* (Lilliput; Viking o/p) completes the project, to form a uniquely challenging travel book.

GUIDES

Kevin Corcoran, *West Cork Walks* (O'Brien; Irish American). A good, accessible guide to ten walks, including a wealth of interesting material on the history and natural history of the county.

David Herman, *Hill Walkers' Donegal* (Shanksmore Publications UK). Over thirty walks in the county described in excellent detail.

Joss Lynam (ed.), *Best Irish Walks* (Gill & MacMillan; Passport). Seventy-six walks through some of the most beautiful and remote parts of the country.

Sally and John McKenna, *Bridgestone Irish Food Guide* (Estragon UK). The best in an almost non-existent field of Irish food writing. The same authors' smaller guides, to restaurants and places to stay, are also popular.

Seán Ó Súilleabháin, *Walk Guide: South West of Ireland – Third Edition* (Gill & MacMillan UK). Forty-seven well-written and clearly illustrated walks; indispensable for anyone planning walking in Kerry and on the Beara Peninsula.

Patrick Simms and Tony Whilde, *West of Ireland Walk Guide* (Gill & MacMillan UK). Detailed descriptions of west and northwest walks from counties Clare to Derry.

Brendan Walsh, *Irish Cycling Guide* (Moorland; Irish Books & Media). This is a grand tour of the country, in 36 stages, taking the roads with least traffic.

Alan Warner, *Walking the Ulster Way* (Appletree Press UK). The first man to walk the entire 500 miles describes his journey in detailed and sometimes whimsical diaries.

LANGUAGE

A visitor to Ireland will probably have little or no contact with the Irish language, unless they seek to do so in the *Gaeltacht* (Irish speaking areas in the west of the country). However, the legacy of the language still pervades many aspects of Irish life, be it in the rhythms of speech patterns in English, the town and townland names throughout the country or in traditional poetry or song. It has been said for decades that Irish is a dying language and although there is little chance of it becoming the first tongue of more than a small minority of the people of Ireland, the recent rebirth of interest has ensured that it will not follow in the linguistic footsteps of its deceased Celtic cousins.

As with all Celtic languages, Irish evolved from a linguistic base, of which ancient Gaulish is the sole written record.

The Celtic settlement of Ireland probably began in the seventh century BC; the later migration of Irish tribes to the Isle of Man and to Scotland established Irish-speaking kingdoms in those areas. With the rise of Rome the Celtic languages survived only in the peripheral western areas – today, Celtic languages are limited to parts of Scotland, Wales and Brittany in addition to Ireland. Cornish, another Celtic derivative, died out in the eighteenth century and, this century, Manx ceased to be a community language.

It is difficult to assess the use of Irish language until the mid-sixteenth century, as Celtic Ireland, at this time, had no written literary tradition. The earliest form of script, known as **ogham**, is found on standing stones dating from the fourth to seventh centuries. Employing a twenty-character alphabet derived from Latin, the letters were represented by varying strokes and notches, and read from the bottom upwards. Following the establishment of monasteries, a written form of the language, more closely resembling its modern-day form, evolved, with monks recording significant events in the areas in which they were based. The best known non-religious text of this period is the *Táin Bó Cúailgnè* ("The cattle raid of Cooley"), which dates back to the seventh century. With the first Viking raid of 795, the world of the monastery was thrown into chaos and the thread of the language, now known as **Old Irish**, was cut, giving way to a less scholastic and more vernacular-based written language referred to as **Middle Irish**. It was in the later part of this era that the **Fenian Cycle** emerged, charting the exploits of Fionn Mac Cumhaill and his Fianna (band), tales which were very popular with the peasantry.

The period from 1200 to 1600 is considered the **Classical Period** in the development of the language, when the grammatical chaos of Middle Irish was brought under control. A succession of invaders speaking Norse, French and English were assimilated into the population, with a resulting cross-fertilization of languages. There were, however, concerted attempts to stamp out the use of the language, one example being in 1367 when the Statutes of Kilkenny declared that, among other things, "the English may not entertain or make gifts to Irish minstrels, rhymers or story tellers". Despite these attempts to preserve an English-speaking culture, the first Anglo-Norman aristocracy became thoroughly Gaelicized, and even as late as 1578 the Lord Chancellor could report that "all English, and most part with delight, even in Dublin, speak Irish and greatly are spotted in manners, habit and conditions with Irish stains".

However, after the Battle of Kinsale in 1601, the Gaelic aristocracy disappeared, as did the king's court, the Brehon system of law and the bardic schools. Poets soon became a class of wandering minstrel, known as "rakarees" (from the Irish *recaire* – "one who recites") and were persecuted since they represented "the old way".

Although the use of Irish was still widespread in the nineteenth century, the language was further weakened by the establishment of the **National School System** in 1831, which decreed that all children should be educated through the medium of English, despite the fact that many of their parents only spoke Irish. A further blow to the language was the **Great Famine** which hit hardest in many Irish-speaking areas and in many places left a psychological legacy that survival itself depended on the mastery of the English language. Even mass movement politics of a vaguely nationalistic nature eschewed the use of Irish, and Daniel O'Connell, despite being a fluent speaker, preferred to use English both at his rallies and in his propaganda.

Despite the language's decline in the nineteenth century, some organizations sprang up to preserve its use: ironically, considering today's political climate, it was northern Protestants who spearheaded this campaign, the most prominent being the Rev William Nelson. In the late-nineteenth century, a catalyst for the revival of Irish was the poet **Thomas Davis** who promoted the use of Irish as a living language. His efforts were followed by the formation of the **Gaelic League** that works to this day in the field of language promotion.

Immediately after Independence in 1921, Irish was installed as the first national language and steps were taken to revive it as a community tongue. Apart from an intensive education programme, the government attempted in other ways to "Gaelicize" Ireland, the most obvious example being the planting of Gaelic-speaking communities in the heart of English-speaking areas (one such community still remains in Raith Cairn, Co. Meath). This enthusiasm has, however, in postwar years, given way to apathy and governments' efforts at promoting the language have been tokenistic at best; Article 8 Section 1 of the constitution states that Irish is the first language, though this is viewed in most political circles as anachronistic and irrelevant.

Despite these factors mitigating against the survival of the language, it is still estimated that in the designated Irish-speaking (*Gaeltacht*) areas – in counties Donegal, Galway and north Mayo, and in counties Kerry, Cork and Waterford – there are around 70,000 speakers of the language, which is 77 percent of the *Gaeltacht* population. In parallel to this, there is growing **grassroots interest** in the promotion and use of Irish. It is in many ways evidence of an increasing national confidence that instead of seeing Irish as backward, it is nowadays embraced by some of the most progressive elements in society and it is becoming trendy in

some areas to converse in Irish. 1967 saw the establishment of the **Irish-language radio station**, Radio na Gaeltachta, and the latter half of this century has seen many fine writers writing in Irish about subjects that are far removed from the rural preoccupations some associate with Irish-language literature: the first staging-post towards modernity in Irish writing was *An Béal Bocht* by Myles na Gopaleen, followed by the poetry of Seán Ó Ríordáin and Máirtín Ó Díreáin, and latterly by the contemporary poetry of Nuala Ní Dhomhnaill, Gabriel Rosentock and Cathal Ó Searcaigh. In the North, the rise in the use of Irish has been both cultural and political: in the 1970s, Republican prisoners began to learn Irish, though owing to the insular nature of its usage and the lack of professional teaching, it mutated into a kind of pidgin that was known as "jailic". Perhaps the most conspicuous evidence of this revived interest came in the form of the new national **television station**, Teilifís na Gaeilge, which, through its progressive and inventive programming and its energetic youth-oriented presentation, presents the contemporary face of the Irish language.

LANGUAGE BOOKS AND RESOURCES

Teach Yourself Irish, Miles Dillon/Donncha Ó Cróinín (Hodder o/p; NTC o/p). Archaic teaching methods; student needs to be a saint; southern dialects favoured.

Learning Irish, Mícheál Ó Siadháil (Yale University Press). Modern guide to language through speaking. Cassettes available. Strong on grammar; Connacht dialect preferred.

Learn Irish – CD ROM Words and Phrases for Beginners. Not the greatest CD ROM ever but is as good a place to start as any.

Irish for Beginners, Angela Wilkes (Usborne). Humorous illustrations and puzzles help make learning more fun.

Now You're Talking (Gael Media). Based on the RTE BBC N.Ireland television programme of the same name, this is a good resource for both the beginner and those wishing to brush up on their language.

Lazy Way to Irish, O Riain, Flann (Y Lolfa; New South Wales University Press). A good introduction to some useful words and phrases.

CLASSES AND COURSES

For information about Irish language classes, contact Conrad na Gaeilge, 6 Harcourt St, Dublin 2. For books relating to the language, Siopa Leabhair (Book Shop) at the same address is the best place in Dublin.

If you want to combine language learning and cultural activities such as walking, *bodhrán* playing or dancing then contact the excellent Oideas Gael (☎073/30248), which runs courses in Gleann Cholm Cille in Donegal.

IRISH WORDS COMMONLY FOUND IN PLACE NAMES

abha	river	**doire**	oak tree	**machaire**	plain
achadh	field	**droichead**	bridge	**mainstir**	abbey
árd	height	**dubh**	black	**maol**	smooth
áth	ford	**eaglais**	church	**móin**	peat bog
baile	town	**eas**	waterfall	**muc**	pig
bán	white	**eó**	yew tree	**mullach**	summit
barr	top	**fál**	hedge	**nead**	nest
beag	small	**fiodh**	wood	**nua**	new
béal	small	**fionn**	white, fair	**ráth**	ring fort
bó	cow	**fraoch**	heather	**reilig**	ring fort
bóthar	road	**gall**	foreigner	**rua**	red-haired
buí	yellow	**garbh**	rough	**sagart**	priest
bun	base	**garraí**	garden	**sean**	old
caisleán	castle	**geal**	bright	**sí**	fairy
caoin	pleasant	**glas**	green	**sliabh**	mountain
caol	narrow	**gleann**	valley	**sráid**	street
carraig	rock	**gort**	field	**suí**	seat
ceann	head	**grian**	sun	**teach, tí**	house, monastery
cill	church	**inis**	island	**teampall**	church
cloch	stone	**iúr**	yew tree	**tír**	country, territory
cluain	meadow	**lag**	hollow	**tobar**	well
conc	hill	**lann**	church	**trá**	beach
coill	wood	**leaba**	bed	**tulach**	small hill
cos	foot, mouth of a river	**leath**	half	**uisce**	water
		léim	leap	**uaimhe**	cave
currach	marsh	**leitir**	hillside		
dearg	red	**loch**	lake		

AN IRISH GLOSSARY

ALLIANCE PARTY A moderate, centrist, non-sectarian Northern Ireland party led by Lord (John) Alderdice, now speaker of the Assembly.

BAWN A castle enclosure or castlefold.

BODHRÁN (pronounced *bore-run*) A hand-held, shallow, goatskin drum.

B-SPECIALS Auxiliary police force of the Stormont government; disbanded in 1971.

CASHEL A kind of rath (see overleaf), distinguished by a circular outer stone wall instead of earthen ramparts.

CLOCHÁN A beehive-shaped, weatherproof hut built of tightly fitted stone without mortar. Clocháns date from the early Christian period.

"THE CRACK" Good conversation, a good time, often accompanying drinking. "What's the crack?" means "what's the gossip?" or "what's going on?"

CRANNÓG An artificial island in the middle of a lake, dating from the Bronze Age.

CURRACH/CURRAGH Small fishing vessel used off the west coast; traditionally made of leather stretched over a light wood frame, modern currachs are of tar-coated canvas.

THE DÁIL Lower house of the Irish parliament.

DOLMEN (or "portal tomb") A chamber formed by standing stones that support a massive capstone. The capstone often slopes to form the entrance of the chamber. Dates from the Copper Age (2000–1750 BC).

DRUMLIN Small, oval, hummocky hill formed from the detritus of a retreating glacier.

DUP The Democratic Unionist Party. A traditionalist, anti-Republican right-wing party founded by Ian Paisley and Desmond Boal in 1971. Paisley has remained leader since then and is the only European political leader this century to have founded his own church. The DUP is fundamentally opposed to the Good Friday Agreement and any loosening of the bonds with the United Kingdom.

ÉIRE Irish name for Ireland, but officially indicates the 26 counties.

FIANNA FÁIL The largest and most successful of Ireland's two main political parties since Independence. Essentially a conservative party, it has its origins in the Republican faction of Sinn Féin, and fought against pro-Treaty forces in the civil war. During the 1930s, the party did much to assert Ireland's separateness from Britain.

FINE GAEL Ireland's second largest political party, Fine Gael sprang from the pro-Treaty faction of Sinn Féin which formed the first Free State government in 1921. Since that time it has not been able to gain a strong majority, and periods in office have been in coalitions. It advocates more liberal policies than Fianna Fáil in terms of social welfare, but in fact there is very little to distinguish the two main parties.

FIR Men (sign on men's public toilets).

GALLERY GRAVE A simple burial chamber of squared stones, generally found under a long mound.

GARDAÍ The police force of the Republic of Ireland.

INLA Irish National Liberation Army. Extreme splinter group of the IRA. Its aim is the creation through physical force of a united socialist 32-county republic.

IRA Irish Republican Army. The upholders of the Irish Fenian tradition, ultimately dedicated to the establishment of a united 32-county republic by whatever means possible and notorious both for its bombing campaigns and the extreme sophistication of its organizational structure.

IRSP Irish Republican Socialist Party. The most revolutionary, if small, party in Northern Ireland and the political wing of the INLA.

LVF Loyalist Volunteer Force. Banned paramilitary organization, led by Billy Wright until his assassination by the INLA in the Maze prison, December 1997.

LOYALIST A person loyal to the British Crown, usually a Northern Irish Protestant.

MARTELLO TOWER Circular coastal tower once used for defence.

MNÁ Women (sign on women's public toilets).

MOTTE A circular mound, flat on top, which the Normans used as a fortification.

NATIONALISTS Those who wish to see a united Ireland.

THE NORTH Term referring to Northern Ireland used by many people.

OGHAM (rhyming with poem) The earliest form of writing used by the Irish (fourth to seventh centuries), and found on the edge of standing stones. Employing a twenty-character alphabet derived from Latin, the letters were represented by varying strokes and notches, and read from the bottom upwards.

ORANGE ORDER A Loyalist Protestant organization, found throughout Northern Ireland, which promotes the Union with Britain. The name comes from William of Orange ("King Billy"), the Protestant king who defeated the Catholic James II at the Battle of the Boyne (1690) and at the Battle of Aughrim (1691). Most Unionist MPs are Orangemen, and outside of Northern Ireland, Orange Lodges (branches) are found amongst Loyalist expats. Also see p.576.

PASSAGE GRAVE A megalithic tomb from the Neolithic period. A simple corridor of large, square, vertical stones lead to a burial chamber, and the whole tomb is covered with earth. The stones are decorated with simple patterns: double spirals, triangles, zigzag lines, and the sun symbol.

POTEEN/POITÍN (pronounced potcheen) Highly alcoholic (and often toxic) and illegal spirit, usually distilled from potatoes.

PUP Progressive Unionist Party. Seen as the political wing of the UVF. Many of its leading lights are former Loyalist paramilitaries, including David Ervine, a major player in ensuring Loyalist support for the Good Friday Agreement..

RATH or RINGFORT A farmstead dating from the first millennium AD. A circular timber enclosure banked by earth and surrounded by a ditch formed the outer walls, within which roofed dwellings were built and, in times of danger, cattle were herded. Today raths are visible as circular earthworks.

REPUBLICANS Supporters of the ideals incorporated in the 1916 Proclamation of the Republic, the overthrow of British rule in Ireland and the promotion of Irish language and culture.

ROUND TOWER Narrow, tall (65–110ft) and circular tower, tapering to a conical roof. Built from the ninth century onwards, they are unique to Ireland. They are found on the sites of early monasteries, and served to call the monks to prayer. The entrance is usually a doorway 10–15ft above the ground, which was reached by a wooden or rope ladder that could be pulled up for safety.

RUC Royal Ulster Constabulary. Northern Ireland's regular, but armed, police force.

SDLP Social Democratic and Labour Party. The largest Nationalist party, centrist left, founded in 1970 and led by John Hume since 1979.

SINN FÉIN ("Ourselves Alone") Sinn Féin's history has been colourful, eventful and characterized by splits. Re-emerging in the 1970s, it subsequently became a major political force in Northern Ireland, aiming to achieve national self-determination and the formation of a 32-county socialist republic, based on the principles of the Proclamation of 1916 and the beliefs of Tone, Pearse and Connolly. It has been labelled by some as the political wing of the IRA. Its leader since 1983 has been Gerry Adams who has gradually steered Republicanism towards democratic resolution of its goals.

SOUTERRAIN Underground passage that served as a hiding place in times of danger; also used to store food and valuables.

TAOISEACH Irish prime minister.

TD Teachta Dála. Member of the Irish parliament.

TRICOLOUR The green, white and orange flag of the Republic.

THE TWENTY-SIX COUNTIES The Republic of Ireland (Éire).

UDA Ulster Defence Association. A Protestant paramilitary organization, the largest in Northern Ireland.

UDF Ulster Defence Force. Illegal paramilitary Protestant organization.

UDP Ulster Democratic Party. Political wing of the LVF, led by Gary McMichael.

UDR Ulster Defence Regiment. A regular regiment of the British army recruited in Northern Ireland.

UFF Ulster Freedom Fighters. Another illegal Protestant paramilitary faction.

UKU United Kingdom Unionists. Virtually a one-person Unionist Party, sharing similar views to the DUP and led by Robert McCartney, MP for North Down.

UNIONISTS Those (predominantly Protestant) who wish to keep Northern Ireland in union with the rest of the United Kingdom.

UUP Ulster Unionist Party. Founded in 1905 by Edward Carson, the UUP was in power in Northern Ireland from 1921 until the dissolution of Stormont in 1972. Known as the Official Unionists, the largest party in the North is led by David Trimble, a key player in the peace process and now First Minister in the Assembly.

UVF Ulster Volunteer Force. Yet another illegal Protestant paramilitary organization, originally formed in 1912 to oppose any British plans to impose a united Ireland on Northern Irish Protestants; banned in 1966 following its random sectarian murders of Catholics.

INDEX

Stay in touch with us!

ROUGH*NEWS* is Rough Guides' free newsletter.
In three issues a year we give you news, travel
issues, music reviews, readers' letters and the
latest dispatches from authors on the road.

Listen!

'If you want to explore the music of another country you need a guide.
Like the useful Rough Guide travel books and television shows,
these discs delve right into the heart and soul of the region they explore'
Rhythm Music (USA)

'Intelligent, authoritative compilations' Folk Roots (UK)

the perfect getaway vehicle

low-price holiday car rental.

rent a car from holiday autos and you'll give yourself real freedom to explore your holiday destination. with great-value, fully-inclusive rates in over 4,000 locations worldwide, wherever you're escaping to, we're there to make sure you get excellent prices and superb service.

what's more, you can book now with complete confidence. our £5 undercut* ensures that you are guaranteed the best value for money in holiday destinations right around the globe.

drive away with a great deal, call holiday autos now on **0990 300 400** and quote ref RG.

holiday autos miles ahead